State Estimates
of Technology,
1963

Volume IV of
Multiregional Input-Output Analysis

Edited by
Karen R. Polenske

This is the fourth volume in a series entitled *Multiregional Input-Output Analysis,* edited by Karen R. Polenske. It contains an explanation of the assembly of 1963 technology data and state estimates of those data. Other volumes in the series contain a presentation of the complete multiregional input-output model and additional explanations of other parts of the data assembly, as well as state estimates of 1947, 1958, and 1963 final demands and outputs, employment, and payrolls; state estimates of 1963 interregional trade flows; and 1970 and 1980 state projections of final demands, outputs, and interregional trade.

State Estimates of Technology, 1963

Karen R. Polenske

Carolyn W. Anderson
Orani Dixon
Roger M. Kubarych
Mary M. Shirley
John V. Wells

Lexington Books
D.C. Heath and Company
Lexington, Massachusetts
Toronto London

The data contained in this book are the result of federally supported research. They may be freely used with the customary crediting of the source.

Library of Congress Cataloging in Publication Data

Polenske, Karen R.
State estimates of technology, 1963.

(Multiregional input-output analysis, v. 4)
Bibliography: p.
1. United States–Economic conditions–1945–
2. Interindustry economics. 3. United States– Economic conditions–
Mathematical models. I. Title. II. Series.
HC101.M85 vol. 4 HC106.6 330.9'73'092s
ISBN 0-669-87007-2 330.9'73'092 73-21702

Published simultaneously in Canada.

Printed in the United States of America.

International Standard Book Number: 0-669-87007-2

Library of Congress Catalog Card Number: 73-21702

Table of Contents

List of Figures

List of Tables

Preface

The 1963 estimates of state technologies presented in this volume were compiled for use in the multiregional input-output model. The model was initially formulated and implemented at the Harvard Economic Research Project for the Economic Development Administration, U.S. Department of Commerce, and it was later used for transportation analyses at the Massachusetts Institute of Technology for the Office of Systems Analysis and Information, U.S. Department of Transportation. The transportation analyses are now being sponsored by the University Research Program, U.S. Department of Transportation. Tabulations of the 1963 state technology estimates, which are contained in Appendix C, have been reconciled with the current account transactions given in the 1963 national input-output table. For the implementation of the multiregional input-output model, three additional sets of data were compiled: base-year and projected final demands; state outputs, employment, and payrolls; and interregional trade flows. The methodology of assembling these estimates and the theoretical structure of the overall multiregional model are described in other volumes of this series.

A considerable amount of reliance was placed throughout this study on the data and documentation from the 450-order 1947 input-output study that was prepared by the Bureau of Labor Statistics in the early 1950s. Because these data are extremely detailed, the composition of purchases of an 80-order industry was often easy to discern by inspecting the subindustry figures in the 1947 table. The data and methodology used to construct the 1947 table are well documented both in a Technical Supplement published with the table and in individual worksheets that were available for reference at the Harvard Economic Research Project. The extensive use made of the 1947 documentation during the multiregional input-output research project, in fact, provided the main impetus for the present series of publications. Since this is the first time that United States data have been assembled for such a comprehensive, large-scale multiregional model, it seemed important to explain the exact procedures used to estimate the state data, thus providing a basis for analyzing, evaluating, and adjusting the figures. All published and unpublished sources used are cited, unless permission to do so was specifically withheld by the agency from which the information was obtained. To make the reading of this technical writing less tedious, only brief references to the sources are given in the text, followed by numbers in square brackets. The numbers refer to the complete bibliographic listing provided at the back of the book.

The original research reports to the Economic Development Administration upon which three of the four chapters in this volume are based are listed below:

Report Number	*Title*	*Author(s)*	*Date*
18	Estimation of 1963 Input Requirements for Agriculture	Carolyn W. Anderson	September 1970
19	Estimation of 1963 Input Requirements for the Mining Industries	Roger M. Kubarych	September 1970
20	State New Construction Technologies, 1963	Orani Dixon and John V. Wells	September 1970

The final methodologies used for the estimates were sometimes altered from those described in the reports listed here. The tabulations presented in the statistical appendix to the present volume are consistent with the data tapes submitted to the Department of Transportation and were calculated using the methodologies described in full detail in the text.

From March 1967, when the overall multiregional research program was officially begun, through June 1972, a major portion of the work was done at the Harvard Economic Research Project. The Project was closed June 30, 1972, and the multiregional research program was transferred to the Department of Urban Studies and Planning, Massachusetts Institute of Technology, where it is being continued. However, a substantial amount of the data assembly, such as that for the state outputs required in the present technology study, was done by the staff of Jack Faucett Associates, Inc., under subcontracts with the Harvard Economic Research Project or under separate contracts with the Office of Business Economics for the interregional trade flows and with the Office of Civil Defense and the Institute of Defense Analyses for an initial set of 1963 output estimates. All of the remaining data were originally assembled at the Harvard Economic Research Project under contract #7-35212 with the Office of Economic Research of the Economic Development Administration, U.S. Department of Commerce. Additional government agencies that had become interested in the overall multiregional project supplied part of the funds to complete the contract in 1970. These agencies are the Office of Systems Analysis and Information, Department of Transportation; the Bureau of Labor Statistics, Department of Labor; the Office of Emergency Preparedness, Executive Office of the President; the Office of Civil Defense, Department of Defense; and the Bureau of Mines, Department of the Interior. During the period 1971–1972, extensive revisions were made to all the data under contract #DOT-OS-10222 between the Office of Systems Analysis and Information, Department of Transportation, and the Harvard Economic Research Project. Additional revisions were made during 1972–1973 under contract #DOT-OS-10058 between the Office of Systems Analysis and Information, Department of Transportation, and the Department of Urban Studies and Planning, Massachusetts Institute of Technology.

Carolyn W. Anderson and Mary M. Shirley, who were members of the staff of the Harvard Economic Research Project when the research for this volume was done, and Margaret C. Feiger, of the Division of Sponsored Research at the Massachusetts Institute of Technology, assisted with making final consistency checks of the tabulations presented in Appendix C. As far as possible, all material in this volume has been checked for accuracy. Some of the chapters, however, were written by staff members of the Harvard Economic Research Project who were no longer available to assist with the final revisions either to the data or to the descriptions presented. I therefore take full responsibility for any errors that may have escaped detection.

Karen R. Polenske

Acknowledgments

I should like to thank all the people who assisted directly or indirectly with the research reported in this volume. Special thanks are extended to the group who met regularly with me in 1971 and 1972 and assisted in refining some of the concepts presented here: Jack G. Faucett, of Jack Faucett Associates, Inc.; Carolyn W. Anderson, formerly a member of the staff at the Harvard Economic Research Project; Albert J. Walderhaug, Bureau of Economic Analysis, U.S. Department of Commerce; John Harman, Office of Systems Analysis and Information, U.S. Department of Transportation; and Wesley H. Long, Economic Development Administration, U.S. Department of Commerce.

I am also grateful for the contributions made by Anne P. Carter and Wassily Leontief.

Staff members of the Harvard Economic Research Project at Harvard University and of the Division of Sponsored Research at the Massachusetts Institute of Technology assisted with the research and programming activities connected with this technology study. In addition to those who are authors of individual chapters in this volume, the following made significant contributions: Charles Cohen, Edward N. Wolff, Douglas W. McMillan, Margaret C. Feiger, Nathaniel K. Ng, and Zdenek Fencl.

Irene S. Raught edited and typed the original reports as well as this manuscript and made substantial improvements in the writing and presentation of the material in this volume.

Finally, none of the research reported here could have been completed without the use of unpublished data, computer programs, and other materials that were available at the Harvard Economic Research Project during the years (1966-1972) the basic research was being done.

K.R.P.

List of Abbreviations

BEA	Bureau of Economic Analysis
BLS	Bureau of Labor Statistics
BPR	Bureau of Public Roads
Census	Bureau of the Census
CMI	Census of Mineral Industries
EO	Establishment Output
FD	Final Demand
FIB	Farm Income Branch
GNI	Gross National Income
GNP	Gross National Product
IO	Input-Output
JAS	Joint Association Survey
JFA	Jack Faucett Associates, Inc.
MRIO	Multiregional Input-Output
N	National
n.e.c.	Not elsewhere classified
OBE	Office of Business Economics
S	State
SIC	Standard Industrial Classification
SIR	Service Industries Residual
STRI	State Transfers-in
STRO	State Transfers-out
TRI	Transfers-in
TRO	Transfers-out
VA	Value Added

State Estimates of Technology, 1963

1 Estimation of Regional Technologies

Karen R. Polenske

Many economic studies have been conducted of the differences in technology between countries and of changes in technology over time within one country. At the regional level, however, sufficient data have not been available to permit economic analysts to explore the technological differences that may occur among regions in the same country. In a few studies of specific areas, technologies unique to the region have been assembled and used. A large number of regional models in the United States, however, have been implemented using national technological coefficients, or, at best, adjusted national data, to represent the regional technologies, the assumption being that national and regional technologies are virtually the same. Variations observed in regional technologies have usually been assumed to be a direct result of the level of industrial aggregation used for the analysis, and national coefficients have been altered (using what is called a product-mix method) to try to account for the differences that occur when the mix of industries varies from region to region.

For the present multiregional input-output (MRIO) study, technology data were assembled for 87 industries and for 51 regions (50 states and the District of Columbia). The industry and regional classifications are given in the appendix, Tables A–1 and B–1, respectively. Because some of the empirical analyses are being conducted for 9 regions, the regional classification shows the way the 51 regions map onto the 9 census regions. For the MRIO analysis, detailed state input requirements were assembled for three large sectors of the economy: agriculture, mining, and construction. Together, these comprise about 13 percent of both the total 1963 gross output and the total 1963 gross national product. Most of the research effort on regional differences in technology was concentrated on these sectors because locational factors are likely to cause significant state-to-state variations in their input requirements. For the remaining industries, namely, the manufacturing and service industries, either variations in the state coefficients were obtained through the product-mix method; or, for a few of those industries, where the components of the industry could not be separated, the national coefficients were used directly.

This is the first time that a major effort has been made to assemble technology data for all states in the United States simultaneously. As discussed in the next section, previous research efforts have generally dealt either with national technologies or with the technologies of a single region.

Research on Variations in Technology

Technology is defined here in the specific terms of the inputs required per unit of output, which is the definition used in input-output literature. In his book *The Structure of American Economy, 1919-1939* [46] and in an article entitled "Structural Change" [45], Leontief discusses the difficulties of measuring changes in technology. One of his findings was that changes in industrial technology were considerably slower during the depression (1929-1939) than during the preceding boom years (1919-1929) [45, p. 28]. He also found that from 1919-1929, the labor input coefficients decreased significantly in the American economy, i.e., that the changes in technology were of the labor-saving type. On the other hand, during the depression, there was a "relative predominance of saving in nonlabor inputs" [45, p. 31]. The most extensive study at the national level for the United States is the historical analysis of structural changes between 1939 and 1962 by Anne P. Carter, reported in her book, *Structural Change in the American Economy* [11], and in articles in *The Review of Economics and Statistics* [9] and *Scientific American* [10]. Beatrice N. Vaccara has supplemented Carter's study by a study of variations that occurred between 1947 and 1958 [156].

The national studies show that although changes in technology do occur in the United States, the infusion of new technologies occurs slowly for most industries, exceptions being aircraft, instruments, and coal mining during the period from 1940 to 1960. The dominant feature of the change in input requirements has been the across-the-board decrease in labor inputs. Another interesting, though not surprising, fact concerning the national input requirements can be observed by looking at the direct coefficients for value added in the 1963 input-output table [122]. (These input coefficients are calculated from gross output data that include both domestic transfers-in and transferred imports.) Input coefficients for value added are large, varying from a low of .234 for IO-31, Petroleum refining & related industries, to a high of .847 for IO-66, Communications, except radio & TV broadcasting. In fact, for 15 of the 17 service industries, the direct input requirements for value added represent more than 50 percent of the total input requirements. (The two exceptions are IO-68, Electric, gas, water, & sanitary services, with a coefficient of .468, and IO-73, Business services, with a coefficient of .489.)

As of the fall of 1973, two sets of technical coefficients have been projected at the national level for the United States and published by the government. One is a set of projections to 1970, first published by the Bureau of Labor Statistics (BLS) in 1966 [152] and published in revised form in 1972 [153]; the other is a set of projections to 1980, published by the BLS in 1970 [151].

For these, information was compiled industry by industry on important changes that might be occurring in technology and on how quickly the new technology would replace the technologies then current. Clopper Almon carried the national input-output studies into the important area of dynamic analysis with his book entitled *The American Economy to 1975: An Interindustry Forecast* [1].

For other countries, numerous studies of changes in national technologies have been conducted. Among these are a comprehensive study for Norway by Sevaldson using annual tables for 1949–1960 [70]; and one for the Netherlands by Tilanus and Rey for the period 1949–1958 [65], which has been extended by Middelhoek in an investigation of the stability of marginal input coefficients using the period 1950–1964 [50]. Researchers in these countries have an advantage over those using U.S. data in that series of national input-output tables have been constructed for the countries on a comparable basis, covering a fairly long time span.

Even at the national level, however, the estimation of actual and future technologies is still in its infancy. As Carter states in *Structural Change in the American Economy:*

> . . . knowledge of the actual underlying technologies is only fragmentary and often qualitative or directional, rather than quantitative. It may therefore be possible to attribute falling steel coefficients in construction to the rise of prestructured concrete but not to specify a mathematical formula (a general production function) relating concrete, steel, and the output of, say, apartment houses. [11, p. 10]

At the regional level, no systematic effort has been made to investigate possible variations in technology from region to region, mainly because of the unavailability of the mass of detailed data required to conduct the investigations. As mentioned earlier, many regional analysts in the United States have assumed that data on national technologies provide approximations sufficiently close to those on regional ones. An attempt to relax this stringent assumption was made by Moore and Petersen in their study of the Utah economy published in 1955 [57]. They adjusted the national input coefficients using information on the differences between Utah and the United States in production techniques, marketing distributions, and product mix. In a later regional study of the St. Louis economy by Hirsch, published in 1959, another technique was used to obtain regional coefficients [39]. For that study, officials in medium- and large-size firms in the city were asked to provide data on input requirements directly to the research team. Now, many state tables are being constructed based upon sample surveys, interspersed with national data when local data are unavailable.

Three recent attempts to construct regional input coefficients from national data should be mentioned in that they all were aimed at eliminating the need for individual regional sample surveys, and all of them made comparisons with the input coefficients for the state of Washington but reached different conclusions.

A 1963 state input-output table for use in making the comparisons was available because a survey in the state had been conducted and reported on by Bourque, Tiebout, and others [8]. Czamanski and Malizia attempted to construct a table for the state using state income and product accounts disaggregated by sector and combining this information with input coefficient data from the national table [17]. They compared their table with the Bourque-Tiebout one, which had been constructed from sample survey data, and found that their approximations to the Washington state data were not very accurate. To reduce the errors, they eliminated the tertiary industries through aggregation (reducing the number of industries from 54 to 34). They proposed that a field survey be conducted, concluding that a complete sample survey was not required. Miernyk looked at their results and concluded instead "that short-cut methods do not work" [51, p. 82]. Schaffer and Chu also tested the Washington data, using a broad range of methods—location quotients, commodity balance, and iterative simulation—to adjust the input coefficients [69]. When they examined the differences between their calculated coefficients for the state and the actual ones, they, too, concluded that a survey-based study is preferable. Finally, Walderhaug made a similar comparison, with considerably better results, by making a variety of adjustments to the national input coefficients [157]. His study, in fact, indicates that a researcher well-informed concerning the national input-output data and willing to make a thorough investigation of the peculiarities of a region can obtain a reasonable approximation to actual regional technologies at a good deal less cost than a survey-based study.

Miernyk is the most vocal advocate of survey-based studies for regions. He has illustrated the use of well-constructed regional input-output tables by his impressive studies of the Colorado River Basin [74], of Boulder, Colorado [54], and of West Virginia [55]. In conducting the surveys, he has worked, then, with regions that comprise parts of states, an entire city, and an entire state. He has also been instrumental in persuading other regional groups to conduct their own surveys. The difficulty, of course, for most regional units is that a survey-based study is costly, so the attempt to find ways to reduce the cost or to develop short-cut methods continues. As Miernyk shows, some progress along these lines has been made by the use of small-sample survey techniques that reduce the cost significantly in most cases [53]. Miernyk has written an article entitled "Regional and Interregional Input-Output Models: A Reappraisal," in which he thoroughly examines and discusses the construction and use of regional input-output coefficients [52].

One severe limitation of the present study is that the causes of changes in the structural and trade coefficients at the regional level cannot be explained because within the multiregional system these coefficients are assumed to be constant. This is not to say that the coefficients must remain constant. For regional growth studies, the fixed coefficients can be made variables and be examined within an even more general dynamic theoretical framework. Dynamic regional models are being developed that will permit the various parameters to change. Structural change depends, however, not only on variations in current inputs, but also on changes in the stock and flow of capital, and regional capital data are extremely scarce. For some industries, such as the metalworking industries, purchases on capital, not current, account comprise a considerable amount of the inputs required to produce a given year's output. Also, variations in patterns of trade occur for many reasons—shifts in the location of industry, price variations, alterations in demand, etc. All of these factors should be incorporated into the regional dynamic models. The development of appropriate dynamic models may be delayed for a number of years because of the masses of data required to implement them.

The present study is a small step in the direction of augmenting the data base that can eventually be used for dynamic analyses of regional economies. In addition, the technology data that have been assembled can be examined to compare differences in technology among the 51 regions. The accounting framework used to assemble the 51-region data is explained in the next section of this chapter.

The Multiregional Input-Output Accounting System

To clarify the basic framework within which the state technologies were assembled, a brief description of the regional input-output tables of the multiregional accounting system is presented here. An important contribution of this system is that it discloses gaps and inconsistencies in the series of available statistics because of the framework used and because of the need to maintain data consistency in three ways: within each region, from region to region, and between the sums of the various sets of data for all regions and the corresponding sets of national aggregates.

Figure 1-1 shows how the purchases and sales of intermediate and final goods and services within each of the 51 regions of the economy are organized. In the figure, each large rectangular block represents a regional input-output table for a particular region. All of the interindustry purchases and sales made by industries on current account and all final purchases by private and public consumers located within that particular region are represented by the rows and columns of the block. Each row of a specific regional table shows the total distribution of a commodity to the intermediate and final users within that region. The rows specify the producing industries but do not designate the region in which the goods were produced. Each column of the table shows the total purchases of goods, services, and value added by the particular intermediate or final user located in that region. It should be noted that these columns provide a detailed specification of all purchases by the region in which they are consumed,

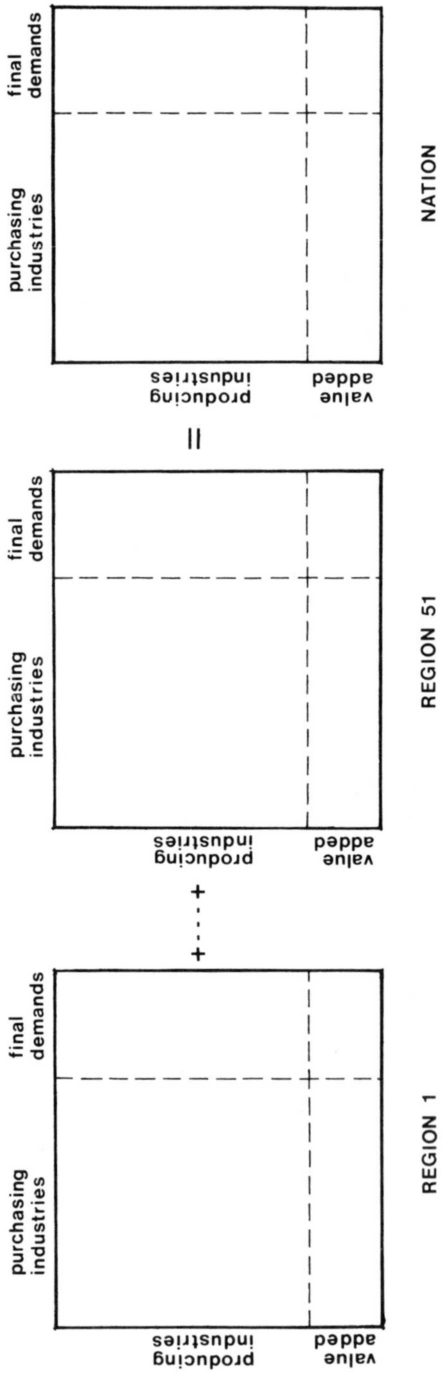

Figure 1–1. Regional Input-Output Tables.

regardless of their region of origin or of the region where the consumer, say, an individual, lives. To obtain the region of production for each item and to complete the multiregional accounting system, the accounts must be expanded to include trade among the regions. This expansion will not be explained in the present volume, because it does not directly relate to the estimation of the regional technologies.[1]

The large square block within each regional table represents the interindustry sales and purchases, with the rows specifying the producing industry and the columns specifying the purchasing industry. In the present study, the number of producing industries exactly equals the number of purchasing industries; therefore, the block is square. (A rectangular block of data will occur if, as in the Canadian input-output table [38], the rows represent the commodities produced and the columns specify the purchasing industries because the number of rows in such a table will exceed the number of columns.) The rectangle along the bottom of each regional table represents the payments to factors of production: wages and salaries, rent, depreciation, taxes, etc. In the national input-output tables, all of these items are usually combined and refered to as value added. They form the income side of the national and regional accounts.

The rectangle at the right of each regional table represents the purchases by final consumers (public and private) in the region. These normally include the six major components of the gross regional product: personal consumption expenditures, gross private capital formation, net inventory change, net foreign exports, net state and local government purchases of goods and services, and federal government purchases. In many regional studies, these components are combined and referred to either as final demand or gross regional product. They form the product or expenditures side of the regional accounts.

The small rectangle in the lower right-hand corner of each regional table represents essentially the wage and salary payments to domestic household employees and government employees. In addition, some balancing items for the foreign sector are included here. For the state estimates, data were compiled for the six basic components of final demand (as explained in *State Estimates of the Gross National Product, 1947, 1958, 1963* [63]) and, wherever possible, estimates were made for these value added (VA) components of the final demand (FD) columns as well.

Because the terms are sometimes confused, a clear distinction must be made between gross regional product and gross regional output. The first term refers to all sales to final consumers; the second term refers to total sales to intermediate and final users. The counterparts on the income side of the accounts are gross regional income and gross regional purchases. Here, the first term refers

---

1. The linkage between the state input-output tables and the interregional trade tables will be explained in the sixth volume of this series, *The United States Multiregional Input-Output Model* [62].

to total payments to the factors of production (land, labor, and capital); the second term refers to total purchases of intermediate goods and services as well as the purchases of the services of the factors of production. Gross regional product (income) is therefore only a part of the total gross regional output (purchases), and the national sum of the 51 gross regional product (income) accounts equals the gross national product (income) for the United States, which is commonly referred to as simply the GNP (GNI).

The user of national input-output tables is accustomed to working with a balanced table, in which the sums of corresponding rows and columns of the table must be equal, since the total consumption of output must equal the total production for each industry in a given year. For a particular regional input-output table, the sum of all elements in each row of the table gives the total consumption only by purchasers within the region, while the sum of all elements in each column gives the total input requirements of each industry within the region. Because in any given year the total amount paid out for inputs by an industry must equal the total amount received for its output, the column sum must also be equal to the total value of production. If none of the good or service produced by the industry in a given region is traded, the corresponding row and column sums will therefore also be identical. (This occurs, for example, for many of the service industries, where the assumption is made that all services produced in a region are also consumed in the region.) The sums of corresponding rows and columns in a regional input-output table will not be equal for most industries, with the differences being attributable to interregional trade.

Although only the interindustry part of the multiregional input-output table will be described later in the book, the entire regional table has been explained here to show how the technology data can be integrated into the complete accounting system.

Interregional Input-Output Tables

The accounting framework that has just been described forms one part of the interregional input-output table, shown in Figure 1-2. The regional input-output tables are shown as the set of *n* rectangular blocks at the bottom of that figure. As was stressed earlier, the regional input-output tables give purchases by the location of the purchaser, not by the location of the producer. However, each total purchase made by an intermediate or final consumer in a particular region can also be separated by the location of the producer. The element x_{12}^{1}, for example, appears in the first row, second column, of the first large block in the lower left-hand corner of the figure. (Industries are denoted by subscripts and regions by superscripts.) It gives the total inputs of the products of industry 1 required by industry 2 located in region 1. The *n* blocks directly above this contain the separate elements that make up the total purchase and specify the

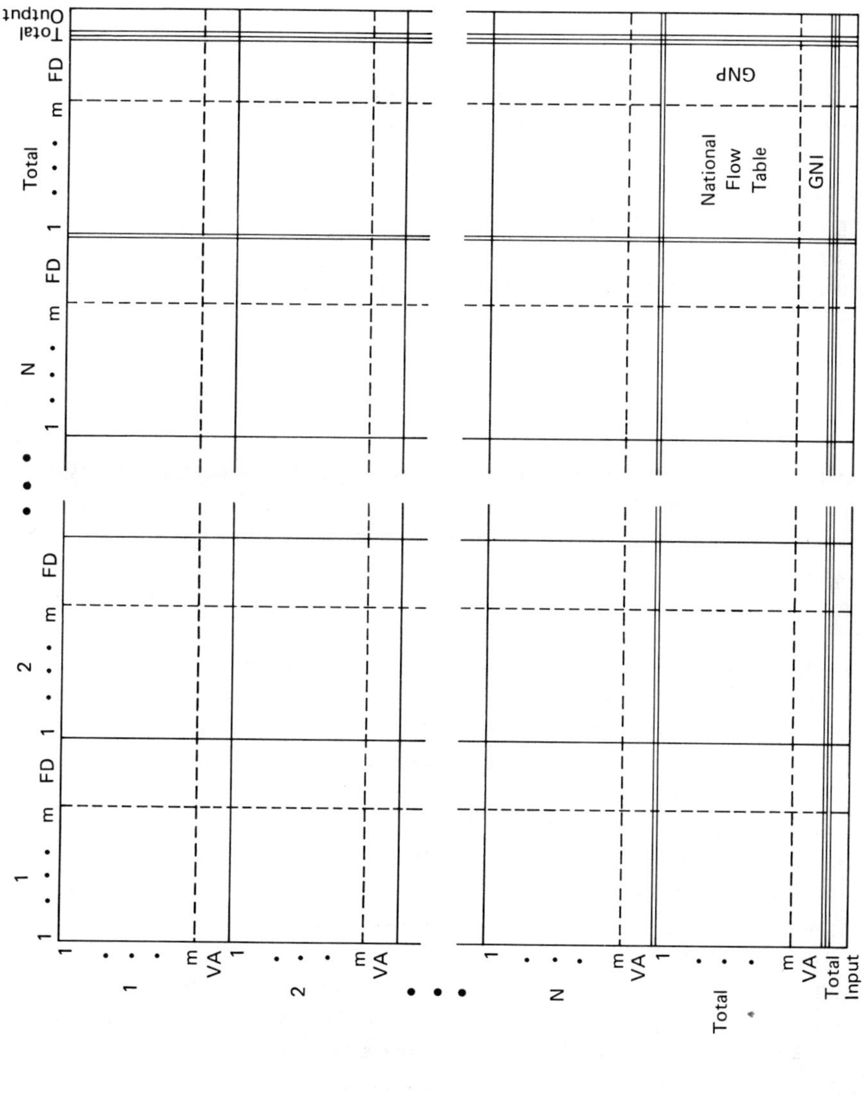

Figure 1–2. Interregional Input-Output Table.

region in which the good is produced as well as the region in which it is purchased (and the industry making the purchase). In other words, the element x^1_{12} can be obtained by summing the respective elements in the n producing regions:

$$\sum_{g=1}^{n} x^{g1}_{12}$$

where g specifies the producing region. These n elements give the purchase by industry 2 located in region 1 of the products of industry 1 located in each of the n producing regions, and they appear in the first row, second column, of each of the n regional blocks in the first column of regional blocks. For the interregional trade table shown in Figure 1-2, n^2 regional blocks are required, while for the regional input-output tables shown in Figure 1-1, only n regional blocks are needed; therefore, $n^2 - n$ more information is required for the interregional input-output accounting system.

Definition of a Regional Input Coefficient

A fundamental difference exists in the way in which regional input coefficients are calculated by different economic analysts. Two basic approaches are used as a result of different interpretations of "regional technology." For the MRIO study, each regional input coefficient is specified as being the total amount of the input of a given product an industry in a particular region requires per unit of its output in that region as given by the element x^h_{ij}. Thus, no regional dimension is given to the production of the input at this point in the analysis. For example, so many units of machinery are required to produce a thousand tons of coal in West Virginia, regardless of where the machinery was manufactured. If machinery for producing coal is considered a homogeneous product and is uniformly priced (for the purchaser) regardless of the region in which it is manufactured, it should not make any difference to the coal industry whether the machinery is obtained from Michigan, Illinois, or any other state.

But it is obvious that even coal machinery is not homogeneous, that strip mining and pit mining require different machinery, that variations do occur from region to region in the cost of manufacturing the machinery, and that, therefore, some means of disaggregating the inputs into the coal-mining industry is desirable. If both production processes are combined in one coal-mining industry and a shift occurs in the mix of processes used, the input coefficients will vary (and the trade coefficients will also vary because of the different states of origin of the two types of equipment). There are at least two possibilities for handling this situation. One is to specify more production processes by separating the coal-mining industry into two parts, one for strip mining and one for pit mining. As noted here, strip mining and pit mining require different machinery, and one type of machinery may be produced in Michigan and the other in Illinois; furthermore, different quantities of machinery per unit of output may be required for the two coal-mining processes. A second possibility is to separate the machinery inputs by location of producer, i.e., into those produced in Michigan, those produced in Illinois, and so on. If the separation is by production process, the assumption of constant input and trade coefficients can be maintained as long as changes occur only in the amount of coal produced by the two processes. If the separation is according to the location of the producer, the input and trade coefficients cannot be assumed to remain constant, because they will vary whenever changes occur in the mix of the two basic techniques used to produce the coal. A separation by location of producer will therefore be less desirable than one by type of production process.[2]

Readers who are familiar with regional input-output literature will recognize the separation by production process as the approach used in the multiregional input-output studies by Leontief and Strout [47], Chenery [12], Moses [58], and Polenske [62] and the separation by location of producer as that described by Isard [40]. Isard's approach requires considerably more information ($n^2 - n$, to be exact) than that required for the MRIO studies. Such detailed data are not only more expensive to assemble, but, as indicated above, disaggregation by state where the input originates may be the wrong type of information to assemble for technology studies. Extra resources for data assembly may be more beneficial if expended on specifying additional industries.[3]

In addition, from the standpoint of data assembly, the "process-specified" coefficient may be easier to obtain than the "region-specified" coefficient. For example, does Heath-Lexington know how many kilowatts of electricity used in producing this book came from power plants in Massachusetts and how many were imported from other states in the East or even from Canada?[4]

Criticisms of the ways in which input-output coefficients are used for regional studies have been made for three reasons. First, some of the regional studies are made at a county or small-area level, and the question arises whether an input-output table can be constructed inexpensively for such areas. Second, in some studies, technology for a region is defined as being the amount an industry within a region consumes of other products of the region, and the question then arises whether an input-output technology matrix has any meaning within this context because a regional economy is so open. All inflows and outflows to and from the region are treated in the same way that imports and

---

2. For a detailed analysis of transportation requirements, specific information on where the inputs are produced must, of course, be taken into account.

3. For some analyses, another dimension–time–may have to be used to separate inputs. Unseasoned wood, for example, cannot be substituted for seasoned wood in certain construction projects.

4. If it is determined, however, that additional information is crucial for regional analyses, ways will certainly be found to organize the appropriate survey or census.

exports are treated at the national level. Third, most of the early regional studies used national input coefficients to approximate regional technology. This section of the chapter discusses these three points.

Technology at a County or Small-Area Level. The development of input-output coefficients for small areas has caused considerable criticism. Some analysts argue that it is too costly to assemble these data for a small area. Although numerous efforts, such as the one reported by Bonner and Fahle in *Technique for Area Planning* [7], have been made to estimate such coefficients in an inexpensive way, the studies have not been notably successful in developing accurate and less costly techniques. As indicated earlier, Miernyk and others still correctly maintain that a survey technique is the only completely reliable method of obtaining the data required for calculating regional input-output coefficients.

Openness of a Regional Economy. Another criticism of small-area studies is that the regions are too open. This refers to the fact that many of the inputs used by industries in the region may be imported, and a considerable amount of the output may be exported. For studies of a single region, the direct inputs from a particular industry are often defined to include only goods produced within the region, and products not produced within that region are lumped together into a single input entry at the bottom of the table in a row called "noncompetitive imports." Then, whenever an industry is established in the region so that goods being imported can be manufactured within the region, the direct input coefficient for the region will be altered. This variation in the input coefficients does not have to occur. If the technology coefficients are calculated using the methods employed for the present MRIO study, the coefficients will reflect the engineering technology used in the region and will not, therefore, depend upon how open or how closed the economy is.[5]

National and Regional Input-Output Coefficients. Finally, criticisms have been made of the use of national input coefficients in regional input-output tables. Differences between national and regional input-output coefficients as they were defined for use in the MRIO study can be caused by three main factors: First, the actual engineering technology may change from region to region. This certainly occurs in the production of agricultural commodities, where soil, climate, topography, and other elements can alter the inputs of fertilizer, farm machinery, electricity, water, and so on, and where differences in relative prices from region to region can cause substitution among inputs used. Second, the inputs are measured in value units, so the same physical quantity of input may be weighted by different regional prices, thus causing variations to

5. It should be noted, however, that shifts from imported to locally produced goods will alter the trade coefficients. This problem can be handled by making a straightforward change to the trade coefficient.

occur in the regional input coefficients measured in terms of dollars. Third, the regional variations in product mix can create different regional input coefficients for an industry. This is of course related to the level of industrial and regional aggregation used for the study. For the MRIO study, it was assumed that actual differences in technology were substantial in the agricultural, mining, and construction industries, and separate studies were made for each of these sectors, as reported in the next three chapters of this book. The differences in product mix were calculated for the manufacturing and service industries. These are described in the last section of this chapter.

National Estimation of Technology

An economic analyst generally must make decisions as to the type of data required for each economic research effort. The region, the industry, the year, and many other specifications will vary from one analysis to another. Particularly, it is not always clear whether an establishment or a product classification would be more appropriate as the unit of analysis for multiregional input-output studies.

In input-output studies, the assumption has generally been made that data should be assembled on a pure-product basis. Some studies, however, obviously should deal with establishments, not products, and establishments frequently produce more than one commodity; for other studies, the choice between an establishment or a product classification as the unit of analysis may not be entirely clear-cut. The study of the effects of property taxation on the location of an industry is an example of a situation in which the establishment may be the appropriate unit for the location part of the analysis and the product may be more relevant for analyzing the impact that changes in the production of the establishment have on the rest of the community. Ideally, then, the economic analyst should be able to manipulate the data from one classification to another as the need arises.

An establishment is classified into a Standard Industrial Classification (SIC) category by the Bureau of the Census (Census) according to the product comprising the largest part of its output—this product being called its primary product. Sometimes an establishment will produce one or more commodities in addition to its primary one—these being called secondary products of the establishment. The SIC categories are used to classify divisions, industries, and products in the economy. In the Census of Manufactures, all data pertaining to the manufacturing division are given. Other economic censuses cover such divisions as mining, retail and wholesale trade, agriculture, and so on. In the *Census of Manufactures, 1963,* there are 21 two-digit SIC major industry groups, 149 three-digit industry groups, and 425 four-digit industries [80, p. 6] ; in addition, there are 1,100 five-digit product classes and 10,000 seven-digit products [80, p. 8].[6]

To determine the SIC code of an establishment, the values of shipments of all seven-digit products of an establishment are aggregated and summed at the four-digit level, and the establishment is assigned the industry code represented by the product with the largest four-digit value of shipments. In some cases, however, the industry code is assigned according to the processes employed or the material used in making the product. Shifts of an establishment from one industry code to another from year to year are restrained (beginning with the 1963 census) by applying a "resistance formula." Prior to the 1963 census, shifts occurred when in one year the production of an establishment was almost evenly distributed among two or more product groups and the establishment was assigned to one product group, but in another year these percentage shares shifted slightly, and as a result, the establishment was assigned to a different product group.

Each country has its own procedure for collecting data from establishments and then in publishing them. In Japan, for example, every establishment is required to submit detailed accounts of the inputs purchased to make each of its products. The Japanese have therefore been able to assemble these data into pure-product input-output tables [56]. In Canada, a different procedure has been adopted for handling multiproduct industries. The Canadian Dominion Bureau of Statistics publishes a rectangular input-output table in which the rows designate products and the columns establishments [49]. Many techniques (at least five major ones) for treating secondary products have been described in the input-output literature.[7] The problem of joint products plagues other than just input-output economists, of course. Many economists ignore the problem, because (as with many other economic concepts) only rather rudimentary methods are available to construct the theoretical economic model so that it conforms with data in the actual world.

In the United States, a special technique has been adopted by the Office of Business Economics (OBE) for the assembly of national input-output data.[8] With this technique, two matrices are constructed. One is called a primary matrix and the other a secondary matrix. However, only the total-transactions (or flows) table is published. It is obtained by adding the primary and the secondary

6. These numbers, which were taken from the 1963 census, vary slightly from one census year to another.

7. These techniques are summarized in an unpublished article by Alan M. Strout [73] and are briefly explained in an unpublished description of the 1958 input-output table [127].

8. Functions previously performed by the Office of Business Economics were transferred in January 1972 to the Bureau of Economic Analysis (BEA) to be a part of the Social and Economic Statistics Administration of the U.S. Department of Commerce. However, for consistency with the previous volumes in this series, OBE will be used rather than BEA. For the multiregional input-output study, most of the conventions of the OBE tables were adopted.

matrices. (The matrices are available from the OBE on computer tape.) Any flow in the published table of national transactions is made up of two elements (one from the primary matrix and the other from the secondary matrix) that represent two entirely different types of transactions. The primary element, which is usually the most important component of the flow, is the amount of purchases of a given good or service required by a particular establishment to produce its primary and secondary outputs. The secondary element is the amount the industry that is supplying the input produces (as a secondary output) of the purchasing industry's output. For example, in 1963 establishments classified in IO-14, Food & kindred products, purchased $15,392 million of IO-1, Livestock & livestock products; but the total flow in the 1963 published OBE table is shown as $16,305 million—the additional $913 million represents the amount of food and kindred products produced by the livestock industry as secondary products. In other words, over 5 percent of the total is secondary production. This method of combining inputs required with goods produced as secondary products leads to a considerable amount of confusion on the part of researchers using the national tables.

In the census, inputs are given by establishments and are not separated into the inputs required to produce primary commodities and those required to produce secondary commodities. On the other hand, complete information is given in the census on the distribution of an establishment's output between its primary commodity and its secondary commodities. The basic source of information on 1963 manufacturing establishments (SIC 20–39), for example, is *Census of Manufactures, 1963,* Vol. II, *Industry Statistics* [81]. Three of the eight basic tables given in the volume are data sources for input-output tables:

1. Table 5, "Industry-Product Analysis," is in two parts and includes value of shipments of primary products, secondary transfers-in (goods of the industry produced by other industries), secondary transfers-out (goods the establishment produces as secondary products), and miscellaneous receipts of the establishment. The information for the transfers-out is frequently aggregated into a single figure. The data are given in terms of value of shipments, which differs from the value of output used in the input-output tables.[9]

2. Table 6, "Products and Product Classes—Value Shipped by All Manufacturing Establishments," gives a detailed listing of the composition and value of shipments of the primary products—generally by seven-digit SIC product code.

3. Tables 7a, "Materials by Kind," and 7b, "Fuels and Electric Energy Consumed and Horsepower Rating of Power Equipment," give details on the

---

9. The differences represent receipts for services provided to foreigners, rents and royalties received, and receipts for research and development performed by auxiliaries and central administrative offices, plus some miscellaneous items. A listing of the differences for the 1947, 1958, and 1963 manufacturing industries (IO-13 through IO-64) is provided in Appendix B of *State Estimates of Outputs, Employment, and Payrolls, 1947, 1958, 1963* [68, pp. 123–127].

inputs consumed by the establishments classified in the particular SIC code. The inputs are not, however, identified by whether they are used to produce the primary or the secondary products of the establishments.

The MRIO model depends upon the use of the national primary and secondary matrices because an accounting balance must be obtained in the base year, but the regional data are treated in a different way from the national data. Since the national primary and secondary matrices are not fully described in any of the published literature, a brief explanation of their composition and meaning is given below.

Primary-Product Matrix

This is a product-by-establishment matrix. In this matrix, the elements in each row show the total amount of a given product purchased by each establishment regardless of which establishment produced the product. The elements in each column, on the other hand, show the total amount of a particular good consumed by establishments (grouped within a particular input-output industry) to produce the total output of the establishments—their primary and secondary products. The corresponding sums of the rows and columns of this matrix will therefore generally not be equal, because, while the row sum is the total amount of a given commodity produced, whether by the primary establishment or by other establishments, the column sum is the total amount of inputs purchased by specific establishments.

Reference to primary-product data given in the appendix, Table C–10, should assist in understanding the composition of the primary matrix. In the table, which is the 1963 primary manufacturing and service industry matrix, the elements in the rows represent the purchases of 80 different products by all manufacturing and service establishments, represented by the 152 columns of the matrix. (A detailed description of the contents of the table is given in Appendix C, pp. 157–161.) Column 47, for example, shows the purchases of SIC 282 establishments, which are classified in IO-28, Plastics & synthetic materials. Row 27, on the other hand, shows the total amount of chemicals and selected chemical products purchased by each of the manufacturing and service industries in the United States.[10] The element in column 47 of that row is $1,778,212 thousand, representing the purchase of chemicals, etc., by the IO-28 establishments. It should be noted that IO-27 establishments produced $543,661 thousand of plastics and synthetic materials as a secondary product. In fact, of the total production of plastics and synthetic materials ($5,691,887 thousand),

10. Table C–10 does not contain all elements of the primary-product matrix because only the intermediate purchases of all manufacturing and some service industries are included. The complete matrix contains all value added and final demand components, as well as the primary purchases of all nonmanufacturing (and the remaining service) industries.

over 13 percent ($768,722 thousand) was produced by other establishments as a secondary product. The establishments classified in IO-28 at the same time produced $649,499 thousand that were not plastics or synthetic materials. The elements in column 47 of the primary matrix, therefore, represent the total purchases by the IO-28 establishments to produce both their primary and secondary products. Their total output of both products was $6,341,386 thousand.

The form of the primary and secondary matrices can be easily illustrated using matrix notations. The primary, secondary, and total-transactions matrices are shown in notational form in Figure 1–3. In the remainder of this chapter, the following notations will be used, where m represents the number of commodities:

p_{ij} = amount of commodity i purchased by establishment j.

$p_{oj} = \sum_{i=1}^{m} p_{ij}$ = total value of establishment output, comprising its primary and secondary production (equals total value of inputs purchased by the establishment).

$p_{io} = \sum_{j=1}^{m} p_{ij}$ = total output of commodity i produced by all establishments, regardless of whether it was produced as primary or secondary output of the establishments.

s_{ij} = total output of commodity j produced by establishment i as a secondary product of the establishment and where s_{ii} is zero by definition.

$s_{oj} = \sum_{i=1}^{m} s_{ij}$ = transfers-in, which is the total amount of commodity j produced by other establishments as secondary outputs.

$s_{io} = \sum_{j=1}^{m} s_{ij}$ = transfers-out, which is the total output of secondary products by establishment i.

x_{ij} = sum of p_{ij} and s_{ij}.

Primary-Product Matrix

$$P = \text{products}\overset{\text{establishments}}{\begin{bmatrix} p_{11} & p_{12} & \cdots & p_{1m} \\ p_{21} & p_{22} & \cdots & p_{2m} \\ \vdots & \vdots & & \vdots \\ p_{m1} & p_{m2} & \cdots & p_{mm} \end{bmatrix}}$$

$$\sum_{i=1}^{m} p_{ij} = p_{oj}$$

$$\sum_{j=1}^{m} p_{ij} = p_{io}$$

Secondary-Product Matrix

$$S = \text{establishments}\overset{\text{products}}{\begin{bmatrix} s_{11} & s_{12} & \cdots & s_{1m} \\ s_{21} & s_{22} & \cdots & s_{2m} \\ \vdots & \vdots & & \vdots \\ s_{m1} & s_{m2} & \cdots & s_{mm} \end{bmatrix}}$$

$$\sum_{i=1}^{m} s_{ij} = s_{oj} = \text{transfers-in}$$

$$\sum_{j=1}^{m} s_{ij} = s_{io} = \text{transfers-out}$$

$$s_{ii} = 0 \text{ (by definition)}$$

Total-Transactions (or Flows) Matrix

$$X = \text{establishments and products}\overset{\text{establishments and products}}{\begin{bmatrix} x_{11} & x_{12} & \cdots & x_{1m} \\ x_{21} & x_{22} & \cdots & x_{2m} \\ \vdots & \vdots & & \vdots \\ x_{m1} & x_{m2} & \cdots & x_{mm} \end{bmatrix}}$$

$$\sum_{i=1}^{m} x_{ij} = \sum_{i=1}^{m} p_{ij} + \sum_{i=1}^{m} s_{ij} = x_{oj}$$

$$\sum_{j=1}^{m} x_{ij} = \sum_{j=1}^{m} p_{ij} + \sum_{j=1}^{m} s_{ij} = x_{io}$$

Figure 1-3. Representation of the Primary, Secondary, and Total-Transactions Matrices for the United States.

$x_{oj} = \sum_{i=1}^{m} x_{ij} = \sum_{i=1}^{m} p_{ij} + \sum_{i=1}^{m} s_{ij}$ = total value of inputs purchased by establishments classified in industry j, plus the total value of commodity j that was produced by other establishments.

$x_{io} = \sum_{j=1}^{m} x_{ij} = \sum_{j=1}^{m} p_{ij} + \sum_{j=1}^{m} s_{ij}$ = total value of products of industry i consumed by intermediate and final users, plus the total value of secondary commodities produced by industry i.

The important facts to note about Figure 1-3 are: (1) The rows of the primary matrix represent unique products, and the row sum, p_{io}, is the total amount of commodity i produced. (2) The columns of the primary matrix represent total inputs required by a specific type of establishment to produce its primary and secondary products, and the column sum, p_{oj}, is the total value of inputs required by establishment j (it can be obtained only if the data are assembled in value, rather than physical, units). (3) The rows of the secondary matrix represent the total amount of secondary commodities produced by a specific type of establishment. (4) The columns of the secondary matrix represent the amounts of a unique product that are produced by establishments other than the primary ones. (It should also be noted that the diagonal of the secondary matrix is zero by definition, since any commodity of an industry i that is produced by industry i is already accounted for in the primary matrix—thus, $s_{ii} = 0$.) The elements in the rows of the primary matrix and the columns of the secondary matrix consequently all refer to a homogeneous product, while the elements in the columns of the primary matrix and the rows of the secondary matrix refer to heterogeneous products. More important, each element of the OBE total-transactions matrix represents a mixture of inputs required and secondary outputs produced. This last statement becomes clearer in the detailed description of the secondary-product and total-transactions matrices given below.

Secondary-Product Matrix

This is an establishment-by-product matrix that provides information on the value of goods produced by each of the establishments in the economy that are actually the products of another industry. It is a matrix that shows the composition of secondary-product output for each industry. The elements in row 1 of the matrix in Figure 1-3, for example, give the value of each of the secondary commodities produced by industry 1 according to the industry of which they are the primary commodity, while the elements in column 1 of the matrix give the value of commodities of industry 1 that are produced by each of the other industries. Thus, element s_{12} in Figure 1-3 represents the quantity of commodities of industry 2 that is produced by industry 1. As mentioned earlier, the diagonal elements of this matrix are zero by definition. (The element s_{22}, for example, is zero because it represents the quantity of goods of industry 2 that is produced by industry 2, which cannot therefore be secondary products of industry 2.) The row sums of the matrix, s_{io}, give the total value of secondary goods produced by each industry. In the OBE tables, these are referred to as transfers-out because they are products that are classified under other industries, and they are therefore transferred out from the industry where they are produced. The column sums, s_{oj}, specify the total amounts of a particular commodity that are produced by other than the primary-producing establishment in the economy. In the OBE tables, these are referred to as transfers-in because the values of these products are transferred into the primary industry and make up part of the input pattern of that industry. These secondary-product data can be compiled from information given in the Census of Manufactures, but it should be stressed that no information is given in the census about the amount of inputs required to produce the secondary commodities exclusively.

Transactions or Flow Matrix

To obtain a balanced national table (that is, a table in which the amount of output of an input-output industry exactly equals the amount of input), the elements of the primary matrix are added to those of the secondary matrix. This results in a total-transactions matrix. The secondary products are thus double-counted. This was the method established at the Bureau of Labor Statistics for use with the 1947 input-output table. As Evans and Hoffenberg note in an article in *The Review of Economics and Statistics,* several methods were used to distribute the secondary products in the 1947 input-output study [20]. The major method, however, was to construct a secondary matrix, which represented products amounting to \$8.4 billion (7 percent of all shipments listed in full detail in the 1947 Census of Manufactures) that could be identified definitely as secondary products. The following is quoted from their article:

> The \$8.4 billion of completely identified secondary products was transferred in the inter-industry accounts from the producing industries to the industries where the products were considered primary and distributed through this channel. In this procedure the secondary product is treated as if it were a "sale" by the industry where it is primary, with a further "sale" by the primary industry to the ultimate user. The value of such secondary products is therefore counted twice. . . . When industries are aggregated to form smaller tables, such secondary transfers as occur in the new broader industrial aggregates may be deleted from the table. [20, p. 106]

By aggregating two industries, some of the double-counting of secondary products can be eliminated. Industry 1 can be combined with industry 2, for example, and the secondary elements s_{12} and s_{21} in Figure 1-3 can be set to zero, because all of s_{12} is already accounted for in row 2 and all of s_{21} is already accounted for in row 1. When the two rows are added, therefore, the two corresponding secondary elements appear on the diagonal of the aggregated matrix and should be set to zero.[11] The aggregation of rows and columns could be continued, of course, until all double-counting of secondary products is eliminated, but aggregation destroys the industrial detail that is needed for economic policy analyses.

The percentage of output that is attributed to secondary production at the national level is shown in Table 1-1 for each of 79 input-output industries for the years 1947, 1958, and 1963. In the first three columns, the percentage of total output of an industry that was produced by other industries (referred to as transfers-in) is given for the three years. In the last three columns, the percentage represents the total amount of an industry's output that was goods or services classified under a different industry (referred to as transfers-out). Both sets of percentages vary tremendously from industry to industry. The high transfers-out percentages for IO-10, Chemical & fertilizer mineral mining, and IO-26, Printing & publishing, certainly indicate that the product classifications used for these industries may not be very useful for economic analyses. Some of the large variations from year to year, such as those for IO-13, Ordnance & accessories, may indicate either real changes in the amount of secondary production or merely variations in the data classification from one year to another.

Pure-Product Matrix

The information in the OBE primary and secondary matrices is useful, but for certain economic analyses, the inputs and outputs of an industry need to be arranged in still other forms. First, each column of the OBE flow matrix is a combination of the products each establishment purchases and the amount other industries produce of commodities of that industry. If an inverse is based upon this matrix, an increase in the final demand for, say, radios, will augment the amounts of each of the inputs purchased by the radio industry; at the same time, all the other industries now producing radios as secondary products will be assumed to increase their production of radios, yet the inputs required to produce the radios as secondary products are not augmented. This may or may not be the effect an increase in demand has on these industries in a real economy.

11. A word of caution to users of input-output tables. With this treatment of secondary products, the diagonal of the aggregated secondary matrix must always be set to zero, but it is also important to subtract the amount of these secondary products that appears on the diagonal from the gross output (or gross domestic output) of the industry. In the present example, this would be done by adding the output figures for industries 1 and 2 and subtracting the amount of the secondary product $s_{12} + s_{21}$.

Table 1–1
1947, 1958, 1963 National Transfers-in and Transfers-out As Percent of Gross Domestic Output

Input-Output Industry		*Transfers-in Percentage*[a]			*Transfers-out Percentage*[a]		
Number	*Title*	*1947*[b]	*1958*[b]	*1963*[c]	*1947*[b]	*1958*[b]	*1963*[c]
1	Livestock & livestock prdts.	–	–	–	10.0	8.6	7.5
2	Other agricultural prdts.	–	–	–	13.6	10.0	9.5
3	Forestry & fishery prdts.	57.6	19.7	18.3	0.4	0.1	0.0
4	Ag., for., & fish. services	31.1	34.9	31.0	0.2	0.4	0.4
5	Iron & ferro. ores mining	–	2.4	2.4	0.4	3.8	1.6
6	Nonferrous metal ores mining	–	1.4	0.6	1.2	2.8	3.1
7	Coal mining	–	–	0.0	1.4	0.7	0.6
8	Crude petro., natural gas	–	–	0.2	2.9	5.5	5.7
9	Stone & clay mining	–	6.8	7.1	0.7	5.1	4.6
10	Chem. & fert. mineral mining	1.3	3.1	0.8	11.4	33.1	37.1
11	New construction	–	–	–	–	–	–
12	Maint. & repair construction	–	–	–	–	–	–
13	Ordnance & accessories	–	10.9	25.0	0.1	16.8	7.1
14	Food & kindred prdts.	3.8	2.4	1.6	0.3	1.1	1.4
15	Tobacco manufactures	–	–	–	0.1	0.1	0.2
16	Fabrics	0.7	1.4	1.4	1.6	4.4	5.8
17	Textile prdts.	4.4	6.9	6.8	3.9	7.9	6.6
18	Apparel	0.1	0.4	0.4	0.3	1.1	1.4
19	Misc. textile prdts.	9.0	18.7	21.5	2.4	5.3	4.9
20	Lumber & wood prdts.	4.5	3.6	3.0	2.0	2.7	2.3
21	Wooden containers	11.1	8.1	8.5	3.0	7.2	8.3
22	Household furniture	3.7	3.7	2.5	3.8	3.8	3.5
23	Other furniture	7.9	9.6	7.0	6.4	7.0	5.3
24	Paper & allied prdts.	0.8	2.4	2.8	0.4	2.8	3.3
25	Paperboard containers	2.5	2.3	2.9	0.7	2.6	2.6
26	Printing & publishing	0.0	1.3	1.2	33.7	44.7	43.7
27	Chemicals, selected prdts.	7.7	12.5	13.2	6.0	7.6	7.8
28	Plastics & synthetics	9.6	11.0	12.3	4.1	8.3	10.4
29	Drugs & cosmetics	4.9	5.6	6.1	6.0	5.9	6.6

30	Paint & allied prdts.	3.3	3.2	3.7	5.1	6.0	6.0
31	Petroleum, related inds.	1.3	2.7	2.5	1.4	4.8	7.8
32	Rubber, misc. plastics	1.0	4.4	6.8	2.9	6.6	6.9
33	Leather tanning & prdts.	0.4	0.8	1.1	1.1	1.3	1.6
34	Footwear, leather prdts.	0.8	1.8	2.0	0.7	2.0	2.4
35	Glass & glass prdts.	2.7	1.0	1.9	0.8	1.5	2.0
36	Stone & clay prdts.	1.9	2.8	2.7	1.3	4.7	5.9
37	Primary iron, steel mfr.	1.7	1.7	1.8	2.9	5.5	5.8
38	Primary nonferrous mfr.	3.5	3.3	2.8	5.1	5.0	5.7
39	Metal containers	3.4	1.6	2.8	4.7	2.1	3.2
40	Fabricated metal prdts.	7.4	8.3	8.6	9.6	7.0	6.7
41	Screw mach. prdts., etc.	13.4	10.1	9.9	7.9	9.8	10.5
42	Other fab. metal prdts.	10.1	14.5	15.6	8.1	7.4	7.7
43	Engines & turbines	15.8	11.2	13.0	18.1	11.6	12.3
44	Farm mach. & equip.	4.8	5.2	4.4	11.1	10.0	11.3
45	Construction mach. & equip.	10.0	7.1	9.0	10.3	10.6	9.8
46	Materials hand. mach. & equip.	12.8	16.2	14.2	11.5	11.3	11.2
47	Metalworking mach. & equip.	9.1	15.1	12.5	6.9	6.1	7.4
48	Special mach. & equip.	10.4	10.2	10.1	7.8	10.3	11.2
49	General mach. & equip.	12.3	13.1	13.0	10.7	9.7	10.9
50	Machine shop prdts.	9.2	7.2	7.3	7.0	6.8	7.8
51	Office, computing machines	5.2	3.8	3.7	6.2	24.6	13.9
52	Service industry machines	6.1	13.6	18.0	13.1	11.7	10.6
53	Elect. transmission equip.	5.9	8.3	10.1	6.6	10.2	11.3
54	Household appliances	9.6	4.8	10.6	10.0	9.6	17.2
55	Electric lighting equip.	6.8	5.9	7.7	7.0	8.6	9.9
56	Radio, TV, etc., equip.	2.5	6.2	4.8	7.5	7.0	8.9
57	Electronic components	3.0	9.6	13.7	6.0	6.6	8.3
58	Misc. electrical mach.	4.9	10.2	11.9	5.9	11.1	12.4
59	Motor vehicles, equip.	1.3	1.2	1.5	1.6	3.7	2.7
60	Aircraft & parts	3.1	5.8	4.3	2.1	6.3	14.1
61	Other transport. equip.	3.8	3.3	3.2	1.3	7.4	7.3
62	Professional, scien. instru.	6.0	12.3	13.0	6.9	10.0	13.7
63	Medical, photo. equip.	2.7	5.2	5.4	4.3	7.4	8.8

(continued)

Table 1-1 (continued)

Input-Output Industry		*Transfers-in Percentage*[a]			*Transfers-out Percentage*[a]		
Number	*Title*	*1947*[b]	*1958*[b]	*1963*[c]	*1947*[b]	*1958*[b]	*1963*[c]
64	Misc. manufacturing	1.9	5.2	5.0	9.5	10.0	10.7
65	Transportation & warehousing	1.8	2.2	2.7	1.9	1.3	0.7
66	Communications, exc. brdcast.	–	–	–	0.9	4.4	4.1
67	Radio & TV broadcasting	–	–	–	97.4	98.9	96.8
68	Elec., gas, water, & san. serv.	20.6	15.2	15.3	0.7	0.3	0.4
69	Wholesale & retail trade	0.8	3.2	3.5	1.0	0.9	0.9
70	Finance & insurance	–	0.2	0.3	2.4	2.9	3.1
71	Real estate & rental	14.0	10.8	9.9	–	–	–
72	Hotels; repair serv., exc. auto	–	–	–	3.8	3.1	2.6
73	Business services	31.1	32.7	29.0	0.3	2.3	1.9
74	Research & development	–	–	–	–	–	–
75	Automobile repair & services	–	0.3	1.4	0.5	0.9	0.9
76	Amusements	–	–	0.2	2.1	2.3	3.1
77	Med., ed. serv., nonprof. org.	–	–	–	1.4	0.1	0.2
78	Federal gov't enterprises	–	–	–	9.3	23.4	20.7
79	State & local gov't enterp.	–	–	–	92.7	84.5	83.1
	National weighted average	3.9	4.7	3.0	3.9	4.7	3.0

[a]To obtain consistency, the secondary matrices for the three years were adjusted by removing all entries in columns 74, 81, 82, and 83. (There are no entries in the rows.)

[b]1958 constant dollars.

[c]1963 current dollars. Intermediate demand deflators were not available in the summer of 1973 to deflate the primary and secondary matrices.

Sources: 1947 [121], 1958 [127], 1963 [128].

An immediate answer appears to be to construct a single matrix in which all the rows and columns represent products rather than establishments. This has been referred to in the literature as a pure-product matrix. In this matrix, the column for the radio industry will contain the total purchases of inputs required to produce all radios regardless of whether they are produced by the primary or the secondary establishment. Each row of the matrix will give the total distribution of radios to intermediate and final users. There is no mixture, in such a matrix, of establishments and products.

Several methods have been adopted to transform the data as published by the OBE into pure-product form. A theoretical article on the subject, "A Treatment of Multiple-Process Industries," was written by J. Harvey Edmonston and published in the November 1952 issue of the *Quarterly Journal of Economics* [18]. A major effort in implementing a similar procedure for use with the 1958 national input-output data was undertaken at the National Planning Association and resulted in the publication of a report entitled "Secondary Product Adjustment with Redistribution (SPAR)," written by Lou P. Koenig and Philip M. Ritz in April 1967 [42]. Other comments on the subject have been written by Chenery and Clark [13], W. van Rijcheghem [66], T. Gigantes [38], and C. Almon [2]. At the University of Maryland, Clopper Almon has employed a pure-product technique for a number of years in the input-output tables that he uses to make forecasts of the American economy.

Anne P. Carter, while at the Harvard Economic Research Project, tested alternative methods of obtaining a pure-product matrix, including the use of Leontief's special aggregation scheme [44]. None of her tests have been described in writing, but one of her research assistants, Frans Kok, made use of a partial pure-product method in a study of paper recycling. His tests led him to the finding that the purchases of pulp by the paper industry were grossly underestimated in the 1963 input-output tables [123]. The Kok analysis indicates that this partial technique could be used industry by industry with the 1963 national 370-order input-output data to identify cells that are not correctly specified. The difficulties are (1) that the 370-order 1963 data must be used, making the computations cumbersome; and (2) that his analysis of the paper industry was relatively simple compared with analyses of other industries, partly because of the concentration of secondary production within the industry. While all of the seven pulp, paper, and paper-converting industries make secondary products, over 97 percent of their output is produced by the seven industries, leaving only 3 percent to be produced by nonpaper industries as secondary products. For other commodities, where the secondary-product output is more dispersed, the analysis would become more difficult.

All of the pure-product methods used with the U.S. data are mechanical means of attempting to transform data that combine primary and secondary products into a matrix in which rows and columns both refer to an individual product or product group. They have, for the most part, been used with national input-output tables. Implementation of the methods requires a considerable amount of intuitive judgment in adjusting the results to maintain plausibility of the input coefficients. One of the major difficulties with most of the methods is the occurrence of negative inputs.

At the regional level, the problem of secondary products appears to have been completely ignored in many studies. Two of the earliest published regional input-output articles for the United States were on the Utah [57] and the St. Louis [39] regions. The problem is not mentioned in either article. For the present MRIO study, the pure-product method was considered too cumbersome, and regional secondary-product data were not readily available. All of the technology data assembled for the MRIO study (as described in this volume) were therefore reconciled with the OBE 1963 national primary-product matrix. The regional secondary products were then estimated and used in a different way from any tried before.[12]

Regional Estimation of Secondary Products

A special technique was developed for estimating the secondary products for the multiregional input-output tables. As explained in the previous section, secondary products are double-counted in the national input-output tables to obtain a balance between total inputs and outputs. This double-counting is accomplished at the national level by estimating a transfer (secondary) matrix. For the multiregional study, the columns of the regional input-output table were first assembled on an establishment basis. The inputs purchased by a particular industry, therefore, consisted of the amounts required to produce its primary and secondary outputs. Secondary products were also double-counted in the state input-output tables to obtain an accounting balance, but with only a single column of transfers-out and a single row of transfers-in being added to each input-output table as an exogenous column and row, respectively. The procedure used for estimating the secondary products for the state input-output tables is described here.

Three sets of data were required to calculate state secondary matrices: the national primary matrix, the national secondary matrix, and the state outputs. The national data were obtained from OBE computer tapes [128]. The 1963 state establishment outputs (revised) are given in Table D-3 in the appendix. A basic assumption was made that the amount an industry produces of another industry's output (referred to in the input-output table as transfers-out) as a

12. The accounting of secondary products in the interregional trade tables in the general MRIO model is described in the sixth volume of this series [62]. The description that is included in this chapter, therefore, concerns only the inclusion of secondary products in the regional input-output tables.

proportion of its total output remains constant from one state to another. For the step-by-step procedure, the following abbreviations will be used:

EO = establishment output

TRI = transfers-in = amount of an industry's output that is produced by other industries

TRO = transfers-out = amount that an industry produces of another industry's product

N = national

S = state

Step 1. Calculate the national ratio of transfers-out to the establishment output for each industry: NTRO/NEO,[13] shown in Figure 1-4.

Step 2. Apply this national ratio for each industry to the state establishment outputs (SEO) of the respective industry to estimate the state transfers-out (STRO), shown in Figure 1-5.

Step 3. Calculate row coefficients for the national secondary matrix and multiply the column of state transfers-out (STRO) for each state by the coefficients to obtain state secondary matrices. Sum the columns of each state secondary matrix to obtain state transfers-in (STRI), shown in Figure 1-6.

Step 4. Insert the calculated STRO (columns), obtained from Step 2, and the STRI (rows), obtained from Step 3, into the state input-output tables (refer to Figure 1-7, page 29).

The advantage of adding a single row and column of secondary products as exogenous components of each regional input-output table over alternative procedures is three-fold.[14] First, the estimated input requirements for each region are not obscured by adding on elements from the transfer matrix. Although the primary and secondary matrices are added element by element in the national table, this is entirely an accounting device to assure a balanced table.

13. Note that before this ratio is calculated, the national secondary and national primary matrices must be adjusted to the MRIO industry definitions. The adjustments required are given in Appendix C.

14. There are at least two alternative ways in which secondary products could have been handled. First, the transfer row and column could have been placed as part of the interindustry flow portion of each regional table and a column of coefficients calculated by dividing each flow in the column by the column sum. Second, an entire transfer matrix could have been used for each region, and the technical coefficients could have been calculated for the primary plus the secondary matrices. The advantage of these two methods is that the transfers are assumed to remain constant from year to year, and no special projections of the transfers are required.

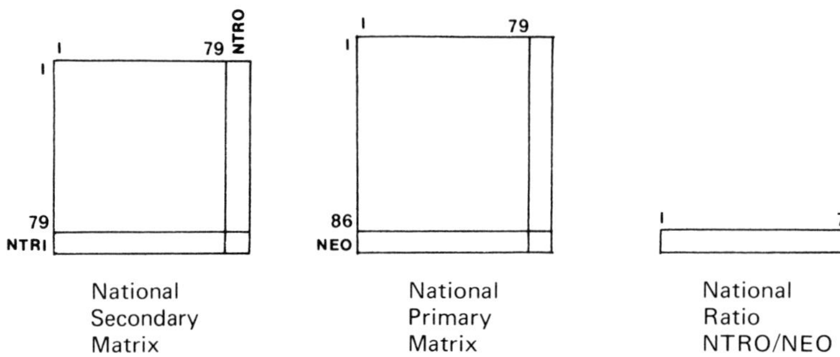

Figure 1-4. Calculation of NTRO/NEO.

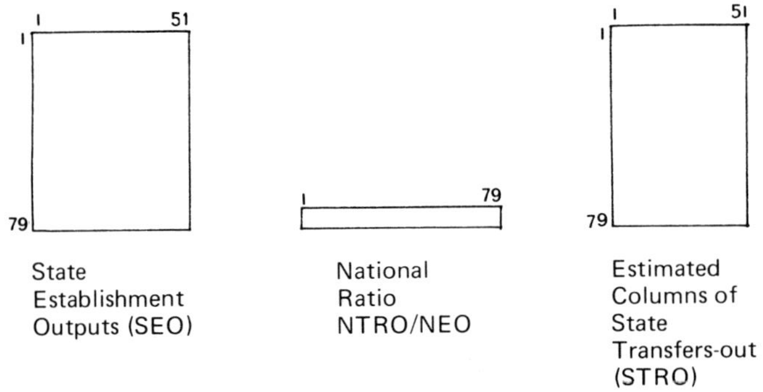

Figure 1-5. Calculation of State Transfers-out.

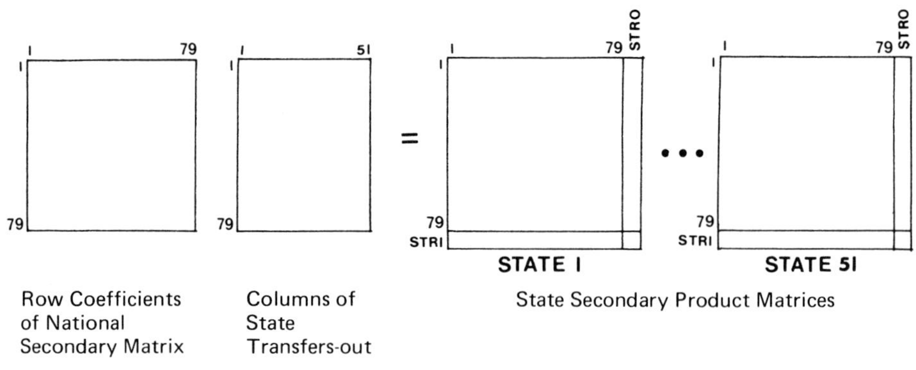

Figure 1-6. Calculation of State Secondary-Product Matrices.

Second, the production of secondary products by establishments may change significantly over time, and this method permits the researcher to alter the secondary product figures without recalculating the inverse matrix. Third, when industries are aggregated, some of the double-counting can be reduced. In the regional input-output tables constructed for this study, alterations to the tables

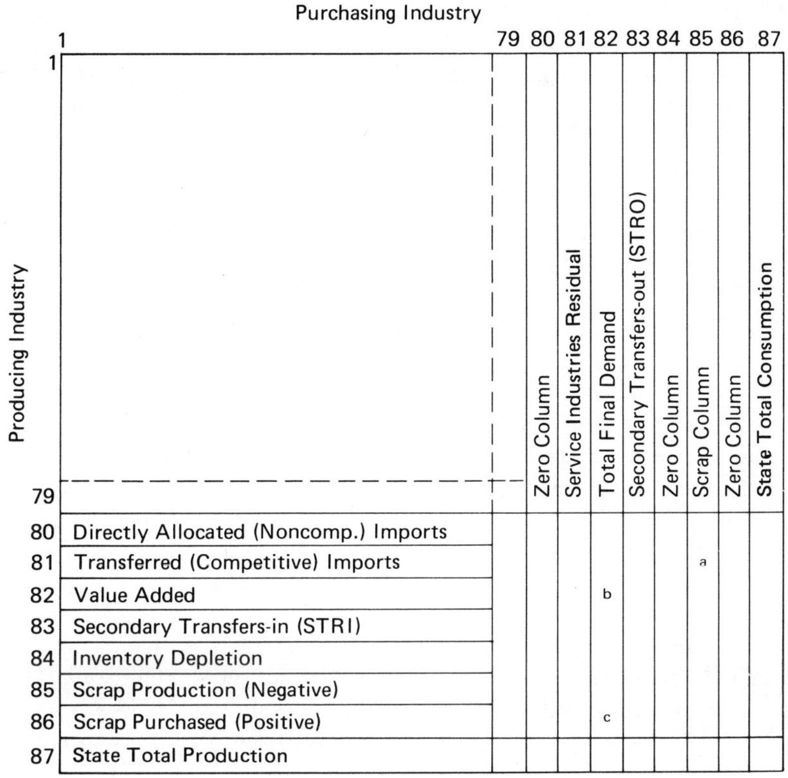

[a]Competitive import of scrap.

[b]Commodity Credit Corporation adjustment figure and rows 84–86 of OBE final demand.

[c]Final demand for scrap.

Figure 1–7. State Input-Output Table.

that result from the reduction of the double-counting are isolated in the secondary row and column of each table. This makes it considerably easier to pinpoint any changes in the table that occur for other reasons.

Procedures Used to Estimate State Technologies

The general organization of the state input-output tables is illustrated in Figure 1-7. For the agricultural (IO-1 and IO-2), mining (IO-5 through IO-10), and new construction (IO-11) sectors, state-by-state data were assembled, as described in Chapters 2, 3, and 4, respectively. All manufacturing industries and some service industries were specially estimated. Separate calculations were then made for all industries to estimate the imports, value added, secondary products, inventory depletions, scrap production, scrap purchases, service industries residual, and total final demand. Although the secondary-product calculations have already been explained, the methods used to make the remainder of the estimates are described here.

Manufacturing and Services

For all manufacturing and for some service industries, a very detailed product-mix approach was used to determine state-by-state input requirements. The national coefficients had to be used for the remaining service industries because of data and time constraints. The basic assumption was made that the input requirements per unit of output remain constant from state to state. This seems to be a reasonable assumption because the data were assembled for industries at the three- and four-digit Standard Industrial Classification (SIC) level of detail. To obtain state inputs, the national direct primary input coefficients for the manufacturing and service industries were therefore weighted by the state establishment outputs, and the industries within each state were aggregated to the 80-order input-output classification. In this way, the resulting regional input requirements for a given industry varied from state to state, reflecting regional variations in the composition of goods produced within the different states.

For 1963, national input flows were available from the 370-order primary input-output table distributed by the OBE [128] and are given in Table C–10 in the appendix. The state outputs for the three- and four-digit SIC industries were obtained from special material prepared at Jack Faucett Associates [21] and are given in Table C–11 in the appendix. These data were assembled under a subcontract with the Harvard Economic Research Project in 1968–69 and were originally used to estimate the 80-order set of state outputs described in *State Estimates of Outputs, Employment, and Payrolls, 1947, 1958, 1963* [68]. Corrections were made to those outputs, and the three corrected output tables are given in the appendix, Tables D–1, D–2, and D–3. For the manufacturing and service industries, the SIC and input-output industry classifications mapped onto each other at the 152-industry level. These 152 industries, together with the SIC and input-output industries within each, are listed in Table A–2 in the appendix.

The step-by-step procedure used to obtain the variations in the state input coefficients is shown in Figure 1–8. Each of the vectors of direct input coefficients, a_{ij}^{n}, from the 370-order 1963 national primary input-output table was weighted by the amount of that output produced in a given state, x_j^h, to obtain vectors of state flows, x_{ij}^h, for each state h ($h = 1, 2, \ldots, 51$). The state flow vectors were then summed to the appropriate 66 manufacturing and service industries given in the OBE 80-order 1963 input-output table. (This step is shown by the arrows in the flow diagram.) When the 80-order flows for each state were

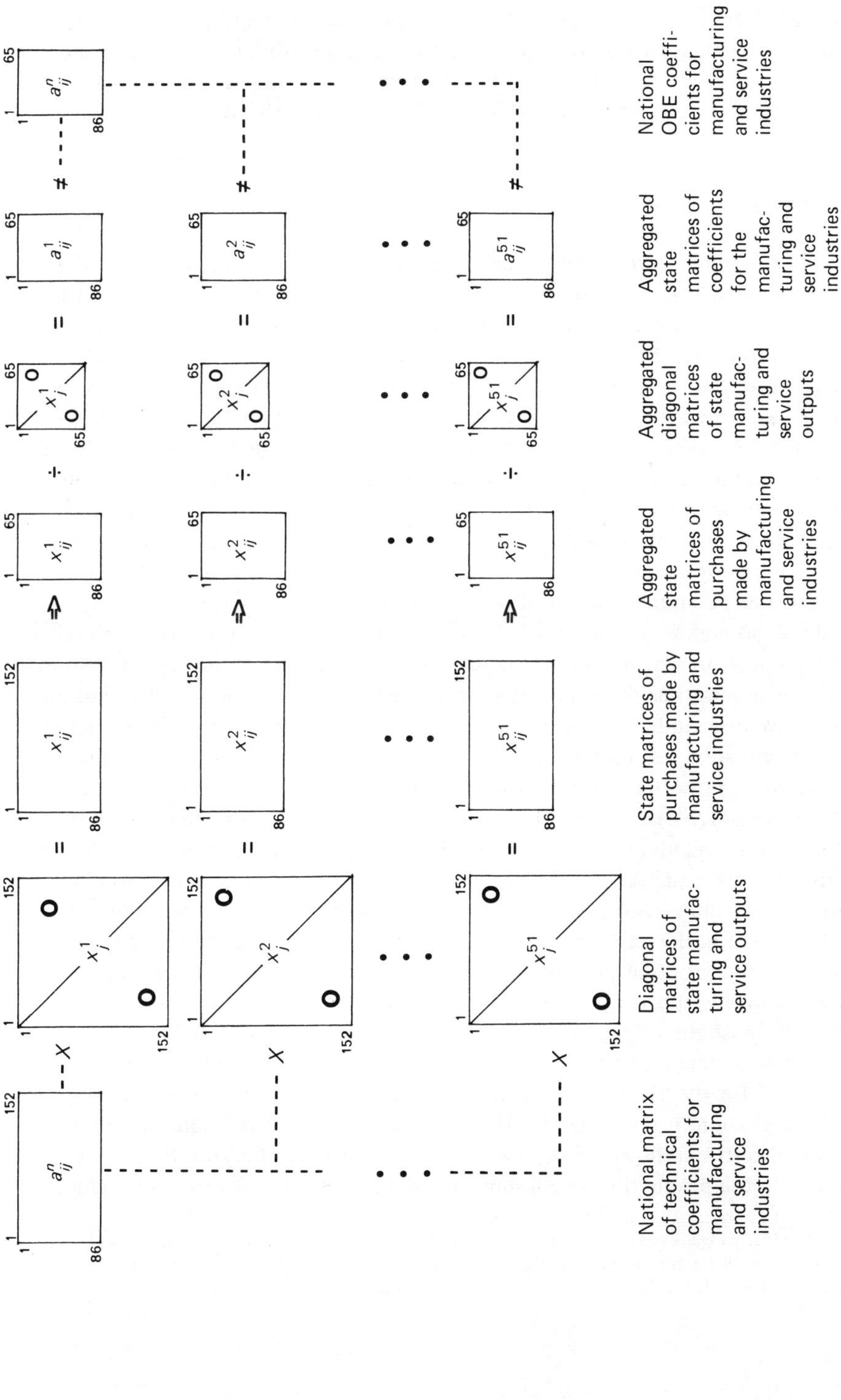

Figure 1–8. Product-Mix Variation in Manufacturing and Service Industries.

divided by the respective 80-order state outputs, the input coefficients for each state, a_{ij}^h, were obtained. These differed from one another and from the national input coefficients because the mix of industries varies from state to state, and the variation in industry mix is taken into account by using the disaggregated state output weights with the detailed national input coefficients.

Foreign Exports and Imports

The original set of interregional trade flows prepared at Jack Faucett Associates (refer to Volume V [67] of this series) represented the total actual shipments of each commodity. Therefore, the original data included shipments of exports designated for foreign countries from the region in which they were produced to the region from which they were exported, as well as shipments of directly allocated (noncompetitive) foreign imports. Shipments of transferred (competitive) foreign imports from their port-of-entry regions to the regions of final consumption were added on to the original data by distributing the transferred imports to regions in proportion to the domestically produced goods.[15]

The regional input-output tables were arranged so as to be consistent with this handling of exports and imports. In each regional input-output table, one row (row 80) contains directly allocated imports that were consumed in a particular region, and one row (row 81) contains transferred imports that entered through ports in that region. The column totals of the table should then sum to the same amounts as the appropriate row sums of the trade-flow tables, and both totals should include directly allocated and transferred imports. Each element in the directly allocated import row represents a heterogeneous mix of products consisting of imported goods and services for which there are no domestic substitutes purchased by an industry. For the assembly of the MRIO data, these imports were calculated with other purchases of goods and services. The elements in the row therefore represent a mix of imported products at the location in which they were consumed, rather than at the port of entry. On the other hand, each element in the transferred import row of the MRIO tables represents a homogeneous group of products consisting of imported goods or services for which domestic substitutes exist. These imports were allocated to the port of entry. Because the original transferred import estimates assembled at Jack Faucett Associates were for only 44 regions, these data had to be separated into 51 regions for the 1973 set of calculations. All imports shown in the final-demand portion of the table are classified as directly allocated imports and were allocated to the state where they were finally consumed. Because they do not enter into the production or consumption data for the industries, interregional

15. In this book, exports and imports always refer to shipments of goods to and from foreign countries, while shipments from one region to another within the United States are called outflows and inflows.

shipments of products were not estimated. (Most of these imports are personal consumption items.)

When the model was first implemented, in 1970, data on transferred imports by port of entry were available for only primary and manufactured commodities. For the service industries (IO-65, Transportation & warehousing, IO-69, Wholesale & retail trade, and IO-70, Finance & insurance) for which the national input-output table contained transferred imports, allocation of the national figures to the regions was made in proportion to the regional consumption of those services. Since that time, special estimates have been made for certain transferred imports of services, and these data are now included in each state input-output table. The estimates were made as follows.

1. *Column 65, transportation ($1,017.4 million).* The competitive import of transportation (IO-65) was separated according to the nature of the imported item being transported by international carriers. Of the $1,017.4 million of transportation services imported in 1963, $240.8 million was for the shipment of noncompetitive imports, $703.6 million was for the shipment of competitive imports by foreign carriers, and $73.0 million was for passenger travel on foreign carriers.

The transportation of noncompetitive imports by foreign carriers was allocated to regions according to the state totals for noncompetitive imports (the sum of row 80 in each state input-output table). This allocates imports of transportation of noncompetitive imports to the state where the import is consumed.

Imports of transportation of competitive imports were allocated to the states according to the transportation margins on these competitive imports in each state. The margins on competitive imports represent a demand for an input of a transportation service, which is thus partially filled by the transportation of imports on foreign carriers. The competitive imports of passenger service were excluded from the allocation and were distributed to the states according to the estimated state consumption of IO-81, Business travel, entertainment, & gifts.

2. *Column 68, gas and electricity ($105.2 million).* The competitive imports of gas and electricity were separated into two parts. The gas imports ($98.2 million) were allocated according to figures from the *Minerals Yearbook, 1963* [138, pp. 347–348] on gas imports by state. The electricity portion ($7.0 million) was distributed to the states according to information on the initial import by transfer points from unpublished statistics of the Federal Power Commission [29].

3. *Column 70, finance and insurance ($15.0 million).* For these imports, no state information could be found because such transactions take place by phone or mail, and the importing state could not be pinpointed. These imports were therefore allocated to all states according to their total consumption of IO-70, Finance & insurance.

In addition, the margins on transferred imports, which were not estimated for the earlier implementation of the model, have been estimated by applying the national margins [130] to the state values of transferred imports for the respective industries. When competitive imports are treated as a positive row, the values of any transportation, wholesaling and retailing, or financing of these imports by domestic firms are allocated to the respective domestic industry (IO-65, IO-69, or IO-70) and are therefore excluded from the value of the import given in the import row. Since these figures represent activities by these service industries, when this allocation has been made, the row and column sums of the interindustry-flow portion of the matrix equal total gross output, rather than gross domestic output.

For scrap, the national figures were distributed to states according to total transferred imports into each state (place of entry into the country). Although scrap imports may belong to relatively few of the import groups, no data were available to allocate these imports using a different criterion. (Most of the scrap imports were previously exported. In 1963, of the total $335.7 million of scrap imports, only $39.0 million represents goods that had not been previously exported.)

The accounting of foreign exports was straightforward. The final-demand column in each state input-output table includes exports by state of exit. This inclusion in final demand of all goods that are shipped abroad from a region means that the total consumption figures for that region are consistent with the shipments into the region shown in the trade flows.[16]

Value Added

The value added elements were calculated as a residual. For each industry, the sum of the inputs of goods and services was subtracted from the total establishment output figure, and the difference was entered in the value added row (row 82) in the state input-output table. The difference in most cases was positive; however, for a few of the states, the difference for the agricultural, mining, or construction industries was negative. The negative figure was eliminated by inserting a value added figure equal to 5 percent of the total establishment figure and reducing the value of the other elements in the particular technology column to make the total still agree with the establishment output value.

In future studies, separate estimates should be made of value added, and special procedures should be developed for adjusting the technology columns when the sums of the input estimates differ from the output totals. Such a

16. Note that the export component of the 1947 and 1958 state final demands is given only for exports by state of production. For 1963, export figures were provided both for exports by state of production and by state of exit. To use the MRIO model for backcasting to 1947 and 1958, a special estimate was made for exports by state of exit: the 1947 and 1958 national export figures were distributed to the regions using the 1963 regional distribution of exports by state of exit. For 1970 and 1980, exports were assembled by state of exit, and no adjustments were required.

detailed study, however, would have required considerably more time and money than were available for the present project.

Inventory Depletions

To balance the data in the interregional trade matrices with those in the state input-output tables, the inventory depletion component of net inventory change had to be estimated, subtracted from the final demands, and added as a row of positive numbers in the value added portion of each state input-output table. This adjustment was required to account for all shipments of a given commodity, regardless of the year in which it was produced.

In the national input-output table, inventory depletions and inventory additions are not given separately. Only a net inventory change figure is published, and even unpublished worksheet information apparently is not available for the two components. Because of this lack of data, the negative inventory elements from the 370-order 1963 national input-output table [123] were aggregated to the 80-order level. The values were distributed to states in proportion to total state commodity output for the industry. (Commodity output equals establishment output minus STRO plus STRI.) The state estimates were placed as positive elements in the inventory depletion row of each respective state input-output table and were subtracted from the respective elements in the total final demand column. (Refer to row 84 in Figure 1-7.)

IO-83, Scrap, Used, & Secondhand Goods

The figures in the columns of the national input-output table are the purchases made by each particular industry, but each number in the scrap column gives the amount of scrap *produced* by the various industries. To use the national matrix for economic impact analyses, the entries in the column are often set equal to zero, and the value of the entries is added to the intraindustry values (the diagonal elements). This procedure prevents an industry's demand for scrap from generating additional industry output. This method of handling scrap, however, combines extremely dissimilar purchases within the intraindustry flows and alters the balance between the row and column sums of the matrix unless the scrap values are also added as a negative row in the table to exactly offset the entries added to the diagonal. The state estimates of scrap consumption and production were made by allocating the national figures to the states on the basis of the Jack Faucett Associates establishment outputs [68].

For the implementation of the MRIO model, an accounting convention slightly different from the national one was introduced to handle the state production and consumption of scrap. The positive elements in the scrap column were simply transferred and became negative elements in a row, given as row 85 in Figure 1-7. In the national control matrix, both the column and row totals for each respective scrap-producing industry are less than the corresponding totals in the published national input-output table by the amount of scrap the industry produces. By using this method, however, scrap production can be estimated in a separate calculation under the assumption that the ratio of scrap produced to total production of an industry remains unchanged over time; or the ratio can be altered to reflect changes that are known to have occurred. Scrap purchases were included as row 86 in the regional input-output tables.

When scrap production is treated as a negative set of figures in the state input-output tables, the control totals used for the adjustment of the interregional trade matrices do not include figures for the amount of scrap the industry produced and shipped. This seems to be an acceptable procedure, but a separate interregional trade matrix should be constructed for the shipment of scrap. An attempt was made to estimate this matrix for the present series of MRIO calculations, but sufficient data could not be found to complete the estimates.

Service Industries Residual

Interregional trade flows were assembled for the agricultural, mining, and manufacturing products. Since there were no interregional trade data for the service industries, it was assumed that services were not traded—that all services produced in a particular state were consumed in the same state. In the state input-output tables, however, the production did not equal the consumption of services, partly because of errors in the estimation of inputs to services within each state. These estimation errors resulted from the general lack of data on services. Some of the differences, however, are attributable to the fact that services are traded a certain extent from state to state; therefore, the assumption is not completely valid.

To balance the figures for the production and consumption of services within each state input-output table, an extra column of numbers, shown as column 81 in Figure 1-7, was added to each table.[17] The column is referred to as the service industries residual (SIR) in the remainder of the book. It was obtained by subtracting total consumption of each service industry (row sum) from total production of that industry (column sum) to obtain the net outflow of services from the state. For the MRIO calculations, this residual column is added to the final demands.

17. The column had entries for IO-3, IO-4, IO-11, IO-12, and IO-65 through IO-79. IO-3, Forestry & fishery products, is not a service industry, but, since its trade-flow matrix has no off-diagonal elements (no shipments outside the region of production), the industry is classified with the service industries as having no interregional trade flows. (Column 81 should be calculated only after the final demand and secondary products columns have been placed in each state input-output table.)

Total Final Demands

The six components of final demands were added to obtain total final demand for each state. (The final demand estimates are described in detail in *State Estimates of the Gross National Product, 1947, 1958, 1963* [63].) As mentioned earlier, under inventory depletions, the net inventory change component of final demand was changed to represent only inventory additions because the inventory depletion values were inserted as row 84 in the state tables. The Commodity Credit Corporation figures were removed from the IO-78 column in the national input-output table, distributed to states, and the state estimates added to the total final demand state figures.

Conclusion

As is evident from the preceding discussion, opinions vary widely among economists on how regional technologies should be defined. Methods for assembling regional technology data other than those used in the present study should be considered and tested. The following three chapters describe the details of the procedures that were employed to assemble state-by-state data for agriculture, mining, and new construction for the MRIO model. The research that was done to obtain those data indicates that, for some industries, statistical sources are available to determine inputs on a region-by-region basis; but even for those industries the information is frequently incomplete. For certain industries, especially some of the service industries, regional data are extremely difficult to obtain. Additional research must be undertaken to determine alternative methods of separating inputs used for primary production from those used for secondary production; to ascertain the exact composition of some of the inputs of all goods and services; to find data sources for assembling comparable information for all industries at the regional level on inputs of primary factors of production and on scrap purchases, scrap production, and inventory depletions; and to develop better sources of data on the amount of imported inputs required by each industry in each region. Another important area of research is to determine ways of overcoming the lack of comparability between the data used to assemble the state technology estimates and those used to construct the interregional shipments tables. All the technology data assembled for this study should therefore be considered as initial estimates subject to revision as new data sources are discovered and as improvements are made to the methods utilized to assemble the statistics.

2 Agricultural Technologies

Carolyn W. Anderson

Any attempt to construct technical coefficients at a regional level for the United States is hampered by lack of suitable data. Ideally, data would be for the particular year and for each of the regions under study and would give input detail by the producing and consuming industries at the given level of industrial aggregation. Since these requirements are rarely met by any one set of statistics, value judgments must be made as to the appropriateness of the available data relative to the study being undertaken, before determining which data will be used. Once a choice has been made, an additional decision is required as to how the figures selected are to be combined to achieve the desired final result. Underlying these decisions are certain basic assumptions as to the nature of regional technical coefficients and their behavior over time.

For this study, a set of criteria was established that prescribes methods for using available data to obtain input coefficients for the agricultural subindustries. Two major assumptions were made: (1) that regional input patterns differ from the national average, that is, the technology for producing a particular commodity varies from region to region; and (2) that technical coefficients for agriculture are relatively more constant over time than over geographic area. Given these assumptions, certain criteria were established that could be used to select from the available sets of data according to how recent (how close to the year under study) they are, how much regional detail is given, and so on. The data selected were then combined in such a way as to preserve the most valuable aspects of each set of data used—that is, the most valuable for the present purpose. The development of these criteria, and the value judgments involved, are discussed in the following section, with specific reference to the estimation of 1963 state technical coefficients for agriculture.

General Methodology

State estimates of inputs to agriculture were made for the ten agricultural subindustries for which data are given in the 370-order 1963 input-output (IO) table published by the Office of Business Economics (OBE) [123]. These ten agricultural subindustries are listed, together with the commodities produced, in Table 2-1. After all figures had been obtained at the subindustry level, they

Table 2-1
Classification of the Ten Agricultural Subindustries According to Commodities Produced

Industry Number	*Subindustry Title*	*Commodities Produced*
1.01	Dairy farm products	Milk, butter, butterfat Manure
1.02	Poultry & eggs	Chickens, turkeys and broilers Eggs and turkey-hatching eggs Other poultry and products Manure
1.03	Meat animals & miscellaneous livestock products	Cattle and calves Hogs Sheep and lambs Wool Goats Mohair Manure Horses and mules Animal work power Honey Package bees Beeswax Miscellaneous animals (rabbits, fur-bearing animals, dogs, etc.)
2.01	Cotton	Cotton Cottonseed
2.02	Food [grains], feed grains, & grass seed	Wheat Rye Rice Buckwheat Corn Hay Pasture

		Oats
		Barley
		Sorghum grain
		Silage
		Cowpeas
		Hayseeds
		Pasture seeds
		Cover-crop seeds
2.03	Tobacco	Tobacco
		Seeds and plants
2.04	Fruits & tree nuts	Citrus fruits
		Noncitrus fruits
		Melons
		Berries
		Other fruits and nuts
		Almonds
		Filberts
		Pecans
		Walnuts
2.05	Vegetables, sugar, & miscellaneous crops	Dry edible beans
		Dry edible peas
		Potatoes
		Sweet potatoes
		Truck crops
		Mung beans
		Sugar beets
		Sugar cane and sirup
		Maple sugar and sirup
		Sorgo sirup
		Hops
		Spearmint and peppermint
		Broomcorn
		Popcorn
		Velvet beans
		Other miscellaneous crops (includes other seeds, flax and hemp fiber, etc.)

(continued)

Table 2-1 (continued)

Industry Number	*Subindustry Title*	*Commodities Produced*
2.06	Oil-bearing crops	Soybeans
		Peanuts
		Flaxseed
		Tung nuts
		Copra (imported)
		Other oil seeds
		Castor beans
2.07	Forest, greenhouse, & nursery products	Stumpage
		Pulpwood
		Gum naval stores
		Fuelwood
		Christmas trees
		Fence posts and other lumber products
		Greenhouse and nursery products

were aggregated to represent inputs to IO-1, Livestock & livestock products, and IO-2, Other agricultural products.

There were two reasons for working with ten instead of only two agricultural industries: (1) many of the state data used, either directly or as allocation factors, are given in greater detail than just for livestock and crops; and (2) since the detailed 1963 national input-output table gives control totals for ten agricultural subindustries, the necessary consistency with national input-output figures can be maintained while taking advantage of available detail in state data. By working with ten subindustries whenever feasible, actual state-to-state differences in technology which might not have been revealed at the two-industry level were pinpointed.

The ideal data for this study would meet the following four requirements:

1. They would be for the year 1963.
2. They would be for each state.
3. They would be for the specific 370-order input-output industry that produces the input.
4. They would be for the specific agricultural subindustry that consumes the input.

Given several sets of data, each of which meets one or more but not all of the above requirements, the "best" set had to be determined. For example, two sets may be available on farmers' purchases of hardware supplies:

(a) Total expenditures for hardware supplies by state in 1963.

(b) Purchases of each component input in the hardware supply category in eight regions of the United States for 1955.

Data set (a) meets the first and second requirements (it is for 1963 and is for each state), but it does not meet the third and fourth requirements (it gives no input detail and is for agriculture as a whole). Data set (b), on the other hand, fulfills the third requirement (the 370-order input-output industries that produce the inputs can be determined), but it is for the year 1955, at the regional level, and for agriculture as a whole. Although data set (b) provides valuable information, for this study the fact that data set (a) is for 1963 and is also by state is more important. Thus, the figures in data set (b) were used to separate control totals from data set (a) into their component parts. Regional figures as percentages of their sum in 1955 were used to distribute 1963 state totals.

Two things should be noted about the case just discussed. First, neither set of data meets the requirement that the consuming agricultural subindustry be identifiable. Therefore, a third set which meets at least this fourth requirement had to be introduced to obtain final data in the desired form. Second, no account is taken of changes in the kinds of commodities produced and/or variations in the level of output of these commodities that have occurred over the period 1955 to 1963, nor of state-to-state differences in production patterns and/or variations in output levels that might occur within a given region.

The regional expenditues figures for 1955, however, can be expressed in terms of some other data that are available both by region in 1955 and by state in 1963. Such a set of data will be called an intermediate data set. It is introduced to convert a highly aggregated set of figures to a more detailed level without distorting the "good" aspects of the original data. The data in this intermediate set, however, may not be directly related to the input being estimated, although the closer the correlation the more accurate the final estimates.

Output data are available for every year, for every state, and for every agricultural commodity. They can be expressed in uniform units. For example, although output of wheat is measured in bushels, output of milk in gallons, and output of cotton in bales, each can be expressed in terms of 1000-lb. units, and thus be made comparable. In addition, inputs are often correlated with levels and kinds of output. Output data, then, successfully fulfill the requirement of an intermediate data set. In the example given of two sets of data on farmers' purchases of hardware supplies, 1955 regional expenditures on individual hardware supplies can be expressed per unit of each region's output in 1955. These coefficients can then be multiplied by 1963 state output data to obtain a matrix of estimated 1963 expenditures for individual hardware supplies by state. This matrix is constructed under the assumption that expenditures on individual hardware supplies per unit of output are constant from 1955 to 1963 and for each state within a given region. To separate 1963 state totals for hardware supply expenditures into purchases of each component input, a percentage distribution of the estimated 1963 expenditures matrix can be used. This method accounts for changes in output levels over time as well as for differences in output levels of states within a region.

In another case, data may be available on purchases of veterinary services for cattle in 1963 at the national level. These figures can be expressed in terms of expenditures per cow and then allocated to the states according to the number of cows in each state in 1963. If, however, additional data provide figures on 1960 state expenditures on veterinary services for cattle, the state expenditures figure can be divided by the number of cows in each state in 1960 to obtain coefficients showing 1960 expenditures for veterinary services per cow in each state. These coefficients can be multiplied by the number of cows in the corresponding states in 1963 to obtain a matrix of figures that can then be used as an allocation series to distribute to the states the 1963 national total for veterinary services purchased for cattle.

The above examples should serve to clarify the ways in which basic criteria were developed to aid in deciding whether given sets of data were to be used as control totals or as allocation factors. The data were combined in many alternative ways to meet the four requirements specified. The following criteria were established to form the basis for choosing both the data sets to be used and the methods in which the chosen data sets were to be combined for this study:

Criterion 1. 1963 data are "better" than data from other years, because all results must be made consistent with available 1963 figures.

Criterion 2. State data are "better" than regional data, subject to constraint (1) above. Thus, 1963 regional data can be allocated to the states using 1959 state figures as allocation factors, but the 1963 regional totals must be preserved.

Criterion 3. Data on specific inputs (both by producing and consuming input-output industries) are "better" than more aggregated data, subject to constraints (1) and (2) above. For example, 1955 data on specific inputs can be used to separate 1963 aggregate expenditures figures into their components, provided the results add to 1963 totals. In another case, detailed data by region can be used to disaggregate state expenditures totals for the same year, but if differences occur, the state totals must be preserved.

Criterion 4. Input data for any year and at any level of detail (regional, producing industry, consuming industry) are "better" than any intermediate set of data that might be introduced, even though the intermediate data are for a year closer to 1963 or at a higher level of disaggregation.

Criterion 1 ensured that all final estimates were consistent with available 1963 data, or at least with the most recent (closest to 1963) data available; criterion 2 ensured that the statistics used for any given year provided greater regional detail than other available data for the same year. These regional figures, however, were not used as controls unless they were the most recent (closest to 1963) available. Criterion 3 ensured that methods used to estimate any individual input took advantage of the most highly disaggregated data available. At the same time, checks were made to assure that the most recent figures were being used as controls and gave all of the relevant regional detail available for that year. And Criterion 4 ensured that any available information on actual regional differences in input patterns, regardless of the year in which the data were collected, was incorporated into the final estimates. As has been said, the assumption was made that technical coefficients are relatively more constant over time than over geographic area.

Major Sources of Data

The three major sources of data used in this study provided statistics on farmers' purchases of inputs for agricultural production.

The 1963 input-output table for the United States, published by the OBE [122; 123], provided national control totals for state estimates of inputs to agriculture. The flows given in the national table were prepared for the OBE by the Farm Income Branch of the Economic Research Service, U.S. Department of Agriculture.

The Farm Income Branch also prepared the second major source of data used in this study: state figures for farm production expenses in 1963 [107].

Since these data are for broad categories of expenditures, they provided state control totals for estimates of 1963 purchased inputs to agriculture. These same national production expense data were used by the Farm Income Branch in preparing the agricultural flows for the 1963 input-output table; hence, the state controls used in this study were consistent with the national control figures.

The survey of *Farmers' Expenditures in 1955 by Regions of Production and Farm Living . . . with Tables on Off-Farm Income* published jointly by the U.S. Bureau of the Census and the U.S. Department of Agriculture [91] was used as the third source of data on inputs for farm production and will be referred to hereafter as *Farmers' Expenditures in 1955*.

The 1963 National Input-Output Table

In the 1963 national input-output table, the flows include not only purchased inputs, but also the imputed value of nonpurchased inputs, transportation and trade margins, competitive imports, and secondary products. (For agriculture, however, secondary products could be disregarded.) Figure 2-1 shows the four major components of the flows into agriculture in the national table. In estimating technical coefficients for agriculture, the primary attention was given to state-to-state variations in purchased as well as nonpurchased inputs, since they show differences in technology. The figures for transportation and trade margins and competitive imports do not reflect actual inputs, but rather result from certain accounting conventions used in the construction of the national input-output table. In order to use the 1963 table most effectively as a control for state estimates of interindustry sales to agriculture, the flows in the national table first had to be separated into their component parts.

Purchased inputs. A detailed account is provided in the last section of this chapter on how these inputs were estimated. The state data are consistent with those given in the national primary matrix. In 1963, no agricultural commodities were produced as secondary products by other industries; therefore, secondary products did not have to be separated from primary products for the ten subindustries.

Imputed value of nonpurchased inputs. The Economic Research Service of the U.S. Department of Agriculture provided unpublished worksheet figures on that portion of flows into the agricultural subindustries in the 1963 table representing nonpurchased inputs such as the imputed value of feed and seed used on farms where grown, manure used for fertilizer, animal work power, etc. [99]. These figures were used as 1963 control totals for state estimates of nonpurchased inputs to agriculture. The methods used to estimate state figures for each specific nonpurchased input are discussed in detail in the last section of this chapter.

Transportation and trade margins. Because the transactions in the national

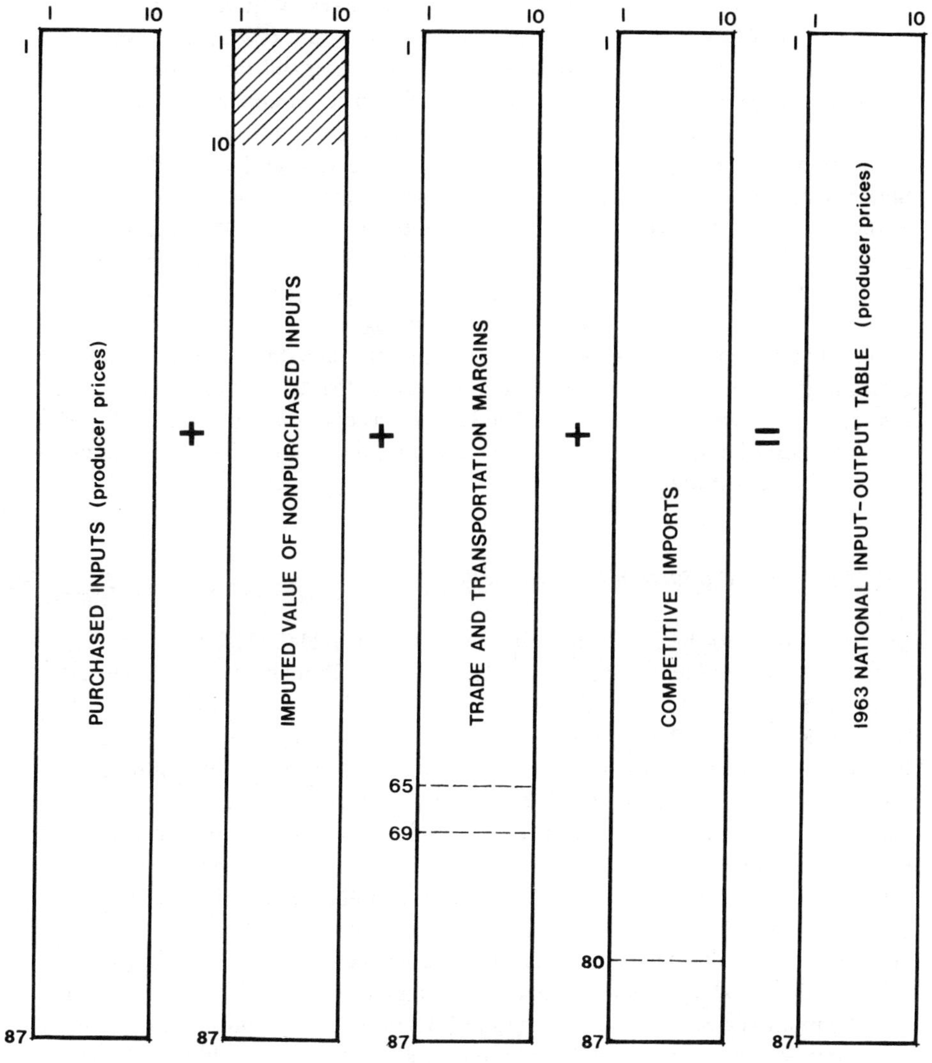

Figure 2–1. Major Components of Inputs into the Ten Agricultural Subindustries in the 1963 National Input-Output Table.

input-output table are valued in producer prices, the difference between the purchaser prices and producer prices (transportation and trade margins) for all inputs purchased were summed and treated as purchases by the agricultural subindustries from IO-65, Transportation & warehousing, and IO-69, Wholesale & retail trade. The OBE provided figures on transportation and trade margins for the 370-order 1963 agricultural flows [130]. The exact methods used to convert purchase price input data to producer prices are discussed later in this chapter.

Competitive imports. Imports of agricultural commodities into the United States were treated as purchases by the agricultural subindustries from IO-80.02, Transferred imports.[1] The transportation, trade, and insurance margins associated with these competitive imports (the difference between the foreign-port value and the domestic-port value of the imported agricultural goods) are included in the input-output table as purchases by agriculture from IO-65, Transportation & warehousing, IO-69, Wholesale & retail trade, and IO-70, Finance & insurance. Information on competitive imports and the margins on them for the ten agricultural subindustries in the 1963 table was provided by the OBE [119]. No allocation of competitive imports of agricultural commodities to the states was made in this study.

State Farm Production Expenses, 1963

In addition to the 370-order 1963 input-output table, which provided control totals at the national level, the Farm Income Branch of the U.S. Department of Agriculture has published control totals at the state level for 1963 farm purchases of inputs. The expense categories for which data are given are shown in Table 2-2. These specific broad expense categories were separated into their component inputs according to both the industry producing the input and the agricultural subindustry consuming it. Figure 2-2 gives a diagrammatic scheme of the overall method used. First, the broad expense categories were separated into their component inputs; second, the agricultural subindustries that purchased the individual inputs were determined; and, third, the inputs consumed by the agricultural subindustries in each state were assigned to the input-output industry that produced them. (A detailed explanation of the derivation of each specific input is given later in this chapter.) These state farm production expense data, however, cover only purchased inputs and were made consistent with the flows in the national input-output table, which had been separated to represent only the purchased inputs shown earlier in Figure 2-1, page 47.

1. Any input-output industry number in the form IO-*xx.yy* referred to in this volume is taken from the 370-order industry classification used by the OBE for the 1963 table [123, pp. 26–29]. The first two digits of the number (*xx*) refer to the 80-order input-output industry of which this particular subindustry is a part. The second pair of digits (*yy*) identifies the subindustry itself.

Table 2–2
1963 State Farm Production Expenditures Data Provided by the Farm Income Branch

Total Farm Production Expenses

I. Current farm operating expenses

A. Total feed
1. Feed for poultry
2. Feed for livestock

B. Total livestock purchases
1. Total purchase of meat animals
(a) Purchase of cattle & calves
(b) Purchase of hogs
(c) Purchase of sheep & lambs
2. Total purchase of chicks and poults
(a) Purchase of turkey poults
(b) Purchase of baby chicks

C. Seed purchased

D. Total fertilizer & lime
1. Fertilizer
2. Lime

E. Repair & maintenance construction
1. Farm dwellings
2. Service buildings & other structures

F. Total expenses for repair & operation of capital items
1. Petroleum, fuel, & oil
2. Auto repairs, tires, antifreeze, etc.
3. Auto license & insurance
4. Truck repairs, tires, antifreeze, etc.
5. Truck license & insurance
6. Tractor repairs, tires, antifreeze, etc.
7. Repairs & parts for farm machinery

G. Total miscellaneous expenditures
1. Blacksmithing & miscellaneous hardware
2. Containers
3. Binding materials
4. Fire, wind, & crop-hail insurance
5. Cotton ginning
6. Pesticides
7. Crop insurance
8. Sugar and sirup tolls
9. Short-term interest on non-real estate debt
10. Electricity
11. Greenhouse & nursery supplies
12. Veterinary fees & medicines
13. Dairy supplies
14. Grazing fees
15. Irrigation
16. Small hand tools
17. Harness & saddlery
18. Telephone

(continued)

Table 2-2 (continued)

G. Total miscellaneous expenditures (continued)
- 19. Marketing expenses for livestock
- 20. Hired hauling of milk
- 21. Other miscellaneous expenditures

H. Hired labor
- 1. Cash wages
- 2. Perquisites
- 3. Social security

II. Depreciation

III. Real estate taxes

IV. Interest on farm mortgage debt

V. Net rent to nonfarm landlords

The Survey of Farmers' Expenditures

In many cases, the most detailed data on specific inputs purchased by farmers (given in the form of average expenditures per farm for each of eight regions in the United States) are for 1955, this being the most recent benchmark year for which the U.S. Department of Agriculture published farm production expenses.[2] For later years, many estimates of farm production expenses were therefore obtained by tying these 1955 expenditures to some appropriate figures (such as value of production), which were used as indices to update them to the year under consideration. This method was used for certain of the estimates made by the Farm Income Branch for the 1963 input-output table.

Other Important Sources of Data

Two other important sources, both of them agricultural input-output studies, provided information on methodology as well as data. The first is the "Agricultural Industrial Relations Study, 1955" [105; 106], an input-output table for agriculture compiled by the Farm Income Branch using data obtained from *Farmers' Expenditures in 1955* [91]. Inputs to agriculture were estimated for the 17 agricultural subindustries shown in Table A-3 in the appendix. The second agricultural input-output table used was compiled by the Economic Research Service of the U.S. Department of Agriculture. Entitled "Interindustry Transactions for Agriculture, 1958" [61], the study gives figures for the 17 agricultural subindustries listed in Table A-3 of the appendix. These flows were aggregated to two agricultural input-output industries for the 1958 input-output table [131].

2. See Table B-2 in the appendix for a listing of the states within each region.

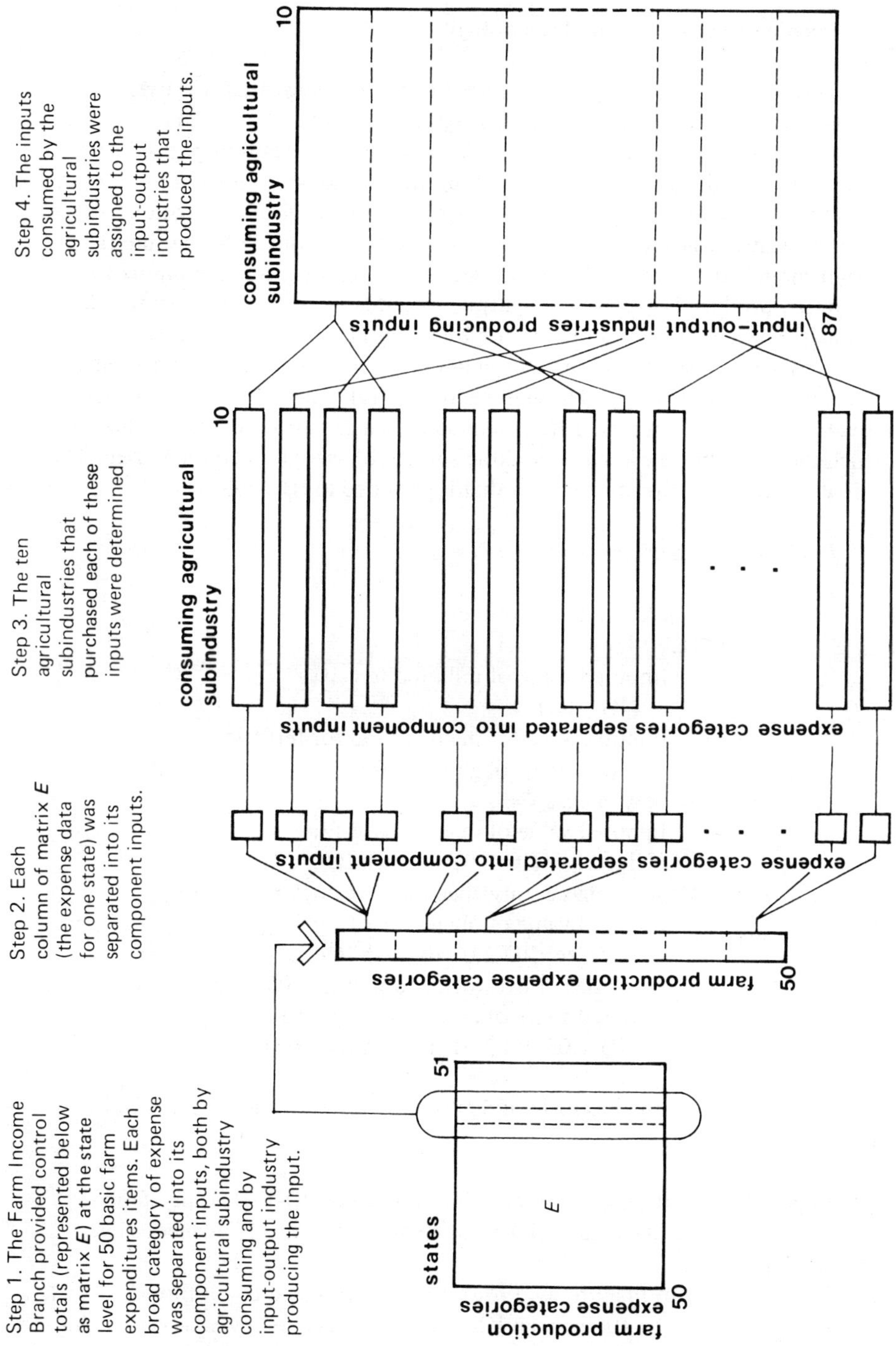

Figure 2–2. A Diagrammatic Representation of the Methods Used to Estimate 1963 Purchased Inputs to Agriculture.

Detailed Explanation of Methodology

This section of the chapter describes the methodology that was used to estimate the individual inputs to the ten agricultural subindustries in each state in 1963. Table 2-3 lists these inputs sequentially by the input-output industry producing the individual input. For each particular industry under consideration, the 80-order input-output industry number and title are given first. Subheadings under an industry give the industry number and title of the 370-order input-output subindustry that produces the agricultural input(s); and the inputs to agriculture produced by this input-output subindustry are listed below the subheadings. The agricultural subindustries that consume these inputs are shown in parentheses after each. For each input, numbers at the right refer to the explanatory notes on methodology. Those notes follow Table 2-3, "Inputs to Agriculture, by Producing Industry, 1963," and contain a discussion of the method by which the inputs were estimated and the sources of the data that were used. The following illustrates the information that is provided in the table:

Producing Industry and Input(s) Produced	*Note*
IO-1 Livestock & livestock products	
1.01 Dairy farm products	
Imputed value of milk fed to calves (IO-1.03)	1
Imputed value of manure used for fertilizer (IO-2.01 through IO-2.07)	2
1.02 Poultry & eggs	
Imputed value of manure used for fertilizer (IO-2.01 through IO-2.07)	2
1.03 Meat animals & miscellaneous livestock products	
Imputed value of manure used for fertilizer (IO-2.01 through IO-2.07)	2
Purchases of livestock and poultry (IO-1.03)	3
Imputed value of animal work power (IO-1.03, IO-2.01 through IO-2.07)	4

This means that the inputs to agriculture produced by IO-1, Livestock & livestock products, are:

(1) Imputed value of milk fed to calves, produced by IO-1.01, Dairy farm products, and consumed by IO-1.03, Meat animals & miscellaneous livestock products.

(2) Imputed value of manure used for fertilizer, produced by all three livestock subindustries, IO-1.01 through IO-1.03, and consumed by all seven of the crop subindustries, IO-2.01 through IO-2.07.

(3) Purchases of livestock, which are intraindustry purchases, that is, the livestock are considered as being both produced and consumed by the same industry, IO-1.03.

(4) Imputed value of animal work power, which is produced by IO-1.03 and consumed by itself as well as by the crop subindustries, IO-2.01 through IO-2.07.

The number under *Note* signifies, for example, that the estimation method used for the imputed value of milk fed to calves is explained in Note 1, for the imputed value of manure used for fertilizer in Note 2, for purchases of livestock in Note 3, and for animal work power in Note 4.

The table listing inputs to agriculture by producing industry and the explanatory notes follow. (The letters "n.e.c." are used in the table as an abbreviation for "not elsewhere classified.")

Table 2–3
Inputs to Agriculture, by Producing Industry, 1963

Producing Industry and Input(s) Produced	*Note*
IO-1 Livestock & livestock products	
1.01 Dairy farm products	
Imputed value of milk fed to calves (IO-1.03)	1
Imputed value of manure used for fertilizer (IO-2.01 through IO-2.07)	2
1.02 Poultry & eggs	
Imputed value of manure used for fertilizer (IO-2.01 through IO-2.07)	2
1.03 Meat animals & miscellaneous livestock products	
Imputed value of manure used for fertilizer (IO-2.01 through IO-2.07)	2
Purchases of livestock and poultry (IO-1.03)	3
Imputed value of animal work power (IO-1.03, IO-2.01 through IO-2.07)	4
IO-2 Other agricultural products	
2.01 Cotton	
Purchased seed (IO-2.01)	5
Imputed value of nonpurchased seed (IO-2.02)	6
2.02 Food [grains], feed grains, & grass seeds	
Purchased seed (IO-2.02)	5
Imputed value of nonpurchased seed (IO-2.02)	6
Purchased feed (IO-1.01 through IO-1.03)	7
Imputed value of nonpurchased feed (IO-1.01 through IO-1.03)	8
2.03 Tobacco	
Total seed, purchased and nonpurchased (IO-2.03)	5
2.04 Fruits and tree nuts	
Purchased seed (IO-2.04)	5
2.05 Vegetables, sugar, & miscellaneous crops	
Purchased seed (IO-2.05)	5
Imputed value of nonpurchased seed (IO-2.05)	6
Imputed value of nonpurchased feed (IO-1.01, IO-1.03)	8
2.06 Oil-bearing crops	
Purchased seed (IO-2.06)	5
Imputed value of nonpurchased seed (IO-2.06)	6
Purchased feed (IO-1.03)	7
Imputed value of nonpurchased feed (IO-1.03)	8
2.07 Forest, greenhouse, & nursery products	
Purchased seed (IO-2.04, IO-2.05, IO-2.07)	5
IO-4 Agricultural, forestry, & fishery services	
4.00 Agricultural, forestry, & fishery services	
Artificial insemination (IO-1.01)	9
Chicks and poults bought from hatcheries (IO-1.02)	3
Seed certification (IO-2.01 through IO-2.07)	10
Soil testing (IO-2.01 through IO-2.07)	10
Machine hire and custom and contract work (IO-2.01 through IO-2.07)	11
Cotton ginning (IO-2.01)	12
Sugar and sirup tolls (IO-2.05)	12
Miscellaneous farm management services (IO-2.01 through IO-2.07)	10
Custom sawing of lumber for sale (IO-2.07)	10

Table 2–3 (continued)

Producing Industry and Input(s) Produced	*Note*
IO-7 Coal mining	
7.00 Coal mining	
Coal for heat, greenhouse (IO-2.07)	13
Coal for heat, incubating chicks, brooding (IO-1.02)	14
IO-9 Stone & clay mining and quarrying	
9.00 Stone & clay mining & quarrying	
Crushed limestone for fertilizer (IO-2.01 through IO-2.07)	15
Mineral salt and other mineral supplements (IO-1.01 through IO-1.03	17
IO-10 Chemical & fertilizer mineral mining	
10.00 Chemical & fertilizer mineral mining	
Potash, soda, borate minerals, phosphate rock (IO-2.01 through IO-2.07)	15
IO-12 Maintenance & repair construction	
12.02 Maintenance & repair construction, all other maintenance construction & other improvements (IO-1.01 through IO-2.07)	16
IO-14 Food & kindred products	
14.14 Flour & cereal preparations	
Millfeeds and other byproduct feeds (IO-1.01 through IO-1.03)	7
14.15 Prepared feeds for animals & fowls	
Prepared animal feeds (IO-1.01 through IO-1.03)	7
14.16 Rice milling	
Millfeeds (IO-1.01 through IO-1.03)	7
14.17 Wet corn milling	
Gluten feed and meal (IO-1.01 through IO-1.03)	7
14.19 Sugar	
Dried and molasses beet pulp (IO-1.01, IO-1.03)	7
14.21 Alcoholic beverages	
Distillers' dried grains (IO-1.01 through IO-1.03)	7
14.24 Cottonseed oil mills	
Oil cake and meal (IO-1.01 through IO-1.03)	7
14.25 Soybean oil mills	
Oil cake and meal (IO-1.01 through IO-1.03)	7
14.26 Vegetable oil mills, n.e.c.	
Oil cake and meal (IO-1.02, IO-1.03)	7
14.27 Animal & marine fats & oils	
Tankage, meat meal, fish meal (IO-1.02, IO-1.03)	7
Inedible tallow and grease (IO-1.02, IO-1.03)	7
14.32 Food preparations, n.e.c.	
Miscellaneous food products (IO-2.05)	24
IO-16 Broad & narrow fabrics, yarn & thread mills	
16.01 Broadwoven fabric mills & fabric finishing plants	
Tobacco cloth (IO-2.03)	18
IO-17 Miscellaneous textile goods & floor coverings	
17.09 Cordage & twine	
Rope (IO-1.01 through IO-2.07)	18
Baler and binder twine (IO-2.02)	19
Cordage and twine (IO-2.07)	13

(continued)

Table 2-3 (continued)

Producing Industry and Input(s) Produced	*Note*
17.10 Textile goods, n.e.c.	
Burlap materials (IO-2.07)	13
Cloth filters (IO-1.01)	20
IO-19 Miscellaneous fabricated textile products	
19.03 Fabricated textile products, n.e.c.	
Canvas (IO-1.01 through IO-2.07)	18
Burlap sacks (IO-1.03, IO-2.02, IO-2.04, IO-2.05)	21
IO-20 Lumber & wood products, except containers	
20.09 Wood products, n.e.c.	
Hand tool handles (IO-1.01 through IO-2.07)	22
Ladders (IO-1.01 through IO-2.07)	18
IO-21 Wooden containers	
21.00 Wooden containers	
Wooden containers (IO-2.04, IO-2.05)	21
IO-24 Paper & allied products, except containers & boxes	
24.02 Paper mills, except building paper	
Miscellaneous paper products (IO-1.01 through IO-2.07)	24
24.04 Envelopes	
Envelopes (IO-1.01 through IO-2.07)	24
24.07 Converted paper products, n.e.c., except containers & boxes	
Egg cartons (IO-1.02)	21
IO-25 Paperboard containers & boxes	
25.00 Paperboard containers & boxes	
Milk cartons (IO-1.01)	20
Paperboard boxes (IO-2.07)	13
IO-26 Printing & publishing	
26.02 Periodicals	
Technical journals (IO-1.01 through IO-2.07)	10
26.03 Book printing & publishing	
Specialized books (IO-1.01 through IO-2.07)	10
IO-27 Chemicals & selected chemical products	
27.01 Industrial inorganic & organic chemicals	
Chemicals for fertilizer (IO-2.01 through IO-2.07)	15
27.02 Fertilizers	
Commercial fertilizers (IO-2.01 through IO-2.07)	15
27.03 Agricultural chemicals, n.e.c.	
Sprays and disinfectants (IO-1.01 through IO-1.03)	26
Pesticides (IO-1.01 through IO-2.07)	27
27.04 Miscellaneous chemical products	
Antifreeze (IO-1.01 through IO-2.07)	28
IO-29 Drugs, cleaning, & toilet preparations	
29.01 Drugs	
Medicines, serums, and tonics (IO-1.01 through IO-1.03)	26
IO-31 Petroleum refining & related industries	
31.01 Petroleum refining & related products	
Gasoline and other petroleum fuel and oil (IO-1.01 through IO-2.07)	29
IO-32 Rubber & miscellaneous plastics products	
32.01 Tires & inner tubes	
Tires and inner tubes (IO-1.01 through IO-2.07)	28

Table 2–3 (continued)

Producing Industry and Input(s) Produced	*Note*
32.03 Reclaimed rubber & miscellaneous rubber products, n.e.c.	
Recapping tires (IO-1.01 through IO-2.07)	23
32.04 Miscellaneous plastics products	
Plastics materials (IO-2.07)	13
IO-34 Footwear & other leather products	
34.03 Other leather products	
Harness and saddlery (IO-1.03)	12
IO-35 Glass & glass products	
35.02 Glass containers	
Glass bottles (IO-1.03)	21
Milk bottles (IO-1.01)	20
IO-36 Stone & clay products	
36.09 Pottery products, n.e.c.	
Clay pots (IO-2.07)	13
36.13 Lime	
Lime (IO-2.01 through IO-2.07)	15
36.17 Asbestos products	
Asbestos products (IO-1.01 through IO-2.07)	24
36.19 Minerals, ground or treated	
Agricultural limestone, ground (IO-2.01 through IO-2.07)	15
IO-38 Primary nonferrous metals manufacturing	
38.10 Nonferrous wire drawing & insulating wire (IO-1.01 through IO-2.07)	18
IO-39 Metal containers	
39.01 Metal cans	
Metal milk cans (IO-1.01)	20
39.02 Metal barrels, drums, & pails	
Fuel barrels, tanks, and pumps (IO-1.01 through IO-2.07)	18
IO-41 Screw machine products, bolts, nuts, etc., & metal stampings	
41.02 Metal stampings	
Milk bottle closures (IO-1.01)	20
IO-42 Other fabricated metal products	
42.02 Hand & edge tools, including saws	
Hand tools (IO-1.01 through IO-2.07)	22
42.05 Miscellaneous fabricated wire products	
Tire chains (IO-1.01 through IO-2.07)	28
Bale ties (IO-2.02)	19
IO-44 Farm machinery & equipment	
44.00 Farm machinery	
Parts and accessories (IO-1.01 through IO-2.07)	28
IO-50 Machine shop products	
50.00 Machine shop products	
Carburetors, pistons, etc. (IO-1.01 through IO-2.07)	31
IO-55 Electric lighting & wiring equipment	
55.01 Electric lamps	
Lamps, lanterns (IO-1.01 through IO-2.07)	31

(continued)

Table 2–3 (continued)

Producing Industry and Input(s) Produced	*Note*
IO-58 Miscellaneous electrical machinery, equipment, & supplies	
58.01 Storage batteries	
Storage batteries (IO-1.01 through IO-2.07)	28
58.04 Engine electrical equipment	
Spark plugs, etc. (IO-1.01 through IO-2.07)	28
IO-59 Motor vehicles & equipment	
59.03 Motor vehicles & parts	
Parts and accessories (IO-1.01 through IO-2.07)	28
IO-61 Other transportation equipment	
61.07 Transportation equipment, n.e.c.	
Parts for wagons, carts, etc. (IO-1.01 through IO-2.07)	31
IO-64 Miscellaneous manufacturing	
64.12 Miscellaneous manufactures, n.e.c.	
Fire extinguishers (IO-1.01 through IO-2.07)	18
IO-65 Transportation & warehousing	
Hired hauling of milk (IO-1.01)	12
Transportation margins on purchased inputs (IO-1.01 through IO-2.07)	25
Miscellaneous trucking charges, n.e.c. (IO-1.01 through IO-2.07)	10
Transportation margins on directly allocated imports (IO-1.02 through IO-2.07)	37
IO 66 Communications, except radio & TV broadcasting	
66.00 Communications, except radio & TV	
Telephone services, business share (IO-1.01 through IO-2.07)	16
Telegraph, teletype (IO-1.01 through IO-2.07)	10
IO-68 Electric, gas, water, & sanitary services	
68.01 Electric utilities	
Electricity, business share (IO-1.01 through IO-2.07)	16
68.02 Gas utilities	
Gas heat (IO-1.03, IO-2.07)	29
68.03 Water & sanitary services	
Piped water for farm business (IO-1.01 through IO-2.07)	10
Irrigation (IO-2.01 through IO-2.07)	30
IO-69 Wholesale & retail trade	
Miscellaneous marketing charges (IO-1.01 through IO-2.07)	32
Trade margins on purchased inputs (IO-1.01 through IO-2.07)	25
Wholesalers, n.e.c. IO-2.07)	13
Livestock marketing costs (IO-1.03)	33
Trade margins on directly allocated imports (IO-1.02 through IO-2.07)	37
IO-70 Finance & insurance	
70.01 Banking	
Banking services (IO-1.01 through IO-2.07)	34
70.04 Insurance carriers	
Auto and truck insurance (IO-1.01 through IO-2.07)	28

Table 2–3 (continued)

Producing Industry and Input(s) Produced	*Note*
Crop-hail insurance (IO-2.01 through IO-2.07)	35
Other insurance	35
Insurance margins on directly allocated imports (IO-1.02 through IO-2.07)	37
IO-71 Real estate & rental	
71.02 Real estate	
Agents' and brokers' fees (IO-1.01 through IO-2.07)	10
Rent payments on service buildings and structures (IO-1.01 through IO-2.07)	36
IO-73 Business services	
73.01 Miscellaneous business services	
Farm machinery repair (IO-1.01 through IO-2.07)	28
Blacksmithing (IO-1.03)	18
73.02 Advertising	
Advertising, livestock (IO-1.03)	10
Advertising, greenhouse (IO-2.07)	13
73.03 Miscellaneous professional services	
Notary public (IO-1.01 through IO-2.07)	10
Legal fees (IO-1.01 through IO-2.07)	10
Accounting services (IO-1.01 through IO-2.07)	10
IO-75 Automobile repair & services	
75.00 Automobile repair & services	
Auto and truck repair (IO-1.01 through IO-2.07)	28
IO-77 Medical, educational services, & nonprofit organizations	
77.03 Other medical & health services	
Veterinary services (IO-1.01 through IO-1.03)	26
77.05 Nonprofit organizations	
Dues to farm organizations, etc. (IO-1.01 through IO-2.07)	10
Herd improvement fees (IO-1.01)	20
IO-78 Federal government enterprises	
78.01 Post office	
Postage (IO-1.01 through IO-2.07)	10
IO-79 State & local government enterprises	
79.03 Other state & local government enterprises	
Truck, auto license fees (IO-1.01 through IO-2.07)	28
Other license fees (IO-1.01 through IO-2.07)	10
IO-80 Gross imports of goods & services	
80.01 Directly allocated imports of goods & services	
Hired foreign labor (IO-1.02 through IO-2.07)	37
IO-81 Business travel, entertainment, & gifts	
81.00 Business travel, entertainment, & gifts	
Business travel (IO-1.01 through IO-2.07)	10
IO-82 Office supplies	
82.00 Office supplies	
Office supplies (IO-1.01 through IO-2.07)	24

1 *Imputed value of milk fed to calves*

State figures on the amount of milk fed to calves in 1963 [89, t. 558, p. 382] were multiplied by the average price of milk in each respective state in 1963 [89, t. 561, p. 386] to obtain an imputed 1963 value by state for milk fed to calves. These figures were allocated to the consuming subindustry, IO-1.03, Meat animals & miscellaneous livestock products.

2 *Imputed value of manure used for fertilizer*

The following data on the amount of manure, with its plant nutrient content, produced by six types of dairy and meat animals were obtained from unpublished worksheets of Jack Faucett Associates [21]:

		Plant Nutrient Content		
Animals Producing Manure	*Manure (tons/yr.)*	*N*	*P_2O_5 (lbs./ton)*	*K_2O*
Horses & mules (2 yrs. +)	6.00	13.2	5.1	12.1
Hogs (6 mos. +)	1.70	9.9	6.7	9.3
Sheep (1 yr. +)	0.75	15.8	6.7	18.0
Cows & heifers (2 yrs. +)	7.80	11.4	3.1	9.9
Dairy cattle (2 yrs. +)	6.60	11.4	3.1	9.9
Steers & bulls (2 yrs. +)	4.25	15.0	6.0	8.0

Using these figures, together with the number of each type of animal in each state in 1963 [108], the plant nutrient content of the manure from each type of livestock was calculated. The value of this manure was imputed in terms of the 1963 market value of the plant nutrients it contains [89, t. 682, p. 475]:

Plant Nutrient	*Price Per Pound*
N	\$.12000
P_2O_5	.10075
K_2O	.04890

The resulting state figures for the imputed value of manure by type of animal were allocated to the appropriate producing subindustries, IO-1.01, Dairy farm products, and IO-1.03, Meat animals & miscellaneous livestock products. These data were distributed to the consuming crop subindustries in each state according to the number of acres of each crop fertilized in 1964 [97, t. 1, pp. 16–281].

According to a study entitled "Interindustry Transactions for Agriculture, 1958," the only poultry product purchased by the crop industries is manure [61]. Therefore, the 1958 value of sales by IO-1.02 to the crop subindustries, obtained from Table 2 of that report, was divided by the total number of chickens and turkeys in 1958 to give a figure for the 1958 value of manure produced per chicken/turkey:

Sales by IO-1.02 to IO-2.00, 1958	$ 86,048,000
Number of chickens and turkeys, 1958	379,893,000
Imputed value of manure produced per chicken/turkey in 1958	$ .2265

On the assumption that the average imputed value of poultry manure had not changed between 1958 and 1963, the value of manure produced per poultry unit was multiplied by the number of poultry units in each state in 1963 to give the 1963 value of poultry manure produced by state. These figures were allocated to the purchasing subindustries in each state in the same proportions as shown for 1958 [61, t. 2].

3 *Purchases of livestock and poultry*
State data on 1963 purchases of poultry [107] consist entirely of purchases of baby chicks and turkey poults from commercial hatcheries. These data needed no adjustments and were considered as inputs produced by IO-4.00, Agricultural, forestry, & fishery services, and consumed by IO-1.02, Poultry & eggs.

The Farm Income Branch (FIB) state data on 1963 purchases of meat animals [107] consist only of interstate transactions and therefore do not include interfarm, intrastate purchases of animals. Since the Census of Agriculture figures do include interfarm, intrastate transactions, the following ratio was used to inflate the 1963 livestock purchases data for each state:

$$\frac{\text{Census livestock \& poultry 1964}}{\text{FIB livestock \& poultry 1964}} = \frac{X}{\text{FIB livestock \& poultry 1963}}$$

where X = livestock & poultry purchased in 1963, including interfarm, intrastate sales. Since both the Census and Farm Income Branch data on poultry purchases contain intrastate as well as interstate transactions, the FIB figures for purchases of poultry were subtracted from X to obtain the desired livestock purchases figure.

The resulting state figures for purchases of livestock include dairy cattle as well as meat animals. The 1955 [106] and the 1958 [61] studies contain no estimate for the purchases of dairy cattle by the dairy subindustry, but all purchases of livestock are included as inputs produced and consumed by IO-1.03, Meat animals & miscellaneous livestock products.

4 *Imputed value of animal work power*
For each subindustry, a value had to be imputed for the work done by horses and mules. The 1958 state outputs estimated by Jack Faucett Associates for IO-1, Meat animals & miscellaneous livestock products, include an estimate of animal work power produced in 1958 for the United States as a

whole [22]. This value was obtained by multiplying the number of horses and mules in each state in 1958 by a factor (112.2) of the value of work power produced per animal, these state values being consistent with a national total of $376,393,000. Since the publication of data on the number of horses and mules by state was discontinued as of the January 1, 1960 enumeration, the number of horses and mules in each state in 1960 was multiplied by the same factor (112.2) to obtain an approximate value of animal work power produced in each state for 1963.

The following percentage distribution of animal work power inputs to ten agricultural subindustries was obtained from the 1955 input-output study [106, t. A]:

Agricultural Subindustries	*Percent*
IO-1.01 (A3)*	–
IO-1.02 (A2)	–
IO-1.03 (A1, A4)	18.93
IO-2.01 (A7)	15.05
IO-2.02 (A5, A6, A13)	45.72
IO-2.03 (A8)	7.40
IO-2.04 (A11, A12)	1.35
IO-2.05 (A10, A14, A15)	6.07
IO-2.06 (A9)	3.47
IO-2.07 (A16, A17)	2.01
	100.00

*The numbers in parentheses represent the 17 agricultural subindustries for which estimates were made in the 1955 study. (See the appendix, Table A-3.)

The national total of animal work power was distributed to the consuming agricultural subindustry using these percentages to obtain the amount of animal work power consumed by each subindustry at the national level.

Only the total figures for animal work power consumed in each state and each subindustry, shown by the shaded areas in Figure 2-3, were available. These data were allocated to the subindustries within each state according to the percentage distribution of a state agricultural subindustry matrix of 1963 outputs [90]. For this calculation, a computer program was used to force a given 1963 output matrix (state-by-agricultural subindustry) to add to specified row sums (1963 animal work power produced in each state) and column sums (1963 animal work power consumed in each subindustry). The result was a matrix of figures for 1963 animal work power inputs to each agricultural subindustry by state.

5 *Purchased seed*

The survey entitled *Farmers' Expenditures in 1955* [91, tt. 14-16] gives data on average expenditures per farm for the following kinds of seed:

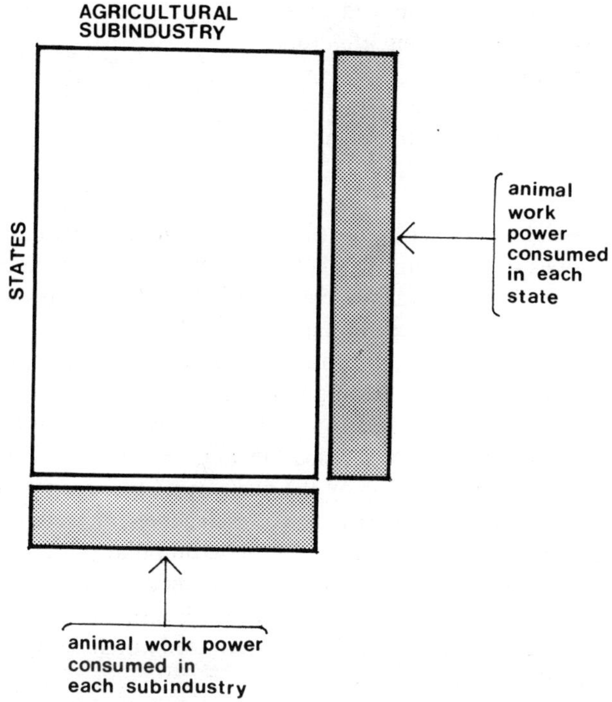

Figure 2–3. Allocation of Animal Work Power by State and Subindustry.

Field crop seeds, total
- Seed corn
- Seed oats
- Seed barley
- Seed wheat
- Seed rye
- Sorghum grain for seed
- Soybean seed
- Dry bean seed
- Irish potatoes for seed
- Cottonseed for seed
- Peanuts for seed
- Tobacco, seed and plants
- Seed rice
- Flax for seed
- Other field crop seeds

Hay, pasture, and cover-crop seeds, total
Vegetable seeds, trees, shrubs, etc., total
    Vegetable seeds
    Fruit and nut trees, etc.
    Other trees, shrubs, bulbs, plants
Total Seeds, Plants, Trees, Etc.

These seed purchases are given for three major regions: North, South, and West. The totals for each crop category, as well as for a few selected individual crops, are given for each of eight subregions. (The states within each region and subregion are listed in Table B–2 in the appendix.)

Using the above data, together with crop production data for each subregion in 1955 [76, ch. VII], seed purchases for each crop in each of the eight subregions were calculated for 1955. Coefficients showing seed purchases per unit of crops produced in 1955 were obtained by dividing the seed expenditures for each crop by the quantity of that crop produced in each subregion. After the coefficients for each subregion were multiplied by the 1963 crop production for each state within that subregion, the resulting estimated state-by-crop matrix of 1963 seed purchases was aggregated to the crop subindustries. The percentage distribution obtained from this matrix was used to allocate actual 1963 state seed purchases figures [104] to the consuming crop subindustries.

The seed purchases of most of the crop subindustries are intraindustry, that is, the seeds are both produced and consumed by the same subindustry. However, the 1958 input-output table giving subindustry detail for agriculture shows that seed purchases for IO-2.04, Fruits & tree nuts, and IO-2.05, Vegetables, sugar, & miscellaneous crops, consist not only of these intraindustry purchases of seed but also of those bought from IO-2.07, Forest, greenhouse, & nursery products [61, t.2]. The seeds purchased from IO-2.07 by IO-2.04 and by IO-2.05 were calculated as a percentage of total seeds purchased by each in 1958. These percentages were applied to the derived 1963 seed purchases figures for IO-2.04 and IO-2.05 to obtain figures for internally consumed seeds, as well as for seeds purchased from IO-2.07.

6 *Imputed value of nonpurchased seed*
State data on the physical amount of seed used on farms where grown in 1963 are available for the following crops [112]:

Nonpurchased Seed	*Nonpurchased Feed & Seed*
Wheat	Corn
Rye	Oats
Flaxseed	Barley
Buckwheat	Sorghums

Nonpurchased Seed

Dry edible beans
Rice
Soybeans
Cottonseed
Dry field peas
Cow peas
Peanuts
Legume & grass seeds
Potatoes
Sweet potatoes

National figures on the imputed value of nonpurchased seed used in 1963 were supplied by the Economic Research Service, U.S. Department of Agriculture, for the above crops, as well as for tobacco, mung beans, sugar cane, broomcorn, velvet beans, and other miscellaneous crops [99]. These national totals for each crop were allocated to the states in proportion to the use of nonpurchased seed in each state in 1963. The distribution for corn, oats, barley, and sorghums was made according to use for feed and seed together on farms where grown. When no state data were available on nonpurchased seed, the allocation was made according to crop output in each state [90].

7 *Purchased feed*
The *Census of Agriculture, 1964* provides state data on 1964 expenditures for three categories of feed: feed grains, feed concentrates (commercially mixed feeds, millfeeds, and feed supplements), and hay and other roughage (harvested forage) [78, t. 10, p. 700]. The 1964 figure for total feed purchased was adjusted to represent feed purchases in 1963 by using the following ratio with Farm Income Branch (FIB) feed expenditures data for 1963 and 1964 [95, t. 10, pp. 72–74]:

$$\frac{\text{Census feed purchased 1964}}{\text{FIB feed purchased 1964}} = \frac{X}{\text{FIB feed purchased 1963}}$$

where X = feed purchased in 1963. The adjusted figures for total feed purchased in 1963 were separated into purchases of feed grains, feed concentrates, and hay and other roughage in proportion to the original 1964 data.

The 1963 purchases of feed grains and feed concentrates by state were allocated to the consuming livestock subindustries in each state according to U.S. Department of Agriculture factors designed to calculate grain and concentrates consumed by various kinds of animals in each state [101, t. A]. Analogous factors were used to assign purchases of hay and roughage to the consuming livestock subindustries [101, t. B]. For each of the three feed categories, the information in these state-by-livestock subindustry expenditures matrices was rearranged to form state-by-feed consumption matrices for the three livestock subindustries: poultry, livestock, and other livestock.

The Farm Income Branch provided 1963 state data on feed expenditures for livestock and poultry [107]. The feed data for poultry were separated into expenditures for grains, for concentrates, and for hay and roughage in proportion to the purchases of each kind of feed obtained from the state-by-feed consumption matrix for poultry.

The dairy and the other livestock matrices were added to obtain a state-by-feed matrix of feed consumed by livestock. For the livestock feed expenditures, the same procedure was followed except that once a state-by-feed consumption matrix had been obtained for total livestock, it was separated into a matrix for dairy and a matrix for other livestock in proportion to the entries in the original dairy and other livestock feed consumption matrices. The resulting matrices for the three livestock subindustries added to the actual 1963 feed-purchase figures. The information in these matrices was rearranged again to form three state-by-livestock subindustry matrices of feed expenditures, one for feed grains, one for feed concentrates, and one for hay and roughage.

These 1963 state-by-livestock subindustry matrices of feed purchases were used as percentage distributions to make state allocations of the feed purchases by each livestock subindustry shown in the national 370-order 1963 input-output table. With the exception of feed purchases from IO-2.02, Food [grains], feed grains, & grass seeds, and IO-2.06, Oil-bearing crops, the flows from the subindustries listed below were assumed to consist entirely of sales of feed:

Kind of Feed	*Producing Industry*	*Allocation Matrix Used*
Grains, hay	IO-2.02	Grains and hay
Oil crops	IO-2.06	Grains
Wheat millfeeds, byproduct feeds	IO-14.14	Concentrates
Prepared animal feeds	IO-14.15	Concentrates
Rice millfeeds	IO-14.16	Concentrates
Gluten feed & meal	IO-14.17	Concentrates
Dried & molasses beet pulp	IO-14.19	Concentrates
Distillers' dried grains	IO-14.21	Concentrates
Cottonseed cake & meal	IO-14.24	Concentrates
Soybean cake & meal	IO-14.25	Concentrates
Other vegetable oil cake & meal	IO-14.26	Concentrates
Tankage, meat & fish meal, inedible tallow & grease	IO-14.27	Concentrates

The value of feed purchased from IO-2.02 and IO-2.06 was determined as a residual obtained by subtracting the imputed value of nonpurchased feed sold to these livestock subindustries [99] from the total flows from IO-2.02 and IO-2.06 to each of the livestock subindustries.

8 *Imputed value of nonpurchased feed*
The Economic Research Service of the U.S. Department of Agriculture provided 1963 national data on the imputed value of thirteen different crops consumed on farms where grown by each of four livestock groups [99]. For each crop, the total value was allocated to the states in proportion to the physical amount of that crop consumed on farms where grown in each state in 1963 [112]. These figures provided row sums and column sums of a state-by-livestock matrix of nonpurchased feed consumption for each crop. For hay and pasture, the allocation factors used were consumption of hay and roughage by each of four livestock groups in each state in 1963. The matrices of feed consumption used as allocation factors were obtained using U.S. Department of Agriculture factors designed to calculate the amount of grains and concentrates (or hay and roughage) consumed per animal in each state [92, tt. A, B]. These figures on consumption of feed per animal were weighted by the number of each kind of animal by state in 1963 [114] and then aggregated to the four livestock groups for which feed data were available. To obtain 1963 state-by-livestock figures for the value of each crop consumed, the resulting state-by-livestock matrices were forced to add to the row and column sums described above and were then aggregated to state-by-livestock subindustry matrices for each crop. The matrices for each crop were summed to obtain the value of nonpurchased feed produced by the seven input-output crop subindustries.

9 *Artificial insemination*
For 1963, information was available by region on the number of milk cows bred artificially as a percentage of total milk cows in each region [92, t. 28, p. 50].[3] These percentages were multiplied by the number of milk cows in the states within each region in 1963 [114, t. 7, p. 8]. For the state allocations, a percentage distribution of this estimated number of milk cows bred artificially in each state was used to obtain the sale from IO-4.00, Agricultural, forestry, & fishery services, to IO-1.01, Dairy farm products, in the 370-order 1963 input-output table [123].

10 *Miscellaneous services and expenses*
Data were available for eight regions of the United States in 1955 on average expenditures per farm [91] for the following expenses (the states in each region are listed in Table B–2 in the appendix):

3. The regions were: North Atlantic, East North Central, West North Central, South Atlantic, South Central, and Western.

Producing Industry	*Expense Category*
IO-4.00	Custom sawing of lumber for sale
IO-4.00	Farm management services (including soil testing & seed certification)
IO-26.01, IO-26.02	Books, periodicals
IO-65.00	Miscellaneous trucking charges, n.e.c.
IO-68.03	Piped water for farm business
IO-71.02	Buying & selling farm real estate
IO-73.02	Promotion fees, other advertising
IO-73.03	Farm record keeping
IO-73.03	Attorney, notary public
IO-77.05	Dues to farm organizations
IO-78.01, IO-66.00	Postage, telegraph & teletype
IO-79.03	License fees (other than motor vehicles)
IO-81.00	Business travel expenses

For some detailed expense categories, data were given for three major regions only. In these cases, estimates were made for the eight subregions by assuming that the average expenditure per farm was constant and then forcing the individual categories to add to given subregional totals.

State data on miscellaneous current farm operating expenses were available for 1955 and 1963 [95, t. 10]. The 1955 state data were used to allocate the individual 1955 expenditures figures given by region to the states within each region. By using the ratio of miscellaneous current farm operating expenses in 1955 to those in 1963, these state figures were then updated to 1963. The resulting 1963 figures for each expenditures category by state were distributed to the consuming agricultural subindustries in proportion to 1963 cash receipts of each [94, t. 16; 95, t. 16], with the following exceptions:

(a) Miscellaneous farm management services (including soil testing and seed certification) were allocated to the crop subindustries, IO-2.01 through IO-2.07, only.

(b) Advertising expenses were consumed by IO-1.03, Meat animals & miscellaneous livestock products, only.

(c) Custom sawing of lumber for sale was allocated to IO-2.07, Forest, greenhouse, & nursery products, only.

11 *Machine hire and custom and contract work*

The *Census of Agriculture, 1964* [77] gives 1964 state data on expenditures for farm machinery rental and for custom and contract work by each of 12 types of farm. These types-of-farm data were aggregated to the two main agricultural input-output industries as follows:

Type of Farm	*Industry*
Poultry Dairy Livestock, other Livestock ranches	IO-1, Livestock & livestock products
Cash grain Tobacco Cotton Other field crops Vegetables Fruit-and-nut General	IO-2, Other agricultural products
Miscellaneous	IO-1 and IO-2

The miscellaneous type of farm produces both crop and livestock products. Each expenditures figure was separated into the crop and livestock components in proportion to the amounts of each produced by miscellaneous farms in each state in 1964 [77, t. 22].

By assuming that expenditures patterns follow income patterns, these 1964 state-by-industry expenditures for machine hire and custom and contract work were allocated to the subindustries within each main agricultural industry according to the cash receipts of each. The resulting matrix was used to distribute the national 1963 figures to the states.

12 *Farm Income Branch data that could be used directly*

The current 1963 operating expense data supplied to the Harvard Economic Research Project by the Farm Income Branch were for all agriculture by state [107]. The following categories needed no further adjustment:

Input	*Producing Industry*	*Consuming Industry*
Harness and saddlery	IO-34.03	IO-1.03
Hired hauling of milk	IO-65.00	IO-1.01
Cotton ginning	IO-4.00	IO-2.01
Sugar and sirup tolls	IO-4.00	IO-2.05

13 *Greenhouse and nursery supplies*

The Farm Income Branch supplied data for 1963 miscellaneous expenses of greenhouses and nurseries by state [107]. According to the 1955 agricultural input-output study: "Greenhouse and nursery miscellaneous expenses consist of expenditures for coal, advertising, commissions, growers' supplies and packing materials" [106, p. 14]. Listed below are the major inputs included in these categories, together with the input-output industry that produces the input:

Input	*Producing Industry*	
Coal	IO-7.00	
Cordage	IO-17.09	Packing materials
Paperboard & paper	IO-25.00	
Burlap materials	IO-17.10	Growers' supplies
Plastics materials	IO-32.04	
Clay pots	IO-36.09	
Commissions	IO-69.01	
Advertising	IO-73.02	

The sales by the above industries to IO-2.07, Forest, greenhouse, & nursery products, constitute the entire flows from those industries to IO-2.07 shown in the 1963 input-output table [123] and are given in producer prices. Using the 1955 ratio of producer to purchaser prices for each input to greenhouses and nurseries, these were converted to purchaser prices [105]. The one exception was plastics materials, which is not listed as an input to greenhouses and nurseries in 1955. The ratio used for plastics was that of producer to purchaser prices for the flow from IO-32, Rubber & miscellaneous plastics products, to IO-2, Other agricultural products, in the 1958 input-output table [131]. The sum of these inputs in purchaser prices, $55.5 million, is extremely close to the national total of the 1963 purchaser price data on miscellaneous expense of greenhouses and nurseries, $55.6 million (Farm Income Branch total).

The 1963 state figures on expenditures for greenhouse and nursery supplies were separated into the component inputs using percentages calculated from the 1963 national figures in purchaser prices:

	1963 Flows ($ millions)		
Producing Industry	*Producer Prices*	*Purchaser Prices*	*Percent of Total*
IO-7.00	$ .7	$ 2.1	3.8
IO-17.09	.7	.8	1.5
IO-17.10	1.4	1.5	2.7
IO-25.00	3.1	3.5	6.3
IO-32.04	4.9	5.8	10.5
IO-36.09	10.3	12.4	22.3
IO-69.00	16.0	16.0	28.8
IO-73.02	13.4	13.4	24.1
	$50.5	$55.5	100.0

14 *Coal for heat (incubating chicks, brooding)*

The figure for purchases of coal from IO-7.00, Coal mining, by IO-1.02,

Poultry & eggs, in the 370-order 1963 input-output table [123] was allocated to the states in proportion to 1963 purchases of baby chicks and turkey poults in each state [107].

15 *Fertilizer and lime*

State data on the amount of fertilizer used in 1963 were available [111, tt. 4–6] for the following kinds of fertilizer:

Producing Industry	*Kind of Fertilizer*
IO-10.00	Phosphate rock Potash materials
IO-27.01	Anhydrous & aqua ammonia Ammonium nitrate Ammonium sulfate Nitrogen solutions Sodium nitrate Urea Other chemical nitrogen materials
IO-27.02	Mixed fertilizers Superphosphates Ammoniated phosphate Other phosphate materials

The total tonnage of fertilizer for each producing input-output industry was allocated to the consuming crop subindustries in proportion to the number of acres of each crop fertilized in each state in 1963 [97, t. 1]. These figures were used as a percentage distribution to allocate the corresponding 370-order 1963 input-output flows to the states [123].

The Farm Income Branch of the U.S. Department of Agriculture provided data on 1963 total purchases of lime by farmers in each state [107]. To obtain the industrial allocation, these total purchases were allocated to the purchasing agricultural subindustries in proportion to acreage fertilized in 1963 [97, t. 1]. The resulting matrix of purchases was used as a percentage distribution to allocate the 370-order 1963 input-output flows to agriculture [123] for IO-9.00, Stone & clay mining & quarrying; IO-36.13, Lime; and IO-36.19, Minerals, ground or treated.

16 *Maintenance and repair construction*
Telephone service (business share)
Electricity (business share)

The Farm Income Branch provided 1963 state data on farmers' expenditures for repair and maintenance construction, telephone service (business share), and electricity (business share). For each state, these totals were allocated to the consuming subindustries in proportion to their 1963 cash receipts [94, t. 16, pp. 90–122; 95, t. 16, pp. 84–85].

17 *Mineral salt and other mineral supplements*

The sale by IO-9, Stone & clay mining & quarrying, to the livestock subindustries, IO-1.01 through IO-1.03, in the 370-order 1963 input-output table [123], was allocated to the consuming livestock subindustries in each state in proportion to the consumption of feed grains and concentrates in each state [101, t. A].

18 *Blacksmithing and miscellaneous hardware supplies*

The Farm Income Branch provided 1963 expenditures data on blacksmithing and miscellaneous supplies by state [107]. In the "Agricultural Industrial Relations Study, 1955" [106, pp. 15–17], this expenditures category was divided into purchases of blacksmith services, $74, 468 thousand, and miscellaneous supplies, $73,092 thousand. The 1955 figure for blacksmith services purchased was divided by the number of horses and mules in the United States in 1954 [76, t. 18, p. 508] to obtain the value of blacksmithing per horse in 1955 ($18.00). Multiplying this value by the number of horses and mules at the national level in 1960 [96, t. 13, p. 33] gave a 1963 estimate of blacksmith services purchased by IO-1.03, Meat animals & miscellaneous livestock products, from IO-73.01, Miscellaneous business services. (Because no enumeration of horses and mules had been conducted since 1960, 1960 figures had to be used for 1963.) Blacksmith services was then assumed to be a constant percentage of total blacksmithing and miscellaneous supplies in 1963 in each state, leaving a residual for purchases of miscellaneous supplies and equipment which had to be separated into its component inputs.

The publication entitled *Farmers' Expenditures in 1955* [91, tt. 14–16, pp. 33–47] gives 1955 expenditures by region for the following inputs to agriculture:

Producing Industry	*Input*
IO-16.01	Tobacco cloth
IO-17.09	Rope
IO-19.03	Canvas
IO-20.09	Ladders
IO-38.10	Wire
IO-39.02	Fuel barrels, tanks and pumps
IO-64.12	Fire extinguishers

For miscellaneous current farm operating expenses, state data were available for 1955 and for 1963 [95, t. 10]. The 1955 state data were used to allocate the regional expenditures figures to the states within each region. By using the ratio of miscellaneous current farm operating expenses in 1955 to those in 1963, these state figures were updated to 1963. The resulting matrix of miscellaneous hardware supplies purchased by state in 1963 was used as a percentage distribution to separate the miscellaneous supplies figure for each state into its component inputs. These inputs, with the exception of tobacco cloth, which is consumed only by IO-2.03, Tobacco, were allocated to the consuming agricultural subindustries in proportion to the 1963 cash receipts of each [94, t. 16; 95, t. 16].

19 *Binding materials*

The Farm Income Branch provided 1963 data on purchases of binding materials by farmers in each state [96]. This category was divided into its component inputs using 1955 regional figures (which had been allocated to the states in each region and updated to 1963 as explained in notes 10 and 18) on farmers' purchases of the following inputs [91, tt. 14–16, pp. 33–47]:

Producing Industry	*Input*
IO-17.09	Baler and binder twine
IO-42.05	Baling wire, bale ties

Because all purchases of binding materials were assumed to be used for baling hay, they were allocated to the consuming subindustry IO-2.02, Food [grains], feed grains, & grass seed, which produces hay.

20 *Miscellaneous dairy supplies*

The Farm Income Branch provided data on 1963 expenditures for miscellaneous dairy supplies by state [107]. These expenditures had to be separated into purchases of the component inputs to dairy farming. In the "Agricultural Industrial Relations Study, 1955" [106, p. 12], the miscellaneous dairy supplies category is divided into expenditures for dairy supplies and for dairy herd improvement fees.

The publication entitled *Farmers' Expenditures in 1955* [91] gives 1955 data on dairy herd improvement fees paid in each of eight regions of the United States. (The states in each region are listed in Table B-2 in the appendix.) These fees paid in each region were divided by the number of dairy cows in the region in 1954 [76, t. 30] to obtain regional figures on fees paid per dairy cow in 1955. The regional coefficients were multiplied by the number of dairy cows in each state within these regions in 1963 [114] to obtain a 1963 matrix of estimated dairy herd improvement fees paid by state. According to information from *Agricultural Statistics, 1965* [90, tt. 543, 552], one in eighteen dairy cows was tested in 1955, whereas in 1963 the rate had doubled to one in nine cows. For this reason, the figures in the 1963 matrix were doubled and were subtracted from the miscellaneous dairy-supplies figures given for each state, the residual representing purchases of dairy supplies by state in 1963.

The following flows into IO-1.01, Dairy farm products, were taken from the 370-order 1963 input-output table [123]:

Input	*Producing Industry*	*1963 Flows ($ thousands)*	
		Producer	*Purchaser*
Cloth filters	IO-17.10	$ 7,616	$11,325
Milk cartons	IO-25.00	1,661	1,764
Milk bottles	IO-35.02	4,113	5,871
Milk cans	IO-39.01	5,691	6,046
Bottle closures	IO-41.02	24,898	27,238

These flows were converted from producer prices to purchaser prices using the 1958 ratio of producer to purchaser prices for each 83-order input-output industry [131]. The residual for each state in 1963 was separated into its components in proportion to the 1963 flows and was converted to the purchaser prices shown here. All inputs were consumed by IO-1.01.

21 *Containers*
State expenditures for containers in 1963 [107] had to be separated into containers purchased by each agricultural subindustry. These state figures do not include containers purchased by dairy farmers since the expenditures category "dairy supplies" includes containers. (See Note 20.) For 1955, expenditures on marketing containers were available by commodity group and were divided by the 1955 output of each commodity group [75, t. 5] to obtain coefficients. To calculate a 1963 state-by-commodity group matrix of expenditures for containers, the 1963 outputs of the commodity groups in each state were multiplied by the 1955 coefficient. The data in this matrix were then aggregated to represent the agricultural subindustries being used in the 1963 input-output table [123] as follows:

IO-1.02	Eggs
IO-1.03	Wool & mohair Honey & other products
IO-2.02	Dry beans, peas, seeds
IO-2.04	Fruits, berries, nuts
IO-2.05	Vegetables, fresh use Vegetables, processing Potatoes

The actual 1963 container expenditures by state were allocated to the purchasing agricultural subindustries according to the percentage distribution of this state-by-subindustry matrix of container purchases.

The types of container purchased by each subindustry were estimated using percentage figures calculated from the 1955 input-output study [106, pp. 14–15].

Type of Container	*Producing Industry*	*Agricultural Subindustry (Percent)*				
		1.02	*1.03*	*2.02*	*2.04*	*2.05*
Textile	IO-19.03	–	45.0	100.0	0.9	30.0
Wooden	IO-21.00	–	–	–	99.1	70.0
Paper	IO-24.07	100.0	–	–	–	–
Glass	IO-35.02	–	55.0	–	–	–
		100.0	100.0	100.0	100.0	100.0

These percentages were used to distribute the 1963 container purchases by subindustry for each state to the appropriate producing industry.

22 *Hand tools and hand tool handles*
Farm Income Branch data on 1963 purchases of hand tools by state [107] were allocated to the consuming agricultural subindustries in each state on the basis of 1963 farm cash receipts [94, t. 16; 95, t. 16]. The 1963 total figure for purchases of hand tools by state was separated into expenditures for hand tools and hand tool handles: IO-42.02, Hand & edge tools, including saws, and IO-20.09, Wood products, n.e.c., respectively. The distribution was made using regional figures on purchases of handles as a percent of total hand-tool purchases (including handles) calculated from data given in *Farmers' Expenditures in 1955* [91, tt. 14, 16] for the states within each region. (The states in each region are listed in Table B–2 in the appendix.)

23 *Recapping tires*
The purchases by each agricultural subindustry from IO-32.03, Reclaimed rubber & miscellaneous rubber products, n.e.c., were allocated to the states in proportion to purchases of tires and inner tubes by each subindustry in 1963. (See Note 28 for method of estimation.)

24 *Inputs for which weighted national coefficients were used*
No 1963 state data on purchases of inputs by farmers were available for five producing industries:

Industry Number	*Industry Title*
IO-14.32	Food preparations, n.e.c.
IO-24.02	Paper mills, except building paper
IO-24.04	Envelopes
IO-36.17	Asbestos products
IO-82.00	Office supplies

Purchases from these industries were estimated by weighting their national inputs to agriculture. To obtain national coefficients for each input, their inputs to each agricultural subindustry in the 370-order 1963 national input-output table [123] were divided by total 1963 cash receipts by each subindustry [94, t. 16; 95, t. 16]. These national coefficients were then multiplied by the 1963 cash receipts of each subindustry in each state to obtain 370-order flows into agriculture for the five industries in each state.

25 *Transportation and trade margins on purchased inputs*
After all state inputs to agriculture had been estimated at the 370-order level (both by producing and by consuming subindustry), they were converted from purchaser to producer prices using ratios developed from the 370-order 1963 transportation and trade margins [130]. The total transportation margins on all inputs for each agricultural subindustry were summed for each state and allocated to producing input-output industry IO-65, Transportation & warehousing. The same process was repeated for the trade margins, which were allocated to IO-69, Wholesale & retail trade.

26 *Sprays and disinfectants, serums and tonics, veterinary services*
The following 1955 data are available on the national level [75, t. 5].

Kind of Animal	*IO-27.03 Sprays & Disinfectants*	*IO-77.03 Veterinary Services*	*IO-29.01 Serums & Tonics*	*IO-77.03 Veterinary Services & Medicines Not Reported Separately*
		($ thousands)		
Cattle & calves	$26,856	$29,520	$17,298	$48,640
Hogs & pigs	3,863	4,006	7,191	23,073
Sheep & lambs	912	585	1,678	799
Chickens	5,251	664	15,776	3,254
Turkeys	236	15	1,863	390
Other	496	1,218	1,045	10,896

The figures for "veterinary services & medicines not reported separately" were separated into their two components in the same proportions as the data that were reported separately.

To obtain coefficients giving expenditures per animal, each expenditures category was divided by the number of each kind of animal in 1955 [90]. The 1955 expenditures per animal for each category was multiplied by the number of animals of that type in each state in 1963 to give estimated 1963 state expenditures figures, by type of animal, for each category.

These figures were then aggregated into the livestock subindustries. The actual 1963 state expenditures data that were available for two of the categories, Veterinary services and Serums & tonics, were allocated to the livestock subindustries in each state according to the percentage distribution of the matrices for these two categories described above.

27 *Pesticides*

Pesticide expenditures figures for 10 regions and 21 commodities were available for 1964 [93, tt. 12–21, pp. 13–17]. These pesticide expenditures were realigned into a region-by-agricultural subindustry matrix and then divided by the output of the subindustries in each region to obtain regional coefficients for pesticide expenditures per unit of output. By multiplying the 1963 output in each state by the pesticide expenditures per unit output coefficient for the region to which it belongs, an estimated state-by-subindustry matrix of 1963 pesticide expenditures was obtained. The state figures for 1963 pesticide expenditures [107] were allocated to the consuming subindustries in each state according to the percentage distribution of the pesticide expenditures matrix.

28 *Repair and operation of motor vehicles and farm machinery*

Regional data on farmers' 1955 expenditures for repair and operation of motor vehicles and farm machinery [91, tt. 15, 16] were available for the following items or services (the states in each region are listed in Table B–2 of the appendix):

	Input-Output Industry Producing Input			
Item or Service	*Autos*	*Trucks*	*Tractors*	*Other Farm Machinery*
Antifreeze	27.04	27.04	27.04	27.04
Tires	32.01	32.01	32.01	32.01
Inner tubes	32.01	32.01	32.01	32.01
Tire chains	42.05	42.05	42.05	42.05
Batteries	58.01	58.01	58.01	58.01
Spark plugs	58.04	58.04	58.04	58.04
Insurance	70.04	70.04	–	–
Lubrication jobs	75.00	75.00	–	–
Brake adjustments	75.00	75.00	–	–
Brake relining	75.00	75.00	73.01	–
Registration & license fees	79.03	79.03	–	–
Other parts/services	59.03/75.00	59.03/75.00	44.00/73.01	44.00/73.01

These 1955 expenditures for automobiles, trucks, tractors, and other farm machinery were divided by the number of automobiles, trucks, tractors, and other farm machinery in each region in 1955 [76, tt. 12, 13, 15, 16] to give 1955 expenditures for each item or service per automobile, per truck, etc., by region. To obtain a matrix of estimated 1963 figures for repair and operation of motor vehicles and farm machinery, these 1955 regional coefficients were multiplied by the 1964 number of automobiles, trucks, etc., in each state within the region [77, t. 22; 78, tt. 1-3].

The Farm Income Branch provided actual 1963 state data for two categories, "Repairs, tires & inner tubes, tire chains, antifreeze & parts" and "License & insurance." These two expenditures figures were given for automobiles, trucks, tractors, and farm machinery within each state [107].

The matrix estimated from the 1955 figures was used to separate the actual 1963 state figures into their component parts, and the resulting figures were allocated to the consuming input-output industries, IO-1, Livestock & livestock products, and IO-2, Other agricultural products, in proportion to the number of automobiles, trucks, etc., in each industry in 1964. (The figures were obtained by aggregating *Census of Agriculture, 1964* figures by type of farm to IO-1 and IO-2 [77, t. 22]). The figures for the two agricultural input-output industries were further allocated to the subindustries within each on the basis of 1963 cash receipts [94, t. 16; 95, t. 16].

29 *Gasoline and other petroleum fuel and oil*

Expenditures for gasoline, kerosene, oil, and grease for the operation of motor vehicles and farm machinery comprise the bulk of farmers' purchases of petroleum products. In addition, petroleum products were used for "drying and curing crops, brooding, killing weeds, heating water and many types of farm buildings, and for frost protection in orchards" [100, p. 11]. *Census of Agriculture, 1964* figures on expenditures for petroleum products in each state are given for twelve types of farm [77, t. 22]. These figures were aggregated to represent 1964 expenditures for gasoline and other petroleum fuel and oil by the two agricultural industries, IO-1, Livestock & livestock products, and IO-2, Other agricultural products.

For petroleum products, total 1963 purchases by farmers in each state [107] were allocated to IO-1 and IO-2 in proportion to the 1964 purchases by each (estimated as described above). The resulting 1963 state petroleum expenditures figures for each industry were allocated to the consuming subindustries within each of the two input-output industries on the basis of 1963 cash receipts [94, t. 16; 95, t. 16].

The total expenditures obtained for IO-1.02, Poultry & eggs, and IO-2.07, Forest, greenhouse, & nursery products, in each state was split between purchases from IO-31.01, Petroleum refining & related products, and IO-68.02, Gas utilities, as follows: The flows from IO-68.02, Gas utilities, to IO-1.02, Poultry & eggs, and IO-2.07, Forest, greenhouse, & nursery products, in the 370-order 1963 input-output table [123] were allocated to the states in proportion to 1963 purchases of baby chicks and turkey poults in each state [107] and the 1964 value of horticultural products sold by state [98], respectively. These figures for gas heat purchased from IO-68.02

by IO-1.02 were subtracted from the petroleum, fuel, and oil purchases, the residuals representing purchases from IO-31.01. Since there is no markup on services sold by IO-68.01, no discrepancy was caused by subtracting sales by IO-68.01 from those of IO-31.01, which are in purchaser prices.

30 *Irrigation*
The Farm Income Branch 1963 data for farmers' expenditures for irrigation, by state [107], were considered as a purchase by agriculture from IO-68.03, Water & sanitary services. Each state figure for irrigation fees paid in 1963 was allocated to the consuming agricultural subindustries according to the number of acres of its crops harvested from irrigated land in each state in 1964 [78, t. 9, pp. 923-927].

31 *Miscellaneous parts for farm machinery and equipment*
No state information was available for 1963 purchases of the following specific inputs by farmers:

Producing Industry	*Input*
IO-50.00	Carburetors, pistons, valves
IO-55.01	Lamps
IO-61.07	Parts for wagons, carts

The sales to agriculture by these three input-output industries consist entirely of the inputs indicated. Therefore, estimates were made by distributing the flows from these producing industries into agriculture in the 1963 input-output table [123] to the purchasing subindustries in each state in proportion to prior estimates of 1963 purchases of parts and accessories for farm machinery from IO-44.00, Farm machinery, by the agricultural subindustries in each state. (See Note 28.)

32 *Miscellaneous marketing charges*
The total 1963 figure for miscellaneous marketing charges paid by farmers in each state [107] was allocated to the purchasing crop subindustries in each state in proportion to the 1963 cash receipts of each [94, t. 16; 95, t. 16]. Allocations were made to the crop subindustries only because livestock marketing costs were given separately [107]. (See Note 33.)

33 *Livestock marketing costs*
For total livestock marketing costs, 1963 state figures were available [107]. The total for each state was separated into marketing costs for each of the livestock subindustries as follows: Marketing cost data for 1955 that were available on the national level for each kind of animal [75, t. 5] were divided by the total number of animals of each respective type [90] to

obtain 1955 marketing costs per animal. The 1955 ratios were multiplied by the number of each kind of animal in each state in 1963 [114], and these estimated 1963 marketing cost figures by kind of animal for each state were aggregated to livestock subindustries. The 1963 marketing cost state-by-industry matrix was used as a percentage distribution to allocate the actual 1963 state livestock marketing cost figures to the livestock subindustries in each state.

34 *Banking services*
The sales by IO-70.01, Banking, to the agricultural subindustries shown in the 1963 input-output table [123] were allocated to the states in proportion to the amount of 1963 farm real estate loans outstanding in each state [89, t. 722, pp. 510–511].

35 *Crop-hail insurance; other insurance*
The 1963 total of fire, wind, and crop-hail insurance paid by farmers in each state [107] was separated into fire and wind insurance and crop-hail insurance using the 1963 national amount of each [89] for a ratio. The state figure for fire and wind insurance was allocated to *purchasing* agricultural subindustries, IO-1.01 through IO-1.03 and IO-2.01 through IO-2.07, on the basis of 1963 cash receipts [94, t. 16; 95, t. 16]. Cash receipts were also used to distribute total crop-hail insurance purchased in each state to the *consuming* crop subindustries, IO-2.01 through IO-2.07.

36 *Rent payments on service buildings and structures*
The flows from IO-71.02, Real estate, into agriculture consist of commissions on real estate transactions paid to agents and brokers and of rent payments on service buildings and structures on farms but not owned by farmers. To obtain a 1963 total rent payment figure for each subindustry, estimates of agents' and brokers' fees paid by each agricultural subindustry in 1963 were subtracted from the total flow from IO-71.02 into each subindustry [123]. (See Note 10.) These agricultural subindustry totals were allocated to the subindustries in each state in proportion to 1963 net rent paid to nonfarm landlords by all farmers in the state [95, t. 10, p. 73].

37 *Directly allocated imports with associated transportation, trade, and insurance margins*
The only directly allocated import used by agriculture is hired foreign labor. The U.S. Department of Labor provided data on 1963 total man-hours of hired foreign labor used on each crop [141, t. 7, p. 17], as well as information on the major states in which labor was used on each crop [141]. Since 95 percent of the 1963 total foreign hired labor was employed in eight states (California, Texas, Florida, Arizona, Michigan, Colorado, Arkansas,

and New Mexico) [141, p. 15], the total man-hours of hired foreign labor for each crop were distributed to these states, using output of each crop by state as an allocation factor. The same Department of Labor source provided figures for Mexican hired labor (97 percent of total) used on crops in each of the eight states, which were used as controls. These state figures for total man-hours of foreign hired labor served as allocation factors for the value of directly allocated imports to IO-1, Livestock & livestock products, and IO-2, Other agricultural products, in the 1963 input-output table [122].

The transportation, trade, and insurance margins associated with these estimated imports of foreign labor were calculated for each state using national figures on margins obtained from the 1963 input-output table [130].

3 Mining Technologies

Roger M. Kubarych and Mary M. Shirley

Attempts to estimate regional inputs are usually hampered by the absence of detailed state data that are consistent with the national input-output classification. The mining sector was no exception. The procedures for estimating state input requirements for the mining industries therefore had to be tailored to fit the data available. Working within these data constraints, state input structures were assembled for each of the six input-output (IO) mining industries: IO-5, Iron & ferroalloy ores mining; IO-6, Nonferrous metal ores mining; IO-7, Coal mining; IO-8, Crude petroleum & natural gas; IO-9, Stone & clay mining & quarrying; and IO-10, Chemical & fertilizer mineral mining. A generally similar methodology was used to construct state estimates for five of the six input-output industries in the mining sector; IO-8 had to be treated in a different way because virtually no regional data were available for this industry.

General Methodology

The methodology used to obtain mining inputs by state was similar to a product-mix procedure, since national coefficients were multiplied by state output figures to calculate state production functions. The usual procedure was modified, however, for five of the six mining industries, as regional and some state data were available for certain broad cost categories by four-digit Standard Industrial Classification (SIC) group. Whenever possible, estimates were constructed for the most important subindustries, with any remaining subindustries being treated as a residual. The regional data were distributed to the states on the basis of state output figures for each SIC group. Some categories corresponded to input-output industries and could be used without change; others were combinations of several industries. The aggregated state cost categories were disaggregated into inputs from relevant input-output industries, using national input coefficients for each SIC group. When the regional data for the five mining industries were assembled from the four-digit SIC information, considerable regional variation in the input structure was assured, particularly in those cases where a mining subindustry is located in only one or two regions. (In effect, the national coefficients for these subindustries will then provide regional production functions, and the input structure will vary from region to region because the national coefficients vary considerably from one subindustry to another.)

This modified product-mix procedure was used for the mining industries with adjustments according to the quality of data available for each SIC subindustry, the extent of aggregation in the cost categories, and the structure of the particular industry. The principal source for the regional cost information for IO-5, IO-6, IO-7, IO-9, and IO-10 was the *Census of Mineral Industries, 1963 (CMI)* [82]. While the *CMI* contained some state data that could be used directly, most of the statistics were for regions only and had to be allocated to states in another step. In addition, the cost categories, which are aggregates of several input-output industries, were combined for some SIC subindustries. Finally, no state-by-state data were available for purchases from the service industries, except for IO-68, Electric, gas, water, & sanitary services. Thus, the techniques used to estimate mining inputs varied according to the quality and quantity of the data.

Detailed Description of the Methodology

To estimate the mining inputs by state, the mining purchases for each of the six mining industries were divided into seven product cost categories, and a separate method was developed to disaggregate each of these categories for the component subindustries. The seven categories are: materials inputs, fuels and purchased electricity, intraindustry purchases, contract mining services, purchased services, transportaton and trade, and value added. For all of the mining industries except IO-8, Crude petroleum & natural gas, regional (and, in some cases, state) data were available in the *CMI* [82] for the first four categories. For example, the *CMI* provided data for SIC 1421, Crushed & broken stone, including riprap, in the format shown in Table 3-1.

The categories and sources used for the estimates were:

1. *Materials inputs.* This category is composed of the products purchased from the manufacturing sector, IO-13 through IO-64 (except IO-31, Petroleum refining & related industries) and IO-82, Office supplies. For most of the mining industries, over half of these purchases come from supplying industries IO-20, Lumber & wood products, except containers; IO-27, Chemicals & selected chemical products; IO-32, Rubber & miscellaneous plastics products; IO-37, Primary iron & steel manufacturing; IO-43, Engines & turbines; IO-45, Construction, mining, oil field machinery & equipment; and IO-50, Machine shop products. Most of the remainder come from only a dozen other industries. Regional (and, in some cases, state) data by SIC subindustries for this broad category of inputs were obtained from *CMI* tables, using the line under "Principal expenses" entitled "Supplies and purchases for resale."

2. *Fuels and purchased electric energy.* This category represents purchases of

Table 3–1
Sample of Data from the *Census of Mineral Industries, 1963* for SIC 1421, Crushed & Broken Stone, Including Riprap

	New England				Middle Atlantic			
	Division	*Massachusetts*	*Connecticut*	. . .	*Division*	*New York*	*New Jersey*	. . .
Principal Expenses ($1000)								
Supplies and purchases for resale / Stone received for preparation	$2650	$788	$1276	. . .	. . .	. . .	. . .	. . .
Purchased fuels	475	103	236	. . .	. . .	. . .	. . .	. . .
Purchased electric energy	531	252	195	. . .	. . .	. . .	. . .	. . .
Contract work	315	165	116	. . .	. . .	. . .	. . .	. . .
Energy Used								
Coal (1000 short tons)	–	–	–	. . .	. . .	. . .	. . .	. . .
Distillate fuel oil (1000 barrels)	21	3	12	. . .	. . .	. . .	. . .	. . .
Residual fuel oil (1000 barrels)	13	12	1	. . .	. . .	. . .	. . .	. . .
Gas (million cubic feet)	17	–	17	. . .	. . .	. . .	. . .	. . .
Gasoline (1000 gallons)	528	80	225	. . .	. . .	. . .	. . .	. . .
Other fuels ($1000)	81	15	51	. . .	. . .	. . .	. . .	. . .
Undistributed ($1000)	104	–	47	. . .	. . .	. . .	. . .	. . .

coal from IO-7, fuel oils and gasoline products from IO-31, and gas and electricity from IO-68. Regional data for this category in the *CMI* were contained in the lines headed "Purchased fuels," "Other fuels," "Undistributed," and "Purchased electric energy."

3. *Intraindustry purchases.* The values for these inputs, taken from the *CMI* lines headed ". . . received for preparation," represent an industry's purchase of its own mined output for further cleaning, preparing, or processing.

4. *Contract mining services.* This category comprises payments by a mining industry to itself or to other mining industries for services directly related to mining operations. The *CMI* gives regional data for this category under the title "Contract work." Information on supplying industries was contained in Wang and Kokat [158].

5. *Purchased services.* This category represents purchases from the service industries, IO-66 through IO-79 (excluding IO-68, Electric, gas, water, & sanitary services, and IO-69, Wholesale & retail trade), and from IO-12, Maintenance & repair construction. Payments for land rentals by mining companies are especially important in this category. As stated earlier, no regional data were available for services, except for IO-68, Electric, gas, water, & sanitary services.

6. *Transportation and trade.* This category contains the imputed payments to IO-65, Transportation & warehousing, and IO-69, Wholesale & retail trade, and represents the margin between producer prices and purchaser prices. The data for this category were calculated for the states using the national transportation and trade margins.

7. *Value added.* This category, which represents the services of labor, capital, interest, etc., was calculated as a residual after the intermediate inputs had been calculated.

The data collection proceeded not at the industry level, but at the subindustry level. Information in each category was gathered for as many important SIC groups within an industry as possible. Table 3–2 indicates which subindustries had sufficient data to be included in the estimation. For some subindustries, the detail given for the materials inputs, category 1, was insufficient to make an estimate, while estimates could be made for the other categories. These SIC groups are listed in the column of partially estimated subindustries. Those subindustries for which no usable data existed were treated as a residual.

Table 3–3 indicates the source of regional information for each SIC group in the first four categories: materials inputs, fuels and purchased electricity, intraindustry purchases, and contract mining services. For each SIC subindustry, the regional figures for the four categories were distributed to the states within the region according to the states' value of output of that SIC subindustry relative to the total regional value of output. The state output figures by three- and four-digit SIC mining group were taken from unpublished worksheets of Jack Faucett Associates, Inc. (JFA) [21]. In those cases where the *CMI* [82] gave one

Table 3–2
SIC Subindustries Used for State Estimates of Mining Input Requirements

Input-Output Industry Number	*SIC Groups Completely Estimated*	*SIC Groups Partially Estimated**	*SIC Groups Not Estimated*	*Total Shipments Represented by SIC Groups Completely Estimated (Percent)*
5	SIC 101	SIC 1064 SIC 1069	SIC 1062	98
6	SIC 102	SIC 103 SIC 104 SIC 105 SIC 108 SIC 109		54
7	SIC 11 SIC 12			100
9	SIC 1421 SIC 1441	SIC 1445	SIC 141 SIC 145 SIC 148 SIC 149	89
10	SIC 1472 SIC 1473 SIC 1474 SIC 1475 SIC 1476 SIC 1477 SIC 1479			100

Note: See the appendix, Table A–4, for names of the SIC subindustries.
*No estimate was made for category 1, Materials inputs.

or more state cost figures in addition to the regional total, the state's (or states') cost figures were subtracted from the regional total first and used without change; the remainder was distributed to the other states in the region for which no figures were given according to the relative value of output of the omitted states. The result was state figures for the SIC subindustries that were estimated for each of the four cost categories. The disaggregation of the data in those broad categories into input-output industries will be described for each category.

Category 1, Materials Inputs

The state estimates of the *CMI* category "costs of supplies" were disaggregated into input-output industries using coefficients from a Bureau of Mines study by Wang and Kokat, *The Interindustry Structure of the U.S. Mining*

Table 3-3
Sources of Regional Mining Data

Industry Number and Title		*Source*
IO-5	Iron & ferroalloy ores mining	
	SIC 101	*CMI* [82, sec. 10B, pp. 6, 7]
	SIC 1064, 1069	*CMI* [82, sec. 10D, p. 8]
IO-6	Nonferrous metal ores mining	
	SIC 102	*CMI* [82, sec. 10C, p. 16]
	SIC 103–105, 108, 109	*
IO-7	Coal mining	
	SIC 11	*CMI* [82, sec. 11B, pp. 8, 9]
	SIC 12	*CMI* [82, sec. 12A, pp. 20–22]
IO-8	Crude petroleum & natural gas	*
IO-9	Stone & clay mining & quarrying	
	SIC 1421	*CMI* [82, sec. 14B, pp. 23–30]
	SIC 1441	*CMI* [82, sec. 14C, pp. 10–14]
	SIC 1445	*CMI* [82, sec. 14D, p. 13]
IO-10	Chemical & fertilizer mineral mining	
	SIC 1472–1477, 1479	*CMI* [82, sec. 14E, pp. 10, 11]

*Estimated by distributing regional output figures from unpublished worksheets of Jack Faucett Associates, Inc. [21].

Industries, 1958 [158]. This work contains direct input coefficient vectors for 48 detailed SIC categories that could be aggregated to input-output industries comparable with the data in the 1958 national input-output table [131]. Because these estimates were based in many cases on actual engineering estimates or process analyses, these coefficients furnished a means of disaggregating the *CMI* cost-of-supplies data to provide detailed technical information that could be directly aggregated to the input-output classification.

Since the *CMI* data are given in purchaser prices, the Wang-Kokat coefficients had to be converted from producer prices, as they appear in that source, to purchaser prices. This was accomplished using 1958 transportation and trade margins for each SIC subindustry, which were calculated from input figures in producer and purchaser values in the Wang-Kokat study. The coefficients for a subindustry were then summed over those input-output industries producing the inputs that fall into the cost-of-supplies category, specifically the manufacturing industries, IO-13 through IO-64 (except IO-31, Petroleum refining & related industries), and IO-82, Office supplies. The coefficients for these input-output industries were then taken as a ratio to this sum and multiplied by the state cost-of-supplies figures for the respective SIC subindustry, to yield input vectors for each state. This process was repeated for each SIC subindustry that was estimated (see Table 3-2). The resulting state vectors for the SIC subindustries within each input-output industry category were then summed to obtain state estimates of materials inputs for the mining sector in purchaser prices.

Category 2, Fuels and Purchased Electric Energy

As explained earlier, the *CMI* information for this category was given as four types of energy costs: purchased fuels, other fuels, undistributed and purchased electric energy. For the last three types, the state allocation was straightforward. The regional data for other fuels and undistributed energy for a given SIC subindustry were distributed to the states in each region according to the state shares of the SIC subindustry output, and the state estimates for each SIC subindustry were then treated as purchases from IO-31, Petroleum refining & related industries. For purchased electric energy, the state figures for each SIC subindustry were calculated in the same way, and the state electricity estimates that resulted were assigned directly to IO-68, Electric, gas, water, & sanitary services.

The purchased-fuels entry was more of a problem, because it represents purchases from both IO-31 and IO-68, as well as purchases of coal from IO-7, Coal mining. To allocate this category among the three input-output industries, the regional totals for purchased fuels were distributed to the states using the JFA output weights for the SIC subindustries. Then the state estimates of purchased fuels were disaggregated whenever sufficient data were available, using the *CMI* [82] information on individual fuels. For some of the SIC subindustries, the *CMI* gave regional data on the quantity purchased of coal (in tons), distillate fuel oil (in barrels), residual fuel oil (in barrels), gas (in millions of cubic feet), and gasoline (in gallons). In addition, a national breakdown of the value of the purchases of these fuels was provided for some SIC subindustries in the *CMI* table entitled "Purchased fuels and electric energy used" [82, sec. 6, t. 3, pp. 8–13]. The national distribution of total fuel among the component types of fuel was determined for each subindustry, and these proportions were applied as standard weights in disaggregating the purchased-fuels category for each state. Next, the regional quantity data for each fuel type were used to adjust the state fuel estimates, which then reflected differences in actual quantities used. The resulting state estimates for coal were treated as purchases from IO-7, Coal mining; the estimates for fuel oil and gasoline were allocated to IO-31, Petroleum refining & related industries; and the estimates for gas were assigned to IO-68, Electric, gas, water, & sanitary services.

Category 3, Intraindustry Purchases

This category represents the purchase by an industry of its own production for further processing and appears in the *CMI* as: minerals received for preparation, coal received for preparation, stone received for preparation, etc. For some regions, the ". . . received for preparation" entry is aggregated with the "cost of supplies" figure. To disaggregate a region's entry, the ratio of the state output to the national total for the appropriate SIC subindustry was applied to the national figures for "cost of supplies" and ". . . received for preparation" to obtain a state figure for each of the two cost categories. These two sets of data were then summed for all the states in the region, and the ratio of the resulting two regional sets of data was applied to the *CMI* regional aggregate figure for these categories. The regional estimate of ". . . received for preparation" was then allocated to the states, using state proportions of regional output, and the state data were placed in the intraindustry cells for the SIC subindustries.

Category 4, Contract Mining Services

The inputs of contract mining services represented by this category were allocated entirely to one supplying industry for each purchasing industry on the basis of information in Wang and Kokat [158] as shown in Table 3-4.

Category 5, Purchased Services

Regional data in a usable form on the inputs of the service industries into the mining sector were unavailable except for IO-68, Electric, gas, water, & sanitary services; therefore, inputs of services were estimated at the input-output industry level. The 1963 Office of Business Economics (OBE) national transactions figures [122] were distributed to states on the basis of each state's value of output relative to the total national value of output for the input-output mining industry in question.

Category 6, Transportation and Trade, and Category 7, Value Added

These two categories were estimated after all other estimates had been made and after the matrices had been initially adjusted to the OBE national totals (the

Table 3–4
Inputs of Contract Mining Services

Supplying Industry	*Purchasing Industry*
IO-6	IO-5
IO-6	IO-6
IO-7	IO-7
IO-8	IO-8
IO-9	IO-9
IO-9	IO-10

Table 3-5
Initial Estimates of 1963 Negative Value Added
(thousands of current dollars)

State	*Industry Number*	*Industry Title*	*Value Added*	*Output*
Maryland	IO-5	Iron & ferroalloy ores mining	$-669	$740
South Dakota	IO-5	Iron & ferroalloy ores mining	-49	27
Georgia	IO-7	Coal mining	-120	146
Washington	IO-10	Chemical & fertilizer mineral mining	-193	51
West Virginia	IO-10	Chemical & fertilizer mineral mining	-130	103

method is described below). The state transportation and trade costs were calculated by multiplying the state inputs by the transportation and trade margin coefficients obtained from the unpublished national OBE margin tables [130]. The value added category was calculated as a residual by subtracting the sum of all intermediate inputs from the JFA state establishment output figures for each input-output industry [68]. In a few instances, the value added figure obtained was negative, indicating that a larger value of output had been allocated to the state intermediate inputs for an industry than had been produced in the state. The states where this occurred are shown in Table 3-5. The negatives occurred in states that are very small producers, indicating relatively minor discrepancies between the estimated regional coefficients and the regional output data. To adjust the value added for these states, the negative figure plus 5 percent of state output was subtracted from the input data for the supplying industries in proportion to their share of state output. This reduced the state inputs by that amount (and insured a positive value added), and the reconciliation described below was again made.

Reconciliation with the National Input-Output Table

After the first four categories had been assembled, the data for each SIC subindustry were aggregated to the input-output industry level, the data were converted from purchaser to producer prices using the national transportation and trade margins,[1] and the estimates for category 5 were inserted into the rows for the service sector inputs. The result was a matrix of inputs by state for mining industries IO-5, Iron & ferroalloy ores mining; IO-6, Nonferrous metal ores

1. This conversion from purchaser to producer prices was made separately from the estimation of data for IO-65, Transportation & warehousing, and IO-69, Wholesale & retail trade, because the state input estimates had to be completely reconciled with the OBE national controls before the data for rows 65 and 69 could be calculated.

mining; IO-7, Coal mining; IO-9, Stone & clay mining & quarrying; and IO-10, Chemical & fertilizer mineral mining. (As explained later, IO-8, Crude petroleum & natural gas, was handled in a different way.) The state estimates were then reconciled with the OBE national 1963 input-output data using the following procedure: The state estimates were summed; each state vector was calculated as a proportion of the resulting national vector of inputs; and the 1963 OBE value (in producer prices) for each respective input-output industry was then distributed to the states according to these proportions. When these estimates had been completed, categories 6 and 7 were calculated, and all inputs into the mining industries were again reconciled with the corresponding data in the OBE national 1963 input-output table. (This second reconciliation with the national data was required because the state inputs were adjusted to eliminate negative value added data for certain states.) At this point, the state estimates for each of the mining industries were in matrix form with inputs from 82 industries for 51 regions. Figure 3–1 illustrates the steps required to obtain state figures for input-output mining indjustry *j*, composed of SIC subindustries *x*, *y*, and *z*.

Since the materials inputs category was allocated to supplying industries on the basis of 1958 Wang-Kokat coefficients, the procedure implicitly assumed that the coefficients were the same in 1963 as in 1958—in other words, that whatever changes in technology occurred over this five-year period had strictly proportionate effects on the distribution of current inputs required to sustain production. For the most part, this assumption seemed justified; however, when the 1963 input-output table was published, it was observed that large changes in transaction costs had occurred between 1958 and 1963 for a few industries.[2]

The most remarkable change took place in the transactions figures for supplying industry IO-43, Engines & turbines. In the 1958 table, the purchases by each mining industry from IO-43 were recorded as being less than $1 million. By 1963, this figure had increased to $36 million for IO-7, to $38 million for IO-9, and to significant amounts for others of the mining industries. The comparisons are shown in terms of the national direct coefficients in Table 3-6. For all mining industries except IO-8, the change in the direct coefficient is significant. Less startling, but, nevertheless, substantial increases also occurred for IO-32, Rubber & miscellaneous plastics products, IO-50, Machine shop products, and IO-59, Motor vehicles & equipment, whereas there were substantial decreases for IO-24, Paper & allied products, except containers & boxes, and IO-46, Materials handling machinery & equipment. For other examples, compare the data in the 1958 [131] and 1963 [122] input-output tables. Clearly, estimates of purchases from these industries based upon 1958 technological requirements would misstate actual purchases based upon 1963 requirements. Consequently,

2. The state mining estimates were initially made in 1968–1969, but the 1963 OBE table was not published until November 1969; therefore, only 1958 data could be used as a guide during the early parts of this study.

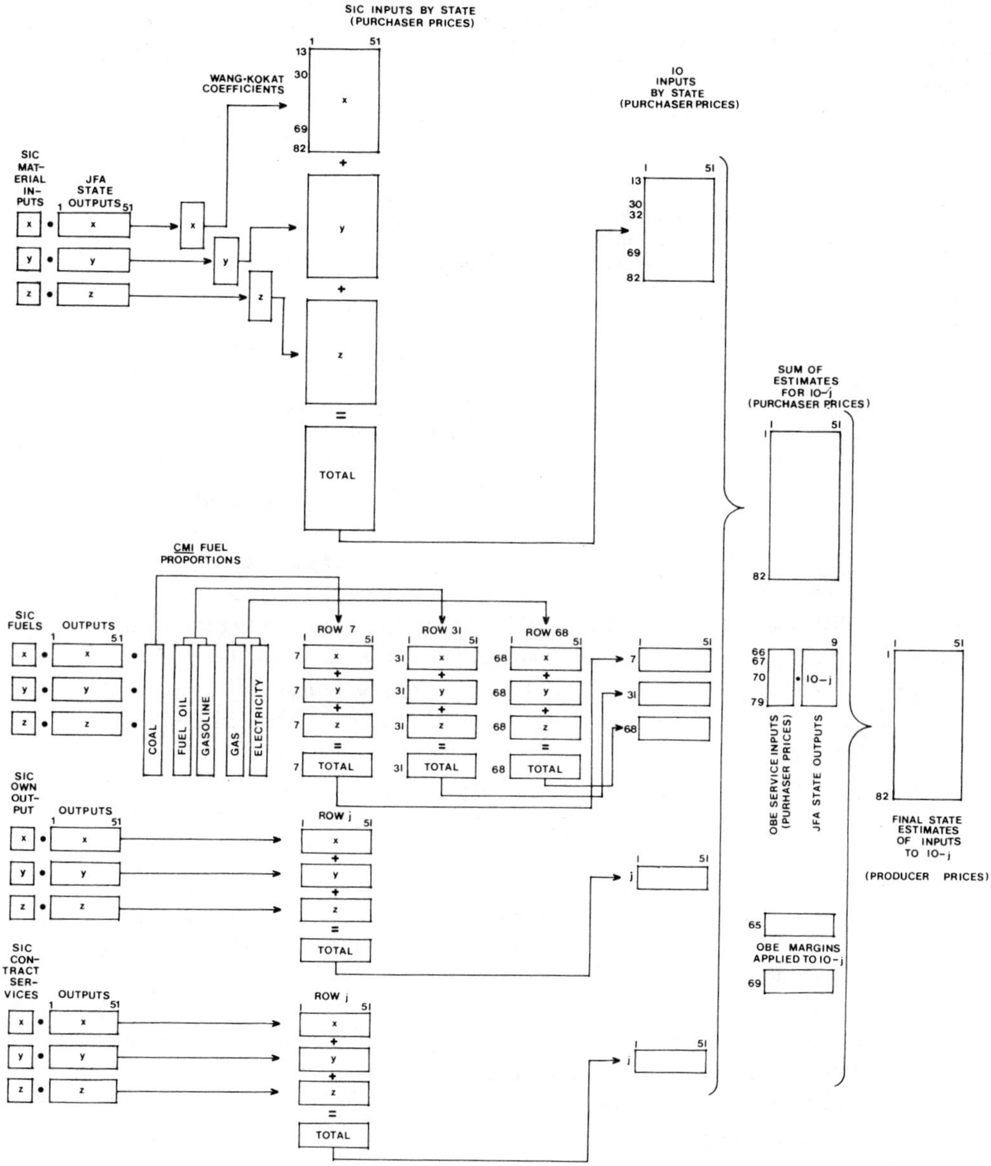

Figure 3-1. Method of Estimating Mining Inputs by State (for Input-Output Industry j, Composed of SIC x, SIC y, and SIC z)

Table 3–6
1958 and 1963 Direct Inputs from IO-43, Engines & Turbines

Purchasing Industry			
Number	*Title*	*1958*	*1963*
IO-5	Iron & ferroalloy ores mining	$.00031	$.00585
IO-6	Nonferrous metal ores mining	.00040	.00719
IO-7	Coal mining	–	.01355
IO-8	Crude petroleum & natural gas	.00137	.00129
IO-9	Stone & clay mining & quarrying	*	.01838
IO-10	Chemical & fertilizer mineral mining	.00030	.00663

*Less than .00001

Sources: For 1958, U.S. Department of Commerce, Office of Business Economics, "The Transactions Table of the 1958 Input-Output Study and Revised Direct and Total Requirements Data," *Survey of Current Business* [131].

For 1963, U.S. Department of Commerce, Office of Business Economics, "Input-Output Structure of the U.S. Economy: 1963," *Survey of Current Business* [122].

to take account of these developments, substantial alterations to the original estimates were made during the reconciliation process.

Comparisons made before adjusting some of the larger discrepancies, summarized in Table 3–7, indicated that many of the estimates differed only slightly from the OBE vectors. For IO-5, 17 of the 29 inputs estimated using the Wang-Kokat coefficients differed less than 10 percent from the OBE totals and 5 between 10 and 25 percent; for IO-7, 11 out of 29 differed less than 10 percent, and 7 differed between 10 and 25 percent; for IO-9, 12 out of the 30 estimated differed less than 10 percent, and 6 less than 25 percent; and for IO-10, 22 out of 29 differed less than 10 percent, and 2 between 10 and 25 percent.[3] IO-6 was omitted from the comparisons because, prior to reconciliation, too large a proportion of costs was undetermined to make it comparable; IO-8 was omitted because the 1963 national coefficients were used for the state estimates.

To reduce some of the larger discrepancies between the sums of the state estimates of this study and the data in the 1963 OBE national table, unestimated or underestimated inputs to mining were allocated by distributing the relevant data from the OBE transactions flow matrix (in producer prices) to the states in proportion to the state value of output. The eight supplying industries for which this was done are given in Table 3–8. In addition, the data for those supplying industries that had very small inputs in 1963, but none in 1958, were allocated to the largest producing states according to their share of 1963 output. In this way, some of the larger deviations between the estimates produced by this study and the 1963 OBE transactions table were eliminated. This problem arose only

3. For these comparisons, estimates representing less than 100 percent of value of output were increased proportionally, and for smaller entries, $1 million was used instead of 10 percent because percentage differences would have been misleading.

Table 3–7
Comparisons of 1963 National Input-Output Data with Multiregional Estimates

Input-Output Mining Industry[a]		*Number of Industries*[b]		
No.	*Title*	*Less than 10 percent*[c]	*10 to 25 percent*	*More than 25 percent*
5	Iron & ferroalloy ores mining	17[d]	5[d]	7[d]
7	Coal mining	11	7	11
9	Stone & clay mining & quarrying	12[d]	6[d]	12[d]
10	Chemical & fertilizer mineral mining	22	2	5

[a] Multiregional totals were obtained by summing appropriate state estimates. IO-6 is omitted because too large a proportion of costs was undetermined prior to reconciliation, and IO-8 is omitted because 1963 national coefficients were used for the state estimates.

[b] The number of industries for which sums of state estimates and national total differ by the percentages shown.

[c] Or $1 million.

[d] Where estimates represented less than 100 percent of value of output, they were increased proportionally for purposes of comparison.

Table 3–8
Unestimated or Underestimated Inputs to Mining

Supplying Industry	*Purchasing Industry*
IO-9	IO-5
IO-46, IO-61	IO-6
IO-43	IO-7
IO-40, IO-43, IO-53	IO-9
IO-55	IO-10

for the materials inputs category since all other categories used 1963 data, and the SIC subindustry outputs from Jack Faucett Associates (JFA) [21] were also for 1963.

After the state estimates had been reconciled with the national data, the resulting mining matrices were adjusted for use in the multiregional input-output model. The data for the six mining industries in the rows for IO-81, Business travel, entertainment, & gifts, and IO-82, Office supplies, were redistributed to other entries in the columns of the mining industries. This was done by taking columns 81 and 82 from the 1963 national input-output transfer (secondary) matrix and dividing the figures in each column by the column totals, to obtain two vectors of coefficients. The values in rows 81 and 82 of the state matrices were then distributed to the other elements in the respective columns in proportion to the calculated coefficients. The values in the original rows 81 and 82 were made zero, and other multiregional data (imports and value added) were assigned to them (refer to Appendix C). When all adjustments had been completed, the state mining vectors were inserted into the state input-output tables as columns 5 through 10 for use in the multiregional model.

Detailed Description of Inputs by Industry

The general methodology just described to obtain state estimates for the mining sector, based upon SIC subindustry data, had to be adapted to fit the limitations of the data available for each input-output industry. The detailed procedure used to estimate the final mining sector inputs is therefore explained for each industry individually.

IO-5, Iron & Ferroalloy Ores Mining

IO-5 is composed of four SIC subindustries: SIC 1011, Iron ores, SIC 1062, Manganese ores, SIC 1064, Tungsten ores, and SIC 1069, Ferroalloy ores, except vanadium, n.e.c. Each of the four subindustries is centered in one or two geographical regions, which makes IO-5 well suited to the procedures used to estimate state input requirements. Unfortunately, few regional data were available for the ferroalloy ores, so they could be only partially estimated. This was not a serious drawback, however, since 91 percent of the 1963 total value of shipments for IO-5, which amounted to $835 million, consisted of iron ore [82, sec. 10B, pp. 6, 7]. Data on the remaining 9 percent attributable to the ferroalloy ores were divided into manganese (1 percent), tungsten (1 percent), and other (7 percent).

Most of the 1963 iron ore was produced in the Lake Superior region, 62 percent of national output in Minnesota alone, an additional 15 percent in Michigan. Another 10 percent was produced in the New York–New Jersey–Pennsylvania region, while the remainder was scattered among a number of other states. Since manganese is generally produced as a secondary product of iron mining in Minnesota, Michigan, and Montana (so its inputs are recorded as part of the purchases of SIC 1011), no attempt was made to obtain a separate distribution for SIC 1062. Some separate estimates were made for tungsten, which is mined primarily in Colorado, and for the other ferroalloy ores, which are mined largely in the western states.

For the materials inputs category, regional data for SIC 1011 were distributed to the states in proportion to their share of regional output of the subindustry and allocated to supplying industries IO-13 through IO-64 (manufacturing industries) and IO-82, Office supplies, according to the Wang-Kokat coefficients for SIC 1011. For the intraindustry purchases and contract mining services, regional data for SIC 1064 and 1069, as well as for SIC 1011, were distributed to the states according to state proportions of regional output of the relevant SIC group and treated as inputs from IO-5 and IO-6, respectively.

Because of the lack of regional data for the ferroalloy ores, the fuels and purchased-electricity category also was estimated only for SIC 1011. For IO-7, Coal mining, the national value of coal purchased by SIC 1011 was divided by the national figure for tons purchased by that subindustry to obtain a price [82, sec. 6, pp. 8–12]. The price was then applied to the regional figure for quantity of coal purchased to calculate the regional value of coal used, and this estimate was allocated to the states according to output. For IO-31, Petroleum refining & related industries, the distribution obtained using the Wang-Kokat coefficients for SIC 1011 was included as that industry's inputs to IO-5. A procedure similar to that used for coal was followed for purchases of gas by SIC 1011 in each state, and these purchases, added to the state purchased-electricity data, were treated as inputs from IO-68, Electric, gas, water, & sanitary services.

All the state data for the first four cost categories were then converted from purchaser to producer prices using national transportation and trade margins. Next, as explained in detail in the first part of this chapter, the data for the services sector were allocated, weighting the 1963 national coefficients from the OBE by JFA state iron and ferroalloy ores outputs. The SIC distributions were then summed to obtain a matrix of inputs by state. The national totals from this matrix were compared with the corresponding elements in the 1963 OBE national vector of inputs for iron and ferroalloy ores. Where large discrepancies occurred, the worksheets for these industries were rechecked, and any errors found in the state elements in the industry rows were corrected. Finally, all elements in the matrix of state estimates were adjusted so that the row sums were consistent with the corresponding elements in the OBE national vector; the national transportation and trade margins were applied to obtain state estimates for rows 65 and 69; and a value added row was obtained as a residual.

Since the iron ore industry is geographically concentrated, the use of the Wang-Kokat coefficients at the regional level should not lead to significant distortions through disregarding variations in regional input patterns. Moreover, the inclusion of the ferroalloy ores in estimating two of the larger categories of inputs increases the amount of regional variation in the estimates.

IO-6, Nonferrous Metal Ores Mining

Over half (52.5 percent) of the value of shipments for the nonferrous metal ores mining industry was composed of SIC 1021, Copper. The second largest industry, SIC 1094, Uranium-vanadium-radium ores, comprised 25.6 percent of the output. The remainder (21.9 percent) is made up of a group of other SIC subindustries that are included in IO-6. They are: SIC 1031, Lead & zinc ores;

SIC 104, Gold & silver; SIC 1051, Bauxite & other aluminum ores; SIC 1081 and 1082, Metal mining services; SIC 1092, Mercury ores; SIC 1093, Titanium; and SIC 1099, Metallic minerals (ores), n.e.c. Table 3-9 gives the 1963 figures for these minerals.

Estimation of the inputs of this industry by state was severely hampered by the disclosure regulations of the Bureau of the Census (Census). In the largest subindustry, copper ores, 5 mines produce 48 percent of output, 10 mines produce 74 percent, and 25 mines produce 97 percent. Such industrial concentration requires frequent enforcement of the Census disclosure regulations; therefore, few data were available at the state or even the regional level. Because many of the smaller subindustries evidenced a similar degree of concentration, state data were virtually unavailable. In addition, when regional figures were given for the noncopper subindustries, the cost-of-supplies category was usually combined with other categories. For these reasons, the estimation process described in the first sections of this chapter was used for copper mining only. The noncopper portion of IO-6 was estimated by distributing detailed OBE national inputs for IO-6.02, Nonferrous metal ores mining, except copper [122], in proportion to state output figures for those minerals [21].

Some consideration was given to using a detailed process analysis made by Cooper and Wang for the Bureau of Mines [16] in estimating state inputs into copper. However, the information in their report was not in a form that could be easily integrated into this study, and the Wang-Kokat coefficients were used instead. The fuels and purchased-electricity category was treated in the same way as was IO-5, Iron & ferroalloy ores mining.

All the state data for the first four cost categories were then converted from purchaser to producer prices using national transportation and trade margins.

Table 3-9
1963 Values of Shipments for Nonferrous Metal Ores

Product	*Values of Shipments ($ thousands)*
Copper ores	$ 670,173
Uranium-vanadium-radium ores	326,370
Lead ores	50,743
Zinc ores	85,222
Gold	34,164
Silver ores	26,060
Bauxite & other aluminum ores	21,491
Metal mining services	32,360
Miscellaneous ores, n.e.c.	28,725
Total	$1,275,308

Source: *Census of Mineral Industries, 1963* [82].

Next, as explained in detail at the beginning of this chapter, the data for the services sector were allocated to the states, weighting the 1963 national coefficients from the OBE by JFA state outputs for nonferrous metal ores. The SIC distributions were then summed to obtain a matrix of inputs by state. The national totals from this matrix were compared with the corresponding elements in the 1963 national vector of inputs for IO-6. Where large discrepancies occurred, the worksheets for these industries were rechecked, and any errors found in the state elements in the industry rows were corrected. Finally, all elements in the matrix of state estimates were adjusted so that the row sums were consistent with the corresponding elements in the OBE national vector; the national transportation and trade margins were applied to obtain state estimates for rows 65 and 69; and a value added row was obtained as a residual.

IO-7, Coal Mining

Two methods were tested for calculating state estimates of IO-7, Coal mining. The first, which was finally used, was essentially the same as the one just outlined. The second was based on a method suggested by a comprehensive study of the mining industry conducted by Cooper and Wang [15]. This latter method derived state-by-state requirements using the *CMI* [82] and the *Minerals Yearbook, 1963* [138], together with an extensive process analysis made for the study. In the initial test, the estimates obtained from the second method were substantially the same as those obtained from the procedure that was finally selected. The Cooper-Wang procedure could not be used for the other mining industries, however, because similar analyses have not been made for them. A consistent method for calculating the estimates for all industries in the mining sector was preferable; therefore, it was decided that the first method would be used. This decision seems justified in view of the marked similarity of the estimates from the two procedures.

One advantage of the Cooper-Wang method is the enormously detailed estimates it produces, detail that would not be put to use in the multiregional input-output (MRIO) model. Since the estimates can be used in many other contexts, the method will be described briefly before the one employed in the present study to estimate coal inputs is explained.

Cooper-Wang Input Estimates. Cooper and Wang made a comprehensive process analysis of the coal industry for 1958, based upon an exhaustive survey of both private and governmental technical literature and complemented by interviews with industry experts. They defined three major mining techniques used by both the bituminous and the anthracite coal subindustries: underground, strip, and auger mining. Within each of these categories, they isolated 16 specific coal-mining processes.[4]

For each type of mining, they estimated national input coefficients by process as well as the volume of coal passing through each process. They could thus determine expenditures on each input, by process and type, and, by summing the value figures, the total cost of the input to the mining industry. On the assumption that the input coefficients for each process remained constant from state to state, this process-mix method was applied in the present study to obtain a set of state inputs for the coal-mining industry that could be compared with the estimates calculated using the general procedure described in the first part of this chapter. The 1963 state inputs were calculated by multiplying the 1958 process input coefficients, obtained from Cooper and Wang [15], by 1963 state tonnage figures, estimated from data in the *Minerals Yearbook, 1963* [138]. The procedure was as follows:

Step 1. Obtain 1963 state costs of an input for one process in one type of mining by multiplying the 1958 national input costs per ton by the relevant 1963 state tonnage figure.

$$V_j^{ptg} = D_j C_j^{pt} Q^{ptg} \qquad (3\text{-}1)$$

where

C_j^{pt} = 1958 cost of input j per ton of coal, using process p in type t mining. ($p = 1, \ldots, 16; t = 1, 2, 3; j = 1, \ldots, 100+$.)

Q^{ptg} = 1963 tons of coal involving process p in type t mining in state g. ($g = 1, \ldots, 51$.)

D_j = deflator to adjust the 1958 price of input j to its 1963 level.

Step 2. Obtain state-by-state total expenditures on each input by aggregating the processes and mining types and by summing inputs to the input-output industry level of detail.

$$V_i^g = \sum_{j \in i}^{82} \sum_{p=1}^{16} \sum_{t=1}^{3} D_j C_j^{pt} Q^{ptg} \qquad \begin{array}{l} g = 1, \ldots, 51 \\ i = 1, \ldots, 100+ \end{array} \qquad (3\text{-}2)$$

4. In this context, the general term "process" is used to refer to any of the following 16 divisions: (1) blasting, (2) cleaning and preparation, (3) drainage, (4) dredging, (5) electrical, (6) face preparation, (7) haulage, (8) materials-handling, (9) mining, (10) outside building, (11) outside supplies, (12) petroleum products, (13) refuse, (14) roof control, (15) safety and ventilation, and (16) tools. These are the typical divisions occurring in any of the mining industries, and as such will display the same general characteristics and use the same kinds of inputs wherever they are employed.

Step 3. Calculate input coefficients for the 82 inputs in each of the 51 states by dividing every element (each represents a particular input i) in the column of state input expenditures for state g, V_i^g, by the total output of coal in that state, X^g.

$$C_i^g = \frac{V_i^g}{X^g} \tag{3-3}$$

Step 4. Obtain total input costs of producing anthracite and bituminous coal in Pennsylvania.

$$C_i^g = \frac{\left[\sum_{j \in i}^{82} \sum_{p=1}^{16} \sum_{t=1}^{3} D_j C_{jb}^{pt} Q_b^t + \sum_{j \in i}^{82} \sum_{p=1}^{16} \sum_{t=1}^{3} D_j C_{ja}^{pt} Q_a^t\right]}{X_b + X_a} \tag{3-4}$$

where b = bituminous and a = anthracite coal mining in Pennsylvania. These input-cost data were inserted into column 37, Pennsylvania, of the matrix of input coefficients for coal mining. This special procedure was required because Pennsylvania is the only producer of anthracite coal.

Data were not available to correct for the effects of technical change between 1958 and 1963 on current purchases of materials inputs. The deflation process therefore allows only for input price changes. The C_j^{pt} is a national input cost figure for a given process in a particular type of mining, and this input cost is assumed to remain constant regardless of the state in which the coal is produced.

The data resulting from *Step 1* consist of state-by-state input requirements for over 100 detailed inputs used in 16 different processes, separated into 3 general types of mining. Because this detail was not required for the MRIO calculations, the data for the 16 processes and the 3 types of mining were summed to obtain total expenditures on each input in each state. These inputs for each state—more than 100—were simultaneously aggregated to the input-output industry classification.

The result of dividing the state input expenditures by state coal-mining output was an 82 × 51 matrix of state input coefficients for bituminous coal. The figures for column 37, Pennsylvania, were calculated in a slightly different way, however, because anthracite coal is produced only in that state. The Cooper-Wang cost figures were therefore applied directly to anthracite tonnages for Pennsylvania, and a combined estimated input cost was calculated for bituminous and anthracite coal mining in that state.

The product-mix estimates are described in the next section and are followed by a comparison of the state estimates obtained from the two procedures.

Modified Product-Mix Estimates. As before, the output weights were used to distribute the regional figures in the *CMI* [82] to the states, and the Wang-Kokat coefficients [158] were applied to the state cost-of-supplies estimates for SIC 12, Bituminous coal. Since the entire output of SIC 11, Anthracite coal, is produced in Pennsylvania, the Wang-Kokat coefficients were applied directly to the *CMI* cost-of-supplies figure for SIC 11, and the results were added to the vector of estimates for Pennsylvania's bituminous coal production. The estimates for the fuels and purchased-electricity category were made using a method different from that described earlier. In the *CMI* table entitled "Fuels and Electric Energy Used, by Geographic Area and Major Industry Group" [82, sec. 6, t. 4, pp. 14–18], both values and quantities were given for five types of fuel used by region and, in the case of some states, for two-digit SIC industry groups. Since IO-7 comprises two such SIC groups (11 and 12), these data could be used directly for certain regions and states. (They could not be used for the other SIC groups, 10 and 14, covered in the table, because 10 and 14 are aggregates of two input-output industries.)

For the other regions and states, detail on quantities purchased was combined with the regional figures for purchased fuels, purchased electricity, and other fuels (undistributed) to yield estimates for inputs from IO-7, Coal mining, IO-31, Petroleum refining & related industries, and IO-68, Electric, gas, water, & sanitary services.

All the state data for the first four cost categories were then converted from purchaser to producer prices using national transportation and trade margins. Next, as explained in detail in the first part of this chapter, the data for the services sector were allocated to the states, weighting the 1963 national coefficients from the OBE by JFA state coal-mining outputs. The SIC distributions were then summed to obtain a matrix of inputs by state. The national totals from this matrix were compared with the corresponding elements in the 1963 OBE national vector of coal-mining inputs. Where large discrepancies occurred, the worksheets for these industries were rechecked, and any errors found in the state elements in the industry rows were corrected. For example, additional estimates had to be made at this point for some industries by distributing 1963 inputs according to state shares of coal-mining output. The largest was IO-43, Engines & turbines, since the IO-43 direct coefficient for coal mining went from zero in 1958 to .0136 in 1963. Finally, all elements in the matrix of state estimates were adjusted so that the row sums were consistent with the corresponding elements in the OBE national vector; the national transportation and trade margins were applied to obtain state estimates for rows 65 and 69; and a value added row was obtained as a residual.

Comparison of Cooper-Wang and Modified Product-Mix Estimates. The Cooper-Wang estimates used in the comparison of the two sets of data were made by separating state tonnage figures by process, but not by type of mining, for bituminous coal only. The inputs were then aggregated to the input-output industry level, and the resulting state vectors were compared with those calculated using the Wang-Kokat coefficient-weighting procedure. The two procedures, however, suffer from the same fundamental defects: the employment of national coefficients as a basis for estimating state technology; the assumption that changes in technology between 1958 and 1963 had strictly proportionate effects on the distribution of current inputs; the failure to take account of some of the relative price changes.

Although the Cooper-Wang estimates were based upon more technological detail and thus have a greater potential for differences in input structure among states, the results obtained from the two methods were actually fairly similar, as shown in Table 3–10. For the six largest coal-producing states, over half of the 27 inputs estimated differed by less than 10 percent. Thus, it was decided to use the estimates obtained from the standard (modified product-mix) method in order to preserve some comparability among the cost estimates for the mining industries.

IO-8, Crude Petroleum & Natural Gas

The problem of nondisclosure of data because of concentration of an industry within one region hampered the estimation of state data for IO-8, Crude petroleum & natural gas. Compilation of state data for cost categories, such as cost of supplies, was not possible for this industry. Even at the national level, the current production costs of the crude petroleum and natural gas industry are

Table 3–10
Comparison of the Cooper-Wang and the Modified Product-Mix Coal Estimates for the Six Largest Coal-Producing States (value of output greater than $100 million)

	Number of Industries[a]		
States	*Less than 10 Percent*[b]	*10 to 25 Percent*	*More than 25 Percent*
West Virginia	15	4	8
Pennsylvania	19	0	8
Kentucky	16	1	10
Illinois	18	0	9
Ohio	17	5	5
Virginia	21	0	6

[a]The number of input-output supplying industries for which estimates by the two methods differ by the percentages shown.
[b]Or $1 million in absolute value.

difficult to determine, since most of the expenditures of IO-8 are for well construction (an input from IO-11, New construction) and for drilling apparatus and similar equipment, all of which are purchases on capital rather than current account. In fact, four-fifths of the current expenditures made by the crude petroleum and natural gas industry are for land rentals (IO-71, Real estate & rental) and value added.

Because of this lack of data, an elementary form of product-mix calculation was used to obtain a set of state inputs for IO-8. State value-of-output figures for three petroleum and natural gas subindustries, SIC 1311, Crude petroleum (component), SIC 1311, Natural gas (component), and SIC 1321, Natural gas liquids, were obtained from worksheets compiled by the staff of Jack Faucett Associates, Inc. [21]. These JFA outputs were applied as weights to the Wang-Kokat direct input coefficient vectors for each of the three subindustries in IO-8, and the results were summed to obtain a single cost vector for each state. Whenever possible, the state estimates were adjusted to the data on fuels and purchased electricity in the *CMI* [82].

The national totals from the final matrix of estimates were compared with the corresponding elements in the 1963 OBE national vector of inputs for crude petroleum and natural gas. To adjust for the differences, all elements in the matrix of state estimates were altered so that the row sums were consistent with the corresponding elements in the OBE national vector. The national transportation and trade margins were applied to obtain state estimates for rows 65 and 69, and a value added row was obtained as a residual.

IO-9, Stone & Clay Mining & Quarrying

The stone and clay mining and quarrying industry, IO-9, has a larger value of shipments than either the iron ore or the nonferrous metal ores mining industries and is the only industry with operations in every state. It is composed of six SIC three-digit industries, which can be further disaggregated into 20 product groups at the SIC four-digit level of detail. The 1963 national values of shipments of these industries are shown in Table 3-11.

Extensive regional information was available in the *CMI* for only two of the subindustries, SIC 1421, Crushed & broken stone, and SIC 1441, Sand & gravel. Since the 1963 value of shipments for these two subindustries comprises 83 percent of the total for IO-9, reliance on the regional data available only for these two product groups should not bias the estimates significantly. The state technology for each of the two industries was assumed to be approximately the same as the national technology. The cost-of-supplies category was separated into industry inputs, using the Wang-Kokat coefficients for SIC 1421 and SIC 1441. The fuel inputs were allocated by disaggregating the purchased-fuels category for

Table 3-11
1963 Values of Shipments for Stone & Clay Mining & Quarrying

SIC Subindustry Title	*SIC Number*	*Values of Shipments ($ thousands)*
1. Dimension stone	1411	$ 19,735
2. Crushed & broken stone	1421	794,860
3. Sand & gravel	1441	678,068
4. Bentonite	1452	18,105
5. Fire clay	1453	17,105
6. Fuller's earth	1454	12,954
7. Kaolin & ball clay	1455	66,077
8. Feldspar	1456	8,459
9. Magnesite & brucite	1457	n.a.
10. Other clay	1459	38,944
11. Nonmetal stripping services	1481 }	13,246
12. Other nonmetal services	1482 }	
13. Gypsum	1492	10,160
14. Mica	1493	5,560
15. Asphalt & bitumens	1494	8,509
16. Pumice & pumicite	1495	5,358
17. Talc, soapstone, pyrophyllite	1496	17,534
18. Natural abrasives	1497	5,002
19. Peat	1498	7,360
20. Miscellaneous nonmetal mining	1499	42,963

Source: *Census of Mineral Industries, 1963* [82].

each region into coal, fuel oils, gas, and gasoline, using the national proportions of these fuels for each SIC group [82] adjusted to reflect the volume of fuels purchased in each region.

All the state data for the first four cost categories were then converted from purchaser to producer prices using national transportation and trade margins. Next, as explained in detail in the first part of this chapter, the data for the services sector were allocated to the states, weighting the 1963 national coefficients from the OBE by JFA state outputs for IO-9. The SIC distributions were then summed to obtain a matrix of inputs by state. The national totals from this matrix were compared with the corresponding elements in the 1963 OBE national vector of inputs for IO-9. Where large discrepancies occurred, the worksheets for these industries were rechecked, and any errors found in the state elements in the industry rows were corrected. Finally, all elements in the matrix of state estimates were adjusted so that the row sums were consistent with the corresponding elements in the OBE national vector; the national transportation and trade margins were applied to obtain state estimates for rows 65 and 69; and a value added row was obtained as a residual.

IO-10, Chemical & Fertilizer Mineral Mining

The chemical and fertilizer mineral mining industry, IO-10, is the best suited of all the mining industries to the coefficient-weighting procedure used. Most of the output of each of the seven SIC subindustries that comprise IO-10 is produced in only two or three states. In fact, six states produce over 80 percent of the total industry output, and almost all of the output of each of these states is accounted for by just one of the seven product groups. For example, in 1963 all of the chemical and fertilizer mineral mining produced in Illinois was SIC 1473, Fluorspar, and 89.5 percent of IO-10 produced in Kentucky was fluorspar. Together, these two states accounted for 85.5 percent of all fluorspar produced in the United States, so the state cost-of-supplies figures could be distributed according to the national Wang-Kokat coefficients for SIC 1473 without causing significant distortion in input costs. Table 3–12 indicates the extent of regional concentration of IO-10.

Because of this marked geographical concentration of the four-digit SIC subindustries, the Wang-Kokat national input coefficients for an SIC subindustry can be taken as being representative of the regional coefficients. The accuracy of

Table 3–12
Locational Distribution Patterns of the Chemical and Fertilizer Mineral Mining Industries

SIC Number	*Subindustry Title*	*U.S. Total ($ millions)*	*Percent of Subindustry Production in Major Producing States*		*Percent of Total State IO-10 Production*
1472	Barite	$ 16.7	Missouri	37.0	100.0
			Arkansas	17.5	89.0
			Georgia	15.0	91.0
1473	Fluorspar	15.8	Illinois	55.5	100.0
			Kentucky	30.0	89.5
1474	Potash, soda, borate minerals	192.1	New Mexico	51.0	98.5
			California	37.0	96.5
1475	Phosphate rock	161.7	Florida	66.5	100.0
			Tennessee	14.5	67.5
1476	Rock salt	59.3	Louisiana	30.2	22.0
			Ohio	22.5	99.5
			New York	19.0	91.0
1477	Sulfur	113.1	Louisiana	51.0	71.0
			Texas	48.0	81.0
1499	Not elsewhere classified	18.3	Tennessee	59.5	31.5

Source: Imputed from Jack Faucett Associates output data [21].

the estimates is also improved by the availability of regional data in the *CMI* on minerals received for preparation, fuel inputs, and contract services [82]. However, data for minerals received for preparation and costs of supplies were combined for some regions and had to be disaggregated using the method described at the beginning of this chapter. Fuel inputs were estimated in the same manner as for IO-9. The result was seven SIC input vectors for each state, but usually only one or two vectors were relevant for a particular state, the others being zero. For each industry, the data in the seven vectors were summed to obtain an estimate for IO-10 in that state for the first four cost categories.

All the state data for the first four cost categories were then converted from purchaser to producer prices using national transportation and trade margins. Next, as explained in detail in the first part of this chapter, the data for the services sector were allocated to the states, weighting the 1963 national coefficients from the OBE by JFA state outputs for chemical and fertilizer mineral mining. The SIC distributions were then summed to obtain a matrix of inputs by state. The national totals from this matrix were compared with the corresponding elements in the 1963 OBE national vector of inputs for IO-10. Where large discrepancies occurred, the worksheets for these industries were rechecked, and any errors found in the state elements in the industry rows were corrected. Finally, all elements in the matrix of state estimates were adjusted so that the row sums were consistent with the corresponding elements in the OBE national vector; the national transportation and trade margins were applied to obtain state estimates for rows 65 and 69; and a value added row was obtained as a residual. The state estimates for chemical and fertilizer mineral mining that resulted from this procedure probably reflect quite accurately the regional variation in the input requirements of the industry.

4 New Construction Technologies

Orani Dixon and
John V. Wells

The construction sector includes both IO-11, New construction, and IO-12, Maintenance & repair construction, but the data for IO-12 are so fragmentary that interregional technologies for that industry were not studied. All of the discussion in this chapter, therefore, concerns IO-11, New construction.

Background to the Present Study

Very little previous research has been done on interregional technological variations within the new construction industry. The Bureau of Labor Statistics (BLS) has published a series of bulletins containing the results of surveys on this subject [142–150], and the Bureau of Public Roads (BPR) has conducted a study of interregional technological variations in highway construction [154]; however, none of these were undertaken within a consistent framework, such as an input-output framework.

As part of the present multiregional input-output research program, in 1968 Pamela King studied purchases by the new construction industry for 1947, 1958, and 1963 [41]. The King study, which was concerned only with product-mix variations from state to state—not with variations in technologies used to produce particular kinds of construction, separated the new construction industry into six major components: private residential, private nonresidential, oil and gas well drilling, state and local government (nonhighway), federal government (nonhighway), and highway. The research reported here is an extension of the King research. Both interregional technological variations and interregional product-mix variations are considered, and the new construction industry has been separated into 24 components, rather than just 6, to increase the accuracy of the estimations of the product-mix variations.

The new construction industry is an extremely important component of the United States economy. Of 87 industries included in the Office of Business Economics (OBE) national 1963 input-output table, IO-11, New construction, ranks fourth in gross output [122]. In 1963, the total final demand (which is

Table 4–1
New Construction As Percent of 1963 Final Demands

Final Demands	*Percentage*
Total final demand	11
Personal consumption expenditures	0
Gross private fixed capital formation	57
Net inventory change	0
Net exports	0
Federal government purchases	6
State and local government purchases	26

Source: U.S. Department of Commerce, Office of Business Economics, "Input-Output Structure of the U.S. Economy: 1963," *Survey of Current Business* [122].

also equal to the total output) of the industry was $65,519 million, representing 11 percent of the total gross national product, as shown in Table 4–1.[1]

Technological variations occur from state to state because of two major factors: the different methods used in building particular kinds of structures, and the different product mixes of structures being built. Variations in the technologies used to construct a given kind of building result from the nature and organization of the construction industry, which is extremely decentralized, with most of the thousands of contractors and subcontractors producing for local markets. Because the structures are immobile, expensive, and long-lasting, they are designed to suit local conditions; and because the inputs to new construction have high weight-to-price ratios, they are produced close to the place of construction wherever possible. Thus, an unusual degree of localization of technologies occurs for new construction as compared with other industries.

The types of new construction demanded (residential, industrial, highway, etc.), the kinds of structures built (wood, concrete, brick, etc.), and the inputs used (window glass, cast-iron pipe, lumber, copper sheets, etc.) vary greatly from state to state, resulting in significant interregional product-mix variations in the new construction industry as a whole. For example, the chief oil-producing states, Texas, Oklahoma, and Louisiana, produce nearly two-thirds of the national total of two oil-related kinds of new construction—Oil & gas well drilling & exploration and Petroleum pipeline construction. Compared with other kinds of new construction, these two in turn purchase a disproportionately large amount of the output of IO-37, Primary iron & steel manufacturing. The purchases of IO-37 per dollar of construction output by the Oil & gas well drilling & exploration industry are nearly three times higher and those by the Petroleum pipeline construction industry nearly nine times higher than for new construction as a whole. The result is an unusually large input coefficient for IO-37 in these three states. Even if the technologies for particular kinds of new construction were

1. All output of new construction is assumed to be consumed by final users and is therefore recorded as part of the final demand (gross national product) of the nation.

constant geographically, the average technology for all new construction would vary from state to state simply because of product-mix variations.

Although several different techniques were used in the present study to estimate coefficients for regional technologies of the new construction industry, the approach, essentially, was to incorporate into these coefficients state-to-state variations in the product mix of the industry by piecing together information from several different sources. The general methodology used is described in the next section of this chapter and the specific methodology used for each of the new construction subindustries is described in the last section of the chapter.

General Methodology

Ideally, the data used for an input-output study would be purchases by one industry of the products of other industries. While these data are available for various types of new construction at the national level, they are not available for the state new construction industries. The general methodology described in this section of the chapter was developed taking into account the scarcity of data on state construction technologies. Data on the industry are fragmentary partly because inadequate resources are spent by government agencies and private trade organizations on collecting them and partly because the extremely decentralized nature of the industry (more than 200,000 firms) inhibits the data-collection efforts that are made. Nevertheless, distinct state technological coefficients were estimated from the available state data for about 3 percent of the industry output. For the remainder of the industry, regional or national technological coefficients were used.

The technology coefficients for the new construction industry in each state were estimated in this study by using a product-mix technique. This technique required the assembly of technological data in terms of input costs per dollar of construction output in a particular state. Because different kinds of construction use different technologies, distinct input coefficients were estimated for each of the 24 new construction subindustries shown in Table 4–2.[2] For one subindustry, #21, Highway construction, distinct input data for each state were assembled, while for the other 23 subindustries, regional or national data were used. In each state, an output total was estimated for all the new construction subindustries, and each element in a particular column of input coefficients was multiplied by the respective state output total to estimate columns of flows. The state-by-state flows for the subindustries were aggregated to obtain one column of flows for total new construction in each state.

A column of input coefficients and an output total were therefore estimated for each of 24 subindustries in each of 51 regions (50 states plus the District of

2. The 24 subindustries are listed in Table 4–2 in the order in which they appear on the OBE worksheets and are numbered sequentially 1 through 24.

Table 4-2
1963 Construction Subindustries

Subindustry		*Value*	
Number[a]	*Title*	*($ millions)*	*Percent*
1	Private one-family nonfarm residential	$14,136	21.6
2	Private two-to-four family nonfarm residential	1,250	1.9
3	Low-rise apartment houses, public & private	3,808	5.8
4	All other private nonfarm residential	6,161	9.4
5	High-rise apartment houses, public & private	1,694	2.6
6	Commercial building	5,801	8.8
7	Industrial building	3,346	5.1
8	Farm building	1,247	1.9
9	Educational building	3,854	5.9
10	Hospital & institutional building	1,426	2.2
11	Religious building	1,001	1.5
12	All other building	2,137	3.3
13	Electric power & light	2,556	3.9
14	Gas	948	1.4
15	Telephone & telegraph	1,128	1.7
16	Petroleum pipeline	272	0.4
17	Oil & gas well drilling & exploration	2,096	3.2
18	Railroad & local transit	315	0.5
19	Military	1,189	1.8
20	Conservation & development	1,569	2.4
21	Highway	6,941	10.7
22	Sewer	1,068	1.6
23	Water system	882	1.3
24	All other	694	1.1
	Total	$65,519	100.0

[a]The subindustries listed above are in the order in which they appear on the OBE worksheets.
Source: U.S. Department of Commerce, Office of Business Economics, "Construction Industries–1963 Input-Output Study" [120].

Columbia)–1224 columns and output totals altogether. These columns were assembled by states, and the final computations were done as illustrated in Figure 4-1. The steps were as follows:

Step 1. For each of the 24 subindustries in each region, shown as matrix *A*, a column of input coefficients (calculated according to the different procedures described at the end of this chapter) was multiplied (arrow #1) by the appropriate state output. The result (arrow #2) for each state was a set of 24 columns of new construction inputs, shown as matrix *B,* for the subindustries in that state.

Step 2. These input columns were added horizontally (arrow #3) to obtain

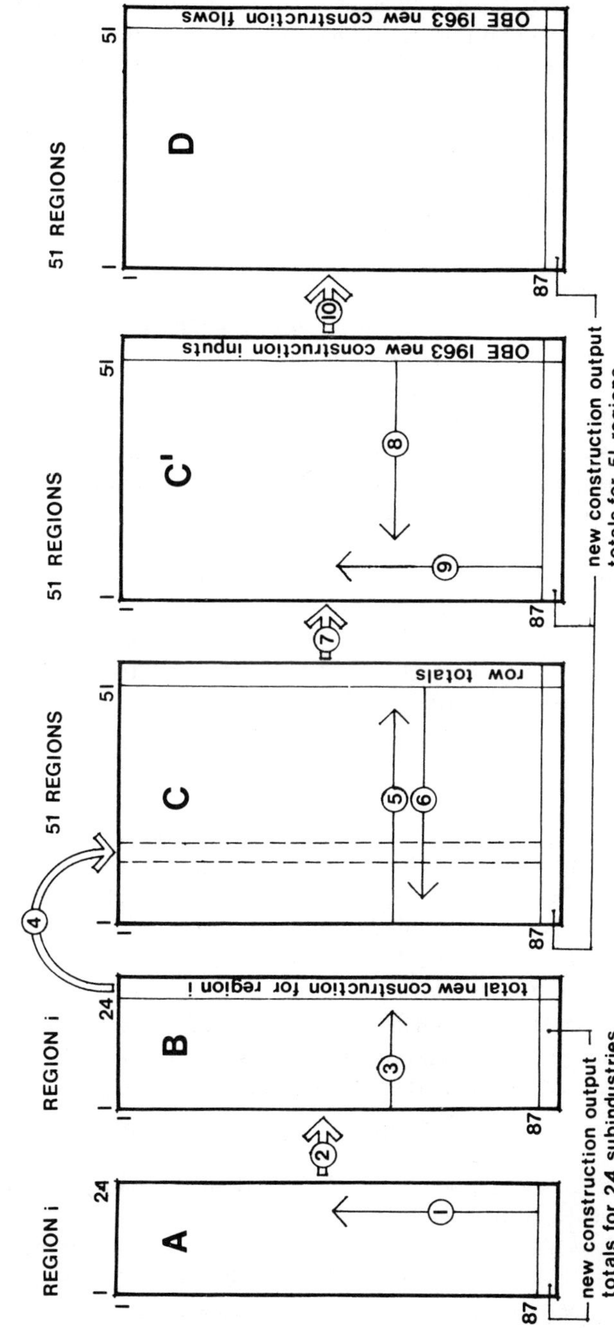

Figure 4–1. Calculation of 1963 Regional New Construction Inputs.

a column of flows of total purchases by all new construction in that state. These flows had to be adjusted so that they would be consistent with the OBE national 1963 input-output table [122].

Step 3. This adjustment was made by reassembling (arrow #4) the state total construction flows into a new matrix, shown as matrix *C.* For each input-output industry, the state flows were added (arrow #5) and then divided (arrow #6) by the row totals to obtain row percentage distributions. These coefficients were placed (arrow #7) in matrix C'.

Step 4. The row coefficients were multiplied (arrow #8) by the total new construction data from the 1963 input-output table to yield adjusted state flows.

Step 5. These flows were further adjusted (arrow #9) to eliminate negative value added figures and were once again adjusted to be consistent with the OBE flows. They were then placed (arrow #10) in matrix *D* and were ready for use in the final computer runs of the multiregional input-output model.

While the specific methodology employed for each of the subindustries is discussed in detail later in this chapter, some common elements of the different procedures are summarized here. Two basic sets of data were required for these calculations: input coefficients for each of the 24 new construction subindustries and state outputs for each subindustry.

Materials Input Coefficient Data

Of the 24 subindustries, distinct state input coefficients could be estimated for only subindustry #21, Highway construction. For six more subindustries, distinct input coefficients were available for the four large multistate regions—Northeast, North Central, South, and West—shown in Table B-4 in the appendix. For the other 17 subindustries, national input coefficients had to be used. Fortunately, the subindustries for which state and regional coefficients could be specifically estimated were among the largest in terms of national output, as shown earlier in Table 4-2. Thus, while state coefficients were estimated for only one of the 24 subindustries—#21, Highway construction—, this subindustry accounted for nearly 11 percent of the 1963 total new construction output. And, while regional coefficients could be estimated for only six subindustries, these accounted for 42 percent of total output.

However, the data base for the state and regional coefficients does not cover all the inputs for these seven subindustries. The state data on highway construction inputs, for example, cover less than one-third of total inputs to that subindustry. National input coefficients were used to estimate inputs for which there were no state data. In the subindustries for which regional coefficients were estimated, the regional data cover slightly less than one-half of all inputs. Again, the remaining inputs were estimated using national input data. This partial coverage means that state input coefficients were used for only about 3 percent of the total new construction input coefficients, and regional coefficients were used for about 19 percent. Therefore, although state and regional data were used for subindustries accounting for over 50 percent of total output, state or regional input data were used for only about 22 percent of the total new construction input coefficients.

The national input coefficients used for the 24 subindustries are from unpublished OBE 1963 input-output computer printouts [120] and are consistent with the 80-order new construction vector in the 1963 input-output table. All state and regional input data were adjusted to be consistent with the national input coefficients for each subindustry. The regional data are from a series of bulletins that give information obtained from BLS surveys of labor and materials requirements for various kinds of construction. Unfortunately, the year in which each survey was taken varies from one type of construction to another. The BLS statistics are for the four regions shown in Table B–4 in the appendix and cover only materials inputs; services and value added inputs had to be estimated by using national input coefficients. Because the materials inputs are not classified according to the input-output industrial classification, the data generally had to be aggregated to fit that classification. However, in one case, plumbing fixtures, the data had to be disaggregated into two input-output industries: IO-36, Stone & clay products, which produces vitreous plumbing fixtures, and IO-40, Heating, plumbing, & fabricated structural metal products, which produces metal plumbing fixtures. The disaggregation was based upon national value of shipments totals from the *Census of Manufactures, 1963* [80] for each kind of plumbing fixture.

Because the national input coefficients are in producer prices, the adjustment from purchaser to producer prices was accomplished implicitly for each subindustry when the regional data were made consistent with the national data. Imported inputs were not a problem because directly allocated (noncompetitive) imports are not used in construction, and all transferred (competitive) imports are included implicitly in the input data.

State Output Totals

National outputs were available for 1963 for all 24 new construction subindustries from the unpublished OBE 1963 input-output computer printout [120] ; but the only available state construction outputs, which had to be obtained from many different sources, were inconsistent with the unpublished OBE totals and were sometimes for years other than 1963. These state outputs were inflated to make them consistent with the unpublished OBE national totals.

No state construction outputs were available for seven of the subindustries, and proxies were used to allocate the OBE figures to states.

All the available state construction outputs were incomplete in that their national totals were less than the unpublished OBE totals (sometimes by as much as 50 percent). Because the extent of undercoverage varied from state to state, erroneous state outputs result when the data for each state are inflated to consistency with the unpublished OBE national totals. While the extent of the error could not be determined, the probable sign of the error in certain states sometimes could be. For example, building-permits data (used in the estimates for subindustries #1, #2, and #3) give the value of permits issued for particular kinds of construction by state in 12,000 permit-issuing places. Some places do not issue building permits, however, so that the building permits total only about 80 to 90 percent of the OBE totals for those kinds of construction. Unfortunately, because the places that do not issue building permits tend to be concentrated in relatively rural states, the use of building-permits data to estimate outputs for construction put-in-place understates the amount of construction being built in rural states. The same understatement occurs when contract-awards data are used, although for a different reason. Contract-awards data exclude contracts below a certain minimum value. Because these low-value contracts, again, tend to be concentrated in relatively rural states, contract-awards data do not reflect the full amount of construction being built in rural states. In neither case were any benchmarks available so that the extent of the error could be estimated and some correction made for it.

Other kinds of distortion occur with other sets of output data. When data on change in the value of structures were used, the ratio between new construction and retirements of old buildings was implicitly assumed to be the same in all states. In fact, however, in older, more settled states (those on the East Coast, in particular), much of new construction replaces old, worn-out structures. In the rapidly growing areas of the Southwest and West, on the other hand, more new construction is built on previously vacant land. Thus, in the East, the value of the new structure is largely concealed because the net value is calculated by subtracting the value of the replaced structure from the value of the new structure. In the Southwest and West, the "netting out" effect is much less, so the use of these data overstates the amount of construction occurring in the newer states relative to that in the older states.

Timing problems also introduce a degree of error. In the case of building-permits data, for example, the date of the building permit precedes by several months the period during which construction is put in place. Thus, a building permit dated November 1963 may have been issued for a building that was actually constructed during the first several months of 1964. Conversely, construction during a particular calendar year will correspond to building permits issued from several months before the beginning of the year to several months before the end of it (the period may be more or less removed from the calendar year itself, depending upon the length of the construction period for the kind of building in question). Theoretically, then, the building-permits data that are used should lead ahead of the calendar year for which construction is being studied. If building-permits data for the calendar year are used to estimate state outputs for the same calendar year, a random distortion occurs, because the calendar-year building-permits data correspond to a somewhat later set of construction output data than those being studied. How the distortion will affect estimates for the different states cannot be predicted, however, unless the secular trend in the interstate distribution of construction output is known.

Contract-awards data involve the same timing problem as do building-permits data. The date of the contract award precedes the date on which the construction is put in place. With the change-in-value-of-structures data, the timing problem is in the opposite direction. Here, the new structure is not added to the total value of structures recorded in the books until it is completed, which is some time after the period during which the construction was put in place. Thus, new structures recorded in 1964 may have been built mainly during 1963.

These timing problems were adjusted for in some cases and not in others, depending upon the difficulty involved in making the adjustment. When the adjustment was made, an average period of construction had to be estimated for the particular kind of building in question. This period may range from a few months to several years. If the data led ahead of a one-year period of construction (as in the case of some building-permits and contract-awards data), the construction was assumed, for example, to have taken place six months after the date of the building permit or contract award. An analogous procedure was used when the data lagged behind the period of construction. In practice, no adjustment was made when building-permits data were used, as monthly data would have had to be used, and time was not available for so laborious a procedure. Adjustments were made in some cases for contract-awards data and for change-in-value-of-structures data, as noted below for certain of the individual subindustries.

Subindustry Methodologies

Two sets of figures were required for each of the 24 subindustries: a column of technological input coefficients and an output total for each state. As discussed earlier, in only one case were different input purchases available for each state. In some cases, different input data were used for each region; but, for most subindustries, the same national inputs were used for all states. When state or regional data were employed, they were made consistent with the national input coefficients for that subindustry.

State outputs were either disaggregated from the 1963 unpublished OBE national total for a subindustry on the basis of a proxy or inflated to the OBE total from actual construction data for a given subindustry. In each of the following sections, the procedure for estimating the input coefficients is discussed first, followed by an explanation of the methodology for estimating state outputs. "National input coefficients" in every case refers to the OBE 1963 input-output computer printouts [120], which will not hereafter be specifically cited. Also, on the traditional assumption that demand equals supply, "national output totals" always refers to the totals of inputs from the OBE printouts.

Subindustry #1, Private One-Family Nonfarm Residential Construction

Regional input coefficients were estimated for subindustry #1, Private one-family nonfarm residential construction, from a BLS survey of private one-family residential construction costs for 1962 [147].

State outputs for this subindustry were estimated by using building-permits data for one-unit housing construction [85], taken from 12,000 permit-issuing places.

Subindustries #2 and #3, Private Two-to Four-Family Nonfarm Residential, and Low-Rise Apartment Houses, Public & Private, Construction

National input coefficients were used for subindustry #2, Private two-to-four-family nonfarm residential construction, and subindustry #3, Low-rise apartment houses, public & private, construction, as no state or regional technological data were available.

State outputs for subindustry #2 were estimated on the basis of building-permits data for two-to-four-unit housing construction [85]. For subindustry #3, state outputs were estimated by using F.W. Dodge residential construction contracts awarded in 1965, which include all new residential construction, additions, and alterations. F.W. Dodge data are not available for subindustry #3 for 1963.

Subindustry #4, All Other Private Nonfarm Residential Construction

Regional input coefficients were estimated for subindustry #4, All other private nonfarm residential construction, from a BLS survey of college housing costs for 1960–61 [143]. This subindustry includes nonhousekeeping forms of residential construction, such as dormitories, hotels, and motels, as well as additions and alterations to all forms of residential construction. The technology of college housing was considered to be broadly representative of the kinds of technologies used in subindustry #4 as a whole.

State outputs for the subindustry were estimated by allocating the national total to states on the basis of 1962 construction contracts for all residential construction [48]. These data were not available for 1963.

Subindustry #5, High-Rise Apartment Houses, Public & Private, Construction

Regional input coefficients were estimated for subindustry #5, High-rise apartment houses, public & private, construction, from a BLS survey of public housing costs for 1959–60 [148].

State outputs for the subindustry were estimated by using 1963 public contract awards for residential construction [85].

Subindustries #6 and #7, Commerical and Industrial Building Construction

National input coefficients were used for subindustry #6, Commercial building construction, and subindustry #7, Industrial building construction, as no state or regional technological data were available.[3]

State outputs for commercial construction and for private (not public) industrial construction were estimated on the basis of 1962 state contract awards for these two types of construction [48]. Data for 1962 were used because 1963 data were not available. In any case, a one-year lag between the time the contract is awarded and the time the construction is put in place did not seem unreasonable. The contract-awards data exclude industrial projects costing less than $110,000 and commercial projects costing less than $400,000. As a result, the industrial data cover 87.5 percent of actual 1963 construction and the commercial data only 50.6 percent; therefore, the degree of error in the state outputs is probably less for private industrial construction than for commercial construction.

State outputs for public industrial construction were estimated by allocating the national output total to states on the basis of 1962 contract-awards data for all nonresidential buildings [48]. Data were not available for 1963.

---

3. Technological data are available for a small number of individual projects in different regions, but since these data represent a very limited sample and would have required laborious tabulation and conversion to the input-output industry classification scheme, they were not used.

Subindustry #8, Farm Building Construction

National input coefficients were used for subindustry #8, Farm building construction, as no state or regional technological data were available.

State outputs were estimated by allocating the national output total to states on the basis of interest on farm mortgage debt in each state in 1963 [95].

Subindustry #9, Educational Building Construction

Regional input coefficients were estimated for subindustry #9, Educational building construction, from a BLS survey of primary and secondary school construction costs in 1964-65 [149]. While the technological data are for primary and secondary schools, they were used to represent all educational construction, including colleges and universities, on the assumption that the technologies used for various kinds of educational construction did not differ significantly.

State outputs were estimated for private and public educational construction and aggregated for educational construction as a whole. The outputs for private educational construction are available by region from *Construction Review* [116]. These regional totals were distributed to states using state data on construction of private colleges and universities [135]. Unfortunately, no state data were available for private primary and secondary educational construction.

State outputs for public educational construction were estimated using state data on new construction and rehabilitation costs for public schools and for public colleges and universities [135]. Because these data are for fiscal year 1963 and fiscal year 1964, they were averaged to yield approximate data for calendar year 1963.

Subindustry #10, Hospital & Institutional Building Construction

National input coefficients were used for subindustry #10, Hospital & institutional building construction, as no state or regional technological data were available.[4]

State outputs for hospital and institutional building construction were

4. A study for 1959 contains man-hour requirements per $1,000 of construction cost for this subindustry for four regions [146]. An estimate of regional technologies could have been made by assuming that, of the different kinds of labor detailed in the study, each used a particular kind of materials input in some constant amount. This seemed to be such a dubious assumption, however, that national technological data were used instead.

estimated separately for private and public construction. Private hospital construction totals are available by region [116]. These regional totals were allocated to states by using data on state and local government payments to private hospitals in fiscal year 1962 in each state [59]. Data for 1963 were not available.

The national output total of public hospital construction was allocated to states on the basis of the total cost of hospital construction from the June 1963 *Hill-Burton Project Register* [133]. For each state, this register gives the total cost of hospital and medical facilities currently under construction that have been approved by the U.S. Department of Health, Education, and Welfare.

Subindustry #11, Religious Building Construction

National input coefficients were used for subindustry #11, Religious building construction, as no state or regional technological data were available.

Regional output totals are available from *Construction Review, 1965* [116], and these were allocated to states on the basis of 1963 state personal-income data [87]. Because no data on state religious construction output were available, personal income was chosen as a proxy. Personal income presumably has a significant impact upon the level of religious construction, since most religious construction is locally financed from private contributions.

Subindustry #12, All Other Building Construction

National input coefficients were used for subindustry #12, All other building construction, as no state or regional technological data were available.

State outputs were estimated by allocating the national output total to states on the basis of 1962 construction-contracts data for nonresidential buildings by state [48]. Data for 1963 were not available.

Subindustry #13, Electric Power & Light Construction

No state or regional technological data were available for subindustry #13, Electric power & light construction, but an extremely detailed product-mix analysis of the subindustry was possible by separating it into the 22 components given in Table 4-3. National input coefficients were estimated for each of the 22 components from unpublished OBE 1963 input-output worksheets [125; 126; 129].

Table 4–3
Electric Power and Light Construction Components

Component	Plant
1. Structures and improvements 2. Boiler plant equipment	Steam production plant
3. Structures and improvements	Nuclear production plant
4. Structures and improvements 5. Reservoirs, dams, and waterways 6. Roads, railroads, and bridges	Hydroelectric production plant
7. Structures and improvements	Other production plant
8. Clearing land and rights-of-way 9. Structures and improvements 10. Towers and fixtures 11. Poles and fixtures 12. Overhead conductors 13. Underground conduit 14. Underground conductors 15. Roads and trails	Transmission plant
16. Structures and improvements 17. Poles, towers, and fixtures 18. Overhead conductors 19. Underground conduit 20. Underground conductors 21. Lights and signals	Distribution plant
22. Structures and improvements	General plant

The national output total for the subindustry was allocated to states and to components on the basis of the change in the value of electrical utility plants during 1964 for each component in each state. The data were deliberately lagged one year, because construction does not appear in the account books as capital plant until after it has been completed. Although the period of construction for electric power and light construction varies from a few months to several years, one year was chosen as a convenient and reasonable lag period. The data were calculated by subtracting the value of capital plant at the end of 1963 [30] from the value at the end of 1964 [31]. Negative changes were regarded as zeros. State totals were aggregated from data for individual utilities. If a utility operated in more than one state, the value of capital plant was allocated to the states in which the plant operated on the basis of data for individual plants of the utility involved [28; 32; 33; 34].

The elements in each of the 22 national input coefficient columns were multiplied by the corresponding state outputs for that particular construction component. All elements in each row of the 22 flow vectors for a given state were then aggregated row by row to yield a total electric power and light flow vector for the state. To obtain the state outputs for electric power and light construction, the elements in the flow vector were summed, and the coefficient vector for the state was calculated by dividing each element in the flow vector by this state output.

Subindustry #14, Gas Construction

National input coefficients were used for subindustry #14, Gas construction, as no state or regional technological data were available.

State outputs were estimated by allocating the national total to states in proportion to a weighted average of four sets of data [3; 4]. These data indicate the change in capacity in physical units by state during 1964 for (1) field and gathering lines, (2) transmission lines, (3) distribution lines, and (4) underground storage plant. A one-year lag was deliberately used because construction that took place in 1963 did not result in a capacity change until 1964. To calculate the four sets of state data, the capacity figure at the end of 1963 [3] was subtracted from the capacity figure at the end of 1964 [4] for each respective set. These data were then weighted by the national construction output total for each of the four kinds of plant [3] and averaged to obtain the final allocative series for each state.

Subindustry #15, Telephone & Telegraph Construction

National input coefficients were used for subindustry #15, Telephone & telegraph construction, as no state or regional technological data were available.

State outputs were estimated by allocating the national output total to states, using three series of data: (1) change in value of telephone utility plant during 1963 for Bell telephone companies, calculated by subtracting the plant value for each state at the beginning of 1963 [24; 26] from the corresponding value at the end of 1963 [25; 27]; (2) change in number of telephones for Bell companies during 1963, calculated by subtracting the number for each state at the beginning of 1963 [86] from the corresponding number at the end of 1963 [87]; and (3) change in number of telephones for all companies, Bell and independent, during 1963, using the same procedure and the same references as for item (2).

The three series of data were used to estimate a fourth series, which was judged to be a better proxy than any of the other three. This fourth series was the change in value of utility plant for all companies during 1963, which was not available directly. (Bell companies are concentrated in cities, so the use of Bell data alone would overstate the amount of construction in urban states.) To estimate these data, the variation between the state distributions calculated from the two series of Bell data was assumed to be the same as the variation between the distribution calculated from the existing series of data for all companies and that which would have been calculated from the unavailable data for all companies. The ratio, for each state, between the Bell change-in-plant-value distribution percentage and the Bell change-in-number-of-telephones percentage was multiplied by the corresponding percentage from the change-in-number-of-telephones data for all companies. The result was an approximation of the percentage that would have been calculated using change-in-plant-value data for all companies:

$$\frac{\left[\begin{array}{l}\text{state percent of}\\ \text{national total cal-}\\ \text{culated from Bell}\\ \text{change-in-plant-}\\ \text{value data}\end{array}\right]}{\left[\begin{array}{l}\text{state percent of}\\ \text{national total cal-}\\ \text{culated from Bell}\\ \text{change-in-number-}\\ \text{of-telephones data}\end{array}\right]} \times \left[\begin{array}{l}\text{state percent of}\\ \text{national total}\\ \text{calculated from}\\ \text{all companies}\\ \text{change-in-number-}\\ \text{of-telephones data}\end{array}\right] = \left[\begin{array}{l}\text{approximation of state}\\ \text{percent of national}\\ \text{total that would have}\\ \text{been calculated from}\\ \text{all companies change-}\\ \text{in-plant-value data}\\ \text{had they been available}\end{array}\right]$$

The result was the final allocating series.

Subindustry #16, Petroleum Pipeline Construction

National input coefficients were used for subindustry #16, Petroleum pipeline construction, as no state or regional technological data were available.

State outputs were calculated by using estimated cost of principal crude gathering lines, principal crude trunk lines, and principal products pipelines for interstate and intrastate construction. These data were assembled for an unpublished study of 1964 state construction outputs [118] from data supplied by the Association of Oil Pipelines. Similar data could not be obtained for 1963.

Subindustry #17, Oil & Gas Well Drilling & Exploration Construction

National input coefficients were used for subindustry #17, Oil & gas well drilling & exploration construction, as no state or regional technological data were available.

State outputs were estimated by allocating the national total to states, using data obtained from the *Joint Association Survey of Industry Drilling Costs,*

1963 (JAS) [5] . The *JAS* list of total costs of wells drilled by state in 1963 was not used because the residual contains the costs for several states. Therefore, the number of wells drilled in each state in 1963, as listed in the *Minerals Yearbook, 1963* [139] , was multiplied by the average cost of wells drilled in each state, as obtained from the *JAS,* to yield state total costs. The results of this calculation were not exactly consistent with the *JAS* total costs, but the discrepancy was negligible. For cases in which states were aggregated in the *JAS,* a common average drilling cost was used for each state in the group. Maryland and New Jersey, which are not listed in the *JAS,* were assigned the average costs of the states adjoining them.

Subindustry #18, Railroad & Local Transit Construction

National input coefficients were used for subindustry #18, Railroad & local transit construction, as no state or regional technological data were available.

State outputs were estimated by allocating the national output total to states, using three sets of data assembled for an unpublished study of 1964 state construction outputs [118] . These data could not be found for 1963, so the 1964 distribution was used. For that study, railroad employment and railroad mileage by state from the *Yearbook of Railroad Facts* [6] were used as allocation factors. The two percentage-distribution series calculated from these data were averaged, giving each series equal weight, and adjusted for consistency with a list of large construction projects for railroads from *Railway Age* [64] .

Subindustry #19, Military Construction

National input coefficients were used for subindustry #19, Military construction, as no state or regional technological data were available.

State outputs were estimated by using the value of military construction projects in each state for which appropriations were made in fiscal year 1962 [132] . These data were not available for 1963. The appropriations list covers about 50 percent of all military construction during the period.

Subindustry #20, Conservation & Development Construction

National input coefficients were used for subindustry #20, Conservation & development construction, as no state or regional technological data were available.

State outputs were estimated by using the total value of construction contracts for earthwork, irrigation, and drainage projects in each state in 1962 [140]. A one-year lag was assumed to have occurred between the date the contract was awarded and the time the construction was put in place. All projects valued at less than $53,000 are excluded from the contract data.

Subindustry #21, Highway Construction

State highway construction technologies were estimated on the basis of data published by the Bureau of Public Roads (BPR) detailing the physical amount of 15 major materials inputs used per thousand dollars of highway construction in each state from 1962-64 [155]. These input coefficients were multiplied by the 1963 highway construction outputs in each state to yield the total physical amount of these inputs used in each state in 1963. These physical units were converted to value units on the basis of national data for costs of the materials per thousand dollars of highway output for federal-aid highway systems [144]. On the assumption that these costs for federal-aid highway systems are representative of all highway construction (which, in general, is true, according to the BPR), national materials expenditures for highway construction were calculated by multiplying these coefficients by the national output total for highway construction. The national totals for materials expenditures were then allocated to states in proportion to the physical input totals for each state, as calculated from the BPR data. The input flows (in value terms) for the materials in each state were then assigned to the appropriate input-output industries. State technological data were estimated from the BPR data for seven input-output industries comprising about 30 percent of total inputs. National input coefficient data were used for all other industries and value added.

State output totals were estimated from BPR state data on 1963 highway construction cost [154].

Subindustries #22 and #23, Sewer and Water-System Construction

Regional input coefficients were directly estimated for sewer construction on the basis of BLS data for 1962-63 [150], but only national input coefficient data were available for water-system construction. While the technology of sewer construction is significantly different from that of water-system construction, the regional variation in water-system construction technologies was assumed to be similar to the regional variation in sewer construction technologies, because both kinds of construction are affected by similar geographic factors. This assumption was used to estimate regional technologies for water-system construction on the basis of the regional variation in sewer construction technologies. The ratio between each of the input coefficients for a particular region for sewer construction and the corresponding national input coefficient for sewer construction was multiplied by the corresponding national input coefficient for water-system construction. The result was an approximation of the regional input coefficients for water-system construction:

$$\frac{\begin{bmatrix}\text{input coefficient}\\ \text{for sewer con-}\\ \text{struction}\\ (\text{industry } i,\\ \text{region } g)\end{bmatrix}}{\begin{bmatrix}\text{input coefficient}\\ \text{for sewer con-}\\ \text{struction}\\ (\text{national}\\ \text{industry } i)\end{bmatrix}} \times \begin{bmatrix}\text{input coefficient}\\ \text{for water-system}\\ \text{construction}\\ (\text{national industry } i)\end{bmatrix} = \begin{bmatrix}\text{approximation}\\ \text{of water-system}\\ \text{construction}\\ (\text{industry } i,\\ \text{region } g)\end{bmatrix}$$

State outputs for subindustries #22 and #23 were estimated on the basis of 1963 state and local government capital expenditures on sewer and water-system construction in each state [84].

Subindustry #24, All Other (Nonbuilding) Construction

National input coefficients were used for subindustry #24, All other (nonbuilding) construction, as no state or regional technological data were available.

State outputs were estimated by allocating the national output total to states on the basis of 1962 F.W. Dodge construction-contracts data for nonbuilding structures by state. No data for 1963 were available.

Appendix A
Industrial Classifications

Table A-1
Input-Output Industry Numbers, Titles, and Related SIC Codes

Industry Number	*Industry Title*	*Related SIC Codes (1957 edition)*[a]
1	Livestock & livestock products	013, pt. 014, 0193, pt. 02, pt. 0729
2	Other agricultural products	011, 012, pt. 014, 0192, 0199, pt. 02
3	Forestry & fishery products	074, 081, 082, 084, 086, 091
4	Agricultural, forestry, & fishery services	071, 0723, pt. 0729, 085, 098
5	Iron & ferroalloy ores mining	1011, 106
6	Nonferrous metal ores mining	102, 103, 104, 105, 108, 109
7	Coal mining	11, 12
8	Crude petroleum & natural gas	1311, 1321
9	Stone & clay mining & quarrying	141, 142, 144, 145, 148, 149
10	Chemical & fertilizer mineral mining	147
11	New construction	138, pt. 15, pt. 16, pt. 17, pt. 6561
12	Maintenance & repair construction	pt. 15, pt. 16, pt. 17
13	Ordnance & accessories	19
14	Food & kindred products	20
15	Tobacco manufactures	21
16	Broad & narrow fabrics, yarn & thread mills	221, 222, 223, 224, 226, 228
17	Miscellaneous textile goods & floor coverings	227, 229
18	Apparel	225, 23 (excluding 239), 3992
19	Miscellaneous fabricated textile products	239
20	Lumber & wood products, except containers	24 (excluding 244)
21	Wooden containers	244
22	Household furniture	251
23	Other furniture & fixtures	25 (excluding 251)
24	Paper & allied products, except containers & boxes	26 (excluding 265)

25	Paperboard containers & boxes	265
26	Printing & publishing	27
27	Chemicals & selected chemical products	281 (excluding alumina pt. of 2819), 286, 287, 289
28	Plastics & synthetic materials	282
29	Drugs, cleaning, & toilet preparations	283, 284
30	Paints & allied products	285
31	Petroleum refining & related industries	29
32	Rubber & miscellaneous plastics products	30
33	Leather tanning & industrial leather products	311, 312
34	Footwear & other leather products	31 (excluding 311, 312)
35	Glass & glass products	321, 322, 323
36	Stone & clay products	324, 325, 326, 327, 328, 329
37	Primary iron & steel manufacturing	331, 332, 3391, 3399
38	Primary nonferrous metals manufacturing	2819 (alumina only), 333, 334, 335, 336, 3392
39	Metal containers	3411, 3491
40	Heating, plumbing, & fabricated structural metal products	343, 344
41	Screw machine products, bolts, nuts, etc., & metal stampings	345, 346
42	Other fabricated metal products	342, 347, 348, 349 (excluding 3491)
43	Engines & turbines	351
44	Farm machinery & equipment	352
45	Construction, mining, oil field machinery & equipment	3531, 3532, 3533
46	Materials handling machinery & equipment	3534, 3535, 3536, 3537
47	Metalworking machinery & equipment	354
48	Special industry machinery & equipment	355
49	General industrial machinery & equipment	356
50	Machine shop products	359
51	Office, computing, & accounting machines	357
52	Service industry machines	358

(continued)

Table A–1 (continued)

Industry Number	*Industry Title*	*Related SIC Codes (1957 edition)*[a]
53	Electric transmission & distribution equipment & electrical industrial apparatus	361, 362
54	Household appliances	363
55	Electric lighting & wiring equipment	364
56	Radio, TV, & communication equipment	365, 366
57	Electronic components & accessories	367
58	Miscellaneous electrical machinery, equipment, & supplies	369
59	Motor vehicles & equipment	371
60	Aircraft & parts	372
61	Other transportation equipment	373, 374, 375, 379
62	Professional, scientific, & controlling instruments & supplies	381, 382, 384, 387
63	Optical, ophthalmic, & photographic equipment & supplies	383, 385, 386
64	Miscellaneous manufacturing	39 (excluding 3992)
65	Transportation & warehousing	40, 41, 42, 44, 45, 46, 47
66	Communications, except radio & TV broadcasting	481, 482, 489
67	Radio & TV broadcasting	483
68	Electric, gas, water, & sanitary services	49
69	Wholesale & retail trade	50 (excluding manufacturers sales offices), 52, 53, 54, 55, 56, 57, 58, 59, pt. 7399
70	Finance & insurance	60, 61, 62, 63, 64, 66, 67
71	Real estate & rental	65 (excluding 6541 and pt. 6561)
72	Hotels & lodging places; personal & repair services, except automobile repair	70, 72, 76 (excluding 7694 and 7699)
73	Business services	6541, 73 (excluding 7361, 7391, and pt. 7399), 7694, 7699, 81, 89 (excluding 8921)

74	Research & development	(eliminated in 1963 study)
75	Automobile repair & services	75
76	Amusements	78, 79
77	Medical, educational services, & nonprofit organizations	0722, 7361, 80, 82, 84, 86, 8921
78	Federal government enterprises	....
79	State & local government enterprises	....
80a	Directly allocated imports of goods & services	....
80b	Transferred imports of goods & services	....
81	Business travel, entertainment, & gifts	....
82	Office supplies	....
83	Scrap, used, & secondhand goods	....

[a]These are the SIC codes assigned to industries in the 1958 input-output study. They differ slightly from those assigned in the 1963 study.

Table A–2
Product-Mix Industrial Classification Scheme

Product-Mix Industry Number	*Input-Output Industry*		*SIC Code (1957 edition)*
	Number	*Title*	
1	3.00	Forestry & fishery products	074, 081, 082, 084, 086, 091
2	4.00	Agricultural, forestry & fishery services	071, 0723, 073, pt. 0729, 085, 098
3	12.01	Maintenance & repair construction, residential buildings (nonfarm)	pt. 15, pt. 17
	12.02	Maintenance & repair construction, all other	pt. 15, pt. 16, pt. 17
4	13.01	Complete guided missiles	1925
	13.02	Ammunition, except for small arms, n.e.c.	1929
	13.03	Tanks & tank components	1931
	13.04	Sighting & fire control equipment	1941
	13.05	Small arms	1951
	13.06	Small arms ammunition	1961
	13.07	Other ordnance & accessories	1911, 1999
5	14.01	Meat products	201
6	14.02	Creamery butter	2021
	14.03	Cheese, natural & processed	2022
	14.04	Condensed & evaporated milk	2023
	14.05	Ice cream & frozen desserts	2024
	14.06	Fluid milk	2026
7	14.07	Canned & cured sea foods	2031
	14.08	Canned specialties	2032
	14.09	Canned fruits & vegetables	2033
	14.10	Dehydrated food products	2034
	14.11	Pickles, sauces & salad dressings	2035
	14.12	Fresh or frozen packaged fish	2036
	14.13	Frozen fruits & vegetables	2037
8	14.14	Flour & cereal preparations	2041, 2043, 2045

	14.15	Prepared feeds for animals & fowls	2042
	14.16	Rice milling	2044
	14.17	Wet corn milling	2046
9	14.18	Bakery products	205
10	14.19	Sugar	206
11	14.20	Confectionery & related products	207
12	14.21	Alcoholic beverages	2082 through 2085
	14.22	Bottled & canned soft drinks	2086
	14.23	Flavoring extracts & sirups, n.e.c.	2087
13	14.24	Cottonseed oil mills	2091
	14.25	Soybean oil mills	2092
	14.26	Vegetable oil mills, n.e.c.	2093
	14.27	Animal & marine fats & oils	2094
	14.28	Roasted coffee	2095
	14.29	Shortening & cooking oils	2096
	14.30	Manufactured ice	2097
	14.31	Macaroni & spaghetti	2098
	14.32	Food preparations, n.e.c.	2099
14	15.01	Cigarettes, cigars, etc.	2111, 2121, 2131
15	15.02	Tobacco stemming & redrying	2141
16	16.01	Broadwoven fabric mills & fabric finishing plants	2211, 2221, 2231, 2261, 2262
	16.03	Yarn mills & finishing of textiles, n.e.c.	2269, 2281 through 2283
	16.04	Thread mills	2284
17	16.02	Narrow fabric mills	2241
18	17.01	Floor coverings	227
19	17.02	Felt goods, n.e.c.	2291
	17.03	Lace goods	2292
	17.04	Paddings & upholstery fillings	2293
	17.05	Processed textile waste	2294
	17.06	Coated fabrics, not rubberized	2295
	17.07	Tire cord & fabric	2296
	17.08	Scouring & combing plants	2297
	17.09	Cordage & twine	2298
	17.10	Textile goods, n.e.c.	2299

(continued)

Table A–2 (continued)

Product-Mix Industry Number	*Input-Output Industry*		*SIC Code (1957 edition)*
	Number	*Title*	
20	18.01	Hosiery	2251, 2252
	18.02	Knit apparel mills	2253, 2254, 2259
	18.03	Knit fabric mills	2256
21	18.04	Apparel made from purchased materials	23 (except 239), 3992
22	19.01	Curtains & draperies	2391
	19.02	Housefurnishings, n.e.c.	2392
	19.03	Fabricated textile products, n.e.c.	2393 through 2399
23	20.01	Logging camps & logging contractors	2411
24	20.02	Sawmills & planing mills, general	2421
	20.03	Hardwood dimension & flooring	2426
	20.04	Special product sawmills, n.e.c.	2429
25	20.05	Millwork	2431
	20.06	Veneer & plywood	2432
	20.07	Prefabricated wood structures	2433
26	20.08	Wood preserving	2491
	20.09	Wood products, n.e.c.	2499
27	21.00	Wooden containers	244
28	22.01	Wood household furniture	2511, 2519
	22.02	Upholstered household furniture	2512
	22.03	Metal household furniture	2514
	22.04	Mattresses & bedsprings	2515
29	23.01	Wood office furniture	2521
	23.02	Metal office furniture	2522
30	23.03	Public building furniture	2531
31	23.04	Wood partitions & fixtures	2541
	23.05	Metal partitions & fixtures	2542
32	23.06	Venetian blinds & shades	2591
	23.07	Furniture & fixtures, n.e.c.	2599

33	24.01	Pulp mills	2611
34	24.02	Paper mills, except building paper	2621
35	24.03	Paperboard mills	2631
36	24.04	Envelopes	2642
	24.05	Sanitary paper products	2647
	24.06	Wallpaper & building paper & board mills	2644, 2661
	24.07	Converted paper products, n.e.c., except containers & boxes	2641, 2643, 2645, 2646, 2649
37	25.00	Paperboard containers & boxes	265
38	26.01	Newspapers	2711
39	26.02	Periodicals	2721
40	26.03	Book printing & publishing	273
41	26.04	Miscellaneous publishing	2741
42	26.05	Commercial printing	2751, 2752
	26.06	Manifold business forms, blankbooks & binders	2761, 2782
	26.08	Miscellaneous printing services	2753, 2789, 279
43	26.07	Greeting card publishing	2771
44	27.01	Industrial inorganic & organic chemicals	281 (except 28195)
45	27.02	Fertilizers	2871, 2872
	27.03	Agricultural chemicals, n.e.c.	2879
46	27.04	Miscellaneous chemical products	2861, 289
47	28.01	Plastics materials & resins	2821
	28.02	Synthetic rubber	2822
	28.03	Cellulosic man-made fibers	2823
	28.04	Organic fibers, noncellulosic	2824
48	29.01	Drugs	283
49	29.02	Cleaning preparations	284 (except 2844)
	29.03	Toilet preparations	2844
50	30.00	Paints & allied products	2851
51	31.01	Petroleum refining & related products	2911, 299
52	31.02	Paving mixtures & blocks	2951
	31.03	Asphalt felts & coatings	2952

(continued)

Table A–2 (continued)

Product-Mix Industry Number	*Input-Output Industry*		*SIC Code (1957 edition)*
	Number	*Title*	
53	32.01	Tires & inner tubes	3011
54	32.02	Rubber footwear	3021
55	32.03	Reclaimed rubber & miscellaneous rubber products, n.e.c.	3031, 3069
56	32.04	Miscellaneous plastics products	3079
57	33.00	Leather tanning & industrial leather products	3111, 3121
58	34.01	Footwear cut stock	3131
59	34.02	Footwear, except rubber	314
60	34.03	Other leather products	3151, 3161, 317, 3199
61	35.01	Glass & glass products, except containers	3211, 3229, 3231
	35.02	Glass containers	3221
62	36.01	Cement, hydraulic	3241
63	36.02	Brick & structural clay tile	3251
	36.03	Ceramic wall & floor tile	3253
	36.04	Clay refractories	3255
	36.05	Structural clay products, n.e.c.	3259
64	36.06	Vitreous plumbing fixtures	3261
	36.07	Food utensils, pottery	3262, 3263
	36.08	Porcelain electrical supplies	3264
	36.09	Pottery products, n.e.c.	3269
65	36.10	Concrete block & brick	3271
	36.11	Concrete products, n.e.c.	3272
	36.12	Ready-mixed concrete	3273
	36.13	Lime	3274
	36.14	Gypsum products	3275
	36.15	Cut stone & stone products	3281
66	36.16	Abrasive products	3291
	36.17	Asbestos products	3292
	36.18	Gaskets & insulations	3293

	36.19	Minerals, ground or treated	3295
	36.20	Mineral wool	3296
	36.21	Nonclay refractories	3297
	36.22	Nonmetallic mineral products, n.e.c.	3299
67	37.01	Blast furnace & basic steel products	331
68	37.02	Iron & steel foundries	332
69	37.03	Iron & steel forgings	3391
70	37.04	Primary metal products, n.e.c.	3399
71	38.01	Primary copper	3331
	38.02	Primary lead	3332
	38.03	Primary zinc	3333
	38.04	Primary aluminum	3334, 28195
	38.05	Primary nonferrous metals, n.e.c.	3339
72	38.06	Secondary nonferrous metals	3341
73	38.07	Copper rolling & drawing	3351
	38.08	Aluminum rolling & drawing	3352
	38.09	Nonferrous rolling & drawing, n.e.c.	3356
	38.10	Nonferrous wire drawing & insulating	3357
74	38.11	Aluminum castings	3361
	38.12	Brass, bronze, & copper castings	3362
	38.13	Nonferrous castings, n.e.c.	3369
75	38.14	Nonferrous forgings	3392
76	39.01	Metal cans	3411
77	39.02	Metal barrels, drums, & pails	3491
78	40.01	Metal sanitary ware	3431
	40.02	Plumbing fittings & brass goods	3432
	40.03	Heating equipment except electric	3433
79	40.04	Fabricated structural steel	3441
	40.05	Metal doors, sash & trim	3442
	40.06	Fabricated plate work (boiler shops)	3443
	40.07	Sheet metal work	3444
	40.08	Architectural metal work	3446
	40.09	Miscellaneous metal work	3449

(continued)

Table A-2 (continued)

Product-Mix Industry Number	*Input-Output Industry*		*SIC Code (1957 edition)*
	Number	*Title*	
80	41.01	Screw machine products & bolts, nuts, rivets, & washers	345
81	41.02	Metal stampings	3461
82	42.01	Cutlery	3421
	42.02	Hand & edge tools including saws	3423, 3425
83	42.03	Hardware, n.e.c.	3429
84	42.04	Coating, engraving, & allied services	3471, 3479
85	42.05	Miscellaneous fabricated wire products	3481
	42.06	Safes & vaults	3492
	42.07	Steel springs	3493
	42.08	Pipe, valves & pipe fittings	3494, 3498
	42.09	Collapsible tubes	3496
	42.10	Metal foil & leaf	3497
	42.11	Fabricated metal products, n.e.c.	3499
86	43.01	Steam engines & turbines	3511
	43.02	Internal combustion engines, n.e.c.	3519
87	44.00	Farm machinery	3522
88	45.01	Construction machinery	3531
89	45.02	Mining machinery	3532
90	45.03	Oil field machinery	3533
91	46.01	Elevators & moving stairways	3534
92	46.02	Conveyors & conveying equipment	3535
93	46.03	Hoists, cranes, & monorails	3536
94	46.04	Industrial trucks & tractors	3537
95	47.01	Machine tools, metal cutting types	3541
	47.02	Machine tools, metal forming types	3542
	47.03	Special dies & tools & machine tool accessories	3544, 3545
	47.04	Metalworking machinery, n.e.c.	3548

96	48.01	Food products machinery	3551
	48.02	Textile machinery	3552
	48.03	Woodworking machinery	3553
	48.04	Paper industries machinery	3554
	48.05	Printing trades machinery	3555
	48.06	Special industry machinery, n.e.c.	3559
97	49.01	Pumps & compressors	3561
	49.02	Ball & roller bearings	3562
	49.03	Blowers & fans	3564
	49.04	Industrial patterns	3565
	49.05	Power transmission equipment	3566
	49.06	Industrial furnaces & ovens	3567
	49.07	General industrial machinery, n.e.c.	3569
98	50.00	Machine shop products	359
99	51.01	Computing & related machines	3571
	51.02	Typewriters	3572
	51.03	Scales & balances	3576
	51.04	Office machines, n.e.c.	3579
100	52.01	Automatic merchandising machines	3581
	52.02	Commercial laundry equipment	3582
	52.03	Refrigeration machinery	3585
	52.04	Measuring & dispensing pumps	3586
	52.05	Service industry machines, n.e.c.	3589
101	53.01	Electric measuring instruments	3611
	53.02	Transformers	3612
	53.03	Switchgear & switchboard apparatus	3613
102	53.04	Motors & generators	3621
	53.05	Industrial controls	3622
	53.06	Welding apparatus	3623
	53.07	Carbon & graphite products	3624
	53.08	Electrical & industrial apparatus, n.e.c.	3629
103	54.01	Household cooking equipment	3631
	54.02	Household refrigerators & freezers	3632

(continued)

Table A–2 (continued)

Product-Mix Industry Number	*Input-Output Industry*		*SIC Code (1957 edition)*
	Number	*Title*	
	54.03	Household laundry equipment	3633
	54.04	Electric housewares & fans	3634
	54.05	Household vacuum cleaners	3635
	54.06	Sewing machines	3636
	54.07	Household appliances, n.e.c.	3639
104	55.01	Electric lamps	3641
	55.02	Lighting fixtures	3642
	55.03	Wiring devices	3643, 3644
105	56.01	Radio & TV receiving sets	3651
	56.02	Phonograph records	3652
106	56.03	Telephone & telegraph apparatus	3661
	56.04	Radio & TV communication equipment	3662
107	57.01	Electron tubes	3671, 3672, 3673
	57.02	Semiconductors	3674
	57.03	Electronic components, n.e.c.	3679
108	58.01	Storage batteries	3691
	58.02	Primary batteries, wet & dry	3692
	58.03	X-ray apparatus & tubes	3693
	58.04	Engine electrical equipment	3694
	58.05	Electrical equipment, n.e.c.	3699
109	59.01	Truck & bus bodies	3713
	59.02	Truck trailers	3715
	59.03	Motor vehicles & parts	3717
110	60.01	Aircraft	3721
	60.02	Aircraft engines & parts	3722
	60.03	Aircraft propellers & parts	3723
	60.04	Aircraft equipment, n.e.c.	3729

111	61.01	Shipbuilding & repairing	3731
	61.02	Boatbuilding & repairing	3732
112	61.03	Locomotives & parts	3741
	61.04	Railroad & street cars	3742
113	61.05	Motorcycles, bicycles, & parts	3751
114	61.06	Trailer coaches	3791
	61.07	Transportation equipment, n.e.c.	3799
115	62.01	Engineering & scientific instruments	3811
116	62.02	Mechanical measuring devices	3821
	62.03	Automatic temperature controls	3822
117	62.04	Surgical & medical instruments	3841
	62.05	Surgical appliances & supplies	3842
	62.06	Dental equipment & supplies	3843
118	62.07	Watches, clocks, & parts	387
119	63.01	Optical instruments & lenses	3831
120	63.02	Ophthalmic goods	3851
121	63.03	Photographic equipment & supplies	3861
122	64.01	Jewelry, including costume & silverware	391, 3961
	64.06	Artificial flowers	3962
	64.07	Buttons, needles, pins, & fasteners	3963, 3964
123	64.02	Musical instruments & parts	3931
124	64.03	Games, toys, etc.	3941
	64.04	Sporting & athletic goods, n.e.c.	3949
125	64.05	Pens, pencils, etc.	395
126	64.08	Brooms & brushes	3981
	64.09	Hard surface floor covering	3982
	64.10	Morticians goods	3988
	64.11	Signs & advertising displays	3993
	64.12	Miscellaneous manufactures, n.e.c.	3983, 3984, 3987, 3995, 3999
127	65.01	Railroads & related services	40, 474
	65.03	Motor freight transportation & warehousing	42, 473
	65.07	Transportation services	47 (except 473, 474)
128	65.02	Local, suburban, & interurban highway passenger transportation	41

(continued)

Table A–2 (continued)

Product-Mix Industry Number	*Input-Output Industry Number*	*Input-Output Industry Title*	*SIC Code (1957 edition)*
129	65.04	Water transportation	44
130	65.05	Air transportation	45
131	65.06	Pipeline transportation	46
132	66.00	Communications, except radio & television	48 (except 483)
133	67.00	Radio & television broadcasting	483
134	68.01	Electric utilities	491, pt. 493
	68.02	Gas utilities	492, pt. 493
	68.03	Water & sanitary services	494, 495, 496, 497, pt. 493
135	69.01	Wholesale trade	50 (except manufacturers' sales offices)
136	69.02	Retail trade	52, 53, 54, 55, 56, 57, 58, 59, 7396
137	70.01	Banking	60
138	70.02	Credit agencies	61, 67
139	70.03	Security & commodity brokers	62
140	70.04	Insurance carriers	63
141	70.05	Insurance agents & brokers	64
142	71.01	Owner-occupied dwellings	Not available
143	71.02	Real estate	65 (except pt. 6561), 66
144	72.01	Hotels & lodging places	70
	72.02	Personal & repair services, except auto repair, barber, & beauty shops	72 (except 723, 724), 76 (except 7694 & pt. 7699)
	72.03	Barber & beauty shops	723, 724
145	73.01	Miscellaneous business services	73 (except 731, 7396), 7694, pt. 7699
	73.02	Advertising	731

146	73.03	Miscellaneous professional services	81, 89 (except 8921)
147	75.00	Automobile repair & services	75
148	76.01	Motion pictures	78
	76.02	Amusement & recreation services	79
149	77.01	Doctors & dentists	801, 802, 803, 804
	77.02	Hospitals	8061
	77.03	Other medical & health services	0722, 807, 809
150	77.04	Educational services	82
	77.05	Nonprofit organizations	84, 86, 8921
151	78.01	Post Office	
	78.02	Federal electric utilities	
	78.03	Commodity Credit Corporation	
	78.04	Other federal government enterprises	
152	79.01	Local government passenger transit	
	79.02	State & local electric utilities	
	79.03	Other state & local government enterprises	

Table A-3
Classification of the Seventeen Agricultural Subindustries According to Commodities Produced

Subindustry Number	*Name of Commodity Group*	*Commodities Produced*
A-1	Meat animals	Cattle and calves Hogs Sheep and lambs Wool Goats Mohair Manure
A-2	Poultry & eggs	Chickens, turkeys, and broilers Eggs and turkey-hatching eggs Other poultry and products Manure
A-3	Farm dairy products	Milk, butter, and butterfat Manure
A-4	Other livestock & products	Horses and mules Animal work power Honey Package bees Beeswax Miscellaneous animals (rabbits, fur-bearing animals, dogs, etc.) Manure
A-5	Food grains	Wheat Rye Rice Buckwheat
A-6	Feed crops	Corn Hay Pasture Oats Barley Sorghum grain Silage
A-7	Cotton	Cotton Cottonseed
A-8	Tobacco	Tobacco Seeds and plants
A-9	Oil-bearing crops	Soybeans Peanuts Flaxseed Tung nuts Copra (imported) Other oil seeds Castor beans
A-10	Vegetables	Dry edible beans Dry edible peas

Table A–3 (continued)

Subindustry Number	*Name of Commodity Group*	*Commodities Produced*
		Potatoes Sweet potatoes Truck crops Mung beans
A-11	Fruits	Citrus fruits Noncitrus fruits Melons Berries Other fruits and nuts
A-12	Tree nuts	Almonds Filberts Pecans Walnuts
A-13	Legume and grass seeds	Cowpeas Hayseeds Pasture seeds Cover-crop seeds
A-14	Sugar and sirup crops	Sugar beets Sugar cane and sirup Maple sugar and sirup Sorgo sirup
A-15	Miscellaneous crops	Hops Spearmint and peppermint Broomcorn Popcorn Velvet beans Other miscellaneous crops (includes other seeds, flax and hemp fiber, etc.)
A-16	Forest products	Stumpage Pulpwood Gum naval stores Fuelwood Christmas trees Fence posts and other lumber products
A-17	Greenhouse & nursery products	Greenhouse and nursery products

Table A-4
List of Mining SIC Subindustries

Input-Output Industry		*SIC Subindustry*	
Number	*Title*	*Number*	*Title*
5	Iron & ferroalloy ores mining	1011	Iron ores
		1062	Manganese ores
		1064	Tungsten ores
		1069	Ferroalloy ores, except vanadium, n.e.c.
6	Nonferrous metal ores mining	1021	Copper ores
		1031	Lead & zinc ores
		1042	Lode gold
		1043	Placer gold
		1044	Silver ores
		1051	Bauxite & other aluminum ores
		1081	Metal mining stripping services
		1082	Metal mining services, except stripping
		1092	Mercury ores
		1093	Titanium ores
		1094	Uranium-radium-vanadium ores
		1099	Metallic minerals (ores), n.e.c.
7	Coal mining	111	Anthracite coal
		121	Bituminous coal
8	Crude petroleum & natural gas	1311	Crude petroleum (subindustry)
		1311	Natural gas (subindustry)
		1321	Natural gas liquids
9	Stone & clay mining & quarrying	1411	Dimension stone
		1421	Crushed & broken stone, including riprap
		1441	Sand & gravel
		1452	Bentonite
		1453	Fire clay
		1454	Fuller's earth
		1455	Kaolin & ball clay
		1456	Feldspar
		1457	Magnesite & brucite
		1459	Clay, ceramic, & refractory minerals, n.e.c.
		1481	Nonmetallic minerals stripping services
		1482	Nonmetallic minerals (except fuel) services, except stripping
		1492	Gypsum
		1493	Mica
		1494	Native asphalt & bitumens
		1495	Pumice & pumicite
		1496	Talc, soapstone, & pyrophyllite
		1497	Natural abrasives, except sand
		1498	Peat

Table A–4 (continued)

Input-Output Industry		SIC Subindustry	
Number	*Title*	*Number*	*Title*
		1499	Miscellaneous nonmetallic minerals, n.e.c.
10	Chemical & fertilizer mineral mining	1472	Barite
		1473	Fluorspar
		1474	Potash, soda, & borate minerals
		1475	Phosphate rock
		1476	Rock salt
		1477	Sulfur
		1479	Chemical & fertilizer mineral mining, n.e.c.

Appendix B
Regional Classifications

Table B–1
Regional Classification

Regions	*States*
9	*51 name*
1	18 Maine
	44 Vermont
	20 Massachusetts
	38 Rhode Island
	28 New Hampshire
	6 Connecticut
2	31 New York
	37 Pennsylvania
	29 New Jersey
3	21 Michigan
	34 Ohio
	13 Indiana
	12 Illinois
	48 Wisconsin
4	22 Minnesota
	14 Iowa
	24 Missouri
	33 North Dakota
	40 South Dakota
	26 Nebraska
	15 Kansas
5	7 Delaware
	19 Maryland
	8 District of Columbia
	45 Virginia
	47 West Virginia
	32 North Carolina
	39 South Carolina
	10 Georgia
	9 Florida
6	16 Kentucky
	41 Tennessee
	1 Alabama
	23 Mississippi
7	3 Arkansas
	17 Louisiana
	35 Oklahoma
	42 Texas
8	25 Montana
	11 Idaho
	49 Wyoming
	5 Colorado
	30 New Mexico
	2 Arizona
	43 Utah
	27 Nevada
9	46 Washington
	36 Oregon
	4 California
	50 Alaska
	51 Hawaii

Table B–2
Regional Classification Used in the 1955 Survey of Farmers' Expenditures

Region	*Subregion*	*State*
North	Northeast	Maryland Delaware New Jersey New York Pennsylvania Maine New Hampshire Vermont Massachusetts Connecticut Rhode Island
	East North Central	Wisconsin Illinois Indiana Michigan Ohio
	West North Central	Minnesota Iowa Missouri North Dakota South Dakota Nebraska Kansas
South	South Atlantic	North Carolina South Carolina Georgia West Virginia Virginia Florida
	East South Central	Mississippi Alabama Tennessee Kentucky
	West South Central	Arkansas Louisiana Oklahoma Texas
West	Mountain	Montana Idaho Wyoming Colorado New Mexico Arizona Nevada Utah
	Pacific	Washington Oregon California

Table B–3
States and Regions for Which Mining Data Were Available

Input-Output Industry: *Number*	Input-Output Industry: *Title*	*SIC Subindustry*	*States and/or Regions Shown*	*Includes ". . . received for preparation"?*
5	Iron & ferroalloy ores mining	SIC 101	Middle Atlantic (New York) East North Central West North Central (Minnesota) East South Central West South Central Mountain (Wyoming, Utah) Pacific	yes
6	Nonferrous metal ores mining	SIC 102	Montana, Arizona	some
7	Coal mining	SIC 11	Pennsylvania	yes
		SIC 12	Middle Atlantic (Pennsylvania) East North Central (Ohio, Indiana, Illinois) West North Central South Atlantic (Maryland, Virginia, West Virginia) East South Central (Tennessee, Kentucky, Alabama) West South Central (Oklahoma) Mountain (Wyoming, Colorado, Utah) Pacific (Alaska)	no
9	Stone & clay mining & quarrying	SIC 1421	New England (Massachusetts, Connecticut) Middle Atlantic (New York, New Jersey, Pennsylvania) East North Central (Ohio, Indiana, Illinois, Michigan, Wisconsin) West North Central (Minnesota, Iowa, Missouri, Nebraska, Kansas) South Atlantic (Georgia, Florida, Virginia, West Virginia, North Carolina, South Carolina) East South Central (Kentucky, Tennessee, Alabama)	some

			West South Central (Oklahoma, Texas) Mountain Pacific (Washington, California, Hawaii)	
		SIC 1441	New England (Massachusetts, Connecticut) Middle Atlantic (New York, New Jersey, Pennsylvania) East North Central (Ohio, Illinois, Indiana, Michigan, Wisconsin) West North Central (Minnesota, Iowa, Missouri, Nebraska, Kansas) South Atlantic (Maryland, Virginia, West Virginia, North Carolina, Florida) East South Central (Kentucky, Tennessee, Alabama, Mississippi) West South Central (Arkansas, Louisiana, Oklahoma, Texas) Mountain (Colorado, Arizona, Utah) Pacific (Washington, Oregon, California)	no
		SIC 1445	Georgia	yes
10	Chemical & fertilizer mineral mining	SIC 1472	West North Central (Missouri) South Central	yes
		SIC 1473	North East North Central South	no
		SIC 1474	West South Central Mountain (New Mexico) Pacific (California)	yes
		SIC 1475	East South (Florida, Tennessee) West	some
		SIC 1476	North East North Central South West	no
		SIC 1477	All United States	no
		SIC 1479	All United States	no

Table B-4
Regional Breakdown for Construction Industries

Regions	*States*
Northeast	Maine, Massachusetts, New Hampshire, Vermont, Rhode Island, Connecticut, New York, New Jersey, Pennsylvania
North Central	Ohio, Indiana, Illinois, Michigan, Wisconsin, Minnesota, Iowa, Missouri, Kansas, Nebraska, South Dakota, North Dakota
South	Delaware, Maryland, District of Columbia, Virginia, West Virginia, North Carolina, South Carolina, Georgia, Florida, Alabama, Mississippi, Louisiana, Texas, Arkansas, Oklahoma, Tennessee, Kentucky
West	Montana, Idaho, Wyoming, Colorado, New Mexico, Arizona, Utah, Nevada, California, Oregon, Washington, Hawaii, Alaska

Note: Input coefficients for the four regions were used for the following new construction subindustries:

Number	*Title*
1	Private one-family nonfarm residential
4	All other private nonfarm residential
5	High-rise apartment houses, public & private
9	Educational building
22	Sewer
23	Water system

Appendix C
1963 State Estimates of Technology (MRIO Data Set 4)

This data set provides estimates of state input-output transactions. A complete and revised description of the methodology used to assemble these data is provided in Chapters 1 through 4 in the main text. All the data have been adjusted for consistency with the national input-output table published by the OBE in the 1963 table [122].

State Input-Output Tables

Figure 1–7 (page 29) shows a sample state input-output table used in the implementation of the multiregional input-output (MRIO) model in 1973. The data listed in the tables in this appendix can be combined to form the 51 state input-output tables. To provide the user with more flexibility, the 51 state tables have not been printed; rather, the various components of the tables are given separately in the next section of this appendix.

Throughout the MRIO calculations, the state tables were checked against a national control matrix. Because several adjustments had to be made to the national accounting framework, the national control matrix used for consistency checks during the computations does not exactly correspond to the OBE 1963 national table. The adjustments made to the state tables and to the OBE national table for the MRIO calculations are explained here. (The row and column numbers refer to those given in Figure 1–7, page 29.)

1. The portion of the matrix in rows and columns 1–79 was adjusted.
   a. Row 74 and column 74 contain zeroes in the national and state tables because IO-74, Research & development, was not included as a separate industry in the 1963 OBE table.
   b. IO-81, Business travel, entertainment, & gifts, and IO-82, Office supplies: These two industries are specially constructed for the input-output accounts. They were eliminated by taking column 81 and column 82 in the 1963 national transfer (secondary) matrix and calculating coefficient vectors from them. The values in rows 81 and 82 of the national (state) table were then distributed to the other elements in the respective columns in proportion to the coefficients formed from columns 81 and 82. Since the row sum is equal to the column sum for industries 81 and 82, none of the row and column sums of the national control matrix are changed by this adjustment. The values in rows and columns 81 and

82 were made zero, and other data were placed in the rows and columns (see below).

2. Row 80a in the national input-output table represents directly allocated (noncompetitive) imports only. These imports were estimated by state at the same time that the other materials and services inputs were estimated and were placed in row 80 of the state (national) tables. The sum of row 80 was placed as a negative figure in column 81. The sum of row 80 then becomes zero, representing the fact that goods imported are not produced in this country.

3. Column 80 contains no entries in the national control and state tables.

4. Row 80b in the national input-output table represents transferred (competitive) imports. These data were estimated for the 51 states in the MRIO model after the other entries in the tables had been assembled. They were placed in row 81. (Refer to pages 32–34 of the main text for a description of the special estimates that were made.) The sum of row 81 was placed as a negative figure in column 81. The sum of row 81 then becomes zero, representing the fact that goods imported are not produced in this country.

5. Column 81 at the state level has entries for the service industries (IO-4, IO-11, IO-12, and IO-65 through IO-79), as well as for IO-3, Forestry & fishery products. As explained in Chapter 1, the trade-flow matrix for IO-3 has entries only on the diagonal (intraregional shipments), indicating that products of that industry are not traded. IO-3 was therefore treated as a service industry.

   Since no interregional trade flows were estimated for the service industries, total production of services should equal total consumption of services in each region. In many cases, however, due to the various methods used in estimating inputs at the state level and the lack of available data, this condition was not fulfilled. The difference between total production of a service in a given region and its total consumption was placed in the appropriate row of column 81 of the state input-output table. This adjustment forces the row sums (total consumption) to equal the column sums (total production) for the service industries in each region. Although the sum for the 51 regions of the elements in column 81 should equal zero (the residuals should cancel at the national level), extremely small values do occur in column 81 of the national control matrix because of rounding errors.

6. Three of the entries in the sum of the state input-output tables differ from corresponding entries in the national control matrix:

a. Row 81, Transferred imports: The sum of row 81 (which was placed as a negative figure in column 81 in the state input-output tables) differs from the corresponding sum in the national table. The sums differ by \$21 million, representing the value that had not been allocated to the states in the net inventory change final demand tables.
b. Row 82, Final demand for value added: The difference between the element in row 82 of column 82 in the state control matrix (\$52,840 million) and the sum of elements in the final demand columns of rows 84, 85, 86, and 87 in the national OBE table (\$61,002 million) was \$8,162 million. This difference represents items that had not been allocated to states in the federal government (\$2,456 million), net foreign export (\$6,208 million), and net inventory change (-\$502 million) final demand tables.
c. Row 86, Final demand for scrap purchased: The difference between the final-demand-for-scrap-purchased entry in row 86, column 82, in the state control matrix (-\$439 million) and the corresponding sum of the final-demand-for-scrap-purchased entry in row 83 of the national OBE table (-\$334 million) was \$105 million. The residual represented an amount that had not been allocated to states in the net inventory change final demand tables.

7. Row 82 contains value added.

8. Column 82 contains total final demand. Before the total final demand elements were inserted into column 82, three adjustments were made:
   a. The entries for IO-82, Office supplies, were redistributed in the manner described under 1b above. (No entries are listed for IO-81, Business travel, entertainment, & gifts, in the final demand figures, so no adjustment was required.)
   b. The Commodity Credit Corporation figures were added to the total final demand figures.
   c. The inventory depletion component of net inventory change was subtracted from the total final demand figures.

9. Row 83 contains the secondary transfers-in (column sums of the secondary matrix) and column 83 contains the secondary transfers-out (row sums of the secondary matrix). The method of obtaining these estimates is described in Chapter 1.

10. Row 84 contains inventory depletions (as positive figures). Because no data were available to separate inventory additions from inventory depletions in the national input-output table, the negative elements in the 370-order OBE 1963 input-output table were aggregated to the 80-order level and were

transposed from a column of negative figures to a row of positive figures. The national total for each industry was distributed to the states in proportion to the amount of total commodity output for the industry in each state. (Refer to page 35.)

11. Column 84 contains no entries.

12. Row 85 contains values for the amount of scrap produced by the particular industry. For the national control matrix, the values in column 83 were simply transposed and placed as a row of negative figures in row 85. This adjustment has the effect of reducing the row and column totals for those industries that produce scrap. The state values were obtained by distributing the national figures in proportion to the state establishment output data for each industry.

13. Column 85 contains values for the competitive import of scrap, placed in row 81, and the margins on these imports, placed in rows 65 and 69. These imports of scrap were allocated to the regions according to the total transferred (competitive) imports into each state. The margins were obtained by applying the national ratio (the margin on the competitive import of scrap as a proportion of the competitive import of scrap) to these regional scrap import figures.

14. Row 86 contains entries for scrap purchased by each industry. These entries correspond with those in row 83 of the OBE national input-output table.

15. Column 86 contains no entries.

16. Row 87 contains the total state output for each establishment plus the total amount of that industry's output produced by other establishments in the state. Secondary products are double-counted in the total.

17. Column 87 contains the total amount of consumption by intermediate and final users in each state (row sums of the state input-output table) plus the total amount that could be classified as secondary products produced by establishments in the industry in the state. Secondary products are double-counted in the total.

Description of the Appendix C Tables

The 23 tables in this appendix contain the data required for the 51 state input-output tables. Because 1020 pages of text would have been required to print the full set of 51 state input-output tables, only the basic components are listed in the following tables. The 51 state tables are available on computer tape from the National Technical Information Service, Springfield, Virginia.

Tables C-1 through C-9 contain the direct primary inputs for the agricultural (IO-1 and IO-2), mining (IO-5 through IO-10), and new construction (IO-11) industries. The detailed methodology of assembling these estimates was described in Chapters 2, 3, and 4, respectively. The sums in column 52 represent the total primary input for each industry and will therefore differ from the values given in the 1963 national input-output table [122] by the values of the secondary products.

Table C-10 contains the 1963 national primary inputs for the manufacturing and service industries (IO-3, IO-4, and IO-12 through IO-79). As described in Chapter 1, pages 30-32, these 152-order national input data were weighted by the state establishment output figures given in Table C-11 and then aggregated to the appropriate 80-order industry.

Tables C-12 through C-21 contain the data for the value added and final demand components of the state input-output tables. The detailed methodology of assembling these estimates is given in Chapter 1.

Tables C-22 and C-23 contain the sums of the data in each column (state total production) and each row (state total consumption) for the 51 input-output tables.

All the state estimates were organized according to the basic format shown in Figure 1-7, page 29. The state input estimates for IO-1 through IO-79 were placed in rows and columns 1 through 79 in each state input-output table. The data from Tables C-12 through C-18 were placed in rows 80 through 86, respectively, in the appropriate state table; and the data from Tables C-19, C-20, and C-21 were placed in columns 81, 82, and 83, respectively.

The 23 tables follow.

MRIO Data Set 4
State Estimates of Technology
(in thousands of current dollars)

Table No.	*Table Title*
C-1	1963 Inputs by State to IO-1, Livestock & livestock products
C-2	1963 Inputs by State to IO-2, Other agricultural products
C-3	1963 Inputs by State to IO-5, Iron & ferroalloy ores mining
C-4	1963 Inputs by State to IO-6, Nonferrous metal ores mining
C-5	1963 Inputs by State to IO-7, Coal mining
C-6	1963 Inputs by State to IO-8, Crude petroleum & natural gas
C-7	1963 Inputs by State to IO-9, Stone & clay mining & quarrying
C-8	1963 Inputs by State to IO-10, Chemical & fertilizer mineral mining
C-9	1963 Inputs by State to IO-11, New construction
C-10	1963 National Primary Inputs to Manufacturing and Services
C-11	1963 State Establishment Outputs for Manufacturing and Services
C-12	1963 Directly Allocated Imports by State
C-13	1963 Transferred Imports by State
C-14	1963 State Value Added
C-15	1963 State Transfers-in
C-16	1963 Inventory Depletions by State
C-17	1963 Scrap Production by State
C-18	1963 Scrap Purchases by State
C-19	1963 Service Industries Residual by State
C-20	1963 State Total Final Demand
C-21	1963 State Transfers-out
C-22	1963 State Total Production
C-23	1963 State Total Consumption

TABLE C-1

1963 INPUTS BY STATE TO
IO-1, LIVESTOCK & LIVESTOCK PRODUCTS

(THOUSANDS OF CURRENT DOLLARS)

INDUSTRY TITLE	1 ALABAMA	2 ARIZONA	3 ARKANSAS	4 CALIFORNIA	5 COLORADO	6 CONNECTICUT	7 DELAWARE	8 DISTRICT OF COLUMBIA	9 FLORIDA
1 LIVESTOCK, PRDTS.	30108	101829	32570	440658	217861	4856	67	0	47638
2 OTHER AGRICULTURE PRDTS.	76381	63895	41772	424033	164447	11918	65311	0	82244
3 FORESTRY, FISHERIES	0	0	0	3	1	0	0	0	0
4 AGRI.,FORES.,FISH. SERV.	27644	754	30977	35405	2196	3573	5808	0	3736
5 IRON, FERRO. ORES MINING	0	0	0	0	0	0	0	0	0
6 NONFERROUS ORES MINING	0	0	0	0	0	0	0	0	0
7 COAL MINING	297	11	327	573	31	52	45	0	81
8 CRUDE PETRO.,NATURAL GAS	0	0	0	0	0	0	0	0	0
9 STONE, CLAY MINING	56	2	54	65	13	8	7	0	15
10 CHEM.,FERT. MIN. MINING	0	0	0	0	0	0	0	0	0
11 NEW CONSTRUCTION	0	0	0	0	0	0	0	0	0
12 MAINT., REPAIR CONSTR.	3111	652	1222	7004	3003	1141	245	0	1709
13 ORDNANCE, ACCESSORIES	0	0	0	3	1	0	0	0	0
14 FOOD, KINDRED PRDTS.	117576	22478	136915	287418	30234	34766	18440	0	63403
15 TOBACCO MANUFACTURES	4	9	3	40	16	1	0	0	3
16 FABRICS	0	0	0	0	0	0	0	0	0
17 TEXTILE PRDTS.	94	42	57	753	41	69	7	0	106
18 APPAREL	0	0	0	3	1	0	0	0	0
19 MISC. TEXTILE PRDTS.	654	61	656	308	368	1	1	0	179
20 LUMBER, WOOD PRDTS.	2	5	9	39	44	3	2	0	3
21 WOODEN CONTAINERS	0	0	0	0	0	0	0	0	0
22 HOUSEHOLD FURNITURE	0	0	0	0	0	0	0	0	0
23 OTHER FURNITURE	0	0	0	0	0	0	0	0	0
24 PAPER, ALLIED PRDTS.	286	62	128	3050	84	148	13	0	393
25 PAPERBOARD CONTAINERS	19	8	11	160	4	14	1	0	22
26 PRINTING, PUBLISHING	37	44	36	229	81	17	5	0	28
27 CHEMICALS,SELECT. PRDTS.	681	389	446	1280	1942	188	52	0	411
28 PLASTICS, SYNTHETICS	0	0	0	0	0	0	0	0	0
29 DRUGS, COSMETICS	2725	244	2965	5496	551	578	536	0	911
30 PAINT, ALLIED PRDTS.	0	0	0	0	0	0	0	0	0
31 PETROLEUM, RELATED INDS.	2223	682	2126	5019	3432	668	258	0	1229
32 RUBBER, MISC. PLASTICS	228	133	248	533	693	95	7	0	202
33 LEATHER TANNING, PRDTS.	0	0	0	0	0	0	0	0	0
34 FOOTWEAR, LEATHER PRDTS.	233	127	192	192	166	9	3	0	66
35 GLASS, GLASS PRDTS.	47	71	27	614	75	33	3	0	128
36 STONE, CLAY PRDTS.	13	14	10	87	32	5	1	0	15
37 PRIMARY IRON, STEEL MFR.	0	0	0	0	0	0	0	0	0
38 PRIMARY NONFERROUS MFR.	8	5	9	34	46	0	0	0	1

39	METAL CONTAINERS	74	34	47	585	53	53	7	0	80
40	FABRICATED METAL PRDTS.	0	0	0	0	0	0	0	0	0
41	SCREW MACH. PRDTS., ETC.	285	128	161	2399	54	217	17	0	343
42	OTHER FAB. METAL PRDTS.	280	50	202	676	360	160	61	0	52
43	ENGINES, TURBINES	0	0	0	0	0	0	0	0	0
44	FARM MACH., EQUIP.	37	23	43	164	151	10	2	0	27
45	CONSTRUC. MACH., EQUIP.	0	0	0	0	0	0	0	0	0
46	MATERIAL HANDLING MACH.	0	0	0	0	0	0	0	0	0
47	METALWORKING MACHINERY	0	0	0	0	0	0	0	0	0
48	SPECIAL MACH., EQUIP.	0	0	0	0	0	0	0	0	0
49	GENERAL MACH., EQUIP.	0	0	0	0	0	0	0	0	0
50	MACHINE SHOP PRDTS.	14	12	14	88	70	6	0	0	16
51	OFFICE, COMPUT. MACHINES	0	0	0	0	0	0	0	0	0
52	SERVICE IND. MACHINES	0	0	0	0	0	0	0	0	0
53	ELECT. TRANSMISS. EQUIP.	0	0	0	0	0	0	0	0	0
54	HOUSEHOLD APPLIANCES	1	2	1	9	4	0	0	0	1
55	ELECTRIC LIGHTING EQUIP.	5	3	5	24	19	2	0	0	5
56	RADIO, TV, ETC., EQUIP.	1	3	1	12	5	0	0	0	1
57	ELECTRONIC COMPONENTS	0	0	0	0	0	0	0	0	0
58	MISC. ELECTRICAL MACH.	42	20	42	118	111	18	2	0	45
59	MOTOR VEHICLES, EQUIP.	38	40	62	196	178	21	1	0	28
60	AIRCRAFT, PARTS	0	0	0	0	0	0	0	0	0
61	OTHER TRANSPORT. EQUIP.	1	0	1	3	3	0	0	0	0
62	PROFESS., SCIEN. INSTRU.	0	1	0	3	1	0	0	0	0
63	MEDICAL, PHOTO. EQUIP.	1	1	1	7	3	0	0	0	1
64	MISC. MANUFACTURING	6	6	7	34	27	2	3	0	3
65	TRANSPORT., WAREHOUSING	8852	7442	8114	46142	15416	2324	4409	0	11218
66	COMMUNICA.,EXC. BRDCAST.	744	225	405	2124	1200	210	80	0	284
67	RADIO, TV BROADCASTING	0	0	0	0	0	0	0	0	0
68	ELEC.,GAS,WATER,SAN.SER.	1518	1017	1315	21725	1681	629	139	0	746
69	WHOLESALE, RETAIL TRADE	17400	7395	17313	63332	13669	4430	6122	0	17796
70	FINANCE, INSURANCE	2073	622	2381	8368	2042	613	202	0	1556
71	REAL ESTATE, RENTAL	1555	5296	964	12132	4549	146	141	0	3167
72	HOTELS, PERSONAL SERV.	22	56	19	246	97	6	2	0	21
73	BUSINESS SERVICES	928	1495	858	6932	5146	184	49	0	840
74	RESEARCH, DEVELOPMENT	0	0	0	0	0	0	0	0	0
75	AUTO. REPAIR, SERVICES	497	427	699	2193	1944	235	16	0	364
76	AMUSEMENTS	4	9	3	40	15	1	0	0	3
77	MED.,EDUC. SERVICES	3513	851	3767	8383	1960	690	612	0	1525
78	FEDERAL GOVT. ENTERPRISE	69	54	28	288	99	17	6	0	42
79	STATE, LOCAL GOVT. ENT.	3	3	2	17	10	2	0	0	2
80	DIRECT ALLOCATED IMPORTS	5	490	5	142	222	2	0	0	5
81	TRANSFERRED IMPORTS	7563	6009	0	17290	0	65	8	0	207
82	VALUE ADDED	157962	26889	109310	336867	123101	49602	478	0	58225
83	SECONDARY TRANSFERS-IN	0	0	0	0	0	0	0	0	0
84	INVENTORY DEPLETION	0	0	0	0	0	0	0	0	0
85	SCRAP PRODUCTION	0	0	0	0	0	0	0	0	0
86	SCRAP PURCHASED	0	0	0	0	0	0	0	0	0
87	STATE TOTAL PRODUCTION	465920	250120	396530	1743539	597553	117787	103170	0	299125

TABLE C-1

1963 INPUTS BY STATE TO
IO-1, LIVESTOCK & LIVESTOCK PRODUCTS

(THOUSANDS OF CURRENT DOLLARS)

INDUSTRY TITLE	10 GEORGIA	11 IDAHO	12 ILLINOIS	13 INDIANA	14 IOWA	15 KANSAS	16 KENTUCKY	17 LOUISIANA	18 MAINE
1 LIVESTOCK, PRDTS.	40818	79387	280907	85007	547001	422597	56651	21735	3850
2 OTHER AGRICULTURE PRDTS.	104064	124903	398171	567257	486529	283498	130982	46438	20387
3 FORESTRY, FISHERIES	0	0	0	0	3	1	0	0	0
4 AGRI.,FORES.,FISH. SERV.	46306	2236	6484	10041	15683	3456	3859	4242	10710
5 IRON, FERRO. ORES MINING	0	0	0	0	0	0	0	0	0
6 NONFERROUS ORES MINING	0	0	0	0	0	0	0	0	0
7 COAL MINING	470	20	116	141	276	59	63	49	112
8 CRUDE PETRO.,NATURAL GAS	0	0	0	0	0	0	0	0	0
9 STONE, CLAY MINING	87	6	102	57	177	31	23	12	17
10 CHEM.,FERT. MIN. MINING	0	0	0	0	0	0	0	0	0
11 NEW CONSTRUCTION	0	0	0	0	0	0	0	0	0
12 MAINT., REPAIR CONSTR.	3013	1481	11790	8030	13355	4675	6014	1302	1066
13 ORDNANCE, ACCESSORIES	0	0	0	0	3	1	0	0	0
14 FOOD, KINDRED PRDTS.	181049	15539	161518	116661	260125	51645	38345	39850	54573
15 TOBACCO MANUFACTURES	5	9	9	5	34	14	4	2	2
16 FABRICS	0	0	0	0	0	0	0	0	0
17 TEXTILE PRDTS.	88	50	387	238	453	213	212	55	64
18 APPAREL	0	0	0	0	3	1	0	0	0
19 MISC. TEXTILE PRDTS.	665	197	113	58	165	120	944	390	3
20 LUMBER, WOOD PRDTS.	19	23	134	71	228	150	2	5	9
21 WOODEN CONTAINERS	0	0	0	0	0	0	0	0	0
22 HOUSEHOLD FURNITURE	0	0	0	0	0	0	0	0	0
23 OTHER FURNITURE	0	0	0	0	0	0	0	0	0
24 PAPER, ALLIED PRDTS.	320	95	317	353	405	168	259	58	295
25 PAPERBOARD CONTAINERS	17	8	58	38	57	17	45	11	12
26 PRINTING, PUBLISHING	43	42	320	179	588	241	39	20	39
27 CHEMICALS,SELECT. PRDTS.	593	942	2672	1696	4985	2656	1074	423	251
28 PLASTICS, SYNTHETICS	0	0	0	0	0	0	0	0	0
29 DRUGS, COSMETICS	5124	576	3786	2563	6266	1684	1143	664	1406
30 PAINT, ALLIED PRDTS.	0	0	0	0	0	0	0	0	0
31 PETROLEUM, RELATED INDS.	3052	2147	8501	4710	14354	6673	2442	981	820
32 RUBBER, MISC. PLASTICS	261	521	1225	781	2280	1229	595	310	85
33 LEATHER TANNING, PRDTS.	0	0	0	0	0	0	0	0	0
34 FOOTWEAR, LEATHER PRDTS.	174	123	175	104	211	171	360	212	19
35 GLASS, GLASS PRDTS.	49	156	164	116	193	67	96	31	32
36 STONE, CLAY PRDTS.	14	14	77	37	133	54	22	10	5
37 PRIMARY IRON, STEEL MFR.	0	0	0	0	0	0	0	0	0
38 PRIMARY NONFERROUS MFR.	9	21	26	14	42	30	7	3	1

39 METAL CONTAINERS	70	50	345	212	424	215	161	43	53
40 FABRICATED METAL PRDTS.	0	0	0	0	0	0	0	0	0
41 SCREW MACH. PRDTS., ETC.	260	129	872	582	861	256	673	173	189
42 OTHER FAB. METAL PRDTS.	260	243	914	784	1622	722	314	127	274
43 ENGINES, TURBINES	0	0	0	0	0	0	0	0	0
44 FARM MACH., EQUIP.	60	78	343	167	570	298	67	36	15
45 CONSTRUC. MACH., EQUIP.	0	0	0	0	0	0	0	0	0
46 MATERIAL HANDLING MACH.	0	0	0	0	0	0	0	0	0
47 METALWORKING MACHINERY	0	0	0	0	0	0	0	0	0
48 SPECIAL MACH., EQUIP.	0	0	0	0	0	0	0	0	0
49 GENERAL MACH., EQUIP.	0	0	0	0	0	0	0	0	0
50 MACHINE SHOP PRDTS.	20	43	168	84	269	141	38	19	7
51 OFFICE, COMPUT. MACHINES	0	0	0	0	0	0	0	0	0
52 SERVICE IND. MACHINES	0	0	0	0	0	0	0	0	0
53 ELECT. TRANSMISS. EQUIP.	0	0	0	0	0	0	0	0	0
54 HOUSEHOLD APPLIANCES	1	2	2	1	8	3	1	0	0
55 ELECTRIC LIGHTING EQUIP.	8	11	47	24	75	40	10	5	2
56 RADIO, TV, ETC., EQUIP.	1	3	3	2	10	4	1	1	1
57 ELECTRONIC COMPONENTS	0	0	0	0	0	0	0	0	0
58 MISC. ELECTRICAL MACH.	54	81	278	166	495	256	111	52	16
59 MOTOR VEHICLES, EQUIP.	43	134	196	159	490	322	94	73	19
60 AIRCRAFT, PARTS	0	0	0	0	0	0	0	0	0
61 OTHER TRANSPORT. EQUIP.	1	1	6	4	12	5	1	1	0
62 PROFESS., SCIEN. INSTRU.	0	1	1	0	3	1	0	0	0
63 MEDICAL, PHOTO. EQUIP.	1	1	4	2	9	3	1	1	1
64 MISC. MANUFACTURING	7	13	130	66	216	145	6	2	7
65 TRANSPORT., WAREHOUSING	13233	8788	32313	27105	46737	27083	7755	4948	3865
66 COMMUNICA., EXC. BRDCAST.	703	704	2131	1448	4354	2259	965	267	387
67 RADIO, TV BROADCASTING	0	0	0	0	0	0	0	0	0
68 ELEC.,GAS,WATER,SAN.SER.	1998	1048	2790	2153	5529	1583	1350	640	649
69 WHOLESALE, RETAIL TRADE	26346	10708	43238	40162	54537	20625	10566	8189	9100
70 FINANCE, INSURANCE	2988	1257	7308	5089	10090	4888	4719	1824	651
71 REAL ESTATE, RENTAL	5249	3568	44064	11547	39921	16453	3137	3927	158
72 HOTELS, PERSONAL SERV.	29	55	54	30	209	86	24	13	13
73 BUSINESS SERVICES	1371	2434	8645	3925	15539	8055	1674	811	348
74 RESEARCH, DEVELOPMENT	0	0	0	0	0	0	0	0	0
75 AUTO. REPAIR, SERVICES	542	1478	2312	1868	5504	3538	1258	842	215
76 AMUSEMENTS	5	9	8	5	34	14	4	2	2
77 MED., EDUC. SERVICES	4771	2654	7049	4006	11467	4588	2783	1753	1551
78 FEDERAL GOVT. ENTERPRISE	69	48	179	96	337	139	70	17	40
79 STATE, LOCAL GOVT. ENT.	4	7	19	15	33	20	4	2	3
80 DIRECT ALLOCATED IMPORTS	7	13	13	8	52	21	6	3	3
81 TRANSFERRED IMPORTS	6972	0	453	0	0	0	0	116	1710
82 VALUE ADDED	151634	9005	402391	6451	921126	154019	208145	85376	52993
83 SECONDARY TRANSFERS-IN	0	0	0	0	0	0	0	0	0
84 INVENTORY DEPLETION	0	0	0	0	0	0	0	0	0
85 SCRAP PRODUCTION	0	0	0	0	0	0	0	0	0
86 SCRAP PURCHASED	0	0	0	0	0	0	0	0	0
87 STATE TOTAL PRODUCTION	602947	271062	1433328	904318	2474082	1025233	487119	226066	166031

TABLE C-1

1963 INPUTS BY STATE TO
IO-1, LIVESTOCK & LIVESTOCK PRODUCTS
(THOUSANDS OF CURRENT DOLLARS)

INDUSTRY TITLE	19 MARYLAND	20 MASSA-CHUSETTS	21 MICHIGAN	22 MINNESOTA	23 MISSISSIPPI	24 MISSOURI	25 MONTANA	26 NEBRASKA	27 NEVADA
1 LIVESTOCK, PRDTS.	9363	4927	44795	165261	30279	141419	85693	483908	20448
2 OTHER AGRICULTURE PRDTS.	159053	14646	384244	439564	77029	310247	139910	342709	20882
3 FORESTRY, FISHERIES	0	0	0	1	0	1	0	1	0
4 AGRI.,FORES.,FISH. SERV.	12297	2981	5186	19175	18364	10885	579	3808	81
5 IRON, FERRO. ORES MINING	0	0	0	0	0	0	0	0	0
6 NONFERROUS ORES MINING	0	0	0	0	0	0	0	0	0
7 COAL MINING	98	42	65	270	221	147	10	83	1
8 CRUDE PETRO.,NATURAL GAS	0	0	0	0	0	0	0	0	0
9 STONE, CLAY MINING	18	7	20	67	42	60	5	66	0
10 CHEM.,FERT. MIN. MINING	0	0	0	0	0	0	0	0	0
11 NEW CONSTRUCTION	0	0	0	0	0	0	0	0	0
12 MAINT., REPAIR CONSTR.	2075	1360	6287	14509	2297	7291	1902	5561	353
13 ORDNANCE, ACCESSORIES	0	0	0	1	0	1	0	1	0
14 FOOD, KINDRED PRDTS.	49439	32369	42898	145581	95518	113782	12494	64145	2833
15 TOBACCO MANUFACTURES	1	1	7	24	4	16	6	16	2
16 FABRICS	0	0	0	0	0	0	0	0	0
17 TEXTILE PRDTS.	97	69	348	663	93	210	30	202	6
18 APPAREL	0	0	0	1	0	1	0	1	0
19 MISC. TEXTILE PRDTS.	6	1	33	158	641	72	375	121	29
20 LUMBER, WOOD PRDTS.	12	4	46	184	2	118	40	146	3
21 WOODEN CONTAINERS	0	0	0	0	0	0	0	0	0
22 HOUSEHOLD FURNITURE	0	0	0	0	0	0	0	0	0
23 OTHER FURNITURE	0	0	0	0	0	0	0	0	0
24 PAPER, ALLIED PRDTS.	59	99	147	644	32	135	47	222	5
25 PAPERBOARD CONTAINERS	19	14	68	110	19	27	1	15	1
26 PRINTING, PUBLISHING	30	26	209	381	38	270	34	280	9
27 CHEMICALS,SELECT. PRDTS.	268	218	1543	3268	752	3076	1434	3140	270
28 PLASTICS, SYNTHETICS	0	0	0	0	0	0	0	0	0
29 DRUGS, COSMETICS	1008	464	1325	4335	1963	3195	433	2147	69
30 PAINT, ALLIED PRDTS.	0	0	0	0	0	0	0	0	0
31 PETROLEUM, RELATED INDS.	1374	648	4035	11584	1900	6842	2939	8554	422
32 RUBBER, MISC. PLASTICS	127	109	743	1881	275	1623	615	1286	70
33 LEATHER TANNING, PRDTS.	0	0	0	0	0	0	0	0	0
34 FOOTWEAR, LEATHER PRDTS.	26	12	73	146	342	254	213	166	39
35 GLASS, GLASS PRDTS.	48	34	173	413	38	103	63	70	14
36 STONE, CLAY PRDTS.	7	6	27	72	13	50	13	56	3
37 PRIMARY IRON, STEEL MFR.	0	0	0	0	0	0	0	0	0
38 PRIMARY NONFERROUS MFR.	2	0	8	35	7	19	47	29	3

39 METAL CONTAINERS	80	53	288	593	73	202	44	205	6
40 FABRICATED METAL PRDTS.	0	0	0	0	0	0	0	0	0
41 SCREW MACH. PRDTS., ETC.	283	219	1014	1658	285	394	15	230	14
42 OTHER FAB. METAL PRDTS.	253	136	558	1405	217	1261	241	743	25
43 ENGINES, TURBINES	0	0	0	0	0	0	0	0	0
44 FARM MACH., EQUIP.	19	11	114	391	42	226	110	328	12
45 CONSTRUC. MACH., EQUIP.	0	0	0	0	0	0	0	0	0
46 MATERIAL HANDLING MACH.	0	0	0	0	0	0	0	0	0
47 METALWORKING MACHINERY	0	0	0	0	0	0	0	0	0
48 SPECIAL MACH., EQUIP.	0	0	0	0	0	0	0	0	0
49 GENERAL MACH., EQUIP.	0	0	0	0	0	0	0	0	0
50 MACHINE SHOP PRDTS.	10	8	81	221	17	112	51	151	6
51 OFFICE, COMPUT. MACHINES	0	0	0	0	0	0	0	0	0
52 SERVICE IND. MACHINES	0	0	0	0	0	0	0	0	0
53 ELECT. TRANSMISS. EQUIP.	0	0	0	0	0	0	0	0	0
54 HOUSEHOLD APPLIANCES	1	0	2	5	1	4	1	4	1
55 ELECTRIC LIGHTING EQUIP.	3	2	21	60	6	32	14	43	2
56 RADIO, TV, ETC., EQUIP.	1	0	2	7	1	5	2	5	1
57 ELECTRONIC COMPONENTS	0	0	0	0	0	0	0	0	0
58 MISC. ELECTRICAL MACH.	27	20	147	390	56	321	101	281	12
59 MOTOR VEHICLES, EQUIP.	24	25	175	458	40	459	153	295	19
60 AIRCRAFT, PARTS	0	0	0	0	0	0	0	0	0
61 OTHER TRANSPORT. EQUIP.	0	0	2	7	1	4	2	6	0
62 PROFESS., SCIEN. INSTRU.	0	0	0	1	0	1	0	1	0
63 MEDICAL, PHOTO. EQUIP.	1	0	2	5	1	4	1	4	0
64 MISC. MANUFACTURING	12	3	42	172	6	100	23	144	3
65 TRANSPORT., WAREHOUSING	8687	2610	17097	27478	7530	20794	8499	31467	1566
66 COMMUNICA.,EXC. BRDCAST.	498	238	1379	3572	496	2534	600	1959	78
67 RADIO, TV BROADCASTING	0	0	0	0	0	0	0	0	0
68 ELEC.,GAS,WATER,SAN.SER.	830	563	2324	4617	1004	2478	522	1833	113
69 WHOLESALE, RETAIL TRADE	13294	6375	27207	41656	14459	30188	8984	24612	1394
70 FINANCE, INSURANCE	1306	803	4597	7988	2326	7750	1257	4270	168
71 REAL ESTATE, RENTAL	264	62	1449	15719	5043	10271	2314	19581	262
72 HOTELS, PERSONAL SERV.	10	9	39	144	23	99	38	100	12
73 BUSINESS SERVICES	360	256	2170	8708	1053	5997	3241	8962	447
74 RESEARCH, DEVELOPMENT	0	0	0	0	0	0	0	0	0
75 AUTO. REPAIR, SERVICES	268	290	2049	5103	526	5100	1675	3270	198
76 AMUSEMENTS	1	1	7	23	4	16	6	16	2
77 MED.,EDUC. SERVICES	2844	727	4586	12152	3476	7219	1313	5013	267
78 FEDERAL GOVT. ENTERPRISE	29	24	97	195	70	150	40	165	11
79 STATE, LOCAL GOVT. ENT.	3	3	14	29	3	30	8	19	1
80 DIRECT ALLOCATED IMPORTS	3	2	223	37	6	24	10	26	3
81 TRANSFERRED IMPORTS	85	11185	10544	0	1836	0	993	0	0
82 VALUE ADDED	1782	56927	2734	404341	129332	290884	22234	104093	936
83 SECONDARY TRANSFERS-IN	0	0	0	0	0	0	0	0	0
84 INVENTORY DEPLETION	0	0	0	0	0	0	0	0	0
85 SCRAP PRODUCTION	0	0	0	0	0	0	0	0	0
86 SCRAP PURCHASED	0	0	0	0	0	0	0	0	0
87 STATE TOTAL PRODUCTION	266404	138588	571244	1345463	397802	986503	299375	1124559	51102

TABLE C-1

1963 INPUTS BY STATE TO
IO-1, LIVESTOCK & LIVESTOCK PRODUCTS

(THOUSANDS OF CURRENT DOLLARS)

INDUSTRY TITLE	28 NEW HAMPSHIRE	29 NEW JERSEY	30 NEW MEXICO	31 NEW YORK	32 NORTH CAROLINA	33 NORTH DAKOTA	34 OHIO	35 OKLAHOMA	36 OREGON
1 LIVESTOCK, PRDTS.	2577	9403	66959	44405	26309	40630	97593	101005	51347
2 OTHER AGRICULTURE PRDTS.	9319	21693	36773	205439	100221	213834	400994	131411	83562
3 FORESTRY, FISHERIES	0	0	0	1	0	0	0	0	0
4 AGRI.,FORES.,FISH. SERV.	1428	3577	338	9362	30189	1273	10199	3331	3848
5 IRON, FERRO. ORES MINING	0	0	0	0	0	0	0	0	0
6 NONFERROUS ORES MINING	0	0	0	0	0	0	0	0	0
7 COAL MINING	23	99	8	104	327	18	162	46	50
8 CRUDE PETRO.,NATURAL GAS	0	0	0	0	0	0	0	0	0
9 STONE, CLAY MINING	4	15	3	28	62	7	52	14	8
10 CHEM.,FERT. MIN. MINING	0	0	0	0	0	0	0	0	0
11 NEW CONSTRUCTION	0	0	0	0	0	0	0	0	0
12 MAINT., REPAIR CONSTR.	575	1859	860	8528	3325	853	11641	3265	1816
13 ORDNANCE, ACCESSORIES	0	0	0	1	0	0	0	0	0
14 FOOD, KINDRED PRDTS.	17494	50809	11935	155824	133845	7696	119143	51714	34732
15 TOBACCO MANUFACTURES	1	2	6	15	4	1	8	5	5
16 FABRICS	0	0	0	0	0	0	0	0	0
17 TEXTILE PRDTS.	30	97	10	741	147	79	446	104	63
18 APPAREL	0	0	0	1	0	0	0	0	0
19 MISC. TEXTILE PRDTS.	1	6	69	47	437	26	68	2655	103
20 LUMBER, WOOD PRDTS.	3	6	11	54	20	45	83	15	19
21 WOODEN CONTAINERS	0	0	0	0	0	0	0	0	0
22 HOUSEHOLD FURNITURE	0	0	0	0	0	0	0	0	0
23 OTHER FURNITURE	0	0	0	0	0	0	0	0	0
24 PAPER, ALLIED PRDTS.	39	850	24	378	235	32	449	45	129
25 PAPERBOARD CONTAINERS	6	20	1	152	31	7	83	19	12
26 PRINTING, PUBLISHING	13	38	31	237	34	24	259	52	33
27 CHEMICALS,SELECT. PRDTS.	134	286	695	1770	473	559	2074	1040	458
28 PLASTICS, SYNTHETICS	0	0	0	0	0	0	0	0	0
29 DRUGS, COSMETICS	288	672	241	2550	3899	560	2769	713	710
30 PAINT, ALLIED PRDTS.	0	0	0	0	0	0	0	0	0
31 PETROLEUM, RELATED INDS.	317	1043	1116	6696	2380	2363	6452	2941	1838
32 RUBBER, MISC. PLASTICS	58	121	226	1204	240	195	1011	891	270
33 LEATHER TANNING, PRDTS.	0	0	0	0	0	0	0	0	0
34 FOOTWEAR, LEATHER PRDTS.	9	19	134	115	360	94	175	213	106
35 GLASS, GLASS PRDTS.	15	52	20	409	68	37	229	43	61
36 STONE, CLAY PRDTS.	3	7	11	52	14	4	44	26	12
37 PRIMARY IRON, STEEL MFR.	0	0	0	0	0	0	0	0	0
38 PRIMARY NONFERROUS MFR.	0	1	8	10	6	9	15	18	15

39 METAL CONTAINERS	25	76	12	593	113	89	379	83	56
40 FABRICATED METAL PRDTS.	0	0	0	0	0	0	0	0	0
41 SCREW MACH. PRDTS., ETC.	91	302	19	2281	467	113	1234	292	180
42 OTHER FAB. METAL PRDTS.	83	224	143	745	274	305	1003	308	327
43 ENGINES, TURBINES	0	0	0	0	0	0	0	0	0
44 FARM MACH., EQUIP.	4	18	35	113	42	54	194	145	57
45 CONSTRUC. MACH., EQUIP.	0	0	0	0	0	0	0	0	0
46 MATERIAL HANDLING MACH.	0	0	0	0	0	0	0	0	0
47 METALWORKING MACHINERY	0	0	0	0	0	0	0	0	0
48 SPECIAL MACH., EQUIP.	0	0	0	0	0	0	0	0	0
49 GENERAL MACH., EQUIP.	0	0	0	0	0	0	0	0	0
50 MACHINE SHOP PRDTS.	3	10	16	98	17	26	113	71	30
51 OFFICE, COMPUT. MACHINES	0	0	0	0	0	0	0	0	0
52 SERVICE IND. MACHINES	0	0	0	0	0	0	0	0	0
53 ELECT. TRANSMISS. EQUIP.	0	0	0	0	0	0	0	0	0
54 HOUSEHOLD APPLIANCES	0	0	1	3	1	0	2	1	1
55 ELECTRIC LIGHTING EQUIP.	1	3	4	24	6	8	31	19	8
56 RADIO, TV, ETC., EQUIP.	0	1	2	5	1	1	2	2	2
57 ELECTRONIC COMPONENTS	0	0	0	0	0	0	0	0	0
58 MISC. ELECTRICAL MACH.	10	24	33	251	47	42	208	149	55
59 MOTOR VEHICLES, EQUIP.	16	24	68	227	44	48	217	221	114
60 AIRCRAFT, PARTS	0	0	0	0	0	0	0	0	0
61 OTHER TRANSPORT. EQUIP.	0	0	1	2	1	1	3	3	1
62 PROFESS., SCIEN. INSTRU.	0	0	0	1	0	0	0	0	0
63 MEDICAL, PHOTO. EQUIP.	0	1	1	3	1	0	2	1	1
64 MISC. MANUFACTURING	2	6	7	51	5	46	76	10	9
65 TRANSPORT., WAREHOUSING	972	4678	4281	15950	10904	9044	22166	10135	6764
66 COMMUNICA.,EXC. BRDCAST.	144	420	378	2601	827	371	2131	971	748
67 RADIO, TV BROADCASTING	0	0	0	0	0	0	0	0	0
68 ELEC.,GAS,WATER,SAN.SER.	373	783	737	3712	1530	222	3542	1093	1785
69 WHOLESALE, RETAIL TRADE	2168	11311	3577	33276	21563	12415	35219	12442	9798
70 FINANCE, INSURANCE	428	1130	768	6439	2560	1205	7526	3677	2057
71 REAL ESTATE, RENTAL	45	271	911	484	9989	2562	5961	4163	623
72 HOTELS, PERSONAL SERV.	5	13	38	91	23	9	46	31	33
73 BUSINESS SERVICES	120	377	1473	2364	987	905	4088	3661	1646
74 RESEARCH, DEVELOPMENT	0	0	0	0	0	0	0	0	0
75 AUTO. REPAIR, SERVICES	182	267	741	2576	552	527	2564	2514	1285
76 AMUSEMENTS	1	2	6	14	4	1	7	5	5
77 MED.,EDUC. SERVICES	462	736	755	11456	3820	1859	5852	2023	1764
78 FEDERAL GOVT. ENTERPRISE	13	37	40	212	50	12	130	47	41
79 STATE, LOCAL GOVT. ENT.	2	3	4	19	4	4	19	4	9
80 DIRECT ALLOCATED IMPORTS	1	3	69	22	6	2	11	8	8
81 TRANSFERRED IMPORTS	0	13356	0	22687	1067	2431	1278	0	388
82 VALUE ADDED	20551	83008	84914	287369	130286	1430	89254	192580	49117
83 SECONDARY TRANSFERS-IN	0	0	0	0	0	0	0	0	0
84 INVENTORY DEPLETION	0	0	0	0	0	0	0	0	0
85 SCRAP PRODUCTION	0	0	0	0	0	0	0	0	0
86 SCRAP PURCHASED	0	0	0	0	0	0	0	0	0
87 STATE TOTAL PRODUCTION	58039	207759	218513	831791	487817	302079	837207	534225	256108

TABLE C-1

1963 INPUTS BY STATE TO
IO-1, LIVESTOCK & LIVESTOCK PRODUCTS
(THOUSANDS OF CURRENT DOLLARS)

INDUSTRY TITLE	37 PENNSYL-VANIA	38 RHODE ISLAND	39 SOUTH CAROLINA	40 SOUTH DAKOTA	41 TENNESSEE	42 TEXAS	43 UTAH	44 VERMONT	45 VIRGINIA
1 LIVESTOCK, PRDTS.	66073	1044	10945	166324	48184	351776	37965	6868	32556
2 OTHER AGRICULTURE PRDTS.	206928	2645	31558	272650	132001	292887	56431	33017	70384
3 FORESTRY, FISHERIES	0	0	0	1	0	1	0	0	0
4 AGRI.,FORES.,FISH. SERV.	15966	355	4752	3422	5984	21520	3203	1477	11003
5 IRON, FERRO. ORES MINING	0	0	0	0	0	0	0	0	0
6 NONFERROUS ORES MINING	0	0	0	0	0	0	0	0	0
7 COAL MINING	212	5	75	81	78	275	46	9	123
8 CRUDE PETRO.,NATURAL GAS	0	0	0	0	0	0	0	0	0
9 STONE, CLAY MINING	45	1	13	32	26	64	3	3	23
10 CHEM.,FERT. MIN. MINING	0	0	0	0	0	0	0	0	0
11 NEW CONSTRUCTION	0	0	0	0	0	0	0	0	0
12 MAINT., REPAIR CONSTR.	10410	205	1190	3628	5264	6223	1379	1610	4602
13 ORDNANCE, ACCESSORIES	0	0	0	1	0	1	0	0	0
14 FOOD, KINDRED PRDTS.	153313	4803	33703	40222	47579	189058	20479	31583	63797
15 TOBACCO MANUFACTURES	10	0	3	11	5	16	6	2	5
16 FABRICS	0	0	0	0	0	0	0	0	0
17 TEXTILE PRDTS.	541	8	54	166	190	231	39	152	190
18 APPAREL	0	0	0	1	0	1	0	0	0
19 MISC. TEXTILE PRDTS.	31	0	469	109	983	4582	77	6	694
20 LUMBER, WOOD PRDTS.	62	0	7	138	2	29	14	11	18
21 WOODEN CONTAINERS	0	0	0	0	0	0	0	0	0
22 HOUSEHOLD FURNITURE	0	0	0	0	0	0	0	0	0
23 OTHER FURNITURE	0	0	0	0	0	0	0	0	0
24 PAPER, ALLIED PRDTS.	351	23	253	66	288	158	53	23	71
25 PAPERBOARD CONTAINERS	108	2	11	8	40	45	7	32	40
26 PRINTING, PUBLISHING	164	3	27	190	41	168	28	34	39
27 CHEMICALS,SELECT. PRDTS.	1863	22	223	2119	1052	2768	704	343	623
28 PLASTICS, SYNTHETICS	0	0	0	0	0	0	0	0	0
29 DRUGS, COSMETICS	3433	65	777	1725	1256	2950	401	338	1591
30 PAINT, ALLIED PRDTS.	0	0	0	0	0	0	0	0	0
31 PETROLEUM, RELATED INDS.	6395	104	717	7740	2201	8340	1327	1076	2199
32 RUBBER, MISC. PLASTICS	1104	16	188	1010	614	1836	278	228	464
33 LEATHER TANNING, PRDTS.	0	0	0	0	0	0	0	0	0
34 FOOTWEAR, LEATHER PRDTS.	136	3	169	147	340	568	75	23	210
35 GLASS, GLASS PRDTS.	276	4	27	43	91	133	55	77	85
36 STONE, CLAY PRDTS.	41	1	14	33	19	71	8	10	16
37 PRIMARY IRON, STEEL MFR.	0	0	0	0	0	0	0	0	0
38 PRIMARY NONFERROUS MFR.	10	0	3	28	8	34	10	2	6

39 METAL CONTAINERS	443	7	41	180	146	183	35	122	146
40 FABRICATED METAL PRDTS.	0	0	0	0	0	0	0	0	0
41 SCREW MACH. PRDTS., ETC.	1619	28	168	124	601	668	107	471	604
42 OTHER FAB. METAL PRDTS.	1123	20	101	615	346	555	225	111	240
43 ENGINES, TURBINES	0	0	0	0	0	0	0	0	0
44 FARM MACH., EQUIP.	115	2	14	277	67	288	36	16	74
45 CONSTRUC. MACH., EQUIP.	0	0	0	0	0	0	0	0	0
46 MATERIAL HANDLING MACH.	0	0	0	0	0	0	0	0	0
47 METALWORKING MACHINERY	0	0	0	0	0	0	0	0	0
48 SPECIAL MACH., EQUIP.	0	0	0	0	0	0	0	0	0
49 GENERAL MACH., EQUIP.	0	0	0	0	0	0	0	0	0
50 MACHINE SHOP PRDTS.	83	1	7	128	38	137	18	15	40
51 OFFICE, COMPUT. MACHINES	0	0	0	0	0	0	0	0	0
52 SERVICE IND. MACHINES	0	0	0	0	0	0	0	0	0
53 ELECT. TRANSMISS. EQUIP.	0	0	0	0	0	0	0	0	0
54 HOUSEHOLD APPLIANCES	2	0	1	2	1	4	1	0	1
55 ELECTRIC LIGHTING EQUIP.	22	0	2	37	10	39	5	4	11
56 RADIO, TV, ETC., EQUIP.	3	0	1	3	1	5	2	1	1
57 ELECTRONIC COMPONENTS	0	0	0	0	0	0	0	0	0
58 MISC. ELECTRICAL MACH.	223	3	39	221	114	318	39	44	94
59 MOTOR VEHICLES, EQUIP.	225	4	33	229	99	414	81	51	76
60 AIRCRAFT, PARTS	0	0	0	0	0	0	0	0	0
61 OTHER TRANSPORT. EQUIP.	2	0	0	5	1	5	1	0	1
62 PROFESS., SCIEN. INSTRU.	1	0	0	1	0	1	0	0	0
63 MEDICAL, PHOTO. EQUIP.	2	0	1	2	1	4	1	0	1
64 MISC. MANUFACTURING	52	0	3	136	6	26	7	9	6
65 TRANSPORT., WAREHOUSING	16183	390	3977	17301	8264	31369	4217	2342	6991
66 COMMUNICA.,EXC. BRDCAST.	2708	35	332	1360	1032	1773	367	533	777
67 RADIO, TV BROADCASTING	0	0	0	0	0	0	0	0	0
68 ELEC.,GAS,WATER,SAN.SER.	3849	64	202	1054	1529	3225	663	713	1499
69 WHOLESALE, RETAIL TRADE	30660	793	8094	18780	12236	40113	5293	4975	12455
70 FINANCE, INSURANCE	7395	98	1000	2813	3941	7396	951	1360	3315
71 REAL ESTATE, RENTAL	456	28	15450	8719	1493	10139	1379	95	658
72 HOTELS, PERSONAL SERV.	59	1	19	69	27	100	34	13	29
73 BUSINESS SERVICES	2173	30	758	7162	1646	7683	1221	316	1769
74 RESEARCH, DEVELOPMENT	0	0	0	0	0	0	0	0	0
75 AUTO. REPAIR, SERVICES	2565	42	410	2526	1322	4728	899	570	973
76 AMUSEMENTS	9	0	3	11	4	16	5	2	5
77 MED., EDUC. SERVICES	8378	96	996	3824	2788	6472	1182	2469	2910
78 FEDERAL GOVT. ENTERPRISE	157	3	45	112	78	152	31	28	63
79 STATE, LOCAL GOVT. ENT.	22	0	2	15	5	9	5	4	5
80 DIRECT ALLOCATED IMPORTS	15	0	5	17	7	937	8	3	7
81 TRANSFERRED IMPORTS	18179	23	6621	0	0	28393	0	2562	3622
82 VALUE ADDED	264157	6409	41743	108584	125951	464243	25968	55283	164173
83 SECONDARY TRANSFERS-IN	0	0	0	0	0	0	0	0	0
84 INVENTORY DEPLETION	0	0	0	0	0	0	0	0	0
85 SCRAP PRODUCTION	0	0	0	0	0	0	0	0	0
86 SCRAP PURCHASED	0	0	0	0	0	0	0	0	0
87 STATE TOTAL PRODUCTION	828353	17386	165246	674202	408000	1493131	165369	149036	389285

TABLE C-1

1963 INPUTS BY STATE TO
IO-1, LIVESTOCK & LIVESTOCK PRODUCTS

(THOUSANDS OF CURRENT DOLLARS)

INDUSTRY TITLE	46 WASHINGTON	47 WEST VIRGINIA	48 WISCONSIN	49 WYOMING	50 ALASKA	51 HAWAII	52 NATIONAL TOTAL
1 LIVESTOCK, PRDTS.	61823	9594	73558	40438	82	2807	4749898
2 OTHER AGRICULTURE PRDTS.	89192	32307	417654	69961	507	5731	7897613
3 FORESTRY, FISHERIES	0	0	1	0	0	0	15
4 AGRI.,FORES.,FISH. SERV.	5114	3744	17183	147	22	856	444759
5 IRON, FERRO. ORES MINING	0	0	0	0	0	0	0
6 NONFERROUS ORES MINING	0	0	0	0	0	0	0
7 COAL MINING	73	39	140	3	0	1	5657
8 CRUDE PETRO.,NATURAL GAS	0	0	0	0	0	0	0
9 STONE, CLAY MINING	12	7	45	2	0	3	1489
10 CHEM.,FERT. MIN. MINING	0	0	0	0	0	0	0
11 NEW CONSTRUCTION	0	0	0	0	0	0	0
12 MAINT., REPAIR CONSTR.	2319	1874	16923	1061	19	247	200124
13 ORDNANCE, ACCESSORIES	0	0	1	0	0	0	15
14 FOOD, KINDRED PRDTS.	47792	18929	119070	7370	665	7505	3558654
15 TOBACCO MANUFACTURES	6	2	14	6	0	0	370
16 FABRICS	0	0	0	0	0	0	0
17 TEXTILE PRDTS.	140	42	1090	11	2	7	9227
18 APPAREL	0	0	1	0	0	0	15
19 MISC. TEXTILE PRDTS.	108	270	98	141	4	11	17314
20 LUMBER, WOOD PRDTS.	21	10	121	16	0	1	2009
21 WOODEN CONTAINERS	0	0	0	0	0	0	0
22 HOUSEHOLD FURNITURE	0	0	0	0	0	0	0
23 OTHER FURNITURE	0	0	0	0	0	0	0
24 PAPER, ALLIED PRDTS.	30	11	384	11	8	237	11972
25 PAPERBOARD CONTAINERS	29	8	215	1	0	2	1655
26 PRINTING, PUBLISHING	34	14	455	29	1	2	5215
27 CHEMICALS,SELECT. PRDTS.	356	273	3318	1032	3	26	56864
28 PLASTICS, SYNTHETICS	0	0	0	0	0	0	0
29 DRUGS, COSMETICS	1002	506	3862	231	3	97	82796
30 PAINT, ALLIED PRDTS.	0	0	0	0	0	0	0
31 PETROLEUM, RELATED INDS.	1738	754	12735	1509	35	195	169826
32 RUBBER, MISC. PLASTICS	293	245	2175	286	4	12	29124
33 LEATHER TANNING, PRDTS.	0	0	0	0	0	0	0
34 FOOTWEAR, LEATHER PRDTS.	89	93	141	123	1	17	7168
35 GLASS, GLASS PRDTS.	75	19	589	19	3	10	5298
36 STONE, CLAY PRDTS.	15	4	84	9	0	2	1290
37 PRIMARY IRON, STEEL MFR.	0	0	0	0	0	0	0
38 PRIMARY NONFERROUS MFR.	19	3	23	17	0	0	651

39 METAL CONTAINERS	118	32	897	16	1	6	7849
40 FABRICATED METAL PRDTS.	0	0	0	0	0	0	0
41 SCREW MACH. PRDTS., ETC.	423	129	3232	8	5	23	24900
42 OTHER FAB. METAL PRDTS.	318	148	1300	122	3	21	20600
43 ENGINES, TURBINES	0	0	0	0	0	0	0
44 FARM MACH., EQUIP.	61	23	356	53	0	0	5388
45 CONSTRUC. MACH., EQUIP.	0	0	0	0	0	0	0
46 MATERIAL HANDLING MACH.	0	0	0	0	0	0	0
47 METALWORKING MACHINERY	0	0	0	0	0	0	0
48 SPECIAL MACH., EQUIP.	0	0	0	0	0	0	0
49 GENERAL MACH., EQUIP.	0	0	0	0	0	0	0
50 MACHINE SHOP PRDTS.	36	12	270	24	0	0	2859
51 OFFICE, COMPUT. MACHINES	0	0	0	0	0	0	0
52 SERVICE IND. MACHINES	0	0	0	0	0	0	0
53 ELECT. TRANSMISS. EQUIP.	0	0	0	0	0	0	0
54 HOUSEHOLD APPLIANCES	1	0	3	1	0	0	81
55 ELECTRIC LIGHTING EQUIP.	10	4	69	7	0	0	792
56 RADIO, TV, ETC., EQUIP.	2	1	4	2	0	0	115
57 ELECTRONIC COMPONENTS	0	0	0	0	0	0	0
58 MISC. ELECTRICAL MACH.	60	42	439	46	1	2	5766
59 MOTOR VEHICLES, EQUIP.	119	55	476	76	0	0	6659
60 AIRCRAFT, PARTS	0	0	0	0	0	0	0
61 OTHER TRANSPORT. EQUIP.	1	0	6	1	0	0	96
62 PROFESS., SCIEN. INSTRU.	0	0	1	0	0	0	19
63 MEDICAL, PHOTO. EQUIP.	1	0	4	1	0	0	83
64 MISC. MANUFACTURING	11	2	111	9	0	0	1775
65 TRANSPORT., WAREHOUSING	7707	2090	20187	4334	55	1600	613373
66 COMMUNICA.,EXC. BRDCAST.	708	568	3392	259	6	32	52317
67 RADIO, TV BROADCASTING	0	0	0	0	0	0	0
68 ELEC.,GAS,WATER,SAN.SER.	1695	673	5809	361	20	56	95983
69 WHOLESALE, RETAIL TRADE	11192	3527	34386	4817	119	2568	870873
70 FINANCE, INSURANCE	2156	1242	10085	797	13	145	155633
71 REAL ESTATE, RENTAL	5114	224	6745	1511	25	787	288771
72 HOTELS, PERSONAL SERV.	36	12	86	35	0	1	2266
73 BUSINESS SERVICES	1541	589	5751	1877	4	20	138589
74 RESEARCH, DEVELOPMENT	0	0	0	0	0	0	0
75 AUTO. REPAIR, SERVICES	1345	693	5566	832	0	0	76090
76 AMUSEMENTS	6	2	14	6	0	0	362
77 MED.,EDUC. SERVICES	2558	1046	19075	658	16	162	180877
78 FEDERAL GOVT. ENTERPRISE	40	24	201	37	0	2	3934
79 STATE, LOCAL GOVT. ENT.	8	3	38	4	0	0	444
80 DIRECT ALLOCATED IMPORTS	9	3	21	9	0	0	2502
81 TRANSFERRED IMPORTS	3361	0	2590	0	53	2177	173824
82 VALUE ADDED	45141	32988	482481	45279	2711	21973	6692430
83 SECONDARY TRANSFERS-IN	0	0	0	0	0	0	0
84 INVENTORY DEPLETION	0	0	0	0	0	0	0
85 SCRAP PRODUCTION	0	0	0	0	0	0	0
86 SCRAP PURCHASED	0	0	0	0	0	0	0
87 STATE TOTAL PRODUCTION	294058	112880	1273475	183605	4391	47344	26684256

TABLE C-2

1963 INPUTS BY STATE TO
IO-2, OTHER AGRICULTURAL PRODUCTS
(THOUSANDS OF CURRENT DOLLARS)

INDUSTRY TITLE	1 ALABAMA	2 ARIZONA	3 ARKANSAS	4 CALIFORNIA	5 COLORADO	6 CONNECTICUT	7 DELAWARE	8 DISTRICT OF COLUMBIA	9 FLORIDA
1 LIVESTOCK, PRDTS.	46974	18332	49067	73592	36596	12845	2119	0	35508
2 OTHER AGRICULTURE PRDTS.	10047	5912	17025	47988	11774	4926	2411	0	15543
3 FORESTRY, FISHERIES	0	1	1	7	1	0	0	0	1
4 AGRI.,FORES.,FISH. SERV.	20465	28289	35218	196246	12836	383	927	0	53492
5 IRON, FERRO. ORES MINING	0	0	0	0	0	0	0	0	0
6 NONFERROUS ORES MINING	0	0	0	0	0	0	0	0	0
7 COAL MINING	5	6	3	49	9	10	3	0	28
8 CRUDE PETRO.,NATURAL GAS	0	0	0	0	0	0	0	0	0
9 STONE, CLAY MINING	3978	0	2602	1530	0	1051	1376	0	6118
10 CHEM.,FERT. MIN. MINING	266	45	1044	501	149	17	36	0	2449
11 NEW CONSTRUCTION	0	0	0	0	0	0	0	0	0
12 MAINT., REPAIR CONSTR.	5280	2131	5451	21553	3061	1015	652	0	8001
13 ORDNANCE, ACCESSORIES	0	1	1	6	1	0	0	0	1
14 FOOD, KINDRED PRDTS.	85	403	152	2178	252	24	19	0	460
15 TOBACCO MANUFACTURES	6	26	12	129	14	1	1	0	21
16 FABRICS	393	20	697	123	102	0	1	0	147
17 TEXTILE PRDTS.	187	290	228	1766	607	103	30	0	133
18 APPAREL	0	1	1	6	1	0	0	0	1
19 MISC. TEXTILE PRDTS.	701	1946	943	13527	852	130	57	0	3334
20 LUMBER, WOOD PRDTS.	3	14	24	104	31	2	3	0	17
21 WOODEN CONTAINERS	184	3160	62	36180	1807	741	240	0	7713
22 HOUSEHOLD FURNITURE	0	0	0	0	0	0	0	0	0
23 OTHER FURNITURE	0	0	0	0	0	0	0	0	0
24 PAPER, ALLIED PRDTS.	15	21	32	138	16	3	2	0	39
25 PAPERBOARD CONTAINERS	22	27	14	232	44	50	15	0	134
26 PRINTING, PUBLISHING	70	175	144	994	75	30	13	0	244
27 CHEMICALS,SELECT. PRDTS.	48268	16800	21179	130133	11233	4579	5896	0	88148
28 PLASTICS, SYNTHETICS	0	0	0	0	0	0	0	0	0
29 DRUGS, COSMETICS	2	8	4	40	4	0	0	0	7
30 PAINT, ALLIED PRDTS.	0	0	0	0	0	0	0	0	0
31 PETROLEUM, RELATED INDS.	8723	8256	28746	46447	14805	1384	1431	0	10902
32 RUBBER, MISC. PLASTICS	1637	740	2832	4510	2116	194	217	0	1868
33 LEATHER TANNING, PRDTS.	0	0	0	0	0	0	0	0	0
34 FOOTWEAR, LEATHER PRDTS.	1	5	2	23	3	0	0	0	4
35 GLASS, GLASS PRDTS.	0	0	0	6	0	0	0	0	0
36 STONE, CLAY PRDTS.	864	134	608	1333	180	301	304	0	1482
37 PRIMARY IRON, STEEL MFR.	0	0	0	0	0	0	0	0	0
38 PRIMARY NONFERROUS MFR.	6	9	15	56	24	0	1	0	4

39 METAL CONTAINERS	38	61	105	325	157	8	17	0	18
40 FABRICATED METAL PRDTS.	0	0	0	0	0	0	0	0	0
41 SCREW MACH. PRDTS., ETC.	0	0	0	0	0	0	0	0	0
42 OTHER FAB. METAL PRDTS.	377	523	521	3544	1110	46	27	0	232
43 ENGINES, TURBINES	0	0	0	0	0	0	0	0	0
44 FARM MACH., EQUIP.	1624	1202	4733	10445	3436	82	252	0	1539
45 CONSTRUC. MACH., EQUIP.	0	0	0	0	0	0	0	0	0
46 MATERIAL HANDLING MACH.	0	0	0	0	0	0	0	0	0
47 METALWORKING MACHINERY	0	0	0	0	0	0	0	0	0
48 SPECIAL MACH., EQUIP.	0	0	0	0	0	0	0	0	0
49 GENERAL MACH., EQUIP.	0	0	0	0	0	0	0	0	0
50 MACHINE SHOP PRDTS.	60	52	132	586	110	7	8	0	156
51 OFFICE, COMPUT. MACHINES	0	0	0	0	0	0	0	0	0
52 SERVICE IND. MACHINES	0	0	0	0	0	0	0	0	0
53 ELECT. TRANSMISS. EQUIP.	0	0	0	0	0	0	0	0	0
54 HOUSEHOLD APPLIANCES	1	6	3	29	3	0	0	0	5
55 ELECTRIC LIGHTING EQUIP.	13	11	29	115	23	1	2	0	30
56 RADIO, TV, ETC., EQUIP.	2	8	4	41	4	0	0	0	7
57 ELECTRONIC COMPONENTS	0	0	0	0	0	0	0	0	0
58 MISC. ELECTRICAL MACH.	347	149	597	1106	390	25	50	0	394
59 MOTOR VEHICLES, EQUIP.	176	102	353	918	298	21	19	0	160
60 AIRCRAFT, PARTS	0	0	0	0	0	0	0	0	0
61 OTHER TRANSPORT. EQUIP.	33	25	94	225	68	2	5	0	39
62 PROFESS., SCIEN. INSTRU.	0	2	1	8	1	0	0	0	1
63 MEDICAL, PHOTO. EQUIP.	1	3	2	20	2	0	0	0	4
64 MISC. MANUFACTURING	8	19	18	110	23	2	4	0	14
65 TRANSPORT., WAREHOUSING	6731	4129	6476	29063	3571	1194	1288	0	14579
66 COMMUNICA.,EXC. BRDCAST.	1010	671	1270	6092	1200	199	169	0	1400
67 RADIO, TV BROADCASTING	0	0	0	0	0	0	0	0	0
68 ELEC.,GAS,WATER,SAN.SER.	1282	12686	2316	70878	7769	384	90	0	1703
69 WHOLESALE, RETAIL TRADE	13742	11055	16077	81265	11788	2210	2324	0	32280
70 FINANCE, INSURANCE	4745	1800	6320	18230	3214	910	902	0	4109
71 REAL ESTATE, RENTAL	10320	35998	6398	79444	28939	854	2199	0	22106
72 HOTELS, PERSONAL SERV.	35	156	71	780	85	8	4	0	129
73 BUSINESS SERVICES	6240	6035	16964	48020	12893	604	986	0	8817
74 RESEARCH, DEVELOPMENT	0	0	0	0	0	0	0	0	0
75 AUTO. REPAIR, SERVICES	2313	1094	3950	10352	3298	231	219	0	2058
76 AMUSEMENTS	6	25	11	126	14	1	1	0	21
77 MED., EDUC. SERVICES	169	243	320	1653	113	43	16	0	313
78 FEDERAL GOVT. ENTERPRISE	56	85	61	473	53	11	9	0	115
79 STATE, LOCAL GOVT. ENT.	12	8	8	84	13	2	2	0	12
80 DIRECT ALLOCATED IMPORTS	8	17148	4294	104986	6437	2	1	0	38526
81 TRANSFERRED IMPORTS	1216	2245	0	19500	0	12	113	0	5861
82 VALUE ADDED	191624	196247	416826	1442993	133748	46171	24542	0	521193
83 SECONDARY TRANSFERS-IN	0	0	0	0	0	0	0	0	0
84 INVENTORY DEPLETION	1365	1320	2296	8733	1107	284	172	0	3106
85 SCRAP PRODUCTION	0	0	0	0	0	0	0	0	0
86 SCRAP PURCHASED	0	0	0	0	0	0	0	0	0
87 STATE TOTAL PRODUCTION	391737	379860	656357	2519541	316460	81103	49174	0	894726

TABLE C-2

1963 INPUTS BY STATE TO
IO-2, OTHER AGRICULTURAL PRODUCTS
(THOUSANDS OF CURRENT DOLLARS)

INDUSTRY TITLE	10 GEORGIA	11 IDAHO	12 ILLINOIS	13 INDIANA	14 IOWA	15 KANSAS	16 KENTUCKY	17 LOUISIANA	18 MAINE
1 LIVESTOCK, PRDTS.	48279	23399	59828	46509	78847	48097	70551	40481	6706
2 OTHER AGRICULTURE PRDTS.	12906	14787	50096	28963	45231	32461	7797	7797	6171
3 FORESTRY, FISHERIES	0	1	1	0	1	1	0	0	0
4 AGRI.,FORES.,FISH. SERV.	19638	12762	38097	18984	41547	37794	6705	16702	848
5 IRON, FERRO. ORES MINING	0	0	0	0	0	0	0	0	0
6 NONFERROUS ORES MINING	0	0	0	0	0	0	0	0	0
7 COAL MINING	4	2	44	19	21	4	4	5	3
8 CRUDE PETRO.,NATURAL GAS	0	0	0	0	0	0	0	0	0
9 STONE, CLAY MINING	5393	0	15315	7441	3710	850	5342	2411	1037
10 CHEM.,FERT. MIN. MINING	161	25	11842	2133	966	51	857	344	39
11 NEW CONSTRUCTION	0	0	0	0	0	0	0	0	0
12 MAINT., REPAIR CONSTR.	5981	4325	32871	21606	12571	11398	10684	6230	837
13 ORDNANCE, ACCESSORIES	0	1	1	1	1	1	0	0	0
14 FOOD, KINDRED PRDTS.	152	361	275	157	342	346	119	176	62
15 TOBACCO MANUFACTURES	10	20	20	11	27	27	9	8	2
16 FABRICS	515	72	43	23	44	40	444	304	1
17 TEXTILE PRDTS.	242	649	1453	811	2065	1238	657	172	141
18 APPAREL	0	1	1	1	1	1	0	0	0
19 MISC. TEXTILE PRDTS.	775	2362	162	150	32	38	379	747	1168
20 LUMBER, WOOD PRDTS.	22	45	183	95	104	169	2	19	7
21 WOODEN CONTAINERS	169	4896	728	729	62	60	186	116	3604
22 HOUSEHOLD FURNITURE	0	0	0	0	0	0	0	0	0
23 OTHER FURNITURE	0	0	0	0	0	0	0	0	0
24 PAPER, ALLIED PRDTS.	25	19	96	47	57	55	19	23	3
25 PAPERBOARD CONTAINERS	20	9	206	92	98	20	20	25	12
26 PRINTING, PUBLISHING	104	106	694	374	423	447	101	97	40
27 CHEMICALS,SELECT. PRDTS.	70840	11688	62434	58419	54364	32109	34109	22541	9838
28 PLASTICS, SYNTHETICS	0	0	0	0	0	0	0	0	0
29 DRUGS, COSMETICS	3	6	6	3	8	9	3	2	1
30 PAINT, ALLIED PRDTS.	0	0	C	0	0	0	0	0	0
31 PETROLEUM, RELATED INDS.	18636	16127	93483	39479	52395	61035	11146	15489	1663
32 RUBBER, MISC. PLASTICS	2417	2379	8743	4599	5777	7271	1682	2586	358
33 LEATHER TANNING, PRDTS.	0	0	0	0	0	0	0	0	0
34 FOOTWEAR, LEATHER PRDTS.	2	4	4	2	5	5	2	1	0
35 GLASS, GLASS PRDTS.	0	0	0	0	0	3	0	0	0
36 STONE, CLAY PRDTS.	1153	75	3961	1898	1194	363	1184	559	218
37 PRIMARY IRON, STEEL MFR.	0	0	C	0	0	0	0	0	0
38 PRIMARY NONFERROUS MFR.	9	31	36	17	19	30	9	7	1

39 METAL CONTAINERS	51	197	1415	662	753	1333	45	47	18
40 FABRICATED METAL PRDTS.	0	0	0	0	0	0	0	0	0
41 SCREW MACH. PRDTS., ETC.	0	0	0	0	0	0	0	0	0
42 OTHER FAB. METAL PRDTS.	428	1360	1433	892	1007	1031	913	469	95
43 ENGINES, TURBINES	0	0	0	0	0	0	0	0	0
44 FARM MACH., EQUIP.	3288	4063	26422	11800	15016	18184	1394	3800	218
45 CONSTRUC. MACH., EQUIP.	0	0	0	0	0	0	0	0	0
46 MATERIAL HANDLING MACH.	0	0	0	0	0	0	0	0	0
47 METALWORKING MACHINERY	0	0	0	0	0	0	0	0	0
48 SPECIAL MACH., EQUIP.	0	0	0	0	0	0	0	0	0
49 GENERAL MACH., EQUIP.	0	0	0	0	0	0	0	0	0
50 MACHINE SHOP PRDTS.	126	140	542	251	300	360	82	133	18
51 OFFICE, COMPUT. MACHINES	0	0	0	0	0	0	0	0	0
52 SERVICE IND. MACHINES	0	0	0	0	0	0	0	0	0
53 ELECT. TRANSMISS. EQUIP.	0	0	0	0	0	0	0	0	0
54 HOUSEHOLD APPLIANCES	2	4	4	2	6	6	2	2	0
55 ELECTRIC LIGHTING EQUIP.	27	29	124	57	69	82	19	28	3
56 RADIO, TV, ETC., EQUIP.	3	6	6	3	8	8	3	2	1
57 ELECTRONIC COMPONENTS	0	0	0	0	0	0	0	0	0
58 MISC. ELECTRICAL MACH.	578	443	2156	1057	1465	1831	337	537	68
59 MOTOR VEHICLES, EQUIP.	243	353	699	461	600	922	226	314	60
60 AIRCRAFT, PARTS	0	0	0	0	0	0	0	0	0
61 OTHER TRANSPORT. EQUIP.	67	82	506	227	288	338	27	77	5
62 PROFESS., SCIEN. INSTRU.	1	1	1	1	2	2	1	0	0
63 MEDICAL, PHOTO. EQUIP.	2	3	6	3	5	5	2	2	0
64 MISC. MANUFACTURING	12	33	189	93	103	173	8	11	8
65 TRANSPORT., WAREHOUSING	10414	3890	25821	13500	13217	10982	6656	5655	1722
66 COMMUNICA.,EXC. BRDCAST.	1118	1852	5037	3184	3461	4662	1445	1040	313
67 RADIO, TV BROADCASTING	0	0	0	0	0	0	0	0	0
68 ELEC.,GAS,WATER,SAN.SER.	1488	12680	3594	2489	2356	1552	1496	8233	147
69 WHOLESALE, RETAIL TRADE	21861	11769	53466	30727	36883	34867	13282	14203	4363
70 FINANCE, INSURANCE	6244	2520	20806	14119	18385	12269	11204	4768	1084
71 REAL ESTATE, RENTAL	36451	24275	309903	96671	278063	115271	21574	27562	707
72 HOTELS, PERSONAL SERV.	63	119	123	66	164	166	55	47	10
73 BUSINESS SERVICES	12509	15435	90022	40427	51570	61569	5556	13819	1038
74 RESEARCH, DEVELOPMENT	0	0	0	0	0	0	0	0	0
75 AUTO. REPAIR, SERVICES	3031	3921	8206	5416	6738	10181	2851	3597	688
76 AMUSEMENTS	10	19	20	11	27	27	9	8	2
77 MED.,EDUC. SERVICES	145	147	839	450	483	487	285	193	39
78 FEDERAL GOVT. ENTERPRISE	74	79	265	141	167	167	73	42	21
79 STATE, LOCAL GOVT. ENT.	16	15	52	34	28	47	11	7	5
80 DIRECT ALLOCATED IMPORTS	16	30	31	16	41	41	14	12	2
81 TRANSFERRED IMPORTS	273	0	906	0	0	0	0	18506	669
82 VALUE ADDED	296340	219602	924491	566992	908897	220194	421023	253142	79833
83 SECONDARY TRANSFERS-IN	0	0	0	0	0	0	0	0	0
84 INVENTORY DEPLETION	2043	1394	6518	3589	5757	2565	2249	1584	432
85 SCRAP PRODUCTION	0	0	0	0	0	0	0	0	0
86 SCRAP PURCHASED	0	0	0	0	0	0	0	0	0
87 STATE TOTAL PRODUCTION	584381	398613	1864226	1025904	1645771	733245	642853	474683	124330

TABLE C-2

1963 INPUTS BY STATE TO
IO-2, OTHER AGRICULTURAL PRODUCTS

(THOUSANDS OF CURRENT DOLLARS)

INDUSTRY TITLE	19 MARYLAND	20 MASSA-CHUSETTS	21 MICHIGAN	22 MINNESOTA	23 MISSISSIPPI	24 MISSOURI	25 MONTANA	26 NEBRASKA	27 NEVADA
1 LIVESTOCK, PRDTS.	11951	4568	26969	57627	57686	67625	35127	53107	7189
2 OTHER AGRICULTURE PRDTS.	7192	5649	22108	42224	8479	26238	12178	21936	2578
3 FORESTRY, FISHERIES	0	0	1	1	1	1	1	1	0
4 AGRI.,FORES.,FISH. SERV.	2835	509	13415	24328	37821	34972	11679	28874	1916
5 IRON, FERRO. ORES MINING	0	0	0	0	0	0	0	0	0
6 NONFERROUS ORES MINING	0	0	0	0	0	0	0	0	0
7 COAL MINING	10	22	36	16	1	15	1	3	0
8 CRUDE PETRO.,NATURAL GAS	0	0	0	0	0	0	0	0	0
9 STONE, CLAY MINING	4168	1028	2781	901	0	0	0	0	0
10 CHEM.,FERT. MIN. MINING	119	16	555	607	622	5214	16	107	0
11 NEW CONSTRUCTION	0	0	0	0	0	0	0	0	0
12 MAINT., REPAIR CONSTR.	3277	1256	14547	16025	8602	10793	7347	10308	299
13 ORDNANCE, ACCESSORIES	0	0	1	1	1	1	1	1	0
14 FOOD, KINDRED PRDTS.	47	38	261	294	152	256	266	332	19
15 TOBACCO MANUFACTURES	2	2	12	20	12	20	20	24	1
16 FABRICS	3	1	14	38	549	24	154	36	7
17 TEXTILE PRDTS.	183	145	955	1933	303	1178	685	1007	112
18 APPAREL	0	0	1	1	1	1	1	1	0
19 MISC. TEXTILE PRDTS.	172	173	942	621	578	106	161	98	53
20 LUMBER, WOOD PRDTS.	11	4	75	104	5	101	75	129	1
21 WOODEN CONTAINERS	960	1171	3910	890	4	179	62	59	93
22 HOUSEHOLD FURNITURE	0	0	0	0	0	0	0	0	0
23 OTHER FURNITURE	0	0	0	0	0	0	0	0	0
24 PAPER, ALLIED PRDTS.	7	3	25	35	27	33	22	45	1
25 PAPERBOARD CONTAINERS	46	103	172	78	5	70	5	13	0
26 PRINTING, PUBLISHING	52	47	520	319	151	352	97	401	6
27 CHEMICALS,SELECT. PRDTS.	16651	5163	48472	26455	37699	38702	5439	31728	876
28 PLASTICS, SYNTHETICS	0	0	0	0	0	0	0	0	0
29 DRUGS, COSMETICS	1	1	4	6	4	6	6	8	0
30 PAINT, ALLIED PRDTS.	0	0	0	0	0	0	0	0	0
31 PETROLEUM, RELATED INDS.	4212	1404	17028	44164	15609	28426	25615	45167	1005
32 RUBBER, MISC. PLASTICS	695	327	2904	4754	2102	3454	3363	4577	114
33 LEATHER TANNING, PRDTS.	0	0	0	0	0	0	0	0	0
34 FOOTWEAR, LEATHER PRDTS.	0	0	2	4	2	4	4	4	0
35 GLASS, GLASS PRDTS.	0	0	0	0	0	0	0	0	0
36 STONE, CLAY PRDTS.	977	533	1132	542	1034	2039	65	337	3
37 PRIMARY IRON, STEEL MFR.	0	0	0	0	0	0	0	0	0
38 PRIMARY NONFERROUS MFR.	2	0	10	18	11	14	76	23	1

39 METAL CONTAINERS	58	9	353	698	79	570	555	997	9
40 FABRICATED METAL PRDTS.	0	0	0	0	0	0	0	0	0
41 SCREW MACH. PRDTS., ETC.	0	0	0	0	0	0	0	0	0
42 OTHER FAB. METAL PRDTS.	122	60	759	921	600	908	1339	719	186
43 ENGINES, TURBINES	0	0	0	0	0	0	0	0	0
44 FARM MACH., EQUIP.	731	110	5460	11641	3007	6707	7794	13616	186
45 CONSTRUC. MACH., EQUIP.	0	0	0	0	0	0	0	0	0
46 MATERIAL HANDLING MACH.	0	0	0	0	0	0	0	0	0
47 METALWORKING MACHINERY	0	0	0	0	0	0	0	0	0
48 SPECIAL MACH., EQUIP.	0	0	0	0	0	0	0	0	0
49 GENERAL MACH., EQUIP.	0	0	0	0	0	0	0	0	0
50 MACHINE SHOP PRDTS.	26	9	207	262	104	151	164	281	4
51 OFFICE, COMPUT. MACHINES	0	0	0	0	0	0	0	0	0
52 SERVICE IND. MACHINES	0	0	0	0	0	0	0	0	0
53 ELECT. TRANSMISS. EQUIP.	0	0	0	0	0	0	0	0	0
54 HOUSEHOLD APPLIANCES	1	0	3	4	3	5	4	5	0
55 ELECTRIC LIGHTING EQUIP.	6	2	42	59	23	34	37	63	1
56 RADIO, TV, ETC., EQUIP.	1	1	4	6	4	6	6	7	0
57 ELECTRONIC COMPONENTS	0	0	0	0	0	0	0	0	0
58 MISC. ELECTRICAL MACH.	148	32	561	1145	532	796	656	1165	22
59 MOTOR VEHICLES, EQUIP.	77	30	368	597	187	495	441	541	15
60 AIRCRAFT, PARTS	0	0	0	0	0	0	0	0	0
61 OTHER TRANSPORT. EQUIP.	15	2	110	227	61	131	146	255	4
62 PROFESS., SCIEN. INSTRU.	0	0	1	1	1	1	1	1	0
63 MEDICAL, PHOTO. EQUIP.	1	0	2	3	2	3	3	4	0
64 MISC. MANUFACTURING	13	4	91	107	15	91	49	138	1
65 TRANSPORT., WAREHOUSING	4285	1435	7933	8447	5334	8815	4002	8363	236
66 COMMUNICA.,EXC. BRDCAST.	641	267	2736	3134	1362	3105	1998	3111	58
67 RADIO, TV BROADCASTING	0	0	0	0	0	0	0	0	0
68 ELEC.,GAS,WATER,SAN.SER.	522	360	1945	2099	1785	1954	4981	4566	1389
69 WHOLESALE, RETAIL TRADE	6918	2996	24220	26153	14401	22275	14616	26902	935
70 FINANCE, INSURANCE	3497	936	10094	13507	5950	11642	2160	9256	221
71 REAL ESTATE, RENTAL	2252	194	11257	108668	35015	70948	16146	136899	1759
72 HOTELS, PERSONAL SERV.	15	12	75	122	71	124	119	148	8
73 BUSINESS SERVICES	2916	999	20780	40168	11466	23773	27201	46410	713
74 RESEARCH, DEVELOPMENT	0	0	0	0	0	0	0	0	0
75 AUTO. REPAIR, SERVICES	875	341	4368	6638	2440	5454	4814	6012	164
76 AMUSEMENTS	2	2	12	20	11	20	19	24	1
77 MED.,EDUC. SERVICES	72	65	530	350	353	380	172	428	10
78 FEDERAL GOVT. ENTERPRISE	29	16	136	124	122	118	76	150	5
79 STATE, LOCAL GOVT. ENT.	7	4	32	28	14	28	20	27	1
80 DIRECT ALLOCATED IMPORTS	4	3	6435	30	18	31	30	37	2
81 TRANSFERRED IMPORTS	4849	1899	19	145	2547	0	334	0	0
82 VALUE ADDED	80118	58181	390994	620682	416918	455932	154394	370438	5481
83 SECONDARY TRANSFERS-IN	0	0	0	0	0	0	0	0	0
84 INVENTORY DEPLETION	548	309	2269	3749	2355	2929	1209	2910	90
85 SCRAP PRODUCTION	0	0	0	0	0	0	0	0	0
86 SCRAP PURCHASED	0	0	0	0	0	0	0	0	0
87 STATE TOTAL PRODUCTION	162322	90441	648648	1071741	676241	837250	345951	831799	25775

TABLE C-2

1963 INPUTS BY STATE TO
IO-2, OTHER AGRICULTURAL PRODUCTS

(THOUSANDS OF CURRENT DOLLARS)

INDUSTRY TITLE	28 NEW HAMPSHIRE	29 NEW JERSEY	30 NEW MEXICO	31 NEW YORK	32 NORTH CAROLINA	33 NORTH DAKOTA	34 OHIO	35 OKLAHOMA	36 OREGON
1 LIVESTOCK, PRDTS.	2546	8511	22247	37004	73131	32435	47322	49421	24055
2 OTHER AGRICULTURE PRDTS.	1193	9059	2439	26746	14065	30451	30840	17870	9780
3 FORESTRY, FISHERIES	0	0	0	0	1	1	0	0	1
4 AGRI.,FORES.,FISH. SERV.	207	1694	8125	8197	14233	15558	14794	34446	9677
5 IRON, FERRO. ORES MINING	0	0	0	0	0	0	0	0	0
6 NONFERROUS ORES MINING	0	0	0	0	0	0	0	0	0
7 COAL MINING	3	25	0	65	7	3	63	3	10
8 CRUDE PETRO.,NATURAL GAS	0	0	0	0	0	0	0	0	0
9 STONE, CLAY MINING	0	0	0	0	0	0	0	0	0
10 CHEM.,FERT. MIN. MINING	6	74	31	159	1077	5	711	109	157
11 NEW CONSTRUCTION	0	0	0	0	0	0	0	0	0
12 MAINT., REPAIR CONSTR.	230	2670	1244	5978	15081	6405	19972	6535	5337
13 ORDNANCE, ACCESSORIES	0	0	0	1	1	1	1	0	1
14 FOOD, KINDRED PRDTS.	9	104	109	223	290	171	185	109	247
15 TOBACCO MANUFACTURES	0	4	8	11	21	12	11	8	15
16 FABRICS	0	1	21	10	549	37	20	956	50
17 TEXTILE PRDTS.	63	165	208	1511	209	1041	1057	550	442
18 APPAREL	0	0	0	1	1	1	1	0	1
19 MISC. TEXTILE PRDTS.	28	1556	127	1756	923	492	324	586	651
20 LUMBER, WOOD PRDTS.	1	8	12	36	53	240	78	17	36
21 WOODEN CONTAINERS	316	5445	176	10449	829	296	1281	9	2224
22 HOUSEHOLD FURNITURE	0	0	0	0	0	0	0	0	0
23 OTHER FURNITURE	0	0	0	0	0	0	0	0	0
24 PAPER, ALLIED PRDTS.	1	8	7	16	48	17	33	23	18
25 PAPERBOARD CONTAINERS	16	117	1	310	31	12	298	15	48
26 PRINTING, PUBLISHING	11	81	49	247	211	262	392	88	100
27 CHEMICALS,SELECT. PRDTS.	2350	14241	6666	35720	91124	8803	52774	15324	17583
28 PLASTICS, SYNTHETICS	0	0	0	0	0	0	0	0	0
29 DRUGS, COSMETICS	0	1	2	3	7	4	3	3	5
30 PAINT, ALLIED PRDTS.	0	0	0	0	0	0	0	0	0
31 PETROLEUM, RELATED INDS.	207	2975	6380	6592	37611	27165	29311	24895	11488
32 RUBBER, MISC. PLASTICS	80	710	622	1563	3157	2438	3943	4142	1389
33 LEATHER TANNING, PRDTS.	0	0	0	0	0	0	0	0	0
34 FOOTWEAR, LEATHER PRDTS.	0	1	1	2	4	2	2	1	3
35 GLASS, GLASS PRDTS.	0	0	0	0	0	0	0	0	0
36 STONE, CLAY PRDTS.	91	934	18	2627	1403	76	2768	219	349
37 PRIMARY IRON, STEEL MFR.	0	0	0	0	0	0	0	0	0
38 PRIMARY NONFERROUS MFR.	0	1	6	4	14	38	13	16	22

39 METAL CONTAINERS	3	25	44	131	76	1379	477	109	136
40 FABRICATED METAL PRDTS.	0	0	0	0	0	0	0	0	0
41 SCREW MACH. PRDTS., ETC.	0	0	0	0	0	0	0	0	0
42 OTHER FAB. METAL PRDTS.	21	113	435	456	707	687	827	811	1022
43 ENGINES, TURBINES	0	0	0	0	0	0	0	0	0
44 FARM MACH., EQUIP.	27	484	1062	1165	3124	5532	8472	7418	2948
45 CONSTRUC. MACH., EQUIP.	0	0	0	0	0	0	0	0	0
46 MATERIAL HANDLING MACH.	0	0	0	0	0	0	0	0	0
47 METALWORKING MACHINERY	0	0	0	0	0	0	0	0	0
48 SPECIAL MACH., EQUIP.	0	0	0	0	0	0	0	0	0
49 GENERAL MACH., EQUIP.	0	0	0	0	0	0	0	0	0
50 MACHINE SHOP PRDTS.	2	34	32	73	173	279	213	167	103
51 OFFICE, COMPUT. MACHINES	0	0	0	0	0	0	0	0	0
52 SERVICE IND. MACHINES	0	0	0	0	0	0	0	0	0
53 ELECT. TRANSMISS. EQUIP.	0	0	0	0	0	0	0	0	0
54 HOUSEHOLD APPLIANCES	0	1	2	2	5	3	2	2	3
55 ELECTRIC LIGHTING EQUIP.	0	7	7	14	39	60	47	37	21
56 RADIO, TV, ETC., EQUIP.	0	1	2	3	6	4	3	3	5
57 ELECTRONIC COMPONENTS	0	0	0	0	0	0	0	0	0
58 MISC. ELECTRICAL MACH.	10	117	124	237	685	580	795	834	311
59 MOTOR VEHICLES, EQUIP.	11	75	89	150	450	472	401	510	322
60 AIRCRAFT, PARTS	0	0	0	0	0	0	0	0	0
61 OTHER TRANSPORT. EQUIP.	1	11	21	25	63	115	164	140	58
62 PROFESS., SCIEN. INSTRU.	0	0	0	1	1	1	1	0	1
63 MEDICAL, PHOTO. EQUIP.	0	1	1	2	4	2	2	2	2
64 MISC. MANUFACTURING	1	11	8	48	19	303	80	13	23
65 TRANSPORT., WAREHOUSING	271	4224	1411	10478	11816	4499	9233	4715	3614
66 COMMUNICA.,EXC. BRDCAST.	68	666	478	1831	2897	2253	3100	1629	2063
67 RADIO, TV BROADCASTING	0	0	0	0	0	0	0	0	0
68 ELEC.,GAS,WATER,SAN.SER.	69	568	3446	1168	2821	1281	2734	1111	5379
69 WHOLESALE, RETAIL TRADE	1014	10512	5317	27457	33005	15239	27672	15756	10450
70 FINANCE, INSURANCE	424	2257	1232	7909	11764	5832	14854	7782	4093
71 REAL ESTATE, RENTAL	174	1575	5188	1237	70172	27233	40895	28707	3767
72 HOTELS, PERSONAL SERV.	3	21	47	65	128	72	66	50	92
73 BUSINESS SERVICES	201	2599	4153	6462	12841	20361	30437	25354	11441
74 RESEARCH, DEVELOPMENT	0	0	0	0	0	0	0	0	0
75 AUTO. REPAIR, SERVICES	122	847	973	1711	5454	4986	4757	5797	3644
76 AMUSEMENTS	0	3	8	10	21	12	11	8	15
77 MED.,EDUC. SERVICES	14	97	76	312	310	256	455	211	178
78 FEDERAL GOVT. ENTERPRISE	3	36	26	104	131	49	129	47	65
79 STATE, LOCAL GOVT. ENT.	1	8	6	17	26	35	30	9	22
80 DIRECT ALLOCATED IMPORTS	0	5	2151	16	32	18	16	12	23
81 TRANSFERRED IMPORTS	0	35341	0	85492	165	816	3618	0	470
82 VALUE ADDED	10492	122000	65069	349120	693117	377173	503682	163627	176630
83 SECONDARY TRANSFERS-IN	0	0	0	0	0	0	0	0	0
84 INVENTORY DEPLETION	71	661	491	1874	3875	2087	3002	1475	1088
85 SCRAP PRODUCTION	0	0	0	0	0	0	0	0	0
86 SCRAP PURCHASED	0	0	0	0	0	0	0	0	0
87 STATE TOTAL PRODUCTION	20361	230685	140398	636801	1108009	597585	862372	421681	311679

TABLE C-2

1963 INPUTS BY STATE TO
IO-2, OTHER AGRICULTURAL PRODUCTS

(THOUSANDS OF CURRENT DOLLARS)

INDUSTRY TITLE	37 PENNSYL-VANIA	38 RHODE ISLAND	39 SOUTH CAROLINA	40 SOUTH DAKOTA	41 TENNESSEE	42 TEXAS	43 UTAH	44 VERMONT	45 VIRGINIA
1 LIVESTOCK, PRDTS.	33158	2050	29571	44737	58357	159483	13663	5889	48276
2 OTHER AGRICULTURE PRDTS.	22742	1844	7515	17340	9125	35441	3825	1004	10237
3 FORESTRY, FISHERIES	0	0	1	0	0	2	0	0	0
4 AGRI.,FORES.,FISH. SERV.	7052	39	8513	18206	19913	153489	3009	574	5326
5 IRON, FERRO. ORES MINING	0	0	0	0	0	0	0	0	0
6 NONFERROUS ORES MINING	0	0	0	0	0	0	0	0	0
7 COAL MINING	63	2	2	1	10	34	1	1	11
8 CRUDE PETRO.,NATURAL GAS	0	0	0	0	0	0	0	0	0
9 STONE, CLAY MINING	0	0	1036	0	3809	2065	0	656	4047
10 CHEM.,FERT. MIN. MINING	214	4	339	19	395	843	3	17	556
11 NEW CONSTRUCTION	0	0	0	0	0	0	0	0	0
12 MAINT., REPAIR CONSTR.	6659	162	9264	4100	9963	20173	1011	319	6108
13 ORDNANCE, ACCESSORIES	0	0	1	0	0	2	0	0	0
14 FOOD, KINDRED PRDTS.	123	5	233	133	119	641	52	9	119
15 TOBACCO MANUFACTURES	7	0	17	10	8	43	3	0	8
16 FABRICS	10	0	324	30	475	2400	20	2	339
17 TEXTILE PRDTS.	992	15	107	812	443	753	277	262	275
18 APPAREL	0	0	1	0	0	2	0	0	0
19 MISC. TEXTILE PRDTS.	274	50	750	37	964	2688	68	19	491
20 LUMBER, WOOD PRDTS.	30	0	24	71	3	64	6	2	16
21 WOODEN CONTAINERS	2012	182	516	3	303	519	245	242	895
22 HOUSEHOLD FURNITURE	0	0	0	0	0	0	0	0	0
23 OTHER FURNITURE	0	0	0	0	0	0	0	0	0
24 PAPER, ALLIED PRDTS.	13	0	42	16	16	97	3	1	13
25 PAPERBOARD CONTAINERS	298	11	9	6	50	163	6	3	54
26 PRINTING, PUBLISHING	155	4	135	163	99	548	18	11	77
27 CHEMICALS,SELECT. PRDTS.	33753	794	44242	5319	31073	67683	2909	5370	37409
28 PLASTICS, SYNTHETICS	0	0	0	0	0	0	0	0	0
29 DRUGS, COSMETICS	2	0	5	3	3	14	1	0	3
30 PAINT, ALLIED PRDTS.	0	0	0	0	0	0	0	0	0
31 PETROLEUM, RELATED INDS.	6705	179	27627	21875	10135	85004	2604	240	8033
32 RUBBER, MISC. PLASTICS	1619	45	3194	1970	1943	9498	516	58	1457
33 LEATHER TANNING, PRDTS.	0	0	0	0	0	0	0	0	0
34 FOOTWEAR, LEATHER PRDTS.	1	0	3	2	2	8	1	0	1
35 GLASS, GLASS PRDTS.	0	0	0	0	0	3	0	0	0
36 STONE, CLAY PRDTS.	2434	57	460	55	936	1143	26	138	1003
37 PRIMARY IRON, STEEL MFR.	0	0	0	0	0	0	0	0	0
38 PRIMARY NONFERROUS MFR.	4	0	10	14	8	47	3	0	6

39 METAL CONTAINERS	124	1	66	585	51	348	23	8	28
40 FABRICATED METAL PRDTS.	0	0	0	0	0	0	0	0	0
41 SCREW MACH. PRDTS., ETC.	0	0	0	0	0	0	0	0	0
42 OTHER FAB. METAL PRDTS.	382	8	434	363	729	1393	502	52	410
43 ENGINES, TURBINES	0	0	0	0	0	0	0	0	0
44 FARM MACH., EQUIP.	1403	22	3342	6930	1986	18812	569	50	1618
45 CONSTRUC. MACH., EQUIP.	0	0	0	0	0	0	0	0	0
46 MATERIAL HANDLING MACH.	0	0	0	0	0	0	0	0	0
47 METALWORKING MACHINERY	0	0	0	0	0	0	0	0	0
48 SPECIAL MACH., EQUIP.	0	0	0	0	0	0	0	0	0
49 GENERAL MACH., EQUIP.	0	0	0	0	0	0	0	0	0
50 MACHINE SHOP PRDTS.	61	2	68	138	80	547	17	3	79
51 OFFICE, COMPUT. MACHINES	0	0	0	0	0	0	0	0	0
52 SERVICE IND. MACHINES	0	0	0	0	0	0	0	0	0
53 ELECT. TRANSMISS. EQUIP.	0	0	0	0	0	0	0	0	0
54 HOUSEHOLD APPLIANCES	2	0	4	2	2	10	1	0	2
55 ELECTRIC LIGHTING EQUIP.	13	0	15	31	18	119	4	1	17
56 RADIO, TV, ETC., EQUIP.	2	0	5	3	3	13	1	0	2
57 ELECTRONIC COMPONENTS	0	0	0	0	0	0	0	0	0
58 MISC. ELECTRICAL MACH.	256	6	800	509	389	2045	85	11	300
59 MOTOR VEHICLES, EQUIP.	157	4	255	218	220	1034	80	8	174
60 AIRCRAFT, PARTS	0	0	0	0	0	0	0	0	0
61 OTHER TRANSPORT. EQUIP.	28	0	63	130	40	365	11	1	33
62 PROFESS., SCIEN. INSTRU.	0	0	1	1	1	3	0	0	0
63 MEDICAL, PHOTO. EQUIP.	1	0	3	2	1	8	0	0	1
64 MISC. MANUFACTURING	33	0	14	75	9	61	5	2	7
65 TRANSPORT., WAREHOUSING	5818	160	7181	3303	5692	19515	751	841	6128
66 COMMUNICA.,EXC. BRDCAST.	1866	40	1909	1288	1616	4713	232	114	949
67 RADIO, TV BROADCASTING	0	0	0	0	0	0	0	0	0
68 ELEC.,GAS,WATER,SAN.SER.	1365	48	172	755	1979	16834	1665	49	1060
69 WHOLESALE, RETAIL TRADE	16333	392	19979	11877	11778	55660	2669	1850	13176
70 FINANCE, INSURANCE	9079	125	3712	4014	8280	17267	1102	1243	6716
71 REAL ESTATE, RENTAL	1683	170	109206	60424	9868	69578	8560	345	4116
72 HOTELS, PERSONAL SERV.	45	1	102	62	51	264	21	3	49
73 BUSINESS SERVICES	6692	142	13006	23445	7736	67677	2201	223	6637
74 RESEARCH, DEVELOPMENT	0	0	0	0	0	0	0	0	0
75 AUTO. REPAIR, SERVICES	1798	51	3285	2423	2863	11708	896	94	2166
76 AMUSEMENTS	7	0	16	10	8	43	3	0	8
77 MED.,EDUC. SERVICES	224	5	201	181	254	1175	30	15	114
78 FEDERAL GOVT. ENTERPRISE	67	2	165	63	79	229	12	4	51
79 STATE, LOCAL GOVT. ENT.	17	0	12	11	13	26	4	1	10
80 DIRECT ALLOCATED IMPORTS	11	0	25	15	13	34283	5	0	12
81 TRANSFERRED IMPORTS	11696	4	2280	0	0	13114	0	861	1889
82 VALUE ADDED	311124	4622	85426	206756	279652	883988	28876	31910	167862
83 SECONDARY TRANSFERS-IN	0	0	0	0	0	0	0	0	0
84 INVENTORY DEPLETION	1667	39	1344	1539	1691	6137	269	181	1180
85 SCRAP PRODUCTION	0	0	0	0	0	0	0	0	0
86 SCRAP PURCHASED	0	0	0	0	0	0	0	0	0
87 STATE TOTAL PRODUCTION	490273	11288	387032	440075	483254	1769819	76864	52686	339553

TABLE C-2

1963 INPUTS BY STATE TO
IO-2, OTHER AGRICULTURAL PRODUCTS
(THOUSANDS OF CURRENT DOLLARS)

INDUSTRY TITLE	46 WASHINGTON	47 WEST VIRGINIA	48 WISCONSIN	49 WYOMING	50 ALASKA	51 HAWAII	52 NATIONAL TOTAL
1 LIVESTOCK, PRDTS.	17841	9841	54461	22436	24	3589	1819627
2 OTHER AGRICULTURE PRDTS.	17295	1744	24073	3210	37	756	769048
3 FORESTRY, FISHERIES	1	0	0	0	0	0	28
4 AGRI.,FORES.,FISH. SERV.	12198	761	13854	3218	10	2790	1053165
5 IRON, FERRO. ORES MINING	0	0	0	0	0	0	0
6 NONFERROUS ORES MINING	0	0	0	0	0	0	0
7 COAL MINING	7	3	15	0	0	2	655
8 CRUDE PETRO.,NATURAL GAS	0	0	0	0	0	0	0
9 STONE, CLAY MINING	523	758	4765	0	1	20	84712
10 CHEM.,FERT. MIN. MINING	270	21	1067	10	0	804	35072
11 NEW CONSTRUCTION	0	0	0	0	0	0	0
12 MAINT., REPAIR CONSTR.	10486	1018	5020	615	3	2066	366520
13 ORDNANCE, ACCESSORIES	1	0	0	0	0	0	30
14 FOOD, KINDRED PRDTS.	384	19	90	52	0	52	10706
15 TOBACCO MANUFACTURES	24	2	3	3	0	2	677
16 FABRICS	78	100	20	34	0	12	9283
17 TEXTILE PRDTS.	492	158	1614	272	0	8	28999
18 APPAREL	1	0	0	0	0	0	30
19 MISC. TEXTILE PRDTS.	293	110	393	41	2	185	43015
20 LUMBER, WOOD PRDTS.	61	5	26	7	0	4	2149
21 WOODEN CONTAINERS	1155	200	1296	5	4	339	96906
22 HOUSEHOLD FURNITURE	0	0	0	0	0	0	0
23 OTHER FURNITURE	0	0	0	0	0	0	0
24 PAPER, ALLIED PRDTS.	31	1	10	2	0	9	1233
25 PAPERBOARD CONTAINERS	33	12	77	1	0	10	3113
26 PRINTING, PUBLISHING	164	16	137	16	0	30	9090
27 CHEMICALS,SELECT. PRDTS.	23833	4153	18901	2110	53	8355	1424305
28 PLASTICS, SYNTHETICS	0	0	0	0	0	0	0
29 DRUGS, COSMETICS	7	0	1	1	0	1	211
30 PAINT, ALLIED PRDTS.	0	0	0	0	0	0	0
31 PETROLEUM, RELATED INDS.	18910	487	6453	2410	11	3864	953938
32 RUBBER, MISC. PLASTICS	2011	246	933	338	1	160	114249
33 LEATHER TANNING, PRDTS.	0	0	0	0	0	0	0
34 FOOTWEAR, LEATHER PRDTS.	4	0	1	0	0	0	122
35 GLASS, GLASS PRDTS.	0	0	0	0	0	0	12
36 STONE, CLAY PRDTS.	275	189	1199	10	0	56	38939
37 PRIMARY IRON, STEEL MFR.	0	0	0	0	0	0	0
38 PRIMARY NONFERROUS MFR.	41	1	4	5	0	1	687

39	METAL CONTAINERS	253	4	128	35	0	8	12620
40	FABRICATED METAL PRDTS.	0	0	0	0	0	0	0
41	SCREW MACH. PRDTS., ETC.	0	0	0	0	0	0	0
42	OTHER FAB. METAL PRDTS.	1258	198	420	463	0	59	31372
43	ENGINES, TURBINES	0	0	0	0	0	0	0
44	FARM MACH., EQUIP.	4521	137	1964	563	0	0	228899
45	CONSTRUC. MACH., EQUIP.	0	0	0	0	0	0	0
46	MATERIAL HANDLING MACH.	0	0	0	0	0	0	0
47	METALWORKING MACHINERY	0	0	0	0	0	0	0
48	SPECIAL MACH., EQUIP.	0	0	0	0	0	0	0
49	GENERAL MACH., EQUIP.	0	0	0	0	0	0	0
50	MACHINE SHOP PRDTS.	167	10	74	19	0	0	6612
51	OFFICE, COMPUT. MACHINES	0	0	0	0	0	0	0
52	SERVICE IND. MACHINES	0	0	0	0	0	0	0
53	ELECT. TRANSMISS. EQUIP.	0	0	0	0	0	0	0
54	HOUSEHOLD APPLIANCES	5	0	1	1	0	0	150
55	ELECTRIC LIGHTING EQUIP.	34	2	15	4	0	0	1434
56	RADIO, TV, ETC., EQUIP.	7	0	1	1	0	1	207
57	ELECTRONIC COMPONENTS	0	0	0	0	0	0	0
58	MISC. ELECTRICAL MACH.	462	40	174	64	0	29	25450
59	MOTOR VEHICLES, EQUIP.	484	38	109	52	0	0	13989
60	AIRCRAFT, PARTS	0	0	0	0	0	0	0
61	OTHER TRANSPORT. EQUIP.	90	3	40	11	0	0	4472
62	PROFESS., SCIEN. INSTRU.	1	0	0	0	0	0	40
63	MEDICAL, PHOTO. EQUIP.	4	0	1	0	0	3	118
64	MISC. MANUFACTURING	45	1	30	5	0	4	2134
65	TRANSPORT., WAREHOUSING	5485	801	5691	556	8	1333	321264
66	COMMUNICA.,EXC. BRDCAST.	2708	338	877	149	1	228	82548
67	RADIO, TV BROADCASTING	0	0	0	0	0	0	0
68	ELEC.,GAS,WATER,SAN.SER.	6807	145	682	2519	1	892	204294
69	WHOLESALE, RETAIL TRADE	15375	1839	10862	2202	14	2468	844476
70	FINANCE, INSURANCE	5862	1377	9891	746	5	526	314986
71	REAL ESTATE, RENTAL	35778	1354	44822	9373	32	5562	2019692
72	HOTELS, PERSONAL SERV.	143	9	20	17	0	10	4116
73	BUSINESS SERVICES	17604	697	7381	2141	1	135	836497
74	RESEARCH, DEVELOPMENT	0	0	0	0	0	0	0
75	AUTO. REPAIR, SERVICES	5485	485	1284	570	0	0	160649
76	AMUSEMENTS	23	2	3	3	0	2	665
77	MED.,EDUC. SERVICES	287	23	135	20	0	37	12908
78	FEDERAL GOVT. ENTERPRISE	100	7	38	11	0	9	4095
79	STATE, LOCAL GOVT. ENT.	35	3	9	2	0	0	814
80	DIRECT ALLOCATED IMPORTS	36	2	5	4	0	2	214881
81	TRANSFERRED IMPORTS	2456	0	3373	0	0	49	220717
82	VALUE ADDED	315337	44384	336795	22812	11	232069	14829530
83	SECONDARY TRANSFERS-IN	0	0	0	0	0	0	0
84	INVENTORY DEPLETION	1841	252	1949	271	1	935	94800
85	SCRAP PRODUCTION	0	0	0	0	0	0	0
86	SCRAP PURCHASED	0	0	0	0	0	0	0
87	STATE TOTAL PRODUCTION	529111	71996	561187	77410	220	267476	27360944

TABLE C-3

1963 INPUTS BY STATE TO
IO-5, IRON & FERROALLOY ORES MINING

(THOUSANDS OF CURRENT DOLLARS)

INDUSTRY TITLE	1 ALABAMA	2 ARIZONA	3 ARKANSAS	4 CALIFORNIA	5 COLORADO	6 CONNECTICUT	7 DELAWARE	8 DISTRICT OF COLUMBIA	9 FLORIDA
1 LIVESTOCK, PRDTS.	0	0	0	0	1	0	0	0	0
2 OTHER AGRICULTURE PRDTS.	1	0	0	1	3	0	0	0	0
3 FORESTRY, FISHERIES	0	0	0	0	0	0	0	0	0
4 AGRI.,FORES.,FISH. SERV.	0	0	0	0	0	0	0	0	0
5 IRON, FERRO. ORES MINING	0	0	0	864	1118	0	0	0	0
6 NONFERROUS ORES MINING	69	5	9	163	588	0	0	0	0
7 COAL MINING	0	0	0	0	0	0	0	0	0
8 CRUDE PETRO.,NATURAL GAS	0	0	0	0	0	0	0	0	0
9 STONE, CLAY MINING	89	3	3	192	361	0	0	0	0
10 CHEM.,FERT. MIN. MINING	0	0	0	0	0	0	0	0	0
11 NEW CONSTRUCTION	0	0	0	0	0	0	0	0	0
12 MAINT., REPAIR CONSTR.	13	0	0	18	61	0	0	0	0
13 ORDNANCE, ACCESSORIES	0	0	0	0	0	0	0	0	0
14 FOOD, KINDRED PRDTS.	12	0	2	28	55	0	0	0	0
15 TOBACCO MANUFACTURES	1	0	0	2	4	0	0	0	0
16 FABRICS	0	0	0	0	0	0	0	0	0
17 TEXTILE PRDTS.	0	0	0	0	0	0	0	0	0
18 APPAREL	0	0	0	0	0	0	0	0	0
19 MISC. TEXTILE PRDTS.	0	0	0	0	0	0	0	0	0
20 LUMBER, WOOD PRDTS.	40	2	1	99	1	0	0	0	0
21 WOODEN CONTAINERS	0	0	0	0	0	0	0	0	0
22 HOUSEHOLD FURNITURE	0	0	0	0	0	0	0	0	0
23 OTHER FURNITURE	0	0	0	0	0	0	0	0	0
24 PAPER, ALLIED PRDTS.	6	0	0	12	0	0	0	0	0
25 PAPERBOARD CONTAINERS	0	0	0	0	0	0	0	0	0
26 PRINTING, PUBLISHING	3	0	0	9	0	0	0	0	0
27 CHEMICALS,SELECT. PRDTS.	355	16	6	871	12	0	0	0	0
28 PLASTICS, SYNTHETICS	0	0	0	0	0	0	0	0	0
29 DRUGS, COSMETICS	0	0	0	1	1	0	0	0	0
30 PAINT, ALLIED PRDTS.	0	0	0	0	0	0	0	0	0
31 PETROLEUM, RELATED INDS.	176	8	3	431	6	0	0	0	0
32 RUBBER, MISC. PLASTICS	110	0	0	274	0	0	0	0	0
33 LEATHER TANNING, PRDTS.	0	0	0	0	0	0	0	0	0
34 FOOTWEAR, LEATHER PRDTS.	0	0	0	0	1	0	0	0	0
35 GLASS, GLASS PRDTS.	0	0	0	0	0	0	0	0	0
36 STONE, CLAY PRDTS.	60	3	0	147	3	0	0	0	0
37 PRIMARY IRON, STEEL MFR.	356	15	7	873	12	0	0	0	0
38 PRIMARY NONFERROUS MFR.	24	1	1	60	1	0	0	0	0

39 METAL CONTAINERS	0	0	0	0	0	0	0	0	0
40 FABRICATED METAL PRDTS.	5	0	0	13	0	0	0	0	0
41 SCREW MACH. PRDTS., ETC.	0	0	0	0	0	0	0	0	0
42 OTHER FAB. METAL PRDTS.	22	1	0	54	1	0	0	0	0
43 ENGINES, TURBINES	148	0	0	345	0	0	0	0	0
44 FARM MACH., EQUIP.	0	0	0	0	0	0	0	0	0
45 CONSTRUC. MACH., EQUIP.	400	17	8	979	14	0	0	0	0
46 MATERIAL HANDLING MACH.	0	0	0	0	0	0	0	0	0
47 METALWORKING MACHINERY	24	0	0	49	0	0	0	0	0
48 SPECIAL MACH., EQUIP.	0	0	0	0	0	0	0	0	0
49 GENERAL MACH., EQUIP.	3	0	0	10	0	0	0	0	0
50 MACHINE SHOP PRDTS.	3	0	0	8	0	0	0	0	0
51 OFFICE, COMPUT. MACHINES	0	0	0	0	0	0	0	0	0
52 SERVICE IND. MACHINES	0	0	0	0	0	0	0	0	0
53 ELECT. TRANSMISS. EQUIP.	1	0	0	2	0	0	0	0	0
54 HOUSEHOLD APPLIANCES	0	0	0	0	1	0	0	0	0
55 ELECTRIC LIGHTING EQUIP.	3	0	0	7	0	0	0	0	0
56 RADIO, TV, ETC., EQUIP.	1	0	0	3	1	0	0	0	0
57 ELECTRONIC COMPONENTS	0	0	0	0	0	0	0	0	0
58 MISC. ELECTRICAL MACH.	4	0	0	10	0	0	0	0	0
59 MOTOR VEHICLES, EQUIP.	37	2	0	92	2	0	0	0	0
60 AIRCRAFT, PARTS	0	0	0	0	0	0	0	0	0
61 OTHER TRANSPORT. EQUIP.	1	0	0	3	0	0	0	0	0
62 PROFESS., SCIEN. INSTRU.	6	0	0	14	0	0	0	0	0
63 MEDICAL, PHOTO. EQUIP.	0	0	0	1	0	0	0	0	0
64 MISC. MANUFACTURING	1	0	0	2	1	0	0	0	0
65 TRANSPORT., WAREHOUSING	7644	43	4	534	413	0	0	0	1
66 COMMUNICA.,EXC. BRDCAST.	23	1	1	51	99	0	0	0	0
67 RADIO, TV BROADCASTING	0	0	0	0	0	0	0	0	0
68 ELEC.,GAS,WATER,SAN.SER.	707	6	55	823	1944	0	0	0	0
69 WHOLESALE, RETAIL TRADE	847	10	6	522	95	0	0	0	0
70 FINANCE, INSURANCE	155	5	4	245	474	0	0	0	0
71 REAL ESTATE, RENTAL	1964	81	69	4373	8464	0	0	0	0
72 HOTELS, PERSONAL SERV.	7	0	1	13	27	0	0	0	0
73 BUSINESS SERVICES	578	24	20	1288	2491	0	0	0	0
74 RESEARCH, DEVELOPMENT	0	0	0	0	0	0	0	0	0
75 AUTO. REPAIR, SERVICES	19	1	1	41	80	0	0	0	0
76 AMUSEMENTS	1	0	0	2	5	0	0	0	0
77 MED.,EDUC. SERVICES	14	1	1	31	60	0	0	0	0
78 FEDERAL GOVT. ENTERPRISE	20	1	1	45	87	0	0	0	0
79 STATE, LOCAL GOVT. ENT.	10	0	0	22	43	0	0	0	0
80 DIRECT ALLOCATED IMPORTS	1	0	0	3	7	0	0	0	0
81 TRANSFERRED IMPORTS	31484	163	0	144	0	0	0	0	3
82 VALUE ADDED	9733	434	340	20863	50141	0	0	0	0
83 SECONDARY TRANSFERS-IN	16	6318	348	121	1303	7	0	0	143
84 INVENTORY DEPLETION	955	435	55	2131	4191	0	0	0	9
85 SCRAP PRODUCTION	0	0	0	0	0	0	0	0	0
86 SCRAP PURCHASED	11	0	0	23	55	0	0	0	0
87 STATE TOTAL PRODUCTION	56165	7597	947	36914	72228	7	0	0	155

TABLE C-3

1963 INPUTS BY STATE TO
IO-5, IRON & FERROALLOY ORES MINING
(THOUSANDS OF CURRENT DOLLARS)

INDUSTRY TITLE	10 GEORGIA	11 IDAHO	12 ILLINOIS	13 INDIANA	14 IOWA	15 KANSAS	16 KENTUCKY	17 LOUISIANA	18 MAINE
1 LIVESTOCK, PRDTS.	0	0	0	0	0	0	0	0	0
2 OTHER AGRICULTURE PRDTS.	0	0	0	0	0	0	0	0	0
3 FORESTRY, FISHERIES	0	0	0	0	0	0	0	0	0
4 AGRI.,FORES.,FISH. SERV.	0	0	0	0	0	0	0	0	0
5 IRON, FERRO. ORES MINING	199	0	0	0	0	0	0	0	0
6 NONFERROUS ORES MINING	9	5	0	0	0	0	0	0	0
7 COAL MINING	0	0	0	0	0	0	0	0	0
8 CRUDE PETRO.,NATURAL GAS	0	0	0	0	0	0	0	0	0
9 STONE, CLAY MINING	9	3	0	0	0	0	0	0	0
10 CHEM.,FERT. MIN. MINING	0	0	0	0	0	0	0	0	0
11 NEW CONSTRUCTION	0	0	0	0	0	0	0	0	0
12 MAINT., REPAIR CONSTR.	1	0	0	0	0	0	0	0	0
13 ORDNANCE, ACCESSORIES	0	0	0	0	0	0	0	0	0
14 FOOD, KINDRED PRDTS.	1	1	0	0	0	0	0	0	0
15 TOBACCO MANUFACTURES	0	0	0	0	0	0	0	0	0
16 FABRICS	0	0	0	0	0	0	0	0	0
17 TEXTILE PRDTS.	0	0	0	0	0	0	0	0	0
18 APPAREL	0	0	0	0	0	0	0	0	0
19 MISC. TEXTILE PRDTS.	0	0	0	0	0	0	0	0	0
20 LUMBER, WOOD PRDTS.	8	2	0	0	0	0	0	0	0
21 WOODEN CONTAINERS	0	0	0	0	0	0	0	0	0
22 HOUSEHOLD FURNITURE	0	0	0	0	0	0	0	0	0
23 OTHER FURNITURE	0	0	0	0	0	0	0	0	0
24 PAPER, ALLIED PRDTS.	0	0	0	0	0	0	0	0	0
25 PAPERBOARD CONTAINERS	0	0	0	0	0	0	0	0	0
26 PRINTING, PUBLISHING	1	0	0	0	0	0	0	0	0
27 CHEMICALS,SELECT. PRDTS.	68	13	0	0	0	0	0	0	0
28 PLASTICS, SYNTHETICS	0	0	0	0	0	0	0	0	0
29 DRUGS, COSMETICS	0	0	0	0	0	0	0	0	0
30 PAINT, ALLIED PRDTS.	0	0	0	0	0	0	0	0	0
31 PETROLEUM, RELATED INDS.	34	6	0	0	0	0	0	0	0
32 RUBBER, MISC. PLASTICS	22	0	0	0	0	0	0	0	0
33 LEATHER TANNING, PRDTS.	0	0	0	0	0	0	0	0	0
34 FOOTWEAR, LEATHER PRDTS.	0	0	0	0	0	0	0	0	0
35 GLASS, GLASS PRDTS.	0	0	0	0	0	0	0	0	0
36 STONE, CLAY PRDTS.	12	3	0	0	0	0	0	0	0
37 PRIMARY IRON, STEEL MFR.	69	13	0	0	0	0	0	0	0
38 PRIMARY NONFERROUS MFR.	5	1	0	0	0	0	0	0	0

39 METAL CONTAINERS	0	0	0	0	0	0	0	0	0
40 FABRICATED METAL PRDTS.	1	0	0	0	0	0	0	0	0
41 SCREW MACH. PRDTS., ETC.	0	0	0	0	0	0	0	0	0
42 OTHER FAB. METAL PRDTS.	5	1	0	0	0	0	0	0	0
43 ENGINES, TURBINES	33	0	0	0	0	0	0	0	0
44 FARM MACH., EQUIP.	0	0	0	0	0	0	0	0	0
45 CONSTRUC. MACH., EQUIP.	77	15	0	0	0	0	0	0	0
46 MATERIAL HANDLING MACH.	0	0	0	0	0	0	0	0	0
47 METALWORKING MACHINERY	0	0	0	0	0	0	0	0	0
48 SPECIAL MACH., EQUIP.	0	0	0	0	0	0	0	0	0
49 GENERAL MACH., EQUIP.	0	0	0	0	0	0	0	0	0
50 MACHINE SHOP PRDTS.	0	0	0	0	0	0	0	0	0
51 OFFICE, COMPUT. MACHINES	0	0	0	0	0	0	0	0	0
52 SERVICE IND. MACHINES	0	0	0	0	0	0	0	0	0
53 ELECT. TRANSMISS. EQUIP.	0	0	0	0	0	0	0	0	0
54 HOUSEHOLD APPLIANCES	0	0	0	0	0	0	0	0	0
55 ELECTRIC LIGHTING EQUIP.	1	0	0	0	0	0	0	0	0
56 RADIO, TV, ETC., EQUIP.	0	0	0	0	0	0	0	0	0
57 ELECTRONIC COMPONENTS	0	0	0	0	0	0	0	0	0
58 MISC. ELECTRICAL MACH.	1	0	0	0	0	0	0	0	0
59 MOTOR VEHICLES, EQUIP.	7	2	0	0	0	0	0	0	0
60 AIRCRAFT, PARTS	0	0	0	0	0	0	0	0	0
61 OTHER TRANSPORT. EQUIP.	0	0	0	0	0	0	0	0	0
62 PROFESS., SCIEN. INSTRU.	1	0	0	0	0	0	0	0	0
63 MEDICAL, PHOTO. EQUIP.	0	0	0	0	0	0	0	0	0
64 MISC. MANUFACTURING	0	0	0	0	0	0	0	0	0
65 TRANSPORT., WAREHOUSING	77	4	6534	594	0	0	0	1894	0
66 COMMUNICA.,EXC. BRDCAST.	3	1	0	0	0	0	0	0	0
67 RADIO, TV BROADCASTING	0	0	0	0	0	0	0	0	0
68 ELEC.,GAS,WATER,SAN.SER.	16	5	0	0	0	0	0	0	0
69 WHOLESALE, RETAIL TRADE	40	7	548	50	0	0	0	159	0
70 FINANCE, INSURANCE	12	4	39	4	0	0	0	11	0
71 REAL ESTATE, RENTAL	216	63	0	0	0	0	0	0	0
72 HOTELS, PERSONAL SERV.	1	0	0	0	0	0	0	0	0
73 BUSINESS SERVICES	64	18	0	0	0	0	0	0	0
74 RESEARCH, DEVELOPMENT	0	0	0	0	0	0	0	0	0
75 AUTO. REPAIR, SERVICES	2	1	0	0	0	0	0	0	0
76 AMUSEMENTS	0	0	0	0	0	0	0	0	0
77 MED.,EDUC. SERVICES	2	0	0	0	0	0	0	0	0
78 FEDERAL GOVT. ENTERPRISE	2	1	0	0	0	0	0	0	0
79 STATE, LOCAL GOVT. ENT.	1	0	0	0	0	0	0	0	0
80 DIRECT ALLOCATED IMPORTS	0	0	0	0	0	0	0	0	0
81 TRANSFERRED IMPORTS	0	0	27269	2479	0	0	0	7904	0
82 VALUE ADDED	705	324	0	0	0	0	0	0	0
83 SECONDARY TRANSFERS-IN	4	667	246	0	0	2	0	0	1
84 INVENTORY DEPLETION	105	72	15	0	0	0	0	0	0
85 SCRAP PRODUCTION	0	0	0	0	0	0	0	0	0
86 SCRAP PURCHASED	1	0	0	0	0	0	0	0	0
87 STATE TOTAL PRODUCTION	1816	1232	34651	3126	0	2	0	9968	2

TABLE C-3

1963 INPUTS BY STATE TO
IO-5, IRON & FERROALLOY ORES MINING

(THOUSANDS OF CURRENT DOLLARS)

INDUSTRY TITLE	19 MARYLAND	20 MASSA-CHUSETTS	21 MICHIGAN	22 MINNESOTA	23 MISSISSIPPI	24 MISSOURI	25 MONTANA	26 NEBRASKA	27 NEVADA
1 LIVESTOCK, PRDTS.	2	0	2	7	0	0	0	0	0
2 OTHER AGRICULTURE PRDTS.	5	0	5	21	0	0	0	0	0
3 FORESTRY, FISHERIES	1	0	0	2	0	0	0	0	0
4 AGRI.,FORES.,FISH. SERV.	0	0	0	0	0	0	0	0	0
5 IRON, FERRO. ORES MINING	44	0	9155	33973	0	5310	0	0	0
6 NONFERROUS ORES MINING	2	0	677	811	0	1001	0	0	43
7 COAL MINING	0	0	1077	3076	0	4	0	0	0
8 CRUDE PETRO.,NATURAL GAS	0	0	0	0	0	0	0	0	0
9 STONE, CLAY MINING	2	0	657	2702	0	23	10	0	26
10 CHEM.,FERT. MIN. MINING	0	0	0	0	0	0	0	0	0
11 NEW CONSTRUCTION	0	0	0	0	0	0	0	0	0
12 MAINT., REPAIR CONSTR.	0	0	139	493	0	5	1	0	4
13 ORDNANCE, ACCESSORIES	1	0	0	2	0	0	0	0	0
14 FOOD, KINDRED PRDTS.	100	0	97	398	0	3	1	0	3
15 TOBACCO MANUFACTURES	8	0	8	34	0	0	0	0	0
16 FABRICS	0	0	5	5	0	0	0	0	0
17 TEXTILE PRDTS.	0	0	3	3	0	0	0	0	0
18 APPAREL	1	0	0	2	0	0	0	0	0
19 MISC. TEXTILE PRDTS.	0	0	0	0	0	0	0	0	0
20 LUMBER, WOOD PRDTS.	2	0	406	1510	0	31	0	0	14
21 WOODEN CONTAINERS	0	0	0	0	0	0	0	0	0
22 HOUSEHOLD FURNITURE	0	0	0	0	0	0	0	0	0
23 OTHER FURNITURE	0	0	0	0	0	0	0	0	0
24 PAPER, ALLIED PRDTS.	0	0	49	176	0	6	0	0	0
25 PAPERBOARD CONTAINERS	0	0	0	0	0	0	0	0	0
26 PRINTING, PUBLISHING	1	0	38	140	0	3	0	0	1
27 CHEMICALS,SELECT. PRDTS.	15	0	3590	13327	0	270	1	0	123
28 PLASTICS, SYNTHETICS	0	0	0	0	0	0	0	0	0
29 DRUGS, COSMETICS	2	0	3	14	0	0	0	0	0
30 PAINT, ALLIED PRDTS.	0	0	1	5	0	0	0	0	0
31 PETROLEUM, RELATED INDS.	7	0	1779	6605	0	133	0	0	61
32 RUBBER, MISC. PLASTICS	6	0	1142	4248	0	88	0	0	44
33 LEATHER TANNING, PRDTS.	0	0	0	0	0	0	0	0	0
34 FOOTWEAR, LEATHER PRDTS.	2	0	3	8	0	0	0	0	0
35 GLASS, GLASS PRDTS.	0	0	0	1	0	0	0	0	0
36 STONE, CLAY PRDTS.	3	0	605	2245	0	45	0	0	21
37 PRIMARY IRON, STEEL MFR.	15	0	3604	13375	0	271	1	0	123
38 PRIMARY NONFERROUS MFR.	1	0	246	912	0	18	0	0	8

39 METAL CONTAINERS	0	0	0	0	0	0	0	0	0
40 FABRICATED METAL PRDTS.	0	0	55	203	0	4	0	0	2
41 SCREW MACH. PRDTS., ETC.	0	0	0	0	0	0	0	0	0
42 OTHER FAB. METAL PRDTS.	1	0	220	818	0	16	0	0	7
43 ENGINES, TURBINES	8	0	1413	5240	0	98	0	0	49
44 FARM MACH., EQUIP.	0	0	0	0	0	0	0	0	0
45 CONSTRUC. MACH., EQUIP.	16	0	4041	14996	0	304	1	0	138
46 MATERIAL HANDLING MACH.	0	0	100	116	0	0	0	0	0
47 METALWORKING MACHINERY	0	0	208	760	0	12	0	0	12
48 SPECIAL MACH., EQUIP.	0	0	0	0	0	0	0	0	0
49 GENERAL MACH., EQUIP.	0	0	39	144	0	3	0	0	3
50 MACHINE SHOP PRDTS.	0	0	35	130	0	3	0	0	1
51 OFFICE, COMPUT. MACHINES	0	0	0	1	0	0	0	0	0
52 SERVICE IND. MACHINES	0	0	0	0	0	0	0	0	0
53 ELECT. TRANSMISS. EQUIP.	0	0	10	37	0	1	0	0	0
54 HOUSEHOLD APPLIANCES	2	0	2	7	0	0	0	0	0
55 ELECTRIC LIGHTING EQUIP.	0	0	30	113	0	2	0	0	1
56 RADIO, TV, ETC., EQUIP.	3	0	12	48	0	1	0	0	0
57 ELECTRONIC COMPONENTS	0	0	0	0	0	0	0	0	0
58 MISC. ELECTRICAL MACH.	1	0	42	156	0	3	0	0	1
59 MOTOR VEHICLES, EQUIP.	2	0	375	1392	0	28	0	0	13
60 AIRCRAFT, PARTS	0	0	0	0	0	0	0	0	0
61 OTHER TRANSPORT. EQUIP.	0	0	15	53	0	1	0	0	0
62 PROFESS., SCIEN. INSTRU.	1	0	61	226	0	4	0	0	2
63 MEDICAL, PHOTO. EQUIP.	1	0	4	19	0	0	0	0	0
64 MISC. MANUFACTURING	3	0	16	46	0	1	0	0	0
65 TRANSPORT., WAREHOUSING	25332	0	16166	15818	0	1644	129	0	34
66 COMMUNICA.,EXC. BRDCAST.	0	0	176	719	0	6	3	0	7
67 RADIO, TV BROADCASTING	0	0	0	0	0	0	0	0	0
68 ELEC.,GAS,WATER,SAN.SER.	3	0	4953	10936	0	331	0	0	47
69 WHOLESALE, RETAIL TRADE	2284	0	3134	8000	0	152	14	0	74
70 FINANCE, INSURANCE	152	0	916	3452	0	28	14	0	32
71 REAL ESTATE, RENTAL	47	0	15116	61683	0	504	239	0	574
72 HOTELS, PERSONAL SERV.	48	0	48	193	0	1	1	0	2
73 BUSINESS SERVICES	14	0	4449	18155	0	148	70	0	169
74 RESEARCH, DEVELOPMENT	0	0	0	0	0	0	0	0	0
75 AUTO. REPAIR, SERVICES	0	0	143	583	0	5	2	0	5
76 AMUSEMENTS	8	0	8	33	0	0	0	0	0
77 MED.,EDUC. SERVICES	3	0	106	434	0	4	2	0	4
78 FEDERAL GOVT. ENTERPRISE	0	0	155	634	0	5	2	0	6
79 STATE, LOCAL GOVT. ENT.	0	0	77	314	0	3	1	0	3
80 DIRECT ALLOCATED IMPORTS	12	0	12	50	0	0	0	0	0
81 TRANSFERRED IMPORTS	105060	0	49038	0	0	0	532	0	0
82 VALUE ADDED	13	0	56494	246011	0	3924	1526	0	2867
83 SECONDARY TRANSFERS-IN	0	0	605	56	0	283	1362	1	851
84 INVENTORY DEPLETION	46	0	7376	29305	0	908	201	0	332
85 SCRAP PRODUCTION	0	0	0	0	0	0	0	0	0
86 SCRAP PURCHASED	0	0	62	272	0	4	2	0	3
87 STATE TOTAL PRODUCTION	133278	0	189007	505247	0	15644	4115	1	5712

TABLE C-3

1963 INPUTS BY STATE TO
IO-5, IRON & FERROALLOY ORES MINING

(THOUSANDS OF CURRENT DOLLARS)

INDUSTRY TITLE	28 NEW HAMPSHIRE	29 NEW JERSEY	30 NEW MEXICO	31 NEW YORK	32 NORTH CAROLINA	33 NORTH DAKOTA	34 OHIO	35 OKLAHOMA	36 OREGON
1 LIVESTOCK, PRDTS.	0	0	0	1	0	0	0	0	0
2 OTHER AGRICULTURE PRDTS.	0	0	0	2	0	0	0	0	0
3 FORESTRY, FISHERIES	0	0	0	0	0	0	0	0	0
4 AGRI.,FORES.,FISH. SERV.	0	0	0	0	0	0	0	0	0
5 IRON, FERRO. ORES MINING	0	458	0	4	79	0	0	0	0
6 NONFERROUS ORES MINING	0	0	5	52	4	0	0	0	0
7 COAL MINING	0	0	0	997	0	0	0	0	0
8 CRUDE PETRO.,NATURAL GAS	0	0	0	0	0	0	0	0	0
9 STONE, CLAY MINING	0	32	14	196	17	0	0	0	12
10 CHEM.,FERT. MIN. MINING	0	0	0	0	0	0	0	0	0
11 NEW CONSTRUCTION	0	0	0	0	0	0	0	0	0
12 MAINT., REPAIR CONSTR.	0	4	3	34	3	0	0	0	2
13 ORDNANCE, ACCESSORIES	0	0	0	0	0	0	0	0	0
14 FOOD, KINDRED PRDTS.	0	4	2	42	2	0	0	0	2
15 TOBACCO MANUFACTURES	0	0	0	3	0	0	0	0	0
16 FABRICS	0	0	0	0	0	0	0	0	0
17 TEXTILE PRDTS.	0	0	0	0	0	0	0	0	0
18 APPAREL	0	0	0	0	0	0	0	0	0
19 MISC. TEXTILE PRDTS.	0	0	0	0	0	0	0	0	0
20 LUMBER, WOOD PRDTS.	0	10	2	70	3	0	0	0	0
21 WOODEN CONTAINERS	0	0	0	0	0	0	0	0	0
22 HOUSEHOLD FURNITURE	0	0	0	0	0	0	0	0	0
23 OTHER FURNITURE	0	0	0	0	0	0	0	0	0
24 PAPER, ALLIED PRDTS.	0	0	0	7	0	0	0	0	0
25 PAPERBOARD CONTAINERS	0	0	0	0	0	0	0	0	0
26 PRINTING, PUBLISHING	0	1	0	6	0	0	0	0	0
27 CHEMICALS,SELECT. PRDTS.	0	90	14	614	27	0	0	0	0
28 PLASTICS, SYNTHETICS	0	0	0	0	0	0	0	0	0
29 DRUGS, COSMETICS	0	0	0	1	0	0	0	0	0
30 PAINT, ALLIED PRDTS.	0	0	0	0	0	0	0	0	0
31 PETROLEUM, RELATED INDS.	0	45	7	304	14	0	0	0	0
32 RUBBER, MISC. PLASTICS	0	33	0	197	11	0	0	0	0
33 LEATHER TANNING, PRDTS.	0	0	0	0	0	0	0	0	0
34 FOOTWEAR, LEATHER PRDTS.	0	0	0	1	0	0	0	0	0
35 GLASS, GLASS PRDTS.	0	0	0	0	0	0	0	0	0
36 STONE, CLAY PRDTS.	0	15	3	105	6	0	0	0	0
37 PRIMARY IRON, STEEL MFR.	0	91	14	616	27	0	0	0	0
38 PRIMARY NONFERROUS MFR.	0	6	1	42	2	0	0	0	0

39 METAL CONTAINERS	0	0	0	0	0	0	0	0	0
40 FABRICATED METAL PRDTS.	0	1	0	9	0	0	0	0	0
41 SCREW MACH. PRDTS., ETC.	0	0	0	0	0	0	0	0	0
42 OTHER FAB. METAL PRDTS.	0	5	1	37	2	0	0	0	0
43 ENGINES, TURBINES	0	33	0	246	16	0	0	0	0
44 FARM MACH., EQUIP.	0	0	0	0	0	0	0	0	0
45 CONSTRUC. MACH., EQUIP.	0	102	16	691	31	0	0	0	0
46 MATERIAL HANDLING MACH.	0	0	0	0	0	0	0	0	0
47 METALWORKING MACHINERY	0	0	0	37	0	0	0	0	0
48 SPECIAL MACH., EQUIP.	0	0	0	0	0	0	0	0	0
49 GENERAL MACH., EQUIP.	0	0	0	8	0	0	0	0	0
50 MACHINE SHOP PRDTS.	0	1	0	6	0	0	0	0	0
51 OFFICE, COMPUT. MACHINES	0	0	0	0	0	0	0	0	0
52 SERVICE IND. MACHINES	0	0	0	0	0	0	0	0	0
53 ELECT. TRANSMISS. EQUIP.	0	0	0	2	0	0	0	0	0
54 HOUSEHOLD APPLIANCES	0	0	0	1	0	0	0	0	0
55 ELECTRIC LIGHTING EQUIP.	0	1	0	5	0	0	0	0	0
56 RADIO, TV, ETC., EQUIP.	0	0	0	3	0	0	0	0	0
57 ELECTRONIC COMPONENTS	0	0	0	0	0	0	0	0	0
58 MISC. ELECTRICAL MACH.	0	1	0	7	0	0	0	0	0
59 MOTOR VEHICLES, EQUIP.	0	9	2	63	4	0	0	0	0
60 AIRCRAFT, PARTS	0	0	0	0	0	0	0	0	0
61 OTHER TRANSPORT. EQUIP.	0	0	0	2	0	0	0	0	0
62 PROFESS., SCIEN. INSTRU.	0	1	0	10	0	0	0	0	0
63 MEDICAL, PHOTO. EQUIP.	0	0	0	1	0	0	0	0	0
64 MISC. MANUFACTURING	0	0	0	2	0	0	0	0	0
65 TRANSPORT., WAREHOUSING	0	3267	6	5251	34	312	7274	0	38
66 COMMUNICA.,EXC. BRDCAST.	0	8	4	53	4	0	0	0	3
67 RADIO, TV BROADCASTING	0	0	0	0	0	0	0	0	0
68 ELEC.,GAS,WATER,SAN.SER.	0	283	6	1506	7	0	0	0	0
69 WHOLESALE, RETAIL TRADE	0	317	9	804	19	26	610	0	6
70 FINANCE, INSURANCE	0	57	17	282	20	2	43	0	16
71 REAL ESTATE, RENTAL	0	695	309	4574	366	0	0	0	279
72 HOTELS, PERSONAL SERV.	0	2	1	20	1	0	0	0	1
73 BUSINESS SERVICES	0	205	91	1347	108	0	0	0	82
74 RESEARCH, DEVELOPMENT	0	0	0	0	0	0	0	0	0
75 AUTO. REPAIR, SERVICES	0	7	3	43	3	0	0	0	3
76 AMUSEMENTS	0	0	0	3	0	0	0	0	0
77 MED.,EDUC. SERVICES	0	5	2	32	3	0	0	0	2
78 FEDERAL GOVT. ENTERPRISE	0	7	3	47	4	0	0	0	3
79 STATE, LOCAL GOVT. ENT.	0	4	2	23	2	0	0	0	1
80 DIRECT ALLOCATED IMPORTS	0	0	0	6	0	0	0	0	0
81 TRANSFERRED IMPORTS	0	12955	0	18247	0	1302	30361	0	151
82 VALUE ADDED	0	3059	1896	22391	2063	0	0	0	1790
83 SECONDARY TRANSFERS-IN	0	96	2641	310	3	20	4	34	6
84 INVENTORY DEPLETION	0	343	315	2240	178	1	0	2	136
85 SCRAP PRODUCTION	0	0	0	0	0	0	0	0	0
86 SCRAP PURCHASED	0	3	2	25	2	0	0	0	2
87 STATE TOTAL PRODUCTION	0	22258	5392	61632	3066	1663	38293	36	2536

TABLE C-3

1963 INPUTS BY STATE TO
IO-5, IRON & FERROALLOY ORES MINING

(THOUSANDS OF CURRENT DOLLARS)

INDUSTRY TITLE	37 PENNSYL-VANIA	38 RHODE ISLAND	39 SOUTH CAROLINA	40 SOUTH DAKOTA	41 TENNESSEE	42 TEXAS	43 UTAH	44 VERMONT	45 VIRGINIA
1 LIVESTOCK, PRDTS.	1	0	0	0	0	0	0	0	0
2 OTHER AGRICULTURE PRDTS.	2	0	0	0	0	0	1	0	0
3 FORESTRY, FISHERIES	0	0	0	0	0	0	0	0	0
4 AGRI.,FORES.,FISH. SERV.	0	0	0	0	0	0	0	0	0
5 IRON, FERRO. ORES MINING	3684	0	0	13	0	0	0	0	0
6 NONFERROUS ORES MINING	0	0	0	2	0	130	218	0	0
7 COAL MINING	0	0	0	0	0	0	0	0	0
8 CRUDE PETRO.,NATURAL GAS	0	0	0	0	0	0	0	0	0
9 STONE, CLAY MINING	250	0	0	0	0	44	76	0	6
10 CHEM.,FERT. MIN. MINING	0	0	0	0	0	0	0	0	0
11 NEW CONSTRUCTION	0	0	0	0	0	0	0	0	0
12 MAINT., REPAIR CONSTR.	42	0	0	0	0	6	8	0	1
13 ORDNANCE, ACCESSORIES	0	0	0	0	0	0	0	0	0
14 FOOD, KINDRED PRDTS.	38	0	0	1	0	7	11	0	1
15 TOBACCO MANUFACTURES	3	0	0	0	0	0	1	0	0
16 FABRICS	0	0	0	0	0	0	0	0	0
17 TEXTILE PRDTS.	0	0	0	0	0	0	0	0	0
18 APPAREL	0	0	0	0	0	0	0	0	0
19 MISC. TEXTILE PRDTS.	0	0	0	0	0	0	0	0	0
20 LUMBER, WOOD PRDTS.	82	0	0	0	0	11	26	0	0
21 WOODEN CONTAINERS	0	0	0	0	0	0	0	0	0
22 HOUSEHOLD FURNITURE	0	0	0	0	0	0	0	0	0
23 OTHER FURNITURE	0	0	0	0	0	0	0	0	0
24 PAPER, ALLIED PRDTS.	12	0	0	0	0	0	1	0	0
25 PAPERBOARD CONTAINERS	0	0	0	0	0	0	0	0	0
26 PRINTING, PUBLISHING	8	0	0	0	0	1	3	0	0
27 CHEMICALS,SELECT. PRDTS.	729	0	0	0	3	94	233	0	0
28 PLASTICS, SYNTHETICS	0	0	0	0	0	0	0	0	0
29 DRUGS, COSMETICS	1	0	0	0	0	0	0	0	0
30 PAINT, ALLIED PRDTS.	0	0	0	0	0	0	0	0	0
31 PETROLEUM, RELATED INDS.	361	0	0	0	2	47	115	0	0
32 RUBBER, MISC. PLASTICS	230	0	0	0	0	33	77	0	0
33 LEATHER TANNING, PRDTS.	0	0	0	0	0	0	0	0	0
34 FOOTWEAR, LEATHER PRDTS.	0	0	0	0	0	0	0	0	0
35 GLASS, GLASS PRDTS.	0	0	0	0	0	0	0	0	0
36 STONE, CLAY PRDTS.	123	0	0	0	0	15	39	0	0
37 PRIMARY IRON, STEEL MFR.	731	0	0	1	2	96	233	0	0
38 PRIMARY NONFERROUS MFR.	50	0	0	0	0	7	16	0	0

39 METAL CONTAINERS	0	0	0	0	0	0	0	0	0
40 FABRICATED METAL PRDTS.	11	0	0	0	0	1	4	0	0
41 SCREW MACH. PRDTS., ETC.	0	0	0	0	0	0	0	0	0
42 OTHER FAB. METAL PRDTS.	45	0	0	0	0	5	15	0	0
43 ENGINES, TURBINES	279	0	0	0	0	33	98	0	0
44 FARM MACH., EQUIP.	0	0	0	0	0	0	0	0	0
45 CONSTRUC. MACH., EQUIP.	820	0	0	1	3	107	262	0	0
46 MATERIAL HANDLING MACH.	0	0	0	0	0	0	0	0	0
47 METALWORKING MACHINERY	37	0	0	0	0	0	12	0	0
48 SPECIAL MACH., EQUIP.	0	0	0	0	0	0	0	0	0
49 GENERAL MACH., EQUIP.	8	0	0	0	0	0	3	0	0
50 MACHINE SHOP PRDTS.	7	0	0	0	0	1	3	0	0
51 OFFICE, COMPUT. MACHINES	0	0	0	0	0	0	0	0	0
52 SERVICE IND. MACHINES	0	0	0	0	0	0	0	0	0
53 ELECT. TRANSMISS. EQUIP.	2	0	0	0	0	0	0	0	0
54 HOUSEHOLD APPLIANCES	1	0	0	0	0	0	0	0	0
55 ELECTRIC LIGHTING EQUIP.	6	0	0	0	0	1	2	0	0
56 RADIO, TV, ETC., EQUIP.	3	0	0	0	0	0	1	0	0
57 ELECTRONIC COMPONENTS	0	0	0	0	0	0	0	0	0
58 MISC. ELECTRICAL MACH.	8	0	0	0	0	1	3	0	0
59 MOTOR VEHICLES, EQUIP.	77	0	0	0	0	9	24	0	0
60 AIRCRAFT, PARTS	0	0	0	0	0	0	0	0	0
61 OTHER TRANSPORT. EQUIP.	3	0	0	0	0	0	1	0	0
62 PROFESS., SCIEN. INSTRU.	12	0	0	0	0	2	4	0	0
63 MEDICAL, PHOTO. EQUIP.	1	0	0	0	0	0	0	0	0
64 MISC. MANUFACTURING	2	0	0	0	0	0	1	0	0
65 TRANSPORT., WAREHOUSING	30157	0	0	4	1	1399	69	329	1366
66 COMMUNICA.,EXC. BRDCAST.	68	0	0	0	0	12	20	0	1
67 RADIO, TV BROADCASTING	0	0	0	0	0	0	0	0	0
68 ELEC.,GAS,WATER,SAN.SER.	2274	0	0	1	6	527	187	0	0
69 WHOLESALE, RETAIL TRADE	2877	0	0	1	1	177	145	28	116
70 FINANCE, INSURANCE	499	0	0	0	1	63	94	2	15
71 REAL ESTATE, RENTAL	5854	0	0	1	14	987	1676	0	119
72 HOTELS, PERSONAL SERV.	19	0	0	0	0	3	6	0	0
73 BUSINESS SERVICES	1723	0	0	0	4	291	493	0	35
74 RESEARCH, DEVELOPMENT	0	0	0	0	0	0	0	0	0
75 AUTO. REPAIR, SERVICES	55	0	0	0	0	9	16	0	1
76 AMUSEMENTS	3	0	0	0	0	0	1	0	0
77 MED.,EDUC. SERVICES	41	0	0	0	0	7	12	0	1
78 FEDERAL GOVT. ENTERPRISE	60	0	0	0	0	10	17	0	1
79 STATE, LOCAL GOVT. ENT.	30	0	0	0	0	5	9	0	1
80 DIRECT ALLOCATED IMPORTS	5	0	0	0	0	1	1	0	0
81 TRANSFERRED IMPORTS	120372	0	1	0	0	5709	0	1373	5698
82 VALUE ADDED	26226	0	0	1	77	5131	8964	0	763
83 SECONDARY TRANSFERS-IN	56	0	5	436	242	83	3873	0	98
84 INVENTORY DEPLETION	2846	0	0	29	22	485	1056	0	64
85 SCRAP PRODUCTION	0	0	0	0	0	0	0	0	0
86 SCRAP PURCHASED	29	0	0	0	0	6	10	0	1
87 STATE TOTAL PRODUCTION	200864	0	6	493	379	15556	18143	1732	8288

TABLE C-3

1963 INPUTS BY STATE TO
IO-5, IRON & FERROALLOY ORES MINING

(THOUSANDS OF CURRENT DOLLARS)

INDUSTRY TITLE	46 WASHINGTON	47 WEST VIRGINIA	48 WISCONSIN	49 WYOMING	50 ALASKA	51 HAWAII	52 NATIONAL TOTAL
1 LIVESTOCK, PRDTS.	1	0	0	0	0	0	15
2 OTHER AGRICULTURE PRDTS.	2	0	0	1	0	0	46
3 FORESTRY, FISHERIES	0	0	0	0	0	0	3
4 AGRI.,FORES.,FISH. SERV.	0	0	0	0	0	0	0
5 IRON, FERRO. ORES MINING	0	0	73	0	0	0	54975
6 NONFERROUS ORES MINING	4	0	72	0	0	0	3871
7 COAL MINING	0	0	6	0	0	0	5160
8 CRUDE PETRO.,NATURAL GAS	0	0	0	0	0	0	0
9 STONE, CLAY MINING	5	0	6	113	0	0	4851
10 CHEM.,FERT. MIN. MINING	0	0	0	0	0	0	0
11 NEW CONSTRUCTION	0	0	0	0	0	0	0
12 MAINT., REPAIR CONSTR.	1	0	1	16	0	0	857
13 ORDNANCE, ACCESSORIES	0	0	0	0	0	0	3
14 FOOD, KINDRED PRDTS.	49	0	1	14	0	0	877
15 TOBACCO MANUFACTURES	4	0	0	1	0	0	71
16 FABRICS	0	0	0	0	0	0	10
17 TEXTILE PRDTS.	0	0	0	0	0	0	6
18 APPAREL	0	0	0	0	0	0	3
19 MISC. TEXTILE PRDTS.	0	0	0	0	0	0	0
20 LUMBER, WOOD PRDTS.	3	0	3	83	0	0	2409
21 WOODEN CONTAINERS	0	0	0	0	0	0	0
22 HOUSEHOLD FURNITURE	0	0	0	0	0	0	0
23 OTHER FURNITURE	0	0	0	0	0	0	0
24 PAPER, ALLIED PRDTS.	0	0	0	12	0	0	281
25 PAPERBOARD CONTAINERS	0	0	0	0	0	0	0
26 PRINTING, PUBLISHING	0	0	0	8	0	0	223
27 CHEMICALS,SELECT. PRDTS.	27	0	28	732	0	0	21258
28 PLASTICS, SYNTHETICS	0	0	0	0	0	0	0
29 DRUGS, COSMETICS	1	0	0	0	0	0	25
30 PAINT, ALLIED PRDTS.	0	0	0	0	0	0	6
31 PETROLEUM, RELATED INDS.	13	0	14	363	0	0	10536
32 RUBBER, MISC. PLASTICS	11	0	11	230	0	0	6768
33 LEATHER TANNING, PRDTS.	0	0	0	0	0	0	0
34 FOOTWEAR, LEATHER PRDTS.	1	0	0	0	0	0	17
35 GLASS, GLASS PRDTS.	0	0	0	0	0	0	1
36 STONE, CLAY PRDTS.	6	0	6	123	0	0	3589
37 PRIMARY IRON, STEEL MFR.	27	0	29	735	0	0	21336
38 PRIMARY NONFERROUS MFR.	2	0	2	50	0	0	1456

39 METAL CONTAINERS	0	0	0	0	0	0	0
40 FABRICATED METAL PRDTS.	0	0	0	11	0	0	320
41 SCREW MACH. PRDTS., ETC.	0	0	0	0	0	0	0
42 OTHER FAB. METAL PRDTS.	2	0	2	45	0	0	1305
43 ENGINES, TURBINES	16	0	16	295	0	0	8367
44 FARM MACH., EQUIP.	0	0	0	0	0	0	0
45 CONSTRUC. MACH., EQUIP.	30	0	33	824	0	0	23926
46 MATERIAL HANDLING MACH.	0	0	0	0	0	0	216
47 METALWORKING MACHINERY	0	0	0	37	0	0	1188
48 SPECIAL MACH., EQUIP.	0	0	0	0	0	0	0
49 GENERAL MACH., EQUIP.	0	0	0	8	0	0	229
50 MACHINE SHOP PRDTS.	0	0	0	7	0	0	205
51 OFFICE, COMPUT. MACHINES	0	0	0	0	0	0	1
52 SERVICE IND. MACHINES	0	0	0	0	0	0	0
53 ELECT. TRANSMISS. EQUIP.	0	0	0	2	0	0	57
54 HOUSEHOLD APPLIANCES	1	0	0	0	0	0	16
55 ELECTRIC LIGHTING EQUIP.	0	0	0	6	0	0	178
56 RADIO, TV, ETC., EQUIP.	1	0	0	2	0	0	80
57 ELECTRONIC COMPONENTS	0	0	0	0	0	0	0
58 MISC. ELECTRICAL MACH.	0	0	0	8	0	0	246
59 MOTOR VEHICLES, EQUIP.	4	0	4	77	0	0	2226
60 AIRCRAFT, PARTS	0	0	0	0	0	0	0
61 OTHER TRANSPORT. EQUIP.	0	0	0	3	0	0	82
62 PROFESS., SCIEN. INSTRU.	0	0	0	12	0	0	356
63 MEDICAL, PHOTO. EQUIP.	0	0	0	1	0	0	29
64 MISC. MANUFACTURING	1	0	0	2	0	0	78
65 TRANSPORT., WAREHOUSING	378	0	346	191	0	1	127288
66 COMMUNICA.,EXC. BRDCAST.	1	0	1	27	0	0	1293
67 RADIO, TV BROADCASTING	0	0	0	0	0	0	0
68 ELEC.,GAS,WATER,SAN.SER.	19	0	40	2010	0	0	26693
69 WHOLESALE, RETAIL TRADE	121	0	43	422	0	0	21664
70 FINANCE, INSURANCE	8	0	9	130	0	0	6805
71 REAL ESTATE, RENTAL	101	0	121	2327	0	0	110817
72 HOTELS, PERSONAL SERV.	23	0	0	8	0	0	428
73 BUSINESS SERVICES	30	0	36	685	0	0	32618
74 RESEARCH, DEVELOPMENT	0	0	0	0	0	0	0
75 AUTO. REPAIR, SERVICES	1	0	1	22	0	0	1048
76 AMUSEMENTS	3	0	0	1	0	0	69
77 MED.,EDUC. SERVICES	2	0	1	16	0	0	786
78 FEDERAL GOVT. ENTERPRISE	1	0	1	24	0	0	1138
79 STATE, LOCAL GOVT. ENT.	1	0	1	12	0	0	565
80 DIRECT ALLOCATED IMPORTS	6	0	0	2	0	0	106
81 TRANSFERRED IMPORTS	1248	0	1300	0	0	4	422800
82 VALUE ADDED	213	0	387	8638	382	0	475355
83 SECONDARY TRANSFERS-IN	181	0	31	1045	102	0	21600
84 INVENTORY DEPLETION	60	0	61	1195	30	0	55200
85 SCRAP PRODUCTION	0	0	0	0	0	0	0
86 SCRAP PURCHASED	0	0	0	10	0	0	525
87 STATE TOTAL PRODUCTION	2612	0	2687	20588	515	5	1484556

TABLE C-4

1963 INPUTS BY STATE TO
IO-6, NONFERROUS METAL ORES MINING
(THOUSANDS OF CURRENT DOLLARS)

INDUSTRY TITLE	1 ALABAMA	2 ARIZONA	3 ARKANSAS	4 CALIFORNIA	5 COLORADO	6 CONNECTICUT	7 DELAWARE	8 DISTRICT OF COLUMBIA	9 FLORIDA
1 LIVESTOCK, PRDTS.	0	8	0	0	1	0	0	0	0
2 OTHER AGRICULTURE PRDTS.	0	20	1	1	4	0	0	0	1
3 FORESTRY, FISHERIES	0	2	0	0	0	0	0	0	0
4 AGRI.,FORES.,FISH. SERV.	0	0	0	0	0	0	0	0	0
5 IRON, FERRO. ORES MINING	0	0	0	0	0	0	0	0	0
6 NONFERROUS ORES MINING	215	68058	4575	1592	17131	92	0	0	1878
7 COAL MINING	1	549	20	7	77	0	0	0	8
8 CRUDE PETRO.,NATURAL GAS	0	0	0	0	0	0	0	0	0
9 STONE, CLAY MINING	0	0	0	0	0	0	0	0	0
10 CHEM.,FERT. MIN. MINING	0	0	0	0	0	0	0	0	0
11 NEW CONSTRUCTION	0	0	0	0	0	0	0	0	0
12 MAINT., REPAIR CONSTR.	12	245	260	90	973	5	0	0	107
13 ORDNANCE, ACCESSORIES	0	2	0	0	0	0	0	0	0
14 FOOD, KINDRED PRDTS.	2	393	24	24	83	1	0	0	17
15 TOBACCO MANUFACTURES	0	32	2	2	7	0	0	0	1
16 FABRICS	0	159	0	0	0	0	0	0	0
17 TEXTILE PRDTS.	0	47	2	1	8	0	0	0	1
18 APPAREL	0	3	0	0	3	0	0	0	0
19 MISC. TEXTILE PRDTS.	0	0	0	0	0	0	0	0	0
20 LUMBER, WOOD PRDTS.	15	752	316	111	1184	7	0	0	131
21 WOODEN CONTAINERS	0	0	0	0	0	0	0	0	0
22 HOUSEHOLD FURNITURE	0	0	0	0	0	0	0	0	0
23 OTHER FURNITURE	0	0	0	0	0	0	0	0	0
24 PAPER, ALLIED PRDTS.	0	123	10	4	38	0	0	0	4
25 PAPERBOARD CONTAINERS	0	0	0	0	0	0	0	0	0
26 PRINTING, PUBLISHING	0	109	5	2	21	0	0	0	2
27 CHEMICALS,SELECT. PRDTS.	57	12935	1208	420	4523	25	0	0	496
28 PLASTICS, SYNTHETICS	0	68	0	0	0	0	0	0	0
29 DRUGS, COSMETICS	0	19	1	1	2	0	0	0	0
30 PAINT, ALLIED PRDTS.	0	8	0	0	0	0	0	0	0
31 PETROLEUM, RELATED INDS.	7	1438	166	57	617	4	0	0	67
32 RUBBER, MISC. PLASTICS	11	2166	218	75	814	5	0	0	89
33 LEATHER TANNING, PRDTS.	0	0	0	0	0	0	0	0	0
34 FOOTWEAR, LEATHER PRDTS.	0	7	1	0	2	0	0	0	0
35 GLASS, GLASS PRDTS.	0	3	0	0	0	0	0	0	0
36 STONE, CLAY PRDTS.	1	781	11	4	42	0	0	0	4
37 PRIMARY IRON, STEEL MFR.	12	11157	261	92	981	5	0	0	107
38 PRIMARY NONFERROUS MFR.	0	136	0	0	0	0	0	0	0

39 METAL CONTAINERS	0	0	0	0	0	0	0	0	0
40 FABRICATED METAL PRDTS.	0	528	21	6	78	0	0	0	9
41 SCREW MACH. PRDTS., ETC.	0	0	0	0	0	0	0	0	0
42 OTHER FAB. METAL PRDTS.	5	373	116	40	433	2	0	0	47
43 ENGINES, TURBINES	16	774	353	122	1324	8	0	0	146
44 FARM MACH., EQUIP.	0	0	0	0	0	0	0	0	0
45 CONSTRUC. MACH., EQUIP.	27	8181	558	195	2088	11	0	0	229
46 MATERIAL HANDLING MACH.	2	1324	40	14	151	1	0	0	16
47 METALWORKING MACHINERY	1	91	14	5	55	0	0	0	6
48 SPECIAL MACH., EQUIP.	0	0	0	0	0	0	0	0	0
49 GENERAL MACH., EQUIP.	1	271	9	3	33	0	0	0	4
50 MACHINE SHOP PRDTS.	52	1054	1102	382	4123	22	0	0	452
51 OFFICE, COMPUT. MACHINES	0	0	0	0	0	0	0	0	0
52 SERVICE IND. MACHINES	0	0	0	0	0	0	0	0	0
53 ELECT. TRANSMISS. EQUIP.	0	279	6	2	22	0	0	0	2
54 HOUSEHOLD APPLIANCES	0	8	0	0	1	0	0	0	0
55 ELECTRIC LIGHTING EQUIP.	1	93	17	5	62	0	0	0	6
56 RADIO, TV, ETC., EQUIP.	0	86	2	1	9	0	0	0	1
57 ELECTRONIC COMPONENTS	0	3	0	0	0	0	0	0	0
58 MISC. ELECTRICAL MACH.	0	46	6	3	26	0	0	0	3
59 MOTOR VEHICLES, EQUIP.	4	360	64	22	238	2	0	0	25
60 AIRCRAFT, PARTS	0	0	0	0	0	0	0	0	0
61 OTHER TRANSPORT. EQUIP.	0	983	3	1	14	0	0	0	1
62 PROFESS., SCIEN. INSTRU.	0	133	11	3	36	0	0	0	6
63 MEDICAL, PHOTO. EQUIP.	0	16	1	0	2	0	0	0	0
64 MISC. MANUFACTURING	2	54	37	13	141	1	0	0	16
65 TRANSPORT., WAREHOUSING	947	10149	94	251	323	2	2	0	64
66 COMMUNICA.,EXC. BRDCAST.	1	511	28	10	105	1	0	0	12
67 RADIO, TV BROADCASTING	0	0	0	0	0	0	0	0	0
68 ELEC.,GAS,WATER,SAN.SER.	34	14905	737	257	2757	15	0	0	303
69 WHOLESALE, RETAIL TRADE	647	10869	46	155	164	2	1	0	33
70 FINANCE, INSURANCE	19	7290	401	140	1503	8	0	0	164
71 REAL ESTATE, RENTAL	32	12236	674	236	2523	14	0	0	277
72 HOTELS, PERSONAL SERV.	1	192	12	12	40	0	0	0	8
73 BUSINESS SERVICES	11	4110	227	79	847	5	0	0	93
74 RESEARCH, DEVELOPMENT	0	0	0	0	0	0	0	0	0
75 AUTO. REPAIR, SERVICES	2	674	37	13	139	1	0	0	15
76 AMUSEMENTS	0	31	2	2	7	0	0	0	1
77 MED.,EDUC. SERVICES	1	312	17	6	64	0	0	0	7
78 FEDERAL GOVT. ENTERPRISE	1	364	20	7	75	0	0	0	8
79 STATE, LOCAL GOVT. ENT.	1	256	14	5	53	0	0	0	6
80 DIRECT ALLOCATED IMPORTS	0	63	3	1	13	0	0	0	2
81 TRANSFERRED IMPORTS	20399	3166	0	3404	0	0	34	0	0
82 VALUE ADDED	406	197529	8796	2972	33050	178	0	0	3560
83 SECONDARY TRANSFERS-IN	33	9	42	902	123	11	3	0	1164
84 INVENTORY DEPLETION	3	988	54	21	204	1	0	0	25
85 SCRAP PRODUCTION	0	0	0	0	0	0	0	0	0
86 SCRAP PURCHASED	4	1653	75	23	280	2	0	0	30
87 STATE TOTAL PRODUCTION	22986	379183	20720	11797	77616	430	39	0	9655

TABLE C-4

1963 INPUTS BY STATE TO
IO-6, NONFERROUS METAL ORES MINING

(THOUSANDS OF CURRENT DOLLARS)

INDUSTRY TITLE	10 GEORGIA	11 IDAHO	12 ILLINOIS	13 INDIANA	14 IOWA	15 KANSAS	16 KENTUCKY	17 LOUISIANA	18 MAINE
1 LIVESTOCK, PRDTS.	0	1	1	0	0	0	0	0	0
2 OTHER AGRICULTURE PRDTS.	0	4	2	0	0	0	0	0	0
3 FORESTRY, FISHERIES	0	0	0	0	0	0	0	0	0
4 AGRI.,FORES.,FISH. SERV.	0	0	0	0	0	0	0	0	0
5 IRON, FERRO. ORES MINING	0	0	0	0	0	0	0	0	0
6 NONFERROUS ORES MINING	57	8768	3233	0	0	22	0	0	20
7 COAL MINING	0	39	14	0	0	0	0	0	0
8 CRUDE PETRO.,NATURAL GAS	0	0	0	0	0	0	0	0	0
9 STONE, CLAY MINING	0	0	0	0	0	0	0	0	0
10 CHEM.,FERT. MIN. MINING	0	0	0	0	0	0	0	0	0
11 NEW CONSTRUCTION	0	0	0	0	0	0	0	0	0
12 MAINT., REPAIR CONSTR.	3	498	184	0	0	1	0	0	1
13 ORDNANCE, ACCESSORIES	0	0	0	0	0	0	0	0	0
14 FOOD, KINDRED PRDTS.	0	79	29	0	0	0	0	0	0
15 TOBACCO MANUFACTURES	0	6	2	0	0	0	0	0	0
16 FABRICS	0	0	0	0	0	0	0	0	0
17 TEXTILE PRDTS.	0	4	1	0	0	0	0	0	0
18 APPAREL	0	1	0	0	0	0	0	0	0
19 MISC. TEXTILE PRDTS.	0	0	0	0	0	0	0	0	0
20 LUMBER, WOOD PRDTS.	4	606	223	0	0	2	0	0	2
21 WOODEN CONTAINERS	0	0	0	0	0	0	0	0	0
22 HOUSEHOLD FURNITURE	0	0	0	0	0	0	0	0	0
23 OTHER FURNITURE	0	0	0	0	0	0	0	0	0
24 PAPER, ALLIED PRDTS.	0	20	7	0	0	0	0	0	0
25 PAPERBOARD CONTAINERS	0	0	0	0	0	0	0	0	0
26 PRINTING, PUBLISHING	0	10	4	0	0	0	0	0	0
27 CHEMICALS,SELECT. PRDTS.	15	2316	853	0	0	7	0	0	5
28 PLASTICS, SYNTHETICS	0	0	0	0	0	0	0	0	0
29 DRUGS, COSMETICS	0	1	1	0	0	0	0	0	0
30 PAINT, ALLIED PRDTS.	0	0	0	0	0	0	0	0	0
31 PETROLEUM, RELATED INDS.	2	316	117	0	0	1	0	0	1
32 RUBBER, MISC. PLASTICS	3	418	154	0	0	2	0	0	2
33 LEATHER TANNING, PRDTS.	0	0	0	0	0	0	0	0	0
34 FOOTWEAR, LEATHER PRDTS.	0	2	1	0	0	0	0	0	0
35 GLASS, GLASS PRDTS.	0	0	0	0	0	0	0	0	0
36 STONE, CLAY PRDTS.	0	21	8	0	0	0	0	0	0
37 PRIMARY IRON, STEEL MFR.	3	502	185	0	0	1	0	0	1
38 PRIMARY NONFERROUS MFR.	0	0	0	0	0	0	0	0	0

39 METAL CONTAINERS	0	0	0	0	0	0	0	0	0
40 FABRICATED METAL PRDTS.	0	39	15	0	0	0	0	0	0
41 SCREW MACH. PRDTS., ETC.	0	0	0	0	0	0	0	0	0
42 OTHER FAB. METAL PRDTS.	1	222	81	0	0	1	0	0	0
43 ENGINES, TURBINES	4	677	249	0	0	2	0	0	2
44 FARM MACH., EQUIP.	0	0	0	0	0	0	0	0	0
45 CONSTRUC. MACH., EQUIP.	7	1070	394	0	0	3	0	0	3
46 MATERIAL HANDLING MACH.	1	77	28	0	0	0	0	0	0
47 METALWORKING MACHINERY	0	28	10	0	0	0	0	0	0
48 SPECIAL MACH., EQUIP.	0	0	0	0	0	0	0	0	0
49 GENERAL MACH., EQUIP.	0	17	6	0	0	0	0	0	0
50 MACHINE SHOP PRDTS.	14	2111	779	0	0	5	0	0	5
51 OFFICE, COMPUT. MACHINES	0	0	0	0	0	0	0	0	0
52 SERVICE IND. MACHINES	0	0	0	0	0	0	0	0	0
53 ELECT. TRANSMISS. EQUIP.	0	11	4	0	0	0	0	0	0
54 HOUSEHOLD APPLIANCES	0	1	1	0	0	0	0	0	0
55 ELECTRIC LIGHTING EQUIP.	0	31	11	0	0	0	0	0	0
56 RADIO, TV, ETC., EQUIP.	0	5	2	0	0	0	0	0	0
57 ELECTRONIC COMPONENTS	0	0	0	0	0	0	0	0	0
58 MISC. ELECTRICAL MACH.	0	13	5	0	0	0	0	0	0
59 MOTOR VEHICLES, EQUIP.	0	122	45	0	0	0	0	0	0
60 AIRCRAFT, PARTS	0	0	0	0	0	0	0	0	0
61 OTHER TRANSPORT. EQUIP.	0	7	2	0	0	0	0	0	0
62 PROFESS., SCIEN. INSTRU.	0	19	8	0	0	0	0	0	0
63 MEDICAL, PHOTO. EQUIP.	0	2	1	0	0	0	0	0	0
64 MISC. MANUFACTURING	0	74	27	0	0	0	0	0	0
65 TRANSPORT., WAREHOUSING	13	309	114	0	0	0	0	1447	152
66 COMMUNICA.,EXC. BRDCAST.	0	54	20	0	0	0	0	0	0
67 RADIO, TV BROADCASTING	0	0	0	0	0	0	0	0	0
68 ELEC.,GAS,WATER,SAN.SER.	9	1412	521	0	0	4	0	0	4
69 WHOLESALE, RETAIL TRADE	9	155	57	0	0	1	0	989	104
70 FINANCE, INSURANCE	5	769	284	0	0	2	0	0	2
71 REAL ESTATE, RENTAL	8	1291	476	0	0	3	0	0	3
72 HOTELS, PERSONAL SERV.	0	39	14	0	0	0	0	0	0
73 BUSINESS SERVICES	3	434	159	0	0	1	0	0	1
74 RESEARCH, DEVELOPMENT	0	0	0	0	0	0	0	0	0
75 AUTO. REPAIR, SERVICES	0	71	26	0	0	0	0	0	0
76 AMUSEMENTS	0	6	2	0	0	0	0	0	0
77 MED.,EDUC. SERVICES	0	34	12	0	0	0	0	0	0
78 FEDERAL GOVT. ENTERPRISE	0	38	14	0	0	0	0	0	0
79 STATE, LOCAL GOVT. ENT.	0	27	10	0	0	0	0	0	0
80 DIRECT ALLOCATED IMPORTS	0	7	3	0	0	0	0	0	0
81 TRANSFERRED IMPORTS	244	0	0	0	0	0	0	31404	3289
82 VALUE ADDED	112	16631	6122	0	0	45	0	0	37
83 SECONDARY TRANSFERS-IN	56	65	126	20	11	20	70	881	1
84 INVENTORY DEPLETION	1	104	39	0	0	0	0	2	0
85 SCRAP PRODUCTION	0	0	0	0	0	0	0	0	0
86 SCRAP PURCHASED	2	144	56	0	0	-1	0	0	0
87 STATE TOTAL PRODUCTION	575	39728	14741	21	11	122	70	34723	3634

TABLE C-4

1963 INPUTS BY STATE TO
IO-6, NONFERROUS METAL ORES MINING

(THOUSANDS OF CURRENT DOLLARS)

INDUSTRY TITLE	19 MARYLAND	20 MASSA-CHUSETTS	21 MICHIGAN	22 MINNESOTA	23 MISSISSIPPI	24 MISSOURI	25 MONTANA	26 NEBRASKA	27 NEVADA
1 LIVESTOCK, PRDTS.	0	0	1	0	0	1	1	0	1
2 OTHER AGRICULTURE PRDTS.	0	0	4	0	0	2	4	0	3
3 FORESTRY, FISHERIES	0	0	0	0	0	0	0	0	0
4 AGRI.,FORES.,FISH. SERV.	0	0	0	0	0	0	0	0	0
5 IRON, FERRO. ORES MINING	0	0	0	0	0	0	0	0	0
6 NONFERROUS ORES MINING	0	0	3685	731	0	3716	43226	1	5357
7 COAL MINING	0	0	90	4	0	17	7	0	34
8 CRUDE PETRO.,NATURAL GAS	0	0	0	0	0	0	0	0	0
9 STONE, CLAY MINING	0	0	0	0	0	0	0	0	0
10 CHEM.,FERT. MIN. MINING	0	0	0	0	0	0	0	0	0
11 NEW CONSTRUCTION	0	0	0	0	0	0	0	0	0
12 MAINT., REPAIR CONSTR.	0	0	0	42	0	211	96	0	20
13 ORDNANCE, ACCESSORIES	0	0	0	0	0	0	0	0	0
14 FOOD, KINDRED PRDTS.	0	0	72	0	0	33	81	0	65
15 TOBACCO MANUFACTURES	0	0	6	0	0	3	6	0	5
16 FABRICS	0	0	10	0	0	0	47	0	15
17 TEXTILE PRDTS.	0	0	0	0	0	1	1	0	0
18 APPAREL	0	0	0	0	0	0	0	0	0
19 MISC. TEXTILE PRDTS.	0	0	0	0	0	0	0	0	0
20 LUMBER, WOOD PRDTS.	0	0	31	51	0	257	252	0	66
21 WOODEN CONTAINERS	0	0	0	0	0	0	0	0	0
22 HOUSEHOLD FURNITURE	0	0	0	0	0	0	0	0	0
23 OTHER FURNITURE	0	0	0	0	0	0	0	0	0
24 PAPER, ALLIED PRDTS.	0	0	9	1	0	9	37	0	11
25 PAPERBOARD CONTAINERS	0	0	0	0	0	0	0	0	0
26 PRINTING, PUBLISHING	0	0	7	1	0	4	31	0	9
27 CHEMICALS,SELECT. PRDTS.	0	0	799	194	0	981	3937	0	1177
28 PLASTICS, SYNTHETICS	0	0	0	0	0	0	0	0	0
29 DRUGS, COSMETICS	0	0	2	0	0	1	5	0	3
30 PAINT, ALLIED PRDTS.	0	0	0	0	0	0	2	0	1
31 PETROLEUM, RELATED INDS.	0	0	87	26	0	134	441	0	131
32 RUBBER, MISC. PLASTICS	0	0	133	34	0	176	660	0	196
33 LEATHER TANNING, PRDTS.	0	0	0	0	0	0	0	0	0
34 FOOTWEAR, LEATHER PRDTS.	0	0	1	0	0	1	1	0	1
35 GLASS, GLASS PRDTS.	0	0	0	0	0	0	0	0	0
36 STONE, CLAY PRDTS.	0	0	52	2	0	9	232	0	72
37 PRIMARY IRON, STEEL MFR.	0	0	737	42	0	214	3324	0	1022
38 PRIMARY NONFERROUS MFR.	0	0	9	0	0	0	40	0	12

39 METAL CONTAINERS	0	0	0	0	0	0	0	0	0
40 FABRICATED METAL PRDTS.	0	0	33	3	0	18	159	0	48
41 SCREW MACH. PRDTS., ETC.	0	0	0	0	0	0	0	0	0
42 OTHER FAB. METAL PRDTS.	0	0	17	18	0	94	121	0	33
43 ENGINES, TURBINES	0	0	30	57	0	286	262	0	69
44 FARM MACH., EQUIP.	0	0	0	0	0	0	0	0	0
45 CONSTRUC. MACH., EQUIP.	0	0	517	89	0	453	2472	0	746
46 MATERIAL HANDLING MACH.	0	0	87	7	0	33	395	0	121
47 METALWORKING MACHINERY	0	0	5	3	0	12	28	0	8
48 SPECIAL MACH., EQUIP.	0	0	0	0	0	0	0	0	0
49 GENERAL MACH., EQUIP.	0	0	18	2	0	7	81	0	25
50 MACHINE SHOP PRDTS.	0	0	1	176	0	894	413	0	87
51 OFFICE, COMPUT. MACHINES	0	0	0	0	0	0	0	0	0
52 SERVICE IND. MACHINES	0	0	0	0	0	0	0	0	0
53 ELECT. TRANSMISS. EQUIP.	0	0	18	1	0	5	83	0	26
54 HOUSEHOLD APPLIANCES	0	0	1	0	0	1	1	0	1
55 ELECTRIC LIGHTING EQUIP.	0	0	5	3	0	14	29	0	8
56 RADIO, TV, ETC., EQUIP.	0	0	2	0	0	2	3	0	2
57 ELECTRONIC COMPONENTS	0	0	0	0	0	0	0	0	0
58 MISC. ELECTRICAL MACH.	0	0	3	1	0	5	15	0	4
59 MOTOR VEHICLES, EQUIP.	0	0	22	11	0	51	113	0	33
60 AIRCRAFT, PARTS	0	0	0	0	0	0	0	0	0
61 OTHER TRANSPORT. EQUIP.	0	0	59	1	0	3	296	0	89
62 PROFESS., SCIEN. INSTRU.	0	0	8	3	0	8	39	0	11
63 MEDICAL, PHOTO. EQUIP.	0	0	2	0	0	1	5	0	2
64 MISC. MANUFACTURING	0	0	2	6	0	31	19	0	5
65 TRANSPORT., WAREHOUSING	65	8	2241	3	3	131	3475	0	980
66 COMMUNICA.,EXC. BRDCAST.	0	0	49	0	0	23	110	0	69
67 RADIO, TV BROADCASTING	0	0	0	0	0	0	0	0	0
68 ELEC.,GAS,WATER,SAN.SER.	0	0	404	117	0	598	2804	0	607
69 WHOLESALE, RETAIL TRADE	45	5	1729	2	2	67	3199	0	1044
70 FINANCE, INSURANCE	0	0	698	0	0	327	1571	0	983
71 REAL ESTATE, RENTAL	0	0	1172	0	0	548	2638	0	1648
72 HOTELS, PERSONAL SERV.	0	0	35	0	0	16	39	0	32
73 BUSINESS SERVICES	0	0	393	0	0	184	886	0	553
74 RESEARCH, DEVELOPMENT	0	0	0	0	0	0	0	0	0
75 AUTO. REPAIR, SERVICES	0	0	64	0	0	30	145	0	90
76 AMUSEMENTS	0	0	6	0	0	3	6	0	5
77 MED.,EDUC. SERVICES	0	0	31	0	0	14	67	0	42
78 FEDERAL GOVT. ENTERPRISE	0	0	35	0	0	16	78	0	49
79 STATE, LOCAL GOVT. ENT.	0	0	24	0	0	11	55	0	34
80 DIRECT ALLOCATED IMPORTS	0	0	6	0	0	3	14	0	9
81 TRANSFERRED IMPORTS	1418	167	28975	63	56	0	2783	0	0
82 VALUE ADDED	0	0	24468	1660	0	7064	8887	32	34537
83 SECONDARY TRANSFERS-IN	15	9	276	739	3	104	106	5	25
84 INVENTORY DEPLETION	0	0	95	11	0	45	213	0	133
85 SCRAP PRODUCTION	0	0	0	0	0	0	0	0	0
86 SCRAP PURCHASED	0	0	208	13	0	59	76	0	290
87 STATE TOTAL PRODUCTION	1542	188	67475	4117	63	16931	84117	38	50650

TABLE C-4

1963 INPUTS BY STATE TO
IO-6, NONFERROUS METAL ORES MINING
(THOUSANDS OF CURRENT DOLLARS)

INDUSTRY TITLE	28 NEW HAMPSHIRE	29 NEW JERSEY	30 NEW MEXICO	31 NEW YORK	32 NORTH CAROLINA	33 NORTH DAKOTA	34 OHIO	35 OKLAHOMA	36 OREGON
1 LIVESTOCK, PRDTS.	0	0	6	1	0	0	0	0	0
2 OTHER AGRICULTURE PRDTS.	0	1	16	2	0	1	0	1	1
3 FORESTRY, FISHERIES	0	0	2	0	0	0	0	0	0
4 AGRI.,FORES.,FISH. SERV.	0	0	0	0	0	0	0	0	0
5 IRON, FERRO. ORES MINING	0	0	0	0	0	0	0	0	0
6 NONFERROUS ORES MINING	0	1257	29573	4078	45	261	58	446	75
7 COAL MINING	0	6	144	19	0	1	0	2	0
8 CRUDE PETRO.,NATURAL GAS	0	0	0	0	0	0	0	0	0
9 STONE, CLAY MINING	0	0	0	0	0	0	0	0	0
10 CHEM.,FERT. MIN. MINING	0	0	0	0	0	0	0	0	0
11 NEW CONSTRUCTION	0	0	0	0	0	0	0	0	0
12 MAINT., REPAIR CONSTR.	0	71	1431	232	2	15	3	25	4
13 ORDNANCE, ACCESSORIES	0	0	2	0	0	0	0	0	0
14 FOOD, KINDRED PRDTS.	0	11	314	37	0	16	1	19	17
15 TOBACCO MANUFACTURES	0	1	25	3	0	1	0	2	1
16 FABRICS	0	0	13	0	0	0	0	0	0
17 TEXTILE PRDTS.	0	0	32	2	0	0	0	0	0
18 APPAREL	0	0	4	0	0	0	0	0	0
19 MISC. TEXTILE PRDTS.	0	0	0	0	0	0	0	0	0
20 LUMBER, WOOD PRDTS.	0	86	1777	283	2	18	4	31	4
21 WOODEN CONTAINERS	0	0	0	0	0	0	0	0	0
22 HOUSEHOLD FURNITURE	0	0	0	0	0	0	0	0	0
23 OTHER FURNITURE	0	0	0	0	0	0	0	0	0
24 PAPER, ALLIED PRDTS.	0	2	66	10	0	1	0	1	0
25 PAPERBOARD CONTAINERS	0	0	0	0	0	0	0	0	0
26 PRINTING, PUBLISHING	0	1	40	5	0	0	0	1	0
27 CHEMICALS,SELECT. PRDTS.	0	331	7598	1077	11	69	15	118	20
28 PLASTICS, SYNTHETICS	0	0	36	0	0	0	0	0	0
29 DRUGS, COSMETICS	0	0	7	1	0	0	0	0	0
30 PAINT, ALLIED PRDTS.	0	0	1	0	0	0	0	0	0
31 PETROLEUM, RELATED INDS.	0	45	1011	147	1	10	2	16	2
32 RUBBER, MISC. PLASTICS	0	59	1356	193	2	12	3	22	3
33 LEATHER TANNING, PRDTS.	0	0	0	0	0	0	0	0	0
34 FOOTWEAR, LEATHER PRDTS.	0	0	7	1	0	0	0	0	0
35 GLASS, GLASS PRDTS.	0	0	0	0	0	0	0	0	0
36 STONE, CLAY PRDTS.	0	3	124	10	0	1	0	1	0
37 PRIMARY IRON, STEEL MFR.	0	71	2324	233	3	15	3	25	4
38 PRIMARY NONFERROUS MFR.	0	0	12	0	0	0	0	0	0

39 METAL CONTAINERS	0	0	0	0	0	0	0	0	0
40 FABRICATED METAL PRDTS.	0	6	156	18	0	0	0	3	0
41 SCREW MACH. PRDTS., ETC.	0	0	0	0	0	0	0	0	0
42 OTHER FAB. METAL PRDTS.	0	32	659	104	1	7	1	11	2
43 ENGINES, TURBINES	0	97	1979	314	4	20	4	34	6
44 FARM MACH., EQUIP.	0	0	0	0	0	0	0	0	0
45 CONSTRUC. MACH., EQUIP.	0	153	3688	497	5	32	7	55	9
46 MATERIAL HANDLING MACH.	0	11	327	36	0	3	1	4	1
47 METALWORKING MACHINERY	0	4	87	13	0	1	0	2	0
48 SPECIAL MACH., EQUIP.	0	0	0	0	0	0	0	0	0
49 GENERAL MACH., EQUIP.	0	3	70	8	0	1	0	1	0
50 MACHINE SHOP PRDTS.	0	303	6057	983	10	63	14	108	16
51 OFFICE, COMPUT. MACHINES	0	0	0	0	0	0	0	0	0
52 SERVICE IND. MACHINES	0	0	0	0	0	0	0	0	0
53 ELECT. TRANSMISS. EQUIP.	0	2	55	5	0	0	0	0	0
54 HOUSEHOLD APPLIANCES	0	0	7	1	0	0	0	0	0
55 ELECTRIC LIGHTING EQUIP.	0	4	97	15	0	1	0	2	0
56 RADIO, TV, ETC., EQUIP.	0	1	52	2	0	0	0	1	0
57 ELECTRONIC COMPONENTS	0	0	1	0	0	0	0	0	0
58 MISC. ELECTRICAL MACH.	0	1	40	6	0	0	0	1	0
59 MOTOR VEHICLES, EQUIP.	0	18	372	56	0	4	0	5	2
60 AIRCRAFT, PARTS	0	0	0	0	0	0	0	0	0
61 OTHER TRANSPORT. EQUIP.	0	1	99	3	0	0	0	0	0
62 PROFESS., SCIEN. INSTRU.	0	3	67	8	0	0	0	0	0
63 MEDICAL, PHOTO. EQUIP.	0	0	6	1	0	0	0	0	0
64 MISC. MANUFACTURING	0	10	214	34	0	2	0	4	1
65 TRANSPORT., WAREHOUSING	0	106	1861	1818	0	376	2	72	169
66 COMMUNICA.,EXC. BRDCAST.	0	8	213	25	0	2	0	3	0
67 RADIO, TV BROADCASTING	0	0	0	0	0	0	0	0	0
68 ELEC.,GAS,WATER,SAN.SER.	0	203	4535	657	7	42	9	72	12
69 WHOLESALE, RETAIL TRADE	0	64	1428	1217	1	246	1	37	104
70 FINANCE, INSURANCE	0	110	3047	358	4	23	5	39	7
71 REAL ESTATE, RENTAL	0	185	5115	601	7	38	8	66	12
72 HOTELS, PERSONAL SERV.	0	5	153	18	0	8	0	9	8
73 BUSINESS SERVICES	0	62	1718	202	2	13	3	22	4
74 RESEARCH, DEVELOPMENT	0	0	0	0	0	0	0	0	0
75 AUTO. REPAIR, SERVICES	0	10	282	33	0	2	0	4	1
76 AMUSEMENTS	0	1	25	3	0	1	0	1	1
77 MED.,EDUC. SERVICES	0	5	134	16	0	1	0	2	1
78 FEDERAL GOVT. ENTERPRISE	0	5	152	18	0	1	0	2	0
79 STATE, LOCAL GOVT. ENT.	0	4	107	12	0	1	0	1	0
80 DIRECT ALLOCATED IMPORTS	0	1	28	3	0	0	0	1	0
81 TRANSFERRED IMPORTS	0	1342	0	36362	0	6814	4	0	2207
82 VALUE ADDED	0	2384	77259	7718	99	392	112	733	43
83 SECONDARY TRANSFERS-IN	1	35	1076	224	53	1	179	6	11
84 INVENTORY DEPLETION	0	15	416	49	1	3	1	5	1
85 SCRAP PRODUCTION	0	0	0	0	0	0	0	0	0
86 SCRAP PURCHASED	0	25	642	66	1	2	3	8	2
87 STATE TOTAL PRODUCTION	1	7165	158144	57839	260	8521	444	2024	2750

TABLE C-4

1963 INPUTS BY STATE TO
IO-6, NONFERROUS METAL ORES MINING

(THOUSANDS OF CURRENT DOLLARS)

INDUSTRY TITLE	37 PENNSYL-VANIA	38 RHODE ISLAND	39 SOUTH CAROLINA	40 SOUTH DAKOTA	41 TENNESSEE	42 TEXAS	43 UTAH	44 VERMONT	45 VIRGINIA
1 LIVESTOCK, PRDTS.	0	0	0	1	1	0	5	0	0
2 OTHER AGRICULTURE PRDTS.	0	0	0	3	3	1	12	0	1
3 FORESTRY, FISHERIES	0	0	0	0	0	0	2	0	0
4 AGRI.,FORES.,FISH. SERV.	0	0	0	0	0	0	0	0	0
5 IRON, FERRO. ORES MINING	0	0	0	0	0	0	0	0	0
6 NONFERROUS ORES MINING	737	0	60	5742	3189	1087	35086	0	1285
7 COAL MINING	4	0	0	26	14	5	187	0	6
8 CRUDE PETRO.,NATURAL GAS	0	0	0	0	0	0	0	0	0
9 STONE, CLAY MINING	0	0	0	0	0	0	0	0	0
10 CHEM.,FERT. MIN. MINING	0	0	0	0	0	0	0	0	0
11 NEW CONSTRUCTION	0	0	0	0	0	0	0	0	0
12 MAINT., REPAIR CONSTR.	42	0	3	327	181	62	1222	0	73
13 ORDNANCE, ACCESSORIES	0	0	0	0	0	0	2	0	0
14 FOOD, KINDRED PRDTS.	7	0	0	52	50	10	229	0	12
15 TOBACCO MANUFACTURES	1	0	0	4	4	1	18	0	1
16 FABRICS	0	0	0	0	0	0	40	0	0
17 TEXTILE PRDTS.	0	0	0	2	1	0	35	0	0
18 APPAREL	0	0	0	1	0	0	4	0	0
19 MISC. TEXTILE PRDTS.	0	0	0	0	0	0	0	0	0
20 LUMBER, WOOD PRDTS.	51	0	4	398	221	75	1602	0	88
21 WOODEN CONTAINERS	0	0	0	0	0	0	0	0	0
22 HOUSEHOLD FURNITURE	0	0	0	0	0	0	0	0	0
23 OTHER FURNITURE	0	0	0	0	0	0	0	0	0
24 PAPER, ALLIED PRDTS.	1	0	0	14	7	2	77	0	2
25 PAPERBOARD CONTAINERS	0	0	0	0	0	0	0	0	0
26 PRINTING, PUBLISHING	1	0	0	7	4	1	52	0	2
27 CHEMICALS,SELECT. PRDTS.	194	0	16	1516	842	287	8619	0	340
28 PLASTICS, SYNTHETICS	0	0	0	0	0	0	36	0	0
29 DRUGS, COSMETICS	0	0	0	1	1	0	8	0	0
30 PAINT, ALLIED PRDTS.	0	0	0	0	0	0	3	0	0
31 PETROLEUM, RELATED INDS.	26	0	2	207	115	39	1095	0	46
32 RUBBER, MISC. PLASTICS	34	0	3	273	151	51	1512	0	61
33 LEATHER TANNING, PRDTS.	0	0	0	0	0	0	0	0	0
34 FOOTWEAR, LEATHER PRDTS.	0	0	0	1	1	0	6	0	0
35 GLASS, GLASS PRDTS.	0	0	0	0	0	0	0	0	0
36 STONE, CLAY PRDTS.	2	0	0	14	8	3	245	0	3
37 PRIMARY IRON, STEEL MFR.	42	0	3	329	182	62	3950	0	73
38 PRIMARY NONFERROUS MFR.	0	0	0	0	0	0	34	0	0

39 METAL CONTAINERS	0	0	0	0	0	0	0	0	0
40 FABRICATED METAL PRDTS.	3	0	0	27	15	6	225	0	6
41 SCREW MACH. PRDTS., ETC.	0	0	0	0	0	0	0	0	0
42 OTHER FAB. METAL PRDTS.	19	0	2	146	80	27	609	0	32
43 ENGINES, TURBINES	57	0	4	444	247	83	1772	0	99
44 FARM MACH., EQUIP.	0	0	0	0	0	0	0	0	0
45 CONSTRUC. MACH., EQUIP.	89	0	8	700	389	132	4531	0	157
46 MATERIAL HANDLING MACH.	7	0	1	51	28	9	511	0	11
47 METALWORKING MACHINERY	3	0	0	19	10	3	88	0	4
48 SPECIAL MACH., EQUIP.	0	0	0	0	0	0	0	0	0
49 GENERAL MACH., EQUIP.	2	0	0	11	6	2	107	0	3
50 MACHINE SHOP PRDTS.	177	0	15	1383	768	262	5180	0	310
51 OFFICE, COMPUT. MACHINES	0	0	0	0	0	0	0	0	0
52 SERVICE IND. MACHINES	0	0	0	0	0	0	0	0	0
53 ELECT. TRANSMISS. EQUIP.	1	0	0	8	4	1	96	0	2
54 HOUSEHOLD APPLIANCES	0	0	0	1	1	0	4	0	0
55 ELECTRIC LIGHTING EQUIP.	3	0	0	21	11	4	96	0	4
56 RADIO, TV, ETC., EQUIP.	0	0	0	3	2	1	54	0	1
57 ELECTRONIC COMPONENTS	0	0	0	0	0	0	1	0	0
58 MISC. ELECTRICAL MACH.	1	0	0	9	5	1	42	0	1
59 MOTOR VEHICLES, EQUIP.	11	0	0	80	44	15	372	0	18
60 AIRCRAFT, PARTS	0	0	0	0	0	0	0	0	0
61 OTHER TRANSPORT. EQUIP.	1	0	0	4	2	1	263	0	1
62 PROFESS., SCIEN. INSTRU.	3	0	0	14	8	3	78	0	3
63 MEDICAL, PHOTO. EQUIP.	0	0	0	1	1	0	7	0	0
64 MISC. MANUFACTURING	6	0	0	48	27	9	184	0	10
65 TRANSPORT., WAREHOUSING	29	0	0	200	195	2269	2871	331	46
66 COMMUNICA.,EXC. BRDCAST.	5	0	0	35	20	7	314	0	8
67 RADIO, TV BROADCASTING	0	0	0	0	0	0	0	0	0
68 ELEC.,GAS,WATER,SAN.SER.	119	0	9	925	514	175	4954	0	207
69 WHOLESALE, RETAIL TRADE	15	0	1	101	98	1545	2946	226	24
70 FINANCE, INSURANCE	65	0	5	503	280	95	4469	0	112
71 REAL ESTATE, RENTAL	108	0	9	845	469	159	7502	0	189
72 HOTELS, PERSONAL SERV.	3	0	0	25	24	5	113	0	6
73 BUSINESS SERVICES	36	0	3	284	157	54	2520	0	63
74 RESEARCH, DEVELOPMENT	0	0	0	0	0	0	0	0	0
75 AUTO. REPAIR, SERVICES	6	0	0	46	26	9	413	0	10
76 AMUSEMENTS	1	0	0	4	4	1	18	0	1
77 MED., EDUC. SERVICES	3	0	0	22	13	4	191	0	5
78 FEDERAL GOVT. ENTERPRISE	3	0	0	25	14	5	223	0	6
79 STATE, LOCAL GOVT. ENT.	2	0	0	18	10	3	157	0	4
80 DIRECT ALLOCATED IMPORTS	1	0	0	5	3	1	39	0	1
81 TRANSFERRED IMPORTS	39	0	4	0	0	48446	0	7184	33
82 VALUE ADDED	1400	0	121	10870	5875	2058	133610	0	2436
83 SECONDARY TRANSFERS-IN	157	3	12	3	389	753	119	3	22
84 INVENTORY DEPLETION	9	0	1	68	39	15	606	0	15
85 SCRAP PRODUCTION	0	0	0	0	0	0	0	0	0
86 SCRAP PURCHASED	10	0	3	91	52	20	1118	0	23
87 STATE TOTAL PRODUCTION	3536	3	289	25958	14805	57868	230484	7744	5865

TABLE C-4

1963 INPUTS BY STATE TO
IO-6, NONFERROUS METAL ORES MINING

(THOUSANDS OF CURRENT DOLLARS)

INDUSTRY TITLE	46 WASHINGTON	47 WEST VIRGINIA	48 WISCONSIN	49 WYOMING	50 ALASKA	51 HAWAII	52 NATIONAL TOTAL
1 LIVESTOCK, PRDTS.	0	0	0	2	0	0	31
2 OTHER AGRICULTURE PRDTS.	1	0	0	6	0	0	95
3 FORESTRY, FISHERIES	0	0	0	0	0	0	6
4 AGRI.,FORES.,FISH. SERV.	0	0	0	0	0	0	0
5 IRON, FERRO. ORES MINING	0	0	0	0	0	0	0
6 NONFERROUS ORES MINING	2374	0	402	13752	1332	0	263196
7 COAL MINING	11	0	2	62	6	0	1362
8 CRUDE PETRO.,NATURAL GAS	0	0	0	0	0	0	0
9 STONE, CLAY MINING	0	0	0	0	0	0	0
10 CHEM.,FERT. MIN. MINING	0	0	0	0	0	0	0
11 NEW CONSTRUCTION	0	0	0	0	0	0	0
12 MAINT., REPAIR CONSTR.	135	0	23	782	75	0	7456
13 ORDNANCE, ACCESSORIES	0	0	0	0	0	0	6
14 FOOD, KINDRED PRDTS.	11	0	4	124	9	0	1826
15 TOBACCO MANUFACTURES	1	0	0	10	1	0	146
16 FABRICS	0	0	0	0	0	0	284
17 TEXTILE PRDTS.	1	0	0	6	1	0	146
18 APPAREL	0	0	0	3	0	0	19
19 MISC. TEXTILE PRDTS.	0	0	0	0	0	0	0
20 LUMBER, WOOD PRDTS.	164	0	29	951	91	0	9889
21 WOODEN CONTAINERS	0	0	0	0	0	0	0
22 HOUSEHOLD FURNITURE	0	0	0	0	0	0	0
23 OTHER FURNITURE	0	0	0	0	0	0	0
24 PAPER, ALLIED PRDTS.	5	0	1	31	2	0	495
25 PAPERBOARD CONTAINERS	0	0	0	0	0	0	0
26 PRINTING, PUBLISHING	3	0	0	17	2	0	341
27 CHEMICALS,SELECT. PRDTS.	627	0	107	3632	351	0	55718
28 PLASTICS, SYNTHETICS	0	0	0	0	0	0	140
29 DRUGS, COSMETICS	0	0	0	3	0	0	57
30 PAINT, ALLIED PRDTS.	0	0	0	0	0	0	15
31 PETROLEUM, RELATED INDS.	86	0	15	495	47	0	7019
32 RUBBER, MISC. PLASTICS	112	0	19	655	62	0	9739
33 LEATHER TANNING, PRDTS.	0	0	0	0	0	0	0
34 FOOTWEAR, LEATHER PRDTS.	0	0	0	3	0	0	36
35 GLASS, GLASS PRDTS.	0	0	0	0	0	0	3
36 STONE, CLAY PRDTS.	6	0	1	34	4	0	1698
37 PRIMARY IRON, STEEL MFR.	137	0	23	786	78	0	26989
38 PRIMARY NONFERROUS MFR.	0	0	0	0	0	0	243

39 METAL CONTAINERS	0	0	0	0	0	0	0
40 FABRICATED METAL PRDTS.	12	0	3	63	6	0	1506
41 SCREW MACH. PRDTS., ETC.	0	0	0	0	0	0	0
42 OTHER FAB. METAL PRDTS.	60	0	10	348	33	0	3787
43 ENGINES, TURBINES	182	0	30	1062	101	0	10920
44 FARM MACH., EQUIP.	0	0	0	0	0	0	0
45 CONSTRUC. MACH., EQUIP.	291	0	49	1677	163	0	29675
46 MATERIAL HANDLING MACH.	21	0	3	122	12	0	3456
47 METALWORKING MACHINERY	8	0	2	44	4	0	558
48 SPECIAL MACH., EQUIP.	0	0	0	0	0	0	0
49 GENERAL MACH., EQUIP.	5	0	1	26	3	0	726
50 MACHINE SHOP PRDTS.	570	0	97	3313	318	0	31619
51 OFFICE, COMPUT. MACHINES	0	0	0	0	0	0	0
52 SERVICE IND. MACHINES	0	0	0	0	0	0	0
53 ELECT. TRANSMISS. EQUIP.	3	0	0	18	2	0	656
54 HOUSEHOLD APPLIANCES	0	0	0	2	0	0	31
55 ELECTRIC LIGHTING EQUIP.	8	0	1	49	5	0	606
56 RADIO, TV, ETC., EQUIP.	1	0	0	8	1	0	242
57 ELECTRONIC COMPONENTS	0	0	0	0	0	0	5
58 MISC. ELECTRICAL MACH.	4	0	0	20	3	0	264
59 MOTOR VEHICLES, EQUIP.	33	0	5	191	18	0	2356
60 AIRCRAFT, PARTS	0	0	0	0	0	0	0
61 OTHER TRANSPORT. EQUIP.	2	0	0	11	1	0	1848
62 PROFESS., SCIEN. INSTRU.	6	0	0	31	3	0	512
63 MEDICAL, PHOTO. EQUIP.	0	0	0	2	0	0	50
64 MISC. MANUFACTURING	20	0	3	115	11	0	1126
65 TRANSPORT., WAREHOUSING	413	0	331	481	37	0	32378
66 COMMUNICA.,EXC. BRDCAST.	15	0	2	84	8	0	1742
67 RADIO, TV BROADCASTING	0	0	0	0	0	0	0
68 ELEC.,GAS,WATER,SAN.SER.	383	0	65	2214	214	0	40804
69 WHOLESALE, RETAIL TRADE	275	0	223	242	21	0	28139
70 FINANCE, INSURANCE	209	0	35	1206	118	0	24856
71 REAL ESTATE, RENTAL	351	0	59	2024	198	0	41724
72 HOTELS, PERSONAL SERV.	5	0	2	60	5	0	889
73 BUSINESS SERVICES	117	0	20	680	66	0	14012
74 RESEARCH, DEVELOPMENT	0	0	0	0	0	0	0
75 AUTO. REPAIR, SERVICES	19	0	3	111	11	0	2293
76 AMUSEMENTS	1	0	0	10	1	0	144
77 MED.,EDUC. SERVICES	9	0	2	53	5	0	1073
78 FEDERAL GOVT. ENTERPRISE	10	0	2	60	6	0	1237
79 STATE, LOCAL GOVT. ENT.	7	0	1	42	4	0	869
80 DIRECT ALLOCATED IMPORTS	2	0	0	11	1	0	221
81 TRANSFERRED IMPORTS	8000	0	6864	0	0	0	212700
82 VALUE ADDED	4603	0	760	26045	2609	0	625211
83 SECONDARY TRANSFERS-IN	12	9	15	222	1	2	8123
84 INVENTORY DEPLETION	28	0	5	164	16	0	3400
85 SCRAP PRODUCTION	0	0	0	0	0	0	0
86 SCRAP PURCHASED	36	0	8	219	22	0	5265
87 STATE TOTAL PRODUCTION	19395	9	9227	62384	6088	2	1521978

TABLE C-5

1963 INPUTS BY STATE TO
IO-7, COAL MINING

(THOUSANDS OF CURRENT DOLLARS)

INDUSTRY TITLE	1 ALABAMA	2 ARIZONA	3 ARKANSAS	4 CALIFORNIA	5 COLORADO	6 CONNECTICUT	7 DELAWARE	8 DISTRICT OF COLUMBIA	9 FLORIDA
1 LIVESTOCK, PRDTS.	1	0	0	0	1	0	0	0	0
2 OTHER AGRICULTURE PRDTS.	3	0	0	0	2	0	0	0	0
3 FORESTRY, FISHERIES	0	0	0	0	0	0	0	0	0
4 AGRI.,FORES.,FISH. SERV.	0	0	0	0	0	0	0	0	0
5 IRON, FERRO. ORES MINING	0	0	0	0	0	0	0	0	0
6 NONFERROUS ORES MINING	0	0	0	0	0	0	0	0	0
7 COAL MINING	7479	5	49	1	1536	0	0	0	0
8 CRUDE PETRO.,NATURAL GAS	0	0	0	0	0	0	0	0	0
9 STONE, CLAY MINING	0	0	0	0	0	0	0	0	0
10 CHEM.,FERT. MIN. MINING	0	0	0	0	0	0	0	0	0
11 NEW CONSTRUCTION	0	0	0	0	0	0	0	0	0
12 MAINT., REPAIR CONSTR.	527	1	15	0	141	0	0	0	0
13 ORDNANCE, ACCESSORIES	0	0	0	0	0	0	0	0	0
14 FOOD, KINDRED PRDTS.	67	9	4	0	34	0	0	0	0
15 TOBACCO MANUFACTURES	5	1	0	0	3	0	0	0	0
16 FABRICS	0	0	0	0	0	0	0	0	0
17 TEXTILE PRDTS.	0	0	0	0	0	0	0	0	0
18 APPAREL	0	0	0	0	0	0	0	0	0
19 MISC. TEXTILE PRDTS.	0	0	0	0	0	0	0	0	0
20 LUMBER, WOOD PRDTS.	661	2	5	0	188	0	0	0	0
21 WOODEN CONTAINERS	0	0	0	0	0	0	0	0	0
22 HOUSEHOLD FURNITURE	0	0	0	0	0	0	0	0	0
23 OTHER FURNITURE	0	0	0	0	0	0	0	0	0
24 PAPER, ALLIED PRDTS.	48	0	0	0	9	0	0	0	0
25 PAPERBOARD CONTAINERS	0	0	0	0	0	0	0	0	0
26 PRINTING, PUBLISHING	26	0	0	0	6	0	0	0	0
27 CHEMICALS,SELECT. PRDTS.	1720	7	13	0	331	0	0	0	0
28 PLASTICS, SYNTHETICS	0	0	0	0	0	0	0	0	0
29 DRUGS, COSMETICS	2	0	0	0	1	0	0	0	0
30 PAINT, ALLIED PRDTS.	0	0	0	0	0	0	0	0	0
31 PETROLEUM, RELATED INDS.	1050	4	8	0	202	0	0	0	0
32 RUBBER, MISC. PLASTICS	1477	7	11	0	284	0	0	0	0
33 LEATHER TANNING, PRDTS.	0	0	0	0	0	0	0	0	0
34 FOOTWEAR, LEATHER PRDTS.	1	0	0	0	0	0	0	0	0
35 GLASS, GLASS PRDTS.	0	0	0	0	0	0	0	0	0
36 STONE, CLAY PRDTS.	152	0	1	0	29	0	0	0	0
37 PRIMARY IRON, STEEL MFR.	1513	3	5	0	583	0	0	0	0
38 PRIMARY NONFERROUS MFR.	4	0	0	0	1	0	0	0	0

39 METAL CONTAINERS	0	0	0	0	0	0	0	0	0
40 FABRICATED METAL PRDTS.	0	0	0	0	0	0	0	0	0
41 SCREW MACH. PRDTS., ETC.	0	0	0	0	0	0	0	0	0
42 OTHER FAB. METAL PRDTS.	575	2	4	0	111	0	0	0	0
43 ENGINES, TURBINES	1314	0	24	0	340	0	0	0	0
44 FARM MACH., EQUIP.	0	0	0	0	0	0	0	0	0
45 CONSTRUC. MACH., EQUIP.	4086	18	31	1	786	0	0	0	0
46 MATERIAL HANDLING MACH.	26	0	0	0	5	0	0	0	0
47 METALWORKING MACHINERY	209	1	2	0	40	0	0	0	0
48 SPECIAL MACH., EQUIP.	0	0	0	0	0	0	0	0	0
49 GENERAL MACH., EQUIP.	94	0	1	0	18	0	0	0	0
50 MACHINE SHOP PRDTS.	432	0	0	0	72	0	0	0	0
51 OFFICE, COMPUT. MACHINES	0	0	0	0	0	0	0	0	0
52 SERVICE IND. MACHINES	0	0	0	0	0	0	0	0	0
53 ELECT. TRANSMISS. EQUIP.	347	1	2	0	67	0	0	0	0
54 HOUSEHOLD APPLIANCES	1	0	0	0	1	0	0	0	0
55 ELECTRIC LIGHTING EQUIP.	475	3	3	0	91	0	0	0	0
56 RADIO, TV, ETC., EQUIP.	2	0	0	0	1	0	0	0	0
57 ELECTRONIC COMPONENTS	0	0	0	0	0	0	0	0	0
58 MISC. ELECTRICAL MACH.	32	0	0	0	6	0	0	0	0
59 MOTOR VEHICLES, EQUIP.	379	1	3	0	73	0	0	0	0
60 AIRCRAFT, PARTS	0	0	0	0	0	0	0	0	0
61 OTHER TRANSPORT. EQUIP.	426	2	3	0	82	0	0	0	0
62 PROFESS., SCIEN. INSTRU.	0	0	0	0	0	0	0	0	0
63 MEDICAL, PHOTO. EQUIP.	3	0	0	0	1	0	0	0	0
64 MISC. MANUFACTURING	8	0	0	0	2	0	0	0	0
65 TRANSPORT., WAREHOUSING	1330	17	14	0	320	0	0	0	0
66 COMMUNICA.,EXC. BRDCAST.	130	0	4	0	35	0	0	0	0
67 RADIO, TV BROADCASTING	0	0	0	0	0	0	0	0	0
68 ELEC.,GAS,WATER,SAN.SER.	2186	0	2	0	641	0	0	0	0
69 WHOLESALE, RETAIL TRADE	2468	32	25	0	552	0	0	0	0
70 FINANCE, INSURANCE	1045	3	29	1	279	0	0	0	0
71 REAL ESTATE, RENTAL	2691	8	74	2	718	0	0	0	0
72 HOTELS, PERSONAL SERV.	33	4	2	0	17	0	0	0	0
73 BUSINESS SERVICES	1049	3	29	1	280	0	0	0	0
74 RESEARCH, DEVELOPMENT	0	0	0	0	0	0	0	0	0
75 AUTO. REPAIR, SERVICES	285	1	8	0	76	0	0	0	0
76 AMUSEMENTS	5	1	0	0	3	0	0	0	0
77 MED.,EDUC. SERVICES	76	0	2	0	21	0	0	0	0
78 FEDERAL GOVT. ENTERPRISE	66	0	2	0	18	0	0	0	0
79 STATE, LOCAL GOVT. ENT.	23	0	1	0	6	0	0	0	0
80 DIRECT ALLOCATED IMPORTS	8	1	0	0	4	0	0	0	0
81 TRANSFERRED IMPORTS	0	0	0	0	0	0	0	0	0
82 VALUE ADDED	62484	160	2293	64	17861	0	0	0	0
83 SECONDARY TRANSFERS-IN	11	84	17	72	23	6	0	0	22
84 INVENTORY DEPLETION	0	0	0	0	0	0	0	0	0
85 SCRAP PRODUCTION	0	0	0	0	0	0	0	0	0
86 SCRAP PURCHASED	35	0	1	0	10	0	0	0	0
87 STATE TOTAL PRODUCTION	97071	381	2688	142	25913	6	0	0	22

TABLE C-5

1963 INPUTS BY STATE TO
IO-7, COAL MINING

(THOUSANDS OF CURRENT DOLLARS)

INDUSTRY TITLE	10 GEORGIA	11 IDAHO	12 ILLINOIS	13 INDIANA	14 IOWA	15 KANSAS	16 KENTUCKY	17 LOUISIANA	18 MAINE
1 LIVESTOCK, PRDTS.	1	0	5	1	0	0	4	0	0
2 OTHER AGRICULTURE PRDTS.	1	0	14	4	0	1	12	0	0
3 FORESTRY, FISHERIES	0	0	1	0	0	0	1	0	0
4 AGRI.,FORES.,FISH. SERV.	0	0	0	0	0	0	0	0	0
5 IRON, FERRO. ORES MINING	0	0	0	0	0	0	0	0	0
6 NONFERROUS ORES MINING	0	0	0	0	0	0	0	0	0
7 COAL MINING	2	0	12871	1651	83	150	70059	0	0
8 CRUDE PETRO.,NATURAL GAS	0	0	0	0	0	0	0	0	0
9 STONE, CLAY MINING	0	0	0	0	0	0	0	0	0
10 CHEM.,FERT. MIN. MINING	0	0	0	0	0	0	0	0	0
11 NEW CONSTRUCTION	0	0	0	0	0	0	0	0	0
12 MAINT., REPAIR CONSTR.	1	0	1138	316	24	44	1965	0	0
13 ORDNANCE, ACCESSORIES	0	0	1	0	0	0	1	0	0
14 FOOD, KINDRED PRDTS.	21	0	279	78	6	11	239	0	0
15 TOBACCO MANUFACTURES	2	0	22	6	0	1	19	0	0
16 FABRICS	0	0	0	0	0	0	0	0	0
17 TEXTILE PRDTS.	0	0	0	0	0	0	0	0	0
18 APPAREL	0	0	1	0	0	0	1	0	0
19 MISC. TEXTILE PRDTS.	0	0	0	0	0	0	0	0	0
20 LUMBER, WOOD PRDTS.	1	0	989	239	8	15	1732	0	0
21 WOODEN CONTAINERS	0	0	0	0	0	0	0	0	0
22 HOUSEHOLD FURNITURE	0	0	0	0	0	0	0	0	0
23 OTHER FURNITURE	0	0	0	0	0	0	0	0	0
24 PAPER, ALLIED PRDTS.	0	0	82	22	1	2	125	0	0
25 PAPERBOARD CONTAINERS	0	0	0	0	0	0	0	0	0
26 PRINTING, PUBLISHING	0	0	45	12	0	1	69	0	0
27 CHEMICALS,SELECT. PRDTS.	1	0	2925	778	31	56	4480	0	0
28 PLASTICS, SYNTHETICS	0	0	0	0	0	0	0	0	0
29 DRUGS, COSMETICS	1	0	7	2	0	0	6	0	0
30 PAINT, ALLIED PRDTS.	0	0	0	0	0	0	1	0	0
31 PETROLEUM, RELATED INDS.	1	0	1787	476	19	34	2737	0	0
32 RUBBER, MISC. PLASTICS	1	0	2513	669	27	48	3847	0	0
33 LEATHER TANNING, PRDTS.	0	0	0	0	0	0	0	0	0
34 FOOTWEAR, LEATHER PRDTS.	1	0	4	1	0	0	3	0	0
35 GLASS, GLASS PRDTS.	0	0	0	0	0	0	0	0	0
36 STONE, CLAY PRDTS.	0	0	258	68	3	5	395	0	0
37 PRIMARY IRON, STEEL MFR.	1	0	3676	650	25	45	4119	0	0
38 PRIMARY NONFERROUS MFR.	0	0	7	2	0	0	10	0	0

39 METAL CONTAINERS	0	0	0	0	0	0	0	0	0
40 FABRICATED METAL PRDTS.	0	0	0	0	0	0	0	0	0
41 SCREW MACH. PRDTS., ETC.	0	0	0	0	0	0	0	0	0
42 OTHER FAB. METAL PRDTS.	1	0	977	260	10	18	1496	0	0
43 ENGINES, TURBINES	0	0	2853	782	48	98	4835	0	0
44 FARM MACH., EQUIP.	0	0	0	0	0	0	0	0	0
45 CONSTRUC. MACH., EQUIP.	3	0	6950	1849	72	132	10646	0	0
46 MATERIAL HANDLING MACH.	0	0	45	12	0	1	68	0	0
47 METALWORKING MACHINERY	0	0	355	95	4	7	544	0	0
48 SPECIAL MACH., EQUIP.	0	0	0	0	0	0	0	0	0
49 GENERAL MACH., EQUIP.	0	0	160	43	2	3	245	0	0
50 MACHINE SHOP PRDTS.	0	0	721	192	0	24	1105	0	0
51 OFFICE, COMPUT. MACHINES	0	0	0	0	0	0	0	0	0
52 SERVICE IND. MACHINES	0	0	0	0	0	0	0	0	0
53 ELECT. TRANSMISS. EQUIP.	0	0	590	157	6	12	905	0	0
54 HOUSEHOLD APPLIANCES	1	0	5	1	0	0	4	0	0
55 ELECTRIC LIGHTING EQUIP.	0	0	809	215	8	15	1238	0	0
56 RADIO, TV, ETC., EQUIP.	1	0	7	2	0	0	6	0	0
57 ELECTRONIC COMPONENTS	0	0	0	0	0	0	0	0	0
58 MISC. ELECTRICAL MACH.	0	0	52	15	0	0	81	0	0
59 MOTOR VEHICLES, EQUIP.	0	0	644	172	6	13	987	0	0
60 AIRCRAFT, PARTS	0	0	0	0	0	0	0	0	0
61 OTHER TRANSPORT. EQUIP.	1	0	724	193	8	14	1109	0	0
62 PROFESS., SCIEN. INSTRU.	0	0	1	0	0	0	1	0	0
63 MEDICAL, PHOTO. EQUIP.	0	0	7	2	0	0	9	0	0
64 MISC. MANUFACTURING	1	0	18	5	0	1	22	0	0
65 TRANSPORT., WAREHOUSING	33	0	2580	534	27	49	7478	0	0
66 COMMUNICA.,EXC. BRDCAST.	0	0	281	78	6	11	476	0	0
67 RADIO, TV BROADCASTING	0	0	0	0	0	0	0	0	0
68 ELEC.,GAS,WATER,SAN.SER.	0	0	7816	1931	3	6	8520	0	0
69 WHOLESALE, RETAIL TRADE	52	0	4664	1219	55	99	6855	0	0
70 FINANCE, INSURANCE	1	0	2255	626	48	87	3813	0	0
71 REAL ESTATE, RENTAL	2	0	5804	1612	124	224	9815	0	0
72 HOTELS, PERSONAL SERV.	10	0	136	38	3	5	117	0	0
73 BUSINESS SERVICES	1	0	2263	629	48	87	3828	0	0
74 RESEARCH, DEVELOPMENT	0	0	0	0	0	0	0	0	0
75 AUTO. REPAIR, SERVICES	0	0	614	171	13	24	1039	0	0
76 AMUSEMENTS	2	0	22	6	0	1	19	0	0
77 MED.,EDUC. SERVICES	1	0	168	47	4	6	277	0	0
78 FEDERAL GOVT. ENTERPRISE	0	0	142	40	3	5	241	0	0
79 STATE, LOCAL GOVT. ENT.	0	0	50	14	1	2	85	0	0
80 DIRECT ALLOCATED IMPORTS	3	0	34	9	1	1	29	0	0
81 TRANSFERRED IMPORTS	0	0	0	0	0	0	0	0	184
82 VALUE ADDED	7	0	140890	42199	3732	6725	198193	0	0
83 SECONDARY TRANSFERS-IN	40	11	38	19	16	9	18	8	1
84 INVENTORY DEPLETION	0	0	0	0	0	0	0	0	0
85 SCRAP PRODUCTION	0	0	0	0	0	0	0	0	0
86 SCRAP PURCHASED	0	0	79	24	2	4	112	0	0
87 STATE TOTAL PRODUCTION	186	11	209382	58167	4477	8096	354044	8	184

TABLE C-5

1963 INPUTS BY STATE TO
IO-7, COAL MINING

(THOUSANDS OF CURRENT DOLLARS)

INDUSTRY TITLE	19 MARYLAND	20 MASSA-CHUSETTS	21 MICHIGAN	22 MINNESOTA	23 MISSISSIPPI	24 MISSOURI	25 MONTANA	26 NEBRASKA	27 NEVADA
1 LIVESTOCK, PRDTS.	0	0	0	0	0	0	0	0	0
2 OTHER AGRICULTURE PRDTS.	0	0	0	0	0	1	0	0	0
3 FORESTRY, FISHERIES	0	0	0	0	0	0	0	0	0
4 AGRI.,FORES.,FISH. SERV.	0	0	0	0	0	0	0	0	0
5 IRON, FERRO. ORES MINING	0	0	0	0	0	0	0	0	0
6 NONFERROUS ORES MINING	0	0	0	0	0	0	0	0	0
7 COAL MINING	188	0	0	0	0	299	41	0	0
8 CRUDE PETRO.,NATURAL GAS	0	0	0	0	0	0	0	0	0
9 STONE, CLAY MINING	0	0	0	0	0	0	0	0	0
10 CHEM.,FERT. MIN. MINING	0	0	0	0	0	0	0	0	0
11 NEW CONSTRUCTION	0	0	0	0	0	0	0	0	0
12 MAINT., REPAIR CONSTR.	28	0	0	0	0	72	12	0	0
13 ORDNANCE, ACCESSORIES	0	0	0	0	0	0	0	0	0
14 FOOD, KINDRED PRDTS.	7	0	0	0	0	17	3	0	0
15 TOBACCO MANUFACTURES	1	0	0	0	0	1	0	0	0
16 FABRICS	0	0	0	0	0	0	0	0	0
17 TEXTILE PRDTS.	0	0	0	0	0	0	0	0	0
18 APPAREL	0	0	0	0	0	0	0	0	0
19 MISC. TEXTILE PRDTS.	0	0	0	0	0	0	0	0	0
20 LUMBER, WOOD PRDTS.	24	0	0	0	0	24	14	0	0
21 WOODEN CONTAINERS	0	0	0	0	0	0	0	0	0
22 HOUSEHOLD FURNITURE	0	0	0	0	0	0	0	0	0
23 OTHER FURNITURE	0	0	0	0	0	0	0	0	0
24 PAPER, ALLIED PRDTS.	2	0	0	0	0	2	2	0	0
25 PAPERBOARD CONTAINERS	0	0	0	0	0	0	0	0	0
26 PRINTING, PUBLISHING	1	0	0	0	0	1	1	0	0
27 CHEMICALS,SELECT. PRDTS.	61	0	0	0	0	90	54	0	0
28 PLASTICS, SYNTHETICS	0	0	0	0	0	0	0	0	0
29 DRUGS, COSMETICS	0	0	0	0	0	0	0	0	0
30 PAINT, ALLIED PRDTS.	0	0	0	0	0	0	0	0	0
31 PETROLEUM, RELATED INDS.	37	0	0	0	0	55	33	0	0
32 RUBBER, MISC. PLASTICS	53	0	0	0	0	77	46	0	0
33 LEATHER TANNING, PRDTS.	0	0	0	0	0	0	0	0	0
34 FOOTWEAR, LEATHER PRDTS.	0	0	0	0	0	0	0	0	0
35 GLASS, GLASS PRDTS.	0	0	0	0	0	0	0	0	0
36 STONE, CLAY PRDTS.	5	0	0	0	0	8	5	0	0
37 PRIMARY IRON, STEEL MFR.	22	0	0	0	0	74	24	0	0
38 PRIMARY NONFERROUS MFR.	0	0	0	0	0	0	0	0	0

39 METAL CONTAINERS	0	0	0	0	0	0	0	0	0
40 FABRICATED METAL PRDTS.	0	0	0	0	0	0	0	0	0
41 SCREW MACH. PRDTS., ETC.	0	0	0	0	0	0	0	0	0
42 OTHER FAB. METAL PRDTS.	20	0	0	0	0	30	18	0	0
43 ENGINES, TURBINES	57	0	0	0	0	166	18	0	0
44 FARM MACH., EQUIP.	0	0	0	0	0	0	0	0	0
45 CONSTRUC. MACH., EQUIP.	145	0	0	0	0	214	129	0	0
46 MATERIAL HANDLING MACH.	1	0	0	0	0	1	1	0	0
47 METALWORKING MACHINERY	7	0	0	0	0	11	6	0	0
48 SPECIAL MACH., EQUIP.	0	0	0	0	0	0	0	0	0
49 GENERAL MACH., EQUIP.	3	0	0	0	0	5	3	0	0
50 MACHINE SHOP PRDTS.	24	0	0	0	0	24	24	0	0
51 OFFICE, COMPUT. MACHINES	0	0	0	0	0	0	0	0	0
52 SERVICE IND. MACHINES	0	0	0	0	0	0	0	0	0
53 ELECT. TRANSMISS. EQUIP.	12	0	0	0	0	18	11	0	0
54 HOUSEHOLD APPLIANCES	0	0	0	0	0	0	0	0	0
55 ELECTRIC LIGHTING EQUIP.	18	0	0	0	0	25	15	0	0
56 RADIO, TV, ETC., EQUIP.	0	0	0	0	0	0	0	0	0
57 ELECTRONIC COMPONENTS	0	0	0	0	0	0	0	0	0
58 MISC. ELECTRICAL MACH.	0	0	0	0	0	3	0	0	0
59 MOTOR VEHICLES, EQUIP.	14	0	0	0	0	20	13	0	0
60 AIRCRAFT, PARTS	0	0	0	0	0	0	0	0	0
61 OTHER TRANSPORT. EQUIP.	15	0	0	0	0	22	13	0	0
62 PROFESS., SCIEN. INSTRU.	0	0	0	0	0	0	0	0	0
63 MEDICAL, PHOTO. EQUIP.	0	0	0	0	0	0	0	0	0
64 MISC. MANUFACTURING	0	0	0	0	0	1	0	0	0
65 TRANSPORT., WAREHOUSING	47	0	0	0	0	84	27	0	0
66 COMMUNICA.,EXC. BRDCAST.	7	0	0	0	0	18	3	0	0
67 RADIO, TV BROADCASTING	0	0	0	0	0	0	0	0	0
68 ELEC.,GAS,WATER,SAN.SER.	71	0	0	0	0	11	2	0	0
69 WHOLESALE, RETAIL TRADE	97	0	0	0	0	162	77	0	0
70 FINANCE, INSURANCE	55	0	0	0	0	142	24	0	0
71 REAL ESTATE, RENTAL	140	0	0	0	0	364	62	0	0
72 HOTELS, PERSONAL SERV.	3	0	0	0	0	8	1	0	0
73 BUSINESS SERVICES	55	0	0	0	0	142	24	0	0
74 RESEARCH, DEVELOPMENT	0	0	0	0	0	0	0	0	0
75 AUTO. REPAIR, SERVICES	15	0	0	0	0	39	7	0	0
76 AMUSEMENTS	1	0	0	0	0	1	0	0	0
77 MED.,EDUC. SERVICES	4	0	0	0	0	11	2	0	0
78 FEDERAL GOVT. ENTERPRISE	3	0	0	0	0	9	2	0	0
79 STATE, LOCAL GOVT. ENT.	1	0	0	0	0	3	1	0	0
80 DIRECT ALLOCATED IMPORTS	1	0	0	0	0	2	0	0	0
81 TRANSFERRED IMPORTS	0	0	0	0	0	0	68	0	0
82 VALUE ADDED	3818	0	0	0	0	10874	1510	0	0
83 SECONDARY TRANSFERS-IN	15	9	35	10	4	25	19	7	16
84 INVENTORY DEPLETION	0	0	0	0	0	0	0	0	0
85 SCRAP PRODUCTION	0	0	0	0	0	0	0	0	0
86 SCRAP PURCHASED	2	0	0	0	0	6	1	0	0
87 STATE TOTAL PRODUCTION	5080	9	35	10	4	13163	2316	7	16

TABLE C-5

1963 INPUTS BY STATE TO
IO-7, COAL MINING

(THOUSANDS OF CURRENT DOLLARS)

INDUSTRY TITLE	28 NEW HAMPSHIRE	29 NEW JERSEY	30 NEW MEXICO	31 NEW YORK	32 NORTH CAROLINA	33 NORTH DAKOTA	34 OHIO	35 OKLAHOMA	36 OREGON
1 LIVESTOCK, PRDTS.	0	0	0	0	0	0	4	0	0
2 OTHER AGRICULTURE PRDTS.	0	0	1	0	0	1	12	0	0
3 FORESTRY, FISHERIES	0	0	0	0	0	0	1	0	0
4 AGRI.,FORES.,FISH. SERV.	0	0	0	0	0	0	0	0	0
5 IRON, FERRO. ORES MINING	0	0	0	0	0	0	0	0	0
6 NONFERROUS ORES MINING	0	0	0	0	0	0	0	0	0
7 COAL MINING	0	0	170	0	0	170	27023	349	0
8 CRUDE PETRO.,NATURAL GAS	0	0	0	0	0	0	0	0	0
9 STONE, CLAY MINING	0	0	0	0	0	0	0	0	0
10 CHEM.,FERT. MIN. MINING	0	0	0	0	0	0	0	0	0
11 NEW CONSTRUCTION	0	0	0	0	0	0	0	0	0
12 MAINT., REPAIR CONSTR.	0	0	50	0	0	50	920	28	0
13 ORDNANCE, ACCESSORIES	0	0	0	0	0	0	1	0	0
14 FOOD, KINDRED PRDTS.	0	0	12	0	0	12	225	7	0
15 TOBACCO MANUFACTURES	0	0	1	0	0	1	18	1	0
16 FABRICS	0	0	0	0	0	0	0	0	0
17 TEXTILE PRDTS.	0	0	0	0	0	0	0	0	0
18 APPAREL	0	0	0	0	0	0	1	0	0
19 MISC. TEXTILE PRDTS.	0	0	0	0	0	0	0	0	0
20 LUMBER, WOOD PRDTS.	0	0	58	0	0	17	991	29	0
21 WOODEN CONTAINERS	0	0	0	0	0	0	0	0	0
22 HOUSEHOLD FURNITURE	0	0	0	0	0	0	0	0	0
23 OTHER FURNITURE	0	0	0	0	0	0	0	0	0
24 PAPER, ALLIED PRDTS.	0	0	6	0	0	2	81	3	0
25 PAPERBOARD CONTAINERS	0	0	0	0	0	0	0	0	0
26 PRINTING, PUBLISHING	0	0	3	0	0	1	45	1	0
27 CHEMICALS,SELECT. PRDTS.	0	0	224	0	0	63	2900	97	0
28 PLASTICS, SYNTHETICS	0	0	0	0	0	0	0	0	0
29 DRUGS, COSMETICS	0	0	0	0	0	0	6	0	0
30 PAINT, ALLIED PRDTS.	0	0	0	0	0	0	0	0	0
31 PETROLEUM, RELATED INDS.	0	0	137	0	0	39	1772	59	0
32 RUBBER, MISC. PLASTICS	0	0	192	0	0	54	2491	82	0
33 LEATHER TANNING, PRDTS.	0	0	0	0	0	0	0	0	0
34 FOOTWEAR, LEATHER PRDTS.	0	0	0	0	0	0	3	0	0
35 GLASS, GLASS PRDTS.	0	0	0	0	0	0	0	0	0
36 STONE, CLAY PRDTS.	0	0	20	0	0	5	256	9	0
37 PRIMARY IRON, STEEL MFR.	0	0	98	0	0	52	2257	99	0
38 PRIMARY NONFERROUS MFR.	0	0	1	0	0	0	7	0	0

39 METAL CONTAINERS	0	0	0	0	0	0	0	0	0
40 FABRICATED METAL PRDTS.	0	0	0	0	0	0	0	0	0
41 SCREW MACH. PRDTS., ETC.	0	0	0	0	0	0	0	0	0
42 OTHER FAB. METAL PRDTS.	0	0	75	0	0	21	969	32	0
43 ENGINES, TURBINES	0	0	113	0	0	113	2304	59	0
44 FARM MACH., EQUIP.	0	0	0	0	0	0	0	0	0
45 CONSTRUC. MACH., EQUIP.	0	0	534	0	0	150	6892	229	0
46 MATERIAL HANDLING MACH.	0	0	3	0	0	1	44	1	0
47 METALWORKING MACHINERY	0	0	27	0	0	8	352	12	0
48 SPECIAL MACH., EQUIP.	0	0	0	0	0	0	0	0	0
49 GENERAL MACH., EQUIP.	0	0	12	0	0	4	159	5	0
50 MACHINE SHOP PRDTS.	0	0	48	0	0	24	721	24	0
51 OFFICE, COMPUT. MACHINES	0	0	0	0	0	0	0	0	0
52 SERVICE IND. MACHINES	0	0	0	0	0	0	0	0	0
53 ELECT. TRANSMISS. EQUIP.	0	0	45	0	0	13	585	20	0
54 HOUSEHOLD APPLIANCES	0	0	0	0	0	0	4	0	0
55 ELECTRIC LIGHTING EQUIP.	0	0	63	0	0	18	801	28	0
56 RADIO, TV, ETC., EQUIP.	0	0	0	0	0	0	6	0	0
57 ELECTRONIC COMPONENTS	0	0	0	0	0	0	0	0	0
58 MISC. ELECTRICAL MACH.	0	0	3	0	0	0	52	3	0
59 MOTOR VEHICLES, EQUIP.	0	0	49	0	0	14	639	21	0
60 AIRCRAFT, PARTS	0	0	0	0	0	0	0	0	0
61 OTHER TRANSPORT. EQUIP.	0	0	56	0	0	15	718	24	0
62 PROFESS., SCIEN. INSTRU.	0	0	0	0	0	0	1	0	0
63 MEDICAL, PHOTO. EQUIP.	0	0	0	0	0	0	7	0	0
64 MISC. MANUFACTURING	0	0	1	0	0	1	16	0	0
65 TRANSPORT., WAREHOUSING	0	0	108	0	0	55	3503	74	0
66 COMMUNICA.,EXC. BRDCAST.	0	0	12	0	0	12	227	7	0
67 RADIO, TV BROADCASTING	0	0	0	0	0	0	0	0	0
68 ELEC.,GAS,WATER,SAN.SER.	0	0	7	0	0	7	2926	4	0
69 WHOLESALE, RETAIL TRADE	0	0	318	0	0	113	4486	147	0
70 FINANCE, INSURANCE	0	0	99	0	0	99	1823	57	0
71 REAL ESTATE, RENTAL	0	0	255	0	0	255	4692	145	0
72 HOTELS, PERSONAL SERV.	0	0	6	0	0	6	110	3	0
73 BUSINESS SERVICES	0	0	99	0	0	100	1830	57	0
74 RESEARCH, DEVELOPMENT	0	0	0	0	0	0	0	0	0
75 AUTO. REPAIR, SERVICES	0	0	27	0	0	27	497	15	0
76 AMUSEMENTS	0	0	1	0	0	1	18	1	0
77 MED.,EDUC. SERVICES	0	0	7	0	0	7	135	4	0
78 FEDERAL GOVT. ENTERPRISE	0	0	6	0	0	6	115	4	0
79 STATE, LOCAL GOVT. ENT.	0	0	2	0	0	2	41	1	0
80 DIRECT ALLOCATED IMPORTS	0	0	1	0	0	1	27	1	0
81 TRANSFERRED IMPORTS	0	0	0	574	0	166	707	0	0
82 VALUE ADDED	0	0	6226	0	0	7664	95458	3504	0
83 SECONDARY TRANSFERS-IN	1	25	37	40	15	2	37	8	10
84 INVENTORY DEPLETION	0	0	0	0	0	0	0	0	0
85 SCRAP PRODUCTION	0	0	0	0	0	0	0	0	0
86 SCRAP PURCHASED	0	0	4	0	0	4	54	2	0
87 STATE TOTAL PRODUCTION	1	25	9217	614	15	9377	169973	5256	10

TABLE C-5

1963 INPUTS BY STATE TO
IO-7, COAL MINING

(THOUSANDS OF CURRENT DOLLARS)

INDUSTRY TITLE	37 PENNSYL-VANIA	38 RHODE ISLAND	39 SOUTH CAROLINA	40 SOUTH DAKOTA	41 TENNESSEE	42 TEXAS	43 UTAH	44 VERMONT	45 VIRGINIA
1 LIVESTOCK, PRDTS.	17	0	0	0	0	0	0	0	4
2 OTHER AGRICULTURE PRDTS.	48	0	0	0	1	0	1	0	11
3 FORESTRY, FISHERIES	3	0	0	0	0	0	0	0	1
4 AGRI.,FORES.,FISH. SERV.	0	0	0	0	0	0	0	0	0
5 IRON, FERRO. ORES MINING	0	0	0	0	0	0	0	0	0
6 NONFERROUS ORES MINING	0	0	0	0	0	0	0	0	0
7 COAL MINING	180568	0	0	2	2842	24	839	0	9360
8 CRUDE PETRO.,NATURAL GAS	0	0	0	0	0	0	0	0	0
9 STONE, CLAY MINING	0	0	0	0	0	0	0	0	0
10 CHEM.,FERT. MIN. MINING	0	0	0	0	0	0	0	0	0
11 NEW CONSTRUCTION	0	0	0	0	0	0	0	0	0
12 MAINT., REPAIR CONSTR.	3759	0	0	0	149	7	182	0	868
13 ORDNANCE, ACCESSORIES	4	0	0	0	0	0	0	0	1
14 FOOD, KINDRED PRDTS.	909	0	0	0	23	4	24	0	212
15 TOBACCO MANUFACTURES	75	0	0	0	2	0	2	0	17
16 FABRICS	0	0	0	0	0	0	0	0	0
17 TEXTILE PRDTS.	0	0	0	0	0	0	0	0	0
18 APPAREL	4	0	0	0	0	0	0	0	1
19 MISC. TEXTILE PRDTS.	0	0	0	0	0	0	0	0	0
20 LUMBER, WOOD PRDTS.	3475	0	0	0	117	2	274	0	871
21 WOODEN CONTAINERS	0	0	0	0	0	0	0	0	0
22 HOUSEHOLD FURNITURE	0	0	0	0	0	0	0	0	0
23 OTHER FURNITURE	0	0	0	0	0	0	0	0	0
24 PAPER, ALLIED PRDTS.	407	0	0	0	10	0	23	0	54
25 PAPERBOARD CONTAINERS	0	0	0	0	0	0	0	0	0
26 PRINTING, PUBLISHING	230	0	0	0	5	0	13	0	30
27 CHEMICALS,SELECT. PRDTS.	9208	0	0	1	363	6	821	0	1924
28 PLASTICS, SYNTHETICS	0	0	0	0	0	0	0	0	0
29 DRUGS, COSMETICS	23	0	0	0	1	0	1	0	5
30 PAINT, ALLIED PRDTS.	1	0	0	0	0	0	0	0	0
31 PETROLEUM, RELATED INDS.	5251	0	0	1	222	3	501	0	1176
32 RUBBER, MISC. PLASTICS	7744	0	0	0	312	5	705	0	1652
33 LEATHER TANNING, PRDTS.	0	0	0	0	0	0	0	0	0
34 FOOTWEAR, LEATHER PRDTS.	15	0	0	0	0	0	0	0	3
35 GLASS, GLASS PRDTS.	2	0	0	0	0	0	0	0	0
36 STONE, CLAY PRDTS.	591	0	0	0	32	0	72	0	170
37 PRIMARY IRON, STEEL MFR.	8228	0	0	1	189	2	747	0	1796
38 PRIMARY NONFERROUS MFR.	17	0	0	0	1	0	2	0	4

39 METAL CONTAINERS	0	0	0	0	0	0	0	0	0
40 FABRICATED METAL PRDTS.	0	0	0	0	0	0	0	0	0
41 SCREW MACH. PRDTS., ETC.	0	0	0	0	0	0	0	0	0
42 OTHER FAB. METAL PRDTS.	2664	0	0	0	121	2	274	0	643
43 ENGINES, TURBINES	9325	0	0	0	360	5	444	0	2171
44 FARM MACH., EQUIP.	0	0	0	0	0	0	0	0	0
45 CONSTRUC. MACH., EQUIP.	16071	0	0	2	864	14	1950	0	4572
46 MATERIAL HANDLING MACH.	134	0	0	0	6	0	13	0	29
47 METALWORKING MACHINERY	1030	0	0	0	44	1	100	0	234
48 SPECIAL MACH., EQUIP.	0	0	0	0	0	0	0	0	0
49 GENERAL MACH., EQUIP.	492	0	0	0	20	0	45	0	105
50 MACHINE SHOP PRDTS.	4060	0	0	0	96	0	192	0	480
51 OFFICE, COMPUT. MACHINES	2	0	0	0	0	0	0	0	0
52 SERVICE IND. MACHINES	0	0	0	0	0	0	0	0	0
53 ELECT. TRANSMISS. EQUIP.	1530	0	0	0	73	1	166	0	389
54 HOUSEHOLD APPLIANCES	17	0	0	0	0	0	0	0	4
55 ELECTRIC LIGHTING EQUIP.	3072	0	0	0	101	3	227	0	531
56 RADIO, TV, ETC., EQUIP.	22	0	0	0	1	0	1	0	5
57 ELECTRONIC COMPONENTS	0	0	0	0	0	0	0	0	0
58 MISC. ELECTRICAL MACH.	265	0	0	0	6	0	15	0	35
59 MOTOR VEHICLES, EQUIP.	1565	0	0	0	80	1	181	0	424
60 AIRCRAFT, PARTS	0	0	0	0	0	0	0	0	0
61 OTHER TRANSPORT. EQUIP.	1744	0	0	0	90	1	203	0	477
62 PROFESS., SCIEN. INSTRU.	5	0	0	0	0	0	0	0	1
63 MEDICAL, PHOTO. EQUIP.	33	0	0	0	1	0	2	0	5
64 MISC. MANUFACTURING	77	0	0	0	2	0	4	0	12
65 TRANSPORT., WAREHOUSING	18600	0	0	0	383	10	406	0	1803
66 COMMUNICA.,EXC. BRDCAST.	917	0	0	0	37	2	45	0	214
67 RADIO, TV BROADCASTING	0	0	0	0	0	0	0	0	0
68 ELEC.,GAS,WATER,SAN.SER.	17374	0	0	0	489	1	919	0	3416
69 WHOLESALE, RETAIL TRADE	14079	0	0	1	540	18	1140	0	3129
70 FINANCE, INSURANCE	7344	0	0	1	294	14	361	0	1719
71 REAL ESTATE, RENTAL	18902	0	0	3	757	36	930	0	4424
72 HOTELS, PERSONAL SERV.	443	0	0	0	11	2	12	0	104
73 BUSINESS SERVICES	7372	0	0	1	295	14	363	0	1725
74 RESEARCH, DEVELOPMENT	0	0	0	0	0	0	0	0	0
75 AUTO. REPAIR, SERVICES	2000	0	0	0	80	4	98	0	468
76 AMUSEMENTS	71	0	0	0	2	0	2	0	17
77 MED.,EDUC. SERVICES	546	0	0	0	22	1	26	0	128
78 FEDERAL GOVT. ENTERPRISE	463	0	0	0	19	1	23	0	108
79 STATE, LOCAL GOVT. ENT.	165	0	0	0	7	0	8	0	38
80 DIRECT ALLOCATED IMPORTS	110	0	0	0	3	1	3	0	26
81 TRANSFERRED IMPORTS	0	0	0	0	0	0	0	175	0
82 VALUE ADDED	330545	0	0	85	18217	1103	21168	0	113910
83 SECONDARY TRANSFERS-IN	38	1	11	9	22	26	52	4	23
84 INVENTORY DEPLETION	0	0	0	0	0	0	0	0	0
85 SCRAP PRODUCTION	0	0	0	0	0	0	0	0	0
86 SCRAP PURCHASED	186	0	0	0	10	1	12	0	64
87 STATE TOTAL PRODUCTION	681847	1	11	107	27323	1314	33592	179	159596

TABLE C-5

1963 INPUTS BY STATE TO IO-7, COAL MINING

(THOUSANDS OF CURRENT DOLLARS)

INDUSTRY TITLE	46 WASHINGTON	47 WEST VIRGINIA	48 WISCONSIN	49 WYOMING	50 ALASKA	51 HAWAII	52 NATIONAL TOTAL
1 LIVESTOCK, PRDTS.	0	11	0	0	0	0	50
2 OTHER AGRICULTURE PRDTS.	0	34	0	1	0	0	148
3 FORESTRY, FISHERIES	0	2	0	0	0	0	10
4 AGRI.,FORES.,FISH. SERV.	0	0	0	0	0	0	0
5 IRON, FERRO. ORES MINING	0	108	0	0	0	0	108
6 NONFERROUS ORES MINING	0	0	0	0	0	0	0
7 COAL MINING	87	92748	0	1608	124	0	410328
8 CRUDE PETRO.,NATURAL GAS	0	0	0	0	0	0	0
9 STONE, CLAY MINING	0	0	0	0	0	0	0
10 CHEM.,FERT. MIN. MINING	0	35	0	0	0	0	35
11 NEW CONSTRUCTION	0	0	0	0	0	0	0
12 MAINT., REPAIR CONSTR.	25	4070	0	57	16	0	14466
13 ORDNANCE, ACCESSORIES	0	2	0	0	0	0	11
14 FOOD, KINDRED PRDTS.	6	632	0	14	4	0	2860
15 TOBACCO MANUFACTURES	0	51	0	1	0	0	230
16 FABRICS	0	0	0	0	0	0	0
17 TEXTILE PRDTS.	0	2	0	0	0	0	2
18 APPAREL	0	2	0	0	0	0	11
19 MISC. TEXTILE PRDTS.	0	0	0	0	0	0	0
20 LUMBER, WOOD PRDTS.	18	6962	0	29	28	0	16773
21 WOODEN CONTAINERS	0	0	0	0	0	0	0
22 HOUSEHOLD FURNITURE	0	0	0	0	0	0	0
23 OTHER FURNITURE	0	0	0	0	0	0	0
24 PAPER, ALLIED PRDTS.	0	326	0	3	2	0	1212
25 PAPERBOARD CONTAINERS	0	0	0	0	0	0	0
26 PRINTING, PUBLISHING	0	182	0	2	1	0	675
27 CHEMICALS,SELECT. PRDTS.	23	11698	0	108	84	0	38067
28 PLASTICS, SYNTHETICS	0	0	0	0	0	0	0
29 DRUGS, COSMETICS	0	18	0	0	0	0	74
30 PAINT, ALLIED PRDTS.	0	3	0	0	0	0	5
31 PETROLEUM, RELATED INDS.	14	7147	0	67	51	0	22884
32 RUBBER, MISC. PLASTICS	20	10047	0	93	72	0	32530
33 LEATHER TANNING, PRDTS.	0	0	0	0	0	0	0
34 FOOTWEAR, LEATHER PRDTS.	0	14	0	0	0	0	44
35 GLASS, GLASS PRDTS.	0	2	0	0	0	0	4
36 STONE, CLAY PRDTS.	2	1032	0	9	7	0	3135
37 PRIMARY IRON, STEEL MFR.	19	14791	0	61	108	0	39187
38 PRIMARY NONFERROUS MFR.	0	26	0	0	0	0	82

39 METAL CONTAINERS	0	0	0	0	0	0	0
40 FABRICATED METAL PRDTS.	0	0	0	0	0	0	0
41 SCREW MACH. PRDTS., ETC.	0	0	0	0	0	0	0
42 OTHER FAB. METAL PRDTS.	7	3908	0	36	28	0	12303
43 ENGINES, TURBINES	52	10096	0	129	25	0	35730
44 FARM MACH., EQUIP.	0	0	0	0	0	0	0
45 CONSTRUC. MACH., EQUIP.	53	27801	0	257	200	0	84652
46 MATERIAL HANDLING MACH.	0	179	0	2	1	0	574
47 METALWORKING MACHINERY	3	1421	0	13	10	0	4536
48 SPECIAL MACH., EQUIP.	0	0	0	0	0	0	0
49 GENERAL MACH., EQUIP.	1	641	0	6	5	0	2072
50 MACHINE SHOP PRDTS.	0	2883	0	24	24	0	11195
51 OFFICE, COMPUT. MACHINES	0	2	0	0	0	0	4
52 SERVICE IND. MACHINES	0	0	0	0	0	0	0
53 ELECT. TRANSMISS. EQUIP.	5	2362	0	22	16	0	7355
54 HOUSEHOLD APPLIANCES	0	12	0	0	0	0	51
55 ELECTRIC LIGHTING EQUIP.	5	3228	0	30	23	0	11045
56 RADIO, TV, ETC., EQUIP.	0	16	0	0	0	0	71
57 ELECTRONIC COMPONENTS	0	0	0	0	0	0	0
58 MISC. ELECTRICAL MACH.	0	215	0	3	3	0	788
59 MOTOR VEHICLES, EQUIP.	5	2579	0	24	19	0	7925
60 AIRCRAFT, PARTS	0	0	0	0	0	0	0
61 OTHER TRANSPORT. EQUIP.	6	2897	0	27	21	0	8892
62 PROFESS., SCIEN. INSTRU.	0	4	0	0	0	0	14
63 MEDICAL, PHOTO. EQUIP.	0	26	0	0	0	0	97
64 MISC. MANUFACTURING	0	59	0	1	0	0	232
65 TRANSPORT., WAREHOUSING	26	13065	0	184	48	0	50806
66 COMMUNICA.,EXC. BRDCAST.	6	994	0	14	4	0	3540
67 RADIO, TV BROADCASTING	0	0	0	0	0	0	0
68 ELEC.,GAS,WATER,SAN.SER.	3	18499	0	215	61	0	65110
69 WHOLESALE, RETAIL TRADE	46	17917	0	183	123	0	58598
70 FINANCE, INSURANCE	51	7957	0	112	30	0	28369
71 REAL ESTATE, RENTAL	130	20478	0	288	78	0	73014
72 HOTELS, PERSONAL SERV.	3	308	0	7	2	0	1394
73 BUSINESS SERVICES	51	7987	0	112	30	0	28476
74 RESEARCH, DEVELOPMENT	0	0	0	0	0	0	0
75 AUTO. REPAIR, SERVICES	14	2167	0	30	8	0	7727
76 AMUSEMENTS	0	49	0	1	0	0	225
77 MED.,EDUC. SERVICES	4	582	0	8	2	0	2092
78 FEDERAL GOVT. ENTERPRISE	3	502	0	7	2	0	1790
79 STATE, LOCAL GOVT. ENT.	1	179	0	3	1	0	635
80 DIRECT ALLOCATED IMPORTS	1	77	0	2	0	0	347
81 TRANSFERRED IMPORTS	159	0	166	0	0	0	2200
82 VALUE ADDED	4003	439379	0	6597	1558	0	1540224
83 SECONDARY TRANSFERS-IN	10	8	19	20	2	3	960
84 INVENTORY DEPLETION	0	0	0	0	0	0	0
85 SCRAP PRODUCTION	0	0	0	0	0	0	0
86 SCRAP PURCHASED	2	247	0	4	1	0	867
87 STATE TOTAL PRODUCTION	4865	738675	185	10414	2821	3	2636841

TABLE C-6

1963 INPUTS BY STATE TO
IO-8, CRUDE PETROLEUM & NATURAL GAS
(THOUSANDS OF CURRENT DOLLARS)

INDUSTRY TITLE	1 ALABAMA	2 ARIZONA	3 ARKANSAS	4 CALIFORNIA	5 COLORADO	6 CONNECTICUT	7 DELAWARE	8 DISTRICT OF COLUMBIA	9 FLORIDA
1 LIVESTOCK, PRDTS.	1	0	2	30	4	0	0	0	0
2 OTHER AGRICULTURE PRDTS.	2	0	6	89	11	0	0	0	0
3 FORESTRY, FISHERIES	0	0	0	6	1	0	0	0	0
4 AGRI.,FORES.,FISH. SERV.	0	0	0	0	0	0	0	0	0
5 IRON, FERRO. ORES MINING	0	0	0	0	0	0	0	0	0
6 NONFERROUS ORES MINING	0	0	0	0	0	0	0	0	0
7 COAL MINING	0	0	0	2	0	0	0	0	0
8 CRUDE PETRO.,NATURAL GAS	53	3	1405	23734	2397	0	0	0	530
9 STONE, CLAY MINING	0	0	0	0	0	0	0	0	0
10 CHEM.,FERT. MIN. MINING	0	0	0	0	0	0	0	0	0
11 NEW CONSTRUCTION	0	0	0	0	0	0	0	0	0
12 MAINT., REPAIR CONSTR.	712	0	2532	36641	4511	0	0	0	79
13 ORDNANCE, ACCESSORIES	0	0	1	6	1	0	0	0	0
14 FOOD, KINDRED PRDTS.	35	1	119	1710	210	0	0	0	3
15 TOBACCO MANUFACTURES	3	0	10	138	17	0	0	0	0
16 FABRICS	0	0	0	0	0	0	0	0	0
17 TEXTILE PRDTS.	3	0	13	194	21	0	0	0	1
18 APPAREL	0	0	1	6	1	0	0	0	0
19 MISC. TEXTILE PRDTS.	0	0	0	0	0	0	0	0	0
20 LUMBER, WOOD PRDTS.	0	0	1	11	1	0	0	0	0
21 WOODEN CONTAINERS	0	0	0	0	0	0	0	0	0
22 HOUSEHOLD FURNITURE	0	0	0	0	0	0	0	0	0
23 OTHER FURNITURE	0	0	0	0	0	0	0	0	0
24 PAPER, ALLIED PRDTS.	5	0	18	258	32	0	0	0	0
25 PAPERBOARD CONTAINERS	0	0	0	0	0	0	0	0	0
26 PRINTING, PUBLISHING	6	0	23	314	38	0	0	0	1
27 CHEMICALS,SELECT. PRDTS.	126	6	645	9281	961	0	0	0	28
28 PLASTICS, SYNTHETICS	0	0	0	0	0	0	0	0	0
29 DRUGS, COSMETICS	1	0	3	44	5	0	0	0	0
30 PAINT, ALLIED PRDTS.	12	0	31	458	64	0	0	0	0
31 PETROLEUM, RELATED INDS.	129	2	434	6222	766	0	0	0	7
32 RUBBER, MISC. PLASTICS	36	0	108	1552	204	0	0	0	1
33 LEATHER TANNING, PRDTS.	0	0	0	0	0	0	0	0	0
34 FOOTWEAR, LEATHER PRDTS.	1	0	2	25	3	0	0	0	0
35 GLASS, GLASS PRDTS.	0	0	0	3	0	0	0	0	0
36 STONE, CLAY PRDTS.	64	0	270	3852	421	0	0	0	8
37 PRIMARY IRON, STEEL MFR.	0	0	132	2327	236	0	0	0	66
38 PRIMARY NONFERROUS MFR.	0	0	0	0	0	0	0	0	0

39 METAL CONTAINERS	0	0	0	0	0	0	0	0	0
40 FABRICATED METAL PRDTS.	24	0	107	1646	202	0	0	0	21
41 SCREW MACH. PRDTS., ETC.	0	0	0	0	0	0	0	0	0
42 OTHER FAB. METAL PRDTS.	18	1	87	1231	126	0	0	0	1
43 ENGINES, TURBINES	36	1	137	1961	230	0	0	0	4
44 FARM MACH., EQUIP.	0	0	0	0	0	0	0	0	0
45 CONSTRUC. MACH., EQUIP.	57	1	170	2428	316	0	0	0	1
46 MATERIAL HANDLING MACH.	0	0	0	0	0	0	0	0	0
47 METALWORKING MACHINERY	0	0	0	0	0	0	0	0	0
48 SPECIAL MACH., EQUIP.	0	0	0	0	0	0	0	0	0
49 GENERAL MACH., EQUIP.	42	1	161	2326	272	0	0	0	6
50 MACHINE SHOP PRDTS.	1	0	3	40	5	0	0	0	0
51 OFFICE, COMPUT. MACHINES	0	0	0	2	0	0	0	0	0
52 SERVICE IND. MACHINES	0	0	0	0	0	0	0	0	0
53 ELECT. TRANSMISS. EQUIP.	141	4	546	7785	891	0	0	0	8
54 HOUSEHOLD APPLIANCES	1	0	2	31	4	0	0	0	0
55 ELECTRIC LIGHTING EQUIP.	0	0	2	26	3	0	0	0	0
56 RADIO, TV, ETC., EQUIP.	10	0	31	444	57	0	0	0	0
57 ELECTRONIC COMPONENTS	19	1	97	1359	140	0	0	0	1
58 MISC. ELECTRICAL MACH.	1	0	5	79	9	0	0	0	0
59 MOTOR VEHICLES, EQUIP.	6	0	22	316	37	0	0	0	0
60 AIRCRAFT, PARTS	0	0	0	0	0	0	0	0	0
61 OTHER TRANSPORT. EQUIP.	0	0	0	0	0	0	0	0	0
62 PROFESS., SCIEN. INSTRU.	0	0	43	428	43	0	0	0	0
63 MEDICAL, PHOTO. EQUIP.	1	0	4	46	6	0	0	0	0
64 MISC. MANUFACTURING	2	0	7	111	14	0	0	0	0
65 TRANSPORT., WAREHOUSING	1001	1057	444	15104	784	18	0	0	431
66 COMMUNICA.,EXC. BRDCAST.	16	0	57	832	104	0	0	0	0
67 RADIO, TV BROADCASTING	0	0	0	0	0	0	0	0	0
68 ELEC.,GAS,WATER,SAN.SER.	229	3	754	11069	1417	0	0	0	43
69 WHOLESALE, RETAIL TRADE	376	187	715	11844	1308	3	0	0	90
70 FINANCE, INSURANCE	198	38	575	8557	1019	1	0	0	27
71 REAL ESTATE, RENTAL	4439	88	15064	216813	26706	0	0	0	350
72 HOTELS, PERSONAL SERV.	17	0	58	834	103	0	0	0	2
73 BUSINESS SERVICES	213	4	725	10427	1284	0	0	0	17
74 RESEARCH, DEVELOPMENT	0	0	0	0	0	0	0	0	0
75 AUTO. REPAIR, SERVICES	84	3	282	4062	499	0	0	0	8
76 AMUSEMENTS	3	0	10	135	17	0	0	0	0
77 MED.,EDUC. SERVICES	10	0	35	502	62	0	0	0	1
78 FEDERAL GOVT. ENTERPRISE	9	0	34	497	60	0	0	0	1
79 STATE, LOCAL GOVT. ENT.	6	0	21	301	37	0	0	0	1
80 DIRECT ALLOCATED IMPORTS	4	0	14	207	26	0	0	0	0
81 TRANSFERRED IMPORTS	3721	4530	0	37681	0	77	0	0	1838
82 VALUE ADDED	13866	293	46582	669497	82603	0	0	0	919
83 SECONDARY TRANSFERS-IN	476	268	206	2133	309	323	69	73	569
84 INVENTORY DEPLETION	0	0	0	0	0	0	0	0	0
85 SCRAP PRODUCTION	0	0	0	0	0	0	0	0	0
86 SCRAP PURCHASED	0	0	0	0	0	0	0	0	0
87 STATE TOTAL PRODUCTION	26215	6494	72756	1097657	128598	422	69	73	5062

TABLE C-6

1963 INPUTS BY STATE TO
IO-8, CRUDE PETROLEUM & NATURAL GAS
(THOUSANDS OF CURRENT DOLLARS)

INDUSTRY TITLE	10 GEORGIA	11 IDAHO	12 ILLINOIS	13 INDIANA	14 IOWA	15 KANSAS	16 KENTUCKY	17 LOUISIANA	18 MAINE
1 LIVESTOCK, PRDTS.	0	0	6	1	0	12	3	68	0
2 OTHER AGRICULTURE PRDTS.	0	0	19	3	0	36	7	204	0
3 FORESTRY, FISHERIES	0	0	2	0	0	3	1	14	0
4 AGRI.,FORES.,FISH. SERV.	0	0	0	0	0	0	0	0	0
5 IRON, FERRO. ORES MINING	0	0	0	0	0	0	0	0	0
6 NONFERROUS ORES MINING	0	0	0	0	0	0	0	104	0
7 COAL MINING	0	0	1	0	0	1	0	6	0
8 CRUDE PETRO.,NATURAL GAS	0	0	2990	83	0	8475	3759	49979	0
9 STONE, CLAY MINING	0	0	0	0	0	0	0	0	0
10 CHEM.,FERT. MIN. MINING	0	0	0	0	0	0	0	0	0
11 NEW CONSTRUCTION	0	0	0	0	0	0	0	0	0
12 MAINT., REPAIR CONSTR.	0	0	8072	1187	0	14957	2770	83886	0
13 ORDNANCE, ACCESSORIES	0	0	2	0	0	3	1	15	0
14 FOOD, KINDRED PRDTS.	0	0	376	55	0	698	131	3920	0
15 TOBACCO MANUFACTURES	0	0	30	4	0	56	11	316	0
16 FABRICS	0	0	0	0	0	0	0	0	0
17 TEXTILE PRDTS.	0	0	33	4	0	82	16	492	0
18 APPAREL	0	0	2	0	0	3	1	15	0
19 MISC. TEXTILE PRDTS.	0	0	0	0	0	0	0	0	0
20 LUMBER, WOOD PRDTS.	0	0	2	0	0	5	1	29	0
21 WOODEN CONTAINERS	0	0	0	0	0	0	0	0	0
22 HOUSEHOLD FURNITURE	0	0	0	0	0	0	0	0	0
23 OTHER FURNITURE	0	0	0	0	0	0	0	0	0
24 PAPER, ALLIED PRDTS.	0	0	56	8	0	105	20	591	0
25 PAPERBOARD CONTAINERS	0	0	0	0	0	0	0	0	0
26 PRINTING, PUBLISHING	0	0	67	9	0	127	27	709	0
27 CHEMICALS,SELECT. PRDTS.	0	0	1447	196	0	4000	780	24491	0
28 PLASTICS, SYNTHETICS	0	0	0	0	0	0	0	0	0
29 DRUGS, COSMETICS	0	0	10	1	0	18	4	99	0
30 PAINT, ALLIED PRDTS.	0	0	125	19	0	178	32	914	0
31 PETROLEUM, RELATED INDS.	0	0	1358	200	0	2555	465	14370	0
32 RUBBER, MISC. PLASTICS	0	0	331	56	0	622	113	3354	0
33 LEATHER TANNING, PRDTS.	0	0	0	0	0	0	0	0	0
34 FOOTWEAR, LEATHER PRDTS.	0	0	5	1	0	10	2	56	0
35 GLASS, GLASS PRDTS.	0	0	1	0	0	1	0	6	0
36 STONE, CLAY PRDTS.	0	0	675	95	0	1660	294	9935	0
37 PRIMARY IRON, STEEL MFR.	0	0	284	0	0	785	407	4559	0
38 PRIMARY NONFERROUS MFR.	0	0	0	0	0	0	0	0	0

39 METAL CONTAINERS	0	0	0	0	0	0	0	0	0
40 FABRICATED METAL PRDTS.	0	0	344	39	0	605	190	3258	0
41 SCREW MACH. PRDTS., ETC.	0	0	0	0	0	0	0	0	0
42 OTHER FAB. METAL PRDTS.	0	0	189	27	0	544	94	3365	0
43 ENGINES, TURBINES	0	0	393	56	0	816	153	0	0
44 FARM MACH., EQUIP.	0	0	0	0	0	0	0	0	0
45 CONSTRUC. MACH., EQUIP.	0	0	592	88	0	979	172	5314	0
46 MATERIAL HANDLING MACH.	0	0	0	0	0	0	0	0	0
47 METALWORKING MACHINERY	0	0	0	0	0	0	0	0	0
48 SPECIAL MACH., EQUIP.	0	0	0	0	0	0	0	0	0
49 GENERAL MACH., EQUIP.	0	0	462	65	0	962	188	5559	0
50 MACHINE SHOP PRDTS.	0	0	9	1	0	17	3	93	0
51 OFFICE, COMPUT. MACHINES	0	0	0	0	0	0	0	6	0
52 SERVICE IND. MACHINES	0	0	0	0	0	0	0	0	0
53 ELECT. TRANSMISS. EQUIP.	0	0	1500	218	0	3294	588	19311	0
54 HOUSEHOLD APPLIANCES	0	0	7	1	0	12	3	69	0
55 ELECTRIC LIGHTING EQUIP.	0	0	5	1	0	11	2	68	0
56 RADIO, TV, ETC., EQUIP.	0	0	106	16	0	180	32	990	0
57 ELECTRONIC COMPONENTS	0	0	211	30	0	600	103	3724	0
58 MISC. ELECTRICAL MACH.	0	0	16	2	0	33	6	193	0
59 MOTOR VEHICLES, EQUIP.	0	0	64	10	0	133	23	773	0
60 AIRCRAFT, PARTS	0	0	0	0	0	0	0	0	0
61 OTHER TRANSPORT. EQUIP.	0	0	0	0	0	0	0	0	0
62 PROFESS., SCIEN. INSTRU.	0	0	86	0	0	171	43	941	0
63 MEDICAL, PHOTO. EQUIP.	0	0	10	1	0	19	4	106	0
64 MISC. MANUFACTURING	0	0	24	3	0	45	9	253	0
65 TRANSPORT., WAREHOUSING	607	0	1413	209	0	2610	457	15497	56376
66 COMMUNICA.,EXC. BRDCAST.	0	0	185	25	0	339	63	1897	0
67 RADIO, TV BROADCASTING	0	0	0	0	0	0	0	0	0
68 ELEC.,GAS,WATER,SAN.SER.	0	0	2572	356	0	4341	941	23535	0
69 WHOLESALE, RETAIL TRADE	106	0	2389	347	0	4160	781	23038	9863
70 FINANCE, INSURANCE	20	0	1817	263	0	3379	634	18983	1829
71 REAL ESTATE, RENTAL	0	0	47642	6890	0	88544	16622	496802	0
72 HOTELS, PERSONAL SERV.	0	0	183	26	0	341	64	1909	0
73 BUSINESS SERVICES	0	0	2291	331	0	4258	799	23892	0
74 RESEARCH, DEVELOPMENT	0	0	0	0	0	0	0	0	0
75 AUTO. REPAIR, SERVICES	0	0	891	128	0	1660	311	9316	0
76 AMUSEMENTS	0	0	30	4	0	55	11	308	0
77 MED.,EDUC. SERVICES	0	0	111	16	0	205	38	1152	0
78 FEDERAL GOVT. ENTERPRISE	0	0	105	15	0	202	41	1135	0
79 STATE, LOCAL GOVT. ENT.	0	0	66	10	0	123	23	691	0
80 DIRECT ALLOCATED IMPORTS	0	0	46	6	0	85	16	475	0
81 TRANSFERRED IMPORTS	2610	0	0	0	0	0	0	3619	242243
82 VALUE ADDED	0	0	147650	21446	0	273784	50831	1540391	0
83 SECONDARY TRANSFERS-IN	474	99	1759	817	400	338	382	468	80
84 INVENTORY DEPLETION	0	0	0	0	0	0	0	0	0
85 SCRAP PRODUCTION	0	0	0	0	0	0	0	0	0
86 SCRAP PURCHASED	0	0	0	0	0	0	0	0	0
87 STATE TOTAL PRODUCTION	3817	99	229122	33369	400	427237	82472	2405264	310391

TABLE C-6

1963 INPUTS BY STATE TO
IO-8, CRUDE PETROLEUM & NATURAL GAS
(THOUSANDS OF CURRENT DOLLARS)

INDUSTRY TITLE	19 MARYLAND	20 MASSA-CHUSETTS	21 MICHIGAN	22 MINNESOTA	23 MISSISSIPPI	24 MISSOURI	25 MONTANA	26 NEBRASKA	27 NEVADA
1 LIVESTOCK, PRDTS.	0	0	2	0	5	0	3	2	0
2 OTHER AGRICULTURE PRDTS.	0	0	5	0	17	0	7	5	0
3 FORESTRY, FISHERIES	0	0	0	0	1	0	1	0	0
4 AGRI.,FORES.,FISH. SERV.	0	0	0	0	0	0	0	0	0
5 IRON, FERRO. ORES MINING	0	0	0	0	0	0	0	0	0
6 NONFERROUS ORES MINING	0	0	0	0	0	0	0	0	0
7 COAL MINING	0	0	0	0	0	0	0	0	0
8 CRUDE PETRO.,NATURAL GAS	4	0	1905	0	1844	1	716	732	1
9 STONE, CLAY MINING	0	0	0	0	0	0	0	0	0
10 CHEM.,FERT. MIN. MINING	0	0	0	0	0	0	0	0	0
11 NEW CONSTRUCTION	0	0	0	0	0	0	0	0	0
12 MAINT., REPAIR CONSTR.	0	0	2137	0	7043	0	2770	2137	0
13 ORDNANCE, ACCESSORIES	0	0	0	0	1	0	1	0	0
14 FOOD, KINDRED PRDTS.	1	0	100	0	328	1	129	100	0
15 TOBACCO MANUFACTURES	0	0	8	0	26	0	11	8	0
16 FABRICS	0	0	0	0	0	0	0	0	0
17 TEXTILE PRDTS.	0	0	11	0	35	0	12	9	0
18 APPAREL	0	0	0	0	1	0	1	0	0
19 MISC. TEXTILE PRDTS.	0	0	0	0	0	0	0	0	0
20 LUMBER, WOOD PRDTS.	0	0	1	0	2	0	1	1	0
21 WOODEN CONTAINERS	0	0	0	0	0	0	0	0	0
22 HOUSEHOLD FURNITURE	0	0	0	0	0	0	0	0	0
23 OTHER FURNITURE	0	0	0	0	0	0	0	0	0
24 PAPER, ALLIED PRDTS.	0	0	15	0	49	0	19	15	0
25 PAPERBOARD CONTAINERS	0	0	0	0	0	0	0	0	0
26 PRINTING, PUBLISHING	0	0	19	0	57	0	23	18	0
27 CHEMICALS,SELECT. PRDTS.	7	0	525	0	1625	3	504	399	1
28 PLASTICS, SYNTHETICS	0	0	0	0	0	0	0	0	0
29 DRUGS, COSMETICS	0	0	3	0	8	0	4	3	0
30 PAINT, ALLIED PRDTS.	0	0	28	0	94	0	42	33	0
31 PETROLEUM, RELATED INDS.	2	0	362	0	1211	3	470	368	1
32 RUBBER, MISC. PLASTICS	0	0	92	0	311	1	130	101	0
33 LEATHER TANNING, PRDTS.	0	0	0	0	0	0	0	0	0
34 FOOTWEAR, LEATHER PRDTS.	0	0	2	0	4	0	2	2	0
35 GLASS, GLASS PRDTS.	0	0	0	0	1	0	0	0	0
36 STONE, CLAY PRDTS.	0	0	214	0	715	0	238	183	0
37 PRIMARY IRON, STEEL MFR.	0	0	199	0	132	0	57	66	0
38 PRIMARY NONFERROUS MFR.	0	0	0	0	0	0	0	0	0

39 METAL CONTAINERS	0	0	0	0	0	0	0	0	0
40 FABRICATED METAL PRDTS.	0	0	119	0	234	0	107	89	0
41 SCREW MACH. PRDTS., ETC.	0	0	0	0	0	0	0	0	0
42 OTHER FAB. METAL PRDTS.	1	0	66	0	228	1	68	53	0
43 ENGINES, TURBINES	0	0	0	0	369	1	135	106	0
44 FARM MACH., EQUIP.	0	0	0	0	0	0	0	0	0
45 CONSTRUC. MACH., EQUIP.	1	0	143	0	491	2	203	158	1
46 MATERIAL HANDLING MACH.	0	0	0	0	0	0	0	0	0
47 METALWORKING MACHINERY	0	0	0	0	0	0	0	0	0
48 SPECIAL MACH., EQUIP.	0	0	0	0	0	0	0	0	0
49 GENERAL MACH., EQUIP.	1	0	137	0	429	1	158	124	0
50 MACHINE SHOP PRDTS.	0	0	2	0	8	0	3	2	0
51 OFFICE, COMPUT. MACHINES	0	0	0	0	0	0	0	0	0
52 SERVICE IND. MACHINES	0	0	0	0	0	0	0	0	0
53 ELECT. TRANSMISS. EQUIP.	4	0	439	0	1483	4	523	408	2
54 HOUSEHOLD APPLIANCES	0	0	2	0	6	0	3	2	0
55 ELECTRIC LIGHTING EQUIP.	0	0	2	0	5	0	2	1	0
56 RADIO, TV, ETC., EQUIP.	0	0	26	0	89	0	36	28	0
57 ELECTRONIC COMPONENTS	1	0	73	0	252	1	76	59	0
58 MISC. ELECTRICAL MACH.	0	0	5	0	15	0	5	4	0
59 MOTOR VEHICLES, EQUIP.	0	0	18	0	62	0	23	18	0
60 AIRCRAFT, PARTS	0	0	0	0	0	0	0	0	0
61 OTHER TRANSPORT. EQUIP.	0	0	0	0	0	0	0	0	0
62 PROFESS., SCIEN. INSTRU.	0	0	43	0	86	0	43	43	0
63 MEDICAL, PHOTO. EQUIP.	0	0	2	0	9	0	4	2	0
64 MISC. MANUFACTURING	0	0	7	0	21	0	8	6	0
65 TRANSPORT., WAREHOUSING	3438	1737	33063	0	1255	4	3629	380	1
66 COMMUNICA.,EXC. BRDCAST.	0	0	50	0	160	0	63	50	0
67 RADIO, TV BROADCASTING	0	0	0	0	0	0	0	0	0
68 ELEC.,GAS,WATER,SAN.SER.	3	0	695	0	2026	6	856	680	1
69 WHOLESALE, RETAIL TRADE	604	304	6335	0	2006	6	1365	637	1
70 FINANCE, INSURANCE	115	56	1548	0	1589	4	724	487	1
71 REAL ESTATE, RENTAL	86	0	12773	0	41651	118	16297	12769	33
72 HOTELS, PERSONAL SERV.	0	0	50	0	160	1	62	50	0
73 BUSINESS SERVICES	4	0	614	0	2003	6	784	614	2
74 RESEARCH, DEVELOPMENT	0	0	0	0	0	0	0	0	0
75 AUTO. REPAIR, SERVICES	3	0	240	0	782	3	306	238	0
76 AMUSEMENTS	0	0	8	0	26	0	10	8	0
77 MED.,EDUC. SERVICES	0	0	29	0	96	0	38	29	0
78 FEDERAL GOVT. ENTERPRISE	0	0	30	0	92	0	36	28	0
79 STATE, LOCAL GOVT. ENT.	0	0	18	0	58	0	23	18	0
80 DIRECT ALLOCATED IMPORTS	0	0	12	0	40	0	16	12	0
81 TRANSFERRED IMPORTS	14760	7465	140502	0	0	0	13497	0	0
82 VALUE ADDED	289	0	39412	0	129343	393	50569	39601	108
83 SECONDARY TRANSFERS-IN	479	741	1237	485	269	574	143	136	76
84 INVENTORY DEPLETION	0	0	0	0	0	0	0	0	0
85 SCRAP PRODUCTION	0	0	0	0	0	0	0	0	0
86 SCRAP PURCHASED	0	0	0	0	0	0	0	0	0
87 STATE TOTAL PRODUCTION	19803	10304	243327	485	198853	1134	94955	61022	229

TABLE C-6

1963 INPUTS BY STATE TO
IO-8, CRUDE PETROLEUM & NATURAL GAS
(THOUSANDS OF CURRENT DOLLARS)

INDUSTRY TITLE	28 NEW HAMPSHIRE	29 NEW JERSEY	30 NEW MEXICO	31 NEW YORK	32 NORTH CAROLINA	33 NORTH DAKOTA	34 OHIO	35 OKLAHOMA	36 OREGON
1 LIVESTOCK, PRDTS.	0	0	13	0	0	2	1	22	0
2 OTHER AGRICULTURE PRDTS.	0	0	39	1	0	6	3	66	0
3 FORESTRY, FISHERIES	0	0	3	0	0	0	0	5	0
4 AGRI.,FORES.,FISH. SERV.	0	0	0	0	0	0	0	0	0
5 IRON, FERRO. ORES MINING	0	0	0	0	0	0	0	0	0
6 NONFERROUS ORES MINING	0	0	0	0	0	0	0	0	0
7 COAL MINING	0	0	1	0	0	0	0	2	0
8 CRUDE PETRO.,NATURAL GAS	0	0	17227	32	0	2618	125	22270	1
9 STONE, CLAY MINING	0	0	0	0	0	0	0	0	0
10 CHEM.,FERT. MIN. MINING	0	0	0	0	0	0	0	0	0
11 NEW CONSTRUCTION	0	0	0	0	0	0	0	0	0
12 MAINT., REPAIR CONSTR.	0	0	15907	317	0	2612	950	27144	0
13 ORDNANCE, ACCESSORIES	0	0	3	0	0	1	0	4	0
14 FOOD, KINDRED PRDTS.	0	0	744	15	0	121	42	1268	1
15 TOBACCO MANUFACTURES	0	0	60	1	0	10	4	102	0
16 FABRICS	0	0	0	0	0	0	0	0	0
17 TEXTILE PRDTS.	0	0	90	1	0	13	5	148	0
18 APPAREL	0	0	3	0	0	1	0	4	0
19 MISC. TEXTILE PRDTS.	0	0	0	0	0	0	0	0	0
20 LUMBER, WOOD PRDTS.	0	0	5	0	0	1	0	9	0
21 WOODEN CONTAINERS	0	0	0	0	0	0	0	0	0
22 HOUSEHOLD FURNITURE	0	0	0	0	0	0	0	0	0
23 OTHER FURNITURE	0	0	0	0	0	0	0	0	0
24 PAPER, ALLIED PRDTS.	0	0	113	2	0	18	6	192	0
25 PAPERBOARD CONTAINERS	0	0	0	0	0	0	0	0	0
26 PRINTING, PUBLISHING	0	0	146	2	0	24	7	240	0
27 CHEMICALS,SELECT. PRDTS.	0	0	4361	69	0	552	253	7141	3
28 PLASTICS, SYNTHETICS	0	0	0	0	0	0	0	0	0
29 DRUGS, COSMETICS	0	0	19	0	0	3	1	32	0
30 PAINT, ALLIED PRDTS.	0	0	187	5	0	37	10	329	0
31 PETROLEUM, RELATED INDS.	0	0	2665	56	0	430	159	4585	3
32 RUBBER, MISC. PLASTICS	0	0	648	15	0	115	37	1130	1
33 LEATHER TANNING, PRDTS.	0	0	0	0	0	0	0	0	0
34 FOOTWEAR, LEATHER PRDTS.	0	0	11	0	0	2	1	19	0
35 GLASS, GLASS PRDTS.	0	0	1	0	0	0	0	2	0
36 STONE, CLAY PRDTS.	0	0	1707	32	0	230	111	2891	0
37 PRIMARY IRON, STEEL MFR.	0	0	1816	0	0	284	0	2270	0
38 PRIMARY NONFERROUS MFR.	0	0	0	0	0	0	0	0	0

39 METAL CONTAINERS	0	0	0	0	0	0	0	0	0
40 FABRICATED METAL PRDTS.	0	0	937	9	0	163	21	1364	0
41 SCREW MACH. PRDTS., ETC.	0	0	0	0	0	0	0	0	0
42 OTHER FAB. METAL PRDTS.	0	0	546	10	0	65	37	926	0
43 ENGINES, TURBINES	0	0	870	16	0	131	50	1467	1
44 FARM MACH., EQUIP.	0	0	0	0	0	0	0	0	0
45 CONSTRUC. MACH., EQUIP.	0	0	1001	24	0	176	61	1760	1
46 MATERIAL HANDLING MACH.	0	0	0	0	0	0	0	0	0
47 METALWORKING MACHINERY	0	0	0	0	0	0	0	0	0
48 SPECIAL MACH., EQUIP.	0	0	0	0	0	0	0	0	0
49 GENERAL MACH., EQUIP.	0	0	1053	19	0	159	59	1755	1
50 MACHINE SHOP PRDTS.	0	0	18	0	0	3	1	30	0
51 OFFICE, COMPUT. MACHINES	0	0	2	0	0	0	0	2	0
52 SERVICE IND. MACHINES	0	0	0	0	0	0	0	0	0
53 ELECT. TRANSMISS. EQUIP.	0	0	3389	67	0	485	214	5790	4
54 HOUSEHOLD APPLIANCES	0	0	13	0	0	2	1	23	0
55 ELECTRIC LIGHTING EQUIP.	0	0	12	0	0	2	1	20	0
56 RADIO, TV, ETC., EQUIP.	0	0	184	4	0	31	11	322	0
57 ELECTRONIC COMPONENTS	0	0	602	11	0	72	41	1048	0
58 MISC. ELECTRICAL MACH.	0	0	35	1	0	5	2	59	0
59 MOTOR VEHICLES, EQUIP.	0	0	133	3	0	20	9	232	0
60 AIRCRAFT, PARTS	0	0	0	0	0	0	0	0	0
61 OTHER TRANSPORT. EQUIP.	0	0	0	0	0	0	0	0	0
62 PROFESS., SCIEN. INSTRU.	0	0	214	0	0	43	0	342	0
63 MEDICAL, PHOTO. EQUIP.	0	0	21	0	0	4	1	35	0
64 MISC. MANUFACTURING	0	0	50	1	0	8	2	84	0
65 TRANSPORT., WAREHOUSING	0	6263	2657	27696	51	8120	165	4631	4
66 COMMUNICA.,EXC. BRDCAST.	0	0	361	6	0	60	22	616	0
67 RADIO, TV BROADCASTING	0	0	0	0	0	0	0	0	0
68 ELEC.,GAS,WATER,SAN.SER.	0	0	5106	94	0	891	235	8384	6
69 WHOLESALE, RETAIL TRADE	0	1096	4437	4929	9	2098	251	7601	6
70 FINANCE, INSURANCE	0	203	3598	971	2	832	206	6133	4
71 REAL ESTATE, RENTAL	0	0	94321	1933	0	15285	5402	160744	108
72 HOTELS, PERSONAL SERV.	0	0	363	7	0	59	21	618	1
73 BUSINESS SERVICES	0	0	4536	93	0	735	260	7731	5
74 RESEARCH, DEVELOPMENT	0	0	0	0	0	0	0	0	0
75 AUTO. REPAIR, SERVICES	0	0	1767	37	0	288	102	3014	3
76 AMUSEMENTS	0	0	58	1	0	10	4	100	0
77 MED.,EDUC. SERVICES	0	0	218	4	0	35	12	372	0
78 FEDERAL GOVT. ENTERPRISE	0	0	226	4	0	36	12	375	0
79 STATE, LOCAL GOVT. ENT.	0	0	131	3	0	21	8	224	0
80 DIRECT ALLOCATED IMPORTS	0	0	90	2	0	15	5	153	0
81 TRANSFERRED IMPORTS	0	26910	0	118754	219	33041	0	0	3
82 VALUE ADDED	0	0	289379	6032	0	46880	16783	495061	359
83 SECONDARY TRANSFERS-IN	82	896	162	2254	416	54	1766	318	160
84 INVENTORY DEPLETION	0	0	0	0	0	0	0	0	0
85 SCRAP PRODUCTION	0	0	0	0	0	0	0	0	0
86 SCRAP PURCHASED	0	0	0	0	0	0	0	0	0
87 STATE TOTAL PRODUCTION	82	35367	462259	163533	696	116910	27480	781209	675

TABLE C-6

1963 INPUTS BY STATE TO
IO-8, CRUDE PETROLEUM & NATURAL GAS
(THOUSANDS OF CURRENT DOLLARS)

INDUSTRY TITLE	37 PENNSYL-VANIA	38 RHODE ISLAND	39 SOUTH CAROLINA	40 SOUTH DAKOTA	41 TENNESSEE	42 TEXAS	43 UTAH	44 VERMONT	45 VIRGINIA
1 LIVESTOCK, PRDTS.	2	0	0	0	0	115	3	0	0
2 OTHER AGRICULTURE PRDTS.	4	0	0	0	0	341	9	0	0
3 FORESTRY, FISHERIES	0	0	0	0	0	24	1	0	0
4 AGRI.,FORES.,FISH. SERV.	0	0	0	0	0	0	0	0	0
5 IRON, FERRO. ORES MINING	0	0	0	0	0	0	0	0	0
6 NONFERROUS ORES MINING	0	0	0	0	0	104	0	0	0
7 COAL MINING	0	0	0	0	0	9	0	0	0
8 CRUDE PETRO.,NATURAL GAS	1085	0	0	0	0	143368	1382	0	7
9 STONE, CLAY MINING	0	0	0	0	0	0	0	0	0
10 CHEM.,FERT. MIN. MINING	0	0	0	0	0	0	0	0	0
11 NEW CONSTRUCTION	0	0	0	0	0	0	0	0	0
12 MAINT., REPAIR CONSTR.	1741	0	0	0	0	140548	3719	0	0
13 ORDNANCE, ACCESSORIES	0	0	0	0	0	25	1	0	0
14 FOOD, KINDRED PRDTS.	81	0	0	0	0	6565	174	0	1
15 TOBACCO MANUFACTURES	6	0	0	0	0	528	14	0	0
16 FABRICS	0	0	0	0	0	0	0	0	0
17 TEXTILE PRDTS.	13	0	0	0	0	780	18	0	0
18 APPAREL	0	0	0	0	0	25	1	0	0
19 MISC. TEXTILE PRDTS.	0	0	0	0	0	0	0	0	0
20 LUMBER, WOOD PRDTS.	1	0	0	0	0	45	1	0	0
21 WOODEN CONTAINERS	0	0	0	0	0	0	0	0	0
22 HOUSEHOLD FURNITURE	0	0	0	0	0	0	0	0	0
23 OTHER FURNITURE	0	0	0	0	0	0	0	0	0
24 PAPER, ALLIED PRDTS.	12	0	0	0	0	999	26	0	0
25 PAPERBOARD CONTAINERS	0	0	0	0	0	0	0	0	0
26 PRINTING, PUBLISHING	14	0	0	0	0	1280	32	0	0
27 CHEMICALS,SELECT. PRDTS.	646	0	0	1	0	37802	802	0	12
28 PLASTICS, SYNTHETICS	0	0	0	0	0	0	0	0	0
29 DRUGS, COSMETICS	2	0	0	0	0	166	4	0	0
30 PAINT, ALLIED PRDTS.	12	0	0	0	0	1674	52	0	0
31 PETROLEUM, RELATED INDS.	300	0	0	1	1	23554	637	0	4
32 RUBBER, MISC. PLASTICS	60	0	0	0	0	5769	168	0	0
33 LEATHER TANNING, PRDTS.	0	0	0	0	0	0	0	0	0
34 FOOTWEAR, LEATHER PRDTS.	1	0	0	0	0	98	3	0	0
35 GLASS, GLASS PRDTS.	0	0	0	0	0	10	0	0	0
36 STONE, CLAY PRDTS.	254	0	0	0	0	14930	357	0	8
37 PRIMARY IRON, STEEL MFR.	95	0	0	0	0	15077	123	0	0
38 PRIMARY NONFERROUS MFR.	0	0	0	0	0	0	0	0	0

39 METAL CONTAINERS	0	0	0	0	0	0	0	0	0
40 FABRICATED METAL PRDTS.	53	0	0	0	0	8008	145	0	0
41 SCREW MACH. PRDTS., ETC.	0	0	0	0	0	0	0	0	0
42 OTHER FAB. METAL PRDTS.	92	0	0	0	0	4759	109	0	2
43 ENGINES, TURBINES	106	0	0	0	0	7632	191	0	1
44 FARM MACH., EQUIP.	0	0	0	0	0	0	0	0	0
45 CONSTRUC. MACH., EQUIP.	97	0	0	1	0	8924	263	0	1
46 MATERIAL HANDLING MACH.	0	0	0	0	0	0	0	0	0
47 METALWORKING MACHINERY	0	0	0	0	0	0	0	0	0
48 SPECIAL MACH., EQUIP.	0	0	0	0	0	0	0	0	0
49 GENERAL MACH., EQUIP.	125	0	0	0	0	9217	224	0	2
50 MACHINE SHOP PRDTS.	2	0	0	0	0	155	4	0	0
51 OFFICE, COMPUT. MACHINES	0	0	0	0	0	9	0	0	0
52 SERVICE IND. MACHINES	0	0	0	0	0	0	0	0	0
53 ELECT. TRANSMISS. EQUIP.	457	0	0	2	0	29771	752	0	8
54 HOUSEHOLD APPLIANCES	2	0	0	0	0	117	4	0	0
55 ELECTRIC LIGHTING EQUIP.	2	0	0	0	0	102	2	0	0
56 RADIO, TV, ETC., EQUIP.	19	0	0	0	0	1634	47	0	0
57 ELECTRONIC COMPONENTS	100	0	0	0	0	5295	120	0	2
58 MISC. ELECTRICAL MACH.	4	0	0	0	0	306	8	0	0
59 MOTOR VEHICLES, EQUIP.	18	0	0	0	0	1177	32	0	0
60 AIRCRAFT, PARTS	0	0	0	0	0	0	0	0	0
61 OTHER TRANSPORT. EQUIP.	0	0	0	0	0	0	0	0	0
62 PROFESS., SCIEN. INSTRU.	0	0	0	0	0	1754	43	0	0
63 MEDICAL, PHOTO. EQUIP.	2	0	0	0	0	186	5	0	0
64 MISC. MANUFACTURING	5	0	0	0	0	437	11	0	0
65 TRANSPORT., WAREHOUSING	56648	7	1195	1	1	28018	657	8107	98
66 COMMUNICA., EXC. BRDCAST.	38	0	0	0	0	3191	85	0	0
67 RADIO, TV BROADCASTING	0	0	0	0	0	0	0	0	0
68 ELEC.,GAS,WATER,SAN.SER.	420	0	0	1	1	44812	1127	0	3
69 WHOLESALE, RETAIL TRADE	10297	1	209	1	1	40045	1076	1418	21
70 FINANCE, INSURANCE	2219	0	39	1	1	31895	841	263	8
71 REAL ESTATE, RENTAL	10238	0	0	33	23	832141	22050	0	128
72 HOTELS, PERSONAL SERV.	39	0	0	0	0	3199	85	0	1
73 BUSINESS SERVICES	492	0	0	2	1	40019	1060	0	6
74 RESEARCH, DEVELOPMENT	0	0	0	0	0	0	0	0	0
75 AUTO. REPAIR, SERVICES	193	0	0	0	0	15594	413	0	3
76 AMUSEMENTS	6	0	0	0	0	516	14	0	0
77 MED.,EDUC. SERVICES	24	0	0	0	0	1927	51	0	0
78 FEDERAL GOVT. ENTERPRISE	24	0	0	0	0	1983	49	0	0
79 STATE, LOCAL GOVT. ENT.	14	0	0	0	0	1158	31	0	0
80 DIRECT ALLOCATED IMPORTS	10	0	0	0	0	796	21	0	0
81 TRANSFERRED IMPORTS	242107	28	5136	0	0	19159	0	34836	402
82 VALUE ADDED	31658	0	0	108	78	2555121	68362	0	415
83 SECONDARY TRANSFERS-IN	1695	98	209	60	175	1373	167	43	498
84 INVENTORY DEPLETION	0	0	0	0	0	0	0	0	0
85 SCRAP PRODUCTION	0	0	0	0	0	0	0	0	0
86 SCRAP PURCHASED	0	0	0	0	0	0	0	0	0
87 STATE TOTAL PRODUCTION	361536	134	6789	212	282	4094266	105576	44668	1631

TABLE C-6

1963 INPUTS BY STATE TO
IO-8, CRUDE PETROLEUM & NATURAL GAS
(THOUSANDS OF CURRENT DOLLARS)

INDUSTRY TITLE	46 WASHINGTON	47 WEST VIRGINIA	48 WISCONSIN	49 WYOMING	50 ALASKA	51 HAWAII	52 NATIONAL TOTAL
1 LIVESTOCK, PRDTS.	0	2	0	11	0	0	310
2 OTHER AGRICULTURE PRDTS.	1	6	0	33	1	0	921
3 FORESTRY, FISHERIES	0	0	0	3	0	0	65
4 AGRI.,FORES.,FISH. SERV.	0	0	0	0	0	0	0
5 IRON, FERRO. ORES MINING	0	0	0	0	0	0	0
6 NONFERROUS ORES MINING	0	0	0	0	0	0	208
7 COAL MINING	0	0	0	1	0	0	23
8 CRUDE PETRO.,NATURAL GAS	21	5187	0	4516	58	0	296508
9 STONE, CLAY MINING	0	0	0	0	0	0	0
10 CHEM.,FERT. MIN. MINING	0	0	0	0	0	0	0
11 NEW CONSTRUCTION	0	0	0	0	0	0	0
12 MAINT., REPAIR CONSTR.	317	2532	0	13532	554	0	379307
13 ORDNANCE, ACCESSORIES	0	1	0	3	0	0	69
14 FOOD, KINDRED PRDTS.	13	118	0	632	25	0	17717
15 TOBACCO MANUFACTURES	1	10	0	51	2	0	1427
16 FABRICS	0	0	0	0	0	0	0
17 TEXTILE PRDTS.	1	22	0	61	3	0	2081
18 APPAREL	0	1	0	3	0	0	69
19 MISC. TEXTILE PRDTS.	0	0	0	0	0	0	0
20 LUMBER, WOOD PRDTS.	0	1	0	4	0	0	122
21 WOODEN CONTAINERS	0	0	0	0	0	0	0
22 HOUSEHOLD FURNITURE	0	0	0	0	0	0	0
23 OTHER FURNITURE	0	0	0	0	0	0	0
24 PAPER, ALLIED PRDTS.	2	19	0	94	4	0	2678
25 PAPERBOARD CONTAINERS	0	0	0	0	0	0	0
26 PRINTING, PUBLISHING	2	26	0	111	3	0	3325
27 CHEMICALS,SELECT. PRDTS.	48	1192	0	2772	123	0	100802
28 PLASTICS, SYNTHETICS	0	0	0	0	0	0	0
29 DRUGS, COSMETICS	0	3	0	16	1	0	450
30 PAINT, ALLIED PRDTS.	5	9	0	196	7	0	4553
31 PETROLEUM, RELATED INDS.	50	416	0	2314	90	0	64200
32 RUBBER, MISC. PLASTICS	14	68	0	620	23	0	15730
33 LEATHER TANNING, PRDTS.	0	0	0	0	0	0	0
34 FOOTWEAR, LEATHER PRDTS.	0	2	0	9	0	0	261
35 GLASS, GLASS PRDTS.	0	0	0	1	0	0	26
36 STONE, CLAY PRDTS.	24	405	0	1255	56	0	40884
37 PRIMARY IRON, STEEL MFR.	0	549	0	397	0	0	29861
38 PRIMARY NONFERROUS MFR.	0	0	0	0	0	0	0

39 METAL CONTAINERS	0	0	0	0	0	0	0
40 FABRICATED METAL PRDTS.	9	184	0	522	15	0	18415
41 SCREW MACH. PRDTS., ETC.	0	0	0	0	0	0	0
42 OTHER FAB. METAL PRDTS.	7	152	0	375	18	0	13198
43 ENGINES, TURBINES	14	168	0	685	28	0	15758
44 FARM MACH., EQUIP.	0	0	0	0	0	0	0
45 CONSTRUC. MACH., EQUIP.	21	106	0	971	36	0	24560
46 MATERIAL HANDLING MACH.	0	0	0	0	0	0	0
47 METALWORKING MACHINERY	0	0	0	0	0	0	0
48 SPECIAL MACH., EQUIP.	0	0	0	0	0	0	0
49 GENERAL MACH., EQUIP.	16	210	0	801	32	0	24567
50 MACHINE SHOP PRDTS.	0	3	0	15	0	0	418
51 OFFICE, COMPUT. MACHINES	0	0	0	0	0	0	21
52 SERVICE IND. MACHINES	0	0	0	0	0	0	0
53 ELECT. TRANSMISS. EQUIP.	53	703	0	2680	113	0	81637
54 HOUSEHOLD APPLIANCES	0	2	0	11	0	0	318
55 ELECTRIC LIGHTING EQUIP.	0	3	0	8	0	0	280
56 RADIO, TV, ETC., EQUIP.	4	22	0	174	7	0	4504
57 ELECTRONIC COMPONENTS	8	165	0	418	19	0	14648
58 MISC. ELECTRICAL MACH.	1	7	0	27	1	0	829
59 MOTOR VEHICLES, EQUIP.	2	25	0	113	5	0	3274
60 AIRCRAFT, PARTS	0	0	0	0	0	0	0
61 OTHER TRANSPORT. EQUIP.	0	0	0	0	0	0	0
62 PROFESS., SCIEN. INSTRU.	0	43	0	128	0	0	4537
63 MEDICAL, PHOTO. EQUIP.	0	4	0	16	1	0	489
64 MISC. MANUFACTURING	1	8	0	40	2	0	1159
65 TRANSPORT., WAREHOUSING	9736	393	7675	2393	94	4321	308446
66 COMMUNICA.,EXC. BRDCAST.	6	57	0	308	13	0	8604
67 RADIO, TV BROADCASTING	0	0	0	0	0	0	0
68 ELEC.,GAS,WATER,SAN.SER.	87	725	0	4134	144	0	115697
69 WHOLESALE, RETAIL TRADE	1779	598	1343	3944	147	756	148529
70 FINANCE, INSURANCE	379	569	249	3059	118	140	93594
71 REAL ESTATE, RENTAL	1689	14904	0	80176	3083	0	2245945
72 HOTELS, PERSONAL SERV.	6	57	0	308	12	0	8636
73 BUSINESS SERVICES	81	717	0	3856	148	0	108010
74 RESEARCH, DEVELOPMENT	0	0	0	0	0	0	0
75 AUTO. REPAIR, SERVICES	31	280	0	1503	58	0	42102
76 AMUSEMENTS	1	10	0	49	2	0	1396
77 MED.,EDUC. SERVICES	4	35	0	186	7	0	5199
78 FEDERAL GOVT. ENTERPRISE	4	40	0	177	7	0	5222
79 STATE, LOCAL GOVT. ENT.	3	20	0	112	4	0	3125
80 DIRECT ALLOCATED IMPORTS	2	14	0	77	3	0	2147
81 TRANSFERRED IMPORTS	41616	0	32979	0	0	18565	1046300
82 VALUE ADDED	5235	45079	0	248722	9574	0	6926423
83 SECONDARY TRANSFERS-IN	187	395	534	97	16	59	25100
84 INVENTORY DEPLETION	0	0	0	0	0	0	0
85 SCRAP PRODUCTION	0	0	0	0	0	0	0
86 SCRAP PURCHASED	0	0	0	0	0	0	0
87 STATE TOTAL PRODUCTION	61482	76267	42781	382720	14657	23841	12264684

TABLE C-7

1963 INPUTS BY STATE TO
IO-9, STONE & CLAY MINING & QUARRYING
(THOUSANDS OF CURRENT DOLLARS)

INDUSTRY TITLE	1 ALABAMA	2 ARIZONA	3 ARKANSAS	4 CALIFORNIA	5 COLORADO	6 CONNECTICUT	7 DELAWARE	8 DISTRICT OF COLUMBIA	9 FLORIDA
1 LIVESTOCK, PRDTS.	2	0	2	6	0	0	0	0	2
2 OTHER AGRICULTURE PRDTS.	3	1	3	17	1	1	0	0	4
3 FORESTRY, FISHERIES	0	0	0	10	0	0	0	0	0
4 AGRI.,FORES.,FISH. SERV.	0	0	0	0	0	0	0	0	0
5 IRON, FERRO. ORES MINING	0	0	0	0	0	0	0	0	0
6 NONFERROUS ORES MINING	0	0	0	0	0	0	0	0	0
7 COAL MINING	0	0	386	0	0	0	0	0	0
8 CRUDE PETRO.,NATURAL GAS	0	0	0	0	0	0	0	0	0
9 STONE, CLAY MINING	716	77	426	1152	258	145	13	0	689
10 CHEM.,FERT. MIN. MINING	0	0	0	0	0	0	0	0	0
11 NEW CONSTRUCTION	0	0	0	0	0	0	0	0	0
12 MAINT., REPAIR CONSTR.	172	78	210	1112	111	93	10	0	319
13 ORDNANCE, ACCESSORIES	0	0	0	11	0	0	0	0	0
14 FOOD, KINDRED PRDTS.	44	20	54	295	29	23	1	0	83
15 TOBACCO MANUFACTURES	3	1	4	24	3	1	0	0	7
16 FABRICS	0	0	0	0	0	0	0	0	0
17 TEXTILE PRDTS.	2	1	3	11	1	1	0	0	3
18 APPAREL	0	0	0	11	0	0	0	0	0
19 MISC. TEXTILE PRDTS.	0	0	0	0	0	0	0	0	0
20 LUMBER, WOOD PRDTS.	0	0	0	41	0	0	0	0	0
21 WOODEN CONTAINERS	0	0	0	0	0	0	0	0	0
22 HOUSEHOLD FURNITURE	0	0	0	0	0	0	0	0	0
23 OTHER FURNITURE	0	0	0	0	0	0	0	0	0
24 PAPER, ALLIED PRDTS.	80	38	151	601	60	49	3	0	122
25 PAPERBOARD CONTAINERS	0	0	0	0	0	0	0	0	0
26 PRINTING, PUBLISHING	8	3	15	60	6	6	0	0	12
27 CHEMICALS,SELECT. PRDTS.	560	83	1479	1354	91	243	7	0	1036
28 PLASTICS, SYNTHETICS	0	0	0	0	0	0	0	0	0
29 DRUGS, COSMETICS	1	0	3	11	1	1	0	0	3
30 PAINT, ALLIED PRDTS.	0	0	1	3	0	0	0	0	1
31 PETROLEUM, RELATED INDS.	581	240	628	2724	338	399	40	0	853
32 RUBBER, MISC. PLASTICS	932	551	1471	8619	885	622	57	0	1293
33 LEATHER TANNING, PRDTS.	0	0	0	0	0	0	0	0	0
34 FOOTWEAR, LEATHER PRDTS.	0	0	2	8	0	0	0	0	2
35 GLASS, GLASS PRDTS.	0	0	0	0	0	0	0	0	0
36 STONE, CLAY PRDTS.	50	29	77	457	47	33	3	0	68
37 PRIMARY IRON, STEEL MFR.	390	155	802	2443	236	221	16	0	624
38 PRIMARY NONFERROUS MFR.	22	18	18	292	33	18	3	0	22

39 METAL CONTAINERS	0	0	0	0	0	0	0	0	0
40 FABRICATED METAL PRDTS.	27	14	31	164	19	14	0	0	47
41 SCREW MACH. PRDTS., ETC.	0	0	0	0	0	0	0	0	0
42 OTHER FAB. METAL PRDTS.	62	29	116	464	45	37	4	0	96
43 ENGINES, TURBINES	578	252	713	3829	362	302	22	0	1097
44 FARM MACH., EQUIP.	0	0	0	0	0	0	0	0	0
45 CONSTRUC. MACH., EQUIP.	744	230	1682	3646	333	387	21	0	1256
46 MATERIAL HANDLING MACH.	191	159	193	2476	263	152	17	0	218
47 METALWORKING MACHINERY	0	0	0	0	0	0	0	0	0
48 SPECIAL MACH., EQUIP.	0	0	0	0	0	0	0	0	0
49 GENERAL MACH., EQUIP.	208	120	331	1877	191	137	13	0	293
50 MACHINE SHOP PRDTS.	102	51	204	792	77	63	0	0	165
51 OFFICE, COMPUT. MACHINES	0	0	0	0	0	0	0	0	0
52 SERVICE IND. MACHINES	0	0	0	0	0	0	0	0	0
53 ELECT. TRANSMISS. EQUIP.	113	49	140	780	71	50	4	0	218
54 HOUSEHOLD APPLIANCES	2	0	2	6	0	0	0	0	2
55 ELECTRIC LIGHTING EQUIP.	13	6	25	100	13	6	0	0	25
56 RADIO, TV, ETC., EQUIP.	1	0	1	8	0	0	0	0	1
57 ELECTRONIC COMPONENTS	0	0	0	0	0	0	0	0	0
58 MISC. ELECTRICAL MACH.	21	8	39	147	13	13	0	0	29
59 MOTOR VEHICLES, EQUIP.	203	95	380	1515	152	124	11	0	309
60 AIRCRAFT, PARTS	0	0	0	0	0	0	0	0	0
61 OTHER TRANSPORT. EQUIP.	1	1	3	13	1	1	0	0	2
62 PROFESS., SCIEN. INSTRU.	0	0	0	3	0	0	0	0	0
63 MEDICAL, PHOTO. EQUIP.	1	0	2	10	1	1	0	0	2
64 MISC. MANUFACTURING	4	1	6	26	2	2	0	0	5
65 TRANSPORT., WAREHOUSING	438	377	901	2543	253	242	210	0	780
66 COMMUNICA.,EXC. BRDCAST.	9	4	11	62	6	5	0	0	17
67 RADIO, TV BROADCASTING	0	0	0	0	0	0	0	0	0
68 ELEC.,GAS,WATER,SAN.SER.	901	445	793	5196	373	579	66	0	2038
69 WHOLESALE, RETAIL TRADE	773	378	1173	5270	554	492	54	0	1168
70 FINANCE, INSURANCE	434	206	536	2911	276	233	28	0	831
71 REAL ESTATE, RENTAL	692	308	853	4610	439	368	26	0	1305
72 HOTELS, PERSONAL SERV.	21	10	27	143	14	11	1	0	40
73 BUSINESS SERVICES	337	150	415	2242	214	179	13	0	635
74 RESEARCH, DEVELOPMENT	0	0	0	0	0	0	0	0	0
75 AUTO. REPAIR, SERVICES	292	130	359	1942	185	155	11	0	550
76 AMUSEMENTS	3	1	4	23	3	1	0	0	7
77 MED.,EDUC. SERVICES	7	3	8	47	5	3	0	0	14
78 FEDERAL GOVT. ENTERPRISE	16	7	19	104	10	8	1	0	29
79 STATE, LOCAL GOVT. ENT.	35	16	43	233	22	19	1	0	66
80 DIRECT ALLOCATED IMPORTS	5	2	7	36	3	3	0	0	10
81 TRANSFERRED IMPORTS	24	2009	0	2655	0	347	1686	0	1620
82 VALUE ADDED	17426	8020	18816	121247	11286	9083	595	0	35141
83 SECONDARY TRANSFERS-IN	2128	2192	809	13846	1544	1552	364	254	3423
84 INVENTORY DEPLETION	0	0	0	0	0	0	0	0	0
85 SCRAP PRODUCTION	0	0	0	0	0	0	0	0	0
86 SCRAP PURCHASED	74	34	80	474	48	39	3	0	149
87 STATE TOTAL PRODUCTION	29454	16602	34459	198704	18879	16465	3303	254	56732

TABLE C-7

1963 INPUTS BY STATE TO
IO-9, STONE & CLAY MINING & QUARRYING

(THOUSANDS OF CURRENT DOLLARS)

INDUSTRY TITLE	10 GEORGIA	11 IDAHO	12 ILLINOIS	13 INDIANA	14 IOWA	15 KANSAS	16 KENTUCKY	17 LOUISIANA	18 MAINE
1 LIVESTOCK, PRDTS.	3	0	3	2	2	0	2	0	0
2 OTHER AGRICULTURE PRDTS.	10	0	7	4	3	1	4	1	0
3 FORESTRY, FISHERIES	0	0	0	0	0	0	0	0	0
4 AGRI.,FORES.,FISH. SERV.	0	0	0	0	0	0	0	0	0
5 IRON, FERRO. ORES MINING	0	0	0	0	0	0	0	0	0
6 NONFERROUS ORES MINING	0	0	0	0	0	0	0	0	0
7 COAL MINING	35	0	366	0	0	0	0	0	0
8 CRUDE PETRO.,NATURAL GAS	0	0	0	0	0	0	0	0	0
9 STONE, CLAY MINING	402	27	734	589	622	399	347	159	26
10 CHEM.,FERT. MIN. MINING	0	0	0	0	0	0	0	0	0
11 NEW CONSTRUCTION	0	0	0	0	0	0	0	0	0
12 MAINT., REPAIR CONSTR.	628	46	553	297	254	145	293	127	16
13 ORDNANCE, ACCESSORIES	0	0	0	0	0	0	0	0	0
14 FOOD, KINDRED PRDTS.	166	11	146	77	66	37	76	33	3
15 TOBACCO MANUFACTURES	13	1	11	6	6	3	6	3	0
16 FABRICS	0	0	0	0	0	0	0	0	0
17 TEXTILE PRDTS.	9	0	6	3	3	2	3	2	0
18 APPAREL	0	0	0	0	0	0	0	0	0
19 MISC. TEXTILE PRDTS.	0	0	0	0	0	0	0	0	0
20 LUMBER, WOOD PRDTS.	0	0	0	0	0	0	0	0	0
21 WOODEN CONTAINERS	0	0	0	0	0	0	0	0	0
22 HOUSEHOLD FURNITURE	0	0	0	0	0	0	0	0	0
23 OTHER FURNITURE	0	0	0	0	0	0	0	0	0
24 PAPER, ALLIED PRDTS.	548	11	302	145	161	86	155	107	6
25 PAPERBOARD CONTAINERS	0	0	0	0	0	0	0	0	0
26 PRINTING, PUBLISHING	34	1	29	15	16	8	15	10	0
27 CHEMICALS,SELECT. PRDTS.	4278	38	1632	829	1150	618	1241	17	22
28 PLASTICS, SYNTHETICS	0	0	0	0	0	0	0	0	0
29 DRUGS, COSMETICS	7	0	5	3	3	1	3	1	0
30 PAINT, ALLIED PRDTS.	2	0	1	1	1	0	1	0	0
31 PETROLEUM, RELATED INDS.	1233	93	1713	1142	1395	821	1095	709	52
32 RUBBER, MISC. PLASTICS	2809	151	3756	1765	1819	986	1690	1681	73
33 LEATHER TANNING, PRDTS.	0	0	0	0	0	0	0	0	0
34 FOOTWEAR, LEATHER PRDTS.	5	0	2	2	2	0	2	0	0
35 GLASS, GLASS PRDTS.	0	0	0	0	0	0	0	0	0
36 STONE, CLAY PRDTS.	249	8	200	94	97	52	89	90	4
37 PRIMARY IRON, STEEL MFR.	2585	47	1386	669	781	423	779	400	24
38 PRIMARY NONFERROUS MFR.	551	3	101	47	40	22	33	61	3

39 METAL CONTAINERS	0	0	0	0	0	0	0	0	0
40 FABRICATED METAL PRDTS.	96	10	84	47	39	23	43	18	0
41 SCREW MACH. PRDTS., ETC.	0	0	0	0	0	0	0	0	2
42 OTHER FAB. METAL PRDTS.	298	8	232	111	124	66	120	82	0
43 ENGINES, TURBINES	2178	149	1915	1019	968	481	1007	419	4
44 FARM MACH., EQUIP.	0	0	0	0	0	0	0	0	42
45 CONSTRUC. MACH., EQUIP.	2815	75	2475	1215	1504	811	1543	500	0
46 MATERIAL HANDLING MACH.	317	41	887	405	363	197	306	528	41
47 METALWORKING MACHINERY	0	0	0	0	0	0	0	0	20
48 SPECIAL MACH., EQUIP.	0	0	0	0	0	0	0	0	0
49 GENERAL MACH., EQUIP.	8051	31	828	389	402	222	376	362	0
50 MACHINE SHOP PRDTS.	498	12	396	191	216	114	204	140	18
51 OFFICE, COMPUT. MACHINES	0	0	0	0	0	0	0	0	12
52 SERVICE IND. MACHINES	0	0	0	0	0	0	0	0	0
53 ELECT. TRANSMISS. EQUIP.	435	29	383	202	172	94	199	83	0
54 HOUSEHOLD APPLIANCES	3	0	3	2	2	0	2	0	8
55 ELECTRIC LIGHTING EQUIP.	63	0	56	25	31	19	31	19	0
56 RADIO, TV, ETC., EQUIP.	5	0	5	1	1	1	1	1	0
57 ELECTRONIC COMPONENTS	0	0	0	0	0	0	0	0	0
58 MISC. ELECTRICAL MACH.	86	4	72	35	39	21	39	25	0
59 MOTOR VEHICLES, EQUIP.	975	27	761	363	403	218	392	272	0
60 AIRCRAFT, PARTS	0	0	0	0	0	0	0	0	15
61 OTHER TRANSPORT. EQUIP.	3	0	6	3	3	2	3	2	0
62 PROFESS., SCIEN. INSTRU.	3	0	0	0	0	0	0	0	0
63 MEDICAL, PHOTO. EQUIP.	5	0	4	2	2	1	2	1	0
64 MISC. MANUFACTURING	14	0	12	6	6	4	6	4	0
65 TRANSPORT., WAREHOUSING	1827	50	1513	639	691	391	618	500	0
66 COMMUNICA.,EXC. BRDCAST.	35	2	31	16	14	8	16	7	2003
67 RADIO, TV BROADCASTING	0	0	0	0	0	0	0	0	1
68 ELEC.,GAS,WATER,SAN.SER.	6490	52	3535	2028	1079	525	1572	1003	0
69 WHOLESALE, RETAIL TRADE	3347	120	2711	1433	1596	895	1438	1040	54
70 FINANCE, INSURANCE	1638	109	1433	762	649	364	751	324	187
71 REAL ESTATE, RENTAL	2593	175	2282	1214	1034	580	1197	505	143
72 HOTELS, PERSONAL SERV.	80	6	72	37	31	19	37	16	49
73 BUSINESS SERVICES	1261	85	1110	590	503	282	582	246	1
74 RESEARCH, DEVELOPMENT	0	0	0	0	0	0	0	0	24
75 AUTO. REPAIR, SERVICES	1092	74	961	511	436	244	505	213	0
76 AMUSEMENTS	13	1	12	6	6	3	6	3	21
77 MED.,EDUC. SERVICES	27	2	24	13	10	6	12	5	0
78 FEDERAL GOVT. ENTERPRISE	58	4	51	27	23	13	27	11	0
79 STATE, LOCAL GOVT. ENT.	131	9	115	61	52	29	61	26	1
80 DIRECT ALLOCATED IMPORTS	20	1	18	9	8	4	9	4	2
81 TRANSFERRED IMPORTS	1668	0	212	3	0	0	0	1032	0
82 VALUE ADDED	54247	5348	56862	30700	23866	13587	30172	10248	17221
83 SECONDARY TRANSFERS-IN	2135	373	8167	4774	1931	2573	1663	3099	1282
84 INVENTORY DEPLETION	0	0	0	0	0	0	0	0	224
85 SCRAP PRODUCTION	0	0	0	0	0	0	0	0	0
86 SCRAP PURCHASED	230	23	242	130	101	58	128	43	0
87 STATE TOTAL PRODUCTION	106304	7257	98427	52662	42728	25460	48904	24183	5
									21609

TABLE C-7

1963 INPUTS BY STATE TO
IO-9, STONE & CLAY MINING & QUARRYING

(THOUSANDS OF CURRENT DOLLARS)

INDUSTRY TITLE	19 MARYLAND	20 MASSA-CHUSETTS	21 MICHIGAN	22 MINNESOTA	23 MISSISSIPPI	24 MISSOURI	25 MONTANA	26 NEBRASKA	27 NEVADA
1 LIVESTOCK, PRDTS.	2	0	2	0	0	2	0	0	0
2 OTHER AGRICULTURE PRDTS.	3	1	6	1	1	4	0	1	1
3 FORESTRY, FISHERIES	0	0	0	0	0	0	0	0	0
4 AGRI.,FORES.,FISH. SERV.	0	0	0	0	0	0	0	0	0
5 IRON, FERRO. ORES MINING	0	0	0	0	0	0	0	0	0
6 NONFERROUS ORES MINING	0	0	0	0	0	0	0	0	0
7 COAL MINING	35	0	68	0	0	0	0	0	0
8 CRUDE PETRO.,NATURAL GAS	0	0	0	0	0	0	0	0	0
9 STONE, CLAY MINING	606	253	640	449	54	770	22	325	31
10 CHEM.,FERT. MIN. MINING	0	0	0	0	0	0	0	0	0
11 NEW CONSTRUCTION	0	0	0	0	0	0	0	0	0
12 MAINT., REPAIR CONSTR.	244	141	440	152	72	346	39	109	90
13 ORDNANCE, ACCESSORIES	0	0	0	0	0	0	0	0	0
14 FOOD, KINDRED PRDTS.	63	36	116	39	19	90	9	27	23
15 TOBACCO MANUFACTURES	6	3	9	3	1	7	1	3	1
16 FABRICS	0	0	0	0	0	0	0	0	0
17 TEXTILE PRDTS.	3	1	4	2	1	3	0	1	0
18 APPAREL	0	0	0	0	0	0	0	0	0
19 MISC. TEXTILE PRDTS.	0	0	0	0	0	0	0	0	0
20 LUMBER, WOOD PRDTS.	0	0	0	0	0	0	0	0	0
21 WOODEN CONTAINERS	0	0	0	0	0	0	0	0	0
22 HOUSEHOLD FURNITURE	0	0	0	0	0	0	0	0	0
23 OTHER FURNITURE	0	0	0	0	0	0	0	0	0
24 PAPER, ALLIED PRDTS.	146	77	161	76	37	156	9	62	13
25 PAPERBOARD CONTAINERS	0	0	0	0	0	0	0	0	0
26 PRINTING, PUBLISHING	15	8	16	8	3	15	1	7	1
27 CHEMICALS,SELECT. PRDTS.	673	151	666	228	1	1319	26	274	13
28 PLASTICS, SYNTHETICS	0	0	0	0	0	0	0	0	0
29 DRUGS, COSMETICS	3	1	4	1	0	3	0	1	0
30 PAINT, ALLIED PRDTS.	1	0	1	0	0	1	0	0	0
31 PETROLEUM, RELATED INDS.	688	658	1274	859	380	1517	66	631	115
32 RUBBER, MISC. PLASTICS	1893	1110	2120	1062	568	1661	120	801	199
33 LEATHER TANNING, PRDTS.	0	0	0	0	0	0	0	0	0
34 FOOTWEAR, LEATHER PRDTS.	2	0	2	0	0	2	0	0	0
35 GLASS, GLASS PRDTS.	0	0	0	0	0	0	0	0	0
36 STONE, CLAY PRDTS.	101	59	112	56	30	88	7	43	10
37 PRIMARY IRON, STEEL MFR.	651	308	703	320	134	796	36	272	52
38 PRIMARY NONFERROUS MFR.	54	40	65	36	22	28	3	25	7

39 METAL CONTAINERS	0	0	0	0	0	0	0	0	0
40 FABRICATED METAL PRDTS.	39	22	67	22	10	51	6	19	14
41 SCREW MACH. PRDTS., ETC.	0	0	0	0	0	0	0	0	0
42 OTHER FAB. METAL PRDTS.	111	57	124	57	29	120	8	45	8
43 ENGINES, TURBINES	831	280	1516	507	230	1180	113	256	292
44 FARM MACH., EQUIP.	0	0	0	0	0	0	0	0	0
45 CONSTRUC. MACH., EQUIP.	1120	450	1179	501	165	1601	58	464	69
46 MATERIAL HANDLING MACH.	475	323	547	293	179	282	33	203	61
47 METALWORKING MACHINERY	0	0	0	0	0	0	0	0	0
48 SPECIAL MACH., EQUIP.	0	0	0	0	0	0	0	0	0
49 GENERAL MACH., EQUIP.	416	244	464	231	124	371	27	177	44
50 MACHINE SHOP PRDTS.	191	102	216	102	51	204	12	77	12
51 OFFICE, COMPUT. MACHINES	0	0	0	0	0	0	0	0	0
52 SERVICE IND. MACHINES	0	0	0	0	0	0	0	0	0
53 ELECT. TRANSMISS. EQUIP.	165	94	304	99	33	237	24	71	58
54 HOUSEHOLD APPLIANCES	2	0	2	0	0	2	0	0	0
55 ELECTRIC LIGHTING EQUIP.	25	13	25	13	6	31	0	13	0
56 RADIO, TV, ETC., EQUIP.	1	1	3	1	0	3	0	0	0
57 ELECTRONIC COMPONENTS	0	0	0	0	0	0	0	0	0
58 MISC. ELECTRICAL MACH.	35	17	39	17	8	39	0	13	4
59 MOTOR VEHICLES, EQUIP.	369	193	405	193	91	394	22	155	33
60 AIRCRAFT, PARTS	0	0	0	0	0	0	0	0	0
61 OTHER TRANSPORT. EQUIP.	3	1	3	1	1	3	0	1	0
62 PROFESS., SCIEN. INSTRU.	0	0	0	0	0	0	0	0	0
63 MEDICAL, PHOTO. EQUIP.	2	1	2	1	0	2	0	1	0
64 MISC. MANUFACTURING	6	4	7	4	1	6	0	2	1
65 TRANSPORT., WAREHOUSING	1604	426	2756	383	142	743	207	289	69
66 COMMUNICA.,EXC. BRDCAST.	13	8	24	8	4	19	2	6	5
67 RADIO, TV BROADCASTING	0	0	0	0	0	0	0	0	0
68 ELEC.,GAS,WATER,SAN.SER.	1190	795	3248	692	194	1483	61	547	63
69 WHOLESALE, RETAIL TRADE	1312	809	1786	885	416	1640	103	675	161
70 FINANCE, INSURANCE	678	363	1249	384	178	888	99	272	224
71 REAL ESTATE, RENTAL	993	568	1812	611	283	1415	144	433	357
72 HOTELS, PERSONAL SERV.	31	17	56	19	9	44	4	13	11
73 BUSINESS SERVICES	483	276	881	297	138	688	70	211	173
74 RESEARCH, DEVELOPMENT	0	0	0	0	0	0	0	0	0
75 AUTO. REPAIR, SERVICES	418	239	763	257	119	596	61	182	150
76 AMUSEMENTS	4	3	9	3	1	7	1	3	1
77 MED.,EDUC. SERVICES	10	6	19	6	2	15	1	5	3
78 FEDERAL GOVT. ENTERPRISE	22	13	41	14	6	32	3	10	8
79 STATE, LOCAL GOVT. ENT.	50	29	92	31	14	72	7	22	18
80 DIRECT ALLOCATED IMPORTS	8	4	14	5	2	11	1	3	3
81 TRANSFERRED IMPORTS	8430	913	17110	82	0	0	1456	0	0
82 VALUE ADDED	24364	14275	49400	15102	7376	36677	4433	10283	11626
83 SECONDARY TRANSFERS-IN	1926	2944	4915	2415	1010	3123	699	669	771
84 INVENTORY DEPLETION	0	0	0	0	0	0	0	0	0
85 SCRAP PRODUCTION	0	0	0	0	0	0	0	0	0
86 SCRAP PURCHASED	103	61	210	64	31	156	19	44	49
87 STATE TOTAL PRODUCTION	50620	26399	95699	26593	12177	58946	8014	17747	14846

TABLE C-7

1963 INPUTS BY STATE TO
IO-9, STONE & CLAY MINING & QUARRYING
(THOUSANDS OF CURRENT DOLLARS)

INDUSTRY TITLE	28 NEW HAMPSHIRE	29 NEW JERSEY	30 NEW MEXICO	31 NEW YORK	32 NORTH CAROLINA	33 NORTH DAKOTA	34 OHIO	35 OKLAHOMA	36 OREGON
1 LIVESTOCK, PRDTS.	0	2	0	3	2	0	3	0	0
2 OTHER AGRICULTURE PRDTS.	0	6	1	7	3	0	10	1	1
3 FORESTRY, FISHERIES	0	0	0	0	0	0	0	0	0
4 AGRI.,FORES.,FISH. SERV.	0	0	0	0	0	0	0	0	0
5 IRON, FERRO. ORES MINING	0	0	0	0	0	0	0	0	0
6 NONFERROUS ORES MINING	0	0	0	0	0	0	0	0	0
7 COAL MINING	0	54	0	210	244	0	27	0	0
8 CRUDE PETRO.,NATURAL GAS	0	0	0	0	0	0	0	0	0
9 STONE, CLAY MINING	45	377	55	607	249	66	645	117	338
10 CHEM.,FERT. MIN. MINING	0	0	0	0	0	0	0	0	0
11 NEW CONSTRUCTION	0	0	0	0	0	0	0	0	0
12 MAINT., REPAIR CONSTR.	23	385	67	570	238	28	583	123	159
13 ORDNANCE, ACCESSORIES	0	0	0	0	0	0	0	0	0
14 FOOD, KINDRED PRDTS.	6	100	17	151	62	6	153	32	42
15 TOBACCO MANUFACTURES	0	9	1	11	4	0	13	3	3
16 FABRICS	0	0	0	0	0	0	0	0	0
17 TEXTILE PRDTS.	0	5	0	5	2	0	6	1	2
18 APPAREL	0	0	0	0	0	0	0	0	0
19 MISC. TEXTILE PRDTS.	0	0	0	0	0	0	0	0	0
20 LUMBER, WOOD PRDTS.	0	0	0	0	0	0	0	0	0
21 WOODEN CONTAINERS	0	0	0	0	0	0	0	0	0
22 HOUSEHOLD FURNITURE	0	0	0	0	0	0	0	0	0
23 OTHER FURNITURE	0	0	0	0	0	0	0	0	0
24 PAPER, ALLIED PRDTS.	8	273	24	250	121	15	290	60	99
25 PAPERBOARD CONTAINERS	0	0	0	0	0	0	0	0	0
26 PRINTING, PUBLISHING	1	27	2	24	12	1	28	6	9
27 CHEMICALS,SELECT. PRDTS.	7	1822	13	1660	898	6	1935	449	449
28 PLASTICS, SYNTHETICS	0	0	0	0	0	0	0	0	0
29 DRUGS, COSMETICS	0	4	0	5	3	0	5	1	1
30 PAINT, ALLIED PRDTS.	0	1	0	1	1	0	1	0	0
31 PETROLEUM, RELATED INDS.	74	1482	212	1293	462	222	2116	254	810
32 RUBBER, MISC. PLASTICS	116	3163	364	2910	1343	237	3380	659	1280
33 LEATHER TANNING, PRDTS.	0	0	0	0	0	0	0	0	0
34 FOOTWEAR, LEATHER PRDTS.	0	2	0	5	2	0	5	0	0
35 GLASS, GLASS PRDTS.	0	0	0	0	0	0	0	0	0
36 STONE, CLAY PRDTS.	7	167	20	154	71	13	179	35	68
37 PRIMARY IRON, STEEL MFR.	29	1304	90	1194	592	58	1389	294	439
38 PRIMARY NONFERROUS MFR.	3	76	15	68	28	7	79	15	36

39 METAL CONTAINERS	0	0	0	0	0	0	0	0	0
40 FABRICATED METAL PRDTS.	6	59	10	88	35	6	88	19	27
41 SCREW MACH. PRDTS., ETC.	0	0	0	0	0	0	0	0	0
42 OTHER FAB. METAL PRDTS.	4	210	17	195	91	12	224	45	74
43 ENGINES, TURBINES	66	1319	213	1973	809	87	2019	407	534
44 FARM MACH., EQUIP.	0	0	0	0	0	0	0	0	0
45 CONSTRUC. MACH., EQUIP.	40	2464	118	2252	1153	74	2624	574	752
46 MATERIAL HANDLING MACH.	36	664	113	615	259	74	711	126	322
47 METALWORKING MACHINERY	0	0	0	0	0	0	0	0	0
48 SPECIAL MACH., EQUIP.	0	0	0	0	0	0	0	0	0
49 GENERAL MACH., EQUIP.	27	704	80	646	300	53	748	146	284
50 MACHINE SHOP PRDTS.	12	357	26	332	153	26	384	77	128
51 OFFICE, COMPUT. MACHINES	0	0	0	0	0	0	0	0	0
52 SERVICE IND. MACHINES	0	0	0	0	0	0	0	0	0
53 ELECT. TRANSMISS. EQUIP.	13	264	42	396	161	17	404	81	103
54 HOUSEHOLD APPLIANCES	0	2	0	3	2	0	3	0	2
55 ELECTRIC LIGHTING EQUIP.	0	50	6	44	19	0	50	13	19
56 RADIO, TV, ETC., EQUIP.	0	3	0	5	1	0	5	1	1
57 ELECTRONIC COMPONENTS	0	0	0	0	0	0	0	0	0
58 MISC. ELECTRICAL MACH.	0	64	4	60	29	4	68	13	25
59 MOTOR VEHICLES, EQUIP.	18	685	60	628	303	40	730	150	249
60 AIRCRAFT, PARTS	0	0	0	0	0	0	0	0	0
61 OTHER TRANSPORT. EQUIP.	0	5	1	5	2	0	5	1	2
62 PROFESS., SCIEN. INSTRU.	0	0	0	3	0	0	3	0	0
63 MEDICAL, PHOTO. EQUIP.	0	4	0	4	1	0	4	1	1
64 MISC. MANUFACTURING	0	10	1	11	5	0	12	2	4
65 TRANSPORT., WAREHOUSING	38	1196	101	3478	661	480	1442	227	429
66 COMMUNICA.,EXC. BRDCAST.	1	21	4	32	13	1	32	7	9
67 RADIO, TV BROADCASTING	0	0	0	0	0	0	0	0	0
68 ELEC.,GAS,WATER,SAN.SER.	69	2540	109	3318	1041	87	4110	926	404
69 WHOLESALE, RETAIL TRADE	87	2332	263	2335	966	228	2782	484	989
70 FINANCE, INSURANCE	49	1001	165	1606	607	86	1524	309	403
71 REAL ESTATE, RENTAL	78	1578	263	2351	967	101	2405	492	640
72 HOTELS, PERSONAL SERV.	3	49	9	73	30	3	74	16	20
73 BUSINESS SERVICES	38	768	128	1143	470	49	1170	239	311
74 RESEARCH, DEVELOPMENT	0	0	0	0	0	0	0	0	0
75 AUTO. REPAIR, SERVICES	33	665	111	990	407	43	1013	207	270
76 AMUSEMENTS	0	9	1	12	4	0	12	3	3
77 MED.,EDUC. SERVICES	1	17	2	25	9	1	25	5	7
78 FEDERAL GOVT. ENTERPRISE	2	36	6	53	22	2	54	11	14
79 STATE, LOCAL GOVT. ENT.	4	80	13	119	49	5	122	25	32
80 DIRECT ALLOCATED IMPORTS	1	12	2	18	7	1	19	4	5
81 TRANSFERRED IMPORTS	0	1520	0	20011	1	3564	2207	0	154
82 VALUE ADDED	2122	35884	7599	63106	25117	2304	61196	12703	15417
83 SECONDARY TRANSFERS-IN	512	6315	1251	8132	1586	161	10322	1560	829
84 INVENTORY DEPLETION	0	0	0	0	0	0	0	0	0
85 SCRAP PRODUCTION	0	0	0	0	0	0	0	0	0
86 SCRAP PURCHASED	9	152	32	268	107	10	260	54	65
87 STATE TOTAL PRODUCTION	3588	70302	11633	123461	39726	8179	107700	20980	26265

TABLE C-7

1963 INPUTS BY STATE TO
IO-9, STONE & CLAY MINING & QUARRYING
(THOUSANDS OF CURRENT DOLLARS)

INDUSTRY TITLE	37 PENNSYL-VANIA	38 RHODE ISLAND	39 SOUTH CAROLINA	40 SOUTH DAKOTA	41 TENNESSEE	42 TEXAS	43 UTAH	44 VERMONT	45 VIRGINIA
1 LIVESTOCK, PRDTS.	3	0	2	0	2	2	0	0	2
2 OTHER AGRICULTURE PRDTS.	10	0	3	1	4	6	0	1	4
3 FORESTRY, FISHERIES	0	0	0	0	0	0	0	0	0
4 AGRI.,FORES.,FISH. SERV.	0	0	0	0	0	0	0	0	0
5 IRON, FERRO. ORES MINING	0	0	0	0	0	0	0	0	0
6 NONFERROUS ORES MINING	0	0	0	0	0	0	0	0	0
7 COAL MINING	101	0	0	0	41	0	0	0	380
8 CRUDE PETRO.,NATURAL GAS	0	0	0	0	0	0	0	0	0
9 STONE, CLAY MINING	1665	42	108	103	343	550	55	62	499
10 CHEM.,FERT. MIN. MINING	0	0	0	0	0	0	0	0	0
11 NEW CONSTRUCTION	0	0	0	0	0	0	0	0	0
12 MAINT., REPAIR CONSTR.	581	20	174	65	308	391	49	71	350
13 ORDNANCE, ACCESSORIES	0	0	0	0	0	0	0	0	0
14 FOOD, KINDRED PRDTS.	153	4	44	16	80	102	11	17	92
15 TOBACCO MANUFACTURES	13	0	4	1	7	9	1	1	7
16 FABRICS	0	0	0	0	0	0	0	0	0
17 TEXTILE PRDTS.	6	0	1	1	3	5	0	0	4
18 APPAREL	0	0	0	0	0	0	0	0	0
19 MISC. TEXTILE PRDTS.	0	0	0	0	0	0	0	0	0
20 LUMBER, WOOD PRDTS.	0	0	0	0	0	0	0	0	0
21 WOODEN CONTAINERS	0	0	0	0	0	0	0	0	0
22 HOUSEHOLD FURNITURE	0	0	0	0	0	0	0	0	0
23 OTHER FURNITURE	0	0	0	0	0	0	0	0	0
24 PAPER, ALLIED PRDTS.	301	9	66	29	153	299	29	13	204
25 PAPERBOARD CONTAINERS	0	0	0	0	0	0	0	0	0
26 PRINTING, PUBLISHING	29	1	7	2	15	29	2	1	20
27 CHEMICALS,SELECT. PRDTS.	2365	41	505	119	1047	1194	63	40	1323
28 PLASTICS, SYNTHETICS	0	0	0	0	0	0	0	0	0
29 DRUGS, COSMETICS	5	0	1	0	3	4	0	0	4
30 PAINT, ALLIED PRDTS.	2	0	0	0	1	1	0	0	1
31 PETROLEUM, RELATED INDS.	2079	89	411	307	982	1594	224	117	938
32 RUBBER, MISC. PLASTICS	3297	123	729	377	1767	3969	421	171	2388
33 LEATHER TANNING, PRDTS.	0	0	0	0	0	0	0	0	0
34 FOOTWEAR, LEATHER PRDTS.	5	0	0	0	2	2	0	0	2
35 GLASS, GLASS PRDTS.	0	0	0	0	0	0	0	0	0
36 STONE, CLAY PRDTS.	174	7	39	20	94	212	22	9	127
37 PRIMARY IRON, STEEL MFR.	1502	42	327	125	738	1301	118	52	969
38 PRIMARY NONFERROUS MFR.	65	3	15	10	40	119	15	7	58

39 METAL CONTAINERS	0	0	0	0	0	0	0	0	0
40 FABRICATED METAL PRDTS.	88	6	26	10	47	58	10	10	55
41 SCREW MACH. PRDTS., ETC.	0	0	0	0	0	0	0	0	0
42 OTHER FAB. METAL PRDTS.	232	8	49	20	120	232	20	8	157
43 ENGINES, TURBINES	2011	56	584	203	1057	1349	147	228	1206
44 FARM MACH., EQUIP.	0	0	0	0	0	0	0	0	0
45 CONSTRUC. MACH., EQUIP.	2964	71	640	210	1402	2164	175	84	1816
46 MATERIAL HANDLING MACH.	606	31	138	98	365	1035	121	47	512
47 METALWORKING MACHINERY	0	0	0	0	0	0	0	0	0
48 SPECIAL MACH., EQUIP.	0	0	0	0	0	0	0	0	0
49 GENERAL MACH., EQUIP.	735	27	164	84	394	872	93	35	531
50 MACHINE SHOP PRDTS.	396	12	89	38	204	396	38	12	267
51 OFFICE, COMPUT. MACHINES	0	0	0	0	0	0	0	0	0
52 SERVICE IND. MACHINES	0	0	0	0	0	0	0	0	0
53 ELECT. TRANSMISS. EQUIP.	403	11	114	40	211	269	28	44	219
54 HOUSEHOLD APPLIANCES	3	0	2	0	2	2	0	0	2
55 ELECTRIC LIGHTING EQUIP.	56	0	13	6	25	50	6	0	38
56 RADIO, TV, ETC., EQUIP.	5	0	1	0	1	3	0	0	3
57 ELECTRONIC COMPONENTS	0	0	0	0	0	0	0	0	0
58 MISC. ELECTRICAL MACH.	72	4	17	8	39	72	8	4	51
59 MOTOR VEHICLES, EQUIP.	758	22	166	73	386	754	73	31	513
60 AIRCRAFT, PARTS	0	0	0	0	0	0	0	0	0
61 OTHER TRANSPORT. EQUIP.	6	0	1	1	3	6	1	0	4
62 PROFESS., SCIEN. INSTRU.	3	0	0	0	0	0	0	0	0
63 MEDICAL, PHOTO. EQUIP.	4	0	1	0	2	4	0	0	2
64 MISC. MANUFACTURING	12	0	2	1	6	11	1	1	9
65 TRANSPORT., WAREHOUSING	1864	45	270	127	643	1886	111	500	1225
66 COMMUNICA.,EXC. BRDCAST.	32	1	9	3	17	21	2	4	19
67 RADIO, TV BROADCASTING	0	0	0	0	0	0	0	0	0
68 ELEC.,GAS,WATER,SAN.SER.	4505	93	732	160	1494	1975	169	118	2153
69 WHOLESALE, RETAIL TRADE	2815	101	607	323	1401	2660	291	176	1714
70 FINANCE, INSURANCE	1525	42	440	159	789	1051	116	200	907
71 REAL ESTATE, RENTAL	2396	67	700	253	1257	1602	186	279	1433
72 HOTELS, PERSONAL SERV.	74	1	21	9	39	50	6	9	44
73 BUSINESS SERVICES	1165	33	341	123	611	779	90	136	697
74 RESEARCH, DEVELOPMENT	0	0	0	0	0	0	0	0	0
75 AUTO. REPAIR, SERVICES	1009	28	295	106	530	675	78	118	604
76 AMUSEMENTS	12	0	3	1	6	9	1	1	7
77 MED.,EDUC. SERVICES	25	1	7	2	13	17	2	2	16
78 FEDERAL GOVT. ENTERPRISE	54	2	16	6	28	36	4	6	32
79 STATE, LOCAL GOVT. ENT.	121	3	35	13	64	81	9	14	72
80 DIRECT ALLOCATED IMPORTS	19	1	5	2	10	12	1	2	11
81 TRANSFERRED IMPORTS	3299	22	44	0	0	6989	0	3758	1093
82 VALUE ADDED	58371	1607	19620	6687	32664	36035	4509	8829	34822
83 SECONDARY TRANSFERS-IN	10007	184	767	281	2150	10720	1809	491	2468
84 INVENTORY DEPLETION	0	0	0	0	0	0	0	0	0
85 SCRAP PRODUCTION	0	0	0	0	0	0	0	0	0
86 SCRAP PURCHASED	248	7	83	28	139	153	19	38	148
87 STATE TOTAL PRODUCTION	108253	2867	28441	10251	51750	81820	9135	15749	60224

TABLE C-7

1963 INPUTS BY STATE TO
IO-9, STONE & CLAY MINING & QUARRYING
(THOUSANDS OF CURRENT DOLLARS)

INDUSTRY TITLE	46 WASHINGTON	47 WEST VIRGINIA	48 WISCONSIN	49 WYOMING	50 ALASKA	51 HAWAII	52 NATIONAL TOTAL
1 LIVESTOCK, PRDTS.	0	0	2	0	0	0	50
2 OTHER AGRICULTURE PRDTS.	1	1	4	1	0	0	149
3 FORESTRY, FISHERIES	0	0	0	0	0	0	10
4 AGRI.,FORES.,FISH. SERV.	0	0	0	0	0	0	0
5 IRON, FERRO. ORES MINING	0	0	0	0	0	0	0
6 NONFERROUS ORES MINING	0	0	0	0	0	0	0
7 COAL MINING	0	74	0	0	0	0	2021
8 CRUDE PETRO.,NATURAL GAS	0	0	0	0	0	0	0
9 STONE, CLAY MINING	382	293	758	50	31	27	17399
10 CHEM.,FERT. MIN. MINING	0	0	0	0	0	0	0
11 NEW CONSTRUCTION	0	0	0	0	0	0	0
12 MAINT., REPAIR CONSTR.	127	133	294	111	12	44	10999
13 ORDNANCE, ACCESSORIES	0	0	0	0	0	0	11
14 FOOD, KINDRED PRDTS.	33	34	77	29	1	10	2862
15 TOBACCO MANUFACTURES	3	3	6	3	0	1	230
16 FABRICS	0	0	0	0	0	0	0
17 TEXTILE PRDTS.	1	1	4	1	0	0	114
18 APPAREL	0	0	0	0	0	0	11
19 MISC. TEXTILE PRDTS.	0	0	0	0	0	0	0
20 LUMBER, WOOD PRDTS.	0	0	0	0	0	0	41
21 WOODEN CONTAINERS	0	0	0	0	0	0	0
22 HOUSEHOLD FURNITURE	0	0	0	0	0	0	0
23 OTHER FURNITURE	0	0	0	0	0	0	0
24 PAPER, ALLIED PRDTS.	72	59	194	21	1	26	5978
25 PAPERBOARD CONTAINERS	0	0	0	0	0	0	0
26 PRINTING, PUBLISHING	7	6	19	1	0	2	567
27 CHEMICALS,SELECT. PRDTS.	189	310	1366	67	0	276	34174
28 PLASTICS, SYNTHETICS	0	0	0	0	0	0	0
29 DRUGS, COSMETICS	1	1	3	1	0	0	100
30 PAINT, ALLIED PRDTS.	0	0	1	0	0	0	27
31 PETROLEUM, RELATED INDS.	413	363	1753	171	1	95	36706
32 RUBBER, MISC. PLASTICS	1030	729	2221	278	24	259	69932
33 LEATHER TANNING, PRDTS.	0	0	0	0	0	0	0
34 FOOTWEAR, LEATHER PRDTS.	0	0	2	0	0	0	62
35 GLASS, GLASS PRDTS.	0	0	0	0	0	0	0
36 STONE, CLAY PRDTS.	55	39	118	14	1	13	3808
37 PRIMARY IRON, STEEL MFR.	301	267	943	87	6	146	27565
38 PRIMARY NONFERROUS MFR.	33	22	50	7	0	3	2339

39 METAL CONTAINERS	0	0	0	0	0	0	0
40 FABRICATED METAL PRDTS.	19	23	43	19	2	6	1693
41 SCREW MACH. PRDTS., ETC.	0	0	0	0	0	0	0
42 OTHER FAB. METAL PRDTS.	57	45	148	17	0	20	4467
43 ENGINES, TURBINES	421	443	1009	362	28	131	37200
44 FARM MACH., EQUIP.	0	0	0	0	0	0	0
45 CONSTRUC. MACH., EQUIP.	459	475	1803	137	7	310	47652
46 MATERIAL HANDLING MACH.	292	173	450	76	8	30	16028
47 METALWORKING MACHINERY	0	0	0	0	0	0	0
48 SPECIAL MACH., EQUIP.	0	0	0	0	0	0	0
49 GENERAL MACH., EQUIP.	226	160	496	62	4	58	22877
50 MACHINE SHOP PRDTS.	102	77	255	26	0	38	7653
51 OFFICE, COMPUT. MACHINES	0	0	0	0	0	0	0
52 SERVICE IND. MACHINES	0	0	0	0	0	0	0
53 ELECT. TRANSMISS. EQUIP.	84	87	201	81	5	27	7424
54 HOUSEHOLD APPLIANCES	0	0	2	0	0	0	51
55 ELECTRIC LIGHTING EQUIP.	13	13	38	6	0	6	1028
56 RADIO, TV, ETC., EQUIP.	1	1	1	0	0	0	71
57 ELECTRONIC COMPONENTS	0	0	0	0	0	0	0
58 MISC. ELECTRICAL MACH.	17	13	47	4	0	8	1399
59 MOTOR VEHICLES, EQUIP.	185	148	488	51	4	69	14656
60 AIRCRAFT, PARTS	0	0	0	0	0	0	0
61 OTHER TRANSPORT. EQUIP.	1	1	4	0	0	1	113
62 PROFESS., SCIEN. INSTRU.	0	0	0	0	0	0	14
63 MEDICAL, PHOTO. EQUIP.	1	1	2	0	0	0	80
64 MISC. MANUFACTURING	2	2	7	1	0	1	237
65 TRANSPORT., WAREHOUSING	893	330	1266	100	12	110	38028
66 COMMUNICA.,EXC. BRDCAST.	7	7	16	6	0	2	600
67 RADIO, TV BROADCASTING	0	0	0	0	0	0	0
68 ELEC.,GAS,WATER,SAN.SER.	440	848	1265	95	15	157	61823
69 WHOLESALE, RETAIL TRADE	705	547	1987	232	13	200	54654
70 FINANCE, INSURANCE	351	335	778	275	20	105	28809
71 REAL ESTATE, RENTAL	508	533	1202	439	32	166	44776
72 HOTELS, PERSONAL SERV.	16	17	37	14	1	6	1395
73 BUSINESS SERVICES	247	259	585	213	16	81	21774
74 RESEARCH, DEVELOPMENT	0	0	0	0	0	0	0
75 AUTO. REPAIR, SERVICES	214	225	506	185	14	70	18865
76 AMUSEMENTS	3	3	6	3	0	1	225
77 MED.,EDUC. SERVICES	5	6	12	5	0	1	463
78 FEDERAL GOVT. ENTERPRISE	11	12	27	10	1	4	1010
79 STATE, LOCAL GOVT. ENT.	26	27	61	22	2	8	2263
80 DIRECT ALLOCATED IMPORTS	4	4	9	3	0	1	347
81 TRANSFERRED IMPORTS	4981	0	3737	0	1	151	108000
82 VALUE ADDED	12654	13819	27218	13966	1015	4027	1122754
83 SECONDARY TRANSFERS-IN	1596	1752	2116	789	98	343	135762
84 INVENTORY DEPLETION	0	0	0	0	0	0	0
85 SCRAP PRODUCTION	0	0	0	0	0	0	0
86 SCRAP PURCHASED	54	59	116	59	4	17	4727
87 STATE TOTAL PRODUCTION	27244	22781	53755	18101	1380	7059	2024071

TABLE C-8

1963 INPUTS BY STATE TO
IO-10, CHEMICAL & FERTILIZER MINERAL MINING

(THOUSANDS OF CURRENT DOLLARS)

INDUSTRY TITLE	1 ALABAMA	2 ARIZONA	3 ARKANSAS	4 CALIFORNIA	5 COLORADO	6 CONNECTICUT	7 DELAWARE	8 DISTRICT OF COLUMBIA	9 FLORIDA
1 LIVESTOCK, PRDTS.	0	0	0	0	0	0	0	0	1
2 OTHER AGRICULTURE PRDTS.	0	0	0	1	0	0	0	0	5
3 FORESTRY, FISHERIES	0	0	0	0	0	0	0	0	0
4 AGRI.,FORES.,FISH. SERV.	0	0	0	0	0	0	0	0	0
5 IRON, FERRO. ORES MINING	0	0	0	0	0	0	0	0	0
6 NONFERROUS ORES MINING	0	0	0	0	0	0	0	0	0
7 COAL MINING	0	0	0	0	0	0	0	0	0
8 CRUDE PETRO.,NATURAL GAS	0	0	0	0	0	0	0	0	0
9 STONE, CLAY MINING	0	0	7	199	3	0	3	0	82
10 CHEM.,FERT. MIN. MINING	0	0	103	42	25	0	25	0	20729
11 NEW CONSTRUCTION	0	0	0	0	0	0	0	0	0
12 MAINT., REPAIR CONSTR.	0	0	14	353	7	0	1	0	513
13 ORDNANCE, ACCESSORIES	0	0	0	0	0	0	0	0	0
14 FOOD, KINDRED PRDTS.	0	0	2	46	3	0	0	0	83
15 TOBACCO MANUFACTURES	0	0	0	2	0	0	0	0	7
16 FABRICS	0	0	6	39	6	0	0	0	0
17 TEXTILE PRDTS.	0	0	0	0	0	0	0	0	0
18 APPAREL	0	0	0	0	0	0	0	0	0
19 MISC. TEXTILE PRDTS.	0	0	0	0	0	0	0	0	0
20 LUMBER, WOOD PRDTS.	0	0	1	57	2	0	0	0	0
21 WOODEN CONTAINERS	0	0	0	0	0	0	0	0	0
22 HOUSEHOLD FURNITURE	0	0	0	0	0	0	0	0	0
23 OTHER FURNITURE	0	0	0	0	0	0	0	0	0
24 PAPER, ALLIED PRDTS.	0	0	67	112	19	0	1	0	238
25 PAPERBOARD CONTAINERS	0	0	0	0	0	0	0	0	0
26 PRINTING, PUBLISHING	0	0	1	12	2	0	0	0	30
27 CHEMICALS,SELECT. PRDTS.	0	0	219	2118	36	0	8	0	3169
28 PLASTICS, SYNTHETICS	0	0	0	0	0	0	0	0	0
29 DRUGS, COSMETICS	0	0	31	2	0	0	0	0	2
30 PAINT, ALLIED PRDTS.	0	0	0	0	0	0	0	0	11
31 PETROLEUM, RELATED INDS.	0	0	35	1454	10	0	1	0	2000
32 RUBBER, MISC. PLASTICS	0	0	14	180	15	0	1	0	208
33 LEATHER TANNING, PRDTS.	0	0	0	0	0	0	0	0	0
34 FOOTWEAR, LEATHER PRDTS.	0	0	0	0	0	0	0	0	6
35 GLASS, GLASS PRDTS.	0	0	0	0	0	0	0	0	0
36 STONE, CLAY PRDTS.	0	0	10	35	2	0	0	0	25
37 PRIMARY IRON, STEEL MFR.	0	0	38	391	78	0	6	0	4202
38 PRIMARY NONFERROUS MFR.	0	0	1	273	4	0	0	0	346

39 METAL CONTAINERS	0	0	0	0	0	0	0	0	0
40 FABRICATED METAL PRDTS.	0	0	0	103	5	0	0	0	19
41 SCREW MACH. PRDTS., ETC.	0	0	0	0	0	0	0	0	0
42 OTHER FAB. METAL PRDTS.	0	0	7	49	10	0	0	0	124
43 ENGINES, TURBINES	0	0	460	15	59	0	0	0	742
44 FARM MACH., EQUIP.	0	0	0	0	0	0	0	0	0
45 CONSTRUC. MACH., EQUIP.	0	0	129	1817	116	0	3	0	3052
46 MATERIAL HANDLING MACH.	0	0	0	745	6	0	0	0	202
47 METALWORKING MACHINERY	0	0	0	0	0	0	0	0	0
48 SPECIAL MACH., EQUIP.	0	0	0	0	0	0	0	0	0
49 GENERAL MACH., EQUIP.	0	0	16	33	9	0	0	0	442
50 MACHINE SHOP PRDTS.	0	0	14	122	27	0	0	0	311
51 OFFICE, COMPUT. MACHINES	0	0	0	0	0	0	0	0	0
52 SERVICE IND. MACHINES	0	0	0	0	0	0	0	0	0
53 ELECT. TRANSMISS. EQUIP.	0	0	14	610	17	0	1	0	276
54 HOUSEHOLD APPLIANCES	0	0	0	0	0	0	0	0	1
55 ELECTRIC LIGHTING EQUIP.	0	0	5	124	2	0	0	0	178
56 RADIO, TV, ETC., EQUIP.	0	0	0	1	0	0	0	0	2
57 ELECTRONIC COMPONENTS	0	0	0	0	0	0	0	0	0
58 MISC. ELECTRICAL MACH.	0	0	2	9	2	0	0	0	22
59 MOTOR VEHICLES, EQUIP.	0	0	9	71	14	0	0	0	181
60 AIRCRAFT, PARTS	0	0	0	0	0	0	0	0	0
61 OTHER TRANSPORT. EQUIP.	0	0	0	72	1	0	0	0	0
62 PROFESS., SCIEN. INSTRU.	0	0	0	0	0	0	0	0	0
63 MEDICAL, PHOTO. EQUIP.	0	0	0	1	0	0	0	0	4
64 MISC. MANUFACTURING	0	0	1	5	1	0	0	0	12
65 TRANSPORT., WAREHOUSING	0	12	96	461	32	0	13	0	12723
66 COMMUNICA.,EXC. BRDCAST.	0	0	16	0	8	0	1	0	615
67 RADIO, TV BROADCASTING	0	0	0	0	0	0	0	0	0
68 ELEC.,GAS,WATER,SAN.SER.	0	0	246	7248	42	0	0	0	7865
69 WHOLESALE, RETAIL TRADE	0	2	108	1210	46	0	3	0	3069
70 FINANCE, INSURANCE	0	0	33	0	17	0	2	0	1256
71 REAL ESTATE, RENTAL	0	0	66	0	33	0	5	0	2477
72 HOTELS, PERSONAL SERV.	0	0	1	13	1	0	0	0	41
73 BUSINESS SERVICES	0	0	36	0	18	0	3	0	1348
74 RESEARCH, DEVELOPMENT	0	0	0	0	0	0	0	0	0
75 AUTO. REPAIR, SERVICES	0	0	6	0	3	0	0	0	210
76 AMUSEMENTS	0	0	0	2	0	0	0	0	7
77 MED.,EDUC. SERVICES	0	0	11	1	5	0	1	0	402
78 FEDERAL GOVT. ENTERPRISE	0	0	9	0	5	0	1	0	352
79 STATE, LOCAL GOVT. ENT.	0	0	5	0	2	0	0	0	187
80 DIRECT ALLOCATED IMPORTS	0	0	0	3	0	0	0	0	10
81 TRANSFERRED IMPORTS	0	52	0	41	0	0	0	0	7638
82 VALUE ADDED	0	0	1037	56419	742	0	127	0	41901
83 SECONDARY TRANSFERS-IN	90	35	14	194	130	51	16	0	74
84 INVENTORY DEPLETION	0	0	3	89	2	0	0	0	128
85 SCRAP PRODUCTION	0	0	0	0	0	0	0	0	0
86 SCRAP PURCHASED	0	0	3	160	2	0	0	0	119
87 STATE TOTAL PRODUCTION	90	101	2898	74938	1571	51	223	0	117649

TABLE C-8

1963 INPUTS BY STATE TO
IO-10, CHEMICAL & FERTILIZER MINERAL MINING

(THOUSANDS OF CURRENT DOLLARS)

INDUSTRY TITLE	10 GEORGIA	11 IDAHO	12 ILLINOIS	13 INDIANA	14 IOWA	15 KANSAS	16 KENTUCKY	17 LOUISIANA	18 MAINE
1 LIVESTOCK, PRDTS.	0	0	0	0	0	0	0	1	0
2 OTHER AGRICULTURE PRDTS.	0	0	0	0	0	0	0	4	0
3 FORESTRY, FISHERIES	0	0	0	0	0	0	0	0	0
4 AGRI.,FORES.,FISH. SERV.	0	0	0	0	0	0	0	0	0
5 IRON, FERRO. ORES MINING	0	0	0	0	0	0	0	0	0
6 NONFERROUS ORES MINING	0	0	0	0	0	0	0	0	0
7 COAL MINING	0	6	38	0	0	0	0	0	0
8 CRUDE PETRO.,NATURAL GAS	0	0	0	0	0	0	0	0	0
9 STONE, CLAY MINING	23	349	44	0	0	1	27	130	0
10 CHEM.,FERT. MIN. MINING	62	283	226	0	0	16	1964	2032	0
11 NEW CONSTRUCTION	0	0	0	0	0	0	0	0	0
12 MAINT., REPAIR CONSTR.	12	27	42	0	0	6	26	388	0
13 ORDNANCE, ACCESSORIES	0	0	0	0	0	0	0	0	0
14 FOOD, KINDRED PRDTS.	2	4	3	0	0	1	2	62	0
15 TOBACCO MANUFACTURES	0	0	0	0	0	0	0	6	0
16 FABRICS	3	0	11	0	0	0	6	0	0
17 TEXTILE PRDTS.	0	0	0	0	0	0	0	0	0
18 APPAREL	0	0	0	0	0	0	0	0	0
19 MISC. TEXTILE PRDTS.	0	0	0	0	0	0	0	0	0
20 LUMBER, WOOD PRDTS.	1	0	19	0	0	0	7	0	0
21 WOODEN CONTAINERS	0	0	0	0	0	0	0	0	0
22 HOUSEHOLD FURNITURE	0	0	0	0	0	0	0	0	0
23 OTHER FURNITURE	0	0	0	0	0	0	0	0	0
24 PAPER, ALLIED PRDTS.	32	16	56	0	0	15	33	280	0
25 PAPERBOARD CONTAINERS	0	0	0	0	0	0	0	0	0
26 PRINTING, PUBLISHING	1	2	3	0	0	0	1	15	0
27 CHEMICALS,SELECT. PRDTS.	96	211	560	0	0	21	228	1065	0
28 PLASTICS, SYNTHETICS	0	0	0	0	0	0	0	0	0
29 DRUGS, COSMETICS	13	0	0	0	0	0	6	1	0
30 PAINT, ALLIED PRDTS.	0	0	0	0	0	0	0	0	0
31 PETROLEUM, RELATED INDS.	43	70	158	0	0	5	52	267	0
32 RUBBER, MISC. PLASTICS	9	14	35	0	0	11	14	196	0
33 LEATHER TANNING, PRDTS.	0	0	0	0	0	0	0	0	0
34 FOOTWEAR, LEATHER PRDTS.	0	0	0	0	0	0	0	1	0
35 GLASS, GLASS PRDTS.	0	0	0	0	0	0	0	0	0
36 STONE, CLAY PRDTS.	4	2	21	0	0	0	10	91	0
37 PRIMARY IRON, STEEL MFR.	27	280	405	0	0	36	137	2554	0
38 PRIMARY NONFERROUS MFR.	1	23	6	0	0	12	2	205	0

39 METAL CONTAINERS	0	0	0	0	0	0	0	0	0
40 FABRICATED METAL PRDTS.	0	0	23	0	0	0	9	0	0
41 SCREW MACH. PRDTS., ETC.	0	0	0	0	0	0	0	0	0
42 OTHER FAB. METAL PRDTS.	4	8	14	0	0	2	7	65	0
43 ENGINES, TURBINES	207	44	0	0	0	0	104	30	0
44 FARM MACH., EQUIP.	0	0	0	0	0	0	0	0	0
45 CONSTRUC. MACH., EQUIP.	75	203	209	0	0	71	95	1171	0
46 MATERIAL HANDLING MACH.	1	13	30	0	0	37	10	533	0
47 METALWORKING MACHINERY	0	0	0	0	0	0	0	0	0
48 SPECIAL MACH., EQUIP.	0	0	0	0	0	0	0	0	0
49 GENERAL MACH., EQUIP.	8	30	6	0	0	19	5	370	0
50 MACHINE SHOP PRDTS.	14	27	41	0	0	0	14	163	0
51 OFFICE, COMPUT. MACHINES	0	0	0	0	0	0	0	0	0
52 SERVICE IND. MACHINES	0	0	0	0	0	0	0	0	0
53 ELECT. TRANSMISS. EQUIP.	9	18	118	0	0	54	41	777	0
54 HOUSEHOLD APPLIANCES	0	0	0	0	0	0	0	1	0
55 ELECTRIC LIGHTING EQUIP.	4	9	14	0	0	2	9	136	0
56 RADIO, TV, ETC., EQUIP.	0	0	0	0	0	0	0	1	0
57 ELECTRONIC COMPONENTS	0	0	0	0	0	0	0	0	0
58 MISC. ELECTRICAL MACH.	2	2	3	0	0	0	2	14	0
59 MOTOR VEHICLES, EQUIP.	7	12	22	0	0	3	9	94	0
60 AIRCRAFT, PARTS	0	0	0	0	0	0	0	0	0
61 OTHER TRANSPORT. EQUIP.	0	0	0	0	0	0	0	0	0
62 PROFESS., SCIEN. INSTRU.	0	0	0	0	0	0	0	0	0
63 MEDICAL, PHOTO. EQUIP.	0	0	0	0	0	0	0	3	0
64 MISC. MANUFACTURING	0	1	1	0	0	0	0	6	0
65 TRANSPORT., WAREHOUSING	89	201	268	0	0	17	1003	1634	285
66 COMMUNICA.,EXC. BRDCAST.	14	32	0	0	0	7	0	467	0
67 RADIO, TV BROADCASTING	0	0	0	0	0	0	0	0	0
68 ELEC.,GAS,WATER,SAN.SER.	107	201	490	0	0	31	182	5160	0
69 WHOLESALE, RETAIL TRADE	71	115	211	0	0	32	161	957	56
70 FINANCE, INSURANCE	29	66	0	0	0	15	0	951	1
71 REAL ESTATE, RENTAL	57	131	0	0	0	29	0	1883	0
72 HOTELS, PERSONAL SERV.	1	2	1	0	0	0	1	31	0
73 BUSINESS SERVICES	31	71	0	0	0	16	0	1025	0
74 RESEARCH, DEVELOPMENT	0	0	0	0	0	0	0	0	0
75 AUTO. REPAIR, SERVICES	5	11	0	0	0	2	0	160	0
76 AMUSEMENTS	0	0	0	0	0	0	0	5	0
77 MED.,EDUC. SERVICES	9	21	0	0	0	5	0	305	0
78 FEDERAL GOVT. ENTERPRISE	8	19	0	0	0	4	0	268	0
79 STATE, LOCAL GOVT. ENT.	4	10	0	0	0	2	0	142	0
80 DIRECT ALLOCATED IMPORTS	0	0	0	0	0	0	0	8	0
81 TRANSFERRED IMPORTS	144	0	0	0	0	0	0	1020	1253
82 VALUE ADDED	1438	3149	5634	0	0	797	1142	58369	0
83 SECONDARY TRANSFERS-IN	71	11	182	57	14	22	58	137	4
84 INVENTORY DEPLETION	3	7	11	0	0	2	6	98	0
85 SCRAP PRODUCTION	0	0	0	0	0	0	0	0	0
86 SCRAP PURCHASED	4	9	16	0	0	2	3	166	0
87 STATE TOTAL PRODUCTION	2746	5711	8972	57	14	1296	5379	83450	1599

TABLE C-8

1963 INPUTS BY STATE TO
IO-10, CHEMICAL & FERTILIZER MINERAL MINING
(THOUSANDS OF CURRENT DOLLARS)

INDUSTRY TITLE	19 MARYLAND	20 MASSA-CHUSETTS	21 MICHIGAN	22 MINNESOTA	23 MISSISSIPPI	24 MISSOURI	25 MONTANA	26 NEBRASKA	27 NEVADA
1 LIVESTOCK, PRDTS.	0	0	0	0	0	0	0	0	0
2 OTHER AGRICULTURE PRDTS.	0	0	0	0	0	0	0	0	0
3 FORESTRY, FISHERIES	0	0	0	0	0	0	0	0	0
4 AGRI.,FORES.,FISH. SERV.	0	0	0	0	0	0	0	0	0
5 IRON, FERRO. ORES MINING	0	0	0	0	0	0	0	0	0
6 NONFERROUS ORES MINING	0	0	0	0	0	0	0	0	0
7 COAL MINING	0	0	0	0	0	1	9	0	0
8 CRUDE PETRO.,NATURAL GAS	0	0	0	0	0	0	0	0	0
9 STONE, CLAY MINING	0	0	17	0	0	181	535	0	21
10 CHEM.,FERT. MIN. MINING	0	0	35	0	0	0	436	0	35
11 NEW CONSTRUCTION	0	0	0	0	0	0	0	0	0
12 MAINT., REPAIR CONSTR.	0	0	30	0	0	30	45	0	6
13 ORDNANCE, ACCESSORIES	0	0	0	0	0	0	0	0	0
14 FOOD, KINDRED PRDTS.	0	0	4	0	0	4	7	0	1
15 TOBACCO MANUFACTURES	0	0	0	0	0	0	1	0	0
16 FABRICS	0	0	0	0	0	14	1	0	2
17 TEXTILE PRDTS.	0	0	0	0	0	0	0	0	0
18 APPAREL	0	0	0	0	0	0	0	0	0
19 MISC. TEXTILE PRDTS.	0	0	0	0	0	0	0	0	0
20 LUMBER, WOOD PRDTS.	0	0	0	0	0	3	1	0	1
21 WOODEN CONTAINERS	0	0	0	0	0	0	0	0	0
22 HOUSEHOLD FURNITURE	0	0	0	0	0	0	0	0	0
23 OTHER FURNITURE	0	0	0	0	0	0	0	0	0
24 PAPER, ALLIED PRDTS.	0	0	38	0	0	143	37	0	28
25 PAPERBOARD CONTAINERS	0	0	0	0	0	0	0	0	0
26 PRINTING, PUBLISHING	0	0	1	0	0	3	3	0	0
27 CHEMICALS,SELECT. PRDTS.	0	0	52	0	0	460	372	0	97
28 PLASTICS, SYNTHETICS	0	0	0	0	0	0	0	0	0
29 DRUGS, COSMETICS	0	0	0	0	0	67	5	0	12
30 PAINT, ALLIED PRDTS.	0	0	0	0	0	0	0	0	0
31 PETROLEUM, RELATED INDS.	0	0	29	0	0	83	116	0	13
32 RUBBER, MISC. PLASTICS	0	0	28	0	0	29	24	0	7
33 LEATHER TANNING, PRDTS.	0	0	0	0	0	0	0	0	0
34 FOOTWEAR, LEATHER PRDTS.	0	0	0	0	0	0	0	0	0
35 GLASS, GLASS PRDTS.	0	0	0	0	0	0	0	0	0
36 STONE, CLAY PRDTS.	0	0	0	0	0	19	6	0	4
37 PRIMARY IRON, STEEL MFR.	0	0	94	0	0	66	439	0	24
38 PRIMARY NONFERROUS MFR.	0	0	31	0	0	0	35	0	1

39 METAL CONTAINERS	0	0	0	0	0	0	0	0	0
40 FABRICATED METAL PRDTS.	0	0	0	0	0	0	5	0	0
41 SCREW MACH. PRDTS., ETC.	0	0	0	0	0	0	0	0	0
42 OTHER FAB. METAL PRDTS.	0	0	6	0	0	13	14	0	3
43 ENGINES, TURBINES	0	0	0	0	0	993	148	0	178
44 FARM MACH., EQUIP.	0	0	0	0	0	0	0	0	0
45 CONSTRUC. MACH., EQUIP.	0	0	179	0	0	268	334	0	57
46 MATERIAL HANDLING MACH.	0	0	93	0	0	0	21	0	2
47 METALWORKING MACHINERY	0	0	0	0	0	0	0	0	0
48 SPECIAL MACH., EQUIP.	0	0	0	0	0	0	0	0	0
49 GENERAL MACH., EQUIP.	0	0	47	0	0	31	47	0	6
50 MACHINE SHOP PRDTS.	0	0	14	0	0	41	41	0	14
51 OFFICE, COMPUT. MACHINES	0	0	0	0	0	0	0	0	0
52 SERVICE IND. MACHINES	0	0	0	0	0	0	0	0	0
53 ELECT. TRANSMISS. EQUIP.	0	0	135	0	0	29	34	0	11
54 HOUSEHOLD APPLIANCES	0	0	0	0	0	0	0	0	0
55 ELECTRIC LIGHTING EQUIP.	0	0	10	0	0	10	15	0	2
56 RADIO, TV, ETC., EQUIP.	0	0	0	0	0	0	0	0	0
57 ELECTRONIC COMPONENTS	0	0	0	0	0	0	0	0	0
58 MISC. ELECTRICAL MACH.	0	0	2	0	0	2	3	0	0
59 MOTOR VEHICLES, EQUIP.	0	0	8	0	0	19	20	0	4
60 AIRCRAFT, PARTS	0	0	0	0	0	0	0	0	0
61 OTHER TRANSPORT. EQUIP.	0	0	0	0	0	0	0	0	0
62 PROFESS., SCIEN. INSTRU.	0	0	0	0	0	0	0	0	0
63 MEDICAL, PHOTO. EQUIP.	0	0	0	0	0	0	0	0	0
64 MISC. MANUFACTURING	0	0	0	0	0	1	1	0	0
65 TRANSPORT., WAREHOUSING	527	4	10043	0	0	101	499	0	37
66 COMMUNICA.,EXC. BRDCAST.	0	0	36	0	0	35	53	0	7
67 RADIO, TV BROADCASTING	0	0	0	0	0	0	0	0	0
68 ELEC.,GAS,WATER,SAN.SER.	0	0	146	0	0	351	329	0	48
69 WHOLESALE, RETAIL TRADE	103	1	2050	0	0	223	233	0	45
70 FINANCE, INSURANCE	3	0	123	0	0	72	109	0	15
71 REAL ESTATE, RENTAL	0	0	145	0	0	143	214	0	30
72 HOTELS, PERSONAL SERV.	0	0	2	0	0	2	3	0	0
73 BUSINESS SERVICES	0	0	79	0	0	78	116	0	16
74 RESEARCH, DEVELOPMENT	0	0	0	0	0	0	0	0	0
75 AUTO. REPAIR, SERVICES	0	0	12	0	0	12	18	0	3
76 AMUSEMENTS	0	0	0	0	0	0	1	0	0
77 MED.,EDUC. SERVICES	0	0	24	0	0	23	35	0	5
78 FEDERAL GOVT. ENTERPRISE	0	0	21	0	0	20	30	0	4
79 STATE, LOCAL GOVT. ENT.	0	0	11	0	0	11	16	0	2
80 DIRECT ALLOCATED IMPORTS	0	0	1	0	0	1	1	0	0
81 TRANSFERRED IMPORTS	2317	17	43957	0	0	0	796	0	0
82 VALUE ADDED	0	0	4773	0	0	2627	5121	0	563
83 SECONDARY TRANSFERS-IN	49	39	346	842	15	107	11	7	19
84 INVENTORY DEPLETION	0	0	8	2	0	8	11	0	2
85 SCRAP PRODUCTION	0	0	0	0	0	0	0	0	0
86 SCRAP PURCHASED	0	0	14	0	0	7	15	0	2
87 STATE TOTAL PRODUCTION	2999	61	62647	844	15	6333	10369	7	1327

TABLE C-8

1963 INPUTS BY STATE TO
IO-10, CHEMICAL & FERTILIZER MINERAL MINING
(THOUSANDS OF CURRENT DOLLARS)

INDUSTRY TITLE	28 NEW HAMPSHIRE	29 NEW JERSEY	30 NEW MEXICO	31 NEW YORK	32 NORTH CAROLINA	33 NORTH DAKOTA	34 OHIO	35 OKLAHOMA	36 OREGON
1 LIVESTOCK, PRDTS.	0	0	1	1	0	0	0	0	0
2 OTHER AGRICULTURE PRDTS.	0	0	5	2	0	0	0	0	0
3 FORESTRY, FISHERIES	0	0	0	0	0	0	0	0	0
4 AGRI.,FORES.,FISH. SERV.	0	0	0	0	0	0	0	0	0
5 IRON, FERRO. ORES MINING	0	0	0	0	0	0	0	0	0
6 NONFERROUS ORES MINING	0	0	0	0	0	0	0	0	0
7 COAL MINING	0	0	0	0	0	0	0	0	0
8 CRUDE PETRO.,NATURAL GAS	0	0	0	0	0	0	0	0	0
9 STONE, CLAY MINING	0	0	947	32	24	0	38	0	0
10 CHEM.,FERT. MIN. MINING	0	0	20	87	795	0	74	0	1
11 NEW CONSTRUCTION	0	0	0	0	0	0	0	0	0
12 MAINT., REPAIR CONSTR.	0	0	476	60	17	0	62	0	0
13 ORDNANCE, ACCESSORIES	0	0	0	0	0	0	0	0	0
14 FOOD, KINDRED PRDTS.	0	0	123	45	2	0	10	0	1
15 TOBACCO MANUFACTURES	0	0	7	4	0	0	1	0	0
16 FABRICS	0	0	101	6	6	0	0	0	0
17 TEXTILE PRDTS.	0	0	0	0	0	0	0	0	0
18 APPAREL	0	0	0	0	0	0	0	0	0
19 MISC. TEXTILE PRDTS.	0	0	0	0	0	0	0	0	0
20 LUMBER, WOOD PRDTS.	0	0	146	2	2	0	0	0	0
21 WOODEN CONTAINERS	0	0	0	0	0	0	0	0	0
22 HOUSEHOLD FURNITURE	0	0	0	0	0	0	0	0	0
23 OTHER FURNITURE	0	0	0	0	0	0	0	0	0
24 PAPER, ALLIED PRDTS.	0	0	240	84	20	0	80	0	0
25 PAPERBOARD CONTAINERS	0	0	0	0	0	0	0	0	0
26 PRINTING, PUBLISHING	0	0	28	4	3	0	3	0	0
27 CHEMICALS,SELECT. PRDTS.	0	0	5316	113	61	0	113	0	0
28 PLASTICS, SYNTHETICS	0	0	0	0	0	0	0	0	0
29 DRUGS, COSMETICS	0	0	3	1	0	0	0	0	0
30 PAINT, ALLIED PRDTS.	0	0	0	0	0	0	0	0	0
31 PETROLEUM, RELATED INDS.	0	0	454	57	50	0	63	0	0
32 RUBBER, MISC. PLASTICS	0	0	427	63	17	0	58	0	1
33 LEATHER TANNING, PRDTS.	0	0	C	0	0	0	0	0	0
34 FOOTWEAR, LEATHER PRDTS.	0	0	6	1	0	0	0	0	0
35 GLASS, GLASS PRDTS.	0	0	0	0	0	0	0	0	0
36 STONE, CLAY PRDTS.	0	0	85	4	2	0	2	0	0
37 PRIMARY IRON, STEEL MFR.	0	0	828	231	120	0	199	0	1
38 PRIMARY NONFERROUS MFR.	0	0	660	57	7	0	65	0	0

39 METAL CONTAINERS	0	0	0	0	0	0	0	0	0
40 FABRICATED METAL PRDTS.	0	0	260	5	5	0	0	0	0
41 SCREW MACH. PRDTS., ETC.	0	0	0	0	0	0	0	0	0
42 OTHER FAB. METAL PRDTS.	0	0	117	19	11	0	11	0	0
43 ENGINES, TURBINES	0	0	15	59	74	0	0	0	0
44 FARM MACH., EQUIP.	0	0	0	0	0	0	0	0	0
45 CONSTRUC. MACH., EQUIP.	0	0	4412	427	150	0	378	0	3
46 MATERIAL HANDLING MACH.	0	0	1798	172	7	0	199	0	0
47 METALWORKING MACHINERY	0	0	0	0	0	0	0	0	0
48 SPECIAL MACH., EQUIP.	0	0	0	0	0	0	0	0	0
49 GENERAL MACH., EQUIP.	0	0	24	94	14	0	101	0	0
50 MACHINE SHOP PRDTS.	0	0	298	41	27	0	27	0	0
51 OFFICE, COMPUT. MACHINES	0	0	0	0	0	0	0	0	0
52 SERVICE IND. MACHINES	0	0	0	0	0	0	0	0	0
53 ELECT. TRANSMISS. EQUIP.	0	0	1404	256	17	0	291	0	0
54 HOUSEHOLD APPLIANCES	0	0	1	1	0	0	0	0	0
55 ELECTRIC LIGHTING EQUIP.	0	0	166	20	6	0	22	0	0
56 RADIO, TV, ETC., EQUIP.	0	0	2	1	0	0	0	0	0
57 ELECTRONIC COMPONENTS	0	0	0	0	0	0	0	0	0
58 MISC. ELECTRICAL MACH.	0	0	22	3	2	0	2	0	0
59 MOTOR VEHICLES, EQUIP.	0	0	170	27	15	0	16	0	1
60 AIRCRAFT, PARTS	0	0	0	0	0	0	0	0	0
61 OTHER TRANSPORT. EQUIP.	0	0	184	1	1	0	0	0	0
62 PROFESS., SCIEN. INSTRU.	0	0	0	0	0	0	0	0	0
63 MEDICAL, PHOTO. EQUIP.	0	0	4	1	0	0	0	0	0
64 MISC. MANUFACTURING	0	0	12	2	1	0	1	0	0
65 TRANSPORT., WAREHOUSING	0	2868	894	1818	441	443	216	0	3
66 COMMUNICA.,EXC. BRDCAST.	0	0	571	71	20	0	77	0	0
67 RADIO, TV BROADCASTING	0	0	0	0	0	0	0	0	0
68 ELEC.,GAS,WATER,SAN.SER.	0	0	5042	289	220	0	314	0	1
69 WHOLESALE, RETAIL TRADE	0	562	1850	587	106	87	217	0	3
70 FINANCE, INSURANCE	0	14	1160	152	41	2	157	0	0
71 REAL ESTATE, RENTAL	0	0	2301	286	81	0	311	0	1
72 HOTELS, PERSONAL SERV.	0	0	38	22	1	0	4	0	1
73 BUSINESS SERVICES	0	0	1252	155	44	0	169	0	0
74 RESEARCH, DEVELOPMENT	0	0	0	0	0	0	0	0	0
75 AUTO. REPAIR, SERVICES	0	0	195	24	7	0	26	0	0
76 AMUSEMENTS	0	0	6	4	0	0	1	0	0
77 MED.,EDUC. SERVICES	0	0	373	47	13	0	50	0	0
78 FEDERAL GOVT. ENTERPRISE	0	0	327	40	11	0	44	0	0
79 STATE, LOCAL GOVT. ENT.	0	0	174	21	6	0	23	0	0
80 DIRECT ALLOCATED IMPORTS	0	0	9	6	0	0	1	0	0
81 TRANSFERRED IMPORTS	0	12612	0	7278	105	1950	510	0	0
82 VALUE ADDED	0	0	66944	8877	1099	0	10214	0	12
83 SECONDARY TRANSFERS-IN	3	384	19	226	39	1	156	7	18
84 INVENTORY DEPLETION	0	1	119	15	4	0	16	0	0
85 SCRAP PRODUCTION	0	0	0	0	0	0	0	0	0
86 SCRAP PURCHASED	0	0	190	25	3	0	29	0	0
87 STATE TOTAL PRODUCTION	3	16442	100227	21929	3698	2484	14353	7	47

TABLE C-8

1963 INPUTS BY STATE TO
IO-10, CHEMICAL & FERTILIZER MINERAL MINING

(THOUSANDS OF CURRENT DOLLARS)

INDUSTRY TITLE	37 PENNSYL-VANIA	38 RHODE ISLAND	39 SOUTH CAROLINA	40 SOUTH DAKOTA	41 TENNESSEE	42 TEXAS	43 UTAH	44 VERMONT	45 VIRGINIA
1 LIVESTOCK, PRDTS.	1	0	0	0	0	1	0	0	0
2 OTHER AGRICULTURE PRDTS.	2	0	0	0	1	2	0	0	0
3 FORESTRY, FISHERIES	0	0	0	0	0	0	0	0	0
4 AGRI.,FORES.,FISH. SERV.	0	0	0	0	0	0	0	0	0
5 IRON, FERRO. ORES MINING	0	0	0	0	0	0	0	0	0
6 NONFERROUS ORES MINING	0	0	0	0	0	0	0	0	0
7 COAL MINING	1	0	0	0	498	0	4	0	0
8 CRUDE PETRO.,NATURAL GAS	0	0	0	0	0	0	0	0	0
9 STONE, CLAY MINING	25	0	5	0	1143	169	408	0	0
10 CHEM.,FERT. MIN. MINING	832	0	11	1	1991	860	168	0	0
11 NEW CONSTRUCTION	0	0	0	0	0	0	0	0	0
12 MAINT., REPAIR CONSTR.	25	0	2	0	159	316	43	0	2
13 ORDNANCE, ACCESSORIES	0	0	0	0	0	0	0	0	0
14 FOOD, KINDRED PRDTS.	33	0	0	0	26	52	8	0	3
15 TOBACCO MANUFACTURES	2	0	0	0	2	5	0	0	0
16 FABRICS	12	0	0	0	54	9	3	0	2
17 TEXTILE PRDTS.	0	0	0	0	0	0	0	0	0
18 APPAREL	0	0	0	0	0	0	0	0	0
19 MISC. TEXTILE PRDTS.	0	0	0	0	0	0	0	0	0
20 LUMBER, WOOD PRDTS.	6	0	0	0	23	6	6	0	1
21 WOODEN CONTAINERS	0	0	0	0	0	0	0	0	0
22 HOUSEHOLD FURNITURE	0	0	0	0	0	0	0	0	0
23 OTHER FURNITURE	0	0	0	0	0	0	0	0	0
24 PAPER, ALLIED PRDTS.	44	0	6	0	198	205	17	0	8
25 PAPERBOARD CONTAINERS	0	0	0	0	0	0	0	0	0
26 PRINTING, PUBLISHING	5	0	0	0	23	12	2	0	1
27 CHEMICALS,SELECT. PRDTS.	95	0	19	0	447	1097	287	0	10
28 PLASTICS, SYNTHETICS	0	0	0	0	0	0	0	0	0
29 DRUGS, COSMETICS	1	0	3	0	6	35	0	0	0
30 PAINT, ALLIED PRDTS.	0	0	0	0	0	0	0	0	0
31 PETROLEUM, RELATED INDS.	59	0	8	0	256	185	88	0	2
32 RUBBER, MISC. PLASTICS	36	0	1	1	156	108	23	0	7
33 LEATHER TANNING, PRDTS.	0	0	0	0	0	0	0	0	0
34 FOOTWEAR, LEATHER PRDTS.	0	0	0	0	0	1	0	0	0
35 GLASS, GLASS PRDTS.	0	0	0	0	0	0	0	0	0
36 STONE, CLAY PRDTS.	4	0	0	0	17	95	4	0	0
37 PRIMARY IRON, STEEL MFR.	214	0	3	1	953	2053	174	0	31
38 PRIMARY NONFERROUS MFR.	12	0	0	0	56	88	34	0	2

39 METAL CONTAINERS	0	0	0	0	0	0	0	0	0
40 FABRICATED METAL PRDTS.	14	0	0	0	56	5	9	0	5
41 SCREW MACH. PRDTS., ETC.	0	0	0	0	0	0	0	0	0
42 OTHER FAB. METAL PRDTS.	23	0	0	0	101	50	8	0	4
43 ENGINES, TURBINES	148	0	44	0	697	519	15	0	30
44 FARM MACH., EQUIP.	0	0	0	0	0	0	0	0	0
45 CONSTRUC. MACH., EQUIP.	299	0	11	3	1327	629	250	0	51
46 MATERIAL HANDLING MACH.	16	0	0	0	66	196	72	0	2
47 METALWORKING MACHINERY	0	0	0	0	0	0	0	0	0
48 SPECIAL MACH., EQUIP.	0	0	0	0	0	0	0	0	0
49 GENERAL MACH., EQUIP.	27	0	2	0	124	186	16	0	5
50 MACHINE SHOP PRDTS.	54	0	0	0	231	122	27	0	14
51 OFFICE, COMPUT. MACHINES	0	0	0	0	0	0	0	0	0
52 SERVICE IND. MACHINES	0	0	0	0	0	0	0	0	0
53 ELECT. TRANSMISS. EQUIP.	37	0	1	0	154	288	63	0	7
54 HOUSEHOLD APPLIANCES	1	0	0	0	0	1	0	0	0
55 ELECTRIC LIGHTING EQUIP.	8	0	1	0	57	112	15	0	1
56 RADIO, TV, ETC., EQUIP.	1	0	0	0	1	1	0	0	0
57 ELECTRONIC COMPONENTS	0	0	0	0	0	0	0	0	0
58 MISC. ELECTRICAL MACH.	5	0	0	0	22	10	2	0	2
59 MOTOR VEHICLES, EQUIP.	33	0	1	1	144	72	12	0	6
60 AIRCRAFT, PARTS	0	0	0	0	0	0	0	0	0
61 OTHER TRANSPORT. EQUIP.	3	0	0	0	11	3	7	0	0
62 PROFESS., SCIEN. INSTRU.	0	0	0	0	0	0	0	0	0
63 MEDICAL, PHOTO. EQUIP.	1	0	0	0	3	1	0	0	0
64 MISC. MANUFACTURING	3	0	0	0	8	5	1	0	0
65 TRANSPORT., WAREHOUSING	728	0	10	1	1562	802	154	467	101
66 COMMUNICA., EXC. BRDCAST.	29	0	3	0	199	384	51	0	3
67 RADIO, TV BROADCASTING	0	0	0	0	0	0	0	0	0
68 ELEC.,GAS,WATER,SAN.SER.	262	0	18	1	1013	4630	494	0	12
69 WHOLESALE, RETAIL TRADE	248	0	11	1	647	640	140	92	42
70 FINANCE, INSURANCE	60	0	5	0	405	780	103	2	6
71 REAL ESTATE, RENTAL	117	0	10	1	803	1546	204	0	12
72 HOTELS, PERSONAL SERV.	16	0	0	0	13	25	3	0	2
73 BUSINESS SERVICES	64	0	6	0	437	842	111	0	6
74 RESEARCH, DEVELOPMENT	0	0	0	0	0	0	0	0	0
75 AUTO. REPAIR, SERVICES	10	0	1	0	68	131	17	0	1
76 AMUSEMENTS	2	0	0	0	2	5	0	0	0
77 MED., EDUC. SERVICES	20	0	2	0	130	250	33	0	2
78 FEDERAL GOVT. ENTERPRISE	17	0	1	0	114	220	29	0	2
79 STATE, LOCAL GOVT. ENT.	9	0	1	0	60	117	15	0	1
80 DIRECT ALLOCATED IMPORTS	5	0	0	0	3	7	1	0	0
81 TRANSFERRED IMPORTS	1013	0	0	0	0	168	0	2055	396
82 VALUE ADDED	1696	0	266	18	20388	49315	5764	0	231
83 SECONDARY TRANSFERS-IN	211	9	15	4	105	580	43	2	65
84 INVENTORY DEPLETION	6	0	1	0	42	81	11	0	1
85 SCRAP PRODUCTION	0	0	0	0	0	0	0	0	0
86 SCRAP PURCHASED	5	0	1	0	58	140	16	0	1
87 STATE TOTAL PRODUCTION	6603	9	469	33	35066	68166	8957	2619	1081

TABLE C-8

1963 INPUTS BY STATE TO
IO-10, CHEMICAL & FERTILIZER MINERAL MINING

(THOUSANDS OF CURRENT DOLLARS)

INDUSTRY TITLE	46 WASHINGTON	47 WEST VIRGINIA	48 WISCONSIN	49 WYOMING	50 ALASKA	51 HAWAII	52 NATIONAL TOTAL
1 LIVESTOCK, PRDTS.	0	1	0	0	0	0	9
2 OTHER AGRICULTURE PRDTS.	0	1	0	1	0	0	26
3 FORESTRY, FISHERIES	0	0	0	0	0	0	0
4 AGRI.,FORES.,FISH. SERV.	0	0	0	0	0	0	0
5 IRON, FERRO. ORES MINING	0	0	0	0	0	0	0
6 NONFERROUS ORES MINING	0	0	0	0	0	0	0
7 COAL MINING	0	0	0	1	0	0	608
8 CRUDE PETRO.,NATURAL GAS	0	0	0	0	0	0	0
9 STONE, CLAY MINING	0	0	0	761	0	0	5176
10 CHEM.,FERT. MIN. MINING	0	1	0	83	0	0	30938
11 NEW CONSTRUCTION	0	0	0	0	0	0	0
12 MAINT., REPAIR CONSTR.	0	0	0	80	0	0	2743
13 ORDNANCE, ACCESSORIES	0	0	0	0	0	0	0
14 FOOD, KINDRED PRDTS.	8	16	0	19	0	0	572
15 TOBACCO MANUFACTURES	1	1	0	1	0	0	41
16 FABRICS	0	0	0	15	0	0	296
17 TEXTILE PRDTS.	0	0	0	0	0	0	0
18 APPAREL	0	0	0	0	0	0	0
19 MISC. TEXTILE PRDTS.	0	0	0	0	0	0	0
20 LUMBER, WOOD PRDTS.	0	0	0	18	0	0	303
21 WOODEN CONTAINERS	0	0	0	0	0	0	0
22 HOUSEHOLD FURNITURE	0	0	0	0	0	0	0
23 OTHER FURNITURE	0	0	0	0	0	0	0
24 PAPER, ALLIED PRDTS.	0	1	0	35	0	0	2056
25 PAPERBOARD CONTAINERS	0	0	0	0	0	0	0
26 PRINTING, PUBLISHING	0	0	0	4	0	0	161
27 CHEMICALS,SELECT. PRDTS.	1	1	0	645	0	0	16918
28 PLASTICS, SYNTHETICS	0	0	0	0	0	0	0
29 DRUGS, COSMETICS	0	0	0	0	0	0	190
30 PAINT, ALLIED PRDTS.	0	0	0	0	0	0	11
31 PETROLEUM, RELATED INDS.	0	0	0	172	0	0	5730
32 RUBBER, MISC. PLASTICS	0	1	0	57	0	0	1743
33 LEATHER TANNING, PRDTS.	0	0	0	0	0	0	0
34 FOOTWEAR, LEATHER PRDTS.	0	0	0	0	0	0	15
35 GLASS, GLASS PRDTS.	0	0	0	0	0	0	0
36 STONE, CLAY PRDTS.	0	0	0	12	0	0	454
37 PRIMARY IRON, STEEL MFR.	0	3	0	158	0	0	13746
38 PRIMARY NONFERROUS MFR.	0	0	0	79	0	0	2000

39 METAL CONTAINERS	0	0	0	0	0	0	0
40 FABRICATED METAL PRDTS.	0	0	0	33	0	0	555
41 SCREW MACH. PRDTS., ETC.	0	0	0	0	0	0	0
42 OTHER FAB. METAL PRDTS.	0	0	0	19	0	0	692
43 ENGINES, TURBINES	3	0	0	30	0	0	4616
44 FARM MACH., EQUIP.	0	0	0	0	0	0	0
45 CONSTRUC. MACH., EQUIP.	1	5	0	577	0	0	16303
46 MATERIAL HANDLING MACH.	0	0	0	206	0	0	4428
47 METALWORKING MACHINERY	0	0	0	0	0	0	0
48 SPECIAL MACH., EQUIP.	0	0	0	0	0	0	0
49 GENERAL MACH., EQUIP.	0	1	0	8	0	0	1672
50 MACHINE SHOP PRDTS.	0	0	0	41	0	0	1724
51 OFFICE, COMPUT. MACHINES	0	0	0	0	0	0	0
52 SERVICE IND. MACHINES	0	0	0	0	0	0	0
53 ELECT. TRANSMISS. EQUIP.	0	0	0	163	0	0	4827
54 HOUSEHOLD APPLIANCES	0	1	0	0	0	0	9
55 ELECTRIC LIGHTING EQUIP.	0	0	0	29	0	0	957
56 RADIO, TV, ETC., EQUIP.	0	0	0	0	0	0	12
57 ELECTRONIC COMPONENTS	0	0	0	0	0	0	0
58 MISC. ELECTRICAL MACH.	0	0	0	3	0	0	136
59 MOTOR VEHICLES, EQUIP.	0	0	0	27	0	0	999
60 AIRCRAFT, PARTS	0	0	0	0	0	0	0
61 OTHER TRANSPORT. EQUIP.	0	0	0	22	0	0	305
62 PROFESS., SCIEN. INSTRU.	0	0	0	0	0	0	0
63 MEDICAL, PHOTO. EQUIP.	0	0	0	0	0	0	19
64 MISC. MANUFACTURING	0	0	0	2	0	0	66
65 TRANSPORT., WAREHOUSING	461	24	443	181	27	31	39724
66 COMMUNICA., EXC. BRDCAST.	0	0	0	101	0	0	2801
67 RADIO, TV BROADCASTING	0	0	0	0	0	0	0
68 ELEC.,GAS,WATER,SAN.SER.	0	1	0	1157	0	0	35901
69 WHOLESALE, RETAIL TRADE	102	29	87	288	5	6	14447
70 FINANCE, INSURANCE	2	0	2	205	0	0	5792
71 REAL ESTATE, RENTAL	0	1	0	408	0	0	11296
72 HOTELS, PERSONAL SERV.	4	8	0	7	0	0	246
73 BUSINESS SERVICES	0	0	0	221	0	0	6145
74 RESEARCH, DEVELOPMENT	0	0	0	0	0	0	0
75 AUTO. REPAIR, SERVICES	0	0	0	34	0	0	956
76 AMUSEMENTS	1	2	0	1	0	0	40
77 MED., EDUC. SERVICES	0	0	0	66	0	0	1836
78 FEDERAL GOVT. ENTERPRISE	0	0	0	58	0	0	1604
79 STATE, LOCAL GOVT. ENT.	0	0	0	31	0	0	850
80 DIRECT ALLOCATED IMPORTS	1	2	0	1	0	0	61
81 TRANSFERRED IMPORTS	1975	0	1946	0	118	138	87500
82 VALUE ADDED	1	2	0	11637	0	0	360303
83 SECONDARY TRANSFERS-IN	52	261	22	38	1	5	4865
84 INVENTORY DEPLETION	0	1	0	21	0	0	700
85 SCRAP PRODUCTION	0	0	0	0	0	0	0
86 SCRAP PURCHASED	0	0	0	33	0	0	1022
87 STATE TOTAL PRODUCTION	2617	364	2500	17791	152	181	697145

TABLE C-9

1963 INPUTS BY STATE TO
IO-11, NEW CONSTRUCTION
(THOUSANDS OF CURRENT DOLLARS)

INDUSTRY TITLE	1 ALABAMA	2 ARIZONA	3 ARKANSAS	4 CALIFORNIA	5 COLORADO	6 CONNECTICUT	7 DELAWARE	8 DISTRICT OF COLUMBIA	9 FLORIDA
1 LIVESTOCK, PRDTS.	23	14	10	268	29	22	6	16	62
2 OTHER AGRICULTURE PRDTS.	5302	2147	2298	46940	3592	6033	1623	1841	19233
3 FORESTRY, FISHERIES	5	3	2	57	6	4	1	3	13
4 AGRI.,FORES.,FISH. SERV.	36	32	16	662	45	46	11	16	134
5 IRON, FERRO. ORES MINING	0	0	0	0	0	0	0	0	0
6 NONFERROUS ORES MINING	0	0	0	0	0	0	0	0	0
7 COAL MINING	0	0	0	0	0	0	0	0	0
8 CRUDE PETRO.,NATURAL GAS	0	0	0	0	0	0	0	0	0
9 STONE, CLAY MINING	7026	6484	4941	46862	5648	5827	1906	2700	18596
10 CHEM.,FERT. MIN. MINING	0	0	0	0	0	0	0	0	0
11 NEW CONSTRUCTION	0	0	0	0	0	0	0	0	0
12 MAINT., REPAIR CONSTR.	237	150	106	2926	310	228	62	156	663
13 ORDNANCE, ACCESSORIES	45	34	24	543	51	135	12	22	101
14 FOOD, KINDRED PRDTS.	1695	1065	755	20807	2107	1728	474	945	4896
15 TOBACCO MANUFACTURES	106	66	48	1239	133	100	28	72	286
16 FABRICS	955	393	250	3798	1108	71	37	95	1215
17 TEXTILE PRDTS.	1180	1135	457	28034	1965	1063	208	1727	3887
18 APPAREL	407	244	214	4426	507	365	110	258	1068
19 MISC. TEXTILE PRDTS.	77	46	34	808	85	158	20	91	151
20 LUMBER, WOOD PRDTS.	46280	28833	19975	620712	66036	50822	13312	16010	159186
21 WOODEN CONTAINERS	0	0	0	0	0	0	0	0	0
22 HOUSEHOLD FURNITURE	4326	3174	1721	66438	4411	4131	1217	1909	16474
23 OTHER FURNITURE	2574	1397	886	30548	3543	2375	630	1815	7330
24 PAPER, ALLIED PRDTS.	3234	1747	1171	36040	3812	2590	746	2565	8835
25 PAPERBOARD CONTAINERS	72	5	5	798	114	45	10	105	174
26 PRINTING, PUBLISHING	169	107	76	2052	218	162	45	113	467
27 CHEMICALS,SELECT. PRDTS.	2619	1584	2011	23672	3180	2238	505	1392	4183
28 PLASTICS, SYNTHETICS	17	1	1	186	27	10	2	25	40
29 DRUGS, COSMETICS	69	24	19	771	96	54	14	73	175
30 PAINT, ALLIED PRDTS.	3935	2947	1932	49857	5299	3372	1291	1772	12834
31 PETROLEUM, RELATED INDS.	18671	11600	14378	134127	18749	12071	4861	5539	41700
32 RUBBER, MISC. PLASTICS	6657	4386	3398	83561	10918	5972	1846	5345	17338
33 LEATHER TANNING, PRDTS.	7	3	4	41	6	5	2	4	14
34 FOOTWEAR, LEATHER PRDTS.	27	16	16	311	35	22	9	40	66
35 GLASS, GLASS PRDTS.	1495	503	633	8238	845	1421	448	618	4729
36 STONE, CLAY PRDTS.	84633	49627	38338	868311	95103	74291	24999	48463	226632
37 PRIMARY IRON, STEEL MFR.	28267	18715	15948	238912	35651	21473	7348	13886	55127
38 PRIMARY NONFERROUS MFR.	18810	10602	8786	182016	20717	18365	4295	9822	49176

39 METAL CONTAINERS	0	0	0	0	0	0	0	0	0
40 FABRICATED METAL PRDTS.	84769	44086	37933	840289	101567	82948	19586	67730	212133
41 SCREW MACH. PRDTS., ETC.	2294	971	1007	12977	2574	1140	222	640	3597
42 OTHER FAB. METAL PRDTS.	14618	7861	6865	149946	18805	10847	3934	10696	39243
43 ENGINES, TURBINES	541	103	120	1900	422	490	47	128	971
44 FARM MACH., EQUIP.	22	13	18	160	24	17	7	9	46
45 CONSTRUC. MACH., EQUIP.	2869	1518	2580	22610	3727	1819	720	951	5012
46 MATERIAL HANDLING MACH.	2818	1832	921	34670	3966	3323	849	4853	7261
47 METALWORKING MACHINERY	145	125	91	1393	182	222	34	70	252
48 SPECIAL MACH., EQUIP.	0	0	0	0	0	0	0	0	0
49 GENERAL MACH., EQUIP.	2542	1423	940	28372	3240	3107	599	2557	6362
50 MACHINE SHOP PRDTS.	200	119	161	933	136	156	71	69	400
51 OFFICE, COMPUT. MACHINES	1	1	0	12	1	1	0	1	3
52 SERVICE IND. MACHINES	5643	2460	1734	61390	6619	4798	1213	6486	14715
53 ELECT. TRANSMISS. EQUIP.	4686	3859	2495	50870	6752	5266	1042	2455	9426
54 HOUSEHOLD APPLIANCES	2549	1897	1187	41429	4102	2077	812	245	9274
55 ELECTRIC LIGHTING EQUIP.	16537	8599	8016	173618	21621	12675	4060	13098	42071
56 RADIO, TV, ETC., EQUIP.	1233	465	596	5473	1066	973	204	643	2488
57 ELECTRONIC COMPONENTS	17	8	8	125	19	13	5	44	29
58 MISC. ELECTRICAL MACH.	498	331	330	5621	618	435	148	190	1365
59 MOTOR VEHICLES, EQUIP.	527	307	437	3659	552	397	161	210	1081
60 AIRCRAFT, PARTS	0	0	0	0	0	0	0	0	0
61 OTHER TRANSPORT. EQUIP.	73	34	34	495	67	54	18	47	152
62 PROFESS., SCIEN. INSTRU.	2412	1667	1023	29829	3453	3238	675	3798	5366
63 MEDICAL, PHOTO. EQUIP.	92	52	42	862	108	90	23	64	216
64 MISC. MANUFACTURING	1348	825	656	18314	2919	1154	348	729	3177
65 TRANSPORT., WAREHOUSING	31769	19866	15518	345783	38513	30019	8482	13092	83676
66 COMMUNICA.,EXC. BRDCAST.	2376	1573	1064	30497	3313	2446	623	1596	6579
67 RADIO, TV BROADCASTING	0	0	0	0	0	0	0	0	0
68 ELEC.,GAS,WATER,SAN.SER.	2772	1752	1245	33885	3602	2701	731	1824	7693
69 WHOLESALE, RETAIL TRADE	72636	48312	37475	924160	98999	69348	20603	40500	213097
70 FINANCE, INSURANCE	5578	3408	3097	57741	7069	4799	1544	3121	14366
71 REAL ESTATE, RENTAL	4230	2616	1931	49889	5358	4024	1121	2874	11514
72 HOTELS, PERSONAL SERV.	642	399	293	7508	806	606	170	437	1735
73 BUSINESS SERVICES	42420	27466	24608	440344	47746	39186	11959	26160	105923
74 RESEARCH, DEVELOPMENT	0	0	0	0	0	0	0	0	0
75 AUTO. REPAIR, SERVICES	3230	2020	1470	38268	4093	3065	853	2185	8799
76 AMUSEMENTS	103	64	47	1212	130	98	27	71	280
77 MED.,EDUC. SERVICES	814	509	370	9658	1033	773	215	550	2219
78 FEDERAL GOVT. ENTERPRISE	244	155	109	3016	319	236	64	161	684
79 STATE, LOCAL GOVT. ENT.	418	246	331	2929	422	324	129	173	876
80 DIRECT ALLOCATED IMPORTS	159	99	73	1865	200	150	42	109	431
81 TRANSFERRED IMPORTS	0	0	0	0	0	0	0	0	0
82 VALUE ADDED	287242	434558	174956	6510493	169804	577451	54023	54435	1149695
83 SECONDARY TRANSFERS-IN	0	0	0	0	0	0	0	0	0
84 INVENTORY DEPLETION	0	0	0	0	0	0	0	0	0
85 SCRAP PRODUCTION	0	0	0	0	0	0	0	0	0
86 SCRAP PURCHASED	492	450	262	7286	497	636	118	226	1538
87 STATE TOTAL PRODUCTION	840568	769136	448501	12453446	848791	1086300	201559	385666	2628530

TABLE C-9

1963 INPUTS BY STATE TO
IO-11, NEW CONSTRUCTION
(THOUSANDS OF CURRENT DOLLARS)

INDUSTRY TITLE	10 GEORGIA	11 IDAHO	12 ILLINOIS	13 INDIANA	14 IOWA	15 KANSAS	16 KENTUCKY	17 LOUISIANA	18 MAINE
1 LIVESTOCK, PRDTS.	37	4	73	35	16	16	19	36	4
2 OTHER AGRICULTURE PRDTS.	8710	329	14928	6613	3054	2667	4068	5647	664
3 FORESTRY, FISHERIES	8	1	15	7	3	3	4	8	1
4 AGRI.,FORES.,FISH. SERV.	63	5	128	56	25	22	28	39	5
5 IRON, FERRO. ORES MINING	0	0	0	0	0	0	0	0	0
6 NONFERROUS ORES MINING	0	0	0	0	0	0	0	0	0
7 COAL MINING	0	0	0	0	0	0	0	0	0
8 CRUDE PETRO.,NATURAL GAS	0	0	0	0	0	0	0	0	0
9 STONE, CLAY MINING	10613	3412	15804	9712	8033	6803	9165	14137	4961
10 CHEM.,FERT. MIN. MINING	0	0	0	0	0	0	0	0	0
11 NEW CONSTRUCTION	0	0	0	0	0	0	0	0	0
12 MAINT., REPAIR CONSTR.	388	38	777	369	162	164	187	378	40
13 ORDNANCE, ACCESSORIES	64	14	340	134	73	57	44	52	31
14 FOOD, KINDRED PRDTS.	2693	273	5357	2536	1203	1137	1383	2449	287
15 TOBACCO MANUFACTURES	170	18	336	160	75	74	88	167	19
16 FABRICS	1550	22	676	228	85	270	209	215	66
17 TEXTILE PRDTS.	2319	134	6408	2603	899	898	658	1506	130
18 APPAREL	649	80	1241	599	334	322	381	784	78
19 MISC. TEXTILE PRDTS.	101	18	448	185	92	75	63	84	38
20 LUMBER, WOOD PRDTS.	87390	8116	166133	80711	43233	33305	32088	51696	6370
21 WOODEN CONTAINERS	0	0	0	0	0	0	0	0	0
22 HOUSEHOLD FURNITURE	9008	464	14926	6006	2466	2309	2575	4792	385
23 OTHER FURNITURE	4401	435	10066	4451	1566	1517	1663	2805	416
24 PAPER, ALLIED PRDTS.	5574	420	9749	4443	1702	1590	1950	3446	449
25 PAPERBOARD CONTAINERS	88	7	333	73	33	19	24	52	10
26 PRINTING, PUBLISHING	276	28	549	261	117	117	136	269	29
27 CHEMICALS,SELECT. PRDTS.	2429	684	5659	2529	1407	3798	7198	17545	621
28 PLASTICS, SYNTHETICS	20	1	79	17	7	4	5	12	2
29 DRUGS, COSMETICS	97	10	267	86	42	34	43	81	11
30 PAINT, ALLIED PRDTS.	7729	861	12773	7343	2678	3164	3691	5525	601
31 PETROLEUM, RELATED INDS.	25090	6383	36617	20147	18328	23712	20512	38216	3938
32 RUBBER, MISC. PLASTICS	10736	1401	19224	10873	5083	4677	5804	9871	1264
33 LEATHER TANNING, PRDTS.	9	2	17	7	8	6	10	10	2
34 FOOTWEAR, LEATHER PRDTS.	39	4	83	38	23	22	25	39	5
35 GLASS, GLASS PRDTS.	2415	123	3490	1841	750	673	1131	1639	199
36 STONE, CLAY PRDTS.	144943	13402	252760	129270	74361	57534	68082	125687	12208
37 PRIMARY IRON, STEEL MFR.	40141	7122	80347	47121	17860	32907	40924	126598	6253
38 PRIMARY NONFERROUS MFR.	32585	3529	56357	29899	13205	9447	13221	19157	3493

39 METAL CONTAINERS	0	0	0	0	0	0	0	0	0
40 FABRICATED METAL PRDTS.	143033	13678	301921	150836	63752	57567	71950	115180	16562
41 SCREW MACH. PRDTS., ETC.	3261	410	4259	2381	1498	1341	1200	3828	329
42 OTHER FAB. METAL PRDTS.	24565	2688	41795	19706	11066	8989	11776	19059	2236
43 ENGINES, TURBINES	604	65	1239	1074	487	137	156	524	105
44 FARM MACH., EQUIP.	30	5	53	29	23	29	31	86	5
45 CONSTRUC. MACH., EQUIP.	3332	592	6432	3413	2609	5672	4087	27543	572
46 MATERIAL HANDLING MACH.	4446	544	15518	7634	1591	2622	2264	3597	697
47 METALWORKING MACHINERY	246	41	441	347	146	100	163	221	56
48 SPECIAL MACH., EQUIP.	0	0	0	0	0	0	0	0	0
49 GENERAL MACH., EQUIP.	3799	473	12843	6759	2611	2251	1737	2993	556
50 MACHINE SHOP PRDTS.	276	63	385	205	257	214	349	383	63
51 OFFICE, COMPUT. MACHINES	2	0	3	1	1	1	1	2	0
52 SERVICE IND. MACHINES	9132	803	23594	9668	2959	2950	3404	6532	988
53 ELECT. TRANSMISS. EQUIP.	7484	1251	13494	9600	4153	2796	4178	6509	1224
54 HOUSEHOLD APPLIANCES	4130	476	8016	3664	2042	1606	1961	2614	217
55 ELECTRIC LIGHTING EQUIP.	26951	2513	53094	23810	11058	10924	12570	20391	2732
56 RADIO, TV, ETC., EQUIP.	1668	534	4642	3763	2387	959	2379	1356	354
57 ELECTRONIC COMPONENTS	24	5	56	43	27	13	25	16	5
58 MISC. ELECTRICAL MACH.	785	95	1367	661	437	495	549	1365	89
59 MOTOR VEHICLES, EQUIP.	707	125	1234	673	562	669	755	1942	126
60 AIRCRAFT, PARTS	0	0	0	0	0	0	0	0	0
61 OTHER TRANSPORT. EQUIP.	102	16	190	78	65	47	78	86	17
62 PROFESS., SCIEN. INSTRU.	3744	459	9858	6059	2464	1938	1873	2795	756
63 MEDICAL, PHOTO. EQUIP.	136	18	311	169	76	68	83	129	21
64 MISC. MANUFACTURING	1981	327	3799	1658	1219	925	1479	1636	306
65 TRANSPORT., WAREHOUSING	50664	6728	101567	50740	26527	24392	29483	55360	6272
66 COMMUNICA.,EXC. BRDCAST.	3812	409	7727	3652	1647	1657	1900	3811	443
67 RADIO, TV BROADCASTING	0	0	0	0	0	0	0	0	0
68 ELEC.,GAS,WATER,SAN.SER.	4533	454	9110	4330	1933	1938	2207	4408	486
69 WHOLESALE, RETAIL TRADE	123322	14013	235079	112959	57877	55102	62783	115658	12297
70 FINANCE, INSURANCE	9059	1060	16278	8213	4432	4766	5461	11672	1060
71 REAL ESTATE, RENTAL	6826	708	13536	6452	2980	2947	3485	6722	749
72 HOTELS, PERSONAL SERV.	1032	108	2038	970	457	447	533	1015	115
73 BUSINESS SERVICES	63509	8834	127924	63149	37236	34011	45065	61315	9030
74 RESEARCH, DEVELOPMENT	0	0	0	0	0	0	0	0	0
75 AUTO. REPAIR, SERVICES	5218	540	10332	4917	2282	2245	2655	5120	572
76 AMUSEMENTS	166	17	328	156	74	72	86	164	19
77 MED.,EDUC. SERVICES	1315	136	2606	1240	575	566	669	1290	144
78 FEDERAL GOVT. ENTERPRISE	401	40	802	381	168	169	193	390	42
79 STATE, LOCAL GOVT. ENT.	573	101	982	526	446	497	596	1350	102
80 DIRECT ALLOCATED IMPORTS	256	27	506	241	114	111	133	252	28
81 TRANSFERRED IMPORTS	0	0	0	0	0	0	0	0	0
82 VALUE ADDED	272423	71831	1244961	260595	169139	246192	289144	613997	59944
83 SECONDARY TRANSFERS-IN	0	0	0	0	0	0	0	0	0
84 INVENTORY DEPLETION	0	0	0	0	0	0	0	0	0
85 SCRAP PRODUCTION	0	0	0	0	0	0	0	0	0
86 SCRAP PURCHASED	693	104	1753	667	360	389	458	898	95
87 STATE TOTAL PRODUCTION	1184579	177637	2996040	1139772	614663	665160	783277	1535151	161994

TABLE C-9

1963 INPUTS BY STATE TO
IO-11, NEW CONSTRUCTION

(THOUSANDS OF CURRENT DOLLARS)

INDUSTRY TITLE	19 MARYLAND	20 MASSA-CHUSETTS	21 MICHIGAN	22 MINNESOTA	23 MISSISSIPPI	24 MISSOURI	25 MONTANA	26 NEBRASKA	27 NEVADA
1 LIVESTOCK, PRDTS.	38	36	52	26	10	26	5	11	11
2 OTHER AGRICULTURE PRDTS.	11301	8351	12444	5915	1804	5915	385	1964	1643
3 FORESTRY, FISHERIES	8	8	11	5	2	5	1	2	2
4 AGRI.,FORES.,FISH. SERV.	84	66	104	50	12	50	6	17	35
5 IRON, FERRO. ORES MINING	0	0	0	0	0	0	0	0	0
6 NONFERROUS ORES MINING	0	0	0	0	0	0	0	0	0
7 COAL MINING	0	0	0	0	0	0	0	0	0
8 CRUDE PETRO.,NATURAL GAS	0	0	0	0	0	0	0	0	0
9 STONE, CLAY MINING	8199	6750	14224	10420	5610	10420	7948	4508	4560
10 CHEM.,FERT. MIN. MINING	0	0	0	0	0	0	0	0	0
11 NEW CONSTRUCTION	0	0	0	0	0	0	0	0	0
12 MAINT., REPAIR CONSTR.	404	390	537	269	97	269	50	115	125
13 ORDNANCE, ACCESSORIES	75	236	234	94	25	94	15	38	15
14 FOOD, KINDRED PRDTS.	2797	2697	4037	1926	687	1926	346	819	1045
15 TOBACCO MANUFACTURES	175	168	239	119	45	119	24	52	53
16 FABRICS	1660	865	968	119	223	119	213	199	301
17 TEXTILE PRDTS.	3720	2531	4099	2388	358	2388	190	726	971
18 APPAREL	633	618	880	466	207	466	112	216	179
19 MISC. TEXTILE PRDTS.	130	280	313	122	36	122	22	54	19
20 LUMBER, WOOD PRDTS.	78661	77308	131265	67470	15584	67470	7858	25799	29996
21 WOODEN CONTAINERS	0	0	0	0	0	0	0	0	0
22 HOUSEHOLD FURNITURE	8791	7453	9444	5413	1171	5413	493	2147	3374
23 OTHER FURNITURE	4158	4250	5177	3026	897	3026	459	1234	1078
24 PAPER, ALLIED PRDTS.	5594	4756	6199	3210	1004	3210	518	1314	1495
25 PAPERBOARD CONTAINERS	104	114	55	86	24	86	12	29	9
26 PRINTING, PUBLISHING	286	275	384	191	70	191	36	82	87
27 CHEMICALS,SELECT. PRDTS.	2670	2972	3909	1690	2110	1690	1434	1088	946
28 PLASTICS, SYNTHETICS	24	27	12	20	5	20	3	7	2
29 DRUGS, COSMETICS	106	108	105	79	27	79	14	31	22
30 PAINT, ALLIED PRDTS.	6442	6137	7767	4172	1681	4172	939	2114	1908
31 PETROLEUM, RELATED INDS.	18295	20118	29833	19847	11625	19847	10446	9855	6163
32 RUBBER, MISC. PLASTICS	11110	10604	14937	7304	2891	7304	1623	3331	2857
33 LEATHER TANNING, PRDTS.	7	8	12	8	5	8	3	4	1
34 FOOTWEAR, LEATHER PRDTS.	50	40	74	28	12	28	7	14	11
35 GLASS, GLASS PRDTS.	2451	2132	2766	1306	486	1306	128	538	288
36 STONE, CLAY PRDTS.	142249	122849	183555	96061	45057	96061	17411	45652	36186
37 PRIMARY IRON, STEEL MFR.	41435	30896	64902	28303	16424	28303	13862	14215	10911
38 PRIMARY NONFERROUS MFR.	30697	31191	41269	22335	6564	22335	2456	8361	8112

39 METAL CONTAINERS	0	0	0	0	0	0	0	0	0
40 FABRICATED METAL PRDTS.	148663	141811	197060	106560	34671	106560	16267	43299	26669
41 SCREW MACH. PRDTS., ETC.	3351	2547	3253	1919	1018	1919	651	895	718
42 OTHER FAB. METAL PRDTS.	23709	19369	29749	14573	5685	14573	3279	6801	6145
43 ENGINES, TURBINES	971	763	584	765	92	765	54	1	181
44 FARM MACH., EQUIP.	29	26	45	23	18	23	10	13	6
45 CONSTRUC. MACH., EQUIP.	3213	2890	5247	2452	3747	2452	1799	1775	689
46 MATERIAL HANDLING MACH.	5502	5782	6916	3170	1116	3170	701	1652	529
47 METALWORKING MACHINERY	210	351	460	254	64	254	31	100	63
48 SPECIAL MACH., EQUIP.	0	0	0	0	0	0	0	0	0
49 GENERAL MACH., EQUIP.	4535	5192	8367	4471	908	4471	506	1655	942
50 MACHINE SHOP PRDTS.	186	193	398	214	169	214	102	137	40
51 OFFICE, COMPUT. MACHINES	2	2	2	1	0	1	0	0	0
52 SERVICE IND. MACHINES	10024	9931	10012	6674	1938	6674	912	2601	1402
53 ELECT. TRANSMISS. EQUIP.	7701	8676	11554	6969	1746	6969	1038	2230	2394
54 HOUSEHOLD APPLIANCES	4148	3181	6315	3199	921	3199	436	1353	2253
55 ELECTRIC LIGHTING EQUIP.	28424	24309	32148	17415	6583	17415	3702	7423	6154
56 RADIO, TV, ETC., EQUIP.	1955	1778	2105	1702	485	1702	460	651	403
57 ELECTRONIC COMPONENTS	37	25	64	18	6	18	6	12	5
58 MISC. ELECTRICAL MACH.	769	699	1063	558	304	558	160	264	247
59 MOTOR VEHICLES, EQUIP.	656	598	1058	549	435	549	238	306	130
60 AIRCRAFT, PARTS	0	0	0	0	0	0	0	0	0
61 OTHER TRANSPORT. EQUIP.	86	83	128	75	41	75	24	39	20
62 PROFESS., SCIEN. INSTRU.	4667	5605	9328	3953	871	3953	527	1793	1002
63 MEDICAL, PHOTO. EQUIP.	148	147	193	111	40	111	23	42	32
64 MISC. MANUFACTURING	1922	1671	2666	1495	746	1495	451	721	526
65 TRANSPORT., WAREHOUSING	49451	48691	69704	37594	15573	37594	8532	16752	14486
66 COMMUNICA.,EXC. BRDCAST.	4036	4243	5404	2679	991	2679	529	1138	1287
67 RADIO, TV BROADCASTING	0	0	0	0	0	0	0	0	0
68 ELEC.,GAS,WATER,SAN.SER.	4684	4585	6356	3184	1142	3184	592	1364	1453
69 WHOLESALE, RETAIL TRADE	120061	118471	163809	86818	32251	86818	17368	38554	39448
70 FINANCE, INSURANCE	8591	8314	11777	6012	2944	6012	1615	2939	2282
71 REAL ESTATE, RENTAL	7066	6779	9611	4752	1800	4752	939	2090	2151
72 HOTELS, PERSONAL SERV.	1061	1019	1447	720	275	720	145	317	322
73 BUSINESS SERVICES	65304	62774	93827	48945	21511	48945	12143	22404	18365
74 RESEARCH, DEVELOPMENT	0	0	0	0	0	0	0	0	0
75 AUTO. REPAIR, SERVICES	5377	5173	7296	3633	1369	3633	718	1590	1639
76 AMUSEMENTS	171	164	233	116	44	116	23	51	52
77 MED.,EDUC. SERVICES	1356	1305	1839	916	344	916	180	400	414
78 FEDERAL GOVT. ENTERPRISE	417	402	555	278	100	278	52	119	129
79 STATE, LOCAL GOVT. ENT.	515	480	845	440	332	440	184	246	109
80 DIRECT ALLOCATED IMPORTS	263	253	360	179	68	179	36	79	80
81 TRANSFERRED IMPORTS	0	0	0	0	0	0	0	0	0
82 VALUE ADDED	620358	1001803	1059113	341005	136877	511418	73999	99507	369385
83 SECONDARY TRANSFERS-IN	0	0	0	0	0	0	0	0	0
84 INVENTORY DEPLETION	0	0	0	0	0	0	0	0	0
85 SCRAP PRODUCTION	0	0	0	0	0	0	0	0	0
86 SCRAP PURCHASED	891	1080	1347	584	229	683	126	226	360
87 STATE TOTAL PRODUCTION	1522868	1845402	2302047	997444	392207	1167957	215578	386080	614917

TABLE C-9

1963 INPUTS BY STATE TO
IO-11, NEW CONSTRUCTION

(THOUSANDS OF CURRENT DOLLARS)

INDUSTRY TITLE	28 NEW HAMPSHIRE	29 NEW JERSEY	30 NEW MEXICO	31 NEW YORK	32 NORTH CAROLINA	33 NORTH DAKOTA	34 OHIO	35 OKLAHOMA	36 OREGON
1 LIVESTOCK, PRDTS.	4	69	11	136	25	5	84	21	18
2 OTHER AGRICULTURE PRDTS.	969	14126	934	27065	5301	711	17372	4905	1942
3 FORESTRY, FISHERIES	1	14	2	28	5	1	17	4	4
4 AGRI.,FORES.,FISH. SERV.	7	118	15	225	37	6	152	33	31
5 IRON, FERRO. ORES MINING	0	0	0	0	0	0	0	0	0
6 NONFERROUS ORES MINING	0	0	0	0	0	0	0	0	0
7 COAL MINING	0	0	0	0	0	0	0	0	0
8 CRUDE PETRO.,NATURAL GAS	0	0	0	0	0	0	0	0	0
9 STONE, CLAY MINING	3015	9713	5394	27884	8678	4853	15879	10995	8314
10 CHEM.,FERT. MIN. MINING	0	0	0	0	0	0	0	0	0
11 NEW CONSTRUCTION	0	0	0	0	0	0	0	0	0
12 MAINT., REPAIR CONSTR.	45	756	114	1400	266	49	896	218	181
13 ORDNANCE, ACCESSORIES	23	304	20	849	68	15	290	40	46
14 FOOD, KINDRED PRDTS.	331	4939	767	9313	1813	336	6164	1563	1314
15 TOBACCO MANUFACTURES	20	319	50	629	116	23	387	98	82
16 FABRICS	170	481	266	1014	967	294	748	936	91
17 TEXTILE PRDTS.	160	5366	585	11131	1174	236	8036	734	1106
18 APPAREL	78	1152	221	2390	437	98	1421	443	343
19 MISC. TEXTILE PRDTS.	28	379	29	1045	106	21	394	54	60
20 LUMBER, WOOD PRDTS.	8224	165873	19162	240865	51183	8706	206978	35387	39089
21 WOODEN CONTAINERS	0	0	0	0	0	0	0	0	0
22 HOUSEHOLD FURNITURE	687	17851	1507	28103	4376	551	23265	3047	2887
23 OTHER FURNITURE	457	7448	843	13005	3531	503	9438	1692	1737
24 PAPER, ALLIED PRDTS.	516	8682	1076	15506	3812	530	10583	2069	1937
25 PAPERBOARD CONTAINERS	9	124	3	353	104	3	184	33	42
26 PRINTING, PUBLISHING	32	530	81	1003	189	35	633	156	130
27 CHEMICALS,SELECT. PRDTS.	562	4212	3753	9840	1903	513	6807	7257	3273
28 PLASTICS, SYNTHETICS	2	29	1	80	24	0	42	7	9
29 DRUGS, COSMETICS	11	160	19	376	86	9	212	49	47
30 PAINT, ALLIED PRDTS.	618	16739	1761	22888	4680	1356	17194	3255	2890
31 PETROLEUM, RELATED INDS.	3334	28505	12709	68538	16121	10133	39253	32903	17474
32 RUBBER, MISC. PLASTICS	1220	20985	2974	36584	8106	1567	20916	5853	5356
33 LEATHER TANNING, PRDTS.	2	7	3	43	6	2	16	8	7
34 FOOTWEAR, LEATHER PRDTS.	5	69	11	156	31	5	92	31	22
35 GLASS, GLASS PRDTS.	252	4067	258	6429	1611	189	4248	1158	462
36 STONE, CLAY PRDTS.	14381	237288	40147	449714	96675	23208	290935	77324	56701
37 PRIMARY IRON, STEEL MFR.	4320	59611	31020	163739	37113	8795	85036	59001	23327
38 PRIMARY NONFERROUS MFR.	3370	58548	8180	104664	23702	2800	62993	11416	13580

39 METAL CONTAINERS	0	0	0	0	0	0	0	0	0
40 FABRICATED METAL PRDTS.	15411	269535	35771	550117	106427	18754	327583	68803	65069
41 SCREW MACH. PRDTS., ETC.	398	3023	1408	6845	2500	642	3920	2460	1342
42 OTHER FAB. METAL PRDTS.	2122	40523	6239	73459	17934	2663	46683	13212	11224
43 ENGINES, TURBINES	52	1568	692	2327	518	30	644	202	809
44 FARM MACH., EQUIP.	4	38	22	123	22	8	56	46	24
45 CONSTRUC. MACH., EQUIP.	474	4069	5307	13219	2434	1186	6872	10605	2713
46 MATERIAL HANDLING MACH.	695	11684	1123	28004	4476	1168	14210	1811	1631
47 METALWORKING MACHINERY	52	391	65	913	221	17	586	80	135
48 SPECIAL MACH., EQUIP.	0	0	0	0	0	0	0	0	0
49 GENERAL MACH., EQUIP.	522	9918	1329	16417	3319	716	13334	1623	2119
50 MACHINE SHOP PRDTS.	51	192	112	1313	146	82	445	288	227
51 OFFICE, COMPUT. MACHINES	0	3	0	6	1	0	4	1	1
52 SERVICE IND. MACHINES	950	16723	1589	35992	7670	901	21941	3024	3359
53 ELECT. TRANSMISS. EQUIP.	1065	12929	3323	25230	6467	542	15377	3079	5618
54 HOUSEHOLD APPLIANCES	344	7277	943	9314	2572	461	10755	2376	2134
55 ELECTRIC LIGHTING EQUIP.	2730	42524	7460	89088	19740	3320	53761	14867	13040
56 RADIO, TV, ETC., EQUIP.	156	3005	983	6771	1691	405	4737	856	1413
57 ELECTRONIC COMPONENTS	3	46	5	99	27	4	77	13	9
58 MISC. ELECTRICAL MACH.	92	1332	362	2880	488	130	1652	771	481
59 MOTOR VEHICLES, EQUIP.	104	859	490	2941	499	181	1307	1062	577
60 AIRCRAFT, PARTS	0	0	0	0	0	0	0	0	0
61 OTHER TRANSPORT. EQUIP.	16	112	27	429	68	20	183	62	58
62 PROFESS., SCIEN. INSTRU.	684	9555	895	18812	3119	487	12181	1450	1761
63 MEDICAL, PHOTO. EQUIP.	18	260	55	544	112	23	300	78	86
64 MISC. MANUFACTURING	292	2309	565	7910	1343	384	3708	1237	1366
65 TRANSPORT., WAREHOUSING	6176	91217	17185	186103	35612	8182	111571	31513	26924
66 COMMUNICA.,EXC. BRDCAST.	485	8364	1185	15178	2620	507	8591	2223	1916
67 RADIO, TV BROADCASTING	0	0	0	0	0	0	0	0	0
68 ELEC.,GAS,WATER,SAN.SER.	530	8834	1330	16639	3096	584	10498	2542	2127
69 WHOLESALE, RETAIL TRADE	13456	237354	35589	421945	81775	16565	278522	72813	61310
70 FINANCE, INSURANCE	1061	16049	3266	32128	6024	1488	19293	6689	4674
71 REAL ESTATE, RENTAL	810	12832	1999	25047	4664	904	15606	3926	3230
72 HOTELS, PERSONAL SERV.	123	1934	304	3816	703	138	2346	593	494
73 BUSINESS SERVICES	8619	101737	21118	253967	44691	10946	136667	44629	38924
74 RESEARCH, DEVELOPMENT	0	0	0	0	0	0	0	0	0
75 AUTO. REPAIR, SERVICES	617	9858	1538	19182	3557	688	11902	2979	2485
76 AMUSEMENTS	20	312	49	616	113	22	379	95	80
77 MED.,EDUC. SERVICES	155	2488	388	4833	897	173	3002	751	627
78 FEDERAL GOVT. ENTERPRISE	46	778	118	1446	274	51	924	225	187
79 STATE, LOCAL GOVT. ENT.	86	689	348	2405	387	143	1062	765	448
80 DIRECT ALLOCATED IMPORTS	30	480	76	948	174	34	583	147	123
81 TRANSFERRED IMPORTS	0	0	0	0	0	0	0	0	0
82 VALUE ADDED	58175	326624	151756	1920906	361779	48527	969400	411585	265476
83 SECONDARY TRANSFERS-IN	0	0	0	0	0	0	0	0	0
84 INVENTORY DEPLETION	0	0	0	0	0	0	0	0	0
85 SCRAP PRODUCTION	0	0	0	0	0	0	0	0	0
86 SCRAP PURCHASED	93	1127	256	2952	586	109	1722	568	414
87 STATE TOTAL PRODUCTION	159572	1927017	437185	5045863	1000997	186738	2943049	970743	707139

TABLE C-9

1963 INPUTS BY STATE TO
IO-11, NEW CONSTRUCTION

(THOUSANDS OF CURRENT DOLLARS)

INDUSTRY TITLE	37 PENNSYL-VANIA	38 RHODE ISLAND	39 SOUTH CAROLINA	40 SOUTH DAKOTA	41 TENNESSEE	42 TEXAS	43 UTAH	44 VERMONT	45 VIRGINIA
1 LIVESTOCK, PRDTS.	69	6	12	4	24	115	13	2	40
2 OTHER AGRICULTURE PRDTS.	11503	1292	2080	552	4819	22974	1336	243	11902
3 FORESTRY, FISHERIES	14	1	3	1	5	24	3	0	8
4 AGRI.,FORES.,FISH. SERV.	94	10	15	5	34	170	20	2	82
5 IRON, FERRO. ORES MINING	0	0	0	0	0	0	0	0	0
6 NONFERROUS ORES MINING	0	0	0	0	0	0	0	0	0
7 COAL MINING	0	0	0	0	0	0	0	0	0
8 CRUDE PETRO.,NATURAL GAS	0	0	0	0	0	0	0	0	0
9 STONE, CLAY MINING	11866	1397	4667	6741	10652	39465	3815	1741	15652
10 CHEM.,FERT. MIN. MINING	0	0	0	0	0	0	0	0	0
11 NEW CONSTRUCTION	0	0	0	0	0	0	0	0	0
12 MAINT., REPAIR CONSTR.	726	57	129	39	242	1235	141	21	417
13 ORDNANCE, ACCESSORIES	445	34	32	16	53	181	22	13	74
14 FOOD, KINDRED PRDTS.	4760	424	843	289	1695	8113	968	147	3091
15 TOBACCO MANUFACTURES	320	26	56	20	110	531	61	11	183
16 FABRICS	597	29	1461	56	1518	1112	221	6	748
17 TEXTILE PRDTS.	3936	234	458	164	1156	7624	850	62	2325
18 APPAREL	1205	92	215	103	436	2187	239	49	690
19 MISC. TEXTILE PRDTS.	547	43	49	18	87	295	42	16	108
20 LUMBER, WOOD PRDTS.	128481	10704	19880	7931	38275	252300	22457	3090	90381
21 WOODEN CONTAINERS	0	0	0	0	0	0	0	0	0
22 HOUSEHOLD FURNITURE	12094	935	1649	422	3475	26639	1814	139	8777
23 OTHER FURNITURE	7095	617	1807	297	3092	14029	1902	181	4227
24 PAPER, ALLIED PRDTS.	7972	651	1938	313	3364	16072	1792	191	5122
25 PAPERBOARD CONTAINERS	112	16	45	7	100	417	72	5	72
26 PRINTING, PUBLISHING	517	41	92	29	174	871	99	16	296
27 CHEMICALS,SELECT. PRDTS.	8307	371	833	567	4238	27584	2024	899	4747
28 PLASTICS, SYNTHETICS	25	4	10	1	23	97	17	1	16
29 DRUGS, COSMETICS	159	16	40	11	84	368	54	6	95
30 PAINT, ALLIED PRDTS.	13934	826	2502	712	4275	24267	2455	357	8311
31 PETROLEUM, RELATED INDS.	37986	2938	11346	10983	20891	92516	11476	3013	30170
32 RUBBER, MISC. PLASTICS	21616	1536	3772	1236	7109	32441	4476	658	11503
33 LEATHER TANNING, PRDTS.	16	1	3	4	10	27	4	2	11
34 FOOTWEAR, LEATHER PRDTS.	80	7	15	7	30	133	17	3	41
35 GLASS, GLASS PRDTS.	3578	333	651	133	1360	6420	427	76	2905
36 STONE, CLAY PRDTS.	244383	19138	50821	18218	91325	404156	42090	6108	144474
37 PRIMARY IRON, STEEL MFR.	90022	5225	18057	5890	28566	229972	20748	4493	49276
38 PRIMARY NONFERROUS MFR.	56333	4316	9335	2509	16049	86703	8625	1497	30797

39 METAL CONTAINERS	0	0	0	0	0	0	0	0	0
40 FABRICATED METAL PRDTS.	293178	20798	51672	14382	91288	427401	47190	9311	150006
41 SCREW MACH. PRDTS., ETC.	3720	279	2101	374	2665	7759	872	142	2483
42 OTHER FAB. METAL PRDTS.	42137	2740	7642	2785	14322	75425	7375	1326	25367
43 ENGINES, TURBINES	1128	56	142	17	22	1417	60	37	1025
44 FARM MACH., EQUIP.	62	4	12	11	27	147	13	4	38
45 CONSTRUC. MACH., EQUIP.	7206	449	1442	1196	3105	36345	2135	455	4145
46 MATERIAL HANDLING MACH.	14335	1305	2666	234	4020	17725	2839	253	5108
47 METALWORKING MACHINERY	622	52	73	30	171	480	120	25	224
48 SPECIAL MACH., EQUIP.	0	0	0	0	0	0	0	0	0
49 GENERAL MACH., EQUIP.	9363	749	1584	418	2566	12315	1713	240	4368
50 MACHINE SHOP PRDTS.	509	41	90	130	283	754	101	60	351
51 OFFICE, COMPUT. MACHINES	3	0	1	0	1	5	1	0	2
52 SERVICE IND. MACHINES	17310	1418	3522	539	6756	32304	4206	448	8519
53 ELECT. TRANSMISS. EQUIP.	15567	1155	2248	762	4276	17811	3581	531	8011
54 HOUSEHOLD APPLIANCES	4962	437	969	392	2182	11062	1385	93	5396
55 ELECTRIC LIGHTING EQUIP.	42891	3314	11012	3413	19102	82058	10004	1422	25827
56 RADIO, TV, ETC., EQUIP.	4752	156	474	313	805	4075	384	141	2756
57 ELECTRONIC COMPONENTS	75	4	8	3	15	65	7	2	30
58 MISC. ELECTRICAL MACH.	1385	103	234	167	525	3066	281	64	918
59 MOTOR VEHICLES, EQUIP.	1444	100	278	263	647	3330	312	105	893
60 AIRCRAFT, PARTS	0	0	0	0	0	0	0	0	0
61 OTHER TRANSPORT. EQUIP.	172	16	39	25	91	264	37	14	109
62 PROFESS., SCIEN. INSTRU.	11235	852	1351	426	2547	10156	1703	348	3710
63 MEDICAL, PHOTO. EQUIP.	289	22	54	20	98	421	57	12	167
64 MISC. MANUFACTURING	3122	295	742	436	1688	5064	933	225	2311
65 TRANSPORT., WAREHOUSING	95553	7362	17232	7367	33884	163209	18615	3838	56782
66 COMMUNICA., EXC. BRDCAST.	7987	614	1282	405	2442	12151	1479	232	4180
67 RADIO, TV BROADCASTING	0	0	0	0	0	0	0	0	0
68 ELEC.,GAS,WATER,SAN.SER.	8662	684	1492	470	2845	14335	1637	256	4876
69 WHOLESALE, RETAIL TRADE	218804	16702	38226	16015	75064	396041	43579	6859	131714
70 FINANCE, INSURANCE	16858	1210	3279	1491	6221	31043	3274	688	9585
71 REAL ESTATE, RENTAL	12831	1027	2275	765	4406	21445	2474	407	7357
72 HOTELS, PERSONAL SERV.	1941	155	342	119	667	3223	372	64	1111
73 BUSINESS SERVICES	122750	9940	22839	13170	48822	186862	25225	5966	73896
74 RESEARCH, DEVELOPMENT	0	0	0	0	0	0	0	0	0
75 AUTO. REPAIR, SERVICES	9796	780	1731	584	3345	16362	1884	312	5616
76 AMUSEMENTS	313	25	55	19	108	521	60	10	179
77 MED., EDUC. SERVICES	2469	196	436	146	842	4128	474	78	1415
78 FEDERAL GOVT. ENTERPRISE	750	59	133	40	250	1273	145	21	431
79 STATE, LOCAL GOVT. ENT.	1142	82	216	206	518	2430	242	86	713
80 DIRECT ALLOCATED IMPORTS	482	38	85	30	166	800	92	16	276
81 TRANSFERRED IMPORTS	0	0	0	0	0	0	0	0	0
82 VALUE ADDED	566072	112497	16288	79215	428158	1136312	147151	8824	636631
83 SECONDARY TRANSFERS-IN	0	0	0	0	0	0	0	0	0
84 INVENTORY DEPLETION	0	0	0	0	0	0	0	0	0
85 SCRAP PRODUCTION	0	0	0	0	0	0	0	0	0
86 SCRAP PURCHASED	1294	139	191	119	590	2364	269	39	944
87 STATE TOTAL PRODUCTION	2211964	237175	327279	203777	1008802	4040992	460565	66006	1614012

TABLE C-9

1963 INPUTS BY STATE TO
IO-11, NEW CONSTRUCTION
(THOUSANDS OF CURRENT DOLLARS)

INDUSTRY TITLE	46 WASHINGTON	47 WEST VIRGINIA	48 WISCONSIN	49 WYOMING	50 ALASKA	51 HAWAII	52 NATIONAL TOTAL
1 LIVESTOCK, PRDTS.	30	11	29	5	8	12	1657
2 OTHER AGRICULTURE PRDTS.	3290	1131	5968	228	613	1344	328011
3 FORESTRY, FISHERIES	6	2	6	1	2	2	344
4 AGRI.,FORES.,FISH. SERV.	60	9	50	3	6	18	2997
5 IRON, FERRO. ORES MINING	0	0	0	0	0	0	0
6 NONFERROUS ORES MINING	0	0	0	0	0	0	0
7 COAL MINING	0	0	0	0	0	0	0
8 CRUDE PETRO.,NATURAL GAS	0	0	0	0	0	0	0
9 STONE, CLAY MINING	8188	2645	8990	5112	5401	1595	477924
10 CHEM.,FERT. MIN. MINING	0	0	0	0	0	0	0
11 NEW CONSTRUCTION	0	0	0	0	0	0	0
12 MAINT., REPAIR CONSTR.	314	107	298	50	74	120	17498
13 ORDNANCE, ACCESSORIES	62	24	110	9	9	18	5361
14 FOOD, KINDRED PRDTS.	2362	655	2125	320	459	812	121673
15 TOBACCO MANUFACTURES	139	48	132	23	35	53	7653
16 FABRICS	204	2634	101	8	845	153	30572
17 TEXTILE PRDTS.	2003	269	2249	106	281	1155	123986
18 APPAREL	535	194	493	117	140	181	29310
19 MISC. TEXTILE PRDTS.	98	39	157	11	25	48	7375
20 LUMBER, WOOD PRDTS.	61829	8738	68305	9574	4959	19621	3553609
21 WOODEN CONTAINERS	0	0	0	0	0	0	0
22 HOUSEHOLD FURNITURE	5332	506	5181	285	249	2174	342377
23 OTHER FURNITURE	3411	1378	3304	319	969	1175	184180
24 PAPER, ALLIED PRDTS.	3738	1654	3575	343	1016	1706	211522
25 PAPERBOARD CONTAINERS	83	11	71	7	4	36	4408
26 PRINTING, PUBLISHING	224	78	213	35	54	86	12412
27 CHEMICALS,SELECT. PRDTS.	3515	2361	2160	1891	972	920	201273
28 PLASTICS, SYNTHETICS	19	3	16	2	1	8	1013
29 DRUGS, COSMETICS	85	21	77	11	14	34	4583
30 PAINT, ALLIED PRDTS.	5234	2186	4635	692	1086	1790	307577
31 PETROLEUM, RELATED INDS.	24906	7614	16438	8876	6665	4016	1119473
32 RUBBER, MISC. PLASTICS	9637	3318	8617	1309	2214	3580	486898
33 LEATHER TANNING, PRDTS.	9	3	7	2	3	1	411
34 FOOTWEAR, LEATHER PRDTS.	41	12	38	5	13	19	1968
35 GLASS, GLASS PRDTS.	911	402	1507	73	210	398	80654
36 STONE, CLAY PRDTS.	95405	51782	104050	21658	22611	36458	5812828
37 PRIMARY IRON, STEEL MFR.	27979	13343	37735	19203	9460	9433	2125213
38 PRIMARY NONFERROUS MFR.	18714	5974	22809	4616	2563	6822	1243718

39 METAL CONTAINERS	0	0	0	0	0	0	0
40 FABRICATED METAL PRDTS.	97537	43566	122162	20153	26333	39221	6158750
41 SCREW MACH. PRDTS., ETC.	1580	3323	1703	821	1107	595	112261
42 OTHER FAB. METAL PRDTS.	17192	4677	17121	3011	4184	7119	975064
43 ENGINES, TURBINES	200	155	535	740	8	176	25851
44 FARM MACH., EQUIP.	30	17	23	14	10	6	1562
45 CONSTRUC. MACH., EQUIP.	3373	3068	2425	3173	1711	805	238236
46 MATERIAL HANDLING MACH.	4173	2546	4942	396	1746	2459	257492
47 METALWORKING MACHINERY	289	70	277	19	40	28	11048
48 SPECIAL MACH., EQUIP.	0	0	0	0	0	0	0
49 GENERAL MACH., EQUIP.	3213	1301	4940	890	951	1437	209557
50 MACHINE SHOP PRDTS.	272	112	203	79	102	29	12071
51 OFFICE, COMPUT. MACHINES	1	0	1	0	0	0	71
52 SERVICE IND. MACHINES	6714	2181	7281	615	2030	3229	404477
53 ELECT. TRANSMISS. EQUIP.	8762	1916	7195	2037	1228	1641	337167
54 HOUSEHOLD APPLIANCES	3942	372	3208	297	159	1075	185412
55 ELECTRIC LIGHTING EQUIP.	20506	10820	18681	3764	6935	9168	1123358
56 RADIO, TV, ETC., EQUIP.	982	949	1468	966	284	376	81318
57 ELECTRONIC COMPONENTS	22	11	30	3	13	15	1260
58 MISC. ELECTRICAL MACH.	684	248	557	199	150	188	36961
59 MOTOR VEHICLES, EQUIP.	703	388	550	310	244	137	36370
60 AIRCRAFT, PARTS	0	0	0	0	0	0	0
61 OTHER TRANSPORT. EQUIP.	80	36	75	17	28	25	4230
62 PROFESS., SCIEN. INSTRU.	3902	1070	5156	268	1376	1810	207961
63 MEDICAL, PHOTO. EQUIP.	115	49	119	37	37	41	6425
64 MISC. MANUFACTURING	1868	721	1463	353	543	646	94020
65 TRANSPORT., WAREHOUSING	41052	14870	39876	9418	11016	13276	2289662
66 COMMUNICA.,EXC. BRDCAST.	3303	1089	2989	523	785	1259	179904
67 RADIO, TV BROADCASTING	0	0	0	0	0	0	0
68 ELEC.,GAS,WATER,SAN.SER.	3664	1261	3527	588	885	1407	204918
69 WHOLESALE, RETAIL TRADE	101508	29808	91653	16547	20593	33686	5473944
70 FINANCE, INSURANCE	7141	3481	6428	1730	2111	2318	400739
71 REAL ESTATE, RENTAL	5590	1933	5293	878	1385	2135	307117
72 HOTELS, PERSONAL SERV.	841	291	801	138	212	322	46388
73 BUSINESS SERVICES	59245	21751	52431	11199	15649	17987	2959130
74 RESEARCH, DEVELOPMENT	0	0	0	0	0	0	0
75 AUTO. REPAIR, SERVICES	4245	1466	4040	691	1054	1627	234627
76 AMUSEMENTS	136	47	129	22	34	52	7484
77 MED.,EDUC. SERVICES	1070	369	1018	174	265	410	59159
78 FEDERAL GOVT. ENTERPRISE	324	111	308	52	77	124	18058
79 STATE, LOCAL GOVT. ENT.	558	286	441	220	191	110	28384
80 DIRECT ALLOCATED IMPORTS	209	82	199	34	53	80	11530
81 TRANSFERRED IMPORTS	0	0	0	0	0	0	0
82 VALUE ADDED	696922	15074	474024	53992	9529	140948	25890208
83 SECONDARY TRANSFERS-IN	0	0	0	0	0	0	0
84 INVENTORY DEPLETION	0	0	0	0	0	0	0
85 SCRAP PRODUCTION	0	0	0	0	0	0	0
86 SCRAP PURCHASED	808	162	692	123	102	222	38333
87 STATE TOTAL PRODUCTION	1381119	276827	1183412	209388	174119	379980	65518976

TABLE C-10

1963 NATIONAL PRIMARY INPUTS TO
MANUFACTURING AND SERVICES

(THOUSANDS OF CURRENT DOLLARS)

INDUSTRY TITLE	1	2	3	4	5	6	7	8	9
1 LIVESTOCK, PRDTS.	81	191843	710	224	11079918	4258942	133	162	91
2 OTHER AGRICULTURE PRDTS.	242	221	2402	669	5392	34535	952541	2332369	52740
3 FORESTRY, FISHERIES	34892	15	148	47	42	37	284689	2283	19
4 AGRI.,FORES.,FISH. SERV.	74288	0	3	0	0	0	0	0	0
5 IRON, FERRO. ORES MINING	0	0	0	0	0	0	0	0	0
6 NONFERROUS ORES MINING	0	0	0	0	0	0	0	0	0
7 COAL MINING	0	0	0	1241	3754	6182	3227	6823	485
8 CRUDE PETRO.,NATURAL GAS	0	0	0	0	0	0	0	0	0
9 STONE, CLAY MINING	0	2	259080	0	0	0	0	7054	0
10 CHEM.,FERT. MIN. MINING	0	0	0	0	3016	0	0	1914	35
11 NEW CONSTRUCTION	0	0	0	0	0	0	0	0	0
12 MAINT., REPAIR CONSTR.	0	0	7191	5728	21748	24159	18873	18182	13208
13 ORDNANCE, ACCESSORIES	18	16	156	160774	44	39	29	35	20
14 FOOD, KINDRED PRDTS.	48934	38505	43502	12883	2142906	1881122	1018560	2065156	1865011
15 TOBACCO MANUFACTURES	374	342	3282	1036	938	824	613	749	420
16 FABRICS	0	0	14	0	0	1734	0	205	0
17 TEXTILE PRDTS.	61917	40673	2735	10	6	1014	2	3	10
18 APPAREL	18	16	13305	3734	20380	3554	6399	2393	4938
19 MISC. TEXTILE PRDTS.	1253	0	126	0	0	0	0	95215	0
20 LUMBER, WOOD PRDTS.	7	6	723528	15956	18	16	1293	2171	1316
21 WOODEN CONTAINERS	0	14137	0	5270	13341	12838	4249	5552	2206
22 HOUSEHOLD FURNITURE	0	0	0	0	0	0	0	0	0
23 OTHER FURNITURE	0	0	4239	0	0	0	0	0	0
24 PAPER, ALLIED PRDTS.	488	137	72506	5232	77989	146372	112616	214144	167590
25 PAPERBOARD CONTAINERS	0	86410	2	7273	145149	377766	145039	94972	80634
26 PRINTING, PUBLISHING	620	275	5398	7236	67685	51000	68492	74380	53371
27 CHEMICALS,SELECT. PRDTS.	1602	907	54195	15586	12275	7825	13069	65239	7445
28 PLASTICS, SYNTHETICS	0	0	23	937	0	0	0	0	62076
29 DRUGS, COSMETICS	118	108	1059	919	2442	1645	7996	135936	940
30 PAINT, ALLIED PRDTS.	4412	1	858595	7	3	5	7	6	2
31 PETROLEUM, RELATED INDS.	34299	3449	540056	13211	18133	64416	14790	12039	47961
32 RUBBER, MISC. PLASTICS	1049	78	139213	99276	157997	35075	20328	2121	13239
33 LEATHER TANNING, PRDTS.	0	0	6	245	297	357	320	416	146
34 FOOTWEAR, LEATHER PRDTS.	68	2823	638	193	172	153	117	141	77
35 GLASS, GLASS PRDTS.	7	6	93363	20	18	21128	229675	14	9
36 STONE, CLAY PRDTS.	495	7	409853	30	49	180	23	64	132
37 PRIMARY IRON, STEEL MFR.	1	1	317383	140364	14	106	17	10	88
38 PRIMARY NONFERROUS MFR.	0	0	208598	178767	0	0	845	0	0

39	METAL CONTAINERS	21297	0	0	0	152889	86738	667030	56181	0
40	FABRICATED METAL PRDTS.	0	0	568592	1	0	0	0	0	1
41	SCREW MACH. PRDTS., ETC.	0	0	18799	5184	0	12967	67474	0	1
42	OTHER FAB. METAL PRDTS.	15080	131814	268776	34000	13773	17277	124285	4090	22880
43	ENGINES, TURBINES	0	0	0	0	0	0	0	0	0
44	FARM MACH., EQUIP.	0	0	641	0	0	0	0	0	0
45	CONSTRUC. MACH., EQUIP.	0	0	71369	0	0	0	0	0	0
46	MATERIAL HANDLING MACH.	0	0	95844	700	1026	940	1045	1001	591
47	METALWORKING MACHINERY	0	0	399	14567	0	0	0	0	0
48	SPECIAL MACH., EQUIP.	0	0	0	0	4099	4989	4533	5892	2040
49	GENERAL MACH., EQUIP.	442	0	43047	12319	766	298	934	159	120
50	MACHINE SHOP PRDTS.	195	23	934	13204	297	1438	124	184	1095
51	OFFICE, COMPUT. MACHINES	2	2	31	42	30	37	18	18	43
52	SERVICE IND. MACHINES	0	0	116043	0	0	0	0	0	0
53	ELECT. TRANSMISS. EQUIP.	0	0	56327	24121	0	0	0	0	0
54	HOUSEHOLD APPLIANCES	83	76	99704	230	208	183	136	166	93
55	ELECTRIC LIGHTING EQUIP.	35815	9	183452	64	59	224	28	35	169
56	RADIO, TV, ETC., EQUIP.	115	105	21011	234428	288	253	188	230	129
57	ELECTRONIC COMPONENTS	0	0	990	82832	0	0	0	0	0
58	MISC. ELECTRICAL MACH.	1839	25	10053	18276	502	2450	196	304	1850
59	MOTOR VEHICLES, EQUIP.	383	55	13967	576	1144	5552	454	696	4192
60	AIRCRAFT, PARTS	0	394	0	590604	0	0	0	0	0
61	OTHER TRANSPORT. EQUIP.	20727	0	77	0	0	0	0	0	0
62	PROFESS., SCIEN. INSTRU.	729	20	70082	28441	1637	825	1443	566	1112
63	MEDICAL, PHOTO. EQUIP.	70	65	969	17622	1113	954	828	550	1103
64	MISC. MANUFACTURING	388	170	79495	2394	2064	2181	1426	1153	2290
65	TRANSPORT., WAREHOUSING	15544	32145	552772	46828	613007	99485	343790	549029	146915
66	COMMUNICA.,EXC. BRDCAST.	0	0	78528	52381	21484	47492	10999	12337	39494
67	RADIO, TV BROADCASTING	0	0	0	0	0	0	0	0	0
68	ELEC.,GAS,WATER,SAN.SER.	159	798	89511	26345	77844	86201	53514	56624	57044
69	WHOLESALE, RETAIL TRADE	48004	43130	1711115	92439	378151	277922	414078	553974	222923
70	FINANCE, INSURANCE	888	5703	161233	26766	48261	102146	27967	31665	36519
71	REAL ESTATE, RENTAL	0	41185	134311	29878	37937	79832	40262	23365	58062
72	HOTELS, PERSONAL SERV.	2270	2072	19893	16032	45483	40780	15582	11802	46489
73	BUSINESS SERVICES	669	32	280913	109648	124039	184025	354896	295933	137258
74	RESEARCH, DEVELOPMENT	0	0	0	0	0	0	0	0	0
75	AUTO. REPAIR, SERVICES	6782	895	101168	9126	13477	65615	5562	8193	49799
76	AMUSEMENTS	366	334	3209	1013	918	805	599	733	411
77	MED.,EDUC. SERVICES	117	107	25522	8032	4118	9007	2218	2397	7406
78	FEDERAL GOVT. ENTERPRISE	313	297	7919	10397	7293	9446	4728	5650	10520
79	STATE, LOCAL GOVT. ENT.	297	46	9847	466	5012	6263	2695	1475	3217
80	DIRECT ALLOCATED IMPORTS	564	614	4945	1561	1414	1241	6431	1129	4983
81	TRANSFERRED IMPORTS	0	0	0	0	0	0	0	0	0
82	VALUE ADDED	598197	581794	11131647	2524938	2705197	2404889	1977130	1572800	2809807
83	STATE TOTAL PRODUCTION	1036518	1221889	19794432	4712321	18037216	10483480	7034584	8338084	6042768

NOTE: The 152 column numbers are identical with the 152 product-mix industry numbers given in Table A-2, pages 134-145, and refer to that industrial classification.

TABLE C-10

1963 NATIONAL PRIMARY INPUTS TO
MANUFACTURING AND SERVICES
(THOUSANDS OF CURRENT DOLLARS)

INDUSTRY TITLE	10	11	12	13	14	15	16	17	18
1 LIVESTOCK, PRDTS.	10	59	230	53444	166	10	46878	9	18
2 OTHER AGRICULTURE PRDTS.	467191	81989	315261	1748395	12295	1112790	1328805	25	54
3 FORESTRY, FISHERIES	2	12	48	16901	34	2	39	2	4
4 AGRI.,FORES.,FISH. SERV.	0	0	0	0	0	0	0	0	0
5 IRON, FERRO. ORES MINING	0	0	0	0	0	0	0	0	0
6 NONFERROUS ORES MINING	0	0	0	0	0	0	0	0	0
7 COAL MINING	6166	1174	5394	5529	1375	425	12671	62	717
8 CRUDE PETRO.,NATURAL GAS	0	0	0	0	0	0	0	0	0
9 STONE, CLAY MINING	0	0	0	273	0	0	441	0	0
10 CHEM.,FERT. MIN. MINING	0	0	0	172	0	0	0	0	0
11 NEW CONSTRUCTION	0	0	0	0	0	0	0	0	0
12 MAINT., REPAIR CONSTR.	4719	3867	26535	17159	4491	2764	27874	1554	3498
13 ORDNANCE, ACCESSORIES	2	13	50	25	36	2	41	2	4
14 FOOD, KINDRED PRDTS.	912574	502952	1236897	1330382	10679	588	42845	491	1048
15 TOBACCO MANUFACTURES	47	271	1063	523	1207542	556805	859	39	84
16 FABRICS	801	0	857	298	0	0	4210561	76785	411975
17 TEXTILE PRDTS.	0	1	8	1489	0	0	412529	0	119076
18 APPAREL	779	1917	3305	2704	36	2	40	2	4
19 MISC. TEXTILE PRDTS.	0	0	0	0	0	0	0	0	0
20 LUMBER, WOOD PRDTS.	478	579	1786	1025	841	1	16	1	2
21 WOODEN CONTAINERS	1645	1176	40958	5285	3903	1057	102	0	0
22 HOUSEHOLD FURNITURE	0	0	0	0	0	0	0	0	0
23 OTHER FURNITURE	0	0	0	0	0	0	0	0	0
24 PAPER, ALLIED PRDTS.	12963	33794	70836	75804	34632	266	54266	314	40916
25 PAPERBOARD CONTAINERS	26962	126445	71781	69309	90858	527	66177	2952	18890
26 PRINTING, PUBLISHING	21535	17867	42400	80094	58075	280	5230	304	502
27 CHEMICALS,SELECT. PRDTS.	46	16184	41811	34093	2213	20	339393	5287	42
28 PLASTICS, SYNTHETICS	0	18199	0	21838	77282	247	1042633	47754	173739
29 DRUGS, COSMETICS	280	381	6655	2446	3110	2717	33878	1010	3440
30 PAINT, ALLIED PRDTS.	6	3	6	9	3	1	6986	1	6
31 PETROLEUM, RELATED INDS.	7197	4301	26652	14447	1268	736	21084	919	2077
32 RUBBER, MISC. PLASTICS	503	175	2650	22548	75	39	6892	22016	40039
33 LEATHER TANNING, PRDTS.	170	86	241	412	40	22	810	11	29
34 FOOTWEAR, LEATHER PRDTS.	13	52	197	103	141	9	167	8	19
35 GLASS, GLASS PRDTS.	1	5	405036	120295	14	1	40265	1379	2
36 STONE, CLAY PRDTS.	372	134	80	25	9	1	21	0	1
37 PRIMARY IRON, STEEL MFR.	1521	5	39	150	2	1	18	1	1
38 PRIMARY NONFERROUS MFR.	0	0	0	0	0	0	0	0	0

39 METAL CONTAINERS	0	43111	433358	153520	9145	0	0	0	0
40 FABRICATED METAL PRDTS.	0	0	0	0	0	0	0	0	0
41 SCREW MACH. PRDTS., ETC.	0	0	101948	18403	0	0	1	0	0
42 OTHER FAB. METAL PRDTS.	1203	11722	2227	18444	41222	817	4001	118	537
43 ENGINES, TURBINES	0	0	0	0	0	0	0	0	0
44 FARM MACH., EQUIP.	0	0	0	0	0	0	0	0	0
45 CONSTRUC. MACH., EQUIP.	0	0	0	0	0	0	0	0	0
46 MATERIAL HANDLING MACH.	401	288	691	1016	178	72	2526	64	116
47 METALWORKING MACHINERY	0	0	0	0	0	0	0	0	0
48 SPECIAL MACH., EQUIP.	2425	1198	3399	5865	0	0	74178	1186	2656
49 GENERAL MACH., EQUIP.	874	20	505	496	20	0	872	99	20
50 MACHINE SHOP PRDTS.	33	37	572	164	12	6	102	6	11
51 OFFICE, COMPUT. MACHINES	2	9	27	15	5	2	33	2	3
52 SERVICE IND. MACHINES	0	0	0	0	0	0	0	0	0
53 ELECT. TRANSMISS. EQUIP.	0	0	0	0	0	0	0	0	0
54 HOUSEHOLD APPLIANCES	11	60	236	116	170	10	191	9	19
55 ELECTRIC LIGHTING EQUIP.	9	9	99	43	3	1	42	1	6
56 RADIO, TV, ETC., EQUIP.	15	83	327	161	235	15	264	12	26
57 ELECTRONIC COMPONENTS	0	0	0	0	0	0	0	0	0
58 MISC. ELECTRICAL MACH.	62	53	949	287	18	11	169	7	14
59 MOTOR VEHICLES, EQUIP.	143	123	2156	660	40	27	360	18	34
60 AIRCRAFT, PARTS	0	0	0	0	0	0	0	0	0
61 OTHER TRANSPORT. EQUIP.	0	0	0	0	0	0	0	0	0
62 PROFESS., SCIEN. INSTRU.	174	437	783	622	406	100	3174	139	206
63 MEDICAL, PHOTO. EQUIP.	96	324	792	501	667	68	1681	83	127
64 MISC. MANUFACTURING	174	613	1780	1040	566	122	2739	139	227
65 TRANSPORT., WAREHOUSING	108318	69688	240415	328330	30373	15586	213931	3644	14788
66 COMMUNICA.,EXC. BRDCAST.	2076	4891	37143	15230	2449	940	24477	1318	2872
67 RADIO, TV BROADCASTING	0	0	0	0	0	0	0	0	0
68 ELEC.,GAS,WATER,SAN.SER.	24062	12798	49415	77701	5777	2273	127849	2974	6567
69 WHOLESALE, RETAIL TRADE	61585	97558	249789	280395	40022	10158	354968	10463	67456
70 FINANCE, INSURANCE	10810	10598	75066	34674	13986	1282	44026	2408	3120
71 REAL ESTATE, RENTAL	14129	18746	54158	42557	6067	6981	58922	2753	7367
72 HOTELS, PERSONAL SERV.	1224	10945	23773	13035	15010	611	8658	239	969
73 BUSINESS SERVICES	19671	109274	665365	309611	305344	7152	117897	4553	16095
74 RESEARCH, DEVELOPMENT	0	0	0	0	0	0	0	0	0
75 AUTO. REPAIR, SERVICES	1636	1646	27975	8010	587	346	4959	247	500
76 AMUSEMENTS	46	265	1039	512	749	46	840	39	82
77 MED., EDUC. SERVICES	397	986	6351	2968	635	167	3190	169	359
78 FEDERAL GOVT. ENTERPRISE	510	2333	6600	4158	9287	3601	9912	539	1388
79 STATE, LOCAL GOVT. ENT.	284	272	4529	1810	86	23	2290	25	262
80 DIRECT ALLOCATED IMPORTS	71	174309	10577	1066027	1153	71	109349	59	227
81 TRANSFERRED IMPORTS	0	0	0	0	0	0	0	0	0
82 VALUE ADDED	636026	743880	5354335	1688980	3269292	340537	3331105	141311	199893
83 STATE TOTAL PRODUCTION	2352448	2127918	9657155	7700530	5262627	2070337	12204230	333552	1142135

NOTE: The 152 column numbers are identical with the 152 product-mix industry numbers given in Table A-2, pages 134-145, and refer to that industrial classification.

TABLE C-10

1963 NATIONAL PRIMARY INPUTS TO MANUFACTURING AND SERVICES
(THOUSANDS OF CURRENT DOLLARS)

INDUSTRY TITLE	19	20	21	22	23	24	25	26	27
1 LIVESTOCK, PRDTS.	181150	51	386	71	20	47	69	37	16
2 OTHER AGRICULTURE PRDTS.	28861	151	1151	213	59	139	205	111	47
3 FORESTRY, FISHERIES	6	11	115481	15	915816	10	14	8	3
4 AGRI.,FORES.,FISH. SERV.	0	0	0	0	0	0	0	0	0
5 IRON, FERRO. ORES MINING	0	0	0	0	0	0	0	0	0
6 NONFERROUS ORES MINING	0	0	0	0	0	0	0	0	0
7 COAL MINING	666	1061	629	268	54	350	663	1051	25
8 CRUDE PETRO.,NATURAL GAS	0	0	0	0	0	0	0	0	0
9 STONE, CLAY MINING	0	0	0	0	0	0	0	37	0
10 CHEM.,FERT. MIN. MINING	0	0	0	0	0	0	0	83	0
11 NEW CONSTRUCTION	0	0	0	0	0	0	0	0	0
12 MAINT., REPAIR CONSTR.	5745	8100	6933	3697	6389	16403	11115	1630	722
13 ORDNANCE, ACCESSORIES	6	11	84	16	4	10	15	8	3
14 FOOD, KINDRED PRDTS.	23000	2911	22172	4243	1129	2682	4064	2139	913
15 TOBACCO MANUFACTURES	133	234	1783	329	91	216	318	172	73
16 FABRICS	123606	913735	3965516	697199	0	0	0	0	0
17 TEXTILE PRDTS.	130876	1	57510	289537	1	2	1	1	0
18 APPAREL	27345	401016	2798319	14104	1976	6567	3781	1791	840
19 MISC. TEXTILE PRDTS.	71554	2219	267367	271552	0	0	0	0	0
20 LUMBER, WOOD PRDTS.	3	4	34	8269	191639	1520435	1134423	325591	126857
21 WOODEN CONTAINERS	0	0	20	0	0	8	122	774	13314
22 HOUSEHOLD FURNITURE	0	0	0	0	0	0	0	0	0
23 OTHER FURNITURE	0	0	0	0	0	0	0	0	0
24 PAPER, ALLIED PRDTS.	1857	2183	12125	1707	534	2524	8376	813	320
25 PAPERBOARD CONTAINERS	10272	42989	84402	27791	0	3102	9161	4640	1389
26 PRINTING, PUBLISHING	727	1633	10106	1545	251	1554	1328	737	245
27 CHEMICALS,SELECT. PRDTS.	15002	10783	3112	677	1435	11821	32057	48335	102
28 PLASTICS, SYNTHETICS	356378	348293	0	28466	0	0	16324	0	0
29 DRUGS, COSMETICS	4420	8174	2749	390	169	564	383	188	87
30 PAINT, ALLIED PRDTS.	9	6	37	8	1	9445	29464	11970	7
31 PETROLEUM, RELATED INDS.	5977	6333	10432	2004	15467	23431	3975	3519	781
32 RUBBER, MISC. PLASTICS	5765	2362	22712	96809	1291	1419	5307	581	76
33 LEATHER TANNING, PRDTS.	95	417	39417	0	221	846	322	120	74
34 FOOTWEAR, LEATHER PRDTS.	33	48	348	67	17	42	60	33	18
35 GLASS, GLASS PRDTS.	3	5	34	6	2	4	11276	2488	1
36 STONE, CLAY PRDTS.	2	7	40	6	34	25630	22641	5	1
37 PRIMARY IRON, STEEL MFR.	2	8	60	2769	25041	21	11552	9383	33649
38 PRIMARY NONFERROUS MFR.	0	0	0	2754	806	0	6449	0	0

39 METAL CONTAINERS	0	0	0	0	0	0	0	0	0
40 FABRICATED METAL PRDTS.	0	0	1	0	0	0	0	0	0
41 SCREW MACH. PRDTS., ETC.	0	0	1	117	0	0	7194	0	641
42 OTHER FAB. METAL PRDTS.	754	1237	16421	2839	8021	30597	103076	22936	2163
43 ENGINES, TURBINES	0	0	0	0	0	0	0	0	0
44 FARM MACH., EQUIP.	0	0	0	0	0	0	0	0	0
45 CONSTRUC. MACH., EQUIP.	0	0	0	0	0	0	0	0	0
46 MATERIAL HANDLING MACH.	293	514	1898	261	707	1988	892	360	203
47 METALWORKING MACHINERY	0	0	1	0	0	0	0	0	0
48 SPECIAL MACH., EQUIP.	8456	7008	0	0	4629	17788	6847	2577	1581
49 GENERAL MACH., EQUIP.	416	1073	1	0	0	487	119	198	0
50 MACHINE SHOP PRDTS.	6	39	200	37	281	304	60	35	14
51 OFFICE, COMPUT. MACHINES	4	10	62	9	1	9	8	5	1
52 SERVICE IND. MACHINES	0	0	0	0	0	0	0	0	0
53 ELECT. TRANSMISS. EQUIP.	0	0	0	0	0	0	0	0	0
54 HOUSEHOLD APPLIANCES	29	52	395	73	20	48	70	38	16
55 ELECTRIC LIGHTING EQUIP.	9	12	84	11	38	46	21	8	7
56 RADIO, TV, ETC., EQUIP.	41	72	548	101	28	66	98	53	23
57 ELECTRONIC COMPONENTS	0	0	0	0	0	0	0	0	0
58 MISC. ELECTRICAL MACH.	34	48	275	59	495	528	97	52	28
59 MOTOR VEHICLES, EQUIP.	76	115	629	135	1116	1195	224	124	62
60 AIRCRAFT, PARTS	0	0	0	0	0	0	0	0	0
61 OTHER TRANSPORT. EQUIP.	0	0	0	0	0	0	0	0	0
62 PROFESS., SCIEN. INSTRU.	375	1327	6785	858	441	1461	849	404	189
63 MEDICAL, PHOTO. EQUIP.	205	628	3441	468	177	649	441	225	93
64 MISC. MANUFACTURING	39768	19804	329544	3857	259	984	748	391	163
65 TRANSPORT., WAREHOUSING	40463	30326	114980	27772	9956	115791	117625	37586	21141
66 COMMUNICA.,EXC. BRDCAST.	5958	11685	64824	11220	3403	11131	10051	4492	1447
67 RADIO, TV BROADCASTING	0	0	0	0	0	0	0	0	0
68 ELEC.,GAS,WATER,SAN.SER.	16571	19511	44343	12053	3516	41435	23196	14590	3583
69 WHOLESALE, RETAIL TRADE	101700	96367	542103	142231	22754	76343	92768	35240	11731
70 FINANCE, INSURANCE	7352	14428	73206	16626	26308	27123	17899	3942	2061
71 REAL ESTATE, RENTAL	14459	31962	183207	25765	5087	26586	31150	18096	3980
72 HOTELS, PERSONAL SERV.	2714	1419	13935	4774	550	1307	1926	1042	703
73 BUSINESS SERVICES	21355	51057	184772	27884	32002	47509	40184	17882	4054
74 RESEARCH, DEVELOPMENT	0	0	0	0	0	0	0	0	0
75 AUTO. REPAIR, SERVICES	1126	1779	9733	1968	11876	13125	2897	1532	739
76 AMUSEMENTS	130	229	1743	322	89	211	311	168	72
77 MED.,EDUC. SERVICES	732	1478	8411	1470	488	1572	1457	662	212
78 FEDERAL GOVT. ENTERPRISE	2288	5684	40506	5109	312	2140	2203	1353	346
79 STATE, LOCAL GOVT. ENT.	235	317	574	424	820	961	251	131	53
80 DIRECT ALLOCATED IMPORTS	47058	353	19161	496	137	325	479	259	111
81 TRANSFERRED IMPORTS	0	0	0	0	0	0	0	0	0
82 VALUE ADDED	456144	1203464	5568235	751243	848183	1450508	1119325	434389	143949
83 STATE TOTAL PRODUCTION	1762241	3254744	14652981	2492698	2144140	3499489	2895933	1015016	378932

NOTE: The 152 column numbers are identical with the 152 product-mix industry numbers given in Table A-2, pages 134-145, and refer to that industrial classification.

TABLE C-10

1963 NATIONAL PRIMARY INPUTS TO
MANUFACTURING AND SERVICES
(THOUSANDS OF CURRENT DOLLARS)

INDUSTRY TITLE	28	29	30	31	32	33	34	35	36
1 LIVESTOCK, PRDTS.	144	14	9	22	9	4	28	17	243
2 OTHER AGRICULTURE PRDTS.	430	42	27	66	28	13	82	50	724
3 FORESTRY, FISHERIES	30	3	2	5	2	1	6	3	50
4 AGRI.,FORES.,FISH. SERV.	0	0	0	0	0	0	0	0	0
5 IRON, FERRO. ORES MINING	0	0	0	0	0	0	0	0	0
6 NONFERROUS ORES MINING	0	0	0	0	0	0	0	0	0
7 COAL MINING	1486	286	140	135	109	2844	38646	30001	4606
8 CRUDE PETRO.,NATURAL GAS	0	0	0	0	0	0	0	0	0
9 STONE, CLAY MINING	0	0	0	0	0	633	36876	4056	14036
10 CHEM.,FERT. MIN. MINING	0	0	0	0	0	3591	6051	2123	0
11 NEW CONSTRUCTION	0	0	0	0	0	0	0	0	0
12 MAINT., REPAIR CONSTR.	4799	1080	413	1429	298	14500	14765	6304	9760
13 ORDNANCE, ACCESSORIES	31	3	2	5	2	1	6	4	53
14 FOOD, KINDRED PRDTS.	8279	813	513	1273	542	6469	60186	22296	50187
15 TOBACCO MANUFACTURES	666	65	41	102	44	21	128	77	1121
16 FABRICS	214109	0	0	0	1740	0	55019	0	15047
17 TEXTILE PRDTS.	104952	6250	6227	819	18133	0	2	1	17900
18 APPAREL	6974	643	399	1036	425	369	3174	1544	4237
19 MISC. TEXTILE PRDTS.	629	0	0	0	0	0	0	0	0
20 LUMBER, WOOD PRDTS.	553838	20183	29527	78639	14929	129161	339617	288256	29324
21 WOODEN CONTAINERS	593	83	227	0	197	0	180	101	86
22 HOUSEHOLD FURNITURE	72209	415	1175	1620	1140	0	0	0	0
23 OTHER FURNITURE	0	2255	1171	18708	20172	0	0	0	0
24 PAPER, ALLIED PRDTS.	4037	368	258	694	743	4181	582979	106755	1567554
25 PAPERBOARD CONTAINERS	52481	9724	3697	8484	7943	0	44555	0	296080
26 PRINTING, PUBLISHING	2959	400	277	775	308	356	2016	969	31485
27 CHEMICALS,SELECT. PRDTS.	7071	635	47	212	297	48730	181736	117041	95696
28 PLASTICS, SYNTHETICS	6898	0	0	0	0	2503	33787	19634	113702
29 DRUGS, COSMETICS	731	70	46	118	50	1108	7047	3966	1082
30 PAINT, ALLIED PRDTS.	90906	10118	4352	18859	2436	1	1	1	9
31 PETROLEUM, RELATED INDS.	6017	981	504	1546	551	8128	30267	31717	35009
32 RUBBER, MISC. PLASTICS	236133	23916	18431	26034	19628	36	7306	4506	135012
33 LEATHER TANNING, PRDTS.	4346	2057	120	28	16	232	1215	595	351
34 FOOTWEAR, LEATHER PRDTS.	125	14	8	20	10	5	24	15	210
35 GLASS, GLASS PRDTS.	26743	7267	6358	26497	1	0	3	2	21
36 STONE, CLAY PRDTS.	21	3	14477	5	1	1968	8641	3289	203
37 PRIMARY IRON, STEEL MFR.	92021	53855	19139	78313	26742	1	733	3	67
38 PRIMARY NONFERROUS MFR.	31736	2634	2760	4209	8060	0	0	0	0

39 METAL CONTAINERS	0	0	0	0	0	0	0	0	0
40 FABRICATED METAL PRDTS.	0	0	0	0	0	0	0	0	0
41 SCREW MACH. PRDTS., ETC.	7175	5177	3676	6800	4193	0	0	0	0
42 OTHER FAB. METAL PRDTS.	259329	27700	10226	25934	3978	25997	92205	26460	8092
43 ENGINES, TURBINES	0	0	0	0	0	0	0	0	0
44 FARM MACH., EQUIP.	0	0	0	0	0	0	0	0	0
45 CONSTRUC. MACH., EQUIP.	0	0	0	0	0	0	0	0	0
46 MATERIAL HANDLING MACH.	793	81	58	118	51	501	2670	1312	974
47 METALWORKING MACHINERY	0	0	0	0	0	0	0	0	0
48 SPECIAL MACH., EQUIP.	0	0	0	0	0	9324	6315	11456	1994
49 GENERAL MACH., EQUIP.	99	0	0	0	594	4296	14090	5212	1356
50 MACHINE SHOP PRDTS.	119	13	6	34	3086	6	57	66	69
51 OFFICE, COMPUT. MACHINES	18	2	2	5	2	1	12	6	15
52 SERVICE IND. MACHINES	0	0	0	0	0	0	0	0	0
53 ELECT. TRANSMISS. EQUIP.	0	0	0	0	199	0	0	0	0
54 HOUSEHOLD APPLIANCES	148	14	9	23	10	5	28	17	248
55 ELECTRIC LIGHTING EQUIP.	482	5	1	1878	2	1	14	14	24
56 RADIO, TV, ETC., EQUIP.	205	20	13	31	13	6	39	24	344
57 ELECTRONIC COMPONENTS	0	0	0	0	0	0	0	0	0
58 MISC. ELECTRICAL MACH.	184	22	14	47	16	10	79	110	110
59 MOTOR VEHICLES, EQUIP.	423	53	31	107	35	26	184	250	259
60 AIRCRAFT, PARTS	0	0	0	0	0	0	0	0	0
61 OTHER TRANSPORT. EQUIP.	0	0	0	0	0	0	0	0	0
62 PROFESS., SCIEN. INSTRU.	1572	145	90	234	97	83	707	345	988
63 MEDICAL, PHOTO. EQUIP.	877	93	61	164	68	53	448	221	671
64 MISC. MANUFACTURING	2575	172	116	310	129	97	788	395	1331
65 TRANSPORT., WAREHOUSING	102325	8946	6965	16491	7913	31582	184613	115897	145940
66 COMMUNICA.,EXC. BRDCAST.	19486	2553	1859	5163	2054	1402	11782	5868	19050
67 RADIO, TV BROADCASTING	0	0	0	0	0	0	0	0	0
68 ELEC.,GAS,WATER,SAN.SER.	23313	3872	2150	5597	1844	30184	129287	67544	47187
69 WHOLESALE, RETAIL TRADE	175472	19233	12249	27276	12075	20013	113471	112976	168161
70 FINANCE, INSURANCE	34958	6771	3179	9539	3563	3299	27645	14568	16668
71 REAL ESTATE, RENTAL	86122	6268	2963	15122	4786	3496	11904	6850	57207
72 HOTELS, PERSONAL SERV.	5608	1143	250	620	264	371	2296	1391	21066
73 BUSINESS SERVICES	83290	16123	4232	8609	3828	7733	74060	38998	81997
74 RESEARCH, DEVELOPMENT	0	0	0	0	0	0	0	0	0
75 AUTO. REPAIR, SERVICES	5405	682	422	1388	465	337	2528	2906	3724
76 AMUSEMENTS	651	64	40	100	43	20	125	76	1096
77 MED.,EDUC. SERVICES	2631	336	245	675	269	186	1556	780	2796
78 FEDERAL GOVT. ENTERPRISE	5243	695	487	1361	544	555	3861	1907	4420
79 STATE, LOCAL GOVT. ENT.	348	49	28	90	71	444	2741	1636	544
80 DIRECT ALLOCATED IMPORTS	1533	98	62	154	66	31	192	117	1689
81 TRANSFERRED IMPORTS	0	0	0	0	0	0	0	0	0
82 VALUE ADDED	1613434	225066	101015	360131	125368	249642	1626821	1105589	1830880
83 STATE TOTAL PRODUCTION	3965210	469576	260795	757655	300179	614557	3765595	2166315	4842757

NOTE: The 152 column numbers are identical with the 152 product-mix industry numbers given in Table A-2, pages 134-145, and refer to that industrial classification.

TABLE C-10

1963 NATIONAL PRIMARY INPUTS TO
MANUFACTURING AND SERVICES
(THOUSANDS OF CURRENT DOLLARS)

INDUSTRY TITLE	37	38	39	40	41	42	43	44	45
1 LIVESTOCK, PRDTS.	80	340	235	234	27	445	16	382	83
2 OTHER AGRICULTURE PRDTS.	238	1014	704	698	82	1328	47	2865	318
3 FORESTRY, FISHERIES	17	71	49	49	6	93	3	3224	17
4 AGRI.,FORES.,FISH. SERV.	0	0	0	0	0	0	0	0	0
5 IRON, FERRO. ORES MINING	0	0	0	0	0	0	0	83008	0
6 NONFERROUS ORES MINING	0	0	0	0	0	0	0	79772	0
7 COAL MINING	792	27	108	68	2	470	42	63870	232
8 CRUDE PETRO.,NATURAL GAS	0	0	0	0	0	0	0	14783	0
9 STONE, CLAY MINING	338	0	0	0	0	0	0	26293	2047
10 CHEM.,FERT. MIN. MINING	0	0	0	0	0	0	0	145585	133397
11 NEW CONSTRUCTION	0	0	0	0	0	0	0	0	0
12 MAINT., REPAIR CONSTR.	12460	10674	2180	2367	313	8881	1236	59517	7965
13 ORDNANCE, ACCESSORIES	17	74	51	51	6	97	3	83	18
14 FOOD, KINDRED PRDTS.	4590	19950	13563	13891	1578	38329	913	53145	17639
15 TOBACCO MANUFACTURES	369	1571	1091	1082	127	2057	73	1765	381
16 FABRICS	0	0	0	0	0	3378	422	2425	0
17 TEXTILE PRDTS.	4	13	5	4	1	22847	529	8	0
18 APPAREL	4787	74	51	51	6	97	3	4751	902
19 MISC. TEXTILE PRDTS.	0	0	0	0	0	0	0	0	14943
20 LUMBER, WOOD PRDTS.	3015	30	21	6802	1304	18077	977	6653	7
21 WOODEN CONTAINERS	165	0	0	0	0	56	0	2747	779
22 HOUSEHOLD FURNITURE	0	0	0	0	0	0	0	0	0
23 OTHER FURNITURE	0	0	0	0	0	0	0	0	0
24 PAPER, ALLIED PRDTS.	1868867	891523	253534	123790	31061	1213992	38266	72644	52195
25 PAPERBOARD CONTAINERS	136338	544	7382	7180	1498	23882	23050	50014	5482
26 PRINTING, PUBLISHING	9105	139856	532173	669276	99184	344378	48464	6391	1061
27 CHEMICALS,SELECT. PRDTS.	81261	37084	4774	19704	660	299278	4550	1848522	692202
28 PLASTICS, SYNTHETICS	33982	572	28	612	0	32957	0	19829	0
29 DRUGS, COSMETICS	503	1079	471	498	83	1437	65	2957	4462
30 PAINT, ALLIED PRDTS.	9	834	45	891	1	21993	1	1383	3
31 PETROLEUM, RELATED INDS.	34715	12975	3220	3592	768	22063	551	50679	15262
32 RUBBER, MISC. PLASTICS	5012	1553	470	14190	99	54523	64	1470	2094
33 LEATHER TANNING, PRDTS.	194	124	18	22	4	186	4	3037	174
34 FOOTWEAR, LEATHER PRDTS.	72	283	197	196	24	379	14	325	71
35 GLASS, GLASS PRDTS.	7	30	21	20	3	39	1	9593	7
36 STONE, CLAY PRDTS.	15	52	21	21	4	38	3	27943	1059
37 PRIMARY IRON, STEEL MFR.	8	26	20	11	4	1672	2	104943	11
38 PRIMARY NONFERROUS MFR.	13192	0	0	0	0	6373	0	153358	0

39	METAL CONTAINERS	0	0	0	0	0	0	0	94352	8822
40	FABRICATED METAL PRDTS.	0	1	1	0	0	1	0	0	0
41	SCREW MACH. PRDTS., ETC.	0	1	1	0	0	1	0	1	0
42	OTHER FAB. METAL PRDTS.	15435	953	331	710	49	15592	787	92423	828
43	ENGINES, TURBINES	0	0	0	0	0	0	0	0	0
44	FARM MACH., EQUIP.	0	0	0	0	0	0	0	0	0
45	CONSTRUC. MACH., EQUIP.	0	0	0	0	0	0	0	0	0
46	MATERIAL HANDLING MACH.	685	548	59	117	25	954	33	6491	415
47	METALWORKING MACHINERY	0	1	0	0	0	1	0	0	0
48	SPECIAL MACH., EQUIP.	7746	6815	512	1919	431	22546	605	148293	0
49	GENERAL MACH., EQUIP.	184	100	1	0	0	160	0	6873	363
50	MACHINE SHOP PRDTS.	106	325	89	71	20	157	13	170	53
51	OFFICE, COMPUT. MACHINES	16	54	41	24	7	51	5	36	6
52	SERVICE IND. MACHINES	0	0	0	0	0	0	0	0	0
53	ELECT. TRANSMISS. EQUIP.	0	0	0	0	0	0	0	14802	0
54	HOUSEHOLD APPLIANCES	82	348	242	240	28	456	16	391	84
55	ELECTRIC LIGHTING EQUIP.	33	84	29	22	7	48	7	53	15
56	RADIO, TV, ETC., EQUIP.	113	483	335	332	39	632	23	542	117
57	ELECTRONIC COMPONENTS	0	0	0	0	0	0	0	0	0
58	MISC. ELECTRICAL MACH.	164	476	121	93	26	226	17	255	87
59	MOTOR VEHICLES, EQUIP.	377	1086	283	219	62	522	42	576	198
60	AIRCRAFT, PARTS	0	0	0	0	0	0	0	0	0
61	OTHER TRANSPORT. EQUIP.	0	0	0	0	0	0	0	0	0
62	PROFESS., SCIEN. INSTRU.	1076	1155	148	338	73	2265	92	1136	218
63	MEDICAL, PHOTO. EQUIP.	657	23849	16002	15592	3674	74353	112	1125	205
64	MISC. MANUFACTURING	1195	3119	1924	1356	345	22208	239	2407	437
65	TRANSPORT., WAREHOUSING	153270	79115	45950	35071	3834	127565	4225	309683	103624
66	COMMUNICA.,EXC. BRDCAST.	20912	109267	22454	15905	4891	34204	3139	44228	7116
67	RADIO, TV BROADCASTING	0	0	0	0	0	0	0	0	0
68	ELEC.,GAS,WATER,SAN.SER.	29199	25588	3667	5394	1343	47527	1782	504417	23208
69	WHOLESALE, RETAIL TRADE	99349	99820	46649	46168	6217	177300	7116	293954	81361
70	FINANCE, INSURANCE	15962	42730	15683	13798	2923	41858	1684	63565	9522
71	REAL ESTATE, RENTAL	46951	154900	262687	268287	20191	149666	26656	54171	6490
72	HOTELS, PERSONAL SERV.	10807	18669	10144	7650	769	26478	1105	18899	2652
73	BUSINESS SERVICES	81547	193154	87478	88793	6754	120242	6209	237910	39534
74	RESEARCH, DEVELOPMENT	0	0	0	0	0	0	0	0	0
75	AUTO. REPAIR, SERVICES	5028	17084	4347	3338	966	7689	646	8080	2401
76	AMUSEMENTS	361	1536	1066	1058	124	2012	72	1726	373
77	MED.,EDUC. SERVICES	2747	9662	10075	2935	840	6227	536	5625	955
78	FEDERAL GOVT. ENTERPRISE	4018	43288	90454	5806	2670	36505	1222	9293	1534
79	STATE, LOCAL GOVT. ENT.	332	866	3249	167	47	702	32	6664	206
80	DIRECT ALLOCATED IMPORTS	556	2367	1643	1630	191	3100	111	26115	4513
81	TRANSFERRED IMPORTS	0	0	0	0	0	0	0	0	0
82	VALUE ADDED	1888232	2537186	776138	730256	198064	3489317	156452	5484280	512812
83	STATE TOTAL PRODUCTION	4597295	4495004	2222235	2112592	391455	6529908	332278	10342500	1760961

NOTE: The 152 column numbers are identical with the 152 product-mix industry numbers given in Table A-2, pages 134-145, and refer to that industrial classification.

TABLE C-10

1963 NATIONAL PRIMARY INPUTS TO
MANUFACTURING AND SERVICES
(THOUSANDS OF CURRENT DOLLARS)

INDUSTRY TITLE	46	47	48	49	50	51	52	53	54
1 LIVESTOCK, PRDTS.	97	168	256	2672	210	115	42	114	21
2 OTHER AGRICULTURE PRDTS.	15852	501	8754	747	626	342	126	339	63
3 FORESTRY, FISHERIES	25034	35	1282	52	44	24	9	24	4
4 AGRI.,FORES.,FISH. SERV.	0	0	0	0	0	0	0	0	0
5 IRON, FERRO. ORES MINING	0	0	0	0	0	0	0	0	0
6 NONFERROUS ORES MINING	0	0	0	0	0	0	0	0	0
7 COAL MINING	4145	24094	2182	1323	330	8958	447	5377	46
8 CRUDE PETRO.,NATURAL GAS	14331	0	0	0	0	9410874	0	0	0
9 STONE, CLAY MINING	4356	300	0	3131	4973	5384	61709	6695	0
10 CHEM.,FERT. MIN. MINING	0	0	0	2139	0	513	0	201	0
11 NEW CONSTRUCTION	0	0	0	0	0	0	0	0	0
12 MAINT., REPAIR CONSTR.	13086	24327	18481	6606	5622	345183	4310	8016	478
13 ORDNANCE, ACCESSORIES	21	37	56	55	46	25	9	25	5
14 FOOD, KINDRED PRDTS.	108266	26284	110891	161204	112461	31671	2428	6522	1213
15 TOBACCO MANUFACTURES	447	776	1184	1156	970	529	195	524	98
16 FABRICS	0	1186	1352	14	382	34	0	10048	37555
17 TEXTILE PRDTS.	1	4	3	3	2	3	0	341952	0
18 APPAREL	1376	3086	1701	1653	1061	2778	539	2011	1174
19 MISC. TEXTILE PRDTS.	0	0	0	0	0	0	0	0	0
20 LUMBER, WOOD PRDTS.	33987	2612	22	22	18	2947	1240	3298	6198
21 WOODEN CONTAINERS	663	1757	599	1258	882	169	11	1120	96
22 HOUSEHOLD FURNITURE	0	0	0	0	0	0	0	0	0
23 OTHER FURNITURE	0	0	0	0	0	0	0	0	0
24 PAPER, ALLIED PRDTS.	31501	209112	18283	57363	1499	3794	100099	2151	308
25 PAPERBOARD CONTAINERS	34648	40808	62786	151321	18873	46275	14179	12838	2964
26 PRINTING, PUBLISHING	1744	2529	4826	32109	2124	5502	466	1498	256
27 CHEMICALS,SELECT. PRDTS.	442811	1778211	138443	550802	457467	539388	109	160495	7843
28 PLASTICS, SYNTHETICS	26439	100017	0	0	212097	0	0	390814	9048
29 DRUGS, COSMETICS	4087	17664	307870	209008	9796	49270	4477	329	87
30 PAINT, ALLIED PRDTS.	16082	4	6	5535	516	6	2	1	1
31 PETROLEUM, RELATED INDS.	52138	22447	10750	26836	102066	1413195	209192	4048	813
32 RUBBER, MISC. PLASTICS	595	4987	50279	220960	552	851	97	76565	27468
33 LEATHER TANNING, PRDTS.	194	520	141	104	85	1969	96	243	14
34 FOOTWEAR, LEATHER PRDTS.	86	143	217	212	175	99	37	95	19
35 GLASS, GLASS PRDTS.	8	454	72630	90240	18	11	4	10	2
36 STONE, CLAY PRDTS.	319	58	5608	4202	5295	897	31756	5156	38
37 PRIMARY IRON, STEEL MFR.	5	8	11	199	5986	32	1007	25093	1
38 PRIMARY NONFERROUS MFR.	1932	2257	0	0	22144	46289	0	0	0

39	METAL CONTAINERS	52510	14361	23963	156320	148254	124042	9640	0	0
40	FABRICATED METAL PRDTS.	0	0	0	0	0	0	0	0	0
41	SCREW MACH. PRDTS., ETC.	831	0	9181	22509	0	1	0	0	0
42	OTHER FAB. METAL PRDTS.	733	1838	12552	45839	958	6132	387	2686	88
43	ENGINES, TURBINES	0	0	0	0	0	0	0	0	0
44	FARM MACH., EQUIP.	0	0	0	0	0	0	0	0	0
45	CONSTRUC. MACH., EQUIP.	0	0	0	0	0	0	0	0	0
46	MATERIAL HANDLING MACH.	466	1255	389	309	237	4189	223	614	81
47	METALWORKING MACHINERY	0	0	0	0	0	0	0	0	0
48	SPECIAL MACH., EQUIP.	0	0	0	0	0	0	0	5213	0
49	GENERAL MACH., EQUIP.	463	1088	40	238	20	1825	79	264	99
50	MACHINE SHOP PRDTS.	81	71	1147	48	47	165	14	39	6
51	OFFICE, COMPUT. MACHINES	10	13	22	14	12	34	3	9	1
52	SERVICE IND. MACHINES	0	0	0	0	0	0	0	0	0
53	ELECT. TRANSMISS. EQUIP.	0	0	0	0	0	0	0	0	0
54	HOUSEHOLD APPLIANCES	99	172	262	256	215	118	43	116	22
55	ELECTRIC LIGHTING EQUIP.	21	22	3125	19	14	36	5	10	1
56	RADIO, TV, ETC., EQUIP.	137	239	364	355	298	163	60	161	30
57	ELECTRONIC COMPONENTS	0	0	0	0	0	0	0	0	0
58	MISC. ELECTRICAL MACH.	144	106	93	66	68	285	30	54	6
59	MOTOR VEHICLES, EQUIP.	331	250	461	150	159	634	70	3072	15
60	AIRCRAFT, PARTS	0	0	0	0	0	0	0	0	0
61	OTHER TRANSPORT. EQUIP.	0	0	0	0	0	0	0	0	0
62	PROFESS., SCIEN. INSTRU.	325	720	4653	422	282	638	127	471	178
63	MEDICAL, PHOTO. EQUIP.	311	531	607	479	384	1264	107	348	92
64	MISC. MANUFACTURING	659	1076	1380	1083	891	1642	224	686	2053
65	TRANSPORT., WAREHOUSING	69052	134927	64033	119582	68894	841813	55089	78131	5332
66	COMMUNICA.,EXC. BRDCAST.	11524	22968	23519	16945	12923	22434	3113	7464	1679
67	RADIO, TV BROADCASTING	0	0	0	0	0	0	0	0	0
68	ELEC.,GAS,WATER,SAN.SER.	27255	70656	18669	17281	11202	365190	16535	27416	2874
69	WHOLESALE, RETAIL TRADE	91718	169569	133252	169620	123169	302195	76635	75018	11422
70	FINANCE, INSURANCE	20197	33556	32607	23656	15882	195054	12980	18497	1950
71	REAL ESTATE, RENTAL	38866	43455	48820	37651	21356	413319	4752	15716	2581
72	HOTELS, PERSONAL SERV.	4548	8197	29486	18541	14467	12006	1514	5642	857
73	BUSINESS SERVICES	83943	163275	423487	863201	66701	463358	23702	102978	9166
74	RESEARCH, DEVELOPMENT	0	0	0	0	0	0	0	0	0
75	AUTO. REPAIR, SERVICES	4040	3704	3380	2377	2350	7565	912	1799	228
76	AMUSEMENTS	437	759	1158	1131	948	518	191	513	95
77	MED.,EDUC. SERVICES	1521	2938	3132	2381	2023	2510	478	1353	230
78	FEDERAL GOVT. ENTERPRISE	2515	3339	9571	8916	3658	13130	806	2597	416
79	STATE, LOCAL GOVT. ENT.	667	1638	761	415	294	2171	233	572	17
80	DIRECT ALLOCATED IMPORTS	40802	1170	3820	4844	14097	798	294	161193	8535
81	TRANSFERRED IMPORTS	0	0	0	0	0	0	0	0	0
82	VALUE ADDED	889737	2555086	2066575	1652027	890985	4842166	258207	1524022	192375
83	STATE TOTAL PRODUCTION	2178193	5501363	3739124	4697604	2367108	19542512	899040	3102256	336242

NOTE: The 152 column numbers are identical with the 152 product-mix industry numbers given in Table A-2, pages 134-145, and refer to that industrial classification.

TABLE C-10

1963 NATIONAL PRIMARY INPUTS TO
MANUFACTURING AND SERVICES
(THOUSANDS OF CURRENT DOLLARS)

INDUSTRY TITLE	55	56	57	58	59	60	61	62	63
1 LIVESTOCK, PRDTS.	149	90	57020	5	73	23	92	42	44
2 OTHER AGRICULTURE PRDTS.	444	268	35	15	216	69	275	126	130
3 FORESTRY, FISHERIES	31	19	2	1	15	5	19	9	9
4 AGRI.,FORES.,FISH. SERV.	0	0	0	0	0	0	0	0	0
5 IRON, FERRO. ORES MINING	0	0	0	0	0	0	0	2382	3624
6 NONFERROUS ORES MINING	0	0	0	0	0	0	89	0	0
7 COAL MINING	3177	613	2070	42	347	19	2816	65633	4288
8 CRUDE PETRO.,NATURAL GAS	0	0	0	0	0	0	0	0	0
9 STONE, CLAY MINING	2728	372	0	0	0	0	36689	98458	57820
10 CHEM.,FERT. MIN. MINING	0	0	327	0	0	0	1348	0	0
11 NEW CONSTRUCTION	0	0	0	0	0	0	0	0	0
12 MAINT., REPAIR CONSTR.	7116	10955	1312	435	2974	936	12893	11965	6201
13 ORDNANCE, ACCESSORIES	32	20	3	1	16	5	20	9	9
14 FOOD, KINDRED PRDTS.	8561	5162	240690	1540	4168	1327	5293	2431	2500
15 TOBACCO MANUFACTURES	688	415	54	23	335	107	426	195	201
16 FABRICS	100035	32861	0	1689	68223	28902	0	411	0
17 TEXTILE PRDTS.	4308	3	0	0	30935	76102	1	1	0
18 APPAREL	3097	4048	3	1	15683	2373	3848	870	1655
19 MISC. TEXTILE PRDTS.	0	0	0	0	0	29573	0	0	0
20 LUMBER, WOOD PRDTS.	6393	10375	872	9277	23455	5869	53681	2570	1475
21 WOODEN CONTAINERS	866	1165	399	17	1002	1506	11374	94	83
22 HOUSEHOLD FURNITURE	0	0	0	0	0	0	0	0	0
23 OTHER FURNITURE	0	0	0	0	0	0	0	0	0
24 PAPER, ALLIED PRDTS.	11679	1923	414	3561	10793	2029	2423	24003	1037
25 PAPERBOARD CONTAINERS	46996	89607	2620	2785	48120	3850	133545	0	3019
26 PRINTING, PUBLISHING	2583	1813	385	214	2455	653	2009	294	783
27 CHEMICALS,SELECT. PRDTS.	145591	38178	31748	43	148	173	130281	81	19116
28 PLASTICS, SYNTHETICS	290537	896653	423	0	0	8397	0	0	0
29 DRUGS, COSMETICS	474	449	39091	35	6797	162	417	129	192
30 PAINT, ALLIED PRDTS.	6286	3772	2	1	2	5	5290	1	4
31 PETROLEUM, RELATED INDS.	9020	6171	3498	325	2043	792	8367	11112	7927
32 RUBBER, MISC. PLASTICS	154796	186560	770	27130	233484	42551	62202	309	11665
33 LEATHER TANNING, PRDTS.	258	218	179432	53821	467096	81730	228	591	177
34 FOOTWEAR, LEATHER PRDTS.	126	76	12	2196	82746	15578	81	36	40
35 GLASS, GLASS PRDTS.	1773	21647	1	0	7	758	189579	4	4
36 STONE, CLAY PRDTS.	620	1527	862	0	7	1	69214	1241	5350
37 PRIMARY IRON, STEEL MFR.	21913	2621	1	6451	11	2	6790	370	8407
38 PRIMARY NONFERROUS MFR.	10633	5187	0	0	0	1373	14855	0	1207

39	METAL CONTAINERS	1883	0	0	0	0	0	0	0	0
40	FABRICATED METAL PRDTS.	0	0	0	0	0	0	1141	0	215
41	SCREW MACH. PRDTS., ETC.	5762	4896	0	0	0	0	1152	0	0
42	OTHER FAB. METAL PRDTS.	30822	17729	1196	4920	2976	21630	674	153	1765
43	ENGINES, TURBINES	0	0	0	0	0	0	0	0	0
44	FARM MACH., EQUIP.	0	0	0	0	0	0	0	0	0
45	CONSTRUC. MACH., EQUIP.	0	0	0	0	0	0	0	0	19262
46	MATERIAL HANDLING MACH.	712	688	176	36	431	133	698	1260	596
47	METALWORKING MACHINERY	283	5016	0	0	0	0	2880	0	8507
48	SPECIAL MACH., EQUIP.	433	0	0	0	0	0	0	0	0
49	GENERAL MACH., EQUIP.	198	99	205	0	0	0	305	285	6128
50	MACHINE SHOP PRDTS.	6220	62	6	6	28	18	54	66	89
51	OFFICE, COMPUT. MACHINES	15	11	2	1	16	4	12	2	5
52	SERVICE IND. MACHINES	0	0	0	0	0	0	0	0	0
53	ELECT. TRANSMISS. EQUIP.	0	0	0	0	0	0	0	0	0
54	HOUSEHOLD APPLIANCES	153	92	12	5	74	24	94	43	45
55	ELECTRIC LIGHTING EQUIP.	19	18	5	1	11	5	19	10	19
56	RADIO, TV, ETC., EQUIP.	212	128	17	7	103	33	131	60	62
57	ELECTRONIC COMPONENTS	0	0	0	0	0	0	0	0	0
58	MISC. ELECTRICAL MACH.	86	84	16	6	44	23	86	113	147
59	MOTOR VEHICLES, EQUIP.	194	191	35	15	98	57	202	259	343
60	AIRCRAFT, PARTS	0	0	0	0	0	0	0	0	0
61	OTHER TRANSPORT. EQUIP.	0	0	0	0	0	0	0	0	0
62	PROFESS., SCIEN. INSTRU.	717	913	197	85	1295	388	870	202	372
63	MEDICAL, PHOTO. EQUIP.	544	518	110	53	725	204	528	110	218
64	MISC. MANUFACTURING	9295	917	187	4610	5940	45133	5452	205	393
65	TRANSPORT., WAREHOUSING	57735	58814	12395	4231	28079	10595	67785	91198	24338
66	COMMUNICA.,EXC. BRDCAST.	11830	11825	2120	875	10051	3694	9627	2901	4994
67	RADIO, TV BROADCASTING	0	0	0	0	0	0	0	0	0
68	ELEC.,GAS,WATER,SAN.SER.	32577	43021	8919	1177	8999	3032	112961	117100	63122
69	WHOLESALE, RETAIL TRADE	92431	113939	29933	7970	74302	30107	94521	15053	16291
70	FINANCE, INSURANCE	13441	14188	5232	1264	14499	6688	20967	15373	11135
71	REAL ESTATE, RENTAL	16378	41198	9893	2030	16112	10130	23786	3638	5680
72	HOTELS, PERSONAL SERV.	7148	7509	348	229	2966	924	4801	1650	1369
73	BUSINESS SERVICES	63358	55662	8206	2284	59882	23528	65977	24897	17668
74	RESEARCH, DEVELOPMENT	0	0	0	0	0	0	0	0	0
75	AUTO. REPAIR, SERVICES	2845	2805	496	199	1524	813	2587	2851	3819
76	AMUSEMENTS	673	406	53	22	328	104	416	191	197
77	MED.,EDUC. SERVICES	2219	2134	323	117	1356	567	1343	446	698
78	FEDERAL GOVT. ENTERPRISE	4028	3155	787	802	8744	2532	3511	377	1118
79	STATE, LOCAL GOVT. ENT.	687	559	385	16	109	66	603	244	271
80	DIRECT ALLOCATED IMPORTS	73324	625	4060	34	1605	161	641	295	303
81	TRANSFERRED IMPORTS	0	0	0	0	0	0	0	0	0
82	VALUE ADDED	1266929	1429790	250784	85928	1109743	308847	1606519	667852	490149
83	STATE TOTAL PRODUCTION	2544064	3139758	898144	226532	2351192	774311	2784489	1170199	816286

NOTE: The 152 column numbers are identical with the 152 product-mix industry numbers given in Table A-2, pages 134-145, and refer to that industrial classification.

TABLE C-10

1963 NATIONAL PRIMARY INPUTS TO MANUFACTURING AND SERVICES
(THOUSANDS OF CURRENT DOLLARS)

INDUSTRY TITLE	64	65	66	67	68	69	70	71	72
1 LIVESTOCK, PRDTS.	27	121	91	279	85	15	6	35	11
2 OTHER AGRICULTURE PRDTS.	79	360	7246	834	254	44	19	104	32
3 FORESTRY, FISHERIES	6	25	19	58	18	3	1	7	2
4 AGRI.,FORES.,FISH. SERV.	0	0	0	0	0	0	0	0	0
5 IRON, FERRO. ORES MINING	0	0	10758	1168468	0	0	0	15090	0
6 NONFERROUS ORES MINING	0	0	273	18	1396	0	0	890146	0
7 COAL MINING	594	9495	2352	463730	3783	1860	109	10182	109
8 CRUDE PETRO.,NATURAL GAS	0	0	0	0	0	0	0	0	0
9 STONE, CLAY MINING	4750	478627	102420	46599	23211	37	0	12493	0
10 CHEM.,FERT. MIN. MINING	0	0	10298	11404	418	0	0	0	0
11 NEW CONSTRUCTION	0	0	0	0	0	0	0	0	0
12 MAINT., REPAIR CONSTR.	1796	16579	6847	161699	9339	1704	652	16185	2034
13 ORDNANCE, ACCESSORIES	6	26	20	61	19	3	1	8	2
14 FOOD, KINDRED PRDTS.	1527	6933	8960	16057	5365	840	362	7863	610
15 TOBACCO MANUFACTURES	123	557	422	1291	393	68	29	161	49
16 FABRICS	108	0	12937	0	0	0	0	1329	0
17 TEXTILE PRDTS.	777	4	15551	8	2	1	0	0	0
18 APPAREL	1067	4037	2285	14042	5137	880	347	1198	342
19 MISC. TEXTILE PRDTS.	0	0	19890	0	0	0	0	0	0
20 LUMBER, WOOD PRDTS.	1147	13094	9383	27525	3369	421	211	95	91
21 WOODEN CONTAINERS	90	1064	598	2152	336	398	70	0	0
22 HOUSEHOLD FURNITURE	0	0	0	0	0	0	0	0	0
23 OTHER FURNITURE	0	0	0	0	0	0	0	0	0
24 PAPER, ALLIED PRDTS.	506	80206	41704	7793	2060	430	322	630	241
25 PAPERBOARD CONTAINERS	19273	0	18438	6929	6021	2472	934	0	0
26 PRINTING, PUBLISHING	492	2427	1937	8145	1775	431	396	647	289
27 CHEMICALS,SELECT. PRDTS.	30179	25027	77426	378256	12855	9987	10571	66807	4248
28 PLASTICS, SYNTHETICS	0	0	71008	283	0	0	0	0	0
29 DRUGS, COSMETICS	121	22704	1951	1496	595	137	38	146	46
30 PAINT, ALLIED PRDTS.	5	6	7	5	6	1	1	5	1
31 PETROLEUM, RELATED INDS.	1786	42005	15543	132854	13556	10318	586	61344	3498
32 RUBBER, MISC. PLASTICS	3123	7513	32851	7631	4350	2256	689	525	145
33 LEATHER TANNING, PRDTS.	34	496	2011	4711	382	117	22	724	32
34 FOOTWEAR, LEATHER PRDTS.	27	106	83	237	75	13	6	34	10
35 GLASS, GLASS PRDTS.	2	11	3	25	7	1	1	3	1
36 STONE, CLAY PRDTS.	28983	716739	312265	24593	4347	4530	0	7344	3
37 PRIMARY IRON, STEEL MFR.	1	57840	43330	4153445	416131	312500	14492	7952	880
38 PRIMARY NONFERROUS MFR.	1163	508	18203	384909	29205	14262	32798	1149603	130098

39 METAL CONTAINERS	0	0	0	0	0	0	535	0	0
40 FABRICATED METAL PRDTS.	9485	689	0	1	0	0	0	0	0
41 SCREW MACH. PRDTS., ETC.	0	1439	0	137001	0	0	0	0	0
42 OTHER FAB. METAL PRDTS.	96	51080	46035	359427	1111	2532	57	1379	508
43 ENGINES, TURBINES	0	1293	0	0	0	0	0	0	0
44 FARM MACH., EQUIP.	0	0	0	0	0	0	0	0	0
45 CONSTRUC. MACH., EQUIP.	0	26772	0	0	0	0	0	0	0
46 MATERIAL HANDLING MACH.	125	10235	694	10519	1088	296	65	1565	79
47 METALWORKING MACHINERY	0	1025	0	0	6368	4812	0	0	0
48 SPECIAL MACH., EQUIP.	0	0	0	0	20752	0	0	0	0
49 GENERAL MACH., EQUIP.	99	1228	482	22557	96206	0	0	688	20
50 MACHINE SHOP PRDTS.	6	360	108	33510	101655	28053	6	16	8
51 OFFICE, COMPUT. MACHINES	3	13	11	48	10	2	3	4	2
52 SERVICE IND. MACHINES	0	0	0	15170	0	0	0	0	0
53 ELECT. TRANSMISS. EQUIP.	0	0	0	117286	20515	0	0	23029	0
54 HOUSEHOLD APPLIANCES	27	124	94	286	87	15	6	36	11
55 ELECTRIC LIGHTING EQUIP.	14086	67	28	63	21	4	1	8	4
56 RADIO, TV, ETC., EQUIP.	38	171	130	397	121	21	9	49	15
57 ELECTRONIC COMPONENTS	0	0	0	0	0	0	0	0	0
58 MISC. ELECTRICAL MACH.	21	596	170	338	141	16	7	39	16
59 MOTOR VEHICLES, EQUIP.	49	1366	397	777	322	38	17	92	35
60 AIRCRAFT, PARTS	0	0	0	0	0	0	0	0	0
61 OTHER TRANSPORT. EQUIP.	0	0	0	0	0	0	0	0	0
62 PROFESS., SCIEN. INSTRU.	240	920	523	20315	1155	197	77	272	77
63 MEDICAL, PHOTO. EQUIP.	138	571	399	1962	586	111	71	164	57
64 MISC. MANUFACTURING	258	1102	14347	24570	976	199	7750	306	112
65 TRANSPORT., WAREHOUSING	7097	358534	64930	1018551	82265	20171	2971	111419	56070
66 COMMUNICA.,EXC. BRDCAST.	3336	23809	12260	74533	20644	5053	2477	6577	2960
67 RADIO, TV BROADCASTING	0	0	0	0	0	0	0	0	0
68 ELEC.,GAS,WATER,SAN.SER.	12299	70751	44521	508123	73788	17319	14051	193348	9042
69 WHOLESALE, RETAIL TRADE	13527	109084	82896	553329	116487	20440	3824	30696	121164
70 FINANCE, INSURANCE	5124	27011	17504	165764	32265	6546	3860	16000	3144
71 REAL ESTATE, RENTAL	3279	32025	16402	33062	13585	2489	5404	4821	4923
72 HOTELS, PERSONAL SERV.	744	4955	4699	17419	3627	1085	287	976	297
73 BUSINESS SERVICES	13484	97590	43427	268712	41919	11696	5772	24673	7460
74 RESEARCH, DEVELOPMENT	0	0	0	0	0	0	0	0	0
75 AUTO. REPAIR, SERVICES	680	15540	4785	13720	4091	575	265	1225	483
76 AMUSEMENTS	120	545	412	1263	384	66	28	158	48
77 MED.,EDUC. SERVICES	469	3334	1704	6832	1935	465	224	623	272
78 FEDERAL GOVT. ENTERPRISE	803	3249	3164	11922	2481	608	668	900	406
79 STATE, LOCAL GOVT. ENT.	92	1083	743	6748	1081	221	51	372	87
80 DIRECT ALLOCATED IMPORTS	185	840	13722	1945	592	102	44	3343	74
81 TRANSFERRED IMPORTS	0	0	0	0	0	0	0	0	0
82 VALUE ADDED	293496	2001685	1141160	8153099	1764893	360939	173612	1132229	216391
83 STATE TOTAL PRODUCTION	477198	4335598	2362868	18604784	2955641	847801	284805	3805668	566539

NOTE: The 152 column numbers are identical with the 152 product-mix industry numbers given in Table A-2, pages 134-145, and refer to that industrial classification.

TABLE C-10

1963 NATIONAL PRIMARY INPUTS TO MANUFACTURING AND SERVICES (THOUSANDS OF CURRENT DOLLARS)

INDUSTRY TITLE	73	74	75	76	77	78	79	80	81
1 LIVESTOCK, PRDTS.	116	49	5	47	9	64	314	83	60
2 OTHER AGRICULTURE PRDTS.	347	146	14	141	28	190	938	247	180
3 FORESTRY, FISHERIES	24	10	1	10	2	13	65	17	13
4 AGRI.,FORES.,FISH. SERV.	0	0	0	0	0	0	0	0	0
5 IRON, FERRO. ORES MINING	0	0	0	0	0	0	0	0	0
6 NONFERROUS ORES MINING	0	0	0	0	0	0	0	0	0
7 COAL MINING	2814	159	59	322	6	543	664	303	556
8 CRUDE PETRO.,NATURAL GAS	0	0	0	0	0	0	0	0	0
9 STONE, CLAY MINING	52	5782	0	0	0	709	0	0	0
10 CHEM.,FERT. MIN. MINING	43	0	0	0	0	0	0	0	0
11 NEW CONSTRUCTION	0	0	0	0	0	0	0	0	0
12 MAINT., REPAIR CONSTR.	21669	4160	378	2620	459	2335	12596	2582	3893
13 ORDNANCE, ACCESSORIES	25	11	1	10	2	14	69	18	13
14 FOOD, KINDRED PRDTS.	6690	3055	267	2712	537	3664	18066	4761	3461
15 TOBACCO MANUFACTURES	538	226	21	218	43	295	1453	383	278
16 FABRICS	10897	0	0	0	0	0	0	0	0
17 TEXTILE PRDTS.	12971	0	0	1	0	2311	7	2	2
18 APPAREL	3935	1763	139	1393	257	1556	7337	2260	3261
19 MISC. TEXTILE PRDTS.	0	0	0	0	0	0	0	0	0
20 LUMBER, WOOD PRDTS.	20870	780	78	2070	1	2710	12193	4024	31789
21 WOODEN CONTAINERS	1913	0	113	140	122	8986	0	1063	1654
22 HOUSEHOLD FURNITURE	0	0	0	0	0	0	0	0	0
23 OTHER FURNITURE	0	0	0	0	0	0	0	0	0
24 PAPER, ALLIED PRDTS.	20407	798	102	656	127	1029	14005	1153	17211
25 PAPERBOARD CONTAINERS	8507	3018	516	43389	0	23377	18281	14493	37545
26 PRINTING, PUBLISHING	2558	765	117	88772	170	1081	5288	1275	1515
27 CHEMICALS,SELECT. PRDTS.	54512	20005	117	7742	460	20536	16673	12028	17993
28 PLASTICS, SYNTHETICS	128253	0	0	0	2531	0	0	0	23960
29 DRUGS, COSMETICS	490	256	28	1592	241	1064	5007	1127	2235
30 PAINT, ALLIED PRDTS.	1260	3	1	49999	18520	12276	77343	5	26830
31 PETROLEUM, RELATED INDS.	11845	5009	690	2968	823	4354	21059	7840	10216
32 RUBBER, MISC. PLASTICS	12614	1893	457	5325	1749	1027	2823	16342	39525
33 LEATHER TANNING, PRDTS.	814	87	26	74	26	87	436	136	183
34 FOOTWEAR, LEATHER PRDTS.	101	44	5	40	9	56	267	72	51
35 GLASS, GLASS PRDTS.	953	4	0	4	1	845	71592	7	1061
36 STONE, CLAY PRDTS.	20652	6903	0	6	1	10555	3288	9059	8431
37 PRIMARY IRON, STEEL MFR.	7328	5329	12165	874783	117904	150112	1824858	356550	598823
38 PRIMARY NONFERROUS MFR.	3192719	348837	62037	34339	713	114143	506161	84505	184152

39 METAL CONTAINERS	0	0	0	536	173	0	0	0	0
40 FABRICATED METAL PRDTS.	0	0	0	0	0	70618	112812	0	0
41 SCREW MACH. PRDTS., ETC.	28777	0	0	0	17794	60544	58643	24754	75264
42 OTHER FAB. METAL PRDTS.	47341	2831	513	3116	985	67197	229350	24106	25426
43 ENGINES, TURBINES	0	0	0	0	0	0	0	0	0
44 FARM MACH., EQUIP.	0	0	0	0	0	0	0	0	0
45 CONSTRUC. MACH., EQUIP.	0	0	0	0	0	0	0	0	0
46 MATERIAL HANDLING MACH.	1911	288	62	236	68	268	1332	414	569
47 METALWORKING MACHINERY	0	67083	922	2483	388	10094	21771	10258	25074
48 SPECIAL MACH., EQUIP.	0	4938	0	0	0	0	0	0	3561
49 GENERAL MACH., EQUIP.	4456	32891	0	99	99	18692	24253	1335	746
50 MACHINE SHOP PRDTS.	4853	80754	10766	23	6	41	176	25	42
51 OFFICE, COMPUT. MACHINES	15	4	1	2	1	6	30	7	8
52 SERVICE IND. MACHINES	0	0	0	0	0	56586	2075	0	0
53 ELECT. TRANSMISS. EQUIP.	0	0	0	0	0	38501	61139	0	2342
54 HOUSEHOLD APPLIANCES	119	50	5	48	10	65	322	85	62
55 ELECTRIC LIGHTING EQUIP.	2714	6	1	7	1	12	54	12	1342
56 RADIO, TV, ETC., EQUIP.	165	70	7	67	13	91	446	118	86
57 ELECTRONIC COMPONENTS	0	0	0	0	0	0	0	0	0
58 MISC. ELECTRICAL MACH.	152	29	4	39	8	70	253	38	58
59 MOTOR VEHICLES, EQUIP.	352	67	9	86	19	154	586	90	135
60 AIRCRAFT, PARTS	0	0	0	0	0	0	0	0	0
61 OTHER TRANSPORT. EQUIP.	0	0	0	0	0	0	0	0	0
62 PROFESS., SCIEN. INSTRU.	897	1478	32	318	60	50236	1692	520	735
63 MEDICAL, PHOTO. EQUIP.	586	224	23	165	35	239	2853	315	401
64 MISC. MANUFACTURING	8613	399	47	286	66	466	2314	591	697
65 TRANSPORT., WAREHOUSING	131848	25805	3098	54358	7635	25878	149368	30135	50939
66 COMMUNICA.,EXC. BRDCAST.	26339	7790	1213	2828	803	9820	44971	15024	10040
67 RADIO, TV BROADCASTING	0	0	0	0	0	0	0	0	0
68 ELEC.,GAS,WATER,SAN.SER.	93926	25309	3574	13787	3146	13305	49204	17661	26410
69 WHOLESALE, RETAIL TRADE	209366	24773	3645	63085	10581	68088	215680	36374	74849
70 FINANCE, INSURANCE	36774	9367	1092	15566	1967	12763	40992	13406	21658
71 REAL ESTATE, RENTAL	32779	11561	2263	14773	1840	13206	96370	20803	30884
72 HOTELS, PERSONAL SERV.	6046	1715	260	2145	382	2609	34656	3733	3451
73 BUSINESS SERVICES	92096	16549	3084	39107	7833	36147	110302	32325	47159
74 RESEARCH, DEVELOPMENT	0	0	0	0	0	0	0	0	0
75 AUTO. REPAIR, SERVICES	4590	971	127	1076	247	2039	8224	1434	2001
76 AMUSEMENTS	526	221	21	213	42	288	1421	374	272
77 MED.,EDUC. SERVICES	2459	750	112	514	141	1142	5657	1358	1579
78 FEDERAL GOVT. ENTERPRISE	4715	1298	167	593	169	1607	7459	2280	2615
79 STATE, LOCAL GOVT. ENT.	1831	354	16	121	29	287	644	292	381
80 DIRECT ALLOCATED IMPORTS	3401	341	32	329	65	444	2189	577	419
81 TRANSFERRED IMPORTS	0	0	0	0	0	0	0	0	0
82 VALUE ADDED	2098771	475670	56437	732202	102392	591471	2779573	1012589	1224667
83 STATE TOTAL PRODUCTION	6392340	1202679	164872	2067580	301738	1516903	6687596	1771367	2648763

NOTE: The 152 column numbers are identical with the 152 product-mix industry numbers given in Table A-2, pages 134-145, and refer to that industrial classification.

TABLE C-10

1963 NATIONAL PRIMARY INPUTS TO MANUFACTURING AND SERVICES
(THOUSANDS OF CURRENT DOLLARS)

INDUSTRY TITLE	82	83	84	85	86	87	88	89	90
1 LIVESTOCK, PRDTS.	26	104	58	171	77	97	97	15	24
2 OTHER AGRICULTURE PRDTS.	77	310	172	511	230	289	289	45	71
3 FORESTRY, FISHERIES	5	22	12	36	16	20	20	3	5
4 AGRI.,FORES.,FISH. SERV.	0	0	0	0	0	0	0	0	0
5 IRON, FERRO. ORES MINING	0	0	0	0	0	0	0	0	0
6 NONFERROUS ORES MINING	0	0	0	0	0	0	0	0	0
7 COAL MINING	356	1007	154	658	2122	1922	1624	220	15
8 CRUDE PETRO.,NATURAL GAS	0	0	0	0	0	0	0	0	0
9 STONE, CLAY MINING	0	0	0	2167	11	109	37	0	0
10 CHEM.,FERT. MIN. MINING	0	0	193	0	0	0	0	0	0
11 NEW CONSTRUCTION	0	0	0	0	0	0	0	0	0
12 MAINT., REPAIR CONSTR.	1416	2574	2149	6573	3899	3308	3342	566	1897
13 ORDNANCE, ACCESSORIES	6	23	13	37	17	21	21	3	5
14 FOOD, KINDRED PRDTS.	1479	5967	3309	9836	4432	5575	5575	862	1376
15 TOBACCO MANUFACTURES	119	480	266	791	356	448	448	69	111
16 FABRICS	0	0	0	422	0	0	0	0	0
17 TEXTILE PRDTS.	1	2	1	43819	2	2	2	0	1
18 APPAREL	1138	2129	1658	4517	1866	2559	2316	357	609
19 MISC. TEXTILE PRDTS.	0	0	0	0	0	0	0	0	0
20 LUMBER, WOOD PRDTS.	31954	2874	5	9677	1818	7358	1595	984	784
21 WOODEN CONTAINERS	0	2906	335	1401	948	1579	1469	0	0
22 HOUSEHOLD FURNITURE	0	0	0	0	0	0	0	0	0
23 OTHER FURNITURE	0	0	0	0	0	2278	0	0	0
24 PAPER, ALLIED PRDTS.	716	7207	717	7294	1313	1949	1516	269	470
25 PAPERBOARD CONTAINERS	4613	23883	0	59014	8447	9232	4607	596	776
26 PRINTING, PUBLISHING	787	1919	626	2967	1591	2387	1834	308	547
27 CHEMICALS,SELECT. PRDTS.	8276	8014	83177	23648	4477	7519	4291	881	1330
28 PLASTICS, SYNTHETICS	0	0	0	0	0	0	0	0	0
29 DRUGS, COSMETICS	1694	1140	481	1523	535	507	547	91	177
30 PAINT, ALLIED PRDTS.	4466	4996	45600	10526	849	15582	9206	1257	1257
31 PETROLEUM, RELATED INDS.	3847	3195	3256	9896	10373	6851	5148	2128	2692
32 RUBBER, MISC. PLASTICS	16583	24554	2115	61427	5400	57495	60254	6574	12886
33 LEATHER TANNING, PRDTS.	58	85	100	246	148	14202	194	47	60
34 FOOTWEAR, LEATHER PRDTS.	9407	87	50	151	66	82	82	13	21
35 GLASS, GLASS PRDTS.	2	8909	5	15	7	9	8	1	2
36 STONE, CLAY PRDTS.	8924	15362	15089	30379	17975	8980	12223	3	136
37 PRIMARY IRON, STEEL MFR.	107931	196850	2	731121	226439	413162	474268	53767	98251
38 PRIMARY NONFERROUS MFR.	26469	141413	48676	338057	91828	20921	31667	2691	5713

39 METAL CONTAINERS	0	0	0	0	0	0	0	0	0
40 FABRICATED METAL PRDTS.	0	0	0	0	3510	0	23408	14521	0
41 SCREW MACH. PRDTS., ETC.	574	37767	0	48076	56714	85849	29398	4316	12973
42 OTHER FAB. METAL PRDTS.	31616	140357	8628	157868	25199	35392	29278	20679	25297
43 ENGINES, TURBINES	0	0	0	0	195236	138143	110404	1815	4214
44 FARM MACH., EQUIP.	0	0	0	0	0	146537	0	0	0
45 CONSTRUC. MACH., EQUIP.	0	0	0	0	0	0	113286	5828	45204
46 MATERIAL HANDLING MACH.	186	307	305	779	7586	436	535	115	162
47 METALWORKING MACHINERY	3611	17542	6808	49195	61278	40633	80130	15053	26239
48 SPECIAL MACH., EQUIP.	0	0	0	0	0	0	0	0	0
49 GENERAL MACH., EQUIP.	1561	2253	0	4719	70429	257810	203495	13591	9743
50 MACHINE SHOP PRDTS.	19	31	19	91	62504	83147	16386	8	20
51 OFFICE, COMPUT. MACHINES	5	8	4	16	9	14	10	2	3
52 SERVICE IND. MACHINES	0	0	0	0	0	0	0	0	0
53 ELECT. TRANSMISS. EQUIP.	0	0	8481	22330	25470	7446	34000	14568	0
54 HOUSEHOLD APPLIANCES	26	106	59	175	79	3920	99	15	25
55 ELECTRIC LIGHTING EQUIP.	6	10	5	938	17	11461	14	4	7
56 RADIO, TV, ETC., EQUIP.	37	147	82	243	109	138	138	21	34
57 ELECTRONIC COMPONENTS	0	0	0	3490	0	0	0	0	0
58 MISC. ELECTRICAL MACH.	28	46	20	141	38080	28570	3851	66	85
59 MOTOR VEHICLES, EQUIP.	60	104	50	332	5097	23467	7560	33	57
60 AIRCRAFT, PARTS	0	0	0	0	0	0	0	0	0
61 OTHER TRANSPORT. EQUIP.	0	0	0	0	0	867	0	0	0
62 PROFESS., SCIEN. INSTRU.	257	495	379	1038	6894	3947	534	81	141
63 MEDICAL, PHOTO. EQUIP.	173	338	209	672	321	978	383	63	109
64 MISC. MANUFACTURING	9233	647	378	5813	642	917	749	129	222
65 TRANSPORT., WAREHOUSING	11628	32713	14037	72215	31851	58080	47541	5249	7675
66 COMMUNICA., EXC. BRDCAST.	4423	7438	4486	19100	9507	10958	10699	1949	3474
67 RADIO, TV BROADCASTING	0	0	0	0	0	0	0	0	0
68 ELEC.,GAS,WATER,SAN.SER.	8684	15825	23583	34056	12870	17762	18236	2827	5547
69 WHOLESALE, RETAIL TRADE	31791	50175	28012	122866	73077	118787	98440	12409	19665
70 FINANCE, INSURANCE	6501	11543	7351	32594	7949	22498	31452	2758	4926
71 REAL ESTATE, RENTAL	5916	17980	17746	43337	3088	12531	15780	2410	4431
72 HOTELS, PERSONAL SERV.	1461	4312	1947	7544	3796	6068	4820	734	1171
73 BUSINESS SERVICES	64677	28234	12154	57478	37988	78990	38762	5979	10851
74 RESEARCH, DEVELOPMENT	0	0	0	0	0	0	0	0	0
75 AUTO. REPAIR, SERVICES	895	1539	796	4648	2582	2887	2757	483	833
76 AMUSEMENTS	116	469	260	773	348	438	438	68	108
77 MED., EDUC. SERVICES	703	1272	760	3154	1673	1893	1894	342	604
78 FEDERAL GOVT. ENTERPRISE	1331	2254	899	4746	2535	4234	3156	539	952
79 STATE, LOCAL GOVT. ENT.	152	431	263	506	508	398	491	40	71
80 DIRECT ALLOCATED IMPORTS	179	723	401	1192	537	676	676	104	167
81 TRANSFERRED IMPORTS	0	0	0	0	0	0	0	0	0
82 VALUE ADDED	519364	935955	489203	1799080	931130	1012968	1096125	193761	316859
83 STATE TOTAL PRODUCTION	935563	1767032	835542	3856087	2063857	2803284	2647607	392314	631085

NOTE: The 152 column numbers are identical with the 152 product-mix industry numbers given in Table A-2, pages 134-145, and refer to that industrial classification.

TABLE C-10

1963 NATIONAL PRIMARY INPUTS TO MANUFACTURING AND SERVICES
(THOUSANDS OF CURRENT DOLLARS)

INDUSTRY TITLE	91	92	93	94	95	96	97	98	99
1 LIVESTOCK, PRDTS.	11	19	8	16	235	150	208	117	238
2 OTHER AGRICULTURE PRDTS.	34	57	24	49	702	448	622	350	709
3 FORESTRY, FISHERIES	2	4	2	3	49	31	43	24	49
4 AGRI.,FORES.,FISH. SERV.	0	0	0	0	0	0	0	0	0
5 IRON, FERRO. ORES MINING	0	0	0	0	0	0	0	0	0
6 NONFERROUS ORES MINING	0	0	0	0	0	0	0	0	0
7 COAL MINING	55	127	108	119	882	627	1221	160	845
8 CRUDE PETRO.,NATURAL GAS	0	0	0	0	0	0	0	0	0
9 STONE, CLAY MINING	0	0	0	0	152	188	190	67	0
10 CHEM.,FERT. MIN. MINING	0	0	0	0	0	0	0	0	0
11 NEW CONSTRUCTION	0	0	0	0	0	0	0	0	0
12 MAINT., REPAIR CONSTR.	132	838	452	904	10590	4979	8909	6781	8533
13 ORDNANCE, ACCESSORIES	2	4	2	4	51	33	45	26	52
14 FOOD, KINDRED PRDTS.	653	1099	469	942	13514	8636	11972	6746	13653
15 TOBACCO MANUFACTURES	52	88	38	76	1087	694	963	542	1098
16 FABRICS	0	1689	0	0	0	2088	0	1689	0
17 TEXTILE PRDTS.	0	1	0	1	6	1072	5	2	1170
18 APPAREL	225	383	206	347	5916	3634	4900	3277	2697
19 MISC. TEXTILE PRDTS.	0	0	0	0	0	0	0	0	0
20 LUMBER, WOOD PRDTS.	1	874	1	1	5103	14333	9229	1639	980
21 WOODEN CONTAINERS	0	0	0	0	763	909	1740	1294	1328
22 HOUSEHOLD FURNITURE	0	0	0	0	0	0	0	0	0
23 OTHER FURNITURE	0	0	0	0	0	0	0	0	0
24 PAPER, ALLIED PRDTS.	235	389	150	305	3560	2683	6815	1675	10276
25 PAPERBOARD CONTAINERS	388	623	364	690	10735	4136	13819	8861	4073
26 PRINTING, PUBLISHING	299	490	249	370	4054	3289	4540	1740	3966
27 CHEMICALS,SELECT. PRDTS.	1373	682	348	586	14013	10865	15914	5154	7119
28 PLASTICS, SYNTHETICS	0	0	0	0	0	4413	0	0	1863
29 DRUGS, COSMETICS	55	89	51	82	1611	2294	1174	994	683
30 PAINT, ALLIED PRDTS.	1257	1257	2517	1	2868	1645	2917	1	1991
31 PETROLEUM, RELATED INDS.	1082	1578	1135	1542	20214	24164	29345	5344	7290
32 RUBBER, MISC. PLASTICS	15266	17424	2238	9703	18498	36290	20177	7113	47082
33 LEATHER TANNING, PRDTS.	11	22	18	14	310	3719	2772	179	66
34 FOOTWEAR, LEATHER PRDTS.	10	17	8	15	200	131	180	98	201
35 GLASS, GLASS PRDTS.	1	2	1	1	20	13	18	10	964
36 STONE, CLAY PRDTS.	1514	3	0	3	49976	8296	38158	20505	20
37 PRIMARY IRON, STEEL MFR.	24848	58546	37581	47903	402007	309338	562174	186620	43989
38 PRIMARY NONFERROUS MFR.	6540	5704	3925	8331	91918	78199	174172	85584	46877

39 METAL CONTAINERS	0	0	0	0	0	0	0	0	0
40 FABRICATED METAL PRDTS.	0	4097	3652	0	20008	62720	37433	0	492
41 SCREW MACH. PRDTS., ETC.	0	7431	4743	8835	49511	29629	32401	15425	53231
42 OTHER FAB. METAL PRDTS.	3165	7336	3678	2832	26100	55240	98414	43788	45483
43 ENGINES, TURBINES	0	233	551	11161	0	24103	14295	0	0
44 FARM MACH., EQUIP.	0	0	0	0	0	0	0	0	0
45 CONSTRUC. MACH., EQUIP.	0	0	0	0	0	0	0	0	0
46 MATERIAL HANDLING MACH.	52941	6072	5265	43826	4124	663	901	558	291
47 METALWORKING MACHINERY	1112	6550	5073	9545	381089	67695	88583	73483	24891
48 SPECIAL MACH., EQUIP.	0	0	0	0	691	224178	0	0	0
49 GENERAL MACH., EQUIP.	5305	43031	10710	17622	175288	163813	399032	3980	18467
50 MACHINE SHOP PRDTS.	6	13	6	29467	95	9320	109	223571	70
51 OFFICE, COMPUT. MACHINES	2	131	1	2	23	19	26	10	661531
52 SERVICE IND. MACHINES	0	0	0	0	0	0	0	0	0
53 ELECT. TRANSMISS. EQUIP.	7657	15426	22178	12383	125637	102436	106668	3651	52002
54 HOUSEHOLD APPLIANCES	12	20	8	17	241	154	213	120	243
55 ELECTRIC LIGHTING EQUIP.	4	7	1	4	36	33	1850	14	29771
56 RADIO, TV, ETC., EQUIP.	16	27	12	23	334	213	296	167	1252
57 ELECTRONIC COMPONENTS	0	0	0	0	0	0	6545	0	238553
58 MISC. ELECTRICAL MACH.	13	62	70	3777	129	104	934	12244	93
59 MOTOR VEHICLES, EQUIP.	30	49	18	38	299	248	364	141	218
60 AIRCRAFT, PARTS	0	0	0	0	1977	0	0	0	0
61 OTHER TRANSPORT. EQUIP.	0	0	0	0	0	0	0	0	0
62 PROFESS., SCIEN. INSTRU.	52	89	46	80	1360	6224	32017	752	1076
63 MEDICAL, PHOTO. EQUIP.	51	85	36	70	925	644	881	460	682
64 MISC. MANUFACTURING	111	182	72	144	2293	1294	1784	852	2335
65 TRANSPORT., WAREHOUSING	5255	7709	3860	9169	57598	47090	66452	33443	37541
66 COMMUNICA.,EXC. BRDCAST.	1904	3114	1076	2343	24631	18005	27618	10290	25491
67 RADIO, TV BROADCASTING	0	0	0	0	0	0	0	0	0
68 ELEC.,GAS,WATER,SAN.SER.	1366	2445	1323	2154	38905	20796	39609	19113	13755
69 WHOLESALE, RETAIL TRADE	8477	20333	7746	18543	136621	119415	150156	57243	81131
70 FINANCE, INSURANCE	2401	3154	1501	2910	33739	25123	25231	19491	24210
71 REAL ESTATE, RENTAL	2430	5251	1252	5568	42002	93181	34865	29379	52025
72 HOTELS, PERSONAL SERV.	533	890	404	804	11535	6781	9616	4882	7777
73 BUSINESS SERVICES	8550	6537	3176	7813	86608	55002	89756	40518	72682
74 RESEARCH, DEVELOPMENT	0	0	0	0	0	0	0	0	0
75 AUTO. REPAIR, SERVICES	449	718	257	552	4713	3882	5613	2164	3511
76 AMUSEMENTS	51	86	37	74	1063	679	941	530	1074
77 MED.,EDUC. SERVICES	327	538	188	406	4314	3444	4766	1885	3404
78 FEDERAL GOVT. ENTERPRISE	504	828	306	661	6763	5353	7466	2838	5714
79 STATE, LOCAL GOVT. ENT.	31	48	20	37	398	299	694	164	466
80 DIRECT ALLOCATED IMPORTS	79	133	57	114	19322	10513	1451	817	1654
81 TRANSFERRED IMPORTS	0	0	0	0	0	0	0	0	0
82 VALUE ADDED	111131	220228	91005	172845	2511570	1540867	2410120	1136409	2019516
83 STATE TOTAL PRODUCTION	268015	454863	218272	435826	4428979	3226458	4609323	2084975	3688446

NOTE: The 152 column numbers are identical with the 152 product-mix industry numbers given in Table A-2, pages 134-145, and refer to that industrial classification.

TABLE C-10

1963 NATIONAL PRIMARY INPUTS TO
MANUFACTURING AND SERVICES
(THOUSANDS OF CURRENT DOLLARS)

INDUSTRY TITLE	100	101	102	103	104	105	106	107	108
1 LIVESTOCK, PRDTS.	97	147	183	165	152	99	470	299	94
2 OTHER AGRICULTURE PRDTS.	289	439	544	492	453	296	1403	892	279
3 FORESTRY, FISHERIES	20	31	38	34	32	21	98	62	19
4 AGRI.,FORES.,FISH. SERV.	0	0	0	0	0	0	0	0	0
5 IRON, FERRO. ORES MINING	0	0	0	0	4540	0	0	0	0
6 NONFERROUS ORES MINING	0	0	0	0	0	0	0	0	0
7 COAL MINING	776	676	991	1967	520	236	1248	431	570
8 CRUDE PETRO.,NATURAL GAS	0	0	0	0	0	0	0	0	0
9 STONE, CLAY MINING	24	0	305	90	0	0	24	304	155
10 CHEM.,FERT. MIN. MINING	0	0	0	0	0	0	0	0	0
11 NEW CONSTRUCTION	0	0	0	0	0	0	0	0	0
12 MAINT., REPAIR CONSTR.	5348	5805	4110	4055	2641	2931	7934	10414	1511
13 ORDNANCE, ACCESSORIES	21	32	40	36	33	22	27654	65	20
14 FOOD, KINDRED PRDTS.	5562	8451	10487	9480	8728	5695	27017	17173	5383
15 TOBACCO MANUFACTURES	447	680	843	762	702	458	2172	1381	433
16 FABRICS	0	3070	0	6743	0	0	1271	0	1535
17 TEXTILE PRDTS.	4735	1300	3004	2	7777	1	24	7	1
18 APPAREL	2354	2785	3545	3518	3166	2244	8187	6390	1977
19 MISC. TEXTILE PRDTS.	0	0	0	0	0	0	0	0	0
20 LUMBER, WOOD PRDTS.	6667	3249	2253	10481	2174	593	2608	260	889
21 WOODEN CONTAINERS	9857	1528	1512	7695	1144	1767	3989	1547	1029
22 HOUSEHOLD FURNITURE	0	0	0	0	0	190805	1534	0	0
23 OTHER FURNITURE	0	0	0	0	0	0	0	0	0
24 PAPER, ALLIED PRDTS.	4061	18056	23303	5461	1624	4566	17517	53794	1406
25 PAPERBOARD CONTAINERS	20687	8328	12576	62837	54220	18136	11492	25383	18165
26 PRINTING, PUBLISHING	2218	11292	2676	6530	1742	24354	13220	4696	1131
27 CHEMICALS,SELECT. PRDTS.	18321	8120	36099	31205	16877	1143	13749	74160	46720
28 PLASTICS, SYNTHETICS	0	9365	11200	20094	29517	33489	11003	23185	9689
29 DRUGS, COSMETICS	461	536	727	605	532	332	1798	1102	320
30 PAINT, ALLIED PRDTS.	21361	10509	11289	41114	16084	2	1915	4558	332
31 PETROLEUM, RELATED INDS.	7618	13790	18403	6988	30663	2799	22232	11295	3224
32 RUBBER, MISC. PLASTICS	69025	47360	40196	238973	73854	39710	61075	81924	90762
33 LEATHER TANNING, PRDTS.	99	125	174	147	85	43	269	96	69
34 FOOTWEAR, LEATHER PRDTS.	85	125	156	3436	131	84	405	253	83
35 GLASS, GLASS PRDTS.	3888	5343	16	9714	103810	28393	9936	134631	1345
36 STONE, CLAY PRDTS.	22399	39949	18495	54259	23812	8	89	27378	14595
37 PRIMARY IRON, STEEL MFR.	211973	147547	238659	342019	170054	15475	57492	63430	61308
38 PRIMARY NONFERROUS MFR.	138973	158802	221933	198385	210374	18132	164983	181300	242513

39 METAL CONTAINERS	0	0	0	0	0	0	0	0	0
40 FABRICATED METAL PRDTS.	5464	10358	3700	1413	0	0	1	0	0
41 SCREW MACH. PRDTS., ETC.	102802	42474	44360	162642	81233	63382	163308	126975	22090
42 OTHER FAB. METAL PRDTS.	128076	38515	82463	181179	62326	44491	125888	72659	25619
43 ENGINES, TURBINES	2623	0	18773	0	0	0	0	0	0
44 FARM MACH., EQUIP.	0	0	0	0	0	0	0	0	0
45 CONSTRUC. MACH., EQUIP.	0	0	0	0	0	0	0	0	0
46 MATERIAL HANDLING MACH.	343	440	574	509	365	221	984	579	259
47 METALWORKING MACHINERY	22473	21216	52321	46841	22573	1760	95917	35400	21877
48 SPECIAL MACH., EQUIP.	0	0	0	0	900	0	0	0	0
49 GENERAL MACH., EQUIP.	37553	4277	51274	24977	794	133	9476	769	29582
50 MACHINE SHOP PRDTS.	59	74	4827	5018	54	25	34972	108	44
51 OFFICE, COMPUT. MACHINES	13	13	14	10	9	5	35823	25	6
52 SERVICE IND. MACHINES	193804	0	0	97998	0	918	0	0	0
53 ELECT. TRANSMISS. EQUIP.	232178	216175	231242	200230	62580	10276	192956	7325	32353
54 HOUSEHOLD APPLIANCES	99	151	187	69979	156	101	482	306	96
55 ELECTRIC LIGHTING EQUIP.	14975	31971	11019	46260	101487	13842	79366	17558	18489
56 RADIO, TV, ETC., EQUIP.	137	7615	259	234	216	157306	619342	4084	133
57 ELECTRONIC COMPONENTS	0	83550	26025	0	637	696742	1209087	212795	8545
58 MISC. ELECTRICAL MACH.	35106	104	10595	74	91694	37	17175	148	98458
59 MOTOR VEHICLES, EQUIP.	182	243	206	164	189	86	882	338	3083
60 AIRCRAFT, PARTS	0	0	0	0	0	0	9622	0	0
61 OTHER TRANSPORT. EQUIP.	0	0	0	0	0	0	0	0	0
62 PROFESS., SCIEN. INSTRU.	47108	8709	822	101436	736	517	6594	1478	1301
63 MEDICAL, PHOTO. EQUIP.	424	491	584	499	460	301	3299	1029	289
64 MISC. MANUFACTURING	6533	2148	1173	45577	883	564	4187	2955	1498
65 TRANSPORT., WAREHOUSING	45698	40149	55054	76741	53383	34187	77408	60863	30550
66 COMMUNICA.,EXC. BRDCAST.	13679	15015	16416	14732	11066	5840	72367	27427	7232
67 RADIO, TV BROADCASTING	0	0	0	0	0	0	0	0	0
68 ELEC.,GAS,WATER,SAN.SER.	16785	17220	32848	31049	19833	8329	40863	37153	14824
69 WHOLESALE, RETAIL TRADE	137689	87647	104283	180130	122982	121323	241665	174374	84159
70 FINANCE, INSURANCE	11637	32814	11042	16801	8507	13873	27438	21349	6382
71 REAL ESTATE, RENTAL	19395	38959	16496	25139	24290	42371	79402	45393	12307
72 HOTELS, PERSONAL SERV.	3312	6136	7513	6275	5550	3809	17320	12740	4021
73 BUSINESS SERVICES	46205	43647	46913	243111	66066	128522	191479	98928	28673
74 RESEARCH, DEVELOPMENT	0	0	0	0	0	0	0	0	0
75 AUTO. REPAIR, SERVICES	2772	3548	3263	2480	2684	1324	15179	5495	1881
76 AMUSEMENTS	437	665	825	745	686	448	2124	1350	423
77 MED.,EDUC. SERVICES	2318	2735	3027	2099	2004	1190	13659	5293	1290
78 FEDERAL GOVT. ENTERPRISE	3831	3238	3543	8640	3044	2280	19282	6596	1720
79 STATE, LOCAL GOVT. ENT.	379	362	582	739	388	248	1159	678	409
80 DIRECT ALLOCATED IMPORTS	674	1718	4721	1149	1058	690	3273	6655	652
81 TRANSFERRED IMPORTS	0	0	0	0	0	0	0	0	0
82 VALUE ADDED	1087840	1322056	1683264	1515274	1278903	941792	4999828	2130597	975360
83 STATE TOTAL PRODUCTION	2779970	2591872	3193965	4177432	2798179	2688765	8884618	3845833	1939164

NOTE: The 152 column numbers are identical with the 152 product-mix industry numbers given in Table A-2, pages 134-145, and refer to that industrial classification.

TABLE C-10

1963 NATIONAL PRIMARY INPUTS TO
MANUFACTURING AND SERVICES
(THOUSANDS OF CURRENT DOLLARS)

INDUSTRY TITLE	109	110	111	112	113	114	115	116	117
1 LIVESTOCK, PRDTS.	518	736	75	40	15	60	52	150	81
2 OTHER AGRICULTURE PRDTS.	1546	2194	225	119	44	179	154	447	4168
3 FORESTRY, FISHERIES	108	153	16	8	3	12	11	31	17
4 AGRI.,FORES.,FISH. SERV.	0	0	0	0	0	0	0	0	0
5 IRON, FERRO. ORES MINING	0	0	0	0	0	0	0	0	0
6 NONFERROUS ORES MINING	0	0	0	0	0	0	0	135	0
7 COAL MINING	15290	1570	418	1316	25	112	19	101	46
8 CRUDE PETRO.,NATURAL GAS	0	0	0	0	0	0	0	0	0
9 STONE, CLAY MINING	2092	0	0	0	0	0	0	0	181
10 CHEM.,FERT. MIN. MINING	0	0	0	0	0	0	0	0	0
11 NEW CONSTRUCTION	0	0	0	0	0	0	0	0	0
12 MAINT., REPAIR CONSTR.	71343	21841	5139	1255	127	562	2116	2713	1788
13 ORDNANCE, ACCESSORIES	113	160	16	9	3	13	11	33	18
14 FOOD, KINDRED PRDTS.	29781	42260	4334	2291	857	3448	2968	8605	18602
15 TOBACCO MANUFACTURES	2395	3398	348	184	69	277	239	692	374
16 FABRICS	14604	6378	0	0	0	1426	0	0	55130
17 TEXTILE PRDTS.	128539	2323	16627	77	0	18357	1	3	1656
18 APPAREL	17233	11863	3536	1056	241	870	676	1913	2927
19 MISC. TEXTILE PRDTS.	396044	0	17502	0	0	0	0	0	0
20 LUMBER, WOOD PRDTS.	23710	2872	30464	13261	50	106698	479	2085	1071
21 WOODEN CONTAINERS	7056	3781	161	0	151	0	573	1723	0
22 HOUSEHOLD FURNITURE	0	0	0	0	0	29188	0	0	0
23 OTHER FURNITURE	1455	39280	5571	210	0	0	0	0	0
24 PAPER, ALLIED PRDTS.	13075	11200	1574	650	125	9980	672	4893	7400
25 PAPERBOARD CONTAINERS	13320	11188	0	1150	507	0	1252	8193	10594
26 PRINTING, PUBLISHING	10639	14179	1513	731	131	380	926	3143	1290
27 CHEMICALS,SELECT. PRDTS.	42045	16102	2205	1384	543	443	1724	4123	10183
28 PLASTICS, SYNTHETICS	11095	18039	13151	0	0	0	941	2264	4998
29 DRUGS, COSMETICS	2854	3123	438	198	47	157	176	485	218
30 PAINT, ALLIED PRDTS.	194336	15453	7477	8516	631	6361	1	2399	2515
31 PETROLEUM, RELATED INDS.	69462	48644	6593	4360	456	1079	2379	4155	1504
32 RUBBER, MISC. PLASTICS	860304	73283	18391	2501	15776	26910	3929	40616	38687
33 LEATHER TANNING, PRDTS.	1255	614	219	104	11	16	26	46	893
34 FOOTWEAR, LEATHER PRDTS.	433	614	65	35	13	52	44	126	70
35 GLASS, GLASS PRDTS.	366003	942	11099	252	1	7657	5	3759	11505
36 STONE, CLAY PRDTS.	79118	29522	8033	4	1	11604	5	535	8473
37 PRIMARY IRON, STEEL MFR.	3437168	315416	141690	374567	19322	48726	7284	46288	54158
38 PRIMARY NONFERROUS MFR.	538647	554766	59445	19677	131	45490	9819	117001	19411

39 METAL CONTAINERS	0	0	0	0	0	0	0	0	11360
40 FABRICATED METAL PRDTS.	4924	1	100091	718	0	79732	0	0	0
41 SCREW MACH. PRDTS., ETC.	1339455	185275	7344	10146	360	10207	11757	38245	15132
42 OTHER FAB. METAL PRDTS.	1122492	195846	84349	10441	9047	13477	3278	51951	5724
43 ENGINES, TURBINES	110842	2921	79105	39285	0	0	0	0	0
44 FARM MACH., EQUIP.	0	0	0	0	0	0	0	0	0
45 CONSTRUC. MACH., EQUIP.	0	0	7170	0	0	0	0	0	0
46 MATERIAL HANDLING MACH.	3596	1963	1143	276	38	76	98	201	107
47 METALWORKING MACHINERY	541061	296352	5457	15562	519	329	10674	30201	2042
48 SPECIAL MACH., EQUIP.	0	0	0	0	0	0	0	0	0
49 GENERAL MACH., EQUIP.	264354	87296	115342	41542	19696	3284	8075	4232	20
50 MACHINE SHOP PRDTS.	391261	569635	23968	19	6	8	18	48	25
51 OFFICE, COMPUT. MACHINES	63	71	9	4	1	2	5	15	7
52 SERVICE IND. MACHINES	197469	1463	7669	1270	0	719	0	0	0
53 ELECT. TRANSMISS. EQUIP.	34666	27853	31193	92880	0	0	25131	29504	500
54 HOUSEHOLD APPLIANCES	531	753	77	41	15	40928	53	153	83
55 ELECTRIC LIGHTING EQUIP.	179803	8998	2618	8	136	9496	9406	12735	1005
56 RADIO, TV, ETC., EQUIP.	111035	486264	1857	57	21	85	73	213	115
57 ELECTRONIC COMPONENTS	29888	123788	310	0	0	0	26999	30088	6241
58 MISC. ELECTRICAL MACH.	316510	33073	718	1063	3018	18	20	69	26
59 MOTOR VEHICLES, EQUIP.	13165786	1325	143	78	13	37345	48	163	65
60 AIRCRAFT, PARTS	0	2262237	0	0	0	0	0	0	0
61 OTHER TRANSPORT. EQUIP.	0	0	23145	296669	26096	40680	0	0	0
62 PROFESS., SCIEN. INSTRU.	226465	213719	2722	241	56	206	44015	103365	19325
63 MEDICAL, PHOTO. EQUIP.	8695	40809	438	166	37	129	2640	461	241
64 MISC. MANUFACTURING	4653	5211	845	320	73	2754	1239	2145	505
65 TRANSPORT., WAREHOUSING	675436	165778	31890	30986	5682	24408	7357	25791	16553
66 COMMUNICA.,EXC. BRDCAST.	66974	113552	6860	4346	702	2070	5779	16617	8026
67 RADIO, TV BROADCASTING	0	0	0	0	0	0	0	0	0
68 ELEC.,GAS,WATER,SAN.SER.	164878	87625	16544	8453	1634	2381	3951	10649	4799
69 WHOLESALE, RETAIL TRADE	920577	295586	60759	46775	14891	26195	18924	58722	31910
70 FINANCE, INSURANCE	118762	51139	9352	8651	981	3369	5374	13549	5432
71 REAL ESTATE, RENTAL	75645	64701	14409	10369	1428	6206	9426	21006	10201
72 HOTELS, PERSONAL SERV.	29397	60776	4012	1736	418	1963	2090	6138	3432
73 BUSINESS SERVICES	481597	318759	31835	17026	6578	9419	24455	64946	68727
74 RESEARCH, DEVELOPMENT	0	0	0	0	0	0	0	0	0
75 AUTO. REPAIR, SERVICES	388002	21156	2054	1077	169	598	782	2492	1064
76 AMUSEMENTS	2342	3323	341	180	67	271	233	677	366
77 MED.,EDUC. SERVICES	8440	19173	1031	697	132	409	758	2181	1066
78 FEDERAL GOVT. ENTERPRISE	39203	20374	2581	1411	237	756	1486	4104	2036
79 STATE, LOCAL GOVT. ENT.	4055	1971	223	299	70	37	99	372	173
80 DIRECT ALLOCATED IMPORTS	3608	5120	525	278	104	418	360	1043	1131
81 TRANSFERRED IMPORTS	0	0	0	0	0	0	0	0	0
82 VALUE ADDED	11892543	6604390	998930	483342	57364	246242	280103	844008	503216
83 STATE TOTAL PRODUCTION	39276576	13630173	2033385	1560366	188871	884275	541186	1632739	978611

NOTE: The 152 column numbers are identical with the 152 product-mix industry numbers given in Table A-2, pages 134-145, and refer to that industrial classification.

TABLE C-10

1963 NATIONAL PRIMARY INPUTS TO MANUFACTURING AND SERVICES

(THOUSANDS OF CURRENT DOLLARS)

INDUSTRY TITLE	118	119	120	121	122	123	124	125	126
1 LIVESTOCK, PRDTS.	18	19	32	73	76	17	80	25	109
2 OTHER AGRICULTURE PRDTS.	53	56	95	217	228	50	238	75	11748
3 FORESTRY, FISHERIES	4	4	7	15	34	3	17	5	3896
4 AGRI.,FORES.,FISH. SERV.	0	0	0	0	0	0	0	0	0
5 IRON, FERRO. ORES MINING	0	0	0	0	0	0	0	0	0
6 NONFERROUS ORES MINING	0	0	0	0	0	0	0	0	0
7 COAL MINING	137	16	1	2692	134	137	162	91	903
8 CRUDE PETRO.,NATURAL GAS	0	0	0	0	0	0	0	0	0
9 STONE, CLAY MINING	0	0	0	0	0	0	0	486	1449
10 CHEM.,FERT. MIN. MINING	0	0	0	0	0	0	0	7	39
11 NEW CONSTRUCTION	0	0	0	0	0	0	0	0	0
12 MAINT., REPAIR CONSTR.	421	554	299	3311	2145	601	4851	1328	6526
13 ORDNANCE, ACCESSORIES	4	4	7	16	17	4	17	5	24
14 FOOD, KINDRED PRDTS.	1024	1070	1821	4176	4384	966	4586	1616	10134
15 TOBACCO MANUFACTURES	82	86	146	336	352	78	369	116	505
16 FABRICS	0	0	0	1689	25770	0	40079	5450	30352
17 TEXTILE PRDTS.	1	0	0	2	522	19163	18290	3165	8900
18 APPAREL	703	253	501	1193	2560	503	7389	698	3766
19 MISC. TEXTILE PRDTS.	0	0	0	0	0	0	0	0	103
20 LUMBER, WOOD PRDTS.	439	26	26	555	62	13286	58647	14988	67315
21 WOODEN CONTAINERS	0	0	0	0	0	557	107	0	2294
22 HOUSEHOLD FURNITURE	0	0	0	0	0	17200	0	0	0
23 OTHER FURNITURE	0	0	0	0	0	0	0	0	0
24 PAPER, ALLIED PRDTS.	778	229	288	53680	10526	298	19777	48058	55282
25 PAPERBOARD CONTAINERS	3737	399	657	14046	36445	0	67059	5019	14928
26 PRINTING, PUBLISHING	478	307	334	1461	1652	322	4052	780	2445
27 CHEMICALS,SELECT. PRDTS.	718	30	1076	152584	13609	234	8109	6909	21758
28 PLASTICS, SYNTHETICS	1214	0	10012	0	24727	9027	63424	9634	79473
29 DRUGS, COSMETICS	93	51	85	230	296	62	335	104	772
30 PAINT, ALLIED PRDTS.	2	1	1	1	1430	3626	22445	5956	21197
31 PETROLEUM, RELATED INDS.	867	412	544	2429	2253	560	2406	4123	13279
32 RUBBER, MISC. PLASTICS	7171	570	4611	28590	31157	196	159938	25342	42650
33 LEATHER TANNING, PRDTS.	8	4	8	64	104	272	15793	20	76
34 FOOTWEAR, LEATHER PRDTS.	2403	679	27	3380	10185	2233	3521	25	100
35 GLASS, GLASS PRDTS.	385	11048	16311	3297	20535	1	7482	178	4512
36 STONE, CLAY PRDTS.	757	755	4733	7	10920	1	3543	423	5787
37 PRIMARY IRON, STEEL MFR.	9684	3722	11064	12944	43021	12226	59393	7124	79065
38 PRIMARY NONFERROUS MFR.	14824	6198	10995	59027	179419	3606	24143	1173	32571

39 METAL CONTAINERS	0	0	0	0	0	0	0	0	0
40 FABRICATED METAL PRDTS.	0	0	0	0	0	0	195	0	0
41 SCREW MACH. PRDTS., ETC.	4747	3025	0	6678	28461	1439	30815	3600	5788
42 OTHER FAB. METAL PRDTS.	10813	2040	73	14008	7764	103	3495	49273	45893
43 ENGINES, TURBINES	0	0	0	0	0	0	0	0	0
44 FARM MACH., EQUIP.	0	0	0	0	0	0	0	0	0
45 CONSTRUC. MACH., EQUIP.	0	0	0	0	0	0	0	0	0
46 MATERIAL HANDLING MACH.	61	20	49	206	245	51	302	85	348
47 METALWORKING MACHINERY	959	71	0	0	0	0	0	0	0
48 SPECIAL MACH., EQUIP.	0	0	0	0	0	0	0	0	0
49 GENERAL MACH., EQUIP.	206	191	0	0	40	0	218	99	99
50 MACHINE SHOP PRDTS.	6	1547	6	39	24	6	32	24	56
51 OFFICE, COMPUT. MACHINES	3	2	2	8	10	2	11	5	15
52 SERVICE IND. MACHINES	0	0	0	0	0	0	0	0	1343
53 ELECT. TRANSMISS. EQUIP.	2816	195	0	12347	0	0	6386	0	22223
54 HOUSEHOLD APPLIANCES	18	19	32	74	78	17	82	26	389
55 ELECTRIC LIGHTING EQUIP.	5	1	1	5068	11	1	157	4	12006
56 RADIO, TV, ETC., EQUIP.	25	26	45	103	108	929	113	36	155
57 ELECTRONIC COMPONENTS	0	2195	0	1117	0	19589	0	0	0
58 MISC. ELECTRICAL MACH.	2034	6	8	54	29	13	33	27	96
59 MOTOR VEHICLES, EQUIP.	30	17	18	124	76	30	77	66	225
60 AIRCRAFT, PARTS	1998	0	0	0	0	0	0	0	0
61 OTHER TRANSPORT. EQUIP.	0	0	0	0	0	0	0	0	0
62 PROFESS., SCIEN. INSTRU.	129088	61	117	279	534	116	756	162	700
63 MEDICAL, PHOTO. EQUIP.	10859	28055	11043	62566	378	77	4723	143	524
64 MISC. MANUFACTURING	9652	118	164	545	182914	14245	75349	18667	234507
65 TRANSPORT., WAREHOUSING	4216	2836	5251	24294	20969	5844	33290	10167	43732
66 COMMUNICA.,EXC. BRDCAST.	3426	1912	2025	12172	9605	1806	9927	4389	11224
67 RADIO, TV BROADCASTING	0	0	0	0	0	0	0	0	0
68 ELEC.,GAS,WATER,SAN.SER.	2262	1346	2376	7492	9243	1787	11652	3135	13188
69 WHOLESALE, RETAIL TRADE	36619	13091	16017	42384	60577	12141	87398	23352	85524
70 FINANCE, INSURANCE	1773	1313	1685	8511	8983	1876	10146	3363	12783
71 REAL ESTATE, RENTAL	3576	4105	4506	19885	17627	3846	28912	7598	37229
72 HOTELS, PERSONAL SERV.	1132	752	1210	4204	4466	1009	2235	1618	5932
73 BUSINESS SERVICES	25031	4518	15309	60317	42837	10681	86964	20700	75481
74 RESEARCH, DEVELOPMENT	0	0	0	0	0	0	0	0	0
75 AUTO. REPAIR, SERVICES	472	264	285	1946	1257	404	1291	901	3044
76 AMUSEMENTS	81	84	143	328	345	76	361	114	494
77 MED.,EDUC. SERVICES	431	254	286	1713	1250	239	1298	566	1806
78 FEDERAL GOVT. ENTERPRISE	811	580	612	2890	5095	954	4879	1247	5192
79 STATE, LOCAL GOVT. ENT.	84	18	25	346	145	27	405	54	194
80 DIRECT ALLOCATED IMPORTS	124	130	221	624	112673	142	556	2775	762
81 TRANSFERRED IMPORTS	0	0	0	0	0	0	0	0	0
82 VALUE ADDED	231591	98967	145518	1185667	727221	174647	786751	278441	900903
83 STATE TOTAL PRODUCTION	530953	194250	270706	1822005	1665529	337326	1785059	573563	2043818

NOTE: The 152 column numbers are identical with the 152 product-mix industry numbers given in Table A-2, pages 134-145, and refer to that industrial classification.

TABLE C-10

1963 NATIONAL PRIMARY INPUTS TO MANUFACTURING AND SERVICES
(THOUSANDS OF CURRENT DOLLARS)

INDUSTRY TITLE	127	128	129	130	131	132	133	134	135
1 LIVESTOCK, PRDTS.	503	49	1246	993	23	445	265	520	4354
2 OTHER AGRICULTURE PRDTS.	1501	146	2433	5198	69	1327	789	1552	12984
3 FORESTRY, FISHERIES	105	10	4	51	5	92	55	108	904
4 AGRI.,FORES.,FISH. SERV.	0	0	0	0	0	0	0	0	169469
5 IRON, FERRO. ORES MINING	0	0	0	0	0	0	0	0	0
6 NONFERROUS ORES MINING	0	0	0	0	0	0	0	0	0
7 COAL MINING	6241	0	2828	0	0	0	0	635460	0
8 CRUDE PETRO.,NATURAL GAS	0	0	0	0	21105	0	0	1819588	0
9 STONE, CLAY MINING	0	0	0	0	0	0	0	0	0
10 CHEM.,FERT. MIN. MINING	404	217	0	0	0	0	0	0	0
11 NEW CONSTRUCTION	0	0	0	0	0	0	0	0	0
12 MAINT., REPAIR CONSTR.	1036921	11799	43120	7478	60000	386000	0	889000	83963
13 ORDNANCE, ACCESSORIES	110	11	4	53	5	97	58	113	949
14 FOOD, KINDRED PRDTS.	47425	2805	48453	80086	1326	25571	15208	29892	250107
15 TOBACCO MANUFACTURES	2325	226	95	1124	107	2056	1223	2403	20110
16 FABRICS	0	0	0	0	0	0	0	0	0
17 TEXTILE PRDTS.	428	435	14342	2042	0	9	1	4	6378
18 APPAREL	12101	2553	4	53	5	4410	58	6734	946
19 MISC. TEXTILE PRDTS.	0	0	0	0	0	0	0	0	5248
20 LUMBER, WOOD PRDTS.	2889	4	2	21	2	41	23	46	8627
21 WOODEN CONTAINERS	0	0	0	0	0	0	0	0	46887
22 HOUSEHOLD FURNITURE	0	0	0	0	0	0	0	0	0
23 OTHER FURNITURE	0	0	0	0	0	0	0	0	0
24 PAPER, ALLIED PRDTS.	16324	1430	1695	2176	1259	20205	832	16512	238400
25 PAPERBOARD CONTAINERS	9751	0	0	0	0	0	0	0	130296
26 PRINTING, PUBLISHING	61137	10573	2175	8895	764	33616	2505	16268	164918
27 CHEMICALS,SELECT. PRDTS.	35971	3617	51	419	16	1842	23	38156	10248
28 PLASTICS, SYNTHETICS	0	0	0	0	0	0	0	0	0
29 DRUGS, COSMETICS	3784	859	36	353	33	644	383	758	14044
30 PAINT, ALLIED PRDTS.	4576	20	6	2	0	1	1	7	1
31 PETROLEUM, RELATED INDS.	787919	218937	130126	386098	20612	85713	1384	221015	710334
32 RUBBER, MISC. PLASTICS	146983	40406	956	9176	46	15279	674	4893	86815
33 LEATHER TANNING, PRDTS.	56	0	0	0	0	0	0	0	0
34 FOOTWEAR, LEATHER PRDTS.	424	44	23	204	19	370	221	439	5453
35 GLASS, GLASS PRDTS.	3427	4	2	21	2	45	23	47	2495
36 STONE, CLAY PRDTS.	4042	592	3	30	3517	122	15	67	968
37 PRIMARY IRON, STEEL MFR.	225398	6	7	12	1	113	5	49	391
38 PRIMARY NONFERROUS MFR.	5168	1962	13362	0	0	6725	0	7935	0

39 METAL CONTAINERS	0	0	0	0	0	0	0	0	0
40 FABRICATED METAL PRDTS.	3	0	0	0	0	3	0	1	10
41 SCREW MACH. PRDTS., ETC.	6675	0	0	0	0	4	0	2	13
42 OTHER FAB. METAL PRDTS.	89811	465	9818	2726	5	236	43	146	1705
43 ENGINES, TURBINES	49154	4852	0	0	1759	0	0	0	0
44 FARM MACH., EQUIP.	0	0	0	0	0	0	0	0	0
45 CONSTRUC. MACH., EQUIP.	0	0	0	0	0	0	0	0	0
46 MATERIAL HANDLING MACH.	1221	0	0	0	0	0	0	0	0
47 METALWORKING MACHINERY	20031	39	0	0	0	2	0	1	2489
48 SPECIAL MACH., EQUIP.	0	0	0	0	0	0	0	0	0
49 GENERAL MACH., EQUIP.	9196	0	0	0	3461	5	0	2	16
50 MACHINE SHOP PRDTS.	8353	1699	6	46	0	720	1	219	2357
51 OFFICE, COMPUT. MACHINES	206	12	14	25	2	233	11	102	809
52 SERVICE IND. MACHINES	605	0	0	0	0	0	0	0	0
53 ELECT. TRANSMISS. EQUIP.	25889	657	0	0	1868	1	0	0	3
54 HOUSEHOLD APPLIANCES	517	50	21	249	24	458	271	533	4462
55 ELECTRIC LIGHTING EQUIP.	11886	1016	14	90	0	279	3	23667	9172
56 RADIO, TV, ETC., EQUIP.	715	69	29	345	371	172380	7324	738	6179
57 ELECTRONIC COMPONENTS	16037	0	0	17868	270	0	0	0	0
58 MISC. ELECTRICAL MACH.	56929	13618	108	12401	14	3147	14	1402	25018
59 MOTOR VEHICLES, EQUIP.	78371	30454	115	863	19	3804	17	1662	37160
60 AIRCRAFT, PARTS	0	0	0	204094	0	0	0	0	0
61 OTHER TRANSPORT. EQUIP.	48244	3230	203535	0	0	0	0	0	0
62 PROFESS., SCIEN. INSTRU.	142	14	6	1068	1817	126	73	145	1215
63 MEDICAL, PHOTO. EQUIP.	3610	221	958	799	47	4687	2076	1923	15348
64 MISC. MANUFACTURING	8480	1078	512	1205	107	8554	755	4245	34136
65 TRANSPORT., WAREHOUSING	2215802	75713	689601	256698	4210	56143	24599	608587	1124768
66 COMMUNICA.,EXC. BRDCAST.	278500	18643	23137	47282	2629	99136	102408	79838	697485
67 RADIO, TV BROADCASTING	0	0	0	0	0	0	13006	0	0
68 ELEC.,GAS,WATER,SAN.SER.	147004	19267	28285	14932	40581	145709	22952	5529063	461348
69 WHOLESALE, RETAIL TRADE	653735	216488	43986	130984	9758	129739	30247	172279	1504931
70 FINANCE, INSURANCE	413438	65180	100310	65954	9322	113375	23745	216391	818030
71 REAL ESTATE, RENTAL	658963	54284	62092	98556	15687	251857	52270	166615	1802903
72 HOTELS, PERSONAL SERV.	19099	2532	574	14003	646	16790	7412	14568	121891
73 BUSINESS SERVICES	448540	74983	52529	104628	10993	234865	93493	492694	2739921
74 RESEARCH, DEVELOPMENT	0	0	0	0	0	0	0	0	0
75 AUTO. REPAIR, SERVICES	515980	79804	3668	7190	1200	103851	544	44091	740022
76 AMUSEMENTS	2274	221	93	1099	104	4011	606798	2350	19666
77 MED.,EDUC. SERVICES	34550	2993	4216	4886	630	12981	2180	9036	72303
78 FEDERAL GOVT. ENTERPRISE	40010	6263	23871	5085	1604	64519	2984	81145	201896
79 STATE, LOCAL GOVT. ENT.	36703	14315	484	1554	77	7414	410	7471	47553
80 DIRECT ALLOCATED IMPORTS	60704	340	523143	179694	161	42198	1843	3622	55903
81 TRANSFERRED IMPORTS	0	0	0	0	0	0	0	0	0
82 VALUE ADDED	16455201	2179965	1914238	2513077	810254	11433017	1288743	13873697	32740144
83 STATE TOTAL PRODUCTION	24832480	3165170	3946337	4191887	1026536	13494967	2307966	25027792	45264144

NOTE: The 152 column numbers are identical with the 152 product-mix industry numbers given in Table A-2, pages 134-145, and refer to that industrial classification.

TABLE C-10

1963 NATIONAL PRIMARY INPUTS TO
MANUFACTURING AND SERVICES
(THOUSANDS OF CURRENT DOLLARS)

INDUSTRY TITLE	136	137	138	139	140	141	142	143	144
1 LIVESTOCK, PRDTS.	1142	170	263	360	1004	304	0	392	1007
2 OTHER AGRICULTURE PRDTS.	3406	508	785	1074	2995	908	26264	8533	3003
3 FORESTRY, FISHERIES	237	35	55	75	209	63	0	81	209
4 AGRI.,FORES.,FISH. SERV.	0	0	0	0	0	0	0	10000	0
5 IRON, FERRO. ORES MINING	0	0	0	0	0	0	0	0	0
6 NONFERROUS ORES MINING	0	0	0	0	0	0	0	0	0
7 COAL MINING	0	0	0	0	0	0	0	0	1201
8 CRUDE PETRO.,NATURAL GAS	0	0	0	0	0	0	0	0	0
9 STONE, CLAY MINING	0	0	0	0	0	0	0	956	1472
10 CHEM.,FERT. MIN. MINING	0	0	0	0	0	0	0	0	0
11 NEW CONSTRUCTION	0	0	0	0	0	0	0	0	0
12 MAINT., REPAIR CONSTR.	312775	58210	29110	1122	21283	2239	3622000	3593384	149718
13 ORDNANCE, ACCESSORIES	249	37	57	78	219	66	0	85	964
14 FOOD, KINDRED PRDTS.	77584	9777	15125	20680	57695	17486	0	22510	59965
15 TOBACCO MANUFACTURES	5275	786	1216	1663	4639	1406	0	1810	4652
16 FABRICS	0	0	0	0	0	0	0	0	44449
17 TEXTILE PRDTS.	2574	22	37	16	14	2	0	41	5787
18 APPAREL	8520	37	57	78	218	66	0	85	63926
19 MISC. TEXTILE PRDTS.	1596	0	0	0	0	0	0	0	87042
20 LUMBER, WOOD PRDTS.	986	18	25	32	103	31	0	36	88
21 WOODEN CONTAINERS	0	0	0	0	0	0	0	0	0
22 HOUSEHOLD FURNITURE	0	0	0	0	0	0	0	0	0
23 OTHER FURNITURE	0	0	0	0	0	0	0	0	0
24 PAPER, ALLIED PRDTS.	563012	52048	59672	20033	151618	27457	0	11888	54106
25 PAPERBOARD CONTAINERS	435738	0	0	0	0	0	0	0	24344
26 PRINTING, PUBLISHING	102595	252727	52683	22322	244933	60001	0	25709	23674
27 CHEMICALS,SELECT. PRDTS.	12822	834	483	200	1787	625	132365	41235	59249
28 PLASTICS, SYNTHETICS	35006	0	0	0	0	0	0	0	0
29 DRUGS, COSMETICS	36348	247	381	521	1461	441	0	567	252302
30 PAINT, ALLIED PRDTS.	2959	1	1	1	12	1	0	1	7489
31 PETROLEUM, RELATED INDS.	583121	12665	10619	8088	32784	19549	0	33856	145250
32 RUBBER, MISC. PLASTICS	127314	1924	2871	1218	2761	1739	31928	16819	58247
33 LEATHER TANNING, PRDTS.	0	0	0	0	0	0	0	0	11621
34 FOOTWEAR, LEATHER PRDTS.	4622	142	219	300	844	254	0	326	150466
35 GLASS, GLASS PRDTS.	29707	23	29	32	128	39	0	39	466
36 STONE, CLAY PRDTS.	22457	18	30	29	64	25	110	47	61808
37 PRIMARY IRON, STEEL MFR.	140	140	104	20	682	207	0	88	55
38 PRIMARY NONFERROUS MFR.	0	0	0	0	0	0	0	0	5043

39	METAL CONTAINERS	0	0	0	0	0	0	0	0	0
40	FABRICATED METAL PRDTS.	4	4	3	1	18	6	25448	1330	1
41	SCREW MACH. PRDTS., ETC.	24980	5	4	1	23	7	0	3	2
42	OTHER FAB. METAL PRDTS.	40316	243	199	79	1206	366	0	190	53148
43	ENGINES, TURBINES	0	0	0	0	0	0	0	0	0
44	FARM MACH., EQUIP.	0	0	0	0	0	0	0	0	0
45	CONSTRUC. MACH., EQUIP.	0	0	0	0	0	0	0	0	0
46	MATERIAL HANDLING MACH.	0	0	0	0	0	0	0	0	0
47	METALWORKING MACHINERY	2250	3	2	0	14	4	0	2	1
48	SPECIAL MACH., EQUIP.	0	0	0	0	0	0	0	0	0
49	GENERAL MACH., EQUIP.	6	6	4	1	28	8	0	4	2
50	MACHINE SHOP PRDTS.	1489	24	61	80	43	38	0	70	1550
51	OFFICE, COMPUT. MACHINES	290	290	215	42	1409	427	0	181	114
52	SERVICE IND. MACHINES	0	0	0	0	0	0	0	0	0
53	ELECT. TRANSMISS. EQUIP.	1	1	1	0	5	1	0	1	32089
54	HOUSEHOLD APPLIANCES	1171	177	271	369	1041	316	0	403	147035
55	ELECTRIC LIGHTING EQUIP.	31572	46	86	61	53	5	0	106	7945
56	RADIO, TV, ETC., EQUIP.	1621	242	374	511	1425	432	0	556	1429
57	ELECTRONIC COMPONENTS	0	0	0	0	0	0	0	0	404230
58	MISC. ELECTRICAL MACH.	25702	397	658	287	256	307	0	1167	4665
59	MOTOR VEHICLES, EQUIP.	25826	444	739	331	292	348	0	1315	5372
60	AIRCRAFT, PARTS	0	0	0	0	0	0	0	0	0
61	OTHER TRANSPORT. EQUIP.	0	0	0	0	0	0	0	0	8505
62	PROFESS., SCIEN. INSTRU.	320	51	76	100	298	90	0	111	2803
63	MEDICAL, PHOTO. EQUIP.	5285	5032	3629	1035	25836	7101	0	3146	132354
64	MISC. MANUFACTURING	57373	10094	7687	1951	49294	14949	0	6733	324330
65	TRANSPORT., WAREHOUSING	233630	27863	29259	34921	107421	31544	13162	102032	189147
66	COMMUNICA.,EXC. BRDCAST.	569949	113373	78967	200613	204534	250218	0	101527	127986
67	RADIO, TV BROADCASTING	0	0	0	0	0	0	0	0	0
68	ELEC.,GAS,WATER,SAN.SER.	1609488	165866	73855	44065	244883	66005	0	127147	224342
69	WHOLESALE, RETAIL TRADE	722720	68518	50513	47498	187148	62913	159037	116958	442969
70	FINANCE, INSURANCE	1078909	193656	779903	419077	4604043	66788	844355	778004	220147
71	REAL ESTATE, RENTAL	4613174	282954	263573	109148	608081	361304	213517	2555376	860870
72	HOTELS, PERSONAL SERV.	290148	4765	7371	10078	28118	8522	0	10971	423569
73	BUSINESS SERVICES	2947082	527988	723827	144622	667519	454678	0	1015223	412867
74	RESEARCH, DEVELOPMENT	0	0	0	0	0	0	0	0	0
75	AUTO. REPAIR, SERVICES	231905	9394	14897	10487	19380	23448	0	39991	126549
76	AMUSEMENTS	91731	769	1189	2126	4537	1375	0	1770	6549
77	MED.,EDUC. SERVICES	55462	22678	10474	6924	291649	29689	0	17814	43800
78	FEDERAL GOVT. ENTERPRISE	331493	267290	174806	30145	59608	95064	196889	83106	41663
79	STATE, LOCAL GOVT. ENT.	33377	3246	2126	1214	4554	1543	0	3658	9497
80	DIRECT ALLOCATED IMPORTS	7949	1185	1833	2506	136990	2119	0	2727	7009
81	TRANSFERRED IMPORTS	0	0	0	0	0	0	0	0	0
82	VALUE ADDED	55707664	8624550	-215253	1672668	5763478	2702074	31830144	29759136	9827716
83	STATE TOTAL PRODUCTION	71113072	10721523	2185171	2818882	13538639	4314599	37095216	38499248	15367859

NOTE: The 152 column numbers are identical with the 152 product-mix industry numbers given in Table A-2, pages 134-145, and refer to that industrial classification.

TABLE C-10

1963 NATIONAL PRIMARY INPUTS TO
MANUFACTURING AND SERVICES
(THOUSANDS OF CURRENT DOLLARS)

INDUSTRY TITLE	145	146	147	148	149	150	151	152	153 TOTAL
1 LIVESTOCK, PRDTS.	1530	2533	225	18669	7642	1023	279	47	15930301
2 OTHER AGRICULTURE PRDTS.	4564	7555	670	2771	41060	3051	831	1735	8695365
3 FORESTRY, FISHERIES	318	526	47	193	321	212	58	57	1410195
4 AGRI.,FORES.,FISH. SERV.	0	0	0	0	90	0	0	572	254422
5 IRON, FERRO. ORES MINING	0	0	0	0	0	0	0	0	1287870
6 NONFERROUS ORES MINING	0	0	0	0	0	0	0	0	971829
7 COAL MINING	0	0	0	0	5067	5660	66890	81359	1674915
8 CRUDE PETRO.,NATURAL GAS	0	0	0	0	0	0	0	38573	11319255
9 STONE, CLAY MINING	0	0	0	0	0	0	0	0	1318919
10 CHEM.,FERT. MIN. MINING	0	0	0	0	0	0	0	1765	325283
11 NEW CONSTRUCTION	0	0	0	0	0	0	0	0	0
12 MAINT., REPAIR CONSTR.	25857	5012	23433	80892	146649	522217	41983	1307367	13870692
13 ORDNANCE, ACCESSORIES	333	552	49	202	337	223	104	18	196409
14 FOOD, KINDRED PRDTS.	89183	145532	12908	53377	390345	58764	16007	2723	16344317
15 TOBACCO MANUFACTURES	7069	11702	1038	4292	7143	4725	1287	219	1919056
16 FABRICS	3121	0	0	0	0	0	2639	0	11252984
17 TEXTILE PRDTS.	49	93	9	22	100	138	3784	2	2096944
18 APPAREL	332	550	5643	202	2890	222	61	627	3688138
19 MISC. TEXTILE PRDTS.	0	0	6413	0	16300	0	6362	1770	1312700
20 LUMBER, WOOD PRDTS.	134	220	20	81	136	92	25	21	6338943
21 WOODEN CONTAINERS	0	0	0	0	0	0	0	0	280961
22 HOUSEHOLD FURNITURE	0	0	0	0	0	0	0	0	315286
23 OTHER FURNITURE	0	0	0	0	0	0	34	0	95373
24 PAPER, ALLIED PRDTS.	87656	15215	4029	3456	52480	24256	14985	24868	10517517
25 PAPERBOARD CONTAINERS	12566	0	0	0	1734	0	628	0	4381884
26 PRINTING, PUBLISHING	243460	109194	2959	53565	59637	471269	19177	11109	4843074
27 CHEMICALS,SELECT. PRDTS.	111848	1254	5434	61539	25053	23079	3010	79477	10764887
28 PLASTICS, SYNTHETICS	0	0	0	0	0	0	1703	0	5057678
29 DRUGS, COSMETICS	120359	3662	325	1353	597793	4695	5231	2900	2016933
30 PAINT, ALLIED PRDTS.	10380	6	74313	14	11	8	119	3	1904276
31 PETROLEUM, RELATED INDS.	60958	55406	119555	17665	55468	90533	16821	55480	7696091
32 RUBBER, MISC. PLASTICS	10697	6782	234124	1825	32847	11487	9077	6673	5905962
33 LEATHER TANNING, PRDTS.	0	0	0	0	0	0	33	0	909759
34 FOOTWEAR, LEATHER PRDTS.	1273	2106	187	5719	1293	854	666	42	327054
35 GLASS, GLASS PRDTS.	133	217	73206	80	2774	1475	336	111	2340241
36 STONE, CLAY PRDTS.	10775	201	108283	70	2538	148	870	19091	2636124
37 PRIMARY IRON, STEEL MFR.	72	59	9	22	106	153	10	11870	20158432
38 PRIMARY NONFERROUS MFR.	0	2144	0	0	0	0	302	0	11497838

39 METAL CONTAINERS	0	0	0	0	0	0	0	0	2270019
40 FABRICATED METAL PRDTS.	2	2	0	1	3	4	0	0	1166853
41 SCREW MACH. PRDTS., ETC.	2	2	121679	1	2257	5	1617	1	3854261
42 OTHER FAB. METAL PRDTS.	12255	946	82953	157	415	2311	319	51	5976136
43 ENGINES, TURBINES	99673	0	32924	0	0	0	0	946	943359
44 FARM MACH., EQUIP.	85845	0	0	0	0	0	0	0	233023
45 CONSTRUC. MACH., EQUIP.	13969	0	0	0	0	0	0	0	302860
46 MATERIAL HANDLING MACH.	0	0	0	0	0	0	10	0	311229
47 METALWORKING MACHINERY	17580	1556	1049	0	2	3	0	517	2409606
48 SPECIAL MACH., EQUIP.	0	0	0	0	0	0	0	0	639968
49 GENERAL MACH., EQUIP.	3	2	0	1	4	6	4	1	2428952
50 MACHINE SHOP PRDTS.	1071	753	109188	197	177	1013	77	1038	1879508
51 OFFICE, COMPUT. MACHINES	64843	122	20	45	219	316	47	64	769111
52 SERVICE IND. MACHINES	102267	0	0	0	0	0	383	0	795782
53 ELECT. TRANSMISS. EQUIP.	116181	0	15943	0	1	1	1	2084	2584337
54 HOUSEHOLD APPLIANCES	1567	2593	230	951	1584	1050	1103	49	395084
55 ELECTRIC LIGHTING EQUIP.	452	459	13106	132	247	584	561	20427	987391
56 RADIO, TV, ETC., EQUIP.	6796	3595	319	1319	2195	1951	395	74	1872056
57 ELECTRONIC COMPONENTS	0	0	0	0	0	3163	152	18	3251744
58 MISC. ELECTRICAL MACH.	26336	1607	192901	434	1836	2642	527	2066	1117147
59 MOTOR VEHICLES, EQUIP.	2052	1911	845711	514	2064	3230	8229	5686	14355812
60 AIRCRAFT, PARTS	564	0	0	0	0	714	0	0	3072204
61 OTHER TRANSPORT. EQUIP.	14907	0	0	0	0	0	11	5250	691943
62 PROFESS., SCIEN. INSTRU.	6507	702	72	257	236164	287	293	347	1446123
63 MEDICAL, PHOTO. EQUIP.	170646	3268	432	112305	61027	11161	896	1500	948962
64 MISC. MANUFACTURING	109311	13054	999	37242	16074	52623	1898	3344	2091797
65 TRANSPORT., WAREHOUSING	194604	235732	103497	99335	200712	142701	672962	85997	19134576
66 COMMUNICA.,EXC. BRDCAST.	247940	129297	69692	53772	170293	232870	9128	31984	5853510
67 RADIO, TV BROADCASTING	0	0	0	0	0	16638	0	0	29644
68 ELEC.,GAS,WATER,SAN.SER.	261906	189255	71078	84275	408004	542184	64381	700875	16164813
69 WHOLESALE, RETAIL TRADE	359151	315188	1277095	143507	387437	233200	43257	39532	22748624
70 FINANCE, INSURANCE	118346	74683	164979	104636	94599	97658	14888	103113	14307694
71 REAL ESTATE, RENTAL	749817	592256	302880	721330	1018913	1675568	136938	50122	22590000
72 HOTELS, PERSONAL SERV.	44384	70925	14291	32536	182703	36498	10999	3280	2295650
73 BUSINESS SERVICES	401073	961128	115876	343499	216294	445916	108098	247409	25020368
74 RESEARCH, DEVELOPMENT	0	0	0	0	0	0	0	0	0
75 AUTO. REPAIR, SERVICES	102338	72150	36814	18951	44761	106064	16090	13487	3413320
76 AMUSEMENTS	6913	11443	1015	1485273	6985	35527	1266	405	2360940
77 MED., EDUC. SERVICES	43858	12019	6131	19914	232734	81717	1141	7773	1329510
78 FEDERAL GOVT. ENTERPRISE	612408	60505	5966	10951	107660	141454	2070	6634	3336590
79 STATE, LOCAL GOVT. ENT.	8359	6811	4681	2189	11635	11707	2207	2766	329131
80 DIRECT ALLOCATED IMPORTS	10652	17633	1564	139787	10764	7120	245539	330	3495810
81 TRANSFERRED IMPORTS	0	0	0	0	0	0	0	0	0
82 VALUE ADDED	9770508	7792737	6427340	3960581	14228472	8951647	4305299	4250349	471847168
83 STATE TOTAL PRODUCTION	14587755	10942856	10693305	7680101	19096048	14063818	5864099	7235999	862910720

NOTE: The 152 column numbers are identical with the 152 product-mix industry numbers given in Table A-2, pages 134-145, and refer to that industrial classification.

TABLE C-11

1963 STATE ESTABLISHMENT OUTPUTS FOR MANUFACTURING AND SERVICES
(THOUSANDS OF CURRENT DOLLARS)

	1	2	3	4	5	6	7	8	9
1 ALABAMA	24887	46562	228615	75367	251351	100184	35791	174771	67541
2 ARIZONA	2987	24822	183255	87384	62802	56822	8854	26530	26047
3 ARKANSAS	17438	69387	183867	93	259710	63028	58397	217406	34679
4 CALIFORNIA	122200	132170	2501539	2612751	1346550	882535	1709765	610323	565372
5 COLORADO	956	7242	265475	35906	470445	88853	18049	63678	75351
6 CONNECTICUT	2408	6627	267749	124882	65023	155832	15873	3891	66176
7 DELAWARE	1976	6199	42874	0	62377	19268	37814	58380	11214
8 DISTRICT OF COLUMBIA	0	0	79517	0	0	54156	0	0	44976
9 FLORIDA	48338	37354	604653	221502	196831	196460	542227	72454	113916
10 GEORGIA	39065	69115	299710	2355	433075	136596	107861	194229	189670
11 IDAHO	6811	7688	97889	3463	74920	93141	99306	38822	8723
12 ILLINOIS	3348	45405	1150129	91903	1144557	521368	384990	999855	501945
13 INDIANA	2153	25182	497800	112980	571626	240804	195895	339407	125485
14 IOWA	919	36892	385352	65945	2009713	295431	57549	494161	72137
15 KANSAS	193	17479	348587	0	585041	118910	8859	376063	57104
16 KENTUCKY	5173	7780	249175	0	168624	154910	28103	84283	61646
17 LOUISIANA	55552	21186	263346	70940	144556	103584	76865	130387	79504
18 MAINE	31869	10452	74507	10648	71211	45621	83973	34258	45406
19 MARYLAND	16695	20993	306326	15408	283518	157617	133921	58314	105582
20 MASSACHUSETTS	49619	3227	459707	86013	241515	299535	133881	52114	185986
21 MICHIGAN	9274	14907	730024	84874	423465	412309	237303	349873	217634
22 MINNESOTA	6110	35068	419101	107973	1070803	596934	121516	311949	82675
23 MISSISSIPPI	24240	62324	168240	0	213991	71059	12200	55161	32838
24 MISSOURI	5364	36918	478527	127716	700848	336003	66318	397482	175285
25 MONTANA	4219	4636	142350	0	61350	32135	1373	26498	12537
26 NEBRASKA	163	15883	244689	949	984131	107276	43872	238676	36587
27 NEVADA	16	777	79482	0	5315	16092	0	400	5444
28 NEW HAMPSHIRE	2905	2729	62198	0	31040	26345	4268	12322	11841
29 NEW JERSEY	14422	5707	571917	1901	412201	244250	367304	83404	337517
30 NEW MEXICO	1314	6518	126501	67886	53657	24387	0	11735	15640
31 NEW YORK	20262	13428	1675894	75332	637668	864283	507749	473910	670828
32 NORTH CAROLINA	35566	43985	385430	33513	270561	152315	49224	203814	156030
33 NORTH DAKOTA	55	7899	136416	0	42063	49972	7754	31333	11161
34 OHIO	4984	22495	1223709	155856	718660	622362	266325	368086	386133
35 OKLAHOMA	1440	21158	259764	255	197608	92308	30957	109768	46191
36 OREGON	166179	10149	244943	342	113240	97972	206587	78436	83420
37 PENNSYLVANIA	9442	24983	899318	97737	744104	674443	342244	218707	577795
38 RHODE ISLAND	4950	2576	58058	73	9439	42046	3550	6266	37069
39 SOUTH CAROLINA	24617	15487	152453	0	146585	55656	15538	32768	34580
40 SOUTH DAKOTA	482	9553	135017	0	341243	71230	547	25755	11432
41 TENNESSEE	7044	14011	262444	57406	336204	184657	47193	257336	109418
42 TEXAS	45990	171192	1234859	50093	791883	331128	173629	495581	250497
43 UTAH	418	3854	105234	117708	109300	65903	15267	65254	22293
44 VERMONT	2389	545	38133	0	7515	64484	171	71748	8510
45 VIRGINIA	42020	17748	345474	681	281521	135574	138789	90770	10870
46 WASHINGTON	94138	12546	368361	7495	236236	165469	256279	129043	76693
47 WEST VIRGINIA	4659	6852	148439	89982	30108	53705	13771	15923	49864
48 WISCONSIN	8337	14631	426113	17009	570936	1072539	166304	125694	112658
49 WYOMING	466	1533	78597	0	22006	14887	689	9760	2465
50 ALASKA	59304	31	23533	0	0	0	71374	0	4849
51 HAWAII	3161	26001	79152	0	30097	21104	128519	11307	13557
52 SUM OF STATE OUTPUTS	1036518	1221889	19794432	4712321	18037216	10483480	7034584	8338084	6042768

NOTE: The 152 column numbers are identical with the 152 product-mix industry numbers given in Table A-2, pages 134-145, and refer to that industrial classification.

TABLE C-11

1963 STATE ESTABLISHMENT OUTPUTS FOR MANUFACTURING AND SERVICES

(THOUSANDS OF CURRENT DOLLARS)

	10	11	12	13	14	15	16	17	18
1 ALABAMA	0	11196	95069	62897	27690	0	589279	12434	18929
2 ARIZONA	0	338	31377	43107	0	0	206	0	0
3 ARKANSAS	0	451	61958	114814	0	0	18158	0	18929
4 CALIFORNIA	337514	149775	1076952	851148	971	0	27022	1007	58375
5 COLORADO	112084	7491	158247	24752	0	0	364	0	0
6 CONNECTICUT	0	16797	100187	17871	3713	10601	197844	11940	15659
7 DELAWARE	0	113	9007	8081	0	0	56758	0	0
8 DISTRICT OF COLUMBIA	0	0	8502	18683	0	0	0	0	0
9 FLORIDA	74670	7292	184375	137826	116922	6567	7656	2264	204
10 GEORGIA	72753	48870	207336	162100	17348	0	1421168	734	488894
11 IDAHO	46930	0	7806	3197	0	0	0	0	0
12 ILLINOIS	31641	394356	835814	1209150	20827	0	42288	5590	16527
13 INDIANA	0	40269	335049	213503	16490	0	0	0	4925
14 IOWA	8305	10624	78043	265917	0	0	3963	0	0
15 KANSAS	0	451	48382	71450	0	0	206	0	0
16 KENTUCKY	0	1481	646247	118759	852356	467244	27913	1629	204
17 LOUISIANA	448057	5155	155466	213084	5192	3545	0	0	0
18 MAINE	0	451	19565	9260	0	0	249479	1305	1309
19 MARYLAND	72753	8680	323232	88416	49	5060	48148	4239	0
20 MASSACHUSETTS	115628	169637	146023	116041	412	2771	518469	30417	34071
21 MICHIGAN	41527	10946	232156	95723	15697	0	5737	230	175
22 MINNESOTA	33221	33903	204021	204966	0	0	16772	0	124
23 MISSISSIPPI	0	338	50953	93652	0	0	30033	1074	34360
24 MISSOURI	7111	22981	479163	202837	20843	0	21378	1074	0
25 MONTANA	34054	0	15983	5138	0	0	0	0	0
26 NEBRASKA	38946	20348	58667	77623	0	0	0	388	0
27 NEVADA	0	0	6757	396	0	0	0	0	0
28 NEW HAMPSHIRE	0	113	20600	1810	0	0	157175	6716	813
29 NEW JERSEY	0	135023	517059	777939	37619	0	280405	18626	19434
30 NEW MEXICO	0	338	14357	8092	0	0	170	0	0
31 NEW YORK	242115	404648	922324	392608	9649	1773	244989	33288	38680
32 NORTH CAROLINA	0	10112	130286	74496	2692154	946429	3559551	42260	38401
33 NORTH DAKOTA	293	113	7038	1388	0	0	0	0	0
34 OHIO	24916	42745	327980	383579	32080	4543	24906	2264	912
35 OKLAHOMA	0	8921	49228	43567	0	0	1518	0	0
36 OREGON	19380	4068	39061	33234	0	0	48861	115	0
37 PENNSYLVANIA	145507	368762	474526	224291	285540	106770	510832	50054	136626
38 RHODE ISLAND	0	9102	45570	16061	49	0	291601	60107	9145
39 SOUTH CAROLINA	0	2209	52661	43367	17298	82367	2945487	23404	117591
40 SOUTH DAKOTA	8305	3629	4588	2155	0	0	0	0	0
41 TENNESSEE	0	18899	156116	332771	45462	13979	251021	3023	32390
42 TEXAS	73046	33132	356710	683896	5406	0	115045	230	204
43 UTAH	27843	8087	23917	11017	0	0	699	0	124
44 VERMONT	0	818	5392	7974	0	0	7784	0	0
45 VIRGINIA	0	54476	121914	111327	1012463	418689	454129	17123	48480
46 WASHINGTON	27685	16126	161835	44806	0	0	10828	0	0
47 WEST VIRGINIA	0	451	40658	2696	25722	0	3678	2016	0
48 WISCONSIN	14834	38175	585710	51727	675	0	12504	0	6314
49 WYOMING	22317	226	3242	760	0	0	0	0	0
50 ALASKA	0	0	4807	0	0	0	0	0	0
51 HAWAII	271013	5800	15240	20575	0	0	206	0	334
52 SUM OF STATE OUTPUTS	2352448	2127918	9657155	7700530	5262627	2070337	12204230	333552	1142135

NOTE: The 152 column numbers are identical with the 152 product-mix industry numbers given in Table A-2, pages 134-145, and refer to that industrial classification.

TABLE C-11

1963 STATE ESTABLISHMENT OUTPUTS FOR MANUFACTURING AND SERVICES

(THOUSANDS OF CURRENT DOLLARS)

	19	20	21	22	23	24	25	26	27
1 ALABAMA	56927	56771	278696	32229	52065	127263	45486	16228	7044
2 ARIZONA	205	722	22818	3459	7297	29403	14122	752	1464
3 ARKANSAS	5583	3315	74935	583	56519	176119	18344	22504	13500
4 CALIFORNIA	81791	34345	777700	169487	253232	506385	338736	93821	64609
5 COLORADO	851	276	15079	7377	5282	17181	6080	3722	1982
6 CONNECTICUT	50344	18124	170036	26533	906	3178	15432	9346	3439
7 DELAWARE	13969	4082	44634	3696	2791	2054	3414	3811	548
8 DISTRICT OF COLUMBIA	0	0	0	900	0	0	1262	0	0
9 FLORIDA	2012	13901	92321	13468	60322	34031	48511	18612	17543
10 GEORGIA	183252	76321	515065	113326	83321	115597	43016	25685	23696
11 IDAHO	0	0	723	648	88023	142043	8319	3468	908
12 ILLINOIS	80693	16331	391290	140674	3081	18028	84434	64186	12995
13 INDIANA	7245	5309	126685	27397	3351	20834	146210	26205	3982
14 IOWA	237	457	27337	7333	1721	4973	40338	3508	2272
15 KANSAS	205	0	30919	9462	1177	2873	5587	915	831
16 KENTUCKY	2618	45372	176501	19781	4960	54469	19030	9381	18223
17 LOUISIANA	7525	0	55634	23047	46417	93404	20366	22426	7570
18 MAINE	11583	5437	33098	8951	111807	30824	8775	35154	1929
19 MARYLAND	1506	6786	296757	29764	4837	19656	26788	9423	7472
20 MASSACHUSETTS	193662	126575	579157	114024	1992	9836	28425	35496	7533
21 MICHIGAN	69629	8390	62421	359023	27477	45772	61581	54443	5922
22 MINNESOTA	15511	18259	72455	25643	27540	8987	69172	22587	4035
23 MISSISSIPPI	7991	30446	240856	15725	28950	99303	27270	95873	22317
24 MISSOURI	27758	4435	332230	55009	4210	34912	24052	18101	8333
25 MONTANA	0	0	0	140	68050	101019	23092	2214	0
26 NEBRASKA	0	0	12324	1613	181	441	10986	7433	651
27 NEVADA	0	0	245	382	453	2837	5397	273	0
28 NEW HAMPSHIRE	11258	36862	17648	6222	25146	13910	22504	9587	4519
29 NEW JERSEY	121295	128282	716520	194256	2355	8742	39388	23389	12300
30 NEW MEXICO	0	0	2468	2321	5269	15672	8866	342	90
31 NEW YORK	165410	670912	5722149	571218	15488	47796	100110	70214	14691
32 NORTH CAROLINA	138012	880850	343296	131029	47206	148865	77978	30907	9456
33 NORTH DAKOTA	0	0	0	304	0	776	622	206	0
34 OHIO	120593	50285	350193	43518	3615	27503	92371	27189	10834
35 OKLAHOMA	205	1802	45732	3962	1177	11374	8067	6469	0
36 OREGON	6363	25746	26629	22821	552002	603466	650799	46911	5108
37 PENNSYLVANIA	128694	486926	1397393	116848	16159	56765	88804	32071	10096
38 RHODE ISLAND	43043	29001	30977	4876	91	415	1985	2395	444
39 SOUTH CAROLINA	97345	60219	210567	33008	37470	64304	59201	17350	8772
40 SOUTH DAKOTA	0	0	0	798	1722	4016	3171	1591	102
41 TENNESSEE	29680	221048	525750	41782	7369	119914	29417	22858	18765
42 TEXAS	13969	3278	407344	53552	18617	85065	95748	33189	8482
43 UTAH	352	6095	18293	1448	1177	7300	5330	342	180
44 VERMONT	2838	2491	19470	404	6814	15139	10919	8243	1550
45 VIRGINIA	24791	92267	208712	23777	36934	120448	62326	26197	13407
46 WASHINGTON	2608	3027	48454	14166	355118	361948	239053	14469	9227
47 WEST VIRGINIA	118	12390	31164	1512	10771	43495	6271	5198	967
48 WISCONSIN	34568	67614	76218	13525	25216	32422	142990	22399	11142
49 WYOMING	0	0	0	69	3314	8626	1139	4393	0
50 ALASKA	0	0	0	0	25152	0	0	0	0
51 HAWAII	0	0	24087	1606	0	105	4649	3537	0
52 SUM OF STATE OUTPUTS	1762241	3254744	14652981	2492698	2144140	3499489	2895933	1015016	378932

NOTE: The 152 column numbers are identical with the 152 product-mix industry numbers given in Table A-2, pages 134-145, and refer to that industrial classification.

TABLE C-11

1963 STATE ESTABLISHMENT OUTPUTS FOR MANUFACTURING AND SERVICES
(THOUSANDS OF CURRENT DOLLARS)

	28	29	30	31	32	33	34	35	36
1 ALABAMA	38599	2805	1252	3843	1945	0	173475	70228	96426
2 ARIZONA	9114	90	538	2680	885	0	10299	0	1490
3 ARKANSAS	90983	622	13204	467	3279	0	63998	55798	61787
4 CALIFORNIA	406707	23697	22394	100085	27492	334	32065	93803	315593
5 COLORADO	14332	90	265	3469	1562	0	0	1990	10673
6 CONNECTICUT	37153	14384	3788	7242	2001	0	31387	37202	41838
7 DELAWARE	316	0	0	1434	67	0	6765	1990	1160
8 DISTRICT OF COLUMBIA	0	0	0	0	0	0	0	0	0
9 FLORIDA	71995	98	1252	12301	3630	49633	67228	158894	80609
10 GEORGIA	92563	2587	2013	5330	2686	62561	2209	284197	133269
11 IDAHO	2034	0	449	0	269	18352	0	10867	2040
12 ILLINOIS	217641	39972	16660	95732	32966	1392	22657	54941	317171
13 INDIANA	277660	26662	10281	22052	2527	0	1147	39643	108183
14 IOWA	20639	13673	3525	1241	731	0	0	9165	28716
15 KANSAS	13904	6761	1516	2595	799	0	0	6572	13397
16 KENTUCKY	65228	1424	715	3959	4110	0	0	0	38425
17 LOUISIANA	14479	0	898	1802	500	0	105693	156377	123832
18 MAINE	5767	0	2116	1486	202	21923	369857	4986	68145
19 MARYLAND	36232	0	715	3626	27045	0	44385	14570	25067
20 MASSACHUSETTS	132254	7174	2085	15887	8926	0	240429	28502	264330
21 MICHIGAN	120015	59597	56092	39660	47581	0	184477	132443	251874
22 MINNESOTA	24216	1155	3568	14661	1850	0	115206	31698	161357
23 MISSISSIPPI	92083	0	1970	3349	135	49735	1147	0	27569
24 MISSOURI	43183	7339	803	17304	11676	0	0	1990	113852
25 MONTANA	616	0	0	479	67	0	0	4583	116
26 NEBRASKA	11283	0	538	8379	366	0	0	0	9330
27 NEVADA	1016	0	0	280	0	0	0	0	116
28 NEW HAMPSHIRE	20672	0	1606	6359	0	20531	72378	5464	57747
29 NEW JERSEY	111721	12813	531	20651	13087	1726	96226	76623	315593
30 NEW MEXICO	1468	98	0	2004	67	0	0	0	0
31 NEW YORK	272248	73490	10599	111682	46459	10264	327276	59413	534589
32 NORTH CAROLINA	583863	24616	16210	10135	1478	49735	141747	73238	34866
33 NORTH DAKOTA	241	0	0	187	0	0	0	0	0
34 OHIO	140777	60855	10000	88134	11495	3571	243810	105301	298946
35 OKLAHOMA	11642	98	626	3876	336	0	0	6572	5458
36 OREGON	32692	0	177	2288	1658	8203	96434	51942	48960
37 PENNSYLVANIA	202054	54934	13931	67536	16774	0	280468	64950	352745
38 RHODE ISLAND	1552	525	0	5907	6268	0	0	0	18404
39 SOUTH CAROLINA	37744	3961	88	1148	202	33460	0	139926	33184
40 SOUTH DAKOTA	874	0	88	93	0	0	0	0	177
41 TENNESSEE	197001	5708	4979	12099	3124	49633	99070	40565	98578
42 TEXAS	103363	5572	20732	19610	5815	334	72334	39973	96963
43 UTAH	8385	0	538	2658	515	0	0	0	4344
44 VERMONT	23055	0	0	187	0	0	14919	10867	36228
45 VIRGINIA	284238	11530	4059	15860	4877	31281	63279	152051	65276
46 WASHINGTON	27878	570	5410	4971	1068	176117	266032	70369	125916
47 WEST VIRGINIA	7595	188	715	3482	336	0	2294	9988	12174
48 WISCONSIN	49927	5332	23866	7914	2558	25769	516906	58636	399164
49 WYOMING	75	0	0	0	67	0	0	0	0
50 ALASKA	0	0	0	0	0	0	0	0	0
51 HAWAII	6136	1156	0	1533	694	0	0	0	7078
52 SUM OF STATE OUTPUTS	3965210	469576	260795	757655	300179	614557	3765595	2166315	4842757

NOTE: The 152 column numbers are identical with the 152 product-mix industry numbers given in Table A-2, pages 134-145, and refer to that industrial classification.

TABLE C-11

1963 STATE ESTABLISHMENT OUTPUTS FOR MANUFACTURING AND SERVICES
(THOUSANDS OF CURRENT DOLLARS)

	37	38	39	40	41	42	43	44	45
1 ALABAMA	19947	41837	1653	3730	125	34980	0	161183	83232
2 ARIZONA	4846	40697	1361	1857	749	18118	0	6839	13869
3 ARKANSAS	41511	21369	1653	4315	494	22168	0	5571	20095
4 CALIFORNIA	442428	529759	48254	50298	27822	561700	17851	307571	97812
5 COLORADO	18326	51886	12077	2326	7637	37208	606	11942	21321
6 CONNECTICUT	75098	65832	49053	9182	7196	143945	2399	203088	1539
7 DELAWARE	9658	13761	92	117	0	10298	0	72543	2429
8 DISTRICT OF COLUMBIA	0	83722	84561	18004	6647	54738	0	0	0
9 FLORIDA	72865	143073	4426	5466	2215	89455	952	32643	241969
10 GEORGIA	153602	64398	6267	6609	2946	81802	136	61456	89612
11 IDAHO	3155	11831	183	1485	187	3459	0	1654	27663
12 ILLINOIS	442796	302556	128046	299692	101592	949444	23761	446688	100062
13 INDIANA	145269	113945	6105	77431	9157	125733	0	153160	51084
14 IOWA	53056	70040	90903	6104	1214	49457	408	2942	39920
15 KANSAS	58615	36359	7846	8649	4175	35527	15193	47428	16787
16 KENTUCKY	46675	41975	2627	11653	2809	63338	1156	221122	20149
17 LOUISIANA	61555	51164	1628	3051	187	24455	0	536961	19557
18 MAINE	7626	18222	458	747	62	9047	0	7217	8186
19 MARYLAND	117677	64329	14779	18462	1981	120751	3419	124203	50375
20 MASSACHUSETTS	208043	191771	12582	168008	7897	223574	33735	89095	11355
21 MICHIGAN	251392	193777	14814	18378	6881	241106	2671	446082	34642
22 MINNESOTA	73488	88892	19104	31858	4974	159114	136	8710	25748
23 MISSISSIPPI	12829	16766	275	117	125	9083	0	859	50291
24 MISSOURI	138402	119164	37123	38917	3297	180009	46724	211547	71751
25 MONTANA	0	13425	1286	0	0	3550	0	4559	1725
26 NEBRASKA	15100	35922	6526	1880	125	32429	0	8060	15728
27 NEVADA	0	12312	275	157	187	4276	0	24829	943
28 NEW HAMPSHIRE	11614	11453	733	1807	125	23469	7026	10920	298
29 NEW JERSEY	320050	156200	22260	139409	13447	255500	5103	1430255	43186
30 NEW MEXICO	202	13348	1378	432	125	5171	0	2398	298
31 NEW YORK	435382	533761	1282157	859361	127303	1168044	77800	523611	35635
32 NORTH CAROLINA	86001	62686	2138	4811	874	62809	136	50321	69316
33 NORTH DAKOTA	202	11592	275	157	250	3582	0	487	1237
34 OHIO	331383	250951	63719	77504	14647	522754	77700	404282	94737
35 OKLAHOMA	16025	46230	4886	3751	931	25984	0	1730	10433
36 OREGON	18628	45324	2768	1769	1051	30319	0	24382	11321
37 PENNSYLVANIA	345027	295040	229079	72990	6618	475525	6723	389761	41957
38 RHODE ISLAND	18302	22432	183	5712	375	25716	2535	38083	895
39 SOUTH CAROLINA	65077	26617	1099	5407	187	11975	0	9807	39379
40 SOUTH DAKOTA	871	12522	1592	0	187	5263	0	1288	1535
41 TENNESSEE	62656	61619	21568	29545	4448	95382	0	367731	38847
42 TEXAS	101800	196183	11941	20089	5660	191185	272	2326321	128902
43 UTAH	2494	22376	2115	6652	187	13649	0	0	11867
44 VERMONT	10077	6774	366	8636	1220	5945	5156	3681	298
45 VIRGINIA	51492	61603	1839	10044	6667	67807	0	157743	71917
46 WASHINGTON	60790	74853	2706	3668	2507	40577	0	199733	7190
47 WEST VIRGINIA	12920	26615	92	1274	0	22734	272	1182072	1583
48 WISCONSIN	168487	93719	14190	70246	3904	177590	272	13043	19520
49 WYOMING	0	5651	92	520	0	2311	0	1288	0
50 ALASKA	0	3901	0	0	0	0	0	0	0
51 HAWAII	3858	14770	1103	315	62	7850	136	5611	12769
52 SUM OF STATE OUTPUTS	4597295	4495004	2222235	2112592	391455	6529908	332278	10342500	1760961

NOTE: The 152 column numbers are identical with the 152 product-mix industry numbers given in Table A-2, pages 134-145, and refer to that industrial classification.

TABLE C-11

1963 STATE ESTABLISHMENT OUTPUTS FOR
MANUFACTURING AND SERVICES
(THOUSANDS OF CURRENT DOLLARS)

	46	47	48	49	50	51	52	53	54
1 ALABAMA	33747	111299	1082	1672	7280	35900	19264	184976	0
2 ARIZONA	7133	0	462	3771	2757	1198	3360	0	0
3 ARKANSAS	10860	874	87	234	3541	129853	15480	27432	0
4 CALIFORNIA	124025	172405	66180	439646	278459	2378668	94001	251398	5169
5 COLORADO	6265	437	7002	2475	9336	75927	6036	85386	0
6 CONNECTICUT	24024	81190	75706	167484	7740	6606	11262	86949	35689
7 DELAWARE	133	186639	735	13518	686	157211	6309	0	0
8 DISTRICT OF COLUMBIA	1940	0	0	0	0	0	0	0	0
9 FLORIDA	38571	136677	8088	11453	38613	14356	19946	267	1787
10 GEORGIA	111318	57577	14546	81819	53413	19260	27025	11020	1787
11 IDAHO	150	0	0	0	229	0	371	0	0
12 ILLINOIS	245282	101875	301815	675296	357115	1212484	108095	13394	29054
13 INDIANA	35725	40473	370922	203149	40576	872148	22801	116777	1765
14 IOWA	2489	86744	20844	27827	34131	6103	3807	174975	0
15 KANSAS	24904	17398	4040	121150	6997	625778	2197	85520	0
16 KENTUCKY	4301	221871	820	1306	75354	158152	5257	27432	0
17 LOUISIANA	69714	181270	1848	8502	10479	1665351	23617	0	0
18 MAINE	2047	437	201	226	458	257	3059	1830	5065
19 MARYLAND	28110	53515	30280	211454	41888	84962	27263	96683	35689
20 MASSACHUSETTS	70806	214840	16955	156506	58408	41658	35059	112951	96896
21 MICHIGAN	131306	113140	298998	60523	169623	340893	23339	170906	0
22 MINNESOTA	82723	13788	4058	130135	18538	144540	17908	3040	0
23 MISSISSIPPI	12374	4325	28717	492	686	79941	4708	34949	0
24 MISSOURI	63497	3625	129149	187345	101414	159832	21133	11831	1765
25 MONTANA	299	0	211	117	0	141796	371	0	0
26 NEBRASKA	598	0	32482	7501	1493	11577	741	0	0
27 NEVADA	150	0	87	1983	229	0	1213	0	0
28 NEW HAMPSHIRE	2150	16961	799	1331	458	471	1112	0	9293
29 NEW JERSEY	231037	290825	697362	786811	276424	1307624	76140	3259	1765
30 NEW MEXICO	7435	0	0	117	458	57429	2746	0	0
31 NEW YORK	149826	242731	734146	526754	132505	196454	55251	27565	19177
32 NORTH CAROLINA	18891	166607	47526	14304	21267	635	6526	267	3404
33 NORTH DAKOTA	1300	0	0	0	0	35880	371	0	0
34 OHIO	173450	284448	96274	428851	221085	857905	76472	972470	419
35 OKLAHOMA	10706	874	1108	2499	5949	747200	8673	89345	0
36 OREGON	17426	4762	3573	2996	11220	5304	12864	1696	22
37 PENNSYLVANIA	128324	394710	526328	101697	155498	1285855	50571	210232	17889
38 RHODE ISLAND	3190	42778	646	7951	7001	29185	1112	0	61207
39 SOUTH CAROLINA	7475	208006	21606	14382	3468	10793	8250	2639	0
40 SOUTH DAKOTA	299	0	850	117	0	0	371	0	0
41 TENNESSEE	50481	530307	72070	36187	21841	30832	12024	104145	1765
42 TEXAS	137494	453889	23197	92084	113658	5666985	47445	105706	0
43 UTAH	4327	0	174	2642	1721	157456	4167	0	0
44 VERMONT	640	3625	174	234	3890	0	371	0	0
45 VIRGINIA	33476	707808	68321	18651	11272	66263	6914	0	0
46 WASHINGTON	13109	17795	2505	2655	15792	211639	10765	1563	0
47 WEST VIRGINIA	15810	312745	87	8002	1721	60254	7999	133	0
48 WISCONSIN	38202	22091	26948	132273	42440	52621	3436	85520	6635
49 WYOMING	0	0	0	0	0	368097	0	0	0
50 ALASKA	0	0	0	0	0	0	0	0	0
51 HAWAII	653	0	115	1484	0	29185	1846	0	0
52 SUM OF STATE OUTPUTS	2178193	5501363	3739124	4697604	2367108	19542512	899040	3102256	336242

NOTE: The 152 column numbers are identical with the 152 product-mix industry numbers given in Table A-2, pages 134-145, and refer to that industrial classification.

TABLE C-11

1963 STATE ESTABLISHMENT OUTPUTS FOR
MANUFACTURING AND SERVICES
(THOUSANDS OF CURRENT DOLLARS)

	55	56	57	58	59	60	61	62	63
1 ALABAMA	4013	30178	0	0	8959	65	6851	48365	22097
2 ARIZONA	1928	4046	0	0	209	246	651	11378	2029
3 ARKANSAS	11584	6471	0	0	66492	3301	13481	11378	10055
4 CALIFORNIA	159910	270037	21695	1604	29131	22455	174281	146459	81469
5 COLORADO	38466	2615	410	0	0	38664	1470	11378	11752
6 CONNECTICUT	108827	72046	2424	118	18844	5212	13192	477	3070
7 DELAWARE	38441	25604	24702	0	0	5959	612	0	518
8 DISTRICT OF COLUMBIA	0	0	0	0	0	0	0	0	1191
9 FLORIDA	2093	19562	1642	1081	9088	9579	16225	27399	12923
10 GEORGIA	36871	16503	9110	0	35973	7685	23711	11915	33837
11 IDAHO	0	221	0	0	0	630	0	3466	591
12 ILLINOIS	148242	372958	58365	5065	109834	32351	231031	36539	24746
13 INDIANA	185117	152656	2469	1081	25867	6488	144758	53713	26914
14 IOWA	1027	28837	0	118	1647	4660	164	44800	13991
15 KANSAS	1627	6296	0	0	1362	211	858	26923	19632
16 KENTUCKY	10976	18779	5608	237	27493	1755	23928	9855	18521
17 LOUISIANA	0	4521	540	0	0	65	24620	21233	2412
18 MAINE	1928	20571	48539	14111	216552	640	1168	5689	1126
19 MARYLAND	23446	43506	3984	118	14353	4063	46099	21199	10539
20 MASSACHUSETTS	257244	188285	191031	93732	355910	39340	3813	0	4235
21 MICHIGAN	90917	160643	27004	560	25197	3113	138061	81176	5943
22 MINNESOTA	19377	43050	9035	0	13386	882	15911	5689	2572
23 MISSISSIPPI	7225	19998	0	0	19364	1525	11977	9155	16257
24 MISSOURI	27525	65677	7736	38230	269124	29672	58797	42301	69232
25 MONTANA	0	221	0	0	0	65	0	9155	455
26 NEBRASKA	42153	3794	1754	0	420	155	164	15544	1843
27 NEVADA	0	0	0	0	0	0	0	0	72
28 NEW HAMPSHIRE	16183	23525	33086	15239	171806	5554	1333	0	1404
29 NEW JERSEY	184775	340242	61305	355	22898	86503	229964	0	17732
30 NEW MEXICO	2835	1919	0	0	1244	129	164	3466	382
31 NEW YORK	98897	321769	89112	23831	214748	338813	168546	72155	13490
32 NORTH CAROLINA	33835	35274	7789	560	14780	926	48241	1445	28847
33 NORTH DAKOTA	0	0	0	0	0	0	0	0	1190
34 OHIO	635113	362408	31050	2947	77973	6854	411782	53314	138967
35 OKLAHOMA	1027	11662	0	118	0	4065	65624	21626	2752
36 OREGON	4668	2453	1536	474	608	3146	8284	17067	1714
37 PENNSYLVANIA	130384	153243	64284	11246	253972	31915	392717	128474	102027
38 RHODE ISLAND	50848	37422	259	2022	630	10065	32534	0	0
39 SOUTH CAROLINA	6547	49159	1059	0	0	0	53581	5689	11819
40 SOUTH DAKOTA	150	3162	0	0	0	0	0	0	382
41 TENNESSEE	42697	29969	37121	6759	164727	17232	108376	31129	10412
42 TEXAS	28251	67494	3115	355	21563	9798	33793	93634	56900
43 UTAH	9768	1324	410	0	0	486	246	9155	5447
44 VERMONT	12747	8368	3854	1641	330	3469	0	0	0
45 VIRGINIA	39308	37452	12278	1681	34337	10036	21473	26922	9494
46 WASHINGTON	2205	6767	821	0	771	2160	7426	16715	3638
47 WEST VIRGINIA	5670	552	12971	0	4040	155	243973	9855	10278
48 WISCONSIN	19219	67526	122044	3245	115951	24044	4115	11744	638
49 WYOMING	0	110	0	0	0	0	0	5689	368
50 ALASKA	0	0	0	0	0	0	0	0	0
51 HAWAII	0	884	0	0	1612	182	493	6932	382
52 SUM OF STATE OUTPUTS	2544064	3139758	898144	226532	2351192	774311	2784489	1170199	816286

NOTE: The 152 column numbers are identical with the 152 product-mix industry numbers given in Table A-2, pages 134-145, and refer to that industrial classification.

TABLE C-11

1963 STATE ESTABLISHMENT OUTPUTS FOR MANUFACTURING AND SERVICES
(THOUSANDS OF CURRENT DOLLARS)

	64	65	66	67	68	69	70	71	72
1 ALABAMA	996	74909	16151	735661	191108	0	1941	96504	7475
2 ARIZONA	221	54049	2247	1419	6962	0	228	378527	637
3 ARKANSAS	347	25179	3827	0	2569	0	114	99082	5010
4 CALIFORNIA	46923	468012	225239	580985	110404	37727	27233	78507	43713
5 COLORADO	11588	52003	9734	150971	9461	0	761	5016	1698
6 CONNECTICUT	10351	57646	54084	164510	31254	12919	10516	4888	2335
7 DELAWARE	0	18462	378	146455	3424	0	114	5386	6387
8 DISTRICT OF COLUMBIA	0	19577	0	0	0	0	0	0	0
9 FLORIDA	608	193382	18588	20184	6743	0	1751	15631	2016
10 GEORGIA	1068	110631	13787	150132	5238	0	875	6431	5352
11 IDAHO	0	13086	662	0	154	992	0	106936	0
12 ILLINOIS	34968	203964	266692	1447336	272894	129532	44998	57667	116701
13 INDIANA	13694	141155	97302	2212921	168767	79840	10159	51793	29716
14 IOWA	84	97826	219	24781	33372	714	990	3997	159
15 KANSAS	343	47980	77360	0	20653	0	343	10927	6387
16 KENTUCKY	3981	42547	19412	231234	2412	0	831	19190	478
17 LOUISIANA	6659	69738	35364	9320	10358	1984	114	113719	2571
18 MAINE	168	11131	0	0	1095	0	0	57	0
19 MARYLAND	5285	84621	28803	462171	8684	143	571	114777	8883
20 MASSACHUSETTS	1659	84298	145629	98773	35932	44093	6258	5096	8911
21 MICHIGAN	8552	188702	83835	1381339	523762	139058	56475	97249	15270
22 MINNESOTA	1465	93326	82442	153060	15138	428	3034	1984	3659
23 MISSISSIPPI	126	27922	24214	5884	1779	0	0	6309	0
24 MISSOURI	1292	97330	27500	112420	51841	143	4999	45580	5147
25 MONTANA	0	11228	2256	325	813	0	114	203118	0
26 NEBRASKA	42	35841	751	0	3629	0	114	38503	3472
27 NEVADA	0	47751	260	0	0	0	533	48357	0
28 NEW HAMPSHIRE	168	15726	24505	10398	6040	143	114	57	159
29 NEW JERSEY	55342	138397	220440	153522	80514	12313	29710	285067	68146
30 NEW MEXICO	0	27221	708	0	0	0	0	39283	0
31 NEW YORK	33599	238809	284044	828375	101302	23897	13196	169936	72248
32 NORTH CAROLINA	1041	72354	18843	9428	18835	428	457	28073	1698
33 NORTH DAKOTA	42	8515	187	0	77	0	0	0	0
34 OHIO	106491	265804	207624	3316425	483773	162706	22661	165973	59537
35 OKLAHOMA	747	55180	1342	12991	9506	3834	1104	71339	1379
36 OREGON	126	46176	1558	35172	23781	0	685	107810	2411
37 PENNSYLVANIA	60499	200898	189413	4984607	307643	60322	21415	166259	52726
38 RHODE ISLAND	128	9456	3514	59155	6028	1963	3112	776	3714
39 SOUTH CAROLINA	866	31425	10875	14047	8620	0	228	12896	159
40 SOUTH DAKOTA	42	14371	596	0	77	0	0	0	0
41 TENNESSEE	15758	86201	14548	53792	42178	4120	3635	173944	3659
42 TEXAS	9238	293315	66709	249806	71898	16366	6524	441259	13340
43 UTAH	42	45636	6614	152318	7772	0	1551	138858	1379
44 VERMONT	34	40125	0	0	2980	0	114	0	0
45 VIRGINIA	168	121835	20238	16401	67745	0	114	10493	2252
46 WASHINGTON	212	83638	9638	35509	12720	1135	457	318814	4201
47 WEST VIRGINIA	22397	21593	15263	498135	10765	992	114	58479	0
48 WISCONSIN	19625	108329	28995	79616	174862	112010	6548	678	3555
49 WYOMING	0	13879	73	0	0	0	0	388	0
50 ALASKA	0	6061	0	0	0	0	0	0	0
51 HAWAII	168	18359	409	5207	77	0	0	57	0
52 SUM OF STATE OUTPUTS	477198	4335598	2362868	18604784	2955641	847801	284805	3805668	566539

NOTE: The 152 column numbers are identical with the 152 product-mix industry numbers given in Table A-2, pages 134-145, and refer to that industrial classification.

TABLE C-11

1963 STATE ESTABLISHMENT OUTPUTS FOR
MANUFACTURING AND SERVICES
(THOUSANDS OF CURRENT DOLLARS)

	73	74	75	76	77	78	79	80	81
1 ALABAMA	113347	22015	0	0	8426	12512	150192	18852	9042
2 ARIZONA	82978	417	0	0	0	256	31357	716	129
3 ARKANSAS	12597	15121	0	8772	0	8392	30393	912	8126
4 CALIFORNIA	331642	117037	22397	352229	26756	122049	653266	139303	100390
5 COLORADO	740	2607	0	19840	400	664	44791	1679	0
6 CONNECTICUT	580960	28472	9463	483	2622	24441	65249	98041	105078
7 DELAWARE	2237	291	0	0	0	5380	16193	188	7584
8 DISTRICT OF COLUMBIA	0	0	0	0	0	0	4408	0	0
9 FLORIDA	30596	2896	222	73346	1161	1963	177767	3599	7991
10 GEORGIA	48493	2650	0	32208	2322	10877	121066	994	38318
11 IDAHO	0	0	0	1448	0	0	9689	0	0
12 ILLINOIS	560930	127262	4945	320252	61665	127053	432451	354599	329826
13 INDIANA	590567	74301	4501	36656	4820	108031	253165	54524	149635
14 IOWA	87623	10033	0	0	400	23870	80677	2054	14587
15 KANSAS	1667	3086	0	483	5781	26601	58782	888	3543
16 KENTUCKY	60901	4369	0	4365	0	52456	50785	3402	28897
17 LOUISIANA	0	454	0	39476	13107	384	84873	0	4703
18 MAINE	5012	781	0	15147	0	1726	12219	106	542
19 MARYLAND	195702	2795	443	114650	961	22013	89797	6000	33265
20 MASSACHUSETTS	180235	24802	35745	21385	1561	21401	141187	91077	48158
21 MICHIGAN	399305	141970	443	9696	1561	68579	324591	247384	376880
22 MINNESOTA	975	19106	0	48731	5020	9316	80485	19139	32579
23 MISSISSIPPI	6584	314	0	0	200	0	50101	3590	16665
24 MISSOURI	48612	30428	1277	93314	3382	23273	190018	17303	34696
25 MONTANA	8404	0	0	0	0	383	5966	0	0
26 NEBRASKA	26249	7785	0	13220	0	3843	70943	700	1473
27 NEVADA	23712	0	0	0	0	0	5605	0	129
28 NEW HAMPSHIRE	12376	6100	0	0	0	0	11249	6149	930
29 NEW JERSEY	596618	55317	443	206742	54337	85517	240578	92879	114411
30 NEW MEXICO	0	179	0	0	0	0	6483	0	1318
31 NEW YORK	731339	108282	0	110825	10480	102760	465252	110495	204096
32 NORTH CAROLINA	57554	1297	0	483	0	1025	97081	13930	3274
33 NORTH DAKOTA	0	0	0	0	0	128	5508	0	259
34 OHIO	451912	196943	35967	94611	38593	280936	592917	287204	358202
35 OKLAHOMA	3889	4032	0	2410	400	3971	142442	5307	776
36 OREGON	194	5606	0	17957	961	3010	73374	1953	1682
37 PENNSYLVANIA	352208	92986	13280	141745	21444	170414	706589	118817	319692
38 RHODE ISLAND	184001	3353	0	0	0	2619	13432	19241	13485
39 SOUTH CAROLINA	2739	1286	0	483	200	1556	44919	106	10713
40 SOUTH DAKOTA	0	0	0	0	0	256	11464	0	0
41 TENNESSEE	123327	2041	0	12106	961	51313	138198	2242	34316
42 TEXAS	63474	14695	35745	85070	25575	27347	371011	10244	14871
43 UTAH	0	618	0	6775	0	1982	51704	0	801
44 VERMONT	10968	112	0	0	0	128	4889	505	259
45 VIRGINIA	62222	3127	0	10216	0	8779	131862	3402	129
46 WASHINGTON	110341	2791	0	48598	200	2696	78007	2763	3879
47 WEST VIRGINIA	153491	2348	0	12143	3022	20927	46751	1131	17370
48 WISCONSIN	75618	62870	0	91283	5420	75950	211424	29952	195522
49 WYOMING	0	0	0	0	0	0	728	0	542
50 ALASKA	0	0	0	0	0	0	0	0	0
51 HAWAII	0	0	0	20433	0	126	5720	0	0
52 SUM OF STATE OUTPUTS	6392340	1202679	164872	2067580	301738	1516903	6687596	1771367	2648763

NOTE: The 152 column numbers are identical with the 152 product-mix industry numbers given in Table A-2, pages 134-145, and refer to that industrial classification.

TABLE C-11

1963 STATE ESTABLISHMENT OUTPUTS FOR MANUFACTURING AND SERVICES
(THOUSANDS OF CURRENT DOLLARS)

	82	83	84	85	86	87	88	89	90
1 ALABAMA	1303	6985	11584	62220	0	19834	8573	671	0
2 ARIZONA	74	6000	1341	1615	0	5196	0	129	0
3 ARKANSAS	3920	2990	1469	16116	0	5055	142	0	368
4 CALIFORNIA	64557	245980	64071	287155	76350	69153	105003	5644	7926
5 COLORADO	2175	6063	2270	25363	4112	8378	3701	38390	36972
6 CONNECTICUT	84709	59564	28075	86808	54822	2209	566	671	123
7 DELAWARE	31	3237	460	6168	0	768	283	0	0
8 DISTRICT OF COLUMBIA	0	0	0	0	0	0	0	0	0
9 FLORIDA	3457	11201	9244	14059	1713	9855	1336	0	693
10 GEORGIA	209	27765	1361	15086	203	35128	27319	0	0
11 IDAHO	37	417	0	130	0	5938	1053	129	0
12 ILLINOIS	92017	269209	120504	525314	210830	598394	1138287	28251	23466
13 INDIANA	29188	56025	42844	175074	71279	114357	85604	3904	1062
14 IOWA	5072	4086	8270	53840	37934	552389	143712	7901	123
15 KANSAS	1103	4065	4120	15559	0	37829	10831	7309	8202
16 KENTUCKY	4492	7344	10472	111694	0	66351	283	1188	123
17 LOUISIANA	1073	8147	812	38838	598	11150	5663	0	15494
18 MAINE	1633	275	176	1738	0	899	10282	671	0
19 MARYLAND	381	21354	22968	32919	0	768	4004	0	0
20 MASSACHUSETTS	80324	62128	19156	137248	186880	1330	4025	129	246
21 MICHIGAN	160977	210995	107238	259413	437144	234621	127034	8368	368
22 MINNESOTA	7908	23187	6444	41759	19209	132135	81970	3362	1560
23 MISSISSIPPI	6414	275	6113	5639	0	28414	4145	0	8956
24 MISSOURI	11282	39562	33323	87170	10948	58865	28428	5121	123
25 MONTANA	31	143	0	260	0	899	142	0	0
26 NEBRASKA	1095	539	900	6507	0	35771	3971	0	0
27 NEVADA	0	285	0	260	0	0	283	0	0
28 NEW HAMPSHIRE	2561	845	176	6631	101	112	0	22488	0
29 NEW JERSEY	61642	80640	45626	257192	3934	3715	20192	22617	246
30 NEW MEXICO	0	560	88	297	0	337	142	129	1062
31 NEW YORK	77270	167646	59637	213319	196443	49633	28950	1601	2130
32 NORTH CAROLINA	9773	5707	14206	13506	101	20208	708	800	0
33 NORTH DAKOTA	0	0	88	130	0	7029	0	0	123
34 OHIO	113420	166923	37239	507213	52534	160836	332714	45555	8939
35 OKLAHOMA	250	29753	5721	18249	101	6900	32739	517	92769
36 OREGON	3325	4558	2973	13902	598	7151	7686	1601	0
37 PENNSYLVANIA	32118	108147	103200	433801	283325	101240	63012	73992	14878
38 RHODE ISLAND	4021	24992	2887	38002	101	112	283	0	0
39 SOUTH CAROLINA	5952	2681	176	4531	0	2752	283	0	123
40 SOUTH DAKOTA	520	132	0	260	0	4246	0	0	0
41 TENNESSEE	12522	8686	9921	26077	101	62636	2854	3550	246
42 TEXAS	2038	36019	28083	176073	17314	26447	46911	1576	372647
43 UTAH	246	2407	724	1220	0	1644	21656	930	8263
44 VERMONT	1105	428	176	1063	0	449	1659	0	0
45 VIRGINIA	11895	3818	2782	28627	0	7951	2367	3128	0
46 WASHINGTON	1573	8421	6039	4936	304	7070	22744	1188	1437
47 WEST VIRGINIA	7067	570	1009	49031	0	8915	283	21516	20366
48 WISCONSIN	24766	35436	11400	53273	396876	287561	265644	79285	1437
49 WYOMING	37	132	0	448	0	0	142	0	614
50 ALASKA	0	0	0	0	0	0	0	0	0
51 HAWAII	0	713	176	308	0	655	0	0	0
52 SUM OF STATE OUTPUTS	935563	1767032	835542	3856037	2063857	2803284	2647607	392314	631085

NOTE: The 152 column numbers are identical with the 152 product-mix industry numbers given in Table A-2, pages 134-145, and refer to that industrial classification.

TABLE C-11

1963 STATE ESTABLISHMENT OUTPUTS FOR MANUFACTURING AND SERVICES

(THOUSANDS OF CURRENT DOLLARS)

	91	92	93	94	95	96	97	98	99
1 ALABAMA	129	3919	0	1684	4673	17236	10050	11108	139
2 ARIZONA	129	0	0	0	2913	809	2093	13153	110453
3 ARKANSAS	0	1058	7147	254	6339	2634	9565	4455	8346
4 CALIFORNIA	18318	20053	9298	25722	183470	153702	377004	291428	551261
5 COLORADO	129	1883	1242	127	1620	6827	18102	15168	1769
6 CONNECTICUT	1275	233	933	2314	256480	87144	356013	65458	207280
7 DELAWARE	0	0	0	0	4593	16803	601	2630	0
8 DISTRICT OF COLUMBIA	0	0	0	0	0	0	0	1670	0
9 FLORIDA	1275	825	154	1287	12340	20081	9991	19636	42446
10 GEORGIA	2890	5193	0	3734	6467	48517	10604	9273	3340
11 IDAHO	0	592	0	127	183	758	0	1718	0
12 ILLINOIS	14327	45429	33095	70413	537980	278291	436010	165140	229318
13 INDIANA	6673	1789	1087	2285	119653	54798	316098	117619	2754
14 IOWA	129	3301	6502	2433	27643	25759	33400	7864	129
15 KANSAS	129	10287	154	1033	7903	17673	23283	27720	282
16 KENTUCKY	4839	14544	1558	381	10587	16586	53449	28881	57373
17 LOUISIANA	0	1589	0	127	897	11506	2845	14623	729
18 MAINE	0	0	0	0	2209	7300	3006	2647	0
19 MARYLAND	8860	350	0	254	62502	64693	16428	30513	9051
20 MASSACHUSETTS	6349	5274	933	20233	210029	331138	155492	65033	129416
21 MICHIGAN	2335	99105	24372	75583	922529	187962	304265	226116	296691
22 MINNESOTA	2108	10537	4635	4096	30549	32115	50335	40852	325180
23 MISSISSIPPI	0	4960	154	7384	179	10712	2301	7537	0
24 MISSOURI	1060	10215	0	2425	48075	42827	48266	90874	21460
25 MONTANA	0	0	0	127	0	0	0	1501	0
26 NEBRASKA	0	1058	0	0	1277	786	21531	2531	139
27 NEVADA	0	0	0	0	0	120	127	1023	0
28 NEW HAMPSHIRE	0	0	0	0	11574	50043	23110	5045	4194
29 NEW JERSEY	83165	34295	617	1970	120597	219467	320873	74527	135982
30 NEW MEXICO	0	0	0	0	1294	757	127	5899	729
31 NEW YORK	63516	23048	15348	21271	285732	289168	463000	189567	1024937
32 NORTH CAROLINA	674	0	0	906	8142	119169	6394	13237	8168
33 NORTH DAKOTA	129	0	0	127	1410	356	124	1126	0
34 OHIO	20404	35062	64685	76151	818267	340484	656218	192547	225651
35 OKLAHOMA	0	1058	933	254	2053	8530	48150	13004	1585
36 OREGON	803	1857	1569	31620	1947	39300	5519	19406	139
37 PENNSYLVANIA	10431	75146	9297	59046	338400	254244	413975	105095	181521
38 RHODE ISLAND	129	350	0	127	55638	46778	15264	8961	282
39 SOUTH CAROLINA	0	3803	0	1303	30438	75416	15964	8499	9791
40 SOUTH DAKOTA	0	4161	0	0	3242	238	3075	3088	0
41 TENNESSEE	7929	5193	4635	4077	9424	19640	23345	17551	0
42 TEXAS	3019	9708	2768	7272	23751	69457	80807	60189	9343
43 UTAH	0	117	0	127	1436	3460	8283	3855	268
44 VERMONT	0	0	0	0	68418	3693	728	1632	25559
45 VIRGINIA	1949	1624	0	1408	1830	11241	15541	9756	48035
46 WASHINGTON	931	1929	18764	652	7378	24983	6357	24757	5223
47 WEST VIRGINIA	129	3803	0	127	15694	2365	912	9114	0
48 WISCONSIN	3856	12515	8389	7238	161033	206379	240443	49553	9482
49 WYOMING	0	0	0	0	0	0	127	1001	0
50 ALASKA	0	0	0	0	0	0	0	0	0
51 HAWAII	0	0	0	127	195	4515	127	1398	0
52 SUM OF STATE OUTPUTS	268015	454863	218272	435826	4428979	3226458	4609323	2084975	3688446

NOTE: The 152 column numbers are identical with the 152 product-mix industry numbers given in Table A-2, pages 134-145, and refer to that industrial classification.

TABLE C-11

1963 STATE ESTABLISHMENT OUTPUTS FOR MANUFACTURING AND SERVICES
(THOUSANDS OF CURRENT DOLLARS)

	100	101	102	103	104	105	106	107	108
1 ALABAMA	15727	16947	2813	199	29920	0	8233	15620	12916
2 ARIZONA	28223	437	1216	162	663	244	78884	68350	492
3 ARKANSAS	16012	7040	44400	128617	22138	85538	10749	137	199
4 CALIFORNIA	125110	309522	134121	204283	178746	121376	1737752	656291	82170
5 COLORADO	1940	29192	12715	432	3523	248	1742	1639	6914
6 CONNECTICUT	25334	75719	66796	197991	144551	13341	104442	140088	34143
7 DELAWARE	3462	132	0	4496	2696	0	109	637	5852
8 DISTRICT OF COLUMBIA	0	0	0	0	0	0	0	0	0
9 FLORIDA	9877	5212	2475	2373	6674	857	176862	25656	26889
10 GEORGIA	16327	94855	1132	4058	22406	551	831	2467	21986
11 IDAHO	698	0	0	0	0	0	0	476	0
12 ILLINOIS	227763	282212	184104	645883	317617	882996	849510	300826	138075
13 INDIANA	110432	75153	193871	324720	143432	574012	221245	161710	435626
14 IOWA	45558	18240	3110	156801	870	21216	67927	47301	14335
15 KANSAS	24729	862	2032	369	1544	373	5076	13862	17027
16 KENTUCKY	67583	47621	14483	296855	53501	9677	3304	26852	8002
17 LOUISIANA	6033	289	1550	786	857	120	217	387	1815
18 MAINE	2855	0	2299	234	6614	3206	109	17622	2802
19 MARYLAND	35500	6533	26846	9428	3855	244	446961	16103	26548
20 MASSACHUSETTS	86414	198166	28118	32294	176020	44532	846154	346620	55653
21 MICHIGAN	281388	51965	129681	264352	44602	25911	45584	59905	200782
22 MINNESOTA	129546	17990	66327	131136	18436	18325	92005	46457	20175
23 MISSISSIPPI	10989	8317	3408	21181	45059	958	7760	7086	2692
24 MISSOURI	142337	78063	81424	48584	95815	1694	108219	8185	31164
25 MONTANA	0	0	0	0	0	0	0	0	0
26 NEBRASKA	1699	78	594	1276	0	0	97129	19741	3103
27 NEVADA	698	211	369	0	0	124	3666	161	120
28 NEW HAMPSHIRE	4827	54383	7904	162	3075	958	54662	45619	760
29 NEW JERSEY	117371	177008	92171	48074	257822	196206	1036129	308192	85741
30 NEW MEXICO	1093	132	101	0	0	0	3040	1170	247
31 NEW YORK	348843	127824	515351	146166	334175	371701	1350298	523182	131514
32 NORTH CAROLINA	21387	59289	38729	46737	22859	1694	230717	42873	62777
33 NORTH DAKOTA	0	0	0	0	0	0	0	0	0
34 OHIO	281049	130494	659257	998776	332004	19746	350996	143122	225599
35 OKLAHOMA	17219	11063	7653	2178	444	3330	169242	4728	5981
36 OREGON	5489	48061	2704	4195	1715	0	1662	830	7976
37 PENNSYLVANIA	217708	486595	262705	100930	310980	89461	191697	513983	108254
38 RHODE ISLAND	2860	3765	1518	3267	51697	0	13871	22410	10155
39 SOUTH CAROLINA	2415	13575	14688	7287	1194	124	1290	37155	387
40 SOUTH DAKOTA	0	0	0	0	0	0	109	2077	0
41 TENNESSEE	34676	1554	61693	142023	21324	88600	57086	16403	15806
42 TEXAS	139344	41587	12419	24181	18362	104441	183288	46099	32816
43 UTAH	9462	5483	286	0	796	0	14547	9368	254
44 VERMONT	4293	1812	0	0	7037	0	0	14572	6838
45 VIRGINIA	23058	12336	100248	606	1348	124	113762	85974	4211
46 WASHINGTON	8481	12700	4194	6983	11416	124	14888	2341	1933
47 WEST VIRGINIA	4113	1521	20634	1576	77662	0	505	7805	0
48 WISCONSIN	119789	77804	387327	167782	24387	6475	182359	33699	88435
49 WYOMING	0	0	499	0	93	0	0	0	0
50 ALASKA	0	0	0	0	0	0	0	0	0
51 HAWAII	258	132	0	0	253	240	0	56	0
52 SUM OF STATE OUTPUTS	2779970	2591872	3193965	4177432	2798179	2688765	8884618	3845833	1939164

NOTE: The 152 column numbers are identical with the 152 product-mix industry numbers given in Table A-2, pages 134-145, and refer to that industrial classification.

TABLE C-11

1963 STATE ESTABLISHMENT OUTPUTS FOR MANUFACTURING AND SERVICES
(THOUSANDS OF CURRENT DOLLARS)

	109	110	111	112	113	114	115	116	117
1 ALABAMA	67035	539385	40823	55428	0	6404	88	95	848
2 ARIZONA	7892	127900	188	0	0	4315	28141	285	1329
3 ARKANSAS	13978	1133	6535	0	15040	8199	0	1338	170
4 CALIFORNIA	2449946	3362601	225991	5376	11902	150606	56827	148765	81274
5 COLORADO	22107	128269	125	0	82	6407	3594	1528	7111
6 CONNECTICUT	226600	1367051	72835	0	1220	1301	8820	85360	54508
7 DELAWARE	446599	7283	2054	0	0	0	1569	95	4985
8 DISTRICT OF COLUMBIA	0	0	0	0	0	0	0	0	0
9 FLORIDA	14697	157740	87670	0	164	30073	2860	3373	13630
10 GEORGIA	797602	213077	12385	3842	1302	47507	495	7529	1410
11 IDAHO	1984	2765	125	0	0	13875	88	0	77
12 ILLINOIS	996182	117313	9682	375431	14410	6743	56672	223428	162289
13 INDIANA	1998485	445968	36777	136429	6517	161634	1113	79704	11934
14 IOWA	33005	6339	692	1293	0	23538	28137	7127	1564
15 KANSAS	239878	690988	956	12650	0	40315	2923	181	442
16 KENTUCKY	246227	1133	4318	3809	8137	2745	88	9275	2549
17 LOUISIANA	16699	112573	155441	0	508	1093	2148	0	2305
18 MAINE	708	17093	77926	0	0	1017	495	95	77
19 MARYLAND	677521	220273	245646	0	0	6000	11738	6851	2390
20 MASSACHUSETTS	303339	200563	96453	0	8137	1567	36407	163458	30165
21 MICHIGAN	15308780	161617	53103	89149	1606	105939	78304	142070	23679
22 MINNESOTA	285963	39680	14191	3102	0	4444	6171	31735	12828
23 MISSISSIPPI	50201	0	2499	0	0	4589	1162	95	641
24 MISSOURI	2519222	344085	5764	84993	0	7583	2191	17252	20052
25 MONTANA	446	0	251	0	0	827	0	1148	679
26 NEBRASKA	54283	121	63	554	13738	17933	177	3199	20657
27 NEVADA	429	121	63	0	0	0	0	0	0
28 NEW HAMPSHIRE	259	0	1588	0	0	297	88	1717	1337
29 NEW JERSEY	745170	345913	141654	30733	328	2075	32105	45255	158161
30 NEW MEXICO	2716	121	63	0	0	474	0	3380	74
31 NEW YORK	1864865	1131283	92051	122060	18053	3789	65886	126623	136899
32 NORTH CAROLINA	38193	18574	13787	0	0	8973	19141	285	5313
33 NORTH DAKOTA	0	0	0	0	0	354	0	0	74
34 OHIO	5231998	1011540	22575	111558	16123	33687	4847	115165	33452
35 OKLAHOMA	61908	482787	1198	0	164	13447	760	7836	394
36 OREGON	86990	18160	43557	0	82	13929	1251	4023	2072
37 PENNSYLVANIA	1004208	792699	94181	420806	246	52018	19029	270470	109229
38 RHODE ISLAND	12361	8328	7741	0	0	0	1834	12883	10533
39 SOUTH CAROLINA	6239	0	8901	0	0	4101	0	95	22943
40 SOUTH DAKOTA	996	0	125	0	0	2726	88	0	74
41 TENNESSEE	90700	66719	23821	0	36031	3645	1746	31364	6204
42 TEXAS	665974	658187	103631	6357	82	46649	22184	9024	11714
43 UTAH	3514	238319	956	0	1466	6178	0	181	1019
44 VERMONT	0	74184	179	0	0	177	265	8772	170
45 VIRGINIA	239645	23690	107609	0	0	4589	6606	1330	1324
46 WASHINGTON	66105	486939	161861	55154	0	3458	495	466	1131
47 WEST VIRGINIA	26618	121	12917	29839	0	0	2923	1148	7169
48 WISCONSIN	2347367	5707	40982	11804	33533	28964	30569	58639	11733
49 WYOMING	0	1828	0	0	0	89	1162	95	0
50 ALASKA	0	0	0	0	0	0	0	0	0
51 HAWAII	900	0	1453	0	0	0	0	0	0
52 SUM OF STATE OUTPUTS	39276576	13630173	2033385	1560366	188871	884275	541186	1632739	978611

NOTE: The 152 column numbers are identical with the 152 product-mix industry numbers given in Table A-2, pages 134-145, and refer to that industrial classification.

TABLE C-11

1963 STATE ESTABLISHMENT OUTPUTS FOR MANUFACTURING AND SERVICES
(THOUSANDS OF CURRENT DOLLARS)

	118	119	120	121	122	123	124	125	126
1 ALABAMA	810	0	0	0	3512	0	10133	308	7546
2 ARIZONA	0	194	0	781	2287	497	766	481	3908
3 ARKANSAS	34266	97	0	0	158	8749	24938	308	6683
4 CALIFORNIA	1555	38790	2171	86343	42144	12551	197159	59732	144289
5 COLORADO	0	291	81	4349	2771	209	4968	6453	8901
6 CONNECTICUT	83076	28272	5775	7279	183355	7151	27730	39663	84177
7 DELAWARE	0	0	0	0	596	0	0	138	732
8 DISTRICT OF COLUMBIA	0	0	0	0	0	0	0	0	2069
9 FLORIDA	111	3257	13311	1112	4182	348	7898	1585	23089
10 GEORGIA	13183	0	414	0	11121	0	15231	25386	15085
11 IDAHO	0	0	0	0	205	0	2562	138	0
12 ILLINOIS	99404	10374	6740	184289	40491	98548	165523	46930	217152
13 INDIANA	7676	194	5147	25269	20162	42826	16771	3849	66831
14 IOWA	12960	0	494	1609	11754	209	21091	27491	22275
15 KANSAS	0	0	0	781	578	1160	1643	1920	2592
16 KENTUCKY	4247	0	1032	221	4426	139	8058	3955	10406
17 LOUISIANA	111	0	81	1720	528	70	7042	779	8293
18 MAINE	0	0	81	0	2005	0	7995	138	5652
19 MARYLAND	1364	1385	5238	442	6908	7221	9059	481	23332
20 MASSACHUSETTS	61575	21138	57916	147096	159202	4044	119025	21477	100766
21 MICHIGAN	3725	6698	1069	4717	8406	23706	134893	10899	63029
22 MINNESOTA	111	1128	4450	19019	14703	70	34586	4470	32235
23 MISSISSIPPI	4136	97	0	0	3980	28103	727	0	3008
24 MISSOURI	0	3421	5355	7562	5802	0	34746	11246	34271
25 MONTANA	0	0	0	0	343	0	536	69	2159
26 NEBRASKA	0	97	81	221	10711	70	1406	984	3464
27 NEVADA	0	0	0	0	246	0	535	69	2388
28 NEW HAMPSHIRE	0	6117	0	0	4868	1090	9766	138	8039
29 NEW JERSEY	7002	2874	10169	106037	116699	5528	130256	54869	138903
30 NEW MEXICO	0	0	0	0	2119	70	70	138	1654
31 NEW YORK	105930	47609	84897	1157732	637794	34461	365102	115784	370637
32 NORTH CAROLINA	7454	0	242	20479	11970	4623	5749	481	15612
33 NORTH DAKOTA	0	0	0	0	4692	0	140	0	126
34 OHIO	810	1225	2633	5214	11755	13952	112279	29253	142697
35 OKLAHOMA	188	97	81	0	2232	0	6587	516	7043
36 OREGON	0	387	0	9399	2288	567	6553	1250	10528
37 PENNSYLVANIA	39546	12127	17764	10136	41135	10134	111984	36200	267321
38 RHODE ISLAND	7084	194	9517	1609	238398	567	22314	5371	9405
39 SOUTH CAROLINA	0	0	4824	9178	13049	5852	22732	206	10814
40 SOUTH DAKOTA	0	0	0	0	644	0	108	69	1169
41 TENNESSEE	7342	0	161	110	2705	9385	26267	25332	26496
42 TEXAS	13183	3354	3003	2335	8015	139	21753	4087	36057
43 UTAH	0	0	161	221	5280	209	333	526	6792
44 VERMONT	0	0	4824	0	612	70	1320	0	5062
45 VIRGINIA	0	0	21961	2288	12080	1160	36475	4300	13788
46 WASHINGTON	111	741	870	331	2994	3106	5489	1449	14467
47 WEST VIRGINIA	0	3707	0	0	238	0	8609	275	1713
48 WISCONSIN	13993	387	161	4016	4297	10673	35936	24236	60050
49 WYOMING	0	0	0	0	78	0	0	0	0
50 ALASKA	0	0	0	0	0	0	0	0	0
51 HAWAII	0	0	0	110	1011	70	218	138	1116
52 SUM OF STATE OUTPUTS	530953	194250	270706	1822005	1665529	337326	1785059	573563	2043818

NOTE: The 152 column numbers are identical with the 152 product-mix industry numbers given in Table A-2, pages 134-145, and refer to that industrial classification.

TABLE C-11

1963 STATE ESTABLISHMENT OUTPUTS FOR MANUFACTURING AND SERVICES

(THOUSANDS OF CURRENT DOLLARS)

	127	128	129	130	131	132	133	134	135
1 ALABAMA	271296	24229	41535	29099	23043	201786	19161	474277	440983
2 ARIZONA	141228	15933	0	21097	0	90878	14158	267713	236585
3 ARKANSAS	195471	9991	1309	3949	6620	87045	9244	205627	204208
4 CALIFORNIA	2152073	354868	505353	742592	28023	1538711	342161	2126718	4540123
5 COLORADO	310233	23062	70	84248	11630	144861	19094	307689	437776
6 CONNECTICUT	267544	49694	10114	9209	0	209037	19772	322354	500493
7 DELAWARE	66603	5703	9548	4308	0	34929	4163	69033	124162
8 DISTRICT OF COLUMBIA	140216	82099	7691	114766	124	111711	51476	72853	272641
9 FLORIDA	412865	60432	98382	437745	0	418738	53742	567611	999227
10 GEORGIA	504286	35814	13544	162813	26910	293385	31846	472985	1027500
11 IDAHO	107009	4347	637	3482	0	42032	5528	98738	96741
12 ILLINOIS	2201342	345944	72073	291456	56109	692073	158161	1754134	3533534
13 INDIANA	716474	41159	19645	22885	9464	340051	35698	814738	812800
14 IOWA	350439	19712	672	5652	10145	157997	25253	399323	518570
15 KANSAS	388740	12932	4403	5272	72069	136425	25519	336602	367741
16 KENTUCKY	356663	38337	24277	14099	11507	174780	22180	380586	398299
17 LOUISIANA	318988	42146	331804	40817	55119	277900	26383	466977	597479
18 MAINE	100200	7251	8877	1238	8785	48568	7346	79975	137259
19 MARYLAND	421124	60582	123315	12237	463	231574	23935	477373	584752
20 MASSACHUSETTS	553899	186372	68571	92918	0	408974	63674	739190	1350635
21 MICHIGAN	952305	55038	24791	65841	7454	624314	77097	1233010	1747227
22 MINNESOTA	514436	55148	8646	54250	16981	222784	30276	483609	985555
23 MISSISSIPPI	139660	7388	21324	3557	7888	115259	10997	267965	227736
24 MISSOURI	803092	77223	39652	201089	35787	307176	42274	571994	1458654
25 MONTANA	118617	6072	0	5663	6155	38173	6953	142364	99762
26 NEBRASKA	283248	14119	0	10427	9063	116226	15493	135409	352276
27 NEVADA	61951	17678	0	15455	0	15637	4819	75819	59243
28 NEW HAMPSHIRE	52060	5045	831	942	0	34202	3646	82031	71519
29 NEW JERSEY	1046072	170429	252553	82142	11320	476454	12197	893730	1669786
30 NEW MEXICO	117371	10360	0	9220	13269	57458	8853	161515	111705
31 NEW YORK	2403906	463708	1048757	780794	6032	1573441	541721	2247913	8613043
32 NORTH CAROLINA	492586	41508	12767	40213	4671	256293	34438	414547	867333
33 NORTH DAKOTA	84630	3629	0	1567	0	45595	5396	54146	129480
34 OHIO	1555144	119758	94545	56917	44324	709944	104323	1760925	2268539
35 OKLAHOMA	222874	16401	70	107694	119177	169959	18982	317367	420570
36 OREGON	306349	24867	118487	14640	0	137271	18948	159845	544093
37 PENNSYLVANIA	1716248	269708	216358	75696	47634	701265	126202	1690451	2345494
38 RHODE ISLAND	79916	16472	10927	3081	0	63906	10305	97706	174685
39 SOUTH CAROLINA	157679	10460	25109	7504	0	118757	15926	208176	268697
40 SOUTH DAKOTA	55682	2871	0	3504	0	33985	6586	59949	104238
41 TENNESSEE	438558	43772	13544	28157	1856	291747	33221	174668	782968
42 TEXAS	1225627	101252	292355	204317	337054	774675	88734	1368715	2247667
43 UTAH	171550	10319	70	10892	371	80983	8130	166411	184025
44 VERMONT	51476	4299	0	1091	0	17842	2936	43331	37806
45 VIRGINIA	494092	68529	77854	103853	6495	259185	31111	496624	558193
46 WASHINGTON	385517	27160	226313	89541	0	228267	28029	186739	678717
47 WEST VIRGINIA	259673	19991	26434	3726	6464	97412	13869	394060	184026
48 WISCONSIN	493054	62057	8417	12237	0	211171	33852	532895	717844
49 WYOMING	73293	3340	0	2476	24529	19939	3347	97124	36082
50 ALASKA	45200	3539	19963	41251	0	5745	3338	15677	29595
51 HAWAII	53930	12423	64752	54271	0	48447	7473	58592	106091
52 SUM OF STATE OUTPUTS	24832480	3165170	3946337	4191887	1026536	13494967	2307966	25027792	45264144

NOTE: The 152 column numbers are identical with the 152 product-mix industry numbers given in Table A-2, pages 134-145, and refer to that industrial classification.

TABLE C-11

1963 STATE ESTABLISHMENT OUTPUTS FOR MANUFACTURING AND SERVICES

(THOUSANDS OF CURRENT DOLLARS)

	136	137	138	139	140	141	142	143	144
1 ALABAMA	904945	100601	14955	9213	210755	37340	432567	348176	159105
2 ARIZONA	581056	76651	17045	10512	78373	31336	248057	419126	156335
3 ARKANSAS	548634	61112	8881	6123	74989	31365	205120	164722	99217
4 CALIFORNIA	7930601	1148306	398725	292075	1269941	491586	4197541	4587406	1779234
5 COLORADO	769333	102791	36969	21665	131704	42399	396156	401717	177808
6 CONNECTICUT	1151303	157961	26474	31085	454537	66020	739581	404161	210906
7 DELAWARE	208981	40410	12145	6535	21658	7674	101907	93945	31984
8 DISTRICT OF COLUMBIA	464968	56767	19065	23502	104091	41057	181318	820332	172012
9 FLORIDA	2180217	232981	70274	52418	370208	144175	1178123	1758203	653524
10 GEORGIA	1285960	178867	26043	25187	315928	79128	544814	555495	261300
11 IDAHO	268159	33272	3809	1455	22199	8973	137758	61418	47567
12 ILLINOIS	4564929	699503	124189	182016	942642	317993	2493130	3157864	992013
13 INDIANA	1870359	214885	42133	16484	323373	94145	957039	537773	328264
14 IOWA	1115403	139683	17069	11687	170147	39114	546811	252126	182794
15 KANSAS	785044	112106	18697	8473	102602	34815	409906	237869	134529
16 KENTUCKY	899795	106182	15913	8943	136983	39265	458396	189630	179038
17 LOUISIANA	973115	127942	22103	15084	190992	75020	537301	404643	173860
18 MAINE	331574	36693	3230	4478	38172	22530	155864	59100	74314
19 MARYLAND	1251791	121582	21684	23388	222125	58450	631421	866881	224574
20 MASSACHUSETTS	2235459	364306	61966	108451	649725	188088	1126024	949803	455466
21 MICHIGAN	3085609	359606	62578	52454	402153	153208	1899457	978298	574872
22 MINNESOTA	1333931	201418	76868	37171	245948	72289	869766	582490	251176
23 MISSISSIPPI	525072	65413	6722	3292	70252	27678	246201	139730	98330
24 MISSOURI	1731229	266950	52476	61238	347602	112675	907928	947629	356472
25 MONTANA	276048	40027	3105	1787	18544	11242	134181	72236	51421
26 NEBRASKA	605468	83984	9799	10525	156611	27829	251398	233184	107335
27 NEVADA	196105	28475	13137	1671	14348	10346	75787	187816	180461
28 NEW HAMPSHIRE	247743	23398	2680	1135	43992	17557	119245	58917	64516
29 NEW JERSEY	2716173	330831	52994	45361	492031	138115	1644125	1301175	561287
30 NEW MEXICO	330233	36603	9202	2589	29644	16946	167398	147512	73256
31 NEW YORK	7447768	2131905	416458	1272762	1978952	702378	3429420	8522246	2050792
32 NORTH CAROLINA	1393617	154663	26967	17863	250821	74409	552479	415796	287442
33 NORTH DAKOTA	247240	34386	4037	2438	21659	6436	110511	35892	36250
34 OHIO	3532868	468622	107983	76665	584888	185047	2447984	1426246	704730
35 OKLAHOMA	781809	125133	30048	18373	116409	42235	370477	427758	148650
36 OREGON	770110	91427	12978	17007	101790	47849	386750	305667	152259
37 PENNSYLVANIA	4099961	652825	84218	138031	774255	201370	2221619	1657137	846450
38 RHODE ISLAND	335936	46761	5417	8167	81487	25185	164327	148791	65057
39 SOUTH CAROLINA	629315	59175	11101	4735	132516	40534	247449	166955	123623
40 SOUTH DAKOTA	247237	37813	2239	904	21252	11557	109479	65549	39703
41 TENNESSEE	1124898	140756	18216	22599	242699	65241	505914	366967	235386
42 TEXAS	3592230	516071	110003	76573	795236	185202	1512660	1525810	750623
43 UTAH	345046	46571	9742	6278	43315	15782	207798	156591	64195
44 VERMONT	151376	17543	578	1121	21387	8198	67402	22954	37364
45 VIRGINIA	1366087	175130	17606	15247	219282	63272	677744	702984	284079
46 WASHINGTON	1190503	141848	29713	27790	157829	70705	681981	693270	219631
47 WEST VIRGINIA	501068	59026	4849	2474	52926	25426	242227	151008	94002
48 WISCONSIN	1534270	174810	27369	27355	246760	79380	942039	450483	279477
49 WYOMING	136797	18687	2631	368	7986	3181	72381	35908	41362
50 ALASKA	87437	13573	956	0	3384	6718	24192	36125	19506
51 HAWAII	228204	65491	11132	6136	31539	16138	126011	265743	74310
52 SUM OF STATE OUTPUTS	71113072	10721523	2185171	2818882	13538639	4314599	37095216	38499248	15367859

NOTE: The 152 column numbers are identical with the 152 product-mix industry numbers given in Table A-2, pages 134-145, and refer to that industrial classification.

TABLE C-11

1963 STATE ESTABLISHMENT OUTPUTS FOR
MANUFACTURING AND SERVICES
(THOUSANDS OF CURRENT DOLLARS)

	145	146	147	148	149	150	151	152	153 TOTAL
1 ALABAMA	84459	93209	146860	34684	114383	84241	162738	143014	10806967
2 ARIZONA	70964	86216	102107	42623	90465	66625	40293	64778	4819213
3 ARKANSAS	31709	34473	85904	32522	51188	37699	50550	31589	5214188
4 CALIFORNIA	1841430	1614624	1352518	1550866	1775066	1307297	611840	736925	85012640
5 COLORADO	99986	115002	136559	70703	165856	122150	62343	65777	6879467
6 CONNECTICUT	146651	156611	161577	57325	438104	322654	64519	67417	14523266
7 DELAWARE	17540	29171	27337	23418	39857	29354	13218	13216	2741042
8 DISTRICT OF COLUMBIA	138247	215387	88294	54657	679778	500642	148710	17944	5066872
9 FLORIDA	337460	319803	342625	249580	323552	238289	167547	236554	17524576
10 GEORGIA	164588	136736	218983	70834	230453	169723	144043	106731	15839377
11 IDAHO	34764	17670	45489	13613	26959	19855	16652	27015	2134297
12 ILLINOIS	1505602	767941	599902	415753	1424992	1049475	311664	395619	61289360
13 INDIANA	145356	146000	247273	91101	370102	272572	98816	128403	25850080
14 IOWA	93836	76852	153951	56446	194427	143191	61915	102838	11439889
15 KANSAS	57858	63707	132485	43297	102925	75802	67703	78833	8227252
16 KENTUCKY	67921	72012	134269	66234	168550	124133	107787	61969	10374667
17 LOUISIANA	141555	130112	148731	72531	197465	145428	67535	80270	11658780
18 MAINE	18452	23352	50686	17993	70590	51988	31128	40543	3444844
19 MARYLAND	209732	157514	212344	124273	407481	300101	91216	91683	13700777
20 MASSACHUSETTS	381923	439678	291799	167345	1408478	1037314	181933	202896	26797872
21 MICHIGAN	701303	487367	500873	212968	534467	393623	161057	353681	48295312
22 MINNESOTA	265055	176435	191688	80397	299073	220260	97516	127521	14737484
23 MISSISSIPPI	37281	41353	86192	21856	52300	38518	47734	33417	4723893
24 MISSOURI	314862	235220	256426	113171	501218	369136	150729	88769	21298128
25 MONTANA	13932	21574	43562	12515	28359	20886	21236	25618	2180084
26 NEBRASKA	65019	57733	90307	40775	97954	72141	47611	160009	5755701
27 NEVADA	24820	39241	33966	248782	14426	10625	16893	10145	1667681
28 NEW HAMPSHIRE	17202	19935	35939	29708	93872	69135	16579	38832	2620794
29 NEW JERSEY	444003	384078	354193	233071	570862	420427	162662	161703	35718464
30 NEW MEXICO	38558	38266	53869	22166	37867	27888	29648	21973	2147581
31 NEW YORK	4026854	2094488	947263	2014204	3544355	2610339	595015	782680	103881120
32 NORTH CAROLINA	105330	110471	202397	70172	310683	228811	110279	171869	20251696
33 NORTH DAKOTA	13141	9599	36238	10382	22940	16895	20678	8746	1346995
34 OHIO	621561	470170	526377	285915	926923	682658	234407	476327	54469696
35 OKLAHOMA	102073	106296	144044	45968	120504	88748	72416	72770	7650377
36 OREGON	87222	90078	133113	45446	134608	99135	58532	102565	8264672
37 PENNSYLVANIA	680400	634276	619574	238807	1429905	1053093	273176	488781	54797216
38 RHODE ISLAND	42579	30790	38633	37079	109362	80543	29606	14346	3843274
39 SOUTH CAROLINA	44615	58912	96281	29124	89190	65687	64929	44276	8374645
40 SOUTH DAKOTA	12515	13005	37091	18282	31588	23264	19060	18355	1684819
41 TENNESSEE	169984	91096	179323	60493	277253	204191	256110	239455	13433572
42 TEXAS	550888	438519	610415	196261	576144	424318	284549	355233	39982480
43 UTAH	43301	32826	57335	28826	114670	84452	24197	40531	3620783
44 VERMONT	7688	10479	22654	14631	81245	59835	11125	17500	1457206
45 VIRGINIA	129420	143124	193657	67051	253543	186729	165269	195412	14459177
46 WASHINGTON	124021	149107	186891	78544	210263	154854	153241	323928	12215204
47 WEST VIRGINIA	81195	31499	62395	47337	94574	69651	31148	55536	6425957
48 WISCONSIN	182734	161517	205854	82200	166911	122927	81729	67792	19933056
49 WYOMING	9455	10275	21573	8984	10789	7946	9314	14506	1252982
50 ALASKA	10500	14094	8795	6640	10715	7892	54178	13428	681452
51 HAWAII	30210	44964	36639	22550	68815	50681	61326	16278	2393760
52 SUM OF STATE OUTPUTS	14587755	10942856	10693305	7680101	19096048	14063818	5864099	7235999	862910720

NOTE: The 152 column numbers are identical with the 152 product-mix industry numbers given in Table A-2, pages 134-145, and refer to that industrial classification.

TABLE C-12

1963 DIRECTLY ALLOCATED IMPORTS BY STATE
(THOUSANDS OF CURRENT DOLLARS)

INDUSTRY TITLE	1 ALABAMA	2 ARIZONA	3 ARKANSAS	4 CALIFORNIA	5 COLORADO	6 CONNECTICUT	7 DELAWARE	8 DISTRICT OF COLUMBIA	9 FLORIDA
1 LIVESTOCK, PRDTS.	5	490	5	142	222	2	0	0	5
2 OTHER AGRICULTURE PRDTS.	8	17148	4294	104986	6437	2	1	0	38526
3 FORESTRY, FISHERIES	14	2	9	67	1	1	1	0	26
4 AGRI.,FORES.,FISH. SERV.	23	12	35	66	4	3	3	0	19
5 IRON, FERRO. ORES MINING	1	0	0	3	7	0	0	0	0
6 NONFERROUS ORES MINING	0	63	3	1	13	0	0	0	2
7 COAL MINING	8	1	0	0	4	0	0	0	0
8 CRUDE PETRO.,NATURAL GAS	4	0	14	207	26	0	0	0	0
9 STONE, CLAY MINING	5	2	7	36	3	3	0	0	10
10 CHEM.,FERT. MIN. MINING	0	0	0	3	0	0	0	0	10
11 NEW CONSTRUCTION	159	99	73	1865	200	150	42	109	431
12 MAINT., REPAIR CONSTR.	57	46	46	625	66	67	11	20	151
13 ORDNANCE, ACCESSORIES	25	29	0	865	12	41	0	0	73
14 FOOD, KINDRED PRDTS.	9872	6074	16138	133610	4352	4053	1197	2639	20520
15 TOBACCO MANUFACTURES	6	0	0	0	0	1	0	0	26
16 FABRICS	5282	2	163	242	3	1775	509	0	69
17 TEXTILE PRDTS.	1524	5	153	2196	23	1347	373	0	54
18 APPAREL	371	30	98	1021	20	224	59	0	122
19 MISC. TEXTILE PRDTS.	6	1	0	34	1	5	1	0	3
20 LUMBER, WOOD PRDTS.	27	6	29	143	4	5	2	0	20
21 WOODEN CONTAINERS	2	0	4	19	1	1	0	0	5
22 HOUSEHOLD FURNITURE	15	4	35	157	6	14	0	0	28
23 OTHER FURNITURE	2	1	4	37	1	6	0	0	4
24 PAPER, ALLIED PRDTS.	46	1	28	117	4	18	1	0	43
25 PAPERBOARD CONTAINERS	2	1	5	54	2	9	1	0	9
26 PRINTING, PUBLISHING	43	33	27	640	60	151	12	150	127
27 CHEMICALS,SELECT. PRDTS.	1252	186	269	3351	202	967	192	36	1425
28 PLASTICS, SYNTHETICS	24	0	0	37	0	17	40	0	29
29 DRUGS, COSMETICS	3	4	0	521	10	250	15	0	20
30 PAINT, ALLIED PRDTS.	43	16	21	1658	56	46	4	0	230
31 PETROLEUM, RELATED INDS.	8	1	10	128	5	4	8	0	7
32 RUBBER, MISC. PLASTICS	9733	56	1761	17857	5546	8575	1113	0	123
33 LEATHER TANNING, PRDTS.	0	0	0	98	2	11	112	0	7
34 FOOTWEAR, LEATHER PRDTS.	6	0	46	25	8	14	1	0	8
35 GLASS, GLASS PRDTS.	2	0	3	40	0	3	0	0	4
36 STONE, CLAY PRDTS.	129	27	34	1484	78	331	6	4	157
37 PRIMARY IRON, STEEL MFR.	116	2	1	92	18	27	16	0	4
38 PRIMARY NONFERROUS MFR.	152	377	99	289	6	324	7	0	31

39 METAL CONTAINERS	2	0	1	62	3	1	0	0	12
40 FABRICATED METAL PRDTS.	53	10	12	250	15	29	7	1	59
41 SCREW MACH. PRDTS., ETC.	8	0	2	61	1	49	1	0	2
42 OTHER FAB. METAL PRDTS.	28	4	8	232	12	81	3	0	14
43 ENGINES, TURBINES	0	0	0	20	1	14	0	0	0
44 FARM MACH., EQUIP.	5	1	1	17	2	1	0	0	2
45 CONSTRUC. MACH., EQUIP.	2	0	0	30	21	0	0	0	1
46 MATERIAL HANDLING MACH.	2	0	2	20	1	1	0	0	1
47 METALWORKING MACHINERY	20	13	28	800	7	1119	20	0	54
48 SPECIAL MACH., EQUIP.	56	3	9	501	22	284	55	0	65
49 GENERAL MACH., EQUIP.	3	1	3	119	6	112	0	0	3
50 MACHINE SHOP PRDTS.	4	5	2	114	6	26	1	1	8
51 OFFICE, COMPUT. MACHINES	0	50	4	247	1	93	0	0	19
52 SERVICE IND. MACHINES	4	7	4	30	0	6	1	0	2
53 ELECT. TRANSMISS. EQUIP.	15	2	70	403	38	149	0	0	7
54 HOUSEHOLD APPLIANCES	0	0	35	56	0	54	1	0	1
55 ELECTRIC LIGHTING EQUIP.	11	0	8	68	1	55	1	0	3
56 RADIO, TV, ETC., EQUIP.	3	29	26	671	1	42	0	0	65
57 ELECTRONIC COMPONENTS	27	118	0	1136	3	242	1	0	44
58 MISC. ELECTRICAL MACH.	4	0	0	28	2	11	2	0	9
59 MOTOR VEHICLES, EQUIP.	6	1	1	225	2	21	41	0	1
60 AIRCRAFT, PARTS	203	48	0	1263	48	514	3	0	59
61 OTHER TRANSPORT. EQUIP.	23	2	14	137	3	20	1	0	37
62 PROFESS., SCIEN. INSTRU.	1	20	9	227	12	143	7	0	20
63 MEDICAL, PHOTO. EQUIP.	0	0	0	57	2	26	0	0	13
64 MISC. MANUFACTURING	245	159	26	3261	224	12639	41	1	302
65 TRANSPORT., WAREHOUSING	7423	1251	823	104128	4383	2395	1614	6291	32823
66 COMMUNICA.,EXC. BRDCAST.	631	284	272	4811	453	654	109	349	1309
67 RADIO, TV BROADCASTING	15	11	7	273	15	16	3	41	43
68 ELEC.,GAS,WATER,SAN.SER.	69	39	30	308	45	47	10	11	82
69 WHOLESALE, RETAIL TRADE	646	357	314	6494	627	747	177	389	1478
70 FINANCE, INSURANCE	2183	841	794	13812	1415	4699	243	1117	3948
71 REAL ESTATE, RENTAL	25	30	12	325	28	29	7	58	125
72 HOTELS, PERSONAL SERV.	73	71	45	812	81	96	15	78	298
73 BUSINESS SERVICES	212	191	79	3946	258	359	60	448	762
74 RESEARCH, DEVELOPMENT	0	0	0	0	0	0	0	0	0
75 AUTO. REPAIR, SERVICES	21	15	13	198	20	24	4	13	50
76 AMUSEMENTS	631	776	592	28228	1287	1043	426	995	4543
77 MED.,EDUC. SERVICES	107	85	48	1662	155	410	37	637	303
78 FEDERAL GOVT. ENTERPRISE	6674	1652	2073	25091	2557	2646	542	6099	6871
79 STATE, LOCAL GOVT. ENT.	7	3	1	34	3	3	1	1	11
80 ZERO ENTRIES	0	0	0	0	0	0	0	0	0
81 SERVICE IND. RESIDUAL	-172238	-109766	-94158	-1454540	-149015	-170947	-33824	-162703	-378563
82 TOTAL FINAL DEMAND	123821	78967	65376	981668	119854	123602	26663	143216	262786
83 SECONDARY TRANSFERS-OUT	0	0	0	0	0	0	0	0	0
84 ZERO ENTRIES	0	0	0	0	0	0	0	0	0
85 SCRAP ENTRIES	0	0	0	0	0	0	0	0	0
86 ZERO ENTRIES	0	0	0	0	0	0	0	0	0
87 STATE TOTAL CONSUMPTION	0	0	0	0	0	0	0	0	0

TABLE C-12

1963 DIRECTLY ALLOCATED IMPORTS BY STATE
(THOUSANDS OF CURRENT DOLLARS)

INDUSTRY TITLE	10 GEORGIA	11 IDAHO	12 ILLINOIS	13 INDIANA	14 IOWA	15 KANSAS	16 KENTUCKY	17 LOUISIANA	18 MAINE
1 LIVESTOCK, PRDTS.	7	13	13	8	52	21	6	3	3
2 OTHER AGRICULTURE PRDTS.	16	30	31	16	41	41	14	12	2
3 FORESTRY, FISHERIES	21	4	2	1	1	0	3	30	17
4 AGRI.,FORES.,FISH. SERV.	35	4	23	13	19	9	4	11	5
5 IRON, FERRO. ORES MINING	0	0	0	0	0	0	0	0	0
6 NONFERROUS ORES MINING	0	7	3	0	0	0	0	0	0
7 COAL MINING	3	0	34	9	1	1	29	0	0
8 CRUDE PETRO.,NATURAL GAS	0	0	46	6	0	85	16	475	0
9 STONE, CLAY MINING	20	1	18	9	8	4	9	4	0
10 CHEM.,FERT. MIN. MINING	0	0	0	0	0	0	0	8	0
11 NEW CONSTRUCTION	256	27	506	241	114	111	133	252	28
12 MAINT., REPAIR CONSTR.	75	24	287	124	96	87	62	66	19
13 ORDNANCE, ACCESSORIES	1	1	30	37	22	0	0	23	4
14 FOOD, KINDRED PRDTS.	27004	573	201662	33624	38140	10147	17389	30282	1470
15 TOBACCO MANUFACTURES	4	0	5	4	0	0	203	1	0
16 FABRICS	12734	0	380	0	36	2	250	0	2236
17 TEXTILE PRDTS.	4991	0	2158	194	6	5	70	201	310
18 APPAREL	682	1	513	166	36	40	236	73	44
19 MISC. TEXTILE PRDTS.	23	0	28	5	1	2	4	5	2
20 LUMBER, WOOD PRDTS.	30	21	32	33	8	1	11	21	20
21 WOODEN CONTAINERS	7	0	4	1	1	0	5	2	1
22 HOUSEHOLD FURNITURE	36	1	84	107	8	5	25	6	2
23 OTHER FURNITURE	3	0	39	13	4	2	2	1	1
24 PAPER, ALLIED PRDTS.	65	2	115	40	11	5	13	57	44
25 PAPERBOARD CONTAINERS	19	0	54	18	6	7	6	7	1
26 PRINTING, PUBLISHING	84	9	994	188	133	56	65	42	15
27 CHEMICALS,SELECT. PRDTS.	2470	78	5979	1187	156	629	691	2712	78
28 PLASTICS, SYNTHETICS	12	0	22	9	18	4	47	39	0
29 DRUGS, COSMETICS	99	0	1005	588	50	129	2	11	0
30 PAINT, ALLIED PRDTS.	318	1	2127	242	203	42	449	62	3
31 PETROLEUM, RELATED INDS.	10	0	85	43	1	26	8	76	1
32 RUBBER, MISC. PLASTICS	1684	0	5780	11478	9127	4492	1745	1	283
33 LEATHER TANNING, PRDTS.	41	0	264	11	0	0	25	2	219
34 FOOTWEAR, LEATHER PRDTS.	26	0	82	19	2	1	19	0	150
35 GLASS, GLASS PRDTS.	5	0	53	33	0	0	6	6	0
36 STONE, CLAY PRDTS.	117	7	1620	621	37	473	132	228	4
37 PRIMARY IRON, STEEL MFR.	17	0	229	276	10	4	25	3	0
38 PRIMARY NONFERROUS MFR.	33	94	401	385	53	12	51	100	3

39 METAL CONTAINERS	6	0	64	7	0	1	1	9	2
40 FABRICATED METAL PRDTS.	43	3	179	114	33	27	32	28	5
41 SCREW MACH. PRDTS., ETC.	6	0	168	41	3	1	6	1	0
42 OTHER FAB. METAL PRDTS.	17	0	348	103	23	9	43	16	1
43 ENGINES, TURBINES	0	0	55	19	10	0	0	0	0
44 FARM MACH., EQUIP.	8	1	144	28	133	9	16	3	0
45 CONSTRUC. MACH., EQUIP.	7	0	304	23	39	7	0	6	3
46 MATERIAL HANDLING MACH.	3	0	45	3	3	3	6	0	0
47 METALWORKING MACHINERY	28	1	2347	522	121	34	46	4	10
48 SPECIAL MACH., EQUIP.	158	2	907	179	84	58	54	37	24
49 GENERAL MACH., EQUIP.	3	0	137	99	11	7	17	1	1
50 MACHINE SHOP PRDTS.	4	1	65	46	3	11	11	6	1
51 OFFICE, COMPUT. MACHINES	1	0	103	1	0	0	26	0	0
52 SERVICE IND. MACHINES	4	0	55	27	11	6	16	1	1
53 ELECT. TRANSMISS. EQUIP.	65	0	459	336	17	4	53	2	3
54 HOUSEHOLD APPLIANCES	1	0	178	89	43	0	82	0	0
55 ELECTRIC LIGHTING EQUIP.	8	0	120	54	0	1	20	0	2
56 RADIO, TV, ETC., EQUIP.	0	0	540	229	30	2	4	0	1
57 ELECTRONIC COMPONENTS	4	1	521	280	82	24	46	1	30
58 MISC. ELECTRICAL MACH.	7	0	46	147	5	6	3	1	1
59 MOTOR VEHICLES, EQUIP.	73	0	92	184	3	22	23	2	0
60 AIRCRAFT, PARTS	80	1	44	168	2	260	0	42	6
61 OTHER TRANSPORT. EQUIP.	27	7	80	114	12	22	8	41	21
62 PROFESS., SCIEN. INSTRU.	10	0	391	67	28	3	10	4	0
63 MEDICAL, PHOTO. EQUIP.	0	0	76	13	1	0	1	1	0
64 MISC. MANUFACTURING	886	15	3140	1431	943	50	325	45	141
65 TRANSPORT., WAREHOUSING	10016	496	27475	5343	1192	1773	4700	46528	1477
66 COMMUNICA.,EXC. BRDCAST.	917	131	2164	1063	494	427	547	869	152
67 RADIO, TV BROADCASTING	25	4	126	28	20	20	18	21	6
68 ELEC.,GAS,WATER,SAN.SER.	68	14	254	118	58	49	55	68	12
69 WHOLESALE, RETAIL TRADE	1413	149	4874	1213	765	542	592	847	207
70 FINANCE, INSURANCE	3300	237	10037	3392	1781	1091	1438	2015	408
71 REAL ESTATE, RENTAL	39	4	224	38	18	17	13	29	4
72 HOTELS, PERSONAL SERV.	119	22	452	150	83	61	82	79	34
73 BUSINESS SERVICES	341	54	2337	341	192	145	166	313	51
74 RESEARCH, DEVELOPMENT	0	0	0	0	0	0	0	0	0
75 AUTO. REPAIR, SERVICES	32	7	88	36	23	19	20	22	7
76 AMUSEMENTS	1289	248	7567	1658	1027	788	1206	1320	327
77 MED.,EDUC. SERVICES	216	25	1335	347	182	96	158	185	66
78 FEDERAL GOVT. ENTERPRISE	5907	683	12781	4052	2539	2776	4420	2770	1277
79 STATE, LOCAL GOVT. ENT.	5	1	18	6	5	4	3	4	2
80 ZERO ENTRIES	0	0	0	0	0	0	0	0	0
81 SERVICE IND. RESIDUAL	-300981	-35768	-760643	-248920	-151411	-146761	-179058	-222808	-59871
82 TOTAL FINAL DEMAND	224896	32758	455595	177059	92990	121942	143036	132668	50623
83 SECONDARY TRANSFERS-OUT	0	0	0	0	0	0	0	0	0
84 ZERO ENTRIES	0	0	0	0	0	0	0	0	0
85 SCRAP ENTRIES	0	0	0	0	0	0	0	0	0
86 ZERO ENTRIES	0	0	0	0	0	0	0	0	0
87 STATE TOTAL CONSUMPTION	0	0	0	0	0	0	0	0	0

TABLE C-12

1963 DIRECTLY ALLOCATED IMPORTS BY STATE
(THOUSANDS OF CURRENT DOLLARS)

INDUSTRY TITLE	19 MARYLAND	20 MASSA-CHUSETTS	21 MICHIGAN	22 MINNESOTA	23 MISSISSIPPI	24 MISSOURI	25 MONTANA	26 NEBRASKA	27 NEVADA
1 LIVESTOCK, PRDTS.	3	2	223	37	6	24	10	26	3
2 OTHER AGRICULTURE PRDTS.	4	3	6435	30	18	31	30	37	2
3 FORESTRY, FISHERIES	9	27	5	3	13	3	2	0	0
4 AGRI.,FORES.,FISH. SERV.	11	2	7	18	31	19	2	8	0
5 IRON, FERRO. ORES MINING	12	0	12	50	0	0	0	0	0
6 NONFERROUS ORES MINING	0	0	6	0	0	3	14	0	9
7 COAL MINING	1	0	0	0	0	2	0	0	0
8 CRUDE PETRO.,NATURAL GAS	0	0	12	0	40	0	16	12	0
9 STONE, CLAY MINING	8	4	14	5	2	11	1	3	3
10 CHEM.,FERT. MIN. MINING	0	0	1	0	0	1	1	0	0
11 NEW CONSTRUCTION	263	253	360	179	68	179	36	79	80
12 MAINT., REPAIR CONSTR.	77	115	182	105	42	120	36	61	20
13 ORDNANCE, ACCESSORIES	5	28	28	36	0	42	0	0	0
14 FOOD, KINDRED PRDTS.	13565	30461	14929	31752	13119	30841	754	12670	69
15 TOBACCO MANUFACTURES	0	0	3	0	0	5	0	0	0
16 FABRICS	432	4651	51	150	269	192	0	0	0
17 TEXTILE PRDTS.	40	5178	1859	414	220	741	0	0	0
18 APPAREL	389	771	83	97	318	435	0	16	0
19 MISC. TEXTILE PRDTS.	6	23	71	5	3	11	0	0	0
20 LUMBER, WOOD PRDTS.	9	15	30	20	40	12	18	4	1
21 WOODEN CONTAINERS	2	2	2	1	7	2	0	0	0
22 HOUSEHOLD FURNITURE	14	51	46	9	36	17	0	4	0
23 OTHER FURNITURE	7	7	44	4	1	8	0	2	0
24 PAPER, ALLIED PRDTS.	12	106	104	64	12	40	0	3	0
25 PAPERBOARD CONTAINERS	14	25	30	9	2	17	0	2	0
26 PRINTING, PUBLISHING	118	361	246	164	13	223	10	41	9
27 CHEMICALS,SELECT. PRDTS.	969	1580	3675	1638	363	1907	22	72	68
28 PLASTICS, SYNTHETICS	11	46	24	3	1	1	0	0	0
29 DRUGS, COSMETICS	249	179	368	138	30	325	0	41	2
30 PAINT, ALLIED PRDTS.	249	348	1010	110	4	604	0	9	1
31 PETROLEUM, RELATED INDS.	12	13	22	12	5	13	6	1	0
32 RUBBER, MISC. PLASTICS	6614	15780	11533	725	2028	1466	0	1216	0
33 LEATHER TANNING, PRDTS.	18	863	122	41	0	35	0	8	0
34 FOOTWEAR, LEATHER PRDTS.	11	265	18	9	14	196	0	0	0
35 GLASS, GLASS PRDTS.	11	1	32	4	3	14	0	0	0
36 STONE, CLAY PRDTS.	195	864	549	500	154	215	18	16	11
37 PRIMARY IRON, STEEL MFR.	50	24	275	20	1	23	0	1	0
38 PRIMARY NONFERROUS MFR.	207	116	340	8	9	75	183	50	55

39 METAL CONTAINERS	18	4	2	9	0	16	0	2	0
40 FABRICATED METAL PRDTS.	36	52	126	29	16	69	2	24	2
41 SCREW MACH. PRDTS., ETC.	7	37	140	11	4	11	0	0	0
42 OTHER FAB. METAL PRDTS.	30	92	249	27	6	61	0	3	0
43 ENGINES, TURBINES	0	49	114	5	0	3	0	0	0
44 FARM MACH., EQUIP.	0	0	57	32	7	14	0	9	0
45 CONSTRUC. MACH., EQUIP.	1	1	35	22	3	9	0	1	0
46 MATERIAL HANDLING MACH.	3	9	56	6	3	4	0	0	0
47 METALWORKING MACHINERY	273	916	4025	133	1	210	0	6	0
48 SPECIAL MACH., EQUIP.	211	1079	612	105	35	140	0	3	0
49 GENERAL MACH., EQUIP.	5	49	96	16	1	15	0	7	0
50 MACHINE SHOP PRDTS.	12	25	89	16	3	36	1	1	0
51 OFFICE, COMPUT. MACHINES	4	58	133	146	0	10	0	0	0
52 SERVICE IND. MACHINES	9	21	68	31	3	35	0	0	0
53 ELECT. TRANSMISS. EQUIP.	44	173	226	110	11	172	0	1	1
54 HOUSEHOLD APPLIANCES	3	9	73	36	6	13	0	0	0
55 ELECTRIC LIGHTING EQUIP.	1	67	17	7	17	36	0	0	0
56 RADIO, TV, ETC., EQUIP.	165	323	23	39	3	40	0	36	1
57 ELECTRONIC COMPONENTS	28	600	104	80	12	14	0	34	0
58 MISC. ELECTRICAL MACH.	9	19	68	7	1	10	0	1	0
59 MOTOR VEHICLES, EQUIP.	62	28	1406	26	5	231	0	5	0
60 AIRCRAFT, PARTS	83	75	61	15	0	129	0	0	0
61 OTHER TRANSPORT. EQUIP.	66	30	81	6	3	20	0	16	0
62 PROFESS., SCIEN. INSTRU.	15	178	171	39	3	36	2	26	0
63 MEDICAL, PHOTO. EQUIP.	5	112	7	11	0	9	0	0	0
64 MISC. MANUFACTURING	484	10950	697	1039	282	471	24	731	18
65 TRANSPORT., WAREHOUSING	17908	14447	8444	4738	3323	15854	534	1142	816
66 COMMUNICA.,EXC. BRDCAST.	724	1279	1952	697	360	961	119	363	49
67 RADIO, TV BROADCASTING	19	51	62	24	9	34	6	12	4
68 ELEC.,GAS,WATER,SAN.SER.	69	107	178	70	39	83	21	20	11
69 WHOLESALE, RETAIL TRADE	862	1918	2503	1366	340	1995	154	503	95
70 FINANCE, INSURANCE	2329	6855	4283	2644	740	3700	202	1625	166
71 REAL ESTATE, RENTAL	61	67	69	41	10	67	5	17	13
72 HOTELS, PERSONAL SERV.	102	208	262	115	45	163	23	49	82
73 BUSINESS SERVICES	407	987	1297	478	94	609	45	141	81
74 RESEARCH, DEVELOPMENT	0	0	0	0	0	0	0	0	0
75 AUTO. REPAIR, SERVICES	31	43	73	28	13	38	6	13	5
76 AMUSEMENTS	2262	3046	3876	1463	398	2060	228	742	4528
77 MED.,EDUC. SERVICES	382	1319	501	280	49	469	27	92	14
78 FEDERAL GOVT. ENTERPRISE	3741	7461	6605	3999	1958	6181	871	1953	693
79 STATE, LOCAL GOVT. ENT.	4	9	16	6	2	4	1	7	0
80 ZERO ENTRIES	0	0	0	0	0	0	0	0	0
81 SERVICE IND. RESIDUAL	-232391	-374313	-389865	-180335	-105167	-263953	-42530	-92897	-32374
82 TOTAL FINAL DEMAND	178317	259394	308254	126023	80492	192070	39099	70929	25458
83 SECONDARY TRANSFERS-OUT	0	0	0	0	0	0	0	0	0
84 ZERO ENTRIES	0	0	0	0	0	0	0	0	0
85 SCRAP ENTRIES	0	0	0	0	0	0	0	0	0
86 ZERO ENTRIES	0	0	0	0	0	0	0	0	0
87 STATE TOTAL CONSUMPTION	0	0	0	0	0	0	0	0	0

TABLE C-12

1963 DIRECTLY ALLOCATED IMPORTS BY STATE

(THOUSANDS OF CURRENT DOLLARS)

INDUSTRY TITLE	28 NEW HAMPSHIRE	29 NEW JERSEY	30 NEW MEXICO	31 NEW YORK	32 NORTH CAROLINA	33 NORTH DAKOTA	34 OHIO	35 OKLAHOMA	36 OREGON
1 LIVESTOCK, PRDTS.	1	3	69	22	6	2	11	8	8
2 OTHER AGRICULTURE PRDTS.	0	5	2151	16	32	18	16	12	23
3 FORESTRY, FISHERIES	2	8	1	11	19	0	3	1	90
4 AGRI.,FORES.,FISH. SERV.	1	3	3	7	22	4	11	11	5
5 IRON, FERRO. ORES MINING	0	0	0	6	0	0	0	0	0
6 NONFERROUS ORES MINING	0	1	28	3	0	0	0	1	0
7 COAL MINING	0	0	1	0	0	1	27	1	0
8 CRUDE PETRO.,NATURAL GAS	0	0	90	2	0	15	5	153	0
9 STONE, CLAY MINING	1	12	2	18	7	1	19	4	5
10 CHEM.,FERT. MIN. MINING	0	0	9	6	0	0	1	0	0
11 NEW CONSTRUCTION	30	480	76	948	174	34	583	147	123
12 MAINT., REPAIR CONSTR.	16	143	32	419	96	34	306	65	61
13 ORDNANCE, ACCESSORIES	0	1	22	25	11	0	52	0	0
14 FOOD, KINDRED PRDTS.	303	120008	1185	89749	11524	239	57704	6924	5266
15 TOBACCO MANUFACTURES	0	8	0	2	623	0	7	0	0
16 FABRICS	1409	2516	2	2201	31901	0	224	14	438
17 TEXTILE PRDTS.	301	3243	0	4425	3693	0	3220	5	170
18 APPAREL	27	951	3	7555	544	0	463	60	38
19 MISC. TEXTILE PRDTS.	1	39	0	114	26	0	9	1	5
20 LUMBER, WOOD PRDTS.	9	13	3	40	38	0	25	4	211
21 WOODEN CONTAINERS	1	4	0	4	3	0	3	0	1
22 HOUSEHOLD FURNITURE	8	43	1	105	226	0	54	5	13
23 OTHER FURNITURE	2	10	0	51	11	0	36	1	1
24 PAPER, ALLIED PRDTS.	25	119	0	207	26	0	123	2	25
25 PAPERBOARD CONTAINERS	1	39	0	53	10	0	40	2	2
26 PRINTING, PUBLISHING	22	336	11	2535	69	8	520	44	42
27 CHEMICALS,SELECT. PRDTS.	69	8050	146	4220	659	29	4513	232	417
28 PLASTICS, SYNTHETICS	4	62	0	52	35	0	60	0	1
29 DRUGS, COSMETICS	2	1524	0	1293	63	0	541	4	7
30 PAINT, ALLIED PRDTS.	3	1646	3	789	127	0	1317	35	67
31 PETROLEUM, RELATED INDS.	0	78	3	26	2	2	60	33	4
32 RUBBER, MISC. PLASTICS	707	5607	82	4834	1082	0	68917	4674	224
33 LEATHER TANNING, PRDTS.	150	277	0	403	35	0	140	0	7
34 FOOTWEAR, LEATHER PRDTS.	121	34	1	221	10	0	55	1	1
35 GLASS, GLASS PRDTS.	0	53	0	39	11	0	95	15	2
36 STONE, CLAY PRDTS.	146	1335	10	1732	135	3	1363	25	23
37 PRIMARY IRON, STEEL MFR.	2	38	0	112	5	0	467	4	9
38 PRIMARY NONFERROUS MFR.	8	592	35	578	56	0	457	66	97

39 METAL CONTAINERS	0	45	0	20	0	0	23	0	3
40 FABRICATED METAL PRDTS.	4	104	2	182	32	2	276	48	25
41 SCREW MACH. PRDTS., ETC.	2	48	0	68	5	0	150	2	1
42 OTHER FAB. METAL PRDTS.	3	146	0	178	15	0	265	21	8
43 ENGINES, TURBINES	0	1	0	51	0	0	14	0	0
44 FARM MACH., EQUIP.	0	1	0	12	5	2	39	2	2
45 CONSTRUC. MACH., EQUIP.	6	11	0	8	0	0	99	33	2
46 MATERIAL HANDLING MACH.	0	35	0	35	0	0	53	1	9
47 METALWORKING MACHINERY	50	526	6	1247	36	6	3570	9	8
48 SPECIAL MACH., EQUIP.	163	715	2	942	388	1	1109	28	128
49 GENERAL MACH., EQUIP.	7	101	0	146	2	0	207	15	2
50 MACHINE SHOP PRDTS.	2	29	2	74	5	0	75	5	8
51 OFFICE, COMPUT. MACHINES	2	61	0	460	4	0	101	1	0
52 SERVICE IND. MACHINES	1	28	0	85	5	0	68	4	1
53 ELECT. TRANSMISS. EQUIP.	48	254	0	846	97	0	1061	19	36
54 HOUSEHOLD APPLIANCES	0	13	0	40	13	0	275	1	1
55 ELECTRIC LIGHTING EQUIP.	1	97	0	126	9	0	125	0	1
56 RADIO, TV, ETC., EQUIP.	20	432	1	593	85	0	134	63	1
57 ELECTRONIC COMPONENTS	79	533	2	905	74	0	248	8	1
58 MISC. ELECTRICAL MACH.	0	29	0	44	21	0	76	2	3
59 MOTOR VEHICLES, EQUIP.	0	68	0	171	4	0	481	6	8
60 AIRCRAFT, PARTS	0	130	0	425	7	0	380	181	7
61 OTHER TRANSPORT. EQUIP.	1	43	0	57	8	0	50	7	18
62 PROFESS., SCIEN. INSTRU.	3	235	2	308	21	0	116	6	6
63 MEDICAL, PHOTO. EQUIP.	4	47	0	497	7	0	5	0	3
64 MISC. MANUFACTURING	337	8255	145	43973	822	317	1031	158	167
65 TRANSPORT., WAREHOUSING	278	39578	685	178425	4626	274	18795	5191	17086
66 COMMUNICA.,EXC. BRDCAST.	107	1490	180	4920	801	143	2220	531	429
67 RADIO, TV BROADCASTING	3	10	7	432	27	4	83	15	15
68 ELEC.,GAS,WATER,SAN.SER.	12	129	23	325	60	8	255	46	23
69 WHOLESALE, RETAIL TRADE	116	2366	175	11470	1227	188	3197	607	758
70 FINANCE, INSURANCE	460	5168	322	22085	2630	232	6220	1254	1090
71 REAL ESTATE, RENTAL	4	92	10	604	29	3	101	30	22
72 HOTELS, PERSONAL SERV.	29	256	33	935	131	17	321	68	69
73 BUSINESS SERVICES	45	943	90	6315	255	25	1211	246	209
74 RESEARCH, DEVELOPMENT	0	0	0	0	0	0	0	0	0
75 AUTO. REPAIR, SERVICES	5	52	8	139	30	5	77	21	19
76 AMUSEMENTS	541	4242	403	36661	1277	189	5204	837	827
77 MED.,EDUC. SERVICES	88	535	35	3319	291	21	868	113	126
78 FEDERAL GOVT. ENTERPRISE	680	6671	1216	24402	4523	848	9613	2970	2400
79 STATE, LOCAL GOVT. ENT.	2	7	1	36	8	0	22	3	5
80 ZERO ENTRIES	0	0	0	0	0	0	0	0	0
81 SERVICE IND. RESIDUAL	-41088	-549544	-69625	-1270623	-296690	-34722	-582473	-150018	-113745
82 TOTAL FINAL DEMAND	34613	328737	62300	806238	227828	32046	382807	124914	82831
83 SECONDARY TRANSFERS-OUT	0	0	0	0	0	0	0	0	0
84 ZERO ENTRIES	0	0	0	0	0	0	0	0	0
85 SCRAP ENTRIES	0	0	0	0	0	0	0	0	0
86 ZERO ENTRIES	0	0	0	0	0	0	0	0	0
87 STATE TOTAL CONSUMPTION	0	0	0	0	0	0	0	0	0

TABLE C-12

1963 DIRECTLY ALLOCATED IMPORTS BY STATE
(THOUSANDS OF CURRENT DOLLARS)

INDUSTRY TITLE	37 PENNSYL- VANIA	38 RHODE ISLAND	39 SOUTH CAROLINA	40 SOUTH DAKOTA	41 TENNESSEE	42 TEXAS	43 UTAH	44 VERMONT	45 VIRGINIA
1 LIVESTOCK, PRDTS.	15	0	5	17	7	937	8	3	7
2 OTHER AGRICULTURE PRDTS.	11	0	25	15	13	34283	5	0	12
3 FORESTRY, FISHERIES	5	3	13	0	4	25	0	1	23
4 AGRI.,FORES.,FISH. SERV.	13	1	8	5	7	86	2	0	9
5 IRON, FERRO. ORES MINING	5	0	0	0	0	1	1	0	0
6 NONFERROUS ORES MINING	1	0	0	5	3	1	39	0	1
7 COAL MINING	110	0	0	0	3	1	3	0	26
8 CRUDE PETRO.,NATURAL GAS	10	0	0	0	0	796	21	0	0
9 STONE, CLAY MINING	19	1	5	2	10	12	1	2	11
10 CHEM.,FERT. MIN. MINING	5	0	0	0	3	7	1	0	0
11 NEW CONSTRUCTION	482	38	85	30	166	800	92	16	276
12 MAINT., REPAIR CONSTR.	225	15	38	34	66	309	26	10	86
13 ORDNANCE, ACCESSORIES	32	0	0	0	19	17	39	0	0
14 FOOD, KINDRED PRDTS.	62738	3059	6307	649	48003	98316	2272	1202	20194
15 TOBACCO MANUFACTURES	66	0	7	0	10	1	0	0	236
16 FABRICS	4586	2623	26396	0	2250	1031	6	70	4072
17 TEXTILE PRDTS.	3464	1151	2623	0	799	373	9	76	672
18 APPAREL	1880	44	282	0	711	533	25	26	283
19 MISC. TEXTILE PRDTS.	23	1	7	0	8	11	0	0	5
20 LUMBER, WOOD PRDTS.	29	1	23	1	22	33	2	6	31
21 WOODEN CONTAINERS	3	0	3	0	5	2	0	0	4
22 HOUSEHOLD FURNITURE	78	1	15	0	76	40	3	9	110
23 OTHER FURNITURE	32	3	1	0	6	11	1	0	8
24 PAPER, ALLIED PRDTS.	141	6	21	0	44	40	2	14	36
25 PAPERBOARD CONTAINERS	42	2	8	0	8	12	0	1	6
26 PRINTING, PUBLISHING	612	30	25	10	119	221	25	16	77
27 CHEMICALS,SELECT. PRDTS.	3495	158	266	13	1974	8780	111	22	1210
28 PLASTICS, SYNTHETICS	84	9	44	0	113	97	0	1	151
29 DRUGS, COSMETICS	643	9	37	1	111	119	3	0	89
30 PAINT, ALLIED PRDTS.	926	42	21	0	130	677	10	23	67
31 PETROLEUM, RELATED INDS.	69	2	3	0	5	247	8	0	5
32 RUBBER, MISC. PLASTICS	15166	3027	336	5	6693	6320	282	369	1140
33 LEATHER TANNING, PRDTS.	291	1	5	0	168	14	2	17	56
34 FOOTWEAR, LEATHER PRDTS.	182	3	0	0	117	17	0	1	26
35 GLASS, GLASS PRDTS.	90	7	12	0	25	8	0	0	5
36 STONE, CLAY PRDTS.	1233	22	75	6	119	492	52	8	151
37 PRIMARY IRON, STEEL MFR.	593	8	3	0	15	43	18	1	15
38 PRIMARY NONFERROUS MFR.	369	100	13	0	219	434	122	6	43

39 METAL CONTAINERS	27	0	0	0	2	19	1	0	2
40 FABRICATED METAL PRDTS.	281	5	15	4	60	129	18	2	46
41 SCREW MACH. PRDTS., ETC.	89	8	2	0	6	6	0	0	1
42 OTHER FAB. METAL PRDTS.	234	24	4	0	19	83	2	1	14
43 ENGINES, TURBINES	74	0	0	0	0	5	0	0	0
44 FARM MACH., EQUIP.	24	0	1	1	15	6	0	0	2
45 CONSTRUC. MACH., EQUIP.	40	0	0	0	2	111	8	0	1
46 MATERIAL HANDLING MACH.	43	0	1	1	6	6	0	0	1
47 METALWORKING MACHINERY	1476	243	133	14	41	104	6	298	8
48 SPECIAL MACH., EQUIP.	828	152	246	1	64	226	11	12	37
49 GENERAL MACH., EQUIP.	130	5	5	1	7	25	3	0	5
50 MACHINE SHOP PRDTS.	41	4	3	1	7	24	2	1	4
51 OFFICE, COMPUT. MACHINES	81	0	4	0	0	4	0	11	22
52 SERVICE IND. MACHINES	53	1	1	0	8	34	2	1	6
53 ELECT. TRANSMISS. EQUIP.	711	5	31	0	92	46	4	1	156
54 HOUSEHOLD APPLIANCES	28	1	2	0	39	7	0	0	0
55 ELECTRIC LIGHTING EQUIP.	118	20	0	0	8	7	0	3	1
56 RADIO, TV, ETC., EQUIP.	94	5	1	0	44	94	5	0	42
57 ELECTRONIC COMPONENTS	889	39	64	4	28	80	16	25	149
58 MISC. ELECTRICAL MACH.	36	3	0	0	5	11	0	2	1
59 MOTOR VEHICLES, EQUIP.	92	1	1	0	8	61	0	0	22
60 AIRCRAFT, PARTS	298	3	0	0	25	247	90	28	9
61 OTHER TRANSPORT. EQUIP.	124	2	4	1	28	50	4	0	30
62 PROFESS., SCIEN. INSTRU.	321	23	27	0	30	37	1	6	7
63 MEDICAL, PHOTO. EQUIP.	26	8	7	0	0	5	0	4	19
64 MISC. MANUFACTURING	3097	16164	897	44	328	582	362	44	855
65 TRANSPORT., WAREHOUSING	36158	1778	4037	287	4080	50574	897	173	15989
66 COMMUNICA.,EXC. BRDCAST.	2193	200	371	106	912	2422	253	56	810
67 RADIO, TV BROADCASTING	101	8	13	5	27	71	6	2	25
68 ELEC.,GAS,WATER,SAN.SER.	245	14	30	9	25	198	24	6	72
69 WHOLESALE, RETAIL TRADE	3355	253	402	156	1093	3177	266	64	842
70 FINANCE, INSURANCE	8199	854	1381	228	2539	8355	465	224	2298
71 REAL ESTATE, RENTAL	117	11	12	5	26	108	11	2	50
72 HOTELS, PERSONAL SERV.	386	30	56	18	107	342	29	17	130
73 BUSINESS SERVICES	1519	81	128	30	271	1109	85	22	325
74 RESEARCH, DEVELOPMENT	0	0	0	0	0	0	0	0	0
75 AUTO. REPAIR, SERVICES	91	6	14	5	26	89	8	3	28
76 AMUSEMENTS	4347	675	530	333	1101	3572	525	266	1220
77 MED.,EDUC. SERVICES	1339	102	84	30	260	540	107	76	237
78 FEDERAL GOVT. ENTERPRISE	11203	1214	2663	782	10503	11669	992	456	6778
79 STATE, LOCAL GOVT. ENT.	22	1	2	1	11	16	2	1	9
80 ZERO ENTRIES	0	0	0	0	0	0	0	0	0
81 SERVICE IND. RESIDUAL	-640105	-73567	-156068	-32000	-213243	-759553	-49441	-21153	-291315
82 TOTAL FINAL DEMAND	463807	41258	108187	29138	129338	520152	42041	17444	231922
83 SECONDARY TRANSFERS-OUT	0	0	0	0	0	0	0	0	0
84 ZERO ENTRIES	0	0	0	0	0	0	0	0	0
85 SCRAP ENTRIES	0	0	0	0	0	0	0	0	0
86 ZERO ENTRIES	0	0	0	0	0	0	0	0	0
87 STATE TOTAL CONSUMPTION	0	0	0	0	0	0	0	0	0

TABLE C-12

1963 DIRECTLY ALLOCATED IMPORTS BY STATE
(THOUSANDS OF CURRENT DOLLARS)

INDUSTRY TITLE	46 WASHINGTON	47 WEST VIRGINIA	48 WISCONSIN	49 WYOMING	50 ALASKA	51 HAWAII	52 NATIONAL TOTAL
1 LIVESTOCK, PRDTS.	9	3	21	9	0	0	2502
2 OTHER AGRICULTURE PRDTS.	36	2	5	4	0	2	214881
3 FORESTRY, FISHERIES	51	3	5	0	32	2	564
4 AGRI.,FORES.,FISH. SERV.	6	3	7	1	0	13	614
5 IRON, FERRO. ORES MINING	6	0	0	2	0	0	106
6 NONFERROUS ORES MINING	2	0	0	11	1	0	221
7 COAL MINING	1	77	0	2	0	0	347
8 CRUDE PETRO.,NATURAL GAS	2	14	0	77	3	0	2147
9 STONE, CLAY MINING	4	4	9	3	0	1	347
10 CHEM.,FERT. MIN. MINING	1	2	0	1	0	0	61
11 NEW CONSTRUCTION	209	82	199	34	53	80	11530
12 MAINT., REPAIR CONSTR.	92	37	106	20	6	20	4945
13 ORDNANCE, ACCESSORIES	2	30	6	0	0	0	1561
14 FOOD, KINDRED PRDTS.	8055	519	11364	135	75	3483	1266183
15 TOBACCO MANUFACTURES	0	6	0	0	0	0	1225
16 FABRICS	97	33	112	0	0	2	109409
17 TEXTILE PRDTS.	70	3	924	0	0	0	47285
18 APPAREL	64	42	107	0	0	31	19514
19 MISC. TEXTILE PRDTS.	3	0	3	0	0	0	496
20 LUMBER, WOOD PRDTS.	99	7	34	2	2	2	1200
21 WOODEN CONTAINERS	3	0	3	0	0	0	111
22 HOUSEHOLD FURNITURE	11	3	19	0	0	2	1533
23 OTHER FURNITURE	3	1	9	0	0	1	380
24 PAPER, ALLIED PRDTS.	70	5	170	0	0	2	2029
25 PAPERBOARD CONTAINERS	7	2	20	0	0	0	556
26 PRINTING, PUBLISHING	65	26	200	5	2	13	9043
27 CHEMICALS,SELECT. PRDTS.	768	3285	799	3	0	59	71430
28 PLASTICS, SYNTHETICS	4	67	5	0	0	0	1170
29 DRUGS, COSMETICS	5	8	164	0	0	2	8664
30 PAINT, ALLIED PRDTS.	94	10	253	0	0	0	14097
31 PETROLEUM, RELATED INDS.	12	5	3	15	0	2	1092
32 RUBBER, MISC. PLASTICS	146	170	5179	0	0	0	243678
33 LEATHER TANNING, PRDTS.	4	59	552	0	0	0	4060
34 FOOTWEAR, LEATHER PRDTS.	1	3	85	0	0	1	1800
35 GLASS, GLASS PRDTS.	2	56	1	0	0	0	641
36 STONE, CLAY PRDTS.	78	108	200	5	1	8	15344
37 PRIMARY IRON, STEEL MFR.	6	54	58	0	0	1	2683
38 PRIMARY NONFERROUS MFR.	340	134	59	0	0	0	7191

39	METAL CONTAINERS	8	3	16	0	0	3	394
40	FABRICATED METAL PRDTS.	26	21	91	0	0	2	2633
41	SCREW MACH. PRDTS., ETC.	2	3	41	0	0	0	996
42	OTHER FAB. METAL PRDTS.	8	17	41	0	0	0	2495
43	ENGINES, TURBINES	0	0	103	0	0	0	537
44	FARM MACH., EQUIP.	2	2	69	0	0	0	676
45	CONSTRUC. MACH., EQUIP.	6	11	89	0	0	0	947
46	MATERIAL HANDLING MACH.	6	1	9	0	0	0	383
47	METALWORKING MACHINERY	32	68	703	0	0	1	19322
48	SPECIAL MACH., EQUIP.	81	8	672	0	0	15	10513
49	GENERAL MACH., EQUIP.	2	0	76	0	0	0	1451
50	MACHINE SHOP PRDTS.	10	4	19	0	0	1	817
51	OFFICE, COMPUT. MACHINES	2	0	4	0	0	0	1654
52	SERVICE IND. MACHINES	2	1	29	0	0	0	674
53	ELECT. TRANSMISS. EQUIP.	15	32	624	1	0	0	6439
54	HOUSEHOLD APPLIANCES	2	0	46	0	0	0	1149
55	ELECTRIC LIGHTING EQUIP.	4	29	9	0	0	0	1058
56	RADIO, TV, ETC., EQUIP.	6	0	69	0	0	0	3963
57	ELECTRONIC COMPONENTS	4	14	58	0	0	0	6655
58	MISC. ELECTRICAL MACH.	1	0	30	0	0	0	652
59	MOTOR VEHICLES, EQUIP.	6	2	216	0	0	0	3608
60	AIRCRAFT, PARTS	183	0	2	1	0	0	5120
61	OTHER TRANSPORT. EQUIP.	53	9	45	0	0	0	1324
62	PROFESS., SCIEN. INSTRU.	2	11	75	1	0	0	2657
63	MEDICAL, PHOTO. EQUIP.	1	2	2	0	0	0	974
64	MISC. MANUFACTURING	218	21	446	5	0	70	116908
65	TRANSPORT., WAREHOUSING	34785	4302	2852	290	4526	11043	764041
66	COMMUNICA.,EXC. BRDCAST.	714	305	660	62	18	151	42198
67	RADIO, TV BROADCASTING	22	11	27	3	3	6	1843
68	ELEC.,GAS,WATER,SAN.SER.	27	57	77	14	2	8	3622
69	WHOLESALE, RETAIL TRADE	971	283	1058	60	46	157	63852
70	FINANCE, INSURANCE	1697	561	2602	87	40	349	144632
71	REAL ESTATE, RENTAL	49	11	32	3	3	19	2727
72	HOTELS, PERSONAL SERV.	100	43	127	19	9	34	7009
73	BUSINESS SERVICES	331	110	394	23	30	95	28285
74	RESEARCH, DEVELOPMENT	0	0	0	0	0	0	0
75	AUTO. REPAIR, SERVICES	27	9	30	3	1	5	1564
76	AMUSEMENTS	1430	862	1496	164	121	410	139787
77	MED.,EDUC. SERVICES	197	89	156	10	10	64	17884
78	FEDERAL GOVT. ENTERPRISE	6284	1277	3352	382	2222	2515	240486
79	STATE, LOCAL GOVT. ENT.	15	3	3	1	1	1	330
80	ZERO ENTRIES	0	0	0	0	0	0	0
81	SERVICE IND. RESIDUAL	-237119	-68061	-179959	-19874	-56610	-92671	-12545066
82	TOTAL FINAL DEMAND	179360	55016	142825	18416	49405	73993	8822167
83	SECONDARY TRANSFERS-OUT	0	0	0	0	0	0	0
84	ZERO ENTRIES	0	0	0	0	0	0	0
85	SCRAP ENTRIES	0	0	0	0	0	0	0
86	ZERO ENTRIES	0	0	0	0	0	0	0
87	STATE TOTAL CONSUMPTION	0	0	0	0	0	0	0

TABLE C-13

1963 TRANSFERRED IMPORTS BY STATE
(THOUSANDS OF CURRENT DOLLARS)

INDUSTRY TITLE	1 ALABAMA	2 ARIZONA	3 ARKANSAS	4 CALIFORNIA	5 COLORADO	6 CONNECTICUT	7 DELAWARE	8 DISTRICT OF COLUMBIA	9 FLORIDA
1 LIVESTOCK, PRDTS.	7563	6009	0	17290	0	65	8	0	207
2 OTHER AGRICULTURE PRDTS.	1216	2245	0	19500	0	12	113	0	5861
3 FORESTRY, FISHERIES	3507	11410	0	33985	0	2387	67	0	2819
4 AGRI.,FORES.,FISH. SERV.	0	0	0	0	0	0	0	0	0
5 IRON, FERRO. ORES MINING	31484	163	0	144	0	0	0	0	3
6 NONFERROUS ORES MINING	20399	3166	0	3404	0	0	34	0	0
7 COAL MINING	0	0	0	0	0	0	0	0	0
8 CRUDE PETRO.,NATURAL GAS	3721	4530	0	37681	0	77	0	0	1838
9 STONE, CLAY MINING	24	2009	0	2655	0	347	1686	0	1620
10 CHEM.,FERT. MIN. MINING	0	52	0	41	0	0	0	0	7638
11 NEW CONSTRUCTION	0	0	0	0	0	0	0	0	0
12 MAINT., REPAIR CONSTR.	0	0	0	0	0	0	0	0	0
13 ORDNANCE, ACCESSORIES	17	0	0	1770	0	0	0	0	17
14 FOOD, KINDRED PRDTS.	4593	4320	0	54764	0	481	1149	0	5572
15 TOBACCO MANUFACTURES	35	18	0	968	0	0	0	0	95
16 FABRICS	244	226	0	14256	0	91	0	0	544
17 TEXTILE PRDTS.	404	13	0	48698	0	1	4138	0	126
18 APPAREL	77	6	0	4263	0	0	0	0	40
19 MISC. TEXTILE PRDTS.	0	0	0	0	0	0	0	0	0
20 LUMBER, WOOD PRDTS.	1165	3030	0	5557	0	55	5689	0	31515
21 WOODEN CONTAINERS	14	12	0	1684	0	0	0	0	23
22 HOUSEHOLD FURNITURE	0	0	0	0	0	0	0	0	0
23 OTHER FURNITURE	0	0	0	0	0	0	0	0	0
24 PAPER, ALLIED PRDTS.	4327	87	0	58630	0	391	25083	0	8874
25 PAPERBOARD CONTAINERS	0	9	0	7	0	0	0	0	0
26 PRINTING, PUBLISHING	0	251	0	198	0	0	0	0	0
27 CHEMICALS,SELECT. PRDTS.	3331	8705	0	13494	0	4473	6	0	15738
28 PLASTICS, SYNTHETICS	76	238	0	500	0	0	0	0	71
29 DRUGS, COSMETICS	2	25	0	640	0	0	3	0	4
30 PAINT, ALLIED PRDTS.	0	0	0	7	0	0	0	0	0
31 PETROLEUM, RELATED INDS.	5458	188	0	55088	0	34556	0	0	67848
32 RUBBER, MISC. PLASTICS	203	0	0	9982	0	0	0	0	136
33 LEATHER TANNING, PRDTS.	23	8	0	2588	0	0	0	0	19
34 FOOTWEAR, LEATHER PRDTS.	2	2	0	305	0	0	0	0	3
35 GLASS, GLASS PRDTS.	51	152	0	9263	0	0	0	0	453
36 STONE, CLAY PRDTS.	78	5354	0	6430	0	59	160	0	179
37 PRIMARY IRON, STEEL MFR.	19952	1330	0	59331	0	3460	2512	0	17762
38 PRIMARY NONFERROUS MFR.	819	3120	0	19993	0	0	22871	0	588

39 METAL CONTAINERS	41	5	0	816	0	0	0	0	64
40 FABRICATED METAL PRDTS.	18	7	0	411	0	0	0	0	28
41 SCREW MACH. PRDTS., ETC.	170	16	0	4591	0	0	0	0	278
42 OTHER FAB. METAL PRDTS.	4946	57	0	29195	0	0	0	0	3380
43 ENGINES, TURBINES	1	1	0	1445	0	0	0	0	118
44 FARM MACH., EQUIP.	162	48	0	1420	0	0	0	0	4810
45 CONSTRUC. MACH., EQUIP.	0	11	0	11	0	0	0	0	0
46 MATERIAL HANDLING MACH.	0	0	0	8358	0	0	0	0	0
47 METALWORKING MACHINERY	215	1	0	713	0	0	0	0	154
48 SPECIAL MACH., EQUIP.	24	28	0	14131	0	0	0	0	767
49 GENERAL MACH., EQUIP.	8	5	0	1445	0	0	0	0	122
50 MACHINE SHOP PRDTS.	0	0	0	0	0	0	0	0	0
51 OFFICE, COMPUT. MACHINES	25	0	0	2469	0	0	0	0	200
52 SERVICE IND. MACHINES	0	0	0	55	0	0	0	0	5
53 ELECT. TRANSMISS. EQUIP.	86	1	0	6345	0	41	0	0	42
54 HOUSEHOLD APPLIANCES	0	0	0	0	0	0	0	0	0
55 ELECTRIC LIGHTING EQUIP.	65	1	0	4822	0	31	0	0	32
56 RADIO, TV, ETC., EQUIP.	340	77	0	27658	0	143	0	0	205
57 ELECTRONIC COMPONENTS	26	0	0	1935	0	12	0	0	30134
58 MISC. ELECTRICAL MACH.	64	1	0	4741	0	31	0	0	74
59 MOTOR VEHICLES, EQUIP.	147	0	0	8515	0	590	6	0	5519
60 AIRCRAFT, PARTS	0	0	0	1175	0	0	0	0	101
61 OTHER TRANSPORT. EQUIP.	110	48	0	10689	0	0	0	0	418
62 PROFESS., SCIEN. INSTRU.	23	14	0	3082	0	0	0	0	32
63 MEDICAL, PHOTO. EQUIP.	64	5	0	9336	0	0	0	0	104
64 MISC. MANUFACTURING	276	0	0	36230	0	0	0	0	389
65 TRANSPORT., WAREHOUSING	14450	2626	2286	71848	3627	6939	6693	3600	24437
66 COMMUNICA.,EXC. BRDCAST.	0	0	0	0	0	0	0	0	0
67 RADIO, TV BROADCASTING	0	0	0	0	0	0	0	0	0
68 ELEC.,GAS,WATER,SAN.SER.	100	0	0	30700	0	198	0	0	0
69 WHOLESALE, RETAIL TRADE	0	0	0	0	0	0	0	0	0
70 FINANCE, INSURANCE	193	106	94	1616	154	286	42	89	401
71 REAL ESTATE, RENTAL	0	0	0	0	0	0	0	0	0
72 HOTELS, PERSONAL SERV.	0	0	0	0	0	0	0	0	0
73 BUSINESS SERVICES	0	0	0	0	0	0	0	0	0
74 RESEARCH, DEVELOPMENT	0	0	0	0	0	0	0	0	0
75 AUTO. REPAIR, SERVICES	0	0	0	0	0	0	0	0	0
76 AMUSEMENTS	0	0	0	0	0	0	0	0	0
77 MED.,EDUC. SERVICES	0	0	0	0	0	0	0	0	0
78 FEDERAL GOVT. ENTERPRISE	0	0	0	0	0	0	0	0	0
79 STATE, LOCAL GOVT. ENT.	0	0	0	0	0	0	0	0	0
80 ZERO ENTRIES	0	0	0	0	0	0	0	0	0
81 SERVICE IND. RESIDUAL	-133756	-61301	-2442	-786978	-3880	-56161	-72101	-3786	-247741
82 TOTAL FINAL DEMAND	0	0	0	0	0	0	0	0	0
83 SECONDARY TRANSFERS-OUT	0	0	0	0	0	0	0	0	0
84 ZERO ENTRIES	0	0	0	0	0	0	0	0	0
85 SCRAP ENTRIES	3418	1566	62	20108	99	1435	1842	97	6330
86 ZERO ENTRIES	0	0	0	0	0	0	0	0	0
87 STATE TOTAL CONSUMPTION	0	0	0	0	0	0	0	0	0

TABLE C-13

1963 TRANSFERRED IMPORTS BY STATE
(THOUSANDS OF CURRENT DOLLARS)

INDUSTRY TITLE	10 GEORGIA	11 IDAHO	12 ILLINOIS	13 INDIANA	14 IOWA	15 KANSAS	16 KENTUCKY	17 LOUISIANA	18 MAINE
1 LIVESTOCK, PRDTS.	6972	0	453	0	0	0	0	116	1710
2 OTHER AGRICULTURE PRDTS.	273	0	906	0	0	0	0	18506	669
3 FORESTRY, FISHERIES	2319	0	1846	0	0	0	0	19610	3092
4 AGRI.,FORES.,FISH. SERV.	0	0	0	0	0	0	0	0	0
5 IRON, FERRO. ORES MINING	0	0	27269	2479	0	0	0	7904	0
6 NONFERROUS ORES MINING	244	0	0	0	0	0	0	31404	3289
7 COAL MINING	0	0	0	0	0	0	0	0	184
8 CRUDE PETRO.,NATURAL GAS	2610	0	0	0	0	0	0	3619	242243
9 STONE, CLAY MINING	1668	0	212	3	0	0	0	1032	17221
10 CHEM.,FERT. MIN. MINING	144	0	0	0	0	0	0	1020	1253
11 NEW CONSTRUCTION	0	0	0	0	0	0	0	0	0
12 MAINT., REPAIR CONSTR.	0	0	0	0	0	0	0	0	0
13 ORDNANCE, ACCESSORIES	17	0	87	0	0	0	0	156	0
14 FOOD, KINDRED PRDTS.	16775	0	5318	0	0	0	0	113239	5249
15 TOBACCO MANUFACTURES	0	0	287	0	0	0	0	637	0
16 FABRICS	2969	0	161	0	0	0	0	1966	18
17 TEXTILE PRDTS.	65362	0	2287	0	0	0	0	68693	80
18 APPAREL	68	0	163	0	0	0	0	349	10
19 MISC. TEXTILE PRDTS.	0	0	0	0	0	0	0	0	0
20 LUMBER, WOOD PRDTS.	27	0	63	0	0	0	0	1075	17419
21 WOODEN CONTAINERS	0	0	54	0	0	0	0	172	28
22 HOUSEHOLD FURNITURE	0	0	0	0	0	0	0	0	0
23 OTHER FURNITURE	0	0	0	0	0	0	0	0	0
24 PAPER, ALLIED PRDTS.	1227	0	40865	0	0	0	0	4951	24047
25 PAPERBOARD CONTAINERS	0	0	0	0	0	0	0	0	1888
26 PRINTING, PUBLISHING	0	0	0	0	0	0	0	0	199
27 CHEMICALS,SELECT. PRDTS.	12859	0	1372	1	0	0	0	19318	752
28 PLASTICS, SYNTHETICS	320	0	39	0	0	0	0	137	1534
29 DRUGS, COSMETICS	2	0	201	0	0	0	0	276	175
30 PAINT, ALLIED PRDTS.	1	0	1	0	0	0	0	366	0
31 PETROLEUM, RELATED INDS.	15869	0	0	0	0	0	0	16888	32775
32 RUBBER, MISC. PLASTICS	592	0	224	0	0	0	0	1318	284
33 LEATHER TANNING, PRDTS.	30	0	100	0	0	0	0	244	31
34 FOOTWEAR, LEATHER PRDTS.	4	0	14	0	0	0	0	27	1
35 GLASS, GLASS PRDTS.	76	0	879	0	0	0	0	368	23
36 STONE, CLAY PRDTS.	217	0	393	3	0	0	0	786	2496
37 PRIMARY IRON, STEEL MFR.	5691	0	28143	44	0	0	0	38811	1933
38 PRIMARY NONFERROUS MFR.	60711	0	608	0	0	0	0	17895	8926

39 METAL CONTAINERS	24	0	273	0	0	0	0	172	4
40 FABRICATED METAL PRDTS.	10	0	120	0	0	0	0	79	3
41 SCREW MACH. PRDTS., ETC.	153	0	1398	0	0	0	0	1182	413
42 OTHER FAB. METAL PRDTS.	2947	0	5182	0	0	0	0	6353	191
43 ENGINES, TURBINES	3	0	94	0	0	0	0	1450	194
44 FARM MACH., EQUIP.	1001	0	933	0	0	0	0	4623	3404
45 CONSTRUC. MACH., EQUIP.	0	0	0	0	0	0	0	0	792
46 MATERIAL HANDLING MACH.	0	0	0	0	0	0	0	0	59
47 METALWORKING MACHINERY	141	0	1391	0	0	0	0	388	151
48 SPECIAL MACH., EQUIP.	761	0	2203	0	0	0	0	3998	230
49 GENERAL MACH., EQUIP.	74	0	666	0	0	0	0	892	273
50 MACHINE SHOP PRDTS.	0	0	0	0	0	0	0	0	0
51 OFFICE, COMPUT. MACHINES	125	0	1148	0	0	0	0	1521	923
52 SERVICE IND. MACHINES	3	0	25	0	0	0	0	34	1
53 ELECT. TRANSMISS. EQUIP.	156	0	439	0	0	0	0	498	112
54 HOUSEHOLD APPLIANCES	0	0	0	0	0	0	0	0	0
55 ELECTRIC LIGHTING EQUIP.	118	0	334	0	0	0	0	379	313
56 RADIO, TV, ETC., EQUIP.	608	0	1800	0	0	0	0	2212	843
57 ELECTRONIC COMPONENTS	47	0	133	0	0	0	0	152	146
58 MISC. ELECTRICAL MACH.	116	0	328	0	0	0	0	372	436
59 MOTOR VEHICLES, EQUIP.	83	0	490	0	0	0	0	3551	87
60 AIRCRAFT, PARTS	0	0	141	0	0	0	0	39	1747
61 OTHER TRANSPORT. EQUIP.	209	0	887	0	0	0	0	2438	94
62 PROFESS., SCIEN. INSTRU.	37	0	153	0	0	0	0	268	46
63 MEDICAL, PHOTO. EQUIP.	114	0	459	0	0	0	0	808	35
64 MISC. MANUFACTURING	446	0	1775	0	0	0	0	3327	552
65 TRANSPORT., WAREHOUSING	15927	918	21844	10980	3940	3551	4265	25826	53322
66 COMMUNICA.,EXC. BRDCAST.	0	0	0	0	0	0	0	0	0
67 RADIO, TV BROADCASTING	0	0	0	0	0	0	0	0	0
68 ELEC.,GAS,WATER,SAN.SER.	0	1800	157	143	0	0	200	1000	2900
69 WHOLESALE, RETAIL TRADE	0	0	0	0	0	0	0	0	0
70 FINANCE, INSURANCE	263	44	982	377	199	159	177	219	61
71 REAL ESTATE, RENTAL	0	0	0	0	0	0	0	0	0
72 HOTELS, PERSONAL SERV.	0	0	0	0	0	0	0	0	0
73 BUSINESS SERVICES	0	0	0	0	0	0	0	0	0
74 RESEARCH, DEVELOPMENT	0	0	0	0	0	0	0	0	0
75 AUTO. REPAIR, SERVICES	0	0	0	0	0	0	0	0	0
76 AMUSEMENTS	0	0	0	0	0	0	0	0	0
77 MED.,EDUC. SERVICES	0	0	0	0	0	0	0	0	0
78 FEDERAL GOVT. ENTERPRISE	0	0	0	0	0	0	0	0	0
79 STATE, LOCAL GOVT. ENT.	0	0	0	0	0	0	0	0	0
80 ZERO ENTRIES	0	0	0	0	0	0	0	0	0
81 SERVICE IND. RESIDUAL	-226191	-2834	-159373	-14397	-4248	-3807	-4764	-444007	-446264
82 TOTAL FINAL DEMAND	0	0	0	0	0	0	0	0	0
83 SECONDARY TRANSFERS-OUT	0	0	0	0	0	0	0	0	0
84 ZERO ENTRIES	0	0	0	0	0	0	0	0	0
85 SCRAP ENTRIES	5779	72	4072	368	109	97	122	11345	11403
86 ZERO ENTRIES	0	0	0	0	0	0	0	0	0
87 STATE TOTAL CONSUMPTION	0	0	0	0	0	0	0	0	0

TABLE C-13

1963 TRANSFERRED IMPORTS BY STATE
(THOUSANDS OF CURRENT DOLLARS)

INDUSTRY TITLE	19 MARYLAND	20 MASSA-CHUSETTS	21 MICHIGAN	22 MINNESOTA	23 MISSISSIPPI	24 MISSOURI	25 MONTANA	26 NEBRASKA	27 NEVADA
1 LIVESTOCK, PRDTS.	85	11185	10544	0	1836	0	993	0	0
2 OTHER AGRICULTURE PRDTS.	4849	1899	19	145	2547	0	334	0	0
3 FORESTRY, FISHERIES	19007	22264	38308	33	0	0	2578	0	0
4 AGRI.,FORES.,FISH. SERV.	0	0	0	0	0	0	0	0	0
5 IRON, FERRO. ORES MINING	105060	0	49038	0	0	0	532	0	0
6 NONFERROUS ORES MINING	1418	167	28975	63	56	0	2783	0	0
7 COAL MINING	0	0	0	0	0	0	68	0	0
8 CRUDE PETRO.,NATURAL GAS	14760	7465	140502	0	0	0	13497	0	0
9 STONE, CLAY MINING	8430	913	17110	82	0	0	1456	0	0
10 CHEM.,FERT. MIN. MINING	2317	17	43957	0	0	0	796	0	0
11 NEW CONSTRUCTION	0	0	0	0	0	0	0	0	0
12 MAINT., REPAIR CONSTR.	0	0	0	0	0	0	0	0	0
13 ORDNANCE, ACCESSORIES	156	295	35	0	0	0	0	0	0
14 FOOD, KINDRED PRDTS.	55286	62070	28187	397	1	0	2525	0	0
15 TOBACCO MANUFACTURES	1247	26	287	0	0	0	0	0	0
16 FABRICS	3527	21355	739	5	122	0	13	0	0
17 TEXTILE PRDTS.	20750	7705	1024	505	5465	0	68	0	0
18 APPAREL	430	802	184	7	0	0	9	0	0
19 MISC. TEXTILE PRDTS.	0	0	0	0	0	0	0	0	0
20 LUMBER, WOOD PRDTS.	29446	5265	158115	0	1807	0	14908	0	0
21 WOODEN CONTAINERS	0	147	278	0	0	0	24	0	0
22 HOUSEHOLD FURNITURE	0	0	0	0	0	0	0	0	0
23 OTHER FURNITURE	0	0	0	0	0	0	0	0	0
24 PAPER, ALLIED PRDTS.	113842	23192	221612	1113	0	0	17891	0	0
25 PAPERBOARD CONTAINERS	0	0	0	0	0	0	247	0	0
26 PRINTING, PUBLISHING	0	0	0	0	0	0	170	0	0
27 CHEMICALS,SELECT. PRDTS.	8233	20962	1080	4	2504	0	0	0	0
28 PLASTICS, SYNTHETICS	121	441	13674	0	0	0	1313	0	0
29 DRUGS, COSMETICS	6033	84	1729	0	0	0	149	0	0
30 PAINT, ALLIED PRDTS.	6	5	1	0	0	0	0	0	0
31 PETROLEUM, RELATED INDS.	50934	111061	2236	0	414	0	177	0	0
32 RUBBER, MISC. PLASTICS	1432	5145	2754	4	0	0	243	0	0
33 LEATHER TANNING, PRDTS.	374	389	351	0	0	0	27	0	0
34 FOOTWEAR, LEATHER PRDTS.	33	170	18	0	0	0	1	0	0
35 GLASS, GLASS PRDTS.	885	1461	2693	6	0	0	19	0	0
36 STONE, CLAY PRDTS.	714	640	23946	85	0	0	2135	0	0
37 PRIMARY IRON, STEEL MFR.	68654	15942	55938	1420	470	0	1277	0	0
38 PRIMARY NONFERROUS MFR.	146906	5119	92836	28	0	0	7640	0	0

39 METAL CONTAINERS	137	230	105	6	0	0	4	0	0
40 FABRICATED METAL PRDTS.	59	108	55	3	0	0	2	0	0
41 SCREW MACH. PRDTS., ETC.	478	804	3900	23	0	0	353	0	0
42 OTHER FAB. METAL PRDTS.	3908	9659	7159	60	0	0	162	0	0
43 ENGINES, TURBINES	210	23	2159	33	0	0	165	0	0
44 FARM MACH., EQUIP.	1116	1298	34749	60	0	0	2913	0	0
45 CONSTRUC. MACH., EQUIP.	0	0	7047	0	0	0	679	0	0
46 MATERIAL HANDLING MACH.	0	0	510	0	0	0	50	0	0
47 METALWORKING MACHINERY	986	1852	2940	0	0	0	128	0	0
48 SPECIAL MACH., EQUIP.	1053	4382	2377	19	0	0	198	0	0
49 GENERAL MACH., EQUIP.	325	673	2680	23	0	0	234	0	0
50 MACHINE SHOP PRDTS.	0	0	0	0	0	0	0	0	0
51 OFFICE, COMPUT. MACHINES	548	1148	8728	50	0	0	798	0	0
52 SERVICE IND. MACHINES	12	26	21	1	0	0	1	0	0
53 ELECT. TRANSMISS. EQUIP.	423	1783	1283	5	0	0	96	0	0
54 HOUSEHOLD APPLIANCES	0	0	0	0	0	0	0	0	0
55 ELECTRIC LIGHTING EQUIP.	322	469	3005	4	0	0	268	0	0
56 RADIO, TV, ETC., EQUIP.	1972	3074	8603	18	0	0	721	0	0
57 ELECTRONIC COMPONENTS	129	187	1381	2	0	0	125	0	0
58 MISC. ELECTRICAL MACH.	316	462	4093	3	0	0	373	0	0
59 MOTOR VEHICLES, EQUIP.	8895	3276	1120	10	0	0	75	0	0
60 AIRCRAFT, PARTS	384	79	16413	0	0	0	1496	0	0
61 OTHER TRANSPORT. EQUIP.	1734	2201	1021	27	0	0	80	0	0
62 PROFESS., SCIEN. INSTRU.	278	518	475	0	0	0	41	0	0
63 MEDICAL, PHOTO. EQUIP.	848	1568	492	0	0	0	30	0	0
64 MISC. MANUFACTURING	3314	6136	5624	8	0	0	473	0	0
65 TRANSPORT., WAREHOUSING	47223	30950	81874	5154	3297	7088	1055	2390	783
66 COMMUNICA.,EXC. BRDCAST.	0	0	0	0	0	0	0	0	0
67 RADIO, TV BROADCASTING	0	0	0	0	0	0	0	0	0
68 ELEC.,GAS,WATER,SAN.SER.	0	495	78	600	200	200	6500	0	100
69 WHOLESALE, RETAIL TRADE	0	0	0	0	0	0	0	0	0
70 FINANCE, INSURANCE	268	494	622	275	95	353	45	115	35
71 REAL ESTATE, RENTAL	0	0	0	0	0	0	0	0	0
72 HOTELS, PERSONAL SERV.	0	0	0	0	0	0	0	0	0
73 BUSINESS SERVICES	0	0	0	0	0	0	0	0	0
74 RESEARCH, DEVELOPMENT	0	0	0	0	0	0	0	0	0
75 AUTO. REPAIR, SERVICES	0	0	0	0	0	0	0	0	0
76 AMUSEMENTS	0	0	0	0	0	0	0	0	0
77 MED.,EDUC. SERVICES	0	0	0	0	0	0	0	0	0
78 FEDERAL GOVT. ENTERPRISE	0	0	0	0	0	0	0	0	0
79 STATE, LOCAL GOVT. ENT.	0	0	0	0	0	0	0	0	0
80 ZERO ENTRIES	0	0	0	0	0	0	0	0	0
81 SERVICE IND. RESIDUAL	-759271	-408517	-1164437	-10551	-19307	-7841	-91272	-2571	-942
82 TOTAL FINAL DEMAND	0	0	0	0	0	0	0	0	0
83 SECONDARY TRANSFERS-OUT	0	0	0	0	0	0	0	0	0
84 ZERO ENTRIES	0	0	0	0	0	0	0	0	0
85 SCRAP ENTRIES	19400	10438	29753	270	493	200	2332	66	24
86 ZERO ENTRIES	0	0	0	0	0	0	0	0	0
87 STATE TOTAL CONSUMPTION	0	0	0	0	0	0	0	0	0

TABLE C-13

1963 TRANSFERRED IMPORTS BY STATE
(THOUSANDS OF CURRENT DOLLARS)

INDUSTRY TITLE	28 NEW HAMPSHIRE	29 NEW JERSEY	30 NEW MEXICO	31 NEW YORK	32 NORTH CAROLINA	33 NORTH DAKOTA	34 OHIO	35 OKLAHOMA	36 OREGON
1 LIVESTOCK, PRDTS.	0	13356	0	22687	1067	2431	1278	0	388
2 OTHER AGRICULTURE PRDTS.	0	35341	0	85492	165	816	3618	0	470
3 FORESTRY, FISHERIES	0	36026	0	124074	5	6312	1829	0	2075
4 AGRI.,FORES.,FISH. SERV.	0	0	0	0	0	0	0	0	0
5 IRON, FERRO. ORES MINING	0	12955	0	18247	0	1302	30361	0	151
6 NONFERROUS ORES MINING	0	1342	0	36362	0	6814	4	0	2207
7 COAL MINING	0	0	0	574	0	166	707	0	0
8 CRUDE PETRO.,NATURAL GAS	0	26910	0	118754	219	33041	0	0	3
9 STONE, CLAY MINING	0	1520	0	20011	1	3564	2207	0	154
10 CHEM.,FERT. MIN. MINING	0	12612	0	7278	105	1950	510	0	0
11 NEW CONSTRUCTION	0	0	0	0	0	0	0	0	0
12 MAINT., REPAIR CONSTR.	0	0	0	0	0	0	0	0	0
13 ORDNANCE, ACCESSORIES	0	1744	0	10660	0	0	35	0	35
14 FOOD, KINDRED PRDTS.	0	129174	0	532736	2072	6184	1043	0	1135
15 TOBACCO MANUFACTURES	0	1571	0	65987	0	0	541	0	0
16 FABRICS	0	52527	0	163752	5137	32	210	0	359
17 TEXTILE PRDTS.	0	14872	0	78428	5529	167	217	0	10252
18 APPAREL	0	4889	0	22616	52	21	83	0	95
19 MISC. TEXTILE PRDTS.	0	0	0	0	0	0	0	0	0
20 LUMBER, WOOD PRDTS.	0	42375	0	138053	295	36497	16	0	238
21 WOODEN CONTAINERS	0	228	0	206	103	60	5	0	85
22 HOUSEHOLD FURNITURE	0	0	0	0	0	0	0	0	0
23 OTHER FURNITURE	0	0	0	0	0	0	0	0	0
24 PAPER, ALLIED PRDTS.	0	33200	0	259734	602	43801	15154	0	298
25 PAPERBOARD CONTAINERS	0	0	0	2099	0	608	2582	0	0
26 PRINTING, PUBLISHING	0	0	0	1437	0	416	1769	0	0
27 CHEMICALS,SELECT. PRDTS.	0	16155	0	66662	15174	0	1218	0	5812
28 PLASTICS, SYNTHETICS	0	2026	0	17107	0	3214	15	0	14
29 DRUGS, COSMETICS	0	3863	0	41802	0	367	5	0	0
30 PAINT, ALLIED PRDTS.	0	8	0	72	0	0	0	0	0
31 PETROLEUM, RELATED INDS.	0	72662	0	133753	5802	433	0	0	343
32 RUBBER, MISC. PLASTICS	0	16184	0	43209	83	596	110	0	330
33 LEATHER TANNING, PRDTS.	0	8448	0	35169	37	66	26	0	29
34 FOOTWEAR, LEATHER PRDTS.	0	696	0	2505	2	2	4	0	6
35 GLASS, GLASS PRDTS.	0	5275	0	28753	40	47	144	0	388
36 STONE, CLAY PRDTS.	0	3375	0	16944	97	5227	1611	0	94
37 PRIMARY IRON, STEEL MFR.	0	95894	0	94709	4345	3127	12586	0	10273
38 PRIMARY NONFERROUS MFR.	0	86089	0	419381	363	18704	10661	0	2499

39 METAL CONTAINERS	0	677	0	5105	30	9	46	0	46
40 FABRICATED METAL PRDTS.	0	348	0	2542	14	6	20	0	21
41 SCREW MACH. PRDTS., ETC.	0	2369	0	20708	138	863	163	0	390
42 OTHER FAB. METAL PRDTS.	0	12741	0	32044	7379	399	1158	0	2619
43 ENGINES, TURBINES	0	218	0	14969	12	405	96	0	87
44 FARM MACH., EQUIP.	0	1500	0	39106	439	7132	93	0	583
45 CONSTRUC. MACH., EQUIP.	0	0	0	5720	0	1655	0	0	0
46 MATERIAL HANDLING MACH.	0	0	0	418	0	121	0	0	0
47 METALWORKING MACHINERY	0	2101	0	40467	8	282	510	0	102
48 SPECIAL MACH., EQUIP.	0	20318	0	21392	1428	482	1053	0	356
49 GENERAL MACH., EQUIP.	0	3857	0	24420	81	571	191	0	140
50 MACHINE SHOP PRDTS.	0	0	0	0	0	0	0	0	0
51 OFFICE, COMPUT. MACHINES	0	6563	0	45014	150	1946	325	0	250
52 SERVICE IND. MACHINES	0	145	0	855	3	3	8	0	5
53 ELECT. TRANSMISS. EQUIP.	0	4458	0	29958	19	236	351	0	208
54 HOUSEHOLD APPLIANCES	0	0	0	0	0	0	0	0	0
55 ELECTRIC LIGHTING EQUIP.	0	3389	0	24420	14	657	268	0	158
56 RADIO, TV, ETC., EQUIP.	0	20922	0	140547	90	1767	1320	0	846
57 ELECTRONIC COMPONENTS	0	1360	0	9936	6	303	106	0	63
58 MISC. ELECTRICAL MACH.	0	3331	0	24930	14	913	263	0	155
59 MOTOR VEHICLES, EQUIP.	0	51507	0	10056	1	183	27	0	1403
60 AIRCRAFT, PARTS	0	2846	0	28244	424	3659	86	0	8
61 OTHER TRANSPORT. EQUIP.	0	4374	0	22908	94	194	109	0	2007
62 PROFESS., SCIEN. INSTRU.	0	2949	0	18771	14	97	52	0	69
63 MEDICAL, PHOTO. EQUIP.	0	9179	0	56253	45	74	159	0	212
64 MISC. MANUFACTURING	0	44173	0	148229	169	1157	615	0	0
65 TRANSPORT., WAREHOUSING	2326	69260	1618	191021	9770	905	31977	2779	5315
66 COMMUNICA.,EXC. BRDCAST.	0	0	0	0	0	0	0	0	0
67 RADIO, TV BROADCASTING	0	0	0	0	0	0	0	0	0
68 ELEC.,GAS,WATER,SAN.SER.	0	675	0	4600	0	500	2622	0	10500
69 WHOLESALE, RETAIL TRADE	0	0	0	0	0	0	0	0	0
70 FINANCE, INSURANCE	47	589	61	1870	267	37	801	165	150
71 REAL ESTATE, RENTAL	0	0	0	0	0	0	0	0	0
72 HOTELS, PERSONAL SERV.	0	0	0	0	0	0	0	0	0
73 BUSINESS SERVICES	0	0	0	0	0	0	0	0	0
74 RESEARCH, DEVELOPMENT	0	0	0	0	0	0	0	0	0
75 AUTO. REPAIR, SERVICES	0	0	0	0	0	0	0	0	0
76 AMUSEMENTS	0	0	0	0	0	0	0	0	0
77 MED.,EDUC. SERVICES	0	0	0	0	0	0	0	0	0
78 FEDERAL GOVT. ENTERPRISE	0	0	0	0	0	0	0	0	0
79 STATE, LOCAL GOVT. ENT.	0	0	0	0	0	0	0	0	0
80 ZERO ENTRIES	0	0	0	0	0	0	0	0	0
81 SERVICE IND. RESIDUAL	-2435	-1027418	-1723	-3667466	-63525	-205780	-134402	-3021	-65092
82 TOTAL FINAL DEMAND	0	0	0	0	0	0	0	0	0
83 SECONDARY TRANSFERS-OUT	0	0	0	0	0	0	0	0	0
84 ZERO ENTRIES	0	0	0	0	0	0	0	0	0
85 SCRAP ENTRIES	62	26252	44	93708	1623	5258	3434	77	1663
86 ZERO ENTRIES	0	0	0	0	0	0	0	0	0
87 STATE TOTAL CONSUMPTION	0	0	0	0	0	0	0	0	0

TABLE C-13

1963 TRANSFERRED IMPORTS BY STATE
(THOUSANDS OF CURRENT DOLLARS)

INDUSTRY TITLE	37 PENNSYL-VANIA	38 RHODE ISLAND	39 SOUTH CAROLINA	40 SOUTH DAKOTA	41 TENNESSEE	42 TEXAS	43 UTAH	44 VERMONT	45 VIRGINIA
1 LIVESTOCK, PRDTS.	18179	23	6621	0	0	28393	0	2562	3622
2 OTHER AGRICULTURE PRDTS.	11696	4	2280	0	0	13114	0	861	1889
3 FORESTRY, FISHERIES	26745	853	550	0	0	40838	0	6655	176
4 AGRI.,FORES.,FISH. SERV.	0	0	0	0	0	0	0	0	0
5 IRON, FERRO. ORES MINING	120372	0	1	0	0	5709	0	1373	5698
6 NONFERROUS ORES MINING	39	0	4	0	0	48446	0	7184	33
7 COAL MINING	0	0	0	0	0	0	0	175	0
8 CRUDE PETRO.,NATURAL GAS	242107	28	5136	0	0	19159	0	34836	402
9 STONE, CLAY MINING	3299	22	44	0	0	6989	0	3758	1093
10 CHEM.,FERT. MIN. MINING	1013	0	0	0	0	168	0	2055	396
11 NEW CONSTRUCTION	0	0	0	0	0	0	0	0	0
12 MAINT., REPAIR CONSTR.	0	0	0	0	0	0	0	0	0
13 ORDNANCE, ACCESSORIES	426	0	17	0	0	208	0	0	52
14 FOOD, KINDRED PRDTS.	98862	157	3602	0	42	32922	0	6519	5637
15 TOBACCO MANUFACTURES	173	0	0	0	0	907	0	0	139
16 FABRICS	11165	32	12746	0	0	2285	0	34	14137
17 TEXTILE PRDTS.	38618	0	3609	0	606	33036	0	176	18554
18 APPAREL	1442	0	72	0	0	437	0	23	149
19 MISC. TEXTILE PRDTS.	0	0	0	0	0	0	0	0	0
20 LUMBER, WOOD PRDTS.	5034	19	48	0	4	10573	0	38480	1154
21 WOODEN CONTAINERS	4	0	257	0	0	315	0	62	38
22 HOUSEHOLD FURNITURE	0	0	0	0	0	0	0	0	0
23 OTHER FURNITURE	0	0	0	0	0	0	0	0	0
24 PAPER, ALLIED PRDTS.	26632	136	2400	0	0	10693	0	46180	4851
25 PAPERBOARD CONTAINERS	0	0	0	0	0	31	0	641	0
26 PRINTING, PUBLISHING	0	0	0	0	0	810	0	438	0
27 CHEMICALS,SELECT. PRDTS.	5209	146	12384	0	0	35015	0	0	23581
28 PLASTICS, SYNTHETICS	6189	0	0	0	0	410	0	3388	1678
29 DRUGS, COSMETICS	1040	0	13	0	0	366	0	387	29
30 PAINT, ALLIED PRDTS.	22	0	0	0	0	109	0	0	2
31 PETROLEUM, RELATED INDS.	52858	1264	11851	0	0	41797	0	457	0
32 RUBBER, MISC. PLASTICS	1714	0	174	0	0	1338	0	628	0
33 LEATHER TANNING, PRDTS.	932	0	13	0	0	145	0	69	462
34 FOOTWEAR, LEATHER PRDTS.	83	0	3	0	0	35	0	3	9
35 GLASS, GLASS PRDTS.	3900	0	117	0	0	1071	0	50	1752
36 STONE, CLAY PRDTS.	1664	0	72	0	0	18372	0	5511	390
37 PRIMARY IRON, STEEL MFR.	58221	0	18723	0	0	73307	0	3297	3485
38 PRIMARY NONFERROUS MFR.	87167	0	5462	0	0	24698	0	19719	2099

39 METAL CONTAINERS	285	0	21	0	0	167	0	11	29
40 FABRICATED METAL PRDTS.	136	0	9	0	0	93	0	6	15
41 SCREW MACH. PRDTS., ETC.	995	0	110	0	0	587	0	911	184
42 OTHER FAB. METAL PRDTS.	7694	0	3888	0	0	13279	0	420	3804
43 ENGINES, TURBINES	181	0	0	0	0	336	0	427	22
44 FARM MACH., EQUIP.	696	0	647	0	0	1629	0	7519	946
45 CONSTRUC. MACH., EQUIP.	0	0	0	0	0	38	0	1747	0
46 MATERIAL HANDLING MACH.	0	0	0	0	0	4	0	125	0
47 METALWORKING MACHINERY	5011	0	15	0	0	1342	0	333	85
48 SPECIAL MACH., EQUIP.	5025	0	5953	0	0	1655	0	508	7138
49 GENERAL MACH., EQUIP.	1138	0	56	0	0	837	0	602	190
50 MACHINE SHOP PRDTS.	0	0	0	0	0	0	0	0	0
51 OFFICE, COMPUT. MACHINES	1942	0	100	0	0	1421	0	2069	325
52 SERVICE IND. MACHINES	43	0	3	0	0	31	0	3	8
53 ELECT. TRANSMISS. EQUIP.	675	15	40	0	0	334	0	249	372
54 HOUSEHOLD APPLIANCES	0	0	0	0	0	0	0	0	0
55 ELECTRIC LIGHTING EQUIP.	514	11	29	0	0	253	0	693	283
56 RADIO, TV, ETC., EQUIP.	3651	51	212	0	0	4225	0	1864	1478
57 ELECTRONIC COMPONENTS	206	5	13	0	0	101	0	320	114
58 MISC. ELECTRICAL MACH.	505	11	29	0	0	251	0	963	279
59 MOTOR VEHICLES, EQUIP.	1047	0	1108	0	0	4116	0	193	422
60 AIRCRAFT, PARTS	366	0	8	0	0	266	0	3862	94
61 OTHER TRANSPORT. EQUIP.	6572	0	56	0	0	1477	0	205	1016
62 PROFESS., SCIEN. INSTRU.	804	0	46	0	0	402	0	101	101
63 MEDICAL, PHOTO. EQUIP.	2219	0	134	0	0	1105	0	79	301
64 MISC. MANUFACTURING	8878	0	552	0	0	4238	0	1220	1169
65 TRANSPORT., WAREHOUSING	99991	649	8973	837	5306	46832	1284	527	12477
66 COMMUNICA.,EXC. BRDCAST.	0	0	0	0	0	0	0	0	0
67 RADIO, TV BROADCASTING	0	0	0	0	0	0	0	0	0
68 ELEC.,GAS,WATER,SAN.SER.	3225	107	0	0	200	1300	0	600	0
69 WHOLESALE, RETAIL TRADE	0	0	0	0	0	0	0	0	0
70 FINANCE, INSURANCE	915	69	125	38	228	764	71	27	268
71 REAL ESTATE, RENTAL	0	0	0	0	0	0	0	0	0
72 HOTELS, PERSONAL SERV.	0	0	0	0	0	0	0	0	0
73 BUSINESS SERVICES	0	0	0	0	0	0	0	0	0
74 RESEARCH, DEVELOPMENT	0	0	0	0	0	0	0	0	0
75 AUTO. REPAIR, SERVICES	0	0	0	0	0	0	0	0	0
76 AMUSEMENTS	0	0	0	0	0	0	0	0	0
77 MED.,EDUC. SERVICES	0	0	0	0	0	0	0	0	0
78 FEDERAL GOVT. ENTERPRISE	0	0	0	0	0	0	0	0	0
79 STATE, LOCAL GOVT. ENT.	0	0	0	0	0	0	0	0	0
80 ZERO ENTRIES	0	0	0	0	0	0	0	0	0
81 SERVICE IND. RESIDUAL	-1003149	-3697	-111168	-898	-6553	-552908	-1391	-216643	-125845
82 TOTAL FINAL DEMAND	0	0	0	0	0	0	0	0	0
83 SECONDARY TRANSFERS-OUT	0	0	0	0	0	0	0	0	0
84 ZERO ENTRIES	0	0	0	0	0	0	0	0	0
85 SCRAP ENTRIES	25632	94	2840	23	167	14127	36	5536	3215
86 ZERO ENTRIES	0	0	0	0	0	0	0	0	0
87 STATE TOTAL CONSUMPTION	0	0	0	0	0	0	0	0	0

TABLE C-13

1963 TRANSFERRED IMPORTS BY STATE
(THOUSANDS OF CURRENT DOLLARS)

INDUSTRY TITLE	46 WASHINGTON	47 WEST VIRGINIA	48 WISCONSIN	49 WYOMING	50 ALASKA	51 HAWAII	52 NATIONAL TOTAL
1 LIVESTOCK, PRDTS.	3361	0	2590	0	53	2177	173824
2 OTHER AGRICULTURE PRDTS.	2456	0	3373	0	0	49	220717
3 FORESTRY, FISHERIES	9987	0	6983	0	432	1127	427900
4 AGRI.,FORES.,FISH. SERV.	0	0	0	0	0	0	0
5 IRON, FERRO. ORES MINING	1248	0	1300	0	0	4	422800
6 NONFERROUS ORES MINING	8000	0	6864	0	0	0	212700
7 COAL MINING	159	0	166	0	0	0	2200
8 CRUDE PETRO.,NATURAL GAS	41616	0	32979	0	0	18565	1046300
9 STONE, CLAY MINING	4981	0	3737	0	1	151	108000
10 CHEM.,FERT. MIN. MINING	1975	0	1946	0	118	138	87500
11 NEW CONSTRUCTION	0	0	0	0	0	0	0
12 MAINT., REPAIR CONSTR.	0	0	0	0	0	0	0
13 ORDNANCE, ACCESSORIES	1267	0	17	0	920	69	18000
14 FOOD, KINDRED PRDTS.	6968	0	8156	0	91	1972	1197200
15 TOBACCO MANUFACTURES	0	0	245	0	0	436	73600
16 FABRICS	180	0	78	0	0	490	309400
17 TEXTILE PRDTS.	1299	0	4093	0	0	126	434900
18 APPAREL	688	0	50	0	1431	133	38600
19 MISC. TEXTILE PRDTS.	0	0	0	0	0	0	0
20 LUMBER, WOOD PRDTS.	89659	0	36736	0	129	652	675100
21 WOODEN CONTAINERS	736	0	79	0	3	12	4629
22 HOUSEHOLD FURNITURE	0	0	0	0	0	0	0
23 OTHER FURNITURE	0	0	0	0	0	0	0
24 PAPER, ALLIED PRDTS.	47488	0	55211	0	0	3487	1096000
25 PAPERBOARD CONTAINERS	582	0	607	0	0	0	9300
26 PRINTING, PUBLISHING	397	0	415	0	0	0	6500
27 CHEMICALS,SELECT. PRDTS.	43543	0	54	0	4	4512	342300
28 PLASTICS, SYNTHETICS	3080	0	3208	0	0	8	58800
29 DRUGS, COSMETICS	388	0	377	0	0	40	58000
30 PAINT, ALLIED PRDTS.	0	0	0	0	0	0	600
31 PETROLEUM, RELATED INDS.	2349	0	432	0	1801	15804	735100
32 RUBBER, MISC. PLASTICS	790	0	624	0	0	203	88300
33 LEATHER TANNING, PRDTS.	77	0	96	0	0	49	49800
34 FOOTWEAR, LEATHER PRDTS.	44	0	5	0	111	10	4100
35 GLASS, GLASS PRDTS.	196	0	102	0	0	437	58600
36 STONE, CLAY PRDTS.	5354	0	5408	0	487	117	108400
37 PRIMARY IRON, STEEL MFR.	3819	0	6281	0	0	4165	714900
38 PRIMARY NONFERROUS MFR.	18007	0	19330	0	1010	48	1103300

39 METAL CONTAINERS	24	0	29	0	4	33	8400
40 FABRICATED METAL PRDTS.	24	0	15	0	33	14	4200
41 SCREW MACH. PRDTS., ETC.	1148	0	931	0	13	331	43600
42 OTHER FAB. METAL PRDTS.	834	0	550	0	145	346	160500
43 ENGINES, TURBINES	401	0	441	0	0	8	23500
44 FARM MACH., EQUIP.	6839	0	7522	0	0	9	131200
45 CONSTRUC. MACH., EQUIP.	1585	0	2615	0	0	0	21900
46 MATERIAL HANDLING MACH.	117	0	238	0	0	0	10000
47 METALWORKING MACHINERY	337	0	940	0	0	8	60600
48 SPECIAL MACH., EQUIP.	534	0	695	0	0	95	96800
49 GENERAL MACH., EQUIP.	581	0	653	0	1	64	40800
50 MACHINE SHOP PRDTS.	0	0	0	0	0	0	0
51 OFFICE, COMPUT. MACHINES	1921	0	2094	0	0	100	81900
52 SERVICE IND. MACHINES	4	0	5	0	0	3	1300
53 ELECT. TRANSMISS. EQUIP.	272	0	271	0	1	132	48900
54 HOUSEHOLD APPLIANCES	0	0	0	0	0	0	0
55 ELECTRIC LIGHTING EQUIP.	664	0	683	0	1	99	42300
56 RADIO, TV, ETC., EQUIP.	5750	0	1927	0	2791	683	236400
57 ELECTRONIC COMPONENTS	303	0	314	0	0	40	47600
58 MISC. ELECTRICAL MACH.	908	0	939	0	0	98	45000
59 MOTOR VEHICLES, EQUIP.	212	0	209	0	11	219	103080
60 AIRCRAFT, PARTS	3502	0	3651	0	0	8	68600
61 OTHER TRANSPORT. EQUIP.	341	0	333	0	14	146	59800
62 PROFESS., SCIEN. INSTRU.	2292	0	120	0	1576	139	32500
63 MEDICAL, PHOTO. EQUIP.	6757	0	139	0	4789	395	95700
64 MISC. MANUFACTURING	27046	0	1409	0	18579	1516	317500
65 TRANSPORT., WAREHOUSING	31259	1741	20151	491	2697	7865	1012943
66 COMMUNICA.,EXC. BRDCAST.	0	0	0	0	0	0	0
67 RADIO, TV BROADCASTING	0	0	0	0	0	0	0
68 ELEC.,GAS,WATER,SAN.SER.	21400	0	14000	0	100	0	105200
69 WHOLESALE, RETAIL TRADE	0	0	0	0	0	0	0
70 FINANCE, INSURANCE	241	105	309	27	15	46	15000
71 REAL ESTATE, RENTAL	0	0	0	0	0	0	0
72 HOTELS, PERSONAL SERV.	0	0	0	0	0	0	0
73 BUSINESS SERVICES	0	0	0	0	0	0	0
74 RESEARCH, DEVELOPMENT	0	0	0	0	0	0	0
75 AUTO. REPAIR, SERVICES	0	0	0	0	0	0	0
76 AMUSEMENTS	0	0	0	0	0	0	0
77 MED.,EDUC. SERVICES	0	0	0	0	0	0	0
78 FEDERAL GOVT. ENTERPRISE	0	0	0	0	0	0	0
79 STATE, LOCAL GOVT. ENT.	0	0	0	0	0	0	0
80 ZERO ENTRIES	0	0	0	0	0	0	0
81 SERVICE IND. RESIDUAL	-426899	-1894	-269628	-532	-38339	-69141	-13138289
82 TOTAL FINAL DEMAND	0	0	0	0	0	0	0
83 SECONDARY TRANSFERS-OUT	0	0	0	0	0	0	0
84 ZERO ENTRIES	0	0	0	0	0	0	0
85 SCRAP ENTRIES	10908	48	6889	14	980	1767	335700
86 ZERO ENTRIES	0	0	0	0	0	0	0
87 STATE TOTAL CONSUMPTION	0	0	0	0	0	0	0

TABLE C-14

1963 STATE VALUE ADDED
(THOUSANDS OF CURRENT DOLLARS)

INDUSTRY TITLE	1 ALABAMA	2 ARIZONA	3 ARKANSAS	4 CALIFORNIA	5 COLORADO	6 CONNECTICUT	7 DELAWARE	8 DISTRICT OF COLUMBIA	9 FLORIDA
1 LIVESTOCK, PRDTS.	157962	26889	109310	336867	123101	49602	478	0	58225
2 OTHER AGRICULTURE PRDTS.	191624	196247	416826	1442993	133748	46171	24542	0	521193
3 FORESTRY, FISHERIES	14363	1724	10064	70524	552	1390	1140	0	27897
4 AGRI.,FORES.,FISH. SERV.	22170	11819	33038	62932	3448	3155	2951	0	17786
5 IRON, FERRO. ORES MINING	9733	434	340	20863	50141	0	0	0	0
6 NONFERROUS ORES MINING	406	197529	8796	2972	33050	178	0	0	3560
7 COAL MINING	62484	160	2293	64	17861	0	0	0	0
8 CRUDE PETRO.,NATURAL GAS	13866	293	46582	669497	82603	0	0	0	919
9 STONE, CLAY MINING	17426	8020	18816	121247	11286	9083	595	0	35141
10 CHEM.,FERT. MIN. MINING	0	0	1037	56419	742	0	127	0	41901
11 NEW CONSTRUCTION	287242	434558	174956	6510493	169804	577451	54023	54435	1149695
12 MAINT., REPAIR CONSTR.	128565	103056	103400	1406771	149293	150572	24111	44717	340034
13 ORDNANCE, ACCESSORIES	40383	46822	50	1399955	19239	66914	0	0	118685
14 FOOD, KINDRED PRDTS.	205531	69028	186650	2190381	269152	146805	47436	42148	448818
15 TOBACCO MANUFACTURES	17202	0	0	603	0	4051	0	0	73715
16 FABRICS	166109	56	4956	7802	99	59059	15492	0	3049
17 TEXTILE PRDTS.	18048	53	4758	31388	220	15772	3616	0	557
18 APPAREL	126898	8938	29702	308231	5832	71316	18471	0	40223
19 MISC. TEXTILE PRDTS.	9713	1043	176	51080	2223	7997	1114	271	4059
20 LUMBER, WOOD PRDTS.	97871	20854	112079	481146	13154	11640	4906	488	64683
21 WOODEN CONTAINERS	2676	556	5128	24544	753	1307	208	0	6664
22 HOUSEHOLD FURNITURE	15706	3708	37021	165488	5832	15117	129	0	29294
23 OTHER FURNITURE	4469	1895	7004	79086	2447	12640	710	0	7895
24 PAPER, ALLIED PRDTS.	147242	5013	79485	181176	5051	48363	4377	0	160774
25 PAPERBOARD CONTAINERS	8193	1990	17050	181717	7527	30845	3967	0	29928
26 PRINTING, PUBLISHING	44236	34149	26226	655891	58340	139154	13343	115626	133562
27 CHEMICALS,SELECT. PRDTS.	123493	10579	13242	242240	15100	117952	39229	793	103529
28 PLASTICS, SYNTHETICS	51692	0	406	80073	203	37709	86684	0	63479
29 DRUGS, COSMETICS	1186	1582	130	191189	4740	100742	5160	0	8498
30 PAINT, ALLIED PRDTS.	2740	1038	1333	104812	3514	2913	258	0	14534
31 PETROLEUM, RELATED INDS.	14428	1262	36620	616374	20546	4871	40765	0	9285
32 RUBBER, MISC. PLASTICS	106612	2803	22192	329064	62294	150137	30803	0	11104
33 LEATHER TANNING, PRDTS.	0	0	0	6058	115	677	6897	0	458
34 FOOTWEAR, LEATHER PRDTS.	4254	197	32700	23315	15422	11018	2377	0	8521
35 GLASS, GLASS PRDTS.	3953	376	7778	100552	848	7611	353	0	9361
36 STONE, CLAY PRDTS.	83869	33887	26218	486220	49387	61217	9018	9754	122030
37 PRIMARY IRON, STEEL MFR.	437685	4918	1604	353191	72273	102665	66295	0	13939
38 PRIMARY NONFERROUS MFR.	77488	140269	41508	202896	3415	207591	4891	0	16687

39 METAL CONTAINERS	2859	0	3107	133816	7162	1061	0	0	26368
40 FABRICATED METAL PRDTS.	67303	13133	15904	319107	18875	36650	8828	1832	74651
41 SCREW MACH. PRDTS., ETC.	14957	469	4278	126047	960	104628	3614	0	5752
42 OTHER FAB. METAL PRDTS.	40235	4758	12138	337615	17581	135513	4879	0	19824
43 ENGINES, TURBINES	0	0	0	34446	1855	24734	0	0	773
44 FARM MACH., EQUIP.	7167	1878	1827	24988	3027	798	277	0	3561
45 CONSTRUC. MACH., EQUIP.	3881	64	244	50239	39056	628	117	0	901
46 MATERIAL HANDLING MACH.	2619	53	3593	31382	1533	1948	0	0	1503
47 METALWORKING MACHINERY	2650	1652	3595	104042	918	145444	2605	0	6998
48 SPECIAL MACH., EQUIP.	8232	386	1258	73404	3260	41618	8025	0	9590
49 GENERAL MACH., EQUIP.	5255	1094	5002	197128	9465	186152	314	0	5224
50 MACHINE SHOP PRDTS.	6054	7169	2428	158842	8267	35678	1433	910	10702
51 OFFICE, COMPUT. MACHINES	76	60476	4569	301829	969	113491	0	0	23240
52 SERVICE IND. MACHINES	6154	11044	6266	48957	759	9913	1355	0	3865
53 ELECT. TRANSMISS. EQUIP.	10127	864	26990	228564	21591	73825	68	0	3963
54 HOUSEHOLD APPLIANCES	72	59	46653	74099	157	71817	1631	0	861
55 ELECTRIC LIGHTING EQUIP.	13675	303	10118	81695	1610	66067	1232	0	3050
56 RADIO, TV, ETC., EQUIP.	4633	44478	36010	1020436	1067	63448	61	0	99829
57 ELECTRONIC COMPONENTS	8653	37866	76	363586	908	77609	353	0	14214
58 MISC. ELECTRICAL MACH.	6496	247	100	41330	3477	17173	2943	0	13525
59 MOTOR VEHICLES, EQUIP.	20298	2390	4232	741818	6694	68612	135225	0	4450
60 AIRCRAFT, PARTS	261355	61973	549	1629321	62152	662394	3529	0	76432
61 OTHER TRANSPORT. EQUIP.	39008	1294	10062	158240	1871	36514	1009	0	51493
62 PROFESS., SCIEN. INSTRU.	884	15396	15726	148783	6307	112955	3425	0	10281
63 MEDICAL, PHOTO. EQUIP.	0	607	49	77117	3022	22246	0	0	9538
64 MISC. MANUFACTURING	9475	3550	18685	204395	10564	152342	649	912	16435
65 TRANSPORT., WAREHOUSING	252241	117206	144636	2382917	281179	221940	55276	222091	625360
66 COMMUNICA.,EXC. BRDCAST.	170955	76992	73745	1303606	122727	177097	29592	94642	354757
67 RADIO, TV BROADCASTING	10700	7906	5162	191059	10662	11040	2324	28744	30009
68 ELEC.,GAS,WATER,SAN.SER.	262907	148402	113986	1178907	170562	178691	38267	40385	314644
69 WHOLESALE, RETAIL TRADE	1027873	626305	577528	9496506	919319	1263906	253517	561446	2430665
70 FINANCE, INSURANCE	198023	119207	103484	1906233	174521	377748	49213	127757	459487
71 REAL ESTATE, RENTAL	640304	536825	303334	7147741	650447	947017	160061	789683	2369964
72 HOTELS, PERSONAL SERV.	101747	99976	63449	1137817	113708	134874	20454	110002	417928
73 BUSINESS SERVICES	122946	108927	45787	2383166	148864	209751	32521	245978	453764
74 RESEARCH, DEVELOPMENT	0	0	0	0	0	0	0	0	0
75 AUTO. REPAIR, SERVICES	88272	61373	51634	812948	82080	97118	16431	53070	205939
76 AMUSEMENTS	17886	21980	16772	799772	36461	29562	12076	28186	128707
77 MED., EDUC. SERVICES	138846	109813	62136	2154699	201328	531801	48381	825162	392751
78 FEDERAL GOVT. ENTERPRISE	117020	28973	36349	439955	44829	46394	9505	106933	120478
79 STATE, LOCAL GOVT. ENT.	84005	38050	18555	432862	38637	39600	7763	10540	138950
80 ZERO ENTRIES	0	0	0	0	0	0	0	0	0
81 SERVICE IND. RESIDUAL	0	0	0	0	0	0	0	0	0
82 TOTAL FINAL DEMAND	898984	427341	353574	6589686	729014	592145	143439	1051472	1465154
83 SECONDARY TRANSFERS-OUT	0	0	0	0	0	0	0	0	0
84 ZERO ENTRIES	0	0	0	0	0	0	0	0	0
85 SCRAP ENTRIES	0	0	0	0	0	0	0	0	0
86 ZERO ENTRIES	0	0	0	0	0	0	0	0	0
87 STATE TOTAL CONSUMPTION	7392346	4172220	3823063	64265200	5370803	9395624	1574858	4567976	14105259

TABLE C-14

1963 STATE VALUE ADDED
(THOUSANDS OF CURRENT DOLLARS)

INDUSTRY TITLE	10 GEORGIA	11 IDAHO	12 ILLINOIS	13 INDIANA	14 IOWA	15 KANSAS	16 KENTUCKY	17 LOUISIANA	18 MAINE
1 LIVESTOCK, PRDTS.	151634	9005	402391	6451	921126	154019	208145	85376	52993
2 OTHER AGRICULTURE PRDTS.	296340	219602	924491	566992	908897	220194	421023	253142	79833
3 FORESTRY, FISHERIES	22545	3931	1932	1242	530	112	2985	32060	18392
4 AGRI.,FORES.,FISH. SERV.	32909	3660	21619	11990	17566	8322	3704	10088	4977
5 IRON, FERRO. ORES MINING	705	324	0	0	0	0	0	0	0
6 NONFERROUS ORES MINING	112	16631	6122	0	0	45	0	0	37
7 COAL MINING	7	0	140890	42199	3732	6725	198193	0	0
8 CRUDE PETRO.,NATURAL GAS	0	0	147650	21446	0	273784	50831	1540391	0
9 STONE, CLAY MINING	54247	5348	56862	30700	23866	13587	30172	10248	1282
10 CHEM.,FERT. MIN. MINING	1438	3149	5634	0	0	797	1142	58369	0
11 NEW CONSTRUCTION	272423	71831	1244961	260595	169139	246192	289144	613997	59944
12 MAINT., REPAIR CONSTR.	168546	55049	646790	279944	216707	196032	140127	148096	41900
13 ORDNANCE, ACCESSORIES	1262	1856	49243	60536	35334	0	0	38011	5705
14 FOOD, KINDRED PRDTS.	438697	89610	1696498	565072	619670	257654	498160	384485	85359
15 TOBACCO MANUFACTURES	10777	0	12938	10244	0	0	606362	3809	0
16 FABRICS	388214	0	13911	0	1082	56	8309	0	68647
17 TEXTILE PRDTS.	132998	0	23779	2737	61	53	713	1948	3227
18 APPAREL	223948	275	154731	50104	10557	11750	83848	21141	14588
19 MISC. TEXTILE PRDTS.	34154	195	42396	8257	2210	2852	5961	6946	2698
20 LUMBER, WOOD PRDTS.	108493	98396	68795	77688	19834	4208	35909	74546	75442
21 WOODEN CONTAINERS	9002	345	4937	1513	863	316	6923	2876	733
22 HOUSEHOLD FURNITURE	37664	828	88553	112979	8398	5657	26541	5891	2346
23 OTHER FURNITURE	5675	286	84883	28298	8814	5395	4557	1413	1610
24 PAPER, ALLIED PRDTS.	221793	13773	158305	61628	15534	8419	14527	172286	197000
25 PAPERBOARD CONTAINERS	63088	1296	181863	59666	21792	24075	19171	25282	3132
26 PRINTING, PUBLISHING	86089	9198	889027	165033	100626	54502	64449	43665	15570
27 CHEMICALS,SELECT. PRDTS.	104155	8994	366195	110685	14202	40210	124878	318904	7047
28 PLASTICS, SYNTHETICS	26742	0	47315	18798	40288	8081	103047	84190	203
29 DRUGS, COSMETICS	36813	0	404294	276447	21306	44838	912	4011	191
30 PAINT, ALLIED PRDTS.	20105	86	134419	15273	12847	2634	28363	3944	172
31 PETROLEUM, RELATED INDS.	12534	106	331470	222646	2606	155684	40696	419417	942
32 RUBBER, MISC. PLASTICS	32313	101	266865	220082	99602	45690	27494	2059	14124
33 LEATHER TANNING, PRDTS.	2544	0	16297	689	0	0	1566	151	13553
34 FOOTWEAR, LEATHER PRDTS.	20044	251	66666	15207	2681	727	13766	26	107819
35 GLASS, GLASS PRDTS.	13680	0	133294	83518	95	495	13806	14205	674
36 STONE, CLAY PRDTS.	85510	8694	280187	167400	79292	86878	48212	66939	9165
37 PRIMARY IRON, STEEL MFR.	69453	514	879789	1110718	31694	12541	103280	11183	654
38 PRIMARY NONFERROUS MFR.	20927	31815	297924	251467	33987	7458	27615	34994	1971

39 METAL CONTAINERS	12194	513	134338	14617	136	2133	1546	18428	5364
40 FABRICATED METAL PRDTS.	54560	4027	229281	147347	42839	34804	41561	35426	5751
41 SCREW MACH. PRDTS., ETC.	18284	0	355200	100352	7918	2146	15305	2174	311
42 OTHER FAB. METAL PRDTS.	22658	302	509317	152645	34941	12437	64626	23506	1966
43 ENGINES, TURBINES	91	0	95118	32158	17114	0	0	270	0
44 FARM MACH., EQUIP.	12694	2146	216230	41323	199606	13669	23976	4029	325
45 CONSTRUC. MACH., EQUIP.	11310	500	496992	37902	63461	12212	766	10124	4588
46 MATERIAL HANDLING MACH.	5194	337	69659	4993	5327	5508	9849	820	0
47 METALWORKING MACHINERY	3667	104	305076	67852	15676	4482	6004	509	1252
48 SPECIAL MACH., EQUIP.	23170	362	132904	26170	12302	8440	7921	5495	3486
49 GENERAL MACH., EQUIP.	5545	0	227981	165281	17464	12174	27948	1488	1572
50 MACHINE SHOP PRDTS.	5054	936	90009	64108	4286	15109	15741	7970	1443
51 OFFICE, COMPUT. MACHINES	1829	0	125557	1508	71	155	31413	399	0
52 SERVICE IND. MACHINES	6389	273	89127	43214	17828	9677	26446	2361	1117
53 ELECT. TRANSMISS. EQUIP.	48980	0	240976	140507	10943	1511	31923	964	1212
54 HOUSEHOLD APPLIANCES	1472	0	234280	117785	56876	134	107678	285	85
55 ELECTRIC LIGHTING EQUIP.	10241	0	145166	65555	397	706	24453	392	3023
56 RADIO, TV, ETC., EQUIP.	660	0	787349	325565	45658	2987	5249	164	1184
57 ELECTRONIC COMPONENTS	1367	264	166658	89587	26205	7680	14876	214	9763
58 MISC. ELECTRICAL MACH.	11058	0	69449	219111	7210	8564	4025	913	1410
59 MOTOR VEHICLES, EQUIP.	241506	601	301633	605121	9994	72632	74555	5056	214
60 AIRCRAFT, PARTS	103245	1340	56843	216090	3071	334813	549	54546	8282
61 OTHER TRANSPORT. EQUIP.	20899	3925	127305	107317	7295	15615	6537	76821	38566
62 PROFESS., SCIEN. INSTRU.	10623	85	271637	51262	24704	1834	8003	2346	345
63 MEDICAL, PHOTO. EQUIP.	222	0	128834	19309	1313	508	698	1162	43
64 MISC. MANUFACTURING	30542	1286	260157	69695	37700	3652	12063	7404	6957
65 TRANSPORT., WAREHOUSING	484249	76300	1950957	533837	257516	328685	292057	469328	83374
66 COMMUNICA.,EXC. BRDCAST.	248558	35610	586329	288093	133856	115580	148075	235438	41147
67 RADIO, TV BROADCASTING	17783	3087	88315	19933	14101	14249	12385	14732	4102
68 ELEC.,GAS,WATER,SAN.SER.	262190	54734	972372	451635	221357	186589	210971	258860	44333
69 WHOLESALE, RETAIL TRADE	1750584	280041	6131868	2053087	1248859	880970	992965	1194471	359026
70 FINANCE, INSURANCE	340311	42322	1258898	375109	214544	158847	172058	237980	62215
71 REAL ESTATE, RENTAL	896873	165680	4580236	1236934	664088	535594	539914	773821	179425
72 HOTELS, PERSONAL SERV.	167101	30419	634390	209924	116896	86031	114494	111183	47524
73 BUSINESS SERVICES	207611	35867	1555288	201326	117578	84120	96773	187467	28988
74 RESEARCH, DEVELOPMENT	0	0	0	0	0	0	0	0	0
75 AUTO. REPAIR, SERVICES	131622	27342	360579	148626	92534	79632	80704	89397	30465
76 AMUSEMENTS	36528	7020	214401	46980	29109	22328	34156	37404	9279
77 MED.,EDUC. SERVICES	279740	32725	1729755	449255	236009	124938	204597	239696	85687
78 FEDERAL GOVT. ENTERPRISE	103577	11974	224108	71056	44521	48683	77506	48562	22383
79 STATE, LOCAL GOVT. ENT.	62693	15869	232383	75423	60406	46306	36400	47150	23814
80 ZERO ENTRIES	0	0	0	0	0	0	0	0	0
81 SERVICE IND. RESIDUAL	0	0	0	0	0	0	0	0	0
82 TOTAL FINAL DEMAND	1464026	165644	2480670	994623	539931	705365	787329	861568	266005
83 SECONDARY TRANSFERS-OUT	0	0	0	0	0	0	0	0	0
84 ZERO ENTRIES	0	0	0	0	0	0	0	0	0
85 SCRAP ENTRIES	0	0	0	0	0	0	0	0	0
86 ZERO ENTRIES	0	0	0	0	0	0	0	0	0
87 STATE TOTAL CONSUMPTION	10324477	1656783	39161552	15000464	8106582	5901478	7618630	9564411	2277954

TABLE C-14

1963 STATE VALUE ADDED
(THOUSANDS OF CURRENT DOLLARS)

INDUSTRY TITLE	19 MARYLAND	20 MASSA-CHUSETTS	21 MICHIGAN	22 MINNESOTA	23 MISSISSIPPI	24 MISSOURI	25 MONTANA	26 NEBRASKA	27 NEVADA
1 LIVESTOCK, PRDTS.	1782	56927	2734	404341	129332	290884	22234	104093	936
2 OTHER AGRICULTURE PRDTS.	80118	58181	390994	620682	416918	455932	154394	370438	5481
3 FORESTRY, FISHERIES	9635	28636	5352	3526	13989	3096	2435	94	9
4 AGRI.,FORES.,FISH. SERV.	9996	1536	7098	16697	29675	17578	2208	7563	370
5 IRON, FERRO. ORES MINING	13	0	56494	246011	0	3924	1526	0	2867
6 NONFERROUS ORES MINING	0	0	24468	1660	0	7064	8887	32	34537
7 COAL MINING	3818	0	0	0	0	10874	1510	0	0
8 CRUDE PETRO.,NATURAL GAS	289	0	39412	0	129343	393	50569	39601	108
9 STONE, CLAY MINING	24364	14275	49400	15102	7376	36677	4433	10283	11626
10 CHEM.,FERT. MIN. MINING	0	0	4773	0	0	2627	5121	0	563
11 NEW CONSTRUCTION	620358	1001803	1059113	341005	136877	511418	73999	99507	369385
12 MAINT., REPAIR CONSTR.	172266	258522	410538	235687	94612	269106	80052	137604	44698
13 ORDNANCE, ACCESSORIES	8256	46087	45477	57854	0	68433	0	509	0
14 FOOD, KINDRED PRDTS.	397724	435852	556750	607880	126408	677425	46982	313768	10929
15 TOBACCO MANUFACTURES	863	712	9751	0	0	12948	0	0	0
16 FABRICS	14938	154401	1663	4578	8653	6290	0	164	0
17 TEXTILE PRDTS.	390	56091	18054	4037	8082	7185	0	0	0
18 APPAREL	115279	266886	26823	34285	102785	127890	0	4683	93
19 MISC. TEXTILE PRDTS.	8970	34364	108202	7728	4739	16578	42	486	115
20 LUMBER, WOOD PRDTS.	24447	31043	76943	51022	104183	33179	78664	7681	3558
21 WOODEN CONTAINERS	2838	2862	2250	1533	8478	3165	0	247	0
22 HOUSEHOLD FURNITURE	14743	53814	48834	9853	37468	17571	251	4591	414
23 OTHER FURNITURE	13296	15525	89015	9676	2411	16930	256	4344	133
24 PAPER, ALLIED PRDTS.	36089	218351	242517	126952	31122	44059	2382	3527	44
25 PAPERBOARD CONTAINERS	48333	85449	103254	30183	5269	56846	0	6202	0
26 PRINTING, PUBLISHING	114990	310063	254430	155464	14517	213537	9924	40597	9480
27 CHEMICALS,SELECT. PRDTS.	92013	79473	300266	45907	20155	159008	3042	9098	13502
28 PLASTICS, SYNTHETICS	24855	99782	52547	6404	2009	1684	0	0	0
29 DRUGS, COSMETICS	91098	64410	186538	48008	16044	137264	158	20590	746
30 PAINT, ALLIED PRDTS.	15767	21985	63846	6978	258	38172	0	562	86
31 PETROLEUM, RELATED INDS.	28882	20391	91168	40957	21160	45672	35240	3081	348
32 RUBBER, MISC. PLASTICS	99404	324774	202390	30747	29874	50437	101	22720	0
33 LEATHER TANNING, PRDTS.	1112	53340	7540	2523	0	2160	0	490	0
34 FOOTWEAR, LEATHER PRDTS.	8440	219232	13347	6670	9748	153361	26	260	0
35 GLASS, GLASS PRDTS.	26597	2200	79655	9180	6910	33923	0	95	0
36 STONE, CLAY PRDTS.	74656	112815	182766	88596	39649	124724	11771	26913	22215
37 PRIMARY IRON, STEEL MFR.	208130	87327	1011719	78146	3640	83329	698	2236	325
38 PRIMARY NONFERROUS MFR.	103051	86141	222170	9865	4163	43959	63189	24478	22172

39 METAL CONTAINERS	40927	8103	3963	18961	68	34194	0	4682	0
40 FABRICATED METAL PRDTS.	45906	67026	161651	37085	20824	88052	2629	30985	2329
41 SCREW MACH. PRDTS., ETC.	18810	74330	315667	26003	9757	25933	0	1081	60
42 OTHER FAB. METAL PRDTS.	40329	152749	384941	39927	9916	87398	214	4456	272
43 ENGINES, TURBINES	0	84313	197222	8666	0	4939	0	0	0
44 FARM MACH., EQUIP.	277	480	84780	47747	10267	21271	325	12926	0
45 CONSTRUC. MACH., EQUIP.	1658	1854	56911	36380	6213	14361	59	1644	117
46 MATERIAL HANDLING MACH.	3944	13599	89088	9533	5394	6347	50	512	0
47 METALWORKING MACHINERY	35443	119102	523145	17324	101	27262	0	724	0
48 SPECIAL MACH., EQUIP.	30896	158142	89765	15337	5116	20453	0	375	57
49 GENERAL MACH., EQUIP.	8590	81303	159094	26319	1203	25237	0	11258	66
50 MACHINE SHOP PRDTS.	16631	35446	123244	22266	4108	49530	818	1379	558
51 OFFICE, COMPUT. MACHINES	4956	70859	162446	178044	0	11750	0	76	0
52 SERVICE IND. MACHINES	13892	33815	110111	50693	4300	55699	0	665	273
53 ELECT. TRANSMISS. EQUIP.	17481	115899	94850	44131	6038	82730	0	353	302
54 HOUSEHOLD APPLIANCES	3420	11714	95888	47567	7683	17623	0	463	0
55 ELECTRIC LIGHTING EQUIP.	1762	80450	20385	8426	20594	43792	0	0	0
56 RADIO, TV, ETC., EQUIP.	251614	491772	34728	58194	4703	61493	0	54659	2106
57 ELECTRONIC COMPONENTS	8921	192028	33187	25737	3926	4535	0	10936	89
58 MISC. ELECTRICAL MACH.	13353	27992	100989	10148	1354	15675	0	1561	60
59 MOTOR VEHICLES, EQUIP.	205146	91863	4635340	86587	15200	762794	135	16436	130
60 AIRCRAFT, PARTS	106731	97181	78310	19226	0	166724	0	59	59
61 OTHER TRANSPORT. EQUIP.	122348	50292	83691	9170	2505	31271	354	9369	31
62 PROFESS., SCIEN. INSTRU.	11440	145708	127769	26243	2785	20363	943	12367	0
63 MEDICAL, PHOTO. EQUIP.	3809	137625	7057	15343	49	9542	0	236	0
64 MISC. MANUFACTURING	21266	178908	108471	38078	17934	38413	1371	7337	1429
65 TRANSPORT., WAREHOUSING	388300	584368	726331	428993	116337	753389	91037	210822	62493
66 COMMUNICA.,EXC. BRDCAST.	196191	346485	528923	188744	97648	260242	32341	98468	13248
67 RADIO, TV BROADCASTING	13365	35555	43050	16906	6141	23605	3882	8651	2691
68 ELEC.,GAS,WATER,SAN.SER.	264623	409756	683497	268079	148541	317074	78917	75061	42029
69 WHOLESALE, RETAIL TRADE	1403571	2728119	3680958	1757823	576049	2411252	288406	729110	196473
70 FINANCE, INSURANCE	240709	745686	581381	326482	101151	464447	47888	156936	35190
71 REAL ESTATE, RENTAL	1211882	1700382	2386065	1196569	319265	1511560	170973	395962	210209
72 HOTELS, PERSONAL SERV.	143614	291270	367629	160626	62882	227963	32883	68641	115404
73 BUSINESS SERVICES	252644	568910	816783	303172	54419	378394	24695	84662	44568
74 RESEARCH, DEVELOPMENT	0	0	0	0	0	0	0	0	0
75 AUTO. REPAIR, SERVICES	127632	175389	301056	115216	51807	154128	26183	54280	20416
76 AMUSEMENTS	64087	86299	109827	41460	11271	58361	6454	21028	128295
77 MED.,EDUC. SERVICES	494629	1709710	648773	363035	63486	608413	34424	118903	17512
78 FEDERAL GOVT. ENTERPRISE	65590	130823	115811	70121	34324	108384	15270	34236	12147
79 STATE, LOCAL GOVT. ENT.	53854	119179	207748	74904	19629	52142	15048	93988	5959
80 ZERO ENTRIES	0	0	0	0	0	0	0	0	0
81 SERVICE IND. RESIDUAL	0	0	0	0	0	0	0	0	0
82 TOTAL FINAL DEMAND	1200371	1471310	1831932	751977	566420	973520	215487	399149	130069
83 SECONDARY TRANSFERS-OUT	0	0	0	0	0	0	0	0	0
84 ZERO ENTRIES	0	0	0	0	0	0	0	0	0
85 SCRAP ENTRIES	0	0	0	0	0	0	0	0	0
86 ZERO ENTRIES	0	0	0	0	0	0	0	0	0
87 STATE TOTAL CONSUMPTION	9648408	17929040	26960784	10346980	3955254	13815560	1750880	4000977	1599381

TABLE C-14

1963 STATE VALUE ADDED

(THOUSANDS OF CURRENT DOLLARS)

INDUSTRY TITLE	28 NEW HAMPSHIRE	29 NEW JERSEY	30 NEW MEXICO	31 NEW YORK	32 NORTH CAROLINA	33 NORTH DAKOTA	34 OHIO	35 OKLAHOMA	36 OREGON
1 LIVESTOCK, PRDTS.	20551	83008	84914	287369	130286	1430	89254	192580	49117
2 OTHER AGRICULTURE PRDTS.	10492	122000	65069	349120	693117	377173	503682	163627	176630
3 FORESTRY, FISHERIES	1676	8323	759	11693	20526	32	2876	831	95905
4 AGRI.,FORES.,FISH. SERV.	1300	2718	3104	6394	20943	3761	10711	10074	4833
5 IRON, FERRO. ORES MINING	0	3059	1896	22391	2063	0	0	0	1790
6 NONFERROUS ORES MINING	0	2384	77259	7718	99	392	112	733	43
7 COAL MINING	0	0	6226	0	0	7664	95458	3504	0
8 CRUDE PETRO.,NATURAL GAS	0	0	289379	6032	0	46880	16783	495061	359
9 STONE, CLAY MINING	2122	35884	7599	63106	25117	2304	61196	12703	15417
10 CHEM.,FERT. MIN. MINING	0	0	66944	8877	1099	0	10214	0	12
11 NEW CONSTRUCTION	58175	326624	151756	1920906	361779	48527	969400	411585	265476
12 MAINT., REPAIR CONSTR.	34978	321625	71139	942460	216751	76715	688168	146081	137747
13 ORDNANCE, ACCESSORIES	0	1018	36375	40364	17957	0	83510	136	183
14 FOOD, KINDRED PRDTS.	31587	898270	32981	1642336	292462	35377	862043	141665	186715
15 TOBACCO MANUFACTURES	0	23370	0	6286	1828115	0	20676	0	0
16 FABRICS	45745	84427	46	80972	989472	0	7757	414	13385
17 TEXTILE PRDTS.	3056	34798	0	49585	42444	0	31374	53	1647
18 APPAREL	20336	319716	933	2422531	456155	0	151669	18044	19639
19 MISC. TEXTILE PRDTS.	1875	58544	700	172152	39489	92	13115	1194	6878
20 LUMBER, WOOD PRDTS.	28514	29789	12154	94681	123744	650	60169	11067	740114
21 WOODEN CONTAINERS	1717	4673	34	5581	3592	0	4116	0	1941
22 HOUSEHOLD FURNITURE	8411	45459	597	110777	237573	98	57282	4737	13302
23 OTHER FURNITURE	3645	21629	1027	111817	23512	89	79734	2272	1849
24 PAPER, ALLIED PRDTS.	64230	200693	0	377992	132000	0	273544	5418	90013
25 PAPERBOARD CONTAINERS	4770	131453	83	178823	35323	83	136108	6582	7651
26 PRINTING, PUBLISHING	23257	289865	10991	1771337	71861	8734	514027	43454	43894
27 CHEMICALS,SELECT. PRDTS.	6755	865366	4396	349231	54586	1149	312815	8329	23343
28 PLASTICS, SYNTHETICS	7878	135072	0	112736	77380	0	132111	406	2212
29 DRUGS, COSMETICS	910	662127	41	591001	31297	0	204026	1491	3028
30 PAINT, ALLIED PRDTS.	172	104047	172	49875	8005	0	83217	2239	4223
31 PETROLEUM, RELATED INDS.	436	345865	15018	64545	2032	8997	234531	187629	5009
32 RUBBER, MISC. PLASTICS	24089	249568	2285	220292	34992	0	959295	49714	4288
33 LEATHER TANNING, PRDTS.	9238	17118	0	24882	2175	0	8670	0	429
34 FOOTWEAR, LEATHER PRDTS.	89087	45445	638	245540	7558	0	40655	1666	1721
35 GLASS, GLASS PRDTS.	769	132679	95	97243	27833	0	237579	37862	4780
36 STONE, CLAY PRDTS.	20041	215043	15117	317380	61291	4761	402359	40578	32918
37 PRIMARY IRON, STEEL MFR.	8294	138707	0	441724	15839	46	1825301	13674	30032
38 PRIMARY NONFERROUS MFR.	6554	328755	11758	361097	28410	0	310698	24623	35277

39 METAL CONTAINERS	0	91653	0	42803	171	0	46601	989	6685
40 FABRICATED METAL PRDTS.	4675	133336	2694	233441	40750	2339	355977	60752	31670
41 SCREW MACH. PRDTS., ETC.	3945	105992	610	157528	9477	120	329794	3393	1894
42 OTHER FAB. METAL PRDTS.	5066	223640	487	266136	23066	112	409825	27762	12486
43 ENGINES, TURBINES	46	1775	0	88627	46	0	23701	46	270
44 FARM MACH., EQUIP.	41	1342	122	17935	7302	2540	58118	2493	2584
45 CONSTRUC. MACH., EQUIP.	11106	19653	656	13846	688	62	164733	60388	3973
46 MATERIAL HANDLING MACH.	0	52127	0	52331	639	104	82606	1002	14426
47 METALWORKING MACHINERY	6563	68387	734	162032	4617	800	464020	1164	1104
48 SPECIAL MACH., EQUIP.	23899	104811	361	138098	56912	170	162606	4074	18769
49 GENERAL MACH., EQUIP.	12084	167778	66	242093	3343	65	343123	25177	2886
50 MACHINE SHOP PRDTS.	2750	40621	3215	103323	7215	614	104947	7088	10577
51 OFFICE, COMPUT. MACHINES	2296	74454	399	561179	4472	0	123550	868	76
52 SERVICE IND. MACHINES	1889	45929	428	136507	8369	0	109979	6738	2148
53 ELECT. TRANSMISS. EQUIP.	31905	138863	121	336797	50653	0	414000	9676	25940
54 HOUSEHOLD APPLIANCES	59	17438	0	53019	16953	0	362285	790	1522
55 ELECTRIC LIGHTING EQUIP.	1405	117837	0	152734	10447	0	151742	203	784
56 RADIO, TV, ETC., EQUIP.	31097	651807	1711	890077	130430	0	204440	96408	935
57 ELECTRONIC COMPONENTS	25273	170739	648	289843	23752	0	79290	2619	460
58 MISC. ELECTRICAL MACH.	382	43126	124	66149	31575	0	113472	3008	4012
59 MOTOR VEHICLES, EQUIP.	79	225630	822	564662	11566	0	1584195	18745	26340
60 AIRCRAFT, PARTS	0	167610	59	548154	9000	0	490134	233931	8799
61 OTHER TRANSPORT. EQUIP.	863	79787	163	89569	9272	99	59924	4383	25302
62 PROFESS., SCIEN. INSTRU.	1621	124393	1785	216155	16037	38	79595	4729	3792
63 MEDICAL, PHOTO. EQUIP.	3117	75934	0	823285	13457	0	5433	93	6314
64 MISC. MANUFACTURING	10605	199090	1788	676822	17269	2166	138944	7233	9428
65 TRANSPORT., WAREHOUSING	38939	991243	100912	2893889	388987	59519	1227964	317649	286379
66 COMMUNICA.,EXC. BRDCAST.	28976	403655	48679	1333029	217133	38628	601469	143991	116297
67 RADIO, TV BROADCASTING	2036	6810	4944	302491	19230	3013	58253	10600	10580
68 ELEC.,GAS,WATER,SAN.SER.	45472	495422	89533	1246089	229797	30015	976136	175927	88607
69 WHOLESALE, RETAIL TRADE	245805	3335540	339491	12064265	1719067	287334	4408398	916647	996829
70 FINANCE, INSURANCE	48954	583778	53306	3711470	285732	41961	776699	184608	155657
71 REAL ESTATE, RENTAL	147861	2416551	257662	9530193	795466	122569	3202991	648542	568131
72 HOTELS, PERSONAL SERV.	41258	358942	46847	1311478	183819	23182	450673	95061	97369
73 BUSINESS SERVICES	25718	570895	53076	4188633	149217	15637	751128	144062	122566
74 RESEARCH, DEVELOPMENT	0	0	0	0	0	0	0	0	0
75 AUTO. REPAIR, SERVICES	21632	212892	32379	569364	121653	21781	316385	86579	80009
76 AMUSEMENTS	15320	120193	11431	1038713	36187	5354	147445	23706	23436
77 MED., EDUC. SERVICES	113949	692953	45965	4302387	377129	27846	1125163	146276	163396
78 FEDERAL GOVT. ENTERPRISE	11921	116965	21319	427857	79298	14869	168555	52072	42089
79 STATE, LOCAL GOVT. ENT.	22810	94983	12907	459738	100954	5137	279790	42744	60246
80 ZERO ENTRIES	0	0	0	0	0	0	0	0	0
81 SERVICE IND. RESIDUAL	0	0	0	0	0	0	0	0	0
82 TOTAL FINAL DEMAND	216952	1599258	410162	4887959	1371703	212762	2045389	817818	466472
83 SECONDARY TRANSFERS-OUT	0	0	0	0	0	0	0	0	0
84 ZERO ENTRIES	0	0	0	0	0	0	0	0	0
85 SCRAP ENTRIES	0	0	0	0	0	0	0	0	0
86 ZERO ENTRIES	0	0	0	0	0	0	0	0	0
87 STATE TOTAL CONSUMPTION	1749028	21432944	2517095	68757536	12699727	1543789	32493696	6430060	5523036

TABLE C-14

1963 STATE VALUE ADDED
(THOUSANDS OF CURRENT DOLLARS)

INDUSTRY TITLE	37 PENNSYL-VANIA	38 RHODE ISLAND	39 SOUTH CAROLINA	40 SOUTH DAKOTA	41 TENNESSEE	42 TEXAS	43 UTAH	44 VERMONT	45 VIRGINIA
1 LIVESTOCK, PRDTS.	264157	6409	41743	108584	125951	464243	25968	55283	164173
2 OTHER AGRICULTURE PRDTS.	311124	4622	85426	206756	279652	883988	28876	31910	167862
3 FORESTRY, FISHERIES	5449	2857	14207	278	4065	26542	241	1379	24251
4 AGRI.,FORES.,FISH. SERV.	11896	1226	7374	4548	6671	81512	1835	260	8451
5 IRON, FERRO. ORES MINING	26226	0	0	1	77	5131	8964	0	763
6 NONFERROUS ORES MINING	1400	0	121	10870	5875	2058	133610	0	2436
7 COAL MINING	330545	0	0	85	18217	1103	21168	0	113910
8 CRUDE PETRO.,NATURAL GAS	31658	0	0	108	78	2555121	68362	0	415
9 STONE, CLAY MINING	58371	1607	19620	6687	32664	36035	4509	8829	34822
10 CHEM.,FERT. MIN. MINING	1696	0	266	18	20388	49315	5764	0	231
11 NEW CONSTRUCTION	566072	112497	16288	79215	428158	1136312	147151	8824	636631
12 MAINT., REPAIR CONSTR.	505742	32650	85734	75928	147589	694438	59179	21445	194281
13 ORDNANCE, ACCESSORIES	52369	39	0	0	30759	26841	63070	0	365
14 FOOD, KINDRED PRDTS.	1152975	62448	100861	84377	371619	832593	84508	38483	245563
15 TOBACCO MANUFACTURES	194947	31	24294	0	30542	3358	0	0	697838
16 FABRICS	160636	105056	813877	0	69796	31499	191	2125	131207
17 TEXTILE PRDTS.	57223	12742	45778	0	13351	3652	113	734	14902
18 APPAREL	711064	22495	102283	0	281523	156006	9205	8320	113429
19 MISC. TEXTILE PRDTS.	35215	1469	9948	241	12592	16139	436	122	7166
20 LUMBER, WOOD PRDTS.	77970	2000	71733	4253	73771	93835	5698	16719	99836
21 WOODEN CONTAINERS	3835	169	3332	39	7128	3222	68	589	5093
22 HOUSEHOLD FURNITURE	82215	631	15358	356	80159	42058	3412	9381	115656
23 OTHER FURNITURE	70833	5677	2563	79	11720	22450	1687	89	16674
24 PAPER, ALLIED PRDTS.	287677	6958	97549	67	120934	88444	1642	25688	142323
25 PAPERBOARD CONTAINERS	141712	7517	26729	358	25735	41812	1024	4139	21149
26 PRINTING, PUBLISHING	532388	29825	23771	10531	105745	227003	23057	13158	78492
27 CHEMICALS,SELECT. PRDTS.	271313	21758	19721	1252	226928	1327271	5223	2300	118263
28 PLASTICS, SYNTHETICS	183322	19868	96607	0	246299	210807	0	1684	328739
29 DRUGS, COSMETICS	326660	3153	16999	511	52558	45204	1025	178	44319
30 PAINT, ALLIED PRDTS.	58530	2635	1305	0	8221	42781	648	1464	4243
31 PETROLEUM, RELATED INDS.	333128	7551	5044	106	11093	1417769	40211	106	18404
32 RUBBER, MISC. PLASTICS	248229	77382	26943	1515	87082	96734	5468	10158	36630
33 LEATHER TANNING, PRDTS.	17950	72	296	0	10365	870	115	1076	3428
34 FOOTWEAR, LEATHER PRDTS.	136868	5079	0	0	87187	14220	194	2162	20847
35 GLASS, GLASS PRDTS.	226579	18771	30913	0	62528	19497	142	0	12389
36 STONE, CLAY PRDTS.	356025	6141	30637	7178	80534	260923	32785	18577	87192
37 PRIMARY IRON, STEEL MFR.	2406821	32255	11443	46	52729	163348	72336	1849	47709
38 PRIMARY NONFERROUS MFR.	226564	63388	5305	0	94446	175263	42083	3645	25648

39	METAL CONTAINERS	57474	0	239	0	4613	38805	2399	0	3618
40	FABRICATED METAL PRDTS.	360128	6604	19277	4865	77447	164867	22262	2082	58229
41	SCREW MACH. PRDTS., ETC.	215732	17234	5014	0	17148	12732	370	408	2004
42	OTHER FAB. METAL PRDTS.	337928	34890	6941	480	29527	118800	2405	1439	23611
43	ENGINES, TURBINES	127825	46	0	0	46	7811	0	0	0
44	FARM MACH., EQUIP.	36583	41	994	1534	22634	9556	594	162	2873
45	CONSTRUC. MACH., EQUIP.	70101	117	179	0	3058	207301	13574	687	2525
46	MATERIAL HANDLING MACH.	68001	273	2358	2015	9352	9506	107	0	2153
47	METALWORKING MACHINERY	191899	31551	17261	1838	5344	13469	814	38798	1038
48	SPECIAL MACH., EQUIP.	121420	22340	36017	114	9380	33171	1652	1764	5369
49	GENERAL MACH., EQUIP.	216459	7981	8347	1608	12207	42252	4331	380	8126
50	MACHINE SHOP PRDTS.	57282	4884	4632	1683	9566	32806	2101	890	5317
51	OFFICE, COMPUT. MACHINES	99387	155	5361	0	0	5116	147	13994	26300
52	SERVICE IND. MACHINES	85192	1119	945	0	13569	54527	3703	1680	9023
53	ELECT. TRANSMISS. EQUIP.	386651	2721	14665	0	33306	27758	2947	924	59124
54	HOUSEHOLD APPLIANCES	36610	1185	2643	0	51516	8771	0	0	220
55	ELECTRIC LIGHTING EQUIP.	142133	23628	546	0	9746	8392	364	3216	616
56	RADIO, TV, ETC., EQUIP.	139213	7806	770	61	63160	139728	8187	0	64063
57	ELECTRONIC COMPONENTS	284747	12415	20584	1150	9087	25539	5190	8073	47630
58	MISC. ELECTRICAL MACH.	54450	5108	194	0	7950	16506	128	3439	2118
59	MOTOR VEHICLES, EQUIP.	304064	3743	1889	302	27463	201650	1064	0	72562
60	AIRCRAFT, PARTS	384096	4035	0	0	32328	318919	115475	35945	11479
61	OTHER TRANSPORT. EQUIP.	191177	3803	5515	821	23661	65895	2635	137	54143
62	PROFESS., SCIEN. INSTRU.	223079	16114	11847	84	23509	27920	618	4759	4787
63	MEDICAL, PHOTO. EQUIP.	22323	6262	8566	0	159	4842	230	2593	13294
64	MISC. MANUFACTURING	207971	120974	23613	878	41594	31037	5809	3116	30116
65	TRANSPORT., WAREHOUSING	1510953	71448	128368	40976	345672	1412237	127642	37725	479759
66	COMMUNICA.,EXC. BRDCAST.	594116	54142	100612	28793	247169	656309	68609	15115	219583
67	RADIO, TV BROADCASTING	70470	5754	8893	3678	18550	49548	4540	1640	17372
68	ELEC.,GAS,WATER,SAN.SER.	937070	54162	115399	33231	96824	758722	92247	24020	275295
69	WHOLESALE, RETAIL TRADE	4908303	389513	687337	269074	1447540	4439803	403406	145929	1473897
70	FINANCE, INSURANCE	1054466	92389	131115	47018	269018	904257	68551	28959	281165
71	REAL ESTATE, RENTAL	3187230	256016	341381	144608	717765	2477384	299346	75578	1124941
72	HOTELS, PERSONAL SERV.	541303	41604	79057	25390	150529	480022	41053	23894	181668
73	BUSINESS SERVICES	907402	50445	71835	17643	178723	681253	52378	12612	188605
74	RESEARCH, DEVELOPMENT	0	0	0	0	0	0	0	0	0
75	AUTO. REPAIR, SERVICES	372402	23221	57871	22294	107785	366897	34462	13616	116400
76	AMUSEMENTS	123152	19121	15019	9428	31196	101211	14865	7545	34578
77	MED.,EDUC. SERVICES	1735719	132751	108266	38344	336549	699364	139194	98621	307768
78	FEDERAL GOVT. ENTERPRISE	196433	21289	46688	13706	184161	204610	17399	8000	118840
79	STATE, LOCAL GOVT. ENT.	287105	8426	26007	10782	140654	208660	23808	10279	114783
80	ZERO ENTRIES	0	0	0	0	0	0	0	0	0
81	SERVICE IND. RESIDUAL	0	0	0	0	0	0	0	0	0
82	TOTAL FINAL DEMAND	2396565	227948	691010	186134	739213	3141060	353323	83733	1705103
83	SECONDARY TRANSFERS-OUT	0	0	0	0	0	0	0	0	0
84	ZERO ENTRIES	0	0	0	0	0	0	0	0	0
85	SCRAP ENTRIES	0	0	0	0	0	0	0	0	0
86	ZERO ENTRIES	0	0	0	0	0	0	0	0	0
87	STATE TOTAL CONSUMPTION	33711984	2460235	4661371	1512516	8873442	29508400	2837898	1002431	10935827

TABLE C-14

1963 STATE VALUE ADDED
(THOUSANDS OF CURRENT DOLLARS)

INDUSTRY TITLE	46 WASHINGTON	47 WEST VIRGINIA	48 WISCONSIN	49 WYOMING	50 ALASKA	51 HAWAII	52 NATIONAL TOTAL
1 LIVESTOCK, PRDTS.	45141	32988	482481	45279	2711	21973	6692430
2 OTHER AGRICULTURE PRDTS.	315337	44384	336795	22812	11	232069	14829530
3 FORESTRY, FISHERIES	54329	2689	4812	269	34225	1824	598197
4 AGRI.,FORES.,FISH. SERV.	5974	3262	6967	730	15	12380	581794
5 IRON, FERRO. ORES MINING	213	0	387	8638	382	0	475355
6 NONFERROUS ORES MINING	4603	0	760	26045	2609	0	625211
7 COAL MINING	4003	439379	0	6597	1558	0	1540224
8 CRUDE PETRO.,NATURAL GAS	5235	45079	0	248722	9574	0	6926423
9 STONE, CLAY MINING	12654	13819	27218	13966	1015	4027	1122754
10 CHEM.,FERT. MIN. MINING	1	2	0	11637	0	0	360303
11 NEW CONSTRUCTION	696922	15074	474024	53992	9529	140948	25890208
12 MAINT., REPAIR CONSTR.	207152	83477	239630	44200	13234	44512	11131648
13 ORDNANCE, ACCESSORIES	4016	48214	9114	0	0	0	2524939
14 FOOD, KINDRED PRDTS.	318100	70187	807947	17973	24981	142177	19893088
15 TOBACCO MANUFACTURES	0	15979	420	0	0	0	3609830
16 FABRICS	2955	1858	3413	0	0	56	3472417
17 TEXTILE PRDTS.	675	31	10053	0	0	59	656037
18 APPAREL	19532	16424	53964	0	0	9153	6771701
19 MISC. TEXTILE PRDTS.	4269	456	4076	21	0	484	751243
20 LUMBER, WOOD PRDTS.	389093	26938	88268	7207	9950	3354	3852407
21 WOODEN CONTAINERS	3505	367	4233	0	0	0	143949
22 HOUSEHOLD FURNITURE	11344	3090	20315	31	0	2497	1613435
23 OTHER FURNITURE	5177	2162	16630	28	0	1572	811580
24 PAPER, ALLIED PRDTS.	269991	10691	414618	0	0	2676	4812935
25 PAPERBOARD CONTAINERS	24968	5307	69202	0	0	1585	1888233
26 PRINTING, PUBLISHING	67414	27772	179137	4636	2202	13122	7887415
27 CHEMICALS,SELECT. PRDTS.	113360	633732	28205	683	0	6961	6886830
28 PLASTICS, SYNTHETICS	8265	145253	10260	0	0	0	2555087
29 DRUGS, COSMETICS	2318	2862	61411	0	0	585	3718604
30 PAINT, ALLIED PRDTS.	5944	648	15975	0	0	0	890985
31 PETROLEUM, RELATED INDS.	55531	17227	14025	91206	0	7762	5100374
32 RUBBER, MISC. PLASTICS	4948	3140	86130	50	0	402	4413119
33 LEATHER TANNING, PRDTS.	229	3622	34078	0	0	0	250784
34 FOOTWEAR, LEATHER PRDTS.	1225	1969	65549	0	0	834	1504519
35 GLASS, GLASS PRDTS.	4285	140761	2374	0	0	284	1606520
36 STONE, CLAY PRDTS.	55123	42911	83173	9911	2798	12963	4594344
37 PRIMARY IRON, STEEL MFR.	23918	225216	190983	0	0	2328	10452545
38 PRIMARY NONFERROUS MFR.	133787	68722	51253	115	0	17	3979500

39 METAL CONTAINERS	17278	5326	34166	0	0	7236	834594
40 FABRICATED METAL PRDTS.	33473	27591	117489	302	0	2427	3371045
41 SCREW MACH. PRDTS., ETC.	3373	8677	107522	251	0	0	2237257
42 OTHER FAB. METAL PRDTS.	11172	27715	64047	300	0	624	3743603
43 ENGINES, TURBINES	137	0	179054	0	0	0	931130
44 FARM MACH., EQUIP.	2555	3222	103910	0	0	237	1012968
45 CONSTRUC. MACH., EQUIP.	10725	20969	149858	367	0	0	1606745
46 MATERIAL HANDLING MACH.	9402	1945	14026	0	0	50	595209
47 METALWORKING MACHINERY	4184	8900	91318	0	0	110	2511571
48 SPECIAL MACH., EQUIP.	11931	1130	98561	0	0	2156	1540868
49 GENERAL MACH., EQUIP.	3324	477	125723	66	0	66	2410121
50 MACHINE SHOP PRDTS.	13494	4968	27009	545	0	762	1136410
51 OFFICE, COMPUT. MACHINES	2860	0	5192	0	0	0	2019517
52 SERVICE IND. MACHINES	3319	1610	46875	0	0	101	1087841
53 ELECT. TRANSMISS. EQUIP.	8688	11650	243813	263	0	68	3005322
54 HOUSEHOLD APPLIANCES	2533	572	60859	0	0	0	1515275
55 ELECTRIC LIGHTING EQUIP.	5218	35495	11146	42	0	116	1278904
56 RADIO, TV, ETC., EQUIP.	8422	284	104891	0	0	84	5941621
57 ELECTRONIC COMPONENTS	1297	4324	18669	0	0	31	2130598
58 MISC. ELECTRICAL MACH.	972	0	44481	0	0	0	975360
59 MOTOR VEHICLES, EQUIP.	20016	8060	710759	0	0	273	11892544
60 AIRCRAFT, PARTS	235943	59	2765	886	0	0	6604391
61 OTHER TRANSPORT. EQUIP.	97564	15588	42040	25	0	714	1785878
62 PROFESS., SCIEN. INSTRU.	1127	5793	58270	651	0	0	1858918
63 MEDICAL, PHOTO. EQUIP.	1061	1889	2897	0	0	72	1430153
64 MISC. MANUFACTURING	12415	4787	61476	34	0	1132	2867968
65 TRANSPORT., WAREHOUSING	437625	205999	380881	71713	66803	108238	23872736
66 COMMUNICA.,EXC. BRDCAST.	193389	82528	178905	16892	4867	41044	11433018
67 RADIO, TV BROADCASTING	15651	7745	18903	1869	1864	4173	1288744
68 ELEC.,GAS,WATER,SAN.SER.	103515	218440	295400	53839	8690	32479	13873698
69 WHOLESALE, RETAIL TRADE	1423527	525629	1721123	133261	89902	255504	88447808
70 FINANCE, INSURANCE	239136	86926	308915	20383	16472	78759	18547520
71 REAL ESTATE, RENTAL	1121068	324573	1156546	89864	48682	313540	61589296
72 HOTELS, PERSONAL SERV.	140454	60114	178725	26451	12474	47521	9827717
73 BUSINESS SERVICES	189250	76814	237412	13650	17070	52254	17563232
74 RESEARCH, DEVELOPMENT	0	0	0	0	0	0	0
75 AUTO. REPAIR, SERVICES	112333	37503	123731	12967	5287	22022	6427341
76 AMUSEMENTS	40505	24411	42390	4633	3424	11629	3960582
77 MED.,EDUC. SERVICES	255232	114800	202609	13097	13007	83532	23180112
78 FEDERAL GOVT. ENTERPRISE	110191	22398	58769	6697	38958	44098	4216693
79 STATE, LOCAL GOVT. ENT.	190272	32621	39820	8521	7887	9562	4250350
80 ZERO ENTRIES	0	0	0	0	0	0	0
81 SERVICE IND. RESIDUAL	0	0	0	0	0	0	0
82 TOTAL FINAL DEMAND	1161404	270300	818535	119873	322411	539538	52840832
83 SECONDARY TRANSFERS-OUT	0	0	0	0	0	0	0
84 ZERO ENTRIES	0	0	0	0	0	0	0
85 SCRAP ENTRIES	0	0	0	0	0	0	0
86 ZERO ENTRIES	0	0	0	0	0	0	0
87 STATE TOTAL CONSUMPTION	9137571	4487522	12187360	1212188	772590	2326756	583062016

TABLE C-15

1963 STATE TRANSFERS-IN
(THOUSANDS OF CURRENT DOLLARS)

INDUSTRY TITLE	1 ALABAMA	2 ARIZONA	3 ARKANSAS	4 CALIFORNIA	5 COLORADO	6 CONNECTICUT	7 DELAWARE	8 DISTRICT OF COLUMBIA	9 FLORIDA
1 LIVESTOCK, PRDTS.	0	0	0	0	0	0	0	0	0
2 OTHER AGRICULTURE PRDTS.	0	0	0	0	0	0	0	0	0
3 FORESTRY, FISHERIES	3701	2699	4580	18370	4006	870	667	0	5145
4 AGRI.,FORES.,FISH. SERV.	7921	7655	13321	50667	6423	1646	995	0	18018
5 IRON, FERRO. ORES MINING	16	6318	348	121	1303	7	0	0	143
6 NONFERROUS ORES MINING	33	9	42	902	123	11	3	0	1164
7 COAL MINING	11	84	17	72	23	6	0	0	22
8 CRUDE PETRO.,NATURAL GAS	476	268	206	2133	309	323	69	73	569
9 STONE, CLAY MINING	2128	2192	809	13846	1544	1552	364	254	3423
10 CHEM.,FERT. MIN. MINING	90	35	14	194	130	51	16	0	74
11 NEW CONSTRUCTION	0	0	0	0	0	0	0	0	0
12 MAINT., REPAIR CONSTR.	0	0	0	0	0	0	0	0	0
13 ORDNANCE, ACCESSORIES	52759	13575	1650	340073	12541	137446	974	6	17061
14 FOOD, KINDRED PRDTS.	18816	9995	16447	75282	22075	7349	4172	21	15040
15 TOBACCO MANUFACTURES	0	0	0	0	0	0	0	0	0
16 FABRICS	3870	125	1029	9818	219	3237	646	22	576
17 TEXTILE PRDTS.	7211	168	570	6639	565	4080	1694	59	1381
18 APPAREL	1793	54	469	2138	300	1459	217	7	247
19 MISC. TEXTILE PRDTS.	28766	215	1894	8444	315	11956	2812	8	1680
20 LUMBER, WOOD PRDTS.	4198	2676	5948	27625	2526	3469	486	33	8066
21 WOODEN CONTAINERS	794	175	924	4198	123	215	44	4	573
22 HOUSEHOLD FURNITURE	1323	292	971	9228	512	2656	217	8	878
23 OTHER FURNITURE	1500	547	1500	11830	464	3672	184	11	1394
24 PAPER, ALLIED PRDTS.	4203	1347	1925	25833	1933	6960	1288	1230	4386
25 PAPERBOARD CONTAINERS	1571	380	865	12208	704	2403	333	517	2657
26 PRINTING, PUBLISHING	3560	340	1991	14092	511	3631	299	6	4174
27 CHEMICALS,SELECT. PRDTS.	19507	5019	11262	197703	8617	21609	19702	726	51597
28 PLASTICS, SYNTHETICS	13502	1209	2693	41971	3388	12425	4298	81	12929
29 DRUGS, COSMETICS	8126	1493	2990	34187	2745	11398	3044	205	9585
30 PAINT, ALLIED PRDTS.	1537	189	250	4703	345	1820	876	19	1540
31 PETROLEUM, RELATED INDS.	2598	648	3335	48618	5448	2090	358	84	2654
32 RUBBER, MISC. PLASTICS	11133	1596	3110	43185	1859	17694	7927	187	10658
33 LEATHER TANNING, PRDTS.	188	10	89	676	131	274	56	0	44
34 FOOTWEAR, LEATHER PRDTS.	656	145	334	4399	294	2167	275	17	382
35 GLASS, GLASS PRDTS.	685	214	688	5306	305	895	61	27	851
36 STONE, CLAY PRDTS.	3057	743	2078	21617	1677	4969	880	32	5546
37 PRIMARY IRON, STEEL MFR.	3623	3173	1697	28642	1496	13390	1384	72	2386
38 PRIMARY NONFERROUS MFR.	5485	642	876	22048	1330	7211	1768	15	1759

39 METAL CONTAINERS	878	192	200	7012	309	2723	99	21	679
40 FABRICATED METAL PRDTS.	13658	3904	3355	59700	3781	20285	1887	25	5532
41 SCREW MACH. PRDTS., ETC.	6400	1688	1344	42405	1865	10588	2323	25	3505
42 OTHER FAB. METAL PRDTS.	31471	9408	6458	82752	6420	37244	5109	78	7644
43 ENGINES, TURBINES	4870	1483	747	43953	1817	11990	459	16	3564
44 FARM MACH., EQUIP.	1315	272	407	9559	760	2689	378	8	920
45 CONSTRUC. MACH., EQUIP.	3051	988	856	24213	994	8793	1226	4	1677
46 MATERIAL HANDLING MACH.	1119	566	369	14884	1760	5404	516	7	870
47 METALWORKING MACHINERY	6509	3731	3499	48128	2332	21746	1911	98	3537
48 SPECIAL MACH., EQUIP.	3418	1842	1603	26911	1884	11270	703	32	2358
49 GENERAL MACH., EQUIP.	6378	2865	3295	52384	3000	18123	2030	70	4397
50 MACHINE SHOP PRDTS.	1799	997	705	15772	681	7257	330	20	1176
51 OFFICE, COMPUT. MACHINES	1050	714	835	15536	410	3321	303	56	1645
52 SERVICE IND. MACHINES	3966	1412	9702	44784	1351	23228	1537	62	3380
53 ELECT. TRANSMISS. EQUIP.	3636	4744	6247	69521	1266	22517	820	9	5404
54 HOUSEHOLD APPLIANCES	3422	1921	2739	42850	2386	14801	714	19	2455
55 ELECTRIC LIGHTING EQUIP.	2953	2141	1320	19352	827	6065	609	32	1536
56 RADIO, TV, ETC., EQUIP.	9326	6316	2455	111740	2880	33310	433	26	7091
57 ELECTRONIC COMPONENTS	3474	2474	5021	65763	1577	18112	343	8	5061
58 MISC. ELECTRICAL MACH.	767	1368	1919	23572	414	5976	923	4	1455
59 MOTOR VEHICLES, EQUIP.	4841	2646	1991	51350	2927	18332	936	31	4512
60 AIRCRAFT, PARTS	5728	6228	2391	154972	2706	15380	653	34	13651
61 OTHER TRANSPORT. EQUIP.	2812	637	270	13734	724	4814	506	8	877
62 PROFESS., SCIEN. INSTRU.	4012	2735	3189	70347	1494	14521	759	8	5811
63 MEDICAL, PHOTO. EQUIP.	877	841	1074	16255	242	4574	512	14	1424
64 MISC. MANUFACTURING	3953	683	2403	25932	1860	10503	802	647	2984
65 TRANSPORT., WAREHOUSING	20138	9641	6193	104679	9643	9155	1895	2692	33789
66 COMMUNICA.,EXC. BRDCAST.	0	0	0	0	0	0	0	0	0
67 RADIO, TV BROADCASTING	0	0	0	0	0	0	0	0	0
68 ELEC.,GAS,WATER,SAN.SER.	91775	38083	21871	454327	41918	42239	8625	20684	139063
69 WHOLESALE, RETAIL TRADE	62628	20727	28998	395310	32337	83700	10037	21392	71973
70 FINANCE, INSURANCE	2311	897	576	10901	1007	1035	205	865	3366
71 REAL ESTATE, RENTAL	102774	66182	83815	825640	89977	93295	23946	36282	194644
72 HOTELS, PERSONAL SERV.	20	9	11	197	22	18	4	18	53
73 BUSINESS SERVICES	65337	54372	37887	1019036	76403	176620	16652	161602	190152
74 RESEARCH, DEVELOPMENT	0	0	0	0	0	0	0	0	0
75 AUTO. REPAIR, SERVICES	2945	1334	650	15174	1354	1388	272	369	4871
76 AMUSEMENTS	470	116	146	1773	180	186	38	429	484
77 MED.,EDUC. SERVICES	0	0	0	0	0	0	0	0	0
78 FEDERAL GOVT. ENTERPRISE	0	0	0	1	0	0	0	0	0
79 STATE, LOCAL GOVT. ENT.	0	0	0	0	0	0	0	0	0
80 ZERO ENTRIES	0	0	0	0	0	0	0	0	0
81 SERVICE IND. RESIDUAL	0	0	0	0	0	0	0	0	0
82 TOTAL FINAL DEMAND	0	0	0	0	0	0	0	0	0
83 SECONDARY TRANSFERS-OUT	0	0	0	0	0	0	0	0	0
84 ZERO ENTRIES	0	0	0	0	0	0	0	0	0
85 SCRAP ENTRIES	0	0	0	0	0	0	0	0	0
86 ZERO ENTRIES	0	0	0	0	0	0	0	0	0
87 STATE TOTAL CONSUMPTION	694920	318391	329464	5067187	383790	1050147	144609	249416	918139

TABLE C-15

1963 STATE TRANSFERS-IN
(THOUSANDS OF CURRENT DOLLARS)

INDUSTRY TITLE	10 GEORGIA	11 IDAHO	12 ILLINOIS	13 INDIANA	14 IOWA	15 KANSAS	16 KENTUCKY	17 LOUISIANA	18 MAINE
1 LIVESTOCK, PRDTS.	0	0	0	0	0	0	0	0	0
2 OTHER AGRICULTURE PRDTS.	0	0	0	0	0	0	0	0	0
3 FORESTRY, FISHERIES	5145	2915	14360	8417	18029	7692	4923	2949	1257
4 AGRI.,FORES.,FISH. SERV.	11854	8090	37813	20821	33401	14881	13047	9189	2507
5 IRON, FERRO. ORES MINING	4	667	246	0	0	2	0	0	1
6 NONFERROUS ORES MINING	56	65	126	20	11	20	70	881	1
7 COAL MINING	40	11	38	19	16	9	18	8	1
8 CRUDE PETRO.,NATURAL GAS	474	99	1759	817	400	338	382	468	80
9 STONE, CLAY MINING	2135	373	8167	4774	1931	2573	1663	3099	224
10 CHEM.,FERT. MIN. MINING	71	11	182	57	14	22	58	137	4
11 NEW CONSTRUCTION	0	0	0	0	0	0	0	0	0
12 MAINT., REPAIR CONSTR.	0	0	0	0	0	0	0	0	0
13 ORDNANCE, ACCESSORIES	21452	460	43736	56198	2710	65509	2667	11544	2203
14 FOOD, KINDRED PRDTS.	25746	11007	66952	40249	92348	39433	20273	11729	6448
15 TOBACCO MANUFACTURES	0	0	0	0	0	0	0	0	0
16 FABRICS	26248	19	7205	1350	245	262	946	829	704
17 TEXTILE PRDTS.	14738	37	5962	2652	1403	602	1926	1402	2650
18 APPAREL	4421	10	2744	714	288	98	367	129	1776
19 MISC. TEXTILE PRDTS.	70897	77	8026	2081	763	292	2245	1055	12467
20 LUMBER, WOOD PRDTS.	6993	2644	20604	10821	11383	5187	6135	4296	1735
21 WOODEN CONTAINERS	938	763	920	844	206	59	333	606	618
22 HOUSEHOLD FURNITURE	1292	403	9140	3721	1541	521	919	589	492
23 OTHER FURNITURE	2685	224	12107	6554	1524	588	1706	617	296
24 PAPER, ALLIED PRDTS.	8664	683	26620	9944	3893	2607	3274	3479	907
25 PAPERBOARD CONTAINERS	2317	189	14756	3717	964	501	1070	2048	1236
26 PRINTING, PUBLISHING	5437	325	11923	4531	1196	1030	1238	4345	3752
27 CHEMICALS,SELECT. PRDTS.	16896	3422	136952	84920	14368	36960	28052	120968	2981
28 PLASTICS, SYNTHETICS	11895	1178	46492	18916	4538	7335	11503	31528	1202
29 DRUGS, COSMETICS	8587	1320	39621	12519	6862	4370	8626	16835	1073
30 PAINT, ALLIED PRDTS.	1321	116	5479	2631	801	784	1531	2699	124
31 PETROLEUM, RELATED INDS.	2806	256	18754	5139	1452	17010	5193	91147	165
32 RUBBER, MISC. PLASTICS	20173	461	37866	14668	6586	4452	11824	11603	3503
33 LEATHER TANNING, PRDTS.	88	1	644	430	178	81	73	7	181
34 FOOTWEAR, LEATHER PRDTS.	936	19	5467	1597	643	193	448	145	358
35 GLASS, GLASS PRDTS.	1009	156	3694	2647	486	359	660	398	153
36 STONE, CLAY PRDTS.	5099	506	16196	8568	3098	2698	3241	6633	452
37 PRIMARY IRON, STEEL MFR.	4262	849	46621	19366	9904	2335	4346	2155	450
38 PRIMARY NONFERROUS MFR.	3494	56	30392	32825	1850	1372	3524	592	220

39 METAL CONTAINERS	946	41	7477	2538	614	817	745	381	58
40 FABRICATED METAL PRDTS.	6331	956	78727	47376	7696	4571	8502	5215	2052
41 SCREW MACH. PRDTS., ETC.	5157	310	39883	27718	7045	2189	4326	2029	421
42 OTHER FAB. METAL PRDTS.	12921	2319	118220	95944	10338	6073	13562	7319	3116
43 ENGINES, TURBINES	3026	199	30062	17861	6994	5419	1649	2330	832
44 FARM MACH., EQUIP.	1298	80	16243	6503	1618	686	921	846	377
45 CONSTRUC. MACH., EQUIP.	4249	331	38459	16805	18699	3493	4427	1540	478
46 MATERIAL HANDLING MACH.	1927	70	34994	8978	5015	1346	1749	845	380
47 METALWORKING MACHINERY	5555	506	65797	30406	8951	3153	9889	2389	486
48 SPECIAL MACH., EQUIP.	2537	310	43953	17772	6766	1819	4134	1565	629
49 GENERAL MACH., EQUIP.	6841	387	68237	31426	9233	5046	8858	3030	902
50 MACHINE SHOP PRDTS.	1517	108	14649	7592	1329	1312	1154	696	285
51 OFFICE, COMPUT. MACHINES	1139	52	14790	8347	1439	870	896	473	259
52 SERVICE IND. MACHINES	4733	238	65265	36392	12916	3394	23115	1813	350
53 ELECT. TRANSMISS. EQUIP.	2947	529	73042	33793	11041	2254	11708	2862	1288
54 HOUSEHOLD APPLIANCES	6810	161	42430	20945	8032	2984	5313	1236	370
55 ELECTRIC LIGHTING EQUIP.	2190	340	18972	13527	2021	861	2595	871	298
56 RADIO, TV, ETC., EQUIP.	4461	478	38470	22967	4650	8509	4530	3185	910
57 ELECTRONIC COMPONENTS	3792	129	72221	34975	4447	1456	6288	924	759
58 MISC. ELECTRICAL MACH.	2360	110	24462	13545	2393	799	3393	310	178
59 MOTOR VEHICLES, EQUIP.	4113	311	63040	45079	11607	3768	5704	1788	951
60 AIRCRAFT, PARTS	2233	480	51793	25751	7195	1384	2558	4995	885
61 OTHER TRANSPORT. EQUIP.	1717	96	13968	8095	5795	1931	1576	547	120
62 PROFESS., SCIEN. INSTRU.	3877	125	56677	29368	4352	3827	2934	1596	977
63 MEDICAL, PHOTO. EQUIP.	686	18	13231	5818	1763	414	2451	755	191
64 MISC. MANUFACTURING	4300	274	31609	14545	5226	2809	4130	2369	2195
65 TRANSPORT., WAREHOUSING	15962	4744	57721	19991	18440	12601	10237	11946	5711
66 COMMUNICA.,EXC. BRDCAST.	0	0	0	0	0	0	0	0	0
67 RADIO, TV BROADCASTING	0	0	0	0	0	0	0	0	0
68 ELEC.,GAS,WATER,SAN.SER.	69115	15820	244192	83874	59933	52309	43272	77585	24370
69 WHOLESALE, RETAIL TRADE	73112	10656	324767	135592	71788	45855	53174	50884	16564
70 FINANCE, INSURANCE	1826	373	5771	1863	1415	1175	1168	1190	588
71 REAL ESTATE, RENTAL	145343	46326	562940	227179	246544	140928	112973	154256	32618
72 HOTELS, PERSONAL SERV.	39	6	154	42	20	25	23	41	7
73 BUSINESS SERVICES	119367	15364	1001716	201180	129968	78789	89103	75389	23186
74 RESEARCH, DEVELOPMENT	0	0	0	0	0	0	0	0	0
75 AUTO. REPAIR, SERVICES	2198	556	8146	2644	2118	1623	1276	1653	835
76 AMUSEMENTS	416	48	899	285	179	195	311	195	90
77 MED.,EDUC. SERVICES	0	0	0	0	0	0	0	0	0
78 FEDERAL GOVT. ENTERPRISE	0	0	0	0	0	0	0	0	0
79 STATE, LOCAL GOVT. ENT.	0	0	0	0	0	0	0	0	0
80 ZERO ENTRIES	0	0	0	0	0	0	0	0	0
81 SERVICE IND. RESIDUAL	0	0	0	0	0	0	0	0	0
82 TOTAL FINAL DEMAND	0	0	0	0	0	0	0	0	0
83 SECONDARY TRANSFERS-OUT	0	0	0	0	0	0	0	0	0
84 ZERO ENTRIES	0	0	0	0	0	0	0	0	0
85 SCRAP ENTRIES	0	0	0	0	0	0	0	0	0
86 ZERO ENTRIES	0	0	0	0	0	0	0	0	0
87 STATE TOTAL CONSUMPTION	813210	140263	4024541	1679244	920615	624858	590927	769155	173937

TABLE C-15

1963 STATE TRANSFERS-IN
(THOUSANDS OF CURRENT DOLLARS)

INDUSTRY TITLE	19 MARYLAND	20 MASSA-CHUSETTS	21 MICHIGAN	22 MINNESOTA	23 MISSISSIPPI	24 MISSOURI	25 MONTANA	26 NEBRASKA	27 NEVADA
1 LIVESTOCK, PRDTS.	0	0	0	0	0	0	0	0	0
2 OTHER AGRICULTURE PRDTS.	0	0	0	0	0	0	0	0	0
3 FORESTRY, FISHERIES	1852	933	5263	10565	4649	7968	2807	8556	337
4 AGRI.,FORES.,FISH. SERV.	3178	1790	13164	21748	13663	16992	7013	16882	523
5 IRON, FERRO. ORES MINING	0	0	605	56	0	283	1362	1	851
6 NONFERROUS ORES MINING	15	9	276	739	3	104	106	5	25
7 COAL MINING	15	9	35	10	4	25	19	7	16
8 CRUDE PETRO.,NATURAL GAS	479	741	1237	485	269	574	143	136	76
9 STONE, CLAY MINING	1926	2944	4915	2415	1010	3123	699	669	771
10 CHEM.,FERT. MIN. MINING	49	39	345	842	15	107	11	7	19
11 NEW CONSTRUCTION	0	0	0	0	0	0	0	0	0
12 MAINT., REPAIR CONSTR.	0	0	0	0	0	0	0	0	0
13 ORDNANCE, ACCESSORIES	25134	35541	29650	6905	1215	36883	271	1009	126
14 FOOD, KINDRED PRDTS.	12328	7500	26670	52063	16818	40853	11665	42418	1965
15 TOBACCO MANUFACTURES	0	0	0	0	0	0	0	0	0
16 FABRICS	1212	11392	9409	1233	2266	2697	7	63	12
17 TEXTILE PRDTS.	1870	10204	6250	1052	839	1483	29	252	33
18 APPAREL	498	5141	2385	392	322	2055	6	66	6
19 MISC. TEXTILE PRDTS.	3659	31494	3785	2153	2824	3286	23	189	13
20 LUMBER, WOOD PRDTS.	2543	5382	10380	8333	6476	7478	2217	5556	215
21 WOODEN CONTAINERS	254	517	804	457	844	364	612	75	30
22 HOUSEHOLD FURNITURE	1367	3935	7262	1217	783	1614	319	404	27
23 OTHER FURNITURE	1380	5641	7496	1611	1443	2347	190	449	43
24 PAPER, ALLIED PRDTS.	5228	14660	15915	4379	1698	6896	696	1169	388
25 PAPERBOARD CONTAINERS	2973	4332	6210	2400	543	3183	153	461	68
26 PRINTING, PUBLISHING	2343	7755	11270	3660	913	3387	65	375	42
27 CHEMICALS,SELECT. PRDTS.	23274	33728	65047	19999	7021	28802	11540	4838	1328
28 PLASTICS, SYNTHETICS	11007	14973	31767	6393	3569	16471	899	1603	1001
29 DRUGS, COSMETICS	7116	14381	23624	7230	2691	11730	784	2878	612
30 PAINT, ALLIED PRDTS.	1462	2366	3651	821	385	1808	81	224	115
31 PETROLEUM, RELATED INDS.	2352	2725	8484	1601	7975	3738	3099	2766	355
32 RUBBER, MISC. PLASTICS	7206	29709	27600	6357	3003	9131	411	982	498
33 LEATHER TANNING, PRDTS.	191	898	398	76	67	330	1	41	1
34 FOOTWEAR, LEATHER PRDTS.	787	5204	2409	691	418	920	21	193	8
35 GLASS, GLASS PRDTS.	619	1703	2048	664	625	1061	135	223	65
36 STONE, CLAY PRDTS.	3658	7521	14860	2637	1168	5032	756	1144	545
37 PRIMARY IRON, STEEL MFR.	6251	13168	64956	5445	1380	10928	1350	1334	517
38 PRIMARY NONFERROUS MFR.	5701	10158	52348	3499	936	9052	68	516	60

39 METAL CONTAINERS	850	1782	5790	810	254	1487	29	183	33
40 FABRICATED METAL PRDTS.	13947	19443	63920	11068	1812	14571	1090	1648	393
41 SCREW MACH. PRDTS., ETC.	7828	12039	75289	5688	959	13507	375	1472	162
42 OTHER FAB. METAL PRDTS.	23156	31256	121156	15037	3243	19153	3752	3082	1234
43 ENGINES, TURBINES	6015	8492	20171	3892	581	6863	32	1128	30
44 FARM MACH., EQUIP.	2263	3991	14192	1560	341	2880	41	379	27
45 CONSTRUC. MACH., EQUIP.	4302	7247	57860	7226	1449	10126	145	1751	47
46 MATERIAL HANDLING MACH.	1932	7367	25620	3890	597	4748	29	508	23
47 METALWORKING MACHINERY	7845	20419	71972	11843	2026	13175	816	1320	442
48 SPECIAL MACH., EQUIP.	4562	10276	36452	6773	1101	6137	352	950	139
49 GENERAL MACH., EQUIP.	9226	24414	80945	12028	1946	16666	372	1500	212
50 MACHINE SHOP PRDTS.	2171	7299	14261	1729	316	2982	145	557	82
51 OFFICE, COMPUT. MACHINES	3157	6683	11473	1967	318	2991	49	740	100
52 SERVICE IND. MACHINES	5066	10314	61694	12778	2474	13263	243	1461	130
53 ELECT. TRANSMISS. EQUIP.	9119	30285	52781	10844	1682	11426	702	2231	265
54 HOUSEHOLD APPLIANCES	4403	15030	40486	10229	1436	12983	73	1021	61
55 ELECTRIC LIGHTING EQUIP.	3333	8519	18057	2637	592	4423	594	798	254
56 RADIO, TV, ETC., EQUIP.	5440	24013	19891	7119	1355	11956	752	1190	265
57 ELECTRONIC COMPONENTS	11521	34040	20134	7130	2128	10636	190	2435	159
58 MISC. ELECTRICAL MACH.	4485	12078	33553	3605	579	7413	192	839	90
59 MOTOR VEHICLES, EQUIP.	5411	23935	51790	9832	1649	8709	266	1560	98
60 AIRCRAFT, PARTS	9768	26259	34841	9106	907	11845	482	1966	281
61 OTHER TRANSPORT. EQUIP.	1789	3706	18162	2900	482	3413	36	493	13
62 PROFESS., SCIEN. INSTRU.	13270	29815	29836	6688	1185	11152	42	2476	110
63 MEDICAL, PHOTO. EQUIP.	1453	6552	5376	1948	460	2063	12	390	12
64 MISC. MANUFACTURING	5248	14183	20196	4618	1573	7960	146	1256	95
65 TRANSPORT., WAREHOUSING	12598	27056	48267	20010	6474	14405	4415	23389	1436
66 COMMUNICA.,EXC. BRDCAST.	0	0	0	0	0	0	0	0	0
67 RADIO, TV BROADCASTING	0	0	0	0	0	0	0	0	0
68 ELEC.,GAS,WATER,SAN.SER.	57484	123285	209306	77607	23940	59930	16398	89294	6800
69 WHOLESALE, RETAIL TRADE	60948	136967	191038	79622	25133	96538	9345	37081	4551
70 FINANCE, INSURANCE	1423	3059	4632	1847	583	1657	378	1982	188
71 REAL ESTATE, RENTAL	98097	187093	292104	212252	83175	206305	47607	134237	18931
72 HOTELS, PERSONAL SERV.	32	47	58	34	9	60	7	16	5
73 BUSINESS SERVICES	134685	381839	342061	196506	29742	245118	17148	55202	18891
74 RESEARCH, DEVELOPMENT	0	0	0	0	0	0	0	0	0
75 AUTO. REPAIR, SERVICES	1888	4178	7283	2626	688	1828	528	3295	209
76 AMUSEMENTS	263	525	465	281	138	435	61	137	49
77 MED.,EDUC. SERVICES	0	0	0	0	0	0	0	0	0
78 FEDERAL GOVT. ENTERPRISE	0	0	0	0	0	0	0	0	0
79 STATE, LOCAL GOVT. ENT.	0	0	0	0	0	0	0	0	0
80 ZERO ENTRIES	0	0	0	0	0	0	0	0	0
81 SERVICE IND. RESIDUAL	0	0	0	0	0	0	0	0	0
82 TOTAL FINAL DEMAND	0	0	0	0	0	0	0	0	0
83 SECONDARY TRANSFERS-OUT	0	0	0	0	0	0	0	0	0
84 ZERO ENTRIES	0	0	0	0	0	0	0	0	0
85 SCRAP ENTRIES	0	0	0	0	0	0	0	0	0
86 ZERO ENTRIES	0	0	0	0	0	0	0	0	0
87 STATE TOTAL CONSUMPTION	672904	1549975	2561634	941858	287165	1099510	154403	473462	66508

TABLE C-15

1963 STATE TRANSFERS-IN
(THOUSANDS OF CURRENT DOLLARS)

INDUSTRY TITLE	28 NEW HAMPSHIRE	29 NEW JERSEY	30 NEW MEXICO	31 NEW YORK	32 NORTH CAROLINA	33 NORTH DAKOTA	34 OHIO	35 OKLAHOMA	36 OREGON
1 LIVESTOCK, PRDTS.	0	0	0	0	0	0	0	0	0
2 OTHER AGRICULTURE PRDTS.	0	0	0	0	0	0	0	0	0
3 FORESTRY, FISHERIES	344	1661	1571	5865	6922	3892	7391	4179	2470
4 AGRI.,FORES.,FISH. SERV.	413	3833	2849	10871	22483	12109	17415	8558	6314
5 IRON, FERRO. ORES MINING	0	96	2641	310	3	20	4	34	6
6 NONFERROUS ORES MINING	1	35	1076	224	53	1	179	6	11
7 COAL MINING	1	25	37	40	15	2	37	8	10
8 CRUDE PETRO.,NATURAL GAS	82	896	162	2254	416	54	1766	318	160
9 STONE, CLAY MINING	512	6315	1251	8132	1586	161	10322	1560	829
10 CHEM.,FERT. MIN. MINING	3	384	19	226	39	1	156	7	18
11 NEW CONSTRUCTION	0	0	0	0	0	0	0	0	0
12 MAINT., REPAIR CONSTR.	0	0	0	0	0	0	0	0	0
13 ORDNANCE, ACCESSORIES	899	51679	120	152728	4539	14	118311	46697	2498
14 FOOD, KINDRED PRDTS.	2333	24183	8125	43904	25423	12667	38654	20224	10340
15 TOBACCO MANUFACTURES	0	0	0	0	0	0	0	0	0
16 FABRICS	651	10195	50	29609	10765	7	6194	198	774
17 TEXTILE PRDTS.	1893	8736	65	13537	35319	12	9427	462	887
18 APPAREL	1388	3065	25	8339	9683	8	1923	106	278
19 MISC. TEXTILE PRDTS.	8123	19851	35	38329	163346	12	7654	421	2861
20 LUMBER, WOOD PRDTS.	990	7012	945	14839	11338	3774	14298	3190	2943
21 WOODEN CONTAINERS	265	509	97	1341	1255	6	763	102	5853
22 HOUSEHOLD FURNITURE	432	4354	103	9620	1755	20	10125	541	3101
23 OTHER FURNITURE	443	6482	76	11612	6387	21	10097	697	1814
24 PAPER, ALLIED PRDTS.	1102	18956	362	46634	5972	127	25942	1657	4029
25 PAPERBOARD CONTAINERS	531	8754	77	15402	1507	35	11517	591	1149
26 PRINTING, PUBLISHING	1476	10454	104	19734	3893	15	12673	536	1987
27 CHEMICALS,SELECT. PRDTS.	2707	142956	37256	101238	17514	2055	129397	37933	5057
28 PLASTICS, SYNTHETICS	1126	80417	713	35849	6615	280	54038	5356	2559
29 DRUGS, COSMETICS	844	47583	545	35643	6138	288	29963	2525	4525
30 PAINT, ALLIED PRDTS.	188	9120	68	5884	1250	21	6669	373	309
31 PETROLEUM, RELATED INDS.	232	12138	17297	9993	1578	2833	9841	29482	781
32 RUBBER, MISC. PLASTICS	3355	36881	375	61587	14975	131	43941	2742	2661
33 LEATHER TANNING, PRDTS.	173	557	6	852	80	0	1705	93	12
34 FOOTWEAR, LEATHER PRDTS.	369	4068	29	17029	1518	11	4464	259	263
35 GLASS, GLASS PRDTS.	289	2270	62	4515	2758	19	4241	379	1242
36 STONE, CLAY PRDTS.	724	12942	2950	15785	2933	217	24915	2815	1697
37 PRIMARY IRON, STEEL MFR.	1138	18332	496	28171	3200	157	50501	2451	2492
38 PRIMARY NONFERROUS MFR.	459	13565	162	25107	3138	16	46974	1107	981

39 METAL CONTAINERS	113	3538	40	4812	438	19	7520	605	218
40 FABRICATED METAL PRDTS.	1716	29592	601	54306	4719	39	89451	4903	4764
41 SCREW MACH. PRDTS., ETC.	673	17601	440	31816	2441	90	56688	2059	1545
42 OTHER FAB. METAL PRDTS.	3104	50548	955	94723	10374	129	176290	7564	8831
43 ENGINES, TURBINES	677	12244	264	22685	2414	77	24514	4799	1068
44 FARM MACH., EQUIP.	400	5645	42	10256	843	18	12913	1279	595
45 CONSTRUC. MACH., EQUIP.	450	11993	64	22641	1568	236	37479	1790	1800
46 MATERIAL HANDLING MACH.	1053	8285	69	14829	1484	31	24383	2944	766
47 METALWORKING MACHINERY	1525	27752	394	53473	4815	102	78556	3111	2325
48 SPECIAL MACH., EQUIP.	894	13840	255	30118	2159	80	45692	2768	1650
49 GENERAL MACH., EQUIP.	2174	26708	282	55415	6250	103	77562	5222	3573
50 MACHINE SHOP PRDTS.	674	8175	93	14937	1306	21	17266	1152	652
51 OFFICE, COMPUT. MACHINES	523	9250	91	15782	1911	22	11280	1345	351
52 SERVICE IND. MACHINES	723	17317	137	36107	5825	83	104160	3716	2134
53 ELECT. TRANSMISS. EQUIP.	1431	30389	735	58173	5706	28	60198	2994	1635
54 HOUSEHOLD APPLIANCES	2733	21166	84	51674	5599	106	56912	2819	3005
55 ELECTRIC LIGHTING EQUIP.	1077	12059	176	20525	2517	27	25095	1297	1254
56 RADIO, TV, ETC., EQUIP.	1654	27655	1383	63625	4157	13	45026	6559	1388
57 ELECTRONIC COMPONENTS	2809	46485	140	75843	8499	11	54544	5165	1849
58 MISC. ELECTRICAL MACH.	1034	14373	94	30072	3045	4	26199	1306	830
59 MOTOR VEHICLES, EQUIP.	1626	23317	460	47466	6318	89	60758	3803	2606
60 AIRCRAFT, PARTS	1295	28756	3230	45943	6027	39	38030	3585	1271
61 OTHER TRANSPORT. EQUIP.	171	3814	28	12286	733	78	15544	1309	562
62 PROFESS., SCIEN. INSTRU.	2219	40872	250	72472	7612	25	40656	5889	1336
63 MEDICAL, PHOTO. EQUIP.	419	8037	160	12526	1739	3	11641	748	187
64 MISC. MANUFACTURING	1817	18316	158	35086	3851	89	36508	2108	1623
65 TRANSPORT., WAREHOUSING	5144	21961	3347	104695	25909	2975	65001	10891	14395
66 COMMUNICA.,EXC. BRDCAST.	0	0	0	0	0	0	0	0	0
67 RADIO, TV BROADCASTING	0	0	0	0	0	0	0	0	0
68 ELEC.,GAS,WATER,SAN.SER.	22112	102835	19522	466201	100911	7090	283883	53565	59747
69 WHOLESALE, RETAIL TRADE	13548	205098	8464	465268	73270	5107	283085	36295	43524
70 FINANCE, INSURANCE	504	2517	376	11321	2395	189	6317	1129	1396
71 REAL ESTATE, RENTAL	20436	243152	37164	872940	175970	55566	385374	112736	79881
72 HOTELS, PERSONAL SERV.	3	81	8	245	31	5	97	24	24
73 BUSINESS SERVICES	26369	320317	21271	2484518	107697	14702	596020	63631	62210
74 RESEARCH, DEVELOPMENT	0	0	0	0	0	0	0	0	0
75 AUTO. REPAIR, SERVICES	800	3330	452	16117	3539	180	9808	1498	2112
76 AMUSEMENTS	48	469	86	1717	318	60	676	209	169
77 MED.,EDUC. SERVICES	0	0	0	0	0	0	0	0	0
78 FEDERAL GOVT. ENTERPRISE	0	0	0	0	0	0	0	0	0
79 STATE, LOCAL GOVT. ENT.	0	0	0	0	0	0	0	0	0
80 ZERO ENTRIES	0	0	0	0	0	0	0	0	0
81 SERVICE IND. RESIDUAL	0	0	0	0	0	0	0	0	0
82 TOTAL FINAL DEMAND	0	0	0	0	0	0	0	0	0
83 SECONDARY TRANSFERS-OUT	0	0	0	0	0	0	0	0	0
84 ZERO ENTRIES	0	0	0	0	0	0	0	0	0
85 SCRAP ENTRIES	0	0	0	0	0	0	0	0	0
86 ZERO ENTRIES	0	0	0	0	0	0	0	0	0
87 STATE TOTAL CONSUMPTION	155434	1985796	181064	6185816	966784	126419	3576623	536430	382190

TABLE C-15

1963 STATE TRANSFERS-IN
(THOUSANDS OF CURRENT DOLLARS)

INDUSTRY TITLE	37 PENNSYL-VANIA	38 RHODE ISLAND	39 SOUTH CAROLINA	40 SOUTH DAKOTA	41 TENNESSEE	42 TEXAS	43 UTAH	44 VERMONT	45 VIRGINIA
1 LIVESTOCK, PRDTS.	0	0	0	0	0	0	0	0	0
2 OTHER AGRICULTURE PRDTS.	0	0	0	0	0	0	0	0	0
3 FORESTRY, FISHERIES	5618	125	2351	4877	3886	14007	1062	868	3155
4 AGRI.,FORES.,FISH. SERV.	9669	229	7800	8931	9808	35604	1560	1049	6846
5 IRON, FERRO. ORES MINING	56	0	5	436	242	83	3873	0	98
6 NONFERROUS ORES MINING	157	3	12	3	389	753	119	3	22
7 COAL MINING	38	1	11	9	22	26	52	4	23
8 CRUDE PETRO.,NATURAL GAS	1695	98	209	60	175	1373	167	43	498
9 STONE, CLAY MINING	10007	184	767	281	2150	10720	1809	491	2468
10 CHEM.,FERT. MIN. MINING	211	9	15	4	105	580	43	2	65
11 NEW CONSTRUCTION	0	0	0	0	0	0	0	0	0
12 MAINT., REPAIR CONSTR.	0	0	0	0	0	0	0	0	0
13 ORDNANCE, ACCESSORIES	97877	2861	904	52	9067	67063	22883	7430	4606
14 FOOD, KINDRED PRDTS.	37319	1347	10023	24992	18697	66751	6100	5277	16644
15 TOBACCO MANUFACTURES	0	0	0	0	0	0	0	0	0
16 FABRICS	15129	2029	8491	16	4350	2413	96	155	3576
17 TEXTILE PRDTS.	11665	3981	28278	30	6374	5081	115	245	8681
18 APPAREL	4420	1377	7616	7	1916	876	32	70	1618
19 MISC. TEXTILE PRDTS.	36335	16779	132993	12	15011	7280	172	618	23175
20 LUMBER, WOOD PRDTS.	11124	1127	3774	2808	6479	14196	716	696	5372
21 WOODEN CONTAINERS	969	74	609	35	709	861	53	146	936
22 HOUSEHOLD FURNITURE	7550	1053	730	42	1559	2429	164	151	1431
23 OTHER FURNITURE	10905	834	1096	43	3031	3299	293	374	3408
24 PAPER, ALLIED PRDTS.	21551	2250	3949	205	6397	12115	782	644	5640
25 PAPERBOARD CONTAINERS	10241	658	1006	48	2546	4129	285	221	2006
26 PRINTING, PUBLISHING	12208	951	2357	22	3784	6821	309	600	3667
27 CHEMICALS,SELECT. PRDTS.	154853	7291	16026	952	53031	330564	13865	1159	50177
28 PLASTICS, SYNTHETICS	35121	3480	3128	181	20021	127035	1482	479	11530
29 DRUGS, COSMETICS	30699	3014	3504	625	14995	64840	1039	607	10786
30 PAINT, ALLIED PRDTS.	5147	503	1014	25	3367	10385	145	82	3149
31 PETROLEUM, RELATED INDS.	9643	498	748	151	2769	161274	4306	249	2221
32 RUBBER, MISC. PLASTICS	48393	6131	14080	153	28019	32726	1482	1132	32496
33 LEATHER TANNING, PRDTS.	658	131	49	3	282	210	11	22	101
34 FOOTWEAR, LEATHER PRDTS.	5249	936	577	10	1412	1082	73	130	729
35 GLASS, GLASS PRDTS.	4323	119	414	39	1381	1703	191	158	1735
36 STONE, CLAY PRDTS.	15431	1798	1938	384	5103	19458	975	795	3622
37 PRIMARY IRON, STEEL MFR.	27283	3288	1724	194	4479	12461	1434	1322	2362
38 PRIMARY NONFERROUS MFR.	40270	1666	464	52	2455	6512	1007	381	1638

39 METAL CONTAINERS	5621	300	184	42	687	1907	284	117	361
40 FABRICATED METAL PRDTS.	89938	3219	1863	166	7790	23358	3794	586	5672
41 SCREW MACH. PRDTS., ETC.	45161	2029	1041	126	4353	11136	1852	434	2901
42 OTHER FAB. METAL PRDTS.	179886	8016	4420	258	15649	36484	7825	1878	9515
43 ENGINES, TURBINES	18771	553	491	103	2671	10795	2113	520	1853
44 FARM MACH., EQUIP.	10742	922	394	34	1069	4921	420	82	1102
45 CONSTRUC. MACH., EQUIP.	24637	819	801	281	3817	6681	692	374	2012
46 MATERIAL HANDLING MACH.	16110	892	850	59	1275	10697	770	301	1271
47 METALWORKING MACHINERY	49362	4084	2240	147	7174	14356	1524	798	3872
48 SPECIAL MACH., EQUIP.	28676	1898	1268	187	3677	10435	1204	1193	2211
49 GENERAL MACH., EQUIP.	54621	2699	2880	268	7055	20775	2078	1056	4713
50 MACHINE SHOP PRDTS.	16960	928	825	62	1537	3663	604	547	1519
51 OFFICE, COMPUT. MACHINES	8997	377	360	40	1584	3905	376	175	1358
52 SERVICE IND. MACHINES	32109	1262	1727	220	13357	11738	1369	479	3373
53 ELECT. TRANSMISS. EQUIP.	47422	2602	1681	99	9292	13337	1944	764	4251
54 HOUSEHOLD APPLIANCES	47980	859	1875	138	5342	7784	1043	595	6571
55 ELECTRIC LIGHTING EQUIP.	25304	1261	1111	69	3088	5550	946	282	2742
56 RADIO, TV, ETC., EQUIP.	44491	3186	1716	71	5810	14634	5495	1482	3637
57 ELECTRONIC COMPONENTS	44396	2880	1334	67	7177	11509	1017	572	5393
58 MISC. ELECTRICAL MACH.	14746	878	876	20	2881	4981	338	195	2259
59 MOTOR VEHICLES, EQUIP.	49923	2434	1663	207	5688	13788	1651	967	3392
60 AIRCRAFT, PARTS	28284	2086	990	113	7605	15473	5969	440	3165
61 OTHER TRANSPORT. EQUIP.	15292	695	338	61	1421	3368	774	243	867
62 PROFESS., SCIEN. INSTRU.	29527	2301	1408	61	6171	13156	1602	764	5495
63 MEDICAL, PHOTO. EQUIP.	10419	833	1022	14	3026	3050	384	195	2370
64 MISC. MANUFACTURING	24364	1812	1545	185	5965	8653	703	493	3348
65 TRANSPORT., WAREHOUSING	65568	1969	7060	3749	33168	52084	5553	2455	26790
66 COMMUNICA.,EXC. BRDCAST.	0	0	0	0	0	0	0	0	0
67 RADIO, TV BROADCASTING	0	0	0	0	0	0	0	0	0
68 ELEC.,GAS,WATER,SAN.SER.	297317	10328	29281	11203	147837	263544	25351	10216	117453
69 WHOLESALE, RETAIL TRADE	273617	21824	31596	8852	93991	186891	16609	8341	67906
70 FINANCE, INSURANCE	6629	291	781	288	3796	5203	557	243	2901
71 REAL ESTATE, RENTAL	399945	23473	68585	60431	135383	549709	36603	17193	124362
72 HOTELS, PERSONAL SERV.	121	6	10	3	27	112	10	3	39
73 BUSINESS SERVICES	655898	49741	44510	17019	141455	315298	32090	18114	114247
74 RESEARCH, DEVELOPMENT	0	0	0	0	0	0	0	0	0
75 AUTO. REPAIR, SERVICES	10065	295	912	378	4931	7315	835	360	4024
76 AMUSEMENTS	788	85	187	55	739	821	70	32	477
77 MED.,EDUC. SERVICES	0	0	0	0	0	0	0	0	0
78 FEDERAL GOVT. ENTERPRISE	0	0	0	0	0	0	0	0	0
79 STATE, LOCAL GOVT. ENT.	0	0	0	0	0	0	0	0	0
80 ZERO ENTRIES	0	0	0	0	0	0	0	0	0
81 SERVICE IND. RESIDUAL	0	0	0	0	0	0	0	0	0
82 TOTAL FINAL DEMAND	0	0	0	0	0	0	0	0	0
83 SECONDARY TRANSFERS-OUT	0	0	0	0	0	0	0	0	0
84 ZERO ENTRIES	0	0	0	0	0	0	0	0	0
85 SCRAP ENTRIES	0	0	0	0	0	0	0	0	0
86 ZERO ENTRIES	0	0	0	0	0	0	0	0	0
87 STATE TOTAL CONSUMPTION	3355498	222663	474485	150759	930500	2691819	231139	98097	757902

TABLE C-15

1963 STATE TRANSFERS-IN
(THOUSANDS OF CURRENT DOLLARS)

INDUSTRY TITLE	46 WASHINGTON	47 WEST VIRGINIA	48 WISCONSIN	49 WYOMING	50 ALASKA	51 HAWAII	52 NATIONAL TOTAL
1 LIVESTOCK, PRDTS.	0	0	0	0	0	0	0
2 OTHER AGRICULTURE PRDTS.	0	0	0	0	0	0	0
3 FORESTRY, FISHERIES	3549	809	8018	1145	20	1349	233790
4 AGRI.,FORES.,FISH. SERV.	10680	1461	11308	1571	4	5427	550000
5 IRON, FERRO. ORES MINING	181	0	31	1045	102	0	21600
6 NONFERROUS ORES MINING	12	9	15	222	1	2	8123
7 COAL MINING	10	8	19	20	2	3	960
8 CRUDE PETRO.,NATURAL GAS	187	395	534	97	16	59	25100
9 STONE, CLAY MINING	1596	1752	2116	789	98	343	135762
10 CHEM.,FERT. MIN. MINING	52	261	22	38	1	5	4865
11 NEW CONSTRUCTION	0	0	0	0	0	0	0
12 MAINT., REPAIR CONSTR.	0	0	0	0	0	0	0
13 ORDNANCE, ACCESSORIES	47552	2334	7448	183	0	29	1567071
14 FOOD, KINDRED PRDTS.	12877	8124	47606	6646	151	2672	1146744
15 TOBACCO MANUFACTURES	0	0	0	0	0	0	2
16 FABRICS	492	162	2032	3	1	89	183118
17 TEXTILE PRDTS.	737	1749	1736	18	4	48	214831
18 APPAREL	143	64	1081	1	0	20	72159
19 MISC. TEXTILE PRDTS.	2006	644	4136	3	1	104	681321
20 LUMBER, WOOD PRDTS.	5214	911	7644	520	6	1757	295076
21 WOODEN CONTAINERS	3087	231	823	55	79	31	35183
22 HOUSEHOLD FURNITURE	1915	420	2545	32	39	71	101814
23 OTHER FURNITURE	1333	786	3193	22	17	80	134346
24 PAPER, ALLIED PRDTS.	4082	3249	6650	154	77	318	333050
25 PAPERBOARD CONTAINERS	2576	1511	5269	22	11	358	139212
26 PRINTING, PUBLISHING	5921	1998	10059	5	2	157	191921
27 CHEMICALS,SELECT. PRDTS.	19301	25549	23629	23419	320	2502	2175586
28 PLASTICS, SYNTHETICS	9975	46103	5915	1648	6	898	768722
29 DRUGS, COSMETICS	7383	25574	8026	537	127	1020	545461
30 PAINT, ALLIED PRDTS.	905	4503	922	68	4	79	91857
31 PETROLEUM, RELATED INDS.	1766	6887	2045	14316	569	192	532661
32 RUBBER, MISC. PLASTICS	6624	15758	14271	186	48	347	661877
33 LEATHER TANNING, PRDTS.	14	11	260	1	0	3	10386
34 FOOTWEAR, LEATHER PRDTS.	191	218	1678	5	1	30	69458
35 GLASS, GLASS PRDTS.	834	287	1743	29	18	61	54550
36 STONE, CLAY PRDTS.	2265	2959	5762	1599	59	321	251859
37 PRIMARY IRON, STEEL MFR.	4114	3093	18717	95	23	136	439144
38 PRIMARY NONFERROUS MFR.	925	3687	13631	47	3	52	362095

39 METAL CONTAINERS	673	252	2290	23	8	49	67048
40 FABRICATED METAL PRDTS.	9211	7623	27205	70	22	252	772306
41 SCREW MACH. PRDTS., ETC.	2388	4177	20510	16	2	251	486269
42 OTHER FAB. METAL PRDTS.	16023	17009	39221	306	36	332	1366843
43 ENGINES, TURBINES	4914	1192	10509	26	0	44	307771
44 FARM MACH., EQUIP.	1160	887	5405	8	1	27	129719
45 CONSTRUC. MACH., EQUIP.	2895	1225	20395	11	1	54	363152
46 MATERIAL HANDLING MACH.	1058	1180	14406	19	0	47	228292
47 METALWORKING MACHINERY	3769	3626	21211	111	24	204	633036
48 SPECIAL MACH., EQUIP.	2737	2677	14019	24	3	57	363969
49 GENERAL MACH., EQUIP.	5310	3338	33796	65	11	232	689996
50 MACHINE SHOP PRDTS.	1406	829	5677	29	5	39	165827
51 OFFICE, COMPUT. MACHINES	788	397	4386	37	10	66	143022
52 SERVICE IND. MACHINES	3382	1533	23937	21	4	122	609894
53 ELECT. TRANSMISS. EQUIP.	4710	2994	27836	39	0	37	651259
54 HOUSEHOLD APPLIANCES	2899	1935	28624	34	1	54	495142
55 ELECTRIC LIGHTING EQUIP.	1860	2367	7500	28	7	61	231921
56 RADIO, TV, ETC., EQUIP.	7660	4220	10478	48	0	25	588132
57 ELECTRONIC COMPONENTS	2715	3495	19039	28	1	40	610201
58 MISC. ELECTRICAL MACH.	945	609	10416	10	0	26	262918
59 MOTOR VEHICLES, EQUIP.	2998	2190	33190	44	9	61	591826
60 AIRCRAFT, PARTS	2869	6738	16689	34	4	82	613188
61 OTHER TRANSPORT. EQUIP.	1329	1022	7467	6	2	29	156662
62 PROFESS., SCIEN. INSTRU.	3586	1130	14496	14	2	56	552284
63 MEDICAL, PHOTO. EQUIP.	431	2141	2626	8	0	9	131395
64 MISC. MANUFACTURING	3336	1797	10721	61	24	196	335256
65 TRANSPORT., WAREHOUSING	44017	7504	10673	2139	1876	3065	1035215
66 COMMUNICA.,EXC. BRDCAST.	0	0	0	0	0	0	0
67 RADIO, TV BROADCASTING	0	0	0	0	0	0	0
68 ELEC.,GAS,WATER,SAN.SER.	184894	35957	45013	13064	11368	13302	4525093
69 WHOLESALE, RETAIL TRADE	72483	30738	104040	4758	7967	14557	4228546
70 FINANCE, INSURANCE	4268	754	1116	202	391	455	106300
71 REAL ESTATE, RENTAL	135769	49203	174968	29305	5757	33208	8292579
72 HOTELS, PERSONAL SERV.	38	16	30	5	6	10	1934
73 BUSINESS SERVICES	94962	41512	204832	8470	5551	20997	10414747
74 RESEARCH, DEVELOPMENT	0	0	0	0	0	0	0
75 AUTO. REPAIR, SERVICES	6670	1144	1396	299	276	335	149000
76 AMUSEMENTS	442	90	236	27	156	177	16931
77 MED.,EDUC. SERVICES	0	0	0	0	0	0	0
78 FEDERAL GOVT. ENTERPRISE	0	0	0	0	0	0	1
79 STATE, LOCAL GOVT. ENT.	0	0	0	0	0	0	0
80 ZERO ENTRIES	0	0	0	0	0	0	0
81 SERVICE IND. RESIDUAL	0	0	0	0	0	0	0
82 TOTAL FINAL DEMAND	0	0	0	0	0	0	0
83 SECONDARY TRANSFERS-OUT	0	0	0	0	0	0	0
84 ZERO ENTRIES	0	0	0	0	0	0	0
85 SCRAP ENTRIES	0	0	0	0	0	0	0
86 ZERO ENTRIES	0	0	0	0	0	0	0
87 STATE TOTAL CONSUMPTION	793093	405004	1193240	113931	35337	107124	52357376

TABLE C-16

1963 INVENTORY DEPLETIONS BY STATE
(THOUSANDS OF CURRENT DOLLARS)

INDUSTRY TITLE	1 ALABAMA	2 ARIZONA	3 ARKANSAS	4 CALIFORNIA	5 COLORADO	6 CONNECTICUT	7 DELAWARE	8 DISTRICT OF COLUMBIA	9 FLORIDA
1 LIVESTOCK, PRDTS.	0	0	0	0	0	0	0	0	0
2 OTHER AGRICULTURE PRDTS.	1365	1320	2296	8733	1107	284	172	0	3106
3 FORESTRY, FISHERIES	0	0	0	0	0	0	0	0	0
4 AGRI.,FORES.,FISH. SERV.	0	0	0	0	0	0	0	0	0
5 IRON, FERRO. ORES MINING	955	435	55	2131	4191	0	0	0	9
6 NONFERROUS ORES MINING	3	988	54	21	204	1	0	0	25
7 COAL MINING	0	0	0	0	0	0	0	0	0
8 CRUDE PETRO.,NATURAL GAS	0	0	0	0	0	0	0	0	0
9 STONE, CLAY MINING	0	0	0	0	0	0	0	0	0
10 CHEM.,FERT. MIN. MINING	0	0	3	89	2	0	0	0	128
11 NEW CONSTRUCTION	0	0	0	0	0	0	0	0	0
12 MAINT., REPAIR CONSTR.	0	0	0	0	0	0	0	0	0
13 ORDNANCE, ACCESSORIES	821	629	12	18367	306	1701	7	0	1477
14 FOOD, KINDRED PRDTS.	91	30	92	845	116	50	23	14	171
15 TOBACCO MANUFACTURES	18	0	0	1	0	9	0	0	81
16 FABRICS	0	0	0	0	0	0	0	0	0
17 TEXTILE PRDTS.	0	0	0	0	0	0	0	0	0
18 APPAREL	75	5	18	181	3	42	11	0	24
19 MISC. TEXTILE PRDTS.	0	0	0	0	0	0	0	0	0
20 LUMBER, WOOD PRDTS.	217	48	247	1077	31	29	11	1	150
21 WOODEN CONTAINERS	0	0	0	0	0	0	0	0	0
22 HOUSEHOLD FURNITURE	0	0	0	0	0	0	0	0	0
23 OTHER FURNITURE	1	0	2	19	1	3	0	0	2
24 PAPER, ALLIED PRDTS.	0	0	0	0	0	0	0	0	0
25 PAPERBOARD CONTAINERS	0	0	0	0	0	0	0	0	0
26 PRINTING, PUBLISHING	26	19	16	376	34	85	7	74	75
27 CHEMICALS,SELECT. PRDTS.	0	0	0	0	0	0	0	0	0
28 PLASTICS, SYNTHETICS	14	0	0	24	0	10	21	0	17
29 DRUGS, COSMETICS	0	0	0	0	0	0	0	0	0
30 PAINT, ALLIED PRDTS.	0	0	0	0	0	0	0	0	0
31 PETROLEUM, RELATED INDS.	0	0	0	0	0	0	0	0	0
32 RUBBER, MISC. PLASTICS	89	3	19	283	50	125	28	0	14
33 LEATHER TANNING, PRDTS.	2	0	1	192	5	23	213	0	14
34 FOOTWEAR, LEATHER PRDTS.	144	9	1043	858	579	392	93	0	299
35 GLASS, GLASS PRDTS.	0	0	0	0	0	0	0	0	0
36 STONE, CLAY PRDTS.	54	23	17	326	32	43	7	7	85
37 PRIMARY IRON, STEEL MFR.	262	3	1	221	46	65	43	0	9
38 PRIMARY NONFERROUS MFR.	602	1138	326	1512	28	1556	40	0	131

39 METAL CONTAINERS	0	0	0	0	0	0	0	0	0
40 FABRICATED METAL PRDTS.	0	0	0	0	0	0	0	0	0
41 SCREW MACH. PRDTS., ETC.	0	0	0	0	0	0	0	0	0
42 OTHER FAB. METAL PRDTS.	0	0	0	0	0	0	0	0	0
43 ENGINES, TURBINES	0	0	0	0	0	0	0	0	0
44 FARM MACH., EQUIP.	0	0	0	0	0	0	0	0	0
45 CONSTRUC. MACH., EQUIP.	4	0	1	50	28	4	1	0	1
46 MATERIAL HANDLING MACH.	10	1	12	127	8	15	1	0	6
47 METALWORKING MACHINERY	0	0	0	0	0	0	0	0	0
48 SPECIAL MACH., EQUIP.	23	3	5	203	10	110	19	0	25
49 GENERAL MACH., EQUIP.	0	0	0	0	0	0	0	0	0
50 MACHINE SHOP PRDTS.	0	0	0	0	0	0	0	0	0
51 OFFICE, COMPUT. MACHINES	0	0	0	0	0	0	0	0	0
52 SERVICE IND. MACHINES	0	0	0	0	0	0	0	0	0
53 ELECT. TRANSMISS. EQUIP.	16	5	39	352	29	113	1	0	9
54 HOUSEHOLD APPLIANCES	0	0	0	0	0	0	0	0	0
55 ELECTRIC LIGHTING EQUIP.	0	0	0	0	0	0	0	0	0
56 RADIO, TV, ETC., EQUIP.	19	88	101	2027	5	158	1	0	190
57 ELECTRONIC COMPONENTS	101	368	29	3774	18	829	5	0	162
58 MISC. ELECTRICAL MACH.	0	0	0	0	0	0	0	0	0
59 MOTOR VEHICLES, EQUIP.	0	0	0	0	0	0	0	0	0
60 AIRCRAFT, PARTS	244	60	2	1581	59	618	4	0	77
61 OTHER TRANSPORT. EQUIP.	1014	50	288	3921	71	773	25	0	1140
62 PROFESS., SCIEN. INSTRU.	0	0	0	0	0	0	0	0	0
63 MEDICAL, PHOTO. EQUIP.	1	1	1	84	3	27	0	0	11
64 MISC. MANUFACTURING	57	19	95	1058	55	772	5	6	88
65 TRANSPORT., WAREHOUSING	0	0	0	0	0	0	0	0	0
66 COMMUNICA., EXC. BRDCAST.	0	0	0	0	0	0	0	0	0
67 RADIO, TV BROADCASTING	0	0	0	0	0	0	0	0	0
68 ELEC., GAS, WATER, SAN. SER.	0	0	0	0	0	0	0	0	0
69 WHOLESALE, RETAIL TRADE	0	0	0	0	0	0	0	0	0
70 FINANCE, INSURANCE	0	0	0	0	0	0	0	0	0
71 REAL ESTATE, RENTAL	0	0	0	0	0	0	0	0	0
72 HOTELS, PERSONAL SERV.	0	0	0	0	0	0	0	0	0
73 BUSINESS SERVICES	0	0	0	0	0	0	0	0	0
74 RESEARCH, DEVELOPMENT	0	0	0	0	0	0	0	0	0
75 AUTO. REPAIR, SERVICES	0	0	0	0	0	0	0	0	0
76 AMUSEMENTS	0	0	0	0	0	0	0	0	0
77 MED., EDUC. SERVICES	0	0	0	0	0	0	0	0	0
78 FEDERAL GOVT. ENTERPRISE	0	0	0	0	0	0	0	0	0
79 STATE, LOCAL GOVT. ENT.	0	0	0	0	0	0	0	0	0
80 ZERO ENTRIES	0	0	0	0	0	0	0	0	0
81 SERVICE IND. RESIDUAL	0	0	0	0	0	0	0	0	0
82 TOTAL FINAL DEMAND	0	0	0	0	0	0	0	0	0
83 SECONDARY TRANSFERS-OUT	0	0	0	0	0	0	0	0	0
84 ZERO ENTRIES	0	0	0	0	0	0	0	0	0
85 SCRAP ENTRIES	0	0	0	0	0	0	0	0	0
86 ZERO ENTRIES	0	0	0	0	0	0	0	0	0
87 STATE TOTAL CONSUMPTION	6227	5246	4777	48433	7019	7838	736	103	7528

TABLE C-16

1963 INVENTORY DEPLETIONS BY STATE
(THOUSANDS OF CURRENT DOLLARS)

INDUSTRY TITLE	10 GEORGIA	11 IDAHO	12 ILLINOIS	13 INDIANA	14 IOWA	15 KANSAS	16 KENTUCKY	17 LOUISIANA	18 MAINE
1 LIVESTOCK, PRDTS.	0	0	0	0	0	0	0	0	0
2 OTHER AGRICULTURE PRDTS.	2043	1394	6518	3589	5757	2565	2249	1584	432
3 FORESTRY, FISHERIES	0	0	0	0	0	0	0	0	0
4 AGRI.,FORES.,FISH. SERV.	0	0	0	0	0	0	0	0	0
5 IRON, FERRO. ORES MINING	105	72	15	0	0	0	0	0	0
6 NONFERROUS ORES MINING	1	104	39	0	0	0	0	2	0
7 COAL MINING	0	0	0	0	0	0	0	0	0
8 CRUDE PETRO.,NATURAL GAS	0	0	0	0	0	0	0	0	0
9 STONE, CLAY MINING	0	0	0	0	0	0	0	0	0
10 CHEM.,FERT. MIN. MINING	3	7	11	0	0	2	6	98	0
11 NEW CONSTRUCTION	0	0	0	0	0	0	0	0	0
12 MAINT., REPAIR CONSTR.	0	0	0	0	0	0	0	0	0
13 ORDNANCE, ACCESSORIES	160	24	862	1076	424	445	18	514	80
14 FOOD, KINDRED PRDTS.	175	43	676	234	376	145	143	152	35
15 TOBACCO MANUFACTURES	11	0	14	11	0	0	864	6	0
16 FABRICS	0	0	0	0	0	0	0	0	0
17 TEXTILE PRDTS.	0	0	0	0	0	0	0	0	0
18 APPAREL	133	0	91	30	6	7	49	12	9
19 MISC. TEXTILE PRDTS.	0	0	0	0	0	0	0	0	0
20 LUMBER, WOOD PRDTS.	243	216	168	183	55	14	83	165	166
21 WOODEN CONTAINERS	0	0	0	0	0	0	0	0	0
22 HOUSEHOLD FURNITURE	0	0	0	0	0	0	0	0	0
23 OTHER FURNITURE	2	0	21	7	2	1	1	0	0
24 PAPER, ALLIED PRDTS.	0	0	0	0	0	0	0	0	0
25 PAPERBOARD CONTAINERS	0	0	0	0	0	0	0	0	0
26 PRINTING, PUBLISHING	51	5	545	102	66	33	38	26	11
27 CHEMICALS,SELECT. PRDTS.	0	0	0	0	0	0	0	0	0
28 PLASTICS, SYNTHETICS	8	0	17	7	10	3	26	24	0
29 DRUGS, COSMETICS	0	0	0	0	0	0	0	0	0
30 PAINT, ALLIED PRDTS.	0	0	0	0	0	0	0	0	0
31 PETROLEUM, RELATED INDS.	0	0	0	0	0	0	0	0	0
32 RUBBER, MISC. PLASTICS	34	0	234	182	82	38	27	7	13
33 LEATHER TANNING, PRDTS.	79	0	507	25	2	1	49	5	418
34 FOOTWEAR, LEATHER PRDTS.	663	10	2273	522	105	26	445	3	3445
35 GLASS, GLASS PRDTS.	0	0	0	0	0	0	0	0	0
36 STONE, CLAY PRDTS.	58	6	192	112	53	58	32	47	6
37 PRIMARY IRON, STEEL MFR.	45	1	546	700	20	7	67	7	0
38 PRIMARY NONFERROUS MFR.	163	263	2206	1925	255	58	217	288	15

39 METAL CONTAINERS	0	0	0	0	0	0	0	0	0
40 FABRICATED METAL PRDTS.	0	0	0	0	0	0	0	0	0
41 SCREW MACH. PRDTS., ETC.	0	0	0	0	0	0	0	0	0
42 OTHER FAB. METAL PRDTS.	0	0	0	0	0	0	0	0	0
43 ENGINES, TURBINES	0	0	0	0	0	0	0	0	0
44 FARM MACH., EQUIP.	0	0	0	0	0	0	0	0	0
45 CONSTRUC. MACH., EQUIP.	11	1	423	38	59	10	2	8	4
46 MATERIAL HANDLING MACH.	20	1	285	31	25	18	33	4	1
47 METALWORKING MACHINERY	0	0	0	0	0	0	0	0	0
48 SPECIAL MACH., EQUIP.	56	1	361	82	37	22	23	15	9
49 GENERAL MACH., EQUIP.	0	0	0	0	0	0	0	0	0
50 MACHINE SHOP PRDTS.	0	0	0	0	0	0	0	0	0
51 OFFICE, COMPUT. MACHINES	0	0	0	0	0	0	0	0	0
52 SERVICE IND. MACHINES	0	0	0	0	0	0	0	0	0
53 ELECT. TRANSMISS. EQUIP.	67	0	370	207	23	4	51	3	3
54 HOUSEHOLD APPLIANCES	0	0	0	0	0	0	0	0	0
55 ELECTRIC LIGHTING EQUIP.	0	0	0	0	0	0	0	0	0
56 RADIO, TV, ETC., EQUIP.	6	1	1815	839	96	15	18	4	4
57 ELECTRONIC COMPONENTS	34	3	1971	1037	270	80	175	7	96
58 MISC. ELECTRICAL MACH.	0	0	0	0	0	0	0	0	0
59 MOTOR VEHICLES, EQUIP.	0	0	0	0	0	0	0	0	0
60 AIRCRAFT, PARTS	96	1	79	212	7	309	2	53	8
61 OTHER TRANSPORT. EQUIP.	642	135	4043	3359	305	537	199	1512	759
62 PROFESS., SCIEN. INSTRU.	0	0	0	0	0	0	0	0	0
63 MEDICAL, PHOTO. EQUIP.	1	0	124	21	2	1	2	2	0
64 MISC. MANUFACTURING	156	7	1318	364	194	24	69	42	40
65 TRANSPORT., WAREHOUSING	0	0	0	0	0	0	0	0	0
66 COMMUNICA.,EXC. BRDCAST.	0	0	0	0	0	0	0	0	0
67 RADIO, TV BROADCASTING	0	0	0	0	0	0	0	0	0
68 ELEC.,GAS,WATER,SAN.SER.	0	0	0	0	0	0	0	0	0
69 WHOLESALE, RETAIL TRADE	0	0	0	0	0	0	0	0	0
70 FINANCE, INSURANCE	0	0	0	0	0	0	0	0	0
71 REAL ESTATE, RENTAL	0	0	0	0	0	0	0	0	0
72 HOTELS, PERSONAL SERV.	0	0	0	0	0	0	0	0	0
73 BUSINESS SERVICES	0	0	0	0	0	0	0	0	0
74 RESEARCH, DEVELOPMENT	0	0	0	0	0	0	0	0	0
75 AUTO. REPAIR, SERVICES	0	0	0	0	0	0	0	0	0
76 AMUSEMENTS	0	0	0	0	0	0	0	0	0
77 MED.,EDUC. SERVICES	0	0	0	0	0	0	0	0	0
78 FEDERAL GOVT. ENTERPRISE	0	0	0	0	0	0	0	0	0
79 STATE, LOCAL GOVT. ENT.	0	0	0	0	0	0	0	0	0
80 ZERO ENTRIES	0	0	0	0	0	0	0	0	0
81 SERVICE IND. RESIDUAL	0	0	0	0	0	0	0	0	0
82 TOTAL FINAL DEMAND	0	0	0	0	0	0	0	0	0
83 SECONDARY TRANSFERS-OUT	0	0	0	0	0	0	0	0	0
84 ZERO ENTRIES	0	0	0	0	0	0	0	0	0
85 SCRAP ENTRIES	0	0	0	0	0	0	0	0	0
86 ZERO ENTRIES	0	0	0	0	0	0	0	0	0
87 STATE TOTAL CONSUMPTION	5068	2297	25724	14895	8230	4422	4889	4590	5554

TABLE C-16

1963 INVENTORY DEPLETIONS BY STATE
(THOUSANDS OF CURRENT DOLLARS)

INDUSTRY TITLE	19 MARYLAND	20 MASSA-CHUSETTS	21 MICHIGAN	22 MINNESOTA	23 MISSISSIPPI	24 MISSOURI	25 MONTANA	26 NEBRASKA	27 NEVADA
1 LIVESTOCK, PRDTS.	0	0	0	0	0	0	0	0	0
2 OTHER AGRICULTURE PRDTS.	548	309	2269	3749	2355	2929	1209	2910	90
3 FORESTRY, FISHERIES	0	0	0	0	0	0	0	0	0
4 AGRI.,FORES.,FISH. SERV.	0	0	0	0	0	0	0	0	0
5 IRON, FERRO. ORES MINING	46	0	7376	29305	0	908	201	0	332
6 NONFERROUS ORES MINING	0	0	95	11	0	45	213	0	133
7 COAL MINING	0	0	0	0	0	0	0	0	0
8 CRUDE PETRO.,NATURAL GAS	0	0	0	0	0	0	0	0	0
9 STONE, CLAY MINING	0	0	0	0	0	0	0	0	0
10 CHEM.,FERT. MIN. MINING	0	0	8	2	0	8	11	0	2
11 NEW CONSTRUCTION	0	0	0	0	0	0	0	0	0
12 MAINT., REPAIR CONSTR.	0	0	0	0	0	0	0	0	0
13 ORDNANCE, ACCESSORIES	265	770	723	710	8	1035	2	13	1
14 FOOD, KINDRED PRDTS.	138	163	227	301	61	270	22	183	4
15 TOBACCO MANUFACTURES	3	2	10	0	0	14	0	0	0
16 FABRICS	0	0	0	0	0	0	0	0	0
17 TEXTILE PRDTS.	0	0	0	0	0	0	0	0	0
18 APPAREL	68	158	16	20	60	75	0	3	0
19 MISC. TEXTILE PRDTS.	0	0	0	0	0	0	0	0	0
20 LUMBER, WOOD PRDTS.	56	72	176	121	228	78	174	22	8
21 WOODEN CONTAINERS	0	0	0	0	0	0	0	0	0
22 HOUSEHOLD FURNITURE	0	0	0	0	0	0	0	0	0
23 OTHER FURNITURE	3	4	22	2	1	4	0	1	0
24 PAPER, ALLIED PRDTS.	0	0	0	0	0	0	0	0	0
25 PAPERBOARD CONTAINERS	0	0	0	0	0	0	0	0	0
26 PRINTING, PUBLISHING	68	194	148	93	8	129	5	23	5
27 CHEMICALS,SELECT. PRDTS.	0	0	0	0	0	0	0	0	0
28 PLASTICS, SYNTHETICS	7	25	16	2	1	2	0	0	0
29 DRUGS, COSMETICS	0	0	0	0	0	0	0	0	0
30 PAINT, ALLIED PRDTS.	0	0	0	0	0	0	0	0	0
31 PETROLEUM, RELATED INDS.	0	0	0	0	0	0	0	0	0
32 RUBBER, MISC. PLASTICS	80	266	175	28	25	45	0	18	0
33 LEATHER TANNING, PRDTS.	36	1648	235	78	1	69	0	15	0
34 FOOTWEAR, LEATHER PRDTS.	288	7350	466	223	317	5025	1	11	0
35 GLASS, GLASS PRDTS.	0	0	0	0	0	0	0	0	0
36 STONE, CLAY PRDTS.	51	80	126	62	26	80	8	18	16
37 PRIMARY IRON, STEEL MFR.	134	56	609	50	3	51	1	1	0
38 PRIMARY NONFERROUS MFR.	807	651	1737	72	35	344	520	188	177

39 METAL CONTAINERS	0	0	0	0	0	0	0	0	0
40 FABRICATED METAL PRDTS.	0	0	0	0	0	0	0	0	0
41 SCREW MACH. PRDTS., ETC.	0	0	0	0	0	0	0	0	0
42 OTHER FAB. METAL PRDTS.	0	0	0	0	0	0	0	0	0
43 ENGINES, TURBINES	0	0	0	0	0	0	0	0	0
44 FARM MACH., EQUIP.	0	0	0	0	0	0	0	0	0
45 CONSTRUC. MACH., EQUIP.	3	4	69	33	5	15	0	0	0
46 MATERIAL HANDLING MACH.	16	58	324	36	18	27	0	2	0
47 METALWORKING MACHINERY	0	0	0	0	0	0	0	2	0
48 SPECIAL MACH., EQUIP.	77	377	252	44	13	55	0	0	0
49 GENERAL MACH., EQUIP.	0	0	0	0	0	0	0	2	0
50 MACHINE SHOP PRDTS.	0	0	0	0	0	0	0	0	0
51 OFFICE, COMPUT. MACHINES	0	0	0	0	0	0	0	0	0
52 SERVICE IND. MACHINES	0	0	0	0	0	0	0	0	0
53 ELECT. TRANSMISS. EQUIP.	30	176	163	65	9	116	1	2	1
54 HOUSEHOLD APPLIANCES	0	0	0	0	0	0	0	0	0
55 ELECTRIC LIGHTING EQUIP.	0	0	0	0	0	0	0	0	0
56 RADIO, TV, ETC., EQUIP.	464	938	96	121	10	126	1	101	4
57 ELECTRONIC COMPONENTS	149	1989	425	281	49	103	1	116	2
58 MISC. ELECTRICAL MACH.	0	0	0	0	0	0	0	0	0
59 MOTOR VEHICLES, EQUIP.	0	0	0	0	0	0	0	0	0
60 AIRCRAFT, PARTS	103	103	90	22	0	160	0	1	0
61 OTHER TRANSPORT. EQUIP.	2433	1057	2585	239	73	979	11	315	1
62 PROFESS., SCIEN. INSTRU.	0	0	0	0	0	0	0	0	0
63 MEDICAL, PHOTO. EQUIP.	5	134	11	15	0	0	0	0	0
64 MISC. MANUFACTURING	115	918	575	199	82	207	7	39	7
65 TRANSPORT., WAREHOUSING	0	0	0	0	0	0	0	0	0
66 COMMUNICA.,EXC. BRDCAST.	0	0	0	0	0	0	0	0	0
67 RADIO, TV BROADCASTING	0	0	0	0	0	0	0	0	0
68 ELEC.,GAS,WATER,SAN.SER.	0	0	0	0	0	0	0	0	0
69 WHOLESALE, RETAIL TRADE	0	0	0	0	0	0	0	0	0
70 FINANCE, INSURANCE	0	0	0	0	0	0	0	0	0
71 REAL ESTATE, RENTAL	0	0	0	0	0	0	0	0	0
72 HOTELS, PERSONAL SERV.	0	0	0	0	0	0	0	0	0
73 BUSINESS SERVICES	0	0	0	0	0	0	0	0	0
74 RESEARCH, DEVELOPMENT	0	0	0	0	0	0	0	0	0
75 AUTO. REPAIR, SERVICES	0	0	0	0	0	0	0	0	0
76 AMUSEMENTS	0	0	0	0	0	0	0	0	0
77 MED.,EDUC. SERVICES	0	0	0	0	0	0	0	0	0
78 FEDERAL GOVT. ENTERPRISE	0	0	0	0	0	0	0	0	0
79 STATE, LOCAL GOVT. ENT.	0	0	0	0	0	0	0	0	0
80 ZERO ENTRIES	0	0	0	0	0	0	0	0	0
81 SERVICE IND. RESIDUAL	0	0	0	0	0	0	0	0	0
82 TOTAL FINAL DEMAND	0	0	0	0	0	0	0	0	0
83 SECONDARY TRANSFERS-OUT	0	0	0	0	0	0	0	0	0
84 ZERO ENTRIES	0	0	0	0	0	0	0	0	0
85 SCRAP ENTRIES	0	0	0	0	0	0	0	0	0
86 ZERO ENTRIES	0	0	0	0	0	0	0	0	0
87 STATE TOTAL CONSUMPTION	5993	17501	19027	35884	3389	12910	2389	3989	784

TABLE C-16

1963 INVENTORY DEPLETIONS BY STATE
(THOUSANDS OF CURRENT DOLLARS)

INDUSTRY TITLE	28 NEW HAMPSHIRE	29 NEW JERSEY	30 NEW MEXICO	31 NEW YORK	32 NORTH CAROLINA	33 NORTH DAKOTA	34 OHIO	35 OKLAHOMA	36 OREGON
1 LIVESTOCK, PRDTS.	0	0	0	0	0	0	0	0	0
2 OTHER AGRICULTURE PRDTS.	71	661	491	1874	3875	2087	3002	1475	1088
3 FORESTRY, FISHERIES	0	0	0	0	0	0	0	0	0
4 AGRI.,FORES.,FISH. SERV.	0	0	0	0	0	0	0	0	0
5 IRON, FERRO. ORES MINING	0	343	315	2240	178	1	0	2	136
6 NONFERROUS ORES MINING	0	15	416	49	1	3	1	5	1
7 COAL MINING	0	0	0	0	0	0	0	0	0
8 CRUDE PETRO.,NATURAL GAS	0	0	0	0	0	0	0	0	0
9 STONE, CLAY MINING	0	0	0	0	0	0	0	0	0
10 CHEM.,FERT. MIN. MINING	0	1	119	15	4	0	16	0	0
11 NEW CONSTRUCTION	0	0	0	0	0	0	0	0	0
12 MAINT., REPAIR CONSTR.	0	0	0	0	0	0	0	0	0
13 ORDNANCE, ACCESSORIES	6	362	418	1500	237	0	1761	319	19
14 FOOD, KINDRED PRDTS.	12	322	15	573	119	18	353	67	76
15 TOBACCO MANUFACTURES	0	25	0	7	2382	0	24	0	0
16 FABRICS	0	0	0	0	0	0	0	0	0
17 TEXTILE PRDTS.	0	0	0	0	0	0	0	0	0
18 APPAREL	12	189	1	1424	275	0	90	11	12
19 MISC. TEXTILE PRDTS.	0	0	0	0	0	0	0	0	0
20 LUMBER, WOOD PRDTS.	64	72	27	220	279	5	146	27	1638
21 WOODEN CONTAINERS	0	0	0	0	0	0	0	0	0
22 HOUSEHOLD FURNITURE	0	0	0	0	0	0	0	0	0
23 OTHER FURNITURE	1	6	0	26	6	0	19	1	1
24 PAPER, ALLIED PRDTS.	0	0	0	0	0	0	0	0	0
25 PAPERBOARD CONTAINERS	0	0	0	0	0	0	0	0	0
26 PRINTING, PUBLISHING	14	182	6	1218	42	5	307	25	25
27 CHEMICALS,SELECT. PRDTS.	0	0	0	0	0	0	0	0	0
28 PLASTICS, SYNTHETICS	2	42	0	31	19	0	38	1	1
29 DRUGS, COSMETICS	0	0	0	0	0	0	0	0	0
30 PAINT, ALLIED PRDTS.	0	0	0	0	0	0	0	0	0
31 PETROLEUM, RELATED INDS.	0	0	0	0	0	0	0	0	0
32 RUBBER, MISC. PLASTICS	20	220	2	206	34	0	780	41	5
33 LEATHER TANNING, PRDTS.	286	531	0	772	68	0	281	1	13
34 FOOTWEAR, LEATHER PRDTS.	2869	1694	21	8845	265	0	1373	66	67
35 GLASS, GLASS PRDTS.	0	0	0	0	0	0	0	0	0
36 STONE, CLAY PRDTS.	14	147	11	217	41	3	263	28	23
37 PRIMARY IRON, STEEL MFR.	5	83	0	280	9	0	1134	8	17
38 PRIMARY NONFERROUS MFR.	47	2504	97	2720	225	0	2353	201	287

39 METAL CONTAINERS	0	0	0	0	0	0	0	0	0
40 FABRICATED METAL PRDTS.	0	0	0	0	0	0	0	0	0
41 SCREW MACH. PRDTS., ETC.	0	0	0	0	0	0	0	0	0
42 OTHER FAB. METAL PRDTS.	0	0	0	0	0	0	0	0	0
43 ENGINES, TURBINES	0	0	0	0	0	0	0	0	0
44 FARM MACH., EQUIP.	0	0	0	0	0	0	0	0	0
45 CONSTRUC. MACH., EQUIP.	8	19	0	20	1	0	147	44	4
46 MATERIAL HANDLING MACH.	2	182	0	197	5	0	315	8	52
47 METALWORKING MACHINERY	0	0	0	0	0	0	0	0	0
48 SPECIAL MACH., EQUIP.	56	258	1	355	134	0	431	13	45
49 GENERAL MACH., EQUIP.	0	0	0	0	0	0	0	0	0
50 MACHINE SHOP PRDTS.	0	0	0	0	0	0	0	0	0
51 OFFICE, COMPUT. MACHINES	0	0	0	0	0	0	0	0	0
52 SERVICE IND. MACHINES	0	0	0	0	0	0	0	0	0
53 ELECT. TRANSMISS. EQUIP.	43	205	1	478	70	0	578	15	35
54 HOUSEHOLD APPLIANCES	0	0	0	0	0	0	0	0	0
55 ELECTRIC LIGHTING EQUIP.	0	0	0	0	0	0	0	0	0
56 RADIO, TV, ETC., EQUIP.	59	1292	5	1833	242	0	430	184	3
57 ELECTRONIC COMPONENTS	252	1861	7	3142	271	0	1053	54	15
58 MISC. ELECTRICAL MACH.	0	0	0	0	0	0	0	0	0
59 MOTOR VEHICLES, EQUIP.	0	0	0	0	0	0	0	0	0
60 AIRCRAFT, PARTS	1	169	2	529	11	0	471	217	9
61 OTHER TRANSPORT. EQUIP.	20	1717	5	2391	226	4	1926	156	558
62 PROFESS., SCIEN. INSTRU.	0	0	0	0	0	0	0	0	0
63 MEDICAL, PHOTO. EQUIP.	4	74	0	751	13	0	13	1	6
64 MISC. MANUFACTURING	57	1019	9	3411	93	11	766	41	50
65 TRANSPORT., WAREHOUSING	0	0	0	0	0	0	0	0	0
66 COMMUNICA.,EXC. BRDCAST.	0	0	0	0	0	0	0	0	0
67 RADIO, TV BROADCASTING	0	0	0	0	0	0	0	0	0
68 ELEC.,GAS,WATER,SAN.SER.	0	0	0	0	0	0	0	0	0
69 WHOLESALE, RETAIL TRADE	0	0	0	0	0	0	0	0	0
70 FINANCE, INSURANCE	0	0	0	0	0	0	0	0	0
71 REAL ESTATE, RENTAL	0	0	0	0	0	0	0	0	0
72 HOTELS, PERSONAL SERV.	0	0	0	0	0	0	0	0	0
73 BUSINESS SERVICES	0	0	0	0	0	0	0	0	0
74 RESEARCH, DEVELOPMENT	0	0	0	0	0	0	0	0	0
75 AUTO. REPAIR, SERVICES	0	0	0	0	0	0	0	0	0
76 AMUSEMENTS	0	0	0	0	0	0	0	0	0
77 MED.,EDUC. SERVICES	0	0	0	0	0	0	0	0	0
78 FEDERAL GOVT. ENTERPRISE	0	0	0	0	0	0	0	0	0
79 STATE, LOCAL GOVT. ENT.	0	0	0	0	0	0	0	0	0
80 ZERO ENTRIES	0	0	0	0	0	0	0	0	0
81 SERVICE IND. RESIDUAL	0	0	0	0	0	0	0	0	0
82 TOTAL FINAL DEMAND	0	0	0	0	0	0	0	0	0
83 SECONDARY TRANSFERS-OUT	0	0	0	0	0	0	0	0	0
84 ZERO ENTRIES	0	0	0	0	0	0	0	0	0
85 SCRAP ENTRIES	0	0	0	0	0	0	0	0	0
86 ZERO ENTRIES	0	0	0	0	0	0	0	0	0
87 STATE TOTAL CONSUMPTION	3925	14193	1972	35324	9126	2139	18071	3008	4187

TABLE C-16

1963 INVENTORY DEPLETIONS BY STATE
(THOUSANDS OF CURRENT DOLLARS)

INDUSTRY TITLE	37 PENNSYL-VANIA	38 RHODE ISLAND	39 SOUTH CAROLINA	40 SOUTH DAKOTA	41 TENNESSEE	42 TEXAS	43 UTAH	44 VERMONT	45 VIRGINIA
1 LIVESTOCK, PRDTS.	0	0	0	0	0	0	0	0	0
2 OTHER AGRICULTURE PRDTS.	1667	39	1344	1539	1691	6137	269	181	1180
3 FORESTRY, FISHERIES	0	0	0	0	0	0	0	0	0
4 AGRI.,FORES.,FISH. SERV.	0	0	0	0	0	0	0	0	0
5 IRON, FERRO. ORES MINING	2846	0	0	29	22	485	1056	0	64
6 NONFERROUS ORES MINING	9	0	1	68	39	15	606	0	15
7 COAL MINING	0	0	0	0	0	0	0	0	0
8 CRUDE PETRO.,NATURAL GAS	0	0	0	0	0	0	0	0	0
9 STONE, CLAY MINING	0	0	0	0	0	0	0	0	0
10 CHEM.,FERT. MIN. MINING	6	0	1	0	42	81	11	0	1
11 NEW CONSTRUCTION	0	0	0	0	0	0	0	0	0
12 MAINT., REPAIR CONSTR.	0	0	0	0	0	0	0	0	0
13 ORDNANCE, ACCESSORIES	1265	20	6	0	414	763	879	50	35
14 FOOD, KINDRED PRDTS.	423	19	44	55	162	362	39	19	107
15 TOBACCO MANUFACTURES	257	0	65	0	39	4	0	0	937
16 FABRICS	0	0	0	0	0	0	0	0	0
17 TEXTILE PRDTS.	0	0	0	0	0	0	0	0	0
18 APPAREL	420	14	52	0	167	92	5	5	67
19 MISC. TEXTILE PRDTS.	0	0	0	0	0	0	0	0	0
20 LUMBER, WOOD PRDTS.	181	5	151	12	164	218	13	37	222
21 WOODEN CONTAINERS	0	0	0	0	0	0	0	0	0
22 HOUSEHOLD FURNITURE	0	0	0	0	0	0	0	0	0
23 OTHER FURNITURE	17	1	1	0	3	6	0	0	4
24 PAPER, ALLIED PRDTS.	0	0	0	0	0	0	0	0	0
25 PAPERBOARD CONTAINERS	0	0	0	0	0	0	0	0	0
26 PRINTING, PUBLISHING	330	17	15	6	65	131	14	9	46
27 CHEMICALS,SELECT. PRDTS.	0	0	0	0	0	0	0	0	0
28 PLASTICS, SYNTHETICS	48	5	23	0	61	66	0	0	79
29 DRUGS, COSMETICS	0	0	0	0	0	0	0	0	0
30 PAINT, ALLIED PRDTS.	0	0	0	0	0	0	0	0	0
31 PETROLEUM, RELATED INDS.	0	0	0	0	0	0	0	0	0
32 RUBBER, MISC. PLASTICS	218	60	28	1	81	91	5	9	43
33 LEATHER TANNING, PRDTS.	558	3	10	0	321	29	4	33	106
34 FOOTWEAR, LEATHER PRDTS.	4498	203	9	0	2828	488	8	83	696
35 GLASS, GLASS PRDTS.	0	0	0	0	0	0	0	0	0
36 STONE, CLAY PRDTS.	229	5	21	5	54	178	22	13	60
37 PRIMARY IRON, STEEL MFR.	1517	21	7	0	30	100	46	1	24
38 PRIMARY NONFERROUS MFR.	1764	475	43	0	750	1413	348	28	196

39 METAL CONTAINERS	0	0	0	0	0	0	0	0	0
40 FABRICATED METAL PRDTS.	0	0	0	0	0	0	0	0	0
41 SCREW MACH. PRDTS., ETC.	0	0	0	0	0	0	0	0	0
42 OTHER FAB. METAL PRDTS.	0	0	0	0	0	0	0	0	0
43 ENGINES, TURBINES	0	0	0	0	0	0	0	0	0
44 FARM MACH., EQUIP.	0	0	0	0	0	0	0	0	0
45 CONSTRUC. MACH., EQUIP.	62	0	0	0	4	147	11	1	3
46 MATERIAL HANDLING MACH.	242	2	9	6	33	48	2	0	9
47 METALWORKING MACHINERY	0	0	0	0	0	0	0	0	0
48 SPECIAL MACH., EQUIP.	315	54	84	0	26	89	5	6	15
49 GENERAL MACH., EQUIP.	0	0	0	0	0	0	0	0	0
50 MACHINE SHOP PRDTS.	0	0	0	0	0	0	0	0	0
51 OFFICE, COMPUT. MACHINES	0	0	0	0	0	0	0	0	0
52 SERVICE IND. MACHINES	0	0	0	0	0	0	0	0	0
53 ELECT. TRANSMISS. EQUIP.	541	6	20	0	50	47	5	2	79
54 HOUSEHOLD APPLIANCES	0	0	0	0	0	0	0	0	0
55 ELECTRIC LIGHTING EQUIP.	0	0	0	0	0	0	0	0	0
56 RADIO, TV, ETC., EQUIP.	338	18	3	0	156	311	21	2	121
57 ELECTRONIC COMPONENTS	2915	132	200	11	126	304	54	79	476
58 MISC. ELECTRICAL MACH.	0	0	0	0	0	0	0	0	0
59 MOTOR VEHICLES, EQUIP.	0	0	0	0	0	0	0	0	0
60 AIRCRAFT, PARTS	368	5	1	0	34	302	109	33	12
61 OTHER TRANSPORT. EQUIP.	5601	81	128	28	624	1539	91	6	1085
62 PROFESS., SCIEN. INSTRU.	0	0	0	0	0	0	0	0	0
63 MEDICAL, PHOTO. EQUIP.	30	7	9	0	2	7	0	3	15
64 MISC. MANUFACTURING	1078	607	119	5	211	174	30	17	156
65 TRANSPORT., WAREHOUSING	0	0	0	0	0	0	0	0	0
66 COMMUNICA.,EXC. BRDCAST.	0	0	0	0	0	0	0	0	0
67 RADIO, TV BROADCASTING	0	0	0	0	0	0	0	0	0
68 ELEC.,GAS,WATER,SAN.SER.	0	0	0	0	0	0	0	0	0
69 WHOLESALE, RETAIL TRADE	0	0	0	0	0	0	0	0	0
70 FINANCE, INSURANCE	0	0	0	0	0	0	0	0	0
71 REAL ESTATE, RENTAL	0	0	0	0	0	0	0	0	0
72 HOTELS, PERSONAL SERV.	0	0	0	0	0	0	0	0	0
73 BUSINESS SERVICES	0	0	0	0	0	0	0	0	0
74 RESEARCH, DEVELOPMENT	0	0	0	0	0	0	0	0	0
75 AUTO. REPAIR, SERVICES	0	0	0	0	0	0	0	0	0
76 AMUSEMENTS	0	0	0	0	0	0	0	0	0
77 MED.,EDUC. SERVICES	0	0	0	0	0	0	0	0	0
78 FEDERAL GOVT. ENTERPRISE	0	0	0	0	0	0	0	0	0
79 STATE, LOCAL GOVT. ENT.	0	0	0	0	0	0	0	0	0
80 ZERO ENTRIES	0	0	0	0	0	0	0	0	0
81 SERVICE IND. RESIDUAL	0	0	0	0	0	0	0	0	0
82 TOTAL FINAL DEMAND	0	0	0	0	0	0	0	0	0
83 SECONDARY TRANSFERS-OUT	0	0	0	0	0	0	0	0	0
84 ZERO ENTRIES	0	0	0	0	0	0	0	0	0
85 SCRAP ENTRIES	0	0	0	0	0	0	0	0	0
86 ZERO ENTRIES	0	0	0	0	0	0	0	0	0
87 STATE TOTAL CONSUMPTION	27743	1802	2413	1767	8198	13624	3655	617	5855

TABLE C-16

1963 INVENTORY DEPLETIONS BY STATE
(THOUSANDS OF CURRENT DOLLARS)

INDUSTRY TITLE	46 WASHINGTON	47 WEST VIRGINIA	48 WISCONSIN	49 WYOMING	50 ALASKA	51 HAWAII	52 NATIONAL TOTAL
1 LIVESTOCK, PRDTS.	0	0	0	0	0	0	0
2 OTHER AGRICULTURE PRDTS.	1841	252	1949	271	1	935	94800
3 FORESTRY, FISHERIES	0	0	0	0	0	0	0
4 AGRI.,FORES.,FISH. SERV.	0	0	0	0	0	0	0
5 IRON, FERRO. ORES MINING	60	0	61	1195	30	0	55200
6 NONFERROUS ORES MINING	28	0	5	164	16	0	3400
7 COAL MINING	0	0	0	0	0	0	0
8 CRUDE PETRO.,NATURAL GAS	0	0	0	0	0	0	0
9 STONE, CLAY MINING	0	0	0	0	0	0	0
10 CHEM.,FERT. MIN. MINING	0	1	0	21	0	0	700
11 NEW CONSTRUCTION	0	0	0	0	0	0	0
12 MAINT., REPAIR CONSTR.	0	0	0	0	0	0	0
13 ORDNANCE, ACCESSORIES	369	569	155	1	0	0	39600
14 FOOD, KINDRED PRDTS.	125	24	309	9	9	58	8100
15 TOBACCO MANUFACTURES	0	17	0	0	0	0	4800
16 FABRICS	0	0	0	0	0	0	0
17 TEXTILE PRDTS.	0	0	0	0	0	0	0
18 APPAREL	11	10	32	0	0	5	4000
19 MISC. TEXTILE PRDTS.	0	0	0	0	0	0	0
20 LUMBER, WOOD PRDTS.	861	59	204	16	22	9	8700
21 WOODEN CONTAINERS	0	0	0	0	0	0	0
22 HOUSEHOLD FURNITURE	0	0	0	0	0	0	0
23 OTHER FURNITURE	1	1	4	0	0	0	200
24 PAPER, ALLIED PRDTS.	0	0	0	0	0	0	0
25 PAPERBOARD CONTAINERS	0	0	0	0	0	0	0
26 PRINTING, PUBLISHING	40	16	113	3	1	7	4900
27 CHEMICALS,SELECT. PRDTS.	0	0	0	0	0	0	0
28 PLASTICS, SYNTHETICS	3	40	3	0	0	0	700
29 DRUGS, COSMETICS	0	0	0	0	0	0	0
30 PAINT, ALLIED PRDTS.	0	0	0	0	0	0	0
31 PETROLEUM, RELATED INDS.	0	0	0	0	0	0	0
32 RUBBER, MISC. PLASTICS	7	9	75	0	0	0	3800
33 LEATHER TANNING, PRDTS.	7	111	1050	0	0	0	7800
34 FOOTWEAR, LEATHER PRDTS.	46	66	2155	0	0	27	50900
35 GLASS, GLASS PRDTS.	0	0	0	0	0	0	0
36 STONE, CLAY PRDTS.	38	27	58	7	2	9	3100
37 PRIMARY IRON, STEEL MFR.	15	144	110	0	0	2	6500
38 PRIMARY NONFERROUS MFR.	1074	536	334	1	0	0	30700

39 METAL CONTAINERS	0	0	0	0	0	0	0
40 FABRICATED METAL PRDTS.	0	0	0	0	0	0	0
41 SCREW MACH. PRDTS., ETC.	0	0	0	0	0	0	0
42 OTHER FAB. METAL PRDTS.	0	0	0	0	0	0	0
43 ENGINES, TURBINES	0	0	0	0	0	0	0
44 FARM MACH., EQUIP.	0	0	0	0	0	0	0
45 CONSTRUC. MACH., EQUIP.	10	15	127	0	0	0	1400
46 MATERIAL HANDLING MACH.	33	8	68	0	0	0	2300
47 METALWORKING MACHINERY	0	0	0	0	0	0	0
48 SPECIAL MACH., EQUIP.	31	6	244	0	0	5	4000
49 GENERAL MACH., EQUIP.	0	0	0	0	0	0	0
50 MACHINE SHOP PRDTS.	0	0	0	0	0	0	0
51 OFFICE, COMPUT. MACHINES	0	0	0	0	0	0	0
52 SERVICE IND. MACHINES	0	0	0	0	0	0	0
53 ELECT. TRANSMISS. EQUIP.	15	17	335	0	0	0	4400
54 HOUSEHOLD APPLIANCES	0	0	0	0	0	0	0
55 ELECTRIC LIGHTING EQUIP.	0	0	0	0	0	0	0
56 RADIO, TV, ETC., EQUIP.	24	5	205	0	0	0	12500
57 ELECTRONIC COMPONENTS	28	60	283	0	0	1	23400
58 MISC. ELECTRICAL MACH.	0	0	0	0	0	0	0
59 MOTOR VEHICLES, EQUIP.	0	0	0	0	0	0	0
60 AIRCRAFT, PARTS	219	4	11	1	0	0	6400
61 OTHER TRANSPORT. EQUIP.	2129	421	1183	1	0	14	46400
62 PROFESS., SCIEN. INSTRU.	0	0	0	0	0	0	0
63 MEDICAL, PHOTO. EQUIP.	1	3	4	0	0	0	1400
64 MISC. MANUFACTURING	68	28	321	0	0	6	14800
65 TRANSPORT., WAREHOUSING	0	0	0	0	0	0	0
66 COMMUNICA.,EXC. BRDCAST.	0	0	0	0	0	0	0
67 RADIO, TV BROADCASTING	0	0	0	0	0	0	0
68 ELEC.,GAS,WATER,SAN.SER.	0	0	0	0	0	0	0
69 WHOLESALE, RETAIL TRADE	0	0	0	0	0	0	0
70 FINANCE, INSURANCE	0	0	0	0	0	0	0
71 REAL ESTATE, RENTAL	0	0	0	0	0	0	0
72 HOTELS, PERSONAL SERV.	0	0	0	0	0	0	0
73 BUSINESS SERVICES	0	0	0	0	0	0	0
74 RESEARCH, DEVELOPMENT	0	0	0	0	0	0	0
75 AUTO. REPAIR, SERVICES	0	0	0	0	0	0	0
76 AMUSEMENTS	0	0	0	0	0	0	0
77 MED., EDUC. SERVICES	0	0	0	0	0	0	0
78 FEDERAL GOVT. ENTERPRISE	0	0	0	0	0	0	0
79 STATE, LOCAL GOVT. ENT.	0	0	0	0	0	0	0
80 ZERO ENTRIES	0	0	0	0	0	0	0
81 SERVICE IND. RESIDUAL	0	0	0	0	0	0	0
82 TOTAL FINAL DEMAND	0	0	0	0	0	0	0
83 SECONDARY TRANSFERS-OUT	0	0	0	0	0	0	0
84 ZERO ENTRIES	0	0	0	0	0	0	0
85 SCRAP ENTRIES	0	0	0	0	0	0	0
86 ZERO ENTRIES	0	0	0	0	0	0	0
87 STATE TOTAL CONSUMPTION	7087	2448	9452	1692	81	1080	444900

TABLE C-17

1963 SCRAP PRODUCTION BY STATE
(THOUSANDS OF CURRENT DOLLARS)

INDUSTRY TITLE	1 ALABAMA	2 ARIZONA	3 ARKANSAS	4 CALIFORNIA	5 COLORADO	6 CONNECTICUT	7 DELAWARE	8 DISTRICT OF COLUMBIA	9 FLORIDA
1 LIVESTOCK, PRDTS.	0	0	0	0	0	0	0	0	0
2 OTHER AGRICULTURE PRDTS.	0	0	0	0	0	0	0	0	0
3 FORESTRY, FISHERIES	0	0	0	0	0	0	0	0	0
4 AGRI.,FORES.,FISH. SERV.	0	0	0	0	0	0	0	0	0
5 IRON, FERRO. ORES MINING	0	0	0	0	0	0	0	0	0
6 NONFERROUS ORES MINING	0	0	0	0	0	0	0	0	0
7 COAL MINING	0	0	0	0	0	0	0	0	0
8 CRUDE PETRO.,NATURAL GAS	0	0	0	0	0	0	0	0	0
9 STONE, CLAY MINING	0	0	0	0	0	0	0	0	0
10 CHEM.,FERT. MIN. MINING	0	0	0	0	0	0	0	0	0
11 NEW CONSTRUCTION	0	0	0	0	0	0	0	0	0
12 MAINT., REPAIR CONSTR.	0	0	0	0	0	0	0	0	0
13 ORDNANCE, ACCESSORIES	0	0	0	0	0	0	0	0	0
14 FOOD, KINDRED PRDTS.	0	0	0	0	0	0	0	0	0
15 TOBACCO MANUFACTURES	-34	0	0	-1	0	-18	0	0	-153
16 FABRICS	-4418	-2	-133	-206	-3	-1540	-417	0	-73
17 TEXTILE PRDTS.	0	0	0	0	0	0	0	0	0
18 APPAREL	-159	-11	-37	-385	-7	-89	-23	0	-50
19 MISC. TEXTILE PRDTS.	-43	-5	-1	-227	-10	-35	-5	-1	-18
20 LUMBER, WOOD PRDTS.	0	0	0	0	0	0	0	0	0
21 WOODEN CONTAINERS	0	0	0	0	0	0	0	0	0
22 HOUSEHOLD FURNITURE	0	0	0	0	0	0	0	0	0
23 OTHER FURNITURE	0	0	0	0	0	0	0	0	0
24 PAPER, ALLIED PRDTS.	-677	-23	-361	-880	-25	-220	-20	0	-709
25 PAPERBOARD CONTAINERS	-155	-38	-323	-3446	-143	-585	-75	0	-568
26 PRINTING, PUBLISHING	-399	-304	-242	-5987	-541	-1345	-118	-1200	-1190
27 CHEMICALS,SELECT. PRDTS.	0	0	0	0	0	0	0	0	0
28 PLASTICS, SYNTHETICS	0	0	0	0	0	0	0	0	0
29 DRUGS, COSMETICS	0	0	0	0	0	0	0	0	0
30 PAINT, ALLIED PRDTS.	0	0	0	0	0	0	0	0	0
31 PETROLEUM, RELATED INDS.	-28	-2	-73	-1239	-41	-9	-82	0	-17
32 RUBBER, MISC. PLASTICS	-286	-8	-59	-894	-165	-395	-83	0	-31
33 LEATHER TANNING, PRDTS.	0	0	0	-198	-4	-22	-225	0	-15
34 FOOTWEAR, LEATHER PRDTS.	-3	0	-25	-19	-14	-9	-2	0	-7
35 GLASS, GLASS PRDTS.	0	0	0	0	0	0	0	0	0
36 STONE, CLAY PRDTS.	0	0	0	0	0	0	0	0	0
37 PRIMARY IRON, STEEL MFR.	-5506	-51	-16	-4484	-956	-1299	-889	0	-170
38 PRIMARY NONFERROUS MFR.	-2653	-5128	-1461	-6578	-112	-6942	-159	0	-569

39 METAL CONTAINERS	-31	0	-33	-1412	-75	-12	0	0	-278
40 FABRICATED METAL PRDTS.	-509	-99	-121	-2425	-142	-280	-67	-14	-562
41 SCREW MACH. PRDTS., ETC.	-281	-9	-91	-2415	-17	-2046	-78	0	-117
42 OTHER FAB. METAL PRDTS.	-271	-30	-81	-2185	-118	-856	-33	0	-125
43 ENGINES, TURBINES	0	0	0	-124	-7	-89	0	0	-3
44 FARM MACH., EQUIP.	-70	-18	-18	-246	-30	-8	-3	0	-35
45 CONSTRUC. MACH., EQUIP.	-33	0	-2	-419	-279	-5	-1	0	-7
46 MATERIAL HANDLING MACH.	0	0	0	0	0	0	0	0	0
47 METALWORKING MACHINERY	-10	-6	-13	-379	-3	-530	-9	0	-26
48 SPECIAL MACH., EQUIP.	-96	-5	-15	-860	-38	-488	-94	0	-112
49 GENERAL MACH., EQUIP.	-66	-14	-63	-2482	-119	-2344	-4	0	-66
50 MACHINE SHOP PRDTS.	-102	-121	-41	-2671	-139	-600	-24	-15	-180
51 OFFICE, COMPUT. MACHINES	0	-28	-2	-142	0	-53	0	0	-11
52 SERVICE IND. MACHINES	-20	-36	-21	-162	-3	-33	-4	0	-13
53 ELECT. TRANSMISS. EQUIP.	-44	-4	-115	-989	-93	-318	0	0	-17
54 HOUSEHOLD APPLIANCES	0	0	-201	-319	-1	-309	-7	0	-4
55 ELECTRIC LIGHTING EQUIP.	0	0	0	0	0	0	0	0	0
56 RADIO, TV, ETC., EQUIP.	-51	-495	-602	-11625	-12	-736	-1	0	-1111
57 ELECTRONIC COMPONENTS	-43	-187	0	-1798	-4	-384	-2	0	-70
58 MISC. ELECTRICAL MACH.	-13	-1	0	-85	-7	-35	-6	0	-28
59 MOTOR VEHICLES, EQUIP.	-274	-32	-57	-10016	-90	-926	-1826	0	-60
60 AIRCRAFT, PARTS	-685	-162	-1	-4268	-163	-1735	-9	0	-200
61 OTHER TRANSPORT. EQUIP.	-477	-21	-138	-1828	-31	-350	-10	0	-547
62 PROFESS., SCIEN. INSTRU.	-5	-85	-102	-820	-35	-659	-19	0	-57
63 MEDICAL, PHOTO. EQUIP.	0	-5	-1	-664	-25	-215	0	0	-92
64 MISC. MANUFACTURING	-56	-21	-107	-1191	-61	-893	-4	-5	-97
65 TRANSPORT., WAREHOUSING	-712	-326	-398	-6925	-786	-616	-158	-631	-1848
66 COMMUNICA.,EXC. BRDCAST.	0	0	0	0	0	0	0	0	0
67 RADIO, TV BROADCASTING	0	0	0	0	0	0	0	0	0
68 ELEC.,GAS,WATER,SAN.SER.	0	0	0	0	0	0	0	0	0
69 WHOLESALE, RETAIL TRADE	0	0	0	0	0	0	0	0	0
70 FINANCE, INSURANCE	0	0	0	0	0	0	0	0	0
71 REAL ESTATE, RENTAL	0	0	0	0	0	0	0	0	0
72 HOTELS, PERSONAL SERV.	0	0	0	0	0	0	0	0	0
73 BUSINESS SERVICES	0	0	0	0	0	0	0	0	0
74 RESEARCH, DEVELOPMENT	0	0	0	0	0	0	0	0	0
75 AUTO. REPAIR, SERVICES	0	0	0	0	0	0	0	0	0
76 AMUSEMENTS	0	0	0	0	0	0	0	0	0
77 MED.,EDUC. SERVICES	0	0	0	0	0	0	0	0	0
78 FEDERAL GOVT. ENTERPRISE	0	0	0	0	0	0	0	0	0
79 STATE, LOCAL GOVT. ENT.	0	0	0	0	0	0	0	0	0
80 ZERO ENTRIES	0	0	0	0	0	0	0	0	0
81 SERVICE IND. RESIDUAL	0	0	0	0	0	0	0	0	0
82 TOTAL FINAL DEMAND	0	0	0	0	0	0	0	0	0
83 SECONDARY TRANSFERS-OUT	0	0	0	0	0	0	0	0	0
84 ZERO ENTRIES	0	0	0	0	0	0	0	0	0
85 SCRAP ENTRIES	-3524	-1615	-64	-20731	-102	-1479	-1899	-100	-6526
86 ZERO ENTRIES	0	0	0	0	0	0	0	0	0
87 STATE TOTAL CONSUMPTION	-21736	-8892	-5019	-101724	-4401	-28511	-6356	-1967	-15762

TABLE C-17

1963 SCRAP PRODUCTION BY STATE
(THOUSANDS OF CURRENT DOLLARS)

INDUSTRY TITLE	10 GEORGIA	11 IDAHO	12 ILLINOIS	13 INDIANA	14 IOWA	15 KANSAS	16 KENTUCKY	17 LOUISIANA	18 MAINE
1 LIVESTOCK, PRDTS.	0	0	0	0	0	0	0	0	0
2 OTHER AGRICULTURE PRDTS.	0	0	0	0	0	0	0	0	0
3 FORESTRY, FISHERIES	0	0	0	0	0	0	0	0	0
4 AGRI.,FORES.,FISH. SERV.	0	0	0	0	0	0	0	0	0
5 IRON, FERRO. ORES MINING	0	0	0	0	0	0	0	0	0
6 NONFERROUS ORES MINING	0	0	0	0	0	0	0	0	0
7 COAL MINING	0	0	0	0	0	0	0	0	0
8 CRUDE PETRO.,NATURAL GAS	0	0	0	0	0	0	0	0	0
9 STONE, CLAY MINING	0	0	0	0	0	0	0	0	0
10 CHEM.,FERT. MIN. MINING	0	0	0	0	0	0	0	0	0
11 NEW CONSTRUCTION	0	0	0	0	0	0	0	0	0
12 MAINT., REPAIR CONSTR.	0	0	0	0	0	0	0	0	0
13 ORDNANCE, ACCESSORIES	0	0	0	0	0	0	0	0	0
14 FOOD, KINDRED PRDTS.	0	0	0	0	0	0	0	0	0
15 TOBACCO MANUFACTURES	-21	0	-26	-20	0	0	-1633	-11	0
16 FABRICS	-10441	0	-352	0	-29	-2	-217	0	-1842
17 TEXTILE PRDTS.	0	0	0	0	0	0	0	0	0
18 APPAREL	-280	0	-193	-63	-13	-15	-105	-26	-18
19 MISC. TEXTILE PRDTS.	-152	-1	-188	-37	-10	-13	-26	-31	-12
20 LUMBER, WOOD PRDTS.	0	0	0	0	0	0	0	0	0
21 WOODEN CONTAINERS	0	0	0	0	0	0	0	0	0
22 HOUSEHOLD FURNITURE	0	0	0	0	0	0	0	0	0
23 OTHER FURNITURE	0	0	0	0	0	0	0	0	0
24 PAPER, ALLIED PRDTS.	-960	-62	-789	-297	-75	-40	-76	-768	-926
25 PAPERBOARD CONTAINERS	-1196	-25	-3449	-1131	-413	-457	-364	-479	-59
26 PRINTING, PUBLISHING	-786	-83	-8746	-1610	-1057	-522	-599	-390	-138
27 CHEMICALS,SELECT. PRDTS.	0	0	0	0	0	0	0	0	0
28 PLASTICS, SYNTHETICS	0	0	0	0	0	0	0	0	0
29 DRUGS, COSMETICS	0	0	0	0	0	0	0	0	0
30 PAINT, ALLIED PRDTS.	0	0	0	0	0	0	0	0	0
31 PETROLEUM, RELATED INDS.	-23	0	-661	-448	-5	-315	-82	-846	-2
32 RUBBER, MISC. PLASTICS	-86	0	-734	-595	-267	-122	-75	-6	-38
33 LEATHER TANNING, PRDTS.	-83	0	-532	-23	0	0	-51	-5	-442
34 FOOTWEAR, LEATHER PRDTS.	-16	0	-53	-12	-2	-1	-11	0	-84
35 GLASS, GLASS PRDTS.	0	0	0	0	0	0	0	0	0
36 STONE, CLAY PRDTS.	0	0	0	0	0	0	0	0	0
37 PRIMARY IRON, STEEL MFR.	-926	-7	-11233	-14653	-355	-124	-1390	-129	-6
38 PRIMARY NONFERROUS MFR.	-698	-1186	-9613	-8321	-1129	-245	-942	-1294	-65

39 METAL CONTAINERS	-129	-5	-1423	-154	-1	-23	-16	-196	-56
40 FABRICATED METAL PRDTS.	-413	-30	-1750	-1130	-327	-267	-323	-267	-44
41 SCREW MACH. PRDTS., ETC.	-396	0	-6895	-2057	-168	-45	-325	-47	-7
42 OTHER FAB. METAL PRDTS.	-147	-2	-3325	-1001	-235	-82	-442	-161	-13
43 ENGINES, TURBINES	0	0	-343	-116	-62	0	0	-1	0
44 FARM MACH., EQUIP.	-125	-21	-2125	-406	-1962	-134	-236	-40	-3
45 CONSTRUC. MACH., EQUIP.	-96	-4	-4200	-320	-536	-93	-6	-75	-39
46 MATERIAL HANDLING MACH.	0	0	0	0	0	0	0	0	0
47 METALWORKING MACHINERY	-13	0	-1112	-247	-57	-16	-22	-2	-5
48 SPECIAL MACH., EQUIP.	-272	-4	-1557	-307	-144	-99	-93	-64	-41
49 GENERAL MACH., EQUIP.	-70	0	-2871	-2081	-220	-153	-352	-19	-20
50 MACHINE SHOP PRDTS.	-85	-16	-1514	-1078	-72	-254	-265	-134	-24
51 OFFICE, COMPUT. MACHINES	-1	0	-59	-1	0	0	-15	0	0
52 SERVICE IND. MACHINES	-21	-1	-294	-143	-59	-32	-87	-8	-4
53 ELECT. TRANSMISS. EQUIP.	-214	0	-1040	-600	-48	-6	-138	-4	-5
54 HOUSEHOLD APPLIANCES	-6	0	-1009	-507	-245	-1	-464	-1	0
55 ELECTRIC LIGHTING EQUIP.	0	0	0	0	0	0	0	0	0
56 RADIO, TV, ETC., EQUIP.	-9	0	-10833	-4973	-557	-34	-81	-2	-21
57 ELECTRONIC COMPONENTS	-7	-1	-824	-443	-130	-38	-74	-1	-48
58 MISC. ELECTRICAL MACH.	-23	0	-143	-452	-15	-18	-8	-2	-3
59 MOTOR VEHICLES, EQUIP.	-3261	-8	-4072	-8170	-135	-981	-1007	-68	-3
60 AIRCRAFT, PARTS	-270	-4	-149	-566	-8	-877	-1	-143	-22
61 OTHER TRANSPORT. EQUIP.	-302	-65	-1886	-1585	-118	-250	-88	-729	-366
62 PROFESS., SCIEN. INSTRU.	-64	0	-1541	-286	-142	-10	-46	-13	-2
63 MEDICAL, PHOTO. EQUIP.	-2	0	-1050	-160	-11	-4	-7	-9	0
64 MISC. MANUFACTURING	-175	-8	-1485	-393	-216	-21	-70	-44	-41
65 TRANSPORT., WAREHOUSING	-1361	-211	-5431	-1482	-708	-885	-814	-1444	-231
66 COMMUNICA.,EXC. BRDCAST.	0	0	0	0	0	0	0	0	0
67 RADIO, TV BROADCASTING	0	0	0	0	0	0	0	0	0
68 ELEC.,GAS,WATER,SAN.SER.	0	0	0	0	0	0	0	0	0
69 WHOLESALE, RETAIL TRADE	0	0	0	0	0	0	0	0	0
70 FINANCE, INSURANCE	0	0	0	0	0	0	0	0	0
71 REAL ESTATE, RENTAL	0	0	0	0	0	0	0	0	0
72 HOTELS, PERSONAL SERV.	0	0	0	0	0	0	0	0	0
73 BUSINESS SERVICES	0	0	0	0	0	0	0	0	0
74 RESEARCH, DEVELOPMENT	0	0	0	0	0	0	0	0	0
75 AUTO. REPAIR, SERVICES	0	0	0	0	0	0	0	0	0
76 AMUSEMENTS	0	0	0	0	0	0	0	0	0
77 MED.,EDUC. SERVICES	0	0	0	0	0	0	0	0	0
78 FEDERAL GOVT. ENTERPRISE	0	0	0	0	0	0	0	0	0
79 STATE, LOCAL GOVT. ENT.	0	0	0	0	0	0	0	0	0
80 ZERO ENTRIES	0	0	0	0	0	0	0	0	0
81 SERVICE IND. RESIDUAL	0	0	0	0	0	0	0	0	0
82 TOTAL FINAL DEMAND	0	0	0	0	0	0	0	0	0
83 SECONDARY TRANSFERS-OUT	0	0	0	0	0	0	0	0	0
84 ZERO ENTRIES	0	0	0	0	0	0	0	0	0
85 SCRAP ENTRIES	-5959	-75	-4198	-379	-112	-100	-125	-11696	-11756
86 ZERO ENTRIES	0	0	0	0	0	0	0	0	0
87 STATE TOTAL CONSUMPTION	-29088	-1820	-97705	-56245	-9643	-6277	-10676	-19156	-16386

TABLE C-17

1963 SCRAP PRODUCTION BY STATE
(THOUSANDS OF CURRENT DOLLARS)

INDUSTRY TITLE	19 MARYLAND	20 MASSA-CHUSETTS	21 MICHIGAN	22 MINNESOTA	23 MISSISSIPPI	24 MISSOURI	25 MONTANA	26 NEBRASKA	27 NEVADA
1 LIVESTOCK, PRDTS.	0	0	0	0	0	0	0	0	0
2 OTHER AGRICULTURE PRDTS.	0	0	0	0	0	0	0	0	0
3 FORESTRY, FISHERIES	0	0	0	0	0	0	0	0	0
4 AGRI.,FORES.,FISH. SERV.	0	0	0	0	0	0	0	0	0
5 IRON, FERRO. ORES MINING	0	0	0	0	0	0	0	0	0
6 NONFERROUS ORES MINING	0	0	0	0	0	0	0	0	0
7 COAL MINING	0	0	0	0	0	0	0	0	0
8 CRUDE PETRO.,NATURAL GAS	0	0	0	0	0	0	0	0	0
9 STONE, CLAY MINING	0	0	0	0	0	0	0	0	0
10 CHEM.,FERT. MIN. MINING	0	0	0	0	0	0	0	0	0
11 NEW CONSTRUCTION	0	0	0	0	0	0	0	0	0
12 MAINT., REPAIR CONSTR.	0	0	0	0	0	0	0	0	0
13 ORDNANCE, ACCESSORIES	0	0	0	0	0	0	0	0	0
14 FOOD, KINDRED PRDTS.	0	0	0	0	0	0	0	0	0
15 TOBACCO MANUFACTURES	-6	-4	-19	0	0	-26	0	0	0
16 FABRICS	-385	-4031	-44	-123	-228	-165	0	-3	0
17 TEXTILE PRDTS.	0	0	0	0	0	0	0	0	0
18 APPAREL	-144	-335	-34	-43	-129	-160	0	-6	0
19 MISC. TEXTILE PRDTS.	-40	-152	-480	-34	-21	-74	0	-2	-1
20 LUMBER, WOOD PRDTS.	0	0	0	0	0	0	0	0	0
21 WOODEN CONTAINERS	0	0	0	0	0	0	0	0	0
22 HOUSEHOLD FURNITURE	0	0	0	0	0	0	0	0	0
23 OTHER FURNITURE	0	0	0	0	0	0	0	0	0
24 PAPER, ALLIED PRDTS.	-167	-1062	-1132	-614	-156	-231	-9	-19	0
25 PAPERBOARD CONTAINERS	-917	-1620	-1958	-572	-100	-1078	0	-118	0
26 PRINTING, PUBLISHING	-1084	-3089	-2314	-1473	-128	-2060	-88	-373	-83
27 CHEMICALS,SELECT. PRDTS.	0	0	0	0	0	0	0	0	0
28 PLASTICS, SYNTHETICS	0	0	0	0	0	0	0	0	0
29 DRUGS, COSMETICS	0	0	0	0	0	0	0	0	0
30 PAINT, ALLIED PRDTS.	0	0	0	0	0	0	0	0	0
31 PETROLEUM, RELATED INDS.	-56	-38	-182	-81	-42	-91	-71	-6	-1
32 RUBBER, MISC. PLASTICS	-260	-854	-550	-85	-81	-139	0	-60	0
33 LEATHER TANNING, PRDTS.	-36	-1741	-246	-82	0	-71	0	-16	0
34 FOOTWEAR, LEATHER PRDTS.	-7	-177	-10	-5	-8	-122	0	0	0
35 GLASS, GLASS PRDTS.	0	0	0	0	0	0	0	0	0
36 STONE, CLAY PRDTS.	0	0	0	0	0	0	0	0	0
37 PRIMARY IRON, STEEL MFR.	-2796	-1097	-12453	-1018	-45	-1004	-7	-22	-3
38 PRIMARY NONFERROUS MFR.	-3577	-2825	-7253	-285	-146	-1453	-2345	-843	-799

39 METAL CONTAINERS	-431	-85	-42	-200	-1	-360	0	-49	0
40 FABRICATED METAL PRDTS.	-350	-508	-1230	-281	-157	-667	-20	-234	-18
41 SCREW MACH. PRDTS., ETC.	-396	-1403	-6289	-521	-204	-524	0	-22	-1
42 OTHER FAB. METAL PRDTS.	-256	-987	-2439	-262	-61	-566	-1	-30	-2
43 ENGINES, TURBINES	0	-304	-711	-31	0	-18	0	0	0
44 FARM MACH., EQUIP.	-3	-5	-833	-469	-101	-209	-3	-127	0
45 CONSTRUC. MACH., EQUIP.	-14	-16	-479	-307	-46	-119	0	-14	-1
46 MATERIAL HANDLING MACH.	0	0	0	0	0	0	0	0	0
47 METALWORKING MACHINERY	-129	-434	-1907	-63	0	-99	0	-3	0
48 SPECIAL MACH., EQUIP.	-362	-1853	-1052	-180	-60	-240	0	-4	-1
49 GENERAL MACH., EQUIP.	-108	-1024	-2003	-331	-15	-318	0	-142	-1
50 MACHINE SHOP PRDTS.	-280	-596	-2073	-374	-69	-833	-14	-23	-9
51 OFFICE, COMPUT. MACHINES	-2	-33	-76	-84	0	-6	0	0	0
52 SERVICE IND. MACHINES	-46	-112	-364	-167	-14	-184	0	-2	-1
53 ELECT. TRANSMISS. EQUIP.	-74	-505	-405	-188	-26	-356	0	-2	-1
54 HOUSEHOLD APPLIANCES	-15	-50	-413	-205	-33	-76	0	-2	0
55 ELECTRIC LIGHTING EQUIP.	0	0	0	0	0	0	0	0	0
56 RADIO, TV, ETC., EQUIP.	-2796	-5569	-447	-690	-55	-687	0	-607	-24
57 ELECTRONIC COMPONENTS	-44	-950	-164	-127	-19	-22	0	-54	0
58 MISC. ELECTRICAL MACH.	-28	-58	-208	-21	-3	-32	0	-3	0
59 MOTOR VEHICLES, EQUIP.	-2770	-1240	-62583	-1169	-205	-10299	-2	-222	-2
60 AIRCRAFT, PARTS	-280	-255	-205	-50	0	-437	0	0	0
61 OTHER TRANSPORT. EQUIP.	-1168	-493	-1160	-101	-33	-456	-5	-150	0
62 PROFESS., SCIEN. INSTRU.	-64	-829	-705	-145	-17	-112	-5	-68	0
63 MEDICAL, PHOTO. EQUIP.	-37	-1179	-65	-128	-1	-85	0	-2	0
64 MISC. MANUFACTURING	-123	-1057	-629	-225	-94	-225	-8	-43	-8
65 TRANSPORT., WAREHOUSING	-1131	-1651	-2024	-1189	-329	-2118	-250	-580	-174
66 COMMUNICA.,EXC. BRDCAST.	0	0	0	0	0	0	0	0	0
67 RADIO, TV BROADCASTING	0	0	0	0	0	0	0	0	0
68 ELEC.,GAS,WATER,SAN.SER.	0	0	0	0	0	0	0	0	0
69 WHOLESALE, RETAIL TRADE	0	0	0	0	0	0	0	0	0
70 FINANCE, INSURANCE	0	0	0	0	0	0	0	0	0
71 REAL ESTATE, RENTAL	0	0	0	0	0	0	0	0	0
72 HOTELS, PERSONAL SERV.	0	0	0	0	0	0	0	0	0
73 BUSINESS SERVICES	0	0	0	0	0	0	0	0	0
74 RESEARCH, DEVELOPMENT	0	0	0	0	0	0	0	0	0
75 AUTO. REPAIR, SERVICES	0	0	0	0	0	0	0	0	0
76 AMUSEMENTS	0	0	0	0	0	0	0	0	0
77 MED.,EDUC. SERVICES	0	0	0	0	0	0	0	0	0
78 FEDERAL GOVT. ENTERPRISE	0	0	0	0	0	0	0	0	0
79 STATE, LOCAL GOVT. ENT.	0	0	0	0	0	0	0	0	0
80 ZERO ENTRIES	0	0	0	0	0	0	0	0	0
81 SERVICE IND. RESIDUAL	0	0	0	0	0	0	0	0	0
82 TOTAL FINAL DEMAND	0	0	0	0	0	0	0	0	0
83 SECONDARY TRANSFERS-OUT	0	0	0	0	0	0	0	0	0
84 ZERO ENTRIES	0	0	0	0	0	0	0	0	0
85 SCRAP ENTRIES	-20001	-10762	-30675	-278	-509	-207	-2404	-68	-25
86 ZERO ENTRIES	0	0	0	0	0	0	0	0	0
87 STATE TOTAL CONSUMPTION	-40380	-48982	-145859	-12204	-3136	-25926	-5235	-3918	-1156

TABLE C-17

1963 SCRAP PRODUCTION BY STATE
(THOUSANDS OF CURRENT DOLLARS)

INDUSTRY TITLE	28 NEW HAMPSHIRE	29 NEW JERSEY	30 NEW MEXICO	31 NEW YORK	32 NORTH CAROLINA	33 NORTH DAKOTA	34 OHIO	35 OKLAHOMA	36 OREGON
1 LIVESTOCK, PRDTS.	0	0	0	0	0	0	0	0	0
2 OTHER AGRICULTURE PRDTS.	0	0	0	0	0	0	0	0	0
3 FORESTRY, FISHERIES	0	0	0	0	0	0	0	0	0
4 AGRI.,FORES.,FISH. SERV.	0	0	0	0	0	0	0	0	0
5 IRON, FERRO. ORES MINING	0	0	0	0	0	0	0	0	0
6 NONFERROUS ORES MINING	0	0	0	0	0	0	0	0	0
7 COAL MINING	0	0	0	0	0	0	0	0	0
8 CRUDE PETRO.,NATURAL GAS	0	0	0	0	0	0	0	0	0
9 STONE, CLAY MINING	0	0	0	0	0	0	0	0	0
10 CHEM.,FERT. MIN. MINING	0	0	0	0	0	0	0	0	0
11 NEW CONSTRUCTION	0	0	0	0	0	0	0	0	0
12 MAINT., REPAIR CONSTR.	0	0	0	0	0	0	0	0	0
13 ORDNANCE, ACCESSORIES	0	0	0	0	0	0	0	0	0
14 FOOD, KINDRED PRDTS.	0	0	0	0	0	0	0	0	0
15 TOBACCO MANUFACTURES	0	-47	0	-14	-4502	0	-45	0	0
16 FABRICS	-1203	-2196	-1	-2043	-26449	0	-200	-11	-360
17 TEXTILE PRDTS.	0	0	0	0	0	0	0	0	0
18 APPAREL	-26	-401	-1	-3032	-581	0	-190	-23	-25
19 MISC. TEXTILE PRDTS.	-8	-260	-3	-764	-175	0	-58	-5	-31
20 LUMBER, WOOD PRDTS.	0	0	0	0	0	0	0	0	0
21 WOODEN CONTAINERS	0	0	0	0	0	0	0	0	0
22 HOUSEHOLD FURNITURE	0	0	0	0	0	0	0	0	0
23 OTHER FURNITURE	0	0	0	0	0	0	0	0	0
24 PAPER, ALLIED PRDTS.	-311	-976	0	-1854	-596	0	-1297	-24	-409
25 PAPERBOARD CONTAINERS	-90	-2493	-2	-3391	-670	-2	-2581	-125	-145
26 PRINTING, PUBLISHING	-216	-2868	-99	-19616	-647	-77	-4881	-396	-394
27 CHEMICALS,SELECT. PRDTS.	0	0	0	0	0	0	0	0	0
28 PLASTICS, SYNTHETICS	0	0	0	0	0	0	0	0	0
29 DRUGS, COSMETICS	0	0	0	0	0	0	0	0	0
30 PAINT, ALLIED PRDTS.	0	0	0	0	0	0	0	0	0
31 PETROLEUM, RELATED INDS.	-1	-693	-30	-126	-4	-18	-468	-379	-9
32 RUBBER, MISC. PLASTICS	-64	-691	-6	-609	-95	0	-2567	-133	-12
33 LEATHER TANNING, PRDTS.	-302	-559	0	-812	-71	0	-283	0	-14
34 FOOTWEAR, LEATHER PRDTS.	-70	-40	0	-209	-6	0	-32	-2	-2
35 GLASS, GLASS PRDTS.	0	0	0	0	0	0	0	0	0
36 STONE, CLAY PRDTS.	0	0	0	0	0	0	0	0	0
37 PRIMARY IRON, STEEL MFR.	-99	-1637	0	-5731	-173	0	-23628	-163	-354
38 PRIMARY NONFERROUS MFR.	-207	-11149	-438	-11994	-983	0	-10093	-894	-1286

39 METAL CONTAINERS	0	-972	0	-452	-2	0	-496	-10	-70
40 FABRICATED METAL PRDTS.	-35	-1020	-20	-1776	-307	-18	-2733	-458	-239
41 SCREW MACH. PRDTS., ETC.	-71	-2088	-13	-3169	-173	-3	-6502	-61	-37
42 OTHER FAB. METAL PRDTS.	-34	-1470	-3	-1710	-143	-1	-2723	-178	-82
43 ENGINES, TURBINES	0	-6	0	-320	0	0	-86	0	-1
44 FARM MACH., EQUIP.	0	-13	-1	-176	-72	-25	-571	-25	-25
45 CONSTRUC. MACH., EQUIP.	-79	-152	-5	-115	-5	0	-1367	-445	-33
46 MATERIAL HANDLING MACH.	0	0	0	0	0	0	0	0	0
47 METALWORKING MACHINERY	-24	-249	-3	-591	-17	-3	-1692	-4	-4
48 SPECIAL MACH., EQUIP.	-280	-1228	-4	-1618	-667	-2	-1905	-48	-220
49 GENERAL MACH., EQUIP.	-152	-2113	-1	-3048	-42	-1	-4320	-317	-36
50 MACHINE SHOP PRDTS.	-46	-683	-54	-1738	-121	-10	-1765	-119	-178
51 OFFICE, COMPUT. MACHINES	-1	-35	0	-264	-2	0	-58	0	0
52 SERVICE IND. MACHINES	-6	-152	-1	-451	-28	0	-363	-22	-7
53 ELECT. TRANSMISS. EQUIP.	-139	-600	-1	-1434	-219	0	-1761	-42	-113
54 HOUSEHOLD APPLIANCES	0	-75	0	-228	-73	0	-1561	-3	-7
55 ELECTRIC LIGHTING EQUIP.	0	0	0	0	0	0	0	0	0
56 RADIO, TV, ETC., EQUIP.	-348	-7706	-19	-10767	-1453	0	-2318	-1079	-10
57 ELECTRONIC COMPONENTS	-125	-845	-3	-1434	-117	0	-392	-13	-2
58 MISC. ELECTRICAL MACH.	-1	-89	0	-136	-65	0	-234	-6	-8
59 MOTOR VEHICLES, EQUIP.	-1	-3046	-11	-7624	-156	0	-21389	-253	-356
60 AIRCRAFT, PARTS	0	-439	0	-1436	-24	0	-1284	-613	-23
61 OTHER TRANSPORT. EQUIP.	-9	-811	-2	-1095	-106	-2	-854	-69	-267
62 PROFESS., SCIEN. INSTRU.	-9	-690	-10	-1238	-92	0	-439	-26	-21
63 MEDICAL, PHOTO. EQUIP.	-32	-621	0	-6727	-108	0	-47	-1	-51
64 MISC. MANUFACTURING	-62	-1166	-11	-3980	-100	-13	-810	-43	-55
65 TRANSPORT., WAREHOUSING	-108	-2860	-275	-8609	-1083	-164	-3424	-853	-850
66 COMMUNICA.,EXC. BRDCAST.	0	0	0	0	0	0	0	0	0
67 RADIO, TV BROADCASTING	0	0	0	0	0	0	0	0	0
68 ELEC.,GAS,WATER,SAN.SER.	0	0	0	0	0	0	0	0	0
69 WHOLESALE, RETAIL TRADE	0	0	0	0	0	0	0	0	0
70 FINANCE, INSURANCE	0	0	0	0	0	0	0	0	0
71 REAL ESTATE, RENTAL	0	0	0	0	0	0	0	0	0
72 HOTELS, PERSONAL SERV.	0	0	0	0	0	0	0	0	0
73 BUSINESS SERVICES	0	0	0	0	0	0	0	0	0
74 RESEARCH, DEVELOPMENT	0	0	0	0	0	0	0	0	0
75 AUTO. REPAIR, SERVICES	0	0	0	0	0	0	0	0	0
76 AMUSEMENTS	0	0	0	0	0	0	0	0	0
77 MED.,EDUC. SERVICES	0	0	0	0	0	0	0	0	0
78 FEDERAL GOVT. ENTERPRISE	0	0	0	0	0	0	0	0	0
79 STATE, LOCAL GOVT. ENT.	0	0	0	0	0	0	0	0	0
80 ZERO ENTRIES	0	0	0	0	0	0	0	0	0
81 SERVICE IND. RESIDUAL	0	0	0	0	0	0	0	0	0
82 TOTAL FINAL DEMAND	0	0	0	0	0	0	0	0	0
83 SECONDARY TRANSFERS-OUT	0	0	0	0	0	0	0	0	0
84 ZERO ENTRIES	0	0	0	0	0	0	0	0	0
85 SCRAP ENTRIES	-64	-27065	-45	-96612	-1673	-5421	-3541	-80	-1715
86 ZERO ENTRIES	0	0	0	0	0	0	0	0	0
87 STATE TOTAL CONSUMPTION	-4225	-80201	-1064	-206945	-41798	-5760	-108957	-6923	-7450

TABLE C-17

1963 SCRAP PRODUCTION BY STATE
(THOUSANDS OF CURRENT DOLLARS)

INDUSTRY TITLE	37 PENNSYL-VANIA	38 RHODE ISLAND	39 SOUTH CAROLINA	40 SOUTH DAKOTA	41 TENNESSEE	42 TEXAS	43 UTAH	44 VERMONT	45 VIRGINIA
1 LIVESTOCK, PRDTS.	0	0	0	0	0	0	0	0	0
2 OTHER AGRICULTURE PRDTS.	0	0	0	0	0	0	0	0	0
3 FORESTRY, FISHERIES	0	0	0	0	0	0	0	0	0
4 AGRI.,FORES.,FISH. SERV.	0	0	0	0	0	0	0	0	0
5 IRON, FERRO. ORES MINING	0	0	0	0	0	0	0	0	0
6 NONFERROUS ORES MINING	0	0	0	0	0	0	0	0	0
7 COAL MINING	0	0	0	0	0	0	0	0	0
8 CRUDE PETRO.,NATURAL GAS	0	0	0	0	0	0	0	0	0
9 STONE, CLAY MINING	0	0	0	0	0	0	0	0	0
10 CHEM.,FERT. MIN. MINING	0	0	0	0	0	0	0	0	0
11 NEW CONSTRUCTION	0	0	0	0	0	0	0	0	0
12 MAINT., REPAIR CONSTR.	0	0	0	0	0	0	0	0	0
13 ORDNANCE, ACCESSORIES	0	0	0	0	0	0	0	0	0
14 FOOD, KINDRED PRDTS.	0	0	0	0	0	0	0	0	0
15 TOBACCO MANUFACTURES	-485	0	-123	0	-74	-7	0	0	-1771
16 FABRICS	-4119	-2583	-21801	0	-1865	-846	-5	-57	-3460
17 TEXTILE PRDTS.	0	0	0	0	0	0	0	0	0
18 APPAREL	-894	-28	-128	0	-354	-195	-12	-10	-143
19 MISC. TEXTILE PRDTS.	-156	-7	-44	-1	-56	-72	-2	-1	-32
20 LUMBER, WOOD PRDTS.	0	0	0	0	0	0	0	0	0
21 WOODEN CONTAINERS	0	0	0	0	0	0	0	0	0
22 HOUSEHOLD FURNITURE	0	0	0	0	0	0	0	0	0
23 OTHER FURNITURE	0	0	0	0	0	0	0	0	0
24 PAPER, ALLIED PRDTS.	-1390	-37	-411	0	-573	-417	-9	-123	-621
25 PAPERBOARD CONTAINERS	-2687	-143	-507	-7	-488	-793	-19	-78	-401
26 PRINTING, PUBLISHING	-5262	-276	-219	-95	-1030	-2061	-218	-136	-717
27 CHEMICALS,SELECT. PRDTS.	0	0	0	0	0	0	0	0	0
28 PLASTICS, SYNTHETICS	0	0	0	0	0	0	0	0	0
29 DRUGS, COSMETICS	0	0	0	0	0	0	0	0	0
30 PAINT, ALLIED PRDTS.	0	0	0	0	0	0	0	0	0
31 PETROLEUM, RELATED INDS.	-669	-15	-10	0	-21	-2862	-81	0	-37
32 RUBBER, MISC. PLASTICS	-667	-195	-76	-4	-233	-262	-14	-28	-100
33 LEATHER TANNING, PRDTS.	-586	-2	-10	0	-338	-28	-4	-35	-112
34 FOOTWEAR, LEATHER PRDTS.	-107	-5	0	0	-68	-11	0	-2	-17
35 GLASS, GLASS PRDTS.	0	0	0	0	0	0	0	0	0
36 STONE, CLAY PRDTS.	0	0	0	0	0	0	0	0	0
37 PRIMARY IRON, STEEL MFR.	-31859	-417	-136	0	-615	-2043	-958	-18	-500
38 PRIMARY NONFERROUS MFR.	-7511	-2127	-189	0	-3359	-6303	-1562	-123	-866

39 METAL CONTAINERS	-608	0	-3	0	-49	-412	-25	0	-38
40 FABRICATED METAL PRDTS.	-2743	-50	-145	-37	-593	-1246	-168	-16	-440
41 SCREW MACH. PRDTS., ETC.	-4418	-330	-109	0	-368	-253	-8	-8	-36
42 OTHER FAB. METAL PRDTS.	-2236	-231	-44	-3	-189	-800	-15	-9	-156
43 ENGINES, TURBINES	-461	0	0	0	0	-28	0	0	0
44 FARM MACH., EQUIP.	-360	0	-10	-15	-222	-94	-6	-2	-28
45 CONSTRUC. MACH., EQUIP.	-536	-1	-1	0	-23	-1486	-109	-6	-19
46 MATERIAL HANDLING MACH.	0	0	0	0	0	0	0	0	0
47 METALWORKING MACHINERY	-700	-115	-63	-7	-19	-49	-3	-141	-4
48 SPECIAL MACH., EQUIP.	-1423	-262	-422	-1	-110	-389	-19	-21	-63
49 GENERAL MACH., EQUIP.	-2726	-100	-105	-20	-154	-532	-55	-5	-102
50 MACHINE SHOP PRDTS.	-963	-82	-78	-28	-161	-552	-35	-15	-89
51 OFFICE, COMPUT. MACHINES	-47	0	-3	0	0	-2	0	-7	-12
52 SERVICE IND. MACHINES	-281	-4	-3	0	-45	-180	-12	-6	-30
53 ELECT. TRANSMISS. EQUIP.	-1671	-12	-63	0	-141	-120	-13	-4	-251
54 HOUSEHOLD APPLIANCES	-158	-5	-11	0	-222	-38	0	0	-1
55 ELECTRIC LIGHTING EQUIP.	0	0	0	0	0	0	0	0	0
56 RADIO, TV, ETC., EQUIP.	-1758	-87	-9	-1	-911	-1799	-91	0	-712
57 ELECTRONIC COMPONENTS	-1409	-61	-102	-6	-45	-126	-26	-40	-236
58 MISC. ELECTRICAL MACH.	-112	-11	0	0	-16	-34	0	-7	-4
59 MOTOR VEHICLES, EQUIP.	-4105	-51	-26	-4	-371	-2723	-14	0	-980
60 AIRCRAFT, PARTS	-1006	-11	0	0	-85	-835	-303	-94	-30
61 OTHER TRANSPORT. EQUIP.	-2633	-36	-60	-13	-295	-727	-40	-2	-521
62 PROFESS., SCIEN. INSTRU.	-1247	-92	-66	0	-133	-160	-3	-26	-26
63 MEDICAL, PHOTO. EQUIP.	-209	-59	-73	0	-1	-45	-2	-25	-126
64 MISC. MANUFACTURING	-1219	-721	-138	-5	-236	-183	-34	-18	-177
65 TRANSPORT., WAREHOUSING	-4257	-202	-367	-114	-963	-3955	-354	-104	-1374
66 COMMUNICA.,EXC. BRDCAST.	0	0	0	0	0	0	0	0	0
67 RADIO, TV BROADCASTING	0	0	0	0	0	0	0	0	0
68 ELEC.,GAS,WATER,SAN.SER.	0	0	0	0	0	0	0	0	0
69 WHOLESALE, RETAIL TRADE	0	0	0	0	0	0	0	0	0
70 FINANCE, INSURANCE	0	0	0	0	0	0	0	0	0
71 REAL ESTATE, RENTAL	0	0	0	0	0	0	0	0	0
72 HOTELS, PERSONAL SERV.	0	0	0	0	0	0	0	0	0
73 BUSINESS SERVICES	0	0	0	0	0	0	0	0	0
74 RESEARCH, DEVELOPMENT	0	0	0	0	0	0	0	0	0
75 AUTO. REPAIR, SERVICES	0	0	0	0	0	0	0	0	0
76 AMUSEMENTS	0	0	0	0	0	0	0	0	0
77 MED., EDUC. SERVICES	0	0	0	0	0	0	0	0	0
78 FEDERAL GOVT. ENTERPRISE	0	0	0	0	0	0	0	0	0
79 STATE, LOCAL GOVT. ENT.	0	0	0	0	0	0	0	0	0
80 ZERO ENTRIES	0	0	0	0	0	0	0	0	0
81 SERVICE IND. RESIDUAL	0	0	0	0	0	0	0	0	0
82 TOTAL FINAL DEMAND	0	0	0	0	0	0	0	0	0
83 SECONDARY TRANSFERS-OUT	0	0	0	0	0	0	0	0	0
84 ZERO ENTRIES	0	0	0	0	0	0	0	0	0
85 SCRAP ENTRIES	-26426	-97	-2928	-24	-173	-14565	-37	-5707	-3315
86 ZERO ENTRIES	0	0	0	0	0	0	0	0	0
87 STATE TOTAL CONSUMPTION	-120102	-8453	-28484	-386	-14598	-47235	-4256	-6874	-17546

TABLE C-17

1963 SCRAP PRODUCTION BY STATE
(THOUSANDS OF CURRENT DOLLARS)

INDUSTRY TITLE	46 WASHINGTON	47 WEST VIRGINIA	48 WISCONSIN	49 WYOMING	50 ALASKA	51 HAWAII	52 NATIONAL TOTAL
1 LIVESTOCK, PRDTS.	0	0	0	0	0	0	0
2 OTHER AGRICULTURE PRDTS.	0	0	0	0	0	0	0
3 FORESTRY, FISHERIES	0	0	0	0	0	0	0
4 AGRI.,FORES.,FISH. SERV.	0	0	0	0	0	0	0
5 IRON, FERRO. ORES MINING	0	0	0	0	0	0	0
6 NONFERROUS ORES MINING	0	0	0	0	0	0	0
7 COAL MINING	0	0	0	0	0	0	0
8 CRUDE PETRO.,NATURAL GAS	0	0	0	0	0	0	0
9 STONE, CLAY MINING	0	0	0	0	0	0	0
10 CHEM.,FERT. MIN. MINING	0	0	0	0	0	0	0
11 NEW CONSTRUCTION	0	0	0	0	0	0	0
12 MAINT., REPAIR CONSTR.	0	0	0	0	0	0	0
13 ORDNANCE, ACCESSORIES	0	0	0	0	0	0	0
14 FOOD, KINDRED PRDTS.	0	0	0	0	0	0	0
15 TOBACCO MANUFACTURES	0	-32	-1	0	0	0	-9073
16 FABRICS	-80	-42	-92	0	0	-2	-92067
17 TEXTILE PRDTS.	0	0	0	0	0	0	0
18 APPAREL	-24	-21	-68	0	0	-11	-8493
19 MISC. TEXTILE PRDTS.	-19	-2	-18	0	0	-2	-3333
20 LUMBER, WOOD PRDTS.	0	0	0	0	0	0	0
21 WOODEN CONTAINERS	0	0	0	0	0	0	0
22 HOUSEHOLD FURNITURE	0	0	0	0	0	0	0
23 OTHER FURNITURE	0	0	0	0	0	0	0
24 PAPER, ALLIED PRDTS.	-1271	-49	-1992	0	0	-14	-22673
25 PAPERBOARD CONTAINERS	-473	-101	-1312	0	0	-30	-35807
26 PRINTING, PUBLISHING	-602	-247	-1744	-42	-19	-117	-77929
27 CHEMICALS,SELECT. PRDTS.	0	0	0	0	0	0	0
28 PLASTICS, SYNTHETICS	0	0	0	0	0	0	0
29 DRUGS, COSMETICS	0	0	0	0	0	0	0
30 PAINT, ALLIED PRDTS.	0	0	0	0	0	0	0
31 PETROLEUM, RELATED INDS.	-111	-34	-28	-184	0	-16	-10239
32 RUBBER, MISC. PLASTICS	-14	-8	-233	0	0	-1	-11885
33 LEATHER TANNING, PRDTS.	-7	-118	-1112	0	0	0	-8187
34 FOOTWEAR, LEATHER PRDTS.	-1	-2	-52	0	0	-1	-1211
35 GLASS, GLASS PRDTS.	0	0	0	0	0	0	0
36 STONE, CLAY PRDTS.	0	0	0	0	0	0	0
37 PRIMARY IRON, STEEL MFR.	-295	-3023	-2211	0	0	-31	-134532
38 PRIMARY NONFERROUS MFR.	-4835	-2376	-1582	-4	0	-1	-134504

39 METAL CONTAINERS	-182	-56	-360	0	0	-76	-8825
40 FABRICATED METAL PRDTS.	-252	-212	-899	-2	0	-18	-25657
41 SCREW MACH. PRDTS., ETC.	-67	-186	-2271	-5	0	0	-44529
42 OTHER FAB. METAL PRDTS.	-69	-191	-412	-2	0	-4	-24415
43 ENGINES, TURBINES	0	0	-646	0	0	0	-3359
44 FARM MACH., EQUIP.	-25	-32	-1021	0	0	-2	-9956
45 CONSTRUC. MACH., EQUIP.	-90	-149	-1223	-3	0	0	-12957
46 MATERIAL HANDLING MACH.	0	0	0	0	0	0	0
47 METALWORKING MACHINERY	-15	-32	-333	0	0	0	-9157
48 SPECIAL MACH., EQUIP.	-140	-13	-1155	0	0	-25	-18056
49 GENERAL MACH., EQUIP.	-42	-6	-1583	-1	0	-1	-30347
50 MACHINE SHOP PRDTS.	-227	-84	-454	-9	0	-13	-19111
51 OFFICE, COMPUT. MACHINES	-1	0	-2	0	0	0	-951
52 SERVICE IND. MACHINES	-11	-5	-155	0	0	0	-3594
53 ELECT. TRANSMISS. EQUIP.	-38	-49	-1037	-1	0	0	-12902
54 HOUSEHOLD APPLIANCES	-11	-2	-262	0	0	0	-6528
55 ELECTRIC LIGHTING EQUIP.	0	0	0	0	0	0	0
56 RADIO, TV, ETC., EQUIP.	-94	-3	-1181	0	0	-2	-72366
57 ELECTRONIC COMPONENTS	-6	-21	-92	0	0	0	-10539
58 MISC. ELECTRICAL MACH.	-2	0	-92	0	0	0	-2011
59 MOTOR VEHICLES, EQUIP.	-270	-109	-9596	0	0	-4	-160565
60 AIRCRAFT, PARTS	-618	0	-7	-2	0	0	-17302
61 OTHER TRANSPORT. EQUIP.	-1023	-198	-535	0	0	-7	-21663
62 PROFESS., SCIEN. INSTRU.	-6	-32	-327	-4	0	0	-10477
63 MEDICAL, PHOTO. EQUIP.	-10	-19	-24	0	0	-1	-11923
64 MISC. MANUFACTURING	-72	-28	-353	0	0	-7	-16730
65 TRANSPORT., WAREHOUSING	-1334	-579	-1054	-190	-201	-339	-68028
66 COMMUNICA.,EXC. BRDCAST.	0	0	0	0	0	0	0
67 RADIO, TV BROADCASTING	0	0	0	0	0	0	0
68 ELEC.,GAS,WATER,SAN.SER.	0	0	0	0	0	0	0
69 WHOLESALE, RETAIL TRADE	0	0	0	0	0	0	0
70 FINANCE, INSURANCE	0	0	0	0	0	0	0
71 REAL ESTATE, RENTAL	0	0	0	0	0	0	0
72 HOTELS, PERSONAL SERV.	0	0	0	0	0	0	0
73 BUSINESS SERVICES	0	0	0	0	0	0	0
74 RESEARCH, DEVELOPMENT	0	0	0	0	0	0	0
75 AUTO. REPAIR, SERVICES	0	0	0	0	0	0	0
76 AMUSEMENTS	0	0	0	0	0	0	0
77 MED.,EDUC. SERVICES	0	0	0	0	0	0	0
78 FEDERAL GOVT. ENTERPRISE	0	0	0	0	0	0	0
79 STATE, LOCAL GOVT. ENT.	0	0	0	0	0	0	0
80 ZERO ENTRIES	0	0	0	0	0	0	0
81 SERVICE IND. RESIDUAL	0	0	0	0	0	0	0
82 TOTAL FINAL DEMAND	0	0	0	0	0	0	0
83 SECONDARY TRANSFERS-OUT	0	0	0	0	0	0	0
84 ZERO ENTRIES	0	0	0	0	0	0	0
85 SCRAP ENTRIES	-11246	-50	-7103	-14	-1010	-1821	-346100
86 ZERO ENTRIES	0	0	0	0	0	0	0
87 STATE TOTAL CONSUMPTION	-23586	-8113	-42624	-464	-1230	-2547	-1517981

TABLE C-18

1963 SCRAP PURCHASES BY STATE
(THOUSANDS OF CURRENT DOLLARS)

INDUSTRY TITLE	1 ALABAMA	2 ARIZONA	3 ARKANSAS	4 CALIFORNIA	5 COLORADO	6 CONNECTICUT	7 DELAWARE	8 DISTRICT OF COLUMBIA	9 FLORIDA
1 LIVESTOCK, PRDTS.	0	0	0	0	0	0	0	0	0
2 OTHER AGRICULTURE PRDTS.	0	0	0	0	0	0	0	0	0
3 FORESTRY, FISHERIES	130	16	91	638	5	13	10	0	252
4 AGRI.,FORES.,FISH. SERV.	0	0	0	0	0	0	0	0	0
5 IRON, FERRO. ORES MINING	11	0	0	23	55	0	0	0	0
6 NONFERROUS ORES MINING	4	1653	75	23	280	2	0	0	30
7 COAL MINING	35	0	1	0	10	0	0	0	0
8 CRUDE PETRO.,NATURAL GAS	0	0	0	0	0	0	0	0	0
9 STONE, CLAY MINING	74	34	80	474	48	39	3	0	149
10 CHEM.,FERT. MIN. MINING	0	0	3	160	2	0	0	0	119
11 NEW CONSTRUCTION	492	450	262	7286	497	636	118	226	1538
12 MAINT., REPAIR CONSTR.	0	0	0	0	0	0	0	0	0
13 ORDNANCE, ACCESSORIES	0	0	0	0	0	0	0	0	0
14 FOOD, KINDRED PRDTS.	0	0	0	0	0	0	0	0	0
15 TOBACCO MANUFACTURES	0	0	0	0	0	0	0	0	0
16 FABRICS	0	0	0	0	0	0	0	0	0
17 TEXTILE PRDTS.	1164	3	376	2152	13	1013	214	0	34
18 APPAREL	0	0	0	0	0	0	0	0	0
19 MISC. TEXTILE PRDTS.	0	0	0	0	0	0	0	0	0
20 LUMBER, WOOD PRDTS.	0	0	0	0	0	0	0	0	0
21 WOODEN CONTAINERS	0	0	0	0	0	0	0	0	0
22 HOUSEHOLD FURNITURE	0	0	0	0	0	0	0	0	0
23 OTHER FURNITURE	0	0	0	0	0	0	0	0	0
24 PAPER, ALLIED PRDTS.	7162	248	3824	9303	267	2325	209	0	7504
25 PAPERBOARD CONTAINERS	0	0	0	0	0	0	0	0	0
26 PRINTING, PUBLISHING	0	0	0	0	0	0	0	0	0
27 CHEMICALS,SELECT. PRDTS.	682	68	90	1298	97	561	184	5	768
28 PLASTICS, SYNTHETICS	0	0	0	0	0	0	0	0	0
29 DRUGS, COSMETICS	1	2	0	191	4	92	5	0	7
30 PAINT, ALLIED PRDTS.	7	3	4	282	9	8	1	0	39
31 PETROLEUM, RELATED INDS.	47	4	124	2105	70	15	139	0	29
32 RUBBER, MISC. PLASTICS	84	2	17	264	49	117	25	0	9
33 LEATHER TANNING, PRDTS.	0	0	0	0	0	0	0	0	0
34 FOOTWEAR, LEATHER PRDTS.	0	0	0	0	0	0	0	0	0
35 GLASS, GLASS PRDTS.	34	3	66	854	7	65	3	0	80
36 STONE, CLAY PRDTS.	42	18	13	247	25	32	5	5	65
37 PRIMARY IRON, STEEL MFR.	27044	251	78	22025	4694	6383	4368	0	835
38 PRIMARY NONFERROUS MFR.	12032	23254	6626	29826	506	31476	719	0	2582

39 METAL CONTAINERS	0	0	0	0	0	0	0	0	0
40 FABRICATED METAL PRDTS.	269	52	64	1282	75	148	36	7	297
41 SCREW MACH. PRDTS., ETC.	0	0	0	0	0	0	0	0	0
42 OTHER FAB. METAL PRDTS.	131	14	39	1055	57	413	16	0	61
43 ENGINES, TURBINES	0	0	0	0	0	0	0	0	0
44 FARM MACH., EQUIP.	67	18	17	234	28	7	3	0	33
45 CONSTRUC. MACH., EQUIP.	5	0	0	59	39	1	0	0	1
46 MATERIAL HANDLING MACH.	0	0	0	0	0	0	0	0	0
47 METALWORKING MACHINERY	11	7	15	430	4	601	11	0	29
48 SPECIAL MACH., EQUIP.	78	4	12	696	31	395	76	0	91
49 GENERAL MACH., EQUIP.	14	3	13	527	25	498	1	0	14
50 MACHINE SHOP PRDTS.	35	41	14	913	48	205	8	5	62
51 OFFICE, COMPUT. MACHINES	0	0	0	0	0	0	0	0	0
52 SERVICE IND. MACHINES	0	0	0	0	0	0	0	0	0
53 ELECT. TRANSMISS. EQUIP.	0	0	0	0	0	0	0	0	0
54 HOUSEHOLD APPLIANCES	0	0	0	0	0	0	0	0	0
55 ELECTRIC LIGHTING EQUIP.	0	0	0	0	0	0	0	0	0
56 RADIO, TV, ETC., EQUIP.	0	0	0	0	0	0	0	0	0
57 ELECTRONIC COMPONENTS	0	0	0	0	0	0	0	0	0
58 MISC. ELECTRICAL MACH.	0	0	0	0	0	0	0	0	0
59 MOTOR VEHICLES, EQUIP.	74	9	15	2691	24	249	491	0	16
60 AIRCRAFT, PARTS	0	0	0	0	0	0	0	0	0
61 OTHER TRANSPORT. EQUIP.	16	1	5	62	1	12	0	0	18
62 PROFESS., SCIEN. INSTRU.	0	0	0	0	0	0	0	0	0
63 MEDICAL, PHOTO. EQUIP.	0	0	0	0	0	0	0	0	0
64 MISC. MANUFACTURING	44	16	83	929	47	697	3	4	76
65 TRANSPORT., WAREHOUSING	0	0	0	0	0	0	0	0	0
66 COMMUNICA.,EXC. BRDCAST.	0	0	0	0	0	0	0	0	0
67 RADIO, TV BROADCASTING	0	0	0	0	0	0	0	0	0
68 ELEC.,GAS,WATER,SAN.SER.	0	0	0	0	0	0	0	0	0
69 WHOLESALE, RETAIL TRADE	87	53	48	802	78	106	21	47	204
70 FINANCE, INSURANCE	0	0	0	0	0	0	0	0	0
71 REAL ESTATE, RENTAL	0	0	0	0	0	0	0	0	0
72 HOTELS, PERSONAL SERV.	0	0	0	0	0	0	0	0	0
73 BUSINESS SERVICES	0	0	0	0	0	0	0	0	0
74 RESEARCH, DEVELOPMENT	0	0	0	0	0	0	0	0	0
75 AUTO. REPAIR, SERVICES	331	230	194	3051	308	365	62	199	773
76 AMUSEMENTS	0	0	0	0	0	0	0	0	0
77 MED.,EDUC. SERVICES	0	0	0	0	0	0	0	0	0
78 FEDERAL GOVT. ENTERPRISE	0	0	0	0	0	0	0	0	0
79 STATE, LOCAL GOVT. ENT.	0	0	0	0	0	0	0	0	0
80 ZERO ENTRIES	0	0	0	0	0	0	0	0	0
81 SERVICE IND. RESIDUAL	0	0	0	0	0	0	0	0	0
82 TOTAL FINAL DEMAND	38955	34650	17248	-143116	42140	-71943	8228	-99454	-63068
83 SECONDARY TRANSFERS-OUT	0	0	0	0	0	0	0	0	0
84 ZERO ENTRIES	0	0	0	0	0	0	0	0	0
85 SCRAP ENTRIES	0	0	0	0	0	0	0	0	0
86 ZERO ENTRIES	0	0	0	0	0	0	0	0	0
87 STATE TOTAL CONSUMPTION	89161	61106	29499	-53234	49542	-25471	14958	-98955	-47353

TABLE C-18

1963 SCRAP PURCHASES BY STATE
(THOUSANDS OF CURRENT DOLLARS)

INDUSTRY TITLE	10 GEORGIA	11 IDAHO	12 ILLINOIS	13 INDIANA	14 IOWA	15 KANSAS	16 KENTUCKY	17 LOUISIANA	18 MAINE
1 LIVESTOCK, PRDTS.	0	0	0	0	0	0	0	0	0
2 OTHER AGRICULTURE PRDTS.	0	0	0	0	0	0	0	0	0
3 FORESTRY, FISHERIES	204	36	17	11	5	1	27	290	166
4 AGRI.,FORES.,FISH. SERV.	0	0	0	0	0	0	0	0	0
5 IRON, FERRO. ORES MINING	1	0	0	0	0	0	0	0	0
6 NONFERROUS ORES MINING	2	144	56	0	0	-1	0	0	0
7 COAL MINING	0	0	79	24	2	4	112	0	0
8 CRUDE PETRO.,NATURAL GAS	0	0	0	0	0	0	0	0	0
9 STONE, CLAY MINING	230	23	242	130	101	58	128	43	5
10 CHEM.,FERT. MIN. MINING	4	9	16	0	0	2	3	166	0
11 NEW CONSTRUCTION	693	104	1753	667	360	389	458	898	95
12 MAINT., REPAIR CONSTR.	0	0	0	0	0	0	0	0	0
13 ORDNANCE, ACCESSORIES	0	0	0	0	0	0	0	0	0
14 FOOD, KINDRED PRDTS.	0	0	0	0	0	0	0	0	0
15 TOBACCO MANUFACTURES	0	0	0	0	0	0	0	0	0
16 FABRICS	0	0	0	0	0	0	0	0	0
17 TEXTILE PRDTS.	10318	0	1492	187	4	3	43	116	198
18 APPAREL	0	0	0	0	0	0	0	0	0
19 MISC. TEXTILE PRDTS.	0	0	0	0	0	0	0	0	0
20 LUMBER, WOOD PRDTS.	0	0	0	0	0	0	0	0	0
21 WOODEN CONTAINERS	0	0	0	0	0	0	0	0	0
22 HOUSEHOLD FURNITURE	0	0	0	0	0	0	0	0	0
23 OTHER FURNITURE	0	0	0	0	0	0	0	0	0
24 PAPER, ALLIED PRDTS.	10155	658	8342	3137	798	420	809	8126	9790
25 PAPERBOARD CONTAINERS	0	0	0	0	0	0	0	0	0
26 PRINTING, PUBLISHING	0	0	0	0	0	0	0	0	0
27 CHEMICALS,SELECT. PRDTS.	643	72	1942	588	111	219	602	1536	43
28 PLASTICS, SYNTHETICS	0	0	0	0	0	0	0	0	0
29 DRUGS, COSMETICS	36	0	368	216	18	47	1	4	0
30 PAINT, ALLIED PRDTS.	54	0	361	41	35	7	76	11	0
31 PETROLEUM, RELATED INDS.	39	0	1124	762	8	535	139	1438	3
32 RUBBER, MISC. PLASTICS	25	0	217	175	79	36	22	2	11
33 LEATHER TANNING, PRDTS.	0	0	0	0	0	0	0	0	0
34 FOOTWEAR, LEATHER PRDTS.	0	0	0	0	0	0	0	0	0
35 GLASS, GLASS PRDTS.	116	0	1132	710	1	4	117	121	6
36 STONE, CLAY PRDTS.	44	5	145	85	40	44	24	35	5
37 PRIMARY IRON, STEEL MFR.	4550	33	55176	71976	1743	611	6828	634	32
38 PRIMARY NONFERROUS MFR.	3163	5376	43611	37733	5118	1109	4270	5869	294

39 METAL CONTAINERS	0	0	0	0	0	0	0	0	0
40 FABRICATED METAL PRDTS.	218	16	925	597	173	141	171	141	23
41 SCREW MACH. PRDTS., ETC.	0	0	0	0	0	0	0	0	0
42 OTHER FAB. METAL PRDTS.	71	1	1605	483	114	40	214	78	6
43 ENGINES, TURBINES	0	0	0	0	0	0	0	0	0
44 FARM MACH., EQUIP.	119	20	2021	386	1866	128	224	38	3
45 CONSTRUC. MACH., EQUIP.	14	1	593	45	76	13	1	11	5
46 MATERIAL HANDLING MACH.	0	0	0	0	0	0	0	0	0
47 METALWORKING MACHINERY	15	0	1261	280	65	19	25	2	5
48 SPECIAL MACH., EQUIP.	220	3	1260	248	117	80	75	52	33
49 GENERAL MACH., EQUIP.	15	0	610	442	47	33	75	4	4
50 MACHINE SHOP PRDTS.	29	5	517	369	25	87	90	46	8
51 OFFICE, COMPUT. MACHINES	0	0	0	0	0	0	0	0	0
52 SERVICE IND. MACHINES	0	0	0	0	0	0	0	0	0
53 ELECT. TRANSMISS. EQUIP.	0	0	0	0	0	0	0	0	0
54 HOUSEHOLD APPLIANCES	0	0	0	0	0	0	0	0	0
55 ELECTRIC LIGHTING EQUIP.	0	0	0	0	0	0	0	0	0
56 RADIO, TV, ETC., EQUIP.	0	0	0	0	0	0	0	0	0
57 ELECTRONIC COMPONENTS	0	0	0	0	0	0	0	0	0
58 MISC. ELECTRICAL MACH.	0	0	0	0	0	0	0	0	0
59 MOTOR VEHICLES, EQUIP.	876	2	1094	2195	36	264	270	18	1
60 AIRCRAFT, PARTS	0	0	0	0	0	0	0	0	0
61 OTHER TRANSPORT. EQUIP.	10	2	63	53	4	8	3	25	12
62 PROFESS., SCIEN. INSTRU.	0	0	0	0	0	0	0	0	0
63 MEDICAL, PHOTO. EQUIP.	0	0	0	0	0	0	0	0	0
64 MISC. MANUFACTURING	136	6	1159	307	169	16	55	34	32
65 TRANSPORT., WAREHOUSING	0	0	0	0	0	0	0	0	0
66 COMMUNICA.,EXC. BRDCAST.	0	0	0	0	0	0	0	0	0
67 RADIO, TV BROADCASTING	0	0	0	0	0	0	0	0	0
68 ELEC.,GAS,WATER,SAN.SER.	0	0	0	0	0	0	0	0	0
69 WHOLESALE, RETAIL TRADE	149	23	521	173	105	74	83	101	30
70 FINANCE, INSURANCE	0	0	0	0	0	0	0	0	0
71 REAL ESTATE, RENTAL	0	0	0	0	0	0	0	0	0
72 HOTELS, PERSONAL SERV.	0	0	0	0	0	0	0	0	0
73 BUSINESS SERVICES	0	0	0	0	0	0	0	0	0
74 RESEARCH, DEVELOPMENT	0	0	0	0	0	0	0	0	0
75 AUTO. REPAIR, SERVICES	494	103	1353	558	347	299	303	336	114
76 AMUSEMENTS	0	0	0	0	0	0	0	0	0
77 MED.,EDUC. SERVICES	0	0	0	0	0	0	0	0	0
78 FEDERAL GOVT. ENTERPRISE	0	0	0	0	0	0	0	0	0
79 STATE, LOCAL GOVT. ENT.	0	0	0	0	0	0	0	0	0
80 ZERO ENTRIES	0	0	0	0	0	0	0	0	0
81 SERVICE IND. RESIDUAL	0	0	0	0	0	0	0	0	0
82 TOTAL FINAL DEMAND	-18639	2523	-87983	113395	93925	67835	43309	39568	2615
83 SECONDARY TRANSFERS-OUT	0	0	0	0	0	0	0	0	0
84 ZERO ENTRIES	0	0	0	0	0	0	0	0	0
85 SCRAP ENTRIES	0	0	0	0	0	0	0	0	0
86 ZERO ENTRIES	0	0	0	0	0	0	0	0	0
87 STATE TOTAL CONSUMPTION	14005	9166	41074	235974	105490	72525	58559	59739	13541

TABLE C-18

1963 SCRAP PURCHASES BY STATE
(THOUSANDS OF CURRENT DOLLARS)

INDUSTRY TITLE	19 MARYLAND	20 MASSA-CHUSETTS	21 MICHIGAN	22 MINNESOTA	23 MISSISSIPPI	24 MISSOURI	25 MONTANA	26 NEBRASKA	27 NEVADA
1 LIVESTOCK, PRDTS.	0	0	0	0	0	0	0	0	0
2 OTHER AGRICULTURE PRDTS.	0	0	0	0	0	0	0	0	0
3 FORESTRY, FISHERIES	87	259	48	32	127	28	22	1	0
4 AGRI.,FORES.,FISH. SERV.	0	0	0	0	0	0	0	0	0
5 IRON, FERRO. ORES MINING	0	0	62	272	0	4	2	0	3
6 NONFERROUS ORES MINING	0	0	208	13	0	59	76	0	290
7 COAL MINING	2	0	0	0	0	6	1	0	0
8 CRUDE PETRO.,NATURAL GAS	0	0	0	0	0	0	0	0	0
9 STONE, CLAY MINING	103	61	210	64	31	156	19	44	49
10 CHEM.,FERT. MIN. MINING	0	0	14	0	0	7	15	0	2
11 NEW CONSTRUCTION	891	1080	1347	584	229	683	126	226	360
12 MAINT., REPAIR CONSTR.	0	0	0	0	0	0	0	0	0
13 ORDNANCE, ACCESSORIES	0	0	0	0	0	0	0	0	0
14 FOOD, KINDRED PRDTS.	0	0	0	0	0	0	0	0	0
15 TOBACCO MANUFACTURES	0	0	0	0	0	0	0	0	0
16 FABRICS	0	0	0	0	0	0	0	0	0
17 TEXTILE PRDTS.	23	3496	1072	240	650	426	0	0	0
18 APPAREL	0	0	0	0	0	0	0	0	0
19 MISC. TEXTILE PRDTS.	0	0	0	0	0	0	0	0	0
20 LUMBER, WOOD PRDTS.	0	0	0	0	0	0	0	0	0
21 WOODEN CONTAINERS	0	0	0	0	0	0	0	0	0
22 HOUSEHOLD FURNITURE	0	0	0	0	0	0	0	0	0
23 OTHER FURNITURE	0	0	0	0	0	0	0	0	0
24 PAPER, ALLIED PRDTS.	1769	11229	11977	6491	1652	2439	99	196	2
25 PAPERBOARD CONTAINERS	0	0	0	0	0	0	0	0	0
26 PRINTING, PUBLISHING	0	0	0	0	0	0	0	0	0
27 CHEMICALS,SELECT. PRDTS.	497	420	1501	287	156	850	16	60	64
28 PLASTICS, SYNTHETICS	0	0	0	0	0	0	0	0	0
29 DRUGS, COSMETICS	91	65	136	51	11	119	0	15	1
30 PAINT, ALLIED PRDTS.	42	59	172	19	1	103	0	2	0
31 PETROLEUM, RELATED INDS.	96	65	310	138	72	154	121	10	1
32 RUBBER, MISC. PLASTICS	77	252	162	25	24	41	0	18	0
33 LEATHER TANNING, PRDTS.	0	0	0	0	0	0	0	0	0
34 FOOTWEAR, LEATHER PRDTS.	0	0	0	0	0	0	0	0	0
35 GLASS, GLASS PRDTS.	226	19	677	78	59	288	0	1	0
36 STONE, CLAY PRDTS.	38	60	94	47	20	61	6	14	12
37 PRIMARY IRON, STEEL MFR.	13732	5389	61171	4999	223	4933	36	109	16
38 PRIMARY NONFERROUS MFR.	16218	12809	32890	1293	664	6588	10634	3821	3623

39 METAL CONTAINERS	0	0	0	0	0	0	0	0	0
40 FABRICATED METAL PRDTS.	185	269	650	148	83	353	10	124	9
41 SCREW MACH. PRDTS., ETC.	0	0	0	0	0	0	0	0	0
42 OTHER FAB. METAL PRDTS.	124	476	1177	126	29	273	1	14	1
43 ENGINES, TURBINES	0	0	0	0	0	0	0	0	0
44 FARM MACH., EQUIP.	3	4	793	446	96	199	3	121	0
45 CONSTRUC. MACH., EQUIP.	2	2	68	43	7	17	0	2	0
46 MATERIAL HANDLING MACH.	0	0	0	0	0	0	0	0	0
47 METALWORKING MACHINERY	146	492	2162	72	0	113	0	3	0
48 SPECIAL MACH., EQUIP.	293	1500	851	145	49	194	0	4	1
49 GENERAL MACH., EQUIP.	23	218	426	70	3	68	0	30	0
50 MACHINE SHOP PRDTS.	96	204	709	128	24	285	5	8	3
51 OFFICE, COMPUT. MACHINES	0	0	0	0	0	0	0	0	0
52 SERVICE IND. MACHINES	0	0	0	0	0	0	0	0	0
53 ELECT. TRANSMISS. EQUIP.	0	0	0	0	0	0	0	0	0
54 HOUSEHOLD APPLIANCES	0	0	0	0	0	0	0	0	0
55 ELECTRIC LIGHTING EQUIP.	0	0	0	0	0	0	0	0	0
56 RADIO, TV, ETC., EQUIP.	0	0	0	0	0	0	0	0	0
57 ELECTRONIC COMPONENTS	0	0	0	0	0	0	0	0	0
58 MISC. ELECTRICAL MACH.	0	0	0	0	0	0	0	0	0
59 MOTOR VEHICLES, EQUIP.	744	333	16817	314	55	2767	0	60	0
60 AIRCRAFT, PARTS	0	0	0	0	0	0	0	0	0
61 OTHER TRANSPORT. EQUIP.	39	17	39	3	1	15	0	5	0
62 PROFESS., SCIEN. INSTRU.	0	0	0	0	0	0	0	0	0
63 MEDICAL, PHOTO. EQUIP.	0	0	0	0	0	0	0	0	0
64 MISC. MANUFACTURING	96	824	491	175	73	175	6	34	7
65 TRANSPORT., WAREHOUSING	0	0	0	0	0	0	0	0	0
66 COMMUNICA.,EXC. BRDCAST.	0	0	0	0	0	0	0	0	0
67 RADIO, TV BROADCASTING	0	0	0	0	0	0	0	0	0
68 ELEC.,GAS,WATER,SAN.SER.	0	0	0	0	0	0	0	0	0
69 WHOLESALE, RETAIL TRADE	118	231	311	149	48	205	24	62	16
70 FINANCE, INSURANCE	0	0	0	0	0	0	0	0	0
71 REAL ESTATE, RENTAL	0	0	0	0	0	0	0	0	0
72 HOTELS, PERSONAL SERV.	0	0	0	0	0	0	0	0	0
73 BUSINESS SERVICES	0	0	0	0	0	0	0	0	0
74 RESEARCH, DEVELOPMENT	0	0	0	0	0	0	0	0	0
75 AUTO. REPAIR, SERVICES	479	658	1130	432	194	578	98	204	77
76 AMUSEMENTS	0	0	0	0	0	0	0	0	0
77 MED.,EDUC. SERVICES	0	0	0	0	0	0	0	0	0
78 FEDERAL GOVT. ENTERPRISE	0	0	0	0	0	0	0	0	0
79 STATE, LOCAL GOVT. ENT.	0	0	0	0	0	0	0	0	0
80 ZERO ENTRIES	0	0	0	0	0	0	0	0	0
81 SERVICE IND. RESIDUAL	0	0	0	0	0	0	0	0	0
82 TOTAL FINAL DEMAND	-56469	-276307	73047	84373	53556	-31807	21648	18728	-27572
83 SECONDARY TRANSFERS-OUT	0	0	0	0	0	0	0	0	0
84 ZERO ENTRIES	0	0	0	0	0	0	0	0	0
85 SCRAP ENTRIES	0	0	0	0	0	0	0	0	0
86 ZERO ENTRIES	0	0	0	0	0	0	0	0	0
87 STATE TOTAL CONSUMPTION	-20228	-235816	210719	101260	58137	-9619	32969	23913	-23034

TABLE C-18

1963 SCRAP PURCHASES BY STATE
(THOUSANDS OF CURRENT DOLLARS)

INDUSTRY TITLE	28 NEW HAMPSHIRE	29 NEW JERSEY	30 NEW MEXICO	31 NEW YORK	32 NORTH CAROLINA	33 NORTH DAKOTA	34 OHIO	35 OKLAHOMA	36 OREGON
1 LIVESTOCK, PRDTS.	0	0	0	0	0	0	0	0	0
2 OTHER AGRICULTURE PRDTS.	0	0	0	0	0	0	0	0	0
3 FORESTRY, FISHERIES	15	75	7	106	186	0	26	8	868
4 AGRI.,FORES.,FISH. SERV.	0	0	0	0	0	0	0	0	0
5 IRON, FERRO. ORES MINING	0	3	2	25	2	0	0	0	2
6 NONFERROUS ORES MINING	0	25	642	66	1	2	3	8	2
7 COAL MINING	0	0	4	0	0	4	54	2	0
8 CRUDE PETRO.,NATURAL GAS	0	0	0	0	0	0	0	0	0
9 STONE, CLAY MINING	9	152	32	268	107	10	260	54	65
10 CHEM.,FERT. MIN. MINING	0	0	190	25	3	0	29	0	0
11 NEW CONSTRUCTION	93	1127	256	2952	586	109	1722	568	414
12 MAINT., REPAIR CONSTR.	0	0	0	0	0	0	0	0	0
13 ORDNANCE, ACCESSORIES	0	0	0	0	0	0	0	0	0
14 FOOD, KINDRED PRDTS.	0	0	0	0	0	0	0	0	0
15 TOBACCO MANUFACTURES	0	0	0	0	0	0	0	0	0
16 FABRICS	0	0	0	0	0	0	0	0	0
17 TEXTILE PRDTS.	185	2160	0	3133	2708	0	1865	3	98
18 APPAREL	0	0	0	0	0	0	0	0	0
19 MISC. TEXTILE PRDTS.	0	0	0	0	0	0	0	0	0
20 LUMBER, WOOD PRDTS.	0	0	0	0	0	0	0	0	0
21 WOODEN CONTAINERS	0	0	0	0	0	0	0	0	0
22 HOUSEHOLD FURNITURE	0	0	0	0	0	0	0	0	0
23 OTHER FURNITURE	0	0	0	0	0	0	0	0	0
24 PAPER, ALLIED PRDTS.	3287	10322	0	19616	6308	0	13722	253	4328
25 PAPERBOARD CONTAINERS	0	0	0	0	0	0	0	0	0
26 PRINTING, PUBLISHING	0	0	0	0	0	0	0	0	0
27 CHEMICALS,SELECT. PRDTS.	33	4180	25	1739	340	7	1649	56	130
28 PLASTICS, SYNTHETICS	0	0	0	0	0	0	0	0	0
29 DRUGS, COSMETICS	1	560	0	475	23	0	198	1	2
30 PAINT, ALLIED PRDTS.	0	280	0	134	22	0	224	6	11
31 PETROLEUM, RELATED INDS.	1	1178	51	214	6	31	795	643	15
32 RUBBER, MISC. PLASTICS	19	204	2	180	28	0	757	39	3
33 LEATHER TANNING, PRDTS.	0	0	0	0	0	0	0	0	0
34 FOOTWEAR, LEATHER PRDTS.	0	0	0	0	0	0	0	0	0
35 GLASS, GLASS PRDTS.	7	1127	1	826	236	0	2018	322	41
36 STONE, CLAY PRDTS.	11	110	8	164	31	3	197	21	17
37 PRIMARY IRON, STEEL MFR.	486	8039	0	28152	849	2	116060	799	1737
38 PRIMARY NONFERROUS MFR.	940	50553	1984	54385	4455	0	45764	4054	5833

39 METAL CONTAINERS	0	0	0	0	0	0	0	0	0
40 FABRICATED METAL PRDTS.	19	539	11	939	162	9	1445	242	126
41 SCREW MACH. PRDTS., ETC.	0	0	0	0	0	0	0	0	0
42 OTHER FAB. METAL PRDTS.	16	709	2	825	69	0	1315	86	39
43 ENGINES, TURBINES	0	0	0	0	0	0	0	0	0
44 FARM MACH., EQUIP.	0	13	1	168	68	24	543	23	24
45 CONSTRUC. MACH., EQUIP.	11	21	1	16	1	0	193	63	5
46 MATERIAL HANDLING MACH.	0	0	0	0	0	0	0	0	0
47 METALWORKING MACHINERY	27	283	3	670	19	3	1918	5	5
48 SPECIAL MACH., EQUIP.	227	994	3	1310	540	2	1542	39	178
49 GENERAL MACH., EQUIP.	32	449	0	648	9	0	918	67	8
50 MACHINE SHOP PRDTS.	16	234	18	594	41	4	603	41	61
51 OFFICE, COMPUT. MACHINES	0	0	0	0	0	0	0	0	0
52 SERVICE IND. MACHINES	0	0	0	0	0	0	0	0	0
53 ELECT. TRANSMISS. EQUIP.	0	0	0	0	0	0	0	0	0
54 HOUSEHOLD APPLIANCES	0	0	0	0	0	0	0	0	0
55 ELECTRIC LIGHTING EQUIP.	0	0	0	0	0	0	0	0	0
56 RADIO, TV, ETC., EQUIP.	0	0	0	0	0	0	0	0	0
57 ELECTRONIC COMPONENTS	0	0	0	0	0	0	0	0	0
58 MISC. ELECTRICAL MACH.	0	0	0	0	0	0	0	0	0
59 MOTOR VEHICLES, EQUIP.	0	819	3	2049	42	0	5747	68	96
60 AIRCRAFT, PARTS	0	0	0	0	0	0	0	0	0
61 OTHER TRANSPORT. EQUIP.	0	27	0	37	4	0	29	2	9
62 PROFESS., SCIEN. INSTRU.	0	0	0	0	0	0	0	0	0
63 MEDICAL, PHOTO. EQUIP.	0	0	0	0	0	0	0	0	0
64 MISC. MANUFACTURING	49	909	8	3105	78	10	631	33	43
65 TRANSPORT., WAREHOUSING	0	0	0	0	0	0	0	0	0
66 COMMUNICA.,EXC. BRDCAST.	0	0	0	0	0	0	0	0	0
67 RADIO, TV BROADCASTING	0	0	0	0	0	0	0	0	0
68 ELEC.,GAS,WATER,SAN.SER.	0	0	0	0	0	0	0	0	0
69 WHOLESALE, RETAIL TRADE	21	282	28	1033	145	24	373	77	85
70 FINANCE, INSURANCE	0	0	0	0	0	0	0	0	0
71 REAL ESTATE, RENTAL	0	0	0	0	0	0	0	0	0
72 HOTELS, PERSONAL SERV.	0	0	0	0	0	0	0	0	0
73 BUSINESS SERVICES	0	0	0	0	0	0	0	0	0
74 RESEARCH, DEVELOPMENT	0	0	0	0	0	0	0	0	0
75 AUTO. REPAIR, SERVICES	81	799	122	2137	457	82	1187	325	300
76 AMUSEMENTS	0	0	0	0	0	0	0	0	0
77 MED.,EDUC. SERVICES	0	0	0	0	0	0	0	0	0
78 FEDERAL GOVT. ENTERPRISE	0	0	0	0	0	0	0	0	0
79 STATE, LOCAL GOVT. ENT.	0	0	0	0	0	0	0	0	0
80 ZERO ENTRIES	0	0	0	0	0	0	0	0	0
81 SERVICE IND. RESIDUAL	0	0	0	0	0	0	0	0	0
82 TOTAL FINAL DEMAND	-3816	-198609	37740	-637623	64925	37768	-5468	58792	25379
83 SECONDARY TRANSFERS-OUT	0	0	0	0	0	0	0	0	0
84 ZERO ENTRIES	0	0	0	0	0	0	0	0	0
85 SCRAP ENTRIES	0	0	0	0	0	0	0	0	0
86 ZERO ENTRIES	0	0	0	0	0	0	0	0	0
87 STATE TOTAL CONSUMPTION	1771	-112436	41143	-511634	82451	38095	196321	66701	39923

TABLE C-18

1963 SCRAP PURCHASES BY STATE
(THOUSANDS OF CURRENT DOLLARS)

INDUSTRY TITLE	37 PENNSYL-VANIA	38 RHODE ISLAND	39 SOUTH CAROLINA	40 SOUTH DAKOTA	41 TENNESSEE	42 TEXAS	43 UTAH	44 VERMONT	45 VIRGINIA
1 LIVESTOCK, PRDTS.	0	0	0	0	0	0	0	0	0
2 OTHER AGRICULTURE PRDTS.	0	0	0	0	0	0	0	0	0
3 FORESTRY, FISHERIES	49	26	129	3	37	240	2	12	219
4 AGRI.,FORES.,FISH. SERV.	0	0	0	0	0	0	0	0	0
5 IRON, FERRO. ORES MINING	29	0	0	0	0	6	10	0	1
6 NONFERROUS ORES MINING	10	0	3	91	52	20	1118	0	23
7 COAL MINING	186	0	0	0	10	1	12	0	64
8 CRUDE PETRO.,NATURAL GAS	0	0	0	0	0	0	0	0	0
9 STONE, CLAY MINING	248	7	83	28	139	153	19	38	148
10 CHEM.,FERT. MIN. MINING	5	0	1	0	58	140	16	0	1
11 NEW CONSTRUCTION	1294	139	191	119	590	2364	269	39	944
12 MAINT., REPAIR CONSTR.	0	0	0	0	0	0	0	0	0
13 ORDNANCE, ACCESSORIES	0	0	0	0	0	0	0	0	0
14 FOOD, KINDRED PRDTS.	0	0	0	0	0	0	0	0	0
15 TOBACCO MANUFACTURES	0	0	0	0	0	0	0	0	0
16 FABRICS	0	0	0	0	0	0	0	0	0
17 TEXTILE PRDTS.	4073	801	3299	0	953	218	7	44	1125
18 APPAREL	0	0	0	0	0	0	0	0	0
19 MISC. TEXTILE PRDTS.	0	0	0	0	0	0	0	0	0
20 LUMBER, WOOD PRDTS.	0	0	0	0	0	0	0	0	0
21 WOODEN CONTAINERS	0	0	0	0	0	0	0	0	0
22 HOUSEHOLD FURNITURE	0	0	0	0	0	0	0	0	0
23 OTHER FURNITURE	0	0	0	0	0	0	0	0	0
24 PAPER, ALLIED PRDTS.	14701	388	4350	4	6061	4414	91	1306	6567
25 PAPERBOARD CONTAINERS	0	0	0	0	0	0	0	0	0
26 PRINTING, PUBLISHING	0	0	0	0	0	0	0	0	0
27 CHEMICALS,SELECT. PRDTS.	1373	103	139	8	1121	6358	40	11	645
28 PLASTICS, SYNTHETICS	0	0	0	0	0	0	0	0	0
29 DRUGS, COSMETICS	237	3	14	0	41	43	1	0	33
30 PAINT, ALLIED PRDTS.	157	7	4	0	22	115	2	4	11
31 PETROLEUM, RELATED INDS.	1138	26	16	0	36	4864	138	0	62
32 RUBBER, MISC. PLASTICS	197	57	22	1	69	77	4	8	29
33 LEATHER TANNING, PRDTS.	0	0	0	0	0	0	0	0	0
34 FOOTWEAR, LEATHER PRDTS.	0	0	0	0	0	0	0	0	0
35 GLASS, GLASS PRDTS.	1925	159	263	0	531	166	1	0	105
36 STONE, CLAY PRDTS.	174	3	15	4	40	133	17	10	46
37 PRIMARY IRON, STEEL MFR.	156491	2046	667	2	3020	10035	4707	90	2454
38 PRIMARY NONFERROUS MFR.	34057	9644	859	0	15231	28580	7081	557	3926

39 METAL CONTAINERS	0	0	0	0	0	0	0	0	0
40 FABRICATED METAL PRDTS.	1450	27	77	19	313	659	89	8	232
41 SCREW MACH. PRDTS., ETC.	0	0	0	0	0	0	0	0	0
42 OTHER FAB. METAL PRDTS.	1080	111	21	1	91	386	7	4	75
43 ENGINES, TURBINES	0	0	0	0	0	0	0	0	0
44 FARM MACH., EQUIP.	342	0	9	14	212	89	6	2	27
45 CONSTRUC. MACH., EQUIP.	76	0	0	0	3	210	15	1	3
46 MATERIAL HANDLING MACH.	0	0	0	0	0	0	0	0	0
47 METALWORKING MACHINERY	793	130	71	8	22	56	3	160	4
48 SPECIAL MACH., EQUIP.	1152	212	342	1	89	315	16	17	51
49 GENERAL MACH., EQUIP.	579	21	22	4	33	113	12	1	22
50 MACHINE SHOP PRDTS.	329	28	27	10	55	189	12	5	31
51 OFFICE, COMPUT. MACHINES	0	0	0	0	0	0	0	0	0
52 SERVICE IND. MACHINES	0	0	0	0	0	0	0	0	0
53 ELECT. TRANSMISS. EQUIP.	0	0	0	0	0	0	0	0	0
54 HOUSEHOLD APPLIANCES	0	0	0	0	0	0	0	0	0
55 ELECTRIC LIGHTING EQUIP.	0	0	0	0	0	0	0	0	0
56 RADIO, TV, ETC., EQUIP.	0	0	0	0	0	0	0	0	0
57 ELECTRONIC COMPONENTS	0	0	0	0	0	0	0	0	0
58 MISC. ELECTRICAL MACH.	0	0	0	0	0	0	0	0	0
59 MOTOR VEHICLES, EQUIP.	1103	14	7	1	100	732	4	0	263
60 AIRCRAFT, PARTS	0	0	0	0	0	0	0	0	0
61 OTHER TRANSPORT. EQUIP.	89	1	2	0	10	24	1	0	18
62 PROFESS., SCIEN. INSTRU.	0	0	0	0	0	0	0	0	0
63 MEDICAL, PHOTO. EQUIP.	0	0	0	0	0	0	0	0	0
64 MISC. MANUFACTURING	951	562	107	4	184	143	27	14	138
65 TRANSPORT., WAREHOUSING	0	0	0	0	0	0	0	0	0
66 COMMUNICA.,EXC. BRDCAST.	0	0	0	0	0	0	0	0	0
67 RADIO, TV BROADCASTING	0	0	0	0	0	0	0	0	0
68 ELEC.,GAS,WATER,SAN.SER.	0	0	0	0	0	0	0	0	0
69 WHOLESALE, RETAIL TRADE	414	33	58	23	123	376	34	12	124
70 FINANCE, INSURANCE	0	0	0	0	0	0	0	0	0
71 REAL ESTATE, RENTAL	0	0	0	0	0	0	0	0	0
72 HOTELS, PERSONAL SERV.	0	0	0	0	0	0	0	0	0
73 BUSINESS SERVICES	0	0	0	0	0	0	0	0	0
74 RESEARCH, DEVELOPMENT	0	0	0	0	0	0	0	0	0
75 AUTO. REPAIR, SERVICES	1398	87	217	84	405	1377	129	51	437
76 AMUSEMENTS	0	0	0	0	0	0	0	0	0
77 MED.,EDUC. SERVICES	0	0	0	0	0	0	0	0	0
78 FEDERAL GOVT. ENTERPRISE	0	0	0	0	0	0	0	0	0
79 STATE, LOCAL GOVT. ENT.	0	0	0	0	0	0	0	0	0
80 ZERO ENTRIES	0	0	0	0	0	0	0	0	0
81 SERVICE IND. RESIDUAL	0	0	0	0	0	0	0	0	0
82 TOTAL FINAL DEMAND	-24748	-24671	35044	28833	12221	183643	50179	-2045	21144
83 SECONDARY TRANSFERS-OUT	0	0	0	0	0	0	0	0	0
84 ZERO ENTRIES	0	0	0	0	0	0	0	0	0
85 SCRAP ENTRIES	0	0	0	0	0	0	0	0	0
86 ZERO ENTRIES	0	0	0	0	0	0	0	0	0
87 STATE TOTAL CONSUMPTION	201351	-10034	46059	29263	41872	246236	64071	350	38972

TABLE C-18

1963 SCRAP PURCHASES BY STATE
(THOUSANDS OF CURRENT DOLLARS)

INDUSTRY TITLE	46 WASHINGTON	47 WEST VIRGINIA	48 WISCONSIN	49 WYOMING	50 ALASKA	51 HAWAII	52 NATIONAL TOTAL
1 LIVESTOCK, PRDTS.	0	0	0	0	0	0	0
2 OTHER AGRICULTURE PRDTS.	0	0	0	0	0	0	0
3 FORESTRY, FISHERIES	491	24	44	2	310	17	5411
4 AGRI.,FORES.,FISH. SERV.	0	0	0	0	0	0	0
5 IRON, FERRO. ORES MINING	0	0	0	10	0	0	525
6 NONFERROUS ORES MINING	36	0	8	219	22	0	5265
7 COAL MINING	2	247	0	4	1	0	867
8 CRUDE PETRO.,NATURAL GAS	0	0	0	0	0	0	0
9 STONE, CLAY MINING	54	59	116	59	4	17	4727
10 CHEM.,FERT. MIN. MINING	0	0	0	33	0	0	1022
11 NEW CONSTRUCTION	808	162	692	123	102	222	38333
12 MAINT., REPAIR CONSTR.	0	0	0	0	0	0	0
13 ORDNANCE, ACCESSORIES	0	0	0	0	0	0	0
14 FOOD, KINDRED PRDTS.	0	0	0	0	0	0	0
15 TOBACCO MANUFACTURES	0	0	0	0	0	0	0
16 FABRICS	0	0	0	0	0	0	0
17 TEXTILE PRDTS.	40	2	628	0	0	5	44583
18 APPAREL	0	0	0	0	0	0	0
19 MISC. TEXTILE PRDTS.	0	0	0	0	0	0	0
20 LUMBER, WOOD PRDTS.	0	0	0	0	0	0	0
21 WOODEN CONTAINERS	0	0	0	0	0	0	0
22 HOUSEHOLD FURNITURE	0	0	0	0	0	0	0
23 OTHER FURNITURE	0	0	0	0	0	0	0
24 PAPER, ALLIED PRDTS.	13444	515	21067	0	0	149	239826
25 PAPERBOARD CONTAINERS	0	0	0	0	0	0	0
26 PRINTING, PUBLISHING	0	0	0	0	0	0	0
27 CHEMICALS,SELECT. PRDTS.	540	2941	174	3	0	47	35023
28 PLASTICS, SYNTHETICS	0	0	0	0	0	0	0
29 DRUGS, COSMETICS	2	3	60	0	0	1	3181
30 PAINT, ALLIED PRDTS.	16	2	43	0	0	0	2396
31 PETROLEUM, RELATED INDS.	189	58	48	313	0	26	17399
32 RUBBER, MISC. PLASTICS	4	2	69	0	0	0	3505
33 LEATHER TANNING, PRDTS.	0	0	0	0	0	0	0
34 FOOTWEAR, LEATHER PRDTS.	0	0	0	0	0	0	0
35 GLASS, GLASS PRDTS.	36	1196	20	0	0	2	13648
36 STONE, CLAY PRDTS.	29	20	43	5	2	7	2340
37 PRIMARY IRON, STEEL MFR.	1451	14851	10863	0	0	154	660823
38 PRIMARY NONFERROUS MFR.	21926	10774	7175	20	0	3	609907

39 METAL CONTAINERS	0	0	0	0	0	0	0
40 FABRICATED METAL PRDTS.	133	112	475	1	0	10	13563
41 SCREW MACH. PRDTS., ETC.	0	0	0	0	0	0	0
42 OTHER FAB. METAL PRDTS.	33	92	199	1	0	2	11786
43 ENGINES, TURBINES	0	0	0	0	0	0	0
44 FARM MACH., EQUIP.	24	30	971	0	0	2	9469
45 CONSTRUC. MACH., EQUIP.	13	21	173	0	0	0	1829
46 MATERIAL HANDLING MACH.	0	0	0	0	0	0	0
47 METALWORKING MACHINERY	17	37	377	0	0	0	10379
48 SPECIAL MACH., EQUIP.	113	11	935	0	0	20	14614
49 GENERAL MACH., EQUIP.	9	1	336	0	0	0	6449
50 MACHINE SHOP PRDTS.	78	29	155	3	0	4	6533
51 OFFICE, COMPUT. MACHINES	0	0	0	0	0	0	0
52 SERVICE IND. MACHINES	0	0	0	0	0	0	0
53 ELECT. TRANSMISS. EQUIP.	0	0	0	0	0	0	0
54 HOUSEHOLD APPLIANCES	0	0	0	0	0	0	0
55 ELECTRIC LIGHTING EQUIP.	0	0	0	0	0	0	0
56 RADIO, TV, ETC., EQUIP.	0	0	0	0	0	0	0
57 ELECTRONIC COMPONENTS	0	0	0	0	0	0	0
58 MISC. ELECTRICAL MACH.	0	0	0	0	0	0	0
59 MOTOR VEHICLES, EQUIP.	73	29	2579	0	0	1	43146
60 AIRCRAFT, PARTS	0	0	0	0	0	0	0
61 OTHER TRANSPORT. EQUIP.	34	7	18	0	0	0	729
62 PROFESS., SCIEN. INSTRU.	0	0	0	0	0	0	0
63 MEDICAL, PHOTO. EQUIP.	0	0	0	0	0	0	0
64 MISC. MANUFACTURING	56	22	275	0	0	5	13050
65 TRANSPORT., WAREHOUSING	0	0	0	0	0	0	0
66 COMMUNICA.,EXC. BRDCAST.	0	0	0	0	0	0	0
67 RADIO, TV BROADCASTING	0	0	0	0	0	0	0
68 ELEC.,GAS,WATER,SAN.SER.	0	0	0	0	0	0	0
69 WHOLESALE, RETAIL TRADE	120	44	145	11	8	21	7483
70 FINANCE, INSURANCE	0	0	0	0	0	0	0
71 REAL ESTATE, RENTAL	0	0	0	0	0	0	0
72 HOTELS, PERSONAL SERV.	0	0	0	0	0	0	0
73 BUSINESS SERVICES	0	0	0	0	0	0	0
74 RESEARCH, DEVELOPMENT	0	0	0	0	0	0	0
75 AUTO. REPAIR, SERVICES	422	141	464	49	20	83	24123
76 AMUSEMENTS	0	0	0	0	0	0	0
77 MED.,EDUC. SERVICES	0	0	0	0	0	0	0
78 FEDERAL GOVT. ENTERPRISE	0	0	0	0	0	0	0
79 STATE, LOCAL GOVT. ENT.	0	0	0	0	0	0	0
80 ZERO ENTRIES	0	0	0	0	0	0	0
81 SERVICE IND. RESIDUAL	0	0	0	0	0	0	0
82 TOTAL FINAL DEMAND	52557	27216	-40998	15976	-5736	-26504	-439417
83 SECONDARY TRANSFERS-OUT	0	0	0	0	0	0	0
84 ZERO ENTRIES	0	0	0	0	0	0	0
85 SCRAP ENTRIES	0	0	0	0	0	0	0
86 ZERO ENTRIES	0	0	0	0	0	0	0
87 STATE TOTAL CONSUMPTION	92750	58648	7154	16832	-5268	-25704	1412517

TABLE C-19

1963 SERVICE INDUSTRIES RESIDUAL BY STATE
(THOUSANDS OF CURRENT DOLLARS)

INDUSTRY TITLE	1 ALABAMA	2 ARIZONA	3 ARKANSAS	4 CALIFORNIA	5 COLORADO	6 CONNECTICUT	7 DELAWARE	8 DISTRICT OF COLUMBIA	9 FLORIDA
1 LIVESTOCK, PRDTS.	0	0	0	0	0	0	0	0	0
2 OTHER AGRICULTURE PRDTS.	0	0	0	0	0	0	0	0	0
3 FORESTRY, FISHERIES	2722	11441	-6827	-47592	-2920	-4523	-1300	-1973	-3570
4 AGRI.,FORES.,FISH. SERV.	2344	2077	14051	-79986	-3541	2258	-315	-1418	-11003
5 IRON, FERRO. ORES MINING	0	0	0	0	0	0	0	0	0
6 NONFERROUS ORES MINING	0	0	0	0	0	0	0	0	0
7 COAL MINING	0	0	0	0	0	0	0	0	0
8 CRUDE PETRO.,NATURAL GAS	0	0	0	0	0	0	0	0	0
9 STONE, CLAY MINING	0	0	0	0	0	0	0	0	0
10 CHEM.,FERT. MIN. MINING	0	0	0	0	0	0	0	0	0
11 NEW CONSTRUCTION	0	0	0	0	0	0	0	0	0
12 MAINT., REPAIR CONSTR.	-23002	25999	69296	301643	54388	4617	-5693	-159273	39928
13 ORDNANCE, ACCESSORIES	0	0	0	0	0	0	0	0	0
14 FOOD, KINDRED PRDTS.	0	0	0	0	0	0	0	0	0
15 TOBACCO MANUFACTURES	0	0	0	0	0	0	0	0	0
16 FABRICS	0	0	0	0	0	0	0	0	0
17 TEXTILE PRDTS.	0	0	0	0	0	0	0	0	0
18 APPAREL	0	0	0	0	0	0	0	0	0
19 MISC. TEXTILE PRDTS.	0	0	0	0	0	0	0	0	0
20 LUMBER, WOOD PRDTS.	0	0	0	0	0	0	0	0	0
21 WOODEN CONTAINERS	0	0	0	0	0	0	0	0	0
22 HOUSEHOLD FURNITURE	0	0	0	0	0	0	0	0	0
23 OTHER FURNITURE	0	0	0	0	0	0	0	0	0
24 PAPER, ALLIED PRDTS.	0	0	0	0	0	0	0	0	0
25 PAPERBOARD CONTAINERS	0	0	0	0	0	0	0	0	0
26 PRINTING, PUBLISHING	0	0	0	0	0	0	0	0	0
27 CHEMICALS,SELECT. PRDTS.	0	0	0	0	0	0	0	0	0
28 PLASTICS, SYNTHETICS	0	0	0	0	0	0	0	0	0
29 DRUGS, COSMETICS	0	0	0	0	0	0	0	0	0
30 PAINT, ALLIED PRDTS.	0	0	0	0	0	0	0	0	0
31 PETROLEUM, RELATED INDS.	0	0	0	0	0	0	0	0	0
32 RUBBER, MISC. PLASTICS	0	0	0	0	0	0	0	0	0
33 LEATHER TANNING, PRDTS.	0	0	0	0	0	0	0	0	0
34 FOOTWEAR, LEATHER PRDTS.	0	0	0	0	0	0	0	0	0
35 GLASS, GLASS PRDTS.	0	0	0	0	0	0	0	0	0
36 STONE, CLAY PRDTS.	0	0	0	0	0	0	0	0	0
37 PRIMARY IRON, STEEL MFR.	0	0	0	0	0	0	0	0	0
38 PRIMARY NONFERROUS MFR.	0	0	0	0	0	0	0	0	0

39 METAL CONTAINERS	0	0	0	0	0	0	0	0	0
40 FABRICATED METAL PRDTS.	0	0	0	0	0	0	0	0	0
41 SCREW MACH. PRDTS., ETC.	0	0	0	0	0	0	0	0	0
42 OTHER FAB. METAL PRDTS.	0	0	0	0	0	0	0	0	0
43 ENGINES, TURBINES	0	0	0	0	0	0	0	0	0
44 FARM MACH., EQUIP.	0	0	0	0	0	0	0	0	0
45 CONSTRUC. MACH., EQUIP.	0	0	0	0	0	0	0	0	0
46 MATERIAL HANDLING MACH.	0	0	0	0	0	0	0	0	0
47 METALWORKING MACHINERY	0	0	0	0	0	0	0	0	0
48 SPECIAL MACH., EQUIP.	0	0	0	0	0	0	0	0	0
49 GENERAL MACH., EQUIP.	0	0	0	0	0	0	0	0	0
50 MACHINE SHOP PRDTS.	0	0	0	0	0	0	0	0	0
51 OFFICE, COMPUT. MACHINES	0	0	0	0	0	0	0	0	0
52 SERVICE IND. MACHINES	0	0	0	0	0	0	0	0	0
53 ELECT. TRANSMISS. EQUIP.	0	0	0	0	0	0	0	0	0
54 HOUSEHOLD APPLIANCES	0	0	0	0	0	0	0	0	0
55 ELECTRIC LIGHTING EQUIP.	0	0	0	0	0	0	0	0	0
56 RADIO, TV, ETC., EQUIP.	0	0	0	0	0	0	0	0	0
57 ELECTRONIC COMPONENTS	0	0	0	0	0	0	0	0	0
58 MISC. ELECTRICAL MACH.	0	0	0	0	0	0	0	0	0
59 MOTOR VEHICLES, EQUIP.	0	0	0	0	0	0	0	0	0
60 AIRCRAFT, PARTS	0	0	0	0	0	0	0	0	0
61 OTHER TRANSPORT. EQUIP.	0	0	0	0	0	0	0	0	0
62 PROFESS., SCIEN. INSTRU.	0	0	0	0	0	0	0	0	0
63 MEDICAL, PHOTO. EQUIP.	0	0	0	0	0	0	0	0	0
64 MISC. MANUFACTURING	0	0	0	0	0	0	0	0	0
65 TRANSPORT., WAREHOUSING	-100015	-44375	-16606	37643	83875	-167746	-29203	91691	155215
66 COMMUNICA.,EXC. BRDCAST.	35769	-4032	6070	48778	8061	-23477	187	11768	73216
67 RADIO, TV BROADCASTING	-1007	138	100	2854	140	-83	30	710	-461
68 ELEC.,GAS,WATER,SAN.SER.	102903	45630	11425	-318693	43978	-60983	-8095	-48555	-41131
69 WHOLESALE, RETAIL TRADE	-208272	-36285	-94122	8720	-33	-239514	981	162550	7517
70 FINANCE, INSURANCE	-91999	-21598	-26593	-8037	-7266	93923	-5673	45007	-25156
71 REAL ESTATE, RENTAL	-40846	92548	-28861	494943	-9572	-194174	22954	495130	1035487
72 HOTELS, PERSONAL SERV.	-43791	30347	-8574	130365	9845	-39352	-8998	36610	90854
73 BUSINESS SERVICES	-157816	-17853	-120073	501121	-62014	-75404	-37635	230850	4213
74 RESEARCH, DEVELOPMENT	0	0	0	0	0	0	0	0	0
75 AUTO. REPAIR, SERVICES	3420	22026	6965	152899	14988	7491	-6603	27421	46411
76 AMUSEMENTS	-34183	-13170	-5677	405128	-9241	-52272	3031	-631	36210
77 MED.,EDUC. SERVICES	-264976	-82946	-145006	-439359	-51399	172440	-24692	982631	-416064
78 FEDERAL GOVT. ENTERPRISE	77922	373	15307	-46459	3386	-23410	-1179	70253	17455
79 STATE, LOCAL GOVT. ENT.	5466	535	-3755	-9937	-3838	-5213	-1232	-28588	6047
80 DIRECT ALLOCATED IMPORTS	-172238	-109766	-94158	-1454540	-149015	-170947	-33824	-162703	-378563
81 TRANSFERRED IMPORTS	-133756	-61301	-2442	-786978	-3880	-56161	-72101	-3786	-247741
82 VALUE ADDED	0	0	0	0	0	0	0	0	0
83 SECONDARY TRANSFERS-IN	0	0	0	0	0	0	0	0	0
84 INVENTORY DEPLETION	0	0	0	0	0	0	0	0	0
85 SCRAP PRODUCTION	0	0	0	0	0	0	0	0	0
86 SCRAP PURCHASED	0	0	0	0	0	0	0	0	0
87 STATE TOTAL PRODUCTION	-1041357	-160212	-429482	-1107485	-84061	-832530	-209361	1747695	388865

TABLE C-19

1963 SERVICE INDUSTRIES RESIDUAL BY STATE
(THOUSANDS OF CURRENT DOLLARS)

INDUSTRY TITLE	10 GEORGIA	11 IDAHO	12 ILLINOIS	13 INDIANA	14 IOWA	15 KANSAS	16 KENTUCKY	17 LOUISIANA	18 MAINE
1 LIVESTOCK, PRDTS.	0	0	0	0	0	0	0	0	0
2 OTHER AGRICULTURE PRDTS.	0	0	0	0	0	0	0	0	0
3 FORESTRY, FISHERIES	-3354	-32781	-32399	-11447	9258	1254	183	49989	-14128
4 AGRI.,FORES.,FISH. SERV.	7213	-66	24631	13522	10983	-10480	8086	1829	-1444
5 IRON, FERRO. ORES MINING	0	0	0	0	0	0	0	0	0
6 NONFERROUS ORES MINING	0	0	0	0	0	0	0	0	0
7 COAL MINING	0	0	0	0	0	0	0	0	0
8 CRUDE PETRO.,NATURAL GAS	0	0	0	0	0	0	0	0	0
9 STONE, CLAY MINING	0	0	0	0	0	0	0	0	0
10 CHEM.,FERT. MIN. MINING	0	0	0	0	0	0	0	0	0
11 NEW CONSTRUCTION	0	0	0	0	0	0	0	0	0
12 MAINT., REPAIR CONSTR.	-30356	32638	-136935	48245	142359	112858	26686	-105980	-1559
13 ORDNANCE, ACCESSORIES	0	0	0	0	0	0	0	0	0
14 FOOD, KINDRED PRDTS.	0	0	0	0	0	0	0	0	0
15 TOBACCO MANUFACTURES	0	0	0	0	0	0	0	0	0
16 FABRICS	0	0	0	0	0	0	0	0	0
17 TEXTILE PRDTS.	0	0	0	0	0	0	0	0	0
18 APPAREL	0	0	0	0	0	0	0	0	0
19 MISC. TEXTILE PRDTS.	0	0	0	0	0	0	0	0	0
20 LUMBER, WOOD PRDTS.	0	0	0	0	0	0	0	0	0
21 WOODEN CONTAINERS	0	0	0	0	0	0	0	0	0
22 HOUSEHOLD FURNITURE	0	0	0	0	0	0	0	0	0
23 OTHER FURNITURE	0	0	0	0	0	0	0	0	0
24 PAPER, ALLIED PRDTS.	0	0	0	0	0	0	0	0	0
25 PAPERBOARD CONTAINERS	0	0	0	0	0	0	0	0	0
26 PRINTING, PUBLISHING	0	0	0	0	0	0	0	0	0
27 CHEMICALS,SELECT. PRDTS.	0	0	0	0	0	0	0	0	0
28 PLASTICS, SYNTHETICS	0	0	0	0	0	0	0	0	0
29 DRUGS, COSMETICS	0	0	0	0	0	0	0	0	0
30 PAINT, ALLIED PRDTS.	0	0	0	0	0	0	0	0	0
31 PETROLEUM, RELATED INDS.	0	0	0	0	0	0	0	0	0
32 RUBBER, MISC. PLASTICS	0	0	0	0	0	0	0	0	0
33 LEATHER TANNING, PRDTS.	0	0	0	0	0	0	0	0	0
34 FOOTWEAR, LEATHER PRDTS.	0	0	0	0	0	0	0	0	0
35 GLASS, GLASS PRDTS.	0	0	0	0	0	0	0	0	0
36 STONE, CLAY PRDTS.	0	0	0	0	0	0	0	0	0
37 PRIMARY IRON, STEEL MFR.	0	0	0	0	0	0	0	0	0
38 PRIMARY NONFERROUS MFR.	0	0	0	0	0	0	0	0	0

39 METAL CONTAINERS	0	0	0	0	0	0	0	0	0
40 FABRICATED METAL PRDTS.	0	0	0	0	0	0	0	0	0
41 SCREW MACH. PRDTS., ETC.	0	0	0	0	0	0	0	0	0
42 OTHER FAB. METAL PRDTS.	0	0	0	0	0	0	0	0	0
43 ENGINES, TURBINES	0	0	0	0	0	0	0	0	0
44 FARM MACH., EQUIP.	0	0	0	0	0	0	0	0	0
45 CONSTRUC. MACH., EQUIP.	0	0	0	0	0	0	0	0	0
46 MATERIAL HANDLING MACH.	0	0	0	0	0	0	0	0	0
47 METALWORKING MACHINERY	0	0	0	0	0	0	0	0	0
48 SPECIAL MACH., EQUIP.	0	0	0	0	0	0	0	0	0
49 GENERAL MACH., EQUIP.	0	0	0	0	0	0	0	0	0
50 MACHINE SHOP PRDTS.	0	0	0	0	0	0	0	0	0
51 OFFICE, COMPUT. MACHINES	0	0	0	0	0	0	0	0	0
52 SERVICE IND. MACHINES	0	0	0	0	0	0	0	0	0
53 ELECT. TRANSMISS. EQUIP.	0	0	0	0	0	0	0	0	0
54 HOUSEHOLD APPLIANCES	0	0	0	0	0	0	0	0	0
55 ELECTRIC LIGHTING EQUIP.	0	0	0	0	0	0	0	0	0
56 RADIO, TV, ETC., EQUIP.	0	0	0	0	0	0	0	0	0
57 ELECTRONIC COMPONENTS	0	0	0	0	0	0	0	0	0
58 MISC. ELECTRICAL MACH.	0	0	0	0	0	0	0	0	0
59 MOTOR VEHICLES, EQUIP.	0	0	0	0	0	0	0	0	0
60 AIRCRAFT, PARTS	0	0	0	0	0	0	0	0	0
61 OTHER TRANSPORT. EQUIP.	0	0	0	0	0	0	0	0	0
62 PROFESS., SCIEN. INSTRU.	0	0	0	0	0	0	0	0	0
63 MEDICAL, PHOTO. EQUIP.	0	0	0	0	0	0	0	0	0
64 MISC. MANUFACTURING	0	0	0	0	0	0	0	0	0
65 TRANSPORT., WAREHOUSING	96572	1819	599473	-190464	-111846	81634	34311	-113751	-38718
66 COMMUNICA.,EXC. BRDCAST.	53408	1049	-173479	13574	-10192	-6294	22034	94715	-9157
67 RADIO, TV BROADCASTING	-794	69	794	-1059	210	355	-969	-946	59
68 ELEC.,GAS,WATER,SAN.SER.	-6521	3276	86986	42640	52375	43154	27714	23196	-19775
69 WHOLESALE, RETAIL TRADE	193644	-44775	1077244	-345441	-12989	-184300	-159430	-280196	-96315
70 FINANCE, INSURANCE	36458	-27194	76455	-150494	-64744	-75464	-84547	-59080	-32037
71 REAL ESTATE, RENTAL	-37600	-28134	746410	-288603	-256312	-257578	-127883	-451094	-128962
72 HOTELS, PERSONAL SERV.	-17126	-2146	75074	-16990	1484	-20837	-15060	-45898	-1498
73 BUSINESS SERVICES	-200852	-36140	646323	-474694	-184260	-215944	-228554	-158795	-54866
74 RESEARCH, DEVELOPMENT	0	0	0	0	0	0	0	0	0
75 AUTO. REPAIR, SERVICES	15904	1492	-39153	-21991	11535	5458	-9398	-16312	5859
76 AMUSEMENTS	-26818	-8525	-28565	-54055	-22588	-24336	-9966	-14496	-10283
77 MED.,EDUC. SERVICES	-190033	-60107	498883	-172333	-97741	-193152	-131815	-138053	-25820
78 FEDERAL GOVT. ENTERPRISE	36287	632	-81589	-21451	-6228	11419	36215	-5639	7335
79 STATE, LOCAL GOVT. ENT.	-5725	-248	-5991	-6493	1743	-80	-6080	-6293	1550
80 DIRECT ALLOCATED IMPORTS	-300981	-35768	-760643	-248920	-151411	-146761	-179058	-222808	-59871
81 TRANSFERRED IMPORTS	-226191	-2834	-159373	-14397	-4248	-3807	-4764	-444007	-446264
82 VALUE ADDED	0	0	0	0	0	0	0	0	0
83 SECONDARY TRANSFERS-IN	0	0	0	0	0	0	0	0	0
84 INVENTORY DEPLETION	0	0	0	0	0	0	0	0	0
85 SCRAP PRODUCTION	0	0	0	0	0	0	0	0	0
86 SCRAP PURCHASED	0	0	0	0	0	0	0	0	0
87 STATE TOTAL PRODUCTION	-606865	-237742	2414145	-1900851	-692610	-882901	-802293	-1893620	-925895

TABLE C-19

1963 SERVICE INDUSTRIES RESIDUAL BY STATE
(THOUSANDS OF CURRENT DOLLARS)

INDUSTRY TITLE	19 MARYLAND	20 MASSA-CHUSETTS	21 MICHIGAN	22 MINNESOTA	23 MISSISSIPPI	24 MISSOURI	25 MONTANA	26 NEBRASKA	27 NEVADA
1 LIVESTOCK, PRDTS.	0	0	0	0	0	0	0	0	0
2 OTHER AGRICULTURE PRDTS.	0	0	0	0	0	0	0	0	0
3 FORESTRY, FISHERIES	22473	53482	12854	-9880	12900	-4369	-20404	3540	-827
4 AGRI.,FORES.,FISH. SERV.	4905	-7070	109	9204	16868	1716	-1328	-1289	-1007
5 IRON, FERRO. ORES MINING	0	0	0	0	0	0	0	0	0
6 NONFERROUS ORES MINING	0	0	0	0	0	0	0	0	0
7 COAL MINING	0	0	0	0	0	0	0	0	0
8 CRUDE PETRO.,NATURAL GAS	0	0	0	0	0	0	0	0	0
9 STONE, CLAY MINING	0	0	0	0	0	0	0	0	0
10 CHEM.,FERT. MIN. MINING	0	0	0	0	0	0	0	0	0
11 NEW CONSTRUCTION	0	0	0	0	0	0	0	0	0
12 MAINT., REPAIR CONSTR.	-38318	-94060	-56585	51630	25682	50969	66273	71902	25723
13 ORDNANCE, ACCESSORIES	0	0	0	0	0	0	0	0	0
14 FOOD, KINDRED PRDTS.	0	0	0	0	0	0	0	0	0
15 TOBACCO MANUFACTURES	0	0	0	0	0	0	0	0	0
16 FABRICS	0	0	0	0	0	0	0	0	0
17 TEXTILE PRDTS.	0	0	0	0	0	0	0	0	0
18 APPAREL	0	0	0	0	0	0	0	0	0
19 MISC. TEXTILE PRDTS.	0	0	0	0	0	0	0	0	0
20 LUMBER, WOOD PRDTS.	0	0	0	0	0	0	0	0	0
21 WOODEN CONTAINERS	0	0	0	0	0	0	0	0	0
22 HOUSEHOLD FURNITURE	0	0	0	0	0	0	0	0	0
23 OTHER FURNITURE	0	0	0	0	0	0	0	0	0
24 PAPER, ALLIED PRDTS.	0	0	0	0	0	0	0	0	0
25 PAPERBOARD CONTAINERS	0	0	0	0	0	0	0	0	0
26 PRINTING, PUBLISHING	0	0	0	0	0	0	0	0	0
27 CHEMICALS,SELECT. PRDTS.	0	0	0	0	0	0	0	0	0
28 PLASTICS, SYNTHETICS	0	0	0	0	0	0	0	0	0
29 DRUGS, COSMETICS	0	0	0	0	0	0	0	0	0
30 PAINT, ALLIED PRDTS.	0	0	0	0	0	0	0	0	0
31 PETROLEUM, RELATED INDS.	0	0	0	0	0	0	0	0	0
32 RUBBER, MISC. PLASTICS	0	0	0	0	0	0	0	0	0
33 LEATHER TANNING, PRDTS.	0	0	0	0	0	0	0	0	0
34 FOOTWEAR, LEATHER PRDTS.	0	0	0	0	0	0	0	0	0
35 GLASS, GLASS PRDTS.	0	0	0	0	0	0	0	0	0
36 STONE, CLAY PRDTS.	0	0	0	0	0	0	0	0	0
37 PRIMARY IRON, STEEL MFR.	0	0	0	0	0	0	0	0	0
38 PRIMARY NONFERROUS MFR.	0	0	0	0	0	0	0	0	0

39 METAL CONTAINERS	0	0	0	0	0	0	0	0	0
40 FABRICATED METAL PRDTS.	0	0	0	0	0	0	0	0	0
41 SCREW MACH. PRDTS., ETC.	0	0	0	0	0	0	0	0	0
42 OTHER FAB. METAL PRDTS.	0	0	0	0	0	0	0	0	0
43 ENGINES, TURBINES	0	0	0	0	0	0	0	0	0
44 FARM MACH., EQUIP.	0	0	0	0	0	0	0	0	0
45 CONSTRUC. MACH., EQUIP.	0	0	0	0	0	0	0	0	0
46 MATERIAL HANDLING MACH.	0	0	0	0	0	0	0	0	0
47 METALWORKING MACHINERY	0	0	0	0	0	0	0	0	0
48 SPECIAL MACH., EQUIP.	0	0	0	0	0	0	0	0	0
49 GENERAL MACH., EQUIP.	0	0	0	0	0	0	0	0	0
50 MACHINE SHOP PRDTS.	0	0	0	0	0	0	0	0	0
51 OFFICE, COMPUT. MACHINES	0	0	0	0	0	0	0	0	0
52 SERVICE IND. MACHINES	0	0	0	0	0	0	0	0	0
53 ELECT. TRANSMISS. EQUIP.	0	0	0	0	0	0	0	0	0
54 HOUSEHOLD APPLIANCES	0	0	0	0	0	0	0	0	0
55 ELECTRIC LIGHTING EQUIP.	0	0	0	0	0	0	0	0	0
56 RADIO, TV, ETC., EQUIP.	0	0	0	0	0	0	0	0	0
57 ELECTRONIC COMPONENTS	0	0	0	0	0	0	0	0	0
58 MISC. ELECTRICAL MACH.	0	0	0	0	0	0	0	0	0
59 MOTOR VEHICLES, EQUIP.	0	0	0	0	0	0	0	0	0
60 AIRCRAFT, PARTS	0	0	0	0	0	0	0	0	0
61 OTHER TRANSPORT. EQUIP.	0	0	0	0	0	0	0	0	0
62 PROFESS., SCIEN. INSTRU.	0	0	0	0	0	0	0	0	0
63 MEDICAL, PHOTO. EQUIP.	0	0	0	0	0	0	0	0	0
64 MISC. MANUFACTURING	0	0	0	0	0	0	0	0	0
65 TRANSPORT., WAREHOUSING	-110951	-57164	-563149	-97380	-46859	359693	4377	56154	18953
66 COMMUNICA.,EXC. BRDCAST.	5251	-45112	58938	-10762	29393	-9764	-3607	20471	-15038
67 RADIO, TV BROADCASTING	-12	52	-466	170	87	-839	87	212	90
68 ELEC.,GAS,WATER,SAN.SER.	11224	22175	57872	31421	61249	-46059	41644	14429	13986
69 WHOLESALE, RETAIL TRADE	-263290	91052	-443728	251027	-111386	549986	-51384	105300	-22014
70 FINANCE, INSURANCE	-151502	260339	-355515	18012	-37953	51099	-25976	32563	-9415
71 REAL ESTATE, RENTAL	260033	-544347	-129476	119820	-85981	149643	-33104	-76982	75071
72 HOTELS, PERSONAL SERV.	-57961	-29057	-27597	-3724	-12308	22533	-1072	8000	73186
73 BUSINESS SERVICES	-84501	161078	-14533	-41262	-98383	-70062	-66621	-103799	-10453
74 RESEARCH, DEVELOPMENT	0	0	0	0	0	0	0	0	0
75 AUTO. REPAIR, SERVICES	6365	3325	-59506	-81	6988	-11740	-1707	11067	7231
76 AMUSEMENTS	-4479	-57898	-66171	-27406	-13803	-30482	-9446	-4146	143111
77 MED.,EDUC. SERVICES	34507	1294127	-488807	-61051	-158326	134448	-56696	-51575	-47209
78 FEDERAL GOVT. ENTERPRISE	-2870	-13339	-69090	-7751	11183	8528	4478	7658	2679
79 STATE, LOCAL GOVT. ENT.	-8242	760	12433	202	-3671	-13370	-949	18284	-1501
80 DIRECT ALLOCATED IMPORTS	-232391	-374313	-389865	-180335	-105167	-263953	-42530	-92897	-32374
81 TRANSFERRED IMPORTS	-759271	-408517	-1164437	-10551	-19307	-7841	-91272	-2571	-942
82 VALUE ADDED	0	0	0	0	0	0	0	0	0
83 SECONDARY TRANSFERS-IN	0	0	0	0	0	0	0	0	0
84 INVENTORY DEPLETION	0	0	0	0	0	0	0	0	0
85 SCRAP PRODUCTION	0	0	0	0	0	0	0	0	0
86 SCRAP PURCHASED	0	0	0	0	0	0	0	0	0
87 STATE TOTAL PRODUCTION	-1369029	256012	-3686722	31304	-528794	870135	-289237	16320	219251

TABLE C-19

1963 SERVICE INDUSTRIES RESIDUAL BY STATE
(THOUSANDS OF CURRENT DOLLARS)

INDUSTRY TITLE	28 NEW HAMPSHIRE	29 NEW JERSEY	30 NEW MEXICO	31 NEW YORK	32 NORTH CAROLINA	33 NORTH DAKOTA	34 OHIO	35 OKLAHOMA	36 OREGON
1 LIVESTOCK, PRDTS.	0	0	0	0	0	0	0	0	0
2 OTHER AGRICULTURE PRDTS.	0	0	0	0	0	0	0	0	0
3 FORESTRY, FISHERIES	-9223	12077	-1495	27934	11646	8519	-27269	-1492	-62615
4 AGRI.,FORES.,FISH. SERV.	931	-3372	147	-28808	15523	2690	5361	-10297	-11231
5 IRON, FERRO. ORES MINING	0	0	0	0	0	0	0	0	0
6 NONFERROUS ORES MINING	0	0	0	0	0	0	0	0	0
7 COAL MINING	0	0	0	0	0	0	0	0	0
8 CRUDE PETRO.,NATURAL GAS	0	0	0	0	0	0	0	0	0
9 STONE, CLAY MINING	0	0	0	0	0	0	0	0	0
10 CHEM.,FERT. MIN. MINING	0	0	0	0	0	0	0	0	0
11 NEW CONSTRUCTION	0	0	0	0	0	0	0	0	0
12 MAINT., REPAIR CONSTR.	1993	-117359	23393	-735774	42610	77622	200942	8043	53157
13 ORDNANCE, ACCESSORIES	0	0	0	0	0	0	0	0	0
14 FOOD, KINDRED PRDTS.	0	0	0	0	0	0	0	0	0
15 TOBACCO MANUFACTURES	0	0	0	0	0	0	0	0	0
16 FABRICS	0	0	0	0	0	0	0	0	0
17 TEXTILE PRDTS.	0	0	0	0	0	0	0	0	0
18 APPAREL	0	0	0	0	0	0	0	0	0
19 MISC. TEXTILE PRDTS.	0	0	0	0	0	0	0	0	0
20 LUMBER, WOOD PRDTS.	0	0	0	0	0	0	0	0	0
21 WOODEN CONTAINERS	0	0	0	0	0	0	0	0	0
22 HOUSEHOLD FURNITURE	0	0	0	0	0	0	0	0	0
23 OTHER FURNITURE	0	0	0	0	0	0	0	0	0
24 PAPER, ALLIED PRDTS.	0	0	0	0	0	0	0	0	0
25 PAPERBOARD CONTAINERS	0	0	0	0	0	0	0	0	0
26 PRINTING, PUBLISHING	0	0	0	0	0	0	0	0	0
27 CHEMICALS,SELECT. PRDTS.	0	0	0	0	0	0	0	0	0
28 PLASTICS, SYNTHETICS	0	0	0	0	0	0	0	0	0
29 DRUGS, COSMETICS	0	0	0	0	0	0	0	0	0
30 PAINT, ALLIED PRDTS.	0	0	0	0	0	0	0	0	0
31 PETROLEUM, RELATED INDS.	0	0	0	0	0	0	0	0	0
32 RUBBER, MISC. PLASTICS	0	0	0	0	0	0	0	0	0
33 LEATHER TANNING, PRDTS.	0	0	0	0	0	0	0	0	0
34 FOOTWEAR, LEATHER PRDTS.	0	0	0	0	0	0	0	0	0
35 GLASS, GLASS PRDTS.	0	0	0	0	0	0	0	0	0
36 STONE, CLAY PRDTS.	0	0	0	0	0	0	0	0	0
37 PRIMARY IRON, STEEL MFR.	0	0	0	0	0	0	0	0	0
38 PRIMARY NONFERROUS MFR.	0	0	0	0	0	0	0	0	0

39 METAL CONTAINERS	0	0	0	0	0	0	0	0	0
40 FABRICATED METAL PRDTS.	0	0	0	0	0	0	0	0	0
41 SCREW MACH. PRDTS., ETC.	0	0	0	0	0	0	0	0	0
42 OTHER FAB. METAL PRDTS.	0	0	0	0	0	0	0	0	0
43 ENGINES, TURBINES	0	0	0	0	0	0	0	0	0
44 FARM MACH., EQUIP.	0	0	0	0	0	0	0	0	0
45 CONSTRUC. MACH., EQUIP.	0	0	0	0	0	0	0	0	0
46 MATERIAL HANDLING MACH.	0	0	0	0	0	0	0	0	0
47 METALWORKING MACHINERY	0	0	0	0	0	0	0	0	0
48 SPECIAL MACH., EQUIP.	0	0	0	0	0	0	0	0	0
49 GENERAL MACH., EQUIP.	0	0	0	0	0	0	0	0	0
50 MACHINE SHOP PRDTS.	0	0	0	0	0	0	0	0	0
51 OFFICE, COMPUT. MACHINES	0	0	0	0	0	0	0	0	0
52 SERVICE IND. MACHINES	0	0	0	0	0	0	0	0	0
53 ELECT. TRANSMISS. EQUIP.	0	0	0	0	0	0	0	0	0
54 HOUSEHOLD APPLIANCES	0	0	0	0	0	0	0	0	0
55 ELECTRIC LIGHTING EQUIP.	0	0	0	0	0	0	0	0	0
56 RADIO, TV, ETC., EQUIP.	0	0	0	0	0	0	0	0	0
57 ELECTRONIC COMPONENTS	0	0	0	0	0	0	0	0	0
58 MISC. ELECTRICAL MACH.	0	0	0	0	0	0	0	0	0
59 MOTOR VEHICLES, EQUIP.	0	0	0	0	0	0	0	0	0
60 AIRCRAFT, PARTS	0	0	0	0	0	0	0	0	0
61 OTHER TRANSPORT. EQUIP.	0	0	0	0	0	0	0	0	0
62 PROFESS., SCIEN. INSTRU.	0	0	0	0	0	0	0	0	0
63 MEDICAL, PHOTO. EQUIP.	0	0	0	0	0	0	0	0	0
64 MISC. MANUFACTURING	0	0	0	0	0	0	0	0	0
65 TRANSPORT., WAREHOUSING	-36937	107101	16975	606565	-18840	-32443	-407138	111328	57540
66 COMMUNICA.,EXC. BRDCAST.	-10709	-55670	1680	-239640	13637	11719	-9812	25056	5242
67 RADIO, TV BROADCASTING	-30	-704	88	8303	-926	49	-59	187	-1020
68 ELEC.,GAS,WATER,SAN.SER.	7770	-93264	34737	-164826	-62010	-9119	231346	19664	-48815
69 WHOLESALE, RETAIL TRADE	-77311	-283247	-81430	3101795	-42084	10221	-535514	-109087	60538
70 FINANCE, INSURANCE	-17683	-256017	-40279	2229816	-68881	-14028	-352969	-34055	-61460
71 REAL ESTATE, RENTAL	-92811	-188591	-96359	2260870	-217159	-22017	28700	-98138	-57353
72 HOTELS, PERSONAL SERV.	2100	-49818	-33	238018	-4160	119	-55948	-32005	452
73 BUSINESS SERVICES	-30724	-351174	-34937	3947695	-409839	-53442	-274747	-105646	-92568
74 RESEARCH, DEVELOPMENT	0	0	0	0	0	0	0	0	0
75 AUTO. REPAIR, SERVICES	4079	-17952	1184	-141225	-7519	3990	-54253	10341	3764
76 AMUSEMENTS	2603	-50170	-9497	597579	-31448	-3811	-73675	-20108	-26017
77 MED.,EDUC. SERVICES	46081	-354170	-88099	2405337	-87800	-42365	-152572	-193719	-104674
78 FEDERAL GOVT. ENTERPRISE	-822	-41727	5393	-302094	6871	6438	-52992	11268	4728
79 STATE, LOCAL GOVT. ENT.	2899	-12722	-3773	10355	5282	-1919	18719	-3434	2413
80 DIRECT ALLOCATED IMPORTS	-41088	-549544	-69625	-1270623	-296690	-34722	-582473	-150018	-113745
81 TRANSFERRED IMPORTS	-2435	-1027418	-1723	-3667466	-63525	-205780	-134402	-3021	-65092
82 VALUE ADDED	0	0	0	0	0	0	0	0	0
83 SECONDARY TRANSFERS-IN	0	0	0	0	0	0	0	0	0
84 INVENTORY DEPLETION	0	0	0	0	0	0	0	0	0
85 SCRAP PRODUCTION	0	0	0	0	0	0	0	0	0
86 SCRAP PURCHASED	0	0	0	0	0	0	0	0	0
87 STATE TOTAL PRODUCTION	-251316	-3333740	-343653	8883811	-1215315	-298279	-2228753	-575131	-456757

TABLE C-19

1963 SERVICE INDUSTRIES RESIDUAL BY STATE
(THOUSANDS OF CURRENT DOLLARS)

INDUSTRY TITLE	37 PENNSYL-VANIA	38 RHODE ISLAND	39 SOUTH CAROLINA	40 SOUTH DAKOTA	41 TENNESSEE	42 TEXAS	43 UTAH	44 VERMONT	45 VIRGINIA
1 LIVESTOCK, PRDTS.	0	0	0	0	0	0	0	0	0
2 OTHER AGRICULTURE PRDTS.	0	0	0	0	0	0	0	0	0
3 FORESTRY, FISHERIES	-18958	3683	6555	3420	-5553	61781	-2040	6846	16524
4 AGRI.,FORES.,FISH. SERV.	1080	1305	6910	-3563	-5585	16831	-1695	-708	1965
5 IRON, FERRO. ORES MINING	0	0	0	0	0	0	0	0	0
6 NONFERROUS ORES MINING	0	0	0	0	0	0	0	0	0
7 COAL MINING	0	0	0	0	0	0	0	0	0
8 CRUDE PETRO.,NATURAL GAS	0	0	0	0	0	0	0	0	0
9 STONE, CLAY MINING	0	0	0	0	0	0	0	0	0
10 CHEM.,FERT. MIN. MINING	0	0	0	0	0	0	0	0	0
11 NEW CONSTRUCTION	0	0	0	0	0	0	0	0	0
12 MAINT., REPAIR CONSTR.	-179422	-17366	3214	76206	-30783	105463	-1168	3650	-44297
13 ORDNANCE, ACCESSORIES	0	0	0	0	0	0	0	0	0
14 FOOD, KINDRED PRDTS.	0	0	0	0	0	0	0	0	0
15 TOBACCO MANUFACTURES	0	0	0	0	0	0	0	0	0
16 FABRICS	0	0	0	0	0	0	0	0	0
17 TEXTILE PRDTS.	0	0	0	0	0	0	0	0	0
18 APPAREL	0	0	0	0	0	0	0	0	0
19 MISC. TEXTILE PRDTS.	0	0	0	0	0	0	0	0	0
20 LUMBER, WOOD PRDTS.	0	0	0	0	0	0	0	0	0
21 WOODEN CONTAINERS	0	0	0	0	0	0	0	0	0
22 HOUSEHOLD FURNITURE	0	0	0	0	0	0	0	0	0
23 OTHER FURNITURE	0	0	0	0	0	0	0	0	0
24 PAPER, ALLIED PRDTS.	0	0	0	0	0	0	0	0	0
25 PAPERBOARD CONTAINERS	0	0	0	0	0	0	0	0	0
26 PRINTING, PUBLISHING	0	0	0	0	0	0	0	0	0
27 CHEMICALS,SELECT. PRDTS.	0	0	0	0	0	0	0	0	0
28 PLASTICS, SYNTHETICS	0	0	0	0	0	0	0	0	0
29 DRUGS, COSMETICS	0	0	0	0	0	0	0	0	0
30 PAINT, ALLIED PRDTS.	0	0	0	0	0	0	0	0	0
31 PETROLEUM, RELATED INDS.	0	0	0	0	0	0	0	0	0
32 RUBBER, MISC. PLASTICS	0	0	0	0	0	0	0	0	0
33 LEATHER TANNING, PRDTS.	0	0	0	0	0	0	0	0	0
34 FOOTWEAR, LEATHER PRDTS.	0	0	0	0	0	0	0	0	0
35 GLASS, GLASS PRDTS.	0	0	0	0	0	0	0	0	0
36 STONE, CLAY PRDTS.	0	0	0	0	0	0	0	0	0
37 PRIMARY IRON, STEEL MFR.	0	0	0	0	0	0	0	0	0
38 PRIMARY NONFERROUS MFR.	0	0	0	0	0	0	0	0	0

39 METAL CONTAINERS	0	0	0	0	0	0	0	0	0
40 FABRICATED METAL PRDTS.	0	0	0	0	0	0	0	0	0
41 SCREW MACH. PRDTS., ETC.	0	0	0	0	0	0	0	0	0
42 OTHER FAB. METAL PRDTS.	0	0	0	0	0	0	0	0	0
43 ENGINES, TURBINES	0	0	0	0	0	0	0	0	0
44 FARM MACH., EQUIP.	0	0	0	0	0	0	0	0	0
45 CONSTRUC. MACH., EQUIP.	0	0	0	0	0	0	0	0	0
46 MATERIAL HANDLING MACH.	0	0	0	0	0	0	0	0	0
47 METALWORKING MACHINERY	0	0	0	0	0	0	0	0	0
48 SPECIAL MACH., EQUIP.	0	0	0	0	0	0	0	0	0
49 GENERAL MACH., EQUIP.	0	0	0	0	0	0	0	0	0
50 MACHINE SHOP PRDTS.	0	0	0	0	0	0	0	0	0
51 OFFICE, COMPUT. MACHINES	0	0	0	0	0	0	0	0	0
52 SERVICE IND. MACHINES	0	0	0	0	0	0	0	0	0
53 ELECT. TRANSMISS. EQUIP.	0	0	0	0	0	0	0	0	0
54 HOUSEHOLD APPLIANCES	0	0	0	0	0	0	0	0	0
55 ELECTRIC LIGHTING EQUIP.	0	0	0	0	0	0	0	0	0
56 RADIO, TV, ETC., EQUIP.	0	0	0	0	0	0	0	0	0
57 ELECTRONIC COMPONENTS	0	0	0	0	0	0	0	0	0
58 MISC. ELECTRICAL MACH.	0	0	0	0	0	0	0	0	0
59 MOTOR VEHICLES, EQUIP.	0	0	0	0	0	0	0	0	0
60 AIRCRAFT, PARTS	0	0	0	0	0	0	0	0	0
61 OTHER TRANSPORT. EQUIP.	0	0	0	0	0	0	0	0	0
62 PROFESS., SCIEN. INSTRU.	0	0	0	0	0	0	0	0	0
63 MEDICAL, PHOTO. EQUIP.	0	0	0	0	0	0	0	0	0
64 MISC. MANUFACTURING	0	0	0	0	0	0	0	0	0
65 TRANSPORT., WAREHOUSING	-17456	-31714	-101990	-34542	17492	93766	19835	-37492	-195725
66 COMMUNICA.,EXC. BRDCAST.	-136689	-567	6478	-388	88913	164166	16596	-15340	20726
67 RADIO, TV BROADCASTING	2	117	-1013	78	-791	-1393	-7	-30	-883
68 ELEC.,GAS,WATER,SAN.SER.	116043	-17093	-46158	-5313	-131927	-64338	27538	779	39844
69 WHOLESALE, RETAIL TRADE	-771494	-17110	-223985	2089	138893	253889	-29088	-130508	-320694
70 FINANCE, INSURANCE	-187332	12491	-29351	-9597	-15910	-23792	-34781	-12606	-103778
71 REAL ESTATE, RENTAL	-1055157	-78656	-244709	-27593	-103065	-833078	-24580	-75523	152055
72 HOTELS, PERSONAL SERV.	-74680	-4553	-14634	392	-2534	-30268	-8217	1753	-34772
73 BUSINESS SERVICES	2269	-14531	-125454	-61453	-134767	-459980	-55043	-17596	-253187
74 RESEARCH, DEVELOPMENT	0	0	0	0	0	0	0	0	0
75 AUTO. REPAIR, SERVICES	26042	-2737	-847	5505	6049	51360	-475	3021	-15166
76 AMUSEMENTS	-170003	-108	-17652	352	-27510	-87821	-7235	236	-41080
77 MED.,EDUC. SERVICES	420192	32268	-147606	-33214	-41138	-647318	37411	77217	-221353
78 FEDERAL GOVT. ENTERPRISE	-59841	3115	17200	4836	134159	18697	-1793	1276	53794
79 STATE, LOCAL GOVT. ENT.	15456	-2263	-3760	-773	18772	-4843	-428	669	8093
80 DIRECT ALLOCATED IMPORTS	-640105	-73567	-156068	-32000	-213243	-759553	-49441	-21153	-291315
81 TRANSFERRED IMPORTS	-1003149	-3697	-111168	-898	-6553	-552908	-1391	-216643	-125845
82 VALUE ADDED	0	0	0	0	0	0	0	0	0
83 SECONDARY TRANSFERS-IN	0	0	0	0	0	0	0	0	0
84 INVENTORY DEPLETION	0	0	0	0	0	0	0	0	0
85 SCRAP PRODUCTION	0	0	0	0	0	0	0	0	0
86 SCRAP PURCHASED	0	0	0	0	0	0	0	0	0
87 STATE TOTAL PRODUCTION	-3733203	-210985	-1184038	-116456	-315082	-2699341	-116000	-432152	-1355095

TABLE C-19

1963 SERVICE INDUSTRIES RESIDUAL BY STATE
(THOUSANDS OF CURRENT DOLLARS)

INDUSTRY TITLE	46 WASHINGTON	47 WEST VIRGINIA	48 WISCONSIN	49 WYOMING	50 ALASKA	51 HAWAII	52 NATIONAL TOTAL
1 LIVESTOCK, PRDTS.	0	0	0	0	0	0	0
2 OTHER AGRICULTURE PRDTS.	0	0	0	0	0	0	0
3 FORESTRY, FISHERIES	-53877	-3195	-2795	-604	49219	-887	0
4 AGRI.,FORES.,FISH. SERV.	-4931	2868	-8037	-429	-4503	26702	0
5 IRON, FERRO. ORES MINING	0	0	0	0	0	0	0
6 NONFERROUS ORES MINING	0	0	0	0	0	0	0
7 COAL MINING	0	0	0	0	0	0	0
8 CRUDE PETRO.,NATURAL GAS	0	0	0	0	0	0	0
9 STONE, CLAY MINING	0	0	0	0	0	0	0
10 CHEM.,FERT. MIN. MINING	0	0	0	0	0	0	0
11 NEW CONSTRUCTION	0	0	0	0	0	0	0
12 MAINT., REPAIR CONSTR.	-19428	6525	61083	21358	-16412	-21464	0
13 ORDNANCE, ACCESSORIES	0	0	0	0	0	0	0
14 FOOD, KINDRED PRDTS.	0	0	0	0	0	0	0
15 TOBACCO MANUFACTURES	0	0	0	0	0	0	0
16 FABRICS	0	0	0	0	0	0	0
17 TEXTILE PRDTS.	0	0	0	0	0	0	0
18 APPAREL	0	0	0	0	0	0	0
19 MISC. TEXTILE PRDTS.	0	0	0	0	0	0	0
20 LUMBER, WOOD PRDTS.	0	0	0	0	0	0	0
21 WOODEN CONTAINERS	0	0	0	0	0	0	0
22 HOUSEHOLD FURNITURE	0	0	0	0	0	0	0
23 OTHER FURNITURE	0	0	0	0	0	0	0
24 PAPER, ALLIED PRDTS.	0	0	0	0	0	0	0
25 PAPERBOARD CONTAINERS	0	0	0	0	0	0	0
26 PRINTING, PUBLISHING	0	0	0	0	0	0	0
27 CHEMICALS,SELECT. PRDTS.	0	0	0	0	0	0	0
28 PLASTICS, SYNTHETICS	0	0	0	0	0	0	0
29 DRUGS, COSMETICS	0	0	0	0	0	0	0
30 PAINT, ALLIED PRDTS.	0	0	0	0	0	0	0
31 PETROLEUM, RELATED INDS.	0	0	0	0	0	0	0
32 RUBBER, MISC. PLASTICS	0	0	0	0	0	0	0
33 LEATHER TANNING, PRDTS.	0	0	0	0	0	0	0
34 FOOTWEAR, LEATHER PRDTS.	0	0	0	0	0	0	0
35 GLASS, GLASS PRDTS.	0	0	0	0	0	0	0
36 STONE, CLAY PRDTS.	0	0	0	0	0	0	0
37 PRIMARY IRON, STEEL MFR.	0	0	0	0	0	0	0
38 PRIMARY NONFERROUS MFR.	0	0	0	0	0	0	0

39 METAL CONTAINERS	0	0	0	0	0	0	0
40 FABRICATED METAL PRDTS.	0	0	0	0	0	0	0
41 SCREW MACH. PRDTS., ETC.	0	0	0	0	0	0	0
42 OTHER FAB. METAL PRDTS.	0	0	0	0	0	0	0
43 ENGINES, TURBINES	0	0	0	0	0	0	0
44 FARM MACH., EQUIP.	0	0	0	0	0	0	0
45 CONSTRUC. MACH., EQUIP.	0	0	0	0	0	0	0
46 MATERIAL HANDLING MACH.	0	0	0	0	0	0	0
47 METALWORKING MACHINERY	0	0	0	0	0	0	0
48 SPECIAL MACH., EQUIP.	0	0	0	0	0	0	0
49 GENERAL MACH., EQUIP.	0	0	0	0	0	0	0
50 MACHINE SHOP PRDTS.	0	0	0	0	0	0	0
51 OFFICE, COMPUT. MACHINES	0	0	0	0	0	0	0
52 SERVICE IND. MACHINES	0	0	0	0	0	0	0
53 ELECT. TRANSMISS. EQUIP.	0	0	0	0	0	0	0
54 HOUSEHOLD APPLIANCES	0	0	0	0	0	0	0
55 ELECTRIC LIGHTING EQUIP.	0	0	0	0	0	0	0
56 RADIO, TV, ETC., EQUIP.	0	0	0	0	0	0	0
57 ELECTRONIC COMPONENTS	0	0	0	0	0	0	0
58 MISC. ELECTRICAL MACH.	0	0	0	0	0	0	0
59 MOTOR VEHICLES, EQUIP.	0	0	0	0	0	0	0
60 AIRCRAFT, PARTS	0	0	0	0	0	0	0
61 OTHER TRANSPORT. EQUIP.	0	0	0	0	0	0	0
62 PROFESS., SCIEN. INSTRU.	0	0	0	0	0	0	0
63 MEDICAL, PHOTO. EQUIP.	0	0	0	0	0	0	0
64 MISC. MANUFACTURING	0	0	0	0	0	0	0
65 TRANSPORT., WAREHOUSING	103088	23557	-268784	25666	43105	33249	0
66 COMMUNICA.,EXC. BRDCAST.	14272	-832	-43884	-739	-14394	-11400	0
67 RADIO, TV BROADCASTING	-985	157	-809	33	54	62	0
68 ELEC.,GAS,WATER,SAN.SER.	-79731	77496	-22951	33567	-7822	-21558	0
69 WHOLESALE, RETAIL TRADE	-119552	-267790	-143760	-43866	-61105	-163470	0
70 FINANCE, INSURANCE	-106735	-84124	-133740	-25979	-9985	26971	0
71 REAL ESTATE, RENTAL	141736	-106671	-25423	-93944	-34060	121809	0
72 HOTELS, PERSONAL SERV.	-26892	-18357	-22337	7050	-5358	8600	0
73 BUSINESS SERVICES	-165707	-77926	-169271	-35873	-25316	-27636	0
74 RESEARCH, DEVELOPMENT	0	0	0	0	0	0	0
75 AUTO. REPAIR, SERVICES	-5770	-23706	-29712	-1597	-6412	2008	0
76 AMUSEMENTS	-41335	-1571	-43877	-3492	-2095	-1079	0
77 MED.,EDUC. SERVICES	-190748	-93476	-398724	-38952	-22074	19650	0
78 FEDERAL GOVT. ENTERPRISE	51781	-3678	-20083	532	35948	30620	0
79 STATE, LOCAL GOVT. ENT.	31626	-1283	-12285	-530	-475	-1559	0
80 DIRECT ALLOCATED IMPORTS	-237119	-68061	-179959	-19874	-56610	-92671	-12545066
81 TRANSFERRED IMPORTS	-426899	-1894	-269628	-532	-38339	-69141	-13138289
82 VALUE ADDED	0	0	0	0	0	0	0
83 SECONDARY TRANSFERS-IN	0	0	0	0	0	0	0
84 INVENTORY DEPLETION	0	0	0	0	0	0	0
85 SCRAP PRODUCTION	0	0	0	0	0	0	0
86 SCRAP PURCHASED	0	0	0	0	0	0	0
87 STATE TOTAL PRODUCTION	-1137205	-641962	-1734975	-178205	-176635	-141195	-25728976

TABLE C-20

1963 STATE TOTAL FINAL DEMAND
(THOUSANDS OF CURRENT DOLLARS)

INDUSTRY TITLE	1 ALABAMA	2 ARIZONA	3 ARKANSAS	4 CALIFORNIA	5 COLORADO	6 CONNECTICUT	7 DELAWARE	8 DISTRICT OF COLUMBIA	9 FLORIDA
1 LIVESTOCK, PRDTS.	31715	10759	27283	207366	21254	23592	4776	13370	65542
2 OTHER AGRICULTURE PRDTS.	158988	39130	709	766354	33894	57320	1967	12254	258105
3 FORESTRY, FISHERIES	2456	2941	769	34273	4518	7314	810	1842	9393
4 AGRI.,FORES.,FISH. SERV.	188	-33	-17	2729	269	-185	95	163	1114
5 IRON, FERRO. ORES MINING	1011	2535	0	43548	4742	0	0	0	1012
6 NONFERROUS ORES MINING	14759	41559	-1265	2267	56768	0	0	0	0
7 COAL MINING	3778	779	1533	8933	1354	3125	328	563	4324
8 CRUDE PETRO.,NATURAL GAS	30	1	104	2663	185	0	0	0	3
9 STONE, CLAY MINING	-43	-596	79	1218	-77	-208	60	-73	2949
10 CHEM.,FERT. MIN. MINING	1312	237	140	10771	232	433	27	127	5759
11 NEW CONSTRUCTION	840568	769136	448501	12453446	848791	1086300	201559	385666	2628530
12 MAINT., REPAIR CONSTR.	71265	46563	29863	655407	59915	63494	8885	97111	128853
13 ORDNANCE, ACCESSORIES	66398	51725	8791	1602682	30246	194975	3625	78940	125402
14 FOOD, KINDRED PRDTS.	702515	406374	368616	5834129	567210	903027	128325	231337	1444441
15 TOBACCO MANUFACTURES	74567	33398	40867	472420	46590	87408	13017	21280	167454
16 FABRICS	12707	5423	5527	79760	7600	10351	2212	3070	36209
17 TEXTILE PRDTS.	13700	7641	5899	114907	10582	25155	3169	5459	28210
18 APPAREL	189168	97411	93302	1397524	135236	259789	38217	66403	401385
19 MISC. TEXTILE PRDTS.	21826	11436	10672	163934	16150	30568	6016	8002	48091
20 LUMBER, WOOD PRDTS.	7379	2394	4851	80454	3103	3584	870	1276	13952
21 WOODEN CONTAINERS	108	5	30	313	64	8	1	19	123
22 HOUSEHOLD FURNITURE	45935	22893	24490	330843	32126	55465	9378	18610	100456
23 OTHER FURNITURE	17187	11774	9520	176083	15898	26075	4577	15327	41194
24 PAPER, ALLIED PRDTS.	30058	11920	12471	227939	15603	23991	3937	12017	104125
25 PAPERBOARD CONTAINERS	2128	1060	1241	21716	1702	2855	447	1135	5863
26 PRINTING, PUBLISHING	51329	34569	24738	481907	45871	67603	10272	17612	116217
27 CHEMICALS,SELECT. PRDTS.	75566	16025	5707	166071	20051	13896	11640	12938	124515
28 PLASTICS, SYNTHETICS	3442	94	99	22907	135	1241	2147	61	8924
29 DRUGS, COSMETICS	92680	45941	49353	657285	64074	95008	16682	33102	195484
30 PAINT, ALLIED PRDTS.	504	226	246	9259	411	695	83	261	2499
31 PETROLEUM, RELATED INDS.	130840	68473	66190	1143114	97130	148583	30672	42044	252340
32 RUBBER, MISC. PLASTICS	32964	16835	15701	266312	24769	39078	9562	11191	68803
33 LEATHER TANNING, PRDTS.	11	5	4	4315	10	2	3	22	1079
34 FOOTWEAR, LEATHER PRDTS.	42476	23533	22683	326246	32642	51145	8215	13032	88389
35 GLASS, GLASS PRDTS.	3889	2288	2247	44567	3325	5001	759	1841	10128
36 STONE, CLAY PRDTS.	5693	2287	2034	44598	3175	5357	767	1258	12375
37 PRIMARY IRON, STEEL MFR.	7712	1149	130	32346	1054	4186	811	321	6553
38 PRIMARY NONFERROUS MFR.	4883	5924	1591	64207	-689	13397	221	-9931	5286

39 METAL CONTAINERS	207	54	180	8085	851	111	212	28	2272
40 FABRICATED METAL PRDTS.	14019	13014	5476	95544	7036	12397	2606	4207	28388
41 SCREW MACH. PRDTS., ETC.	4341	2428	2332	42531	3476	8180	989	1910	8448
42 OTHER FAB. METAL PRDTS.	13300	7434	6680	123422	9739	19879	2733	6109	28748
43 ENGINES, TURBINES	8992	11928	4958	88292	7782	52012	1597	9547	25981
44 FARM MACH., EQUIP.	31374	23247	38153	193021	30958	9517	5350	2184	55572
45 CONSTRUC. MACH., EQUIP.	26408	24819	13064	306669	24695	22843	4245	10200	74935
46 MATERIAL HANDLING MACH.	8198	6257	5785	86340	7135	18872	2452	4200	15901
47 METALWORKING MACHINERY	19633	15355	12434	210520	11435	50940	8883	6339	34463
48 SPECIAL MACH., EQUIP.	35119	13925	20852	212165	15325	34185	9514	8767	54632
49 GENERAL MACH., EQUIP.	19863	14650	10462	206273	12353	52120	6659	8529	36408
50 MACHINE SHOP PRDTS.	821	540	355	14844	835	4033	184	348	1952
51 OFFICE, COMPUT. MACHINES	20155	19718	11651	292875	18287	46669	81507	28317	54222
52 SERVICE IND. MACHINES	22240	10162	12122	171691	14340	23506	6084	13712	56294
53 ELECT. TRANSMISS. EQUIP.	28622	33391	19616	307983	29467	40629	5872	18185	70611
54 HOUSEHOLD APPLIANCES	45920	23885	31964	332205	32798	56045	8477	12805	96852
55 ELECTRIC LIGHTING EQUIP.	7664	4574	4209	68744	6092	10184	1625	2492	16376
56 RADIO, TV, ETC., EQUIP.	63902	71539	50161	1631675	51480	119989	11507	77425	225991
57 ELECTRONIC COMPONENTS	4017	14344	2118	165084	3583	19556	926	6563	14697
58 MISC. ELECTRICAL MACH.	8466	5077	4592	89413	7727	12156	2465	4898	19442
59 MOTOR VEHICLES, EQUIP.	300738	172423	165562	2459937	247560	327221	91390	123387	635566
60 AIRCRAFT, PARTS	155627	71402	7338	1676321	36905	795279	9204	51464	106352
61 OTHER TRANSPORT. EQUIP.	41449	22040	23072	442695	40204	158121	16213	62573	91486
62 PROFESS., SCIEN. INSTRU.	15940	17913	10331	233478	15446	57966	3891	20153	38702
63 MEDICAL, PHOTO. EQUIP.	13601	9279	6494	155321	12672	19940	4488	15256	31453
64 MISC. MANUFACTURING	50888	33746	26091	508712	46592	70580	11517	22324	117583
65 TRANSPORT., WAREHOUSING	181172	95898	74442	1614549	138002	231676	37757	149534	394091
66 COMMUNICA., EXC. BRDCAST.	88535	53317	44612	749026	73992	115550	17447	43585	188095
67 RADIO, TV BROADCASTING	1412	156	99	4615	219	222	45	54	1595
68 ELEC.,GAS,WATER,SAN.SER.	189969	96826	99739	1308326	133666	177387	34298	49739	385165
69 WHOLESALE, RETAIL TRADE	1204990	676603	641548	9401260	930288	1495162	235229	446909	2501020
70 FINANCE, INSURANCE	260974	128438	111083	1905979	179635	316149	51054	83205	478745
71 REAL ESTATE, RENTAL	674020	436034	333422	6290463	611220	1070359	134599	264614	1463026
72 HOTELS, PERSONAL SERV.	172523	106856	92163	1343945	141522	201224	34303	109427	487401
73 BUSINESS SERVICES	78149	50525	33416	745878	71984	77679	13413	87224	160412
74 RESEARCH, DEVELOPMENT	0	0	0	0	0	0	0	0	0
75 AUTO. REPAIR, SERVICES	104371	57784	53684	807249	81171	105538	20997	32920	216736
76 AMUSEMENTS	53442	40769	27016	678933	56599	86580	13343	26861	136950
77 MED., EDUC. SERVICES	444216	230201	222868	3357298	323765	555693	90005	177068	942455
78 FEDERAL GOVT. ENTERPRISE	16105	10508	7961	147631	14670	19571	2837	11003	33217
79 STATE, LOCAL GOVT. ENT.	14244	8038	6726	98578	11306	11288	2383	28535	25655
80 DIRECT ALLOCATED IMPORTS	123821	78967	65376	981668	119854	123602	26663	143216	262786
81 TRANSFERRED IMPORTS	0	0	0	0	0	0	0	0	0
82 VALUE ADDED	898984	427341	353574	6589686	729014	592145	143439	1051472	1465154
83 SECONDARY TRANSFERS-IN	0	0	0	0	0	0	0	0	0
84 INVENTORY DEPLETION	0	0	0	0	0	0	0	0	0
85 SCRAP PRODUCTION	0	0	0	0	0	0	0	0	0
86 SCRAP PURCHASED	38955	34650	17248	-143116	42140	-71943	8228	-99454	-63068
87 STATE TOTAL PRODUCTION	8269079	4969868	3965728	73960608	6559731	10460441	1690763	4225484	17537840

TABLE C-20

1963 STATE TOTAL FINAL DEMAND
(THOUSANDS OF CURRENT DOLLARS)

INDUSTRY TITLE	10 GEORGIA	11 IDAHO	12 ILLINOIS	13 INDIANA	14 IOWA	15 KANSAS	16 KENTUCKY	17 LOUISIANA	18 MAINE
1 LIVESTOCK, PRDTS.	50506	21977	102592	45086	32400	52065	48832	41222	7428
2 OTHER AGRICULTURE PRDTS.	146255	15544	279673	155134	367878	4567	188652	958585	2814
3 FORESTRY, FISHERIES	3160	658	25146	10144	5503	4890	4620	3761	-1720
4 AGRI.,FORES.,FISH. SERV.	547	-73	-713	-96	-241	8	186	1110	-37
5 IRON, FERRO. ORES MINING	0	0	4047	0	0	0	0	9106	0
6 NONFERROUS ORES MINING	0	12159	9956	-258	0	8411	164	0	0
7 COAL MINING	3146	452	23438	6790	3855	2975	7241	2548	1547
8 CRUDE PETRO.,NATURAL GAS	0	0	327	47	0	615	118	5767	0
9 STONE, CLAY MINING	1289	-60	617	33	-277	-68	125	3938	-86
10 CHEM.,FERT. MIN. MINING	1357	114	2714	484	366	293	299	6465	140
11 NEW CONSTRUCTION	1184579	177637	2996040	1139772	614663	665160	783277	1535151	161994
12 MAINT., REPAIR CONSTR.	102799	19020	244581	86763	57844	61803	60754	68306	25905
13 ORDNANCE, ACCESSORIES	22148	4669	178640	280029	59024	29802	10309	71221	18665
14 FOOD, KINDRED PRDTS.	881434	203578	3020162	1275150	721945	600342	652339	997374	279178
15 TOBACCO MANUFACTURES	94963	16158	282239	120893	66385	56987	75864	76751	28094
16 FABRICS	22489	2698	37577	15638	8474	7325	10105	14555	4724
17 TEXTILE PRDTS.	33992	3437	69636	29769	14892	13109	10416	13985	5943
18 APPAREL	237166	45217	847805	354595	180199	160439	174469	195977	66445
19 MISC. TEXTILE PRDTS.	28992	5472	89592	36840	19130	16803	20272	24086	7393
20 LUMBER, WOOD PRDTS.	8911	2800	15489	7193	3727	2768	5371	14997	3753
21 WOODEN CONTAINERS	53	3	35	10	93	3	41	397	5
22 HOUSEHOLD FURNITURE	59259	10458	204634	85976	42222	37379	43838	47684	14702
23 OTHER FURNITURE	25612	4680	102298	37828	19582	15600	17930	21975	6403
24 PAPER, ALLIED PRDTS.	46958	5436	81711	33622	18277	15794	19960	94039	12709
25 PAPERBOARD CONTAINERS	3914	510	10833	4206	2119	2042	2070	4823	731
26 PRINTING, PUBLISHING	71125	14112	247332	99378	53487	48199	48164	54871	20603
27 CHEMICALS,SELECT. PRDTS.	60137	30524	104496	34387	14603	17485	72625	129621	4305
28 PLASTICS, SYNTHETICS	2874	45	6994	766	1147	341	2683	28250	1071
29 DRUGS, COSMETICS	120216	22523	347688	153039	78318	68563	86001	111323	27708
30 PAINT, ALLIED PRDTS.	1411	85	7557	1362	932	462	1604	2718	175
31 PETROLEUM, RELATED INDS.	150552	32210	522946	251724	132338	127246	124117	336728	50404
32 RUBBER, MISC. PLASTICS	42314	8055	138475	65737	28759	23987	28862	38942	10878
33 LEATHER TANNING, PRDTS.	23	1	1080	5	1	8	12	2131	5
34 FOOTWEAR, LEATHER PRDTS.	52161	11297	186452	80528	42124	36861	40415	43359	14560
35 GLASS, GLASS PRDTS.	6259	1022	23843	10697	3657	3192	4028	8490	1291
36 STONE, CLAY PRDTS.	6222	977	20221	9516	4432	4115	3905	10331	1307
37 PRIMARY IRON, STEEL MFR.	3071	52	19832	15968	824	411	1750	31348	1097
38 PRIMARY NONFERROUS MFR.	1282	1039	20686	14805	1823	-25	1114	41312	914

39 METAL CONTAINERS	848	70	6957	772	262	170	173	1941	228
40 FABRICATED METAL PRDTS.	17469	2337	47250	21209	8175	9246	13975	38388	4113
41 SCREW MACH. PRDTS., ETC.	5918	1034	28902	9927	3952	3248	4766	5331	1325
42 OTHER FAB. METAL PRDTS.	16336	3175	70034	26595	11577	9851	14260	23220	4945
43 ENGINES, TURBINES	15936	1898	40020	24148	6071	6601	11077	30301	1825
44 FARM MACH., EQUIP.	45230	23677	148669	70310	141818	58785	41837	39720	10075
45 CONSTRUC. MACH., EQUIP.	35207	6339	177330	37610	22010	25931	34583	162257	5449
46 MATERIAL HANDLING MACH.	11946	2354	63021	21541	7567	6278	9167	15291	3650
47 METALWORKING MACHINERY	28293	4868	154695	84381	22330	15177	24501	19685	7987
48 SPECIAL MACH., EQUIP.	69447	7430	142507	51385	23484	17818	28936	58463	26574
49 GENERAL MACH., EQUIP.	26390	4892	117951	66681	15969	15826	28478	46443	8053
50 MACHINE SHOP PRDTS.	3679	199	5763	3339	944	1390	898	969	249
51 OFFICE, COMPUT. MACHINES	29191	5717	146193	51180	22179	18066	22266.	31460	9279
52 SERVICE IND. MACHINES	35116	4784	115082	39169	20935	16855	22042	33514	6484
53 ELECT. TRANSMISS. EQUIP.	60763	7571	147316	68902	24832	22874	36508	40253	7261
54 HOUSEHOLD APPLIANCES	59040	12171	202408	91369	48280	34312	59753	51282	14966
55 ELECTRIC LIGHTING EQUIP.	9943	2177	38231	16202	7891	6638	7844	10159	2527
56 RADIO, TV, ETC., EQUIP.	93663	20051	636433	268646	121472	53559	53435	67906	16945
57 ELECTRONIC COMPONENTS	6467	1239	30859	13260	7058	4308	5881	6990	3302
58 MISC. ELECTRICAL MACH.	12474	2485	43411	36788	8411	7534	8241	9618	2778
59 MOTOR VEHICLES, EQUIP.	399039	92907	1585676	760105	345271	285265	292008	373062	95736
60 AIRCRAFT, PARTS	399711	5906	120379	199013	14975	330233	8934	54579	8382
61 OTHER TRANSPORT. EQUIP.	59362	17451	191880	57863	26230	34368	30803	95440	23657
62 PROFESS., SCIEN. INSTRU.	24521	3951	112362	38581	15944	13644	17980	30292	7313
63 MEDICAL, PHOTO. EQUIP.	17894	4011	79069	27055	14027	12031	12591	17300	5573
64 MISC. MANUFACTURING	65860	15512	251330	100169	51419	44285	48468	59551	18976
65 TRANSPORT., WAREHOUSING	222389	45451	855210	289714	144948	137404	146202	466201	62224
66 COMMUNICA.,EXC. BRDCAST.	123446	23550	390873	157152	86256	77747	83103	94834	34403
67 RADIO, TV BROADCASTING	1432	53	2132	1677	286	228	1406	1469	73
68 ELEC.,GAS,WATER,SAN.SER.	248149	45724	768765	337373	186017	163215	180843	196217	58553
69 WHOLESALE, RETAIL TRADE	1525179	324715	5204152	2222185	1229327	1038267	1148147	1420342	440754
70 FINANCE, INSURANCE	284169	56938	1061113	435851	228013	195473	210010	237088	81399
71 REAL ESTATE, RENTAL	863780	191069	3373228	1375604	724331	629908	614014	714467	298921
72 HOTELS, PERSONAL SERV.	231940	42935	721406	273836	144208	129102	162181	186186	65123
73 BUSINESS SERVICES	114775	20980	409884	129382	71664	69997	70141	79071	22865
74 RESEARCH, DEVELOPMENT	0	0	0	0	0	0	0	0	0
75 AUTO. REPAIR, SERVICES	128911	28639	380591	166920	89545	77294	99109	106562	32167
76 AMUSEMENTS	69139	16965	290330	108506	56350	48845	52703	60316	21362
77 MED.,EDUC. SERVICES	560746	101266	1862923	776549	406606	355126	406918	459813	141963
78 FEDERAL GOVT. ENTERPRISE	23218	4473	68449	27242	15166	14318	14760	16472	6003
79 STATE, LOCAL GOVT. ENT.	16970	3717	47424	19051	10687	9626	12017	13150	3755
80 DIRECT ALLOCATED IMPORTS	224896	32758	455595	177059	92990	121942	143036	132668	50623
81 TRANSFERRED IMPORTS	0	0	0	0	0	0	0	0	0
82 VALUE ADDED	1464026	165644	2480670	994623	539931	705365	787329	861568	266005
83 SECONDARY TRANSFERS-IN	0	0	0	0	0	0	0	0	0
84 INVENTORY DEPLETION	0	0	0	0	0	0	0	0	0
85 SCRAP PRODUCTION	0	0	0	0	0	0	0	0	0
86 SCRAP PURCHASED	-18639	2523	-87983	113395	93925	67835	43309	39568	2615
87 STATE TOTAL PRODUCTION	11111443	2036094	33265152	14255879	7713838	6985938	7567168	11462651	2667506

TABLE C-20

1963 STATE TOTAL FINAL DEMAND
(THOUSANDS OF CURRENT DOLLARS)

INDUSTRY TITLE	19 MARYLAND	20 MASSA-CHUSETTS	21 MICHIGAN	22 MINNESOTA	23 MISSISSIPPI	24 MISSOURI	25 MONTANA	26 NEBRASKA	27 NEVADA
1 LIVESTOCK, PRDTS.	30698	51002	70493	48486	25890	58521	26457	61139	9989
2 OTHER AGRICULTURE PRDTS.	166372	96188	347555	294223	178234	52343	18290	9689	11674
3 FORESTRY, FISHERIES	6151	7988	19642	7491	129	8819	1010	2917	950
4 AGRI.,FORES.,FISH. SERV.	307	-371	1679	-435	-69	-27	-10	-142	-1
5 IRON, FERRO. ORES MINING	1011	1012	18209	3024	1012	-1	1216	0	0
6 NONFERROUS ORES MINING	645	0	3842	0	0	6676	-4258	0	4221
7 COAL MINING	76356	6084	51279	11342	1790	5910	470	1933	201
8 CRUDE PETRO.,NATURAL GAS	1	0	1245	0	286	1	112	88	0
9 STONE, CLAY MINING	1051	-546	1321	-295	-131	132	-8	-165	-298
10 CHEM.,FERT. MIN. MINING	1377	903	5236	1551	235	425	100	259	70
11 NEW CONSTRUCTION	1522868	1845402	2302047	997444	392207	1167957	215578	386080	614917
12 MAINT., REPAIR CONSTR.	90827	150624	186479	84274	47975	86352	19394	44161	12970
13 ORDNANCE, ACCESSORIES	72261	113809	331474	232003	11480	174790	4472	6144	3825
14 FOOD, KINDRED PRDTS.	907546	1713799	2298270	945420	412763	1160896	206576	377436	116629
15 TOBACCO MANUFACTURES	129057	165659	207055	84648	42725	110614	18182	34407	9047
16 FABRICS	21002	22613	34545	11918	5940	13808	2651	4319	1510
17 TEXTILE PRDTS.	20684	49119	52932	19831	6643	25767	3434	7571	2249
18 APPAREL	272738	466087	616195	240294	99308	309164	44945	92604	27790
19 MISC. TEXTILE PRDTS.	32439	51123	79546	25511	12497	33084	5420	9764	3214
20 LUMBER, WOOD PRDTS.	10283	10788	18570	5904	6275	5805	7571	1869	636
21 WOODEN CONTAINERS	19	20	16	53	48	22	1	2	0
22 HOUSEHOLD FURNITURE	65479	100709	146779	56685	25589	72874	10345	21846	6936
23 OTHER FURNITURE	25070	51340	71749	28906	9858	37553	4970	10718	4277
24 PAPER, ALLIED PRDTS.	35347	53757	70091	26792	17610	30607	9327	9536	3027
25 PAPERBOARD CONTAINERS	4852	7340	9137	2967	1300	3504	487	927	315
26 PRINTING, PUBLISHING	77801	130829	188363	73173	28825	88718	15572	28394	8980
27 CHEMICALS,SELECT. PRDTS.	61092	27777	116443	28547	40891	41821	8050	7290	10973
28 PLASTICS, SYNTHETICS	29224	4841	27815	4370	1148	314	1046	86	25
29 DRUGS, COSMETICS	126322	174380	263378	104180	55167	132502	23417	39723	12666
30 PAINT, ALLIED PRDTS.	2304	2018	5088	794	229	2314	84	227	57
31 PETROLEUM, RELATED INDS.	177875	270985	405985	166945	80827	208841	37403	67254	18413
32 RUBBER, MISC. PLASTICS	52703	75143	123481	38924	18601	44486	8978	13837	4875
33 LEATHER TANNING, PRDTS.	1078	1082	3194	3	6	10	3	5	2
34 FOOTWEAR, LEATHER PRDTS.	57056	92359	138098	54402	23509	70745	11175	21660	6536
35 GLASS, GLASS PRDTS.	8364	9713	25347	7393	2377	7251	1026	1795	631
36 STONE, CLAY PRDTS.	8401	10251	25181	8066	2398	7036	1011	3019	849
37 PRIMARY IRON, STEEL MFR.	29405	6877	47900	6559	2161	2052	1054	178	32
38 PRIMARY NONFERROUS MFR.	21458	6381	31684	2729	2880	1115	7183	1308	861

39 METAL CONTAINERS	1811	506	3965	899	62	1508	23	267	8
40 FABRICATED METAL PRDTS.	18404	20055	51739	13277	7951	18397	3953	4328	2496
41 SCREW MACH. PRDTS., ETC.	6357	10934	36603	7750	2849	6886	1051	1886	647
42 OTHER FAB. METAL PRDTS.	20755	32993	71169	18845	8140	22281	4324	5567	2382
43 ENGINES, TURBINES	13608	13265	101179	13199	6933	15260	4739	1872	3744
44 FARM MACH., EQUIP.	21447	14809	121117	94642	40114	65072	23196	64375	4160
45 CONSTRUC. MACH., EQUIP.	41870	39872	192437	45162	19005	38468	16584	11593	10690
46 MATERIAL HANDLING MACH.	11447	22787	65127	12261	6127	14883	3475	3497	2322
47 METALWORKING MACHINERY	37034	63318	211558	30532	13125	45331	5539	8112	3463
48 SPECIAL MACH., EQUIP.	38509	68569	131799	38718	22981	39679	7688	11247	4111
49 GENERAL MACH., EQUIP.	28093	54477	122557	26556	12683	34896	7355	7676	4751
50 MACHINE SHOP PRDTS.	1295	3170	6444	1691	545	3487	234	401	99
51 OFFICE, COMPUT. MACHINES	36203	82789	123580	82918	11753	46254	7061	11561	4778
52 SERVICE IND. MACHINES	37474	47276	89838	34895	12028	42134	5385	10860	3589
53 ELECT. TRANSMISS. EQUIP.	42415	67415	96899	37518	19389	68548	9317	10116	17260
54 HOUSEHOLD APPLIANCES	58023	84348	151566	59204	28086	67516	11872	20707	6546
55 ELECTRIC LIGHTING EQUIP.	11379	18077	31195	11115	4921	13618	2128	3913	1346
56 RADIO, TV, ETC., EQUIP.	306439	529900	208127	124602	34034	162598	19019	62440	27800
57 ELECTRONIC COMPONENTS	10356	46969	35493	10275	2608	7822	2126	3218	960
58 MISC. ELECTRICAL MACH.	14966	22378	44586	11819	4870	15591	3247	3831	1854
59 MOTOR VEHICLES, EQUIP.	439039	595925	1817918	508289	173993	608996	92195	178068	60684
60 AIRCRAFT, PARTS	73737	186549	127310	34469	7559	799064	4089	4359	4497
61 OTHER TRANSPORT. EQUIP.	65963	73397	134761	55923	81730	98477	13858	14200	13334
62 PROFESS., SCIEN. INSTRU.	26017	85728	94994	26690	9642	29853	6884	8086	3488
63 MEDICAL, PHOTO. EQUIP.	20426	40814	53395	21364	6983	26662	5110	7285	3261
64 MISC. MANUFACTURING	77833	126734	188254	71752	27471	88831	16299	26290	13216
65 TRANSPORT., WAREHOUSING	353819	438535	600091	345019	95197	268590	48871	80281	28199
66 COMMUNICA.,EXC. BRDCAST.	122040	223484	276294	112944	49561	150217	24107	47398	16055
67 RADIO, TV BROADCASTING	288	399	2032	367	157	1516	71	111	24
68 ELEC.,GAS,WATER,SAN.SER.	241031	336639	575952	236648	111071	307381	46819	97954	25737
69 WHOLESALE, RETAIL TRADE	1625247	2724316	3883232	1570558	687882	2006136	333687	635256	197931
70 FINANCE, INSURANCE	343391	548191	763204	299105	119115	385012	58369	117398	39682
71 REAL ESTATE, RENTAL	950015	1978991	2402853	965887	354197	1272377	192579	376918	122739
72 HOTELS, PERSONAL SERV.	239386	390611	485077	206641	95660	266464	45814	79873	93710
73 BUSINESS SERVICES	107380	168582	269384	105824	44543	139254	20680	40781	15484
74 RESEARCH, DEVELOPMENT	0	0	0	0	0	0	0	0	0
75 AUTO. REPAIR, SERVICES	145178	185379	281758	114512	56523	145967	28361	46214	16717
76 AMUSEMENTS	90126	160659	199586	77164	26451	100722	16657	29920	47943
77 MED.,EDUC. SERVICES	645105	1084812	1358754	542751	238686	692451	101540	205845	68657
78 FEDERAL GOVT. ENTERPRISE	22284	39407	49141	20644	9512	26246	4582	8910	2945
79 STATE, LOCAL GOVT. ENT.	17949	22356	32104	14379	7182	19385	4058	5979	2270
80 DIRECT ALLOCATED IMPORTS	178317	259394	308254	126023	80492	192070	39099	70929	25458
81 TRANSFERRED IMPORTS	0	0	0	0	0	0	0	0	0
82 VALUE ADDED	1200371	1471310	1831932	751977	566420	973520	215487	399149	130069
83 SECONDARY TRANSFERS-IN	0	0	0	0	0	0	0	0	0
84 INVENTORY DEPLETION	0	0	0	0	0	0	0	0	0
85 SCRAP PRODUCTION	0	0	0	0	0	0	0	0	0
86 SCRAP PURCHASED	-56469	-276307	73047	84373	53556	-31807	21648	18728	-27572
87 STATE TOTAL PRODUCTION	11833880	17886896	26053648	10593298	4720399	13270411	2191915	4015276	1906583

TABLE C-20

1963 STATE TOTAL FINAL DEMAND
(THOUSANDS OF CURRENT DOLLARS)

INDUSTRY TITLE	28 NEW HAMPSHIRE	29 NEW JERSEY	30 NEW MEXICO	31 NEW YORK	32 NORTH CAROLINA	33 NORTH DAKOTA	34 OHIO	35 OKLAHOMA	36 OREGON
1 LIVESTOCK, PRDTS.	5876	58196	17129	173861	48623	39156	74145	46366	30702
2 OTHER AGRICULTURE PRDTS.	7033	137752	19379	473464	104930	-52247	244466	789	123477
3 FORESTRY, FISHERIES	1265	16484	1940	58268	4345	2086	22662	4623	-15884
4 AGRI.,FORES.,FISH. SERV.	59	-148	153	-746	312	-65	11	285	45
5 IRON, FERRO. ORES MINING	0	0	1569	13152	15	3035	3035	0	1012
6 NONFERROUS ORES MINING	0	4148	-33327	2999	-418	0	-1383	9324	43457
7 COAL MINING	974	8900	643	26314	3822	7912	20510	1969	1161
8 CRUDE PETRO.,NATURAL GAS	0	0	665	2325	0	107	37	1124	1
9 STONE, CLAY MINING	-49	-344	-26	7467	428	-300	-95	-134	973
10 CHEM.,FERT. MIN. MINING	91	945	78	19944	1454	1141	2189	209	1319
11 NEW CONSTRUCTION	159572	1927017	437185	5045863	1000997	186738	2943049	970743	707139
12 MAINT., REPAIR CONSTR.	19454	156809	29003	547390	104801	22036	198839	61166	50046
13 ORDNANCE, ACCESSORIES	3288	71759	31041	210598	36739	2698	477462	13937	12298
14 FOOD, KINDRED PRDTS.	195324	2189231	253912	6053628	971226	170929	2718668	583212	605210
15 TOBACCO MANUFACTURES	19826	209995	21015	864690	123837	13001	258650	63554	54545
16 FABRICS	2669	23935	3500	280198	33286	2697	34193	8965	9215
17 TEXTILE PRDTS.	4744	58291	4790	162315	19153	2898	65790	10725	11097
18 APPAREL	50982	626183	61876	1691497	262080	34662	768463	166273	141058
19 MISC. TEXTILE PRDTS.	5570	75338	7330	201427	38015	3616	80157	18647	16954
20 LUMBER, WOOD PRDTS.	1517	8150	1600	59355	10389	1784	13230	3880	30621
21 WOODEN CONTAINERS	10	2818	1	2100	22	1	28	2	261
22 HOUSEHOLD FURNITURE	11614	129061	14061	345048	73360	7750	180853	40588	33360
23 OTHER FURNITURE	4762	55381	6421	212252	29797	4369	82158	15779	15580
24 PAPER, ALLIED PRDTS.	6401	58427	7217	247217	46147	5755	76783	18556	27233
25 PAPERBOARD CONTAINERS	616	7533	781	29204	3441	391	9135	2019	1629
26 PRINTING, PUBLISHING	15180	162805	21061	561348	74587	13424	217127	46372	45732
27 CHEMICALS,SELECT. PRDTS.	2414	73148	5089	472654	44209	10450	101407	8677	17094
28 PLASTICS, SYNTHETICS	240	4921	60	241760	4142	5035	8988	168	2192
29 DRUGS, COSMETICS	19769	243856	29807	809611	132442	17421	308997	79108	69862
30 PAINT, ALLIED PRDTS.	135	5900	134	22999	894	83	5144	441	424
31 PETROLEUM, RELATED INDS.	34651	361215	45872	1020951	177015	39821	496092	131348	100884
32 RUBBER, MISC. PLASTICS	7942	87701	10667	367268	46774	9256	178861	27062	27600
33 LEATHER TANNING, PRDTS.	4	15	6	21258	19	2	16	11	1064
34 FOOTWEAR, LEATHER PRDTS.	11468	120389	15045	323260	59295	8138	170966	36771	34172
35 GLASS, GLASS PRDTS.	981	16469	1475	86482	6343	2714	27397	4909	4432
36 STONE, CLAY PRDTS.	1190	14041	1370	96897	6478	2727	21366	3365	4066
37 PRIMARY IRON, STEEL MFR.	326	3248	67	234077	2443	6042	31965	400	3657
38 PRIMARY NONFERROUS MFR.	298	17005	-152	218865	1980	3791	21067	434	14175

39 METAL CONTAINERS	14	4431	22	16585	163	39	2440	312	340
40 FABRICATED METAL PRDTS.	1954	42007	4776	177471	17571	4770	50809	11793	10423
41 SCREW MACH. PRDTS., ETC.	1090	14901	1514	46505	6125	3911	27086	3668	3402
42 OTHER FAB. METAL PRDTS.	2944	39761	4125	226935	18970	6180	62488	10805	12739
43 ENGINES, TURBINES	1168	42613	4546	177841	17696	8792	41253	10253	13050
44 FARM MACH., EQUIP.	3098	19428	12489	154471	62633	44026	81136	33353	25388
45 CONSTRUC. MACH., EQUIP.	3842	56185	27898	529569	32853	25018	120160	40029	32897
46 MATERIAL HANDLING MACH.	1926	29588	3012	116540	16849	3336	52827	6919	10559
47 METALWORKING MACHINERY	5646	76139	4659	420121	25081	7569	175595	14345	16394
48 SPECIAL MACH., EQUIP.	8202	100324	4918	493906	101166	10692	131736	15097	37307
49 GENERAL MACH., EQUIP.	5515	81014	6186	339291	32680	7585	132364	16662	18777
50 MACHINE SHOP PRDTS.	167	3190	351	8119	1237	239	11423	970	754
51 OFFICE, COMPUT. MACHINES	5680	105829	7143	578451	33488	7304	119470	18411	20202
52 SERVICE IND. MACHINES	3957	58438	5283	309352	35583	7147	92058	20657	17143
53 ELECT. TRANSMISS. EQUIP.	9971	88012	11561	463772	59534	10558	147523	31314	33701
54 HOUSEHOLD APPLIANCES	10579	106322	15272	355698	73646	10196	207572	39166	36392
55 ELECTRIC LIGHTING EQUIP.	1805	22800	2789	105119	11132	2691	35087	6671	7326
56 RADIO, TV, ETC., EQUIP.	40341	703015	26353	1468126	187270	17465	315321	111931	56237
57 ELECTRONIC COMPONENTS	5690	35574	1777	187492	12572	2768	24513	4002	7270
58 MISC. ELECTRICAL MACH.	2024	28957	2856	112621	16432	2417	46124	7203	9270
59 MOTOR VEHICLES, EQUIP.	69020	744991	107084	2536554	438916	146081	1529796	270447	258530
60 AIRCRAFT, PARTS	2067	186259	5800	1115119	27180	5926	776892	121857	47177
61 OTHER TRANSPORT. EQUIP.	6803	122346	17449	365612	59612	10500	164235	38497	49742
62 PROFESS., SCIEN. INSTRU.	4049	84136	6922	432995	27840	7085	82506	15490	19992
63 MEDICAL, PHOTO. EQUIP.	3564	46755	5628	305711	18777	3845	64323	11633	13629
64 MISC. MANUFACTURING	13894	161548	20413	565418	72317	11771	221799	44946	50143
65 TRANSPORT., WAREHOUSING	46087	555973	63339	1952144	216615	54560	937082	143329	166368
66 COMMUNICA.,EXC. BRDCAST.	25938	277556	34385	801990	125385	18584	345754	79980	69627
67 RADIO, TV BROADCASTING	44	528	112	2882	1563	73	2000	208	1402
68 ELEC.,GAS,WATER,SAN.SER.	42073	422035	62547	1141505	273067	39820	706528	165716	132666
69 WHOLESALE, RETAIL TRADE	318805	3505549	425176	9892628	1710575	275580	4718924	1044013	979611
70 FINANCE, INSURANCE	61673	721387	79022	1894775	307860	43963	943024	197084	182585
71 REAL ESTATE, RENTAL	221579	2501314	266748	6810344	892721	134079	3030935	595609	618597
72 HOTELS, PERSONAL SERV.	53200	497475	64055	1446047	237507	30949	608941	154799	128157
73 BUSINESS SERVICES	19409	196982	34773	795279	110328	17299	303627	72260	63125
74 RESEARCH, DEVELOPMENT	0	0	0	0	0	0	0	0	0
75 AUTO. REPAIR, SERVICES	23682	237920	37019	625881	146508	18042	350486	91079	85079
76 AMUSEMENTS	18600	217199	23469	784816	71902	9895	253330	48304	53897
77 MED.,EDUC. SERVICES	111404	1291123	148480	3509993	598378	77665	1679930	388026	324545
78 FEDERAL GOVT. ENTERPRISE	4628	47064	6813	136096	22373	3552	60354	14515	13562
79 STATE, LOCAL GOVT. ENT.	2652	26162	5730	75596	17271	2489	41807	11910	10999
80 DIRECT ALLOCATED IMPORTS	34613	328737	62300	806238	227828	32046	382807	124914	82831
81 TRANSFERRED IMPORTS	0	0	0	0	0	0	0	0	0
82 VALUE ADDED	216952	1599258	410162	4887959	1371703	212762	2045389	817818	466472
83 SECONDARY TRANSFERS-IN	0	0	0	0	0	0	0	0	0
84 INVENTORY DEPLETION	0	0	0	0	0	0	0	0	0
85 SCRAP PRODUCTION	0	0	0	0	0	0	0	0	0
86 SCRAP PURCHASED	-3816	-198609	37740	-637623	64925	37768	-5468	58792	25379
87 STATE TOTAL PRODUCTION	2008729	22168784	3091135	67743200	11277254	1956090	30984400	7296452	6441548

TABLE C-20

1963 STATE TOTAL FINAL DEMAND
(THOUSANDS OF CURRENT DOLLARS)

INDUSTRY TITLE	37 PENNSYL-VANIA	38 RHODE ISLAND	39 SOUTH CAROLINA	40 SOUTH DAKOTA	41 TENNESSEE	42 TEXAS	43 UTAH	44 VERMONT	45 VIRGINIA
1 LIVESTOCK, PRDTS.	86691	7532	23766	64953	40299	107050	10977	16	29523
2 OTHER AGRICULTURE PRDTS.	295784	13981	73119	34583	125409	498018	17551	7113	132472
3 FORESTRY, FISHERIES	28425	1634	1758	1136	5410	19750	2106	597	3755
4 AGRI.,FORES.,FISH. SERV.	381	32	190	-85	-160	1655	91	-74	814
5 IRON, FERRO. ORES MINING	1040	0	0	0	0	6975	0	1012	2024
6 NONFERROUS ORES MINING	11350	0	0	0	7708	17265	24423	0	2203
7 COAL MINING	73186	1035	1902	965	3238	8275	1028	678	103301
8 CRUDE PETRO.,NATURAL GAS	72	0	0	0	0	10481	152	0	1
9 STONE, CLAY MINING	935	-51	1006	-55	-27	5621	-497	119	1127
10 CHEM.,FERT. MIN. MINING	2262	106	1198	114	416	9273	113	83	2422
11 NEW CONSTRUCTION	2211964	237175	327279	203777	1008802	4040992	460565	66006	1614012
12 MAINT., REPAIR CONSTR.	221139	20384	49325	20600	73565	257678	26323	10315	121340
13 ORDNANCE, ACCESSORIES	240972	8642	5742	3748	114771	173523	53123	19886	92811
14 FOOD, KINDRED PRDTS.	3460206	267485	479987	159550	773884	2662832	260143	116769	1017847
15 TOBACCO MANUFACTURES	371918	27024	56267	13927	85739	259979	22243	12381	158586
16 FABRICS	44921	4472	24664	1768	13932	36978	3657	4161	26894
17 TEXTILE PRDTS.	88973	7267	12875	2967	14583	45529	5062	3235	21887
18 APPAREL	927435	70247	125906	35337	220177	675208	64537	27877	281668
19 MISC. TEXTILE PRDTS.	105587	7495	15375	3831	29081	78166	7688	2956	35365
20 LUMBER, WOOD PRDTS.	20908	993	5898	870	6711	17192	1412	5194	15148
21 WOODEN CONTAINERS	82	39	20	1	43	114	1	3	30
22 HOUSEHOLD FURNITURE	200376	15167	30875	8150	55162	162356	15606	8219	72049
23 OTHER FURNITURE	89818	6684	12048	4224	23960	26018	4518	19112	24396
24 PAPER, ALLIED PRDTS.	98577	6920	30281	4047	26267	91394	7234	9393	41996
25 PAPERBOARD CONTAINERS	11974	745	1862	353	2591	8727	740	1416	4477
26 PRINTING, PUBLISHING	252554	19869	37196	11693	55914	198984	21366	8916	85901
27 CHEMICALS,SELECT. PRDTS.	70967	3450	43835	2268	159473	349656	7734	4369	77102
28 PLASTICS, SYNTHETICS	24262	268	4478	35	6209	121826	63	2069	44287
29 DRUGS, COSMETICS	367079	26517	66261	16329	107562	347908	30088	12295	137385
30 PAINT, ALLIED PRDTS.	4616	273	327	85	777	7549	149	131	1865
31 PETROLEUM, RELATED INDS.	610466	42343	86886	29365	144049	845293	51209	21406	201337
32 RUBBER, MISC. PLASTICS	132797	11968	24652	5462	37224	114698	11096	7794	49913
33 LEATHER TANNING, PRDTS.	21	2	10	2	7	1105	5	1062	1092
34 FOOTWEAR, LEATHER PRDTS.	187600	14252	28875	8560	48891	148484	15764	5808	61016
35 GLASS, GLASS PRDTS.	28220	2044	3817	746	6891	18301	1542	1516	8853
36 STONE, CLAY PRDTS.	23239	1216	3670	781	4831	24778	1707	1806	10872
37 PRIMARY IRON, STEEL MFR.	50499	1143	2267	63	951	42688	1030	2081	35700
38 PRIMARY NONFERROUS MFR.	21079	4070	1129	-344	4153	44810	1268	2547	22503

39 METAL CONTAINERS	3136	29	67	31	351	2927	98	133	257
40 FABRICATED METAL PRDTS.	56656	2300	9611	1418	13892	37866	2027	15351	18919
41 SCREW MACH. PRDTS., ETC.	25245	1866	2948	768	5629	16975	1661	559	5823
42 OTHER FAB. METAL PRDTS.	65129	4433	9491	2154	15506	60959	3751	7971	22872
43 ENGINES, TURBINES	41147	1188	9173	1009	5832	31668	1827	11005	12742
44 FARM MACH., EQUIP.	56324	1858	22930	35800	33978	22759	6478	27666	37324
45 CONSTRUC. MACH., EQUIP.	117497	4679	16326	5944	26235	146893	7329	37647	45520
46 MATERIAL HANDLING MACH.	54461	2463	7437	1217	10634	13455	1222	13041	12802
47 METALWORKING MACHINERY	135888	8699	12063	1965	30284	44377	5189	25144	32075
48 SPECIAL MACH., EQUIP.	131362	9864	73627	3329	36796	55065	4071	62356	46079
49 GENERAL MACH., EQUIP.	117321	6335	17614	2292	29502	66085	2784	32267	24835
50 MACHINE SHOP PRDTS.	3513	477	549	236	2077	4669	1658	668	968
51 OFFICE, COMPUT. MACHINES	138726	7671	14588	4128	29411	26343	4403	32727	27061
52 SERVICE IND. MACHINES	92362	5825	16449	3894	29580	62407	3528	20339	36690
53 ELECT. TRANSMISS. EQUIP.	160160	6267	28863	4046	27190	43863	4635	42713	39048
54 HOUSEHOLD APPLIANCES	180541	12919	35368	8472	60899	153688	15839	8635	65259
55 ELECTRIC LIGHTING EQUIP.	36128	2812	5203	1677	8625	29239	2718	3054	11373
56 RADIO, TV, ETC., EQUIP.	348763	23283	43974	13627	103658	250088	24579	43733	133599
57 ELECTRONIC COMPONENTS	59175	3413	9548	931	6864	33436	3117	5245	23379
58 MISC. ELECTRICAL MACH.	43947	3026	5835	1459	11041	26414	2671	5394	12389
59 MOTOR VEHICLES, EQUIP.	1283335	85047	193339	75092	347751	927810	97805	128683	452465
60 AIRCRAFT, PARTS	320627	3462	11873	2956	28610	658843	48410	37631	28303
61 OTHER TRANSPORT. EQUIP.	221162	7832	20835	7101	43307	94119	11789	27471	256475
62 PROFESS., SCIEN. INSTRU.	134901	8914	14414	2754	21032	52646	4759	19479	23489
63 MEDICAL, PHOTO. EQUIP.	64840	4694	8561	3017	16223	42121	5115	8055	19915
64 MISC. MANUFACTURING	245682	20542	35268	10200	60160	175002	21166	16498	78194
65 TRANSPORT., WAREHOUSING	909426	64333	110854	34958	174290	814681	63717	37674	587130
66 COMMUNICA.,EXC. BRDCAST.	432837	34816	62094	19185	97375	306204	32992	21265	137501
67 RADIO, TV BROADCASTING	2077	59	1355	68	1425	3229	121	37	1482
68 ELEC.,GAS,WATER,SAN.SER.	696564	55157	135578	41564	211429	672271	63363	23351	279269
69 WHOLESALE, RETAIL TRADE	5617629	421552	831065	263362	1366401	4162692	426805	262067	1767883
70 FINANCE, INSURANCE	1090602	81150	147604	46142	255413	829937	84713	33557	336559
71 REAL ESTATE, RENTAL	3959841	312926	442648	145122	764552	2436000	282692	139367	984045
72 HOTELS, PERSONAL SERV.	750681	57453	117962	32967	196105	657008	60045	29619	273469
73 BUSINESS SERVICES	303354	21818	53954	17230	81712	292502	32742	8943	129344
74 RESEARCH, DEVELOPMENT	0	0	0	0	0	0	0	0	0
75 AUTO. REPAIR, SERVICES	389278	28239	70925	18942	118826	366145	38899	13291	151762
76 AMUSEMENTS	305553	24934	34154	11508	62175	204753	26209	9768	80814
77 MED.,EDUC. SERVICES	1962683	150377	291135	81410	497140	1574594	153424	58020	636911
78 FEDERAL GOVT. ENTERPRISE	73074	5785	11408	3560	17106	58370	6505	2296	25984
79 STATE, LOCAL GOVT. ENT.	44545	3231	8334	2874	15691	45580	5341	1601	18817
80 DIRECT ALLOCATED IMPORTS	463807	41258	108187	29138	129338	520152	42041	17444	231922
81 TRANSFERRED IMPORTS	0	0	0	0	0	0	0	0	0
82 VALUE ADDED	2396565	227948	691010	186134	739213	3141060	353323	83733	1705103
83 SECONDARY TRANSFERS-IN	0	0	0	0	0	0	0	0	0
84 INVENTORY DEPLETION	0	0	0	0	0	0	0	0	0
85 SCRAP PRODUCTION	0	0	0	0	0	0	0	0	0
86 SCRAP PURCHASED	-24748	-24671	35044	28833	12221	183643	50179	-2045	21144
87 STATE TOTAL PRODUCTION	33880160	2578682	5364011	1798322	8953972	30835664	3143554	1761721	13380969

TABLE C-20

1963 STATE TOTAL FINAL DEMAND
(THOUSANDS OF CURRENT DOLLARS)

INDUSTRY TITLE	46 WASHINGTON	47 WEST VIRGINIA	48 WISCONSIN	49 WYOMING	50 ALASKA	51 HAWAII	52 NATIONAL TOTAL
1 LIVESTOCK, PRDTS.	43346	12442	41583	22513	5822	11510	2192511
2 OTHER AGRICULTURE PRDTS.	190305	19110	-22556	16040	4871	9114	7096348
3 FORESTRY, FISHERIES	-2918	2524	7710	743	-4740	1090	340340
4 AGRI.,FORES.,FISH. SERV.	1217	-176	-603	-23	129	218	9457
5 IRON, FERRO. ORES MINING	2024	0	1012	0	0	0	127387
6 NONFERROUS ORES MINING	-1617	0	0	0	0	0	241777
7 COAL MINING	1759	11285	6875	308	1315	389	519811
8 CRUDE PETRO.,NATURAL GAS	11	109	0	551	21	0	27251
9 STONE, CLAY MINING	724	-17	-407	52	-79	-144	26107
10 CHEM.,FERT. MIN. MINING	2609	186	717	50	82	166	88595
11 NEW CONSTRUCTION	1381119	276827	1183412	209388	174119	379980	65518976
12 MAINT., REPAIR CONSTR.	109750	29699	101470	10639	26193	43634	4923784
13 ORDNANCE, ACCESSORIES	32766	210956	81396	2207	3410	2249	5693572
14 FOOD, KINDRED PRDTS.	1022224	380087	1103126	99259	79925	197582	53179056
15 TOBACCO MANUFACTURES	92229	42702	101652	8260	5722	14808	5479279
16 FABRICS	15085	6132	14266	1389	965	2253	1004948
17 TEXTILE PRDTS.	17623	6971	24345	1839	1361	4226	1196674
18 APPAREL	233240	105749	298563	23787	17148	39314	14059141
19 MISC. TEXTILE PRDTS.	27340	12786	33412	2838	1964	4701	1633508
20 LUMBER, WOOD PRDTS.	43210	3338	6220	677	664	1140	510674
21 WOODEN CONTAINERS	22	3	26	0	1	74	7194
22 HOUSEHOLD FURNITURE	53172	27673	67827	5504	3828	12174	3267423
23 OTHER FURNITURE	16374	24811	10040	2140	4359	31393	1540380
24 PAPER, ALLIED PRDTS.	53200	11879	36705	2730	2427	5308	1948757
25 PAPERBOARD CONTAINERS	4195	1140	3985	321	328	674	198503
26 PRINTING, PUBLISHING	79198	26573	86690	7774	8318	17901	4224529
27 CHEMICALS,SELECT. PRDTS.	38717	107774	22608	1847	1772	2779	2886970
28 PLASTICS, SYNTHETICS	4423	3646	2508	23	16	40	633753
29 DRUGS, COSMETICS	116077	52544	122489	11734	8685	20615	6351163
30 PAINT, ALLIED PRDTS.	1762	224	1293	44	56	105	99012
31 PETROLEUM, RELATED INDS.	175422	77240	193459	24606	16347	30255	10099714
32 RUBBER, MISC. PLASTICS	45952	17554	48259	4208	5020	7471	2539451
33 LEATHER TANNING, PRDTS.	2137	2	7	1	7	10	41965
34 FOOTWEAR, LEATHER PRDTS.	55849	24517	67412	5836	4110	9666	3057798
35 GLASS, GLASS PRDTS.	7770	8151	6905	576	379	960	448297
36 STONE, CLAY PRDTS.	7019	2481	7595	591	334	6366	453569
37 PRIMARY IRON, STEEL MFR.	6680	3297	4737	24	1779	90	660086
38 PRIMARY NONFERROUS MFR.	36561	3538	3116	-203	1313	433	666870

39 METAL CONTAINERS	1725	519	1339	12	73	530	68045
40 FABRICATED METAL PRDTS.	18422	12905	8793	1105	1974	12755	1021014
41 SCREW MACH. PRDTS., ETC.	5655	2842	10078	600	951	969	404777
42 OTHER FAB. METAL PRDTS.	22071	10794	16492	1569	2151	8239	1223020
43 ENGINES, TURBINES	26317	9363	13920	963	2649	13024	1021803
44 FARM MACH., EQUIP.	16480	58792	17879	582	12734	63674	2269705
45 CONSTRUC. MACH., EQUIP.	72251	28137	30580	7103	6389	36879	2888133
46 MATERIAL HANDLING MACH.	10912	17376	3918	1224	1860	14545	846004
47 METALWORKING MACHINERY	31385	56869	11302	1233	2040	39641	2333636
48 SPECIAL MACH., EQUIP.	26002	57881	7335	2865	6395	39297	2659498
49 GENERAL MACH., EQUIP.	32142	29038	19104	1810	4170	32593	2055011
50 MACHINE SHOP PRDTS.	2843	2070	3723	142	102	369	109219
51 OFFICE, COMPUT. MACHINES	28504	35795	9962	4774	5452	39685	2621039
52 SERVICE IND. MACHINES	18183	28684	16593	1841	3798	30631	1828035
53 ELECT. TRANSMISS. EQUIP.	36424	41526	38679	1260	10311	57283	2737746
54 HOUSEHOLD APPLIANCES	56736	29133	71931	5999	4232	12912	3279804
55 ELECTRIC LIGHTING EQUIP.	12129	6548	11173	1087	996	3270	652716
56 RADIO, TV, ETC., EQUIP.	86003	50486	99364	6307	13804	66052	9344121
57 ELECTRONIC COMPONENTS	14047	5310	6684	532	1970	2770	888157
58 MISC. ELECTRICAL MACH.	13538	7523	12718	1240	1566	6868	792647
59 MOTOR VEHICLES, EQUIP.	398394	245128	463833	48009	47503	233508	24357072
60 AIRCRAFT, PARTS	447925	11319	14357	5174	3607	27378	9232389
61 OTHER TRANSPORT. EQUIP.	162219	33936	45089	16628	6921	80800	3857029
62 PROFESS., SCIEN. INSTRU.	31496	20240	20788	2266	3320	16268	2027577
63 MEDICAL, PHOTO. EQUIP.	20921	11527	17036	2128	2417	10405	1354192
64 MISC. MANUFACTURING	80892	35224	77696	8209	6697	24351	4238315
65 TRANSPORT., WAREHOUSING	287595	97531	368917	24919	32073	67233	15356294
66 COMMUNICA.,EXC. BRDCAST.	119021	52571	125160	12089	14462	40828	6755222
67 RADIO, TV BROADCASTING	1540	126	1555	46	25	75	44173
68 ELEC.,GAS,WATER,SAN.SER.	228519	103500	281179	23283	22448	50092	12512728
69 WHOLESALE, RETAIL TRADE	1589975	756514	1776367	163150	139771	408441	88574848
70 FINANCE, INSURANCE	304157	127738	367639	31313	22212	52821	17221712
71 REAL ESTATE, RENTAL	1004467	381593	1144971	99908	74888	215603	56140176
72 HOTELS, PERSONAL SERV.	209556	94543	244339	29726	22121	56789	12603032
73 BUSINESS SERVICES	116858	35701	117780	10785	18587	34223	6107968
74 RESEARCH, DEVELOPMENT	0	0	0	0	0	0	0
75 AUTO. REPAIR, SERVICES	138857	60966	140242	14660	10800	24501	6812825
76 AMUSEMENTS	91452	32856	93605	9184	6234	15951	5084800
77 MED., EDUC. SERVICES	534483	247829	644542	55246	39504	95270	31506192
78 FEDERAL GOVT. ENTERPRISE	24405	8068	24425	2421	3265	6334	1219238
79 STATE, LOCAL GOVT. ENT.	17545	7241	16148	2066	2209	3270	857914
80 DIRECT ALLOCATED IMPORTS	179360	55016	142825	18416	49405	73993	8822167
81 TRANSFERRED IMPORTS	0	0	0	0	0	0	0
82 VALUE ADDED	1161404	270300	818535	119873	322411	539538	52840832
83 SECONDARY TRANSFERS-IN	0	0	0	0	0	0	0
84 INVENTORY DEPLETION	0	0	0	0	0	0	0
85 SCRAP PRODUCTION	0	0	0	0	0	0	0
86 SCRAP PURCHASED	52557	27216	-40998	15976	-5736	-26504	-439417
87 STATE TOTAL PRODUCTION	11651945	4722030	10985449	1225991	1306733	3391701	609125888

TABLE C-21

1963 STATE TRANSFERS-OUT
(THOUSANDS OF CURRENT DOLLARS)

INDUSTRY TITLE	1 ALABAMA	2 ARIZONA	3 ARKANSAS	4 CALIFORNIA	5 COLORADO	6 CONNECTICUT	7 DELAWARE	8 DISTRICT OF COLUMBIA	9 FLORIDA
1 LIVESTOCK, PRDTS.	34334	18255	29804	129482	44914	8847	7754	0	22464
2 OTHER AGRICULTURE PRDTS.	37061	35817	62325	237052	30050	7700	4657	0	84300
3 FORESTRY, FISHERIES	0	0	0	0	0	0	0	0	0
4 AGRI.,FORES.,FISH. SERV.	270	144	402	766	42	38	36	0	217
5 IRON, FERRO. ORES MINING	252	10	9	560	1085	0	0	0	0
6 NONFERROUS ORES MINING	30	11783	648	227	2430	13	0	0	266
7 COAL MINING	601	2	17	0	160	0	0	0	0
8 CRUDE PETRO.,NATURAL GAS	1196	24	4138	59732	7317	0	0	0	122
9 STONE, CLAY MINING	1352	601	1667	9007	859	719	51	0	2550
10 CHEM.,FERT. MIN. MINING	0	0	1078	27931	539	0	77	0	40331
11 NEW CONSTRUCTION	0	0	0	0	0	0	0	0	0
12 MAINT., REPAIR CONSTR.	0	0	0	0	0	0	0	0	0
13 ORDNANCE, ACCESSORIES	7132	8269	9	247237	3398	11817	0	0	20960
14 FOOD, KINDRED PRDTS.	11467	3673	11634	108092	14627	6340	2961	1813	21906
15 TOBACCO MANUFACTURES	42	0	0	1	0	22	0	0	187
16 FABRICS	35516	12	1072	1654	22	12383	3350	0	586
17 TEXTILE PRDTS.	5479	15	1771	10125	61	4768	1009	0	160
18 APPAREL	4647	326	1084	11248	213	2606	675	0	1471
19 MISC. TEXTILE PRDTS.	2027	218	37	10659	464	1669	232	57	847
20 LUMBER, WOOD PRDTS.	5697	1219	6464	28178	763	682	285	30	3817
21 WOODEN CONTAINERS	640	133	1227	5874	180	313	50	0	1595
22 HOUSEHOLD FURNITURE	1382	326	3257	14559	513	1330	11	0	2577
23 OTHER FURNITURE	566	241	1010	9986	310	1576	86	0	994
24 PAPER, ALLIED PRDTS.	11731	407	6263	15237	437	3809	342	0	12291
25 PAPERBOARD CONTAINERS	533	130	1110	11830	490	2008	258	0	1948
26 PRINTING, PUBLISHING	36396	27757	22105	546307	49401	122733	10729	109498	108577
27 CHEMICALS,SELECT. PRDTS.	25169	2519	3305	47902	3577	20689	6796	176	28337
28 PLASTICS, SYNTHETICS	13140	0	103	20354	52	9585	22035	0	16136
29 DRUGS, COSMETICS	195	299	23	35763	670	17194	1008	0	1382
30 PAINT, ALLIED PRDTS.	451	171	219	17242	578	479	42	0	2391
31 PETROLEUM, RELATED INDS.	4427	366	11663	198434	6578	1434	13123	0	2753
32 RUBBER, MISC. PLASTICS	16116	439	3345	50481	9299	22318	4709	0	1743
33 LEATHER TANNING, PRDTS.	0	0	0	350	7	39	399	0	27
34 FOOTWEAR, LEATHER PRDTS.	220	11	1704	1299	944	590	145	0	482
35 GLASS, GLASS PRDTS.	141	13	278	3596	30	272	13	0	335
36 STONE, CLAY PRDTS.	9833	4231	3073	58572	5836	7601	1171	1257	15301
37 PRIMARY IRON, STEEL MFR.	56793	526	164	46253	9857	13405	9173	0	1754
38 PRIMARY NONFERROUS MFR.	14833	28668	8169	36770	624	38804	886	0	3183

39 METAL CONTAINERS	276	0	287	12413	663	102	0	0	2440
40 FABRICATED METAL PRDTS.	11925	2317	2843	56825	3332	6574	1581	323	13173
41 SCREW MACH. PRDTS., ETC.	3248	98	1052	27910	196	23651	905	0	1350
42 OTHER FAB. METAL PRDTS.	7516	827	2243	60589	3284	23728	906	0	3476
43 ENGINES, TURBINES	0	0	0	10771	580	7734	0	0	242
44 FARM MACH., EQUIP.	2344	614	597	8172	990	261	91	0	1164
45 CONSTRUC. MACH., EQUIP.	992	14	55	12727	8486	146	30	0	218
46 MATERIAL HANDLING MACH.	747	17	1103	9569	441	620	0	0	462
47 METALWORKING MACHINERY	395	246	536	15504	137	21674	388	0	1043
48 SPECIAL MACH., EQUIP.	2152	101	329	19189	852	10880	2098	0	2507
49 GENERAL MACH., EQUIP.	1260	262	1199	47273	2270	44641	75	0	1253
50 MACHINE SHOP PRDTS.	933	1105	374	24480	1274	5498	221	140	1649
51 OFFICE, COMPUT. MACHINES	20	15972	1207	79716	256	29974	0	0	6138
52 SERVICE IND. MACHINES	2034	3651	2071	16182	251	3277	448	0	1278
53 ELECT. TRANSMISS. EQUIP.	2478	207	6451	55637	5255	17873	17	0	964
54 HOUSEHOLD APPLIANCES	38	31	24786	39368	83	38155	866	0	457
55 ELECTRIC LIGHTING EQUIP.	3220	71	2382	19235	379	15555	290	0	718
56 RADIO, TV, ETC., EQUIP.	766	7364	8961	173018	185	10961	10	0	16539
57 ELECTRONIC COMPONENTS	1497	6550	13	62897	157	13426	61	0	2459
58 MISC. ELECTRICAL MACH.	1816	69	28	11553	972	4800	823	0	3781
59 MOTOR VEHICLES, EQUIP.	1825	215	380	66683	602	6168	12155	0	400
60 AIRCRAFT, PARTS	79204	18781	166	493770	18835	200740	1070	0	23163
61 OTHER TRANSPORT. EQUIP.	7697	338	2232	29532	496	5650	154	0	8841
62 PROFESS., SCIEN. INSTRU.	291	4702	5654	45582	1933	36628	1051	0	3157
63 MEDICAL, PHOTO. EQUIP.	0	91	9	11872	440	3854	0	0	1649
64 MISC. MANUFACTURING	2415	892	4587	51210	2618	38427	165	232	4168
65 TRANSPORT., WAREHOUSING	2812	1288	1570	27328	3101	2431	622	2492	7292
66 COMMUNICA.,EXC. BRDCAST.	8267	3723	3566	63040	5935	8564	1431	4577	17156
67 RADIO, TV BROADCASTING	18549	13706	8948	331218	18484	19140	4029	49830	52023
68 ELEC.,GAS,WATER,SAN.SER.	2493	1407	1081	11177	1617	1694	363	383	2983
69 WHOLESALE, RETAIL TRADE	12247	7440	6851	113477	10984	15030	3031	6712	28931
70 FINANCE, INSURANCE	11545	6624	5650	111489	10389	22792	2738	7570	26940
71 REAL ESTATE, RENTAL	140	119	66	1570	143	204	35	179	525
72 HOTELS, PERSONAL SERV.	4197	4124	2617	46930	4690	5563	844	4537	17238
73 BUSINESS SERVICES	4675	4136	1741	90938	5657	7980	1229	9305	17294
74 RESEARCH, DEVELOPMENT	0	0	0	0	0	0	0	0	0
75 AUTO. REPAIR, SERVICES	1318	916	771	12134	1225	1450	245	792	3074
76 AMUSEMENTS	1087	1336	1019	48601	2216	1796	734	1713	7821
77 MED.,EDUC. SERVICES	358	283	160	5556	519	1371	125	2128	1013
78 FEDERAL GOVT. ENTERPRISE	33671	8337	10459	127120	12899	13349	2735	30768	34665
79 STATE, LOCAL GOVT. ENT.	118803	53811	26241	612169	54642	56003	10979	14906	196508
80 DIRECT ALLOCATED IMPORTS	0	0	0	0	0	0	0	0	0
81 TRANSFERRED IMPORTS	0	0	0	0	0	0	0	0	0
82 VALUE ADDED	0	0	0	0	0	0	0	0	0
83 SECONDARY TRANSFERS-IN	0	0	0	0	0	0	0	0	0
84 INVENTORY DEPLETION	0	0	0	0	0	0	0	0	0
85 SCRAP PRODUCTION	0	0	0	0	0	0	0	0	0
86 SCRAP PURCHASED	0	0	0	0	0	0	0	0	0
87 STATE TOTAL PRODUCTION	694920	318391	329464	5067187	383790	1050147	144609	249416	918139

TABLE C-21

1963 STATE TRANSFERS-OUT
(THOUSANDS OF CURRENT DOLLARS)

INDUSTRY TITLE	10 GEORGIA	11 IDAHO	12 ILLINOIS	13 INDIANA	14 IOWA	15 KANSAS	16 KENTUCKY	17 LOUISIANA	18 MAINE
1 LIVESTOCK, PRDTS.	44687	20374	107691	67970	185957	77059	36613	16981	12324
2 OTHER AGRICULTURE PRDTS.	55459	37850	176916	97415	156274	69625	61042	42995	11731
3 FORESTRY, FISHERIES	0	0	0	0	0	0	0	0	0
4 AGRI.,FORES.,FISH. SERV.	401	45	263	146	214	101	45	123	61
5 IRON, FERRO. ORES MINING	28	8	0	0	0	0	0	0	0
6 NONFERROUS ORES MINING	8	1244	458	0	0	3	0	0	3
7 COAL MINING	1	0	1296	360	28	50	2191	0	0
8 CRUDE PETRO.,NATURAL GAS	0	0	12968	1857	0	24349	4682	136898	0
9 STONE, CLAY MINING	5066	341	4459	2372	2021	1134	2340	987	96
10 CHEM.,FERT. MIN. MINING	932	2132	3287	0	0	476	1990	30669	0
11 NEW CONSTRUCTION	0	0	0	0	0	0	0	0	0
12 MAINT., REPAIR CONSTR.	0	0	0	0	0	0	0	0	0
13 ORDNANCE, ACCESSORIES	223	328	8697	10691	6240	0	0	6713	1008
14 FOOD, KINDRED PRDTS.	22286	5352	86470	29600	47255	18177	18145	19475	4446
15 TOBACCO MANUFACTURES	26	0	32	25	0	0	1999	13	0
16 FABRICS	83929	0	2826	0	234	12	1744	0	14803
17 TEXTILE PRDTS.	48553	0	7023	879	17	15	204	544	931
18 APPAREL	8191	10	5646	1828	385	428	3073	771	534
19 MISC. TEXTILE PRDTS.	7127	41	8847	1723	461	595	1244	1449	563
20 LUMBER, WOOD PRDTS.	6325	5716	4012	4647	1195	249	2076	4316	4409
21 WOODEN CONTAINERS	2154	83	1181	362	207	76	1657	688	175
22 HOUSEHOLD FURNITURE	3313	73	7791	9939	739	498	2335	518	206
23 OTHER FURNITURE	725	41	10656	3538	1102	671	587	184	219
24 PAPER, ALLIED PRDTS.	16632	1078	13664	5138	1307	689	1325	13310	16035
25 PAPERBOARD CONTAINERS	4107	84	11840	3884	1419	1567	1248	1646	204
26 PRINTING, PUBLISHING	71691	7580	798048	146944	96435	47637	54626	35583	12616
27 CHEMICALS,SELECT. PRDTS.	23741	2666	71665	21713	4103	8064	22220	56663	1579
28 PLASTICS, SYNTHETICS	6798	0	12027	4778	10241	2054	26194	21401	52
29 DRUGS, COSMETICS	6813	0	69084	40588	3441	8851	150	732	30
30 PAINT, ALLIED PRDTS.	3307	14	22113	2512	2113	433	4666	649	28
31 PETROLEUM, RELATED INDS.	3714	30	105978	71821	795	50396	13114	135541	266
32 RUBBER, MISC. PLASTICS	4866	16	41446	33554	15062	6871	4205	332	2161
33 LEATHER TANNING, PRDTS.	147	0	943	40	0	0	91	9	784
34 FOOTWEAR, LEATHER PRDTS.	1066	15	3595	816	157	38	720	2	5647
35 GLASS, GLASS PRDTS.	489	0	4766	2987	3	18	494	508	24
36 STONE, CLAY PRDTS.	10360	1077	34299	20134	9494	10421	5706	8192	1096
37 PRIMARY IRON, STEEL MFR.	9555	70	115870	151151	3660	1284	14339	1332	67
38 PRIMARY NONFERROUS MFR.	3900	6627	53765	46518	6310	1368	5264	7235	363

39 METAL CONTAINERS	1131	47	12509	1358	13	205	143	1722	496
40 FABRICATED METAL PRDTS.	9670	710	41007	26473	7663	6258	7567	6249	1022
41 SCREW MACH. PRDTS., ETC.	4577	0	79694	23772	1938	516	3761	548	75
42 OTHER FAB. METAL PRDTS.	4067	53	92202	27754	6525	2275	12269	4474	350
43 ENGINES, TURBINES	29	0	29743	10056	5352	0	0	84	0
44 FARM MACH., EQUIP.	4151	702	70710	13513	65274	4470	7840	1318	106
45 CONSTRUC. MACH., EQUIP.	2932	127	127733	9722	16287	2828	171	2271	1176
46 MATERIAL HANDLING MACH.	1541	94	21287	1543	1612	1513	2780	224	0
47 METALWORKING MACHINERY	547	15	45462	10111	2336	668	895	76	187
48 SPECIAL MACH., EQUIP.	6057	95	34744	6841	3216	2206	2071	1436	911
49 GENERAL MACH., EQUIP.	1330	0	54672	39636	4188	2920	6702	357	377
50 MACHINE SHOP PRDTS.	779	144	13872	9880	661	2328	2426	1228	222
51 OFFICE, COMPUT. MACHINES	483	0	33161	398	19	41	8297	105	0
52 SERVICE IND. MACHINES	2112	90	29460	14284	5893	3199	8742	780	369
53 ELECT. TRANSMISS. EQUIP.	12038	0	58481	33738	2678	363	7788	231	288
54 HOUSEHOLD APPLIANCES	782	0	124469	62577	30217	71	57207	151	45
55 ELECTRIC LIGHTING EQUIP.	2411	0	34179	15435	94	166	5757	92	712
56 RADIO, TV, ETC., EQUIP.	129	0	161235	74010	8296	507	1208	31	308
57 ELECTRONIC COMPONENTS	236	46	28830	15498	4533	1329	2573	37	1689
58 MISC. ELECTRICAL MACH.	3091	0	19413	61248	2015	2394	1125	255	394
59 MOTOR VEHICLES, EQUIP.	21709	54	27114	54395	898	6529	6702	455	19
60 AIRCRAFT, PARTS	31289	406	17226	65487	931	101466	166	16530	2510
61 OTHER TRANSPORT. EQUIP.	4876	1050	30462	25595	1914	4043	1425	11775	5919
62 PROFESS., SCIEN. INSTRU.	3574	26	85625	15872	7869	560	2554	721	105
63 MEDICAL, PHOTO. EQUIP.	39	0	18783	2855	196	73	117	168	8
64 MISC. MANUFACTURING	7506	326	63878	16899	9303	887	3031	1877	1774
65 TRANSPORT., WAREHOUSING	5370	834	21433	5849	2793	3492	3214	5699	913
66 COMMUNICA.,EXC. BRDCAST.	12020	1722	28354	13932	6473	5589	7161	11385	1990
67 RADIO, TV BROADCASTING	30828	5351	153102	34556	24445	24703	21471	25539	7111
68 ELEC.,GAS,WATER,SAN.SER.	2486	519	9219	4282	2099	1769	2000	2454	420
69 WHOLESALE, RETAIL TRADE	21051	3320	73692	24415	14868	10490	11812	14292	4266
70 FINANCE, INSURANCE	19357	2158	70174	21396	11695	8567	9515	13350	3254
71 REAL ESTATE, RENTAL	197	36	1010	267	143	116	116	168	38
72 HOTELS, PERSONAL SERV.	6892	1255	26166	8658	4821	3548	4722	4586	1960
73 BUSINESS SERVICES	7929	1380	59823	7666	4491	3199	3682	7148	1100
74 RESEARCH, DEVELOPMENT	0	0	0	0	0	0	0	0	0
75 AUTO. REPAIR, SERVICES	1965	408	5382	2218	1381	1189	1205	1334	455
76 AMUSEMENTS	2220	427	13029	2855	1769	1357	2076	2273	564
77 MED.,EDUC. SERVICES	721	84	4460	1158	609	322	528	618	221
78 FEDERAL GOVT. ENTERPRISE	29803	3445	64483	20445	12810	14008	22301	13973	6440
79 STATE, LOCAL GOVT. ENT.	88662	22442	328644	106666	85429	65487	51478	66681	33679
80 DIRECT ALLOCATED IMPORTS	0	0	0	0	0	0	0	0	0
81 TRANSFERRED IMPORTS	0	0	0	0	0	0	0	0	0
82 VALUE ADDED	0	0	0	0	0	0	0	0	0
83 SECONDARY TRANSFERS-IN	0	0	0	0	0	0	0	0	0
84 INVENTORY DEPLETION	0	0	0	0	0	0	0	0	0
85 SCRAP PRODUCTION	0	0	0	0	0	0	0	0	0
86 SCRAP PURCHASED	0	0	0	0	0	0	0	0	0
87 STATE TOTAL PRODUCTION	813210	140263	4024541	1679244	920615	624858	590927	769155	173937

TABLE C-21

1963 STATE TRANSFERS-OUT
(THOUSANDS OF CURRENT DOLLARS)

INDUSTRY TITLE	19 MARYLAND	20 MASSA-CHUSETTS	21 MICHIGAN	22 MINNESOTA	23 MISSISSIPPI	24 MISSOURI	25 MONTANA	26 NEBRASKA	27 NEVADA
1 LIVESTOCK, PRDTS.	20016	9403	41981	101128	29734	74148	22412	84524	3841
2 OTHER AGRICULTURE PRDTS.	14869	8375	61590	101751	63926	79501	32813	78984	2448
3 FORESTRY, FISHERIES	0	0	0	0	0	0	0	0	0
4 AGRI.,FORES.,FISH. SERV.	122	19	86	203	361	214	27	92	5
5 IRON, FERRO. ORES MINING	12	0	1937	7736	0	235	31	0	74
6 NONFERROUS ORES MINING	0	0	1128	104	0	528	2540	1	1588
7 COAL MINING	31	0	0	0	0	81	14	0	0
8 CRUDE PETRO.,NATURAL GAS	24	0	3543	0	11327	32	4422	3473	9
9 STONE, CLAY MINING	1941	1111	3540	1193	553	2765	281	846	697
10 CHEM.,FERT. MIN. MINING	0	0	2369	0	0	2328	3494	0	489
11 NEW CONSTRUCTION	0	0	0	0	0	0	0	0	0
12 MAINT., REPAIR CONSTR.	0	0	0	0	0	0	0	0	0
13 ORDNANCE, ACCESSORIES	1458	8139	8031	10217	0	12085	0	90	0
14 FOOD, KINDRED PRDTS.	17686	20963	29010	38184	7611	34280	2714	23056	494
15 TOBACCO MANUFACTURES	8	5	24	0	0	32	0	0	0
16 FABRICS	3092	32398	352	990	1836	1325	0	23	0
17 TEXTILE PRDTS.	109	16450	5042	1129	3059	2005	0	0	0
18 APPAREL	4204	9775	981	1256	3758	4663	0	171	3
19 MISC. TEXTILE PRDTS.	1872	7171	22579	1613	989	3459	9	101	24
20 LUMBER, WOOD PRDTS.	1435	1790	4474	3032	5942	1921	4594	450	212
21 WOODEN CONTAINERS	679	685	538	367	2029	758	0	59	0
22 HOUSEHOLD FURNITURE	1297	4734	4296	867	3296	1546	22	404	36
23 OTHER FURNITURE	1805	1959	11669	1221	314	2135	31	534	16
24 PAPER, ALLIED PRDTS.	2898	18392	19618	10632	2706	3995	162	322	4
25 PAPERBOARD CONTAINERS	3147	5563	6722	1965	343	3701	0	404	0
26 PRINTING, PUBLISHING	98909	281875	211163	134435	11657	188000	8074	33990	7608
27 CHEMICALS,SELECT. PRDTS.	18340	15496	55378	10603	5748	31379	596	2206	2345
28 PLASTICS, SYNTHETICS	6318	25364	13357	1628	511	428	0	0	0
29 DRUGS, COSMETICS	17091	12264	25419	9488	2065	22377	23	2827	146
30 PAINT, ALLIED PRDTS.	2594	3617	10503	1148	42	6280	0	92	14
31 PETROLEUM, RELATED INDS.	9006	6157	29230	13037	6793	14523	11409	989	97
32 RUBBER, MISC. PLASTICS	14657	48191	31065	4814	4572	7853	16	3379	0
33 LEATHER TANNING, PRDTS.	64	3085	436	146	0	125	0	28	0
34 FOOTWEAR, LEATHER PRDTS.	453	11939	705	348	510	8229	2	14	0
35 GLASS, GLASS PRDTS.	951	79	2848	328	247	1213	0	3	0
36 STONE, CLAY PRDTS.	9102	14268	22277	11223	4699	14379	1397	3268	2909
37 PRIMARY IRON, STEEL MFR.	28838	11317	128460	10497	469	10359	77	229	33
38 PRIMARY NONFERROUS MFR.	19993	15791	40547	1594	818	8122	13109	4711	4467

39 METAL CONTAINERS	3787	752	369	1761	7	3167	0	433	0
40 FABRICATED METAL PRDTS.	8195	11916	28816	6582	3672	15633	465	5481	411
41 SCREW MACH. PRDTS., ETC.	4572	16213	72689	6022	2358	6055	0	253	15
42 OTHER FAB. METAL PRDTS.	7107	27363	67626	7260	1688	15687	40	828	50
43 ENGINES, TURBINES	0	26364	61670	2710	0	1544	0	0	0
44 FARM MACH., EQUIP.	91	157	27724	15614	3358	6956	106	4227	0
45 CONSTRUC. MACH., EQUIP.	430	472	14573	9327	1406	3614	15	426	30
46 MATERIAL HANDLING MACH.	1234	4275	26259	2787	1630	1786	17	138	0
47 METALWORKING MACHINERY	5282	17748	77957	2582	15	4063	0	108	0
48 SPECIAL MACH., EQUIP.	8077	41342	23467	4009	1337	5347	0	98	15
49 GENERAL MACH., EQUIP.	2060	19497	38152	6312	289	6052	0	2700	16
50 MACHINE SHOP PRDTS.	2563	5463	18993	3432	633	7633	126	213	86
51 OFFICE, COMPUT. MACHINES	1309	18715	42904	47023	0	3103	0	20	0
52 SERVICE IND. MACHINES	4592	11177	36396	16756	1421	18411	0	220	90
53 ELECT. TRANSMISS. EQUIP.	4186	28378	22780	10574	1470	20001	0	84	73
54 HOUSEHOLD APPLIANCES	1817	6223	50944	25271	4082	9363	0	246	0
55 ELECTRIC LIGHTING EQUIP.	415	18942	4800	1984	4849	10311	0	0	0
56 RADIO, TV, ETC., EQUIP.	41619	82891	6654	10268	811	10229	0	9039	353
57 ELECTRONIC COMPONENTS	1543	33219	5741	4452	679	784	0	1892	15
58 MISC. ELECTRICAL MACH.	3733	7825	28229	2837	379	4382	0	436	17
59 MOTOR VEHICLES, EQUIP.	18441	8258	416674	7783	1366	68568	12	1477	12
60 AIRCRAFT, PARTS	32345	29451	23732	5827	0	50526	0	18	18
61 OTHER TRANSPORT. EQUIP.	18868	7960	18730	1630	531	7373	81	2421	5
62 PROFESS., SCIEN. INSTRU.	3531	46085	39159	8035	954	6242	289	3798	0
63 MEDICAL, PHOTO. EQUIP.	659	21091	1164	2294	9	1524	0	37	0
64 MISC. MANUFACTURING	5280	45440	27065	9668	4024	9668	349	1869	364
65 TRANSPORT., WAREHOUSING	4462	6514	7986	4692	1299	8357	986	2289	687
66 COMMUNICA.,EXC. BRDCAST.	9487	16756	25578	9127	4722	12585	1564	4762	641
67 RADIO, TV BROADCASTING	23170	61637	74632	29308	10645	40922	6730	14998	4665
68 ELEC.,GAS,WATER,SAN.SER.	2509	3885	6480	2542	1408	3006	748	712	398
69 WHOLESALE, RETAIL TRADE	16712	32632	43976	21106	6850	29026	3420	8715	2324
70 FINANCE, INSURANCE	13848	42499	31893	19621	5368	26039	2313	8941	2105
71 REAL ESTATE, RENTAL	268	371	514	259	69	332	37	87	47
72 HOTELS, PERSONAL SERV.	5923	12014	15163	6625	2594	9402	1356	2831	4760
73 BUSINESS SERVICES	9663	21618	31277	11617	2069	14474	934	3230	1686
74 RESEARCH, DEVELOPMENT	0	0	0	0	0	0	0	0	0
75 AUTO. REPAIR, SERVICES	1905	2618	4494	1720	773	2301	391	810	305
76 AMUSEMENTS	3895	5244	6674	2519	685	3547	392	1278	7796
77 MED.,EDUC. SERVICES	1275	4408	1673	936	164	1569	89	307	45
78 FEDERAL GOVT. ENTERPRISE	18872	37642	33323	20176	9876	31186	4394	9851	3495
79 STATE, LOCAL GOVT. ENT.	76162	168548	293805	105933	27760	73741	21281	132921	8428
80 DIRECT ALLOCATED IMPORTS	0	0	0	0	0	0	0	0	0
81 TRANSFERRED IMPORTS	0	0	0	0	0	0	0	0	0
82 VALUE ADDED	0	0	0	0	0	0	0	0	0
83 SECONDARY TRANSFERS-IN	0	0	0	0	0	0	0	0	0
84 INVENTORY DEPLETION	0	0	0	0	0	0	0	0	0
85 SCRAP PRODUCTION	0	0	0	0	0	0	0	0	0
86 SCRAP PURCHASED	0	0	0	0	0	0	0	0	0
87 STATE TOTAL PRODUCTION	672904	1549975	2561634	941858	287165	1099510	154403	473462	66508

TABLE C-21

1963 STATE TRANSFERS-OUT
(THOUSANDS OF CURRENT DOLLARS)

INDUSTRY TITLE	28 NEW HAMPSHIRE	29 NEW JERSEY	30 NEW MEXICO	31 NEW YORK	32 NORTH CAROLINA	33 NORTH DAKOTA	34 OHIO	35 OKLAHOMA	36 OREGON
1 LIVESTOCK, PRDTS.	4362	14406	16424	60464	36569	22485	62811	40154	19215
2 OTHER AGRICULTURE PRDTS.	1933	17935	13332	50864	105192	56652	81480	40041	29543
3 FORESTRY, FISHERIES	0	0	0	0	0	0	0	0	0
4 AGRI.,FORES.,FISH. SERV.	16	33	38	78	255	46	130	123	59
5 IRON, FERRO. ORES MINING	0	89	40	586	47	0	0	0	36
6 NONFERROUS ORES MINING	0	178	4925	578	7	37	8	63	11
7 COAL MINING	0	0	57	0	0	57	1048	32	0
8 CRUDE PETRO.,NATURAL GAS	0	0	26357	522	0	4251	1467	44540	29
9 STONE, CLAY MINING	152	3084	514	4593	1889	198	4700	962	1251
10 CHEM.,FERT. MIN. MINING	0	0	37473	4651	1318	0	5066	0	11
11 NEW CONSTRUCTION	0	0	0	0	0	0	0	0	0
12 MAINT., REPAIR CONSTR.	0	0	0	0	0	0	0	0	0
13 ORDNANCE, ACCESSORIES	0	180	6424	7128	3171	0	14748	24	32
14 FOOD, KINDRED PRDTS.	1555	41266	1840	73442	15027	2169	45086	8305	9695
15 TOBACCO MANUFACTURES	0	57	0	17	5512	0	55	0	0
16 FABRICS	9674	17650	10	16425	212599	0	1604	90	2891
17 TEXTILE PRDTS.	872	10166	0	14743	12743	0	8777	15	460
18 APPAREL	755	11701	34	88550	16956	0	5547	658	725
19 MISC. TEXTILE PRDTS.	391	12217	146	35924	8240	19	2737	249	1435
20 LUMBER, WOOD PRDTS.	1682	1746	713	5521	7208	38	3561	640	43801
21 WOODEN CONTAINERS	411	1118	8	1336	860	0	985	0	464
22 HOUSEHOLD FURNITURE	740	3999	53	9745	20900	9	5039	417	1170
23 OTHER FURNITURE	458	2707	125	13928	3015	11	9803	284	237
24 PAPER, ALLIED PRDTS.	5385	16906	0	32129	10333	0	22475	415	7089
25 PAPERBOARD CONTAINERS	311	8558	5	11642	2300	5	8861	428	498
26 PRINTING, PUBLISHING	19724	261693	9043	1789848	59001	7010	445326	36157	35913
27 CHEMICALS,SELECT. PRDTS.	1210	154225	917	64158	12534	274	60846	2069	4807
28 PLASTICS, SYNTHETICS	2002	34335	0	28657	19670	0	33582	103	562
29 DRUGS, COSMETICS	151	104934	8	89148	4372	0	37127	255	464
30 PAINT, ALLIED PRDTS.	28	17116	28	8205	1317	0	13690	368	695
31 PETROLEUM, RELATED INDS.	127	111049	4829	20200	575	2909	74985	60660	1458
32 RUBBER, MISC. PLASTICS	3603	38975	350	34370	5352	0	144888	7503	650
33 LEATHER TANNING, PRDTS.	534	990	0	1439	126	0	501	0	25
34 FOOTWEAR, LEATHER PRDTS.	4702	2680	34	14097	397	0	2143	102	103
35 GLASS, GLASS PRDTS.	27	4744	3	3477	995	0	8496	1354	171
36 STONE, CLAY PRDTS.	2529	26132	1923	38848	7413	601	46720	4940	4032
37 PRIMARY IRON, STEEL MFR.	1021	16882	0	59121	1782	5	243729	1678	3647
38 PRIMARY NONFERROUS MFR.	1158	62323	2446	67046	5492	0	56419	4998	7191

39 METAL CONTAINERS	0	8551	0	3973	16	0	4363	92	620
40 FABRICATED METAL PRDTS.	824	23900	475	41631	7190	413	64047	10731	5598
41 SCREW MACH. PRDTS., ETC.	824	24137	154	36631	2003	30	75151	708	423
42 OTHER FAB. METAL PRDTS.	935	40752	86	47415	3954	20	75516	4942	2267
43 ENGINES, TURBINES	14	555	0	27713	14	0	7411	14	84
44 FARM MACH., EQUIP.	13	439	40	5865	2388	831	19005	815	845
45 CONSTRUC. MACH., EQUIP.	2414	4621	143	3508	162	13	41562	13527	997
46 MATERIAL HANDLING MACH.	0	15652	0	16061	206	33	25595	293	4674
47 METALWORKING MACHINERY	978	10191	109	24146	688	119	69147	174	165
48 SPECIAL MACH., EQUIP.	6248	27400	94	36102	14878	44	42509	1065	4907
49 GENERAL MACH., EQUIP.	2898	40235	16	58056	802	16	82284	6038	692
50 MACHINE SHOP PRDTS.	424	6260	496	15923	1112	95	16174	1092	1630
51 OFFICE, COMPUT. MACHINES	606	19664	105	148214	1181	0	32631	229	20
52 SERVICE IND. MACHINES	624	15181	141	45121	2766	0	36352	2227	710
53 ELECT. TRANSMISS. EQUIP.	7811	33758	29	80661	12292	0	99043	2347	6366
54 HOUSEHOLD APPLIANCES	31	9264	0	28168	9007	0	192476	420	809
55 ELECTRIC LIGHTING EQUIP.	331	27744	0	35961	2460	0	35727	48	185
56 RADIO, TV, ETC., EQUIP.	5176	114686	283	160257	21629	0	34503	16060	155
57 ELECTRONIC COMPONENTS	4372	29536	112	50140	4109	0	13716	453	80
58 MISC. ELECTRICAL MACH.	107	12055	35	18491	8826	0	31719	841	1121
59 MOTOR VEHICLES, EQUIP.	7	20282	74	50758	1040	0	142404	1685	2368
60 AIRCRAFT, PARTS	0	50794	18	166119	2727	0	148536	70893	2667
61 OTHER TRANSPORT. EQUIP.	141	13106	40	17692	1707	27	13792	1110	4316
62 PROFESS., SCIEN. INSTRU.	497	38328	546	68801	5088	12	24381	1451	1161
63 MEDICAL, PHOTO. EQUIP.	570	11105	0	120329	1932	0	846	17	913
64 MISC. MANUFACTURING	2685	50129	455	171171	4318	557	34816	1840	2380
65 TRANSPORT., WAREHOUSING	425	11288	1085	33976	4275	649	13514	3368	3354
66 COMMUNICA.,EXC. BRDCAST.	1401	19520	2354	64463	10500	1868	29086	6963	5624
67 RADIO, TV BROADCASTING	3529	11807	8570	524395	33337	5223	100987	18375	18342
68 ELEC.,GAS,WATER,SAN.SER.	431	4697	849	11814	2179	285	9255	1668	840
69 WHOLESALE, RETAIL TRADE	2905	39910	4021	146145	20573	3428	52790	10941	11959
70 FINANCE, INSURANCE	2748	32801	2941	201340	16247	2135	44068	10286	8393
71 REAL ESTATE, RENTAL	32	526	56	2135	173	26	692	143	124
72 HOTELS, PERSONAL SERV.	1702	14805	1932	54093	7582	956	18588	3921	4016
73 BUSINESS SERVICES	977	21789	2021	161069	5678	598	28726	5483	4665
74 RESEARCH, DEVELOPMENT	0	0	0	0	0	0	0	0	0
75 AUTO. REPAIR, SERVICES	323	3178	483	8498	1816	325	4722	1292	1194
76 AMUSEMENTS	931	7304	695	63122	2199	325	8960	1441	1424
77 MED.,EDUC. SERVICES	294	1787	119	11094	972	72	2901	377	421
78 FEDERAL GOVT. ENTERPRISE	3430	33655	6134	123109	22817	4278	48499	14983	12110
79 STATE, LOCAL GOVT. ENT.	32258	134328	18253	650178	142773	7265	395689	60451	85201
80 DIRECT ALLOCATED IMPORTS	0	0	0	0	0	0	0	0	0
81 TRANSFERRED IMPORTS	0	0	0	0	0	0	0	0	0
82 VALUE ADDED	0	0	0	0	0	0	0	0	0
83 SECONDARY TRANSFERS-IN	0	0	0	0	0	0	0	0	0
84 INVENTORY DEPLETION	0	0	0	0	0	0	0	0	0
85 SCRAP PRODUCTION	0	0	0	0	0	0	0	0	0
86 SCRAP PURCHASED	0	0	0	0	0	0	0	0	0
87 STATE TOTAL PRODUCTION	155434	1985796	181064	6185816	966784	126419	3576623	536430	382190

TABLE C-21

1963 STATE TRANSFERS-OUT
(THOUSANDS OF CURRENT DOLLARS)

INDUSTRY TITLE	37 PENNSYL- VANIA	38 RHODE ISLAND	39 SOUTH CAROLINA	40 SOUTH DAKOTA	41 TENNESSEE	42 TEXAS	43 UTAH	44 VERMONT	45 VIRGINIA
1 LIVESTOCK, PRDTS.	60614	1305	11820	50675	30666	109655	12430	10970	28931
2 OTHER AGRICULTURE PRDTS.	45240	1071	36495	41787	45887	166580	7299	4906	32030
3 FORESTRY, FISHERIES	0	0	0	0	0	0	0	0	0
4 AGRI.,FORES.,FISH. SERV.	145	15	90	55	81	993	22	3	103
5 IRON, FERRO. ORES MINING	750	0	0	0	2	127	215	0	15
6 NONFERROUS ORES MINING	105	0	9	814	452	154	7224	0	182
7 COAL MINING	4221	0	0	1	169	8	208	0	988
8 CRUDE PETRO.,NATURAL GAS	2835	0	0	9	6	232047	6012	0	35
9 STONE, CLAY MINING	4682	132	1368	494	2457	3131	363	546	2800
10 CHEM.,FERT. MIN. MINING	1908	0	170	11	13074	25193	3333	0	191
11 NEW CONSTRUCTION	0	0	0	0	0	0	0	0	0
12 MAINT., REPAIR CONSTR.	0	0	0	0	0	0	0	0	0
13 ORDNANCE, ACCESSORIES	9249	7	0	0	5432	4740	11138	0	64
14 FOOD, KINDRED PRDTS.	54124	2427	5503	6731	20708	45785	5008	2392	13569
15 TOBACCO MANUFACTURES	594	0	151	0	90	8	0	0	2168
16 FABRICS	33107	20760	175240	0	14995	6804	41	459	27816
17 TEXTILE PRDTS.	19166	3770	15526	0	4484	1024	34	205	5293
18 APPAREL	26100	831	3751	0	10344	5688	338	304	4169
19 MISC. TEXTILE PRDTS.	7349	307	2076	50	2628	3368	91	25	1495
20 LUMBER, WOOD PRDTS.	4581	115	4215	248	4244	5498	334	972	5812
21 WOODEN CONTAINERS	918	40	797	9	1706	771	16	141	1219
22 HOUSEHOLD FURNITURE	7233	56	1351	31	7052	3700	300	825	10175
23 OTHER FURNITURE	8808	730	310	10	1490	2974	213	11	2089
24 PAPER, ALLIED PRDTS.	24080	635	7125	6	9928	7229	150	2139	10757
25 PAPERBOARD CONTAINERS	9226	489	1740	23	1675	2722	67	269	1377
26 PRINTING, PUBLISHING	480120	25179	20021	8650	93976	188043	19886	12422	65415
27 CHEMICALS,SELECT. PRDTS.	50674	3815	5127	282	41356	234595	1465	418	23809
28 PLASTICS, SYNTHETICS	46600	5050	24557	0	62609	53587	0	428	83565
29 DRUGS, COSMETICS	44403	608	2544	68	7654	8151	199	29	6149
30 PAINT, ALLIED PRDTS.	9629	434	215	0	1352	7038	107	241	698
31 PETROLEUM, RELATED INDS.	107250	2431	1528	30	3439	458589	12970	30	5873
32 RUBBER, MISC. PLASTICS	37630	10991	4290	244	13131	14813	816	1553	5644
33 LEATHER TANNING, PRDTS.	1038	4	17	0	600	50	7	62	198
34 FOOTWEAR, LEATHER PRDTS.	7255	310	0	0	4608	774	12	133	1124
35 GLASS, GLASS PRDTS.	8102	671	1105	0	2236	697	5	0	443
36 STONE, CLAY PRDTS.	41221	792	3671	931	9562	31449	4047	2433	10809
37 PRIMARY IRON, STEEL MFR.	328634	4296	1400	5	6343	21073	9885	189	5153
38 PRIMARY NONFERROUS MFR.	41986	11890	1059	0	18777	35234	8730	687	4840

39 METAL CONTAINERS	5345	0	22	0	428	3624	222	0	335
40 FABRICATED METAL PRDTS.	64278	1176	3406	859	13890	29197	3935	368	10308
41 SCREW MACH. PRDTS., ETC.	51060	3811	1260	0	4257	2924	93	89	411
42 OTHER FAB. METAL PRDTS.	62009	6400	1221	84	5238	22176	421	254	4314
43 ENGINES, TURBINES	39970	14	0	0	14	2443	0	0	0
44 FARM MACH., EQUIP.	11963	13	325	502	7402	3125	194	53	939
45 CONSTRUC. MACH., EQUIP.	16303	30	44	0	714	45204	3311	178	590
46 MATERIAL HANDLING MACH.	20069	79	666	543	2847	2838	32	0	649
47 METALWORKING MACHINERY	28596	4702	2572	274	796	2007	121	5782	155
48 SPECIAL MACH., EQUIP.	31742	5840	9416	30	2452	8672	432	461	1403
49 GENERAL MACH., EQUIP.	51909	1914	2002	386	2927	10132	1039	91	1949
50 MACHINE SHOP PRDTS.	8828	753	714	259	1474	5056	324	137	819
51 OFFICE, COMPUT. MACHINES	26249	41	1416	0	0	1351	39	3696	6946
52 SERVICE IND. MACHINES	28160	370	312	0	4485	18023	1224	555	2982
53 ELECT. TRANSMISS. EQUIP.	93970	663	3545	0	7932	6773	723	227	14119
54 HOUSEHOLD APPLIANCES	19450	630	1404	0	27369	4660	0	0	117
55 ELECTRIC LIGHTING EQUIP.	33465	5563	128	0	2295	1976	86	757	145
56 RADIO, TV, ETC., EQUIP.	26166	1291	132	10	13558	26777	1354	0	10599
57 ELECTRONIC COMPONENTS	49259	2148	3561	199	1572	4418	898	1397	8240
58 MISC. ELECTRICAL MACH.	15220	1428	54	0	2222	4614	36	961	592
59 MOTOR VEHICLES, EQUIP.	27332	336	170	27	2469	18126	96	0	6523
60 AIRCRAFT, PARTS	116401	1223	0	0	9797	96649	34995	10893	3479
61 OTHER TRANSPORT. EQUIP.	42532	580	975	214	4761	11751	645	27	8413
62 PROFESS., SCIEN. INSTRU.	69265	5110	3641	26	7373	8867	190	1455	1463
63 MEDICAL, PHOTO. EQUIP.	3733	1056	1306	0	25	811	36	450	2261
64 MISC. MANUFACTURING	52434	31010	5915	224	10131	7869	1476	793	7616
65 TRANSPORT., WAREHOUSING	16801	798	1450	448	3799	15608	1396	411	5424
66 COMMUNICA.,EXC. BRDCAST.	28731	2618	4865	1392	11953	31738	3318	731	10619
67 RADIO, TV BROADCASTING	122165	9976	15416	6376	32159	85896	7870	2843	30116
68 ELEC.,GAS,WATER,SAN.SER.	8884	514	1094	315	918	7193	875	228	2610
69 WHOLESALE, RETAIL TRADE	58650	4646	8171	3198	17361	53140	4814	1721	17510
70 FINANCE, INSURANCE	57304	5171	7681	2284	15157	52114	3768	1512	15189
71 REAL ESTATE, RENTAL	693	56	74	31	156	543	65	16	247
72 HOTELS, PERSONAL SERV.	22326	1716	3261	1047	6209	19799	1693	986	7493
73 BUSINESS SERVICES	34593	1931	2724	671	6870	26034	2003	478	7171
74 RESEARCH, DEVELOPMENT	0	0	0	0	0	0	0	0	0
75 AUTO. REPAIR, SERVICES	5558	347	864	333	1609	5476	514	203	1737
76 AMUSEMENTS	7484	1162	913	573	1896	6150	903	458	2101
77 MED.,EDUC. SERVICES	4475	342	279	99	868	1803	359	254	794
78 FEDERAL GOVT. ENTERPRISE	56520	6126	13434	3944	52989	58873	5006	2302	34194
79 STATE, LOCAL GOVT. ENT.	406034	11917	36780	15248	198917	295095	33669	14538	162331
80 DIRECT ALLOCATED IMPORTS	0	0	0	0	0	0	0	0	0
81 TRANSFERRED IMPORTS	0	0	0	0	0	0	0	0	0
82 VALUE ADDED	0	0	0	0	0	0	0	0	0
83 SECONDARY TRANSFERS-IN	0	0	0	0	0	0	0	0	0
84 INVENTORY DEPLETION	0	0	0	0	0	0	0	0	0
85 SCRAP PRODUCTION	0	0	0	0	0	0	0	0	0
86 SCRAP PURCHASED	0	0	0	0	0	0	0	0	0
87 STATE TOTAL PRODUCTION	3355498	222663	474485	150759	930500	2691819	231139	98097	757902

TABLE C-21

1963 STATE TRANSFERS-OUT
(THOUSANDS OF CURRENT DOLLARS)

INDUSTRY TITLE	46 WASHINGTON	47 WEST VIRGINIA	48 WISCONSIN	49 WYOMING	50 ALASKA	51 HAWAII	52 NATIONAL TOTAL
1 LIVESTOCK, PRDTS.	21798	8484	95483	13800	325	3361	1989905
2 OTHER AGRICULTURE PRDTS.	49966	6836	52909	7351	21	25393	2573268
3 FORESTRY, FISHERIES	0	0	0	0	0	0	0
4 AGRI.,FORES.,FISH. SERV.	73	40	85	9	0	151	7086
5 IRON, FERRO. ORES MINING	13	0	16	298	6	0	14216
6 NONFERROUS ORES MINING	337	0	57	1949	191	0	40284
7 COAL MINING	29	4572	0	64	17	0	16303
8 CRUDE PETRO.,NATURAL GAS	455	4328	0	21824	835	0	621664
9 STONE, CLAY MINING	992	1042	2349	857	63	324	87489
10 CHEM.,FERT. MIN. MINING	19	38	0	6639	0	0	217216
11 NEW CONSTRUCTION	0	0	0	0	0	0	0
12 MAINT., REPAIR CONSTR.	0	0	0	0	0	0	0
13 ORDNANCE, ACCESSORIES	709	8515	1610	0	0	0	445913
14 FOOD, KINDRED PRDTS.	15994	2974	39312	1096	1163	7425	1030315
15 TOBACCO MANUFACTURES	0	39	1	0	0	0	11109
16 FABRICS	639	336	738	0	0	12	740049
17 TEXTILE PRDTS.	188	9	2953	0	0	24	209800
18 APPAREL	713	603	1992	0	0	334	248040
19 MISC. TEXTILE PRDTS.	891	95	851	4	0	101	156765
20 LUMBER, WOOD PRDTS.	22940	1554	5271	413	594	196	225828
21 WOODEN CONTAINERS	839	88	1013	0	0	0	34449
22 HOUSEHOLD FURNITURE	998	272	1787	3	0	220	141939
23 OTHER FURNITURE	691	271	2281	4	0	194	102822
24 PAPER, ALLIED PRDTS.	22020	844	34506	0	0	244	392813
25 PAPERBOARD CONTAINERS	1625	345	4505	0	0	103	122928
26 PRINTING, PUBLISHING	54959	22542	159125	3790	1725	10715	7110658
27 CHEMICALS,SELECT. PRDTS.	19909	108530	6403	117	0	1722	1292236
28 PLASTICS, SYNTHETICS	2101	36923	2608	0	0	0	649499
29 DRUGS, COSMETICS	365	572	11257	0	0	113	596493
30 PAINT, ALLIED PRDTS.	978	107	2628	0	0	0	146573
31 PETROLEUM, RELATED INDS.	17848	5477	4499	29540	0	2490	1640457
32 RUBBER, MISC. PLASTICS	775	467	13155	8	0	65	670783
33 LEATHER TANNING, PRDTS.	13	209	1971	0	0	0	14506
34 FOOTWEAR, LEATHER PRDTS.	72	102	3497	0	0	44	81841
35 GLASS, GLASS PRDTS.	153	5033	85	0	0	10	57447
36 STONE, CLAY PRDTS.	6888	4803	10245	1211	367	1588	554330
37 PRIMARY IRON, STEEL MFR.	3047	31188	22812	0	0	323	1387743
38 PRIMARY NONFERROUS MFR.	27031	13283	8845	24	0	4	751901

39 METAL CONTAINERS	1598	497	3167	0	0	669	77604
40 FABRICATED METAL PRDTS.	5915	4960	21062	53	0	428	601329
41 SCREW MACH. PRDTS., ETC.	773	2154	26254	63	0	0	514681
42 OTHER FAB. METAL PRDTS.	1920	5285	11433	57	0	110	676995
43 ENGINES, TURBINES	43	0	55989	0	0	0	291158
44 FARM MACH., EQUIP.	835	1054	33980	0	0	77	331255
45 CONSTRUC. MACH., EQUIP.	2723	4526	37178	81	0	0	394038
46 MATERIAL HANDLING MACH.	2904	529	4172	0	0	17	179537
47 METALWORKING MACHINERY	623	1326	13608	0	0	16	374267
48 SPECIAL MACH., EQUIP.	3119	295	25766	0	0	564	402816
49 GENERAL MACH., EQUIP.	797	114	30149	16	0	16	577969
50 MACHINE SHOP PRDTS.	2080	766	4162	84	0	117	175135
51 OFFICE, COMPUT. MACHINES	755	0	1371	0	0	0	533377
52 SERVICE IND. MACHINES	1097	532	15494	0	0	33	359576
53 ELECT. TRANSMISS. EQUIP.	2119	2779	58332	63	0	17	725603
54 HOUSEHOLD APPLIANCES	1346	304	32334	0	0	0	805039
55 ELECTRIC LIGHTING EQUIP.	1229	8357	2624	10	0	27	301113
56 RADIO, TV, ETC., EQUIP.	1397	47	17574	0	0	22	1077069
57 ELECTRONIC COMPONENTS	224	748	3230	0	0	5	368575
58 MISC. ELECTRICAL MACH.	272	0	12434	0	0	0	272642
59 MOTOR VEHICLES, EQUIP.	1799	724	63891	0	0	25	1069028
60 AIRCRAFT, PARTS	71503	18	838	268	0	0	2001477
61 OTHER TRANSPORT. EQUIP.	16531	3206	8644	7	0	109	349920
62 PROFESS., SCIEN. INSTRU.	348	1776	18164	199	0	0	582138
63 MEDICAL, PHOTO. EQUIP.	181	346	426	0	0	10	213284
64 MISC. MANUFACTURING	3090	1217	15187	9	0	287	719529
65 TRANSPORT., WAREHOUSING	5263	2285	4159	749	794	1339	268464
66 COMMUNICA.,EXC. BRDCAST.	9352	3991	8652	817	235	1985	552884
67 RADIO, TV BROADCASTING	27132	13426	32769	3239	3232	7234	2234150
68 ELEC.,GAS,WATER,SAN.SER.	981	2071	2801	510	82	308	131536
69 WHOLESALE, RETAIL TRADE	17009	6234	20493	1573	1065	3042	1058969
70 FINANCE, INSURANCE	13249	4480	17206	1017	763	4039	1039722
71 REAL ESTATE, RENTAL	246	70	249	19	11	70	13507
72 HOTELS, PERSONAL SERV.	5793	2479	7372	1091	514	1960	405350
73 BUSINESS SERVICES	7187	2965	9058	519	647	1978	671778
74 RESEARCH, DEVELOPMENT	0	0	0	0	0	0	0
75 AUTO. REPAIR, SERVICES	1677	560	1847	194	79	329	95934
76 AMUSEMENTS	2461	1483	2576	282	208	707	240681
77 MED.,EDUC. SERVICES	658	296	522	34	34	215	59769
78 FEDERAL GOVT. ENTERPRISE	31705	6445	16910	1927	11209	12688	1213811
79 STATE, LOCAL GOVT. ENT.	269089	46134	56315	12050	11154	13522	6011000
80 DIRECT ALLOCATED IMPORTS	0	0	0	0	0	0	0
81 TRANSFERRED IMPORTS	0	0	0	0	0	0	0
82 VALUE ADDED	0	0	0	0	0	0	0
83 SECONDARY TRANSFERS-IN	0	0	0	0	0	0	0
84 INVENTORY DEPLETION	0	0	0	0	0	0	0
85 SCRAP PRODUCTION	0	0	0	0	0	0	0
86 SCRAP PURCHASED	0	0	0	0	0	0	0
87 STATE TOTAL PRODUCTION	793093	405004	1193240	113931	35337	107124	52357376

TABLE C-22

1963 STATE TOTAL PRODUCTION
(THOUSANDS OF CURRENT DOLLARS)

INDUSTRY TITLE	1 ALABAMA	2 ARIZONA	3 ARKANSAS	4 CALIFORNIA	5 COLORADO	6 CONNECTICUT	7 DELAWARE	8 DISTRICT OF COLUMBIA	9 FLORIDA
1 LIVESTOCK, PRDTS.	465920	250120	396530	1743539	597553	117787	103170	0	299125
2 OTHER AGRICULTURE PRDTS.	391737	379860	656357	2519541	316460	81103	49174	0	894726
3 FORESTRY, FISHERIES	32614	18376	22109	178957	4966	5942	2728	0	56866
4 AGRI.,FORES.,FISH. SERV.	54483	32478	82708	182837	13665	8273	7194	0	55372
5 IRON, FERRO. ORES MINING	56165	7597	947	36914	72228	7	0	0	155
6 NONFERROUS ORES MINING	22986	379183	20720	11797	77616	430	39	0	9655
7 COAL MINING	97071	381	2688	142	25913	6	0	0	22
8 CRUDE PETRO.,NATURAL GAS	26215	6494	72756	1097657	128598	422	69	0	5062
9 STONE, CLAY MINING	29454	16602	34459	198704	18879	16465	3303	73	56732
10 CHEM.,FERT. MIN. MINING	90	101	2898	74938	1571	51	223	254	117649
11 NEW CONSTRUCTION	840568	769136	448501	12453446	848791	1086300	201559	0	2628530
12 MAINT., REPAIR CONSTR.	228615	183255	183867	2501539	265475	267749	42874	385666	604653
13 ORDNANCE, ACCESSORIES	128969	101589	1755	2973394	48753	264028	981	79517	240062
14 FOOD, KINDRED PRDTS.	822856	270744	826983	7667468	1041141	449588	211739	6	1547510
15 TOBACCO MANUFACTURES	27717	22	0	2175	0	14306	0	126353	123535
16 FABRICS	601488	630	19054	56514	581	211600	56987	0	11143
17 TEXTILE PRDTS.	84699	392	25458	205415	1428	71098	20674	22	3778
18 APPAREL	337275	23595	78699	819436	15651	189572	48921	59	106493
19 MISC. TEXTILE PRDTS.	60952	3670	2476	177705	7682	38454	6503	7	15130
20 LUMBER, WOOD PRDTS.	246844	57908	279681	1227498	34822	32425	19345	907	207242
21 WOODEN CONTAINERS	7854	1652	14423	70709	2105	3654	592	1296	18142
22 HOUSEHOLD FURNITURE	39921	9406	91955	415935	14845	39809	533	4	72873
23 OTHER FURNITURE	11347	4741	19075	185517	5851	31091	1685	8	18676
24 PAPER, ALLIED PRDTS.	355385	13453	186970	537951	14838	119905	37873	11	376913
25 PAPERBOARD CONTAINERS	21363	5199	42053	451199	18887	76916	9916	1230	74954
26 PRINTING, PUBLISHING	85511	63142	51764	1244405	111742	279978	24457	517	248647
27 CHEMICALS,SELECT. PRDTS.	302255	43130	47877	744225	48242	256063	94998	246551	383993
28 PLASTICS, SYNTHETICS	124907	1498	3568	215007	3826	93626	190958	2671	149708
29 DRUGS, COSMETICS	10884	5758	3310	540951	12226	254679	17306	81	29139
30 PAINT, ALLIED PRDTS.	8824	2949	3794	283452	9690	9569	1563	205	40192
31 PETROLEUM, RELATED INDS.	64057	5424	148719	2585494	87440	59696	163935	19	114977
32 RUBBER, MISC. PLASTICS	230424	7567	48574	741030	128260	321051	71941	84	34518
33 LEATHER TANNING, PRDTS.	217	19	89	25405	542	2699	24746	187	1707
34 FOOTWEAR, LEATHER PRDTS.	9823	611	71144	58815	39523	26725	6324	0	20427
35 GLASS, GLASS PRDTS.	7639	1075	14235	192975	1782	14151	675	17	17768
36 STONE, CLAY PRDTS.	165766	77188	52895	998074	98189	130744	20443	27	258811
37 PRIMARY IRON, STEEL MFR.	977164	13521	4444	871238	166474	241731	157798	20813	52240
38 PRIMARY NONFERROUS MFR.	255673	485767	138177	661263	11813	659420	40871	72	55885

39	METAL CCNTAINERS	9314	197	8940	385421	20473	5816	99	21	74974
40	FABRICATEC METAL PRDTS.	176146	35480	42083	834411	49169	109844	23428	4427	185035
41	SCREW MACH. PRDTS., FTC.	34205	2543	10291	284843	3527	211662	10017	25	15291
42	OTHER FAB. METAL PRDTS.	119293	18491	30910	778037	42229	295958	14988	78	49553
43	ENGINES, TURBINES	4871	1484	747	121808	5922	66723	459	16	5408
44	FARM MACH., EQUIP.	21316	5518	5461	80186	9137	4897	1146	8	15807
45	CONSTRUC. MACH., EQUIP.	12272	1130	1365	142489	79845	10153	1509	4	3702
46	MATERIAL HANDLING MACH.	6861	696	8841	97929	5148	10175	516	7	4417
47	METALWORKING MACHINERY	11436	6645	9840	232492	3952	278296	6505	98	16062
48	SPECIAL MACH., EQUIP.	20686	2685	4238	196899	8714	98432	17508	32	23325
49	GENERAL MACH., EQUIP.	16386	4953	12810	429141	21008	372290	2628	70	14481
50	MACHINE SHOP PRDTS.	12840	14070	5134	305442	15757	72321	2944	1679	20694
51	OFFICE, COMPUT. MACHINES	1217	111139	9179	569461	2178	210548	303	56	44307
52	SERVICE IND. MACHINES	19673	29598	25693	169799	3289	48529	4994	62	13250
53	ELECT. TRANSMISS. EQUIP.	23471	6400	57611	520079	43108	164877	953	9	13132
54	HOUSEHOLD APPLIANCES	3621	2082	131155	246813	2817	212482	5203	19	4824
55	ELECTRIC LIGHTING EQUIP.	32951	2805	23458	203888	4350	150653	3305	32	8248
56	RADIO, TV, ETC., EQUIP.	17926	85129	98241	1993819	4863	150683	541	26	184130
57	ELECTRONIC COMPONENTS	19182	71004	5187	726285	3229	158659	984	8	65944
58	MISC. ELECTRICAL MACH.	13746	1861	2118	111368	7321	40120	6769	4	28406
59	MOTOR VEHICLES, EQUIP.	71846	10514	15927	2503834	24968	244938	446207	31	25557
60	AIRCRAFT, PARTS	544673	134026	3525	3516147	130871	1381314	7931	34	171377
61	OTHER TRANSPORT. EQUIP.	106149	5226	30199	422258	7380	80605	2576	8	119883
62	PROFESS., SCIEN. INSTRU.	5879	32424	38863	362120	13693	245626	7389	8	25772
63	MEDICAL, PHOTO. EQUIP.	955	1817	1171	154295	4940	45712	512	14	19148
64	MISC. MANUFACTURING	25842	8637	43310	528110	25203	353155	2271	2721	40643
65	TRANSPORT., WAREHOUSING	423077	190199	225420	3952511	441726	352039	94592	350558	1065802
66	COMMUNICA.,EXC. BRDCAST.	201786	90878	87045	1538712	144861	209037	34929	111711	418738
67	RADIO, TV BROADCASTING	19161	14158	9244	342161	19094	19772	4163	51476	53742
68	ELEC.,GAS,WATER,SAN.SER.	566154	305796	227498	2612388	349607	364795	77658	93537	706674
69	WHOLESALE, RETAIL TRADE	1408643	838420	781939	12866838	1239524	1735602	343202	759049	3251621
70	FINANCE, INSURANCE	375368	214921	183139	3613152	336690	737396	88669	245437	873825
71	REAL ESTATE, RENTAL	883515	733364	453657	9610564	887847	1237032	219798	1037930	3130964
72	HOTELS, PERSONAL SERV.	159125	156344	99228	1779432	177830	210923	31988	172030	653577
73	BUSINESS SERVICES	243006	211553	104069	4475091	291391	479882	63363	515236	847416
74	RESEARCH, DEVELOPMENT	0	0	0	0	0	0	0	0	0
75	AUTO. REPAIR, SERVICES	150136	103671	86749	1370744	138221	163330	27671	88862	348269
76	AMUSEMENTS	35154	42739	32668	1552639	70883	57512	23456	55086	250064
77	MED.,EDUC. SERVICES	198624	157090	88887	3082363	288006	760758	69211	1180420	561842
78	FEDERAL GOVT. ENTERPRISE	159389	39463	49509	599249	61060	63191	12946	145649	164099
79	STATE, LOCAL GOVT. ENT.	143014	64778	31589	736925	65777	67417	13216	17944	236554
80	ZERO ENTRIES	0	0	0	0	0	0	0	0	0
81	SERVICE IND. RESIDUAL	-1041357	-160212	-429482	-1107485	-84061	-832530	-209361	1747695	388865
82	TOTAL FINAL DEMAND	8269079	4969868	3965728	73960608	6559731	10460441	1690763	4225484	17537840
83	SECONDARY TRANSFERS-OUT	694920	318391	329464	5067187	383790	1050147	144609	249416	918139
84	ZERO ENTRIES	0	0	0	0	0	0	0	0	0
85	SCRAP ENTRIES	0	0	0	0	0	0	0	0	0
86	ZERO ENTRIES	0	0	0	0	0	0	0	0	0
87	STATE TOTAL CONSUMPTION	21457280	12132210	11054361	186923712	16213117	27638320	4944659	11923685	41554416

TABLE C-22

1963 STATE TOTAL PRODUCTION
(THOUSANDS OF CURRENT DOLLARS)

INDUSTRY TITLE	10 GEORGIA	11 IDAHO	12 ILLINOIS	13 INDIANA	14 IOWA	15 KANSAS	16 KENTUCKY	17 LOUISIANA	18 MAINE
1 LIVESTOCK, PRDTS.	602947	271062	1433328	904318	2474082	1025233	487119	226066	166031
2 OTHER AGRICULTURE PRDTS.	584381	398613	1864226	1025904	1645771	733245	642853	474683	124330
3 FORESTRY, FISHERIES	46990	9762	19776	10581	18953	7886	10123	80574	36727
4 AGRI.,FORES.,FISH. SERV.	80969	15778	83219	46003	70294	32360	20826	30375	12960
5 IRON, FERRO. ORES MINING	1816	1232	34651	3126	0	2	0	9968	2
6 NONFERROUS ORES MINING	575	39728	14741	21	11	122	70	34723	3634
7 COAL MINING	186	11	209382	58167	4477	8096	354044	8	184
8 CRUDE PETRO.,NATURAL GAS	3817	99	229122	33369	400	427237	82472	2405264	310391
9 STONE, CLAY MINING	106304	7257	98427	52662	42728	25460	48904	24183	21609
10 CHEM.,FERT. MIN. MINING	2746	5711	8972	57	14	1296	5379	83450	1599
11 NEW CONSTRUCTION	1184579	177637	2996040	1139772	614663	665160	783277	1535151	161994
12 MAINT., REPAIR CONSTR.	299710	97889	1150130	497800	385352	348587	249175	263346	74507
13 ORDNANCE, ACCESSORIES	23988	3948	136609	170254	69078	65954	2686	83193	12931
14 FOOD, KINDRED PRDTS.	1597219	383893	6097267	2102520	3384606	1305839	1284469	1495513	322114
15 TOBACCO MANUFACTURES	17338	0	21173	16481	0	0	1318831	9524	0
16 FABRICS	1441639	19	54945	1350	4178	467	30271	3431	249669
17 TEXTILE PRDTS.	772978	37	107326	15009	1643	811	4792	88681	15832
18 APPAREL	595746	732	410472	132675	28076	31010	222183	56196	40314
19 MISC. TEXTILE PRDTS.	184072	724	148511	29442	8086	9742	22000	24071	21406
20 LUMBER, WOOD PRDTS.	274888	244713	190575	207603	61977	15754	94058	188355	209216
21 WOODEN CONTAINERS	24634	1672	13976	4826	2478	890	18556	8370	2578
22 HOUSEHOLD FURNITURE	93855	2437	226782	281380	22180	14425	66147	15068	6258
23 OTHER FURNITURE	15303	942	197457	68084	20697	12260	11915	3818	4100
24 PAPER, ALLIED PRDTS.	501390	32539	473478	161757	42496	22957	42432	401965	500069
25 PAPERBOARD CONTAINERS	154723	3320	454104	147855	53607	58660	47382	63124	11197
26 PRINTING, PUBLISHING	166860	17392	1808814	335393	218330	108289	124235	84466	32402
27 CHEMICALS,SELECT. PRDTS.	294997	32961	932535	325479	59830	126297	274227	771377	21355
28 PLASTICS, SYNTHETICS	69868	1178	148431	59396	91292	24736	233400	212988	3499
29 DRUGS, COSMETICS	104990	1320	1017334	586806	55551	129607	10753	27511	1705
30 PAINT, ALLIED PRDTS.	54789	345	362956	43247	34967	7789	76961	13615	582
31 PETROLEUM, RELATED INDS.	67352	627	1339796	900401	11365	645205	168660	1800124	41167
32 RUBBER, MISC. PLASTICS	87020	682	601491	470746	211319	97848	68984	17669	33215
33 LEATHER TANNING, PRDTS.	9230	1	59101	2901	179	82	5679	834	48732
34 FOOTWEAR, LEATHER PRDTS.	45247	658	154955	35542	7172	1792	30367	246	235024
35 GLASS, GLASS PRDTS.	24940	156	237047	148114	652	1222	24706	25638	1358
36 STONE, CLAY PRDTS.	176701	18321	583917	341547	160111	175039	97613	143073	21597
37 PRIMARY IRON, STEEL MFR.	170745	2022	2018355	2549127	71169	23824	244329	69242	3802
38 PRIMARY NONFERROUS MFR.	133292	111445	934739	814740	107907	24362	92007	141135	15759

39	METAL CCNTAINERS	35372	1484	388250	43860	1013	7057	5094	52945	15153
40	FABRICATED METAL PRDTS.	138093	10631	637562	408040	112089	89828	111590	90450	15980
41	SCREW MACH. PRDTS., ETC.	44244	310	718984	229820	23518	6575	36300	8013	1527
42	OTHER FAB. METAL PRDTS.	60764	2902	1129693	398556	81484	30878	147335	63646	7159
43	ENGINES, TURBINES	3231	199	240655	89024	44866	5419	1649	4562	1051
44	FARM MACH., EQUIP.	37467	6017	615511	120840	553912	38508	67261	16832	4838
45	CCNSTRUC. MACH., EQUIP.	31496	1510	1225280	107138	170034	29766	6018	22641	12329
46	MATERIAL HANDLING MACH.	13764	789	198543	20844	17405	12967	23104	2565	448
47	METALWORKING MACHINERY	12191	689	605569	150092	36602	11058	20479	3745	2874
48	SPECIAL MACH., EQUIP.	51934	1068	324841	72593	32535	19495	20725	17670	8194
49	GENERAL MACH., EQUIP.	17477	387	502773	345885	42460	28209	62030	6913	4215
50	MACHINE SHOP PRCTS.	10734	1815	178792	124501	9146	28865	29860	15231	2917
51	OFFICE, CCMPUT. MACHINES	4620	52	245353	11100	1568	1152	58255	2932	1308
52	SERVICE IND. MACHINES	21043	935	292764	146682	58415	28091	90611	7879	3203
53	ELECT. TRANSMISS. EQUIP.	98971	529	539212	302425	32367	5145	73724	5293	3718
54	HOUSEHOLD APPLIANCES	10861	161	687303	345158	164588	3353	301704	2020	604
55	ELECTRIC LIGHTING EQUIP.	24737	340	336990	156959	2890	2406	56097	2183	7288
56	RADIO, TV, ETC., EQUIP.	6556	479	1764077	814092	93332	13939	17448	6127	5201
57	ELECTRONIC COMPCNENTS	6341	607	374348	197279	51888	15361	33241	1493	18599
58	MISC. ELECTRICAL MACH.	24462	110	162789	448719	16714	17808	11387	2571	3503
59	MOTOR VEHICLES, EQUIP.	799427	2289	1056811	2037590	44514	242929	251195	22550	1757
60	AIRCRAFT, PARTS	215135	3244	169188	471366	13532	691803	3692	117519	19839
61	OTHER TRANSPORT. EQUIP.	67347	14169	423491	351281	31508	56148	20699	161246	79578
62	PROFESS., SCIEN. INSTRU.	26480	289	597136	129510	53999	7363	19047	6511	1704
63	MEDICAL, PHOTO. EQUIP.	1236	18	214265	36290	3857	1191	3699	3527	314
64	MISC. MANUFACTURING	71802	3184	603474	165262	88192	10721	31168	23292	18708
65	TRANSPORT., WAREHOUSING	773896	120926	3041057	839116	408292	498681	458570	825203	185153
66	COMMUNICA.,EXC. BRDCAST.	293385	42032	692073	340051	157997	136425	174780	277900	48568
67	RADIO, TV BROADCASTING	31846	5528	158161	35698	25253	25519	22180	26383	7346
68	ELEC.,GAS,WATER,SAN.SER.	542100	116395	1998486	898758	459256	388912	424062	545582	107305
69	WHOLESALE, RETAIL TRADE	2386721	375579	8423752	2818923	1705865	1198714	1351352	1621579	485428
70	FINANCE, INSURANCE	627241	70126	2273097	693260	379314	278028	308632	432550	105751
71	REAL ESTATE, RENTAL	1245649	245502	6213920	1722036	1045478	788700	760997	1096197	247581
72	HOTELS, PERSONAL SERV.	261339	47573	992167	328306	182814	134554	179061	173901	74320
73	BUSINESS SERVICES	420691	67798	3275259	492535	300657	200354	229036	347056	64989
74	RESEARCH, DEVELOPMENT	0	0	0	0	0	0	0	0	0
75	AUTO. REPAIR, SERVICES	221674	46148	609402	250475	156416	134408	135848	150720	51635
76	AMUSEMENTS	71249	13661	416653	91386	56625	43493	66545	72726	18082
77	MED.,EDUC. SERVICES	400176	46814	2474468	642673	337617	178727	292683	342893	122578
78	FEDERAL GOVT. ENTERPRISE	141079	16310	305250	96783	60641	66309	105568	66145	30488
79	STATE, LOCAL GOVT. ENT.	106731	27015	395619	128403	102838	78833	61969	80270	40543
80	ZERO ENTRIES	0	0	0	0	0	0	0	0	0
81	SERVICE IND. RESIDUAL	-606865	-237742	2414145	-1900851	-692610	-882901	-802293	-1893620	-925895
82	TOTAL FINAL DEMAND	11111443	2036094	33265152	14255879	7713838	6985938	7567168	11462651	2667506
83	SECONDARY TRANSFERS-OUT	813210	140263	4024541	1679244	920615	624858	590927	769155	173937
84	ZERO ENTRIES	0	0	0	0	0	0	0	0	0
85	SCRAP ENTRIES	0	0	0	0	0	0	0	0	0
86	ZERO ENTRIES	0	0	0	0	0	0	0	0	0
87	STATE TOTAL CONSUMPTION	30696176	5121097	112081024	44862032	25089024	18465120	20732368	27984656	6517169

TABLE C-22

1963 STATE TOTAL PRODUCTION
(THOUSANDS OF CURRENT DOLLARS)

INDUSTRY TITLE	19 MARYLAND	20 MASSA-CHUSETTS	21 MICHIGAN	22 MINNESOTA	23 MISSISSIPPI	24 MISSOURI	25 MONTANA	26 NEBRASKA	27 NEVADA
1 LIVESTOCK, PRDTS.	266404	138588	571244	1345463	397802	986503	299375	1124559	51102
2 OTHER AGRICULTURE PRDTS.	162322	90441	648648	1071741	676241	837250	345951	831799	25775
3 FORESTRY, FISHERIES	39748	75541	57138	16744	29015	13360	9912	8719	353
4 AGRI.,FORES.,FISH. SERV.	24171	5017	28071	56816	75987	53911	11650	32765	1301
5 IRON, FERRO. ORES MINING	133278	0	189007	505247	0	15644	4115	1	5712
6 NONFERROUS ORES MINING	1542	188	67475	4117	63	16931	84117	38	50650
7 COAL MINING	5080	9	35	10	4	13163	2316	7	16
8 CRUDE PETRO.,NATURAL GAS	19803	10304	243327	485	198853	1134	94955	61022	229
9 STONE, CLAY MINING	50620	26399	95699	26593	12177	58946	8014	17747	14846
10 CHEM.,FERT. MIN. MINING	2999	61	62647	844	15	6333	10369	7	1327
11 NEW CONSTRUCTION	1522868	1845402	2302047	997444	392207	1167957	215578	386080	614917
12 MAINT., REPAIR CONSTR.	306326	459707	730024	419101	168240	478527	142350	244689	79482
13 ORDNANCE, ACCESSORIES	41001	122691	115290	115588	1223	165634	273	1971	127
14 FOOD, KINDRED PRDTS.	1306491	1537622	2079437	2712798	547074	2429150	203588	1648728	36374
15 TOBACCO MANUFACTURES	6659	3213	16045	0	0	20831	0	0	0
16 FABRICS	57883	584518	16310	17889	33306	24985	25	448	12
17 TEXTILE PRDTS.	27456	250366	78313	17513	50175	29667	107	252	33
18 APPAREL	304514	711722	73414	91092	271556	338636	17	12387	251
19 MISC. TEXTILE PRDTS.	33384	145366	362329	27762	18528	58221	163	1800	395
20 LUMBER, WOOD PRDTS.	98389	87476	388227	136739	260253	88831	214529	24618	9183
21 WOODEN CONTAINERS	7725	8216	7039	4492	23161	8697	639	726	30
22 HOUSEHOLD FURNITURE	37599	136188	127277	25433	92866	44797	935	11687	1043
23 OTHER FURNITURE	32770	39717	210448	22846	6897	39473	736	9733	324
24 PAPER, ALLIED PRDTS.	211042	582573	829522	319692	81645	124947	24372	10677	506
25 PAPERBOARD CONTAINERS	119733	210754	255644	75316	13272	140508	466	15443	68
26 PRINTING, PUBLISHING	225048	642428	486731	306356	27160	426690	18450	76908	17172
27 CHEMICALS,SELECT. PRDTS.	236109	229973	679845	137473	73635	376448	18140	29283	27313
28 PLASTICS, SYNTHETICS	64676	230373	161505	20183	7895	20098	2491	1603	1001
29 DRUGS, COSMETICS	255983	188005	385300	141474	31910	328344	1286	42876	2683
30 PAINT, ALLIED PRDTS.	43399	60840	173446	19378	1072	103325	81	1718	344
31 PETROLEUM, RELATED INDS.	173179	207164	375414	164105	93130	184767	145518	15089	1568
32 RUBBER, MISC. PLASTICS	208102	690767	453075	71795	65144	115876	916	46905	498
33 LEATHER TANNING, PRDTS.	4615	192292	27803	9107	68	8064	32	1795	1
34 FOOTWEAR, LEATHER PRDTS.	19644	501575	31757	15176	21617	342849	88	780	8
35 GLASS, GLASS PRDTS.	48142	7512	144429	16662	12660	60146	160	388	65
36 STONE, CLAY PRDTS.	155058	244258	412270	188345	78887	242827	26447	55196	48656
37 PRIMARY IRON, STEEL MFR.	568138	220972	2279485	182774	9765	184310	4106	5165	1062
38 PRIMARY NONFERROUS MFR.	497203	281000	832199	30334	14695	145576	228484	79691	75131

39 METAL CONTAINERS	116169	24878	17112	54368	453	97824	33	13354	33
40 FABRICATED METAL PRDTS.	125669	181933	456583	100741	51839	227548	7432	76324	5989
41 SCREW MACH. PRDTS., ETC.	47234	150775	697648	56910	21009	64982	771	3623	290
42 OTHER FAB. METAL PRDTS.	105284	341067	867014	94270	21652	190198	4378	12108	1778
43 ENGINES, TURBINES	6252	195094	459039	23108	581	17793	218	1128	30
44 FARM MACH., EQUIP.	4198	6678	285137	133735	28750	61735	3989	36144	27
45 CONSTRUC. MACH., EQUIP.	8296	11638	201526	93887	14516	43712	1080	5712	329
46 MATERIAL HANDLING MACH.	11412	40214	227921	25303	13114	18475	214	1569	23
47 METALWORKING MACHINERY	71528	232693	998229	42400	2205	61263	967	2598	442
48 SPECIAL MACH., EQUIP.	70473	346476	227199	38919	11815	48974	579	1737	259
49 GENERAL MACH., EQUIP.	25953	179894	386798	62128	4235	64682	648	22919	339
50 MACHINE SHOP PRDTS.	32500	71939	239013	42335	7807	93308	1637	3073	1099
51 OFFICE, COMPUT. MACHINES	12828	137370	318009	327119	318	24446	957	879	100
52 SERVICE IND. MACHINES	40535	96649	342745	142157	13449	155417	244	3157	827
53 ELECT. TRANSMISS. EQUIP.	42957	258363	235712	95044	13390	170674	816	2904	844
54 HOUSEHOLD APPLIANCES	13816	47273	304424	141160	22585	61491	73	2295	61
55 ELECTRIC LIGHTING EQUIP.	7574	185103	66268	21078	45651	100238	916	798	254
56 RADIO, TV, ETC., EQUIP.	452634	913685	101158	116901	10030	121307	1602	97812	4035
57 ELECTRONIC COMPONENTS	27879	381917	81911	53743	9244	18902	337	22238	321
58 MISC. ELECTRICAL MACH.	31386	68230	239057	23762	3269	38544	641	3938	210
59 MOTOR VEHICLES, EQUIP.	691209	330211	15316101	294952	51699	2520400	798	55680	525
60 AIRCRAFT, PARTS	230276	226755	213953	48758	907	355653	2087	2088	402
61 OTHER TRANSPORT. EQUIP.	256765	113016	270616	24810	7611	102291	1213	32951	76
62 PROFESS., SCIEN. INSTRU.	35925	321290	277552	57389	7202	50535	1920	26440	110
63 MEDICAL, PHOTO. EQUIP.	9514	233558	18403	26432	557	18327	49	787	12
64 MISC. MANUFACTURING	56500	427088	268630	90841	37453	94183	3852	17920	3338
65 TRANSPORT., WAREHOUSING	676411	958115	1233547	673436	189260	1176218	141727	342056	97129
66 COMMUNICA.,EXC. BRDCAST.	231574	408974	624314	222784	115259	307176	38173	116226	15637
67 RADIO, TV BROADCASTING	23935	63674	77097	30276	10997	42274	6953	15493	4819
68 ELEC.,GAS,WATER,SAN.SER.	534857	862981	1442396	561828	292109	632128	165399	224703	82721
69 WHOLESALE, RETAIL TRADE	1897609	3723293	5024186	2399257	777990	3286627	385179	994887	259915
70 FINANCE, INSURANCE	448919	1376089	1035253	635816	174035	842951	75128	290846	68199
71 REAL ESTATE, RENTAL	1596395	2262914	3169849	1664503	469104	2061857	254023	618817	282534
72 HOTELS, PERSONAL SERV.	224606	455513	574929	251209	98339	356532	51428	107352	180465
73 BUSINESS SERVICES	501931	1203439	1530730	637997	108377	795199	52655	177955	82952
74 RESEARCH, DEVELOPMENT	0	0	0	0	0	0	0	0	0
75 AUTO. REPAIR, SERVICES	214711	296635	509286	194746	87074	258832	44188	93806	34252
76 AMUSEMENTS	124536	167870	213433	80678	21993	113606	12576	40913	248831
77 MED.,EDUC. SERVICES	707581	2445793	928090	519333	90818	870353	49245	170095	25051
78 FEDERAL GOVT. ENTERPRISE	89338	178189	157742	95509	46752	147627	20799	46631	16545
79 STATE, LOCAL GOVT. ENT.	91683	202896	353681	127521	33417	88769	25618	160009	10145
80 ZERO ENTRIES	0	0	0	0	0	0	0	0	0
81 SERVICE IND. RESIDUAL	-1369029	256012	-3686722	31304	-528794	870135	-289237	16320	219251
82 TOTAL FINAL DEMAND	11833880	17886896	26053648	10593298	4720399	13270411	2191915	4015276	1906583
83 SECONDARY TRANSFERS-OUT	672904	1549975	2561634	941858	287165	1099510	154403	473462	66508
84 ZERO ENTRIES	0	0	0	0	0	0	0	0	0
85 SCRAP ENTRIES	0	0	0	0	0	0	0	0	0
86 ZERO ENTRIES	0	0	0	0	0	0	0	0	0
87 STATE TOTAL CONSUMPTION	28355712	50592288	80918768	31208528	11183835	40746448	5538378	13158324	4692849

TABLE C-22

1963 STATE TOTAL PRODUCTION
(THOUSANDS OF CURRENT DOLLARS)

INDUSTRY TITLE	28 NEW HAMPSHIRE	29 NEW JERSEY	30 NEW MEXICO	31 NEW YORK	32 NORTH CAROLINA	33 NORTH DAKOTA	34 OHIO	35 OKLAHOMA	36 OREGON
1 LIVESTOCK, PRDTS.	58039	207759	218513	831791	487817	302079	837207	534225	256108
2 OTHER AGRICULTURE PRDTS.	20361	230685	140398	636801	1108009	597585	862372	421681	311679
3 FORESTRY, FISHERIES	3264	56175	2892	164050	42679	10959	14432	5626	171821
4 AGRI.,FORES.,FISH. SERV.	3143	9541	9368	24300	66469	20007	39911	29716	16464
5 IRON, FERRO. ORES MINING	0	22258	5392	61632	3066	1663	38293	36	2536
6 NONFERROUS ORES MINING	1	7165	158144	57839	260	8521	444	2024	2750
7 COAL MINING	1	25	9217	614	15	9377	169973	5256	10
8 CRUDE PETRO.,NATURAL GAS	82	35367	462259	163533	696	116910	27480	781209	675
9 STONE, CLAY MINING	3588	70302	11633	123461	39726	8179	107700	20980	26265
10 CHEM.,FERT. MIN. MINING	3	16442	100227	21929	3698	2484	14353	7	47
11 NEW CONSTRUCTION	159572	1527017	437185	5045863	1000997	186738	2943049	970743	707139
12 MAINT., REPAIR CONSTR.	62198	571917	126501	1675894	385430	136416	1223710	259764	244943
13 ORDNANCE, ACCESSORIES	905	56113	68424	242825	38289	14	275970	47270	2902
14 FOOD, KINDRED PRDTS.	110685	3044042	136346	5757958	1074703	170735	3180964	598838	687087
15 TOBACCO MANUFACTURES	0	39552	0	93540	3636463	0	37276	0	0
16 FABRICS	163338	376568	219	522626	3592927	49	33443	1705	49866
17 TEXTILE PRDTS.	14150	168868	65	311685	220850	205	133048	670	19234
18 APPAREL	55884	853912	2493	6428736	1233590	34	402406	47627	52761
19 MISC. TEXTILE PRDTS.	14336	213848	2354	608783	294200	316	51114	4377	25651
20 LUMBER, WOOD PRDTS.	72201	131450	31122	413161	316926	48870	165142	30305	1858043
21 WOODEN CONTAINERS	4783	13066	187	16265	10828	73	11602	102	11058
22 HOUSEHOLD FURNITURE	21104	116075	1571	281868	585619	261	150902	12182	35793
23 OTHER FURNITURE	8409	53570	2245	253867	58833	207	180601	5634	5938
24 PAPER, ALLIED PRDTS.	160199	553522	362	1270151	311907	46370	705994	13917	213801
25 PAPERBOARD CONTAINERS	12054	326312	277	450055	86838	1007	343595	16491	19632
26 PRINTING, PUBLISHING	45886	599687	20465	4051508	136742	16305	1017524	81948	82848
27 CHEMICALS,SELECT. PRDTS.	16108	1870549	47412	890181	174167	5085	804942	60859	65128
28 PLASTICS, SYNTHETICS	18090	373740	713	299355	173241	4177	338543	6232	7339
29 DRUGS, COSMETICS	2975	1536825	662	1345812	67992	717	555292	6133	11096
30 PAINT, ALLIED PRDTS.	646	285833	526	138607	22539	21	227978	6328	11540
31 PETROLEUM, RELATED INDS.	1815	1479932	77493	415572	15412	39594	944545	785620	19349
32 RUBBER, MISC. PLASTICS	52331	585590	5126	579322	87820	829	2013450	104724	11884
33 LEATHER TANNING, PRDTS.	33242	71758	6	131237	7909	77	32784	94	1581
34 FOOTWEAR, LEATHER PRDTS.	195769	116361	1422	606235	18046	14	93586	4508	4563
35 GLASS, GLASS PRDTS.	1628	240500	227	212798	51289	82	418236	66324	10092
36 STONE, CLAY PRDTS.	42551	449194	34747	678770	125652	16483	799524	84510	68492
37 PRIMARY IRON, STEEL MFR.	18225	411564	496	1126965	38050	3845	4144161	30530	75389
38 PRIMARY NONFERROUS MFR.	19931	1152163	41268	1595807	95842	19808	1006611	85107	124481

39 METAL CONTAINERS	113	264338	40	130891	950	29	140275	3404	19112
40 FABRICATED METAL PRDTS.	12948	355662	7074	624811	102699	5675	962041	151101	81063
41 SCREW MACH. PRDTS., ETC.	7681	225464	1745	366510	19626	1316	695775	8081	5583
42 OTHER FAB. METAL PRDTS.	13300	510009	1898	649745	62249	819	1001052	61444	36654
43 ENGINES, TURBINES	778	16418	264	235689	2528	534	77070	4900	1763
44 FARM MACH., EQUIP.	513	10929	379	100804	21506	14509	173819	8178	8355
45 CONSTRUC. MACH., EQUIP.	22877	54936	1393	61929	3072	2293	423661	127478	11063
46 MATERIAL HANDLING MACH.	1055	128514	70	138686	3068	425	221000	5198	36667
47 METALWORKING MACHINERY	13102	150864	1688	387096	12968	1846	897652	5165	4393
48 SPECIAL MACH., EQUIP.	50940	256692	1012	343928	122977	990	387454	11301	41363
49 GENERAL MACH., EQUIP.	25164	350475	408	544864	12706	901	730604	53123	9228
50 MACHINE SHOP PRDTS.	5688	82252	5957	203361	14462	1140	208652	14078	19941
51 OFFICE, COMPUT. MACHINES	4716	152658	820	1091624	10248	2234	237242	2929	774
52 SERVICE IND. MACHINES	5543	134715	1228	385551	27187	86	384856	20912	7623
53 ELECT. TRANSMISS. EQUIP.	63623	304478	968	736047	103599	308	849184	21683	52569
54 HOUSEHOLD APPLIANCES	2894	69165	84	197611	52263	106	1054128	4994	7194
55 ELECTRIC LIGHTING EQUIP.	4152	273951	176	384027	25392	816	357421	1741	3160
56 RADIO, TV, ETC., EQUIP.	56985	1278196	4409	1942088	235463	2093	415433	178236	4040
57 ELECTRONIC COMPONENTS	48555	357279	1313	612318	51532	365	198450	9934	2766
58 MISC. ELECTRICAL MACH.	1793	104037	341	191477	65773	1104	251881	7281	8985
59 MOTOR VEHICLES, EQUIP.	1885	825911	3168	1918402	44404	301	5277147	65526	90961
60 AIRCRAFT, PARTS	1296	377453	3353	1206622	25043	3964	1048851	485976	19425
61 OTHER TRANSPORT. EQUIP.	2067	184650	568	276349	23726	662	200715	16208	60776
62 PROFESS., SCIEN. INSTRU.	5352	286698	3694	531983	39732	230	194562	15042	8754
63 MEDICAL, PHOTO. EQUIP.	6508	137695	160	1364975	22420	93	20870	926	10185
64 MISC. MANUFACTURING	25761	520819	4215	1747585	42570	6507	347805	18519	22846
65 TRANSPORT., WAREHOUSING	66239	1650878	154910	4990305	626341	93541	1964243	479033	483202
66 COMMUNICA.,EXC. BRDCAST.	34202	476454	57458	1573442	256293	45595	709944	169959	137271
67 RADIO, TV BROADCASTING	3646	12197	8853	541721	34438	5396	104323	18982	18948
68 ELEC.,GAS,WATER,SAN.SER.	104143	997254	181036	2718811	515458	61746	2047485	370932	230312
69 WHOLESALE, RETAIL TRADE	332831	4591339	450430	16527113	2334366	381851	6084866	1238752	1357812
70 FINANCE, INSURANCE	89312	1062438	95421	6515646	527384	69183	1430322	333493	272598
71 REAL ESTATE, RENTAL	198597	3188444	352073	12824585	1144242	201968	4259590	910969	772295
72 HOTELS, PERSONAL SERV.	64519	561368	73264	2051037	287473	36254	704827	148674	152283
73 BUSINESS SERVICES	63506	1148397	98096	8605861	323498	37442	1687751	272000	239510
74 RESEARCH, DEVELOPMENT	0	0	0	0	0	0	0	0	0
75 AUTO. REPAIR, SERVICES	36870	358322	54443	965517	206392	36500	537373	145867	135525
76 AMUSEMENTS	29756	233540	22252	2015922	70490	10442	286591	46177	45615
77 MED.,EDUC. SERVICES	163007	991290	65755	6154695	539494	39835	1609580	209252	233743
78 FEDERAL GOVT. ENTERPRISE	16238	159315	29038	582769	108009	20253	229583	70925	57328
79 STATE, LOCAL GOVT. ENT.	38832	161703	21973	782680	171869	8746	476327	72770	102565
80 ZERO ENTRIES	0	0	0	0	0	0	0	0	0
81 SERVICE IND. RESIDUAL	-251316	-3333740	-343653	8883811	-1215315	-298279	-2228753	-575131	-456757
82 TOTAL FINAL DEMAND	2008729	22168784	3091135	67743200	11277254	1956090	30984400	7296452	6441548
83 SECONDARY TRANSFERS-OUT	155434	1985796	181064	6185816	966784	126419	3576623	536430	382190
84 ZERO ENTRIES	0	0	0	0	0	0	0	0	0
85 SCRAP ENTRIES	0	0	0	0	0	0	0	0	0
86 ZERO ENTRIES	0	0	0	0	0	0	0	0	0
87 STATE TOTAL CONSUMPTION	4937331	62103280	6797930	203569312	34938160	4658427	95570832	18182192	16397215

TABLE C-22

1963 STATE TOTAL PRODUCTION
(THOUSANDS OF CURRENT DOLLARS)

INDUSTRY TITLE	37 PENNSYL-VANIA	38 RHODE ISLAND	39 SOUTH CAROLINA	40 SOUTH DAKOTA	41 TENNESSEE	42 TEXAS	43 UTAH	44 VERMONT	45 VIRGINIA
1 LIVESTOCK, PRDTS.	828353	17386	165246	674202	408000	1493131	165369	149036	389285
2 OTHER AGRICULTURE PRDTS.	490273	11288	387032	440075	483254	1769819	76864	52686	339553
3 FORESTRY, FISHERIES	44817	6049	27707	5361	10966	105599	1483	10662	45590
4 AGRI.,FORES.,FISH. SERV.	34653	2805	23287	18484	23819	206796	5414	1594	24594
5 IRON, FERRO. ORES MINING	200864	0	6	493	379	15556	18143	1732	8288
6 NONFERROUS ORES MINING	3536	3	289	25958	14805	57868	230484	7744	5865
7 COAL MINING	681847	1	11	107	27323	1314	33592	179	159596
8 CRUDE PETRO.,NATURAL GAS	361536	134	6789	212	282	4094266	105576	44668	1631
9 STONE, CLAY MINING	108253	2867	28441	10251	51750	81820	9135	15749	60224
10 CHEM.,FERT. MIN. MINING	6603	9	469	33	35066	68166	8957	2619	1081
11 NEW CONSTRUCTION	2211964	237175	327279	203777	1008802	4040992	460565	66006	1614012
12 MAINT., REPAIR CONSTR.	899318	58058	152453	135017	262444	1234860	105234	38133	345474
13 ORDNANCE, ACCESSORIES	197410	2954	931	52	66887	118178	141470	7480	5388
14 FOOD, KINDRED PRDTS.	3918974	170645	397470	493930	1461501	3293531	355020	179218	968312
15 TOBACCO MANUFACTURES	392296	49	99607	0	59406	6532	0	0	1430491
16 FABRICS	586677	351196	2972455	16	256529	119867	790	7927	490083
17 TEXTILE PRDTS.	325829	56971	250698	30	70100	57772	599	3330	104587
18 APPAREL	1890111	61340	278428	7	748526	411955	24414	22056	302713
19 MISC. TEXTILE PRDTS.	153026	21649	165957	809	56737	60761	1618	1021	46920
20 LUMBER, WOOD PRDTS.	211101	6040	182317	13320	186205	259631	14878	87699	252874
21 WOODEN CONTAINERS	11069	518	9671	137	19473	9700	233	1767	14387
22 HOUSEHOLD FURNITURE	209604	2605	38474	916	198560	105792	8549	23206	285669
23 OTHER FURNITURE	164097	13535	6496	225	28945	55033	4005	561	39739
24 PAPER, ALLIED PRDTS.	761141	21149	216990	386	299731	237003	5209	112595	328594
25 PAPERBOARD CONTAINERS	352581	18818	65576	912	64715	105176	2759	11033	53098
26 PRINTING, PUBLISHING	1093252	57645	47438	19498	215382	431206	45084	29103	150956
27 CHEMICALS,SELECT. PRDTS.	722375	49733	87341	4081	511210	2970680	30099	5789	341596
28 PLASTICS, SYNTHETICS	437383	46263	211157	181	550389	581487	1482	8213	721452
29 DRUGS, COSMETICS	660176	11614	39520	1592	123292	180591	3856	1466	97825
30 PAINT, ALLIED PRDTS.	160828	7511	4485	25	25229	124286	1868	3976	14435
31 PETROLEUM, RELATED INDS.	1407311	32259	33423	522	45640	5925762	165986	1145	75424
32 RUBBER, MISC. PLASTICS	561894	155531	72603	3463	206512	235649	12569	22971	109229
33 LEATHER TANNING, PRDTS.	66008	392	1123	3	37386	3496	422	3955	12917
34 FOOTWEAR, LEATHER PRDTS.	306878	13852	590	11	192890	33318	566	5655	47473
35 GLASS, GLASS PRDTS.	404243	32812	54416	39	110288	37111	439	226	25685
36 STONE, CLAY PRDTS.	699160	14904	62735	15784	163245	561801	67909	47698	182857
37 PRIMARY IRON, STEEL MFR.	5594623	75196	46770	273	110640	449765	166869	8295	92623
38 PRIMARY NONFERROUS MFR.	838278	201502	24037	52	318047	624850	147730	32790	85209

39 METAL CONTAINERS	168494	300	885	42	13705	112311	7034	127	10569
40 FABRICATED METAL PRDTS.	965826	19247	48282	11869	197022	421251	57401	5604	146125
41 SCREW MACH. PRDTS., ETC.	480370	34425	11875	126	40543	36657	2644	2213	6604
42 OTHER FAB. METAL PRDTS.	865129	77799	22352	1168	72757	294044	12414	5143	61073
43 ENGINES, TURBINES	301839	654	491	103	2772	28459	2113	1001	1877
44 FARM MACH., EQUIP.	112693	1034	3822	4279	63695	33068	2063	8400	10042
45 CONSTRUC. MACH., EQUIP.	176119	1101	1206	281	10451	426730	31458	4071	7493
46 MATERIAL HANDLING MACH.	170272	1500	5964	4226	23142	32515	1015	444	6261
47 METALWORKING MACHINERY	393776	59738	32704	3390	16601	39699	2960	69628	5803
48 SPECIAL MACH., EQUIP.	288741	48680	83532	425	23323	81809	4666	5472	21663
49 GENERAL MACH., EQUIP.	467794	17884	18828	3327	30279	102151	10318	2491	20398
50 MACHINE SHOP PRDTS.	121421	9835	9273	3132	18982	63488	4436	2169	11216
51 OFFICE, COMPUT. MACHINES	192678	659	10262	40	1584	14862	644	28079	49749
52 SERVICE IND. MACHINES	249589	4118	4142	220	47989	150940	10819	4770	26411
53 ELECT. TRANSMISS. EQUIP.	796396	7897	29950	99	72447	67667	7705	2870	117106
54 HOUSEHOLD APPLIANCES	148752	4121	9151	138	147143	31927	1043	595	7176
55 ELECTRIC LIGHTING EQUIP.	336901	52971	2340	69	24412	24216	1743	8151	4429
56 RADIO, TV, ETC., EQUIP.	328525	17048	3375	179	150742	305846	19973	3677	118670
57 ELECTRONIC COMPONENTS	560125	25367	38602	2149	23661	57903	10414	15556	91740
58 MISC. ELECTRICAL MACH.	123496	11035	1298	20	18671	38065	592	8185	6803
59 MOTOR VEHICLES, EQUIP.	1052341	14758	9166	1200	96116	682538	5155	1191	242809
60 AIRCRAFT, PARTS	820738	10409	999	113	74273	673412	244094	78707	26938
61 OTHER TRANSPORT. EQUIP.	593281	8482	13475	2928	65257	162649	9425	843	114834
62 PROFESS., SCIEN. INSTRU.	467643	34542	24442	222	52694	69646	2799	10083	14865
63 MEDICAL, PHOTO. EQUIP.	52956	12100	15122	14	3299	13042	764	5093	26873
64 MISC. MANUFACTURING	503098	278316	54981	2179	96308	84161	13864	9102	72736
65 TRANSPORT., WAREHOUSING	2486946	112811	216417	66530	563398	2255566	199686	59743	788716
66 COMMUNICA.,EXC. BRDCAST.	701265	63906	118757	33985	291747	774675	80983	17842	259185
67 RADIO, TV BROADCASTING	126202	10305	15926	6586	33221	88734	8130	2936	31111
68 ELEC.,GAS,WATER,SAN.SER.	1991061	108143	237457	71152	322709	1633587	191762	54160	614077
69 WHOLESALE, RETAIL TRADE	6719487	532477	929666	360349	2001980	6027164	545714	197536	1992311
70 FINANCE, INSURANCE	1858242	167376	248967	74092	493534	1689051	122315	49098	493707
71 REAL ESTATE, RENTAL	4278689	336590	482988	235459	1008260	3588172	400991	107549	1505086
72 HOTELS, PERSONAL SERV.	846571	65063	123634	39707	235413	750735	64205	37367	284118
73 BUSINESS SERVICES	1970574	123110	148037	42538	402534	1304705	108217	36282	386791
74 RESEARCH, DEVELOPMENT	0	0	0	0	0	0	0	0	0
75 AUTO. REPAIR, SERVICES	631036	39016	97410	37552	184659	619107	58299	23065	198118
76 AMUSEMENTS	239596	37164	29311	18337	61232	197083	28896	14663	67528
77 MED.,EDUC. SERVICES	2482999	189905	154877	54852	481443	1000462	199121	141081	440271
78 FEDERAL GOVT. ENTERPRISE	267554	28997	63592	18668	250840	278693	23699	10896	161868
79 STATE, LOCAL GOVT. ENT.	488781	14346	44276	18355	239455	355233	40531	17500	195412
80 ZERO ENTRIES	0	0	0	0	0	0	0	0	0
81 SERVICE IND. RESIDUAL	-3733203	-210985	-1184038	-116456	-315082	-2699341	-116000	-432152	-1355095
82 TOTAL FINAL DEMAND	33880160	2578682	5364011	1798322	8953972	30835664	3143554	1761721	13380969
83 SECONDARY TRANSFERS-OUT	3355498	222663	474485	150759	930500	2691819	231139	98097	757902
84 ZERO ENTRIES	0	0	0	0	0	0	0	0	0
85 SCRAP ENTRIES	0	0	0	0	0	0	0	0	0
86 ZERO ENTRIES	0	0	0	0	0	0	0	0	0
87 STATE TOTAL CONSUMPTION	97328800	6936048	14512011	5022962	25982032	85611280	8224034	3501033	30708064

TABLE C-22

1963 STATE TOTAL PRODUCTION
(THOUSANDS OF CURRENT DOLLARS)

INDUSTRY TITLE	46 WASHINGTON	47 WEST VIRGINIA	48 WISCONSIN	49 WYOMING	50 ALASKA	51 HAWAII	52 NATIONAL TOTAL
1 LIVESTOCK, PRDTS.	294058	112880	1273475	183605	4391	47344	26684256
2 OTHER AGRICULTURE PRDTS.	529111	71996	561187	77410	220	267476	27360944
3 FORESTRY, FISHERIES	109271	5493	24155	1614	60113	5778	1751019
4 AGRI.,FORES.,FISH. SERV.	23226	8313	25940	3104	36	31428	1771890
5 IRON, FERRO. ORES MINING	2612	0	2687	20588	515	5	1484556
6 NONFERROUS ORES MINING	19395	9	9227	62384	6088	2	1521978
7 COAL MINING	4865	738675	185	10414	2821	3	2636841
8 CRUDE PETRO.,NATURAL GAS	61482	76267	42781	382720	14657	23841	12264684
9 STONE, CLAY MINING	27244	22781	53755	18101	1380	7059	2024071
10 CHEM.,FERT. MIN. MINING	2617	364	2500	17791	152	181	697145
11 NEW CONSTRUCTION	1381119	276827	1183412	209388	174119	379980	65518976
12 MAINT., REPAIR CONSTR.	368361	148439	426113	78597	23533	79152	19794432
13 ORDNANCE, ACCESSORIES	56993	92885	24633	184	1145	115	6341393
14 FOOD, KINDRED PRDTS.	1134988	215325	2795639	83007	81291	522154	74271440
15 TOBACCO MANUFACTURES	0	25707	980	0	0	542	7420295
16 FABRICS	11479	5815	14548	3	1	942	13038434
17 TEXTILE PRDTS.	4891	1869	47991	18	4	533	3667991
18 APPAREL	52492	43608	144954	1	1831	24270	18024784
19 MISC. TEXTILE PRDTS.	16153	2154	17644	73	1	1708	3170687
20 LUMBER, WOOD PRDTS.	1083495	66705	274648	18009	25334	10834	10662755
21 WOODEN CONTAINERS	13146	1198	12055	55	82	45	419344
22 HOUSEHOLD FURNITURE	29793	8015	52472	107	39	6207	4067025
23 OTHER FURNITURE	13353	5507	42868	89	17	3463	1922751
24 PAPER, ALLIED PRDTS.	704824	28172	1084490	154	77	11213	13096528
25 PAPERBOARD CONTAINERS	63631	14330	173213	22	11	4187	4712501
26 PRINTING, PUBLISHING	130152	52754	368853	8539	3885	24283	16210268
27 CHEMICALS,SELECT. PRDTS.	290909	1227956	94631	24710	325	26871	16893456
28 PLASTICS, SYNTHETICS	31509	358888	31899	1648	6	908	6342086
29 DRUGS, COSMETICS	12997	33666	167748	537	127	2666	9053071
30 PAINT, ALLIED PRDTS.	16713	6226	43405	68	4	79	2462062
31 PETROLEUM, RELATED INDS.	226949	75163	58619	382542	2640	49406	21826576
32 RUBBER, MISC. PLASTICS	18080	22116	193813	296	48	1467	9882920
33 LEATHER TANNING, PRDTS.	924	12974	122354	1	0	60	966643
34 FOOTWEAR, LEATHER PRDTS.	3223	4477	147028	5	142	1863	3476383
35 GLASS, GLASS PRDTS.	8561	245457	6017	29	18	1147	2931988
36 STONE, CLAY PRDTS.	122652	82392	181740	21620	6713	26729	9550651
37 PRIMARY IRON, STEEL MFR.	59513	525071	407765	95	23	10353	24490160
38 PRIMARY NONFERROUS MFR.	474291	226939	182785	451	1073	161	14167797

39	METAL CONTAINERS	49314	15361	98664	23	13	20439	2436142
40	FABRICATED METAL PRDTS.	89826	75201	314175	796	64	6108	8970211
41	SCREW MACH. PRDTS., ETC.	10254	22491	244759	553	16	623	4910872
42	OTHER FAB. METAL PRDTS.	37946	74637	164536	922	207	1937	8938939
43	ENGINES, TURBINES	5670	1192	407235	26	0	53	2394770
44	FARM MACH., EQUIP.	15387	9801	300788	8	1	692	3069817
45	CONSTRUC. MACH., EQUIP.	30050	43277	368894	764	1	54	4050031
46	MATERIAL HANDLING MACH.	23500	5246	46743	19	0	175	1618968
47	METALWORKING MACHINERY	11547	19324	183399	111	24	408	5134837
48	SPECIAL MACH., EQUIP.	28337	5045	221221	24	3	4681	3702286
49	GENERAL MACH., EQUIP.	12320	4245	273764	192	12	434	5323622
50	MACHINE SHOP PRDTS.	26014	9888	54932	1024	5	1428	2238225
51	OFFICE, COMPUT. MACHINES	8192	397	16246	37	10	180	3923617
52	SERVICE IND. MACHINES	11857	5641	143577	21	4	382	3387871
53	ELECT. TRANSMISS. EQUIP.	21904	25117	492587	537	2	326	6486795
54	HOUSEHOLD APPLIANCES	9871	3509	196144	34	1	54	4666047
55	ELECTRIC LIGHTING EQUIP.	14074	80029	32707	121	8	432	3080901
56	RADIO, TV, ETC., EQUIP.	29369	4726	200605	48	3285	1068	12379851
57	ELECTRONIC COMPONENTS	5431	11339	53295	28	1	143	4524396
58	MISC. ELECTRICAL MACH.	3970	609	99890	10	0	144	2254272
59	MOTOR VEHICLES, EQUIP.	69151	28728	2373783	44	21	1213	39870368
60	AIRCRAFT, PARTS	493165	6862	26317	1860	4	91	14306059
61	OTHER TRANSPORT. EQUIP.	223341	44006	123806	96	18	1660	4918926
62	PROFESS., SCIEN. INSTRU.	8886	12338	129266	1268	2135	244	4269297
63	MEDICAL, PHOTO. EQUIP.	10554	5832	7339	8	5805	598	2523834
64	MISC. MANUFACTURING	64865	12654	147926	139	23360	4656	7150474
65	TRANSPORT., WAREHOUSING	802473	324955	605535	106077	114325	195967	39142544
66	COMMUNICA.,EXC. BRDCAST.	228267	97412	211171	19939	5745	48447	13494968
67	RADIO, TV BROADCASTING	28029	13869	33852	3347	3338	7473	2307967
68	ELEC.,GAS,WATER,SAN.SER.	393481	430017	592201	110188	27148	71894	29660288
69	WHOLESALE, RETAIL TRADE	1941824	715876	2356300	177648	125006	348873	120613248
70	FINANCE, INSURANCE	432394	145559	557098	33081	25037	130936	33700112
71	REAL ESTATE, RENTAL	1511016	442437	1567485	137593	66074	424962	83886832
72	HOTELS, PERSONAL SERV.	219669	94019	279507	41367	19511	74319	15369794
73	BUSINESS SERVICES	368091	154206	549083	28199	30145	96171	35945360
74	RESEARCH, DEVELOPMENT	0	0	0	0	0	0	0
75	AUTO. REPAIR, SERVICES	193983	63680	207714	21921	9092	37057	10866429
76	AMUSEMENTS	78986	47427	82436	9011	6796	22727	7697033
77	MED.,EDUC. SERVICES	365117	164225	289838	18735	18607	119496	33159856
78	FEDERAL GOVT. ENTERPRISE	150087	30507	80047	9122	53063	60064	5743413
79	STATE, LOCAL GOVT. ENT.	323928	55536	67792	14506	13428	16278	7236000
80	ZERO ENTRIES	0	0	0	0	0	0	0
81	SERVICE IND. RESIDUAL	-1137205	-641962	-1734975	-178205	-176635	-141195	-25728976
82	TOTAL FINAL DEMAND	11651945	4722030	10985449	1225991	1306733	3391701	609125888
83	SECONDARY TRANSFERS-OUT	793093	405004	1193240	113931	35337	107124	52357376
84	ZERO ENTRIES	0	0	0	0	0	0	0
85	SCRAP ENTRIES	0	0	0	0	0	0	0
86	ZERO ENTRIES	0	0	0	0	0	0	0
87	STATE TOTAL CONSUMPTION	27065040	12639707	34944576	3509146	2130612	6634972	1703690496

TABLE C-23

1963 STATE TOTAL CONSUMPTION
(THOUSANDS OF CURRENT DOLLARS)

INDUSTRY TITLE	1 ALABAMA	2 ARIZONA	3 ARKANSAS	4 CALIFORNIA	5 COLORADO	6 CONNECTICUT	7 DELAWARE	8 DISTRICT OF COLUMBIA	9 FLORIDA
1 LIVESTOCK, PRDTS.	354597	215395	336463	2081910	647660	161660	65277	36172	380592
2 OTHER AGRICULTURE PRDTS.	427540	167929	224503	2260385	300224	132852	106600	21787	616857
3 FORESTRY, FISHERIES	32614	18376	22109	178957	4966	5942	2728	0	56866
4 AGRI.,FORES.,FISH. SERV.	54483	32478	82708	182837	13665	8273	7194	0	55372
5 IRON, FERRO. ORES MINING	49461	4234	568	86216	16668	12477	9810	5	2812
6 NONFERROUS ORES MINING	38982	209999	27188	25081	78188	2844	1821	0	6059
7 COAL MINING	55876	11713	11997	121856	18367	22380	8114	4829	31819
8 CRUDE PETRO.,NATURAL GAS	54737	20471	83512	1391977	69481	27425	80900	5408	50396
9 STONE, CLAY MINING	39336	17906	19781	191200	20008	23668	7382	5957	68050
10 CHEM.,FERT. MIN. MINING	11194	1498	4262	53508	2994	3993	1524	140	88845
11 NEW CONSTRUCTION	840568	769136	448501	12453446	848791	1086300	201559	385666	2628530
12 MAINT., REPAIR CONSTR.	228615	183255	183867	2501539	265475	267749	42874	79517	604653
13 ORDNANCE, ACCESSORIES	76258	63304	8904	1945879	34995	211661	3657	79035	154754
14 FOOD, KINDRED PRDTS.	1011910	494428	677414	7910874	819045	1083186	201520	291686	1870958
15 TOBACCO MANUFACTURES	82747	34400	41720	491108	48030	94187	13436	22696	199805
16 FABRICS	375003	15310	52491	450235	20942	185794	43220	4080	84414
17 TEXTILE PRDTS.	79452	11783	24247	279677	29605	66509	10705	7835	46227
18 APPAREL	261122	104748	112977	1611740	142334	307535	49463	67975	431524
19 MISC. TEXTILE PRDTS.	41503	16168	17802	276610	23110	46048	13823	10060	64810
20 LUMBER, WOOD PRDTS.	193122	64336	171974	1413608	99750	112056	22433	21230	310948
21 WOODEN CONTAINERS	4094	4656	4313	71409	4347	5356	1013	442	14327
22 HOUSEHOLD FURNITURE	52582	26769	37987	434210	37566	63028	10616	20520	121967
23 OTHER FURNITURE	22314	13954	11776	232147	20377	34633	5386	17160	50905
24 PAPER, ALLIED PRDTS.	179227	49104	105666	1166908	81429	190087	32227	68743	334792
25 PAPERBOARD CONTAINERS	51962	14907	39223	406612	28705	75992	12290	8842	78151
26 PRINTING, PUBLISHING	120738	81159	68213	1443004	132184	264246	29213	193718	306992
27 CHEMICALS,SELECT. PRDTS.	343621	78469	78701	1041021	88564	213425	118538	25438	473286
28 PLASTICS, SYNTHETICS	137542	5910	21527	315554	21225	126440	48658	1287	55258
29 DRUGS, COSMETICS	111279	54403	61614	865514	78044	149937	24625	59436	230872
30 PAINT, ALLIED PRDTS.	24573	14046	18117	278523	22246	34748	6590	6636	56952
31 PETROLEUM, RELATED INDS.	249496	132446	174953	2365732	209168	252503	78873	93352	483455
32 RUBBER, MISC. PLASTICS	107655	44026	72682	940178	83466	190711	36687	27091	155657
33 LEATHER TANNING, PRDTS.	3609	454	14425	26549	4650	6758	6281	170	5882
34 FOOTWEAR, LEATHER PRDTS.	45392	25540	28736	353766	36714	57970	8928	15071	96999
35 GLASS, GLASS PRDTS.	22529	10682	16317	305145	16575	43501	8956	4660	58110
36 STONE, CLAY PRDTS.	133412	75310	61531	1240552	126662	142043	33986	57960	317139
37 PRIMARY IRON, STEEL MFR.	417876	64893	76135	1765601	150373	410694	105017	18540	220020
38 PRIMARY NONFERROUS MFR.	213988	225468	86262	1217731	52801	594205	26847	1518	141959

39 METAL CONTAINERS	18398	5172	17430	333757	18098	18986	8325	1277	78508
40 FABRICATED METAL PRDTS.	124098	66485	54269	1122567	123685	122745	26125	74774	282796
41 SCREW MACH. PRDTS., ETC.	38557	16381	20563	428347	18852	120032	21311	4221	41249
42 OTHER FAB. METAL PRDTS.	106726	38996	59711	884463	63346	180443	31277	21306	147819
43 ENGINES, TURBINES	18153	14537	8569	164539	14555	73991	3538	11301	37943
44 FARM MACH., EQUIP.	36942	25794	44001	226494	36594	10874	5847	3009	60869
45 CONSTRUC. MACH., EQUIP.	37994	35911	19418	372609	45590	27040	5337	11719	89122
46 MATERIAL HANDLING MACH.	15183	11004	9798	160678	13909	26891	3929	9529	28848
47 METALWORKING MACHINERY	41012	23428	19171	456539	21746	159313	17163	6853	48672
48 SPECIAL MACH., EQUIP.	48834	14714	23966	261772	17882	57619	14518	9187	62936
49 GENERAL MACH., EQUIP.	48008	21233	21012	449743	27049	172211	12618	11355	60285
50 MACHINE SHOP PRDTS.	39904	12058	5814	296537	17085	87661	6475	1889	21557
51 OFFICE, COMPUT. MACHINES	20691	56174	14576	487377	19376	115032	81602	28996	70350
52 SERVICE IND. MACHINES	34686	19902	21827	309467	23923	43287	11048	21649	79569
53 ELECT. TRANSMISS. EQUIP.	58531	50397	46083	638316	53760	130058	10685	22693	101857
54 HOUSEHOLD APPLIANCES	51886	28637	62522	456808	40614	103666	10839	15401	118018
55 ELECTRIC LIGHTING EQUIP.	35409	19070	21296	361439	33626	59306	9090	17084	73816
56 RADIO, TV, ETC., EQUIP.	93129	95660	67214	2226010	62033	199920	13872	80199	281404
57 ELECTRONIC COMPONENTS	19065	51133	30366	719117	12896	99316	2509	11832	71088
58 MISC. ELECTRICAL MACH.	20392	10204	10113	213109	16020	37579	8534	8697	40743
59 MOTOR VEHICLES, EQUIP.	341777	186108	180920	3496437	271110	426627	256270	133004	677020
60 AIRCRAFT, PARTS	335253	123491	8065	3093957	85646	1239577	11698	57082	205004
61 OTHER TRANSPORT. EQUIP.	64456	24182	28891	521691	42145	166343	17126	63623	110713
62 PROFESS., SCIEN. INSTRU.	33324	32000	31253	463612	27779	166099	9930	32891	60088
63 MEDICAL, PHOTO. EQUIP.	21406	14700	10475	288287	20375	46051	6157	24446	55142
64 MISC. MANUFACTURING	75392	44331	43443	752602	66758	170530	16398	33508	160992
65 TRANSPORT., WAREHOUSING	423077	190199	225420	3952511	441726	352039	94592	350558	1065802
66 COMMUNICA.,EXC. BRDCAST.	201786	90878	87045	1538712	144861	209037	34929	111711	418738
67 RADIO, TV BROADCASTING	19161	14158	9244	342161	19094	19772	4163	51476	53742
68 ELEC.,GAS,WATER,SAN.SER.	566154	305796	227498	2612388	349607	364795	77658	93537	706674
69 WHOLESALE, RETAIL TRADE	1408643	838420	781939	12866838	1239524	1735602	343202	759049	3251621
70 FINANCE, INSURANCE	375368	214921	183139	3613152	336690	737396	88669	245437	873825
71 REAL ESTATE, RENTAL	883515	733364	453657	9610564	887847	1237032	219798	1037930	3130964
72 HOTELS, PERSONAL SERV.	159125	156344	99228	1779432	177830	210923	31988	172030	653577
73 BUSINESS SERVICES	243006	211553	104069	4475091	291391	479882	63363	515236	847416
74 RESEARCH, DEVELOPMENT	0	0	0	0	0	0	0	0	0
75 AUTO. REPAIR, SERVICES	150136	103671	86749	1370744	138221	163330	27671	88862	348269
76 AMUSEMENTS	35154	42739	32668	1552639	70883	57512	23456	55086	250064
77 MED.,EDUC. SERVICES	198624	157090	88887	3082363	288006	760758	69211	1180420	561842
78 FEDERAL GOVT. ENTERPRISE	159389	39463	49509	599249	61060	63191	12946	145649	164099
79 STATE, LOCAL GOVT. ENT.	143014	64778	31589	736925	65777	67417	13216	17944	236554
80 DIRECT ALLOCATED IMPORTS	0	0	0	0	0	0	0	0	0
81 TRANSFERRED IMPORTS	0	0	0	0	0	0	0	0	0
82 VALUE ADDED	7392346	4172220	3823063	64265200	5370803	9395624	1574858	4567976	14105259
83 SECONDARY TRANSFERS-IN	694920	318391	329464	5067187	383790	1050147	144609	249416	918139
84 INVENTORY DEPLETION	6227	5246	4777	48433	7019	7838	736	103	7528
85 SCRAP PRODUCTION	-21736	-8892	-5019	-101724	-4401	-28511	-6356	-1967	-15762
86 SCRAP PURCHASED	89161	61106	29499	-53234	49542	-25471	14958	-98955	-47353
87 STATE TOTAL PRODUCTION	21457280	12132210	11054361	186923712	16213117	27638320	4944659	11923685	41554416

TABLE C-23

1963 STATE TOTAL CONSUMPTION
(THOUSANDS OF CURRENT DOLLARS)

INDUSTRY TITLE	10 GEORGIA	11 IDAHO	12 ILLINOIS	13 INDIANA	14 IOWA	15 KANSAS	16 KENTUCKY	17 LOUISIANA	18 MAINE
1 LIVESTOCK, PRDTS.	543525	230332	1498041	701223	2207002	1011258	382529	257722	99692
2 OTHER AGRICULTURE PRDTS.	619856	228777	1605384	1045906	1274648	519929	727185	1257201	94012
3 FORESTRY, FISHERIES	46990	9762	19776	10581	18953	7886	10123	80574	36727
4 AGRI.,FORES.,FISH. SERV.	80969	15778	83219	46003	70294	32360	20826	30375	12960
5 IRON, FERRO. ORES MINING	10448	458	100674	141321	1752	921	16651	14668	85
6 NONFERROUS ORES MINING	2058	47201	30768	13142	974	11376	6363	30854	92
7 COAL MINING	32463	4642	147078	98737	22968	17354	102072	28789	9664
8 CRUDE PETRO.,NATURAL GAS	45604	7326	733213	482544	32748	361393	113300	1031347	6359
9 STONE, CLAY MINING	47741	7666	115082	66572	36762	27482	30934	42795	13004
10 CHEM.,FERT. MIN. MINING	11180	4824	35245	10924	4943	3413	10074	49183	1682
11 NEW CONSTRUCTION	1184579	177637	2996040	1139772	614663	665160	783277	1535151	161994
12 MAINT., REPAIR CONSTR.	299710	97889	1150130	497800	385352	348587	249175	263346	74507
13 ORDNANCE, ACCESSORIES	22651	5146	194061	295604	67894	29947	10451	80511	20094
14 FOOD, KINDRED PRDTS.	1445663	302384	4642653	1856945	1565423	918305	936506	1443263	423577
15 TOBACCO MANUFACTURES	101696	16502	299359	128963	68283	58436	400726	81106	28610
16 FABRICS	992241	3638	275928	95139	24748	21658	96416	41572	134021
17 TEXTILE PRDTS.	228880	5591	158741	81817	44020	30522	26244	28972	24643
18 APPAREL	363978	46644	967251	398274	193199	171187	222117	213022	77545
19 MISC. TEXTILE PRDTS.	80633	9273	158981	73043	29165	27843	33752	35546	12999
20 LUMBER, WOOD PRDTS.	284838	102792	421715	285104	98200	65145	107753	183695	101468
21 WOODEN CONTAINERS	7937	5566	24504	10867	5702	2607	8956	4508	4678
22 HOUSEHOLD FURNITURE	74906	11493	299809	155395	48140	41878	50749	53316	15673
23 OTHER FURNITURE	31843	5211	129053	48383	22965	20055	20697	25862	7377
24 PAPER, ALLIED PRDTS.	312270	23699	957088	291136	153761	104297	128659	270022	132369
25 PAPERBOARD CONTAINERS	99850	11227	373543	144416	72219	41329	66960	60226	27383
26 PRINTING, PUBLISHING	204258	30352	1505036	355908	222294	133254	150957	135951	45419
27 CHEMICALS,SELECT. PRDTS.	373936	68515	960783	421096	178120	154220	320766	517493	59477
28 PLASTICS, SYNTHETICS	286476	825	308019	140094	56747	22810	79986	69941	39739
29 DRUGS, COSMETICS	164644	26311	588792	268335	112218	100406	103092	133734	38248
30 PAINT, ALLIED PRDTS.	42441	6554	182056	77764	34308	26186	33021	28798	6798
31 PETROLEUM, RELATED INDS.	331732	76719	1328009	612309	291704	376801	255582	758789	82160
32 RUBBER, MISC. PLASTICS	168068	19503	683035	363219	142676	91245	112272	89441	52607
33 LEATHER TANNING, PRDTS.	12593	264	49799	10109	4443	1074	8440	3363	57380
34 FOOTWEAR, LEATHER PRDTS.	58360	12026	210956	87807	45328	38857	45047	45882	28914
35 GLASS, GLASS PRDTS.	48276	6372	212828	114544	24078	17463	48527	30915	9114
36 STONE, CLAY PRDTS.	204597	22457	504492	259951	127015	107526	109774	186716	21808
37 PRIMARY IRON, STEEL MFR.	282959	18832	2146058	1420145	242132	143595	268317	269595	35064
38 PRIMARY NONFERROUS MFR.	133728	46937	1029484	780928	125605	75384	130792	147057	16864

39	METAL CONTAINERS	43268	12179	216770	71271	42567	24513	48120	45452	11931
40	FABRICATED METAL PRDTS.	188634	21141	466782	246017	98619	91053	106559	180726	28468
41	SCREW MACH. PRDTS., ETC.	64457	4200	408643	230256	53018	34025	58478	22311	6263
42	OTHER FAB. METAL PRDTS.	137480	17400	627777	354688	92158	68144	114383	97244	32957
43	ENGINES, TURBINES	28202	3791	210080	69699	52243	13722	23713	40772	6077
44	FARM MACH., EQUIP.	55574	29043	286374	102668	252141	84096	55045	46383	10577
45	CONSTRUC. MACH., EQUIP.	48380	8949	380386	61264	51173	39661	53015	202529	8347
46	MATERIAL HANDLING MACH.	22598	3898	125078	39508	14666	13374	18089	23182	5369
47	METALWORKING MACHINERY	52761	5502	412864	195801	50648	40866	43454	27023	10359
48	SPECIAL MACH., EQUIP.	95637	9129	215883	68958	31002	23189	37112	71483	31447
49	GENERAL MACH., EQUIP.	61877	6841	480928	221803	99110	41311	60466	72254	17357
50	MACHINE SHOP PRDTS.	28645	3891	131717	96015	27373	42794	15875	14444	3408
51	OFFICE, COMPUT. MACHINES	31139	5886	231104	53778	22994	18496	41241	32422	9386
52	SERVICE IND. MACHINES	55223	6572	228405	99028	40718	29539	51246	44551	8989
53	ELECT. TRANSMISS. EQUIP.	102314	10652	485572	232408	61466	41220	88118	77315	12278
54	HOUSEHOLD APPLIANCES	70834	14312	364720	177203	89080	41245	127433	57554	16473
55	ELECTRIC LIGHTING EQUIP.	52932	6561	200475	98473	31381	25297	40255	37813	8881
56	RADIO, TV, ETC., EQUIP.	110763	21627	940799	429267	144892	83486	61843	82497	19905
57	ELECTRONIC COMPONENTS	21248	2754	494672	244325	37673	18534	24058	18414	9280
58	MISC. ELECTRICAL MACH.	34626	4749	139804	159390	26776	22449	21254	18623	5583
59	MOTOR VEHICLES, EQUIP.	714785	99558	2027997	1521109	381218	390039	398358	397987	101372
60	AIRCRAFT, PARTS	474678	7380	184446	354142	25656	546661	10011	100693	15131
61	OTHER TRANSPORT. EQUIP.	70547	19711	308546	121608	31054	44291	37794	128461	31919
62	PROFESS., SCIEN. INSTRU.	50830	5445	322632	115139	44227	33470	40417	41993	10489
63	MEDICAL, PHOTO. EQUIP.	29474	5592	174416	47411	22760	19081	19595	25783	7890
64	MISC. MANUFACTURING	113243	19112	462921	166249	82629	56759	73771	77611	27858
65	TRANSPORT., WAREHOUSING	773896	120926	3041057	839116	408292	498681	458570	825203	185153
66	COMMUNICA.,EXC. BRDCAST.	293385	42032	692073	340051	157997	136425	174780	277900	48568
67	RADIO, TV BROADCASTING	31846	5528	158161	35698	25253	25519	22180	26383	7346
68	ELEC.,GAS,WATER,SAN.SER.	542100	116395	1998486	898758	459256	388912	424062	545582	107305
69	WHOLESALE, RETAIL TRADE	2386721	375579	8423752	2818923	1705865	1198714	1351352	1621579	485428
70	FINANCE, INSURANCE	627241	70126	2273097	693260	379314	278028	308632	432550	105751
71	REAL ESTATE, RENTAL	1245649	245502	6213920	1722036	1045478	788700	760997	1096197	247581
72	HOTELS, PERSONAL SERV.	261339	47573	992167	328306	182814	134554	179061	173901	74320
73	BUSINESS SERVICES	420691	67798	3275259	492535	300657	200354	229036	347056	64989
74	RESEARCH, DEVELOPMENT	0	0	0	0	0	0	0	0	0
75	AUTO. REPAIR, SERVICES	221674	46148	609402	250475	156416	134408	135848	150720	51635
76	AMUSEMENTS	71249	13661	416653	91386	56625	43493	66545	72726	18082
77	MED.,EDUC. SERVICES	400176	46814	2474468	642673	337617	178727	292683	342893	122578
78	FEDERAL GOVT. ENTERPRISE	141079	16310	305250	96783	60641	66309	105568	66145	30488
79	STATE, LOCAL GOVT. ENT.	106731	27015	395619	128403	102838	78833	61969	80270	40543
80	DIRECT ALLOCATED IMPORTS	0	0	0	0	0	0	0	0	0
81	TRANSFERRED IMPORTS	0	0	0	0	0	0	0	0	0
82	VALUE ADDED	10324477	1656783	39161552	15000464	8106582	5901478	7618630	9564411	2277954
83	SECONDARY TRANSFERS-IN	813210	140263	4024541	1679244	920615	624858	590927	769155	173937
84	INVENTORY DEPLETION	5068	2297	25724	14895	8230	4422	4889	4590	5554
85	SCRAP PRODUCTION	-29088	-1820	-97705	-56245	-9643	-6277	-10676	-19156	-16386
86	SCRAP PURCHASED	14005	9166	41074	235974	105490	72525	58559	59739	13541
87	STATE TOTAL PRODUCTION	30696176	5121097	112081024	44862032	25089024	18465120	20732368	27984656	6517169

TABLE C-23

1963 STATE TOTAL CONSUMPTION
(THOUSANDS OF CURRENT DOLLARS)

INDUSTRY TITLE	19 MARYLAND	20 MASSA-CHUSETTS	21 MICHIGAN	22 MINNESOTA	23 MISSISSIPPI	24 MISSOURI	25 MONTANA	26 NEBRASKA	27 NEVADA
1 LIVESTOCK, PRDTS.	315831	377485	626060	1282878	315518	920761	221301	1334264	52075
2 OTHER AGRICULTURE PRDTS.	451639	299425	1010688	1057650	374518	669584	220244	558183	40165
3 FORESTRY, FISHERIES	39748	75541	57138	16744	29015	13360	9912	8719	353
4 AGRI.,FORES.,FISH. SERV.	24171	5017	28071	56816	75987	53911	11650	32765	1301
5 IRON, FERRO. ORES MINING	31773	8918	120667	54852	1687	15158	2140	261	466
6 NONFERROUS ORES MINING	28461	1927	35794	2197	1486	24245	89053	9072	22711
7 COAL MINING	108283	42379	149270	38600	11708	35077	6179	9956	2923
8 CRUDE PETRO.,NATURAL GAS	76510	75477	264036	106350	71858	120517	84154	20767	5613
9 STONE, CLAY MINING	38927	38451	83334	40002	15334	46434	13590	14822	11699
10 CHEM.,FERT. MIN. MINING	7789	4437	19229	5280	5162	16964	4285	1946	1023
11 NEW CONSTRUCTION	1522868	1845402	2302047	997444	392207	1167957	215578	386080	614917
12 MAINT., REPAIR CONSTR.	306326	459707	730024	419101	168240	478527	142350	244689	79482
13 ORDNANCE, ACCESSORIES	75830	128035	343142	246424	11571	191861	4505	6656	3879
14 FOOD, KINDRED PRDTS.	1245497	2237695	2891723	1622984	619278	1802649	267413	734637	133128
15 TOBACCO MANUFACTURES	132990	172373	218078	87478	43548	119390	18530	35428	9507
16 FABRICS	145901	551658	195862	61319	117305	151269	3519	12794	2722
17 TEXTILE PRDTS.	54228	158641	203629	38908	31419	66483	4975	11861	3646
18 APPAREL	342056	622591	660934	265973	155919	390630	46099	98458	29097
19 MISC. TEXTILE PRDTS.	55771	101492	311013	42384	23836	85001	6742	14852	4492
20 LUMBER, WOOD PRDTS.	152793	218969	379882	167118	156679	155813	86500	50602	37886
21 WOODEN CONTAINERS	6379	8634	18051	7604	4846	9470	444	2306	255
22 HOUSEHOLD FURNITURE	77001	118952	169828	64928	33403	81100	10900	25236	10375
23 OTHER FURNITURE	34343	59539	94848	34023	11237	45228	5509	12804	5396
24 PAPER, ALLIED PRDTS.	203001	507331	540162	270755	62651	293479	21599	66389	14021
25 PAPERBOARD CONTAINERS	70573	169851	194708	100497	29473	117742	6392	31603	3246
26 PRINTING, PUBLISHING	246774	608534	534027	295014	55459	397319	30570	92503	23446
27 CHEMICALS,SELECT. PRDTS.	263786	349069	655993	203087	139798	320785	35100	74491	27848
28 PLASTICS, SYNTHETICS	90167	295804	207277	48202	30829	60973	1960	9205	930
29 DRUGS, COSMETICS	180119	270780	369181	150044	67965	214911	26985	58496	17163
30 PAINT, ALLIED PRDTS.	40910	56271	176289	39630	16885	65012	8333	16954	6027
31 PETROLEUM, RELATED INDS.	319139	492116	781550	384638	159058	459714	120840	176035	42096
32 RUBBER, MISC. PLASTICS	165567	380059	746656	160867	60174	254010	20915	58035	12521
33 LEATHER TANNING, PRDTS.	6934	143894	20337	6606	5195	69863	170	942	176
34 FOOTWEAR, LEATHER PRDTS.	61147	127014	149566	58977	26688	94453	11999	23283	8595
35 GLASS, GLASS PRDTS.	54774	73812	238354	43591	14874	84585	3425	13790	2165
36 STONE, CLAY PRDTS.	201208	225844	392825	168867	70622	175631	27813	67596	51223
37 PRIMARY IRON, STEEL MFR.	429518	463767	2820265	307809	74701	562734	26478	71539	17286
38 PRIMARY NONFERROUS MFR.	296180	390951	963440	118281	35112	232115	91479	60645	42131

39	METAL CONTAINERS	52286	45526	74723	54694	10193	68065	3598	22570	845
40	FABRICATED METAL PRDTS.	201802	206271	338064	144998	53325	163458	25355	63680	32095
41	SCREW MACH. PRDTS., ETC.	73843	131902	780655	71218	17178	148231	3030	14262	2414
42	OTHER FAB. METAL PRDTS.	145039	239272	850205	128811	51762	215491	16272	36864	13090
43	ENGINES, TURBINES	30967	71879	285988	40287	10635	40876	6021	5742	4972
44	FARM MACH., EQUIP.	23601	17445	170876	130792	48248	83930	31350	84819	4512
45	CONSTRUC. MACH., EQUIP.	49909	46860	228698	78647	26841	52960	22209	15796	13040
46	MATERIAL HANDLING MACH.	23532	42094	120652	23104	11191	24990	5623	7077	3591
47	METALWORKING MACHINERY	75186	157346	670744	62841	17569	118434	5882	13068	3799
48	SPECIAL MACH., EQUIP.	55181	142760	184604	48300	27601	54504	8634	12448	4567
49	GENERAL MACH., EQUIP.	68258	148222	456784	78623	21308	96391	8846	21551	6132
50	MACHINE SHOP PRDTS.	33043	52018	280210	26350	5521	73424	1968	5533	936
51	OFFICE, COMPUT. MACHINES	41975	130092	223297	189939	11986	55220	7137	12338	4916
52	SERVICE IND. MACHINES	63670	83479	252473	76793	18192	97166	7255	16186	5779
53	ELECT. TRANSMISS. EQUIP.	90737	201806	307157	101882	31301	153564	13232	19314	21354
54	HOUSEHOLD APPLIANCES	68634	102295	229190	95350	35650	87980	13622	25670	11004
55	ELECTRIC LIGHTING EQUIP.	55092	96608	169512	47093	22344	69292	7950	16742	8704
56	RADIO, TV, ETC., EQUIP.	396066	697152	286313	156136	38181	213904	20270	81239	29252
57	ELECTRONIC COMPONENTS	85207	263859	119982	67668	10015	47878	3702	22905	6392
58	MISC. ELECTRICAL MACH.	35920	61572	244118	33001	11428	62315	5687	10720	3379
59	MOTOR VEHICLES, EQUIP.	707230	738918	7426179	637155	201802	1552613	97828	209593	64507
60	AIRCRAFT, PARTS	145716	265903	192236	63201	7780	932677	4368	5141	5293
61	OTHER TRANSPORT. EQUIP.	96003	90324	181195	61041	84595	127058	14844	20573	13724
62	PROFESS., SCIEN. INSTRU.	53641	200666	284437	57746	15640	77691	8901	17646	5085
63	MEDICAL, PHOTO. EQUIP.	34520	101642	88835	38230	9975	48377	6447	11735	9158
64	MISC. MANUFACTURING	112961	270442	286809	112040	45996	142671	20219	38237	20645
65	TRANSPORT., WAREHOUSING	676411	958115	1233547	673436	189260	1176218	141727	342056	97129
66	COMMUNICA.,EXC. BRDCAST.	231574	408974	624314	222784	115259	307176	38173	116226	15637
67	RADIO, TV BROADCASTING	23935	63674	77097	30276	10997	42274	6953	15493	4819
68	ELEC.,GAS,WATER,SAN.SER.	534857	862981	1442396	561828	292109	632128	165399	224703	82721
69	WHOLESALE, RETAIL TRADE	1897609	3723293	5024186	2399257	777990	3286627	385179	994887	259915
70	FINANCE, INSURANCE	448919	1376089	1035253	635816	174035	842951	75128	290846	68199
71	REAL ESTATE, RENTAL	1596395	2262914	3169849	1664503	469104	2061857	254023	618817	282534
72	HOTELS, PERSONAL SERV.	224606	455513	574929	251209	98339	356532	51428	107352	180465
73	BUSINESS SERVICES	501931	1203439	1530730	637997	108377	795199	52655	177955	82952
74	RESEARCH, DEVELOPMENT	0	0	0	0	0	0	0	0	0
75	AUTO. REPAIR, SERVICES	214711	296635	509286	194746	87074	258832	44188	93806	34252
76	AMUSEMENTS	124536	167870	213433	80678	21993	113606	12576	40913	248831
77	MED.,EDUC. SERVICES	707581	2445793	928090	519333	90818	870353	49245	170095	25051
78	FEDERAL GOVT. ENTERPRISE	89338	178189	157742	95509	46752	147627	20799	46631	16545
79	STATE, LOCAL GOVT. ENT.	91683	202896	353681	127521	33417	88769	25618	160009	10145
80	DIRECT ALLOCATED IMPORTS	0	0	0	0	0	0	0	0	0
81	TRANSFERRED IMPORTS	0	0	0	0	0	0	0	0	0
82	VALUE ADDED	9648408	17929040	26960784	10346980	3955254	13815560	1750880	4000977	1599381
83	SECONDARY TRANSFERS-IN	672904	1549975	2561634	941858	287165	1099510	154403	473462	66508
84	INVENTORY DEPLETION	5993	17501	19027	35884	3389	12910	2389	3989	784
85	SCRAP PRODUCTION	-40380	-48982	-145859	-12204	-3136	-25926	-5235	-3918	-1156
86	SCRAP PURCHASED	-20228	-235816	210719	101260	58137	-9619	32969	23913	-23034
87	STATE TOTAL PRODUCTION	28355712	50592288	80918768	31208528	11183835	40746448	5538378	13158324	4692849

TABLE C-23

1963 STATE TOTAL CONSUMPTION
(THOUSANDS OF CURRENT DOLLARS)

INDUSTRY TITLE	28 NEW HAMPSHIRE	29 NEW JERSEY	30 NEW MEXICO	31 NEW YORK	32 NORTH CAROLINA	33 NORTH DAKOTA	34 OHIO	35 OKLAHOMA	36 OREGON
1 LIVESTOCK, PRDTS.	49632	469351	166879	1098848	449357	182180	1000098	399971	237927
2 OTHER AGRICULTURE PRDTS.	43767	521076	79298	1241059	1324665	260388	1044296	244412	319268
3 FORESTRY, FISHERIES	3264	56175	2892	164050	42679	10959	14432	5626	171821
4 AGRI.,FORES.,FISH. SERV.	3143	9541	9368	24300	66469	20007	39911	29716	16464
5 IRON, FERRO. ORES MINING	864	24299	1795	72687	1502	3045	217435	1176	3932
6 NONFERROUS ORES MINING	103	83366	10384	51591	6604	302	40901	26541	68960
7 COAL MINING	5702	60406	6262	150327	29230	10031	210329	15318	12476
8 CRUDE PETRO.,NATURAL GAS	6427	699334	84089	266943	31653	28247	547954	453739	14903
9 STONE, CLAY MINING	8084	66056	12296	127883	31147	7715	125505	25974	23934
10 CHEM.,FERT. MIN. MINING	663	26451	37683	38199	11471	1266	25303	1296	3055
11 NEW CONSTRUCTION	159572	1927017	437185	5045863	1000997	186738	2943049	970743	707139
12 MAINT., REPAIR CONSTR.	62198	571917	126501	1675894	385430	136416	1223710	259764	244943
13 ORDNANCE, ACCESSORIES	3505	75856	39836	226577	41990	2727	499377	14609	12463
14 FOOD, KINDRED PRDTS.	252510	2982654	297615	7771354	1386130	212521	3651652	770773	808730
15 TOBACCO MANUFACTURES	20304	225502	21532	892224	1004256	13271	276938	65087	55949
16 FABRICS	96801	489006	5873	2409317	1924333	3340	239256	27951	55338
17 TEXTILE PRDTS.	17518	152028	6543	393847	207110	4683	253583	25745	32102
18 APPAREL	62534	814307	63541	3006533	463246	35278	883602	179755	156006
19 MISC. TEXTILE PRDTS.	8594	148348	8714	471947	80522	4869	165559	26808	26261
20 LUMBER, WOOD PRDTS.	55493	309328	40159	633911	322120	16744	471433	68192	733214
21 WOODEN CONTAINERS	1477	21425	639	40057	8304	686	21729	2124	4769
22 HOUSEHOLD FURNITURE	13581	167505	15672	416874	110082	8326	215336	44986	38513
23 OTHER FURNITURE	5860	68533	7471	249466	37076	4922	108265	19335	17957
24 PAPER, ALLIED PRDTS.	66381	606504	21264	1689964	253656	16303	756377	73807	126477
25 PAPERBOARD CONTAINERS	19448	258517	6572	504935	148065	6176	309582	30017	34420
26 PRINTING, PUBLISHING	46654	617049	38595	3516171	214882	26302	899008	112206	111215
27 CHEMICALS,SELECT. PRDTS.	37097	1049468	43433	1405157	412975	25578	973270	95746	100183
28 PLASTICS, SYNTHETICS	37563	332624	1756	675247	535423	5416	473020	19472	23470
29 DRUGS, COSMETICS	28011	493215	33713	1202726	184093	20346	447616	92923	82924
30 PAINT, ALLIED PRDTS.	6023	108956	8544	209234	48341	7868	183922	21791	29400
31 PETROLEUM, RELATED INDS.	55063	866875	100219	1889290	341706	99564	1087392	374762	209803
32 RUBBER, MISC. PLASTICS	49204	435471	25713	1033144	167096	18312	884064	79361	66457
33 LEATHER TANNING, PRDTS.	45888	32972	374	148575	7789	81	30951	1076	2793
34 FOOTWEAR, LEATHER PRDTS.	23342	134637	16139	387154	64551	8707	187700	39078	36420
35 GLASS, GLASS PRDTS.	6954	169977	4014	310841	48597	4767	208596	21934	22940
36 STONE, CLAY PRDTS.	29091	400176	54285	798379	149104	31906	579610	112492	94177
37 PRIMARY IRON, STEEL MFR.	39076	755722	46135	1714013	159645	21515	2890966	179236	124368
38 PRIMARY NONFERROUS MFR.	28223	853530	29165	1467004	128850	9403	1177350	96290	97774

39 METAL CONTAINERS	2351	174585	2285	186319	26879	3845	115057	15633	30694
40 FABRICATED METAL PRDTS.	22650	379482	46328	852506	148712	28249	533696	105350	94426
41 SCREW MACH. PRDTS., ETC.	9375	191701	4917	401069	36787	5975	520260	29844	20218
42 OTHER FAB. METAL PRDTS.	23542	354879	18896	822337	161424	14424	752768	71999	94028
43 ENGINES, TURBINES	2322	66024	9184	288438	24410	9903	119528	17210	19975
44 FARM MACH., EQUIP.	3255	23233	13897	188083	69897	50899	120968	42747	30157
45 CONSTRUC. MACH., EQUIP.	7480	73072	43872	563619	39497	27243	204118	76277	39170
46 MATERIAL HANDLING MACH.	3334	82074	7142	192931	26144	5369	121779	11181	23103
47 METALWORKING MACHINERY	12630	169919	5960	626680	39317	8142	533797	37114	23550
48 SPECIAL MACH., EQUIP.	20155	171499	5305	574659	153125	10874	217299	17611	52952
49 GENERAL MACH., EQUIP.	16381	218724	9613	573608	54453	9652	503229	42358	33790
50 MACHINE SHOP PRDTS.	2796	60636	9009	159001	11344	1622	216118	28659	12776
51 OFFICE, COMPUT. MACHINES	7357	156299	7584	934883	37658	7374	197125	20125	20703
52 SERVICE IND. MACHINES	6384	114047	8124	471336	51963	8950	245044	29996	24537
53 ELECT. TRANSMISS. EQUIP.	30121	254511	21912	840666	108054	12471	556209	57582	58974
54 HOUSEHOLD APPLIANCES	12000	133444	17675	429230	91776	11767	444191	45668	43033
55 ELECTRIC LIGHTING EQUIP.	7668	138692	12494	325031	46941	7725	212288	28379	31609
56 RADIO, TV, ETC., EQUIP.	50398	928634	32473	1833613	234125	18713	452903	161529	61496
57 ELECTRONIC COMPONENTS	24339	313979	6351	705171	64165	3871	165115	39506	14005
58 MISC. ELECTRICAL MACH.	3740	80928	5608	232668	39321	4444	180041	17305	18012
59 MOTOR VEHICLES, EQUIP.	72796	1055769	114777	3325360	475683	150527	3490553	309688	305873
60 AIRCRAFT, PARTS	2182	299946	14804	1518739	39460	6007	1116436	278356	53627
61 OTHER TRANSPORT. EQUIP.	7282	159583	18263	476174	64792	10906	213890	41218	65631
62 PROFESS., SCIEN. INSTRU.	7735	176151	10354	673698	50642	8463	244071	31391	28464
63 MEDICAL, PHOTO. EQUIP.	7438	91000	7986	644656	32371	4906	108534	18724	20618
64 MISC. MANUFACTURING	24374	316061	25762	1197039	116042	15766	368174	59857	65956
65 TRANSPORT., WAREHOUSING	66239	1650878	154910	4990305	626341	93541	1964243	479033	483202
66 COMMUNICA.,EXC. BRDCAST.	34202	476454	57458	1573442	256293	45595	709944	169959	137271
67 RADIO, TV BROADCASTING	3646	12197	8853	541721	34438	5396	104323	18982	18948
68 ELEC.,GAS,WATER,SAN.SER.	104143	997254	181036	2718811	515458	61746	2047485	370932	230312
69 WHOLESALE, RETAIL TRADE	332831	4591339	450430	16527113	2334366	381851	6084866	1238752	1357812
70 FINANCE, INSURANCE	89312	1062438	95421	6515646	527384	69183	1430322	333493	272598
71 REAL ESTATE, RENTAL	198597	3188444	352073	12824585	1144242	201968	4259590	910969	772295
72 HOTELS, PERSONAL SERV.	64519	561368	73264	2051037	287473	36254	704827	148674	152283
73 BUSINESS SERVICES	63506	1148397	98096	8605861	323498	37442	1687751	272000	239510
74 RESEARCH, DEVELOPMENT	0	0	0	0	0	0	0	0	0
75 AUTO. REPAIR, SERVICES	36870	358322	54443	965517	206392	36500	537373	145867	135525
76 AMUSEMENTS	29756	233540	22252	2015922	70490	10442	286591	46177	45615
77 MED.,EDUC. SERVICES	163007	991290	65755	6154695	539494	39835	1609580	209252	233743
78 FEDERAL GOVT. ENTERPRISE	16238	159315	29038	582769	108009	20253	229583	70925	57328
79 STATE, LOCAL GOVT. ENT.	38832	161703	21973	782680	171869	8746	476327	72770	102565
80 DIRECT ALLOCATED IMPORTS	0	0	0	0	0	0	0	0	0
81 TRANSFERRED IMPORTS	0	0	0	0	0	0	0	0	0
82 VALUE ADDED	1749028	21432944	2517095	68757536	12699727	1543789	32493696	6430060	5523036
83 SECONDARY TRANSFERS-IN	155434	1985796	181064	6185816	966784	126419	3576623	536430	382190
84 INVENTORY DEPLETION	3925	14193	1972	35324	9126	2139	18071	3008	4187
85 SCRAP PRODUCTION	-4225	-80201	-1064	-206945	-41798	-5760	-108957	-6923	-7450
86 SCRAP PURCHASED	1771	-112436	41143	-511634	82451	38095	196321	66701	39923
87 STATE TOTAL PRODUCTION	4937331	62103280	6797930	203569312	34938160	4658427	95570832	18182192	16397215

TABLE C-23

1963 STATE TOTAL CONSUMPTION
(THOUSANDS OF CURRENT DOLLARS)

INDUSTRY TITLE	37 PENNSYL-VANIA	38 RHODE ISLAND	39 SOUTH CAROLINA	40 SOUTH DAKOTA	41 TENNESSEE	42 TEXAS	43 UTAH	44 VERMONT	45 VIRGINIA
1 LIVESTOCK, PRDTS.	1005653	41169	213191	566865	470692	1385008	169951	55384	376738
2 OTHER AGRICULTURE PRDTS.	938088	62406	542085	377374	517351	1386143	117322	69995	613624
3 FORESTRY, FISHERIES	44817	6049	27707	5361	10966	105599	1483	10662	45590
4 AGRI.,FORES.,FISH. SERV.	34653	2805	23287	18484	23819	206796	5414	1594	24594
5 IRON, FERRO. ORES MINING	324401	4124	1128	28	7232	43987	10406	1053	4568
6 NONFERROUS ORES MINING	54293	481	3167	6568	54898	139938	99434	31	7376
7 COAL MINING	461744	6838	16232	3273	29906	89134	12642	2858	142680
8 CRUDE PETRO.,NATURAL GAS	751094	21310	20632	4469	29725	3227445	95721	3253	69680
9 STONE, CLAY MINING	112489	4518	17599	10783	42024	131279	13443	8486	49352
10 CHEM.,FERT. MIN. MINING	19010	799	5311	351	24874	79893	4693	235	11538
11 NEW CONSTRUCTION	2211964	237175	327279	203777	1008802	4040992	460565	66006	1614012
12 MAINT., REPAIR CONSTR.	899318	58058	152453	135017	262444	1234860	105234	38133	345474
13 ORDNANCE, ACCESSORIES	255096	8765	5838	3779	122514	181087	68378	19914	93449
14 FOOD, KINDRED PRDTS.	4619286	321754	614536	279100	1161231	3628798	365506	192800	1303272
15 TOBACCO MANUFACTURES	476765	27768	83718	14221	102454	268716	22957	12673	508013
16 FABRICS	927750	179360	1361414	2370	372001	231138	12961	16239	347446
17 TEXTILE PRDTS.	235333	29722	157564	4752	67636	104792	7606	5993	72807
18 APPAREL	1316137	83682	182038	36341	366951	778472	71054	33181	345103
19 MISC. TEXTILE PRDTS.	181399	11998	32086	4774	56578	124153	10003	4820	53524
20 LUMBER, WOOD PRDTS.	410929	22580	134926	18995	206026	465400	39513	32437	302350
21 WOODEN CONTAINERS	19609	1305	3183	644	7603	12759	1203	788	6577
22 HOUSEHOLD FURNITURE	232317	16254	35013	8710	76238	203730	18100	9613	96496
23 OTHER FURNITURE	111754	8659	14287	4567	29470	46510	7450	19531	31958
24 PAPER, ALLIED PRDTS.	843752	49534	139453	16934	233361	462068	34154	41797	231340
25 PAPERBOARD CONTAINERS	325298	27766	51255	9507	88046	170916	12815	11560	87454
26 PRINTING, PUBLISHING	1027781	61497	78565	28106	219097	541689	58147	31882	213165
27 CHEMICALS,SELECT. PRDTS.	866437	62781	295622	16298	589513	1665123	50098	22219	512066
28 PLASTICS, SYNTHETICS	411954	83335	354874	1404	183072	272725	4430	10799	249987
29 DRUGS, COSMETICS	556323	34808	89309	20775	151423	434936	38341	17854	176640
30 PAINT, ALLIED PRDTS.	136055	7226	16230	7295	34466	126007	9799	3870	42599
31 PETROLEUM, RELATED INDS.	1259780	73216	176179	84018	278987	2231010	123125	36310	359961
32 RUBBER, MISC. PLASTICS	556834	61582	73148	18030	166087	336400	34983	19919	151997
33 LEATHER TANNING, PRDTS.	80401	2283	1689	80	47200	11572	423	2890	14048
34 FOOTWEAR, LEATHER PRDTS.	216493	17210	30817	9210	63373	160516	16715	6518	67471
35 GLASS, GLASS PRDTS.	191330	17328	28879	2640	46190	95778	6389	4110	45187
36 STONE, CLAY PRDTS.	482456	31606	75779	26267	146427	600275	62443	20167	209934
37 PRIMARY IRON, STEEL MFR.	2764985	79180	73585	15217	209664	863069	114324	23131	234573
38 PRIMARY NONFERROUS MFR.	958728	165938	37447	5448	223044	564270	88946	20136	148858

39 METAL CONTAINERS	123332	5106	9674	4877	35432	140988	6630	2154	36222
40 FABRICATED METAL PRDTS.	489799	28130	72808	21194	134784	559490	58702	26724	198843
41 SCREW MACH. PRDTS., ETC.	322956	20615	15407	2653	47298	120513	11412	5498	38450
42 OTHER FAB. METAL PRDTS.	591571	33356	46203	11672	117706	373590	31170	18367	142554
43 ENGINES, TURBINES	163309	2687	12135	2222	16069	68815	6603	11661	26038
44 FARM MACH., EQUIP.	79192	2157	27034	43820	47743	49795	7635	27859	41182
45 CONSTRUC. MACH., EQUIP.	174080	5577	19587	8653	36201	277634	22573	38828	59725
46 MATERIAL HANDLING MACH.	112513	4696	13079	2941	23184	48398	5792	13801	22972
47 METALWORKING MACHINERY	320317	23070	21667	3041	45704	110630	13767	39460	44919
48 SPECIAL MACH., EQUIP.	201304	22146	109614	3618	51960	107447	5141	63633	57521
49 GENERAL MACH., EQUIP.	351102	16929	31443	4808	60306	155488	12322	36930	50856
50 MACHINE SHOP PRDTS.	129471	4475	4688	3238	18414	71786	19920	4656	15305
51 OFFICE, COMPUT. MACHINES	201768	8042	18021	4198	30508	32890	4770	41053	43761
52 SERVICE IND. MACHINES	182198	8780	21996	5337	51933	139417	10814	21940	54775
53 ELECT. TRANSMISS. EQUIP.	513211	16464	44122	6013	69685	159959	16984	47593	85085
54 HOUSEHOLD APPLIANCES	223959	15111	40256	10111	97181	186901	18798	9346	75968
55 ELECTRIC LIGHTING EQUIP.	172901	15565	20494	6869	40952	143450	15459	6730	49306
56 RADIO, TV, ETC., EQUIP.	449681	27207	46870	14640	137580	343138	43169	46906	161160
57 ELECTRONIC COMPONENTS	258468	11274	20509	2381	50369	130677	12980	11085	65466
58 MISC. ELECTRICAL MACH.	122857	8513	10310	3586	25582	70382	6568	8060	24791
59 MOTOR VEHICLES, EQUIP.	1721874	93779	205947	80051	401860	1239056	106467	131200	561785
60 AIRCRAFT, PARTS	585126	6299	12264	3133	58162	881316	138266	60924	40999
61 OTHER TRANSPORT. EQUIP.	365671	9441	24455	7777	55958	130793	13922	27717	273269
62 PROFESS., SCIEN. INSTRU.	315477	20586	23574	4232	49172	114014	13756	24424	38134
63 MEDICAL, PHOTO. EQUIP.	118278	9688	14614	4298	27218	74960	9140	10269	33063
64 MISC. MANUFACTURING	450396	88065	60576	13684	109853	250950	30052	21036	115104
65 TRANSPORT., WAREHOUSING	2486946	112811	216417	66530	563398	2255566	199686	59743	788716
66 COMMUNICA.,EXC. BRDCAST.	701265	63906	118757	33985	291747	774675	80983	17842	259185
67 RADIO, TV BROADCASTING	126202	10305	15926	6586	33221	88734	8130	2936	31111
68 ELEC.,GAS,WATER,SAN.SER.	1991061	108143	237457	71152	322709	1633587	191762	54160	614077
69 WHOLESALE, RETAIL TRADE	6719487	532477	929666	360349	2001980	6027164	545714	197536	1992311
70 FINANCE, INSURANCE	1858242	167376	248967	74092	493534	1689051	122315	49098	493707
71 REAL ESTATE, RENTAL	4278689	336590	482988	235459	1008260	3588172	400991	107549	1505086
72 HOTELS, PERSONAL SERV.	846571	65063	123634	39707	235413	750735	64205	37367	284118
73 BUSINESS SERVICES	1970574	123110	148037	42538	402534	1304705	108217	36282	386791
74 RESEARCH, DEVELOPMENT	0	0	0	0	0	0	0	0	0
75 AUTO. REPAIR, SERVICES	631036	39016	97410	37552	184659	619107	58299	23065	198118
76 AMUSEMENTS	239596	37164	29311	18337	61232	197083	28896	14663	67528
77 MED.,EDUC. SERVICES	2482999	189905	154877	54852	481443	1000462	199121	141081	440271
78 FEDERAL GOVT. ENTERPRISE	267554	28997	63592	18668	250840	278693	23699	10896	161868
79 STATE, LOCAL GOVT. ENT.	488781	14346	44276	18355	239455	355233	40531	17500	195412
80 DIRECT ALLOCATED IMPORTS	0	0	0	0	0	0	0	0	0
81 TRANSFERRED IMPORTS	0	0	0	0	0	0	0	0	0
82 VALUE ADDED	33711984	2460235	4661371	1512516	8873442	29508400	2837898	1002431	10935827
83 SECONDARY TRANSFERS-IN	3355498	222663	474485	150759	930500	2691819	231139	98097	757902
84 INVENTORY DEPLETION	27743	1802	2413	1767	8198	13624	3655	617	5855
85 SCRAP PRODUCTION	-120102	-8453	-28484	-386	-14598	-47235	-4256	-6874	-17546
86 SCRAP PURCHASED	201351	-10034	46059	29263	41872	246236	64071	350	38972
87 STATE TOTAL PRODUCTION	97328800	6936048	14512011	5022962	25982032	85611280	8224034	3501033	30708064

TABLE C-23

1963 STATE TOTAL CONSUMPTION
(THOUSANDS OF CURRENT DOLLARS)

INDUSTRY TITLE	46 WASHINGTON	47 WEST VIRGINIA	48 WISCONSIN	49 WYOMING	50 ALASKA	51 HAWAII	52 NATIONAL TOTAL
1 LIVESTOCK, PRDTS.	360562	83011	1066517	119072	6327	52752	26684352
2 OTHER AGRICULTURE PRDTS.	447681	71976	581399	104627	16098	122955	27361008
3 FORESTRY, FISHERIES	109271	5493	24155	1614	60113	5778	1751019
4 AGRI.,FORES.,FISH. SERV.	23226	8313	25940	3104	36	31428	1771890
5 IRON, FERRO. ORES MINING	7247	41374	6407	324	6	390	1484557
6 NONFERROUS ORES MINING	77217	22811	881	15802	1523	57	1521165
7 COAL MINING	22508	142654	37377	5427	2700	4317	2635467
8 CRUDE PETRO.,NATURAL GAS	118079	69511	64715	211796	2125	18413	12264679
9 STONE, CLAY MINING	33156	20033	46107	10136	6397	5752	2024067
10 CHEM.,FERT. MIN. MINING	8018	17585	4960	6821	87	2037	697139
11 NEW CONSTRUCTION	1381119	276827	1183412	209388	174119	379980	65518976
12 MAINT., REPAIR CONSTR.	368361	148439	426113	78597	23533	79152	19794432
13 ORDNANCE, ACCESSORIES	33942	222621	84423	2228	3426	2289	6341398
14 FOOD, KINDRED PRDTS.	1328325	468321	1807512	129300	99892	366791	74271104
15 TOBACCO MANUFACTURES	94317	49763	105065	8500	5891	15248	7420262
16 FABRICS	45919	25833	91608	1616	1894	10410	13038373
17 TEXTILE PRDTS.	34533	10695	68735	2452	5338	7523	3667902
18 APPAREL	250548	117560	337244	24393	17537	45351	18024784
19 MISC. TEXTILE PRDTS.	37027	15493	68104	3433	2258	6523	3170547
20 LUMBER, WOOD PRDTS.	515138	63169	275640	20731	9492	28419	10662749
21 WOODEN CONTAINERS	5153	2819	11868	147	103	1265	419510
22 HOUSEHOLD FURNITURE	60334	28601	77835	5796	4077	14707	4067025
23 OTHER FURNITURE	22639	26653	16668	2490	5333	32875	1922754
24 PAPER, ALLIED PRDTS.	261347	71301	496377	8520	7275	27386	13096204
25 PAPERBOARD CONTAINERS	56766	38450	156747	3620	2592	14031	4712479
26 PRINTING, PUBLISHING	180625	66816	342933	15046	12925	42978	16209876
27 CHEMICALS,SELECT. PRDTS.	212617	593560	221437	27325	4423	25558	16893408
28 PLASTICS, SYNTHETICS	29106	58703	92802	194	126	1163	6342049
29 DRUGS, COSMETICS	135917	62712	171610	14400	9703	25502	9052968
30 PAINT, ALLIED PRDTS.	36018	13841	64103	4660	2514	6625	2462054
31 PETROLEUM, RELATED INDS.	364479	153991	364992	106908	34641	64988	21826224
32 RUBBER, MISC. PLASTICS	100655	58907	269179	10693	8969	17493	9882723
33 LEATHER TANNING, PRDTS.	3804	4567	56168	84	32	541	966640
34 FOOTWEAR, LEATHER PRDTS.	58867	26170	79794	6424	4352	10701	3476373
35 GLASS, GLASS PRDTS.	34384	39853	80822	1495	3347	7664	2931977
36 STONE, CLAY PRDTS.	148503	85756	192176	29566	25156	50339	9550630
37 PRIMARY IRON, STEEL MFR.	177670	262910	848780	24478	12617	25370	24490160
38 PRIMARY NONFERROUS MFR.	288986	175318	303943	6870	4242	10124	14167780

39 METAL CCNTAINERS	47454	18117	73109	3026	8276	15573	2436138
40 FABRICATED METAL PRDTS.	143984	70037	191362	24294	29025	55050	8970215
41 SCREW MACH. PRDTS., ETC.	32078	23346	207502	2071	2982	4021	4910847
42 OTHER FAB. METAL PRDTS.	121353	67678	252971	8754	9495	25074	8938933
43 ENGINES, TURBINES	39121	23700	151060	4607	3034	13910	2394762
44 FARM MACH., EQUIP.	23039	60971	70323	1271	12806	63972	3069832
45 CCNSTRUC. MACH., EQUIP.	82915	66942	87255	15236	8638	38437	4050035
46 MATERIAL HANDLING MACH.	22645	23149	21412	2547	3778	17614	1618963
47 METALWORKING MACHINERY	50486	67499	135324	1592	2153	40056	5134839
48 SPECIAL MACH., EQUIP.	41614	76050	54618	3011	6504	40754	3702282
49 GENERAL MACH., EQUIP.	61548	40116	204210	4039	5270	34887	5323633
50 MACHINE SHOP PRDTS.	35505	10401	80084	4237	683	1249	2238217
51 OFFICE, COMPUT. MACHINES	30901	36201	14714	4823	5504	39839	3923623
52 SERVICE IND. MACHINES	31003	34578	70446	2986	6044	34613	3387862
53 ELECT. TRANSMISS. EQUIP.	67862	65557	210744	6986	11931	60044	6486809
54 HCUSEHCLD APPLIANCES	66692	31726	117506	7133	4730	15184	4666023
55 ELECTRIC LIGHTING EQUIP.	44963	35589	62090	6063	10376	13711	3080886
56 RADIO, TV, ETC., EQUIP.	111515	57902	143685	7923	14248	67318	12379858
57 ELECTRCNIC CCMPCNENTS	28620	11557	58589	2193	2724	5103	4524387
58 MISC. ELECTRICAL MACH.	24469	14085	72986	2388	2343	8493	2254265
59 MOTOR VEHICLES, EQUIP.	443300	265013	1343548	51140	48898	237741	39870192
60 AIRCRAFT, PARTS	605582	22833	19210	5867	5616	30033	14306071
61 OTHER TRANSPORT. EQUIP.	206237	48060	64638	16929	9309	84556	4918930
62 PROFESS., SCIEN. INSTRU.	49765	27975	86187	3541	5006	19405	4269285
63 MEDICAL, PHOTO. EQUIP.	31016	16981	31457	3033	3007	12599	2523811
64 MISC. MANUFACTURING	103057	46003	130362	10462	8185	29489	7150429
65 TRANSPCRT., WAREHCUSING	802473	324955	605535	106077	114325	195967	39142544
66 COMMUNICA.,EXC. BRDCAST.	228267	97412	211171	19939	5745	48447	13494968
67 RADIO, TV BROADCASTING	28029	13869	33852	3347	3338	7473	2307967
68 ELEC.,GAS,WATER,SAN.SER.	393481	430017	592201	110188	27148	71894	29660288
69 WHOLESALE, RETAIL TRADE	1941824	715876	2356300	177648	125006	348873	120613248
70 FINANCE, INSURANCE	432394	145559	557098	33081	25037	130936	33700112
71 REAL ESTATE, RENTAL	1511016	442437	1567485	137593	66074	424962	83886832
72 HOTELS, PERSONAL SERV.	219669	94019	279507	41367	19511	74319	15369794
73 BUSINESS SERVICES	368091	154206	549083	28199	30145	96171	35945360
74 RESEARCH, DEVELCPMENT	0	0	0	0	0	0	0
75 AUTO. REPAIR, SERVICES	193983	63680	207714	21921	9092	37057	10866429
76 AMUSEMENTS	78986	47427	82436	9011	6796	22727	7697033
77 MED.,EDUC. SERVICES	365117	164225	289838	18735	18607	119496	33159856
78 FEDERAL GCVT. ENTERPRISE	150087	30507	80047	9122	53063	60064	5743413
79 STATE, LOCAL GOVT. ENT.	323928	55536	67792	14506	13428	16278	7236000
80 DIRECT ALLOCATED IMPORTS	0	0	0	0	0	0	0
81 TRANSFERRED IMPCRTS	0	0	0	0	0	0	0
82 VALUE ADDED	9137571	4487522	12187360	1212188	772590	2326756	583062016
83 SECCNDARY TRANSFERS-IN	793093	405004	1193240	113931	35337	107124	52357376
84 INVENTORY DEPLETION	7087	2448	9452	1692	81	1080	444900
85 SCRAP PRODUCTION	-23586	-8113	-42624	-464	-1230	-2547	-1517981
86 SCRAP PURCHASED	92750	58648	7154	16832	-5268	-25704	1412517
87 STATE TOTAL PRODUCTION	27065040	12639707	34944576	3509146	2130612	6634972	1703690496

Appendix D:
1947, 1958, and 1963 State Estimates of Outputs, Employment, and Payrolls (MRIO Data Set 2)

This data set provides state estimates of output, employment, and payrolls for the three base years, 1947, 1958, and 1963, for 87 industries. The data for each year were constructed on a basis consistent with the industry definitions of the national input-output tables prepared by the Office of Business Economics (OBE). The procedures used to estimate the state values are described earlier in this volume.

The state output estimates sum to a figure that is exactly equal to the national output values of the primary matrix (column sums of that table) in the OBE input-output tables listed below:

1. 1947: OBE computer listing of the table [121].
2. 1958: *Survey of Current Business*, September 1965 [131, pp. 34–39].
3. 1963: *Survey of Current Business*, November 1969 [122, pp. 30–35].

For the published national table, a secondary product matrix is added to the primary matrix to obtain a balanced table of total transactions, which double-counts secondary products. The national control used for the multiregional input-output (MRIO) calculations can be obtained by taking the value listed in the row marked "Total" in the OBE table and subtracting from it the respective value in the row marked "Transfers." The result represents the total value of goods and services produced by domestic establishments of the establishment's "own" product plus the value of its secondary products. It therefore excludes transferred imports (and the transportation, trade, and insurance margins on those imports) and the double-counting of secondary products that are included in the national input-output table. For the multiregional calculations, these values that are called "transfers" were estimated at the 51-region level and added as row 81 (imports) and row and column 83 (secondary products) of the regional tables. (The transportation, trade, and insurance margins on the imports were added to the entries in rows 65, 69, and 70, respectively.)

Note: This appendix is included to provide corrected 1947, 1958, and 1963 outputs. The output data in Volume II, *State Estimates of Outputs, Employment, and Payrolls, 1947, 1958, 1963* [68] are incorrect. The entire description from Volume II is given here, although only the output tables are included.

Notes About the State Estimates of Outputs, Employment, and Payrolls

1. Throughout the estimation process, an attempt was made to construct the state figures on a basis comparable with the national input-output tables. Whenever an unreconcilable discrepancy occurred between the state figures and the national controls, the discrepancy was allocated to the states in proportion to the original entries in the state tables.
   a. The rows are the 87 industries listed in the OBE tables plus a row 88 of state totals.
   b. The columns are the 51 regions (50 states plus the District of Columbia), arranged in alphabetical order, plus a column 52 of residuals and a column 53 of industry totals. Only the first 49 of the 51 regional columns contain values for 1947 and 1958 (columns 50 and 51 are zero) because Alaska and Hawaii did not become states until 1958. For 1963, all 51 regional columns contain values.
   c. Column 52 contains values for data that were not allocated to the states. These represent figures for which purchases or payments were made outside the 51 regions (such as purchases for the Panama Canal, wage payments to overseas military employees, etc.).

2. The data for the three years are given in thousands of current dollars and are in producer prices.
   a. Deflators. For comparisons of the data for the three years, the output and payroll figures must be deflated to constant dollars. The national output deflators were used for deflation of the outputs in the multiregional calculations. (National value added deflators could be used as an approximation for the payrolls.) The output deflators are given in *State Estimates of Outputs, Employment, and Payrolls, 1947, 1958, 1963* [68, pp. 17–19].
   b. Significant digits. The final adjustments to the three sets of data were made in double precision on the IBM 360/65 at Harvard.
   c. Producer prices. It is customary for the input-output data to be given in producer prices. The margins on the goods (the differences between the producer prices and the purchaser prices) are then recorded as parts of IO-65, Transportation & warehousing; IO-69, Wholesale & retail trade; and IO-70, Finance & insurance.

3. IO-11, New construction. All purchases of new construction are recorded in the final demand sector of the input-output table, that is, no purchases from this industry are considered to be intermediate purchases. Because the output of new construction is assumed to be used in the region in which it is produced, the total output must equal the total consumption in each state. The total output of the industry, given state-by-state in row

11 of Tables D–1, D–2, and D–3, should be consistent with the respective state elements obtained by adding the figures in row 11 of the state final demand tables for gross private capital formation, net foreign exports, state and local government net purchases of goods and services, and federal government purchases. For 1947, however, a discrepancy exists between the two sets of data, and no immediate way of reconciling the differences could be found.

4. IO-74, Research & development. For 1947 and 1958, values of research and development were estimated for each state because the industry was given in the national input-output table. For 1963, this industry was eliminated in the national input-output table, and the values were included as part of the industries where the research and development was actually performed, and SIC 7391, Research, development, and testing laboratories, was added to IO-73, Business services; therefore, no separate state estimates were made for IO-74 in the 1963 output, employment, or payroll tables given in this appendix. To use the 1947 and 1958 state data for the multiregional calculations, the values given in the appendix tables for IO-74 (the SIC 7391 portion) must be added to the values for IO-73 for the respective year.

5. IO-78, Federal government enterprises. For this industry, a value appears in the residual column 52 of the output matrices only. This value represents output of federal government enterprises that are located outside the states, such as the Panama Canal or the Alaska Railroad in 1947 and 1958 (before Alaska became a state). In the payroll and employment matrices, the entry in column 52 is zero, and the total for industry 78 excludes these values because of lack of information, although these enterprises had employees.

6. IO-80, Imports. State values were estimated for this industry. For the multiregional input-output calculations, imports were inserted in the state input-output tables before implementing the model.

7. IO-81, Business travel, entertainment, & gifts, and IO-82, Office supplies. These two industries are especially constructed for the national input-output tables, and the values appear in the transfer (secondary) matrix; therefore, no state estimates were made for these industries.

8. IO-83, Scrap, used & secondhand goods. The values for this industry are given in the transfer (secondary) matrix of the national input-output table; therefore, no state output, employment, or payroll estimates were made for this industry.

9. Value added in final demand: IO-84, Government industry, IO-85, Rest of the world industry, and IO-86, Household industry. For these industries, figures appear only in the value added portion of the final demand sector of the input-output table and represent payments to government employees; purchases by foreigners and foreign interest payments and receipts; and payments to household employees, respectively. The following balances exist between the final demand values given in MRIO DATA SET 1 and the payroll and output values given in MRIO DATA SET 2:[1]

IO-84 PAYROLLS = IO-84 OUTPUT = IO-84 SLG + IO-84 FG
IO-85 OUTPUT = IO-85 PCE + IO-85 NEXP + IO-85 FG
IO-86 PAYROLLS = IO-86 OUTPUT = IO-86 PCE

Part of the value of IO-84 represents wages paid to government military employees overseas. This value appears in column 52 of the payrolls, outputs, and federal government final demand tables.

10. IO-87, Inventory valuation adjustment. No state estimates were made for this industry. The total value appears in columns 52 and 53 of the output tables. Because the item represents an adjustment of the total of net inventory change for the differences in the value of the goods when they are placed in inventory compared with their value when they are withdrawn from inventory, no figure is given in either the employment or payrolls tables.

11. Row 88 is the state total for either outputs, employment, or payrolls, obtained by summing all elements in each column.

12. Column 52 contains values for data that were not allocated to the states (explained above under 1).

13. Column 53 contains the industry total for the particular table of outputs, employment, or payrolls. As explained under 1 above, this total was forced to equal the respective national figure for the industry.

14. For certain regional analyses, an additional adjustment would have to be made to the state outputs. To balance the data in the interregional trade matrices with the regional input-output tables, the inventory depletion component of net inventory change must be subtracted from the final

1. For a detailed description of the methodology of constructing the state final demands given in MRIO DATA SET 1, refer to the first volume of this series, *State Estimates of the Gross National Product, 1947, 1958, 1963* [63].

demands and added as a row in the regional input-output tables. (These tables are described in the first volume of this series.) This adjustment is required to account for all shipments of a given commodity, regardless of the year in which it was produced, and essentially augments each of the output figures presented in the accompanying tables by the value of commodities that are withdrawn from inventories in the given year.

The three tables of state outputs follow.

MRIO Data Set 2
1947, 1958, and 1963 State Estimates of Outputs, Employment, and Payrolls (88 x 53)
(in thousands of current dollars)

Table No.	*Table Title*
D-1	State Estimates of 1947 Outputs—Revised
D-2	State Estimates of 1958 Outputs—Revised
D-3	State Estimates of 1963 Outputs—Revised

TABLE D-1

STATE ESTIMATES OF 1947 OUTPUTS - REVISED
(THOUSANDS OF CURRENT DOLLARS)

INDUSTRY TITLE	1 ALABAMA	2 ARIZONA	3 ARKANSAS	4 CALIFORNIA	5 COLORADO	6 CONNECTICUT	7 DELAWARE	8 DISTRICT OF COLUMBIA	9 FLORIDA
1 LIVESTOCK, PRDTS.	261034	90915	279000	817605	300804	110528	81007	0	135578
2 OTHER AGRICULTURE PRDTS.	349387	168955	423440	1786540	378700	66448	28648	0	225988
3 FORESTRY, FISHERIES	10674	73	6302	64227	587	3112	5627	0	24862
4 AGRI.,FORES.,FISH. SERV.	15948	6962	21609	51242	6781	7328	8200	0	6788
5 IRON, FERRO. ORES MINING	25722	25	50	2001	105	0	0	0	0
6 NONFERROUS ORES MINING	0	164776	10593	25156	19760	0	0	0	3711
7 COAL MINING	124966	0	14934	0	34465	0	0	0	0
8 CRUDE PETRO.,NATURAL GAS	614	0	61968	696855	30840	0	0	0	403
9 STONE, CLAY MINING	8079	1803	2343	50122	3624	3698	535	0	10190
10 CHEM.,FERT. MIN. MINING	0	255	2808	5109	1116	0	0	0	38655
11 NEW CONSTRUCTION	257488	133106	220613	2714845	194842	236076	36753	108491	653795
12 MAINT., REPAIR CONSTR.	102971	53558	76089	1033378	120532	126937	23944	43596	239651
13 ORDNANCE, ACCESSORIES	86	5	0	999	570	66310	0	21	11
14 FOOD, KINDRED PRDTS.	305277	77015	256320	3617824	438578	174516	148080	99240	355243
15 TOBACCO MANUFACTURES	5658	0	2655	22143	93	6596	8403	0	73083
16 FABRICS	550519	19	12421	20221	3674	303484	8379	52	130
17 TEXTILE PRDTS.	70284	0	3449	19975	544	65503	3149	19	1014
18 APPAREL	73665	1492	14984	344193	8899	175897	10733	5714	12942
19 MISC. TEXTILE PRDTS.	14394	271	549	45900	3537	16257	208	1230	2278
20 LUMBER, WOOD PRDTS.	236253	23692	174284	428388	17816	14513	5277	1402	92788
21 WOODEN CONTAINERS	6973	1080	15065	50063	1877	4819	3703	243	17765
22 HOUSEHOLD FURNITURE	9714	1663	23193	129785	3540	10640	428	542	10358
23 OTHER FURNITURE	2146	681	1078	44393	2601	5528	182	770	4000
24 PAPER, ALLIED PRDTS.	82375	5104	45641	85398	6252	59278	12250	3214	114918
25 PAPERBOARD CONTAINERS	3261	459	1835	69107	7542	38561	3638	3825	11522
26 PRINTING, PUBLISHING	29012	12095	15195	379937	33325	102220	4943	81767	48344
27 CHEMICALS,SELECT. PRDTS.	87935	4496	48124	212949	12387	46956	38644	1937	62982
28 PLASTICS, SYNTHETICS	0	0	21300	29268	0	18718	62090	0	11094
29 DRUGS, COSMETICS	2608	1166	565	144230	2579	42660	757	1817	2137
30 PAINT, ALLIED PRDTS.	3094	730	332	121976	4697	7908	342	664	3432
31 PETROLEUM, RELATED INDS.	9275	3288	56333	1103828	13022	2628	5063	14	5072
32 RUBBER, MISC. PLASTICS	80882	63	4041	217730	7208	171770	16553	286	7044
33 LEATHER TANNING, PRDTS.	0	0	0	16777	182	5653	23231	0	3636
34 FOOTWEAR, LEATHER PRDTS.	2307	346	5952	33051	9102	9111	0	0	1441
35 GLASS, GLASS PRDTS.	381	81	10228	49776	3908	13268	0	0	336
36 STONE, CLAY PRDTS.	61156	6428	11745	216748	15932	39496	2004	1288	25809
37 PRIMARY IRON, STEEL MFR.	494067	2898	1690	215702	59474	105263	13245	5	1017
38 PRIMARY NONFERROUS MFR.	94744	82588	61181	216305	29530	460172	1008	0	10817

39 METAL CONTAINERS	2980	0	2974	117480	2183	1421	996	0	20885
40 FABRICATED METAL PRDTS.	73044	8836	3724	280255	18315	73487	6332	2956	15030
41 SCREW MACH. PRDTS., ETC.	8223	1	99	53369	308	98905	7531	0	268
42 OTHER FAB. METAL PRDTS.	18938	635	2980	129644	5164	194331	2617	770	4921
43 ENGINES, TURBINES	46	1	0	36576	357	6781	0	0	46
44 FARM MACH., EQUIP.	7145	133	5668	32853	4937	2634	151	0	2024
45 CONSTRUC. MACH., EQUIP.	3942	0	2996	98835	18141	11745	0	0	2346
46 MATERIAL HANDLING MACH.	1899	0	2171	13396	4632	5634	0	0	393
47 METALWORKING MACHINERY	530	166	10	22818	338	110959	7020	13	177
48 SPECIAL MACH., EQUIP.	4517	399	1261	68228	6103	60663	15370	50	4316
49 GENERAL MACH., EQUIP.	7771	0	981	86915	4957	165281	1140	827	4942
50 MACHINE SHOP PRDTS.	949	268	251	25129	1371	9934	784	64	784
51 OFFICE, COMPUT. MACHINES	80	0	0	25201	630	113442	0	80	113
52 SERVICE IND. MACHINES	1451	1680	796	33409	660	17627	443	0	43
53 ELECT. TRANSMISS. EQUIP.	2651	0	0	74120	1811	47717	160	0	976
54 HOUSEHOLD APPLIANCES	5756	1382	595	76973	297	134792	469	0	372
55 ELECTRIC LIGHTING EQUIP.	3504	117	142	43750	943	76426	5	13	627
56 RADIO, TV, ETC., EQUIP.	4741	258	0	42444	2930	52261	0	1196	632
57 ELECTRONIC COMPONENTS	1572	86	0	10595	86	12956	0	377	209
58 MISC. ELECTRICAL MACH.	604	0	0	31754	1150	14126	0	607	4357
59 MOTOR VEHICLES, EQUIP.	8388	6032	1227	506582	4347	48522	4919	206	11607
60 AIRCRAFT, PARTS	0	164	0	491116	332	189694	515	7	515
61 OTHER TRANSPORT. EQUIP.	43306	2186	1786	153937	11979	16552	10434	0	38624
62 PROFESS., SCIEN. INSTRU.	763	547	2423	37990	1002	118916	756	1379	933
63 MEDICAL, PHOTO. EQUIP.	3	1	6	12556	2081	5383	0	110	268
64 MISC. MANUFACTURING	3441	765	4982	98827	11719	211901	10220	1257	7027
65 TRANSPORT., WAREHOUSING	282209	90155	139474	1831202	184107	155814	86651	89356	293865
66 COMMUNICA.,EXC. BRDCAST.	29078	10190	11593	311839	23351	128378	8209	43708	37179
67 RADIO, TV BROADCASTING	4575	2536	2332	42846	3429	3978	582	14234	6830
68 ELEC.,GAS,WATER,SAN.SER.	72819	21019	38728	439247	19093	110279	12456	42284	67356
69 WHOLESALE, RETAIL TRADE	606542	236828	385382	4423170	489862	701666	115051	398041	882542
70 FINANCE, INSURANCE	111052	31496	42965	874674	73270	292189	61122	95550	157171
71 REAL ESTATE, RENTAL	238487	102527	141876	2108198	198019	323827	46347	224303	471134
72 HOTELS, PERSONAL SERV.	76323	38421	49864	637109	67488	99349	13796	90675	174533
73 BUSINESS SERVICES	34953	15595	17316	538319	34627	53561	8990	80890	82695
74 RESEARCH, DEVELOPMENT	1205	77	62	24065	206	1096	616	696	1040
75 AUTO. REPAIR, SERVICES	55102	19704	35410	380906	45120	57010	10082	28981	77042
76 AMUSEMENTS	27735	14162	20119	919228	26791	40600	9982	30280	88058
77 MED.,EDUC. SERVICES	71860	29595	46536	885175	75447	149986	16732	150501	105857
78 FEDERAL GOVT. ENTERPRISE	36687	6607	15455	138596	15635	19194	2560	26772	26167
79 STATE, LOCAL GOVT. ENT.	29026	6191	2460	230548	12182	4764	2068	6360	35416
80 IMPORTS	0	0	0	0	0	0	0	0	0
81 BUS.TRAVEL, ENT., GIFTS.	0	0	0	0	0	0	0	0	0
82 OFFICE SUPPLIES	0	0	0	0	0	0	0	0	0
83 SCRAP, USED GOODS	0	0	0	0	0	0	0	0	0
84 GOVERNMENT INDUSTRY	192850	82978	87318	1651514	164426	139833	21092	532746	341895
85 REST OF WORLD INDUSTRY	-5412	-6248	-3354	-93911	-5734	-8136	-1288	-6951	-15741
86 HOUSEHOLD INDUSTRY	57455	11501	19527	197836	14325	43508	10065	38124	84713
87 INVENTORY VALUATION ADJ.	0	0	0	0	0	0	0	0	0
88 STATE TOTAL	5511739	1583077	2996041	33229056	3327441	6640839	1052004	2252598	5259022

TABLE D-1

STATE ESTIMATES OF 1947 OUTPUTS - REVISED
(THOUSANDS OF CURRENT DOLLARS)

INDUSTRY TITLE	10 GEORGIA	11 IDAHO	12 ILLINOIS	13 INDIANA	14 IOWA	15 KANSAS	16 KENTUCKY	17 LOUISIANA	18 MAINE
1 LIVESTOCK, PRDTS.	317016	205570	1392447	989654	2350492	714999	474092	195050	89510
2 OTHER AGRICULTURE PRDTS.	450106	306537	2240497	722051	1552708	957484	433694	259972	123214
3 FORESTRY, FISHERIES	3450	589	1949	1236	908	522	5384	30633	20290
4 AGRI.,FORES.,FISH. SERV.	22002	4894	34545	27288	34363	15971	6931	10584	3684
5 IRON, FERRO. ORES MINING	762	94	0	0	0	0	0	0	0
6 NONFERROUS ORES MINING	596	42341	1386	0	0	7559	125	0	0
7 COAL MINING	281	0	255559	98062	7697	10971	442375	0	0
8 CRUDE PETRO.,NATURAL GAS	0	0	152302	13074	0	221545	36654	371877	0
9 STONE, CLAY MINING	28963	2223	36549	20737	13128	8376	10572	3031	2311
10 CHEM.,FERT. MIN. MINING	744	4789	7220	0	0	6715	3186	34552	0
11 NEW CONSTRUCTION	322689	79582	1081651	446256	357300	331817	245884	359417	62297
12 MAINT., REPAIR CONSTR.	125123	52024	584807	258350	210358	156174	110234	125064	35669
13 ORDNANCE, ACCESSORIES	86	20591	6670	2870	199	10	0	0	0
14 FOOD, KINDRED PRDTS.	665994	179202	4929322	1255630	2023956	1303132	805529	1329631	120568
15 TOBACCO MANUFACTURES	8739	0	5966	13105	115	0	340374	7556	167
16 FABRICS	1116939	0	37429	13050	2775	328	28771	7237	298648
17 TEXTILE PRDTS.	116021	0	85226	6857	61	217	3123	6324	21604
18 APPAREL	183191	0	463604	147901	28480	8981	84767	34837	14547
19 MISC. TEXTILE PRDTS.	41461	218	51560	11228	4241	7521	4725	21381	19449
20 LUMBER, WOOD PRDTS.	216615	82553	122538	88769	46902	8584	73518	180581	65355
21 WOODEN CONTAINERS	16867	592	29089	9598	2278	1661	22685	15516	11474
22 HOUSEHOLD FURNITURE	36774	440	181633	142259	13341	5770	47603	8745	1495
23 OTHER FURNITURE	5390	311	100444	21615	8213	2012	2736	1459	2206
24 PAPER, ALLIED PRDTS.	92653	4	178449	63851	8991	12203	5747	218945	245906
25 PAPERBOARD CONTAINERS	16153	459	151206	64568	10724	9025	8150	27454	1377
26 PRINTING, PUBLISHING	48076	6420	824679	122623	81809	36830	41981	32436	13205
27 CHEMICALS,SELECT. PRDTS.	113480	2778	294868	61346	10820	40053	21201	180151	12272
28 PLASTICS, SYNTHETICS	26765	0	20940	7980	3208	0	16401	56521	1177
29 DRUGS, COSMETICS	15978	699	299892	346857	22784	67062	2283	3562	605
30 PAINT, ALLIED PRDTS.	10277	10	190667	27352	15583	1008	35509	7074	866
31 PETROLEUM, RELATED INDS.	12062	2752	565457	374515	2397	295327	58180	545362	1354
32 RUBBER, MISC. PLASTICS	11275	0	107718	108344	39314	17044	32273	547	1353
33 LEATHER TANNING, PRDTS.	4965	0	88765	7935	0	0	6303	390	7771
34 FOOTWEAR, LEATHER PRDTS.	15754	200	190693	16653	5662	963	25009	2296	101428
35 GLASS, GLASS PRDTS.	217	0	116289	88305	997	46	1280	6937	798
36 STONE, CLAY PRDTS.	54673	4275	195567	99266	52042	35411	26532	18453	5108
37 PRIMARY IRON, STEEL MFR.	24703	449	955229	1041151	19431	6709	81116	3351	1435
38 PRIMARY NONFERROUS MFR.	15813	29751	543076	261148	7565	15133	71785	18875	3749

39 METAL CONTAINERS	1092	0	187880	18813	2984	0	733	16047	2857
40 FABRICATED METAL PRDTS.	19448	1660	290191	152690	48384	39831	85924	20871	7880
41 SCREW MACH. PRDTS., ETC.	5709	0	272689	71294	2629	1056	3819	2010	374
42 OTHER FAB. METAL PRDTS.	3629	24	395814	80879	17284	1731	17145	9717	4029
43 ENGINES, TURBINES	0	0	81370	83943	1339	462	0	0	0
44 FARM MACH., EQUIP.	8550	1407	507641	71860	104723	12725	12353	1860	315
45 CONSTRUC. MACH., EQUIP.	10918	584	245786	44236	78205	18586	6327	5493	1544
46 MATERIAL HANDLING MACH.	5291	50	84136	10550	9793	3561	6570	323	378
47 METALWORKING MACHINERY	574	6	221512	40507	11462	1136	3781	291	416
48 SPECIAL MACH., EQUIP.	18126	4	161939	41450	16076	7547	4420	3437	46888
49 GENERAL MACH., EQUIP.	2563	579	179380	109089	11980	1167	10559	2054	83
50 MACHINE SHOP PRDTS.	244	102	35156	34532	3521	2759	2561	978	260
51 OFFICE, COMPUT. MACHINES	160	0	77061	1972	155	0	729	0	60
52 SERVICE IND. MACHINES	3832	0	97651	171728	5711	2731	4245	785	250
53 ELECT. TRANSMISS. EQUIP.	6242	0	149227	133776	12314	2091	2357	0	0
54 HOUSEHOLD APPLIANCES	4235	0	375306	143425	78419	16264	8308	469	518
55 ELECTRIC LIGHTING EQUIP.	553	0	163839	57671	1633	2812	7357	0	0
56 RADIO, TV, ETC., EQUIP.	7413	0	679033	164824	14025	640	333	60	0
57 ELECTRONIC COMPONENTS	1572	0	105688	61643	3654	195	10765	0	0
58 MISC. ELECTRICAL MACH.	12353	0	67772	141211	13518	3457	3834	644	176
59 MOTOR VEHICLES, EQUIP.	45189	181	318232	942054	11652	49789	41173	1764	117
60 AIRCRAFT, PARTS	5	0	14416	78652	8865	37224	9	0	1
61 OTHER TRANSPORT. EQUIP.	10739	929	371925	137530	10785	13804	9551	49009	18824
62 PROFESS., SCIEN. INSTRU.	1594	17	179615	21367	1484	1263	3409	495	1156
63 MEDICAL, PHOTO. EQUIP.	6	313	80342	2341	2400	14	7	59	528
64 MISC. MANUFACTURING	10929	1071	274447	70835	41014	5162	9517	5172	20012
65 TRANSPORT., WAREHOUSING	347341	76670	1678322	564248	310303	495405	314848	409951	90576
66 COMMUNICA.,EXC. BRDCAST.	40975	14587	286186	144458	39503	22462	28101	41334	20478
67 RADIO, TV BROADCASTING	10476	1571	27296	5938	6820	3168	4140	5530	1825
68 ELEC.,GAS,WATER,SAN.SER.	75248	16371	403801	181020	100413	86052	66309	91416	26386
69 WHOLESALE, RETAIL TRADE	809184	178926	3872452	1277060	895853	636377	618921	748633	246984
70 FINANCE, INSURANCE	179473	17641	820961	197478	125591	76074	93449	116779	36296
71 REAL ESTATE, RENTAL	301470	65213	1759581	483963	306793	217151	255972	269737	91579
72 HOTELS, PERSONAL SERV.	110547	21103	549126	158381	88051	64957	84704	74935	31653
73 BUSINESS SERVICES	56673	10534	475303	67453	51116	43119	29310	63340	11791
74 RESEARCH, DEVELOPMENT	203	146	9805	308	165	143	112	411	440
75 AUTO. REPAIR, SERVICES	72380	18692	246093	109887	77995	63204	53145	52014	22474
76 AMUSEMENTS	35878	10324	237987	62319	39389	26717	35026	38304	11069
77 MED.,EDUC. SERVICES	104627	23517	715401	203733	131659	82294	86188	100887	38573
78 FEDERAL GOVT. ENTERPRISE	33648	4942	119380	32636	24820	22845	26103	17666	10024
79 STATE, LOCAL GOVT. ENT.	11207	4856	44288	17474	21629	2660	8696	11517	10130
80 IMPORTS	0	0	0	0	0	0	0	0	0
81 BUS.TRAVEL, ENT., GIFTS.	0	0	0	0	0	0	0	0	0
82 OFFICE SUPPLIES	0	0	0	0	0	0	0	0	0
83 SCRAP, USED GOODS	0	0	0	0	0	0	0	0	0
84 GOVERNMENT INDUSTRY	256486	47726	726715	257145	152630	159222	173175	191614	69810
85 REST OF WORLD INDUSTRY	-6671	-4183	-48419	-13777	-9140	-5726	-6790	-7725	-4074
86 HOUSEHOLD INDUSTRY	76212	4194	100426	37690	24135	18796	28180	51941	12688
87 INVENTORY VALUATION ADJ.	0	0	0	0	0	0	0	0	0
88 STATE TOTAL	6838974	1550102	34168624	13657769	9840574	6548090	5772086	6525660	2126263

TABLE D-1

STATE ESTIMATES OF 1947 OUTPUTS - REVISED
(THOUSANDS OF CURRENT DOLLARS)

INDUSTRY TITLE	19 MARYLAND	20 MASSA-CHUSETTS	21 MICHIGAN	22 MINNESOTA	23 MISSISSIPPI	24 MISSOURI	25 MONTANA	26 NEBRASKA	27 NEVADA
1 LIVESTOCK, PRDTS.	199368	137549	596119	1245211	251346	1120180	268944	859591	55796
2 OTHER AGRICULTURE PRDTS.	142116	76546	422090	959525	440895	429981	321177	1051806	17705
3 FORESTRY, FISHERIES	9667	41246	10686	3096	6954	4457	1339	609	50
4 AGRI.,FORES.,FISH. SERV.	13317	6705	13744	26123	24093	31448	3721	14231	583
5 IRON, FERRO. ORES MINING	0	0	51347	227257	0	639	4601	0	3244
6 NONFERROUS ORES MINING	0	0	9428	0	0	36801	41210	0	28588
7 COAL MINING	11781	3192	841	0	0	16168	7797	0	0
8 CRUDE PETRO.,NATURAL GAS	0	0	47593	0	64872	540	19230	431	0
9 STONE, CLAY MINING	8658	10327	27856	8268	1463	17130	2368	2878	5110
10 CHEM.,FERT. MIN. MINING	0	0	4124	0	0	2824	1844	0	559
11 NEW CONSTRUCTION	308340	523790	915393	367909	194326	391054	91238	165776	48687
12 MAINT., REPAIR CONSTR.	136422	207823	393690	173939	68139	222793	60016	113106	25132
13 ORDNANCE, ACCESSORIES	494	17778	1079	6563	0	54	0	57	0
14 FOOD, KINDRED PRDTS.	721228	952017	1115117	2119160	209241	1680756	124519	1082209	18571
15 TOBACCO MANUFACTURES	1610	25388	14368	229	0	59616	0	0	0
16 FABRICS	26830	1317980	17140	10311	44068	8289	0	653	0
17 TEXTILE PRDTS.	6640	210926	45128	10160	5417	15587	0	776	0
18 APPAREL	233120	390256	64485	88592	72800	281585	273	4345	0
19 MISC. TEXTILE PRDTS.	13409	46204	19809	17464	989	44758	0	7965	69
20 LUMBER, WOOD PRDTS.	26388	47230	130305	61932	198129	51837	45915	2728	6662
21 WOODEN CONTAINERS	7775	19172	23811	7036	16666	12468	0	959	0
22 HOUSEHOLD FURNITURE	14286	67934	85086	17649	6698	31885	311	8486	0
23 OTHER FURNITURE	6796	18263	65682	5930	1143	20230	249	3775	0
24 PAPER, ALLIED PRDTS.	38559	277735	314678	108315	77048	45792	0	4137	448
25 PAPERBOARD CONTAINERS	25102	105872	79043	27600	1577	51005	0	2746	0
26 PRINTING, PUBLISHING	82397	267109	200143	147112	10371	161879	7968	30589	3028
27 CHEMICALS,SELECT. PRDTS.	115717	104890	264801	15335	36290	125642	5501	4568	5079
28 PLASTICS, SYNTHETICS	68626	60395	26291	0	0	0	0	103	0
29 DRUGS, COSMETICS	67958	137156	149311	36385	4223	107879	30	35540	0
30 PAINT, ALLIED PRDTS.	15023	31053	96344	4643	141	49227	0	294	0
31 PETROLEUM, RELATED INDS.	78761	63398	109309	71975	4777	44312	33343	8496	9
32 RUBBER, MISC. PLASTICS	59077	321374	287574	75954	28081	28187	0	7465	4
33 LEATHER TANNING, PRDTS.	4266	314812	36553	5333	309	4661	0	2683	0
34 FOOTWEAR, LEATHER PRDTS.	19487	475814	13524	10170	17	337515	73	1645	22
35 GLASS, GLASS PRDTS.	13366	11701	17129	8798	3205	18468	37	46	0
36 STONE, CLAY PRDTS.	43138	101148	149253	26566	8488	100750	6981	11171	5884
37 PRIMARY IRON, STEEL MFR.	294101	154595	661931	55062	1028	85279	9740	2917	9
38 PRIMARY NONFERROUS MFR.	89855	118588	309846	27905	930	93377	81376	12817	12456

39 METAL CONTAINERS	65565	11400	2567	7473	769	28299	0	2872	0
40 FABRICATED METAL PRDTS.	56491	76979	241600	58221	2873	100724	2591	13510	877
41 SCREW MACH. PRDTS., ETC.	46838	63391	282820	18016	0	18259	0	82	0
42 OTHER FAB. METAL PRDTS.	12396	156335	315512	14113	2592	59845	466	3391	0
43 ENGINES, TURBINES	109	35406	137845	9862	0	12402	2	359	0
44 FARM MACH., EQUIP.	9652	2718	108068	59377	693	12266	171	10228	65
45 CONSTRUC. MACH., EQUIP.	7175	3365	81398	42807	2015	11285	584	2560	0
46 MATERIAL HANDLING MACH.	2432	15739	63966	9914	124	2985	1751	402	35
47 METALWORKING MACHINERY	9606	94972	292824	14086	14	13554	15	821	0
48 SPECIAL MACH., EQUIP.	21723	230335	79915	19123	3699	26256	47	353	0
49 GENERAL MACH., EQUIP.	9415	75145	133037	8753	2582	20046	6	1866	4
50 MACHINE SHOP PRDTS.	9142	11112	61061	4292	140	16751	102	199	205
51 OFFICE, COMPUT. MACHINES	60	11732	53839	250	0	1636	0	0	0
52 SERVICE IND. MACHINES	8742	55861	150306	45198	0	36072	149	3391	0
53 ELECT. TRANSMISS. EQUIP.	8539	226840	91879	71057	364	89226	0	2850	0
54 HOUSEHOLD APPLIANCES	11276	44697	218016	47721	0	52666	340	3362	0
55 ELECTRIC LIGHTING EQUIP.	3622	95940	23610	1169	2952	36630	7	1227	0
56 RADIO, TV, ETC., EQUIP.	53974	79374	42382	32898	0	6227	0	11138	0
57 ELECTRONIC COMPONENTS	9046	44769	12427	1511	0	979	0	1045	0
58 MISC. ELECTRICAL MACH.	4197	25116	24881	13822	0	8678	0	1226	0
59 MOTOR VEHICLES, EQUIP.	61694	86326	6217893	41455	7390	542449	371	6585	190
60 AIRCRAFT, PARTS	93077	40925	13106	7848	0	7727	13	0	0
61 OTHER TRANSPORT. EQUIP.	87559	63363	83897	21344	19374	54436	106	2254	0
62 PROFESS., SCIEN. INSTRU.	5656	78658	39840	12722	163	12362	260	3088	0
63 MEDICAL, PHOTO. EQUIP.	577	45090	11616	3587	116	5650	1	1305	0
64 MISC. MANUFACTURING	26732	251622	100055	34385	2675	59848	1352	6676	664
65 TRANSPORT., WAREHOUSING	334498	472468	588485	436634	117772	679924	126007	217552	44230
66 COMMUNICA.,EXC. BRDCAST.	54671	148091	124243	54079	16837	56010	8155	36393	7301
67 RADIO, TV BROADCASTING	4777	20920	23114	6630	1903	10777	1608	3943	455
68 ELEC.,GAS,WATER,SAN.SER.	92864	240861	265232	88583	31675	121248	29010	20863	4931
69 WHOLESALE, RETAIL TRADE	732397	1824797	2216634	1217400	375839	1599989	200272	499550	66485
70 FINANCE, INSURANCE	149134	494001	308320	191138	40374	262808	21749	87591	6063
71 REAL ESTATE, RENTAL	284700	738047	932396	413779	145898	568086	71163	149774	29979
72 HOTELS, PERSONAL SERV.	98451	239326	284817	114027	45882	185269	24697	51086	23799
73 BUSINESS SERVICES	63114	180616	223380	65094	23631	115757	9770	27292	5747
74 RESEARCH, DEVELOPMENT	2257	3709	823	1047	174	729	22	120	118
75 AUTO. REPAIR, SERVICES	53747	108427	199254	87401	34269	111729	20014	44822	7376
76 AMUSEMENTS	56783	123120	129083	48960	14389	72030	8944	20585	32242
77 MED.,EDUC. SERVICES	138853	402694	319426	174128	42070	223692	28315	67140	6604
78 FEDERAL GOVT. ENTERPRISE	22373	62328	53226	25969	14838	58219	5479	15332	1757
79 STATE, LOCAL GOVT. ENT.	14509	79614	115374	11352	1333	27393	588	1679	35
80 IMPORTS	0	0	0	0	0	0	0	0	0
81 BUS.TRAVEL, ENT., GIFTS.	0	0	0	0	0	0	0	0	0
82 OFFICE SUPPLIES	0	0	0	0	0	0	0	0	0
83 SCRAP, USED GOODS	0	0	0	0	0	0	0	0	0
84 GOVERNMENT INDUSTRY	370410	431444	480222	227160	122703	260915	56548	112524	22590
85 REST OF WORLD INDUSTRY	-9727	-22448	-38714	-19754	-2974	-15788	-5728	-5292	-3309
86 HOUSEHOLD INDUSTRY	56251	76411	66751	23589	30913	41912	4029	11178	1985
87 INVENTORY VALUATION ADJ.	0	0	0	0	0	0	0	0	0
88 STATE TOTAL	6049037	14217602	21967072	9745723	2889783	11353012	1758780	4888523	498125

TABLE D-1

STATE ESTIMATES OF 1947 OUTPUTS - REVISED
(THOUSANDS OF CURRENT DOLLARS)

INDUSTRY TITLE	28 NEW HAMPSHIRE	29 NEW JERSEY	30 NEW MEXICO	31 NEW YORK	32 NORTH CAROLINA	33 NORTH DAKOTA	34 OHIO	35 OKLAHOMA	36 OREGON
1 LIVESTOCK, PRDTS.	60928	196302	126985	733465	325679	309876	977673	468291	244098
2 OTHER AGRICULTURE PRDTS.	21449	144242	100838	379866	709362	878925	588726	443609	314234
3 FORESTRY, FISHERIES	2319	11301	230	19800	6754	69	5115	2254	11444
4 AGRI.,FORES.,FISH. SERV.	6028	9048	4328	15793	18788	6266	21159	15533	6594
5 IRON, FERRO. ORES MINING	0	4050	481	14791	831	0	0	0	0
6 NONFERROUS ORES MINING	0	10563	31650	7528	568	0	0	10658	943
7 COAL MINING	0	0	7805	0	0	6341	157262	18054	0
8 CRUDE PETRO.,NATURAL GAS	0	0	82881	21479	0	14	24796	316180	0
9 STONE, CLAY MINING	556	21638	1189	34888	14579	640	46886	6412	10016
10 CHEM.,FERT. MIN. MINING	0	0	20394	8247	0	0	0	0	0
11 NEW CONSTRUCTION	47695	654072	120686	1315556	372243	76611	1047457	391148	272780
12 MAINT., REPAIR CONSTR.	29933	272327	51160	751329	160555	64146	508150	121187	105772
13 ORDNANCE, ACCESSORIES	0	2003	0	16432	257	0	959	0	9
14 FOOD, KINDRED PRDTS.	52207	1499541	38462	3862557	303058	154739	1894322	480885	404605
15 TOBACCO MANUFACTURES	5628	102021	0	24547	2033596	0	46074	0	11
16 FABRICS	211280	491527	121	448900	1819159	0	82317	6329	10011
17 TEXTILE PRDTS.	11981	137808	0	266335	130208	822	52308	690	2178
18 APPAREL	24717	472937	1125	5084874	373310	0	291334	11294	20180
19 MISC. TEXTILE PRDTS.	1801	65749	625	271423	94895	155	31056	1345	4848
20 LUMBER, WOOD PRDTS.	39268	65660	16762	142889	194842	295	97380	24871	711536
21 WOODEN CONTAINERS	11929	17397	250	27602	15267	0	26003	650	9611
22 HOUSEHOLD FURNITURE	8221	50634	1589	207843	177248	66	95606	5198	21905
23 OTHER FURNITURE	742	16193	208	134384	12476	155	116704	2252	4285
24 PAPER, ALLIED PRDTS.	71336	198673	4	557412	104314	0	293865	3281	78696
25 PAPERBOARD CONTAINERS	1995	121353	0	244069	17258	0	143749	6221	4893
26 PRINTING, PUBLISHING	14260	162758	4984	1824456	37348	6171	465448	35531	33860
27 CHEMICALS,SELECT. PRDTS.	-3822	616589	6288	415933	44722	1444	279052	8312	12222
28 PLASTICS, SYNTHETICS	1224	142804	0	63346	31318	0	73055	0	0
29 DRUGS, COSMETICS	1247	517904	0	474327	12459	0	218122	1050	2473
30 PAINT, ALLIED PRDTS.	295	173067	0	156284	5246	730	139792	3040	6639
31 PETROLEUM, RELATED INDS.	158	675227	14203	204541	639	894	324744	306313	9261
32 RUBBER, MISC. PLASTICS	8019	203235	0	187089	11614	0	903858	31660	2411
33 LEATHER TANNING, PRDTS.	17988	58623	0	148591	20485	0	47546	0	536
34 FOOTWEAR, LEATHER PRDTS.	160777	53397	557	546800	2917	0	109921	1409	2488
35 GLASS, GLASS PRDTS.	0	79175	0	83090	3789	46	161556	29847	490
36 STONE, CLAY PRDTS.	6903	162686	2158	294703	33574	1276	323453	18610	12395
37 PRIMARY IRON, STEEL MFR.	2376	201640	390	649977	7855	110	2119190	15174	47107
38 PRIMARY NONFERROUS MFR.	8458	709738	26094	667146	15396	0	305450	70976	22249

39 METAL CONTAINERS	0	72593	0	49440	0	0	78395	2974	2548
40 FABRICATED METAL PRDTS.	3796	118283	3734	296827	20924	1259	455439	39588	27987
41 SCREW MACH. PRDTS., ETC.	4290	42414	0	158876	446	35	354447	1388	822
42 OTHER FAB. METAL PRDTS.	2855	163076	7	209237	6279	308	289001	5431	5233
43 ENGINES, TURBINES	42	26904	1	63030	28	2	91867	356	0
44 FARM MACH., EQUIP.	118	10263	126	68943	5178	543	103114	3066	2045
45 CONSTRUC. MACH., EQUIP.	5379	33023	0	22300	2346	0	253031	42421	6053
46 MATERIAL HANDLING MACH.	467	48618	0	58204	2660	0	102556	1076	19918
47 METALWORKING MACHINERY	8412	72076	230	114242	754	14	364039	729	1483
48 SPECIAL MACH., EQUIP.	28963	110158	572	214505	15261	1	219178	1091	8134
49 GENERAL MACH., EQUIP.	1120	152485	4	203338	1658	118	289970	8589	2785
50 MACHINE SHOP PRDTS.	634	21576	0	27775	1841	6	32414	784	4276
51 OFFICE, COMPUT. MACHINES	0	21166	0	184133	60	0	142331	160	0
52 SERVICE IND. MACHINES	219	24861	0	96903	1394	5164	224580	1212	987
53 ELECT. TRANSMISS. EQUIP.	7579	132248	0	232056	725	0	429521	1619	4198
54 HOUSEHOLD APPLIANCES	176	82417	0	123742	1146	0	410910	2103	5168
55 ELECTRIC LIGHTING EQUIP.	335	108549	3	172386	485	7	144515	344	250
56 RADIO, TV, ETC., EQUIP.	0	337126	0	284278	14208	0	74800	0	518
57 ELECTRONIC COMPONENTS	0	76328	0	97909	4713	0	19351	0	172
58 MISC. ELECTRICAL MACH.	1811	78168	0	98341	2368	604	186555	1207	3457
59 MOTOR VEHICLES, EQUIP.	113	357739	3793	677834	8933	0	1095238	6743	5795
60 AIRCRAFT, PARTS	1	79827	0	102934	4	0	116622	1203	0
61 OTHER TRANSPORT. EQUIP.	82	125588	0	269269	2849	75	122859	2318	14211
62 PROFESS., SCIEN. INSTRU.	4827	104181	17	355447	828	0	57359	3159	1065
63 MEDICAL, PHOTO. EQUIP.	598	34703	0	391652	75	1	13329	355	967
64 MISC. MANUFACTURING	14997	293415	2082	799989	4875	539	223314	6427	8869
65 TRANSPORT., WAREHOUSING	38647	507655	92070	3088762	196924	66901	1240960	597658	215279
66 COMMUNICA.,EXC. BRDCAST.	13138	137517	3401	472642	39874	7001	181438	28900	37182
67 RADIO, TV BROADCASTING	1120	3287	1721	60804	7656	1482	27847	4604	4640
68 ELEC.,GAS,WATER,SAN.SER.	22063	246155	29636	795834	62103	13329	399170	75594	44333
69 WHOLESALE, RETAIL TRADE	143242	1612955	168320	8266947	859021	203716	2932592	623266	623045
70 FINANCE, INSURANCE	29858	432182	14699	2363468	132557	20924	465238	76124	78162
71 REAL ESTATE, RENTAL	60886	802146	73316	3510785	315354	59158	1238501	229313	223884
72 HOTELS, PERSONAL SERV.	26536	289617	26099	1079607	121609	16251	359029	79283	76484
73 BUSINESS SERVICES	7381	139092	12385	1355792	43845	7559	225663	61437	46452
74 RESEARCH, DEVELOPMENT	166	3395	409	9828	103	1025	1908	771	123
75 AUTO. REPAIR, SERVICES	13045	124527	16433	360167	72345	18751	219221	63880	58627
76 AMUSEMENTS	16443	130794	9597	642108	38094	7290	161536	31376	29071
77 MED.,EDUC. SERVICES	33080	297296	18593	1387324	104882	22293	448053	75007	88864
78 FEDERAL GOVT. ENTERPRISE	5276	44246	6490	226521	27713	6837	79492	23066	13203
79 STATE, LOCAL GOVT. ENT.	6598	25565	986	342874	15471	291	131636	8313	24303
80 IMPORTS	0	0	0	0	0	0	0	0	0
81 BUS.TRAVEL, ENT., GIFTS.	0	0	0	0	0	0	0	0	0
82 OFFICE SUPPLIES	0	0	0	0	0	0	0	0	0
83 SCRAP, USED GOODS	0	0	0	0	0	0	0	0	0
84 GOVERNMENT INDUSTRY	45173	432574	77011	1517543	281387	44126	602355	176799	133473
85 REST OF WORLD INDUSTRY	-3672	-25340	-3625	-157074	-5762	-4149	-34335	-5737	-6619
86 HOUSEHOLD INDUSTRY	6624	95593	6034	357779	67217	3578	93418	22719	17700
87 INVENTORY VALUATION ADJ.	0	0	0	0	0	0	0	0	0
88 STATE TOTAL	1380313	16388924	1226591	51363584	9593036	2014829	26688544	5169979	4225926

TABLE D-1

STATE ESTIMATES OF 1947 OUTPUTS - REVISED
(THOUSANDS OF CURRENT DOLLARS)

INDUSTRY TITLE	37 PENNSYL-VANIA	38 RHODE ISLAND	39 SOUTH CAROLINA	40 SOUTH DAKOTA	41 TENNESSEE	42 TEXAS	43 UTAH	44 VERMONT	45 VIRGINIA
1 LIVESTOCK, PRDTS.	720761	18388	157009	542256	403165	1151746	138991	114770	378435
2 OTHER AGRICULTURE PRDTS.	351088	7370	329848	701981	362365	1689961	86297	35255	293410
3 FORESTRY, FISHERIES	7958	2806	2575	94	3983	8199	42	1295	23974
4 AGRI.,FORES.,FISH. SERV.	20773	775	11642	8738	12771	77344	2869	1893	12786
5 IRON, FERRO. ORES MINING	13977	0	0	0	3553	1079	3207	0	80
6 NONFERROUS ORES MINING	71	0	0	17049	8671	42	145658	655	3506
7 COAL MINING	1242715	0	0	397	35726	72	34938	0	116585
8 CRUDE PETRO.,NATURAL GAS	76994	0	0	0	17	1838971	381	0	100
9 STONE, CLAY MINING	54621	455	6493	7531	18193	18445	2083	9989	20467
10 CHEM.,FERT. MIN. MINING	0	0	0	0	9470	82018	144	0	0
11 NEW CONSTRUCTION	1089593	84805	170157	84654	313404	1751403	92855	31534	407729
12 MAINT., REPAIR CONSTR.	447227	30653	62740	63464	119058	658243	47153	17650	172804
13 ORDNANCE, ACCESSORIES	4038	34	0	0	0	362	0	34	86
14 FOOD, KINDRED PRDTS.	2221640	81663	144607	295048	756020	1853911	197459	108909	422992
15 TOBACCO MANUFACTURES	236549	156	21799	0	36743	14693	41	0	833162
16 FABRICS	684514	699596	1405273	0	141413	65660	2477	39982	336246
17 TEXTILE PRDTS.	256703	81499	112249	0	12569	16226	0	1141	31576
18 APPAREL	1253137	21984	48067	0	202214	137621	11631	18062	143714
19 MISC. TEXTILE PRDTS.	54556	7211	34369	238	20150	38749	488	896	37980
20 LUMBER, WOOD PRDTS.	110524	3506	149500	7141	109040	213830	4679	37271	140145
21 WOODEN CONTAINERS	25596	1440	7633	236	22360	13228	368	4647	12928
22 HOUSEHOLD FURNITURE	100579	3051	13272	0	52533	29634	2585	7629	97037
23 OTHER FURNITURE	32000	2823	664	0	1719	16744	698	2739	2470
24 PAPER, ALLIED PRDTS.	309799	15235	63931	0	57981	46301	0	40143	146231
25 PAPERBOARD CONTAINERS	154496	8070	12781	644	16659	23460	905	3175	14793
26 PRINTING, PUBLISHING	521667	23304	14148	7374	69944	132629	13635	6680	42862
27 CHEMICALS,SELECT. PRDTS.	313355	7237	38684	640	126368	240860	7045	2219	110402
28 PLASTICS, SYNTHETICS	126345	3678	34	0	143315	94180	0	1502	255968
29 DRUGS, COSMETICS	171354	7138	1361	560	27173	42302	1216	3050	18958
30 PAINT, ALLIED PRDTS.	95325	5642	953	0	8545	28973	808	320	5445
31 PETROLEUM, RELATED INDS.	716386	16922	3739	546	13042	1919751	38322	3490	5213
32 RUBBER, MISC. PLASTICS	254969	51312	3968	0	79916	18498	116	10753	13105
33 LEATHER TANNING, PRDTS.	142017	3582	229	0	7596	4024	0	1313	15434
34 FOOTWEAR, LEATHER PRDTS.	181872	3624	318	0	90075	10173	146	1829	24405
35 GLASS, GLASS PRDTS.	218107	2503	436	0	10411	11833	81	798	8643
36 STONE, CLAY PRDTS.	366091	2044	14302	3542	50889	89584	10469	22129	31509
37 PRIMARY IRON, STEEL MFR.	2888071	42821	7641	101	78922	80110	77240	2350	31291
38 PRIMARY NONFERROUS MFR.	385768	72897	452	0	81258	113885	64072	598	10311

39 METAL CONTAINERS	63820	0	0	0	4426	49312	4381	0	2007
40 FABRICATED METAL PRDTS.	480405	10987	3128	4327	84797	101252	6951	4868	34938
41 SCREW MACH. PRDTS., ETC.	276502	19626	0	0	6564	3551	37	97	101
42 OTHER FAB. METAL PRDTS.	278513	31300	432	425	8255	29942	522	2482	9316
43 ENGINES, TURBINES	87836	0	12	0	91	807	1	4015	399
44 FARM MACH., EQUIP.	65666	309	307	1403	7186	14226	268	103	1616
45 CONSTRUC. MACH., EQUIP.	131562	0	0	175	5859	148256	5491	0	2346
46 MATERIAL HANDLING MACH.	48469	375	529	0	6374	1907	2177	0	2056
47 METALWORKING MACHINERY	140840	43136	103	195	584	1968	251	22905	150
48 SPECIAL MACH., EQUIP.	178301	33951	8827	460	6881	19404	556	6908	6579
49 GENERAL MACH., EQUIP.	176093	2494	1935	114	6878	15968	4	211	1332
50 MACHINE SHOP PRDTS.	45892	7858	64	31	2390	5198	103	582	826
51 OFFICE, COMPUT. MACHINES	1951	60	0	0	80	120	320	8694	60
52 SERVICE IND. MACHINES	118083	2888	6	301	6664	11267	464	92	233
53 ELECT. TRANSMISS. EQUIP.	525899	1330	0	594	2824	5040	0	0	5093
54 HOUSEHOLD APPLIANCES	160693	1902	5	312	20794	13394	180	1025	3499
55 ELECTRIC LIGHTING EQUIP.	98865	18484	70	0	3447	5499	247	357	438
56 RADIO, TV, ETC., EQUIP.	149805	1851	0	0	2946	948	273	1851	4860
57 ELECTRONIC COMPONENTS	84757	614	0	0	0	219	0	614	1572
58 MISC. ELECTRICAL MACH.	60188	17609	36	0	6506	16361	0	50	1295
59 MOTOR VEHICLES, EQUIP.	425709	1757	2068	172	68333	39234	371	95	11742
60 AIRCRAFT, PARTS	30176	0	2	0	179	79221	0	0	2
61 OTHER TRANSPORT. EQUIP.	373424	746	4286	66	10586	34367	1242	203	105536
62 PROFESS., SCIEN. INSTRU.	155868	6399	164	119	10551	2841	250	831	851
63 MEDICAL, PHOTO. EQUIP.	11240	7732	151	1242	113	1905	1	6	6134
64 MISC. MANUFACTURING	261311	162153	6370	873	19904	21767	2998	4928	10154
65 TRANSPORT., WAREHOUSING	1756610	44972	98498	54913	277391	1890970	105715	35663	378883
66 COMMUNICA.,EXC. BRDCAST.	229373	21710	15251	6752	54736	158426	7640	8669	54027
67 RADIO, TV BROADCASTING	18900	2057	3241	1514	8662	19103	2516	494	5765
68 ELEC.,GAS,WATER,SAN.SER.	512850	41304	35157	13202	9600	293170	18723	17940	89696
69 WHOLESALE, RETAIL TRADE	3451503	275918	415155	203253	978429	2557597	226373	101463	786580
70 FINANCE, INSURANCE	727183	58898	71730	20405	135799	345946	32646	18299	142505
71 REAL ESTATE, RENTAL	1252636	103478	145240	63021	298786	812596	90056	36415	373523
72 HOTELS, PERSONAL SERV.	446147	38683	53803	18356	110611	329798	30076	13466	117776
73 BUSINESS SERVICES	278575	20365	19038	8853	40557	268057	11923	3483	39637
74 RESEARCH, DEVELOPMENT	2286	107	436	55	804	2636	38	120	1154
75 AUTO. REPAIR, SERVICES	252739	19257	38560	18698	69706	228378	18853	10307	68745
76 AMUSEMENTS	203246	29534	16055	8645	36585	113467	13677	5012	44646
77 MED.,EDUC. SERVICES	708754	50430	48514	23713	112650	255937	29365	22014	121330
78 FEDERAL GOVT. ENTERPRISE	82100	9622	13534	7837	64625	76442	5972	4673	79588
79 STATE, LOCAL GOVT. ENT.	109091	6124	3958	898	72014	72999	9547	1714	50949
80 IMPORTS	0	0	0	0	0	0	0	0	0
81 BUS.TRAVEL, ENT., GIFTS.	0	0	0	0	0	0	0	0	0
82 OFFICE SUPPLIES	0	0	0	0	0	0	0	0	0
83 SCRAP, USED GOODS	0	0	0	0	0	0	0	0	0
84 GOVERNMENT INDUSTRY	819149	99948	171675	50917	178517	668294	95808	24857	646517
85 REST OF WORLD INDUSTRY	-40244	-3432	-2791	-2415	-7954	-35567	-2456	-1918	-8277
86 HOUSEHOLD INDUSTRY	155760	11757	42820	4339	50966	132116	4011	6670	55894
87 INVENTORY VALUATION ADJ.	0	0	0	0	0	0	0	0	0
88 STATE TOTAL	31249760	2518515	4059240	2255997	6292930	21349072	1716669	904956	7484855

TABLE D-1

STATE ESTIMATES OF 1947 OUTPUTS - REVISED
(THOUSANDS OF CURRENT DOLLARS)

INDUSTRY TITLE	46 WASHINGTON	47 WEST VIRGINIA	48 WISCONSIN	49 WYOMING	50 ALASKA	51 HAWAII	52 NO STATE ALLOCATION	53 NATIONAL TOTAL
1 LIVESTOCK, PRDTS.	260150	171959	1172846	161675	0	0	0	22374848
2 OTHER AGRICULTURE PRDTS.	472041	52282	319132	66154	0	0	0	22684640
3 FORESTRY, FISHERIES	27825	5133	6253	82	0	0	0	408035
4 AGRI.,FORES.,FISH. SERV.	8732	2870	15682	1573	0	0	0	701068
5 IRON, FERRO. ORES MINING	8	0	5756	2430	0	0	0	366087
6 NONFERROUS ORES MINING	5800	0	1976	62	0	0	0	637428
7 COAL MINING	8014	944378	0	32467	0	0	0	3633843
8 CRUDE PETRO.,NATURAL GAS	0	47336	0	82062	0	0	0	4210010
9 STONE, CLAY MINING	10869	13307	22070	2918	0	0	0	614590
10 CHEM.,FERT. MIN. MINING	0	212	0	341	0	0	0	235328
11 NEW CONSTRUCTION	481194	220681	390033	63399	0	0	0	20329104
12 MAINT., REPAIR CONSTR.	148075	70708	193417	26681	0	0	0	9001948
13 ORDNANCE, ACCESSORIES	9	0	187	0	0	0	0	148861
14 FOOD, KINDRED PRDTS.	642522	112298	1850941	36528	0	0	0	43522784
15 TOBACCO MANUFACTURES	11	13885	5409	0	0	0	0	3970191
16 FABRICS	2189	18013	20925	0	0	0	0	10315281
17 TEXTILE PRDTS.	1329	0	18253	0	0	0	0	1831877
18 APPAREL	19057	21794	111834	0	0	0	0	11019170
19 MISC. TEXTILE PRDTS.	6551	208	11780	0	0	0	0	1082151
20 LUMBER, WOOD PRDTS.	577516	48217	128743	9277	0	0	0	5283847
21 WOODEN CONTAINERS	5698	3149	17765	125	0	0	0	523114
22 HOUSEHOLD FURNITURE	22973	5772	74668	399	0	0	0	1838700
23 OTHER FURNITURE	3971	987	15338	0	0	0	0	695385
24 PAPER, ALLIED PRDTS.	248465	18874	379267	0	0	0	0	4741702
25 PAPERBOARD CONTAINERS	24351	8683	67986	0	0	0	0	1597349
26 PRINTING, PUBLISHING	56851	18817	142517	3265	0	0	0	6464000
27 CHEMICALS,SELECT. PRDTS.	24335	272399	34167	2714	0	0	0	4492364
28 PLASTICS, SYNTHETICS	1806	56662	1607	0	0	0	0	1427720
29 DRUGS, COSMETICS	4422	3358	37984	0	0	0	0	3043181
30 PAINT, ALLIED PRDTS.	4804	707	33063	376	0	0	0	1298299
31 PETROLEUM, RELATED INDS.	9354	40007	28373	78279	0	0	0	7879711
32 RUBBER, MISC. PLASTICS	772	3394	55086	35	0	0	0	3470974
33 LEATHER TANNING, PRDTS.	205	22914	107168	0	0	0	0	1132475
34 FOOTWEAR, LEATHER PRDTS.	3254	3319	131738	73	0	0	0	2607327
35 GLASS, GLASS PRDTS.	4525	138809	3648	0	0	0	0	1123383
36 STONE, CLAY PRDTS.	28577	71165	46247	3019	0	0	0	2920637
37 PRIMARY IRON, STEEL MFR.	31650	262420	184940	8	0	0	0	11022980
38 PRIMARY NONFERROUS MFR.	129866	42655	117684	44	0	0	0	5515384

39	METAL CONTAINERS	10543	17435	5912	0	0	0	0	862057
40	FABRICATED METAL PRDTS.	24973	40450	205750	716	0	0	0	3674097
41	SCREW MACH. PRDTS., ETC.	1396	26524	88440	0	0	0	0	1943241
42	OTHER FAB. METAL PRDTS.	6978	11048	52076	0	0	0	0	2567616
43	ENGINES, TURBINES	723	0	148239	0	0	0	0	831260
44	FARM MACH., EQUIP.	3381	2160	149538	268	0	0	0	1420045
45	CONSTRUC. MACH., EQUIP.	16498	18104	191210	132	0	0	0	1585059
46	MATERIAL HANDLING MACH.	4211	970	19457	0	0	0	0	566147
47	METALWORKING MACHINERY	3412	366	73240	4	0	0	0	1696737
48	SPECIAL MACH., EQUIP.	9231	2448	101832	3	0	0	0	1815490
49	GENERAL MACH., EQUIP.	3255	521	89687	3	0	0	0	1799685
50	MACHINE SHOP PRDTS.	3259	1009	11158	57	0	0	0	390382
51	OFFICE, COMPUT. MACHINES	117	0	1721	0	0	0	0	648173
52	SERVICE IND. MACHINES	1045	254	27162	120	0	0	0	1166658
53	ELECT. TRANSMISS. EQUIP.	2854	1440	154221	364	0	0	0	2431801
54	HOUSEHOLD APPLIANCES	9087	2147	83609	124	0	0	0	2148090
55	ELECTRIC LIGHTING EQUIP.	1615	7209	12601	0	0	0	0	1100254
56	RADIO, TV, ETC., EQUIP.	3189	0	4214	0	0	0	0	2077650
57	ELECTRONIC COMPONENTS	172	3208	1340	0	0	0	0	570142
58	MISC. ELECTRICAL MACH.	3413	496	37624	0	0	0	0	889573
59	MOTOR VEHICLES, EQUIP.	20523	11721	445226	0	0	0	0	12189471
60	AIRCRAFT, PARTS	46031	166	4974	164	0	0	0	1445718
61	OTHER TRANSPORT. EQUIP.	44086	12480	53928	3	0	0	0	2412429
62	PROFESS., SCIEN. INSTRU.	1290	314	58814	0	0	0	0	1293032
63	MEDICAL, PHOTO. EQUIP.	348	386	2503	0	0	0	0	647845
64	MISC. MANUFACTURING	9107	9279	66416	200	0	0	0	3202274
65	TRANSPORT., WAREHOUSING	433451	255051	324744	165216	0	0	0	22324992
66	COMMUNICA., EXC. BRDCAST.	68898	23395	98646	1995	0	0	0	3418000
67	RADIO, TV BROADCASTING	6814	4101	5896	543	0	0	0	415000
68	ELEC., GAS, WATER, SAN. SER.	62265	94347	121931	10034	0	0	0	5774000
69	WHOLESALE, RETAIL TRADE	956184	480985	1163247	100372	0	0	0	53392000
70	FINANCE, INSURANCE	153198	52173	177195	8402	0	0	0	10522000
71	REAL ESTATE, RENTAL	379608	162436	472222	35641	0	0	0	21678992
72	HOTELS, PERSONAL SERV.	111857	56139	130756	15648	0	0	0	7046000
73	BUSINESS SERVICES	62630	23381	68562	7347	0	0	0	5142000
74	RESEARCH, DEVELOPMENT	583	581	630	168	0	0	0	77121
75	AUTO. REPAIR, SERVICES	74367	35746	88509	10859	0	0	0	3974000
76	AMUSEMENTS	46872	28491	51299	5058	0	0	0	3849000
77	MED., EDUC. SERVICES	160529	69223	183001	9658	0	0	0	8692000
78	FEDERAL GOVT. ENTERPRISE	56316	12543	37114	3877	0	0	51226	1777571
79	STATE, LOCAL GOVT. ENT.	75784	21313	13014	1209	0	0	0	1708000
80	IMPORTS	0	0	0	0	0	0	0	0
81	BUS. TRAVEL, ENT., GIFTS.	0	0	0	0	0	0	0	0
82	OFFICE SUPPLIES	0	0	0	0	0	0	0	0
83	SCRAP, USED GOODS	0	0	0	0	0	0	0	0
84	GOVERNMENT INDUSTRY	396134	110343	234451	33295	0	0	1556000	15730037
85	REST OF WORLD INDUSTRY	-16138	-4543	-17120	-1820	0	0	1592000*	823998*
86	HOUSEHOLD INDUSTRY	22121	17736	26662	2151	0	0	0	2348000
87	INVENTORY VALUATION ADJ.	0	0	0	0	0	0	-763965	-763965
88	STATE TOTAL	6559982	4330951	11026133	985803	0	0	2435261	443469312

*These figures exclude the value of secondary production. They therefore differ from those obtained by adding the corresponding values of final demand given in Appendix C of Volume I of this series. {63, p. 216, Note 9}

TABLE D-2

STATE ESTIMATES OF 1958 OUTPUTS - REVISED
(THOUSANDS OF CURRENT DOLLARS)

INDUSTRY TITLE	1 ALABAMA	2 ARIZONA	3 ARKANSAS	4 CALIFORNIA	5 COLORADO	6 CONNECTICUT	7 DELAWARE	8 DISTRICT OF COLUMBIA	9 FLORIDA
1 LIVESTOCK, PRDTS.	439590	142353	329719	1220290	419318	129759	98808	0	281067
2 OTHER AGRICULTURE PRDTS.	261262	363739	443536	2339777	345540	61286	55387	0	544676
3 FORESTRY, FISHERIES	24063	2430	16042	130756	904	1214	6845	0	44024
4 AGRI.,FORES.,FISH. SERV.	35070	17631	46099	90587	7855	11176	15974	0	12149
5 IRON, FERRO. ORES MINING	73419	7891	1711	29042	26246	0	0	0	0
6 NONFERROUS ORES MINING	2331	229971	18023	7787	112145	428	0	0	7391
7 COAL MINING	89591	51	3089	0	19718	0	0	0	0
8 CRUDE PETRO.,NATURAL GAS	16560	54	91385	1165224	170351	0	0	0	1035
9 STONE, CLAY MINING	15426	4826	13985	126161	13936	13091	1090	0	40821
10 CHEM.,FERT. MIN. MINING	0	458	2019	55970	5139	0	291	0	105199
11 NEW CONSTRUCTION	758078	632967	399123	6223625	716830	833604	176361	250707	2005218
12 MAINT., REPAIR CONSTR.	200900	103415	159175	1899336	228461	232324	44069	78754	449855
13 ORDNANCE, ACCESSORIES	21986	121062	101	1491071	88630	132824	0	830	66908
14 FOOD, KINDRED PRDTS.	581016	187553	463768	6434439	791999	403136	204544	157971	1140307
15 TOBACCO MANUFACTURES	14526	0	0	650	0	57583	0	0	134014
16 FABRICS	499881	0	15610	36855	392	187640	24827	0	2856
17 TEXTILE PRDTS.	41840	0	11529	76267	0	41582	6264	0	2630
18 APPAREL	212438	12538	44134	594192	15756	190575	40483	264	53694
19 MISC. TEXTILE PRDTS.	39609	989	186	116223	3505	23078	876	1530	9759
20 LUMBER, WOOD PRDTS.	202711	43871	179243	968531	32288	18813	7362	1416	128729
21 WOODEN CONTAINERS	5441	1090	9223	54802	1125	2008	1083	0	16464
22 HOUSEHOLD FURNITURE	28166	7458	64631	303976	12706	28439	333	1416	63751
23 OTHER FURNITURE	3607	2732	7563	106670	7337	16571	89	1295	13502
24 PAPER, ALLIED PRDTS.	231266	1940	105655	353903	8486	85192	11739	9315	303356
25 PAPERBOARD CONTAINERS	3308	1477	28455	312157	9838	73384	3267	3700	45410
26 PRINTING, PUBLISHING	66038	36755	36861	899077	84221	184990	15509	194053	158985
27 CHEMICALS,SELECT. PRDTS.	197596	16586	93745	489616	23662	79347	78636	1667	190661
28 PLASTICS, SYNTHETICS	74261	0	0	122126	0	67927	73398	0	154138
29 DRUGS, COSMETICS	8723	3235	814	349868	10042	119259	19073	1544	10104
30 PAINT, ALLIED PRDTS.	6661	2717	2874	202307	7707	6766	2596	589	17284
31 PETROLEUM, RELATED INDS.	32144	6144	122907	2271499	67975	12845	61585	0	19712
32 RUBBER, MISC. PLASTICS	209608	5411	26024	465872	104996	264016	28101	915	8181
33 LEATHER TANNING, PRDTS.	0	0	0	20252	87	4050	27748	0	784
34 FOOTWEAR, LEATHER PRDTS.	7490	1099	35644	49117	24084	33005	2069	0	7225
35 GLASS, GLASS PRDTS.	8127	285	18166	120606	1039	9218	188	119	11906
36 STONE, CLAY PRDTS.	130966	44911	32809	725633	72148	82406	13552	17069	210723
37 PRIMARY IRON, STEEL MFR.	906968	7150	2330	694957	172861	118809	41749	0	7594
38 PRIMARY NONFERROUS MFR.	215523	192827	86409	443247	34050	480025	9973	0	69656

39 METAL CONTAINERS	7928	0	3577	362434	8304	190	1412	0	73362
40 FABRICATED METAL PRDTS.	135172	25660	18093	694627	47553	76251	25818	6905	165895
41 SCREW MACH. PRDTS., ETC.	28780	217	3097	206818	3129	157136	6466	129	5623
42 OTHER FAB. METAL PRDTS.	48826	2089	19398	451235	21920	301390	12418	843	28009
43 ENGINES, TURBINES	0	577	0	68921	0	14446	0	0	799
44 FARM MACH., EQUIP.	9575	376	865	47977	5947	1180	818	0	4920
45 CONSTRUC. MACH., EQUIP.	3461	42	108	129613	39773	1788	156	0	1764
46 MATERIAL HANDLING MACH.	8801	47	5977	64228	6308	3034	0	0	707
47 METALWORKING MACHINERY	1687	4041	1951	124437	1034	182157	4178	0	5925
48 SPECIAL MACH., EQUIP.	13569	168	604	111147	2562	63958	14639	101	6711
49 GENERAL MACH., EQUIP.	6063	560	5571	213969	9308	262350	806	0	6631
50 MACHINE SHOP PRDTS.	8150	6329	3686	218421	16622	52475	1490	1545	15150
51 OFFICE, COMPUT. MACHINES	157	5066	0	145547	198	165141	0	135	1602
52 SERVICE IND. MACHINES	5729	22123	2127	97004	1210	19471	2736	141	4423
53 ELECT. TRANSMISS. EQUIP.	7903	474	25968	372588	22653	111424	118	538	12392
54 HOUSEHOLD APPLIANCES	507	0	10368	185511	576	137892	1234	0	2557
55 ELECTRIC LIGHTING EQUIP.	19035	954	8742	169755	1106	118856	965	281	3967
56 RADIO, TV, ETC., EQUIP.	0	20800	6314	379037	447	75018	191	194	17069
57 ELECTRONIC COMPONENTS	24018	5714	476	250955	609	50411	0	1646	12659
58 MISC. ELECTRICAL MACH.	0	540	233	47685	3727	16537	0	131	18125
59 MOTOR VEHICLES, EQUIP.	38610	2819	5371	1415745	12510	51435	222948	0	7975
60 AIRCRAFT, PARTS	104803	75698	0	3016609	20658	1104980	5299	303	24480
61 OTHER TRANSPORT. EQUIP.	55179	1047	12673	243122	7400	163590	2484	123	74391
62 PROFESS., SCIEN. INSTRU.	841	7230	20214	237933	4252	178084	5174	766	3498
63 MEDICAL, PHOTO. EQUIP.	82	0	92	48440	2479	19806	0	117	3143
64 MISC. MANUFACTURING	9448	5813	20516	263941	20678	220952	10202	1954	32233
65 TRANSPORT., WAREHOUSING	317221	142666	212297	3020348	349634	270907	96115	177122	783335
66 COMMUNICA.,EXC. BRDCAST.	99543	23785	38716	1036715	44043	311136	27532	77742	185744
67 RADIO, TV BROADCASTING	13541	9324	7928	225674	15100	13337	3536	30788	33770
68 ELEC.,GAS,WATER,SAN.SER.	213982	121624	148981	1571326	164469	271962	42581	74683	308585
69 WHOLESALE, RETAIL TRADE	1092252	544038	565831	8999704	927442	1208689	268220	565884	2416440
70 FINANCE, INSURANCE	249728	127390	117292	2661028	265677	552083	87041	223102	585004
71 REAL ESTATE, RENTAL	618181	414003	288979	6171118	574792	907303	157227	451816	1849482
72 HOTELS, PERSONAL SERV.	131599	101269	80066	1285581	132679	163192	27310	133839	497737
73 BUSINESS SERVICES	94946	73548	36711	1890511	122896	173546	19940	242470	348464
74 RESEARCH, DEVELOPMENT	5342	716	267	141101	2570	5661	7618	3103	6019
75 AUTO. REPAIR, SERVICES	105749	68470	61648	884444	101296	115417	22689	51633	252173
76 AMUSEMENTS	27822	27461	22150	1026862	84942	42194	18128	47993	183297
77 MED.,EDUC. SERVICES	204460	108697	101986	2324967	226279	404044	61305	343442	466342
78 FEDERAL GOVT. ENTERPRISE	117469	26008	36692	368338	42101	46684	8626	68312	100264
79 STATE, LOCAL GOVT. ENT.	84246	43297	24352	489777	53539	42091	19404	12640	147337
80 IMPORTS	0	0	0	0	0	0	0	0	0
81 BUS.TRAVEL, ENT., GIFTS.	0	0	0	0	0	0	0	0	0
82 OFFICE SUPPLIES	0	0	0	0	0	0	0	0	0
83 SCRAP, USED GOODS	0	0	0	0	0	0	0	0	0
84 GOVERNMENT INDUSTRY	636079	336200	224938	4413723	504465	400313	104858	798802	1004931
85 REST OF WORLD INDUSTRY	-11593	-14357	-6221	-194382	-11786	-14096	-2693	-13523	-39019
86 HOUSEHOLD INDUSTRY	95071	21052	36181	307555	24096	62988	13481	47779	166266
87 INVENTORY VALUATION ADJ.	0	0	0	0	0	0	0	0	0
88 STATE TOTAL	10300152	4567191	5087402	77184544	7526579	12533777	2376339	4076634	16169952

TABLE D-2

STATE ESTIMATES OF 1958 OUTPUTS - REVISED
(THOUSANDS OF CURRENT DOLLARS)

INDUSTRY TITLE	10 GEORGIA	11 IDAHO	12 ILLINOIS	13 INDIANA	14 IOWA	15 KANSAS	16 KENTUCKY	17 LOUISIANA	18 MAINE
1 LIVESTOCK, PRDTS.	597087	267832	1655270	1059438	2648758	716074	493258	257002	145140
2 OTHER AGRICULTURE PRDTS.	422842	287897	1740665	685850	1215080	1144776	352128	229381	107924
3 FORESTRY, FISHERIES	41533	7176	3801	2353	1402	146	5541	37844	26702
4 AGRI.,FORES.,FISH. SERV.	71115	6522	25342	28971	35867	14145	9830	12557	14286
5 IRON, FERRO. ORES MINING	1404	7964	0	0	0	0	0	0	0
6 NONFERROUS ORES MINING	151	32973	3693	0	0	443	0	0	28
7 COAL MINING	53	3	186964	61199	4969	3357	366764	0	0
8 CRUDE PETRO.,NATURAL GAS	77	23	256783	32973	0	414309	75302	1472545	0
9 STONE, CLAY MINING	50528	5698	98220	38953	39696	19976	28647	15003	2903
10 CHEM.,FERT. MIN. MINING	6476	4907	9718	0	0	4492	3409	67804	0
11 NEW CONSTRUCTION	955492	234559	2639793	1064012	612442	795350	730432	1569160	221924
12 MAINT., REPAIR CONSTR.	242243	103147	1072560	485999	395981	301503	212463	236666	67201
13 ORDNANCE, ACCESSORIES	3077	1012	86869	44154	42757	21	0	13300	23180
14 FOOD, KINDRED PRDTS.	1320710	267346	5695959	1817487	2703406	1042724	1187908	1008578	258123
15 TOBACCO MANUFACTURES	21096	0	23725	12086	0	0	1075832	10533	0
16 FABRICS	1081488	0	27644	607	2784	3297	11481	389	205738
17 TEXTILE PRDTS.	362612	0	91883	9488	143	218	2235	10422	13365
18 APPAREL	367827	87	409104	104045	26460	18390	145154	43200	28678
19 MISC. TEXTILE PRDTS.	78648	3476	107695	17728	11578	7477	10651	18370	9110
20 LUMBER, WOOD PRDTS.	240230	202996	140959	148125	60992	11656	77696	162475	163620
21 WOODEN CONTAINERS	27804	412	17411	6575	3169	586	27993	11740	2109
22 HOUSEHOLD FURNITURE	67669	700	247016	197686	22468	10708	54569	12995	4433
23 OTHER FURNITURE	8697	746	126355	39128	16768	5809	2784	2872	3011
24 PAPER, ALLIED PRDTS.	389369	27718	329580	123689	29287	8986	14561	339213	383119
25 PAPERBOARD CONTAINERS	106361	1575	336767	105768	44430	37308	19490	53475	5518
26 PRINTING, PUBLISHING	126504	13592	1457693	239949	144133	77619	90865	70388	21761
27 CHEMICALS,SELECT. PRDTS.	181856	52681	543927	201475	34092	87323	221410	456791	14072
28 PLASTICS, SYNTHETICS	34520	0	85856	22550	55304	0	160734	110960	0
29 DRUGS, COSMETICS	42800	332	650465	504371	56283	103803	10351	9666	433
30 PAINT, ALLIED PRDTS.	30723	247	297357	23922	23582	4436	51313	10449	50
31 PETROLEUM, RELATED INDS.	25357	588	1120685	786601	6040	527337	175839	1451887	4558
32 RUBBER, MISC. PLASTICS	27043	142	331362	280014	105012	47664	15402	3770	14069
33 LEATHER TANNING, PRDTS.	5715	87	63225	5408	0	0	4110	663	19516
34 FOOTWEAR, LEATHER PRDTS.	30843	459	166043	24848	1667	1226	22129	1306	179162
35 GLASS, GLASS PRDTS.	12904	106	243757	123800	244	3863	13059	15813	0
36 STONE, CLAY PRDTS.	107629	15287	487584	303025	132673	128517	64625	118025	16918
37 PRIMARY IRON, STEEL MFR.	29281	669	1550027	1983655	63647	8675	185390	25181	507
38 PRIMARY NONFERROUS MFR.	30113	72024	657686	465005	108039	27988	43133	128669	2416

39 METAL CONTAINERS	6953	0	359400	38409	272	4670	11628	54266	10655
40 FABRICATED METAL PRDTS.	77155	8715	573349	298596	101035	77547	108072	61718	13701
41 SCREW MACH. PRDTS., ETC.	22781	609	534655	159485	14831	3034	19602	2221	0
42 OTHER FAB. METAL PRDTS.	10013	577	772046	217091	54746	20599	67206	24923	9523
43 ENGINES, TURBINES	0	0	186339	104878	36350	0	0	1025	0
44 FARM MACH., EQUIP.	23225	3550	597180	96484	366195	41941	5167	5167	1076
45 CONSTRUC. MACH., EQUIP.	21055	621	892884	78645	103469	25556	10642	13351	6536
46 MATERIAL HANDLING MACH.	13959	127	117443	10746	16456	6511	1803	1297	0
47 METALWORKING MACHINERY	5538	264	375893	87956	16000	4055	7837	792	1310
48 SPECIAL MACH., EQUIP.	32209	139	209971	40241	19201	11876	6328	6155	21155
49 GENERAL MACH., EQUIP.	12044	6444	333705	184349	9640	17654	32190	2703	333
50 MACHINE SHOP PRDTS.	6965	944	115846	83590	5630	18215	27730	11256	3270
51 OFFICE, COMPUT. MACHINES	1626	0	137854	3378	190	209	136572	0	0
52 SERVICE IND. MACHINES	9325	194	161253	82011	9340	30674	47595	2588	0
53 ELECT. TRANSMISS. EQUIP.	59632	0	372461	227231	23439	758	25749	266	0
54 HOUSEHOLD APPLIANCES	227	0	513573	195021	145686	1717	322244	611	929
55 ELECTRIC LIGHTING EQUIP.	8131	0	290779	94161	937	668	53592	81	4274
56 RADIO, TV, ETC., EQUIP.	203	0	1420726	412548	93213	312	13648	734	2090
57 ELECTRONIC COMPONENTS	1525	0	214391	134027	25021	6003	28614	275	1997
58 MISC. ELECTRICAL MACH.	15529	0	79986	204336	10983	15292	1647	531	644
59 MOTOR VEHICLES, EQUIP.	580678	2296	670907	1328164	23707	183051	252703	9436	1471
60 AIRCRAFT, PARTS	255987	0	393871	457744	29317	832411	3542	0	27057
61 OTHER TRANSPORT. EQUIP.	17736	1512	287788	237054	16093	18198	24467	74860	60180
62 PROFESS., SCIEN. INSTRU.	16640	2304	348665	39679	15385	1228	4064	1068	749
63 MEDICAL, PHOTO. EQUIP.	354	66	149082	6704	3339	610	174	2609	1673
64 MISC. MANUFACTURING	57581	5119	490948	117586	52542	8768	20114	19026	16070
65 TRANSPORT., WAREHOUSING	552049	107413	2775677	798669	365275	455195	452447	609716	160357
66 COMMUNICA.,EXC. BRDCAST.	138560	45410	717462	385802	103726	67094	96094	157225	39393
67 RADIO, TV BROADCASTING	22344	4088	112613	22766	17566	9544	12846	16653	6413
68 ELEC.,GAS,WATER,SAN.SER.	257904	62579	1404287	655946	262951	237951	159871	328487	61785
69 WHOLESALE, RETAIL TRADE	1741146	295405	6538669	2040890	1358413	913686	1047800	1430639	401499
70 FINANCE, INSURANCE	427371	55576	1864027	516425	278291	192589	198831	284741	83841
71 REAL ESTATE, RENTAL	792525	160948	4163872	1190670	675860	526248	587386	754625	203560
72 HOTELS, PERSONAL SERV.	210564	39350	866424	258955	136396	114419	145369	162880	58244
73 BUSINESS SERVICES	154126	21974	1650714	184134	107579	80850	86694	184372	28574
74 RESEARCH, DEVELOPMENT	875	246	61817	1726	802	620	793	2117	1259
75 AUTO. REPAIR, SERVICES	153587	34287	456030	194161	123834	105192	102760	113272	43587
76 AMUSEMENTS	57687	9527	326197	75188	42960	32877	48394	62802	13559
77 MED.,EDUC. SERVICES	297341	54069	1738899	521943	285895	216090	236132	247488	99886
78 FEDERAL GOVT. ENTERPRISE	91721	13426	231328	68049	45433	54477	70017	44962	23454
79 STATE, LOCAL GOVT. ENT.	69911	11169	278368	109225	58937	58180	49792	72946	19559
80 IMPORTS	0	0	0	0	0	0	0	0	0
81 BUS.TRAVEL, ENT., GIFTS.	0	0	0	0	0	0	0	0	0
82 OFFICE SUPPLIES	0	0	0	0	0	0	0	0	0
83 SCRAP, USED GOODS	0	0	0	0	0	0	0	0	0
84 GOVERNMENT INDUSTRY	977744	113731	1642824	636045	361691	534679	569086	558480	182604
85 REST OF WORLD INDUSTRY	-14269	-7192	-74976	-22730	-13564	-10372	-12717	-13769	-9033
86 HOUSEHOLD INDUSTRY	132510	8318	144407	59194	35605	31316	43620	99282	17989
87 INVENTORY VALUATION ADJ.	0	0	0	0	0	0	0	0	0
88 STATE TOTAL	14470645	2684788	58489072	23688096	14089820	10532394	11094634	13402971	3580798

TABLE D-2

STATE ESTIMATES OF 1958 OUTPUTS - REVISED
(THOUSANDS OF CURRENT DOLLARS)

INDUSTRY TITLE	19 MARYLAND	20 MASSA-CHUSETTS	21 MICHIGAN	22 MINNESOTA	23 MISSISSIPPI	24 MISSOURI	25 MONTANA	26 NEBRASKA	27 NEVADA
1 LIVESTOCK, PRDTS.	236742	128746	544706	1401335	399696	1117323	364930	1008570	68949
2 OTHER AGRICULTURE PRDTS.	138242	63756	476006	855465	346300	593491	312656	1132348	16392
3 FORESTRY, FISHERIES	15586	44204	9564	5987	21179	4960	3373	129	113
4 AGRI.,FORES.,FISH. SERV.	20769	7299	16666	33192	37667	35092	5079	14324	830
5 IRON, FERRO. ORES MINING	242	0	78903	383866	0	3745	20337	0	8337
6 NONFERROUS ORES MINING	35	0	33116	1342	0	23489	56510	27	61255
7 COAL MINING	8454	0	0	0	0	11951	1580	0	0
8 CRUDE PETRO.,NATURAL GAS	906	0	28851	0	138801	373	83482	66504	23
9 STONE, CLAY MINING	24576	14247	60517	27017	11542	34891	6919	16190	14939
10 CHEM.,FERT. MIN. MINING	0	0	9677	0	0	5029	5301	0	847
11 NEW CONSTRUCTION	915977	1232527	1826682	947991	372083	1167733	266835	385958	155074
12 MAINT., REPAIR CONSTR.	250647	380367	729238	335022	132000	410053	122015	219190	62709
13 ORDNANCE, ACCESSORIES	85654	211515	226112	92700	0	190522	0	13240	0
14 FOOD, KINDRED PRDTS.	1092429	1321682	1843891	2458901	412015	2202106	142536	1458952	24705
15 TOBACCO MANUFACTURES	6552	5447	17863	437	0	11592	0	0	0
16 FABRICS	45806	644352	8339	6383	10010	17290	0	152	0
17 TEXTILE PRDTS.	2758	191388	29571	13998	18495	17396	694	198	0
18 APPAREL	252442	596189	46926	81931	165816	291277	87	11914	175
19 MISC. TEXTILE PRDTS.	28717	96324	150506	23017	11307	44786	287	1025	81
20 LUMBER, WOOD PRDTS.	54470	59212	134401	122211	189983	65927	114407	10409	9819
21 WOODEN CONTAINERS	8212	8432	7795	5033	21805	7434	261	351	0
22 HOUSEHOLD FURNITURE	28079	111868	108130	22479	56379	51929	488	10344	391
23 OTHER FURNITURE	29839	20005	157191	13192	2685	27790	118	6227	773
24 PAPER, ALLIED PRDTS.	64462	462833	478042	248755	103279	112224	1812	12070	234
25 PAPERBOARD CONTAINERS	95861	174226	191906	56347	7718	117116	0	6141	197
26 PRINTING, PUBLISHING	154936	489475	388418	240227	20800	374300	20015	61714	8592
27 CHEMICALS,SELECT. PRDTS.	150360	129456	474006	93103	76353	277683	25277	25661	21558
28 PLASTICS, SYNTHETICS	57095	134152	132941	9367	1909	1635	0	179	0
29 DRUGS, COSMETICS	135987	178864	312558	85928	31142	229362	0	22802	0
30 PAINT, ALLIED PRDTS.	33847	45826	122093	19900	1797	74575	646	2197	0
31 PETROLEUM, RELATED INDS.	124375	106463	274213	118618	26078	179027	124481	13843	294
32 RUBBER, MISC. PLASTICS	147979	537959	317272	27277	37794	47605	0	15841	142
33 LEATHER TANNING, PRDTS.	3933	216551	27638	8114	219	5812	109	0	0
34 FOOTWEAR, LEATHER PRDTS.	18208	527869	13753	11925	16286	342325	62	963	0
35 GLASS, GLASS PRDTS.	44228	3757	59992	6697	18786	33810	370	499	158
36 STONE, CLAY PRDTS.	121459	185200	304626	179760	44237	216333	9396	41704	25126
37 PRIMARY IRON, STEEL MFR.	759639	205817	1263292	83789	2588	168242	4904	3735	0
38 PRIMARY NONFERROUS MFR.	180416	192995	384508	20718	10248	103594	211512	72910	32240

39 METAL CONTAINERS	124888	16558	2777	47312	137	96336	0	15111	0
40 FABRICATED METAL PRDTS.	98516	135129	341690	96129	31237	209652	7278	54736	1542
41 SCREW MACH. PRDTS., ETC.	41462	113902	394043	27794	1153	38117	0	2048	0
42 OTHER FAB. METAL PRDTS.	52594	294210	557416	54381	9886	102060	95	10005	1028
43 ENGINES, TURBINES	0	151627	233626	21579	0	8353	0	0	0
44 FARM MACH., EQUIP.	4736	1269	195640	99302	8496	52700	855	31045	0
45 CONSTRUC. MACH., EQUIP.	3803	7854	120416	51541	5819	14321	90	3313	0
46 MATERIAL HANDLING MACH.	3940	17712	121522	17995	5035	8411	0	354	0
47 METALWORKING MACHINERY	39784	167188	599732	28429	480	28630	37	759	0
48 SPECIAL MACH., EQUIP.	40757	220133	122162	22105	6388	24769	0	753	0
49 GENERAL MACH., EQUIP.	20459	129655	229371	30349	1470	29070	0	14501	0
50 MACHINE SHOP PRDTS.	13849	43095	159218	26885	5466	63523	872	2450	837
51 OFFICE, COMPUT. MACHINES	10047	36683	143186	112939	0	1214	0	135	0
52 SERVICE IND. MACHINES	29332	88995	228931	84315	1499	116183	0	1967	86
53 ELECT. TRANSMISS. EQUIP.	24224	235006	137441	55367	2840	176227	0	271	158
54 HOUSEHOLD APPLIANCES	30124	25632	251518	99529	25076	40957	0	0	0
55 ELECTRIC LIGHTING EQUIP.	5232	123825	23774	2916	27969	63933	0	0	0
56 RADIO, TV, ETC., EQUIP.	262015	342930	61199	33357	1660	9085	0	35111	3269
57 ELECTRONIC COMPONENTS	5235	293107	55272	25882	2513	7896	119	14942	119
58 MISC. ELECTRICAL MACH.	13060	33196	86270	8811	67	19547	0	1078	0
59 MOTOR VEHICLES, EQUIP.	196197	140784	8420038	189992	41296	1317996	497	16640	403
60 AIRCRAFT, PARTS	510119	138858	149999	34690	8623	463554	0	0	152
61 OTHER TRANSPORT. EQUIP.	193530	164471	190945	30064	101896	59428	599	20800	0
62 PROFESS., SCIEN. INSTRU.	24329	175622	118871	122402	277	35681	256	4158	0
63 MEDICAL, PHOTO. EQUIP.	3377	143304	28818	39084	241	10156	0	615	0
64 MISC. MANUFACTURING	42264	337761	178100	70405	9582	87535	3709	16307	1820
65 TRANSPORT., WAREHOUSING	596993	745283	1029545	705384	154220	1130975	157188	296171	71920
66 COMMUNICA.,EXC. BRDCAST.	159235	327433	399874	159397	53537	141684	14327	64840	21807
67 RADIO, TV BROADCASTING	14764	35275	62663	21633	7528	40451	4986	11042	4786
68 ELEC.,GAS,WATER,SAN.SER.	252251	519444	820550	287315	120964	393519	64898	58631	33466
69 WHOLESALE, RETAIL TRADE	1375574	2916960	3940640	1878706	582780	2515418	326986	766850	150767
70 FINANCE, INSURANCE	327449	1150823	814061	460699	105242	613676	60122	227642	28732
71 REAL ESTATE, RENTAL	978211	1732605	2307389	1061415	329675	1352215	177997	352553	117240
72 HOTELS, PERSONAL SERV.	174815	362883	464791	195907	83788	309838	39903	80645	113113
73 BUSINESS SERVICES	201333	523205	843504	261601	44936	359657	23128	75195	22382
74 RESEARCH, DEVELOPMENT	10024	19474	5846	7599	460	4928	156	656	379
75 AUTO. REPAIR, SERVICES	155868	202667	348191	144097	55598	215998	33040	69611	18225
76 AMUSEMENTS	89372	139907	188939	61880	16102	91792	10171	30591	147408
77 MED.,EDUC. SERVICES	366528	994636	974024	434080	98164	569659	63641	159352	23851
78 FEDERAL GOVT. ENTERPRISE	56784	124289	114020	70603	31951	119404	16438	31214	6954
79 STATE, LOCAL GOVT. ENT.	57274	145921	209979	74502	31209	73807	12302	120643	7867
80 IMPORTS	0	0	0	0	0	0	0	0	0
81 BUS.TRAVEL, ENT., GIFTS.	0	0	0	0	0	0	0	0	0
82 OFFICE SUPPLIES	0	0	0	0	0	0	0	0	0
83 SCRAP, USED GOODS	0	0	0	0	0	0	0	0	0
84 GOVERNMENT INDUSTRY	893113	1062862	1235594	512162	328302	711785	142306	285879	105825
85 REST OF WORLD INDUSTRY	-18804	-34761	-78334	-38601	-5506	-26923	-9788	-8440	-10679
86 HOUSEHOLD INDUSTRY	71787	83583	110989	48651	63845	64359	9015	19955	4452
87 INVENTORY VALUATION ADJ.	0	0	0	0	0	0	0	0	0
88 STATE TOTAL	12896363	23359984	38234144	15822607	5148901	20387392	3067702	7526441	1391860

TABLE D-2

STATE ESTIMATES OF 1958 OUTPUTS - REVISED
(THOUSANDS OF CURRENT DOLLARS)

INDUSTRY TITLE	28 NEW HAMPSHIRE	29 NEW JERSEY	30 NEW MEXICO	31 NEW YORK	32 NORTH CAROLINA	33 NORTH DAKOTA	34 OHIO	35 OKLAHOMA	36 OREGON
1 LIVESTOCK, PRDTS.	64304	228563	189073	767721	519760	338496	901806	475098	279246
2 OTHER AGRICULTURE PRDTS.	16148	151434	127754	335636	882115	710269	635415	447946	291400
3 FORESTRY, FISHERIES	2291	10669	1244	15440	36698	207	6517	1978	143856
4 AGRI.,FORES.,FISH. SERV.	4495	9982	7277	17209	38982	6750	22836	14290	10303
5 IRON, FERRO. ORES MINING	0	9065	3816	34894	3024	0	0	0	1706
6 NONFERROUS ORES MINING	0	808	111802	10683	1379	272	252	2273	4961
7 COAL MINING	0	0	784	0	0	6918	167575	12572	0
8 CRUDE PETRO.,NATURAL GAS	0	0	406217	8128	0	46873	24783	703994	1
9 STONE, CLAY MINING	2807	38723	7727	82575	46850	2906	84114	14596	13387
10 CHEM.,FERT. MIN. MINING	58	0	76870	7504	1543	0	0	217	29
11 NEW CONSTRUCTION	182164	1701927	577544	4626994	762662	331669	3043851	969831	592934
12 MAINT., REPAIR CONSTR.	56437	496504	102569	1375313	308612	122832	930500	232496	206357
13 ORDNANCE, ACCESSORIES	426	13038	79157	613673	178456	61	76585	40	384
14 FOOD, KINDRED PRDTS.	82634	2806909	89991	4941692	792010	140038	2903697	506703	640937
15 TOBACCO MANUFACTURES	3511	49877	0	9146	2827509	0	32179	0	0
16 FABRICS	174077	356924	557	334593	2637968	0	29169	16812	32290
17 TEXTILE PRDTS.	5703	130258	0	203022	115687	0	102094	233	10622
18 APPAREL	50119	688822	1383	5660208	801241	0	299964	29189	30676
19 MISC. TEXTILE PRDTS.	1226	144622	2873	455577	88854	287	49627	2852	18440
20 LUMBER, WOOD PRDTS.	66105	65385	22678	218156	259740	340	118941	21178	1396068
21 WOODEN CONTAINERS	7636	12520	0	13670	11070	0	17727	170	13950
22 HOUSEHOLD FURNITURE	13413	88914	926	283405	369623	77	130934	10363	19463
23 OTHER FURNITURE	4236	41288	1113	214479	37410	47	162958	2298	5102
24 PAPER, ALLIED PRDTS.	141818	380754	0	849678	186603	172	532315	11277	177992
25 PAPERBOARD CONTAINERS	5355	244452	0	421924	51589	197	266442	11069	21863
26 PRINTING, PUBLISHING	35927	432614	16577	3190648	98494	12666	801615	68107	65137
27 CHEMICALS,SELECT. PRDTS.	960	1077309	9682	557480	91053	233	696495	39904	30894
28 PLASTICS, SYNTHETICS	182	234564	0	158808	161394	0	174772	0	1040
29 DRUGS, COSMETICS	3130	1076712	78	1037755	32217	415	348548	2813	7235
30 PAINT, ALLIED PRDTS.	257	237239	59	119618	14181	308	171333	2784	6597
31 PETROLEUM, RELATED INDS.	1221	1022121	54379	219835	5849	28095	793968	694205	14100
32 RUBBER, MISC. PLASTICS	18264	366444	0	395354	37247	243	1589272	59201	6055
33 LEATHER TANNING, PRDTS.	29920	58903	0	97852	6995	0	31301	0	1007
34 FOOTWEAR, LEATHER PRDTS.	176400	88614	791	563502	10678	61	84881	4042	1696
35 GLASS, GLASS PRDTS.	114	173315	238	130676	13981	0	344602	49360	3952
36 STONE, CLAY PRDTS.	20385	338739	17808	540365	83860	8396	641300	60153	48482
37 PRIMARY IRON, STEEL MFR.	11477	238642	0	810038	14258	244	3114253	14195	63783
38 PRIMARY NONFERROUS MFR.	23770	791776	9030	740896	33747	0	654504	44720	56450

39	METAL CONTAINERS	0	193634	0	106758	245	0	74275	1113	28293
40	FABRICATED METAL PRDTS.	7622	280070	9170	572030	60738	5711	789041	115134	59185
41	SCREW MACH. PRDTS., ETC.	4510	153606	0	250967	12450	0	488296	3288	2250
42	OTHER FAB. METAL PRDTS.	5640	341481	434	402903	24183	70	622658	24781	16431
43	ENGINES, TURBINES	0	32658	0	248115	813	0	92042	201	0
44	FARM MACH., EQUIP.	155	4575	124	67282	11926	6669	113228	3007	4691
45	CONSTRUC. MACH., EQUIP.	10902	42917	2133	15954	2367	166	310603	96911	6479
46	MATERIAL HANDLING MACH.	0	102947	0	54227	2630	165	126978	1348	17346
47	METALWORKING MACHINERY	6767	89443	540	204132	2059	701	587710	1820	1644
48	SPECIAL MACH., EQUIP.	43369	156810	0	248701	62165	0	216687	8359	20851
49	GENERAL MACH., EQUIP.	13837	252196	378	339847	4785	0	471843	26539	3788
50	MACHINE SHOP PRDTS.	1924	61174	3584	109982	11148	741	116779	13224	13319
51	OFFICE, COMPUT. MACHINES	2270	54692	820	715438	7247	0	347728	145	378
52	SERVICE IND. MACHINES	700	91822	159	273939	7602	136	158678	5093	2411
53	ELECT. TRANSMISS. EQUIP.	34478	264887	135	548031	71371	0	639253	5117	36289
54	HOUSEHOLD APPLIANCES	131	73666	0	131682	23801	0	784462	984	4912
55	ELECTRIC LIGHTING EQUIP.	218	184163	0	271874	16388	140	240164	206	1316
56	RADIO, TV, ETC., EQUIP.	23691	764473	1060	963860	130606	0	115770	14752	1404
57	ELECTRONIC COMPONENTS	24431	275087	3542	314271	26857	0	102132	6505	3138
58	MISC. ELECTRICAL MACH.	0	54111	181	142564	38109	0	231286	2687	3737
59	MOTOR VEHICLES, EQUIP.	258	542921	1812	1206019	21073	2618	2783158	14487	25644
60	AIRCRAFT, PARTS	0	351064	0	702371	1912	0	1049936	69623	12299
61	OTHER TRANSPORT. EQUIP.	822	184863	0	226791	8411	0	132190	16017	31145
62	PROFESS., SCIEN. INSTRU.	928	355852	1806	676836	16658	128	118376	6813	2429
63	MEDICAL, PHOTO. EQUIP.	1798	68618	0	850368	0	0	7190	92	5963
64	MISC. MANUFACTURING	24815	323178	3252	1294549	17813	3389	309405	12279	14751
65	TRANSPORT., WAREHOUSING	49714	1337559	131266	3774183	498667	97470	1846048	348360	401726
66	COMMUNICA.,EXC. BRDCAST.	24434	394034	17915	1107453	150457	19138	423574	81944	114482
67	RADIO, TV BROADCASTING	2576	8857	6009	343556	20110	3034	62260	18449	13785
68	ELEC.,GAS,WATER,SAN.SER.	76094	619330	109922	1762413	245315	28288	1190905	216237	110364
69	WHOLESALE, RETAIL TRADE	243601	3192876	355512	13398103	1691166	307650	4882607	992905	967968
70	FINANCE, INSURANCE	79325	877536	67030	6186160	326272	57986	1068443	228712	201067
71	REAL ESTATE, RENTAL	148699	2205945	252688	7970873	801964	138910	3128847	563983	499306
72	HOTELS, PERSONAL SERV.	38827	452856	59753	1677682	218184	25777	598588	136914	114525
73	BUSINESS SERVICES	20218	461670	50687	4533046	115463	15721	766258	125431	127741
74	RESEARCH, DEVELOPMENT	1317	19235	11222	58748	532	2303	11336	3397	602
75	AUTO. REPAIR, SERVICES	28596	261270	44526	685611	160525	27034	431218	111219	95066
76	AMUSEMENTS	17598	167404	15692	1426345	52224	6844	240231	38130	33801
77	MED.,EDUC. SERVICES	85408	774431	66671	3407509	314138	50175	1276637	213558	212703
78	FEDERAL GOVT. ENTERPRISE	11805	102179	22883	433975	71638	14015	167045	53117	48589
79	STATE, LOCAL GOVT. ENT.	12907	124972	16297	604184	88860	20357	293067	49142	51932
80	IMPORTS	0	0	0	0	0	0	0	0	0
81	BUS.TRAVEL, ENT., GIFTS.	0	0	0	0	0	0	0	0	0
82	OFFICE SUPPLIES	0	0	0	0	0	0	0	0	0
83	SCRAP, USED GOODS	0	0	0	0	0	0	0	0	0
84	GOVERNMENT INDUSTRY	171005	1104783	338723	3169294	880519	106151	1439665	598372	314236
85	REST OF WORLD INDUSTRY	-7517	-39568	-8594	-329286	-13145	-6721	-56373	-10782	-10423
86	HOUSEHOLD INDUSTRY	10194	102495	12671	426124	110247	7943	140449	34219	25373
87	INVENTORY VALUATION ADJ.	0	0	0	0	0	0	0	0	0
88	STATE TOTAL	2431039	31677200	3519996	91639600	17879824	2701781	48927792	8780791	7861331

TABLE D-2

STATE ESTIMATES OF 1958 OUTPUTS – REVISED
(THOUSANDS OF CURRENT DOLLARS)

INDUSTRY TITLE	37 PENNSYL-VANIA	38 RHODE ISLAND	39 SOUTH CAROLINA	40 SOUTH DAKOTA	41 TENNESSEE	42 TEXAS	43 UTAH	44 VERMONT	45 VIRGINIA
1 LIVESTOCK, PRDTS.	773209	18729	185251	713902	453390	1359721	164593	123559	424299
2 OTHER AGRICULTURE PRDTS.	303740	7390	273838	429598	291072	2456900	49305	21018	280204
3 FORESTRY, FISHERIES	5847	4529	23402	500	9274	48104	310	2486	45964
4 AGRI.,FORES.,FISH. SERV.	25957	763	13051	8934	20676	120740	3876	1584	26450
5 IRON, FERRO. ORES MINING	20028	0	0	35	19927	4574	24368	0	1790
6 NONFERROUS ORES MINING	2253	0	391	25320	5909	2268	205482	50	2696
7 COAL MINING	773635	0	0	223	29986	3638	49790	0	155712
8 CRUDE PETRO.,NATURAL GAS	52157	0	0	3	135	3551792	79604	0	925
9 STONE, CLAY MINING	88241	1631	20291	8614	34550	64445	19111	8960	40020
10 CHEM.,FERT. MIN. MINING	3004	0	554	0	16133	60311	3486	0	1443
11 NEW CONSTRUCTION	2277212	157022	495846	248430	604056	3603421	444817	117068	1029925
12 MAINT., REPAIR CONSTR.	826682	56098	125519	125034	229267	1228864	92462	33825	322618
13 ORDNANCE, ACCESSORIES	132723	4656	0	304	38910	21419	25893	142	2611
14 FOOD, KINDRED PRDTS.	3296433	132832	252488	376328	1129172	2669318	293458	148126	820412
15 TOBACCO MANUFACTURES	301066	201	38016	0	125503	7959	0	0	1103954
16 FABRICS	556058	365729	2229217	0	217450	83300	1340	10829	556196
17 TEXTILE PRDTS.	199879	56051	122312	0	50278	11723	370	1514	45073
18 APPAREL	1500758	53911	175480	118	465074	254700	10772	13909	207486
19 MISC. TEXTILE PRDTS.	91995	10695	19908	718	29773	58406	2667	74	34277
20 LUMBER, WOOD PRDTS.	138657	6174	135848	11919	138905	179692	7993	36594	177658
21 WOODEN CONTAINERS	10793	88	5883	36	18923	12519	52	184	13985
22 HOUSEHOLD FURNITURE	193555	2011	25583	412	117549	90138	5662	15699	199146
23 OTHER FURNITURE	105791	6060	1915	80	9035	45991	2436	0	24608
24 PAPER, ALLIED PRDTS.	596692	13041	131751	0	211214	174374	1766	52251	241500
25 PAPERBOARD CONTAINERS	275294	12986	41601	885	44045	65710	2922	6014	38974
26 PRINTING, PUBLISHING	904748	44678	31773	15050	150930	318633	28410	20248	103070
27 CHEMICALS,SELECT. PRDTS.	402846	19671	220416	2675	477342	1320423	17089	2009	235099
28 PLASTICS, SYNTHETICS	293532	11604	69166	0	370833	326316	0	1272	494471
29 DRUGS, COSMETICS	473078	8821	11326	2356	62489	76773	2564	2191	59126
30 PAINT, ALLIED PRDTS.	130113	5849	2267	0	10649	66945	1101	838	8650
31 PETROLEUM, RELATED INDS.	1263701	12995	14827	0	44440	4458370	143358	2124	41012
32 RUBBER, MISC. PLASTICS	401159	114911	15563	1304	132770	125017	6165	13017	29794
33 LEATHER TANNING, PRDTS.	82740	155	972	219	15042	2057	87	4340	11049
34 FOOTWEAR, LEATHER PRDTS.	249195	18965	97	72	129204	19755	403	5321	30740
35 GLASS, GLASS PRDTS.	329222	19350	29265	0	45060	29793	178	3257	11360
36 STONE, CLAY PRDTS.	645559	9936	46990	8578	108696	378418	51710	38169	127006
37 PRIMARY IRON, STEEL MFR.	4597506	29304	10980	121	89449	312651	237389	911	48925
38 PRIMARY NONFERROUS MFR.	553836	165896	4359	0	221947	349755	161154	7616	81228

39	METAL CONTAINERS	154376	0	0	0	5163	107302	4304	0	0
40	FABRICATED METAL PRDTS.	951731	16288	31825	9326	152995	311937	51130	5014	85493
41	SCREW MACH. PRDTS., ETC.	353633	24285	779	545	9916	14724	1165	89	235
42	OTHER FAB. METAL PRDTS.	479279	52449	2273	531	48869	155277	1356	3001	27486
43	ENGINES, TURBINES	414623	145	0	0	0	2612	0	0	0
44	FARM MACH., EQUIP.	92029	0	111	1061	38023	19570	924	1392	4226
45	CONSTRUC. MACH., EQUIP.	166417	134	83	0	9217	348929	29395	3578	2456
46	MATERIAL HANDLING MACH.	106059	164	973	943	9982	9803	413	0	3049
47	METALWORKING MACHINERY	269202	43355	254	1560	3261	11377	0	38203	1730
48	SPECIAL MACH., EQUIP.	184683	25695	32118	222	10905	48737	1280	5579	8368
49	GENERAL MACH., EQUIP.	315835	13326	2173	246	8219	58783	540	1580	3516
50	MACHINE SHOP PRDTS.	80024	3663	4595	2200	18620	47898	2376	1027	5414
51	OFFICE, COMPUT. MACHINES	65837	116	108	0	0	608	292	13824	12512
52	SERVICE IND. MACHINES	116093	7218	1538	310	12802	86018	3484	1538	16659
53	ELECT. TRANSMISS. EQUIP.	718873	5361	127	554	37010	26147	1157	6187	10597
54	HOUSEHOLD APPLIANCES	99572	0	16677	0	108823	10644	0	0	3921
55	ELECTRIC LIGHTING EQUIP.	260274	24407	0	0	16209	9978	174	5381	446
56	RADIO, TV, ETC., EQUIP.	190692	268	7428	191	92098	62489	0	0	44051
57	ELECTRONIC COMPONENTS	326059	3246	9907	0	7428	40196	6045	5761	46055
58	MISC. ELECTRICAL MACH.	76863	12917	0	0	11713	24955	1216	2491	5170
59	MOTOR VEHICLES, EQUIP.	622538	7512	3696	403	84859	380209	1991	403	74195
60	AIRCRAFT, PARTS	248299	2256	0	0	1938	855026	18159	1136	3921
61	OTHER TRANSPORT. EQUIP.	371926	3689	2752	4242	41510	125775	3103	588	203454
62	PROFESS., SCIEN. INSTRU.	304891	17561	4159	164	30566	67891	193	6074	5352
63	MEDICAL, PHOTO. EQUIP.	21909	8142	445	0	496	8528	75	0	14517
64	MISC. MANUFACTURING	336120	240947	10918	1227	61609	43308	6057	4159	50068
65	TRANSPORT., WAREHOUSING	2329003	92253	152038	64768	473705	1896026	205129	42707	751034
66	COMMUNICA.,EXC. BRDCAST.	537084	52647	57496	20831	154958	558059	24910	14555	165043
67	RADIO, TV BROADCASTING	95877	5583	10308	3485	26382	58415	6122	2102	21383
68	ELEC.,GAS,WATER,SAN.SER.	1376785	78086	115811	31307	59746	997032	82514	44907	328363
69	WHOLESALE, RETAIL TRADE	5596877	406934	708726	298578	1489998	4716197	403154	152919	1444396
70	FINANCE, INSURANCE	1541025	135079	156201	51344	307297	1157520	87921	41183	331100
71	REAL ESTATE, RENTAL	3042161	245277	356984	143345	696250	2229305	252968	79691	1030153
72	HOTELS, PERSONAL SERV.	675455	51226	95071	30847	187643	628716	52035	22292	226006
73	BUSINESS SERVICES	836259	43779	51907	16184	138109	607712	46873	8807	141128
74	RESEARCH, DEVELOPMENT	11348	676	2705	751	25795	12400	351	216	67703
75	AUTO. REPAIR, SERVICES	503239	31964	75373	28627	130930	484109	41389	17768	143178
76	AMUSEMENTS	200504	27123	20100	12348	45266	150888	19477	5742	47491
77	MED.,EDUC. SERVICES	1666666	135344	127359	56301	289130	993522	82841	56155	280016
78	FEDERAL GOVT. ENTERPRISE	200308	20001	42255	14356	230685	203398	16485	8865	124436
79	STATE, LOCAL GOVT. ENT.	247298	11072	32326	17021	171969	250529	24312	7509	96684
80	IMPORTS	0	0	0	0	0	0	0	0	0
81	BUS.TRAVEL, ENT., GIFTS.	0	0	0	0	0	0	0	0	0
82	OFFICE SUPPLIES	0	0	0	0	0	0	0	0	0
83	SCRAP, USED GOODS	0	0	0	0	0	0	0	0	0
84	GOVERNMENT INDUSTRY	1684320	179111	560596	141753	513668	2279378	239456	59127	1308059
85	REST OF WORLD INDUSTRY	-63243	-4703	-6594	-3673	-17545	-70071	-4326	-4059	-17215
86	HOUSEHOLD INDUSTRY	196240	12451	68255	9959	81617	225883	7088	9496	88359
87	INVENTORY VALUATION ADJ.	0	0	0	0	0	0	0	0	0
88	STATE TOTAL	50883936	3409779	7536004	2943626	11996888	44622672	3865674	1372185	14289666

TABLE D-2

STATE ESTIMATES OF 1958 OUTPUTS - REVISED
(THOUSANDS OF CURRENT DOLLARS)

INDUSTRY TITLE	46 WASHINGTON	47 WEST VIRGINIA	48 WISCONSIN	49 WYOMING	50 ALASKA	51 HAWAII	52 NO STATE ALLOCATION	53 NATIONAL TOTAL
1 LIVESTOCK, PRDTS.	292606	149075	1280861	209978	0	0	0	26084992
2 OTHER AGRICULTURE PRDTS.	466117	39148	244686	46465	0	0	0	23044000
3 FORESTRY, FISHERIES	92203	3418	8740	452	0	0	0	922000
4 AGRI.,FORES.,FISH. SERV.	11375	4206	21114	2056	0	0	0	1019000
5 IRON, FERRO. ORES MINING	66	35	7277	3288	0	0	0	777000
6 NONFERROUS ORES MINING	13886	0	2253	32924	0	0	0	1017000
7 COAL MINING	2538	780062	0	7824	0	0	0	2749000
8 CRUDE PETRO.,NATURAL GAS	6	57931	0	319890	0	0	0	9668000
9 STONE, CLAY MINING	16477	20193	35278	12706	0	0	0	1404000
10 CHEM.,FERT. MIN. MINING	29	0	0	11083	0	0	0	469000
11 NEW CONSTRUCTION	925063	420995	994075	217947	0	0	0	52415984
12 MAINT., REPAIR CONSTR.	277874	133224	366299	70321	0	0	0	16874992
13 ORDNANCE, ACCESSORIES	426	749	1822	0	0	0	0	4148999
14 FOOD, KINDRED PRDTS.	928959	188578	2540556	41521	0	0	0	62346976
15 TOBACCO MANUFACTURES	0	25307	1835	0	0	0	0	5917999
16 FABRICS	7881	19123	17664	0	0	0	0	10480999
17 TEXTILE PRDTS.	2618	0	25588	0	0	0	0	2027999
18 APPAREL	32506	24015	146891	0	0	0	0	14200999
19 MISC. TEXTILE PRDTS.	14208	569	11669	143	0	0	0	1855999
20 LUMBER, WOOD PRDTS.	845743	50070	183370	10233	0	0	0	7643999
21 WOODEN CONTAINERS	8345	1693	10399	0	0	0	0	408000
22 HOUSEHOLD FURNITURE	32326	8273	50064	260	0	0	0	3176999
23 OTHER FURNITURE	7342	2644	52707	104	0	0	0	1350999
24 PAPER, ALLIED PRDTS.	495815	14143	843524	234	0	0	0	9296999
25 PAPERBOARD CONTAINERS	46295	11089	149093	0	0	0	0	3558999
26 PRINTING, PUBLISHING	101935	35236	289522	6515	0	0	0	12449999
27 CHEMICALS,SELECT. PRDTS.	184364	626067	53188	200	0	0	0	10303999
28 PLASTICS, SYNTHETICS	6627	150403	11962	0	0	0	0	3765999
29 DRUGS, COSMETICS	7828	8803	97856	76	0	0	0	6219999
30 PAINT, ALLIED PRDTS.	11266	1429	31054	0	0	0	0	1814999
31 PETROLEUM, RELATED INDS.	158904	34720	38940	161738	0	0	0	16869984
32 RUBBER, MISC. PLASTICS	7060	7589	144955	142	0	0	0	6540999
33 LEATHER TANNING, PRDTS.	385	10116	106836	0	0	0	0	874000
34 FOOTWEAR, LEATHER PRDTS.	4478	4116	136179	0	0	0	0	3047999
35 GLASS, GLASS PRDTS.	6943	178187	2653	0	0	0	0	2122999
36 STONE, CLAY PRDTS.	93296	65482	123198	9133	0	0	0	7297999
37 PRIMARY IRON, STEEL MFR.	78436	494360	325619	0	0	0	0	18783984
38 PRIMARY NONFERROUS MFR.	411581	202611	98026	172	0	0	0	8888999

39	METAL CONTAINERS	33751	5962	98244	0	0	0	0	2059999
40	FABRICATED METAL PRDTS.	73272	52500	237341	1673	0	0	0	7370999
41	SCREW MACH. PRDTS., ETC.	10306	22617	175207	0	0	0	0	3315999
42	OTHER FAB. METAL PRDTS.	17561	44378	93334	98	0	0	0	5508999
43	ENGINES, TURBINES	160	0	334111	0	0	0	0	1953999
44	FARM MACH., EQUIP.	5288	4940	328092	0	0	0	0	2312999
45	CONSTRUC. MACH., EQUIP.	12408	21476	245582	272	0	0	0	2864999
46	MATERIAL HANDLING MACH.	8937	2376	25245	0	0	0	0	906000
47	METALWORKING MACHINERY	4987	16626	105448	87	0	0	0	3080999
48	SPECIAL MACH., EQUIP.	19490	1030	161146	0	0	0	0	2253999
49	GENERAL MACH., EQUIP.	9941	3182	164252	0	0	0	0	3253999
50	MACHINE SHOP PRDTS.	27671	7814	25270	1044	0	0	0	1472999
51	OFFICE, COMPUT. MACHINES	808	0	7296	0	0	0	0	2131999
52	SERVICE IND. MACHINES	2747	3478	100916	406	0	0	0	1942999
53	ELECT. TRANSMISS. EQUIP.	8022	18671	351450	158	0	0	0	4678999
54	HOUSEHOLD APPLIANCES	6095	1347	162795	0	0	0	0	3420999
55	ELECTRIC LIGHTING EQUIP.	6025	70556	19986	158	0	0	0	2151999
56	RADIO, TV, ETC., EQUIP.	1372	208	29417	0	0	0	0	5634999
57	ELECTRONIC COMPONENTS	1044	5015	22854	0	0	0	0	2392999
58	MISC. ELECTRICAL MACH.	1796	288	188960	0	0	0	0	1376999
59	MOTOR VEHICLES, EQUIP.	41738	17489	1192290	0	0	0	0	22558976
60	AIRCRAFT, PARTS	943293	1257	27620	1136	0	0	0	11949999
61	OTHER TRANSPORT. EQUIP.	99396	11858	73579	263	0	0	0	3601999
62	PROFESS., SCIEN. INSTRU.	6863	2330	70763	0	0	0	0	3065999
63	MEDICAL, PHOTO. EQUIP.	3195	591	5706	0	0	0	0	1461999
64	MISC. MANUFACTURING	25392	12045	114984	757	0	0	0	5031999
65	TRANSPORT., WAREHOUSING	529039	352063	547839	114281	0	0	0	32568992
66	COMMUNICA.,EXC. BRDCAST.	194496	67815	165709	7110	0	0	0	9292000
67	RADIO, TV BROADCASTING	20140	12023	25086	2499	0	0	0	1549000
68	ELEC.,GAS,WATER,SAN.SER.	117770	264076	365243	55500	0	0	0	17176992
69	WHOLESALE, RETAIL TRADE	1535970	627260	1841264	137011	0	0	0	92202992
70	FINANCE, INSURANCE	366736	105282	442678	26620	0	0	0	26400992
71	REAL ESTATE, RENTAL	981787	341903	1170583	94483	0	0	0	55274000
72	HOTELS, PERSONAL SERV.	185674	80306	208702	30365	0	0	0	12169000
73	BUSINESS SERVICES	181599	61308	227711	13399	0	0	0	16448000
74	RESEARCH, DEVELOPMENT	3515	3499	3932	505	0	0	0	534262
75	AUTO. REPAIR, SERVICES	131998	58304	150354	16178	0	0	0	7892000
76	AMUSEMENTS	63082	32906	64728	5874	0	0	0	5620000
77	MED.,EDUC. SERVICES	344439	139771	480705	26321	0	0	0	22702992
78	FEDERAL GOVT. ENTERPRISE	101282	24012	61671	6936	0	0	96087	4105041
79	STATE, LOCAL GOVT. ENT.	193492	25113	59432	7251	0	0	0	4784000
80	IMPORTS	0	0	0	0	0	0	0	0
81	BUS.TRAVEL, ENT., GIFTS.	0	0	0	0	0	0	0	0
82	OFFICE SUPPLIES	0	0	0	0	0	0	0	0
83	SCRAP, USED GOODS	0	0	0	0	0	0	0	0
84	GOVERNMENT INDUSTRY	870250	175494	512591	73528	0	0	3030000	39029088
85	REST OF WORLD INDUSTRY	-33966	-7016	-24191	-2661	0	0	3489800*	2030000*
86	HOUSEHOLD INDUSTRY	42743	21020	42026	4802	0	0	0	3503000
87	INVENTORY VALUATION ADJ.	0	0	0	0	0	0	-311000	-311000
88	STATE TOTAL	12795410	6486832	19163696	1791459	0	0	6304887	822573312

*These figures exclude the value of secondary production. They therefore differ from those obtained by adding the corresponding values of final demand given in Appendix C of Volume I of this series. {63, p. 216, Note 9}

TABLE D-3

STATE ESTIMATES OF 1963 OUTPUTS – REVISED
(THOUSANDS OF CURRENT DOLLARS)

INDUSTRY TITLE	1 ALABAMA	2 ARIZONA	3 ARKANSAS	4 CALIFORNIA	5 COLORADO	6 CONNECTICUT	7 DELAWARE	8 DISTRICT OF COLUMBIA	9 FLORIDA
1 LIVESTOCK, PRDTS.	456804	242880	396533	1722698	597555	117709	103163	0	298879
2 OTHER AGRICULTURE PRDTS.	388933	375885	654064	2487742	315355	80805	48870	0	884690
3 FORESTRY, FISHERIES	25017	3003	17529	122838	961	2420	1986	0	48590
4 AGRI.,FORES.,FISH. SERV.	46562	24822	69387	132170	7242	6627	6199	0	37354
5 IRON, FERRO. ORES MINING	15489	639	544	34480	66734	0	0	0	0
6 NONFERROUS ORES MINING	968	374775	20624	7205	77289	418	0	0	8466
7 COAL MINING	97061	297	2671	70	25890	0	0	0	0
8 CRUDE PETRO.,NATURAL GAS	20973	422	72550	1047255	128289	0	0	0	2139
9 STONE, CLAY MINING	27299	12142	33650	181862	17335	14521	1037	0	51481
10 CHEM.,FERT. MIN. MINING	0	0	2880	74603	1439	0	206	0	107723
11 NEW CONSTRUCTION	840568	769136	448501	12453446	848791	1086300	201559	385666	2628530
12 MAINT., REPAIR CONSTR.	228615	183255	183867	2501539	265475	267749	42874	79517	604653
13 ORDNANCE, ACCESSORIES	75367	87384	93	2612751	35906	124882	0	0	221502
14 FOOD, KINDRED PRDTS.	792070	257022	816436	7599117	988442	433528	209948	129214	1564158
15 TOBACCO MANUFACTURES	27938	0	0	979	0	14107	0	0	124387
16 FABRICS	600542	204	18000	28114	361	211866	56264	0	10575
17 TEXTILE PRDTS.	76227	203	25563	142554	839	66268	13784	0	2202
18 APPAREL	335424	23503	78137	810877	15329	187994	48668	0	106166
19 MISC. TEXTILE PRDTS.	32229	3459	583	169487	7377	26533	3696	900	13468
20 LUMBER, WOOD PRDTS.	242111	53891	276018	1199930	33316	31869	12020	1417	148463
21 WOODEN CONTAINERS	7044	1464	13500	64609	1982	3439	548	0	17543
22 HOUSEHOLD FURNITURE	38599	9114	90983	406707	14332	37153	316	0	71995
23 OTHER FURNITURE	9829	4185	18031	173596	5344	27481	1497	0	17205
24 PAPER, ALLIED PRDTS.	348615	11973	186988	450668	12860	113840	10178	0	368949
25 PAPERBOARD CONTAINERS	19947	4846	41511	442428	18326	75098	9658	0	72865
26 PRINTING, PUBLISHING	82128	62652	49887	1233177	111698	277832	24204	248855	245029
27 CHEMICALS,SELECT. PRDTS.	282217	28938	38215	536149	40964	226358	74001	2033	329722
28 PLASTICS, SYNTHETICS	111299	0	874	172405	437	81190	186639	0	136677
29 DRUGS, COSMETICS	2757	4248	321	507428	9455	243568	14308	0	19554
30 PAINT, ALLIED PRDTS.	7287	2759	3545	278741	9345	7748	687	0	38652
31 PETROLEUM, RELATED INDS.	58333	5148	147141	2472040	82483	19825	163495	0	37748
32 RUBBER, MISC. PLASTICS	204058	6257	43846	684346	120623	305851	67039	0	24811
33 LEATHER TANNING, PRDTS.	0	0	0	21695	410	2424	24702	0	1642
34 FOOTWEAR, LEATHER PRDTS.	9036	455	69885	53211	33672	24199	5960	0	19747
35 GLASS, GLASS PRDTS.	6885	655	13547	175135	1477	13256	615	0	16304
36 STONE, CLAY PRDTS.	162673	70033	50826	968487	96503	125585	19388	20800	253226
37 PRIMARY IRON, STEEL MFR.	959546	9124	2861	778432	165475	225487	153748	0	29635
38 PRIMARY NONFERROUS MFR.	246708	446395	131063	644459	11103	663392	18495	0	53800

39 METAL CONTAINERS	8427	0	8772	378981	20239	3105	0	0	74505
40 FABRICATED METAL PRDTS.	163146	31721	38837	776806	45607	89761	21595	4424	180336
41 SCREW MACH. PRDTS., ETC.	27881	845	9042	239615	1678	203090	7777	0	11592
42 OTHER FAB. METAL PRDTS.	67251	5866	26470	593137	30732	370784	6762	0	36830
43 ENGINES, TURBINES	0	0	0	76350	4112	54822	0	0	1713
44 FARM MACH., EQUIP.	19901	5213	5072	69387	8407	2216	770	0	9888
45 CONSTRUC. MACH., EQUIP.	9249	130	510	118625	79138	1362	283	0	2030
46 MATERIAL HANDLING MACH.	5585	146	8175	74024	3299	4803	0	0	3635
47 METALWORKING MACHINERY	4684	2919	6354	183900	1623	257081	4604	0	12369
48 SPECIAL MACH., EQUIP.	17314	812	2645	154398	6858	87539	16879	0	20172
49 GENERAL MACH., EQUIP.	10065	2096	9579	377531	18127	356510	602	0	10005
50 MACHINE SHOP PRDTS.	11143	13194	4469	292341	15215	65663	2638	1675	19697
51 OFFICE, COMPUT. MACHINES	139	110453	8346	551261	1769	207280	0	0	42446
52 SERVICE IND. MACHINES	15727	28223	16012	125110	1940	25334	3462	0	9877
53 ELECT. TRANSMISS. EQUIP.	19688	1656	51582	442654	41813	142409	132	0	7671
54 HOUSEHOLD APPLIANCES	199	162	128617	204283	432	197991	4496	0	2373
55 ELECTRIC LIGHTING EQUIP.	29920	663	22138	178746	3523	144551	2696	0	6674
56 RADIO, TV, ETC., EQUIP.	8366	80392	91889	1880748	2005	118759	110	0	180534
57 ELECTRONIC COMPONENTS	15620	68350	137	656291	1639	140088	637	0	25656
58 MISC. ELECTRICAL MACH.	12916	492	199	82170	6914	34142	5852	0	26889
59 MOTOR VEHICLES, EQUIP.	67109	7900	13993	2452637	22131	226849	447089	0	14713
60 AIRCRAFT, PARTS	539385	127900	1133	3362600	128269	1367051	7283	0	157740
61 OTHER TRANSPORT. EQUIP.	100039	4672	31009	409809	6862	78773	2148	0	123025
62 PROFESS., SCIEN. INSTRU.	1837	29616	35744	288471	12190	231782	6619	0	19912
63 MEDICAL, PHOTO. EQUIP.	0	974	98	127579	4708	41833	0	0	17954
64 MISC. MANUFACTURING	21732	7954	41076	461755	23606	337742	1463	2126	37704
65 TRANSPORT., WAREHOUSING	389201	178258	217339	3782908	429242	336561	86162	344897	1009424
66 COMMUNICA.,EXC. BRDCAST.	201786	90878	87045	1538712	144861	209037	34929	111711	418738
67 RADIO, TV BROADCASTING	19161	14158	9244	342161	19094	19772	4163	51476	53742
68 ELEC.,GAS,WATER,SAN.SER.	474277	267713	205627	2126719	307689	322354	69033	72853	567611
69 WHOLESALE, RETAIL TRADE	1346014	817693	752941	12471528	1207187	1651902	333165	737657	3179648
70 FINANCE, INSURANCE	372864	213918	182470	3600634	335529	736076	88421	244483	870057
71 REAL ESTATE, RENTAL	780741	667181	369841	8784924	797871	1143737	195852	1001649	2936320
72 HOTELS, PERSONAL SERV.	159105	156335	99217	1779235	177808	210906	31984	172012	653524
73 BUSINESS SERVICES	177668	157180	66182	3456055	214988	303262	46711	353634	657264
74 RESEARCH, DEVELOPMENT	0	0	0	0	0	0	0	0	0
75 AUTO. REPAIR, SERVICES	147191	102337	86098	1355570	136867	161941	27399	88493	343398
76 AMUSEMENTS	34684	42623	32522	1550866	70703	57325	23418	54657	249580
77 MED., EDUC. SERVICES	198624	157090	88887	3082363	288006	760758	69211	1180420	561842
78 FEDERAL GOVT. ENTERPRISE	159389	39463	49509	599248	61060	63191	12946	145649	164099
79 STATE, LOCAL GOVT. ENT.	143014	64778	31589	736925	65777	67417	13216	17944	236554
80 IMPORTS	0	0	0	0	0	0	0	0	0
81 BUS.TRAVEL, ENT., GIFTS.	0	0	0	0	0	0	0	0	0
82 OFFICE SUPPLIES	0	0	0	0	0	0	0	0	0
83 SCRAP, USED GOODS	0	0	0	0	0	0	0	0	0
84 GOVERNMENT INDUSTRY	841379	489433	333848	6857313	754904	554375	133629	1185957	1461282
85 REST OF WORLD INDUSTRY	-20450	-27203	-10042	-306954	-21689	-18468	-3526	-96118	-53483
86 HOUSEHOLD INDUSTRY	99704	27229	40748	376514	27732	67637	14727	51286	189220
87 INVENTORY VALUATION ADJ.	0	0	0	0	0	0	0	0	0
88 STATE TOTAL	13588835	7072578	7225619	110087360	9685882	16586424	3251089	6595285	23173280

TABLE D-3

STATE ESTIMATES OF 1963 OUTPUTS – REVISED
(THOUSANDS OF CURRENT DOLLARS)

INDUSTRY TITLE	10 GEORGIA	11 IDAHO	12 ILLINOIS	13 INDIANA	14 IOWA	15 KANSAS	16 KENTUCKY	17 LOUISIANA	18 MAINE
1 LIVESTOCK, PRDTS.	594546	271066	1432787	904317	2474083	1025238	487122	225929	163971
2 OTHER AGRICULTURE PRDTS.	582017	397221	1856639	1022318	1640015	730680	640608	451206	123107
3 FORESTRY, FISHERIES	39269	6846	3366	2164	923	194	5200	55842	32035
4 AGRI.,FORES.,FISH. SERV.	69115	7688	45405	25182	36892	17479	7780	21186	10452
5 IRON, FERRO. ORES MINING	1707	493	0	0	0	0	0	0	0
6 NONFERROUS ORES MINING	256	39559	14576	0	0	102	0	0	89
7 COAL MINING	146	0	209343	58148	4461	8087	354026	0	0
8 CRUDE PETRO.,NATURAL GAS	0	0	227363	32552	0	426899	82090	2400160	0
9 STONE, CLAY MINING	102287	6884	90020	47884	40797	22887	47241	19919	1947
10 CHEM.,FERT. MIN. MINING	2489	5694	8779	0	0	1272	5314	81916	0
11 NEW CONSTRUCTION	1184579	177637	2996040	1139772	614663	665160	783277	1535151	161994
12 MAINT., REPAIR CONSTR.	299710	97889	1150130	497800	385352	348587	249175	263346	74507
13 ORDNANCE, ACCESSORIES	2355	3463	91903	112980	65945	0	0	70940	10648
14 FOOD, KINDRED PRDTS.	1537311	391278	6044241	2039245	3299443	1267514	1135964	1376991	315781
15 TOBACCO MANUFACTURES	17503	0	21013	16638	0	0	1316594	8703	0
16 FABRICS	1409755	0	49291	0	3928	204	29818	0	249026
17 TEXTILE PRDTS.	698789	0	97135	12367	234	203	2799	7425	12816
18 APPAREL	591064	722	407025	131801	27747	30862	221924	55530	38518
19 MISC. TEXTILE PRDTS.	113326	648	140673	27397	7333	9462	19781	23047	8951
20 LUMBER, WOOD PRDTS.	254998	223565	188596	218748	55780	11200	95796	179614	148675
21 WOODEN CONTAINERS	23696	908	12995	3982	2272	831	18223	7570	1929
22 HOUSEHOLD FURNITURE	92563	2034	217641	277660	20639	13904	65228	14479	5767
23 OTHER FURNITURE	12608	729	184823	61807	19273	11696	10103	3221	3885
24 PAPER, ALLIED PRDTS.	502858	31918	402091	152383	38684	20508	38621	399538	471782
25 PAPERBOARD CONTAINERS	153602	3155	442797	145269	53056	58615	46675	61555	7626
26 PRINTING, PUBLISHING	161810	17106	1801848	331447	219547	107644	123233	80312	28473
27 CHEMICALS,SELECT. PRDTS.	272290	31190	802287	242231	47937	90542	243197	621443	17939
28 PLASTICS, SYNTHETICS	57577	0	101875	40473	86744	17398	221871	181270	437
29 DRUGS, COSMETICS	96653	0	978652	573247	48696	125697	2128	10379	427
30 PAINT, ALLIED PRDTS.	53467	229	357477	40617	34166	7004	75430	10489	458
31 PETROLEUM, RELATED INDS.	50956	437	1330974	892641	10543	623797	163191	1681013	3859
32 RUBBER, MISC. PLASTICS	67754	232	588630	461661	190436	86079	56111	4739	30557
33 LEATHER TANNING, PRDTS.	9110	0	58366	2469	0	0	5608	540	48539
34 FOOTWEAR, LEATHER PRDTS.	43709	630	147333	33457	6427	1574	29520	65	231389
35 GLASS, GLASS PRDTS.	23827	0	232163	145467	165	862	24046	24741	1174
36 STONE, CLAY PRDTS.	171353	17833	566641	332847	157160	172171	94322	135481	18143
37 PRIMARY IRON, STEEL MFR.	160216	1167	1949914	2537374	62761	22419	240201	22735	1170
38 PRIMARY NONFERROUS MFR.	69203	100855	983198	806479	107356	26048	87983	112052	6180

39 METAL CONTAINERS	34529	1448	381920	41476	400	6265	4365	52585	15146
40 FABRICATED METAL PRDTS.	132294	9723	560195	361386	104675	85417	103082	85550	13976
41 SCREW MACH. PRDTS., ETC.	39338	0	684279	204207	16649	4432	32316	4706	648
42 OTHER FAB. METAL PRDTS.	26601	401	928223	292359	66536	21624	112078	36811	6344
43 ENGINES, TURBINES	203	0	210829	71279	37934	0	0	598	0
44 FARM MACH., EQUIP.	35247	5958	600417	114743	554256	37957	66575	11187	902
45 CONSTRUC. MACH., EQUIP.	27330	1183	1190516	90612	151808	26361	1597	21160	10959
46 MATERIAL HANDLING MACH.	11925	698	160315	12540	11983	11301	21495	1669	0
47 METALWORKING MACHINERY	6482	183	539241	119933	27708	7921	10612	859	2214
48 SPECIAL MACH., EQUIP.	48737	761	279551	55046	25876	17753	16661	11558	7333
49 GENERAL MACH., EQUIP.	10619	0	436619	316540	33447	23316	53524	2849	3010
50 MACHINE SHOP PRDTS.	9302	1723	165657	117988	7889	27807	28971	14669	2656
51 OFFICE, COMPUT. MACHINES	3340	0	229317	2754	129	282	57373	729	0
52 SERVICE IND. MACHINES	16327	698	227763	110432	45558	24729	67583	6033	2855
53 ELECT. TRANSMISS. EQUIP.	95524	0	465662	269429	21273	2898	61927	1844	2308
54 HOUSEHOLD APPLIANCES	4058	0	645883	324721	156801	369	296855	786	234
55 ELECTRIC LIGHTING EQUIP.	22406	0	317617	143432	870	1544	53501	857	6614
56 RADIO, TV, ETC., EQUIP.	1365	0	1699050	768155	89108	5511	12517	334	3145
57 ELECTRONIC COMPONENTS	2467	476	300826	161710	47301	13862	26852	387	17622
58 MISC. ELECTRICAL MACH.	21986	0	138075	435626	14335	17027	8002	1815	2802
59 MOTOR VEHICLES, EQUIP.	798478	1986	997276	2000680	33041	240141	246498	16718	709
60 AIRCRAFT, PARTS	213077	2765	117313	445968	6339	690988	1133	112573	17093
61 OTHER TRANSPORT. EQUIP.	67093	14521	375635	337712	26319	54388	19326	164184	82531
62 PROFESS., SCIEN. INSTRU.	22629	164	541715	100735	49667	3531	16186	4544	664
63 MEDICAL, PHOTO. EQUIP.	421	0	200905	30595	2105	778	1269	1794	82
64 MISC. MANUFACTURING	67431	2940	572463	150087	83718	7951	27277	17041	15994
65 TRANSPORT., WAREHOUSING	743368	115476	2966923	809628	386620	483415	444883	788875	126352
66 COMMUNICA.,EXC. BRDCAST.	293385	42032	692073	340051	157997	136425	174780	277900	48568
67 RADIO, TV BROADCASTING	31846	5528	158161	35698	25253	25519	22180	26383	7346
68 ELEC.,GAS,WATER,SAN.SER.	472985	98738	1754134	814738	399323	336602	380586	466977	79975
69 WHOLESALE, RETAIL TRADE	2313609	364923	8098984	2683332	1634078	1152859	1298178	1570695	468863
70 FINANCE, INSURANCE	625152	69708	2266344	691020	377700	276694	307286	431140	105102
71 REAL ESTATE, RENTAL	1100306	199175	5650980	1494857	798934	647772	648023	941941	214963
72 HOTELS, PERSONAL SERV.	261300	47567	992013	328264	182794	134529	179038	173860	74314
73 BUSINESS SERVICES	301324	52434	2273543	291356	170689	121565	139933	271667	41804
74 RESEARCH, DEVELOPMENT	0	0	0	0	0	0	0	0	0
75 AUTO. REPAIR, SERVICES	219477	45592	601256	247831	154299	132784	134572	149067	50800
76 AMUSEMENTS	70834	13613	415753	91101	56446	43297	66234	72531	17993
77 MED.,EDUC. SERVICES	400176	46814	2474468	642673	337617	178727	292683	342893	122578
78 FEDERAL GOVT. ENTERPRISE	141079	16310	305250	96783	60641	66309	105568	66145	30488
79 STATE, LOCAL GOVT. ENT.	106731	27015	395619	128403	102838	78833	61969	80270	40543
80 IMPORTS	0	0	0	0	0	0	0	0	0
81 BUS.TRAVEL, ENT., GIFTS.	0	0	0	0	0	0	0	0	0
82 OFFICE SUPPLIES	0	0	0	0	0	0	0	0	0
83 SCRAP, USED GOODS	0	0	0	0	0	0	0	0	0
84 GOVERNMENT INDUSTRY	1365581	171852	2479015	961739	536242	696498	768868	791726	257846
85 REST OF WORLD INDUSTRY	-24565	-10023	-96343	-9934	-17857	-14235	-17775	-19455	-10719
86 HOUSEHOLD INDUSTRY	149186	8663	145791	62554	39229	33022	46393	101618	18016
87 INVENTORY VALUATION ADJ.	0	0	0	0	0	0	0	0	0
88 STATE TOTAL	19815456	3200122	70775248	30161056	16782016	11817586	13431175	17256640	4142923

TABLE D-3

STATE ESTIMATES OF 1963 OUTPUTS - REVISED
(THOUSANDS OF CURRENT DOLLARS)

INDUSTRY TITLE	19 MARYLAND	20 MASSA-CHUSETTS	21 MICHIGAN	22 MINNESOTA	23 MISSISSIPPI	24 MISSOURI	25 MONTANA	26 NEBRASKA	27 NEVADA
1 LIVESTOCK, PRDTS.	266299	125106	558535	1345468	395593	986507	298180	1124560	51099
2 OTHER AGRICULTURE PRDTS.	156039	87887	646356	1067824	670875	834324	344351	828892	25686
3 FORESTRY, FISHERIES	16783	49878	9323	6142	24366	5392	4241	164	16
4 AGRI.,FORES.,FISH. SERV.	20993	3227	14907	35068	62324	36918	4636	15883	777
5 IRON, FERRO. ORES MINING	740	0	119183	475886	0	14454	1881	0	4529
6 NONFERROUS ORES MINING	0	0	35880	3299	0	16782	80799	33	50492
7 COAL MINING	5065	0	0	0	0	13138	2228	0	0
8 CRUDE PETRO.,NATURAL GAS	417	0	62109	0	198584	560	77523	60886	153
9 STONE, CLAY MINING	39179	22425	71472	24086	11167	55823	5671	17078	14075
10 CHEM.,FERT. MIN. MINING	0	0	6328	0	0	6219	9333	0	1307
11 NEW CONSTRUCTION	1522868	1845402	2302047	997444	392207	1167957	215578	386080	614917
12 MAINT., REPAIR CONSTR.	306326	459707	730024	419101	168240	478527	142350	244689	79482
13 ORDNANCE, ACCESSORIES	15408	86013	84874	107973	0	127716	0	949	0
14 FOOD, KINDRED PRDTS.	1187194	1488463	2030197	2686421	530346	2321624	189446	1600945	34044
15 TOBACCO MANUFACTURES	4994	3123	15837	0	0	21030	0	0	0
16 FABRICS	53319	554065	5990	16626	31188	22609	0	512	0
17 TEXTILE PRDTS.	1486	227195	68893	15437	44288	27350	0	0	0
18 APPAREL	303043	705714	70765	90732	271108	336079	0	12300	245
19 MISC. TEXTILE PRDTS.	29764	114024	359023	25643	15725	55009	140	1613	382
20 LUMBER, WOOD PRDTS.	65456	83808	197310	128991	266011	88832	181160	21248	9807
21 WOODEN CONTAINERS	7472	7533	5922	4035	22317	8333	0	651	0
22 HOUSEHOLD FURNITURE	36232	132254	120015	24216	92083	43183	616	11283	1016
23 OTHER FURNITURE	30573	33851	203688	21306	5528	36760	543	9283	280
24 PAPER, ALLIED PRDTS.	85953	540761	582718	313323	78257	116566	5027	9377	116
25 PAPERBOARD CONTAINERS	117677	208043	251393	73488	12829	138402	0	15100	0
26 PRINTING, PUBLISHING	223348	635879	476534	303532	26304	424870	18247	76810	17172
27 CHEMICALS,SELECT. PRDTS.	205046	173805	612721	122608	67273	350672	6627	25266	25556
28 PLASTICS, SYNTHETICS	53515	214840	113140	13788	4325	3625	0	0	0
29 DRUGS, COSMETICS	242512	174062	358409	134739	29078	316713	328	39866	2078
30 PAINT, ALLIED PRDTS.	41930	58468	169794	18557	687	101517	0	1494	229
31 PETROLEUM, RELATED INDS.	116459	82656	365899	164581	84904	183562	141197	12365	1429
32 RUBBER, MISC. PLASTICS	195499	670772	418899	68153	60303	110240	232	48059	0
33 LEATHER TANNING, PRDTS.	3984	191031	27004	9035	0	7736	0	1754	0
34 FOOTWEAR, LEATHER PRDTS.	18553	488074	28896	14287	20916	336829	65	576	0
35 GLASS, GLASS PRDTS.	46325	3832	138738	15989	12035	59085	0	165	0
36 STONE, CLAY PRDTS.	150546	235635	368503	185479	77655	237709	23128	54111	48164
37 PRIMARY IRON, STEEL MFR.	483273	190408	2171626	176396	7926	175695	1317	3993	535
38 PRIMARY NONFERROUS MFR.	333843	273367	689560	29083	13252	136332	200470	78112	70722

39 METAL CONTAINERS	115607	22946	11257	53751	200	96695	0	13219	0
40 FABRICATED METAL PRDTS.	111982	162942	393861	90021	50275	213803	6367	75008	5624
41 SCREW MACH. PRDTS., ETC.	39282	139172	624269	51720	20263	52005	0	2173	129
42 OTHER FAB. METAL PRDTS.	63271	386155	885869	72579	30163	156114	350	9333	328
43 ENGINES, TURBINES	0	186880	437142	19209	0	10948	0	0	0
44 FARM MACH., EQUIP.	770	1334	235414	132582	28510	59064	902	35892	0
45 CONSTRUC. MACH., EQUIP.	4005	4402	135837	86931	13104	33693	142	3973	283
46 MATERIAL HANDLING MACH.	10602	32740	195558	21064	12103	13479	123	1030	0
47 METALWORKING MACHINERY	62648	210521	924691	30620	179	48187	0	1280	0
48 SPECIAL MACH., EQUIP.	64986	332637	188813	32260	10760	43021	0	790	121
49 GENERAL MACH., EQUIP.	16451	155709	304690	50405	2304	48334	0	21561	127
50 MACHINE SHOP PRDTS.	30608	65237	226825	40980	7560	91158	1506	2539	1026
51 OFFICE, COMPUT. MACHINES	9051	129416	296691	325179	0	21460	0	139	0
52 SERVICE IND. MACHINES	35500	86414	281388	129546	10989	142337	0	1699	698
53 ELECT. TRANSMISS. EQUIP.	33454	225420	181908	84493	11698	159428	0	675	580
54 HOUSEHOLD APPLIANCES	9428	32294	264352	131136	21181	48584	0	1276	0
55 ELECTRIC LIGHTING EQUIP.	3855	176020	44602	18436	45059	95815	0	0	0
56 RADIO, TV, ETC., EQUIP.	454422	901992	70848	110838	8793	111572	0	98700	3842
57 ELECTRONIC COMPONENTS	16103	346620	59905	46457	7086	8185	0	19741	161
58 MISC. ELECTRICAL MACH.	26548	55653	200782	20175	2692	31164	0	3103	120
59 MOTOR VEHICLES, EQUIP.	678266	303722	15325593	286277	50256	2521988	447	54343	429
60 AIRCRAFT, PARTS	220273	200563	161617	39680	0	344085	0	121	121
61 OTHER TRANSPORT. EQUIP.	263057	110951	248638	22285	7372	91656	1120	33488	66
62 PROFESS., SCIEN. INSTRU.	22306	291996	247961	50905	6022	39473	1829	23951	0
63 MEDICAL, PHOTO. EQUIP.	7174	226854	12587	24611	98	16451	0	400	0
64 MISC. MANUFACTURING	47228	402931	243740	86978	34639	87508	3161	16330	3302
65 TRANSPORT., WAREHOUSING	617721	901760	1105429	649460	179818	1156843	136507	316857	95084
66 COMMUNICA.,EXC. BRDCAST.	231574	408974	624314	222784	115259	307176	38173	116226	15637
67 RADIO, TV BROADCASTING	23935	63674	77097	30276	10997	42274	6953	15493	4819
68 ELEC.,GAS,WATER,SAN.SER.	477373	739190	1233011	483609	267965	571994	142364	135409	75819
69 WHOLESALE, RETAIL TRADE	1836661	3586326	4833148	2319635	752856	3190089	375834	957806	255364
70 FINANCE, INSURANCE	447229	1372536	1029999	633694	173357	840941	74705	288748	67976
71 REAL ESTATE, RENTAL	1498298	2075821	2877745	1452251	385929	1855551	206416	484580	263603
72 HOTELS, PERSONAL SERV.	224574	455466	574872	251176	98330	356472	51421	107335	180461
73 BUSINESS SERVICES	367246	821601	1188670	441491	78635	550082	35506	122753	64061
74 RESEARCH, DEVELOPMENT	0	0	0	0	0	0	0	0	0
75 AUTO. REPAIR, SERVICES	212823	292457	502003	192120	86386	257005	43660	90511	34043
76 AMUSEMENTS	124273	167345	212968	80397	21856	113171	12515	40775	248782
77 MED.,EDUC. SERVICES	707581	2445793	928090	519333	90818	870353	49245	170095	25051
78 FEDERAL GOVT. ENTERPRISE	89338	178189	157742	95509	46752	147627	20799	46631	16545
79 STATE, LOCAL GOVT. ENT.	91683	202896	353681	127521	33417	88769	25618	160009	10145
80 IMPORTS	0	0	0	0	0	0	0	0	0
81 BUS.TRAVEL, ENT., GIFTS.	0	0	0	0	0	0	0	0	0
82 OFFICE SUPPLIES	0	0	0	0	0	0	0	0	0
83 SCRAP, USED GOODS	0	0	0	0	0	0	0	0	0
84 GOVERNMENT INDUSTRY	1171873	1459191	1850911	776146	513072	965960	218526	399222	145206
85 REST OF WORLD INDUSTRY	-30124	-47903	-91435	-46166	-9423	-37367	-4138	-12129	-18571
86 HOUSEHOLD INDUSTRY	75073	86259	118488	49273	73454	67734	8325	21766	6846
87 INVENTORY VALUATION ADJ.	0	0	0	0	0	0	0	0	0
88 STATE TOTAL	16902112	30572400	54274080	19476352	6998479	25335600	3413688	8586948	2562137

TABLE D-3

STATE ESTIMATES OF 1963 OUTPUTS - REVISED
(THOUSANDS OF CURRENT DOLLARS)

INDUSTRY TITLE	28 NEW HAMPSHIRE	29 NEW JERSEY	30 NEW MEXICO	31 NEW YORK	32 NORTH CAROLINA	33 NORTH DAKOTA	34 OHIO	35 OKLAHOMA	36 OREGON
1 LIVESTOCK, PRDTS.	58039	191662	218518	804447	486531	299154	835670	534229	255643
2 OTHER AGRICULTURE PRDTS.	20291	188219	139910	533789	1103939	594535	855092	420207	310036
3 FORESTRY, FISHERIES	2920	14497	1321	20367	35751	55	5010	1448	167046
4 AGRI.,FORES.,FISH. SERV.	2729	5707	6518	13428	43985	7899	22495	21158	10149
5 IRON, FERRO. ORES MINING	0	5481	2436	36069	2885	0	0	0	2203
6 NONFERROUS ORES MINING	0	5668	156652	18383	207	1174	260	2013	359
7 COAL MINING	0	0	9180	0	0	9209	169229	5248	0
8 CRUDE PETRO.,NATURAL GAS	0	0	462097	9156	0	74530	25714	780891	511
9 STONE, CLAY MINING	3076	62271	10381	92743	38138	3995	94887	19420	25263
10 CHEM.,FERT. MIN. MINING	0	0	100089	12421	3521	0	13531	0	29
11 NEW CONSTRUCTION	159572	1927017	437185	5045863	1000997	186738	2943049	970743	707139
12 MAINT., REPAIR CONSTR.	62198	571917	126501	1675894	385430	136416	1223710	259764	244943
13 ORDNANCE, ACCESSORIES	0	1901	67886	75332	33513	0	155856	255	342
14 FOOD, KINDRED PRDTS.	105684	2876505	126362	5085737	1035210	154510	3166463	580019	695807
15 TOBACCO MANUFACTURES	0	37956	0	11468	3641148	0	36807	0	0
16 FABRICS	164662	302525	168	286753	3584272	0	27675	1505	48587
17 TEXTILE PRDTS.	11971	140279	0	204200	176869	0	119963	203	6279
18 APPAREL	54787	844542	2463	6387995	1230940	0	400245	47463	52542
19 MISC. TEXTILE PRDTS.	6222	194256	2321	571218	131029	304	43518	3962	22821
20 LUMBER, WOOD PRDTS.	66186	81553	30963	253514	316403	1798	167042	29728	1780096
21 WOODEN CONTAINERS	4519	12300	90	14691	9456	0	10834	0	5108
22 HOUSEHOLD FURNITURE	20672	111721	1468	272248	583863	241	140777	11642	32692
23 OTHER FURNITURE	8026	46651	2164	240970	53029	187	170337	4947	4076
24 PAPER, ALLIED PRDTS.	157897	498898	0	944046	307078	0	664837	12529	211098
25 PAPERBOARD CONTAINERS	11614	320051	202	435382	86001	202	331383	16025	18628
26 PRINTING, PUBLISHING	44507	590472	20433	4064028	133115	15824	1005682	81672	81071
27 CHEMICALS,SELECT. PRDTS.	13299	1693328	10464	709359	142927	3155	679693	24009	54250
28 PLASTICS, SYNTHETICS	16961	290825	0	242731	166607	0	284448	874	4762
29 DRUGS, COSMETICS	2132	1484379	117	1259808	61674	0	526542	3612	6566
30 PAINT, ALLIED PRDTS.	458	276704	458	132639	21288	0	221308	5955	11231
31 PETROLEUM, RELATED INDS.	1777	1387774	60244	260108	8318	36055	941729	751961	20420
32 RUBBER, MISC. PLASTICS	51333	554693	4976	485896	76173	0	1928927	94555	9019
33 LEATHER TANNING, PRDTS.	33086	61305	0	89113	7789	0	31051	C	1536
34 FOOTWEAR, LEATHER PRDTS.	192609	109800	1374	577400	16279	0	87839	4183	4221
35 GLASS, GLASS PRDTS.	1339	231092	165	169373	48477	0	413800	65945	8325
36 STONE, CLAY PRDTS.	41772	431527	31830	641957	122553	9945	771838	81780	66751
37 PRIMARY IRON, STEEL MFR.	17363	285549	0	993960	30678	82	4100400	28447	62124
38 PRIMARY NONFERROUS MFR.	19822	1073781	37237	1169835	91647	0	978619	77947	111817

39 METAL CONTAINERS	0	261085	0	121304	483	0	133209	2810	18918
40 FABRICATED METAL PRDTS.	11288	326384	6505	568973	98437	5654	874119	146883	76620
41 SCREW MACH. PRDTS., ETC.	7074	207272	1319	314618	17191	259	645355	6078	3634
42 OTHER FAB. METAL PRDTS.	12929	462027	591	532482	57991	202	828083	35247	25656
43 ENGINES, TURBINES	101	3934	0	196443	101	0	52534	101	598
44 FARM MACH., EQUIP.	113	3727	338	49801	20276	7053	161379	6923	7175
45 CONSTRUC. MACH., EQUIP.	22529	43104	1333	32696	1510	123	387426	126047	9293
46 MATERIAL HANDLING MACH.	0	129884	0	129579	1636	268	193131	2176	34750
47 METALWORKING MACHINERY	11601	120879	1297	286401	8161	1413	820185	2058	1952
48 SPECIAL MACH., EQUIP.	50270	220461	760	290477	119709	358	342025	8568	39478
49 GENERAL MACH., EQUIP.	23142	321322	127	463647	6403	124	657135	48217	5526
50 MACHINE SHOP PRDTS.	5061	74760	5917	190161	13278	1129	193150	13044	19467
51 OFFICE, COMPUT. MACHINES	4194	135982	729	1024937	8168	0	225651	1585	139
52 SERVICE IND. MACHINES	4827	117371	1093	348843	21387	0	281049	17219	5489
53 ELECT. TRANSMISS. EQUIP.	62051	268676	233	644604	97881	0	791743	18692	50539
54 HOUSEHOLD APPLIANCES	162	48074	0	146166	46737	0	998777	2178	4195
55 ELECTRIC LIGHTING EQUIP.	3075	257822	0	334175	22859	0	332004	444	1715
56 RADIO, TV, ETC., EQUIP.	56453	1238606	3089	1723972	236052	0	375364	175131	1689
57 ELECTRONIC COMPONENTS	45619	308192	1170	523182	42873	0	143122	4728	830
58 MISC. ELECTRICAL MACH.	760	85741	247	131514	62777	0	225599	5981	7976
59 MOTOR VEHICLES, EQUIP.	260	745988	2719	1866914	38240	0	5237744	61976	87086
60 AIRCRAFT, PARTS	0	345913	121	1131283	18574	0	1011540	482787	18160
61 OTHER TRANSPORT. EQUIP.	1968	178719	557	230665	23722	367	177413	15370	60074
62 PROFESS., SCIEN. INSTRU.	3144	241840	3470	434870	32069	73	154638	9210	7349
63 MEDICAL, PHOTO. EQUIP.	6212	118853	0	1287567	20639	0	9114	180	9753
64 MISC. MANUFACTURING	24042	448084	4010	1514466	38296	4773	315091	16596	21484
65 TRANSPORT., WAREHOUSING	58877	1562516	150221	4703198	591745	89826	1870690	466217	464342
66 COMMUNICA.,EXC. BRDCAST.	34202	476454	57458	1573442	256293	45595	709944	169959	137271
67 RADIO, TV BROADCASTING	3646	12197	8853	541721	34438	5396	104323	18982	18948
68 ELEC.,GAS,WATER,SAN.SER.	82031	893730	161515	2247914	414547	54146	1760925	317367	159845
69 WHOLESALE, RETAIL TRADE	319283	4386241	441966	16061845	2261095	376744	5801781	1202456	1314288
70 FINANCE, INSURANCE	88762	1059332	94984	6502456	524723	68956	1423204	332199	271052
71 REAL ESTATE, RENTAL	178161	2945292	314909	11951645	968272	146402	3874216	798233	692414
72 HOTELS, PERSONAL SERV.	64516	561287	73256	2050793	287442	36250	704730	148650	152259
73 BUSINESS SERVICES	37137	828080	76824	6121343	215801	22740	1091731	208369	177300
74 RESEARCH, DEVELOPMENT	0	0	0	0	0	0	0	0	0
75 AUTO. REPAIR, SERVICES	36070	354992	53991	949400	202853	36319	527564	144369	133413
76 AMUSEMENTS	29708	233071	22166	2014205	70172	10382	285915	45968	45446
77 MED.,EDUC. SERVICES	163007	591290	65755	6154695	539494	39835	1609580	209252	233743
78 FEDERAL GOVT. ENTERPRISE	16238	159315	29038	582769	108009	20253	229583	70925	57328
79 STATE, LOCAL GOVT. ENT.	38832	161703	21973	782680	171869	8746	476327	72770	102565
80 IMPORTS	0	0	0	0	0	0	0	0	0
81 BUS.TRAVEL, ENT., GIFTS.	0	0	0	0	0	0	0	0	0
82 OFFICE SUPPLIES	0	0	0	0	0	0	0	0	0
83 SCRAP, USED GOODS	0	0	0	0	0	0	0	0	0
84 GOVERNMENT INDUSTRY	216995	1580420	424222	4904783	1293308	216859	2023815	809486	481283
85 REST OF WORLD INDUSTRY	-9151	-53643	-16385	-354838	-21222	-8625	-73885	-17569	-18588
86 HOUSEHOLD INDUSTRY	11328	119459	14220	451466	129142	8109	143230	37888	27685
87 INVENTORY VALUATION ADJ.	0	0	0	0	0	0	0	0	0
88 STATE TOTAL	3084036	39899232	4102769	115601568	24321152	2735739	61726512	11190090	10013630

TABLE D-3

STATE ESTIMATES OF 1963 OUTPUTS - REVISED
(THOUSANDS OF CURRENT DOLLARS)

INDUSTRY TITLE	37 PENNSYL-VANIA	38 RHODE ISLAND	39 SOUTH CAROLINA	40 SOUTH DAKOTA	41 TENNESSEE	42 TEXAS	43 UTAH	44 VERMONT	45 VIRGINIA
1 LIVESTOCK, PRDTS.	806437	17360	157263	674203	408001	1458908	165371	145950	384917
2 OTHER AGRICULTURE PRDTS.	474773	11244	382994	438535	481564	1748170	76595	51488	336142
3 FORESTRY, FISHERIES	9491	4976	24745	485	7081	46230	420	2402	42240
4 AGRI.,FORES.,FISH. SERV.	24983	2576	15487	9553	14011	171192	3854	545	17748
5 IRON, FERRO. ORES MINING	46159	0	0	27	114	7789	13213	0	940
6 NONFERROUS ORES MINING	3328	0	272	25887	14377	4897	229759	0	5792
7 COAL MINING	681809	0	0	98	27301	1288	33540	0	159572
8 CRUDE PETRO.,NATURAL GAS	49704	0	0	152	107	4068350	105409	0	618
9 STONE, CLAY MINING	94522	2659	27624	9970	49600	63212	7326	11016	56523
10 CHEM.,FERT. MIN. MINING	5096	0	453	29	34919	67291	8903	0	511
11 NEW CONSTRUCTION	2211964	237175	327279	203777	1008802	4040992	460565	66006	1614012
12 MAINT., REPAIR CONSTR.	899318	58058	152453	135017	262444	1234860	105234	38133	345474
13 ORDNANCE, ACCESSORIES	97737	73	0	0	57406	50093	117708	0	681
14 FOOD, KINDRED PRDTS.	3783077	163354	378163	468469	1455395	3209082	352451	173548	954580
15 TOBACCO MANUFACTURES	392436	50	97944	0	59530	5454	0	0	1430686
16 FABRICS	572390	368326	2950691	0	252821	114346	693	7716	472754
17 TEXTILE PRDTS.	271740	52163	220640	0	63603	14000	479	2800	75826
18 APPAREL	1885810	60165	270900	0	747679	409885	24405	21946	301367
19 MISC. TEXTILE PRDTS.	116848	4876	33008	798	41782	53552	1448	404	23777
20 LUMBER, WOOD PRDTS.	208586	5426	179713	10842	197294	250783	15232	42409	255742
21 WOODEN CONTAINERS	10096	444	8772	102	18765	8482	180	1550	13407
22 HOUSEHOLD FURNITURE	202054	1552	37744	874	197001	103363	8385	23055	284238
23 OTHER FURNITURE	153067	12497	5389	186	26000	52394	3714	187	36308
24 PAPER, ALLIED PRDTS.	709408	18498	216519	178	292593	214194	4367	63232	323965
25 PAPERBCARC CONTAINERS	345027	18302	65077	871	62657	101801	2494	10077	51492
26 PRINTING, PUBLISHING	1087762	56791	45188	19551	212369	424363	44898	28028	147557
27 CHEMICALS,SELECT. PRDTS.	562033	41713	59332	3210	455515	2566892	17150	4604	266524
28 PLASTICS, SYNTHETICS	394710	42778	208006	0	530307	453889	0	3625	707808
29 DRUGS, COSMETICS	626046	8628	35951	964	108082	115574	2826	408	86738
30 PAINT, ALLIED PRDTS.	155656	7008	3471	0	21863	113773	1723	3894	11283
31 PETROLEUM, RELATED INDS.	1336042	30282	20433	437	44771	5681500	161216	437	73925
32 RUBBER, MISC. PLASTICS	506951	156622	60776	3471	172633	196429	11604	22101	80365
33 LEATHER TANNING, PRDTS.	64284	259	1059	0	37121	3115	410	3854	12278
34 FOOTWEAR, LEATHER PRDTS.	297320	12690	0	0	188847	31742	486	5417	46078
35 GLASS, GLASS PRDTS.	394642	32693	53843	0	108907	33959	248	C	21579
36 STONE, CLAY PRDTS.	681207	13106	60690	15414	158185	520229	66967	40278	178863
37 PRIMARY IRON, STEEL MFR.	5515649	72128	23828	82	107981	355750	165841	3300	89318
38 PRIMARY NONFERROUS MFR.	729594	205369	16679	0	302962	557920	133929	11734	82862

39 METAL CONTAINERS	163190	0	683	0	13067	110648	6775	0	10216
40 FABRICATED METAL PRDTS.	878370	16081	46621	11758	189664	399473	53852	5033	141043
41 SCREW MACH. PRDTS., ETC.	438612	32715	10827	0	36580	25115	802	763	3528
42 OTHER FAB. METAL PRDTS.	590386	55159	22016	1756	71535	187603	3627	4391	60747
43 ENGINES, TURBINES	283324	101	0	0	101	17314	0	0	0
44 FARM MACH., EQUIP.	101582	113	2761	4260	62848	26536	1649	451	7977
45 CONSTRUC. MACH., EQUIP.	152043	283	406	0	6657	421185	30860	1660	5502
46 MATERIAL HANDLING MACH.	150881	609	4958	4049	22427	21576	236	0	5143
47 METALWORKING MACHINERY	339194	55769	30509	3250	9446	23807	1439	68578	1834
48 SPECIAL MACH., EQUIP.	255395	46990	75758	239	19729	69771	3475	3710	11292
49 GENERAL MACH., EQUIP.	414554	15285	15987	3079	23378	80920	8295	729	15562
50 MACHINE SHOP PRDTS.	105424	8989	8526	3098	17606	60377	3867	1637	9786
51 OFFICE, COMPUT. MACHINES	181521	282	9791	0	0	9343	268	25559	48035
52 SERVICE IND. MACHINES	217708	2860	2415	0	34676	139344	9462	4293	23058
53 ELECT. TRANSMISS. EQUIP.	747953	5271	28255	0	63485	53851	5743	1803	112923
54 HOUSEHOLD APPLIANCES	100930	3267	7287	0	142023	24181	0	0	606
55 ELECTRIC LIGHTING EQUIP.	310980	51697	1194	0	21324	18362	796	7037	1348
56 RADIO, TV, ETC., EQUIP.	279476	14095	1429	110	141875	285111	14783	0	115719
57 ELECTRONIC COMPONENTS	513983	22410	37155	2077	16403	46099	9368	14572	85974
58 MISC. ELECTRICAL MACH.	108254	10155	387	0	15806	32816	254	6838	4211
59 MOTOR VEHICLES, EQUIP.	1005311	12374	6246	997	90799	666705	3518	0	239908
60 AIRCRAFT, PARTS	792699	8328	0	0	66719	658187	238318	74184	23690
61 OTHER TRANSPORT. EQUIP.	537696	8093	13560	2959	66233	162637	8935	371	117271
62 PROFESS., SCIEN. INSTRU.	438911	32328	22931	161	46759	55973	1196	9247	9228
63 MEDICAL, PHOTO. EQUIP.	40477	11480	14047	0	274	8785	384	4907	24617
64 MISC. MANUFACTURING	474397	267084	52562	1999	91251	71123	13116	7196	68304
65 TRANSPORT., WAREHOUSING	2325645	110395	200751	62057	525887	2160606	193203	56865	750823
66 COMMUNICA.,EXC. BRDCAST.	701265	63906	118757	33985	291747	774675	80983	17842	259185
67 RADIO, TV BROADCASTING	126202	10305	15926	6586	33221	88734	8130	2936	31111
68 ELEC.,GAS,WATER,SAN.SER.	1690452	97706	208176	59949	174668	1368716	166411	43331	496624
69 WHOLESALE, RETAIL TRADE	6445870	510654	898070	351497	1907989	5840274	529106	189195	1924405
70 FINANCE, INSURANCE	1850699	167016	248062	73765	489511	1683084	121687	48827	490538
71 REAL ESTATE, RENTAL	3878744	313118	414403	175028	872878	3038462	364388	90356	1380724
72 HOTELS, PERSONAL SERV.	846450	65057	123623	39703	235386	750623	64195	37364	284079
73 BUSINESS SERVICES	1314676	73369	103527	25520	261079	989407	76127	18167	272544
74 RESEARCH, DEVELOPMENT	0	0	0	0	0	0	0	0	0
75 AUTO. REPAIR, SERVICES	620972	38721	96499	37174	179728	611792	57465	22705	194094
76 AMUSEMENTS	238807	37079	29124	18282	60493	196261	28826	14631	67051
77 MED.,EDUC. SERVICES	2482999	189905	154877	54852	481443	1000462	199121	141081	440271
78 FEDERAL GOVT. ENTERPRISE	267554	28997	63592	18668	250840	278693	23699	10896	161868
79 STATE, LOCAL GOVT. ENT.	488781	14346	44276	18355	239455	355233	40531	17500	195412
80 IMPORTS	0	0	0	0	0	0	0	0	0
81 BUS.TRAVEL, ENT., GIFTS.	0	0	0	0	0	0	0	0	0
82 OFFICE SUPPLIES	0	0	0	0	0	0	0	0	0
83 SCRAP, USED GOODS	0	0	0	0	0	0	0	0	0
84 GOVERNMENT INDUSTRY	2335309	223339	645406	191708	696642	3105681	360050	78809	1644651
85 REST OF WORLD INDUSTRY	-82654	-6053	-9469	-6712	-24428	-104693	-8444	-6080	-25989
86 HOUSEHOLD INDUSTRY	188151	13830	72732	10416	86632	247775	8979	12126	101645
87 INVENTORY VALUATION ADJ.	0	0	0	0	0	0	0	0	0
88 STATE TOTAL	61750928	4353349	9987027	3233805	16264226	54618368	5084518	1829651	18811040

TABLE D-3

STATE ESTIMATES OF 1963 OUTPUTS - REVISED
(THOUSANDS OF CURRENT DOLLARS)

INDUSTRY TITLE	46 WASHINGTON	47 WEST VIRGINIA	48 WISCONSIN	49 WYOMING	50 ALASKA	51 HAWAII	52 NO STATE ALLOCATION	53 NATIONAL TOTAL
1 LIVESTOCK, PRDTS.	290008	112882	1270359	183608	4330	44721	0	26474832
2 OTHER AGRICULTURE PRDTS.	524369	71745	555249	77140	220	266485	0	27005120
3 FORESTRY, FISHERIES	94630	4684	8381	468	59613	3177	0	1041926
4 AGRI.,FORES.,FISH. SERV.	12546	6852	14631	1533	31	26001	0	1221886
5 IRON, FERRO. ORES MINING	796	0	955	18347	382	0	0	874555
6 NONFERROUS ORES MINING	10734	0	1810	61998	6072	0	0	1281254
7 COAL MINING	4695	738667	0	10394	2820	0	0	2633681
8 CRUDE PETRO.,NATURAL GAS	7985	75872	0	382623	14641	0	0	10899284
9 STONE, CLAY MINING	20026	21029	47421	17312	1281	6545	0	1766409
10 CHEM.,FERT. MIN. MINING	51	103	0	17732	0	0	0	580181
11 NEW CONSTRUCTION	1381119	276827	1183412	209388	174119	379980	0	65518976
12 MAINT., REPAIR CONSTR.	368361	148439	426113	78597	23533	79152	0	19794432
13 ORDNANCE, ACCESSORIES	7495	89982	17009	0	0	0	0	4712321
14 FOOD, KINDRED PRDTS.	1118501	201777	2715187	77950	86632	543328	0	71774176
15 TOBACCO MANUFACTURES	0	25953	681	0	0	0	0	7332962
16 FABRICS	10733	6305	12395	0	0	204	0	12537783
17 TEXTILE PRDTS.	2574	117	40801	0	0	354	0	2948958
18 APPAREL	51416	43601	144260	0	0	24041	0	17907728
19 MISC. TEXTILE PRDTS.	14166	1512	13525	69	0	1606	0	2492695
20 LUMBER, WOOD PRDTS.	896514	67867	236565	17789	14608	9294	0	9554575
21 WOODEN CONTAINERS	9227	967	11142	0	0	0	0	378932
22 HOUSEHOLD FURNITURE	27878	7595	49927	75	0	6136	0	3965210
23 OTHER FURNITURE	12208	4736	40587	65	0	3357	0	1788204
24 PAPER, ALLIED PRDTS.	647407	25273	1015364	0	0	7114	0	11629046
25 PAPERBOARD CONTAINERS	60790	12920	168487	0	0	3858	0	4597298
26 PRINTING, PUBLISHING	124042	50847	359048	8552	3894	24199	0	16083474
27 CHEMICALS,SELECT. PRDTS.	217632	1179726	73595	1266	0	19773	0	14316678
28 PLASTICS, SYNTHETICS	17795	312745	22091	0	0	0	0	5501363
29 DRUGS, COSMETICS	5160	8123	159671	0	0	1604	0	8439908
30 PAINT, ALLIED PRDTS.	15808	1723	42483	0	0	0	0	2369504
31 PETROLEUM, RELATED INDS.	222776	69237	56285	365410	0	31147	0	20458960
32 RUBBER, MISC. PLASTICS	10821	6629	175620	116	0	926	0	9125821
33 LEATHER TANNING, PRDTS.	821	12971	122045	0	0	0	0	898147
34 FOOTWEAR, LEATHER PRDTS.	2932	4201	143355	0	0	1797	0	3352034
35 GLASS, GLASS PRDTS.	7463	245169	4135	0	0	495	0	2798137
36 STONE, CLAY PRDTS.	113993	79350	169445	20045	6071	26296	0	9164490
37 PRIMARY IRON, STEEL MFR.	51563	522724	388234	0	0	5415	0	23353840
38 PRIMARY NONFERROUS MFR.	427538	220179	152598	366	0	53	0	12742000

39 METAL CONTAINERS	48797	15166	96702	0	0	20432	0	2369323
40 FABRICATED METAL PRDTS.	80956	67706	287624	730	0	5865	0	8218053
41 SCREW MACH. PRDTS., ETC.	6642	18512	225583	543	0	0	0	4420131
42 OTHER FAB. METAL PRDTS.	19447	58366	141512	503	0	778	0	7406004
43 ENGINES, TURBINES	304	0	396874	0	0	0	0	2063848
44 FARM MACH., EQUIP.	7094	8946	288532	0	0	658	0	2812757
45 CONSTRUC. MACH., EQUIP.	25381	42206	346618	756	0	0	0	3672838
46 MATERIAL HANDLING MACH.	21673	3968	31622	0	0	123	0	1376975
47 METALWORKING MACHINERY	7395	15731	161410	0	0	195	0	4439360
48 SPECIAL MACH., EQUIP.	25096	2376	207314	0	0	4536	0	3241066
49 GENERAL MACH., EQUIP.	6366	914	240779	127	0	127	0	4615765
50 MACHINE SHOP PRDTS.	24835	9143	49708	1004	0	1403	0	2091507
51 OFFICE, COMPUT. MACHINES	5223	0	9482	0	0	0	0	3688444
52 SERVICE IND. MACHINES	8481	4113	119788	0	0	258	0	2779966
53 ELECT. TRANSMISS. EQUIP.	16847	22230	466295	501	0	132	0	5785834
54 HOUSEHOLD APPLIANCES	6983	1576	167782	0	0	0	0	4177434
55 ELECTRIC LIGHTING EQUIP.	11416	77662	24387	93	0	253	0	2798179
56 RADIO, TV, ETC., EQUIP.	15247	513	191437	0	0	227	0	11573377
57 ELECTRONIC COMPONENTS	2341	7805	33699	0	0	56	0	3845834
58 MISC. ELECTRICAL MACH.	1933	0	88435	0	0	0	0	1939163
59 MOTOR VEHICLES, EQUIP.	66178	26647	2349945	0	0	901	0	39319712
60 AIRCRAFT, PARTS	486939	121	5707	1828	0	0	0	13630170
61 OTHER TRANSPORT. EQUIP.	223284	40806	118633	92	0	1519	0	4667622
62 PROFESS., SCIEN. INSTRU.	2198	11199	114995	1252	0	0	0	3683492
63 MEDICAL, PHOTO. EQUIP.	1967	3764	4556	0	0	110	0	2286958
64 MISC. MANUFACTURING	27767	11017	137200	75	0	2544	0	6418357
65 TRANSPORT., WAREHOUSING	728530	316289	575765	103638	109953	185376	0	37162416
66 COMMUNICA.,EXC. BRDCAST.	228267	97412	211171	19939	5745	48447	0	13494969
67 RADIO, TV BROADCASTING	28029	13869	33852	3347	3338	7473	0	2307966
68 ELEC.,GAS,WATER,SAN.SER.	186739	394060	532895	97124	15677	58592	0	25027808
69 WHOLESALE, RETAIL TRADE	1869341	685138	2252259	172890	117039	334316	0	116384704
70 FINANCE, INSURANCE	427885	144700	555673	32852	24631	130435	0	33578816
71 REAL ESTATE, RENTAL	1375247	393234	1392517	108288	60317	391754	0	75594256
72 HOTELS, PERSONAL SERV.	219631	94002	279477	41362	19506	74310	0	15367863
73 BUSINESS SERVICES	273128	112694	344251	19730	24594	75174	0	25530608
74 RESEARCH, DEVELOPMENT	0	0	0	0	0	0	0	0
75 AUTO. REPAIR, SERVICES	187313	62536	206318	21622	8815	36722	0	10717427
76 AMUSEMENTS	78544	47337	82200	8984	6640	22550	0	7680104
77 MED.,EDUC. SERVICES	365117	164225	289838	18735	18607	119496	0	33159856
78 FEDERAL GOVT. ENTERPRISE	150087	30507	80047	9122	53063	60064	120588	5864002
79 STATE, LOCAL GOVT. ENT.	323928	55536	67792	14506	13428	16278	0	7235996
80 IMPORTS	0	0	0	0	0	0	0	0
81 BUS.TRAVEL, ENT., GIFTS.	0	0	0	0	0	0	0	0
82 OFFICE SUPPLIES	0	0	0	0	0	0	0	0
83 SCRAP, USED GOODS	0	0	0	0	0	0	0	0
84 GOVERNMENT INDUSTRY	1157883	263669	829711	123142	287290	537477	2456000	55029520
85 REST OF WORLD INDUSTRY	-42252	-10387	-30760	-4626	-5212	-7239	5284000*	3259001*
86 HOUSEHOLD INDUSTRY	45668	19738	46432	4550	3287	13025	0	3824000
87 INVENTORY VALUATION ADJ.	0	0	0	0	0	0	-502000	-502000
88 STATE TOTAL	15546448	7994373	23898912	2353550	1164965	3661425	7358588	1063356416

*These figures exclude the value of secondary production. They therefore differ from those obtained by adding the corresponding values of final demand given in Appendix C of Volume I of this series. {63, p. 216, Note 9}

Bibliography*

1. Almon, Clopper, Jr. *The American Economy to 1975: An Interindustry Forecast.* New York: Harper & Row, 1966.
2. Almon, Clopper, Jr. "Investment in Input-Output Models and the Treatment of Secondary Products." *Contributions to Input-Output Analysis.* Edited by A.P. Carter and A. Brody. Amsterdam: North-Holland Publishing Co., 1970.
3. American Gas Association, Inc. Department of Statistics. *Gas Facts, 1964.* New York: American Gas Association, 1965.
4. American Gas Association, Inc. Department of Statistics. *Gas Facts, 1965.* New York: American Gas Association, 1966.
5. American Petroleum Institute. Independent Petroleum Association of America and Mid-Continent Oil & Gas Association. *Joint Association Survey of Industry Drilling Costs (Section 1).* 1963.
6. Association of American Railroads. Bureau of Railway Economics. *Yearbook of Railroad Facts, 1965.* Washington, D.C.: Association of American Railroads, May 1965.
7. Bonner, Ernest R., and Fahle, Vernon L. *Technique for Area Planning.* Prepared for the Office of Economic Research, U.S. Department of Commerce. Pittsburgh, Penn.: Regional Economic Development Institute, Inc. (December 1967).
8. Bourque, Philip J.; Chambers, Edward J.; Chiu, John S.Y.; Denman, Frederick L.; Dowdle, Barney; Gordon, Guy G.; Thomas, Morgan; Tiebout, Charles M.; Weeks, Eldon E. "The Washington Interindustry Study for 1963." *University of Washington Business Review* 25, no. 3 (February 1966): 5–10.
9. Carter, Anne P. "Changes in the Structure of the American Economy, 1947 to 1958 and 1962." *Review of Economics and Statistics* 49, no. 2 (May 1967): 209–224.
10. Carter, Anne P. "The Economics of Technological Change." *Scientific American* 214, no. 4 (April 1966): 25–31.
11. Carter, Anne P. *Structural Change in the American Economy.* Cambridge, Mass.: Harvard University Press, 1970.
12. Chenery, Hollis. "Regional Analysis." *The Structure and Growth of the Italian Economy.* Edited by H. Chenery and P. Clark. Rome: United States Mutual Security Agency (1953): 97–129.
13. Chenery, Hollis B., and Clark, Paul G. *Interindustry Economics.* New York: John Wiley & Sons, Inc., 1959: 138–139, 206–211.
14. Chenery, H.B., and Watanabe, T. "Interregional Comparison of the Structure of Production." *Econometrica* 26, no. 4 (October 1958): 487–521.
15. Cooper, Franklin D., and Wang, Kung-Lee. *Process Analysis of the U.S.*

*Material published by the U.S. Government Printing Office, Washington, D.C. 20402, is cited as: GPO, [date].

Coal Industry in 1958. U.S. Department of the Interior, Bureau of Mines, 1964. Open file report.

16. Cooper, Franklin D., and Wang, Kung-Lee. *Process Analysis of the U.S. Copper Industry in 1958.* U.S. Department of the Interior, Bureau of Mines, n.d. Open file report.
17. Czamanski, Stanislaw, and Malizia, Emil E. "Applicability and Limitations in the Use of National Input-Output Tables for Regional Studies." *Papers of the Regional Science Association* 23 (1969): 65–77.
18. Edmonston, J. Harvey. "A Treatment of Multiple-Process Industries." *Quarterly Journal of Economics* 66 (November 1952): 557–571.
19. Emerson, Jarvin M. "An Interindustry Comparison of Regional and National Economic Structure." *Papers of the Regional Science Association* 26 (1971): 165–177.
20. Evans, Duane W., and Hoffenberg, Marvin. "The Interindustry Relations Study for 1947." *Review of Economics and Statistics* 34, no. 2 (May 1952): 97–142.
21. [Jack] Faucett Associates, Inc. "Development of Input-Output Measures by State, 1947, 1958, and 1963." Unpublished worksheets.
22. [Jack] Faucett Associates, Inc. "Development of Input-Output Measures by State, 1947, 1958, and 1963. Appendix B: Detailed Notes on the Construction of Output Measures for Nonmanufacturing Sectors." Prepared for the Harvard Economic Research Project. February 1969.
23. [Jack] Faucett Associates, Inc. "Projections to 1970 of Input Coefficients for Selected Construction Activities." Prepared for the U.S. Bureau of Labor Statistics. July 1964.
24. Federal Communications Commission. "Bell Telephone System Selected Earnings and Balance Sheet Data, 1962." Unpublished worksheets.
25. Federal Communications Commission. "Bell Telephone System Selected Earnings and Balance Sheet Data, 1963." Unpublished worksheets.
26. Federal Communications Commission. "Bell Telephone System Selected Earnings and Balance Sheet Data of Multi-State Companies by States, 1962." Unpublished worksheets.
27. Federal Communications Commission. "Bell Telephone System Selected Earnings and Balance Sheet Data of Multi-State Companies by States, 1963." Unpublished worksheets.
28. Federal Power Commission. *Hydroelectric Plant Construction Cost and Annual Production Expenses, 1960.* GPO, 1961.
29. Federal Power Commission. "Imports of Electricity." Unpublished worksheets, n.d.
30. Federal Power Commission. *Statistics of Electric Utilities in the United States, 1963, Privately Owned.* GPO, 1965.
31. Federal Power Commission. *Statistics of Electric Utilities in the United States, 1964, Privately Owned.* GPO, 1966.
32. Federal Power Commission. *Steam-Electric Plant Construction Cost and Annual Production Expenses, 1962, 1963.* GPO, 1964.
33. Federal Power Commission. *Steam-Electric Plant Construction Cost and Annual Production Expenses, 1964.* GPO, 1966.

34. Federal Power Commission. *Steam-Electric Plant Construction Cost and Annual Production Expenses, 1965.* GPO, 1966.
35. Federal Power Commission. *Uniform System of Accounts.* GPO, 1965.
36. Frumkin, Norman. "Construction Activity in the 1958 Input-Output Study." *Survey of Current Business* 45, no. 5 (May 1965): 13–24.
37. Frumkin, Norman. "New and Maintenance Construction: Concepts and Methodology in the 1958 Interindustry Sales and Purchases Study." Unpublished.
38. Gigantes, T. "The Representation of Technology in Input-Output Systems." *Contributions to Input-Output Analysis.* Edited by A.P. Carter and A. Brody. Amsterdam: North-Holland Publishing Co., 1970.
39. Hirsch, Werner Z. "Interindustry Relations of a Metropolitan Area." *Review of Economics and Statistics* 41, no. 3 (November 1959): 360–369.
40. Isard, Walter. *Methods of Regional Analysis: An Introduction to Regional Science.* Cambridge, Mass.: M.I.T. Press, 1960, 316–319.
— Jack Faucett Associates, Inc.: See entries 21–23.
41. King, Pamela M. "State Estimates of Purchases by the New Construction Industry, 1947, 1958, 1963." EDA Report No. 10 (Harvard Economic Research Project), August 1968.
42. Koenig, Lou P., and Ritz, Philip M. *Secondary Product Adjustment with Redistribution (SPAR).* NRAC Technical Report No. 67. Prepared for U.S. Army Engineer Mathematical Computation Agency, Corps of Engineers. Washington, D.C.: National Planning Association, April 1967.
43. Kok, Frans. "Paper Recycling." Harvard Economic Research Project. Unpublished, 1971.
44. Leontief, Wassily. "An Alternative to Aggregation in Input-Output Analysis and National Accounts." *Review of Economics and Statistics* 49 (August 1967): 412–419.
45. Leontief, Wassily. "Structural Change." In Wassily Leontief and others, *Studies in the Structure of the American Economy.* New York: Oxford University Press, 1953: 17–52.
46. Leontief, Wassily. *The Structure of American Economy.* 2d ed. enlarged. New York: Oxford University Press, 1951.
47. Leontief, Wassily, and Strout, Alan. "Multiregional Input-Output Analysis." *Input-Output Economics.* Edited by Wassily Leontief. New York: Oxford University Press, 1966: 223–257.
48. McGraw-Hill, Inc. "ENR Heavy Construction Awards and Owner-Builds Projects." *Engineering News-Record* 170, no. 4 (January 24, 1963): 54.
49. Matuszewski, T. "Partly Disaggregated Input-Output Models and Their Use for the Purpose of a Large Corporation." *Input-Output Techniques.* Edited by A. Brody and A.P. Carter. Amsterdam: North-Holland Publishing Co., 1972.
50. Middelhoek, A.J. "Tests of the Marginal Stability of Input-Output Coefficients." *Contributions to Input-Output Analysis.* Edited by A.P. Carter and A. Brody. Amsterdam: North-Holland Publishing Co., 1970.
51. Miernyk, William H. "Comments on Czamanski and Malizia." *Papers of the Regional Science Association* 23 (1969): 81–82.

52. Miernyk, William H. "Regional and Interregional Input-Output Models: A Reappraisal." *Spatial, Regional, and Population Economics: Essays in Honor of Edgar M. Hoover.* Edited by Mark Perlman, Charles J. Leven, and Benjamin Chinitz. New York: Gordon and Breach, 1972: 263–292.
53. Miernyk, William H. "Sampling Techniques in Making Regional Industry Forecasts." *Contributions to Input-Output Analysis.* Edited by A.P. Carter and A. Brody. Amsterdam: North-Holland Publishing Co., 1970.
54. Miernyk, William H.; Bonner, Ernest R.; Chapman, John H., Jr.; and Shellhammer, Kenneth. *Impact of the Space Program on a Local Economy: An Input-Output Analysis.* Morgantown, West Virginia: West Virginia University Library, 1967.
55. Miernyk, William H.; Shellhammer, Kenneth L.; Brown, Douglas M.; Coccari, Ronald L.; Gallagher, Charles J.; and Wineman, Wesley H. *Simulating Regional Economic Development: An Interindustry Analysis of the West Virginia Economy.* Lexington: Lexington Books, D.C. Heath and Company, 1970.
56. MITI [Ministry of International Trade and Industry]. "Inter-regional Input-Output Table for Japan." *Trade and Industry of Japan,* no. 108, n.d.: 23.
57. Moore, Frederick T., and Petersen, James W. "Regional Analysis: An Interindustry Model of Utah." *Review of Economics and Statistics* 37 (November 1955): 368–381.
58. Moses, Leon N. "The Stability of Interregional Trading Patterns and Input-Output Analysis." *American Economic Review* 45, no. 5 (December 1955): 803–832.
59. Mushkin, Selma J. *Health and Hospital Expenditures of State and Local Governments: 1970 Projections.* Chicago: The Council of State Governments, May 1965.
60. Mushkin, Selma J., and Harris, Robert. *Transportation Outlays of States and Cities: 1970 Projections.* Chicago: The Council of State Governments, May 1965.
61. Nelson, Frederick J. "Interindustry Transactions for Agriculture, 1958." Economic Research Service, U.S. Department of Agriculture. Unpublished, n.d.
62. Polenske, Karen R. *The United States Multiregional Input-Output Model.* Lexington: Lexington Books, D.C. Heath and Company, forthcoming.
63. Polenske, Karen R., and others. *State Estimates of the Gross National Product, 1947, 1958, 1963.* Lexington: Lexington Books, D.C. Heath and Company, 1972.
64. *Railway Age* 156, no. 2 (January 18, 1964).
65. Rey, G., and Tilanus, C.G. "Input-Output Forecasts for the Netherlands, 1949–1958." *Econometrica* 31, no. 3 (July 1963): 454–463.
66. Rijcheghem, W. van. "Exact Method for Determining the Technology Matrix in a Situation with Secondary Products." Unpublished, n.d.
67. Rodgers, John M. *State Estimates of Interregional Commodity Trade, 1963.* Lexington: Lexington Books, D.C. Heath and Company, 1973.
68. Rodgers, John M. *State Estimates of Outputs, Employment, and Payrolls,*

1947, 1958, 1963. Lexington: Lexington Books, D.C. Heath and Company, 1972.

69. Schaffer, William A., and Chu, Kong. "Nonsurvey Techniques for Constructing Interindustry Models." *Papers of the Regional Science Association* 23 (1969): 83–101.
70. Sevaldson, Per. "The Stability of Input-Output Coefficients." *Contributions to Input-Output Analysis.* Edited by A.P. Carter and A. Brody. Amsterdam: North-Holland Publishing Co., 1970.
71. Simpson, David, and Tsukui, Jinkichi. "The Fundamental Structure of Input-Output Tables, An International Comparison." *Review of Economics and Statistics* 47 (November 1965): 434–448.
72. Siskind, David I. "Input-Output N-244. New and Maintenance Construction: Construction in the 1947 Interindustry Study." U.S. Bureau of Labor Statistics. Unpublished, August 1952.
73. Strout, Alan. "A Flexible Input-Output Convention for Secondary Product Transactions." Harvard Economic Research Project. Unpublished, January 14, 1963.
74. Udis, Bernard, (Ed.) "An Interindustry Analysis of the Colorado River Basin in 1960 with Projections to 1980 and 2010." Boulder: Bureau of Economic Research, University of Colorado. Unpublished, June 1968.
75. U.S. Bureau of the Census. *Census of Agriculture, 1954.* Vol. III, *Special Reports:* Part 11, *Farmers' Expenditures.* GPO, 1956.
76. U.S. Bureau of the Census. *Census of Agriculture, 1959.* Vol. II, *General Report.* GPO, 1962.
77. U.S. Bureau of the Census. *Census of Agriculture, 1964.* Vol. I, *State and County Statistics.* GPO, 1967.
78. U.S. Bureau of the Census. *Census of Agriculture, 1964.* Vol. II, *General Report.* GPO, 1967.
79. U.S. Bureau of the Census. *Census of Agriculture, 1964.* Vol. III, *Special Reports.* GPO, 1968.
80. U.S. Bureau of the Census. *Census of Manufactures, 1963.* GPO, 1966.
81. U.S. Bureau of the Census. *Census of Manufactures, 1963.* Vol. II, *Industry Statistics.* GPO, 1966.
82. U.S. Bureau of the Census. *Census of Mineral Industries, 1963.* Vol. I, *Summary and Industry Statistics.* Vol. II, *Area Reports.* GPO, 1967.
83. U.S. Bureau of the Census. *Compendium of State Government Finances in 1963.* (State Finances, 1963, No. 2.) GPO, 1964.
84. U.S. Bureau of the Census. *Governmental Finances in 1963.* (Series G-GF63, No. 2.) GPO, November 1964.
85. U.S. Bureau of the Census. *Housing Construction Statistics, 1884 to 1964.* GPO, 1966.
86. U.S. Bureau of the Census. *Statistical Abstract of the United States, 1964.* GPO, 1964.
87. U.S. Bureau of the Census. *Statistical Abstract of the United States, 1965.* GPO, 1965.
88. U.S. Bureau of the Census. *Statistical Abstract of the United States, 1968.* GPO, 1968.

89. U.S. Department of Agriculture. *Agricultural Statistics, 1964.* GPO, 1964.
90. U.S. Department of Agriculture. *Agricultural Statistics, 1965.* GPO, 1965.
91. U.S. Department of Agriculture. Agricultural Marketing Service and Agricultural Research Service, U.S. Department of Commerce. Bureau of the Census. *Farmers' Expenditures in 1955 by Regions for Production and Farm Living . . . with Tables on Off-Farm Income.* Statistical Bulletin No. 224, April 1958.
92. U.S. Department of Agriculture. Economic Research Service. *Dairy Statistics, 1960–67.* Statistical Bulletin No. 430, July 1968.
93. U.S. Department of Agriculture. Economic Research Service. *Farmers' Pesticide Expenditure for Crops, Livestock, and Other Selected Uses in 1964.* Agricultural Economic Report No. 145, October 1968.
94. U.S. Department of Agriculture. Economic Research Service. *Farm Income: State Estimates, 1949–1964.* FIS-199 Supplement, August 1966.
95. U.S. Department of Agriculture. Economic Research Service. *Farm Income: State Estimates, 1949–1965.* FIS-203 Supplement, August 1966.
96. U.S. Department of Agriculture. Economic Research Service. *Feed Consumed by Various Classes of Livestock, by States, 1949–1950 and 1959–1960 with 1964–65 National Estimates and Comparisons.* Statistical Bulletin No. 379, October 1966.
97. U.S. Department of Agriculture. Economic Research Service. *Fertilizer Use in the United States, by Crops and Areas, 1964 Estimates.* Statistical Bulletin No. 408, August 1967.
98. U.S. Department of Agriculture. Economic Research Service. *Horticultural Specialty Crops.* Statistical Bulletin No. 122, April 1968.
99. U.S. Department of Agriculture. Economic Research Service. "Imputed Value of Items Produced and Consumed by Agriculture, 1963." Unpublished worksheets.
100. U.S. Department of Agriculture. Economic Research Service. *Liquid Petroleum Fuel Used by Farmers in 1959 and Related Data.* Statistical Bulletin No. 344, May 1964.
101. U.S. Department of Agriculture. Economic Research Service. *Livestock-Feed Relationships 1909–1963.* Statistical Bulletin No. 337, November 1963.
102. U.S. Department of Agriculture. Economic Research Service. *Statistics on Cotton and Related Data, 1930–67.* Statistical Bulletin No. 417, March 1968.
103. U.S. Department of Agriculture. Economic Research Service. *Supplement for 1964 to Grain and Feed Statistics.* Statistical Bulletin No. 159 (supplement), March 1965.
104. U.S. Department of Agriculture. Economic Research Service. *Supplement for 1967 to Livestock-Feed Relationships 1909–1963.* Statistical Bulletin No. 337 (supplement), November 1967.
105. U.S. Department of Agriculture. Farm Income Branch. "Agricultural Industrial Relations Study, 1955." Unpublished, January 1959.
106. U.S. Department of Agriculture. Farm Income Branch. "Agricultural Industrial Relations Study, 1955: Explanatory Notes to Input Tables." Unpublished, January 1959.

107. U.S. Department of Agriculture. Farm Income Branch. "Repair and Operation of Capital Items; Miscellaneous Production Expenses; Feed; Livestock; Seed; Fertilizer and Lime; Hired Labor." Unpublished worksheets, n.d.
108. U.S. Department of Agriculture. Statistical Reporting Service. *Calf Crop, Lamb Crop, Wool Production, Mohair Production: Revised Estimates, by States, 1960–64.* Statistical Bulletin No. 392, February 1967.
109. U.S. Department of Agriculture. Statistical Reporting Service. *Cattle and Calves and Sheep and Lambs on Feed: Selected States, 1959–65, Revised Estimates.* Statistical Bulletin No. 387, January 1967.
110. U.S. Department of Agriculture. Statistical Reporting Service. *Chickens and Eggs: Production, Disposition, Cash Receipts, Gross Income; Commercial Broilers: Production, Gross Income.* Statistical Bulletin No. 399, April 1967.
111. U.S. Department of Agriculture. Statistical Reporting Service. *Consumption of Commercial Fertilizers and Primary Plant Nutrients in the United States, 1850–1964, and by States, 1945–64.* Statistical Bulletin No. 375, June 1966.
112. U.S. Department of Agriculture. Statistical Reporting Service. *Field and Seed Crops: Production, Farm Use, Sales, Value . . . Revised Estimates, by States, 1959–64.* Statistical Bulletin No. 404, May 1967.
113. U.S. Department of Agriculture. Statistical Reporting Service. *Honey and Beeswax: Number of Colonies, Yield Per Colony, Production, Price Per Pound, Value of Production, by States, 1955–64. (Revised.)* Statistical Bulletin No. 388, January 1967.
114. U.S. Department of Agriculture. Statistical Reporting Service. *Livestock and Poultry Inventory, January 1, Revised Estimates 1961–65: Number, Value and Classes, by State.* Statistical Bulletin No. 389, February 1967.
115. U.S. Department of Agriculture. Statistical Reporting Service. *Potatoes and Sweet Potatoes, by States and Seasonal Groups: Crops of 1959–1964.* Statistical Bulletin No. 409, July 1967.
116. U.S. Department of Commerce. Business and Defense Services Administration. *Construction Review, 1965* 11, no. 10. GPO, October 1965.
117. U.S. Department of Commerce. Business and Defense Services Administration. *Regional Construction Requirements for Water and Wastewater Facilities, 1955–1967–1980.* GPO, October 1967.
118. U.S. Department of Commerce. Business and Defense Services Administration. Building Materials and Construction Industries Division. "1964 Construction Data." Unpublished research materials.
119. U.S. Department of Commerce. Office of Business Economics. "Competitive Imports in the 1963 Input-Output Table, with Associated Trade, Transportation, and Insurance Margins." Unpublished worksheets.
120. U.S. Department of Commerce. Office of Business Economics. "Construction Industries—1963 Input-Output Study." Unpublished printout.
121. U.S. Department of Commerce. Office of Business Economics. "The Input-Output Structure of the United States Economy: 1947." March 1970.
122. U.S. Department of Commerce. Office of Business Economics. "Input-Output Structure of the U.S. Economy: 1963." *Survey of Current Business* 49, no. 11 (November 1969): 16–47.

123. U.S. Department of Commerce. Office of Business Economics. *Input-Output Structure of the U.S. Economy: 1963.* Vol. I, *Transactions Data for Detailed Industries.* GPO, 1969.
124. U.S. Department of Commerce. Office of Business Economics. *The National Income and Product Accounts of the United States, 1929–1965: Statistical Tables.* GPO, 1966.
125. U.S. Department of Commerce. Office of Business Economics. "New Electric Utility Construction Breakdown of Types of Work." Unpublished worksheets.
126. U.S. Department of Commerce. Office of Business Economics. "New Electric Utility Construction 1963 Establishment Spread." Unpublished worksheets.
127. U.S. Department of Commerce. Office of Business Economics. "The 1958 Interindustry Relations Study." Unpublished, November 1964: 9–12.
128. U.S. Department of Commerce. Office of Business Economics. "1963 Input-Output Data." Computer tapes, 1970.
129. U.S. Department of Commerce. Office of Business Economics. "1963 Spread Sheet New Electric Utility Construction." Unpublished worksheets.
130. U.S. Department of Commerce. Office of Business Economics. "Trade, Transportation, and Insurance Margins for the 370-Order Flows in the 1963 Input-Output Table." Unpublished worksheets.
131. U.S. Department of Commerce. Office of Business Economics. "The Transactions Table of the 1958 Input-Output Study and Revised Direct and Total Requirements Data." *Survey of Current Business* 45, no. 9 (September 1965): 33–49.
132. U.S. Department of Defense. "Funds Appropriated by the Congress for Military Construction: Fiscal Year 1962." Unpublished worksheet.
133. U.S. Department of Health, Education, and Welfare. Division of Hospital and Medical Facilities. "Hospital and Medical Facilities Projects Approved through June 1963." *Hill-Burton Project Register.* n.d.
134. U.S. Department of Health, Education, and Welfare. Office of Education. *Digest of Educational Statistics, 1964.* Statistical Abstract. 1965.
135. U.S. Department of Health, Education, and Welfare. Office of Education. *New Construction and Rehabilitation on College Campuses, 1961–62, 1962–63, and 1963–64.* GPO, 1966.
136. U.S. Department of Health, Education, and Welfare. Office of Education. *School Management.* GPO, July 1965.
137. U.S. Department of the Interior. Bureau of Mines. *Minerals Yearbook, 1958.* Vols. I, II, III. GPO, 1959.
138. U.S. Department of the Interior. Bureau of Mines. *Minerals Yearbook, 1963.* Vols. I, III. GPO, 1964.
139. U.S. Department of the Interior. Bureau of Mines. *Minerals Yearbook, 1963.* Vol. II, *Fuels.* GPO, 1964.
140. U.S. Department of the Interior. Bureau of Reclamation. "Estimated Distribution by Annual Appropriations and Allotments by States." Tables VI–1, VI–2, WR–126. Photocopy, n.d.
141. U.S. Department of Labor. Bureau of Employment Security. *Farm Labor Market Developments, Review and Outlook.* January 1964.

142. U.S. Department of Labor. Bureau of Labor Statistics. *Labor and Material Requirements for Civil Works Construction by the Corps of Engineers.* Bulletin No. 1390. GPO, March 1964.
143. U.S. Department of Labor. Bureau of Labor Statistics. *Labor and Material Requirements for College Housing Construction.* Bulletin No. 1441. GPO, May 1965.
144. U.S. Department of Labor. Bureau of Labor Statistics. *Labor and Material Requirements for Construction of Federally Aided Highways, 1958, 1961, and 1964.* Report No. 299. GPO, 1966.
145. U.S. Department of Labor. Bureau of Labor Statistics. *Labor and Material Requirements for Federal Office Building Construction.* Bulletin No. 1331. GPO, 1962.
146. U.S. Department of Labor. Bureau of Labor Statistics. *Labor and Material Requirements for Hospital Construction.* Bulletin No. 1340. GPO, 1962.
147. U.S. Department of Labor. Bureau of Labor Statistics. *Labor and Material Requirements for Private One-Family House Construction.* Bulletin No. 1404. GPO, June 1964.
148. U.S. Department of Labor. Bureau of Labor Statistics. *Labor and Material Requirements for Public Housing Construction.* Bulletin No. 1402. GPO, May 1964.
149. U.S. Department of Labor. Bureau of Labor Statistics. *Labor and Material Requirements for School Construction.* Bulletin No. 1586. GPO, June 1968.
150. U.S. Department of Labor. Bureau of Labor Statistics. *Labor and Material Requirements for Sewer Works Construction.* Bulletin No. 1490. GPO, 1966.
151. U.S. Department of Labor. Bureau of Labor Statistics. *Patterns of U.S. Economic Growth.* BLS Bulletin No. 1672. GPO, 1970.
152. U.S. Department of Labor. Bureau of Labor Statistics. *Projections 1970: Interindustry Relationships, Potential Demand, Employment.* BLS Bulletin No. 1536. GPO, 1966.
153. U.S. Department of Labor. Bureau of Labor Statistics. *Projections of the Post-Vietnam Economy, 1975.* BLS Bulletin No. 1733. GPO, 1972.
154. U.S. Department of Transportation. Bureau of Public Roads. *Highway Statistics, 1964.* GPO, March 1966.
155. U.S. Senate. Committee on Public Works. *Study and Investigations of Use of Materials and New Designs and Methods in Public Works.* Prepared by U.S. Department of Army, Corps of Engineers. Committee Print No. 1. GPO, 1962.
156. Vaccara, Beatrice N. "Changes over Time in Input-Output Coefficients for the United States." *Contributions to Input-Output Analysis.* Edited by A.P. Carter and A. Brody. Amsterdam: North-Holland Publishing Co., 1970.
157. Walderhaug, Albert J. "State Input-Output Tables Derived from National Data." *Proceedings of the American Statistical Association.*
158. Wang, Kung-Lee, and Kokat, Robert G. *The Interindustry Structure of the U.S. Mining Industries, 1958.* Bureau of Mines Information Circular No. 8338. GPO, 1967.

About the Authors

Karen R. Polenske is an associate professor in the Department of Urban Studies and Planning at the Massachusetts Institute of Technology. She received the B.A. in 1959 from Oregon State College in home economics, the M.A. in 1961 from the Maxwell School, Syracuse University, in the joint program of public administration and economics, and the Ph.D. in 1966 from Harvard University in economics. After receiving the Ph.D., she taught for four years in the Department of Economics at Harvard University and was a research associate at the Harvard Economic Research Project until 1972. In 1970–1971, she spent the year at the University of Cambridge as a Senior Visitor at the Faculty of Economics and a Member of High Table at King's College. She belongs to the American Economic Association and the Regional Science Association.

Other contributors to this volume worked with Dr. Polenske on the multiregional input-output program and were all staff members of the Harvard Economic Research Project when the research was done. Carolyn W. Anderson, Orani Dixon, and Mary M. Shirley were full-time research assistants at the Project. Roger M. Kubarych was a graduate student at Harvard University, and John V. Wells was an undergraduate at Harvard College.